COLLINS
ITALIAN ★ ENGLISH
ENGLISH ★ ITALIAN
DICTIONARY

CATHERINE E. LOVE

D0972552

BERKLEY BOOKS, NEW YORK

General Editor
R. H. Thomas

The text of this dictionary has been
adapted from the Collins Gem
Italian–English, English–Italian
Dictionary prepared for Collins
Publishers by Lexus
1982

First published in this edition 1982

Contributors
Paolo L. Rossi with Davina M. Chaplin,
Fernando Villa, Ennio Bilucaglia

This Berkley book contains the complete
text of the original edition.
It has been completely reset in a type face
designed for easy reading, and was printed
from new film.

COLLINS ITALIAN/ENGLISH ENGLISH/ITALIAN
DICTIONARY

A Berkley Book / published by arrangement with
Collins Publishers

PRINTING HISTORY
Collins Gem edition published 1982
Berkley edition / August 1982

ISBN: 0-425-05451-9

INTRODUCTION

The user whose aim is to read and understand Italian will find in this dictionary a comprehensive and up-to-date wordlist including numerous phrases in current use. He will also find listed alphabetically the main irregular forms with a cross-reference to the basic form where a translation is given, as well as some of the most common abbreviations, acronyms and geographical names.

The user who wishes to communicate and to express himself in Italian will find clear and detailed treatment of all the basic words, with numerous indications pointing to the appropriate translation, and helping him to use it correctly.

INTRODUZIONE

Questo dizionario offre a chi deve leggere e comprendere l'inglese una nomenclatura dettagliata e aggiornata, con vocaboli e locuzioni idiomatiche parlate e scritte della lingua inglese contemporanea. Vi figurano anche, in ordine alfabetico, le principali forme irregolari, con un rimando alla forma di base dove si trova la traduzione, così come i più comuni nomi di luogo, le sigle e le abbreviazioni.

A loro volta, quanti hanno la necessità di esprimersi in inglese trovano in questo dizionario una trattazione chiara ed essenziale di tutti i vocaboli di base, con numerose indicazioni per una esatta traduzione e un uso corretto ed appropriato.

Abbreviations

Abbreviazioni

adjective	**a**	aggettivo
abbreviation	**abbr**	abbreviazione
adverb	**ad**	avverbio
administration	**ADMIN**	amministrazione
flying, air travel	**AER**	aeronautica, viaggi aerei
adjective	**ag**	aggettivo
agriculture	**AGR**	agricoltura
administration	**AMM**	amministrazione
anatomy	**ANAT**	anatomia
architecture	**ARCHIT**	architettura
astronomy, astrology	**ASTR**	astronomia, astrologia
the motor car and motoring	**AUT**	l'automobile
adverb	**av**	avverbio
flying, air travel	**AVIAT**	aeronautica, viaggi aerei
biology	**BIOL**	biologia
botany	**BOT**	botania
British English	**Brit**	inglese di Gran Bretagna
consonant	**C**	consonante
conjunction	**cj**	congiunzione
colloquial usage (! particularly offensive)	**col(!)**	familiare (! da evitare)
commerce, finance, banking	**COMM**	commercio, finanza, banca
conjunction	**cong**	congiunzione
compound element: noun used as adjective and which cannot follow the noun it qualifies	**cpd**	sostantivo usato come aggettivo, non può essere usato né come attributo, né dopo il sostantivo qualificato
cookery	**CULIN, CUC**	cucina
before	**dav**	davanti a
determiner: article, demonstrative etc	**det**	determinativo: articolo, aggettivo dimostrativo o indefinito etc
law	**DIR**	diritto
economics	**ECON**	economia
building	**EDIL**	edilizia
electricity, electronics	**ELEC, ELETTR**	elettricità, elettronica
exclamation	**excl, escl**	esclamazione

iv

feminine	**f**	femminile
colloquial usage (! particularly offensive)	**fam(!)**	familiare (! da evitare)
railways	**FERR**	ferrovia
figurative use	**fig**	figurato
physiology	**FISIOL**	fisiologia
photography	**FOT**	fotografia
(phrasal verb) where the particle cannot be separated from main verb	**fus**	(verbo inglese) la cui particella è inseparabile dal verbo
in most or all senses; generally	**gen**	nella maggior parte dei sensi; generalmente
geography, geology	**GEO**	geografia, geologia
geometry	**GEOM**	geometria
computers	**INFORM**	informatica
schooling, schools and universities	**INS**	insegnamento, sistema scolastico e universitario
invariable	**inv**	invariabile
irregular	**irg**	irregolare
grammar, linguistics	**LING**	grammatica, linguistica
masculine	**m**	maschile
mathematics	**MAT(H)**	matematica
medical term, medicine	**MED**	termine medico, medicina
the weather, meteorology	**METEOR**	il tempo, meteorologia
either masculine or feminine depending on sex	**m/f**	maschile o femminile, secondo il sesso
military matters	**MIL**	esercito, lingua militare
music	**MUS**	musica
noun	**n**	sostantivo
sailing, navigation	**NAUT**	nautica
numeral adjective or noun	**num**	numerale (aggettivo, sostantivo)
oneself	**o.s.**	
derogatory, pejorative	**pej, peg**	peggiorativo
photography	**PHOT**	fotografia
physiology	**PHYSIOL**	fisiologia
plural	**pl**	plurale
politics	**POL**	politica
past participle	**pp**	participio passato
preposition	**prep**	preposizione
psychology, psychiatry	**PSYCH, PSIC**	psicologia, psichiatria

past tense	pt	tempo del passato
uncountable noun: not used in the plural	q	sostantivo che non si usa al plurale
	qc	qualcosa
	qd	qualcuno
religions, church service	REL	religione, liturgia
noun	s	sostantivo
somebody	sb	
schooling, schools and universities	SCOL	insegnamento, sistema scolastico e universitario
singular	sg	singolare
(grammatical) subject	sog	soggetto (grammaticale)
something	sth	
subjunctive	sub	congiuntivo
(grammatical) subject	subj	soggetto (grammaticale)
technical term, technology	TECH, TECN	termine tecnico, tecnologia
telecommunications	TEL	telecomunicazioni
typography, printing	TIP	tipografia
television	TV	televisione
typography, printing	TYP	tipografia
American English	US	inglese degli Stati Uniti
vowel	V	vocale
verb	vb	verbo
verb or phrasal verb used intransitively	vi	verbo o gruppo verbale con funzione intransitiva
reflexive verb	vr	verbo riflessivo
verb or phrasal verb used transitively	vt	verbo o gruppo verbale con funzione transitiva
zoology	ZOOL	zoologia
registered trademark	®	marca depositata
introduces a cultural equivalent	≈	introduce un'equivalenza culturale
auxiliary verb 'essere' in compound tenses	2	verbo ausiliare 'essere' nei tempi composti

TRASCRIZIONE FONETICA

PHONETIC TRANSCRIPTION

CONSONANTS CONSONANTI

VOWELS VOCALI

NB. The pairing of some vowel sounds only indicates approximate equivalence/La messa in equivalenza di certi suoni indica solo una rassomiglianza approssimativa.

NB. **p, b, t, d, k, g** are not aspirated in Italian/sono seguiti da un'aspirazione in inglese.

*pu*ppy	p	*p*adre	
*b*aby	b	*b*ambino	
*t*ent	t	*t*u*tt*o	
*d*addy	d	*d*a*d*o	
*c*ork *k*iss *ch*ord	k	*c*ane *ch*e	
*g*a*g g*uess	g	*g*ola *gh*iro	
*s*o ri*c*e ki*ss*	s	*s*ano	
cou*s*in bu*zz*	z	*s*vago e*s*ame	
*sh*eep *s*ugar	∫	*sc*ena	
plea*s*ure bei*ge*	ʒ		
*ch*ur*ch*	t∫	pe*ce* lan*ci*are	
*j*u*dge g*eneral	dʒ	*gi*ro *gi*oco	
*f*arm ra*ff*le	f	a*f*a *f*aro	
*v*ery re*v*	v	*v*ero *b*ravo·	
*th*in ma*th*s	θ		
*th*at o*th*er	ð		
*l*ittle ba*ll*	l	*l*etto a*l*a	
	ʎ	g*l*i	
*r*at b*r*at	r	*r*ete a*r*co	
*m*ummy co*mb*	m	*r*amo *m*adre	
*n*o ra*n*	n	*n*o fuma*n*te	
	ɲ	*gn*omo	
si*ng*ing ba*n*k	ŋ		
*h*at re*h*eat	h		
*y*et	j	*bui*o p*i*acere	
*w*all be*w*ail	w	*uo*mo g*ua*io	
lo*ch*	x		

Vowels:

*hee*l *bea*d	iː i	v*i*no *i*dea
h*i*t p*i*ty	ɪ	
	e	st*e*lla *e*dera
s*e*t t*e*nt	ɛ	*e*poca
		e*cce*tto
*a*pple b*a*t	æ a	m*a*mma
		*a*more
*a*fter c*a*r c*a*lm	ɑː	
f*u*n c*ou*sin	ʌ	
*o*ver *a*bove	ə	
*u*rn f*er*n w*or*k	əː	
w*a*sh p*o*t	ɔ	r*o*sa *o*cchio
b*or*n c*or*k	ɔː	p*o*nte
		*o*gnuno
f*u*ll s*oo*t	u	*u*tile z*u*cca
b*oo*n l*ew*d	uː	

DIPHTHONGS DITTONGHI

ɪə	b*ee*r t*ie*r
ɛə	t*ear* f*air* th*ere*
eɪ	d*a*te pl*ai*ce d*ay*
aɪ	l*i*fe b*uy* cr*y*
au	*ow*l f*ou*l n*ow*
əu	l*ow* n*o*
ɔɪ	b*oi*l b*oy* *oi*ly
uə	p*oo*r t*our*

MISCELLANEOUS

VARIE

* per l'inglese: la 'r' finale viene pronunciata se seguita da una vocale.

' precedes the stressed syllable/precede la sillaba accentata.

ITALIAN PRONUNCIATION

Vowels

Where the vowel **e** or the vowel **o** appears in a stressed syllable it can be either open [ɛ], [ɔ] or closed [e], [o]. As the open or closed pronunciation of these vowels is subject to regional variation, the distinction is of little importance to the user of this dictionary. Phonetic transcription for headwords containing these vowels will therefore only appear where other pronunciation difficulties are present.

Consonants

c before 'e' or 'i' is pronounced *tch*.

ch is pronounced like the 'k' in 'kit'.

g before 'e' or 'i' is pronounced like the 'j' in 'jet'.

gl before 'e' or 'i' is normally pronounced like the 'lli' in 'million', and in a few cases only like the 'gl' in 'glove'.

gn is pronounced like the 'ny' in 'canyon'.

sc before 'e' or 'i' is pronounced *sh*.

z is pronounced like the 'ts' in 'stetson', or like the 'd's' in 'bird's-eye'.

Headwords containing the above consonants and consonantal groups have been given full phonetic transcription in this dictionary.

NB. All double written consonants in Italian are fully sounded: eg. the *tt* in 'tutto' is pronounced as in 'hat *t*rick'.

ITALIANO - INGLESE
ITALIAN - ENGLISH

A

a *prep* (*a + il* = **al**, *a + lo* = **allo**, *a + l'* = **all'**, *a + la* = **alla**, *a + i* = **ai**, *a + gli* = **agli**, *a + le* = **alle**) (*stato in luogo, tempo*) at; in; (*moto a luogo, complemento di termine*) to; (*mezzo*) with, by; **essere ~ Roma/alla posta/~ casa** to be in Rome/at the post office/at home; **~ 18 anni** at 18 (years of age); **~ mezzanotte/Natale** at midnight/ Christmas; **alle 3** at 3 (o'clock); **~ maggio** in May; **~ piedi/cavallo** on foot/horseback; **una barca ~ motore** a motorboat; **alla milanese** the Milanese way, in the Milanese fashion; **~ 500 lire il chilo** 500 lire *a o* per kilo; **viaggiare ~ 100 chilometri l'ora** to travel at 100 kilometres an *o* per hour; **~ 10 chilometri da Firenze** 10 kilometres from Florence; **~ domani!** see you tomorrow!; **~ uno ~ uno** one by one.

a'bate *sm* abbot.

abbacchi'ato, a [abbak'kjato] *ag* downhearted, in low spirits.

abbagli'ante [abbaʎ'ʎante] *ag* dazzling; **~i** *smpl* (*AUT*): **accendere gli ~i** to put one's headlights on full beam.

abbagli'are [abbaʎ'ʎare] *vt* to dazzle; (*illudere*) to delude; **ab'baglio** *sm* blunder; **prendere un abbaglio** to blunder, make a blunder.

abbai'are *vi* to bark.

abba'ino *sm* dormer window; (*soffitta*) attic room.

abbando'nare *vt* to leave, abandon, desert; (*trascurare*) to neglect; (*rinunciare a*) to abandon, give up; **~rsi** *vr* to let o.s. go; **~rsi a** (*ricordi, vizio*) to give o.s. up to; **abban'dono** *sm* abandoning; neglecting; (*stato*) abandonment; neglect; (*SPORT*) withdrawal; (*fig*) abandon.

abbas'sare *vt* to lower; (*radio*) to turn down; **~rsi** *vr* (*chinarsi*) to stoop; (*livello, sole*) to go down; (*fig: umiliarsi*) to demean o.s.; **~ i fari** (*AUT*) to dip one's lights.

ab'basso *escl*: **~ il re!** down with the king!

abbas'tanza [abbas'tantsa] *av* (*a sufficienza*) enough; (*alquanto*) quite, rather, fairly; **un vino ~ dolce** quite a sweet wine, a fairly sweet wine; **averne ~ di qd/qc** to have had enough of sb/sth.

ab'battere *vt* (*muro, casa*) to pull down; (*ostacolo*) to knock down; (*albero*) to fell; (: *sog: vento*) to bring down; (*bestie da macello*) to slaughter; (*cane, cavallo*) to destroy, put down; (*selvaggina, aereo*) to shoot down; (*fig: sog: malattia*) to leave prostrate; **~rsi** *vr* (*avvilirsi*) to lose heart.

abba'zia [abbat'tsia] *sf* abbey.

abbece'dario [abbetʃe'darjo] *sm* primer.

abbel'lire *vt* to make beautiful; (*ornare*) to embellish.

abbeve'rare *vt* to water; **abbevera'toio** *sm* drinking trough.

'abbi, 'abbia, abbi'amo, 'abbiano, abbi'ate *forme del vb* avere.

abbicci [abbit'tʃi] *sm inv* alphabet; (*sillabario*) primer; (*fig*) rudiments *pl*.

abbi'ente *ag* well-to-do, well-off.

abbi'etto, a *ag* = abietto.

abbiglia'mento [abbiʎʎa'mento] *sm* dress *q*; (*indumenti*) clothes *pl*; (*industria*) clothing industry.

abbigli'are [abbiʎ'ʎare] *vt* to dress up.

abbi'nare *vt* to combine, put together.

abbindo'lare *vt* (*fig*) to cheat, trick.

abbocca'mento *sm* talks *pl*, meeting.

abboc'care *vt* (*tubi, canali*) to connect, join up // *vi* (*pesce*) to bite; (*fig*) to swallow the bait; (*tubi*) to join.

abbona'mento *sm* subscription; (*alle ferrovie etc*) season ticket; **fare l'~** to take out a subscription (*o* season ticket).

abbo'nare *vt* = **abbuonare**; **~rsi** *vr*: **~rsi a un giornale** to take out a subscription to a newspaper; **~rsi al teatro/alle ferrovie** to take out a season ticket for the theatre/the train; **abbo'nato, a** *sm/f* subscriber; season-ticket holder.

abbon'dante *ag* abundant, plentiful; (*giacca*) roomy.

abbon'danza [abbon'dantsa] *sf* abundance.

abbon'dare *vi* to abound, be plentiful; **~ in** *o* **di** to be full of, abound in.

abbor'dabile *ag* (*persona*) approachable; (*prezzo*) reasonable.

abbor'dare *vt* (*nave*) to board; (*persona*) to approach; (*argomento*) to tackle; **~ una curva** to take a bend.

abbotto'nare *vt* to button up, do up.

abboz'zare [abbot'tsare] *vt* to sketch, outline; (*SCULTURA*) to rough-hew; **~ un sorriso** to give a ghost of a smile; **ab'bozzo** *sm* sketch, outline; (*DIR*) draft.

abbracci'are [abbrat'tʃare] *vt* to embrace; (*persona*) to hug, embrace; (*professione*) to take up; (*contenere*) to include; **~rsi** *vr* to hug *o* embrace (one another); **~rsi a qd/qc** to cling to sb/sth; **ab'braccio** *sm* hug, embrace.

abbrevi'are *vt* to shorten; (*parola*) to abbreviate, shorten; **abbreviazi'one** *sf* abbreviation.

abbron'zante [abbron'dzante] *ag* tanning, sun *cpd*.

abbron'zare [abbron'dzare] *vt* (*pelle*) to tan; (*metalli*) to bronze; **~rsi** *vr* to tan, get a tan; **abbronza'tura** *sf* tan, suntan.

abbrusto'lire *vt* (*pane*) to toast; (*caffè*) to roast.

abbui'are *vi* (*annottare*) to grow dark; **~rsi** *vr* to grow dark; (*vista*) to grow dim; (*fig*) to grow sad.

abbuo'nare *vt* (*perdonare*) to forgive.

abbu'ono *sm* (COMM) allowance, discount; (SPORT) handicap.

abdi'care *vi* to abdicate; **~ a** to give up, renounce; **abdicazi'one** *sf* abdication.

aberrazi'one [aberrat'tsjone] *sf* aberration.

a'bete *sm* fir (tree); **~ rosso** spruce.

abi'etto, a *ag* despicable, abject.

'abile *ag* (*idoneo*) suitable, fit; (*capace*) able; (*astuto*) clever; (*accorto*) skilful; (MIL): **~ alla leva** fit for military service; **abilità** *sf inv* ability; cleverness; skill.

abili'tato, a *ag* qualified; **abilitazi'one** *sf* qualification.

a'bisso *sm* abyss, gulf.

abi'tante *sm/f* inhabitant.

abi'tare *vt* to live in, dwell in // *vi*: **~ in campagna/a Roma** to live in the country/in Rome; **abi'tato, a** *ag* inhabited; lived in // *sm* built-up area; **abitazi'one** *sf* residence; house.

'abito *sm* dress *q*; (*da uomo*) suit; (*da donna*) dress; (*abitudine, disposizione, REL*) habit; **~i** *smpl* clothes; **in ~ da sera** in evening dress.

abitu'ale *ag* usual, habitual.

abitu'are *vt*: **~ qd a** to get sb used o accustomed to; **~rsi a** to get used to, accustom o.s. to.

abitudi'nario, a *ag* of fixed habits; **~i** *smpl* regular customers.

abi'tudine *sf* habit; **d'~** usually; **per ~** from o out of habit.

abiu'rare *vt* to renounce.

abnegazi'one [abnegat'tsjone] *sf* (self-)abnegation, self-denial.

abo'lire *vt* to abolish; (DIR) to repeal; **abolizi'one** *sf* abolition; repeal.

abomi'nevole *ag* abominable.

abo'rigeno [abo'ridʒeno] *sm* aborigine.

abor'rire *vt* to abhor, detest.

abor'tire *vi* (MED: *accidentalmente*) to miscarry, have a miscarriage; (: *deliberatamente*) to have an abortion; (*fig*) to miscarry, fail; **a'borto** *sm* miscarriage; abortion; (*fig*) freak.

abrasi'one *sf* abrasion; **abra'sivo, a** *ag*, *sm* abrasive.

abro'gare *vt* to repeal, abrogate.

A'bruzzo *sm*: **l'~, gli ~i** the Abruzzi.

'abside *sf* apse.

abu'sare *vi*: **~ di** to abuse, misuse; (*alcool*) to take to excess; (*approfittare, violare*) to take advantage of; **~ dei cibi** to eat to excess; **a'buso** *sm* abuse, misuse; excessive use.

a.C. (*abbr di* **avanti Cristo**) B.C.

'acca *sf* letter H.

acca'demia *sf* (*società*) learned society; (*scuola: d'arte, militare*) academy; **acca-'demico, a, ci, che** *ag* academic // *sm* academician.

acca'dere *vb impers* (2) to happen, occur; **acca'duto** *sm* event; **raccontare l'accaduto** to describe what has happened.

accalappi'are *vt* to catch; (*fig*) to trick, dupe.

accal'care *vt* to crowd, throng.

accal'darsi *vr* to grow hot.

accalo'rarsi *vr* (*fig*) to get excited.

accampa'mento *sm* camp.

accam'pare *vt* to encamp; (*fig*) to put forward, advance; **~rsi** *vr* to camp.

accani'mento *sm* fury; (*tenacia*) tenacity, perseverance.

acca'nirsi *vr* (*infierire*) to rage; (*ostinarsi*): **~ in** to persist in; **acca'nito, a** *ag* (*odio, gelosia*) fierce, bitter; (*lavoratore*) assiduous, dogged; (*fumatore*) inveterate.

ac'canto *av* near, nearby; **~ a** *prep* near, beside, close to.

accanto'nare *vt* (*problema*) to shelve; (*somma*) to set aside.

accaparra'mento *sm* (COMM) cornering, buying up.

accapar'rare *vt* to corner, buy up; (*versare una caparra*) to pay a deposit on; **~rsi qc** (*fig: simpatia, voti*) to secure sth (for o.s.).

accapigli'arsi [akkapiʎ'ʎarsi] *vr* to come to blows; (*fig*) to quarrel.

accappa'toio *sm* bathrobe.

accappo'nare *vi*: **mi si accappona la pelle per il freddo** the cold is giving me goosepimples o gooseflesh.

accarez'zare [akkaret'tsare] *vt* to caress, stroke, fondle; (*fig*) to toy with.

acca'sarsi *vr* to set up house; to get married.

accasci'arsi [akkaʃ'ʃarsi] *vr* to collapse; (*fig*) to lose heart.

accatto'naggio [akkatto'naddʒo] *sm* begging.

accat'tone *a, sm/f* beggar.

accaval'lare *vt* (*gambe*) to cross; **~rsi** *vr* (*sovrapporsi*) to overlap; (*addensarsi*) to gather.

acce'care [attʃe'kare] *vt* to blind // *vi* (2) to go blind.

ac'cedere [at'tʃedere] *vi* (2): **~ a** to enter; (*richiesta*) to grant, accede to.

accele'rare [attʃele'rare] *vt* to speed up // *vi* (AUT) to accelerate; **~ il passo** to quicken one's pace; **accele'rato, a** *ag* quick, rapid; accelerated // *sm* (FERR) slow train; **accelera'tore** *sm* (AUT) accelerator; **accelerazi'one** *sf* acceleration.

ac'cendere [at'tʃendere] *vt* (*fuoco, sigaretta*) to light; (*luce, televisione*) to put o switch o turn on; (AUT: *motore*) to switch on; (COMM: *conto*) to open; (*fig: suscitare*) to inflame, stir up; **~rsi** *vr* (*luce*) to come o go on; (*legna*) to catch fire, ignite; **accen-**

'dino *sm*, **accendi'sigaro** *sm* (cigarette) lighter.

accen'nare [attʃen'nare] *vt* to indicate, point out; (*disegno*) to sketch; (*mus*) to pick out the notes of; to hum // *vi*: ~ **a** to beckon to; (*col capo*) to nod to; (*fig: alludere a*) to hint at; (: *parlare brevemente di*) to touch on; (: *far vista di*) to look as if; (: *far atto di*) to make as if.

ac'cenno [at'tʃenno] *sm* (*cenno*) sign; nod; (*allusione*) hint.

accensi'one [attʃen'sjone] *sf* (*vedi accendere*) lighting; switching on; opening; (*aut*) ignition.

accen'tare [attʃen'tare] *vt* (*parlando*) to stress; (*scrivendo*) to accent.

ac'cento [at'tʃento] *sm* accent; (*fonetica, fig*) stress; (*inflessione*) tone (of voice).

accen'trare [attʃen'trare] *vt* to centralize.

accentu'are [attʃentu'are] *vt* to stress, emphasize; ~**rsi** *vr* to become more noticeable.

accerchi'are [attʃer'kjare] *vt* to surround, encircle.

accerta'mento [attʃerta'mento] *sm* check; assessment.

accer'tare [attʃer'tare] *vt* to ascertain; (*verificare*) to check; (*reddito*) to assess.

ac'ceso, a [at'tʃeso] *pp di* **accendere** // *ag* lit; on; open; (*colore*) bright.

acces'sibile [attʃes'sibile] *ag* (*luogo*) accessible; (*persona*) approachable; (*prezzo*) reasonable; (*idea*): ~ **a qd** within the reach of sb.

ac'cesso [at'tʃesso] *sm* access; (*med*) attack, fit; (*impulso violento*) fit, outburst.

acces'sorio, a [attʃes'sɔrjo] *ag* secondary, of secondary importance; ~**i** *smpl* accessories.

ac'cetta [at'tʃetta] *sf* hatchet.

accet'tabile [attʃet'tabile] *ag* acceptable.

accet'tare [attʃet'tare] *vt* to accept; ~ **di fare qc** to agree to do sth; **accettazi'one** *sf* acceptance; (*locale di servizio pubblico*) reception.

ac'cetto, \a [at'tʃetto] *ag* agreeable; (*persona*) liked.

accezi'one [attʃet'tsjone] *sf* meaning.

acchiap'pare [akkjap'pare] *vt* to catch.

acci'acco, chi [at'tʃakko] *sm* ailment.

acciaie'ria [attʃaje'ria] *sf* steelworks *sg*.

acci'aio [at'tʃajo] *sm* steel.

acci'dentale [attʃiden'tale] *ag* accidental.

acciden'tato, a [attʃiden'tato] *ag* (*terreno etc*) uneven.

acci'dente [attʃi'dɛnte] *sm* (*caso imprevisto*) accident; (*disgrazia*) mishap; (*med*) stroke; ~**!** (*fam: per rabbia*) damn (it)!; (: *per meraviglia*) good heavens!

ac'cidia [at'tʃidja] *sf* (*rel*) sloth.

accigli'ato, a [attʃiʎ'ʎato] *ag* frowning.

ac'cingersi [at'tʃindʒersi] *vr*: ~ **a fare** to be about to do.

acciuf'fare [attʃuf'fare] *vt* to seize, catch.

acci'uga, ghe [at'tʃuga] *sf* anchovy.

accla'mare *vt* (*applaudire*) to applaud; (*eleggere*) to acclaim; **acclamazi'one** *sf* applause; acclamation.

acclima'tare *vt* to acclimatize; ~**rsi** *vr* to become acclimatized.

ac'cludere *vt* to enclose; **ac'cluso, a** *pp di* **accludere** // *ag* enclosed.

accocco'larsi *vr* to crouch.

accogli'ente [akkoʎ'ʎɛnte] *ag* welcoming, friendly; **accogli'enza** *sf* reception; welcome.

ac'cogliere [ak'kɔʎʎere] *vt* (*ricevere*) to receive; (*dare il benvenuto*) to welcome; (*approvare*) to agree to, accept; (*contenere*) to hold, accommodate.

accol'lato, a *ag* (*vestito*) high-necked.

accoltel'lare *vt* to knife, stab.

ac'colto, a *pp di* **accogliere**.

accoman'dita *sf* (*dir*) limited partnership.

accomia'tare *vt* to dismiss; ~**rsi** *vr*: ~**rsi (da)** to take one's leave (of).

accoda'mento *sm* agreement, settlement.

accomo'dante *ag* accommodating.

accomo'dare *vt* (*aggiustare*) to repair, mend; (*riordinare*) to tidy; (*conciliare*) to settle; ~**rsi** *vr* to make o.s. comfortable *o* at home; (*adattarsi*) to make do; ~**rsi a sedere/in casa** to sit down/come in.

accompagna'mento [akkompaɲ-ɲa'mento] *sm* (*mus*) accompaniment.

accompa'gnare [akkompaɲ'ɲare] *vt* to accompany, come *o* go with; (*mus*) to accompany; (*unire*) to couple.

accomu'nare *vt* to pool, share; (*avvicinare*) to unite.

acconcia'tura [akkontʃa'tura] *sf* hairstyle.

ac'concio, a, ci, ce [ak'kontʃo] *ag* suitable.

accondi'scendere [akkondiʃ'ʃendere] *vi*: ~ **a** to agree *o* consent to; **accondi'sceso, a** *pp di* **accondiscendere**.

acconsen'tire *vi*: ~ **(a)** to agree *o* consent (to).

acconten'tare *vt* to satisfy; ~**rsi di** to be satisfied with, content o.s. with.

ac'conto *sm* part payment; **pagare una somma in** ~ to pay a sum of money as a deposit.

accoppia'mento *sm* coupling, pairing off; mating.

accoppi'are *vt* to couple, pair off; (*biol*) to mate; ~**rsi** *vr* to pair off; to mate.

accorci'are [akkor'tʃare] *vt* to shorten; ~**rsi** *vr* to become shorter.

accor'dare *vt* to reconcile; (*colori*) to match; (*mus*) to tune; (*ling*): to make sth agree with sth; (*dir*) to grant; ~**rsi** *vr* to agree, come to an agreement; (*colori*) to match.

ac'cordo *sm* agreement; (*armonia*) harmony; (*mus*) chord; **essere d'**~ to agree; **andare d'**~ to get on well together; **d'**~**!** all right!, agreed!

ac'corgersi [ak'kɔrdʒersi] *vr*: ~ **di** to notice; (*fig*) to realize; **accorgi'mento** *sm* shrewdness *q*; (*espediente*) trick, device.

ac'correre *vi* (*2*) to run up.

ac'corto, a *pp di* **accorgersi** // *ag* shrewd; **stare ~ to be** on one's guard.

accos'tare *vt* (*avvicinare*): **~ qc a** to bring sth near to, put sth near to; (*avvicinarsi a*) to approach; (*socchiudere: imposte*) to half-close; (*: porta*) to leave ajar // *vi* (*NAUT*) to come alongside; **~rsi a** to draw near, approach; (*fig*) to support.

accovacci'arsi [akkovat'tʃarsi] *vr* to crouch.

accoz'zaglia [akkot'tsaʎʎa] *sf* jumble, hotchpotch; (*peg: di persone*) mob.

accredi'tare *vt* (*notizia*) to confirm the truth of; (*COMM*) to credit; (*diplomato*) to accredit; **~rsi** *vr* (*fig*) to gain credit.

ac'crescere [ak'kreʃʃere] *vt* to increase; **~rsi** *vr* to increase, grow; **accresci'mento** *sm* increase, growth; **accresci'uto, a** *pp di* **accrescere**.

accucci'arsi [akkut'tʃarsi] *vr* (*cane*) to lie down.

accu'dire *vt* (*anche: vi:* **~ a**) to attend to.

accumu'lare *vt* to accumulate; **accumu-la'tore** *sm* (*ELETTR*) accumulator; **accumulazi'one** *sf* accumulation.

accura'tezza [akkura'tettsa] *sf* care; accuracy.

accu'rato, a *ag* (*diligente*) careful; (*preciso*) accurate.

ac'cusa *sf* accusation; (*DIR*) charge.

accu'sare *vt*: **~ qd di qc** to accuse sb of sth; (*DIR*) to charge sb with sth; **~ ricevuta di** (*COMM*) to acknowledge receipt of.

accu'sato, a *sm/f* accused; defendant.

accusa'tore, 'trice *sm/f* accuser // *sm* (*DIR*) prosecutor.

a'cerbo, a [a'tʃerbo] *ag* bitter; (*frutta*) sour, unripe.

'acero ['atʃero] *sm* maple.

a'cerrimo, a [a'tʃerrimo] *ag* very fierce.

a'ceto [a'tʃeto] *sm* vinegar.

A.C.I. *sm* (*abbr di* Automobile Club d'Italia) ≈ A.A.

acidità [atʃidi'ta] *sf* acidity; sourness.

'acido, a ['atʃido] *ag* (*sapore*) acid, sour; (*CHIM*) acid // *sm* (*CHIM*) acid.

'acino ['atʃino] *sm* berry; **~ d'uva** grape.

'acne *sf* acne.

'acqua *sf* water; (*pioggia*) rain; **~e** *sfpl* waters; **fare ~** (*NAUT*) to leak, take in water; **~ corrente** running water; **~ dolce** fresh water; **~ minerale** mineral water; **~ potabile** drinking water; **~ salata** salt water; **~ tonica** tonic water.

acqua'forte, *pl* **acque'forti** *sf* etching.

a'cquaio *sm* sink.

acqua'ragia [akkwa'radʒa] *sf* turpentine.

a'cquario *sm* aquarium; (*dello zodiaco*): **A ~** Aquarius.

acqua'santa *sf* holy water.

acqua'vite *sf* brandy.

acquaz'zone [akkwat'tsone] *sm* cloudburst, heavy shower.

acque'dotto *sm* aqueduct; waterworks *pl*, water system.

acque'rello *sm* watercolour.

acque'rugiola [akkwe'rudʒola] *sf* drizzle.

acquie'tare *vt* to appease; (*dolore*) to ease; **~rsi** *vr* to calm down.

acqui'rente *sm/f* purchaser, buyer.

acqui'sire *vt* to acquire.

acquis'tare *vt* to purchase, buy; (*fig*) to gain; **a'cquisto** *sm* purchase; **fare acquisti** to go shopping.

acqui'trino *sm* bog, marsh.

acquo'lina *sf*: **far venire l'~ in bocca a qd** to make sb's mouth water.

a'cquoso, a *ag* watery.

'acre *ag* acrid, pungent; (*fig*) harsh, biting.

a'crobata, i, e *sm/f* acrobat.

acro'batica *sf* acrobatics *sg*.

acroba'zia [akrobat'tsia] *sf* acrobatic feat.

acu'ire *vt* to sharpen.

a'culeo *sm* (*ZOOL*) sting; (*BOT*) prickle.

a'cume *sm* acumen, perspicacity.

a'custica *sf* (*scienza*) acoustics *sg*; (*di una sala*) acoustics *pl*.

a'cuto, a *ag* (*appuntito*) sharp, pointed; (*suono, voce*) shrill, piercing; (*MAT, LING, MED*) acute; (*MUS*) high-pitched; (*fig: dolore, desiderio*) intense; (*: perspicace*) acute, keen.

ad *prep* (*dav V*) = **a**.

adagi'are [ada'dʒare] *vt* to lay o set down carefully; **~rsi** *vr* to lie down, stretch out.

a'dagio [a'dadʒo] *av* slowly // *sm* (*MUS*) adagio; (*proverbio*) adage, saying.

adatta'mento *sm* adaptation.

adat'tare *vt* to adapt; (*applicare*) to fit; **~rsi (a)** (*ambiente, tempi*) to adapt (to).

a'datto, a *ag*: **~ (a)** suitable (for), right (for).

addebi'tare *vt*: **~ qc a qd** to debit sb with sth; (*fig: incolpare*) to blame sb for sth.

adden'sare *vt* to thicken; **~rsi** *vr* to thicken; (*folla, nuvole*) to gather.

adden'tare *vt* to bite into.

adden'trarsi *vr*: **~ in** to penetrate, go into.

ad'dentro *av* inside, within; (*fig*) deeply; **essere molto ~ in qc** to be well-versed in sth.

addestra'mento *sm* training.

addes'trare *vt*, **~rsi** *vr* to train; **~rsi in qc** to practise sth.

ad'detto, a *ag*: **~ a** assigned to; (*occupato in un lavoro*) employed in, attached to // *sm* employee; (*funzionario*) attaché; **~ commerciale/stampa** commercial/press attaché.

addì *av* (*AMM*): **~ 3 luglio 1978** on the 3rd of July 1978.

addi'etro *av* (*indietro*) behind; (*nel passato, prima*) before, ago.

ad'dio *sm, escl* goodbye, farewell.

addirit'tura *av* (*veramente*) really, absolutely; (*perfino*) even; (*direttamente*) directly, right away.

ad'dirsi *vr*: **~ a** to suit, be suitable for.

addi'tare *vt* to point out; (*fig*) to expose.

addi'tivo *sm* additive.

addizio'nare [additsjo'nare] *vt* (MAT) to add (up); **addizi'one** *sf* addition.

addob'bare *vt* to decorate; **ad'dobbo** *sm* decoration.

addol'cire [addol'tʃire] *vt* (*caffè etc*) to sweeten; (*acqua, fig: carattere*) to soften; ~**rsi** *vr* (*fig*) to mellow, soften.

addolo'rare *vt* to pain, grieve; ~**rsi (per)** to be distressed (by).

ad'dome *sm* abdomen.

addomesti'care *vt* to tame.

addormen'tare *vt* to put to sleep; ~**rsi** *vr* to fall asleep.

addos'sare *vt* (*appoggiare*): ~ **qc a qc** to lean sth against sth; (*fig*): ~ **qc a qd** to saddle sb with sth; ~ **la colpa a qd** to lay the blame on sb; ~**rsi qc** (*responsabilità etc*) to shoulder.

ad'dosso *av* (*sulla persona*) on; **mettersi** ~ **il cappotto** to put one's coat on; ~ **a** *prep* (*sopra*) on; (*molto vicino*) right next to.

ad'durre *vt* (DIR) to produce; (*citare*) to cite.

adegu'are *vt*: ~ **qc a** to adjust *o* relate sth to; ~**rsi** *vr* to adapt; **adegu'ato, a** *ag* adequate; (*conveniente*) suitable; (*equo*) fair.

a'dempiere, adem'pire *vt* to fulfil, carry out.

ade'rente *ag* adhesive; (*vestito*) close-fitting // *sm/f* follower; **ade'renza** *sf* adhesion; **aderenze** *sfpl* (*fig*) connections, contacts.

ade'rire *vi* (*stare attaccato*) to adhere, stick; ~ **a** to adhere to, stick to; (*fig: società, partito*) to join; (: *opinione*) to support; (*richiesta*) to agree to; **adesi'one** *sf* adhesion; (*fig*) agreement, acceptance; **ade'sivo, a** *ag*, *sm* adhesive.

a'desso *av* (*ora*) now; (*or ora, poco fa*) just now; (*tra poco*) any moment now.

adia'cente [adja'tʃente] *ag* adjacent.

adi'bire *vt* (*usare*): ~ **qc a** to turn sth into.

adi'rarsi *vr*: ~ (**con** *o* **contro qd per qc**) to get angry (with sb over sth).

a'dire *vt* (*tribunale*) to resort to; ~ **le vie legali** to take legal proceedings.

'adito *sm* entrance; access.

adocchi'are [adok'kjare] *vt* (*scorgere*) to catch sight of; (*occhieggiare*) to eye.

adole'scente [adole'ʃʃente] *ag*, *sm/f* adolescent; **adole'scenza** *sf* adolescence.

adom'brare *vt* (*fig*) to veil, conceal; ~**rsi** *vr* (*cavallo*) to shy; (*persona*) to grow suspicious; (: *aversene a male*) to be offended.

adope'rare *vt* to use; ~**rsi** *vr* to strive; ~**rsi per qd/qc** to do one's best for sb/sth.

ado'rare *vt* to adore; (REL) to adore, worship; **adorazi'one** *sf* adoration; worship.

ador'nare *vt* to adorn.

adot'tare *vt* to adopt; (*decisione, provvedimenti*) to pass; **adot'tivo, a** *ag*

(*genitori*) adoptive; (*figlio, patria*) adopted; **adozi'one** *sf* adoption.

adri'atico, a, ci, che *ag* Adriatic // *sm*: **l'A~, il mare A~** the Adriatic, the Adriatic Sea.

adu'lare *vt* to adulate, flatter.

adulte'rare *vt* to adulterate.

adul'terio *sm* adultery; **a'dultero, a** *ag* adulterous // *sm/f* adulterer/adulteress.

a'dulto, a *ag* adult; (*fig*) mature // *sm* adult, grown-up.

adu'nanza [adu'nantsa] *sf* assembly, meeting.

adu'nare *vt*, ~**rsi** *vr* to assemble, gather; **adu'nata** *sf* (MIL) parade, muster.

a'dunco, a, chi, che *ag* hooked.

a'ereo, a *ag* air *cpd*; (*radice*) aerial // *sm* aerial; (*abbr di aeroplano*) plane; **aerodi-'namico, a, ci, che** *ag* aerodynamic; (*affusolato*) streamlined // *sf* aerodynamics *sg*; **aero'nautica** *sf* (*scienza*) aeronautics *sg*; **aeronautica militare** air force; **aero'plano** *sm* aeroplane; **aero'porto** *sm* airport; **aero-'sol** *sm inv* aerosol; **aerospazi'ale** *ag* aerospace.

'afa *sf* sultriness.

af'fabile *ag* affable.

affaccen'darsi [affattʃen'darsi] *vr*: ~**intorno a qc** to busy o.s. with sth; **affaccen'dato, a** *ag* busy.

affacci'arsi [affat'tʃarsi] *vr*: ~ (**a**) to appear (at).

affa'mare *vt* to starve; **affa'mato, a** *ag* starving; (*fig*): **affamato (di)** eager (for).

affan'nare *vt* to leave breathless; (*fig*) to worry; ~**rsi** *vr*: ~**rsi per qd/qc** to worry about sb/sth; **af'fanno** *sm* breathlessness; (*fig*) anxiety, worry; **affan'noso, a** *ag* (*respiro*) difficult; (*fig*) troubled, anxious.

af'fare *sm* (*cosa, faccenda*) matter, affair; (COMM) piece of business, (business) deal; (DIR) case; (*fam: cosa*) thing; ~**i** *smpl* (COMM) business *sg*; **ministro degli A~i esteri** Foreign Secretary; **affa'rista, i** *sm* profiteer, unscrupulous businessman.

affasci'nare [affaʃʃi'nare] *vt* to bewitch; (*fig*) to charm, fascinate.

affati'care *vt* to tire; ~**rsi** *vr* (*durar fatica*) to tire o.s. out.

af'fatto *av* completely; **non ... ~** not ... at all.

affer'mare *vi* (*dire di sì*) to say yes // *vt* (*dichiarare*) to maintain, affirm; ~**rsi** *vr* to assert o.s., make one's name known; **affermazi'one** *sf* affirmation, assertion; (*successo*) achievement.

affer'rare *vt* to seize, grasp; (*fig: idea*) to grasp; ~**rsi** *vr*: ~**rsi a** to cling to.

affet'tare *vt* (*tagliare a fette*) to slice; (*ostentare*) to affect; **affet'tato, a** *ag* sliced; affected // *sm* sliced cold meat; **affettazi'one** *sf* affectation.

affet'tivo, a *ag* emotional, affective.

af'fetto *sm* affection; **affettu'oso, a** *ag* affectionate.

affezio'narsi [affettsjo'narsi] *vr*: ~ **a** to grow fond of.

affezi'one [affet'tsjone] *sf* (*affetto*) affection; (*MED*) ailment, disorder.

affian'care *vt* to place side by side; (*MIL*) to flank; (*fig*) to support; ~ **qc a qc** to place sth next to *o* beside sth; ~**rsi a qd** to stand beside sb.

affia'tarsi *vr* to get on well together.

affibbi'are *vt* to buckle, do up; (*fig: dare*) to give.

affida'mento *sm* (*fiducia*) confidence, trust; (*garanzia*) assurance; **fare** ~ **su qd** to rely on sb.

affi'dare *vt*: ~ **qc a qd** to entrust sb with sth; ~**rsi** *vr*: ~**rsi a** to place one's trust in.

affievo'lirsi *vr* to grow weak.

af'figgere [af'fiddʒere] *vt* to stick up, post up.

affi'lare *vt* to sharpen.

affili'are *vt* to affiliate; ~**rsi** *vr*: ~**rsi a** to become affiliated to.

affi'nare *vt* to sharpen.

affinché [affin'ke] *cong* in order that, so that.

af'fine *ag* similar; **affinità** *sf inv* affinity.

affio'rare *vi* to emerge.

affissi'one *sf* bill-posting.

af'fisso, a *pp di* **affiggere** // *sm* bill, poster; (*LING*) affix.

affit'tare *vt* (*dare in affitto*) to let, rent (out); (*prendere in affitto*) to rent; **af'fitto** *sm* rent; (*contratto*) lease.

af'fliggere [af'fliddʒere] *vt* to torment; ~**rsi** *vr* to grieve; **af'flitto, a** *pp di* **affliggere**; **afflizi'one** *sf* distress, torment.

afflosci'arsi [afflof'farsi] *vr* to go limp; (*frutta*) to go soft.

afflu'ente *sm* tributary; **afflu'enza** *sf* flow; (*di persone*) crowd.

afflu'ire *vi* (2) to flow; (*fig: merci, persone*) to pour in; **af'flusso** *sm* influx.

affo'gare *vt, vi* to drown; ~**rsi** *vr* to drown; (*deliberatamente*) to drown o.s.

affol'lare *vt*, ~**rsi** *vr* to crowd; **affol-'lato, a** *ag* crowded.

affon'dare *vt* to sink.

affran'care *vt* to free, liberate; (*AMM*) to redeem; (*lettera*) to stamp; (*automaticamente*) to frank; ~**rsi** *vr* to free o.s.; **affranca'tura** *sf* (*di francobollo*) stamping; franking; (*tassa di spedizione*) postage.

af'franto, a *ag* (*esausto*) worn out; (*abbattuto*) overcome.

af'fresco, schi *sm* fresco.

affret'tare *vt* to quicken, speed up; ~**rsi** *vr* to hurry; ~**rsi a fare qc** to hurry *o* hasten to do sth.

affron'tare *vt* (*pericolo etc*) to face; (*assalire: nemico*) to confront; ~**rsi** *vr* (*reciproco*) to come to blows.

af'fronto *sm* affront, insult.

affumi'care *vt* to fill with smoke; to blacken with smoke; (*alimenti*) to smoke.

affuso'lato, a *ag* tapering.

a'foso, a *ag* sultry, close.

'Africa *sf*: l'~ Africa; **afri'cano, a** *ag, sm/f* African.

afrodi'siaco, a, ci, che *ag, sm* aphrodisiac.

a'genda [a'dʒenda] *sf* diary.

a'gente [a'dʒente] *sm* agent; ~ **di cambio** stockbroker; ~ **di polizia** police officer; ~ **di vendita** sales agent; **agen-'zia** *sf* agency; (*succursale*) branch; **agenzia immobiliare** estate agent's (office); **agenzia pubblicitaria/viaggi** advertising/travel agency.

agevo'lare [adʒevo'lare] *vt* to facilitate, make easy.

a'gevole [a'dʒevole] *ag* easy; (*strada*) smooth.

aggnci'are [aggan'tʃare] *vt* to hook up; (*FERR*) to couple.

ag'geggio [ad'dʒeddʒo] *sm* gadget, contraption.

agget'tivo [addʒet'tivo] *sm* adjective.

agghiacci'are [aggjat'tʃare] *vt* to freeze; (*fig*) to make one's blood run cold; ~**rsi** *vr* to freeze.

aggior'nare [addʒor'nare] *vt* (*opera, manuale*) to bring up-to-date; (*seduta etc*) to postpone; ~**rsi** *vr* to bring (*o* keep) o.s. up-to-date.

aggi'rare [addʒi'rare] *vt* to go round; (*fig: ingannare*) to trick; ~**rsi** *vr* to wander about; **il prezzo s'aggira sul milione** the price is around the million mark.

aggiudi'care [addʒudi'kare] *vt* to award; (*all'asta*) to knock down; ~**rsi qc** to win sth.

ag'giungere [ad'dʒundʒere] *vt* to add; **aggi'unto, a** *pp di* **aggiungere** // *ag* assistant *cpd* // *sm* assistant / *sf* addition; **sindaco aggiunto** deputy mayor.

aggius'tare [addʒus'tare] *vt* (*accomodare*) to mend, repair; (*riassettare*) to adjust; (*fig: lite*) to settle; ~**rsi** *vr* (*arrangiarsi*) to make do; (*con senso reciproco*) to come to an agreement.

agglome'rato *sm* (*di rocce*) conglomerate; (*di legno*) chipboard; ~ **urbano** built-up area.

aggrap'parsi *vr*: ~ **a** to cling to.

aggra'vare *vt* (*aumentare*) to increase; (*appesantire: anche fig*) to weigh down, make heavy; (*fig: pena*) to make worse; ~**rsi** *vr* (*fig*) to worsen, become worse.

aggrazi'ato, a [aggrat'tsjato] *ag* graceful.

aggre'dire *vt* to attack, assault.

aggre'gare *vt*: ~ **qd a qc** to admit sb to sth; ~**rsi** *vr* to join; ~**rsi a** to join, become a member of; **aggre'gato, a** *ag* associated // *sm* aggregate; **aggregato di case** block of houses.

aggressi'one *sf* aggression; (*atto*) attack, assault.

aggres'sivo, a *ag* aggressive.

aggres'sore *sm* aggressor, attacker.

aggrot'tare *vt*: ~ **le sopracciglia** to frown.

aggrovigli'are [aggroviʎ'ʎare] *vt* to

tangle; **~rsi** *vr* (*fig*) to become complicated.

aggru'marsi *vr* to clot.

agguan'tare *vt* to catch, seize.

aggu'ato *sm* trap; (*imboscata*) ambush; **tendere un ~ a qd** to set a trap for sb.

agi'ato, a [a'dʒato] *ag* (*vita*) easy; (*persona*) well-off, well-to-do.

'agile ['adʒile] *ag* agile, nimble; **agilità** *sf* agility, nimbleness.

'agio ['adʒo] *sm* ease, comfort; **~i** *smpl* comforts; **mettersi a proprio ~** to make o.s. at home o comfortable.

a'gire [a'dʒire] *vi* to act; (*esercitare un'azione*) to take effect; (TECN) to work, function; **~ su** (*influire su*) to affect; **~ contro qd** (DIR) to take action against sb.

agi'tare [adʒi'tare] *vt* (*bottiglia*) to shake; (*mano, fazzoletto*) to wave; (*fig: turbare*) to disturb; (*: incitare*) to stir (up); (*: dibattere*) to discuss; **~rsi** *vr* (*mare*) to be rough; (*malato, dormitore*) to toss and turn; (*bambino*) to fidget; (*emozionarsi*) to get upset; (POL) to agitate; **agi'tato, a** *ag* rough; restless; fidgety; upset, perturbed; **agitazi'one** *sf* agitation, (POL) unrest, agitation; **mettere in agitazione qd** to upset o distress sb.

'agli ['aʎʎi] *prep + det vedi* **a**.

'aglio ['aʎʎo] *sm* garlic.

a'gnello [aɲ'ɲɛllo] *sm* lamb.

'ago, *pl* aghi *sm* needle.

ago'nia *sf* agony.

ago'nistico, a, ci, che *ag* athletic; (*fig*) competitive.

agoniz'zare [agonid'dzare] *vi* to be dying.

agopun'tura *sf* acupuncture.

a'gosto *sm* August.

a'grario, a *ag* agrarian, agricultural; (*riforma*) land *cpd* // *sm* landowner // *sf* agriculture.

a'gricolo, a *ag* agricultural, farm *cpd*; **agricol'tore** *sm* farmer; **agricol'tura** *sf* agriculture, farming.

agri'foglio [agri'fɔʎʎo] *sm* holly.

agrimen'sore *sm* land surveyor.

'agro, a *ag* sour, sharp.

a'grume *sm* (*spesso al pl: pianta*) citrus; (*: frutto*) citrus fruit.

aguz'zare [agut'tsare] *vt* to sharpen; **~ gli orecchi** to prick up one's ears.

a'guzzo, a [a'guttso] *ag* sharp.

'ai *prep + det vedi* **a**.

'aia *sf* threshing-floor.

'Aia *sf*: **l'~** the Hague.

ai'rone *sm* heron.

aiu'ola *sf* flower bed.

aiu'tante *sm/f* assistant // *sm* (MIL) adjutant; (NAUT) master-at-arms; **~ di campo** aide-de-camp.

aiu'tare *vt* to help.

ai'uto *sm* help, assistance, aid; (*aiutante*) assistant; **venire in ~ di qd** to come to sb's aid; **~ chirurgo** assistant surgeon.

aiz'zare [ait'tsare] *vt* to incite; **~ i cani contro qd** to set the dogs on sb.

al *prep + det vedi* **a**.

'ala, *pl* 'ali *sf* wing; **fare ~** to fall back, make way; **~ destra/sinistra** (SPORT) right/left wing.

ala'bastro *sm* alabaster.

'alacre *ag* quick, brisk.

a'lano *sm* Great Dane.

a'lare *ag* wing *cpd*; **~i** *smpl* firedogs.

'alba *sf* dawn.

Alba'nia *sf*: **l'~** Albania.

'albatro *sm* albatross.

albeggi'are [albed'dʒare] (2) *vi*, *vb impers* to dawn.

albera'tura *sf* (NAUT) masts *pl*.

alberga'tore, 'trice *sm/f* hotelier, hotel-keeper.

alberghi'ero, a [alber'gjɛro] *ag* hotel *cpd*.

al'bergo, ghi *sm* hotel.

'albero *sm* tree; (NAUT) mast; (TECN) shaft; **~ di Natale** Christmas tree; **~ maestro** mainmast; **~ di trasmissione** transmission shaft.

albi'cocca, che *sf* apricot; **albi'cocco, chi** *sm* apricot tree.

'albo *sm* (*registro*) register, roll; (AMM) notice board.

'album *sm* album; **~ da disegno** sketch book.

al'bume *sm* albumen.

albu'mina *sf* albumin.

'alce *sf* [alt̮ʃe] *sm* elk.

al'chimia [al'kimia] *sf* alchemy; **alchi'mista, i** *sm* alchemist.

al'colico, a, ci, che *ag* alcoholic // *sm* alcoholic drink.

alcoliz'zato, a [alkolid'dzato] *sm/f* alcoholic.

'alcool *sm* alcohol; **alco'olico** *etc vedi* **alcolico** *etc*.

al'cova *sf* alcove.

al'cuno, a *det* (*dav sm:* **alcun** +C, V, **alcuno** + *s impura*, *gn*, *pn*, *ps*, *x*, *z*; *dav sf:* **alcuna** +C, **alcun'** +V) (*nessuno*): **non ... ~** no, not any; **~i(e)** *det pl*, *pronome pl* some, a few; **non c'è ~a fretta** there's no hurry, there isn't any hurry; **senza alcun riguardo** without any consideration.

a'letta *sf* (TECN) fin; tab.

alfa'beto *sm* alphabet.

alfi'ere *sm* standard-bearer; (MIL) ensign; (SCACCHI) bishop.

al'fine *av* finally, in the end.

'alga, ghe *sf* seaweed *q*, alga.

'algebra ['aldʒebra] *sf* algebra.

Alge'ria [aldʒe'ria] *sf*: **l'~** Algeria.

ali'ante *sm* (AER) glider.

'alibi *sm inv* alibi.

alie'nare *vt* (DIR) to alienate, transfer; (*rendere ostile*) to alienate; **~rsi qd** to alienate sb; **alie'nato, a** *ag* alienated; transferred; (*fuor di senno*) insane // *sm* lunatic, insane person; **alienazi'one** *sf* alienation; transfer; insanity.

ali'eno, a *ag* (*avverso*): **~ (da)** opposed (to), averse (to).

alimen'tare *vt* to feed; (TECN) to feed; to supply; (*fig*) to sustain // *ag* food *cpd*;

alimentazi'one sf feeding; supplying; sustaining; (gli alimenti) diet.

ali'mento sm food; ~i smpl food sg; (DIR) alimony.

a'liquota sf share; (d'imposta) rate.

alis'cafo sm hydrofoil.

'alito sm breath.

all. (abbr di allegato) encl.

'alla prep + det vedi **a.**

allacci'are [allat'tʃare] vt (scarpe) to tie, lace (up); (cintura) to do up, fasten; (due località) to link; (luce, gas) to connect; (amicizia) to form.

allaga'mento sm flooding q; flood.

allar'gare vt to widen; (vestito) to let out; (aprire) to open; (fig: dilatare) to extend.

allar'mare vt to alarm.

al'larme sm alarm; ~ aereo air-raid warning.

allat'tare vt to feed.

'alle prep + det vedi **a.**

alle'anza [alle'antsa] sf alliance.

alle'arsi vr to form an alliance; **alle'ato, a** ag allied // sm/f ally.

alle'gare vt (accludere) to enclose; (DIR: citare) to cite, adduce; (denti) to set on edge; **alle'gato, a** ag enclosed // sm enclosure; **in allegato** enclosed.

allegge'rire [alleddʒe'rire] vt to lighten, make lighter; (fig: sofferenza) to alleviate, lessen; (: lavoro, tasse) to reduce; ~rsi vr to put on lighter clothes.

allego'ria sf allegory.

alle'gria sf gaiety, cheerfulness.

al'legro, a ag cheerful, merry; (un po' brillo) merry, tipsy; (vivace: colore) bright // sm (MUS) allegro.

allena'mento sm training.

alle'nare vt, ~rsi vr to train; **allena'tore** sm (SPORT) trainer, coach.

allen'tare vt to slacken; (disciplina) to relax; ~rsi vr to become slack; (ingranaggio) to work loose.

aller'gia, 'gie [aller'dʒia] sf allergy; **al'lergico, a, ci, che** ag allergic.

alles'tire vt (cena) to prepare; (esercito, nave) to equip, fit out; (spettacolo) to stage.

allet'tare vt to lure, entice.

alleva'mento sm breeding, rearing; (luogo) stock farm.

alle'vare vt (animale) to breed, rear; (bambino) to bring up.

allevi'are vt to alleviate.

alli'bire vi (2) to be astounded.

allie'tare vt to cheer up, gladden.

alli'evo sm pupil; (apprendista) apprentice; (MIL) cadet.

alliga'tore sm alligator.

alline'are vt (persone, cose) to line up; (TIP) to align; (fig: economia, salari) to adjust, align; ~rsi vr to line up; (fig: a idee): ~rsi **a** to come into line with.

'allo prep + det vedi **a.**

al'locco, a, chi, che sm tawny owl // sm/f dolt.

allocuzi'one [allokut'tsjone] sf address, solemn speech.

al'lodola sf (sky)lark.

alloggi'are [allod'dʒare] vt to put up, give accommodation to; (MIL) to quarter; to billet // vi to live; (MIL) to be quartered; to be billeted; **al'loggio** sm lodging, accommodation; (appartamento) flat; (MIL) quarters pl; billet.

allontana'mento sm removal; dismissal.

allonta'nare vt to send away, send off; (impiegato) to dismiss; (pericolo) to avert, remove; (estraniare) to alienate; ~rsi vr: ~rsi (da) to go away (from); (estraniarsi) to become estranged (from).

al'lora av (in quel momento) then // cong (in questo caso) well then; (dunque) well then, so; **la gente d'~** people then o in those days; **da ~ in poi** from then on.

al'loro sm laurel.

'alluce ['allutʃe] sm big toe.

allucinazi'one [allutʃinat'tsjone] sf hallucination.

al'ludere vi: ~ **a** to allude to, hint at.

allu'minio sm aluminium.

allun'gare vt to lengthen; (distendere) to prolong, extend; (diluire) to water down; ~rsi vr to lengthen; (ragazzo) to stretch, grow taller; (sdraiarsi) to lie down, stretch out.

allusi'one sf hint, allusion.

alluvi'one sf flood.

alma'nacco, chi sm almanac.

al'meno av at least // cong if only; ~ **piovesse!** if only it would rain!

a'lone sm halo.

'Alpi sfpl: **le ~** the Alps.

alpi'nismo sm mountaineering, climbing; **alpi'nista, i, e** sm/f mountaineer, climber.

al'pino, a ag Alpine; mountain cpd.

al'quanto av rather, a little; ~, **a** det a certain amount of, some // pronome a certain amount, some; ~i(e) det pl, pronome pl several, quite a few.

alt escl halt!, stop!

alta'lena sf (a funi) swing; (in bilico, anche fig) seesaw.

al'tare sm altar.

alte'rare vt to alter, change; (cibo) to adulterate; (registro) to falsify; (persona) to irritate; ~rsi vr to alter; (cibo) to go bad; (persona) to lose one's temper; **alterazi'one** sf alteration, change; adulteration; falsification; annoyance.

al'terco, chi sm altercation, wrangle.

alter'nare vt, ~rsi vr to alternate; **alterna'tivo, a** ag alternating // sf (avvicendamento) alternation; (scelta) alternative; **alterna'tore** sm alternator.

al'terno, a ag alternate; **a giorni** ~i on alternate days, every other day.

al'tezza [al'tettsa] sf height; width, breadth; depth; pitch; (GEO) latitude; (titolo) highness; (fig: nobiltà) greatness; **essere all'~ di** to be on a level with; (fig) to be up to o equal to; **altez'zoso, a** ag haughty.

alti'tudine sf altitude.

'alto, a ag high; (persona) tall; (tessuto)

wide, broad; (sonno, acque) deep; (suono) high(-pitched); (GEO) upper; (: settentrionale) northern // sm top (part) // av high; (parlare) aloud, loudly; **il palazzo è ~ 20 metri** the building is 20 metres high; **il tessuto è ~ 70 cm** the material is 70 cm wide; **ad ~a voce** aloud; **a notte ~a** in the dead of night; **in ~** up, upwards; at the top; **dall'~ in o al basso** up and down; **degli ~i e bassi** (fig) ups and downs; **~a fedeltà** high fidelity, hi-fi; **~a moda** haute couture.

alto'forno sm blast furnace.

altopar'lante sm loudspeaker.

altret'tanto, a ag, pronome as much; (pl) as many // av equally; **tanti auguri! — grazie, ~** all the best! — thank you, the same to you.

'altri pronome inv (qualcuno) somebody; (: in espressioni negative) anybody; (un'altra persona) another (person).

altri'menti av otherwise.

'altro, a det other; **un ~ libro** (supplementare) another book, one more book; (diverso) another book, a different book; **un ~ another (one); l'~** the other (one); **gli ~i** (la gente) others, other people; **desidera ~?** do you want anything else?; **aiutarsi l'un l'~** to help one another; **l'uno e l'~** both (of them); **l'~ giorno** the other day; **l'~ ieri** the day before yesterday; **domani l'~** the day after tomorrow; **quest'~ mese** next month; **da un giorno all'~** from day to day; (qualsiasi giorno) any day now; **d'~a parte** on the other hand; **tra l'~** among other things; **ci mancherebbe ~!** that's all we need!; **non faccio ~ che studiare** I do nothing but study; **sei contento? — ~ che!/tutt'~!** are you pleased? — and how!/on the contrary!; **noi/voi ~i** us/you (lot).

al'tronde av: **d'~** on the other hand.

al'trove av elsewhere, somewhere else.

al'trui ag inv other people's // sm other people's belongings pl.

altru'ista, i, e ag altruistic.

al'tura sf (rialto) height, high ground; (alto mare) open sea; **pesca d'~** deep-sea fishing.

a'lunno, a sm/f pupil.

alve'are sm hive.

al'zare [al'tsare] vt to raise, lift; (issare) to hoist; (costruire) to build, erect; **~rsi** vr to rise; (dal letto) to get up; (crescere) to grow tall (o taller); **~ le spalle** to shrug one's shoulders; **~ le carte** to cut the cards; **~rsi in piedi** to stand up, get to one's feet; **al'zata** sf lifting, raising; **un'alzata di spalle** a shrug.

a'mabile ag lovable; (vino) sweet.

a'maca, che sf hammock.

amalga'mare vt, **~rsi** vr to amalgamate.

a'mante ag: **~ di** (musica etc) fond of // sm/f lover/mistress.

a'mare vt to love; (amico, musica, sport) to like.

ama'rena sf sour black cherry.

ama'rezza [ama'rettsa] sf bitterness.

a'maro, a ag bitter // sm bitterness; (liquore) bitters pl.

ambasce'ria [ambaʃʃe'ria] sf embassy.

am'bascia, sce [am'baʃʃa] sf (MED) difficulty in breathing; (fig) anguish.

ambasci'ata [ambaʃ'ʃata] sf embassy; (messaggio) message; **ambascia'tore, 'trice** sm/f ambassador/ambassadress.

ambe'due ag inv: **~ i ragazzi** both boys // pronome inv both.

ambien'tare vt to acclimatize; (romanzo, film) to set; **~rsi** vr to get used to one's surroundings.

ambi'ente sm environment; (fig: insieme di persone) milieu; (stanza) room.

ambiguità sf inv ambiguity.

am'biguo, a ag ambiguous; (persona) shady.

am'bire vt (anche: vi: **~ a**) to aspire to.

'ambito sm sphere, field.

ambizi'one [ambit'tsjone] sf ambition; **ambizi'oso, a** ag ambitious.

'ambra sf amber; **~ grigia** ambergris.

ambu'lante ag travelling, itinerant.

ambu'lanza [ambu'lantsa] sf ambulance.

ambula'torio sm (studio medico) surgery.

amenità sf inv pleasantness q; (facezia) pleasantry.

a'meno, a ag pleasant; (strano) funny, strange; (spiritoso) amusing.

A'merica sf: **l'~** America; **l'~ latina** Latin America; **ameri'cano, a** ag, sm/f American.

ame'tista sf amethyst.

a'mica sf vedi **amico**.

ami'chevole [ami'kevole] ag friendly.

ami'cizia [ami'tʃittsja] sf friendship; **~e** sfpl (amici) friends.

a'mico, a, ci, che sm/f friend; (amante) boyfriend/girlfriend; **~ del cuore o intimo** bosom friend.

'amido sm starch.

ammac'care vt (pentola) to dent; (persona) to bruise; **~rsi** vr to bruise; **ammacca'tura** sf dent; bruise.

ammae'strare vt (animale) to train; (persona) to teach.

ammai'nare vt to lower, haul down.

amma'larsi vr to fall ill; **amma'lato, a** ag ill, sick // sm/f sick person; (paziente) patient.

ammali'are vt (fig) to enchant, charm; **ammalia'tore, 'trice** sm/f enchanter/enchantress.

am'manco, chi sm (ECON) deficit.

ammanet'tare vt to handcuff.

ammas'sare vt (ammucchiare) to amass; (raccogliere) to gather together; **~rsi** vr to pile up; to gather; **am'masso** sm mass; (mucchio) pile, heap; (ECON) stockpile.

ammat'tire vi (2) to go mad.

ammaz'zare [ammat'tsare] vt to kill; **~rsi** vr (uccidersi) to kill o.s.; (rimanere ucciso) to be killed; **~rsi di lavoro** to work o.s. to death.

am'menda sf amends pl; (DIR, SPORT) fine; **fare ~ di qc** to make amends for sth.

am'messo, a pp di **ammettere** // cong: **~ che** supposing that.

am'mettere vt to admit; (riconoscere: fatto) to acknowledge, admit; (permettere) to allow, accept; (supporre) to suppose; **ammettiamo che ...** let us suppose that ... .

ammic'care vi: **~ (a)** to wink (at).

amminis'trare vt to run, manage; (REL, DIR) to administer; **amministra'tivo, a** ag administrative; **amministra'tore** sm administrator; (direttore di azienda) manager; (consigliere di società) director; **amministratore delegato** managing director; **amministrazi'one** sf management; administration.

ammiragli'ato [ammiraʎ'ʎato] sm admiralty.

ammi'raglio [ammi'raʎʎo] sm admiral.

ammi'rare vt to admire; **ammira'tore, 'trice** sm/f admirer; **ammirazi'one** sf admiration.

ammis'sibile ag admissible, acceptable.

ammissi'one sf admission; (approvazione) acknowledgment.

ammobili'are vt to furnish.

am'modo, a 'modo av properly // ag inv respectable, nice.

ammol'lare vt (panni etc) to soak.

ammo'niaca sf ammonia.

ammoni'mento sm warning; admonishment.

ammo'nire vt (avvertire) to warn; (rimproverare) to admonish; (DIR) to caution.

ammon'tare vi (2): **~ a** to amount to // sm (total) amount.

ammonticchi'are [ammontik'kjare] vt to pile up, heap up.

ammorbi'dire vt to soften.

ammortiz'zare [ammortid'dzare] vt (ECON) to pay off, amortize; (: spese d'impianto) to write off; (AUT, TECN) to absorb, deaden; **ammortizza'tore** sm (AUT, TECN) shock-absorber.

ammucchi'are [ammuk'kjare] vt, **~rsi** vr to pile up, accumulate.

ammuf'fire vi (2) to go mouldy.

ammutina'mento sm mutiny.

ammuti'narsi vr to mutiny.

ammuto'lire vi to be struck dumb.

amne'sia sf amnesia.

amnis'tia sf amnesty.

'amo sm (PESCA) hook; (fig) bait.

a'more sm love; **~i** smpl love affairs; **il tuo bambino è un ~** your baby's a darling; **fare l'~ o all'~** to make love; **per ~ o per forza** by hook or by crook; **amor proprio** self-esteem, pride; **amo'revole** ag loving, affectionate.

a'morfo, a ag amorphous; (fig: persona) lifeless.

amo'roso, a ag (affettuoso) loving, affectionate; (d'amore: sguardo) amorous; (: poesia, relazione) love cpd.

ampi'ezza [am'pjettsa] sf width, breadth; spaciousness; (fig: importanza) scale, size.

'ampio, a ag wide, broad; (spazioso) spacious; (abbondante: vestito) loose; (: gonna) full; (: spiegazione) ample, full.

am'plesso sm (eufemismo) embrace.

ampli'are vt (ingrandire) to enlarge; (allargare) to widen.

amplifi'care vt to amplify; (magnificare) to extol; **amplifica'tore** sm (TECN, MUS) amplifier.

am'polla sf (vasetto) cruet.

ampol'loso, a ag bombastic, pompous.

ampu'tare vt (MED) to amputate; **amputazi'one** sf amputation.

anabbagli'ante [anabbaʎ'ʎante] ag (AUT) dipped; **~i** smpl dipped headlights.

a'nagrafe sf (registro) register of births, marriages and deaths; (ufficio) registry office.

analfa'beta, i, e ag, sm/f illiterate.

a'nalisi sf inv analysis; (MED: esame) test; **~ grammaticale** parsing; **ana'lista, i, e** sm/f analyst; (PSIC) (psycho)analyst.

analiz'zare [analid'dzare] vt to analyse; (MED) to test.

analo'gia, 'gie [analo'dʒia] sf analogy.

a'nalogo, a, ghi, ghe ag analogous.

'ananas sm inv pineapple.

anar'chia [anar'kia] sf anarchy; **a'narchico, a, ci, che** ag anarchic(al) // sm/f anarchist.

ana'tema, i sm anathema.

anato'mia sf anatomy; **ana'tomico, a, ci, che** ag anatomical; (sedile) contoured.

'anatra sf duck.

'anca, che sf (ANAT) hip; (ZOOL) haunch.

'anche ['anke] av also; (perfino) even; **vengo anch'io!** I'm coming too!; **~ se** even if.

an'cora av still; (di nuovo) again; (di più) some more; (: in frasi negative) any more; (persino): **~ più forte** even stronger; **non ~ not yet**; **~ un po'** a little more; (di tempo) a little longer.

'ancora sf anchor; **gettare/levare l'~** to cast/weigh anchor; **anco'raggio** sm anchorage; **anco'rare** vt, **ancorarsi** vr to anchor.

anda'mento sm progress, movement; course; state.

an'dante ag (corrente) current; (di poco pregio) cheap, second-rate // sm (MUS) andante.

an'dare sm (l'andatura) walk, gait; **a lungo ~** in the long run // vi (2) to go; (essere adatto): **~ a** to suit; (moneta) to be legal tender; (piacere): **il suo comportamento non mi va** I don't like the way he behaves; **ti va di andare al cinema?** do you feel like going to the cinema?; **andarsene** to go away; **questa camicia va lavata** this shirt needs a wash o should be washed; **~ a cavallo** to ride; **~ in macchina/aereo** to go by car/plane; **~ a male** to go bad; **come va? — bene, grazie!** how are you? — fine, thanks!; **ne va della nostra vita** our lives are at stake; **an'data** *sf* going; (*viaggio*) outward journey; **biglietto di sola andata/di andata e ritorno** single/return ticket; **anda'tura** *sf* (*modo di andare*) walk, gait; (*SPORT*) pace; (*NAUT*) tack.

an'dazzo [an'dattso] *sm* (*peg*) current (bad) practice.

andirivi'eni *sm inv* coming and going.

'andito *sm* corridor, passage.

an'drone *sm* entrance-hall.

a'neddoto *sm* anecdote.

ane'lare *vi*: ~ **a** (*fig*) to long for, yearn for.

a'nelito *sm* (*fig*): ~ **di** longing *o* yearning for.

a'nello *sm* ring; (*di catena*) link.

ane'mia *sf* anaemia; **a'nemico, a, ci, che** *ag* anaemic.

a'nemone *sm* anemone.

aneste'sia *sf* anaesthesia; **anes'tetico, a, ci, che** *ag, sm* anaesthetic.

an'fibio, a *ag* amphibious.

anfite'atro *sm* amphitheatre.

an'fratto *sm* ravine.

an'gelico, a, ci, che [an'dʒeliko] *ag* angelic(al).

'angelo ['andʒelo] *sm* angel; ~ **custode** guardian angel.

anghe'ria [ange'ria] *sf* vexation.

an'gina [an'dʒina] *sf* angina.

angli'cano, a *ag* Anglican.

angli'cismo [angli'tʃizmo] *sm* anglicism.

anglo'sassone *ag* Anglo-Saxon.

ango'lare *ag* angular.

'angolo *sm* corner; (*MAT*) angle.

an'goscia, sce [an'gɔʃʃa] *sf* deep anxiety, anguish *q*; (*d'angoscia*) anguished; (*che dà angoscia*) distressing, painful.

angu'illa *sf* eel.

an'guria *sf* watermelon.

an'gustia *sf* (*ansia*) anguish, distress; (*povertà*) poverty, want.

angusti'are *vt* to distress; ~**rsi** *vr*: ~**rsi (per)** to worry (about).

an'gusto, a *ag* (*stretto*) narrow; (*fig*) mean, petty.

'anice ['anitʃe] *sm* (*CUC*) aniseed; (*BOT*) anise.

'anima *sf* soul; (*fig: persona*) person, soul; (: *abitante*) inhabitant.

ani'male *sm, ag* animal.

ani'mare *vt* to give life to, liven up; (*incoraggiare*) to encourage; ~**rsi** *vr* to become animated, come to life; **ani'mato, a** *ag* animate; (*vivace*) lively, animated; (: *strada*) busy; **anima'tore, 'trice** *sm/f* guiding spirit; (*CINEMA*) animator; (*di festa*) life and soul; **animazi'one** *sf* liveliness; (*di strada*) bustle; (*CINEMA*) animation.

'animo *sm* (*mente*) mind; (*cuore*) heart; (*coraggio*) courage; (*disposizione*) character, disposition; (*inclinazione*) inclination; (*proposito*) intention; **avere in ~ di fare qc** to intend *o* have a mind to do sth; **fare qc di buon/mal ~** to do sth

willingly/unwillingly; **perdersi d'~** to lose heart; **animosità** *sf* animosity; **ani'moso, a** *ag* hostile; (*coraggioso*) spirited, bold.

'anitra *sf* = **anatra.**

anna'cquare *vt* to water down, dilute.

annaffi'are *vt* to water; **annaffia'toio** *sm* watering can.

an'nali *smpl* annals.

an'nata *sf* year; (*importo annuo*) annual amount.

annebbi'are *vt* (*fig*) to cloud; ~**rsi** *vr* (*tempo*) to become foggy, become misty; (*vista*) to become dim.

annega'mento *sm* drowning.

anne'gare *vt, vi* (*2*) to drown; ~**rsi** *vr* (*accidentalmente*) to drown; (*deliberatamente*) to drown o.s.

anne'rire *vt* to blacken // *vi* (*2*) to become black.

an'nessi *smpl* (*edifici*) outbuildings; ~ **e connessi** appurtenances.

annessi'one *sf* (*POL*) annexation.

an'nesso, a *pp di* **annettere.**

an'nettere *vt* (*POL*) to annex; (*accludere*) to attach.

annichi'lare, annichi'lire [anniki'lare, anniki'lire] *vt* to annihilate.

anni'darsi *vr* to nest.

annienta'mento *sm* annihilation, destruction.

annien'tare *vt* to annihilate, destroy.

anniver'sario, a *ag*: **giorno ~** anniversary // *sm* anniversary.

'anno *sm* year; ~**i fa** years ago.

anno'dare *vt* to knot, tie; (*fig: rapporto*) to form.

annoi'are *vt* to bore; (*seccare*) to annoy; ~**rsi** *vr* to be bored; to be annoyed.

anno'tare *vt* (*registrare*) to note, note down; (*commentare*) to annotate; **annotazi'one** *sf* note; annotation.

annove'rare *vt* to number.

annu'ale *ag* annual.

annu'ario *sm* yearbook.

annu'ire *vi* to nod; (*acconsentire*) to agree.

annulla'mento *sm* annihilation, destruction; cancellation; annulment; quashing.

annul'lare *vt* to annihilate, destroy; (*contratto, francobollo*) to cancel; (*matrimonio*) to annul; (*sentenza*) to quash; (*risultati*) to declare void.

annunci'are [annun'tʃare] *vt* to announce; (*dar segni rivelatori*) to herald; **annuncia'tore, 'trice** *sm/f* (*RADIO, TV*) announcer; **l'Annunciazi'one** *sf* the Annunciation.

an'nuncio [an'nuntʃo] *sm* announcement; (*fig*) sign; ~ **pubblicitario** advertisement; ~**i economici** classified advertisements, small ads.

'annuo, a *ag* annual, yearly.

annu'sare *vt* to sniff, smell; (*fig*) to smell, suspect.

anoma'lia *sf* anomaly.

a'nomalo, a *ag* anomalous.

a'nonimo, a *ag* anonymous // *sm* (*autore*) anonymous writer (*o* painter *etc*).

anor'male *ag* abnormal // *sm/f* subnormal person; (*eufemismo*) homosexual; **anormalità** *sf inv* abnormality.

'ansa *sf* (*manico*) handle; (*di fiume*) bend, loop.

'ansia, ansietà *sf* anxiety.

ansi'mare *vi* to pant.

ansi'oso, a *ag* anxious.

antago'nismo *sm* antagonism; **antago-'nista, i, e** *sm/f* antagonist.

an'tartico, a, ci, che *ag* Antarctic // *sm*: l'A~ the Antarctic.

antece'dente [antetʃe'dɛnte] *ag* preceding, previous.

ante'fatto *sm* previous events *pl*; previous history.

antegu'erra *sm* pre-war period.

ante'nato *sm* ancestor, forefather.

an'tenna *sf* (*RADIO*, *TV*) aerial; (*ZOOL*) antenna, feeler; (*NAUT*) yard.

ante'prima *sf* preview.

anteri'ore *ag* (*ruota*, *zampa*) front; (*fatti*) previous, preceding.

antia'ereo, a *ag* anti-aircraft.

antibi'otico, a, ci, che *ag*, *sm* antibiotic.

anti'camera *sf* anteroom; **fare** ~ to wait (for an audience).

antichità [antiki'ta] *sf inv* antiquity; (*oggetto*) antique.

antici'clone [antitʃi'klone] *sm* anticyclone.

antici'pare [antitʃi'pare] *vt* (*consegna*, *visita*) to bring forward, anticipate; (*somma di denaro*) to pay in advance; (*notizia*) to disclose // *vi* to be ahead of time; **anticipazi'one** *sf* anticipation; (*di notizia*) advance information; (*somma di denaro*) advance; **an'ticipo** *sm* anticipation; (*di denaro*) advance; **in anticipo** early, in advance.

an'tico, a, chi, che *ag* (*quadro*, *mobili*) antique; (*dell'antichità*) ancient.

anticoncezio'nale [antikontʃettsjo'nale] *sm* contraceptive.

an'tidoto *sm* antidote.

An'tille *sfpl*: le ~ the West Indies.

an'tilope *sf* antelope.

anti'pasto *sm* hors d'œuvre.

antipa'tia *sf* antipathy, dislike; **anti-'patico, a, ci, che** *ag* unpleasant, disagreeable.

an'tipodi *smpl*: gli ~ the antipodes.

antiquari'ato *sm* antique trade.

anti'quario *sm* antique dealer.

anti'quato, a *ag* antiquated, old-fashioned.

anti'settico, a, ci, che *ag*, *sm* antiseptic.

an'titesi *sf* antithesis.

antolo'gia, 'gie [antolo'dʒia] *sf* anthology.

'antro *sm* cavern; (*fig*) hole.

antro'pofago, gi *sm* cannibal.

antropolo'gia [antropolo'dʒia] *sf* anthropology.

anu'lare *ag* ring *cpd* // *sm* ring finger.

'anzi ['antsi] *av* (*invece*) on the contrary; (*o meglio*) or rather, or better still; (*di più*) indeed; ~ **che** = **anziché**.

anzianità [antsjani'ta] *sf* old age; (*AMM*) seniority.

anzi'ano, a [an'tsjano] *ag* old; (*AMM*) senior // *sm/f* old person; senior member.

anziché [antsi'ke] *cong* rather than.

anzi'tutto [antsi'tutto] *av* first of all.

apa'tia *sf* apathy, indifference; **a'patico, a, ci, che** *ag* apathetic, indifferent.

'ape *sf* bee.

aperi'tivo *sm* aperitif.

a'perto, a *pp di* aprire // *ag* open; **all'**~ in the open (air).

aper'tura *sf* opening; (*ampiezza*) width, spread; (*POL*) approach; (*FOT*) aperture; ~ **alare** wing span; ~ **mentale** open-mindedness.

'apice ['apitʃe] *sm* apex; (*fig*) height.

apicol'tore *sm* beekeeper.

a'polide *ag* stateless.

apoples'sia *sf* (*MED*) apoplexy.

a'postolo *sm* apostle.

a'postrofo *sm* apostrophe.

appa'gare *vt* to satisfy; ~**rsi** *vr*: ~**rsi di** to be satisfied with.

appai'are *vt* to couple, pair.

ap'palto *sm* (*COMM*) contract; **dare/prendere in** ~ **un lavoro** to let out/undertake a job on contract.

appan'nare *vt* (*vetro*) to mist; (*metallo*) to tarnish; (*vista*) to dim; ~**rsi** *vr* to mist over; to tarnish; to grow dim.

appa'rato *sm* (*messinscena*) display; (*ANAT*, *TECN*) apparatus; ~ **scenico** (*TEATRO*) props *pl*.

apparecchi'are [apparek'kjare] *vt* to prepare; (*tavola*) to set // *vi* to set the table.

appa'recchio [appa'rekkjo] *sm* piece of apparatus, device; (*aeroplano*) aircraft *inv*; ~ **televisivo/telefonico** television set/telephone.

appa'rente *ag* apparent; **appa'renza** *sf* appearance; **in** *o* **all'apparenza** apparently, to all appearances.

appa'rire *vi* (2) to appear; (*sembrare*) to seem, appear; **appari'scente** *ag* (*colore*) garish, gaudy; (*bellezza*) striking; **appari-zi'one** *sf* apparition.

apparta'mento *sm* flat, apartment (*US*).

appar'tarsi *vr* to withdraw; **appar'tato, a** *ag* secluded.

apparte'nere *vi*: ~ **a** to belong to.

appassio'nare *vt* to thrill; (*commuovere*) to move; ~**rsi a qc** to take a great interest in sth; to be deeply moved by sth; **appassio'nato, a** *ag* passionate; **appassionato per la musica** passionately fond of music.

appas'sire *vi* (2) to wither.

appel'lare *vi* (*DIR*) to appeal; ~**rsi** *vr* (*ricorrere*): ~**rsi a** to appeal to; (*DIR*): ~**rsi contro** to appeal against; **ap'pello** *sm* roll-call; (*implorazione*, *DIR*) appeal;

fare **appello a** to appeal to.

ap'pena av (a stento) hardly, scarcely; (solamente, da poco) just // cong as soon as; ~ **furono arrivati ...** as soon as they had arrived ...; ~ ... **che** o **quando** no sooner ... than.

ap'pendere vt to hang (up).

appen'dice [appen'ditʃe] sf appendix.

appendi'cite [appendi'tʃite] sf appendicitis.

Appen'nini smpl: **gli** ~ the Apennines.

appesan'tire vt to make heavy; ~**rsi** vr to grow stout.

ap'peso, a pp di **appendere**.

appe'tito sm appetite; **appeti'toso, a** ag appetising; (fig) attractive, desirable.

appia'nare vt to level; (fig) to smooth away, iron out.

appiat'tire vt to flatten; ~**rsi** vr to become flatter; (farsi piatto) to flatten o.s.; ~**rsi al suolo** to lie flat on the ground.

appicci'care [appittʃi'kare] vt to stick; (fig): ~ **qc a qd** to palm sth off on sb; ~**rsi** vt to stick; (fig: persona) to cling.

appigli'arsi [appiʎ'ʎarsi] vr: ~ **a** (afferrarsi) to take hold of; (fig) to cling to; **ap'piglio** sm hold; (fig) pretext.

appiso'larsi vr to doze off.

applau'dire vt, vi to applaud; **ap'plauso** sm applause.

appli'care vt to apply; (regolamento) to enforce; ~**rsi** vr to apply o.s.; **applica-zi'one** sf application; enforcement.

appoggi'are [appod'dʒare] vt (mettere contro): ~ **qc a qc** to lean o rest sth against sth; (fig: sostenere) to support; ~**rsi** vr: ~**rsi a** to lean against; (fig) to rely upon; **ap'poggio** sm support.

ap'porre vt to affix.

appor'tare vt to bring.

ap'posito, a ag appropriate.

ap'posta av on purpose, deliberately.

appos'tare vt to lie in wait for; ~**rsi** vr to lie in wait.

ap'prendere vt (imparare) to learn; (comprendere) to grasp.

appren'dista, i, e sm/f apprentice.

apprensi'one sf apprehension; **appren-'sivo, a** ag apprehensive.

ap'presso av (accanto, vicino) close by, near; (dietro) behind; (dopo, più tardi) after, later; ~ **a** prep (vicino a) near, close to.

appres'tare vt to prepare, get ready; ~**rsi** vr: ~**rsi a fare qc** to prepare o get ready to do sth.

apprez'zabile [appret'tsabile] ag noteworthy, significant.

apprezza'mento [apprettsa'mento] sm appreciation; (giudizio) opinion.

apprez'zare [appret'tsare] vt to appreciate.

ap'proccio [ap'prottʃo] sm approach.

appro'dare vi (NAUT) to land; (fig): **non** ~ **a nulla** to come to nothing; **ap'prodo** sm landing; (luogo) landing-place.

approfit'tare vi: ~ **di** to make the most of, profit by.

approfon'dire vt to deepen; (fig) to study in depth.

appropri'ato, a ag appropriate.

approssi'marsi vr: ~ **a** to approach.

approssima'tivo, a ag approximate, rough; (impreciso) inexact, imprecise.

appro'vare vt (condotta, azione) to approve of; (candidato) to pass; (progetto di legge) to approve; **approvazi'one** sf approval.

approvvigiona'mento [approvvidʒona-'mento] sm supplying; stocking up; ~**i** smpl (MIL) supplies.

approvvigio'nare [approvvidʒo'nare] vt to supply; ~**rsi** vr to lay in provisions, stock up; ~ **qd di qc** to supply sb with sth.

appunta'mento sm appointment; (amoroso) date; **darsi** ~ to arrange to meet (one another).

appun'tare vt (rendere aguzzo) to sharpen; (fissare) to pin, fix; (annotare) to note down.

ap'punto sm note; (rimprovero) reproach // av (proprio) exactly, just; **per l'** ~!, ~! exactly!

appu'rare vt to check, verify.

apribot'tiglie [apribot'tiʎʎe] sm inv bottleopener.

a'prile sm April.

a'prire vt to open; (via, cadavere) to open up; (gas, luce, acqua) to turn on // vi to open; ~**rsi** vr to open; ~**rsi a qd** to confide in sb, open one's heart to sb.

apris'catole sm inv tin opener.

a'quario sm = **acquario**.

'aquila sf (ZOOL) eagle; (fig) genius.

aqui'lone sm (giocattolo) kite; (vento) North wind.

A'rabia 'Saudita sf: l'~ Saudi Arabia.

'arabo, a ag, sm/f Arab // sm Arabic.

a'rachide [a'rakide] sf peanut.

ara'gosta sf crayfish; lobster.

a'raldica sf heraldry.

a'raldo sm herald.

a'rancia, ce [a'rantʃa] sf orange; **aran-ci'ata** sf orangeade; **a'rancio** sm (BOT) orange tree; (colore) orange // ag inv (colore) orange.

a'rare vt to plough.

a'ratro sm plough.

a'razzo [a'rattso] sm tapestry.

arbi'traggio [arbi'traddʒo] sm (SPORT) refereeing; umpiring; (DIR) arbitration.

arbi'trare vt (SPORT) to referee; to umpire; (DIR) to arbitrate.

arbi'trario, a ag arbitrary.

ar'bitrio sm will; (abuso, sopruso) arbitrary act.

'arbitro sm arbiter, judge; (DIR) arbitrator; (SPORT) referee; (: TENNIS, CRICKET) umpire.

ar'busto sm shrub.

'arca, che sf (sarcofago) sarcophagus; l'~ **di Noè** Noah's ark.

ar'caico, a, ci, che *ag* archaic.
ar'cangelo [ar'kandʒelo] *sm* archangel.
ar'cano, a *ag* arcane, mysterious.
ar'cata *sf* (ARCHIT, ANAT) arch; (*ordine di archi*) arcade.
archeolo'gia [arkeolo'dʒia] *sf* archaeology; **arche'ologo, a, gi, ghe** *sm/f* archaeologist.
ar'chetto [ar'ketto] *sm* (MUS) bow.
archi'tetto [arki'tetto] *sm* architect; **architet'tura** *sf* architecture.
ar'chivio [ar'kivjo] *sm* archives *pl*.
arci'ere [ar'tʃɛre] *sm* archer.
ar'cigno, a [ar'tʃiɲɲo] *ag* grim, severe.
arci'pelago, ghi [artʃi'pɛlago] *sm* archipelago.
arci'vescovo [artʃi'veskovo] *sm* archbishop.
'arco *sm* (arma, MUS) bow; (ARCHIT) arch; (MAT) arc.
arcoba'leno *sm* rainbow.
arcu'ato, a *ag* curved, bent; **dalle gambe ~e** bow-legged.
ar'dente *ag* burning; (*fig*) burning, ardent.
'ardere *vt, vi* (2) to burn.
ar'desia *sf* slate.
ar'dire *vi* to dare; **ar'dito, a** *ag* brave, daring, bold; (*sfacciato*) bold.
ar'dore *sm* blazing heat; (*fig*) ardour, fervour.
'arduo, a *ag* arduous, difficult.
'area *sf* area; (EDIL) land, ground.
a'rena *sf* arena; (*sabbia*) sand.
are'narsi *vr* to run aground.
areo'plano *sm* = **aeroplano.**
'argano *sm* winch.
argente'ria [ardʒente'ria] *sf* silverware, silver.
argenti'ere [ardʒen'tjɛre] *sm* silversmith.
Argen'tina [ardʒen'tina] *sf*: **l'~** Argentina.
ar'gento [ar'dʒɛnto] *sm* silver; **~ vivo** quicksilver.
ar'gilla [ar'dʒilla] *sf* clay.
'argine ['ardʒine] *sm* embankment, bank; (*diga*) dyke.
argomen'tare *vi* to argue.
argo'mento *sm* argument; (*motivo*) motive; (*materia, tema*) subject.
argu'ire *vt* to deduce.
ar'guto, a *ag* sharp, quick-witted; (*spiritoso*) witty; **ar'guzia** *sf* wit; (*battuta*) witty remark.
'aria *sf* air; (*espressione, aspetto*) air, look; (MUS: *melodia*) tune; (: *di opera*) aria; **mandare all'~** qc to ruin o upset sth; **all'~ aperta** in the open (air).
'arido, a *ag* arid.
arieggi'are [arjed'dʒare] *vt* (*cambiare aria*) to air; (*imitare*) to imitate.
ari'ete *sm* ram; (MIL) battering ram; (*dello zodiaco*): A~ Aries.
a'ringa, ghe *sf* herring *inv*.
'arista *sf* (CUC) chine of pork.
aristo'cratico, a, ci, che *ag* aristocratic.
aristocra'zia [aristokrat'tsia] *sf* aristocracy.

arit'metica *sf* arithmetic.
arlec'chino [arlek'kino] *sm* harlequin.
'arma, i *sf* weapon, arm; (*parte dell'esercito*) arm; **chiamare alle ~i** to call up; **sotto le ~i** in the army (*o* forces); **alle ~i!** to arms!; **~ da fuoco** firearm.
ar'madio *sm* cupboard; (*per abiti*) wardrobe.
armamen'tario *sm* equipment, instruments *pl*.
arma'mento *sm* (MIL) armament; (: *materiale*) arms *pl*, weapons *pl*; (NAUT) fitting out; manning.
ar'mare *vt* to arm; (*arma da fuoco*) to cock; (NAUT: *nave*) to rig, fit out; to man; (EDIL: *volta, galleria*) to prop up, shore up; **~rsi** *vr* to arm o.s.; (MIL) to take up arms; **ar'mata** *sf* (MIL) army; (NAUT) fleet; **arma'tore** *sm* shipowner; **arma'tura** *sf* (*struttura di sostegno*) framework; (*impalcatura*) scaffolding; (STORIA) armour *q*, suit of armour.
armis'tizio [armis'tittsjo] *sm* armistice.
armo'nia *sf* harmony; **ar'monico, a, ci, che** *ag* harmonic; (*fig*) harmonious; **armoni'oso, a** *ag* harmonious.
armoniz'zare [armonid'dzare] *vt* to harmonize; (*colori, abiti*) to match // *vi* to be in harmony; to match.
ar'nese *sm* tool, implement; (*oggetto indeterminato*) thing, contraption; **male in ~** (*malvestito*) badly dressed; (*di salute malferma*) in poor health; (*di condizioni economiche*) down-at-heel.
'arnia *sf* hive.
a'roma, i *sm* aroma; fragrance; **~i** *smpl* herbs and spices; **aro'matico, a, ci, che** *ag* aromatic; (*cibo*) spicy.
'arpa *sf* (MUS) harp.
ar'peggio [ar'pedd3o] *sm* (MUS) arpeggio.
ar'pia *sf* (*anche fig*) harpy.
arpi'one *sm* (*gancio*) hook; (*cardine*) hinge; (PESCA) harpoon.
arrabat'tarsi *vr* to do all one can, strive.
arrabbi'are *vi* (2) (*cane*) to be affected with rabies; **~rsi** *vr* (*essere preso dall'ira*) to get angry, fly into a rage; **arrabbi'ato, a** *ag* rabid, with rabies; furious, angry.
arrampi'carsi *vr* to climb (up).
arran'giare [arran'dʒare] *vt* to arrange; **~rsi** *vr* to manage, do the best one can.
arre'care *vt* to bring; (*causare*) to cause.
arreda'mento *sm* (*studio*) interior design; (*mobili etc*) furnishings *pl*.
arre'dare *vt* to furnish; **ar'redo** *sm* fittings *pl*, furnishings *pl*.
ar'rendersi *vr* to surrender.
arres'tare *vt* (*fermare*) to stop, halt; (*catturare*) to arrest; **~rsi** *vr* (*fermarsi*) to stop; **ar'resto** *sm* (*cessazione*) stopping; (*fermata*) stop; (*cattura, MED*) arrest; **subire un arresto** to come to a stop *o* standstill; **mettere agli arresti** to place under arrest.
arre'trare *vt, vi* (2) to withdraw; **arre'trato, a** *ag* (*lavoro*) behind schedule;

(*paese, bambino*) backward; (*numero di giornale*) back *cpd*.

arric'chire [arrik'kire] *vt* to enrich; **~rsi** *vr* to become rich.

arricci'are [arrit'tʃare] *vt* to curl; **~ il naso** to turn up one's nose.

ar'ringa, ghe *sf* harangue; (*DIR*) address by counsel.

arrischi'are [arris'kjare] *vt* to risk; **~rsi** *vr* to venture, dare; **arrischi'ato, a** *ag* risky; (*temerario*) reckless, rash.

arri'vare *vi* (2) to arrive; (*accadere*) to happen, occur; **~ a** (*livello, grado etc*) to reach; **lui arriva a Roma alle 7** he gets to *o* arrives at Rome at 7; **non ci arrivo** I can't reach it; (*fig: non capisco*) I can't understand it.

arrive'derci [arrive'dertʃi] *escl* goodbye!

arrive'derla *escl* (*forma di cortesia*) goodbye!

arri'vista, i, e *sm/f* go-getter.

ar'rivo *sm* arrival; (*SPORT*) finish, finishing-line.

arro'gante *ag* arrogant.

arro'lare *vb* **= arruolare.**

arros'sire *vi* (*per vergogna, timidità*) to blush, flush; (*per gioia, rabbia*) to flush.

arros'tire *vt* to roast; (*pane*) to toast; (*ai ferri*) to grill.

ar'rosto *sm, ag inv* roast.

arro'tare *vt* to sharpen; (*investire con un veicolo*) to run over.

arroto'lare *vt* to roll up.

arroton'dare *vt* (*forma, oggetto*) to round; (*stipendio*) to add to; (*somma*) to round off.

arruf'fare *vt* to ruffle; (*fili*) to tangle; (*fig: questione*) to confuse.

arruggi'nire [arruddʒi'nire] *vt* to rust; **~rsi** *vr* to rust; (*fig*) to become rusty.

arruola'mento *sm* (*MIL*) enlistment.

arruo'lare (*MIL*) *vt* to enlist; **~rsi** *vr* to enlist, join up.

arse'nale *sm* (*MIL*) arsenal; (*cantiere navale*) dockyard.

ar'senico *sm* arsenic.

'arso, a *pp di* **ardere** // *ag* (*bruciato*) burnt; (*arido*) dry; **ar'sura** *sf* (*calore opprimente*) burning heat; (*siccità*) drought.

'arte *sf* art; (*abilità*) skill.

ar'tefice [ar'tefitʃe] *sm/f* crafts-man/woman; (*autore*) author.

ar'teria *sf* artery.

'artico, a, ci, che *ag* Arctic.

artico'lare *ag* (*ANAT*) of the joints, articular // *vt* to articulate; (*suddividere*) to divide, split up.

ar'ticolo *sm* article; **~ di fondo** (*STAMPA*) leader, leading article.

'Artide *sf*: **l'~** the Arctic.

artifici'ale [artifi'tʃale] *ag* artificial.

arti'ficio [arti'fitʃo] *sm* (*espediente*) trick, artifice; (*ricerca di effetto*) artificiality; **artifi'cioso, a** *ag* cunning; (*non spontaneo*) affected.

artigia'nato [artidʒa'nato] *sm* craftsmanship; craftsmen *pl*.

artigi'ano, a [arti'dʒano] *sm/f* craftsman/woman.

artiglie'ria [artiʎʎe'ria] *sf* artillery.

ar'tiglio [ar'tiʎʎo] *sm* claw; (*di rapaci*) talon.

ar'tista, i, e *sm/f* artist; **ar'tistico, a, ci, che** *ag* artistic.

'arto *sm* (*ANAT*) limb.

ar'trite *sf* (*MED*) arthritis.

ar'zillo, a [ar'dzillo] *ag* lively, sprightly.

a'scella [aʃ'ʃɛlla] *sf* (*ANAT*) armpit.

ascen'dente [aʃʃen'dɛnte] *sm* ancestor; (*fig*) ascendancy.

ascensi'one [aʃʃen'sjone] *sf* (*ALPINISMO*) ascent; (*REL*): **l'A~** the Ascension.

ascen'sore [aʃʃen'sore] *sm* lift.

a'scesa [aʃ'ʃesa] *sf* ascent; (*al trono*) accession.

a'scesso [aʃ'ʃɛsso] *sm* (*MED*) abscess.

a'sceta, i [aʃ'ʃɛta] *sm* ascetic.

'ascia, pl 'asce [ˈaʃʃa] *sf* axe.

asciugaca'pelli [aʃʃugaka'pelli] *sm* hair-drier.

asciuga'mano [aʃʃuga'mano] *sm* towel.

asciu'gare [aʃʃu'gare] *vt* to dry; **~rsi** *vr* to dry o.s.; (*diventare asciutto*) to dry.

asci'utto, a [aʃ'ʃutto] *ag* dry; (*fig: magro*) lean; (*: burbero*) curt; **restare a bocca ~a** (*fig*) to be disappointed; **restare all'~** (*fig*) to be left penniless.

ascol'tare *vt* to listen to; **ascolta'tore, 'trice** *sm/f* listener; **as'colto** *sm*: **essere** *o* **stare in ascolto** to be listening; **dare** *o* **prestare ascolto (a)** to pay attention (to).

as'falto *sm* asphalt.

asfis'sia *sf* asphyxia, asphyxiation.

'Asia *sf*: **l'A~** Asia; **asi'atico, a, ci, che** *ag, sm/f* Asiatic, Asian.

a'silo *sm* refuge, sanctuary; **~ (d'infanzia)** nursery(-school); **~ politico** political asylum.

'asino *sm* donkey, ass.

'asma *sf* asthma.

'asola *sf* buttonhole.

as'parago, gi *sm* asparagus *q*.

asperità *sf inv* roughness *q*; (*fig*) harshness *q*.

aspet'tare *vt* to wait for; (*anche COMM*) to await; (*aspettarsi*) to expect // *vi* to wait; **~rsi** *vr* to expect; **~ un bambino** to be expecting (a baby); **questo non me l'aspettavo** I wasn't expecting this; **aspetta'tiva** *sf* wait; expectation; **inferiore all'aspettativa** worse than expected.

as'petto *sm* (*apparenza*) aspect, appearance, look; (*punto di vista*) point of view.

aspi'rante *ag* (*attore etc*) aspiring // *sm/f* candidate, applicant.

aspira'polvere *sm inv* vacuum cleaner.

aspi'rare *vt* (*respirare*) to breathe in, inhale; (*sog: apparecchi*) to suck (up) // *vi*: **~ a** to aspire to; **aspira'tore** *sm* extractor fan.

aspi'rina *sf* aspirin.

aspor'tare *vt* (*anche* MED) to remove, take away.

as'prezza [as'prettsa] *sf* sourness, tartness; pungency; harshness; roughness; rugged nature.

'aspro, a *ag* (*sapore*) sour, tart; (*odore*) acrid, pungent; (*voce, clima, fig*) harsh; (*superficie*) rough; (*paesaggio*) rugged.

assaggi'are [assad'dʒare] *vt* to taste; **as-'saggio** *sm* tasting; (*piccola quantità*) taste; (*campione*) sample.

as'sai *av* (*abbastanza*) enough; (*molto*) a lot, much // *ag inv* (*quantità*) a lot of, much; (*numero*) a lot of, many; ~ **contento** very pleased.

assa'lire *vt* to attack, assail.

as'salto *sm* attack, assault.

assassi'nare *vt* to murder; to assassinate; (*fig*) to ruin; **assas'sinio** *sm* murder; assassination; **assas'sino, a** *ag* murderous // *sm/f* murderer; assassin.

'asse *sm* (TECN) axle; (MAT) axis // *sf* board; ~ **f da stiro** ironing board.

assedi'are *vt* to besiege; **as'sedio** *sm* siege.

asse'gnare [assep'ɲare] *vt* to assign, allot.

as'segno [as'seɲɲo] *sm* allowance; (*anche*: ~ **bancario**) cheque; **contro** ~ cash on delivery; ~ **circolare** bank draft; ~ **sbarrato** crossed cheque; ~ **a vuoto** dud cheque; ~**i familiari** family allowance *sg*.

assem'blea *sf* assembly.

assen'nato, a *ag* sensible.

as'senso *sm* assent, consent.

as'sente *ag* absent; (*fig*) faraway, vacant; **as'senza** *sf* absence.

asses'sore *sm* (POL) councillor.

assesta'mento *sm* (*sistemazione*) arrangement; (EDIL) settlement.

asses'tare *vt* (*mettere in ordine*) to put in order, arrange; ~**rsi** *vr* to settle in; ~ **un colpo a qd** to deal sb a blow.

asse'tato, a *ag* thirsty, parched.

as'setto *sm* order, arrangement; (NAUT, AER) trim.

assicu'rare *vt* (*accertare*) to ensure; (*infondere certezza*) to assure; (*fermare, legare*) to make fast, secure; (*fare un contratto di assicurazione*) to insure; ~**rsi** *vr* (*accertarsi*): ~**rsi (di)** to make sure (of); (*contro il furto etc*): ~**rsi (contro)** to insure o.s. (against); **assicurazi'one** *sf* assurance; insurance.

assidera'mento *sm* exposure.

as'siduo, a *ag* (*costante*) assiduous; (*regolare*) regular.

assi'eme *av* (*insieme*) together; ~ **a** *prep* (together) with.

assil'lare *vt* to pester, torment.

as'sillo *sm* (*fig*) worrying thought.

assimi'lare *vt* to assimilate.

as'sise *sfpl* (DIR) assizes; **Corte f d'A~** Court of Assizes.

assis'tente *sm/f* assistant; ~ **sociale** social worker.

assis'tenza [assis'tɛntsa] *sf* assistance, help; treatment; (*presenza*) presence; ~ **sociale** welfare services *pl*.

as'sistere *vt* (*aiutare*) to assist, help; (*curare*) to treat // *vi*: ~ **(a qc)** (*essere presente*) to be present (at sth), to attend (sth).

'asso *sm* ace; **piantare qd in** ~ to leave sb in the lurch.

associ'are [asso'tʃare] *vt* to associate; (*rendere partecipe*): ~ **qd a** (*affari*) to take sb into partnership in; (*partito*) to make sb a member of; ~**rsi** *vr* to enter into partnership; ~**rsi a** to become a member of, join; (*dolori, gioie*) to share in.

associazi'one [assotʃat'tsjone] *sf* association; (COMM) association, society.

assogget'tare [assoddʒet'tare] *vt* to subject, subjugate.

asso'lato, a *ag* sunny.

assol'dare *vt* to recruit.

as'solto, a *pp di* **assolvere.**

assoluta'mente *av* absolutely.

asso'luto, a *ag* absolute.

assoluzi'one [assolut'tsjone] *sf* (DIR) acquittal; (REL) absolution.

as'solvere *vt* (DIR) to acquit; (REL) to absolve; (*adempiere*) to carry out, perform.

assomigli'are [assomiʎ'ʎare] *vi*: ~ **a** to resemble, look like.

asso'pirsi *vr* to doze off.

assor'bente *ag* absorbent // *sm*: ~ **igienico** sanitary towel.

assor'bire *vt* to absorb; (*fig: far proprio*) to assimilate.

assor'dare *vt* to deafen.

assorti'mento *sm* assortment.

assor'tito, a *ag* assorted; matched; matching.

as'sorto, a *ag* absorbed, engrossed.

assottigli'are [assottiʎ'ʎare] *vt* to make thin, to thin; (*aguzzare: anche fig*) to sharpen; (*ridurre*) to reduce; ~**rsi** *vr* to grow thin; (*fig: ridursi*) to be reduced.

assue'fare *vt* to accustom; ~**rsi a** to get used to, accustom o.s. to.

as'sumere *vt* (*impiegato*) to take on, engage; (*responsabilità*) to assume, take upon o.s.; (*contegno, espressione*) to assume, put on; **as'sunto, a** *pp di* **assumere** // *sm* (*tesi*) proposition.

assurdità *sf inv* absurdity; **dire delle** ~ to talk nonsense.

as'surdo, a *ag* absurd.

'asta *sf* pole; (*modo di vendita*) auction.

as'temio, a *ag* abstemious.

aste'nersi *vr*: ~ **(da)** to abstain (from), refrain (from); (POL) to abstain (from); **astensi'one** *sf* abstention.

aste'risco, schi *sm* asterisk.

asti'nenza [asti'nɛntsa] *sf* abstinence.

'astio *sm* rancour, resentment.

as'tratto, a *ag* abstract.

'astro *sm* star.

'astro... *prefisso*: **astrolo'gia** [astrolo'dʒia] *sf* astrology; **as'trologo, a, ghi, ghe** *sm/f* astrologer; **astro'nauta, i, e** *sm/f* astronaut; **astro'nave** *sf* space ship; **astrono'mia** *sf* astronomy; **astro-'nomico, a, ci, che** *ag* astronomic(al); **as-'tronomo** *sm* astronomer.

as'tuccio [as'tuttʃo] *sm* case, box, holder.

as'tuto, a *ag* astute, cunning, shrewd; **as-'tuzia** *sf* astuteness, shrewdness; (*azione*) trick.

ate'ismo *sm* atheism.

A'tene *sf* Athens.

'ateo, a *ag, sm/f* atheist.

at'lante *sm* atlas.

at'lantico, a, ci, che *ag* Atlantic // *sm*: **l'A~, l'Oceano A~** the Atlantic, the Atlantic Ocean.

at'leta, i, e *sm/f* athlete; **at'letica** *sf* athletics *sg*.

atmos'fera *sf* atmosphere; **atmos'ferico, a, ci, che** *ag* atmospheric.

a'tomico, a, ci, che *ag* atomic; (*nucleare*) atomic, atom *cpd*, nuclear.

'atomo *sm* atom.

'atrio *sm* entrance-hall, lobby.

a'troce [a'trotʃe] *ag* (*che provoca orrore*) dreadful; (*terribile*) atrocious; **atrocità** *sf inv* atrocity.

attacca'mento *sm* (*fig*) attachment, affection.

attacca'panni *sm* hook, peg; (*mobile*) hall stand.

attac'care *vt* (*unire*) to attach; (*far aderire*) to stick (on); (*appendere*) to hang (up); (*assalire: anche fig*) to attack; (*iniziare*) to begin, start; (*fig: contagiare*) to pass on // *vi* to stick, adhere; **~rsi** *vr* to stick, adhere; (*trasmettersi per contagio*) to be contagious; (*afferrarsi*): **~rsi (a)** to cling (to); (*fig: affezionarsi*): **~rsi (a)** to become attached (to); **~ discorso** to start a conversation; **at'tacco, chi** *sm* (*punto di unione*) junction; (*azione offensiva: anche fig*) attack; (*MED*) attack, fit.

atteggia'mento [atteddʒa'mento] *sm* attitude.

atteggi'arsi [atted'dʒarsi] *vr*: **~ a** to pose as.

at'tendere *vt* to wait for, await // *vi*: **~ a** to attend to.

atte'nersi *vr*: **~ a** to keep *o* stick to.

atten'tare *vi*: **~ a** to make an attempt on; **atten'tato** *sm* attack; **attentato alla vita di qd** attempt on sb's life.

at'tento, a *ag* attentive; (*accurato*) careful, thorough; **stare ~ a qc** to pay attention to sth // *escl* be careful!

attenu'ante *sf* (*DIR*) extenuating circumstance.

attenu'are *vt* to attenuate; (*dolore, rumore*) to lessen, deaden; (*pena, tasse*) to alleviate; **~rsi** *vr* to ease, abate.

attenzi'one [atten'tsjone] *sf* attention // *escl* watch out!, be careful!

atter'raggio [atter'raddʒo] *sm* landing.

atter'rare *vt* to bring down // *vi* to land.

atter'rire *vt* to terrify; **~rsi** *vr* to be terrified.

at'teso, a *pp di* **attendere** // *sf* waiting; (*tempo trascorso aspettando*) wait.

attes'tato *sm* certificate.

'attico, ci *sm* attic.

at'tiguo, a *ag* adjacent, adjoining.

attil'lato, a *ag* (*vestito*) close-fitting, tight; (*persona*) dressed up.

'attimo *sm* moment; **in un ~** in a moment.

atti'nente *ag*: **~ a** relating to, concerning.

atti'rare *vt* to attract.

atti'tudine *sf* (*disposizione*) aptitude; (*atteggiamento*) attitude.

atti'vare *vt* to activate; (*far funzionare*) to set going, start.

attività *sf inv* activity; (*COMM*) assets *pl*.

at'tivo, a *ag* active; (*COMM*) profit-making, credit *cpd* // *sm* (*COMM*) assets *pl*.

attiz'zare [attit'tsare] *vt* (*fuoco*) to poke; (*fig*) to stir up.

'atto *sm* act; (*azione, gesto*) action, act, deed; (*DIR: documento*) deed, document; **~i** *smpl* (*di congressi etc*) proceedings; **mettere in ~** to put into action.

at'tonito, a *ag* dumbfounded, astonished.

attorcigli'are [attortʃiʎ'ʎare] *vt*, **~rsi** *vr* to twist.

at'tore, 'trice *sm/f* actor/actress.

at'torno *av*, **~ a** *prep* round, around, about.

attra'ente *ag* attractive.

at'trarre *vt* to attract; **attrat'tiva** *sf* (*fig: fascino*) attraction, charm; **at'tratto, a** *pp di* **attrarre**.

attraver'sare *vt* to cross; (*città, bosco, fig: periodo*) to go through; (*sog: fiume*) to run through.

attra'verso *prep* through; (*da una parte all'altra*) across.

attrazi'one [attrat'tsjone] *sf* attraction.

attrez'zare [attret'tsare] *vt* to equip; (*NAUT*) to rig; **attrezza'tura** *sf* equipment *q*; rigging; **at'trezzo** *sm* tool, instrument; (*SPORT*) piece of equipment.

attribu'ire *vt*: **~ qc a qd** (*assegnare*) to give *o* award sth to sb; (*quadro etc*) to attribute sth to sb; **attri'buto** *sm* attribute.

at'trice [at'tritʃe] *sf vedi* **attore.**

attu'ale *ag* (*presente*) present; (*di attualità*) topical; (*che è in atto*) actual; **attualità** *sf inv* topicality; (*avvenimento*) current event; **essere di attualità** to be topical; to be fashionable.

attu'are *vt* to carry out; **~rsi** *vr* to be realized.

attu'tire *vt* to deaden, reduce; **~rsi** *vr* to die down.

au'dace [au'datʃe] *ag* audacious, daring, bold; (*provocante*) provocative; (*sfacciato*) impudent, bold; **au'dacia** *sf* audacity, daring; boldness; provocativeness; impudence.

audiovi'sivo, a *ag* audiovisual.

audi'torio *sm* auditorium.

audizi'one [audit'tsjone] *sf* hearing; (*MUS*) audition.

augu'rare *vt* to wish; **~rsi qc** to hope for sth.

au'gurio *sm* (*presagio*) omen; (*voto di benessere etc*) (good) wish; **fare gli ~i a qd** to give sb one's best wishes; **tanti ~i!** all the best!

'aula *sf* (*scolastica*) classroom; (*universitaria*) lecture-theatre; (*di edificio pubblico*) hall.

aumen'tare *vt, vi* (2) to increase; **au-'mento** *sm* increase.

au'reola *sf* halo.

au'rora *sf* dawn.

ausili'are *ag, sm, sm/f* auxiliary.

aus'picio [aus'pitʃo] *sm* omen; (*protezione*) patronage; **sotto gli ~i di** under the auspices of.

austerità *sf inv* austerity.

aus'tero, a *ag* austere.

Aus'tralia *sf*: **l'A~** Australia; **australi'ano, a** *ag, sm/f* Australian.

'Austria *sf*: **l'A~** Austria; **aus'triaco, a, ci, che** *ag, sm/f* Austrian.

autenti'care *vt* to authenticate.

au'tentico, a, ci, che *ag* (*quadro, firma*) authentic, genuine; (*fatto*) true, genuine.

au'tista, i *sm* driver.

'auto *sf inv* car.

autobiogra'fia *sf* autobiography.

'autobus *sm inv* bus.

auto'carro *sm* lorry.

au'tografo, a *ag, sm* autograph.

auto'linea *sf* bus route.

au'toma, i *sm* automaton.

auto'matico, a, ci, che *ag* automatic // *sm* (*bottone*) snap fastener; (*fucile*) automatic.

auto'mezzo [auto'mɛddzo] *sm* motor vehicle.

auto'mobile *sf* (motor) car.

autono'mia *sf* autonomy; (*di volo*) range.

au'tonomo, a *ag* autonomous.

autop'sia *sf* post-mortem (examination), autopsy.

auto'radio *sf inv* (*apparecchio*) car radio; (*autoveicolo*) radio car.

au'tore, 'trice *sm/f* author; **l'~ del furto** the person who committed the robbery.

auto'revole *ag* authoritative; (*persona*) influential.

autori'messa *sf* garage.

autorità *sf inv* authority.

autoriz'zare [autorid'dzare] *vt* (*permettere*) to authorize; (*giustificare*) to allow, sanction; **autorizzazi'one** *sf* authorization.

autoscu'ola *sf* driving school.

autos'top *sm* hitchhiking; **autostop-'pista, i, e** *sm/f* hitchhiker.

autos'trada *sf* motorway.

auto'treno *sm* articulated lorry.

autove'icolo *sm* motor vehicle.

au'tunno *sm* autumn.

avam'braccio, *pl(f)* **cia** [avam'brattʃo] *sm* forearm.

avangu'ardia *sf* vanguard.

a'vanti *av* (*stato in luogo*) in front; (*moto: andare, venire*) forward; (*tempo: prima*) before // *escl* (*entrate*) come (*o* go) in!; (*MIL*) forward!; (*suvvia*) come on! // *ag inv* (*precedente*) before; **il giorno ~** the day before; (*che si trova davanti*) front *cpd* // *sm inv* (*SPORT*) forward; **~ e indietro** backwards and forwards; **andare ~** to go forward; (*precedere*) to go ahead; (*continuare*) to go on; (*orologio*) to be fast; **essere ~ negli studi** to be well advanced with one's studies.

avanza'mento [avantsa'mento] *sm* progress; promotion.

avan'zare [avan'tsare] *vt* (*spostare in avanti*) to move forward, advance; (*domanda*) to put forward; (*superare*) to surpass; (*vincere*) to beat; (*promuovere*) to promote; (*essere creditore*): **~ qc da qd** to be owed sth by sb // *vi* (2) (*andare avanti*) to move forward, advance; (*fig: progredire*) to make progress; (*essere d'avanzo*) to be left, remain; **~rsi** *vr* to move forward, advance; **avan'zata** *sf* (*MIL*) advance; **a'vanzo** *sm* (*residuo*) remains *pl*, left-overs *pl*; (*MAT*) remainder; (*COMM*) surplus; **averne d'avanzo di qc** to have more than enough of sth.

ava'ria *sf* (*guasto*) damage; (*: meccanico*) breakdown.

ava'rizia [ava'rittsja] *sf* avarice.

a'varo, a *ag* avaricious, miserly // *sm* miser.

a'vena *sf* oats *pl*.

a'vere *sm* (*COMM*) credit; **~i** *smpl* (*ricchezza*) wealth *sg*, possessions // *vt, vb ausiliare* to have; *vedi* **freddo, fame** *etc*; **~ da mangiare/bere** to have something to eat/drink; **~ da** *o* **a fare qc** to have to do sth; **~ (a) che fare** *o* **vedere con qd/qc** to have to do with sb/sth; **ho 28 anni** I am 28 (years old); **avercela con qd** to have something against sb.

avia'tore, 'trice *sm/f* aviator, pilot.

aviazi'one [avjat'tsjone] *sf* aviation; (*MIL*) air force.

avidità *sf* eagerness; greed.

'avido, a *ag* eager; (*peg*) greedy.

'avi *smpl* ancestors, forefathers.

avo'cado *sm* avocado.

a'vorio *sm* ivory.

Avv. *abbr di* **avvocato**.

avvalla'mento *sm* sinking *q*; (*effetto*) depression.

avvalo'rare *vt* to confirm.

avvantaggi'are [avvantad'dʒare] *vt* to favour; **~rsi** *vr* (*trarre vantaggio*): **~rsi di** to take advantage of; (*prevalere*): **~rsi negli affari/sui concorrenti** to get ahead in business/of one's competitors.

avvelena'mento *sm* poisoning.

avvele'nare *vt* to poison.

avve'nente *ag* attractive, charming.

avveni'mento *sm* event.

avve'nire *vi, vb impers* (2) to happen, occur // *sm* future.

avven'tarsi *vr*: **~ su** *o* **contro qd/qc** to hurl o.s. *o* rush at sb/sth.

avven'tato, a *ag* rash, reckless.

av'vento *sm* advent, coming; (*REL*): **l'A~** Advent.

avven'tura *sf* adventure; (*amorosa*) affair.

avventu'rarsi *vr* to venture.

avventuri'ero, a *sm/f* adventurer/adventuress.

avventu'roso, a *ag* adventurous.

avve'rarsi *vr* to come true.

av'verbio *sm* adverb.

avver'sare *vt* to oppose.

avver'sario, a *ag* opposing // *sm* opponent, adversary.

avversi'one *sf* aversion.

avversità *sf inv* adversity, misfortune.

av'verso, a *ag* (*contrario*) contrary; (*sfavorevole*) unfavourable.

avver'tenza [avver'tɛntsa] *sf* (*ammonimento*) warning; (*cautela*) care; (*premessa*) foreword; **~e** *sfpl* (*istruzioni per l'uso*) instructions.

avverti'mento *sm* warning.

avver'tire *vt* (*avvisare*) to warn; (*rendere consapevole*) to inform, notify; (*percepire*) to feel.

av'vezzo, a [av'vettso] *ag:* **~ a** used to.

avvia'mento *sm* (*atto*) starting; (*effetto*) start; (*AUT*) starting; (: *dispositivo*) starter; (*COMM*) goodwill.

avvi'are *vt* (*mettere sul cammino*) to direct; (*impresa*) to begin, start; (*motore*) to start; **~rsi** *vr* to set off, set out.

avvicina'mento [avvitʃina'mento] *sm* approach.

avvici'nare [avvitʃi'nare] *vt* to bring near; (*trattare con: persona*) to approach; **~rsi** *vr:* **~rsi (a qd/qc)** to approach (sb/sth), draw near (to sb/sth).

avvili'mento *sm* humiliation; disgrace; discouragement.

avvi'lire *vt* (*umiliare*) to humiliate; (*degradare*) to disgrace; (*scoraggiare*) to dishearten, discourage; **~rsi** *vr* (*abbattersi*) to lose heart.

avvinaz'zato, a [avvinat'tsato] *ag* drunk.

av'vincere [av'vintʃere] *vt* to charm, enthral.

avvinghi'are [avvin'gjare] *vt* to clasp; **~rsi** *vr:* **~rsi a** to cling to.

avvi'sare *vt* (*far sapere*) to inform; (*mettere in guardia*) to warn; **av'viso** *sm* warning; (*annuncio*) announcement; (: *affisso*) notice; (*inserzione pubblicitaria*) advertisement; **a mio avviso** in my opinion.

avvi'tare *vt* to screw down (*o* in).

avviz'zire [avvit'tsire] *vi* (*2*) to wither.

avvo'cato, 'essa *sm/f* (*DIR*) barrister; (*fig*) defender, advocate.

av'volgere [av'voldʒere] *vt* to roll up; (*avviluppare*) to wrap up; **~rsi** *vr* (*avvilupparsi*) to wrap o.s. up; **avvol-'gibile** *sm* roller blind.

avvol'toio *sm* vulture.

azi'enda [ad'dzjɛnda] *sf* business, firm, concern; **~ agricola** farm.

azi'one [at'tsjone] *sf* action; (*COMM*) share; **azio'nista, i, e** *sm/f* (*COMM*) shareholder.

azzan'nare [attsan'nare] *vt* to sink one's teeth into.

azzar'darsi [addzar'darsi] *vr* to dare; **azzar'dato, a** *ag* (*impresa*) risky; (*risposta*) rash.

az'zardo [ad'dzardo] *sm* risk.

azzuf'farsi [attsuf'farsi] *vr* to come to blows.

az'zurro, a [ad'dzurro] *ag* blue // *sm* (*colore*) blue; **gli ~i** (*SPORT*) the Italian national team.

B

bab'beo *sm* simpleton.

'babbo *sm* (*fam*) dad, daddy; **B~ natale** Father Christmas.

bab'buccia, ce [bab'buttʃa] *sf* slipper; (*per neonati*) bootee.

ba'bordo *sm* (*NAUT*) port side.

ba'cato, a *ag* worm-eaten, rotten.

'bacca, che *sf* berry.

baccalà *sm* dried salted cod.

bac'cano *sm* din, clamour.

bac'cello [bat'tʃello] *sm* pod.

bac'chetta [bak'ketta] *sf* (*verga*) stick, rod; (*di direttore d'orchestra*) baton; (*di tamburo*) drumstick; **~ magica** magic wand.

baci'are [ba'tʃare] *vt* to kiss; **~rsi** *vr* to kiss (one another).

baci'nella [batʃi'nɛlla] *sf* basin.

ba'cino [ba'tʃino] *sm* basin; (*MINERALOGIA*) field, bed; (*ANAT*) pelvis; (*NAUT*) dock.

'bacio [ˈbatʃo] *sm* kiss.

'baco, chi *sm* worm; **~ da seta** silkworm.

ba'dare *vi* (*fare attenzione*) to take care, be careful; (*occuparsi di*): **~ a** to look after, take care of; (*dar ascolto*): **~ a** to pay attention to; **bada ai fatti tuoi!** mind your own business!

ba'dia *sf* abbey.

ba'dile *sm* shovel.

'baffi *smpl* moustache *sg*; (*di animale*) whiskers; **ridere sotto i ~** to laugh up one's sleeve; **leccarsi i ~** to lick one's lips.

bagagli'aio [bagaʎ'ʎajo] *sm* luggage-van; (*AUT*) boot.

ba'gagli [ba'gaʎʎi] *smpl* luggage *sg*.

bagat'tella *sf* trifle, trifling matter.

bagli'ore [baʎ'ʎore] *sm* flash, dazzling light; **un ~ di speranza** a sudden ray of hope.

ba'gnante [ban'nante] *sm/f* bather.

ba'gnare [ban'nare] *vt* to wet; (*inzuppare*) to soak; (*innaffiare*) to water; (*sog: fiume*) to flow through; (: *mare*) to wash, bathe; **~rsi** *vr* (*al mare*) to go swimming *o* bathing; (*in vasca*) to have a bath.

ba'gnino [ban'nino] *sm* lifeguard.

'bagno [ˈbanno] *sm* bath; (*locale*) bathroom; **~i** *smpl* (*stabilimento*) baths; **fare il ~** to have a bath; (*nel mare*) to go swimming *o* bathing; **fare il ~ a qd** to give sb a bath.

'baia *sf* bay.

baio'netta *sf* bayonet.

balaus'trata *sf* balustrade.

balbet'tare *vi* to stutter, stammer; (*bimbo*) to babble // *vt* to stammer out.

balbuzi'ente [balbut'tsjɛnte] *ag* stuttering, stammering.

bal'cone *sm* balcony.

baldac'chino [baldak'kino] *sm* canopy.

bal'danza [bal'dantsa] *sf* self-confidence, boldness.

'baldo, a *ag* bold, daring.

bal'doria *sf* merrymaking *q*; noisy party.

ba'lena *sf* whale.

bale'nare (2) *vb impers*: **balena** there's lightning // *vi* to flash; **mi balenò un'idea** an idea flashed through my mind; **ba'leno** *sm* flash of lightning; **in un baleno** in a flash.

ba'lestra *sf* crossbow.

'balia *sf* wet-nurse.

ba'lìa *sf*: **in ~ di** at the mercy of; **cadere in ~ di qd** to fall into sb's hands.

'balla *sf* (*di merci*) bale; (*fandonia*) (tall) story.

bal'lare *vt, vi* to dance; **bal'lata** *sf* ballad.

balle'rina *sf* dancer; ballet dancer; (*scarpa*) ballet shoe.

balle'rino *sm* dancer; ballet dancer.

bal'letto *sm* ballet.

'ballo *sm* dance; (*azione*) dancing *q*; **essere in ~** (*fig: persona*) to be involved; (*: cosa*) to be at stake.

ballot'taggio [ballot'taddʒo] *sm* (*POL*) second ballot.

balne'are *ag* seaside *cpd*; (*stagione*) bathing.

ba'locco, chi *sm* toy.

ba'lordo, a *ag* stupid, senseless; (*stordito*) stupefied, dopey.

'balsamo *sm* (*aroma*) balsam; (*lenimento, fig*) balm.

'Baltico *sm*: **il (mar) ~** the Baltic (Sea).

balu'ardo *sm* bulwark.

'balza ['baltsa] *sf* (*dirupo*) crag; (*di stoffa*) frill.

bal'zare [bal'tsare] *vi* to bounce; (*lanciarsi*) to jump, leap; **'balzo** *sm* bounce; jump, leap; (*del terreno*) crag.

bam'bagia [bam'badʒa] *sf* (*ovatta*) cotton wool; (*cascame*) cotton waste.

bam'bina *ag, sf vedi* **bambino**.

bambi'naia *sf* nanny, nurse(maid).

bam'bino, a *ag* child *cpd*; (*non sviluppato*) immature // *sm/f* child.

bam'boccio [bam'bottʃo] *sm* plump child; (*pupazzo*) rag doll.

'bambola *sf* doll.

bambù *sm* bamboo.

ba'nale *ag* banal, commonplace; **banalità** *sf inv* banality.

ba'nana *sf* banana; **ba'nano** *sm* banana tree.

'banca, che *sf* bank.

banca'rella *sf* stall.

ban'cario, a *ag* banking, bank *cpd* // *sm* bank clerk.

banca'rotta *sf* bankruptcy; **fare ~** to go bankrupt.

ban'chetto [ban'ketto] *sm* banquet.

banchi'ere [ban'kjɛre] *sm* banker.

ban'china [ban'kina] *sf* (*di porto*) quay; (*per pedoni, ciclisti*) path; (*di stazione*) platform; **~ spartitraffico** (*AUT*) central reservation; **~e non transitabili** (*AUT*) soft verges.

'banco, chi *sm* bench; (*di negozio*) counter; (*di mercato*) stall; (*di officina*) (work-)bench; (*GEO, banca*) bank; **~ degli imputati** dock; **~ di prova** (*fig*) testing ground; **~ dei testimoni** witness box.

banco'nota *sf* banknote.

'banda *sf* band; (*di stoffa*) band, stripe; (*lato, parte*) side.

banderu'ola *sf* pennant; (*METEOR*) weathercock, weathervane.

bandi'era *sf* flag, banner.

ban'dire *vt* to proclaim; (*esiliare*) to exile; (*fig*) to dispense with.

ban'dito *sm* outlaw, bandit.

bandi'tore *sm* (*di aste*) auctioneer.

'bando *sm* proclamation; (*esilio*) exile, banishment.

bar *sm inv* bar.

'bara *sf* bier.

ba'racca, che *sf* shed, hut; (*peg*) hovel; **mandare avanti la ~** to keep things going; **far ~** to make merry.

bara'onda *sf* hubbub, bustle.

ba'rare *vi* to cheat.

'baratro *sm* abyss.

barat'tare *vt*: **~ qc con** to barter sth for, swap sth for; **ba'ratto** *sm* barter.

ba'rattolo *sm* (*di latta*) tin; (*di vetro*) jar; (*di coccio*) pot.

'barba *sf* beard; **farsi la ~** to shave; **farla in ~ a qd** (*fig*) to do sth to sb's face; **che ~!** what a bore!

barbabi'etola *sf* beetroot; **~ da zucchero** sugar beet.

bar'barico, a, ci, che *ag* barbarian; barbaric.

bar'barie *sf* barbarity.

'barbaro, a *ag* barbarous; **~i** *smpl* barbarians.

barbi'ere *sm* barber.

bar'bone *sm* (*cane*) poodle; (*vagabondo*) tramp.

bar'buto, a *ag* bearded.

'barca, che *sf* boat; **~ a remi** rowing boat; **barcai'olo** *sm* boatman; (*noleggiatore*) boat hirer.

barcol'lare *vi* to stagger.

bar'cone *sm* (*per ponti di barche*) pontoon.

ba'rella *sf* (*lettiga*) stretcher.

ba'rile *sm* barrel, cask.

ba'rista, i, e *sm/f* barman/maid; bar owner.

ba'ritono *sm* baritone.

bar'lume *sm* glimmer, gleam.

ba'rocco, a, chi, che *ag, sm* baroque.

ba'rometro *sm* barometer.

ba'rone *sm* baron; **baro'nessa** *sf* baroness.

'barra sf bar; (NAUT) helm; (linea grafica) line, stroke.

barri'care vt to barricade; **barri'cata** sf barricade.

barri'era sf barrier; (GEO) reef.

ba'ruffa sf scuffle.

barzel'letta [bardzel'letta] sf joke, funny story.

ba'sare vt to base, found; **~rsi** vr: **~rsi su** (sog: fatti, prove) to be based o founded on; (: persona) to base one's arguments on.

'basco, schi sm (copricapo) beret.

'base sf base; (fig: fondamento) basis; (POL) rank and file; **di ~** basic; **in ~ a** on the basis of, according to; **a ~ di caffè** coffee-based.

ba'setta sf sideburn.

ba'silica, che sf basilica.

ba'silico sm basil.

'basso, a ag low; (di statura) short; (meridionale) southern // sm bottom, lower part; (MUS) bass; **la ~a Italia** southern Italy.

basso'fondo, pl **bassifondi** sm (GEO) shallows pl; **bassifondi** smpl (fig) dregs.

bassorili'evo sm bas-relief.

'basta escl (that's) enough!, that will do!

bas'tardo, a ag (animale, pianta) hybrid, crossbreed; (persona) illegitimate, bastard (peg) // sm/f illegitimate child, bastard (peg).

bas'tare vi, vb impers (2) to be enough, be sufficient; **~ a qd** to be enough for sb; **basta chiedere a un vigile** you have only to o need only ask a policeman.

basti'mento sm ship, vessel.

basto'nare vt to beat, thrash.

bas'tone sm stick; **~ da passeggio** walking stick.

bat'taglia [bat'taλλa] sf battle; fight.

bat'taglio [bat'taλλo] sm (di campana) clapper; (di porta) knocker.

battagli'one [battaλ'λone] sm battalion.

bat'tello sm boat.

bat'tente sm (imposta: di porta) wing, flap; (: di finestra) shutter; (batacchio: di porta) knocker; (: di orologio) hammer.

'battere vt to beat; (grano) to thresh; (percorrere) to scour // vi (bussare) to knock; (urtare): **~ contro** to hit o strike against; (pioggia, sole) to beat down; (cuore) to beat; (TENNIS) to serve; **~rsi** vr to fight; **~ le mani** to clap; **~ i piedi** to stamp one's feet; **~ le ore** to strike the hours; **~ su un argomento** to hammer home an argument; **~ a macchina** to type; **~ bandiera italiana** to fly the Italian flag; **~ in testa** (AUT) to knock; **in un batter d'occhio** in the twinkling of an eye.

bat'teri smpl bacteria.

batte'ria sf battery; (MUS) drums pl.

bat'tesimo sm baptism; christening.

battez'zare [batted'dzare] vt to baptize; to christen.

batticu'ore sm palpitations pl; **avere il ~** to be frightened to death.

batti'mano sm applause.

batti'panni sm inv carpet-beater.

battis'tero sm baptistry.

battis'trada sm inv (di pneumatico) tread; (di gara) pacemaker.

'battito sm beat, throb; **~ cardiaco** heartbeat; **~ della pioggia/dell'orologio** beating of the rain/ticking of the clock.

bat'tuta sf blow; (di macchina da scrivere) stroke; (MUS) bar; beat; (TEATRO) cue; (di caccia) beating; (POLIZIA) combing, scouring; (TENNIS) service.

ba'ule sm trunk; (AUT) boot.

'bava sf dribble; (di cane etc) slaver, slobber; (di vento) breath.

bava'glino [bavaλ'λino] sm bib.

ba'vaglio [ba'vaλλo] sm gag.

'bavero sm collar.

ba'zar [bad'dzar] sm inv bazaar.

baz'zecola [bad'dzekola] sf trifle.

bazzi'care [battsi'kare] vt to frequent // vi: **~ in/con** to frequent.

beati'tudine sf bliss.

be'ato, a ag blessed; (fig) happy; **~ te!** lucky you!

bec'caccia, ce [bek'kattʃa] sf woodcock.

bec'care vt to peck; (fig: raffreddore) to pick up, catch; **~rsi** vr (fig) to squabble.

beccheggi'are [bekked'dʒare] vi to pitch.

bec'chino [bek'kino] sm gravedigger.

'becco, chi sm beak, bill; (di caffettiera etc) spout; lip.

Be'fana sf old woman who, according to legend, brings children their presents at the Epiphany; (Epifania) Epiphany; (donna brutta): **b~** hag, witch.

'beffa sf practical joke; **bef'fardo, a** ag scornful, mocking; **bef'fare** vt (anche: **beffarsi di**) to make a fool of, mock.

'bega, ghe sf quarrel.

'begli ['beλλi] **'bei, bel** ag vedi **bello**.

be'lare vi to bleat.

'belga, gi, ghe ag, sm/f Belgian.

'Belgio ['bɛldʒo] sm: **il ~** Belgium.

bel'lezza [bel'lettsa] sf beauty.

belli'coso, a ag warlike.

bellige'rante [bellidʒe'rante] ag belligerent.

'bello, a ag (dav sm bel +C, bell' +V, bello +s impura, gn, pn, ps, x, z, pl bei +C, begli +s impura etc o V) beautiful, fine, lovely; (uomo) handsome // sm (bellezza) beauty; (tempo) fine weather // sf (SPORT) decider // av: **fa ~** the weather is fine, it's fine; **una ~a cifra** a considerable sum of money; **un bel niente** absolutely nothing; **è una truffa ~a e buona!** it's a real fraud!; **è bell'e finito** it's already finished; **sul più ~** at the crucial point; **belle arti** fine arts.

'belva sf wild animal.

belve'dere sm inv panoramic viewpoint.

benché [ben'ke] cong although.

'benda sf bandage; (per gli occhi) blindfold; **ben'dare** vt to bandage; to blindfold.

'bene av well; (completamente, affatto): è

ben difficile it's very difficult // ag inv: **gente** ~ well-to-do people // sm good; ~**i** smpl (averi) property sg, estate sg; **io sto** ~**/poco** ~ I'm well/not very well; **va** ~ all right; **volere un** ~ **dell'anima a qd** to love sb very much; **un uomo per** ~ a respectable man; **fare** ~ to do the right thing; **fare** ~ **a** (salute) to be good for; **fare del** ~ **a qd** to do sb a good turn; ~**i di consumo** consumer goods.

bene'detto, a pp di **benedire** // ag blessed, holy.

bene'dire vt to bless; to consecrate; **benedizi'one** sf blessing.

benedu'cato, a ag well-mannered.

benefat'tore, 'trice sm/f benefactor/benefactress.

benefi'care vt to help, benefit.

benefi'cenza [benefi'tʃɛntsa] sf charity.

bene'ficio [bene'fitʃo] sm benefit.

be'nefico, a, ci, che ag beneficial; charitable.

bene'merito, a ag meritorious.

be'nessere sm well-being.

benes'tante ag well-to-do.

benes'tare sm consent, approval.

benevo'lenza [benevo'lɛntsa] sf benevolence.

be'nevolo, a ag benevolent.

be'nigno, a [be'ninno] ag kind, kindly; (critica etc) favourable; (MED) benign.

benin'teso av of course.

bensì cong but (rather).

benve'nuto, a ag, sm welcome; **dare il** ~ **a qd** to welcome sb.

ben'zina [ben'dzina] sf petrol; **fare** ~ to get petrol; **benzi'naio** sm petrol pump attendant.

'**bere** vt to drink; (assorbire) to soak up.

ber'lina sf (AUT) saloon (car).

Ber'lino sf Berlin.

ber'noccolo sm bump; (inclinazione) bent, flair.

ber'retto sm cap.

bersagli'are [bersaʎ'ʎare] vt to shoot at; (colpire ripetutamente, fig) to bombard; **bersagliato dalla sfortuna** dogged by ill fortune.

ber'saglio [ber'saʎʎo] sm target.

bes'temmia sf blasphemy; oath, curse, swearword.

bestemmi'are vi to blaspheme; to curse, swear // vt to blaspheme; to curse, swear at.

'**bestia** sf animal; ~ **da soma** beast of burden; **besti'ale** ag bestial; brutal; **besti'ame** sm livestock; (bovino) cattle pl.

'**bettola** sf (peg) dive.

be'tulla sf birch.

be'vanda sf drink, beverage.

bevi'tore, 'trice sm/f drinker.

be'vuto, a pp di **bere** // sf drink.

bi'ada sf fodder.

bianche'ria [bjanke'ria] sf linen; ~ **intima** underwear; ~ **da donna** ladies' underwear, lingerie.

bi'anco, a, chi, che ag white; (non scritto) blank // sm white; blank, blank space; (intonaco) whitewash // sm/f white, white man/woman; **in** ~ (foglio, assegno) blank; **mangiare in** ~ to follow a bland diet; **pesce in** ~ boiled fish; ~ **dell'uovo** egg-white.

biasi'mare vt to disapprove of, censure; **bi'asimo** sm disapproval, censure.

'**bibbia** sf bible.

bibe'ron sm inv feeding bottle.

'**bibita** sf (soft) drink.

biblio'teca, che sf library; (mobile) bookcase; **bibliote'cario, a** sm/f librarian.

bicarbo'nato sm: ~ **(di sodio)** bicarbonate (of soda).

bicchi'ere [bik'kjɛre] sm glass.

bici'cletta [bitʃi'kletta] sf bicycle.

bidé sm inv bidet.

bi'dello, a sm/f (INS) janitor.

bi'done sm drum, can; (anche: ~ **dell'immondizia**) (dust)bin; (fam: truffa) swindle.

bien'nale ag biennial.

bi'etola sf beet.

bifor'carsi vr to fork; **biforcazi'one** sf fork.

biga'mia sf bigamy.

bighello'nare [bigello'nare] vi to loaf (about).

bigiotte'ria [bidʒotte'ria] sf costume jewellery; (negozio) jeweller's (selling only costume jewellery).

bigli'ardo [biʎ'ʎardo] sm = **biliardo.**

bigliette'ria [biʎʎette'ria] sf (di stazione) ticket office; booking office; (di teatro) box office.

bigli'etto [biʎ'ʎetto] sm (per viaggi, spettacoli etc) ticket; (cartoncino) card; (anche: ~ **di banca**) (bank)note; ~ **d'auguri/da visita** greetings/visiting card.

bigo'dino sm roller, curler.

bi'gotto, a ag over-pious // sm/f church fiend.

bi'lancia, ce [bi'lantʃa] sf (pesa) scales pl; (: di precisione) balance; (dello zodiaco): **B**~ Libra; ~ **commerciale/dei pagamenti** balance of trade/payments; **bilanci'are** vt (pesare) to weigh; (: fig) to weigh up; (pareggiare) to balance.

bi'lancio [bi'lantʃo] sm (COMM) balance(-sheet); (statale) budget; **fare il** ~ **di** (fig) to assess; ~ **consuntivo** (final) balance; ~ **preventivo** budget.

'**bile** sf bile; (fig) rage, anger.

bili'ardo sm billiards sg; billiard table.

'**bilico, chi** sm unstable equilibrium; **in** ~ in the balance; **tenere qd in** ~ to keep sb in suspense.

bi'lingue ag bilingual.

bili'one sm (mille milioni) thousand million; (milione di milioni) billion.

'**bimbo, a** sm/f little boy/girl.

bimen'sile ag fortnightly.

bimes'trale ag two-monthly, bimonthly.

bi'nario sm (railway) track o line;

(*piattaforma*) platform; ~ **morto** dead-end track.

bi'nocolo *sm* binoculars *pl.*

bio... *prefisso:* **bio'chimica** [bio'kimika] *sf* biochemistry; **biodegra'dabile** *ag* biodegradable; **biogra'fia** *sf* biography; **biolo'gia** *sf* biology; **bio'logico, a, ci, che** *ag* biological.

bi'ondo, a *ag* blond, fair.

bir'bante *sm* rogue, rascal.

biri'chino, a [biri'kino] *ag* mischievous // *sm/f* scamp, little rascal.

bi'rillo *sm* skittle; ~**i** *smpl* (*gioco*) skittles *sg.*

'birra *sf* beer; **a tutta** ~ (*fig*) at top speed; **birre'ria** *sf* ≈ bierkeller.

bis *escl, sm inv* encore.

bisbigli'are [bisbiʎ'ʎare] *vt, vi* to whisper; **bis'biglio** *sm* whisper; (*notizia*) rumour; **bisbi'glio** *sm* whispering.

'bisca, sche *sf* gambling-house.

'biscia, sce ['biʃʃa] *sf* snake; ~ **d'acqua** grass snake.

bis'cotto *sm* biscuit.

bises'tile *ag:* **anno** ~ leap year.

bis'lungo, a, ghi, ghe *ag* oblong.

bis'nonno, a *sm/f* great-grandfather/grandmother.

biso'gnare [bizoɲ'ɲare] *vb impers:* **bisogna che tu parta/lo faccia** you'll have to go/do it; **bisogna parlargli** we'll (*o* I'll) have to talk to him // *vi* (*esser utile*) to be necessary; **mi bisognano quei fogli** I need those sheets of paper.

bi'sogno [bi'zoɲɲo] *sm* need; ~**i** *smpl:* **fare i propri** ~**i** to relieve o.s.; **avere** ~ **di qc/di fare qc** to need sth/to do sth; **al** ~, **in caso di** ~ if need be; **biso'gnoso, a** *ag* needy, poor; **bisognoso di** in need of, needing.

bis'tecca, che *sf* steak, beefsteak.

bisticci'are [bistit'tʃare] *vi*, ~**rsi** *vr* to quarrel, bicker; **bis'ticcio** *sm* quarrel, squabble; (*gioco di parole*) pun.

'bisturi *sm* scalpel.

bi'sunto, a *ag* very greasy.

'bitter *sm inv* bitters *pl.*

bi'vacco, chi *sm* bivouac.

'bivio *sm* fork; (*fig*) dilemma.

'bizza ['biddza] *sf* tantrum; **fare le** ~**e** (*bambino*) to be naughty.

biz'zarro, a [bid'dzarro] *ag* bizarre, strange.

biz'zeffe [bid'dzɛffe]: **a** ~ *av* in plenty, galore.

blan'dire *vt* to soothe; to flatter.

'blando, a *ag* mild, gentle.

bla'sone *sm* coat of arms.

blate'rare *vi* to chatter, blether.

'blatta *sf* cockroach.

blin'dato, a *ag* armoured.

bloc'care *vt* to block; (*isolare*) to isolate, cut off; (*porto*) to blockade; (*prezzi, beni*) to freeze; (*meccanismo*) to jam.

'blocco, chi *sm* block; (*MIL*) blockade; (*dei fitti*) restriction; (*quadernetto*) pad; (*fig: unione*) coalition; (*il bloccare*) blocking;

---

isolating, cutting-off; blockading; freezing; jamming; **in** ~ (*nell'insieme*) as a whole; (*COMM*) in bulk.

blu *ag inv, sm* dark blue.

'blusa *sf* (*camiciotto*) smock; (*camicetta*) blouse.

'boa *sm inv* (*ZOOL*) boa constrictor; (*sciarpa*) feather boa // *sf* buoy.

bo'ato *sm* rumble, roar.

bo'bina *sf* reel, spool; (*di pellicola*) spool; (*di film*) reel; (*ELETTR*) coil.

'bocca, che *sf* mouth; **in** ~ **al lupo!** good luck!

boc'caccia, ce [bok'kattʃa] *sf* (*smorfia*) grimace.

boc'cale *sm* jug; ~ **da birra** tankard.

boc'cetta [bot'tʃetta] *sf* small bottle.

boccheggi'are [bokked'dʒare] *vi* to gasp.

boc'chino [bok'kino] *sm* (*di sigaretta, sigaro: cannella*) cigarette-holder; cigar-holder; (*di pipa, strumenti musicali*) mouthpiece; ~ **con filtro** filter tip.

'boccia, ce ['bottʃa] *sf* bottle; (*da vino*) decanter, carafe; (*palla*) bowl; **gioco di** ~ **ce** bowls *sg.*

bocci'are [bot'tʃare] *vt* (*respingere*) to reject; (: *INS*) to fail; (*nel gioco delle bocce*) to hit; **boccia'tura** *sf* failure.

bocci'olo [bot'tʃolo] *sm* bud.

boc'cone *sm* mouthful, morsel.

boc'coni *av* face downwards.

'boia *sm inv* executioner; hangman.

boi'ata *sf* botch.

boicot'tare *vt* to boycott.

Bo'livia *sf:* **la** ~ Bolivia.

'bolla *sf* bubble; (*MED*) blister; ~ **papale** papal bull.

bol'lare *vt* to stamp; (*fig*) to brand.

bol'lente *ag* boiling; boiling hot.

bol'letta *sf* bill; (*ricevuta*) receipt; **essere in** ~ to be hard up.

bollet'tino *sm* bulletin; (*COMM*) note; ~ **di spedizione** consignment note.

bol'lire *vt, vi* to boil; **bol'lito** *sm* (*CUC*) boiled meat; **bolli'tura** *sf* boiling.

'bollo *sm* stamp.

bol'lore *sm* boiling (point); (*caldo intenso*) torrid heat; ~**i di gioventù** youthful enthusiasm *sg.*

'bomba *sf* bomb; **tornare a** ~ (*fig*) to get back to the point; ~ **atomica** atom bomb.

bombarda'mento *sm* bombardment; bombing.

bombar'dare *vt* to bombard; (*da aereo*) to bomb.

bombardi'ere *sm* bomber.

bom'betta *sf* bowler (hat).

'bombola *sf* cylinder.

bo'naccia, ce [bo'nattʃa] *sf* dead calm.

bo'nario, a *ag* good-natured, kind.

bo'nifica, che *sf* reclamation; reclaimed land.

bo'nifico, ci *sm* (*COMM: abbuono*) discount; (: *versamento*) credit transfer.

bontà *sf* goodness; (*cortesia*) kindness; **aver la** ~ **di fare qc** to be good *o* kind enough to do sth.

borbot'tare *vi* to mumble; (*stomaco*) to rumble.

'borchia ['borkja] *sf* stud.

borda'tura *sf* (*SARTORIA*) border, trim.

'bordo *sm* (*NAUT*) ship's side; (*orlo*) edge; (*striscia di guarnizione*) border, trim; **prendere a ~** to take on board; **a ~ della macchina** inside the car.

bor'dura *sf* border.

bor'gata *sf* hamlet.

bor'ghese [bor'geze] *ag* (*spesso peg*) middle-class; bourgeois; **abito ~** civilian dress; **borghe'sia** *sf* middle classes *pl*; bourgeoisie.

'borgo, ghi *sm* (*paesino*) village; (*quartiere*) district.

'boria *sf* self-conceit, arrogance; **bori'oso, a** *ag* arrogant.

boro'talco *sm* talcum powder.

bor'raccia, ce [bor'rattʃa] *sf* canteen, water-bottle.

'borsa *sf* bag; (*anche*: **~ da signora**) handbag; (*ECON*): **la B~** (*valori*) the Stock Exchange; **~ nera** black market; **~ della spesa** shopping bag; **~ di studio** grant; **borsai'olo** *sm* pickpocket; **borsel'lino** *sm* purse; **bor'setta** *sf* handbag; **bor'sista, i, e** *sm/f* (*ECON*) speculator; (*INS*) grant-holder.

bos'caglia [bos'kaʎʎa] *sf* woodlands *pl*.

boscai'olo *sm* woodcutter; forester.

'bosco, schi *sm* wood; **bos'coso, a** *ag* wooded.

'bossolo *sm* cartridge-case.

bo'tanico, a, ci, che *ag* botanical // *sm* botanist // *sf* botany.

'botola *sf* trap door.

'botta *sf* blow; (*rumore*) bang.

'botte *sf* barrel, cask.

bot'tega, ghe *sf* shop; (*officina*) workshop; **botte'gaio, a** *sm/f* shopkeeper; **botte'ghino** *sm* ticket office; (*del lotto*) public lottery office.

bot'tiglia [bot'tiʎʎa] *sf* bottle; **bottiglie'ria** *sf* wine shop.

bot'tino *sm* (*di guerra*) booty; (*di rapina, furto*) loot.

'botto *sm* bang; crash; **di ~** suddenly.

bot'tone *sm* button; (*BOT*) bud; **botton d'oro** buttercup.

bo'vino, a *ag* bovine; **~i** *smpl* cattle.

boxe [bɔks] *sf* boxing.

'bozza ['bɔttsa] *sf* draft; sketch; (*TIP*) proof; **boz'zetto** *sm* sketch.

'bozzolo ['bɔttsolo] *sm* cocoon.

brac'care *vt* to hunt.

brac'cetto [brat'tʃetto] *sm*: **a ~** arm in arm.

bracci'ale [brat'tʃale] *sm* bracelet; (*distintivo*) armband; **braccia'letto** *sm* bracelet, bangle.

bracci'ante [brat'tʃante] *sm* (*AGR*) day labourer.

bracci'ata [brat'tʃata] *sf* armful; (*nel nuoto*) stroke.

'braccio ['brattʃo] *sm* (*pl(f)* **braccia**: *ANAT*) arm; (*pl(m)* **bracci**: *di gru, fiume*) arm; (: *di edificio*) wing; **~ di mare** sound; **~ di terra** promontory; **bracci'olo** *sm* (*appoggio*) arm.

'bracco, chi *sm* hound.

bracconi'ere *sm* poacher.

'brace ['bratʃe] *sf* embers *pl*; **braci'ere** *sm* brazier.

braci'ola [bra'tʃɔla] *sf* (*CUC*) chop.

'branca, che *sf* branch.

'branchia ['brankja] *sf* (*ZOOL*) gill.

'branco, chi *sm* (*di cani, lupi*) pack; (*di uccelli, pecore*) flock; (*mandria*) herd; (*peg: di persone*) gang, pack.

branco'lare *vi* to grope, feel one's way.

'branda *sf* camp bed.

bran'dello *sm* scrap, shred; **a ~i** in tatters, in rags.

bran'dire *vt* to brandish.

'brano *sm* piece; (*di libro*) passage.

bra'sare *vt* to braise.

Bra'sile *sm*: **il ~** Brazil; **brasili'ano, a** *ag, sm/f* Brazilian.

'bravo, a *ag* (*abile*) clever, capable, skilful; (*buono*) good, honest; (: *bambino*) good; (*coraggioso*) brave; **~!** well done!; (*al teatro*) bravo!

bra'vura *sf* cleverness, skill.

'breccia, ce ['brettʃa] *sf* breach.

bre'tella *sf* (*AUT*) link; **~e** *sfpl* braces.

'breve *ag* brief, short; **in ~** in short.

brevet'tare *vt* to patent.

bre'vetto *sm* patent; **~ di pilotaggio** pilot's licence.

brevità *sf* brevity.

'brezza ['breddza] *sf* breeze.

'bricco, chi *sm* jug, pot; **~ del caffè** coffeepot.

bric'cone, a *sm/f* rogue, rascal.

'briciola ['britʃola] *sf* crumb.

'briciolo ['britʃolo] *sm* bit.

'briga, ghe *sf* (*fastidio*) trouble, bother; **pigliarsi la ~ di fare qc** to take the trouble to do sth.

brigadi'ere *sm* (*dei carabinieri etc*) ≈ sergeant.

bri'gante *sm* bandit.

bri'gare *vi* to scheme.

bri'gata *sf* (*MIL*) brigade; (*gruppo*) group, party.

'briglia ['briʎʎa] *sf* rein; **a ~ sciolta** at full gallop; (*fig*) at full speed.

bril'lante *ag* bright; brilliant; (*che luccica*) shining // *sm* diamond.

bril'lare *vi* to shine; (*mina*) to blow up.

'brillo, a *ag* merry, tipsy.

'brina *sf* hoarfrost.

brin'dare *vi*: **~ a qd/qc** to drink to o toast sb/sth.

'brindisi *sm inv* toast.

'brio *sm* liveliness, go; **bri'oso, a** *ag* lively.

bri'tannico, a, ci, che *ag* British.

'brivido *sm* shiver; (*di ribrezzo*) shudder; (*fig*) thrill.

brizzo'lato, a [brittso'lato] *ag* (*persona*) going grey; (*barba, capelli*) greying.

'brocca, che *sf* jug.

broc'cato *sm* brocade.

'broccolo *sm* broccoli *sg*.

'brodo *sm* broth; (*per cucinare*) stock; ~ **ristretto** consommé.

'brogli ['brɔʎʎi] *smpl* (*DIR*) malpractices.

brogli'accio [broʎ'ʎattʃo] *sm* scribbling pad.

bron'chite [bron'kite] *sf* (*MED*) bronchitis.

'broncio ['brontʃo] *sm* sulky expression; **fare il** ~ to sulk.

bronto'lare *vi* to grumble; (*stomaco*) to rumble.

'bronzo ['brondzo] *sm* bronze.

bru'care *vt* to browse on, nibble at.

brucia'pelo [brutʃa'pelo]: **a** ~ *av* point-blank.

bruci'are [bru'tʃare] *vt* to burn; (*scottare*) to scald // *vi* (2) to burn; **brucia'tore** *sm* burner; **brucia'tura** *sf* burning *q*; burn; (*scottatura*) scald; **bruci'ore** *sm* burning *o* smarting sensation.

'bruco, chi *sm* caterpillar; grub.

brughi'era [bru'gjɛra] *sf* heath, moor.

bruli'care *vi* to swarm.

'brullo, a *ag* bare, bleak.

'bruma *sf* mist.

'bruno, a *ag* brown, dark; (*persona*) dark(-haired).

'brusco, a, schi, sche *ag* (*sapore*) sharp; (*modi, persona*) brusque, abrupt; (*movimento*) abrupt, sudden.

bru'sio *sm* buzz, buzzing.

bru'tale *ag* brutal; **brutalità** *sf inv* brutality.

'bruto, a *ag* brute *cpd*; brutal // *sm* brute.

brut'tezza [brut'tettsa] *sf* ugliness.

'brutto, a *ag* ugly; (*cattivo*) bad; (*malattia, strada, affare*) nasty, bad; ~ **tempo** bad weather; **brut'tura** *sf* (*cosa brutta*) ugly thing; (*sudiciume*) filth; (*azione meschina*) mean action.

Bru'xelles [bry'sɛl] *sf* Brussels.

'buca, che *sf* hole; (*avvallamento*) hollow; ~ **delle lettere** letterbox.

buca'neve *sm inv* snowdrop.

bu'care *vt* (*forare*) to make a hole (*o* holes) in; (*pungere*) to pierce; (*biglietto*) to punch; ~ **una gomma** to have a puncture.

bu'cato *sm* (*operazione*) washing; (*panni*) wash, washing.

'buccia, ce ['buttʃa] *sf* skin, peel; (*corteccia*) bark.

bucherel'lare [bukerel'lare] *vt* to riddle with holes.

'buco, chi *sm* hole.

bu'dello *sm* intestine; (*fig: tubo*) tube; ~**a** *sfpl* bowels, guts.

bu'dino *sm* pudding.

'bue *sm* ox; (*anche:* **carne di** ~) beef.

'bufalo *sm* buffalo.

bu'fera *sf* storm; ~ **di vento** gale.

'buffo, a *ag* funny; (*TEATRO*) comic.

buf'fone *sm* buffoon.

bu'gia, 'gie [bu'dʒia] *sf* lie; (*candeliere*) candleholder; **bugi'ardo, a** *ag* lying, deceitful // *sm/f* liar.

bugi'gattolo [budʒi'gattolo] *sm* poky little room.

'buio, a *ag* dark // *sm* dark, darkness; **fa** ~ **pesto** it's pitch-dark.

'bulbo *sm* (*BOT*) bulb; ~ **oculare** eyeball.

Bulga'ria *sf*: **la** ~ Bulgaria.

bul'lone *sm* bolt.

buongus'taio, a *sm/f* gourmet.

buon'gusto *sm* good taste.

bu'ono, a *ag* (*dav sm* **buon** + *C o V,* **buono** + *s impura, gn, pn, ps, x, z; dav sf* **buon'** + *V*) good; (*benevolo*): ~ (**con**) good (to), kind (to); (*adatto*): ~ **a/da** fit for/to // *sm* good; (*COMM*) voucher, coupon; **alla buona** *ag* simple // *av* in a simple way, without any fuss; **buona fortuna** good luck; **buona notte** good night; **buona sera** good evening; **buon compleanno** happy birthday; **buon divertimento** have a nice time; **buon giorno** good morning (*o* afternoon); **a buon mercato** cheap; **di buon'ora** early; ~ **di cassa** cash voucher; ~ **fruttifero** bond bearing interest; ~ **a nulla** good-for-nothing; ~ **del tesoro** Treasury bill; **buon riposo** sleep well; **buon senso** common sense; **buon viaggio** bon voyage, have a good trip.

buontem'pone, a *sm/f* jovial person.

burat'tino *sm* puppet.

'burbero, a *ag* surly, gruff.

'burla *sf* prank, trick; **bur'lare** *vt*: **burlare qc/qd, burlarsi di qc/qd** to make fun of sth/sb.

bu'rocrate *sm* bureaucrat; **buro'cratico, a, ci, che** *ag* bureaucratic; **burocra'zia** *sf* bureaucracy.

bur'rasca, sche *sf* storm; **burras'coso, a** *ag* stormy.

'burro *sm* butter.

bur'rone *sm* ravine.

bus'care *vt* (*anche:* ~**rsi:** *raffreddore*) to get, catch; **buscarle** (*fam*) to get a hiding.

bus'sare *vi* to knock.

'bussola *sf* compass; **perdere la** ~ (*fig*) to lose one's bearings.

'busta *sf* (*da lettera*) envelope; (*astuccio*) case; **in** ~ **aperta** in an unsealed envelope; ~ **paga** pay packet.

busta'rella *sf* bribe, backhander.

'busto *sm* bust; (*indumento*) corset, girdle.

but'tare *vt* to throw; (*anche:* ~ **via**) to throw away; ~ **giù** (*scritto*) to scribble down, dash off; (*cibo*) to gulp down; (*edificio*) to pull down, demolish; (*pasta, verdura*) to put into boiling water; ~**rsi dalla finestra** to jump *o* throw o.s. out of the window.

C

ca'bina *sf* (*di nave*) cabin; (*da spiaggia*) beach hut; (*di autocarro, treno*) cab; (*di aereo*) cockpit; (*di ascensore*) cage; ~ **telefonica** call box, (tele)phone box *o* booth.

ca'cao *sm* cocoa.

'caccia ['kattʃa] *sf* hunting; (*con fucile*)

shooting; (inseguimento) chase; (cacciagione) game; ~ **grossa** big-game hunting; ~ **all'uomo** manhunt // *sm inv* (aereo) fighter; (nave) destroyer.

cacciabombardi'ere [kattʃabombar-'djɛre] *sm* fighter-bomber.

cacciagi'one [kattʃa'dʒone] *sf* game.

cacci'are [kat'tʃare] *vt* to hunt; (mandar via) to chase away; (ficcare) to shove, stick // *vi* to hunt; **~rsi** *vr* (mettersi): **~rsi tra la folla** to plunge into the crowd; **dove s'è cacciata la mia borsa?** where has my bag got to?; ~ **fuori qc** to whip o pull sth out; ~ **un urlo** to let out a yell; **caccia'tore** *sm* hunter; **cacciatore di frodo** poacher.

caccia'vite [kattʃa'vite] *sm inv* screwdriver.

'cactus *sm inv* cactus.

ca'davere *sm* (dead) body, corpse.

ca'dente ag falling; (casa) tumbledown; (persona) decrepit.

ca'denza [ka'dɛntsa] *sf* cadence; (andamento ritmico) rhythm; (MUS) cadenza.

ca'dere *vi* (2) to fall; (denti, capelli) to fall out; (tetto) to fall in; **questa gonna cade bene** this skirt hangs well; **lasciar cadere** (anche fig) to drop; ~ **dal sonno** to be falling asleep on one's feet; ~ **ammalato** to fall ill.

ca'detto *sm* cadet.

ca'duta *sf* fall; ~ **di temperatura** drop in temperature.

caffè *sm inv* coffee; (locale) café; ~ **macchiato** coffee with a dash of milk; ~ **macinato** ground coffee.

caffel'latte *sm inv* white coffee.

caffetti'era *sf* coffeepot.

cagio'nare [kadʒo'nare] *vt* to cause, be the cause of.

cagio'nevole [kadʒo'nevole] ag delicate, weak.

cagli'are [kaʎ'ʎare] *vi* (2) to curdle.

'cagna ['kaɲɲa] *sf* (ZOOL, peg) bitch.

ca'gnesco, a, schi, sche [kaɲ'nesko] ag (fig): **guardare qd in** ~ to scowl at sb.

cala'brone *sm* hornet.

cala'maio *sm* inkpot; inkwell.

cala'maro *sm* squid.

cala'mita *sf* magnet.

calamità *sf inv* calamity, disaster.

ca'lare *vt* (far discendere) to lower; (MAGLIA) to decrease // *vi* (2) (discendere) to go (o come) down; (tramontare) to set, go down; ~ **di peso** to lose weight.

'calca *sf* throng, press.

cal'cagno [kal'kaɲɲo] *sm* heel.

cal'care *sm* limestone // *vt* (premere coi piedi) to tread, press down; (premere con forza) to press down; (mettere in rilievo) to stress.

'calce ['kaltʃe] *sm*: **in** ~ at the foot of the page // *sf* lime; ~ **viva** quicklime.

calces'truzzo [kaltʃes'truttso] *sm* concrete.

calci'are [kal'tʃare] *vt, vi* to kick; **calcia-'tore** *sm* footballer.

cal'cina [kal'tʃina] *sf* (lime) mortar.

'calcio ['kaltʃo] *sm* (pedata) kick; (sport) football, soccer; (di pistola, fucile) butt; (CHIM) calcium; ~ **di punizione** (SPORT) free kick.

'calco, chi *sm* (ARTE) casting, moulding; cast, mould.

calco'lare *vt* to calculate, work out, reckon; (ponderare) to weigh (up); **calcola'tore, 'trice** ag calculating // *sm* calculator; (fig) calculating person // *sf* calculator; **calcolatore elettronico** computer.

'calcolo *sm* (anche MAT) calculation; (infinitesimale etc) calculus; (MED) stone; **fare i propri** ~**i** (fig) to weigh the pros and cons; **per** ~ out of self-interest.

cal'daia *sf* boiler.

caldeggi'are [kalded'dʒare] *vt* to support warmly, favour.

'caldo, a ag warm; (molto caldo) hot; (fig: appassionato) keen; hearty // *sm* heat; **ho** ~ I'm warm; I'm hot; **fa** ~ it's warm; it's hot.

calen'dario *sm* calendar.

'calibro *sm* (di arma) calibre, bore; (TECN) callipers *pl*; (fig) calibre; **i grossi** ~**i** (anche fig) the big guns.

'calice ['kalitʃe] *sm* goblet; (REL) chalice.

ca'ligine [ka'lidʒine] *sf* fog; (mista con fumo) smog.

'callo *sm* callus; (ai piedi) corn; **fare il** ~ **a qc** to get used to sth.

'calma *sf* calm.

cal'mante *sm* sedative, tranquillizer.

cal'mare *vt* to calm; (lenire) to soothe; **~rsi** *vr* to grow calm, calm down; (vento) to abate; (dolore) to ease.

calmi'ere *sm* controlled price.

'calmo, a ag calm, quiet.

'calo *sm* (COMM: di prezzi) fall; (: di volume) shrinkage; (: di peso) loss.

ca'lore *sm* warmth; heat; **essere in** ~ (ZOOL) to be on heat.

calo'ria *sf* calorie.

calo'roso, a ag warm.

calpes'tare *vt* to tread on, trample on; **'è vietato** ~ **l'erba'** 'keep off the grass'.

ca'lunnia *sf* slander; (scritta) libel.

cal'vario *sm* (fig) affliction, cross.

cal'vizie [kal'vittsje] *sf* baldness.

'calvo, a ag bald.

'calza ['kaltsa] *sf* (da donna) stocking; (da uomo) sock.

cal'zare [kal'tsare] *vt* (scarpe, guanti: mettersi) to put on; (: portare) to wear // *vi* (2) to fit; **calza'tura** *sf* footwear.

calzet'tone [kaltset'tone] *sm* heavy knee-length sock.

cal'zino [kal'tsino] *sm* sock.

calzo'laio [kaltso'lajo] *sm* shoemaker; (che ripara scarpe) cobbler; **calzole'ria** *sf* (negozio) shoe shop.

calzon'cini [kaltson'tʃini] *smpl* shorts.

cal'zone [kal'tsone] *sm* trouser leg; (CUC)

savoury turnover made with pizza dough; ~**i** *smpl* trousers.

camale'onte *sm* chameleon.

cambi'ale *sf* bill (of exchange); *(pagherò cambiario)* promissory note.

cambia'mento *sm* change.

cambi'are *vt* to change; *(modificare)* to alter, change; *(barattare)* to exchange // *vi* (2) to change, alter; ~**rsi** *vr (variare abito)* to change; ~ **casa** to move (house); ~ **idea** to change one's mind; ~ **aspetto** to change (in appearance); ~ **treno** to change trains.

'cambio *sm* change; *(modifica)* alteration, change; *(scambio, COMM)* exchange; *(corso dei cambi)* rate (of exchange); *(TECN, AUT)* gears *pl;* **in** ~ **di** in exchange for; **dare il** ~ **a qd** to take over from sb.

'camera *sf* room; *(anche:* ~ *da letto)* bedroom; *(COMM, TECN)* chamber; *(POL)* chamber, house; *(FOT)* camera; ~ **ardente** mortuary chapel; ~ **d'aria** inner tube; *(di pallone)* bladder; **C**~ **dei Deputati** Chamber of Deputies, ≈ House of Commons; ~ **a gas** gas chamber; ~ **a un letto/a due letti/matrimoniale** single/twin-bedded/double room; ~ **oscura** *(FOT)* dark room.

came'rata, i, e *sm/f* companion, mate // *sf* dormitory; **camera'tismo** *sm* comradeship.

cameri'era *sf (domestica)* maid; *(che serve a tavola)* waitress; *(che fa le camere)* chambermaid.

cameri'ere *sm* (man)servant; *(di ristorante)* waiter.

came'rino *sm (TEATRO)* dressing room.

'camice ['kamit∫e] *sm (REL)* alb; *(per medici etc)* white coat.

cami'cetta [kami't∫etta] *sf* blouse.

ca'micia, cie [ka'mit∫a] *sf (da uomo)* shirt; *(da donna)* blouse; ~ **di forza** straitjacket; **camici'otto** *sm* smock; workman's top.

ca'mino *sm* chimney; *(focolare)* fireplace, hearth.

'camion *sm inv* lorry; **camion'cino** *sm* van.

cam'mello *sm (ZOOL)* camel; *(tessuto)* camel hair.

cam'meo *sm* cameo.

cammi'nare *vi* to walk; *(funzionare)* to work, go.

cam'mino *sm* walk; *(sentiero)* path; *(itinerario, direzione, tragitto)* way; **mettersi in** ~ to set o start off; **cammin facendo** on the way.

camo'milla *sf* camomile; *(infuso)* camomile tea.

ca'morra *sf* camorra; racket.

ca'moscio [ka'moʃʃo] *sm* chamois.

cam'pagna [kam'paɲɲa] *sf* country, countryside; *(POL, COMM, MIL)* campaign; **in** ~ in the country; **fare una** ~ to campaign; **campa'gnolo, a** *ag* country *cpd* // *sf (AUT)* land rover.

cam'pale *ag* field *cpd;* *(fig):* **una giornata** ~ a hard day.

cam'pana *sf* bell; *(anche:* ~ **di vetro)** bell jar; **campa'nella** *sf* small bell; *(di tenda)* curtain ring; *(di porta)* (ring-shaped) knocker; **campa'nello** *sm (all'uscio, da tavola)* bell.

campa'nile *sm* bell tower, belfry; **campani'lismo** *sm* parochialism.

cam'pare *vi* (2) to live; *(tirare avanti)* to get by, manage; ~ **alla giornata** to live from day to day.

cam'pato, a *ag:* ~ **in aria** unsound, unfounded.

campeggi'are [kamped'dʒare] *vi* to camp; *(risaltare)* to stand out; **cam'peggio** *sm* camping; *(terreno)* camp site; **fare (del) campeggio** to go camping.

cam'pestre *ag* country *cpd,* rural.

campio'nario, a *ag:* **fiera** ~ a trade fair // *sm* collection of samples.

campio'nato *sm* championship.

campio'ne, 'essa *sm/f (SPORT)* champion // *sm (COMM)* sample.

'campo *sm* field; *(MIL)* field; *(: accampamento)* camp; *(spazio delimitato: sportivo etc)* ground; field; *(di quadro)* background; **i** ~**i** *(campagna)* the countryside; ~ **da aviazione** airfield; ~ **di concentramento** concentration camp; ~ **di golf** golf course; ~ **da tennis** tennis court; ~ **visivo** field of vision.

campo'santo, *pl* **campi'santi** *sm* cemetery.

camuf'fare *vt* to disguise.

'Canada *sm:* **il** ~ Canada; **cana'dese** *ag, sm/f* Canadian.

ca'naglia [ka'naʎʎa] *sf* rabble, mob; *(persona)* scoundrel, rogue.

ca'nale *sm (anche fig)* channel; *(artificiale)* canal.

'canapa *sf* hemp.

cana'rino *sm* canary.

cancel'lare [kant∫el'lare] *vt (con la gomma)* to rub out, erase; *(con la penna)* to strike out; *(annullare)* to annul, cancel; *(disdire)* to cancel.

cancelle'ria [kant∫elle'ria] *sf* chancery; *(quanto necessario per scrivere)* stationery.

cancelli'ere [kant∫el'ljere] *sm* chancellor; *(di tribunale)* clerk of the court.

can'cello [kan't∫ello] *sm* gate.

can'crena *sf* gangrene.

'cancro *sm (MED)* cancer; *(dello zodiaco):* **C**~ Cancer.

can'dela *sf* candle; ~ **(di accensione)** *(AUT)* sparking plug.

cande'labro *sm* candelabra.

candeli'ere *sm* candlestick.

candi'dato, a *sm/f* candidate; *(aspirante a una carica)* applicant.

'candido, a *ag* white as snow; *(puro)* pure; *(sincero)* sincere, candid.

can'dito, a *ag* candied.

can'dore *sm* brilliant white; purity; sincerity, candour.

'cane *sm* dog; *(di pistola, fucile)* cock; **fa un freddo** ~ it's bitterly cold; **non c'era un** ~ there wasn't a soul; **quell'attore è un**

~ he's a rotten actor; ~ **da guardia** guard dog; ~ **lupo** alsatian.

ca'nestro *sm* basket.

cangi'ante [kan'dʒante] *ag* iridescent; **seta** ~ shot silk.

can'guro *sm* kangaroo.

ca'nile *sm* kennel; (*di allevamento*) kennels *pl*; ~ **municipale** dog pound.

ca'nino, a *ag, sm* canine.

'canna *sf* (*pianta*) reed; (: *indica, da zucchero*) cane; (*bastone*) stick, cane; (*di fucile*) barrel; (*di organo*) pipe; ~ **fumaria** chimney flue; ~ **da pesca** (fishing) rod; ~ **da zucchero** sugar cane.

can'nella *sf* (*CUC*) cinnamon.

can'nibale *sm* cannibal.

cannocchi'ale [kannok'kjale] *sm* telescope.

can'none *sm* (*MIL*) gun; (: *STORIA*) cannon; (*tubo*) pipe, tube; (*piega*) box pleat; (*fig*) ace.

can'nuccia, ce [kan'nuttʃa] *sf* (drinking) straw.

ca'noa *sf* canoe.

'canone *sm* canon, criterion; (*mensile, annuo*) rent; fee; **ca'nonico, ci** *sm* (*REL*) canon.

canoniz'zare [kanonid'dzare] *vt* to canonize.

ca'noro, a *ag* (*uccello*) singing, song *cpd*.

canot'taggio [kanot'taddʒo] *sm* rowing.

canotti'era *sf* vest.

ca'notto *sm* small boat, dinghy; canoe.

cano'vaccio [kano'vattʃo] *sm* (*tela*) canvas; (*strofinaccio*) duster; (*trama*) plot.

can'tante *sm/f* singer.

can'tare *vt, vi* to sing; **cantau'tore, 'trice** *sm/f* singer-composer.

canterel'lare *vt* to hum, sing to oneself.

canti'ere *sm* (*EDIL*) (building) site; (*anche:* ~ **navale**) shipyard.

canti'lena *sf* (*filastrocca*) lullaby; (*fig*) sing-song voice.

can'tina *sf* (*locale*) cellar; (*bottega*) wine shop.

'canto *sm* song; (*arte*) singing; (*REL*) chant; chanting; (*poesia*) poem, lyric; (*parte di una poesia*) canto; (*angolo di due muri*) corner; (*parte, lato*) side; **d'altro** ~ on the other hand.

can'tone *sm* (*in Svizzera*) canton.

can'tuccio [kan'tuttʃo] *sm* corner, nook.

ca'nuto, a *ag* white, whitehaired.

canzo'nare [kantso'nare] *vt* to tease.

can'zone [kan'tsone] *sf* song; (*POESIA*) canzone; **canzoni'ere** *sm* (*MUS*) songbook; (*LETTERATURA*) collection of poems.

'caos *sm inv* chaos; **ca'otico, a, ci, che** *ag* chaotic.

C.A.P. *abbr vedi* **codice.**

ca'pace [ka'patʃe] *ag* able, capable; (*ampio, vasto*) large, capacious; **sei** ~ **di farlo?** can you *o* are you able to do it?; **capacità** *sf inv* ability; (*DIR, di recipiente*) capacity; **capaci'tarsi** *vr*: **capacitarsi di** to make out, understand.

ca'panna *sf* hut.

capan'none *sm* (*AGR*) barn; (*fabbricato industriale*) (factory) shed.

ca'parbio, a *ag* stubborn.

ca'parra *sf* deposit, down payment.

ca'pello *sm* hair; ~**i** *smpl* (*capigliatura*) hair *sg*; **capel'luto, a** *ag* having thick hair.

capez'zale [kapet'tsale] *sm* bolster; (*fig*) bedside.

ca'pezzolo [ka'pettsolo] *sm* nipple.

capi'enza [ka'pjentsa] *sf* capacity.

capiglia'tura [kapiʎʎa'tura] *sf* hair.

ca'pire *vt* to understand.

capi'tale *ag* (*mortale*) capital; (*fondamentale*) main, chief // *sf* (*città*) capital // *sm* (*ECON*) capital; **capita'lismo** *sm* capitalism; **capita'lista, i, e** *ag, sm/f* capitalist.

capi'tano *sm* captain.

capi'tare (2) *vi* (*giungere casualmente*) to happen to go, find o.s.; (*accadere*) to happen; (*presentarsi: cosa*) to turn up, present itself // *vb impers* to happen.

capi'tello *sm* (*ARCHIT*) capital.

capito'lare *vi* to capitulate.

ca'pitolo *sm* chapter.

capi'tombolo *sm* headlong fall, tumble.

'capo *sm* head; (*persona*) head, leader; (: *in ufficio*) head, boss; (: *in tribù*) chief; (*di oggetti*) head; top; end; (*GEO*) cape; **andare a** ~ to start a new paragraph; **da** ~ over again; ~ **di bestiame** head *inv* of cattle; ~ **di vestiario** item of clothing.

'capo... *prefisso*: **Capo'danno** *sm* New Year; **capo'fitto: a capofitto** *av* headfirst, headlong; **capo'giro** *sm* dizziness *q*; **capola'voro, i** *sm* masterpiece; **capo'linea, i** *sm* **capi'linea** *sm* terminus; **capolu'ogo, pl ghi** *o* **capi-lu'oghi** *sm* chief town, administrative centre; **capo'mastro, pl i** *o* **capi'mastri** *sm* master builder.

capo'rale *sm* (*MIL*) lance corporal.

'capo... *prefisso*: **capo'saldo, pl capi'saldi** *sm* stronghold; (*fig: fondamento*) basis, cornerstone; **capostazi'one, pl capistazi'one** *sm* station master; **capo'treno, pl capi'treno** *o* **capo'treni** *sm* guard.

capo'volgere [kapo'voldʒere] *vt* to overturn; (*fig*) to reverse; ~**rsi** *vr* to overturn; (*barca*) to capsize; (*fig*) to be reversed.

capo'volto, a *pp di* **capovolgere.**

'cappa *sf* (*mantello*) cape, cloak; (*del camino*) hood.

cap'pella *sf* (*REL*) chapel; **cappel'lano** *sm* chaplain.

cap'pello *sm* hat.

'cappero *sm* caper.

cap'pone *sm* capon.

cap'potto *sm* (over)coat.

cappuc'cino [kapput'tʃino] *sm* (*frate*) Capuchin monk; (*bevanda*) frothy white coffee.

cap'puccio [kap'puttʃo] *sm* (*copricapo*) hood; (*della biro*) cap.

'**capra** sf (she-)goat; **ca'pretto** sm kid.

ca'priccio [ka'prittʃo] sm caprice, whim; (bizza) tantrum; **fare i ~i** to be very naughty; **capricci'oso, a** ag capricious, whimsical; naughty.

Capri'corno sm Capricorn.

capri'ola sf somersault.

capri'olo sm roe ĝeer.

'**capro** sm billy-goat; **~ espiatorio** (fig) scapegoat.

'**capsula** sf capsule; (di proiettile) primer; cap.

cap'tare vt (RADIO, TV) to pick up; (cattivarsi) to gain, win.

carabini'ere sm carabiniere.

ca'raffa sf carafe.

cara'mella sf sweet.

ca'rattere sm character; (caratteristica) characteristic, trait; **avere un buon ~** to be good-natured; **caratte'ristico, a, ci, che** ag characteristic // sf characteristic, trait, peculiarity; **caratteriz'zare** vt to characterize, distinguish.

car'bone sm coal.

carbu'rante sm (motor) fuel.

carbura'tore sm carburettor.

car'cassa sf carcass.

carce'rato, a [kartʃe'rato] sm/f prisoner.

'**carcere** ['kartʃere] sm prison; (pena) imprisonment.

carci'ofo [kar'tʃɔfo] sm artichoke.

car'diaco, a, ci, che ag cardiac, heart cpd.

cardi'nale ag, sm cardinal.

'**cardine** sm hinge.

'**cardo** sm thistle.

ca'rena sf (NAUT) bottom, hull.

ca'renza [ka'rɛntsa] sf lack, scarcity; (vitaminica) deficiency.

cares'tia sf famine; (penuria) scarcity, dearth.

ca'rezza [ka'rettsa] sf caress; **carez'zare** vt to caress, stroke, fondle.

'**carica** sf vedi **carico**.

cari'care vt to load; (aggravare: anche fig) to weigh down; (orologio) to wind up; (batteria, MIL) to charge.

carica'tura sf caricature.

'**carico, a, chi, che** ag (che porta un peso): **~ di** loaded o laden with; (fucile) loaded; (orologio) wound up; (batteria) charged; (colore) deep; (caffè, tè) strong // sm (il caricare) loading; (ciò che si carica, ELETTR) load; (fig: peso) burden, weight // sf (mansione ufficiale) office, position; (MIL, TECN, ELETTR) charge; (fig: energia) drive; **persona a ~** dependent; **essere a ~ di qd** (spese etc) to be charged to sb.

'**carie** sf (dentaria) decay.

ca'rino, a ag lovely, pretty, nice; (simpatico) nice.

carità sf charity; **per ~!** (escl di rifiuto) good heavens, no!

carnagi'one [karna'dʒone] sf complexion.

car'nale ag (amore) carnal; (fratello) blood cpd.

'**carne** sf flesh; (bovina, ovina etc) meat; **~ di manzo/maiale/pecora** beef/pork/mutton; **~ tritata** mince, minced meat.

car'nefice [kar'nefitʃe] sm executioner; hangman.

carne'vale sm carnival.

car'nivoro, a ag carnivorous.

car'noso, a ag fleshy.

'**caro, a** ag (amato) dear; (costoso) dear, expensive.

ca'rogna [ka'roɲɲa] sf carrion; (fig: fam) swine.

caro'sello sm merry-go-round.

ca'rota sf carrot.

caro'vana sf caravan.

caro'vita sm high cost of living.

carpenti'ere sm carpenter.

car'pire vt: **~ qc a qd** (segreto etc) to get sth out of sb.

car'poni av on all fours.

car'rabile ag suitable for vehicles.

car'raio, a ag: **passo ~** vehicle entrance.

carreggi'ata [karred'dʒata] sf carriageway.

car'rello sm trolley; (AER) undercarriage; (CINEMA) dolly; (di macchina da scrivere) carriage.

car'retto sm cart.

carri'era sf career; **fare ~** to get on; **a gran ~** at full speed.

carri'ola sf wheelbarrow.

'**carro** sm cart, wagon; **~ armato** tank.

car'rozza [kar'rɔttsa] sf carriage.

carrozze'ria [karrottse'ria] sf body, coachwork; (officina) coachbuilder's workshop.

carroz'zina [karrot'tsina] sf pram.

'**carta** sf paper; (al ristorante) menu; (GEO) map; plan; (documento, da gioco) card; (costituzione) charter; **~e** sfpl (documenti) papers, documents; **~ assorbente** blotting paper; **~ di credito** credit card; **~ (geografica)** map; **~ d'identità** identity card; **~ igienica** toilet paper; **~ da lettere** writing paper; **~ da parati** wallpaper; **~ verde** (AUT) green card; **~ vetrata** sandpaper.

cartacar'bone, pl **cartecar'bone** sf carbon paper.

car'taccia, ce [kar'tattʃa] sf waste paper.

cartamo'neta sf paper money.

carta'pecora sf parchment.

carta'pesta sf papier-mâché.

car'teggio [kar'teddʒo] sm correspondence.

car'tella sf (scheda) card; (custodia: di cartone) folder; (: di uomo d'affari etc) briefcase; (: di scolaro) schoolbag, satchel.

car'tello sm sign; (pubblicitario) poster; (stradale) sign, signpost; (ECON) cartel; (in dimostrazioni) placard; **cartel'lone** sm (pubblicitario) advertising poster; (della tombola) scoring frame; (TEATRO) playbill; **tenere il cartellone** (spettacolo) to have a long run.

carti'era *sf* paper mill.
carti'lagine [karti'ladʒine] *sf* cartilage.
car'toccio [kar'tɔttʃo] *sm* paper bag.
cartole'ria *sf* stationer's (shop).
carto'lina *sf* postcard.
car'tone *sm* cardboard; (*ARTE*) cartoon; **~i animati** *smpl* (*CINEMA*) cartoons.
car'tuccia, ce [kar'tuttʃa] *sf* cartridge.
'casa *sf* house; (*specialmente la propria casa*) home; (*COMM*) firm, house; **essere a ~** to be at home; **vado a ~ mia/tua** I'm going home/to your house; **~ di cura** nursing home; **~ dello studente** student hostel; **~e popolari** ≈ council houses (*o* flats).
ca'sacca, che *sf* military coat; (*di fantino*) blouse.
casalingo, a, ghi, ghe *ag* household, domestic; (*fatto a casa*) home-made; (*semplice*) homely; (*amante della casa*) home-loving // *sf* housewife; **~ghi** *smpl* household articles; **cucina ~a** a plain home cooking.
cas'care *vi* to fall; **cas'cata** *sf* fall; (*d'acqua*) cascade, waterfall.
'casco, schi *sm* helmet; (*del parrucchiere*) hair-drier.
ca'sella *sf* pigeon-hole; **~ postale (C.P.)** post office box (P.O. box).
ca'sello *sm* (*di autostrada*) toll-house.
ca'serma *sf* barracks *pl*.
ca'sino *sm* (*confusione*) row, racket; (*casa di prostituzione*) brothel.
casinò *sm inv* casino.
'caso *sm* chance; (*fatto, vicenda*) event, incident; (*possibilità*) possibility; (*MED, LING*) case; **a ~** at random; **per ~** by chance; by accident; **in ogni ~, in tutti i ~i** in any case, at any rate; **al ~** should the opportunity arise; **nel ~ che** in case; **~ mai** if by chance; **~ limite** borderline case.
'cassa *sf* case, crate, box; (*bara*) coffin; (*mobile*) chest; (*involucro: di orologio etc*) case; (*macchina*) cash register; (*luogo di pagamento*) cash desk; (*fondo*) fund; (*istituto bancario*) bank; **~ mutua** *o* **malattia** health insurance scheme; **~ toracica** (*ANAT*) chest; **~ di risparmio** savings bank.
cassa'forte, *pl* **casseforti** *sf* safe.
cassa'panca, *pl* **cassapanche** *o* **cassepanche** *sf* settle.
casseru'ola, casse'rola *sf* saucepan.
cas'setta *sf* box; (*per registratore*) cassette; (*CINEMA, TEATRO*) box-office takings *pl*; **~ di sicurezza** strongbox; **~ delle lettere** letterbox.
cas'setto *sm* drawer; **casset'tone** *sm* chest of drawers.
cassi'ere, a *sm/f* cashier; (*di banca*) teller.
'casta *sf* caste.
cas'tagna [kas'taɲɲa] *sf* chestnut.
cas'tagno [kas'taɲɲo] *sm* chestnut (tree).
cas'tello *sm* castle; (*TECN*) scaffolding.
casti'gare *vt* to punish; **cas'tigo, ghi** *sm* punishment.

castità *sf* chastity.
'casto, a *ag* chaste, pure.
cas'toro *sm* beaver.
cas'trare *vt* to castrate; to geld; to doctor.
casu'ale *ag* chance *cpd*.
cata'comba *sf* catacomb.
ca'talogo, ghi *sm* catalogue.
catarifran'gente [catarifran'dʒente] *sm* (*AUT*) reflector.
ca'tarro *sm* catarrh.
ca'tasta *sf* stack, pile.
ca'tasto *sm* land register; land registry office.
ca'tastrofe *sf* catastrophe, disaster.
cate'chismo [kate'kizmo] *sm* catechism.
catego'ria *sf* category; **cate'gorico, a, ci, che** *ag* categorical.
ca'tena *sf* chain; **~ di montaggio** assembly line; **~e da neve** (*AUT*) snow chains; **cate'naccio** *sm* bolt.
cate'ratta *sf* cataract; (*chiusa*) sluice-gate.
cati'nella *sf*: **piovere a ~e** to pour, rain cats and dogs.
ca'tino *sm* basin.
ca'trame *sm* tar.
'cattedra *sf* teacher's desk; (*di università*) chair.
catte'drale *sf* cathedral.
catti'veria *sf* malice, spite; naughtiness; (*atto*) spiteful act; (*parole*) malicious *o* spiteful remark.
cattività *sf* captivity.
cat'tivo, a *ag* bad; (*malvagio*) bad, wicked; (*turbolento: bambino*) bad, naughty; (*: mare*) rough; (*odore, sapore*) nasty, bad.
cattoli'cesimo [kattoli'tʃezimo] *sm* Catholicism.
cat'tolico, a, ci, che *ag, sm/f* (Roman) Catholic.
cat'tura *sf* capture.
cattu'rare *vt* to capture.
cauc'ciù [kaut'tʃu] *sm* rubber.
'causa *sf* cause; (*DIR*) lawsuit, case, action; **fare** *o* **muovere ~ a qd** to take legal action against sb.
cau'sare *vt* to cause.
'caustico, a, ci, che *ag* caustic.
cau'tela *sf* caution, prudence.
caute'lare *vt* to protect.
'cauto, a *ag* cautious, prudent.
cauzi'one [kaut'tsjone] *sf* security; (*DIR*) bail.
cav. *abbr di* **cavaliere.**
'cava *sf* quarry; (*di carbone*) open-cast mine.
caval'care *vt* (*cavallo*) to ride; (*muro*) to sit astride; (*sog: ponte*) to span; **caval'cata** *sf* ride; (*gruppo di persone*) riding party.
cavalca'via *sm inv* flyover.
cavalcioni [kaval'tʃoni]: **a ~ di** *prep* astride.
cavali'ere *sm* rider; (*feudale, titolo*) knight; (*soldato*) cavalryman; (*che accompagna una donna*) escort; (*: al ballo*) partner; **cavalle'resco, a, schi, sche** *ag*

chivalrous; **cavalle'ria** *sf* chivalry; (*milizia a cavallo*) cavalry.

cavalle'rizzo, a [kavalle'rittso] *sm/f* horseman/woman.

caval'letta *sf* grasshopper.

caval'letto *sm* (FOT) tripod; (*da pittore*) easel.

ca'vallo *sm* horse; (SCACCHI) knight; (AUT: *anche*: ~ **vapore**) horsepower; (*dei pantaloni*) crotch; **a** ~ **on** horseback; **a** ~ **di** astride, straddling; ~ **di corsa** racehorse.

ca'vare *vt* (*togliere*) to draw out, extract, take out; (*: giacca, scarpe*) to take off; (*: fame, sete, voglia*) to satisfy; **cavarsela** to get away with it; to manage, get on all right.

cava'tappi *sm inv* corkscrew.

ca'verna *sf* cave.

ca'vezza [ka'vettsa] *sf* halter.

'cavia *sf* guinea pig.

cavi'ale *sm* caviar.

ca'viglia [ka'viʎʎa] *sf* ankle.

cavil'lare *vi* to quibble.

cavità *sf inv* cavity.

'cavo, a *ag* hollow // *sm* (ANAT) cavity; (*grossa corda*) rope, cable; (ELETTR, TEL) cable.

cavolfi'ore *sm* cauliflower.

'cavolo *sm* cabbage; ~ **di Bruxelles** Brussels sprout.

cazzu'ola [kat'tswɔla] *sf* trowel.

c/c *abbr di* **conto corrente.**

ce [tʃe] *pron, av vedi* **ci.**

cecità [tʃetʃi'ta] *sf* blindness.

Cecoslo'vacchia [tʃekoslo'vakkja] *sf*: **la** ~ Czechoslovakia; **cecoslo'vacco, a, chi, che** *ag, sm/f* Czechoslovakian.

'cedere ['tʃɛdere] *vt* (*concedere: posto*) to give up; (DIR) to transfer, make over // *vi* (*cadere*) to give way, subside; ~ **(a)** to surrender (to), yield (to), give in (to); **ce-'devole** *ag* (*terreno*) soft; (*fig*) yielding.

'cedola ['tʃɛdola] *sf* (COMM) coupon; voucher.

'cedro ['tʃɛdro] *sm* cedar; (*albero da frutto*) lime tree.

C.E.E. *abbr f vedi* **comunità.**

cef'fone [tʃef'fone] *sm* slap, smack.

ce'larsi [tʃe'larsi] *vr* to hide.

cele'brare [tʃele'brare] *vt* to celebrate; **celebrazi'one** *sf* celebration.

'celebre ['tʃelebre] *ag* famous, celebrated; **celebrità** *sf inv* fame; (*persona*) celebrity.

'celere ['tʃelere] *ag* fast, swift; (*corso*) crash *cpd.*

ce'leste [tʃe'lɛste] *ag* celestial; heavenly; (*colore*) sky-blue.

celi'bato [tʃeli'bato] *sm* bachelorhood; (REL) celibacy.

'celibe ['tʃelibe] *ag* single, unmarried // *sm* bachelor.

'cella ['tʃella] *sf* cell.

'cellula ['tʃellula] *sf* (BIOL, ELETTR, POL) cell.

cemen'tare [tʃemen'tare] *vt* (*anche fig*) to cement.

ce'mento [tʃe'mento] *sm* cement; ~ **armato** reinforced concrete.

'cena ['tʃena] *sf* dinner; (*leggera*) supper.

ce'nare [tʃe'nare] *vi* to dine, have dinner.

'cencio ['tʃentʃo] *sm* piece of cloth, rag; (*da spolverare*) duster.

'cenere ['tʃenere] *sf* ash.

'cenno ['tʃenno] *sm* (*segno*) sign, signal; (*gesto*) gesture; (*col capo*) nod; (*con la mano*) wave; (*allusione*) hint, mention; (*spiegazione sommaria*) short account; **far** ~ **di sì/no** to nod (one's head)/shake one's head.

censi'mento [tʃensi'mento] *sm* census.

cen'sore [tʃen'sore] *sm* censor.

cen'sura [tʃen'sura] *sf* censorship; censor's office; (*fig*) censure; **censu'rare** *vt* to censor; to censure.

cente'nario, a [tʃente'narjo] *ag* (*che ha cento anni*) hundred-year-old; (*che ricorre ogni cento anni*) centennial, centenary *cpd* // *sm/f* centenarian // *sm* centenary.

cen'tesimo, a [tʃen'tezimo] *ag, sm* hundredth.

cen'tigrado, a [tʃen'tigrado] *ag* centigrade; **20 gradi** ~**i** 20 degrees centigrade.

cen'timetro [tʃen'timetro] *sm* centimetre.

centi'naio, pl(f) **aia** [tʃenti'najo] *sm*: **un** ~ **(di)** a hundred; about a hundred.

'cento ['tʃɛnto] *num* a hundred, one hundred.

cen'trale [tʃen'trale] *ag* central // *sf*: ~ **telefonica** (telephone) exchange; ~ **elettrica** electric power station; **centra-'lino** *sm* (telephone) exchange; (*di albergo etc*) switchboard; **centrali'nista** *sm/f* operator; **centraliz'zare** *vt* to centralize.

cen'trare [tʃen'trare] *vt* to hit the centre of; (TECN) to centre.

cen'trifuga [tʃen'trifuga] *sf* spin-drier.

'centro ['tʃentro] *sm* centre.

'ceppo ['tʃeppo] *sm* (*di albero*) stump; (*pezzo di legno*) log.

'cera ['tʃera] *sf* wax; (*aspetto*) appearance, look.

ce'ramica, che [tʃe'ramika] *sf* ceramic; (ARTE) ceramics *sg.*

'cerca ['tʃerka] *sf*: **in** *o* **alla** ~ **di** in search of.

cer'care [tʃer'kare] *vt* to look for, search for // *vi*: ~ **di fare qc** to try to do sth.

'cerchia ['tʃerkja] *sf* circle.

'cerchio ['tʃerkjo] *sm* circle; (*giocattolo, di botte*) hoop.

cere'ale [tʃere'ale] *sm* cereal.

cere'brale [tʃere'brale] *ag* cerebral.

ceri'monia [tʃeri'mɔnja] *sf* ceremony; **cerimoni'ale** *sm* etiquette, ceremonial; **cerimoni'oso, a** *ag* formal, ceremonious.

ce'rino [tʃe'rino] *sm* wax match.

'cernia ['tʃɛrnja] *sf* (ZOOL) stone bass.

cerni'era [tʃer'njɛra] *sf* hinge; ~ **lampo** zip (fastener).

'cernita ['tʃɛrnita] *sf* selection.

'cero ['tʃero] *sm* (church) candle.

ce'rotto [tʃe'rɔtto] *sm* sticking plaster.

cer'tezza [tʃer'tettsa] sf certainty.
certifi'care [tʃertifi'kare] vt to certify.
certifi'cato sm certificate; ~ medico/di nascita medical/birth certificate.
'certo, a ['tʃɛrto] ag certain; (sicuro): ~ (di/che) certain o sure (of/that) // det certain // av certainly, of course; ~i pronome pl some; un ~ non so che an indefinable something; di una ~a età past one's prime, not so young; sì ~ yes indeed; no ~ certainly not; di ~ certainly.
cer'tuni [tʃer'tuni] pronome pl some (people).
cer'vello [tʃer'vɛllo] sm (anche: pl(f) a o e) [tʃer'vɛllo] sm brain.
'cervo, a ['tʃɛrvo] sm/f stag/hind // sm deer; ~ volante stag beetle.
cesel'lare [tʃezel'lare] vt to chisel; (fig) to polish, finish with care.
ce'sello [tʃe'zɛllo] sm chisel.
ce'soie [tʃe'zoje] sfpl shears.
'cespite ['tʃɛspite] sm source of income.
ces'puglio [tʃes'puʎʎo] sm bush.
ces'sare [tʃes'sare] vi (2), vt to stop, cease; ~ di fare qc to stop doing sth; cessate il fuoco sm ceasefire.
'cesso ['tʃɛsso] sm (fam) bog.
'cesta ['tʃesta] sf (large) basket.
ces'tino [tʃes'tino] sm basket; (per la carta straccia) wastepaper basket.
'cesto ['tʃesto] sm basket.
'ceto ['tʃeto] sm (social) class.
cetrio'lino [tʃetrio'lino] sm gherkin.
cetri'olo [tʃetri'ɔlo] sm cucumber.
cfr. (abbr di confronta) cf.
che [ke] pronome (relativo: persona: soggetto) who; (: oggetto) whom; (: cosa) which, that; (tempo) ~ l'uomo ~ io vedo the man (whom) I see; il libro ~ è sul tavolo the book which o that is on the table; il giorno ~ ... the day (that) ...; la sera ~ ti ho visto the evening I saw you; (interrogativo, esclamativo) what; ~ (cosa) fai? what are you doing?; a ~ (cosa) pensi? what are you thinking about?; non sa ~ fare he doesn't know what to do // det what; (di numero limitato) which; ~ vestito ti vuoi mettere? what (o which) dress do you want to put on?; ~ tipo di film hai visto? what sort of film did you see?; ~ bel vestito! what a lovely dress!; ~ buono! how delicious! // cong that; so ~ tu c'eri I know (that) you were there; voglio ~ tu studi I want you to study; (affinché): vieni qua, ~ ti veda come here, so that I can see you; (temporale): arrivai ~ eri già partito you had already left when I arrived; sono anni ~ non lo vedo I haven't seen him in years; (in frasi imperative): ~ venga pure let him come by all means; non ~ sia stupido not that he's stupid; vedi non, più, meno etc.
cheru'bino [keru'bino] sm cherub.
cheti'chella [keti'kɛlla] alla ~ av stealthily, unobtrusively.
'cheto, a ['keto] ag quiet, silent.

chi [ki] pronome (interrogativo: soggetto) who; (: oggetto): di ~ è questo libro? whose book is this?; con ~ parli? to whom are you talking?, who are you talking to?; (relativo: colui/colei che) he/she who; (: complemento): dillo a ~ vuoi tell it to whoever you like; ~ dice una cosa ~ un'altra some say one thing some another.
chiacchie'rare [kjakkje'rare] vi to chat; (discorrere futilmente) to chatter; (far pettegolezzi) to gossip; chi'acchiere sfpl chatter q; gossip q; fare due o quattro chiacchiere to have a chat; chiacchie-'rone, a ag talkative, chatty; gossipy.
chia'mare [kja'mare] vt to call; (rivolgersi a qd) to call (in), send for; ~rsi vr (aver nome) to be called; mi chiamo Paolo my name is Paolo, I'm called Paolo; ~ alle armi to call up; ~ in giudizio to summon; chia'mata sf call; (MIL) call-up; chiamata interurbana (TEL) trunk call.
chia'rezza [kja'rettsa] sf clearness; clarity.
chiarifi'care [kjarifi'kare] vt (anche fig) to clarify.
chia'rire [kja'rire] vt to make clear; (fig: spiegare) to clear up, explain; ~rsi vr to become clear.
chi'aro, a ['kjaro] ag clear; (luminoso) clear, bright; (colore) pale, light.
chiaroveg'gente [kjaroved'dʒɛnte] sm/f clairvoyant.
chi'asso ['kjasso] sm uproar, row; chias-'soso, a ag noisy, rowdy.
chi'ave ['kjave] sf key // ag inv key cpd; ~ inglese monkey wrench; chiavis-'tello sm bolt.
chi'azza ['kjattsa] sf stain; splash.
chic [ʃik] ag inv chic, elegant.
'chicco, chi ['kikko] sm (di cereale, riso) grain; (di caffè) bean; ~ d'uva grape.
chi'edere ['kjɛdere] vt (per sapere) to ask; (per avere) to ask for // vi: ~ di qd to ask after sb; (chiamare: al telefono) to ask for o want sb; ~ qc a qd to ask sb sth; to ask sb for sth.
chi'erico, ci ['kjɛriko] sm cleric; altar boy.
chi'esa ['kjɛza] sf church.
chi'esto, a pp di chiedere.
'chiglia ['kiʎʎa] sf keel.
'chilo ['kilo] sm (abbr di chilogrammo) kilo; chilo'grammo sm kilogram(me); chi'lometro sm kilometre.
'chimico, a, ci, che ['kimiko] ag chemical // sm/f chemist // sf chemistry.
'china ['kina] sf (pendio) slope, descent; (inchiostro di) ~ Indian ink.
chi'nare [ki'nare] vt to lower, bend; ~rsi vr to stoop, bend.
chincaglie'ria [kinkaʎʎe'ria] sf fancy-goods shop; ~e sfpl fancy goods, knick-knacks.
chi'nino [ki'nino] sm quinine.
chi'occia, ce ['kjɔttʃa] sf brooding hen.
chi'occiola ['kjɔttʃola] sf snail.
chi'odo ['kjɔdo] sm nail; (fig) obsession.

chi'oma ['kjɔma] sf (capelli) head of hair; (di albero) foliage.

chi'osco, schi ['kjɔsko] sm kiosk.

chi'ostro ['kjɔstro] sm cloister.

chirur'gia [kirur'dʒia] sf surgery; **chi-'rurgo, ghi** o **gi** sm surgeon.

chissà [kis'sa] av who knows, I wonder.

chi'tarra [ki'tarra] sf guitar; **chitar-'rista, i, e** sm/f guitarist, guitar player.

chi'udere ['kjudere] vt to close, shut; (luce, acqua) to put off, turn off; (definitivamente: fabbrica) to close down, shut down; (strada) to close; (recingere) to enclose; (porre termine) to end // vi to close, shut; to close down, shut down; to end; **~rsi** vr to shut close; (ritirarsi: anche fig) to shut o.s. away; (ferita) to close up.

chi'unque [ki'unkwe] pronome (relativo) whoever; (indefinito) anyone, anybody.

chi'uso, a ['kjuso] pp di **chiudere** // sf (di corso d'acqua) sluice, lock; (recinto) enclosure; (di discorso etc) conclusion, ending; **chiu'sura** sf closing; shutting; closing o shutting down; enclosing; putting o turning off; ending; (dispositivo) catch; fastening; fastener.

ci [tʃi] (dav lo, la, li, le, ne diventa **ce**) pronome (personale) us; (: complemento di termine) (to) us; (: riflessivo) ourselves; (: reciproco) one another; (dimostrativo: di ciò, su ciò, in ciò etc) about (o on o of) it; **non so cosa far~** I don't know what to do about it; **che c'entro io?** what have I got to do with it? // av (qui) here; (lì) there; **esser~** vedi **essere**.

C.ia (abbr di **compagnia**) Co.

cia'batta [tʃa'batta] sf mule, slipper.

ci'alda ['tʃalda] sf (CUC) wafer.

ciam'bella [tʃam'bella] sf (CUC) ring-shaped cake; (salvagente) rubber ring.

ci'ao ['tʃao] escl (all'arrivo) hello!; (alla partenza) cheerio!, bye!

ciarla'tano [tʃarla'tano] sm charlatan.

cias'cuno, a [tʃas'kuno] (dav sm: **ciascun** +C, V, **ciascuno** +s impura, gn, pn, ps, x, z; dav sf: **ciascuna** +C, **ciascun'** +V) det, pronome each.

'cibo ['tʃibo] sm food.

ci'cala [tʃi'kala] sf cicada.

cica'trice [tʃika'tritʃe] sf scar; **cicatriz-'zarsi** vr to form a scar, heal (up).

'cicca ['tʃikka] sf cigarette end.

'ciccia ['tʃittʃa] sf (fam: carne) meat; (: grasso umano) fat, flesh.

cice'rone [tʃitʃe'rone] sm guide.

cicla'mino [tʃikla'mino] sm cyclamen.

ci'clismo [tʃi'klizmo] sm cycling; **ci'clista, i, e** sm/f cyclist.

'ciclo ['tʃiklo] sm cycle; (di malattia) course.

ciclomo'tore [tʃiklomo'tore] sm moped.

ci'clone [tʃi'klone] sm cyclone.

ciclos'tile [tʃiklos'tile] sm cyclostyle.

ci'cogna [tʃi'koɲɲa] sf stork.

ci'coria [tʃi'kɔria] sf chicory.

ci'eco, a, chi, che ['tʃɛko] ag blind // sm/f blind man/woman.

ci'elo ['tʃɛlo] sm sky; (REL) heaven.

'cifra ['tʃifra] sf (numero) figure; numeral; (somma di denaro) sum, figure; (monogramma) monogram, initials pl; (codice) code, cipher; **ci'frare** vt to embroider with a monogram; to code.

'ciglio ['tʃiʎʎo] sm (margine) edge, verge; (pl(f) **ciglia**: delle palpebre) eye(lash); eye(lid); (sopracciglio) eyebrow.

'cigno ['tʃiɲɲo] sm swan.

cigo'lare [tʃigo'lare] vi to squeak, creak.

'Cile ['tʃile] sm: **il ~** Chile.

cilecca [tʃi'lekka] sf: **far ~** to fail.

cili'egia, gie o **ge** [tʃi'ljedʒa] sf cherry; **cili'egio** sm cherry tree.

cilin'drata [tʃilin'drata] sf (AUT) (cubic) capacity; **una macchina di grossa ~** a big-engined car.

ci'lindro [tʃi'lindro] sm cylinder; (cappello) top hat.

'cima ['tʃima] sf (sommità) top; (di monte) top, summit; (estremità) end; **da ~ a fondo** from top to bottom; (fig) from beginning to end.

cimen'tare [tʃimen'tare] vt to put to the test.

'cimice ['tʃimitʃe] sf (ZOOL) bug; (puntina) drawing pin.

cimini'era [tʃimi'njɛra] sf chimney; (di nave) funnel.

cimi'tero [tʃimi'tɛro] sm cemetery.

ci'murro [tʃi'murro] sm (di cani) distemper.

'Cina ['tʃina] sf: **la ~** China.

'cinema ['tʃinema] sm inv cinema; **cinematogra'fare** vt to film; **cine'presa** sf cine-camera.

ci'nese [tʃi'nese] ag, sm/f, sm Chinese inv.

ci'netico, a, ci, che [tʃi'nɛtiko] ag kinetic.

'cingere ['tʃindʒere] vt (attorniare) to surround, encircle; **~ la vita con una cintura** to put a belt round one's waist.

'cinghia ['tʃiŋgja] sf strap; (cintura, TECN) belt.

cinghi'ale [tʃin'gjale] sm wild boar.

cinguet'tare [tʃiŋgwet'tare] vi to twitter.

'cinico, a, ci, che ['tʃiniko] ag cynical // sm/f cynic.

cin'quanta [tʃin'kwanta] num fifty; **cinquan'tesimo, a** num fiftieth.

cinquan'tina [tʃinkwan'tina] sf (serie): **una ~ (di)** about fifty; (età): **essere sulla ~** to be about fifty.

'cinque ['tʃinkwe] num five; **avere ~ anni** to be five (years old); **il ~ dicembre 1982** the fifth of December 1982; **alle ~ (ora)** at five (o'clock).

cinque'cento [tʃinkwe'tʃento] num five hundred // sm: **il C~** the sixteenth century.

'cinto, a ['tʃinto] pp di **cingere**.

cin'tura [tʃin'tura] sf belt; **~ di salvataggio** lifebelt; **~ di sicurezza** (AUT, AER) safety belt.

ciò [tʃɔ] pronome this; that; **~ che** what; **~ nondimeno** in spite of this (o that).

ci'occa, che ['tʃɔkka] sf (di capelli) lock.

ciocco'lata [tʃokko'lata] sf chocolate; (bevanda) (hot) chocolate; **cioccola'tino** sm chocolate; **ciocco'lato** sm chocolate.

cioè [tʃo'ɛ] av that is (to say).

ciondo'lare [tʃondo'lare] vi to dangle; (fig) to loaf (about); **ci'ondolo** sm pendant.

ci'otola ['tʃɔtola] sf bowl.

ci'ottolo ['tʃɔttolo] sm pebble; (di strada) cobble(stone).

ci'polla [tʃi'polla] sf onion; (di tulipano etc) bulb.

ci'presso [tʃi'prɛsso] sm cypress (tree).

'cipria ['tʃiprja] sf (face) powder.

cipri'ota, i, e [tʃipri'ɔta] ag, sm/f Cypriot.

'Cipro ['tʃipro] sm Cyprus.

'circa ['tʃirka] av about, roughly // prep about, concerning; **a mezzogiorno ~** about midday.

'circo, chi ['tʃirko] sm circus.

circo'lare [tʃirko'lare] vi to circulate; (AUT) to drive (along), move (along) // ag circular // sf (AMM) circular; (di autobus) circle (line); **circolazi'one** sf circulation; (AUT): **la circolazione** (the) traffic.

'circolo ['tʃirkolo] sm circle.

circon'dare [tʃirkon'dare] vt to surround.

circonfe'renza [tʃirkonfe'rɛntsa] sf circumference.

circonvallazi'one [tʃirkonvallat'tsjone] sf ring road; (per evitare una città) by-pass.

circos'critto, a [tʃirkos'kritto] pp di **circoscrivere**.

circos'crivere [tʃirkos'krivere] vt to circumscribe; (fig) to limit, restrict; **circoscrizi'one** sf (AMM) district, area; **circoscrizione elettorale** constituency.

circos'petto, a [tʃirkos'pɛtto] ag circumspect, cautious.

circos'tante [tʃirkos'tante] ag surrounding, neighbouring.

circos'tanza [tʃirkos'tantsa] sf circumstance; (occasione) occasion.

cir'cuito [tʃir'kuito] sm circuit.

'ciste ['tʃiste] sf = **cisti**.

cis'terna [tʃis'tɛrna] sf tank, cistern.

'cisti ['tʃisti] sf cyst.

C.I.T. [tʃit] abbr f di Compagnia Italiana Turismo.

ci'tare [tʃi'tare] vt (DIR) to summon; (autore) to quote; (a esempio, modello) to cite; **citazi'one** sf summons sg; quotation; (di persona) mention.

ci'tofono [tʃi'tɔfono] sm entry phone; (in uffici) intercom.

città [tʃit'ta] sf inv town; (importante) city; **~ universitaria** university campus.

cittadi'nanza [tʃittadi'nantsa] sf citizens pl, inhabitants pl of a town (o city); (DIR) citizenship.

citta'dino, a [tʃitta'dino] ag town cpd; city cpd // sm/f (di uno Stato) citizen; (abitante di città) towndweller.

ci'uco, a, chi, che ['tʃuko] sm/f ass, donkey.

ci'uffo ['tʃuffo] sm tuft.

ci'vetta [tʃi'vetta] sf (ZOOL) owl; (fig: donna) coquette, flirt.

'civico, a, ci, che ['tʃiviko] ag civic; (museo) municipal, town cpd; municipal, city cpd.

ci'vile [tʃi'vile] ag civil; (non militare) civilian; (nazione) civilized // sm civilian.

civiliz'zare [tʃivilid'dzare] vt to civilize; **civilizzazi'one** sf civilization.

civiltà [tʃivil'ta] sf civilization; (cortesia) civility.

ci'vismo [tʃi'vizmo] sm public spirit.

'clacson sm inv (AUT) horn.

cla'more sm (frastuono) din, uproar, clamour; (fig) outcry; **clamo'roso, a** ag noisy; (fig) sensational.

clandes'tino, a ag clandestine; (POL) underground, clandestine // sm/f stowaway.

clari'netto sm clarinet.

'classe sf class; **di ~** (fig) with class; of excellent quality.

classi'cismo [klassi'tʃizmo] sm classicism.

'classico, a, ci, che ag classical; (tradizionale: moda) classic(al) // sm classic; classical author.

clas'sifica sf classification; (SPORT) placings pl.

classifi'care vt to classify; (candidato, concorrente) to grade; (compito) to mark; **~rsi** vr to be placed; **classificazi'one** sf classification; grading; marking.

'clausola sf (DIR) clause.

'clava sf club.

clavi'cembalo [klavi'tʃembalo] sm harpsichord.

cla'vicola sf (ANAT) collar bone.

cle'mente ag merciful; (clima) mild; **cle'menza** sf mercy, clemency; mildness.

cleri'cale ag clerical.

'clero sm clergy.

cli'ente sm/f customer, client; **clien'tela** sf customers pl, clientèle.

'clima, i sm climate; **cli'matico, a, ci, che** ag climatic; **climatizzazi'one** sf (TECN) air conditioning.

'clinico, a, ci, che ag clinical // sm (medico) clinician // sf (scienza) clinical medicine; (casa di cura) clinic, nursing home; (ospedale) clinic.

clo'aca, che sf sewer.

cloro'filla sf chlorophyll.

cloro'formio sm chloroform.

club sm inv club.

coabi'tare vi to live together, live under the same roof.

coagu'lare vt to coagulate // vi (2), **~rsi** vr to coagulate; (latte) to curdle.

coalizi'one [koalit'tsjone] sf coalition.

co'atto, a ag (DIR) compulsory, forced.

'cobra sm inv cobra.

coca'ina sf cocaine.

cocci'nella [kottʃi'nɛlla] sf ladybird.

'coccio ['kɔttʃo] sm earthenware; (vaso) earthenware pot; **~i** smpl fragments (of pottery).

cocci'uto, a [kot'tʃuto] *ag* stubborn, pigheaded.

'cocco, chi *sm* (*pianta*) coconut palm; (*frutto*): **noce di ~** coconut // *sm/f* (*fam*) darling.

cocco'drillo *sm* crocodile.

cocco'lare *vt* to cuddle, fondle.

co'cente [ko'tʃɛnte] *ag* (*anche fig*) burning.

co'comero *sm* watermelon.

co'cuzzolo [ko'kuttsolo] *sm* top; (*di capo, cappello*) crown.

'coda *sf* tail; (*fila di persone, auto*) queue; (*di abiti*) train; (*dell'occhio*) corner; **mettersi in ~** to queue (up); to join the queue; **~ di cavallo** (*acconciatura*) ponytail.

co'dardo, a *ag* cowardly // *sm/f* coward.

'codice ['koditʃe] *sm* code; **~ di avviamento postale (C.A.P.)** postal code; **~ della strada** highway code.

codifi'care *vt* (*DIR*) to codify; (*cifrare*) to code.

coe'rente *ag* coherent; **coe'renza** *sf* coherence.

coesi'one *sf* cohesion.

coe'sistere *vi* (2) to coexist.

coe'taneo, a *ag*, *sm/f* contemporary.

'cofano *sm* (*AUT*) bonnet; (*forziere*) chest.

'cogli ['kɔʎʎi] *prep + det vedi* **con**.

'cogliere ['kɔʎʎere] *vt* (*fiore, frutto*) to pick, gather; (*sorprendere*) to catch, surprise; (*bersaglio*) to hit; (*fig: momento opportuno etc*) to grasp, seize, take; (*: capire*) to grasp; **~ qd in flagrante** *o* **in fallo** to catch sb red-handed.

co'gnato, a [koɲ'ɲato] *sm/f* brother-/sister-in-law.

cognizi'one [koɲɲit'tsjone] *sf* knowledge.

co'gnome [koɲ'ɲome] *sm* surname.

'coi *prep + det vedi* **con**.

coinci'denza [kointʃi'dɛntsa] *sf* coincidence; (*FERR, AER, di autobus*) connection.

coin'volgere [koin'vɔldʒere] *vt*: **~ in** to involve in.

col *prep + det vedi* **con**.

cola'brodo *sm inv* strainer.

cola'pasta *sm inv* colander.

co'lare *vt* (*liquido*) to strain; (*pasta*) to drain; (*oro fuso*) to pour // *vi* (*sudore*) to drip; (*botte*) to leak; (*cera*) to melt; **~ a picco** *vt, vi* (*nave*) to sink.

co'lata *sf* (*di lava*) flow; (*FONDERIA*) casting.

colazi'one [kolat'tsjone] *sf* (*anche*: **prima ~**) breakfast; (*anche*: **seconda ~**) lunch; **fare ~** to have breakfast (*o* lunch).

co'lei *pronome vedi* **colui**.

co'lera *sm* (*MED*) cholera.

'colica *sf* (*MED*) colic.

'colla *sf* glue; (*di farina*) paste.

collabo'rare *vi* to collaborate; **~ a** to collaborate on; (*giornale*) to contribute to; **collabora'tore, 'trice** *sm/f* collaborator; contributor; **collaborazi'one** *sf* collaboration; contribution.

col'lana *sf* necklace; (*collezione*) collection, series.

col'lant [kɔ'lã] *sm inv* tights *pl*.

col'lare *sm* collar.

col'lasso *sm* (*MED*) collapse.

collau'dare *vt* to test, try out; **col'laudo** *sm* testing *q*; test.

'colle *sm* hill.

col'lega, ghi, ghe *sm/f* colleague.

collega'mento *sm* connection; (*MIL*) liaison.

colle'gare *vt* to connect, join, link; **~rsi** *vr* (*RADIO, TV*) to link up; **~rsi con** (*TEL*) to get through to.

col'legio [kol'lɛdʒo] *sm* college; (*convitto*) boarding school; **~ elettorale** (*POL*) constituency.

'collera *sf* anger.

col'lerico, a, ci, che *ag* quick-tempered, irascible.

col'letta *sf* collection.

collettività *sf* community.

collet'tivo, a *ag* collective; (*interesse*) general, everybody's; (*biglietto, visita etc*) group *cpd* // *sm* (*POL*) (political) group.

col'letto *sm* collar.

collezio'nare [kollettsjo'nare] *vt* to collect.

collezi'one [kollet'tsjone] *sf* collection.

colli'mare *vi* to correspond, coincide.

col'lina *sf* hill.

col'lirio *sm* eyewash.

collisi'one *sf* collision.

'collo *sm* neck; (*di abito*) neck, collar; (*pacco*) parcel; **~ del piede** instep.

colloca'mento *sm* (*impiego*) employment; (*disposizione*) placing, arrangement.

collo'care *vt* (*libri, mobili*) to place; (*persona: trovare un lavoro per*) to find a job for, place; (*COMM: merce*) to find a market for; **~rsi** *vr* to take one's place; to find a job.

col'loquio *sm* conversation, talk; (*ufficiale*) interview, talk; (*INS*) preliminary oral exam.

col'mare *vt*: **~ di** (*anche fig*) to fill with; (*dare in abbondanza*) to load *o* overwhelm with; **'colmo, a** *ag*: **colmo (di)** full (of) // *sm* summit, top; (*fig*) height; **al colmo della disperazione** in the depths of despair; **è il colmo!** it's the last straw!

co'lombo, a *sm/f* dove; pigeon.

co'lonia *sf* colony; (*per bambini*) holiday camp; **acqua di ~** (eau de) cologne; **coloni'ale** *ag* colonial // *sm/f* colonist, settler.

coloniz'zare [kolonid'dzare] *vt* to colonize.

co'lonna *sf* column; **~ vertebrale** spine, spinal column.

colon'nello *sm* colonel.

co'lono *sm* (*coltivatore*) tenant farmer.

colo'rante *sm* colouring.

colo'rare *vt* to colour; (*disegno*) to colour in.

co'lore *sm* colour; **a ~i** in colour, colour

cpd; **farne di tutti i ~i** to get up to all sorts of mischief.

colo'rito, a ag coloured; (*viso*) rosy, pink; (*linguaggio*) colourful // sm (*tinta*) colour; (*carnagione*) complexion.

co'loro pronome pl vedi **colui.**

colos'sale ag colossal, enormous.

co'losso sm colossus.

'colpa sf fault; (*biasimo*) blame; (*colpevolezza*) guilt; (*azione colpevole*) offence; (*peccato*) sin; **di chi è la ~?** whose fault is it?; **per ~ di** through, owing to; **col'pevole** ag guilty.

col'pire vt to hit, strike; (*fig*) to strike; **rimanere colpito da qc** to be amazed o struck by sth.

'colpo sm (*urto*) knock; (: *affettivo*) blow, shock; (: *aggressivo*) blow; (*di pistola*) shot; (*SPORT*) stroke; shot; blow; (*MED*) stroke; **di ~** suddenly; **fare ~** to make a strong impression; **~ di grazia** coup de grâce; **~ di sole** sunstroke; **~ di Stato** coup d'état; **~ di telefono** phone call; **~ di testa** (sudden) impulse o whim; **~ di vento** gust (of wind).

coltel'lata sf stab.

col'tello sm knife; **~ a serramanico** clasp knife.

colti'vare vt to cultivate; (*verdura*) to grow, cultivate; (*MINERALOGIA*) to work; **coltiva'tore** sm farmer; **coltivazi'one** sf cultivation; growing; working.

'colto, a pp di **cogliere** // ag (*istruito*) cultured, educated.

'coltre sf blanket.

col'tura sf (*di terra*) cultivation; (*di verdura*) growing; cultivation.

co'lui, co'lei, pl **co'loro** pronome the one; **~ che parla** the one o the man o the person who is speaking; **colei che amo** the one o the woman o the person (whom) I love.

'coma sm inv coma.

comanda'mento sm (*REL*) commandment.

coman'dante sm (*MIL*) commander, commandant; (*di reggimento*) commanding officer; (*NAUT, AER*) captain.

coman'dare vt to command; (*imporre*) to order, command; (*meccanismo*) to control; **co'mando** sm (*ingiunzione*) order, command; (*autorità*) command; (*TECN*) control.

combaci'are [kombat'tʃare] vi to meet; (*fig: coincidere*) to coincide, correspond.

combat'tente ag fighting // sm combatant; **ex-~** ex-serviceman.

com'battere vt to fight; (*fig*) to combat, fight against // vi to fight; **combatti'mento** sm fight; fighting q; (*di pugilato*) match.

combi'nare vt to combine; (*organizzare*) to arrange; (*fam: fare*) to make, cause; **~rsi** vr to combine; (*mettersi d'accordo*) to come to an agreement; **combinazi'one** sf combination; (*caso fortuito*) coincidence; (*biancheria*) combinations pl; (*tuta: da aviatore*) flying suit; (: *da operaio*) boiler

suit; **per combinazione** by chance.

combus'tibile ag combustible // sm fuel.

combusti'one sf combustion.

com'butta sf (*peg*) gang; **in ~** in league.

'come av like; (*in qualità di*) as; (*interrogativo, esclamativo*) how; (*che cosa, prego*): **~?** pardon?, sorry? // cong as; (*che, in quale modo*) how; (*appena che, quando*) as soon as; **~ stai?** how are you?; **~ sei cresciuto!** how you've grown!; **~ se** as if, as though; vedi **così, tanto.**

co'meta sf comet.

'comico, a, ci, che ag (*TEATRO*) comic; (*buffo*) comical // sm (*attore*) comedian, comic actor; (*comicità*) comic spirit, comedy.

co'mignolo [ko'miɲnolo] sm chimney top.

cominci'are [komin'tʃare] vt, vi to begin, start; **~ a fare/col fare** to begin to do/by doing.

comi'tato sm committee.

comi'tiva sf party, group.

co'mizio [ko'mittsjo] sm (*POL*) meeting, assembly.

com'mando sm inv commando (squad).

com'media sf comedy; (*opera teatrale*) play; (: *che fa ridere*) comedy; (*fig*) playacting q; **commedi'ante** sm/f (*peg*) third-rate actor/actress; (: *fig*) sham.

commemo'rare vt to commemorate; **commemorazi'one** sf commemoration.

commen'tare vt to comment on; (*testo*) to annotate; (*RADIO, TV*) to give a commentary on; **commenta'tore, 'trice** sm/f commentator; **com'mento** sm comment; (*a un testo*) commentary, notes pl; (*RADIO, TV*) commentary.

commerci'ale [kommer'tʃale] ag commercial, trading; (*peg*) commercial.

commerci'ante [kommer'tʃante] sm/f trader, dealer; (*bottegaio*) shopkeeper.

commerci'are [kommer'tʃare] vi: **~ in** to deal o trade in.

com'mercio [kom'mertʃo] sm trade, commerce; **essere in ~** (*prodotto*) to be on the market o on sale; **essere nel ~** (*persona*) to be in business; **all'ingrosso/al minuto** wholesale/retail trade.

com'messo, a pp di **commettere** // sm/f shop assistant // sm (*impiegato subalterno*) clerk // sf (*COMM*) order; **~ viaggiatore** commercial traveller.

commes'tibile ag edible.

com'mettere vt to commit.

commi'nare vt (*DIR*) to threaten; to inflict.

commise'rare vt to sympathize with, commiserate with.

commissari'ato sm (*AMM*) commissionership; (: *sede*) commissioner's office; (: *di polizia*) police station.

commis'sario sm commissioner; (*di pubblica sicurezza*) ≈ police superintendent; (*SPORT*) steward; (*membro di commissione*) member of a committee o board.

commissio'nario sm (COMM) selling agent.

commissi'one sf (incarico) message; errand; (comitato, percentuale) commission; (per: ordinazione) order; ~i sfpl (acquisti) shopping sg.

commit'tente sm/f (COMM) purchaser, buyer.

com'mosso, a pp di **commuovere.**

commo'vente ag moving.

commozi'one [kommot'tsjone] sf emotion, deep feeling; ~ **cerebrale** concussion.

commu'overe vt to move, affect; ~rsi vr to be moved.

commu'tare vt (pena) to commute; (ELETTR) to change o switch over.

comò sm inv chest of drawers.

como'dino sm bedside table.

comodità sf inv comfort; convenience.

'comodo, a ag comfortable; (facile) easy; (conveniente) convenient; (utile) useful, handy; (persona) easy-going // sm comfort; convenience; con ~ at one's convenience o leisure; **fare il proprio** ~ to do as one pleases; **far** ~ to be useful o handy.

compae'sano, a sm/f fellow-countryman; person from the same town.

com'pagine [kom'padʒine] sf (squadra) team.

compa'gnia [kompaɲ'ɲia] sf company; (gruppo) gathering.

com'pagno, a [kom'paɲɲo] sm/f (di classe, gioco) companion; (POL) comrade; (COMM: socio) partner; ~ **di squadra** team mate.

compa'rare vt to compare.

compara'tivo, a ag, sm comparative.

comparazi'one [komparat'tsjone] sf comparison.

compa'rire vi (2) to appear; (spiccare: persona) to stand out; **com'parso, a** pp di **comparire** // sf appearance; (TEATRO) walk-on; (CINEMA) extra.

compartecipazi'one [kompartet ʃipat'tsjone] sf sharing; (quota) share; ~ **agli utili** profit-sharing.

comparti'mento sm (suddivisione) division, compartment; (FERR) compartment; (AMM) department.

compassi'one sf compassion, pity; **avere ~ di qd** to feel sorry for sb, to pity sb; **compassio'nevole** ag compassionate.

com'passo sm (pair of) compasses pl; callipers pl.

compa'tibile ag (scusabile) excusable; (conciliabile) compatible.

compati'mento sm compassion; indulgence.

compa'tire vt (aver compassione di) to sympathize with, feel sorry for; (scusare) to make allowances for.

compatri'ota, i, e sm/f compatriot.

com'patto, a ag compact; (roccia) solid; (folla) dense; (fig: partito) united, close-knit.

compendi'are vt to summarize.

com'pendio sm summary; (libro) compendium.

compene'trare vt to permeate.

compen'sare vt (equilibrare) to compensate for, make up for; ~ **qd di** (rimunerare) to pay o remunerate sb for; (risarcire) to pay compensation to sb for; (fig: fatiche, dolori) to reward sb for; **com'penso** sm compensation; payment, remuneration; reward; **in compenso** in compensation; (in cambio) in return.

'compera etc = **compra** etc.

compe'tente ag competent; (mancia) apt, suitable; **compe'tenza** sf competence; **competenze** sfpl (onorari) fees.

com'petere vi to compete, vie; (DIR: spettare): ~ **a** to lie within the competence of; **competi'tore, 'trice** sm/f competitor; **competizi'one** sf competition.

compia'cente [kompja'tʃɛnte] ag courteous, obliging; **compia'cenza** sf courtesy.

compia'cere [kompja'tʃere] vi: ~ **a** to gratify, please // vt to humour; ~rsi vr (provare soddisfazione): ~rsi di o per qc to be delighted at sth; (rallegrarsi): ~rsi **con qd** to congratulate sb; (degnarsi): ~rsi **di fare** to be so good as to do; **compiaci'uto, a** pp di **compiacere.**

compi'angere [kom'pjandʒere] vt to sympathize with, feel sorry for; **com'pianto, a** pp di **compiangere.**

'compiere vt (concludere) to finish, end, complete; (adempiere) to carry out, fulfil; ~rsi vr (avverarsi) to be fulfilled, come true; ~ **gli anni** to have one's birthday.

compi'lare vt to compile.

com'pire vb = **compiere.**

compi'tare vt to spell out.

'compito sm (incarico) task, duty; (dovere) duty; (INS) exercise; (: a casa) homework.

com'pito, a ag well-mannered, polite.

complemen'tare ag complementary; (INS: materia) subsidiary.

comple'mento sm complement; (MIL) reserve (troops); ~ **oggetto** (LING) direct object.

complessità sf complexity.

comples'sivo, a ag (globale) comprehensive, overall; (totale: cifra) total.

com'plesso, a ag complex // sm (PSIC, EDIL) complex; (MUS: corale) ensemble; (: orchestrina) band; (: di musica pop) group; **in** o **nel** ~ on the whole.

comple'tare vt to complete.

com'pleto, a ag complete; (teatro, autobus) full // sm suit; **al** ~ full; (tutti presenti) all present.

compli'care vt to complicate; ~rsi vr to become complicated; **complicazi'one** sf complication.

'complice ['kɔmplitʃe] sm/f accomplice.

complimen'tarsi vr: ~ **con** to congratulate.

compli'mento sm compliment; ~i smpl

(cortesia eccessiva) ceremony sg; (ossequi) regards, compliments; ~i! congratulations!; senza ~i! don't stand on ceremony!; make yourself at home!; help yourself!

complot'tare vi to plot, conspire.

com'plotto sm plot, conspiracy.

compo'nente sm/f member // sm o f component (part).

componi'mento sm (DIR) settlement; (INS) composition; (poetico, teatrale) work.

com'porre vt (musica, testo) to compose; (formare) to make up, form; (motore) to make up, put together; (mettere in ordine) to arrange; (DIR: lite) to settle; (TIP) to set.

comporta'mento sm behaviour.

compor'tare vt (implicare) to involve; (consentire) to permit, allow (of); ~rsi vr (condursi) to behave.

composi'tore, 'trice sm/f composer; (TIP) compositor, typesetter.

composizi'one [kompozit'tsjone] sf composition; (DIR) settlement.

com'posta sf vedi composto.

compos'tezza [kompos'tettsa] sf composure; decorum.

com'posto, a pp di comporre // ag (persona) composed, self-possessed; (: decoroso) dignified; (formato da più elementi) compound cpd // sm compound // sf (CUC) stewed fruit q; (AGR) compost.

'compra sf purchase.

com'prare vt to buy; compra'tore, 'trice sm/f buyer, purchaser.

com'prendere vt (contenere) to comprise, consist of; (capire) to understand.

comprensi'one sf understanding.

compren'sivo, a ag (prezzo): ~ di inclusive of; (indulgente) understanding.

com'preso, a pp di comprendere // ag (incluso) included.

com'pressa sf vedi compresso.

compressi'one sf compression; (pressione) pressure.

com'presso, a pp di comprimere // ag pressed; compressed; repressed // sf (MED: garza) compress; (: pastiglia) tablet.

com'primere vt (premere) to press; (FISICA) to compress; (fig) to repress.

compro'messo, a pp di compromettere // sm compromise.

compro'mettere vt to compromise.

compro'vare vt to confirm.

com'punto, a ag contrite; compunzi'one sf compunction.

compu'tare vt to calculate; (addebitare): ~ qc a qd to debit sb with sth; computiste'ria sf accounting, book-keeping; 'computo sm calculation.

comu'nale ag municipal; town cpd, ≈ borough cpd.

comu'nanza [komu'nantsa] sf community.

co'mune ag common; (consueto) common, everyday; (di livello medio) average; (ordinario) ordinary // sm (AMM) commune, ≈ town council; (: sede) town hall // sf (di persone) commune; fuori del ~ out of the ordinary; mettere in ~ to share.

comuni'care vt (notizia) to pass on, convey; (malattia) to pass on; (ansia etc) to communicate; (trasmettere: calore etc) to transmit, communicate; (REL) to administer communion to // vi to communicate; ~rsi vr (propagarsi): ~rsi a to spread to; (REL) to receive communion; comunica-'tivo, a ag (sentimento) infectious; (persona) communicative.

comuni'cato sm communiqué.

comunicazi'one [komunikat'tsjone] sf communication; (TEL): ~ (telefonica) (telephone) call; dare la ~ a qd to put sb through; ottenere la ~ to get through.

comuni'one sf communion.

comu'nismo sm communism; comu-'nista, i, e ag, sm/f communist.

comunità sf inv community; C~ Economica Europea (C.E.E.) European Economic Community (EEC).

co'munque cong however, no matter how // av (in ogni modo) in any case; (tuttavia) however, nevertheless.

con prep (nei seguenti casi con può fondersi con l'articolo definito: con + il = col, con + gli = cogli, con + i = coi) with; partire col treno to leave by train; ~ mio grande stupore to my great astonishment; ~ tutto ciò for all that.

co'nato sm: ~ di vomito retching.

'conca, che sf (GEO) valley.

'concavo, a ag concave.

con'cedere [kon'tʃɛdere] vt (accordare) to grant; (ammettere) to admit, concede; ~rsi qc to treat o.s. to sth, to allow o.s. sth.

concentra'mento [kontʃentra'mento] sm concentration.

concen'trare [kontʃen'trare] vt, ~rsi vr to concentrate; concentrazi'one sf concentration.

concepi'mento [kontʃepi'mento] sm conception.

conce'pire [kontʃe'pire] vt (bambino) to conceive, (progetto, idea) to conceive (of); (metodo, piano) to devise; (affetto, speranze) to entertain.

con'cernere [kon'tʃɛrnere] vt to concern.

concer'tare [kontʃer'tare] vt (MUS) to harmonize; (ordire) to devise, plan; ~rsi vr to agree.

con'certo [kon'tʃɛrto] sm (MUS) concert; (: componimento) concerto.

concessio'nario [kontʃessjo'narjo] sm (COMM) agent, dealer.

concessi'one [kontʃes'sjone] sf concession.

con'cesso, a [kon'tʃɛsso] pp di concedere.

con'cetto [kon'tʃɛtto] sm (pensiero, idea) concept; (opinione) opinion.

concezi'one [kontʃet'tsjone] sf conception.

con'chiglia [kon'kiʎʎa] sf shell.

'concia ['kɔntʃa] sf (di pelle) tanning; (di

tabacco) curing; (*sostanza*) tannin.

conci'are [kon'tʃare] *vt* (*pelle*) to tan; (*tabacco*) to cure; (*fig: ridurre in cattivo stato*) to beat up; ~**rsi** *vr* (*sporcarsi*) to get in a mess; (*vestirsi male*) to dress badly.

concili'abolo [kontʃi'ljabolo] *sm* clandestine meeting.

concili'are [kontʃi'ljare] *vt* to reconcile; (*contravvenzione*) to pay on the spot; (*favorire: sonno*) to be conducive to, induce; (*procurare: simpatia*) to gain; ~**rsi qc** to gain *o* win sth (for o.s.); ~**rsi qd** to win sb over; ~**rsi con** to be reconciled with; **conciliazi'one** *sf* reconciliation; (*DIR*) settlement.

con'cilio [kon'tʃiljo] *sm* (*REL*) council.

con'cime [kon'tʃime] *sm* manure; (*chimico*) fertilizer.

con'ciso, a [kon'tʃizo] *ag* concise, succinct.

conci'tato, a [kontʃi'tato] *ag* excited, emotional.

concitta'dino, a [kontʃitta'dino] *sm/f* fellow citizen.

con'clave *sm* conclave.

con'cludere *vt* to conclude; (*portare a compimento*) to conclude, finish, bring to an end; (*operare positivamente*) to achieve // *vi* (*essere convincente*) to be conclusive; ~**rsi** *vr* to come to an end, close; **conclusi'one** *sf* conclusion; (*risultato*) result; **conclu'sivo, a** *ag* conclusive; (*finale*) final; **con'cluso, a** *pp di* **concludere**.

concor'danza [konkor'dantsa] *sf* (*anche LING*) agreement.

concor'dare *vt* (*tregua*) to agree on; (*LING*) to make agree // *vi* to agree; **concor'dato** *sm* agreement; (*DIR*) composition; (*REL*) concordat.

con'corde *ag* (*d'accordo*) in agreement; (*simultaneo*) simultaneous.

con'cordia *sf* harmony, concord.

concor'rente *ag* competing; (*MAT*) concurrent // *sm/f* competitor; (*INS*) candidate; **concor'renza** *sf* competition.

con'correre *vi*: ~ **(in)** (*MAT*) to converge *o* meet (in); ~ **(a)** (*competere*) to compete (for); (: *INS: a una cattedra*) to apply (for); (*partecipare: a un'impresa*) to take part (in), contribute (to); **con'corso, a** *pp di* **concorrere** // **con'corso** *sm* competition; (*INS*) competitive examination.

con'creto, a *ag* concrete.

concussi'one *sf* (*DIR*) extortion.

con'danna *sf* sentence; conviction; condemnation.

condan'nare *vt* (*DIR*): ~ **a** to sentence to; ~ **per** to convict of; (*disapprovare*) to condemn; **condan'nato, a** *sm/f* convict.

conden'sare *vt*, ~**rsi** *vr* to condense; **condensazi'one** *sf* condensation.

condi'mento *sm* seasoning; dressing.

con'dire *vt* to season; (*insalata*) to dress.

condiscen'dente [kondiʃʃen'dɛnte] *ag* compliant; indulgent, easy-going.

condi'scendere [kondiʃ'ʃendere] *vi*: ~ **a**

to agree to; **condi'sceso, a** *pp di* **condiscendere.**

condi'videre *vt* to share; **condi'viso, a** *pp di* **condividere.**

condizio'nale [kondittsjo'nale] *ag* conditional // *sm* (*LING*) conditional // *sf* (*DIR*) suspended sentence.

condizio'nare [kondittsjo'nare] *vt* to condition; (*determinare*) to determine.

condizi'one [kondit'tsjone] *sf* condition; ~**i** *sfpl* (*di pagamento etc*) terms, conditions; **a ~ che** on condition that, provided that.

condogli'anze [kondoʎ'ʎantse] *sfpl* condolences.

condo'minio *sm* joint ownership; (*edificio*) jointly-owned building.

condo'nare *vt* (*DIR*) to remit; **con'dono** *sm* remission.

con'dotta *sf vedi* **condotto.**

con'dotto, a *pp di* **condurre** // *ag*: **medico** ~ local authority doctor (*in country district*) // *sm* (*canale, tubo*) pipe, conduit; (*ANAT*) duct // *sf* (*modo di comportarsi*) conduct, behaviour; (*di un affare etc*) handling; (*di acqua*) piping; (*incarico sanitario*) country medical practice controlled by a local authority.

condu'cente [kondu'tʃɛnte] *sm* driver.

con'durre *vt* to conduct; (*azienda*) to manage; (*accompagnare: bambino*) to take; (*automobile*) to drive; (*trasportare: acqua, gas*) to convey, conduct; (*fig*) to lead // *vi* to lead; **condursi** *vr* to behave, conduct o.s.; ~ **una vita felice** to lead a happy life.

condut'tore *sm* (*conducente*) driver; (*FERR*) guard; (*ELETTR, FISICA*) conductor.

con'farsi *vr*: ~ **a** to suit, agree with.

confederazi'one [konfederat'tsjone] *sf* confederation.

confe'renza [konfe'rɛntsa] *sf* (*discorso*) lecture; (*riunione*) conference; **conferenzi'ere, a** *sm/f* lecturer.

confe'rire *vt*: ~ **qc a qd** to give sth to sb, bestow sth on sb // *vi* to confer.

con'ferma *sf* confirmation.

confer'mare *vt* to confirm.

confes'sare *vt*, ~**rsi** *vr* to confess; **confessio'nale** *ag*, *sm* confessional; **confessi'one** *sf* confession; (*setta religiosa*) denomination; **confes'sore** *sm* confessor.

con'fetto *sm* sugared almond; (*MED*) pill.

confezio'nare [konfettsjo'nare] *vt* (*vestito*) to make (up); (*merci, pacchi*) to package.

confezi'one [konfet'tsjone] *sf* tailoring; dressmaking; packaging; ~**i** *sfpl* garments, clothes; ~ **regalo** gift pack.

confic'care *vt*: ~ **qc in** to hammer *o* drive sth into; ~**rsi** *vr* to stick.

confi'dare *vi*: ~ **in** to confide in, rely on // *vt* to confide; ~**rsi con qd** to confide in sb; **confi'dente** *sm/f* (*persona amica*) confidant/confidante; (*spia*) informer; **confi'denza** *sf* (*familiarità*) intimacy, familiarity; (*fiducia*) trust, confidence; (*rivelazione*) confidence; **confidenzi'ale** ag familiar, friendly; (notizia) confidential.

configu'rarsi vr: ~ a to assume the shape o form of; **configurazi'one** sf configuration.

confi'nare vi: ~ con to border on // vt (POL) to intern; (fig) to confine; ~rsi vr (isolarsi): ~rsi in to shut o.s. up in; (fig: limitarsi): ~rsi a to confine o.s. to.

con'fine sm boundary; (di paese) border, frontier.

con'fino sm internment.

confis'care vt to confiscate.

conflagrazi'one [konflagrat'tsjone] sf conflagration.

con'flitto sm conflict.

conflu'enza [konflu'entsa] sf (di fiumi) confluence; (di strade) junction.

conflu'ire vi (fiumi) to flow into each other, meet; (strade) to meet.

con'fondere vt to mix up, confuse; (imbarazzare) to embarrass; ~rsi vr (mescolarsi) to mingle; (turbarsi) to be confused; (sbagliare) to get mixed up.

confor'mare vt (adeguare): ~ a to adapt o conform to // vr: ~rsi (a) to conform (to).

conforme'mente av accordingly; ~ a in accordance with.

confor'mista, i, e sm/f conformist.

confor'tare vt to comfort, console; **confor'tevole** ag (consolante) comforting; (comodo) comfortable; **con'forto** sm comfort, consolation; comfort.

confron'tare vt to compare.

con'fronto sm comparison; **in** o a ~ **di** in comparison with, compared to; **nei miei** (o tuoi etc) ~**i** towards me (o you etc).

confusi'one sf confusion; (imbarazzo) embarrassment.

con'fuso, a pp di **confondere** // ag (vedi confondere) confused; embarrassed.

confu'tare vt to refute.

conge'dare [kondʒe'dare] vt to dismiss; (MIL) to demob; ~rsi vr to take one's leave; **con'gedo** sm (anche MIL) leave; **prendere congedo da qd** to take one's leave of sb; **congedo assoluto** (MIL) discharge.

conge'gnare [kondʒeɲ'ɲare] vt to construct, put together; **con'gegno** sm device, mechanism.

conge'lare [kondʒe'lare] vt to freeze; **congela'tore** sm freezer.

con'genito, a [kon'dʒɛnito] ag congenital.

congestio'nare [kondʒestjo'nare] vt to congest.

congesti'one [kondʒes'tjone] sf congestion.

conget'tura [kondʒet'tura] sf conjecture, supposition.

con'giungere [kon'dʒundʒere] vt to join (together); (porre in comunicazione) to connect, link (up); ~rsi vr to join (together); to connect, link (up).

congiunti'vite [kondʒunti'vite] sf conjunctivitis.

congiun'tivo [kondʒun'tivo] sm (LING) subjunctive.

congi'unto, a [kon'dʒunto] pp di **congiungere** // ag (unito) joined; (: da parentela) related.

congiun'tura [kondʒun'tura] sf (giuntura) junction, join; (ANAT) joint; (circostanza) juncture; (ECON) economic situation.

congiunzi'one [kondʒun'tsjone] sf (LING) conjunction.

congi'ura [kon'dʒura] sf conspiracy; **congiu'rare** vi to conspire.

conglome'rato sm (GEO) conglomerate; (fig) conglomeration; (EDIL) concrete.

congratu'larsi vr: ~ **con qd per qc** to congratulate sb on sth.

congratulazi'oni [kongratulat'tsjoni] sfpl congratulations.

congrega, ghe sf band, bunch.

congregazi'one [kongregat'tsjone] sf congregation.

con'gresso sm congress.

conguagli'are [kongwaʎ'ʎare] vt to balance; **congu'aglio** sm balancing, adjusting; (somma di denaro) balance.

coni'are vt to mint, coin; (fig) to coin.

'conico, a, ci, che ag conical.

co'nifera sf conifer.

co'niglio [ko'niʎʎo] sm rabbit.

coniu'gare vt (LING) to conjugate; ~rsi vr to get married; **coniugazi'one** sf (LING) conjugation.

'coniuge ['kɔnjudʒe] sm/f spouse.

connazio'nale [konnattsjo'nale] sm/f fellow-countryman/woman.

connessi'one sf connection.

con'nesso, a pp di **connettere**.

con'nettere vt to connect, join // vi (fig) to think straight.

conni'vente ag conniving.

conno'tati smpl distinguishing marks.

'cono sm cone; ~ **gelato** ice-cream cone.

cono'scente [konoʃ'ʃɛnte] sm/f acquaintance.

cono'scenza [konoʃ'ʃɛntsa] sf (il sapere) knowledge q; (persona) acquaintance; (facoltà sensoriale) consciousness q; **perdere** ~ to lose consciousness.

co'noscere [ko'noʃʃere] vt to know; **ci siamo conosciuti a Firenze** we (first) met in Florence; **conosci'tore, 'trice** sm/f connoisseur; **conosci'uto, a** pp di **conoscere** // ag well-known.

con'quista sf conquest.

conquis'tare vt to conquer; (fig) to gain, win.

consa'crare vt (REL) to consecrate; (: sacerdote) to ordain; (dedicare) to dedicate; (fig: uso etc) to sanction; ~rsi a to dedicate o.s. to.

consangu'ineo, a sm/f blood relation.

consa'pevole ag: ~ **di** aware o conscious of; **consapevo'lezza** sf awareness, consciousness.

'conscio, a, sci, sce ['kɔnʃo] ag: ~ **di** aware o conscious of.

consecu'tivo, a ag consecutive;

(*successivo: giorno*) following, next.

con'segna [kon'seɲɲa] *sf* delivery; (*merce consegnata*) consignment; (*custodia*) trust, custody; (MIL: *ordine*) orders *pl*; (*: punizione*) confinement to barracks; (DIR: *di malfattore*) handing over; **alla ~** on delivery; **dare qc in ~ a qd** to entrust sth to sb.

conse'gnare [konseɲ'ɲare] *vt* to deliver; (*affidare*) to entrust, hand over; (MIL) to confine to barracks.

consegu'ente *ag* consequent.

consegu'enza [konse'gwentsa] *sf* consequence; **per o di ~** consequently.

consegu'ire *vt* to achieve // *vi* (2) to follow, result.

con'senso *sm* consent; (*fra due o più persone*) agreement.

consen'tire *vi*: **~ a** to consent o agree to // *vt* to allow, permit.

con'serva *sf* (CUC) preserve; **~ di frutta** jam; **~ di pomodoro** tomato purée.

conser'vare *vt* (CUC) to preserve; (*custodire*) to keep; (*: dalla distruzione etc*) to preserve, conserve; **~rsi** *vr* to keep; **~rsi sano** to keep healthy.

conserva'tore, 'trice *sm/f* (POL) conservative.

conservazi'one [konservat'tsjone] *sf* preservation.

conside'rare *vt* to consider; (*reputare*) to consider, regard; **~ molto qd** to think highly of sb; **considerazi'one** *sf* consideration; regard, esteem; **conside-'revole** *ag* considerable.

consigli'are [konsiʎ'ʎare] *vt* (*persona*) to advise; (*metodo, azione*) to recommend, advise, suggest; **~rsi con qd** to ask sb for advice; **consigli'ere, a** *sm/f* adviser // *sm*: **consigliere d'amministrazione** board member; **consigliere comunale** town councillor; **con'siglio** *sm* (*suggerimento*) advice q, piece of advice; (*assemblea*) council; **consiglio d'amministrazione** board; **il Consiglio dei Ministri** (POL) ≈ the Cabinet.

consis'tente *ag* thick; solid; (*fig*) sound, valid; **consis'tenza** *sf* consistency, thickness; solidity; validity.

consis'tere *vi*: **~ in** to consist of; **consis-'tito, a** *pp* di **consistere**.

conso'lare *ag* consular // *vt* (*confortare*) to console, comfort; (*rallegrare*) to cheer up; **~rsi** *vr* to be comforted; to cheer up.

conso'lato *sm* consulate.

consolazi'one [konsolat'tsjone] *sf* consolation q, comfort q.

'console *sm* consul.

consoli'dare *vt* to strengthen, reinforce; (MIL: *terreno*) to consolidate; **~rsi** *vr* to consolidate.

conso'nante *sf* consonant.

conso'nanza [konso'nantsa] *sf* consonance.

con'sorte *sm/f* consort.

con'sorzio [kon'sɔrtsjo] *sm* consortium.

con'stare (2) *vi*: **~ di** to consist of // *vb impers*: **mi consta che** it has come to my knowledge that, it appears that.

consta'tare *vt* to establish, verify; (*notare*) to notice, observe.

consu'eto, a *ag* habitual, usual; **consue-'tudine** *sf* habit, custom; (*usanza*) custom.

consu'lente *sm/f* consultant; **consu-'lenza** *sf* consultancy.

consul'tare *vt* to consult; **~rsi con qd** to seek the advice of sb; **consultazi'one** *sf* consultation; **consultazioni** *sfpl* (POL) talks.

consu'mare *vt* (*logorare: abiti, scarpe*) to wear out; (*usare*) to consume, use up; (*mangiare, bere*) to consume; (DIR) to consummate; **~rsi** *vr* to wear out; to be used up; (*anche fig*) to be consumed; (*combustibile*) to burn out; **consuma'tore** *sm* consumer; **consumazi'one** *sf* consumption; (*bibita*) drink; (*spuntino*) snack; (DIR) consummation; **con'sumo** *sm* consumption; wear; use.

consun'tivo *sm* (ECON) final balance.

con'sunto, a *ag* worn-out; (*viso*) wasted.

con'tabile *ag* accounts *cpd*, accounting // *sm/f* accountant; **contabilità** *sf* (*attività, tecnica*) accounting, accountancy; (*insieme dei libri etc*) books *pl*, accounts *pl*; (*ufficio*) accounts department.

conta'dino, a *sm/f* countryman/woman; farm worker; (*peg*) peasant.

contagi'are [konta'dʒare] *vt* to infect.

con'tagio [kon'tadʒo] *sm* infection; (*per contatto diretto*) contagion; **contagi'oso, a** *ag* infectious; contagious.

contami'nare *vt* to contaminate; **contaminazi'one** *sf* contamination.

con'tante *sm* cash; **pagare in ~i** to pay cash.

con'tare *vt* to count; (*considerare*) to consider // *vi* to count; to be of importance; **~ su qd** to count o rely on sb; **~ di fare qc** to intend to do sth; **conta'tore** *sm* meter.

contat'tare *vt* to contact.

con'tatto *sm* contact.

'conte *sm* count.

conteggi'are [konted'dʒare] *vt* to charge, put on the bill; **con'teggio** *sm* calculation; **conteggio alla rovescia** countdown.

con'tegno [kon'teɲɲo] *sm* (*comportamento*) behaviour; (*atteggiamento*) attitude; **con'gnoso, a** *ag* reserved, dignified.

contem'plare *vt* to contemplate, gaze at; (DIR) to make provision for.

contempo'raneo, a *ag*, *sm/f* contemporary.

conten'dente *sm/f* opponent, adversary.

con'tendere *vi* (*competere*) to compete; (*litigare*) to quarrel // *vt* to contest.

conte'nere *vt* to contain; **conteni'tore** *sm* container.

conten'tare *vt* to please, satisfy; **~rsi di** to be satisfied with, content o.s. with.

conten'tezza [konten'tettsa] *sf* contentment.

con'tento, a *ag* pleased, glad; **~ di** pleased with.

conte'nuto *sm* contents *pl*; *(argomento)* content.

con'teso, a *pp di* **contendere** // *sf* dispute, argument.

con'tessa *sf* countess.

contes'tare *vt* *(DIR)* to notify; *(fig)* to dispute.

con'testo *sm* context.

con'tiguo, a *ag*: ∼ **(a)** adjacent (to).

continen'tale *ag, sm/f* continental.

conti'nente *ag* continent // *sm* *(GEO)* continent; *(: terra ferma)* mainland; **conti'nenza** *sf* continence.

contin'gente [kontin'dʒɛnte] *sm* *(COMM)* quota; *(MIL)* contingent; **contin'genza** *sf* circumstance.

continu'are *vt* to continue (with), go on with // *vi* to continue, go on; ∼ **a fare qc** to go on o continue doing sth; **continua-zi'one** *sf* continuation.

continuità *sf* continuity.

con'tinuo, a *ag* *(numerazione)* continuous; *(pioggia)* continual, constant; *(ELETTR)*: **corrente** ∼**a** direct current; **di** ∼ continually.

'conto *sm* *(calcolo)* calculation; *(COMM, ECON)* account; *(di ristorante, albergo)* bill; *(fig: stima)* consideration, esteem; **fare i** ∼**i con qd** to settle one's account with sb; **fare** ∼ **su qd/qc** to count o rely on sb; **rendere** ∼ **a qd di qc** to be accountable to sb for sth; **tener** ∼ **di qd/qc** to take sb/sth into account; **per** ∼ **di** on behalf of; **per** ∼ **mio** as far as I'm concerned; ∼ **corrente** current account; **a** ∼**i fatti, in fin dei** ∼**i** all things considered.

con'torcere [kon'tortʃere] *vt* to twist; *(panni)* to wring (out); ∼**rsi** *vr* to twist, writhe.

contor'nare *vt* to surround.

con'torno *sm* *(linea)* outline, contour; *(ornamento)* border; *(CUC)* vegetables *pl*.

contorsi'one *sf* contortion.

con'torto, a *pp di* **contorcere**.

contrabbandi'ere, a *sm/f* smuggler.

contrab'bando *sm* smuggling, contraband; **merce di** ∼ contraband, smuggled goods *pl*.

contraccambi'are *vt* *(favore etc)* to return; **contrac'cambio** *sm* return; **in contraccambio di** in return o exchange for.

contrac'colpo *sm* rebound; *(di arma da fuoco)* recoil; *(fig)* repercussion.

contrad'detto, a *pp di* **contraddire**.

contrad'dire *vt* to contradict; **contraddit'torio, a** *ag* contradictory // *sm* debate; **contraddizi'one** *sf* contradiction.

contraf'fare *vt* *(persona)* to mimic; *(alterare: voce)* to disguise; *(firma)* to forge, counterfeit; **contraf'fatto, a** *pp di* **contraffare** // *ag* counterfeit; **contraffazi'one** *sf* mimicking *q*; disguising *q*; forging *q*; *(cosa contraffatta)* forgery.

con'tralto *sm* *(MUS)* contralto.

contrap'peso *sm* counterbalance, counterweight.

contrap'porre *vt* *(opporre)* to oppose, set against; **contrap'posto, a** *pp di* **contrapporre**.

contraria'mente *av*: ∼ **a** contrary to.

contrari'are *vt* *(contrastare)* to thwart, oppose; *(irritare)* to annoy, bother; ∼**rsi** *vr* to get annoyed.

contrarietà *sf* adversity; *(fig)* aversion.

con'trario, a *ag* opposite; *(sfavorevole)* unfavourable // *sm* opposite; ∼ **a** contrary to; **al** ∼ on the contrary.

con'trarre *vt*, **contrarsi** *vr* to contract.

contrasse'gnare [kontrassen'ɲare] *vt* to mark; **contras'segno** *sm* mark; *(distintivo)* distinguishing mark.

contras'tante *ag* contrasting.

contras'tare *vt* *(avversare)* to oppose; *(impedire)* to bar; *(negare: diritto)* to contest, dispute // *vi*: ∼ **(con)** *(essere in disaccordo)* to contrast (with); *(lottare)* to struggle (with); **con'trasto** *sm* contrast; *(conflitto)* conflict; *(litigio)* dispute.

contrat'tacco *sm* counterattack.

contrat'tare *vt, vi* to negotiate.

contrat'tempo *sm* hitch.

con'tratto, a *pp di* **contrarre** // *sm* contract; **contrattu'ale** *ag* contractual.

contravve'leno *sm* antidote.

contravve'nire *vi*: ∼ **a** *(legge)* to contravene; *(obbligo)* to fail to meet; **contravvenzi'one** *sf* contravention; *(ammenda)* fine.

contrazi'one [kontrat'tsjone] *sf* contraction; *(di prezzi etc)* reduction.

contribu'ente *sm/f* taxpayer; ratepayer.

contribu'ire *vi* to contribute; **contri'buto** *sm* contribution; *(tassa)* tax.

con'trito, a *ag* contrite, penitent.

'contro *prep* against; ∼ **di me/lui** against me/him; ∼ **pagamento** *(COMM)* on payment // *prefisso*: **contro'battere** *vt* *(fig: a parole)* to answer back; *(: confutare)* to refute; **controfi'gura** *sf* *(CINEMA)* double; **controfir'mare** *vt* to countersign.

control'lare *vt* *(accertare)* to check; *(sorvegliare)* to watch, control; *(tenere nel proprio potere, fig: dominare)* to control; **con'trollo** *sm* check; watch; control; **controllo delle nascite** birth control; **control'lore** *sm* *(FERR, AUTOBUS)* (ticket) inspector.

controprodu'cente [kontroprodu'tʃɛnte] *ag* producing the opposite effect.

contro'senso *sm* *(contraddizione)* contradiction in terms; *(assurdità)* nonsense.

controspio'naggio [kontrospio'naddʒo] *sm* counterespionage.

contro'versia *sf* controversy.

contro'verso, a *ag* controversial.

contro'voglia [kontro'vɔʎʎa] *av* unwillingly.

contu'macia [kontu'matʃa] *sf* *(DIR)* default.

contur'bare *vt* to disturb, upset.

contusi'one *sf* (MED) bruise.
convale'scente [konvaleʃ'ʃɛnte] *ag, sm/f* convalescent;   **convale'scenza** *sf* convalescence.
convali'dare *vt* to confirm.
con'vegno [kon'veɲɲo] *sm* (*incontro*) meeting; (*congresso*) convention, congress; (*luogo*) meeting place.
conve'nevoli *smpl* civilities.
conveni'ente *ag* suitable; (*pratico*) convenient, handy; (*vantaggioso*) profitable, advantageous; (*prezzo*) cheap; **conveni'enza** *sf* suitability; convenience; advantage; **le convenienze** *sfpl* social conventions.
conve'nire *vi* (2: *riunirsi*) to gather, assemble; (*concordare*) to agree; (*essere opportuno, addirsi*) to be suitable; (*tornare utile*) to be worthwhile // *vb impers* (2): **conviene fare questo** it is advisable to do this; **conviene andarsene** we should go; **ne convengo** I agree.
con'vento *sm* (*di frati*) monastery; (*di suore*) convent.
convenzio'nale [konventsjo'nale] *ag* conventional.
convenzi'one [konven'tsjone] *sf* (DIR) agreement; (*nella società*) convention; **le ∼ i** *sfpl* convention sg, social conventions.
conver'gente [konver'dʒɛnte] *ag* convergent.
con'vergere [kon'vɛrdʒere] *vi* (2) to converge.
conver'sare *vi* to converse.
conversazi'one [konversat'tsjone] *sf* conversation.
conversi'one *sf* conversion.
con'verso, a *pp di* **convergere**.
conver'tire *vt* (*trasformare*) to change; (POL, REL) to convert; **∼rsi** *vr*: **∼rsi (in)** to change (to); **∼rsi (a)** to be converted (to); **conver'tito, a** *sm/f* convert.
con'vesso, a *ag* convex.
con'vincere [kon'vintʃere] *vt* to convince; **∼ qd di qc** to convince sb of sth; **∼ qd a fare qc** to persuade sb to do sth; **con'vinto, a** *pp di* **convincere**; **convinzi'one** *sf* conviction, firm belief.
convis'suto, a *pp di* **convivere**.
con'vitto *sm* (INS) boarding school; **convit'tore, 'trice** *sm/f* boarder.
con'vivere *vi* to live together.
convo'care *vt* to call, convene; (DIR) to summon; **convocazi'one** *sf* meeting; summons *sg*.
convogli'are [konvoʎ'ʎare] *vt* to convey; (*dirigere*) to direct, send; **con'voglio** *sm* (*di veicoli*) convoy; (FERR) train; **convoglio funebre** funeral procession.
convulsi'one *sf* convulsion.
con'vulso, a *ag* (*pianto*) violent, convulsive; (*attività*) feverish.
coope'rare *vi*: **∼ (a)** to cooperate (in); **coopera'tiva** *sf* cooperative; **coopera-zi'one** *sf* cooperation.
coordi'nare *vt* to coordinate; **coordi-'nate** *sfpl* (MAT, GEO) coordinates; **coordinazi'one** *sf* coordination.

co'perchio [ko'pɛrkjo] *sm* cover; (*di pentola*) lid.
co'perta *sf* cover; (*di lana*) blanket; (*da viaggio*) rug; (NAUT) deck.
coper'tina *sf* (STAMPA) cover, jacket.
co'perto, a *pp di* **coprire** // *ag* covered; (*cielo*) overcast // *sm* place setting; (*posto a tavola*) place; (*al ristorante*) cover charge; **∼ di** covered in *o* with.
coper'tone *sm* (*telo impermeabile*) tarpaulin; (AUT) rubber tyre.
coper'tura *sf* (*anche* ECON, MIL) cover; (*di edificio*) roofing.
'copia *sf* copy; (*stesura*) draught, copy; **brutta/bella ∼** rough/final draft.
copi'are *vt* to copy; **copia'trice** *sf* copier, copying machine.
copi'one *sm* (CINEMA, TEATRO) script.
'coppa *sf* (*bicchiere*) goblet; (*per frutta, gelato*) dish; (*trofeo*) cup, trophy; **∼ dell'olio** oil sump.
'coppia *sf* couple.
coprifu'oco, chi *sm* curfew.
copri'letto *sm* bedspread.
co'prire *vt* to cover; (*occupare: carica, posto*) to hold; **∼rsi** *vr* (*cielo*) to cloud over; (*vestirsi*) to wrap up, cover up; (ECON) to cover o.s.; **∼rsi di** (*fiori, muffa*) to become covered in.
co'raggio [ko'raddʒo] *sm* courage, bravery; **coraggi'oso, a** *ag* courageous, brave.
co'rale *ag* choral; (*approvazione*) unanimous.
co'rallo *sm* coral.
co'rano *sm* (REL) Koran.
co'razza [ko'rattsa] *sf* armour; (*di animali*) carapace, shell; (MIL) armour(-plating); **coraz'zata** *sf* battleship.
corbelle'ria *sf* stupid action; howler; **∼e** *sfpl* nonsense *q*.
'corda *sf* cord; (*fune*) rope; (*spago, MUS*) string; **tenere sulla ∼ qd** to keep sb on tenterhooks; **tagliare la ∼** to slip away, sneak off; **∼e vocali** vocal cords.
cordi'ale *ag* cordial, warm // *sm* (*bevanda*) cordial.
cor'doglio [kor'dɔʎʎo] *sm* grief; (*lutto*) mourning.
cor'done *sm* cord, string; (*linea: di polizia*) cordon; **∼ ombelicale** umbilical chord.
coreogra'fia *sf* choreography.
core'ografo, a *sm/f* choreographer.
cori'andoli *smpl* confetti *sg*.
cori'care *vt* to put to bed; **∼rsi** *vr* to go to bed.
'corna *sfpl vedi* **corno**.
cor'nacchia [kor'nakkja] *sf* crow.
corna'musa *sf* bagpipes *pl*.
'cornea *sf* (ANAT) cornea.
cor'netta *sf* (MUS) cornet; (TEL) receiver.
cor'netto *sm* (CUC) croissant; **∼ acustico** ear trumpet.
cor'nice [kor'nitʃe] *sf* frame.
'corno *sm* (ZOOL: *pl(f)* **∼a**, MUS) horn; **fare le ∼a a qd** to be unfaithful to sb; **cor'nuto, a** *ag* (*con corna*) horned; (*faml!*

marito) cuckolded // *sm* (*fam!*) cuckold; (:
insulto) bastard (!).

'co'ro *sm* chorus; (REL) choir.

co'rona *sf* crown; (*di fiori*) wreath; ~ **del
rosario** rosary, rosary beads *pl*; **coro-
'nare** *vt* to crown.

'corpo *sm* body; (*cadavere*) (dead) body;
(*militare, diplomatico*) corps *inv*; (*di opere*)
corpus; **prendere** ~ to take shape; **a** ~
a ~ hand-to-hand; ~ **di ballo** corps de
ballet; ~ **di guardia** guardroom; ~
insegnante teaching staff.

corpo'rale *ag* bodily; (*punizione*) corporal.

corpora'tura *sf* build, physique.

corporazi'one [korporat'tsjone] *sf*
corporation.

cor'poreo, a *ag* bodily, physical.

corpu'lento, a *ag* stout.

corre'dare *vt*: ~ **di** to provide *o* furnish
with; **cor'redo** *sm* equipment; (*di sposa*)
trousseau.

cor'reggere [kor'rɛddʒere] *vt* to correct;
(*compiti*) to correct, mark.

cor'rente *ag* (*fiume*) flowing; (*acqua del
rubinetto*) running; (*moneta, prezzo*)
current; (*comune*) everyday // *sm*: **essere
al** ~ to be well-informed // *sf* (*movimento
di liquido*) current, stream; (*spiffero*)
draught; (ELETTR, METEOR) current; (*fig*)
trend, tendency.

'correre *vi* (2) to run; (*precipitarsi*) to
rush; (*partecipare a una gara*) to race, run;
(*fig: diffondersi*) to go round // *vt* (SPORT:
gara) to compete in; (*rischio*) to run;
(*pericolo*) to face; ~ **dietro a qd** to run
after sb.

cor'retto, a *pp di* **correggere** // *ag*
(*comportamento*) correct, proper.

correzi'one [korret'tsjone] *sf* correction;
marking; ~ **di bozze** proofreading.

corri'doio *sm* corridor.

corri'dore *sm* (SPORT) runner; (: *su
veicolo*) racer.

corri'era *sf* coach, bus.

corri'ere *sm* (*diplomatico, di guerra*)
courier; (*posta*) mail, post; (COMM) carrier.

corri'gendo [korri'dʒendo] *sm/f* (DIR)
young offender.

corrispon'dente *ag* corresponding //
sm/f correspondent.

corrispon'denza [korrispon'dɛntsa] *sf*
correspondence.

corris'pondere *vi* to correspond; (*stanze*)
to communicate; (*fig: contraccambiare*): ~
a to return; **corris'posto, a** *pp di*
corrispondere.

corrobo'rare *vt* to strengthen, fortify;
(*fig*) to corroborate, bear out.

cor'rodere *vt*, ~**rsi** *vr* to corrode.

cor'rompere *vt* to corrupt; (*comprare*) to
bribe.

corrosi'one *sf* corrosion.

corro'sivo, a *ag* corrosive.

cor'roso, a *pp di* **corrodere.**

cor'rotto, a *pp di* **corrompere** // *ag*
corrupt.

corrucci'arsi [korrut'tʃarsi] *vr* to grow
angry *o* vexed.

corru'gare *vt* to wrinkle; ~ **la fronte** to
knit one's brows.

corruzi'one [korrut'tsjone] *sf* corruption;
bribery.

'corsa *sf* running *q*; (*gara*) race; (*di
autobus, taxi*) journey, trip; **fare una** ~ to
run, dash; (SPORT) to run a race.

cor'sia *sf* (AUT, SPORT) lane; (*di ospedale*)
ward.

cor'sivo *sm* cursive (writing); (TIP) italics
pl.

'corso, a *pp di* **correre** // *sm* course;
(*strada cittadina*) main street; (*di unità
monetaria*) circulation; (*di titoli, valori*)
rate, price; **dar libero** ~ **a** to give free
expression to; **in** ~ in progress, under
way; (*annata*) current; ~ **serale** evening
class.

'corte *sf* (court)yard; (DIR, *regale*) court;
fare la ~ **a qd** to court sb; ~ **marziale**
court-martial.

cor'teccia, ce [kor'tettʃa] *sf* bark.

corteggi'are [korted'dʒare] *vt* to court.

cor'teo *sm* procession.

cor'tese *ag* courteous; **corte'sia** *sf*
courtesy.

cortigi'ano, a [korti'dʒano] *sm/f* courtier
// *sf* courtesan.

cor'tile *sm* (court)yard.

cor'tina *sf* curtain; (*anche fig*) screen.

'corto, a *ag* short; **essere a** ~ **di qc** to be
short of sth; ~ **circuito** short-circuit.

'corvo *sm* raven.

'cosa *sf* thing; (*faccenda*) affair, matter,
business *q*; (**che**) ~? what?; **a** ~ **pensi?**
what are you thinking about?; **a** ~ **e fatte**
when it's all over.

'coscia, sce ['kɔʃʃa] *sf* thigh.

cosci'ente [koʃ'ʃɛnte] *ag* conscious; ~ **di**
conscious *o* aware of; **cosci'enza** *sf*
conscience; (*consapevolezza*) consciou-
ness; **coscienzi'oso, a** *ag* conscientious.

cosci'otto [koʃ'ʃɔtto] *sm* (CUC) leg.

cos'critto *sm* (MIL) conscript.

coscrizi'one [koskrit'tsjone] *sf*
conscription.

così *av* so; (*in questo modo*) like this, like
that; ~ **lontano** so far away; **un ragazzo**
~ **intelligente** such an intelligent boy //
ag *inv* (*tale*) **non ho mai visto un film**
~ I've never seen such a film // *cong*
(*perciò*) so, therefore; ~ **... come** as ... as;
non è ~ **bravo come te** he's not as good
as you; **come stai?** — ~ ~ how are you? —
so-so; **non ho detto** ~ I didn't say that;
e ~ **via** and so on; **per** ~ **dire** so to
speak.

cosid'detto, a *ag* so-called.

cos'metico, a, ci, che *ag, sm* cosmetic.

'cosmo *sm* cosmos.

cosmo'nauta, i, e *sm/f* cosmonaut.

cosmopo'lita, i, e *ag* cosmopolitan.

cos'pargere [kos'pardʒere] *vt*: ~ **di** to
sprinkle with; **cos'parso, a** *pp di*
cospargere.

cos'petto *sm*: **al** ~ **di** in front of; in the
presence of.

cos'picuo, a *ag* conspicuous, remarkable; (*grande*) considerable, large.

cospi'rare *vi* to conspire; cospira'tore, 'trice *sm/f* conspirator; cospirazi'one *sf* conspiracy.

'costa *sf* (*tra terra e mare*) coast(line); (*litorale*) shore; (*pendio*) slope; (ANAT) rib.

costà *av* there.

cos'tante *ag* constant; (*persona*) steadfast // *sf* constant.

cos'tare *vi* (2), *vt* to cost; ~ caro to be expensive, cost a lot.

costeggi'are [kosted'dʒare] *vt* to be close to; to run alongside.

cos'tei *pronome vedi* costui.

costellazi'one [kostellat'tsjone] *sf* constellation.

costernazi'one [kosternat'tsjone] *sf* dismay, consternation.

costi'ero, a *ag* coastal, coast *cpd* // *sf* stretch of coast.

costitu'ire *vt* (*comitato, gruppo*) to set up, form; (*collezione*) to put together, build up; (*sog: elementi, parti: comporre*) to make up, constitute; (*rappresentare*) to constitute; (DIR) to appoint; ~rsi alla polizia to give o.s. up to the police.

costituzio'nale [kostituttsjo'nale] *ag* constitutional.

costituzi'one [kostitut'tsjone] *sf* setting up; building up; constitution.

'costo *sm* cost; a ogni o qualunque ~, a tutti i ~i at all costs.

'costola *sf* (ANAT) rib; (*di libro, pettine*) spine.

costo'letta *sf* (CUC) cutlet.

cos'toro *pronome pl vedi* costui.

cos'toso, a *ag* expensive, costly.

cos'tretto, a *pp di* costringere.

cos'tringere [kos'trindʒere] *vt*: ~ qd a fare qc to force sb to do sth; costrizi'one *sf* coercion.

costru'ire *vt* to construct, build; costru-zi'one *sf* construction, building.

cos'tui, cos'tei, *pl* cos'toro *pronome* (*soggetto*) he/she; *pl* they; (*complemento*) him/her; *pl* them.

cos'tume *sm* (*uso*) custom; (*foggia di vestire, indumento*) costume; (~i) *smpl* morals, morality *sg*; il buon ~ public morality; ~ da bagno bathing o swimming costume, swimsuit; (*da uomo*) bathing o swimming trunks *pl*.

co'tenna *sf* hide; (*di maiale*) pigskin; (*del lardo*) rind.

co'togna [ko'toɲɲa] *sf* quince.

co'tone *sm* cotton; ~ idrofilo cotton wool.

'cotta *sf* (REL) surplice; (*fam: innamoramento*) crush.

'cottimo *sm* piecework; lavorare a ~ to do piecework.

'cotto, a *pp di* cuocere // *ag* cooked; (*fam: innamorato*) head-over-heels in love.

cot'tura *sf* cooking; (*in forno*) baking; (*in umido*) stewing.

co'vare *vt* to hatch; (*fig: malattia*) to be sickening for; (: *odio, rancore*) to nurse // *vi* (*fuoco, fig*) to smoulder.

'covo *sm* den.

co'vone *sm* sheaf.

'cozza ['kɔttsa] *sf* mussel.

coz'zare [kot'tsare] *vi*: ~ contro to bang into, collide with; 'cozzo *sm* collision.

C.P. *abbr vedi* casella.

'crampo *sm* cramp.

'cranio *sm* skull.

cra'tere *sm* crater.

cra'vatta *sf* tie.

cre'anza [kre'antsa] *sf* manners *pl*.

cre'are *vt* to create; cre'ato *sm* creation; crea'tore, 'trice *ag* creative // *sm* creator; crea'tura *sf* creature; (*bimbo*) baby, infant; creazi'one *sf* creation; (*fondazione*) foundation, establishment.

cre'dente *sm/f* (REL) believer.

cre'denza [kre'dɛntsa] *sf* belief; (*credito*) credit; (*armadio*) sideboard.

credenzi'ali [kreden'tsjali] *sfpl* credentials.

'credere *vt* to believe // *vi*: ~ in, ~ a to believe in; ~ qd onesto to believe sb (to be) honest; ~ che to believe o think that; ~rsi furbo to think one is clever; cre-'dibile *ag* credible, believable.

'credito *sm* (*anche* COMM) credit; (*reputazione*) esteem, repute; comprare a ~ to buy on credit.

'credo *sm inv* credo.

'credulo, a *ag* credulous.

'crema *sf* cream; (*con uova, zucchero etc*) custard.

cre'mare *vt* to cremate; cremazi'one *sf* cremation.

Crem'lino *sm*: il ~ the Kremlin.

'crepa *sf* crack.

cre'paccio [kre'pattʃo] *sm* large crack, fissure; (*di ghiacciaio*) crevasse.

crepacu'ore *sm* broken heart.

cre'pare *vi* (2) (*fam!: morire*) to snuff it, kick the bucket; (*spaccarsi*) to crack; ~ dalle risa to split one's sides laughing; ~ dall'invidia to be green with envy.

crepi'tare *vi* (*fuoco*) to crackle; (*pioggia*) to patter.

cre'puscolo *sm* twilight, dusk.

cre'scendo [kreʃʃendo] *sm* (MUS) crescendo.

'crescere ['kreʃʃere] *vi* (2) to grow; 'crescita *sf* growth; cresci'uto, a *pp di* crescere.

'cresima *sf* (REL) confirmation; cresi-'mare *vt* to confirm.

'crespo, a *ag* (*capelli*) frizzy; (*vestito*) wrinkled // *sm* crêpe.

'cresta *sf* crest; (*di polli, uccelli*) crest, comb.

'creta *sf* chalk; clay.

'Creta *sf* Crete.

cre'tino, a *sm/f* idiot, fool.

'cric *sm inv* (TECN) jack.

'cricca, che *sf* clique.

'cricco, chi *sm* = cric.

crimi'nale *ag, sm/f* criminal.

'crimine sm (DIR) crime.

'crine sm horsehair; **crini'era** sf mane.

'cripta sf crypt.

crisan'temo sm chrysanthemum.

'crisi sf inv crisis; (MED) attack, fit; ~ **di nervi** attack o fit of nerves.

cristalliz'zare [kristalid'dʒare] vi (2), ~**rsi** vr to crystallize; (fig) to become fossilized.

cris'tallo sm crystal.

cristia'nesimo sm Christianity.

cristianità sf Christianity; (i cristiani) Christendom.

cristi'ano, a ag, sm/f Christian.

'Cristo sm Christ.

cri'terio sm criterion; (buon senso) (common) sense.

'critica, che sf vedi **critico**.

criti'care vt to criticize.

'critico, a, ci, che ag critical // sm critic // sf criticism; **la** ~**a** (attività) criticism; (persone) the critics pl.

cri'vello sm riddle.

'croce ['krotʃe] sf cross; **in** ~ (di traverso) crosswise; (fig) on tenterhooks; **la C**~ **Rossa** the Red Cross.

croce'figgere [krotʃe'fiddʒere] etc = **crocifiggere** etc.

croce'via [krotʃe'via] sm inv crossroads sg.

croci'ata [kro'tʃata] sf crusade.

cro'cicchio [kro'tʃikkjo] sm crossroads sg.

croci'era [kro'tʃɛra] sf (viaggio) cruise; (ARCHIT) transept.

croci'figgere [krotʃi'fiddʒere] vt to crucify; **crocifissi'one** sf crucifixion; **croci'fisso, a** pp di **crocifiggere**.

crogi'olo, crogiu'olo [kro'dʒɔlo] sm crucible; (fig) melting pot.

crol'lare vi (2) to collapse; **'crollo** sm collapse; (di prezzi) slump, sudden fall.

cro'mato, a ag chromium-plated.

'cromo sm chrome, chromium.

cromo'soma, i sm chromosome.

'cronaca, che sf chronicle; (STAMPA) news sg; (: rubrica) column; (TV, RADIO) commentary; **fatto** o **episodio di** ~ news item; ~ **nera** crime news sg; crime column.

'cronico, a, ci, che ag chronic.

cro'nista, i sm (STAMPA) reporter, columnist.

cronolo'gia [kronolo'dʒia] sf chronology.

'crosta sf crust.

cros'tacei [kros'tatʃei] smpl shellfish.

'cruccio ['kruttʃo] sm worry, torment.

cruci'verba sm inv crossword (puzzle).

cru'dele ag cruel; **crudeltà** sf cruelty.

'crudo, a ag (non cotto) raw; (aspro) harsh, severe.

cru'miro sm (peg) blackleg, scab.

'crusca sf bran.

crus'cotto sm (AUT) dashboard.

'Cuba sf: **la** ~ Cuba.

'cubico, a, ci, che ag cubic.

'cubo, a ag cubic // sm cube; **elevare al** ~ (MAT) to cube.

cuc'cagna [kuk'kaɲɲa] sf: **paese della** ~ land of plenty; **albero della** ~ greasy pole (fig).

cuc'cetta [kut'tʃetta] sf (FERR) couchette; (NAUT) berth.

cucchiai'ata [kukkja'jata] sf spoonful.

cucchia'ino [kukkja'ino] sm teaspoon; coffee spoon.

cucchi'aio [kuk'kjajo] sm spoon.

'cuccia, ce ['kuttʃa] sf dog's bed; **a** ~! down!

'cucciolo ['kuttʃolo] sm puppy.

cu'cina [ku'tʃina] sf (locale) kitchen; (arte culinaria) cooking, cookery; (le vivande) food, cooking; (apparecchio) cooker; **fare da** ~ to cook; ~ **componibile** fitted kitchen; **cuci'nare** vt to cook.

cu'cire [ku'tʃire] vt to sew, stitch; **cuci'tura** sf sewing, stitching; (costura) seam.

cucù sm inv, **cu'culo** sm cuckoo.

'cuffia sf bonnet, cap; (da bagno) (bathing) cap; (per ascoltare) headphones pl, headset.

cu'gino, a [ku'dzino] sm/f cousin.

'cui pronome (nei complementi indiretti): **la persona a** ~ **accennava** the person you were referring to o to whom you referred; **il libro di** ~ **parlavo** the book I was talking about o about which I was talking; **il quartiere in** ~ **abito** the district where I live; (inserito tra l'articolo e il sostantivo) whose; **il** ~ **nome** whose name; **la** ~ **madre** whose mother.

culi'naria sf cookery.

'culla sf (anche fig) cradle.

cul'lare vt to rock.

culmi'nare vi to culminate.

'culmine sm top, summit.

'culo sm (fam!) arse (!), bum.

'culto sm (religione) religion; (adorazione) worship, adoration; (venerazione: anche fig) cult.

cul'tura sf culture; education, learning; **cultu'rale** ag cultural.

cumu'lare vt to accumulate, amass; **cumula'tivo, a** ag cumulative; (prezzo) inclusive; (biglietto) group cpd.

'cumulo sm (mucchio) pile, heap; (METEOR) cumulus.

'cuneo sm wedge.

cu'ocere ['kwɔtʃere] vt (alimenti) to cook; (mattoni etc) to fire // vi (2) to cook; **cu'oco, a, chi, che** sm/f cook; **primo cuoco** chef.

cu'oio sm leather; ~ **capelluto** scalp.

cu'ore sm heart; ~**i** smpl (CARTE) hearts; **avere buon** ~ to be kind-hearted; **di (buon)** ~ willingly.

cupi'digia [kupi'didʒa] sf greed, covetousness.

'cupo, a ag dark; (fig) gloomy, dismal.

'cupola sf dome; cupola.

'cura sf care; (MED: trattamento) (course of) treatment; **aver** ~ **di** (occuparsi di) to look after; **a** ~ **di** (libro) edited by.

cu'rare vt (malato, malattia) to treat; (: guarire) to cure; (aver cura di) to take care

of; (*testo*) to edit; ~**rsi** *vr* to take care of
o.s.; (*MED*) to follow a course of treatment;
~ **rsi di** to pay attention to.

cu'**rato** *sm* parish priest; (*protestante*)
vicar.

cura'**tore**, '**trice** *sm/f* (*DIR*) trustee; (*di
antologia etc*) editor.

'**curia** *sf* (*REL*): **la** ~ **romana** the Roman
curia.

curiosità *sf inv* curiosity; (*cosa rara*) curio,
curiosity.

curi'**oso**, **a** *a*' *ag* (*che vuol sapere*) curious,
inquiring; (*ficcanaso*) curious, inquisitive;
(*bizzarro*) strange, curious.

'**curva** *sf* curve; (*stradale*) bend, curve.

cur'**vare** *vt* to bend // *vi* (*veicolo*) to take
a bend; (*strada*) to bend, curve; ~**rsi** *vr* to
bend; (*legno*) to warp.

'**curvo**, **a** *ag* curved; (*piegato*) bent.

cusci'**netto** [kuʃʃi'netto] *sm* pad; (*TECN*)
bearing // *ag inv*: **stato** ~ buffer state; ~
a sfere ball bearing.

cu'**scino** [kuʃ'ʃino] *sm* cushion; (*guanciale*)
pillow.

'**cuspide** *sf* (*ARCHIT*) spire.

cus'**tode** *sm/f* keeper, custodian.

cus'**todia** *sf* care; (*DIR*) custody; (*astuccio*)
case, holder.

custo'**dire** *vt* (*conservare*) to keep;
(*assistere*) to look after, take care of; (*fare
la guardia*) to guard.

'**cute** *sf* (*ANAT*) skin.

cu'**ticola** *sf* cuticle.

C.V. (*abbr di* **cavallo vapore**) h.p.

D

da *prep* (*da + il* = **dai**, *da + lo* = **dallo**, *da
+ l'* = **dall'**, *da + la* = **dalla**, *da + i* = **dai**,
da + gli = **dagli**, *da + le* = **dalle**) (*agente*)
by; (*provenienza*) from; (*causale*) with;
(*moto a luogo: riferito a persone*): **vado** ~
Pietro/dal giornalaio I'm going to
Pietro's (house)/to the newsagent's; (*stato
in luogo: riferito a persone*): **sono** ~ **Pietro**
I'm at Pietro's (house); (*moto per luogo*)
through; (*fuori da*) out of, from; (*tempo*):
vivo qui ~ **un anno** I have been living
here for a year; **è dalle 3 che ti aspetto**
I've been waiting for you since 3 (o'clock);
comportarsi ~ **bambino** to behave like
a child; ~ **bambino piangevo molto** I
cried a lot as a *o* when I was a child; **una
ragazza dai capelli biondi** a girl with
blonde hair; **un vestito** ~ **100,000 lire** a
100,000 lire dress; ~ ... **a** from ... to; ~
oggi in poi from today onwards; **l'ho
fatto** ~ **me** I did it myself; **macchina** ~
corsa racing car.

dab'**bene** *ag inv* honest, decent.

dac'**capo**, **da** '**capo** *av* (*di nuovo*) (once)
again; (*dal principio*) all over again, from
the beginning.

dacché [dak'ke] *cong* since.

'**dado** *sm* (*da gioco*) dice *o* die (*pl* **dice**);
(*CUC*) stock cube; ~**i** *smpl* (*game of*) dice.

daf'**fare**, **da** '**fare** *sm* work, toil.

'**dagli** ['daʎʎi], '**dai** *prep + det vedi* **da**.

'**daino** *sm* (*fallow*) deer *inv*; (*pelle*)
buckskin.

dal, dall', dalla, dalle, dallo *prep +
det vedi* **da**.

'**dama** *sf* lady; (*nei balli*) partner; (*gioco*)
draughts *sg*.

damigi'**ana** [dami'dʒana] *sf* demijohn.

da'**naro** *sm* = **denaro**.

da'**nese** *ag* Danish // *sm/f* Dane // *sm*
(*LING*) Danish.

Dani'**marca** *sf*: **la** ~ Denmark.

dan'**nare** *vt* (*REL*) to damn; **far** ~ **qd** to
drive sb mad; **dannazi'one** *sf* damnation.

danneggi'**are** [danned'dʒare] *vt* to
damage; (*rovinare*) to spoil; (*nuocere*) to
harm.

'**danno** *sm* damage; (*a persona*) harm,
injury; ~**i** *smpl* (*DIR*) damages; **dan'noso,
a** *ag*: **dannoso (a)** harmful (to), bad (for).

Da'**nubio** *sm*: **il** ~ the Danube.

'**danza** ['dantsa] *sf*: **la** ~ dancing; **una** ~
a dance.

dan'**zare** [dan'tsare] *vt, vi* to dance.

dapper'**tutto** *av* everywhere.

dap'**poco** *ag inv* inept, worthless.

dap'**presso** *av* (*vicino*) near, close at
hand; (*da vicino*) closely.

dap'**prima** *av* at first.

'**dardo** *sm* dart.

'**dare** *sm* (*COMM*) debit // *vt* to give;
(*produrre: frutti, suono*) to produce // *vi*
(*guardare*): ~ **su** to look (out) onto; ~**rsi**
vr: ~**rsi a** to dedicate o.s. to; ~**rsi al
commercio** to go into business; ~**rsi al
bere** to take to drink; ~**rsi a correre** to
start to run; ~ **per certo qc** to consider
sth certain; ~ **per morto qd** to give sb up
for dead.

'**darsena** *sf* dock; dockyard.

'**data** *sf* date.

da'**tare** *vt* to date // *vi*: ~ **da** to date
from.

'**dato, a** *ag* given // *sm* datum; ~**i** *smpl*
data *pl*; ~ **che** given that.

'**dattero** *sm* date.

dattilogra'**fare** *vt* to type; **dattilogra'fia**
sf typing; **datti'lografo, a** *sm/f* typist.

da'**vanti** *av* in front; (*dirimpetto*) opposite
// *ag inv* front // *sm* front; ~ **a** *prep* in
front of; facing, opposite; (*in presenza di*)
before, in front of.

davan'**zale** [davan'tsale] *sm* windowsill.

da'**vanzo, d'a'vanzo** [da'vantso] *av* more
than enough.

dav'**vero** *av* really, indeed.

'**dazio** ['dattsjo] *sm* (*somma*) duty; (*luogo*)
customs *pl*.

d. C. (*abbr di* **dopo Cristo**) A.D.

'**dea** *sf* goddess.

'**debito, a** *ag* due, proper // *sm* debt;
(*COMM: dare*) debit; **a tempo** ~ at the
right time; **debi'tore, 'trice** *sm/f* debtor.

'**debole** *ag* weak, feeble; (*suono*) faint;
(*luce*) dim; **debo'lezza** *sf* weakness.

debut'**tare** *vi* to make one's début; **dé-
butto** *sm* début.

deca'**dente** *ag* decadent, in decline; **deca-**

'denza *sf* decline; (*DIR*) loss, forfeiture.

decaffei'nare *vt* to decaffeinate.

de'cano *sm* (*REL*) dean.

decapi'tare *vt* to decapitate, behead.

decappot'tabile *ag, sf* convertible.

dece'duto, a [detʃe'duto] *ag* deceased.

de'cenne [de'tʃɛnne] *ag* ten-year-old; (*predicativo*) ten years old; **de'cennio** *sm* decade.

de'cente [de'tʃɛnte] *ag* decent, respectable, proper; (*accettabile*) satisfactory, decent; **de'cenza** *sf* decency, propriety.

de'cesso [de'tʃɛsso] *sm* death; **atto di ~** death certificate.

de'cidere [de'tʃidere] *vt*: ~ **qc** to decide on sth; (*questione, lite*) to settle sth; ~ **di fare/che** to decide to do/that; ~ **di qc** (*sog: cosa*) to determine sth; **~rsi (a fare)** to decide (to do), make up one's mind (to do).

deci'frare [detʃi'frare] *vt* to decode; (*fig*) to decipher, make out.

deci'male [detʃi'male] *ag* decimal.

deci'mare [detʃi'mare] *vt* to decimate.

'decimo, a ['dɛtʃimo] *num* tenth.

de'cina [de'tʃina] *sf* ten; (*circa dieci*): **una ~ (di)** about ten.

decisi'one [detʃi'zjone] *sf* decision; **prendere una ~** to make a decision.

de'ciso, a [de'tʃizo] *pp di* **decidere**.

declas'sare *vt* to downgrade; to lower in status.

decli'nare *vi* to go down; (*fig: diminuire*) to decline; (*tramontare*) to set, go down // *vt* to decline; **declinazi'one** *sf* (*LING*) declension; **de'clino** *sm* decline.

de'clivio *sm* (downward) slope.

decol'lare *vi* (*AER*) to take off; **de'collo** *sm* take-off.

decolo'rare *vt* to bleach.

decom'porre *vt,* **decomporsi** *vr* to decompose; **decomposizi'one** *sf* decomposition; **decom'posto, a** *pp di* **decomporre**.

deconge'lare [dekondʒe'lare] *vt* to defrost.

deco'rare *vt* to decorate; **decora'tore, 'trice** *sm/f* (interior) decorator; **decora-zi'one** *sf* decoration.

de'coro *sm* decorum; **deco'roso, a** *ag* decorous, dignified.

de'correre *vi* (2) to pass, elapse; (*avere effetto*) to run, have effect; **de'corso, a** *pp di* **decorrere** // *sm* passing; (*evoluzione: anche MED*) course.

de'crepito, a *ag* decrepit.

de'crescere [de'kreʃʃere] *vi* (2) (*diminuire*) to decrease, diminish; (*acque*) to subside, go down; (*prezzi*) to go down; **decresci'uto, a** *pp di* **decrescere**.

de'creto *sm* decree.

'dedalo *sm* maze, labyrinth.

'dedica, che *sf* dedication.

dedi'care *vt* to dedicate.

'dedito, a *ag*: ~ **a** (*studio etc*) dedicated *o* devoted to; (*vizio*) addicted to.

de'dotto, a *pp di* **dedurre**.

de'durre *vt* (*concludere*) to deduce; (*defalcare*) to deduct; **deduzi'one** *sf* deduction.

defal'care *vt* to deduct.

defe'rente *ag* respectful, deferential.

defe'rire *vt* (*DIR*) to refer.

defezi'one [defet'tsjone] *sf* defection, desertion.

defici'ente [defi'tʃɛnte] *ag* (*mancante*) insufficient; (*minorato*) mentally deficient; (*stupido*) idiotic // *sm/f* mental defective; idiot; **defici'enza** *sf* shortage; (*lacuna*) gap; (*MED*) mental deficiency.

'deficit ['dɛfitʃit] *sm inv* (*ECON*) deficit.

defi'nire *vt* to define; (*risolvere*) to settle; **defini'tivo, a** *ag* definitive, final; **defini-zi'one** *sf* definition; settlement.

deflazi'one [deflat'tsjone] *sf* (*ECON*) deflation.

de'flusso *sm* (*della marea*) ebb.

defor'mare *vt* (*alterare*) to put out of shape; (*corpo*) to deform; (*pensiero, fatto*) to distort; **~rsi** *vr* to lose its shape.

de'forme *ag* deformed; disfigured; **deformità** *sf inv* deformity.

defrau'dare *vt*: ~ **qd di qc** to defraud sb of sth, cheat sb out of sth.

de'funto, a *ag* late *cpd* // *sm/f* deceased.

degene'rare *vi* to degenerate; **de'genere** *ag* degenerate.

de'gente [de'dʒɛnte] *ag* bedridden.

'degli ['deʎʎi] *prep + det vedi* **di**.

de'gnarsi [deɲ'ɲarsi] *vr*: ~ **di fare** to deign o condescend to do.

'degno, a *ag* dignified; ~ **di** worthy of; ~ **di lode** praiseworthy.

degra'dare *vt* (*MIL*) to demote; (*privare della dignità*) to degrade; **~rsi** *vr* to demean o.s.

degus'tare *vt* to sample, taste; **degusta-zi'one** *sf* sampling, tasting.

'dei, dei *prep + det vedi* **di**.

dela'tore, 'trice *sm/f* police informer.

'delega, ghe *sf* (*procura*) proxy.

dele'gare *vt* to delegate; **dele'gato** *sm* delegate; **delegazi'one** *sf* delegation.

del'fino *sm* dolphin.

delibe'rare *vt, vi* to deliberate.

delica'tezza [delika'tettsa] *sf* (*anche CUC*) delicacy; frailty; thoughtfulness; tactfulness.

deli'cato, a *ag* delicate; (*salute*) delicate, frail; (*fig: gentile*) thoughtful, considerate; (: *pieno di tatto*) tactful.

delimi'tare *vt* to circumscribe, define.

deline'are *vt* to outline; **~rsi** *vr* to be outlined; (*fig*) to emerge.

delin'quente *sm/f* criminal, delinquent; **delin'quenza** *sf* criminality, delinquency; **delinquenza minorile** juvenile delinquency.

deli'rare *vi* to be delirious, rave; (*fig*) to rave.

de'lirio *sm* delirium; (*ragionamento insensato*) raving; (*fig*) frenzy.

de'litto sm crime; **delittu'oso, a** ag criminal.

de'lizia [de'littsja] sf delight; **delizi'oso, a** ag delightful; (cibi) delicious.

dell', 'della, 'delle, 'dello prep + det vedi **di**.

'delta sm inv delta.

delta'plano sm hang-glider; **volo col ~** hang gliding.

de'ludere vt to disappoint; **delusi'one** sf disappointment; **de'luso, a** pp di **deludere**.

dema'gogo, ghi sm demagogue.

de'manio sm state property.

de'mente ag (MED) demented, mentally deranged; **de'menza** sf dementia; (stupidità) foolishness.

demo'cratico, a, ci, che ag democratic.

democra'zia [demokrat'tsia] sf democracy.

democristi'ano, a ag, sm/f Christian Democrat.

demo'lire vt to demolish; **demolizi'one** sf demolition.

'demone sm demon.

de'monio sm demon, devil; **il D~** the Devil.

demoraliz'zare [demoralid'dzare] vt to demoralize.

de'naro sm money.

deni'grare vt to denigrate, run down.

denomi'nare vt to name; **~rsi** vr to be named o called; **denomina'tore** sm (MAT) denominator; **denominazi'one** sf name; denomination.

deno'tare vt to denote, indicate.

densità sf inv density.

'denso, a ag thick, dense.

den'tale ag dental.

den'tario, a ag dental.

'dente sm tooth; (di forchetta) prong; (GEO: cima) jagged peak; **al ~** (CUC: pasta) cooked so as to be firm when eaten; **~i del giudizio** wisdom teeth; **denti'era** sf (set of) false teeth pl.

denti'fricio [denti'fritʃo] sm toothpaste.

den'tista, i, e sm/f dentist.

'dentro av in, inside; (fig: nell'intimo) inwardly, in one's mind // prep in, inside; (entro) within; **~ a, ~ in** in, inside; within; **qui/là ~** in here/there; **~ di sé** (pensare, brontolare) to oneself; **di ~** from inside.

de'nuncia, ce o **cie** [de'nuntʃa], **de-'nunzia** [de'nuntsja] sf denunciation; accusation; declaration; **~ del reddito** (income) tax return.

denunci'are [denun'tʃare], **denunzi'are** [denun'tsjare] vt to denounce; (accusare) to accuse; (dichiarare) to declare.

denutrizi'one [denutrit'tsjone] sf malnutrition.

deodo'rante sm deodorant.

depe'rire vi to waste away.

depila'torio sm depilatory.

deplo'rare vt to deplore; to lament; **deplo'revole** ag deplorable.

de'porre vt (depositare) to put down; (rimuovere: da una carica) to remove; (: re) to depose; (DIR) to testify.

depor'tare vt to deport.

deposi'tare vt (GEO, ECON) to deposit; (lasciare) to leave; (merci) to store.

de'posito sm deposit; (luogo) warehouse; depot; (: MIL) depot; **~ bagagli** left-luggage office.

deposizi'one [depozit'tsjone] sf deposition; (da una carica) removal.

de'posto, a pp di **deporre**.

depra'vare vt to corrupt, deprave.

depre'care vt to deprecate, disapprove of.

depre'dare vt to rob, plunder.

depressi'one sf depression.

de'presso, a pp di **deprimere** // ag depressed.

deprez'zare [depret'tsare] vt (ECON) to depreciate.

de'primere vt to depress.

depu'rare vt to purify.

depu'tare vt to delegate; **~ qd a** to send sb (as a representative) to; **depu'tato, a** o **'essa** sm/f (POL) deputy, ≈ Member of Parliament; **deputazi'one** sf deputation; (POL) position of deputy, ≈ parliamentary seat.

deraglia'mento [deraλλa'mento] sm derailment.

deragli'are [deraʎ'ʎare] vi to be derailed; **far ~** to derail.

dere'litto, a ag derelict.

dere'tano sm bottom, buttocks pl.

de'ridere vt to mock, deride; **derisi'one** sf derision, mockery; **de'riso, a** pp di **deridere**.

de'riva sf (NAUT, AER) drift; **andare alla ~** (anche fig) to drift.

deri'vare vi (2): **~ da** to derive from // vt to derive; (corso d'acqua) to divert; **derivazi'one** sf derivation; diversion.

dero'gare vi: **~ a** to go against, depart from; (legge) to repeal in part.

der'rate sfpl commodities; **~ alimentari** foodstuffs.

deru'bare vt to rob.

des'critto, a pp di **descrivere**.

des'crivere vt to describe; **descrizi'one** sf description.

de'serto, a ag deserted // sm (GEO) desert; **isola ~a** desert island.

deside'rare vt to want, wish for; (sessualmente) to desire; **~ fare/che qd faccia** to want o wish to do/sb to do; **desidera fare una passeggiata?** would you like to go for a walk?

desi'derio sm wish; (forte, carnale) desire.

deside'roso, a ag: **~ di** longing o eager for.

desi'gnare [desiɲ'pare] vt to designate, appoint; (data) to fix.

desi'nare vi to dine, have dinner // sm dinner.

de'sistere vi: **~ da** to give up, desist from; **desis'tito, a** pp di **desistere**.

deso'lare vt (affliggere) to distress, grieve.

deso'lato, a ag (paesaggio) desolate; (persona: spiacente) sorry; **desolazi'one** sf desolation.

'despota, i sm despot.

des'tare vt to wake (up); (fig) to awaken, arouse; ~**rsi** vr to wake (up).

desti'nare vt to destine; (assegnare) to appoint, assign; (indirizzare) to address; ~ **qc a qd** to intend to give sth to sb, intend sb to have sth.

destinazi'one [destinat'tsjone] sf destination; (uso) purpose.

des'tino sm destiny, fate.

destitu'ire vt to dismiss, remove.

'desto, a ag (wide) awake.

'destra sf vedi **destro**.

destreggi'arsi [destred'dʒarsi] vr to manoeuvre.

des'trezza [des'trettsa] sf skill, dexterity.

'destro, a ag right, right-hand; (abile) skilful, adroit // sf (mano) right hand; (parte) right (side); (POL): **la** ~ the Right; **a** ~ **a** on the right.

dete'nere vt (incarico, primato) to hold; (un bene) to be in possession of; (in prigione) to detain, hold; **dete'nuto, a** sm/f prisoner; **detenzi'one** sf holding; possession; detention.

deter'gente [deter'dʒɛnte] sm detergent.

deterio'rare vt to damage; ~**rsi** vr to deteriorate.

determi'nare vt to determine; ~**rsi a fare qc** to make up one's mind to do sth; **determinazi'one** sf determination; (decisione) decision.

deter'sivo sm detergent.

detes'tare vt to detest, hate.

deto'nare vi to detonate.

de'trarre vt: ~ (**da**) to deduct (from), take away (from); **de'tratto, a** pp di **detrarre**.

detri'mento sm detriment, harm; **a** ~ **di** to the detriment of.

de'trito sm (GEO) detritus.

dettagli'ante [dettaʎ'ʎante] sm/f (COMM) retailer.

dettagli'are [dettaʎ'ʎare] vt to detail, give full details of.

det'taglio [det'taʎʎo] sm detail; (COMM): **il** ~ retail; **al** ~ (COMM) retail; separately.

det'tare vt to dictate; **det'tato** sm dictation; **detta'tura** sf dictation.

'detto, a pp di **dire** // ag (soprannominato) called, known as; (già nominato) above-mentioned // sm saying; ~ **fatto** no sooner said than done.

detur'pare vt to disfigure; (moralmente) to sully.

devas'tare vt to devastate; (fig) to ravage; **devastazi'one** sf devastation; ravages pl.

devi'are vi to swerve, veer off // vt to divert; **deviazi'one** sf (anche AUT) diversion.

devo'luto, a pp di **devolvere**.

devoluzi'one [devolut'tsjone] sf (DIR) devolution, transfer.

de'volvere vt (DIR) to transfer, devolve.

de'voto, a ag (REL) devout, pious; (affezionato) devoted.

devozi'one [devot'tsjone] sf devoutness; (anche REL) devotion.

di prep (di + il = **del**, di + lo = **dello**, di + l' = **dell'**, di + la = **della**, di + i = **dei**, di + gli = **degli**, di + le = **delle**) of; (causa) with; for; of; (mezzo) with; (provenienza) from // det: **del pane** (some) bread; **dei libri** (some) books; **la sorella** ~ **mio padre** my father's sister; **un sacchetto** ~ **plastica/orologio d'oro** a plastic bag/gold watch; **tremare** ~ **paura** to tremble with fear; **un bambino** ~ **tre anni** a child of three, a three-year-old child; ~ **primavera/giugno** in spring/June; ~ **mattina/sera** in the morning/evening; ~ **notte** by night; at night; **in the night**; ~ **domenica** on Sundays; ~ **... in** from ... to; vedi **più**, **meno** etc.

dia'bete sm diabetes sg.

dia'bolico, a, ci, che ag diabolical.

di'acono sm (REL) deacon.

dia'dema, i sm diadem; (di donna) tiara.

dia'framma, i sm (divisione) screen; (ANAT, FOT) diaphragm.

di'agnosi [di'aɲɲozi] sf diagnosis sg; **diagnosti'care** vt to diagnose.

diago'nale ag, sf diagonal.

dia'gramma, i sm diagram.

dia'letto sm dialect.

di'alogo, ghi sm dialogue.

dia'mante sm diamond.

di'ametro sm diameter.

di'amine escl: **che** ~ **... ?** what on earth ... ?

diaposi'tiva sf transparency, slide.

di'ario sm diary.

diar'rea sf diarrhoea.

di'avolo sm devil.

di'battere vt to debate, discuss; ~**rsi** vr to struggle; **di'battito** sm debate, discussion.

di'cembre [di'tʃɛmbre] sm December.

dicas'tero sm ministry.

dichia'rare [dikja'rare] vt to declare; **dichiarazi'one** sf declaration.

dician'nove [ditʃan'nɔve] num nineteen.

dicias'sette [ditʃas'sɛtte] num seventeen.

dici'otto [di'tʃɔtto] num eighteen.

dici'tura [ditʃi'tura] sf words pl, wording.

di'dattico, a, ci, che ag didactic.

di'eci ['djɛtʃi] num ten; **die'cina** sf = **decina**.

'diesel ['dizəl] sm inv diesel engine.

di'eta sf diet; **essere a** ~ to be on a diet.

di'etro av behind // prep behind; (tempo: dopo) after // sm back, rear; **le zampe di** ~ the back legs, the hind legs; ~ **richiesta** on demand; (scritta) on application.

di'fendere vt to defend; **difen'sivo, a** ag defensive // sf: **stare sulla difensiva**

(*anche fig*) to be on the defensive; **difen-'sore, a** *sm/f* defender; **avvocato difensore** counsel for the defence; **di'feso, a** *pp di* **difendere** // *sf* defence.
difet'tare *vi* to be defective; ~ **di** to be lacking in, lack; **difet'tivo, a** *ag* defective.
di'fetto *sm* (*mancanza*): ~ **di** lack of; shortage of; (*di fabbricazione*) fault, flaw, defect; (*morale*) fault, failing, defect; (*fisico*) defect; **far** ~ to be lacking; **in** ~ at fault; in the wrong; **difet'toso, a** *ag* defective, faulty.
diffa'mare *vt* to defame, slander; to libel.
diffe'rente *ag* different.
diffe'renza [diffe'rɛntsa] *sf* difference; a ~ **di** unlike.
differenzi'ale [differen'tsjale] *ag, sm* differential.
differenzi'are [differen'tsjare] *vt* to differentiate; ~**rsi da** to differentiate o.s. from; to differ from.
diffe'rire [dif'firʃile] *vt* to postpone, defer // *vi* to be different.
dif'ficile [dif'fitʃile] *ag* difficult; (*persona*) hard to please, difficult (to please); (*poco probabile*): **è** ~ **che sia libero** it is unlikely that he'll be free // *sm* difficult part, difficulty; **difficoltà** *sf inv* difficulty.
dif'fida (*DIR*) warning, notice.
diffi'dare *vi*: ~ **di** to be suspicious o distrustful of // *vt* (*DIR*) to warn; **diffi-'dente** *ag* suspicious, distrustful; **diffi-'denza** *sf* suspicion, distrust.
dif'fondere *vt* (*calore*) to diffuse; (*notizie*) to spread, circulate; ~**rsi** *vr* to spread; **diffusi'one** *sf* diffusion; spread; (*anche di giornale*) circulation; (*FISICA*) scattering; **dif'fuso, a** *pp di* **diffondere**.
difi'lato *av* (*direttamente*) straight, directly; (*subito*) straight away.
difte'rite (*MED*) diphtheria.
'diga, ghe *sf* dam; (*argine litoraneo*) dyke.
dige'rire [didʒe'rire] *vt* to digest; **diges-ti'one** *sf* digestion; **diges'tivo, a** *ag* digestive // *sm* (*after-dinner*) liqueur.
digi'tale [didʒi'tale] *ag* digital; (*delle dita*) finger *cpd*, digital // *sf* (*BOT*) foxglove.
digiu'nare [didʒu'nare] *vi* to starve o.s.; (*REL*) to fast; **digi'uno, a** *ag*: **essere digiuno** not to have eaten // *sm* fast; **a digiuno** on an empty stomach.
dignità [diɲɲi'ta] *sf inv* dignity; **digni-'tario** *sm* dignitary; **digni'toso, a** *ag* dignified.
digressi'one *sf* digression.
digri'gnare [digriɲ'ɲare] *vt*: ~ **i denti** to grind one's teeth.
dila'gare *vi* to flood; (*fig*) to spread.
dilapi'dare *vt* to squander, waste.
dila'tare *vt* to dilate; (*gas*) to cause to expand; (*passaggio, cavità*) to open (up); ~**rsi** *vr* to dilate; (*FISICA*) to expand.
dilazio'nare [dilattsjo'nare] *vt* to delay, defer; **dilazi'one** *sf* delay; (*COMM: di pagamento etc*) extension; (*rinvio*) postponement.
dileggi'are [diled'dʒare] *vt* to mock, deride.

dilegu'are *vi*, ~**rsi** *vr* to vanish, disappear.
di'lemma, i *sm* dilemma.
dilet'tante *sm/f* dilettante; (*anche SPORT*) amateur.
dilet'tare *vt* to give pleasure to, delight; ~**rsi** *vr*: ~**rsi di** to take pleasure in, enjoy.
di'letto, a *ag* dear, beloved // *sm* pleasure, delight.
dili'gente [dili'dʒɛnte] *ag* (*scrupoloso*) diligent; (*accurato*) careful, accurate; **dili-'genza** *sf* diligence; care; (*carrozza*) stagecoach.
dilu'ire *vt* to dilute.
dilun'garsi *vr* (*fig*): ~ **su** to talk at length on o about.
diluvi'are *vb impers* to pour (down).
di'luvio *sm* downpour; (*inondazione, fig*) flood.
dima'grire *vi* (2) to get thinner, lose weight.
dime'nare *vt* to wave, shake; ~**rsi** *vr* to toss and turn; (*fig*) to struggle; ~ **la coda** (*sog: cane*) to wag its tail.
dimensi'one *sf* dimension; (*grandezza*) size.
dimenti'canza [dimenti'kantsa] *sf* forgetfulness; (*errore*) oversight, slip; **per** ~ inadvertently.
dimenti'care *vt* to forget; ~**rsi di qc** to forget sth.
di'messo, a *pp di* **dimettere** // *ag* (*voce*) subdued; (*uomo, abito*) modest, humble.
dimesti'chezza [dimesti'kettsa] *sf* familiarity.
di'mettere *vt*: ~ **qd** to dismiss sb from; (*dall'ospedale*) to discharge sb from; ~**rsi (da)** to resign (from).
dimez'zare [dimed'dzare] *vt* to halve.
diminu'ire *vt* to reduce, diminish // *vi* (2) to decrease, diminish, go down; **diminu-zi'one** *sf* decreasing, diminishing.
dimissi'oni *sfpl* resignation *sg*; **dare o presentare le** ~ to resign, hand in one's resignation.
di'mora *sf* residence.
dimo'rare *vi* to reside.
dimos'trare *vt* to demonstrate, show; (*provare*) to prove, demonstrate; ~**rsi** *vr*: ~**rsi molto abile** to show o.s. o prove to be very clever; **dimostra'tivo, a** *ag* (*anche LING*) demonstrative; **dimostra-zi'one** *sf* demonstration; proof.
di'namico, a, ci, che *ag* dynamic // *sf* dynamics *sg*.
dina'mismo *sm* dynamism.
dina'mite *sf* dynamite.
'dinamo *sf inv* dynamo.
di'nanzi [di'nantsi]: ~ **a** *prep* in front of.
dinas'tia *sf* dynasty.
dini'ego, ghi *sm* refusal; denial.
din'torno *av* round, (round) about; ~**i** *smpl* outskirts; **nei** ~**i di** in the vicinity o neighbourhood of.
'dio, pl 'dei *sm* god; **D**~ God; **gli dei** the gods.

di'ocesi [di'ɔtʃezi] *sf* diocese.

dipa'nare *vt* (*lana*) to wind into a ball; (*fig*) to disentangle, sort out.

diparti'mento *sm* department.

dipen'dente *ag* dependent // *sm/f* employee; **dipen'denza** *sf* dependence; **essere alle dipendenze di qd** to be employed by sb *o* in sb's employ.

di'pendere *vi* (2): ~ **da** to depend on; (*finanziariamente*) to be dependent on; (*derivare*) to come from, be due to; **di'peso, a** *pp di* **dipendere**.

di'pingere [di'pindʒere] *vt* to paint; ~**rsi** *vr* to make up, put on makeup; **di'pinto, a** *pp di* **dipingere** // *sm* painting.

di'ploma, i *sm* diploma.

diplo'matico, a, ci, che *ag* diplomatic // *sm* diplomat.

diploma'zia [diplomat'tsia] *sf* diplomacy.

di'porto *sm*: **imbarcazione** *f* **da** ~, pleasure craft.

dira'dare *vt* to thin (out); (*visite*) to reduce, make less frequent; ~**rsi** *vr* to disperse; (*nebbia*) to clear (up).

dira'mare *vt* to issue, send out // *vi*, ~**rsi** *vr* to branch.

'dire *vt* to say; (*segreto, fatto*) to tell; ~ **qc a qd** to tell sb sth; ~ **a qd di fare qc** to tell sb to do sth; ~ **di sì/no** to say yes/no; **si dice che ...** they say that ...; **si direbbe che ...** it looks (*o* sounds) as though ... ; **dica, signora?** (*in un negozio*) yes, Madam, can I help you?

diret'tissimo *sm* (*FERR*) fast (through) train.

di'retto, a *pp di* **dirigere** // *ag* direct // *sm* (*FERR*) through train.

diret'tore, 'trice *sm/f* (*d'impresa*) director; manager/ess; (*di scuola elementare*) headmaster/mistress; ~ **d'orchestra** conductor.

direzi'one [diret'tsjone] *sf* board of directors; management; (*senso di movimento*) direction; **in** ~ **di** in the direction of, towards.

diri'gente [diri'dʒɛnte] *sm/f* executive; (*POL*) leader.

di'rigere [di'ridʒere] *vt* to direct; (*impresa*) to run, manage; (*MUS*) to conduct; ~**rsi** *vr*: ~**rsi verso** *o* **a** to make *o* head for.

diri'gibile [diri'dʒibile] *sm* dirigible.

dirim'petto *av* opposite; ~ **a** *prep* opposite, facing.

di'ritto, a *ag* straight; (*onesto*) straight, upright; (*destro*) right // *av* straight, directly; (*prerogativa*) right; (*leggi, scienza*): **il** ~ law; ~**i** *smpl* (*tasse*) duty *sg*; **stare** ~ to stand upright.

dirit'tura *sf* (*SPORT*) straight; (*fig*) rectitude.

diroc'cato, a *ag* tumbledown, in ruins.

dirot'tare *vt* (*nave, aereo*) to change the course of; (*aereo: sotto minaccia*) to hijack; (*traffico*) to divert // *vi* (*nave, aereo*) to change course; **dirotta'tore, 'trice** *sm/f* hijacker.

di'rotto, a *ag* (*pioggia*) torrential; (*pianto*) unrestrained; **piovere a** ~ to pour, rain cats and dogs; **piangere a** ~ to cry one's heart out.

di'rupo *sm* crag, precipice.

disabi'tato, a *ag* uninhabited.

disabitu'arsi *vr*: ~ **a** to get out of the habit of.

disac'cordo *sm* disagreement.

disadat'tato, a *ag* (*PSIC*) maladjusted.

disa'datto, a *ag*: ~ **(a** *o* **per)** unsuited (to).

disa'dorno, a *ag* plain, unadorned.

disagi'ato, a [diza'dʒato] *ag* poor, needy; (*vita*) hard.

di'sagio [di'zadʒo] *sm* discomfort; (*disturbo*) inconvenience; (*fig: imbarazzo*) embarrassment; ~**i** *smpl* hardship *sg*, poverty *sg*; **essere a** ~ to be ill at ease.

disappro'vare *vt* to disapprove of; **disapprovazi'one** *sf* disapproval.

disap'punto *sm* disappointment.

disar'mare *vt, vi* to disarm; **di'sarmo** *sm* (*MIL*) disarmament.

di'sastro *sm* disaster; **disas'troso, a** *ag* disastrous.

disat'tento, a *ag* inattentive.

disa'vanzo [diza'vantso] *sm* (*ECON*) deficit.

disavve'duto, a *ag* careless, thoughtless.

disavven'tura *sf* misadventure, mishap.

dis'brigo, ghi *sm* (*prompt*) clearing up *o* settlement.

dis'capito *sm* disadvantage, detriment; **a** ~ **di qd** to sb's cost.

discen'dente [diʃʃen'dɛnte] *ag* descending // *sm/f* descendant.

di'scendere [diʃ'ʃendere] *vt* to go (*o* come) down // *vi* (2) to go (*o* come) down; (*strada*) to go down; (*smontare*) to get off; ~ **da** (*famiglia*) to be descended from; ~ **dalla macchina/dal treno** to get out of the car/out of *o* off the train; ~ **da cavallo** to dismount, get off one's horse.

di'scepolo, a [diʃ'ʃepolo] *sm/f* disciple.

di'scernere [diʃ'ʃernere] *vt* to discern, make out; **discerni'mento** *sm* judgment, discernment.

di'sceso, a [diʃ'ʃeso] *pp di* **discendere** // *sf* descent; (*pendio*) slope; **in** ~**a** (*strada*) downhill.

disci'ogliere [diʃ'ʃɔʎʎere] *vt*, ~**rsi** *vr* to dissolve; (*fondere*) to melt; **disci'olto, a** *pp di* **disciogliere**.

disci'plina [diʃʃi'plina] *sf* discipline; **discipli'nare** *ag* disciplinary // *vt* to discipline.

'disco, schi *sm* disc; (*SPORT*) discus; (*fonografico*) record, disc; ~ **orario** (*AUT*) parking disc; ~ **volante** flying saucer.

discol'pare *vt* to clear of blame.

disco'noscere [disko'noʃʃere] *vt* to refuse to acknowledge; (*figlio*) to disown; **disconosci'uto, a** *pp di* **disconoscere**.

dis'corde *ag* conflicting, clashing; **dis'cordia** *sf* discord; (*dissidio*) disagreement, clash.

dis'correre *vi*: ~ **(di)** to talk (about).
dis'corso, a *pp di* **discorrere** // *sm* speech; (*conversazione*) conversation, talk.
dis'costo, a *ag* faraway, distant // *av* far away; ~ **da** *prep* far from.
disco'teca, che *sf* (*raccolta*) record library; (*luogo di ballo*) discothèque.
discredi'tare *vt* to discredit.
discre'panza [diskre'pantsa] *sf* disagreement.
dis'creto, a *ag* discreet; (*abbastanza buono*) reasonable, fair; **discrezi'one** *sf* discretion; (*giudizio*) judgment, discernment; **a discrezione di** at the discretion of.
discriminazi'one [diskriminat'tsjone] *sf* discrimination.
discussi'one *sf* discussion; (*litigio*) argument.
dis'cusso, a *pp di* **discutere**.
dis'cutere *vt* to discuss, debate; (*contestare*) to question, dispute // *vi* to talk; (*contrastare*) to argue; ~ **di** to discuss.
disde'gnare [disdeɲ'ɲare] *vt* to scorn; **dis'degno** *sm* scorn, disdain.
dis'detto, a *pp di* **disdire** // *sf* retraction; cancellation; (*sfortuna*) bad luck.
dis'dire *vt* (*ritrattare*) to retract, take back; (*annullare*) to cancel.
dise'gnare [diseɲ'ɲare] *vt* to draw; (*progettare*) to design; (*fig*) to outline; **disegna'tore, 'trice** *sm/f* designer.
di'segno [di'seɲɲo] *sm* drawing; design; outline.
diser'tare *vt, vi* to desert; **diser'tore** *sm* (MIL) deserter; **diserzi'one** *sf* (MIL) desertion.
dis'fare *vt* to undo; (*valigie*) to unpack; (*lavoro, paese*) to destroy; (*neve*) to melt; ~**rsi** *vr* to melt; ~ **il letto** to strip the bed; ~**rsi in lacrime** to dissolve into tears; ~**rsi di qd** (*liberarsi*) to get rid of sb; **dis'fatto, a** *pp di* **disfare** // *sf* (*sconfitta*) rout.
disfunzi'one [disfun'tsjone] *sf* (MED) disorder.
disge'lare [dizdʒe'lare] *vt, vi*, ~**rsi** *vr* to thaw; **dis'gelo** *sm* thaw.
dis'grazia [diz'grattsja] *sf* (*sventura*) misfortune; (*incidente*) accident, mishap; **disgrazi'ato, a** *ag* unfortunate // *sm/f* wretch.
disgre'gare *vt*, ~**rsi** *vr* to break up.
disgu'ido *sm*: ~ **postale** error in postal delivery.
disgus'tare *vt* to disgust; ~**rsi** *vr*: ~**rsi di** to be disgusted by.
dis'gusto *sm* disgust; **disgus'toso, a** *ag* disgusting.
disidra'tare *vt* to dehydrate.
disil'ludere *vt* to disillusion, disenchant; **disillusi'one** *sf* disillusion, disenchantment.
disimpa'rare *vt* to forget.
disimpe'gnare [dizimpeɲ'ɲare] *vt* (*oggetto dato in pegno*) to redeem, get out of pawn; (*liberare*) to release, free;

(*sbrigare: ufficio*) to carry out; ~**rsi** *vr* to free o.s.; (*cavarsela*) to manage.
disinfet'tante *ag, sm* disinfectant.
disinfet'tare *vt* to disinfect; **disinfezi'one** *sf* disinfection.
disingan'nare *vt* to disabuse, disillusion.
disinte'grare *vt, vi* (2) to disintegrate.
disinteres'sarsi *vr*: ~ **di** to take no interest in.
disinte'resse *sm* indifference; (*generosità*) unselfishness.
disin'volto, a *ag* casual, free and easy; **disinvol'tura** *sf* casualness, ease.
dislo'care *vt* to station, position.
dismi'sura *sf* excess; **a** ~ to excess, excessively.
disobbe'dire *etc* = **disubbidire** *etc*.
disoccu'pato, a *ag* unemployed // *sm/f* unemployed person; **disoccupazi'one** *sf* unemployment.
disonestà *sf* dishonesty.
diso'nesto, a *ag* dishonest.
disono'rare *vt* to dishonour, bring disgrace upon.
diso'nore *sm* dishonour, disgrace.
di'sopra *av* (*con contatto*) on top; (*senza contatto*) above; (*al piano superiore*) upstairs // *ag inv* (*superiore*) upper; **la gente** ~ the people upstairs; **il piano** ~ the floor above // *sm inv* top, upper part.
disordi'nare *vt* to mess up, disarrange; (*fig*) to upset, confuse; (MIL) to throw into disorder // *vi*: ~ **nel bere** *etc* to take drink *etc* to excess; **disordi'nato, a** *ag* untidy; (*privo di misura*) irregular, wild.
di'sordine *sm* (*confusione*) disorder, confusion; (*sregolatezza*) debauchery.
disorien'tare *vt* to disorientate; ~**rsi** *vr* (*fig*) to get confused, lose one's bearings.
di'sotto *av* below, underneath; (*in fondo*) at the bottom; (*al piano inferiore*) downstairs // *ag inv* (*inferiore*) lower; bottom *cpd*; **la gente** ~ the people downstairs; **il piano** ~ the floor below // *sm inv* (*parte inferiore*) lower part; bottom.
dis'paccio [dis'pattʃo] *sm* dispatch.
dispa'rato, a *ag* disparate.
'dispari *ag inv* odd, uneven.
disparità *sf inv* disparity.
dis'parte: in ~ *av* (*da lato*) aside, apart; **tenersi** *o* **starsene in** ~ to keep to o.s., hold aloof.
dispendi'oso, a *ag* expensive.
dis'pensa *sf* pantry, larder; (*mobile*) sideboard; (DIR) exemption; (REL) dispensation; (*fascicolo*) number, issue.
dispen'sare *vt* (*elemosine, favori*) to distribute; (*esonerare*) to exempt.
dispe'rare *vi*: ~ **(di)** to despair (of); ~**rsi** *vr* to despair; **dispe'rato, a** *ag* desperate; **disperazi'one** *sf* desperation.
dis'perdere *vt* (*disseminare*) to disperse; (MIL) to scatter, rout; (*fig: consumare*) to waste, squander; ~**rsi** *vr* to disperse; to scatter; **dispersi'one** *sf* dispersion, dispersal; (FISICA, CHIM) dispersion; **dis'perso, a** *pp di* **disperdere** // *sm* missing soldier.

dis'petto sm (spite q, spitefulness q; **fare un ~ a qd** to play a (nasty) trick on sb; **a ~ di** in spite of; **dispet'toso, a** ag spiteful.

dispia'cere [dispja'tʃere] sm (rammarico) regret, sorrow; (dolore) grief; **~i** smpl troubles, worries // vi: **~ a** to displease // vb impers: **mi dispiace (che)** I am sorry (that); **se non le dispiace, me ne vado adesso** if you don't mind, I'll go now; **dispiaci'uto, a** pp di **dispiacere**.

dispo'nibile ag available.

dis'porre vt (sistemare) to arrange; (preparare) to prepare; (DIR) to order; (persuadere): **~ qd a** to incline o dispose sb towards // vi (decidere) to decide; (usufruire): **~ di** to use, have at one's disposal; (essere dotato): **~ di** to have; **disporsi** vr (ordinarsi) to place o.s., arrange o.s.; **disporsi a fare** to get ready to do; **disposizi'one** sf arrangement, layout; (stato d'animo) mood; (tendenza) bent, inclination; (comando) order; (DIR) provision, regulation; **a disposizione di qd** at sb's disposal; **dis'posto, a** pp di **disporre**.

dis'potico, a, ci, che ag despotic.

disprez'zare [dispret'tsare] vt to despise.

dis'prezzo [dis'prɛttso] sm contempt.

'disputa sf dispute, quarrel.

dispu'tare vt (contendere) to dispute, contest; (SPORT: partita) to play; (: gareggiare) to take part in // vi to quarrel; **~ di** to discuss; **~rsi qc** to fight for sth.

dissangua'mento sm loss of blood.

disse'care vt to dissect.

dissec'care vt, **~rsi** vr to dry up.

dissemi'nare vt to scatter; (fig: notizie) to spread.

dis'senso sm dissent; (disapprovazione) disapproval.

dissente'ria sf dysentery.

dissen'tire vi: **~ (da)** to disagree (with).

dissertazi'one [dissertat'tsjone] sf dissertation.

disser'vizio [disser'vittsjo] sm inefficiency.

disses'tare vt (ECON) to ruin; **dis'sesto** sm (financial) ruin.

disse'tante ag refreshing.

disse'tare vt to quench the thirst of.

dissezi'one [disset'tsjone] sf dissection.

dissi'dente ag, sm/f dissident.

dis'sidio sm disagreement.

dis'simile ag different, dissimilar.

dissimu'lare vt (fingere) to dissemble; (nascondere) to conceal.

dissi'pare vt to dissipate; (scialacquare) to squander, waste; **dissipa'tezza** sf dissipation; **dissipazi'one** sf squandering.

dissoci'are [disso'tʃare] vt to dissociate.

dis'solto, a pp di **dissolvere**.

disso'lubile ag soluble.

disso'luto, a pp di **dissolvere** // ag dissolute, licentious.

dis'solvere vt to dissolve; (neve) to melt; (fumo) to disperse; **~rsi** vr to dissolve; to melt; to disperse.

disso'nante ag discordant.

dissu'adere vt: **~ qd da** to dissuade sb from; **dissu'aso, a** pp di **dissuadere**.

distac'care vt to detach, separate; (SPORT) to leave behind; **~rsi** vr to be detached; (fig) to stand out; **~rsi da** (fig: allontanarsi) to grow away from.

dis'tacco, chi sm (separazione) separation; (fig: indifferenza) detachment; (SPORT): **è arrivato con un ~ di 10 minuti dai primi** he came in 10 minutes behind the leaders.

dis'tante av far away // ag distant, far away.

dis'tanza [dis'tantsa] sf distance.

distanzi'are [distan'tsjare] vt to space out, place at intervals; (SPORT) to outdistance; (fig: superare) to outstrip, surpass.

dis'tare vi: **distiamo pochi chilometri da Roma** we are only a few kilometres (away) from Rome.

dis'tendere vt (coperta) to spread out; (gambe) to stretch (out); (mettere a giacere) to lay; (rilassare: muscoli, nervi) to relax; **~rsi** vr (rilassarsi) to relax; (sdraiarsi) to lie down; **distensi'one** sf stretching; relaxation; (POL) détente.

dis'teso, a pp di **distendere** // sf expanse, stretch.

distil'lare vt to distil.

distille'ria sf distillery.

dis'tinguere vt to distinguish.

dis'tinta sf (nota) note; (elenco) list.

distin'tivo, a ag distinctive; distinguishing // sm badge.

dis'tinto, a pp di **distinguere** // ag (dignitoso ed elegante) distinguished; **"~i saluti"** "Yours faithfully".

distinzi'one [distin'tsjone] sf distinction.

dis'togliere [dis'tɔʎʎere] vt: **~ da** to take away from; (fig) to dissuade from; **dis'tolto, a** pp di **distogliere**.

distorsi'one sf (MED) sprain; (alterazione) distortion.

dis'trarre vt to distract; (divertire) to entertain, amuse; **distrarsi** vr (svagarsi) to amuse o enjoy o.s.; **dis'tratto, a** pp di **distrarre** // ag absent-minded; (disattento) inattentive; **distrazi'one** sf absent-mindedness; inattention; (svago) distraction, entertainment.

dis'tretto sm district.

distribu'ire vt to distribute; (CARTE) to deal (out); (consegnare: posta) to deliver; **distribu'tore** sm (di benzina) petrol pump; (AUT, ELETTR) distributor; (automatico) vending o slot machine; **distribuzi'one** sf distribution; delivery.

distri'care vt to disentangle, unravel.

dis'truggere [dis'truddʒere] vt to destroy; **distrut'tivo, a** ag destructive; **dis'trutto, a** pp di **distruggere**; **distruzi'one** sf destruction.

distur'bare vt to disturb, trouble; (sonno,

lezioni) to disturb, interrupt; ~**rsi** *vr* to put o.s. out.

dis'turbo *sm* trouble, bother, inconvenience; (*indisposizione*) (slight) disorder, ailment; ~**i** *smpl* (RADIO, TV) static *sg*.

disubbidi'ente *ag* disobedient; **disubbidi'enza** *sf* disobedience.

disubbi'dire *vi*: ~ (**a qd**) to disobey (sb).

disugu'ale *ag* unequal; (*diverso*) different; (*irregolare*) uneven.

disu'mano, a *ag* inhuman.

disu'nire *vt* to divide, disunite.

di'suso *sm* disuse; **andare** *o* **cadere in** ~ to fall into disuse.

'dita *fpl di* **dito**.

di'tale *sm* thimble.

'dito, *pl(f)* **'dita** *sm* finger; (*misura*) finger, finger's breadth; ~ (**del piede**) toe.

'ditta *sf* firm, business.

ditta'tore *sm* dictator.

ditta'tura *sf* dictatorship.

dit'tongo, ghi *sm* diphthong.

di'urno, a *ag* day *cpd*, daytime *cpd* // *sm* (*anche*: **albergo** ~) public toilets with washing and shaving facilities etc.

'diva *sf vedi* **divo**.

diva'gare *vi* to digress; **divagazi'one** *sf* digression.

divam'pare *vi* (2) to flare up, blaze up.

di'vano *sm* sofa; divan.

divari'care *vt* to open wide.

di'vario *sm* difference.

dive'nire *vi* (2) = **diventare**; **dive'nuto, a** *pp di* **divenire**.

diven'tare *vi* (2) to become; ~ **famoso/professore** to become famous/a teacher.

di'verbio *sm* altercation.

diver'gente [diver'dʒɛnte] *ag* divergent.

di'vergere [di'vɛrdʒere] *vi* to diverge.

diversifi'care *vt* to diversify, vary; to differentiate.

diversi'one *sf* diversion.

diversità *sf inv* difference, diversity; (*varietà*) variety.

diver'sivo *sm* diversion, distraction.

di'verso, a *ag* (*differente*): ~ (**da**) different (from); ~**i, e** *det pl* several, various; (COMM) sundry // *pronome pl* several (people), many (people).

diver'tente *ag* amusing.

diverti'mento *sm* amusement, pleasure; (*passatempo*) pastime, recreation.

diver'tire *vt* to amuse, entertain; ~**rsi** *vr* to amuse *o* enjoy o.s.

divi'dendo *sm* dividend.

di'videre *vt* (*anche* MAT) to divide; (*distribuire, ripartire*) to divide (up), split (up).

divi'eto *sm* prohibition; "~ **di sosta**" (AUT) "no parking".

divinco'larsi *vr* to wriggle, writhe.

divinità *sf inv* divinity.

di'vino, a *ag* divine.

di'visa *sf* (MIL *etc*) uniform; (COMM) foreign currency.

divisi'one *sf* division.

di'viso, a *pp di* **dividere**.

'divo, a *sm/f* star.

divo'rare *vt* to devour.

divorzi'are [divor'tsjare] *vi*: ~ (**da qd**) to divorce (sb).

di'vorzio [di'vɔrtsjo] *sm* divorce.

divul'gare *vt* to divulge, disclose; (*rendere comprensibile*) to popularize; ~**rsi** *vr* to spread.

dizio'nario [ditsjo'narjo] *sm* dictionary.

dizi'one [dit'tsjone] *sf* diction; pronunciation.

do *sm* (MUS) C; (: *solfeggiando la scala*) do(h).

'doccia, ce ['dɔttʃa] *sf* shower; (*condotto*) pipe.

do'cente [do'tʃɛnte] *ag* teaching // *sm/f* teacher; (*di università*) lecturer; **do'cenza** *sf* university teaching *o* lecturing.

docile ['dɔtʃile] *ag* docile.

documen'tare *vt* to document; ~**rsi** *vr*: ~**rsi (su)** to gather information *o* material (about).

documen'tario, a *ag*, *sm* documentary.

documentazi'one [dokumentat'tsjone] *sf* documentation.

docu'mento *sm* document; ~**i** *smpl* (*d'identità etc*) papers.

'dodici ['dɔditʃi] *num* twelve.

do'gana *sf* (*ufficio*) customs *pl*; (*tassa*) (customs) duty; **passare la** ~ to go through customs; **doga'nale** *ag* customs *cpd*; **dogani'ere** *sm* customs officer.

'doglie ['dɔʎʎe] *sfpl* (MED) labour *sg*, labour pains.

'dogma, i *sm* dogma.

'dolce ['doltʃe] *ag* sweet; (*colore*) soft; (*fig: mite: clima*) mild; (*non ripido: pendio*) gentle // *sm* (*sapore dolce*) sweetness, sweet taste; (CUC: *portata*) sweet, dessert; (: *torta*) cake; **dol'cezza** *sf* sweetness; softness; mildness; gentleness; **dolci'umi** *smpl* sweets.

do'lente *ag* sorrowful, sad.

do'lere *vi* (2) to be sore, hurt, ache; ~**rsi** *vr* to complain; (*essere spiacente*): ~**rsi di** to be sorry for; **mi duole la testa** my head aches, I've got a headache.

'dollaro *sm* dollar.

'dolo *sm* (DIR) malice.

Dolo'miti *sfpl*: **le** ~ the Dolomites.

do'lore *sm* (*fisico*) pain; (*morale*) sorrow, grief; **dolo'roso, a** *ag* painful; sorrowful, sad.

do'loso, a *ag* (DIR) malicious.

do'manda *sf* (*interrogazione*) question; (*richiesta*) demand; (: *cortese*) request; (DIR: *richiesta scritta*) application; (ECON): **la** ~ demand; **fare una** ~ **a qd** to ask sb a question.

doman'dare *vt* (*per avere*) to ask for; (*per sapere*) to ask; (*esigere*) to demand; ~**rsi** *vr* to wonder; to ask o.s.; ~ **qc a qd** to ask sb for sth; to ask sb sth.

do'mani *av* tomorrow // *sm*: **il** ~ (*il futuro*) the future; (*il giorno successivo*) the next day; ~ **l'altro** the day after tomorrow.

do'mare *vt* to tame.

domat'tina *av* tomorrow morning.

do'menica, che *sf* Sunday; **di o la** ~ on Sundays; **domeni'cale** *ag* Sunday *cpd*.

do'mestica, che *sf vedi* **domestico**.

domesti'chezza [domesti'kettsa] *sf* = **dimestichezza**.

do'mestico, a, ci, che *ag* domestic // *sm/f* servant, domestic.

domi'cilio [domi't∫iljo] *sm* (*DIR*) domicile, place of residence.

domi'nare *vt* to dominate; (*fig: sentimenti*) to control, master // *vi* to be in the dominant position; ~**rsi** *vr* (*controllarsi*) to control o.s.; ~ **su** (*fig*) to surpass, outclass; **dominazi'one** *sf* domination.

do'minio *sm* dominion; (*fig: campo*) field, domain.

do'nare *vt* to give, present; (*per beneficenza etc*) to donate // *vi* (*fig*): ~ **a** to suit, become; **dona'tore, 'trice** *sm/f* donor; **donatore di sangue** blood donor; **donazi'one** *sf* donation.

dondo'lare *vt* (*cullare*) to rock; ~**rsi** *vr* to swing, sway; **'dondolo** *sm*: **sedia/cavallo a dondolo** rocking chair/horse.

'donna *sf* woman; ~ **di casa** housewife; home-loving woman; ~ **di servizio** maid.

donnai'olo *sm* ladykiller.

don'nesco, a, schi, sche *ag* women's, woman's.

'donnola *sf* weasel.

'dono *sm* gift.

'dopo *av* (*tempo*) afterwards; (*luogo*) after, next // *prep* after // *cong* (*temporale*): ~ **aver studiato** after having studied; ~ **mangiato va a dormire** after having eaten *o* after a meal he goes for a sleep // *ag inv*: **il giorno** ~ the following day; **un anno** ~ a year later; ~ **di me/lui** after me/him.

dopodo'mani *av* the day after tomorrow.

dopogu'erra *sm* postwar years *pl*.

dopo'pranzo [dopo'prandzo] *av* after lunch (*o* dinner).

dopo'sci [dopo'∫i] *sm inv* après-ski outfit.

doposcu'ola *sm inv* sort of school club offering extra tuition and recreational facilities.

dopo'tutto *av* after all.

doppi'aggio [dop'pjadd3o] *sm* (*CINEMA*) dubbing.

doppi'are *vt* (*NAUT*) to round; (*SPORT*) to lap; (*CINEMA*) to dub.

'doppio, a *ag* double; (*fig: falso*) double-dealing, deceitful // *sm* (*quantità*): **il** ~ **(di)** twice as much (*o* many), double the amount (*o* number) of; (*SPORT*) doubles *pl* // *av* double.

doppi'one *sm* duplicate (copy).

doppio'petto *sm* double-breasted jacket.

do'rare *vt* to gild; (*CUC*) to brown; **dora-'tura** *sf* gilding.

dormicchi'are [dormik'kjare] *vi* to doze.

dormigli'one, a [dormiλ'λone] *sm/f* sleepyhead.

dor'mire *vt, vi* to sleep; **dor'mita** *sf* (good) sleep.

dormi'torio *sm* dormitory.

dormi'veglia [dormi've λλa] *sm* drowsiness.

'dorso *sm* back; (*di montagna*) ridge, crest; (*di libro*) spine; **a** ~ **di cavallo** on horseback.

do'sare *vt* to measure out; (*MED*) to dose.

'dose *sf* quantity, amount; (*MED*) dose.

'dosso *sm* (*dorso*) back; **levarsi di** ~ **i vestiti** to take one's clothes off.

do'tare *vt*: ~ **di** to provide *o* supply with; (*fig*) to endow with; **dotazi'one** *sf* (*insieme di beni*) endowment; (*di macchine etc*) equipment.

'dote *sf* (*di sposa*) dowry; (*assegnata a un ente*) endowment; (*fig*) gift, talent.

Dott. (*abbr di dottore*) Dr.

'dotto, a *ag* (*colto*) learned // *sm* (*sapiente*) scholar; (*ANAT*) duct.

dotto'rato *sm* degree; (*di ricerca*) doctorate, doctor's degree.

dot'tore, essa *sm/f* doctor.

dot'trina *sf* doctrine.

Dott.ssa (*abbr di dottoressa*) Dr.

'dove *av* where; (*in cui*) where, in which; (*dovunque*) wherever; **di** ~ **sei?** where are you from?; **da** ~ **abito vedo tutta la città** I can see the whole city from where I stay; **per** ~ **si passa?** which way should we go?

do'vere *sm* (*obbligo*) duty // *vt* (*essere debitore*): ~ **qc (a qd)** to owe (sb) sth // *vi* (*seguito dall'infinito: obbligo*) to have to; **lui deve farlo** he has to do it, he must do it; **è dovuto partire** he had to leave; **ha dovuto pagare** he had to pay; (: *intenzione*): **devo partire domani** I'm (due) to leave tomorrow; (: *probabilità*) **dev'essere tardi** it must be late.

dove'roso, a *ag* (right and) proper.

do'vunque *av* (*in qualunque luogo*) wherever; (*dappertutto*) everywhere; ~ **io vada** wherever I go.

do'vuto, a *ag* (*causato*): ~ **a** due to.

doz'zina [dod'dzina] *sf* dozen; **una** ~ **di uova** a dozen eggs.

dozzi'nale [doddzi'nale] *ag* cheap, second-rate.

dra'gare *vt* to dredge.

'drago, ghi *sm* dragon.

'dramma, i *sm* drama; **dram'matico, a, ci, che** *ag* dramatic; **drammatiz'zare** *vt* to dramatize; **dramma'turgo, ghi** *sm* playwright, dramatist.

drappeggi'are [draped'd3are] *vt* to drape.

drap'pello *sm* (*MIL*) squad; (*gruppo*) band, group.

dre'naggio [dre'nadd3o] *sm* drainage.

dre'nare *vt* to drain.

'dritto, a *ag, av* = **diritto**.

driz'zare [drit'tsare] *vt* (*far tornare diritto*) to straighten; (*volgere: sguardo, occhi*) to turn, direct; (*innalzare*: *antenna*, *muro*) to erect; ~**rsi** *vr* to stand up; ~ **le orecchie** to prick up one's ears.

'**droga, ghe** *sf* (*sostanza aromatica*) spice; (*stupefacente*) drug; **dro'gare** *vt* to season, spice; to drug; **drogarsi** *vr* to take drugs; **dro'gato, a** *sm/f* drug addict.

droghe'ria [droge'ria] *sf* grocer's shop.

drome'dario *sm* dromedary.

'**dubbio, a** *ag* (*incerto*) doubtful, dubious; (*ambiguo*) dubious // *sm* (*incertezza*) doubt; **avere il ~ che** to be afraid that, suspect that; **mettere in ~ qc** to question sth; **dubbi'oso, a** *ag* doubtful, dubious.

dubi'tare *vi*: ~ **di** to doubt; (*risultato*) to be doubtful of; **dubita'tivo, a** *ag* doubtful, dubious.

'**duca, chi** *sm* duke.

du'chessa [du'kessa] *sf* duchess.

'**due** *num* two.

due'cento [due'tʃɛnto] *num* two hundred // *sm*: **il D**~ the thirteenth century.

du'ello *sm* duel.

due'pezzi [due'pɛttsi] *sm* (*costume da bagno*) two-piece swimsuit; (*abito femminile*) two-piece suit *o* costume.

du'etto *sm* duet.

'**duna** *sf* dune.

'**dunque** *cong* (*perciò*) so, therefore; (*riprendendo il discorso*) well (then).

du'omo *sm* cathedral.

dupli'cato *sm* duplicate.

'**duplice** ['duplitʃe] *ag* double, twofold; **in ~** in duplicate.

du'rante *prep* during.

du'rare *vi* to last; (*perseverare*): ~ **in qc/a fare qc** to persist *o* persevere in sth/in doing sth; ~ **fatica a** to have difficulty in; **du'rata** *sf* length (of time); duration; **dura'turo, a** *ag*, **du'revole** *ag* lasting.

du'rezza [du'rettsa] *sf* hardness; stubbornness; harshness; toughness.

'**duro, a** *ag* (*pietra, lavoro, materasso, problema*) hard; (*persona*: *ostinato*) stubborn, obstinate; (*: severo*) harsh, hard; (*voce*) harsh; (*carne*) tough // *sm* (*persona*) tough guy; ~ **d'orecchi** hard of hearing; ~ **di testa** (*fig: fam*) slow-witted.

du'rone *sm* hard skin.

E

e, *dav* V *spesso* **ed** *cong* and.

E. (*abbr di* **est**) E.

è *forma del vb* **essere**.

'**ebano** *sm* ebony.

eb'bene *cong* well (then).

eb'brezza [eb'brettsa] *sf* intoxication.

'**ebbro, a** *ag* drunk; ~ **di** (*gioia etc*) beside o.s. *o* wild with.

'**ebete** *ag* stupid, idiotic.

ebollizi'one [ebolli'tsjone] *sf* boiling; **punto di ~** boiling point.

e'braico, a, ci, che *ag* Hebrew, Hebraic // *sm* (*LING*) Hebrew.

e'breo, a *ag* Jewish // *sm/f* Jew/Jewess.

ecc *av* (*abbr di* **eccetera**) etc.

ecce'denza [ettʃe'dɛntsa] *sf* excess, surplus.

ec'cedere [et'tʃɛdere] *vt* to exceed // *vi* to go too far; ~ **nel bere/mangiare** to indulge in drink/food to excess.

eccel'lente [ettʃel'lɛnte] *ag* excellent; **eccel'lenza** *sf* excellence; (*titolo*) Excellency.

ec'cellere [et'tʃɛllere] *vi* to excel; ~ **su tutti** to surpass everyone; **ec'celso, a** *pp di* **eccellere**.

ec'centrico, a, ci, che [et'tʃɛntriko] *ag* eccentric; (*quartiere*) outlying.

ecces'sivo, a [ettʃes'sivo] *ag* excessive.

ec'cesso [et'tʃɛsso] *sm* excess; **all'~** (*gentile, generoso*) to excess, excessively; **dare in ~i** to fly into a rage.

ec'cetera [et'tʃɛtera] *av* et cetera, and so on.

ec'cetto [et'tʃɛtto] *prep* except, with the exception of; ~ **che** *cong* except, other than; ~ **che (non)** unless.

eccettu'are [ettʃettu'are] *vt* to except.

eccezio'nale [ettʃetsjo'nale] *ag* exceptional.

eccezi'one [ettʃet'tsjone] *sf* exception; (*DIR*) objection; **a ~ di** with the exception of, except for; **d'~** exceptional.

ecci'tare [ettʃi'tare] *vt* (*curiosità, interesse*) to excite, arouse; (*folla*) to incite; ~**rsi** *vr* to get excited; **eccita-zi'one** *sf* excitement.

ecclesi'astico, a, ci, che *ag* ecclesiastical, church *cpd*; clerical // *sm* ecclesiastic.

'**ecco** *av* (*per dimostrare*): ~ **il treno!** here's *o* here comes the train!; (*dav pronome*): ~**mi!** here I am!; ~**ne uno!** here's one (of them)!; (*dav pp*): ~ **fatto!** there, that's it done!

echeggi'are [eked'dʒare] *vi* to echo.

e'clissi *sf* eclipse.

'**eco**, *pl*(*m*) '**echi** *sm o f* echo.

ecolo'gia [ekolo'dʒia] *sf* ecology.

econo'mia *sf* economy; (*scienza*) economics *sg*; (*risparmio*: *azione*) saving; ~**e** *sfpl* (*denari risparmiati*) savings; **fare ~e** to save; **eco'nomico, a, ci, che** *ag* (*ECON*) economic; (*poco costoso*) economical; **econo'mista, i** *sm* economist; **economiz'zare** *vt, vi* to save; **e'conomo, a** *ag* thrifty // *sm/f* (*INS*) bursar.

ed *cong vedi* **e**.

'**edera** *sf* ivy.

e'dicola *sf* newspaper kiosk.

edifi'care *vt* to build; (*fig: teoria, azienda*) to establish; (*indurre al bene*) to edify.

edi'ficio [edi'fitʃo] *sm* building; (*fig*) structure.

e'dile *ag* building *cpd*; **edi'lizio, a** *ag* building *cpd* // *sf* building, building trade.

edi'tore, 'trice *ag* publishing *cpd* // *sm/f* publisher; (*curatore*) editor; **edito'ria** *sf* publishing; **editori'ale** *ag* publishing *cpd* // *sm* editorial, leader.

edizi'one [edit'tsjone] *sf* edition; (*tiratura*) printing; (*di manifestazioni, feste etc*) production.

edu'care *vt* to educate; (*abituare*): ~ **(a)** to train (for); **edu'cato, a** *ag* polite, well-mannered; **educazi'one** *sf* education; (*comportamento*) (good) manners *pl*; **educazione fisica** (*INS*) physical training *o* education.

effemi'nato, a *ag* effeminate.

efferve'scente [efferveʃ'ʃɛnte] *ag* effervescent.

effet'tivo, a *ag* (*reale*) real, actual; (*operaio, professore*) permanent; (*MIL*) regular // *sm* (*MIL*) strength; (*di patrimonio etc*) sum total.

ef'fetto *sm* effect; (*fig: impressione*) impression; **cercare l'~** to look for attention; **in ~i** in fact, actually; **effettu'are** *vt* to effect, carry out.

effi'cace [effi'katʃe] *ag* effective.

effici'ente [effi'tʃɛnte] *ag* efficient; **efficienza** *sf* efficiency; **in piena efficienza** (*persona*) fit; (*macchina*) in perfect working order.

ef'figie [ef'fidʒe] *sf inv* effigy.

ef'fimero, a *ag* ephemeral.

effusi'one *sf* effusion.

E'geo [e'dʒɛo] *sm*: **l'~, il mare ~** the Aegean (Sea).

E'gitto [e'dʒitto] *sm*: **l'~** Egypt.

'egli ['eʎʎi] *pronome* he; ~ **stesso** he himself.

ego'ismo *sm* selfishness, egoism; **ego'ista, i, e** *ag* selfish, egoistic // *sm/f* egoist.

egr. *abbr di* **egregio.**

e'gregio, a, gi, gie [e'grɛdʒo] *ag* distinguished; (*nelle lettere*): **E~ Signore** Dear Sir.

eguagli'anza [egwaʎ'ʎantsa] *etc vedi* **uguaglianza** *etc*.

elabo'rare *vt* (*progetto*) to work out, elaborate; (*dati*) to process; (*digerire*) to digest; **elaborazi'one** *sf* elaboration; digestion; **elaborazione dei dati** data processing.

e'lastico, a, ci, che *ag* elastic // *sm* (*gommino*) rubber band; (*per il cucito*) elastic *q*.

ele'fante *sm* elephant.

ele'gante *ag* elegant; **ele'ganza** *sf* elegance.

e'leggere [e'lɛddʒere] *vt* to elect.

elemen'tare *ag* elementary; ~**i** *sfpl* primary school.

ele'mento *sm* element; (*parte componente*) element, component, part; ~**i** *smpl* (*della scienza etc*) elements, rudiments.

ele'mosina *sf* charity, alms *pl*.

elen'care *vt* to list.

e'lenco, chi *sm* list; ~ **telefonico** telephone directory.

e'letto, a *pp di* **eleggere** // *sm/f* (*nominato*) elected member; **eletto'rale** *ag* electoral, election *cpd*; **eletto'rato** *sm*

electorate; **elet'tore, 'trice** *sm/f* voter, elector.

elet'trauto *sm inv* workshop for car electrical repairs; (*tecnico*) car electrician.

elettri'cista, i [elettri'tʃista] *sm* electrician.

elettricità [elettritʃi'ta] *sf* electricity.

e'lettrico, a, ci, che *ag* electric(al).

elettrifi'care *vt* to electrify.

elettriz'zare [elettrid'dzare] *vt* to electrify.

e'lettro... *prefisso*: **elettrocardio'gramma, i** *sm* electrocardiogram; **e'lettrodo** *sm* electrode; **elettrodo'mestico, a, ci, che** *ag*: **apparecchi elettrodomestici** domestic (electrical) appliances; **elettroma'gnetico, a, ci, che** *ag* electromagnetic; **elet'trone** *sm* electron; **elet'tronico, a, ci, che** *ag* electronic // *sf* electronics *sg*; **elettro'treno** *sm* electric train.

ele'vare *vt* to raise; (*edificio*) to erect; (*multa*) to impose; **elevazi'one** *sf* elevation; (*l'elevare*) raising.

elezi'one [elet'tsjone] *sf* election; ~**i** *sfpl* (*POL*) election(s).

'elica, che *sf* propeller.

eli'cottero *sm* helicopter.

elimi'nare *vt* to eliminate; **elimina'toria** *sf* eliminating round.

'elio *sm* helium.

'ella *pronome* she; (*forma di cortesia*) you; ~ **stessa** she herself; you yourself.

el'metto *sm* helmet.

e'logio [e'lɔdʒo] *sm* (*discorso, scritto*) eulogy; (*lode*) praise (*di solito q*).

elo'quente *ag* eloquent; **elo'quenza** *sf* eloquence.

e'ludere *vt* to evade; **elu'sivo, a** *ag* evasive.

ema'nare *vt* to send out, give out; (*fig: leggi, decreti*) to issue // *vi* (*2*): ~ **da** to come from.

emanci'pare [emantʃi'pare] *vt* to emancipate; ~**rsi** *vr* (*fig*) to become liberated *o* emancipated; **emancipazi'one** *sf* emancipation.

em'blema, i *sm* emblem.

embri'one *sm* embryo.

emenda'mento *sm* amendment.

emen'dare *vt* to amend.

emer'genza [emer'dʒentsa] *sf* emergency; **in caso di** ~ in an emergency.

e'mergere [e'mɛrdʒere] *vi* to emerge; (*sommergibile*) to surface; (*fig: distinguersi*) to stand out; **e'merso, a** *pp di* **emergere.**

e'messo, a *pp di* **emettere.**

e'mettere *vt* (*suono, luce*) to give out, emit; (*onde radio*) to send out; (*assegno, francobollo*) to issue; (*fig: giudizio*) to express, voice.

emi'crania *sf* migraine.

emi'grante *ag, sm/f* emigrant.

emi'grare *vi* to emigrate; **emigrazi'one** *sf* emigration.

emi'nente *ag* eminent, distinguished; emi'nenza *sf* eminence.

emis'fero *sm* hemisphere; ~ boreale/australe northern/southern hemisphere.

emissi'one *sf* emission; sending out; issue; (*RADIO*) broadcast.

emit'tente *ag* (*banca*) issuing; (*RADIO*) broadcasting, transmitting // *sf* (*RADIO*) transmitter.

emorra'gia, 'gie [emorra'dʒia] *sf* haemorrhage.

emo'tivo, a *ag* emotional.

emozio'nante [emottsjo'nante] *ag* exciting, thrilling.

emozio'nare [emottsjo'nare] *vt* (*eccitare*) to excite; (*commuovere*) to move; (*turbare*) to upset; ~rsi *vr* to be excited; to be moved; to be upset.

emozi'one [emot'tsjone] *sf* emotion; (*agitazione*) excitement.

'empio, a *ag* (*sacrilego*) impious; (*spietato*) cruel, pitiless; (*malvagio*) wicked, evil.

em'pire *vt* to fill (up).

em'porio *sm* market, commercial centre; (*grande magazzino*) department store.

emu'lare *vt* to emulate.

emulsi'one *sf* emulsion.

en'ciclica, che [en'tʃiklika] *sf* (*REL*) encyclical.

enciclope'dia [entʃiklope'dia] *sf* encyclopaedia.

endove'noso, a *ag* (*MED*) intravenous.

ener'gia, 'gie [ener'dʒia] *sf* (*FISICA*) energy; (*fig*) energy, strength, vigour; e'nergico, a, ci, che *ag* energetic, vigorous; (*efficace*) powerful, strong.

'enfasi *sf* emphasis; (*peg*) bombast, pomposity; en'fatico, a, ci, che *ag* pompous.

e'nigma, i *sm* enigma; enig'matico, a, ci, che *ag* enigmatic.

E.N.I.T. *abbr di Ente Nazionale Italiano per il Turismo*.

en'nesimo, a *ag* (*MAT, fig*) nth; per l' ~ a volta for the umpteenth time.

e'norme *ag* enormous, huge; enormità *sf inv* enormity, huge size; (*assurdità*) absurdity; non dire ~! don't talk nonsense!

'ente *sm* (*istituzione*) body, board, corporation; (*FILOSOFIA*) being.

en'trambi, e *pronome pl* both (of them) // *ag pl:* ~ i ragazzi both boys, both of the boys.

en'trare *vi* (2) to enter, go (*o come*) in; ~ in (*luogo*) to enter, go (*o come*) into; (*trovar posto, poter stare*) to fit into; (*essere ammesso a: club etc*) to join, become a member of; ~ in automobile to get into the car; questo non c'entra (*fig*) that's got nothing to do with it; en'trata *sf* entrance, entry; entrate *sf pl* (*COMM*) receipts, takings; (*ECON*) income *sg*.

'entro *prep* (*temporale*) within.

entusias'mare *vt* to excite, fill with enthusiasm; ~rsi (per qc/qd) to become enthusiastic (about sth/sb); entusi'asmo

sm enthusiasm; entusi'asta, i, e *ag* enthusiastic // *sm/f* enthusiast; entusi'astico, a, ci, che *ag* enthusiastic.

enume'rare *vt* to enumerate, list.

enunci'are [enun'tʃare] *vt* (*teoria*) to enunciate, set out.

'epico, a, ci, che *ag* epic.

epide'mia *sf* epidemic.

Epifa'nia *sf* Epiphany.

epiles'sia *sf* epilepsy.

e'pilogo, ghi *sm* conclusion.

epi'sodio *sm* episode.

e'pistola *sf* epistle.

e'piteto *sm* epithet.

'epoca, che *sf* (*periodo storico*) age, era; (*tempo*) time; (*GEO*) age.

ep'pure *cong* and yet, nevertheless.

epu'rare *vt* (*POL*) to purge; (: *persona*) to expel, remove.

equa'tore *sm* equator.

equazi'one [ekwat'tsjone] *sf* (*MAT*) equation.

e'questre *ag* equestrian.

equi'latero, a *ag* equilateral.

equili'brare *vt* to balance; equi'librio *sm* balance; (*bilancia*) equilibrium.

e'quino, a *ag* horse *cpd*, equine.

equi'nozio [ekwi'nɔttsjo] *sm* equinox.

equipaggi'are [ekwipad'dʒare] *vt* (*di persone*) to man; (*di mezzi*) to equip; equi'paggio *sm* crew.

equipa'rare *vt* to make equal.

equità *sf* equity, fairness.

equitazi'one [ekwitat'tsjone] *sf* (horse-)riding.

equiva'lente *ag, sm* equivalent; equiva'lenza *sf* equivalence.

equivo'care *vi* to misunderstand; e'quivoco, a, ci, che *ag* equivocal, ambiguous; (*sospetto*) dubious // *sm* misunderstanding; a scanso di equivoci to avoid any misunderstanding; giocare sull'equivoco to equivocate.

'equo, a *ag* fair, just.

'era *sf* era.

'erba *sf* grass; (*aromatica, medicinale*) herb; in ~ (*fig*) budding; er'baccia, ce *sf* weed; er'boso, a *ag* grassy.

e'rede *sm/f* heir; eredità *sf* (*DIR*) inheritance; (*BIOL*) heredity; lasciare qc in eredità a qd to leave *o* bequeath sth to sb; eredi'tare *vt* to inherit; eredi'tario, a *ag* hereditary.

ere'mita, i *sm* hermit.

ere'sia *sf* heresy; e'retico, a, ci, che *ag* heretical // *sm/f* heretic.

e'retto, a *pp di* erigere // *ag* erect, upright; erezi'one *sf* (*FISIOL*) erection.

er'gastolo *sm* (*DIR: pena*) life imprisonment; (: *luogo di pena*) prison.

'erica *sf* heather.

e'rigere [e'ridʒere] *vt* to erect, raise; (*fig: fondare*) to found.

ermel'lino *sm* ermine.

er'metico, a, ci, che *ag* hermetic.

'ernia *sf* (*MED*) hernia.

e'roe *sm* hero.

ero'gare vt (somme) to distribute; (: per beneficenza) to donate; (gas, servizi) to supply.

e'roico, a, ci, che ag heroic.

ero'ina sf heroine; (droga) heroin.

ero'ismo sm heroism.

erosi'one sf erosion.

e'rotico, a, ci, che ag erotic.

'erpice ['erpitʃe] sm (AGR) harrow.

er'rare vi (vagare) to wander, roam; (sbagliare) to be mistaken; er'roneo, a ag erroneous, wrong; er'rore sm error, mistake; (morale) error; per errore by mistake.

'erta sf steep slope; stare all'~ to be on the alert.

eru'dito, a ag learned, erudite.

erut'tare vi to belch // vt (sog: vulcano) to throw out.

eruzi'one [erut'tsjone] sf eruption.

esacer'bare [ezatʃer'bare] vt to exacerbate.

esage'rare [ezadʒe'rare] vt to exaggerate // vi to exaggerate; (eccedere) to go too far; esagerazi'one sf exaggeration.

e'sagono sm hexagon.

esal'tare vt to exalt; (entusiasmare) to excite, stir; esal'tato sm fanatic.

e'same sm examination; (INS) exam, examination; dare un ~ to sit an exam; ~ del sangue blood test.

esami'nare vt to examine.

e'sanime ag lifeless.

esaspe'rare vt to exasperate; to exacerbate; ~rsi vr to become annoyed o exasperated; esasperazi'one sf exasperation.

esat'tezza [ezat'tettsa] sf exactitude, accuracy, precision.

e'satto, a pp di esigere // ag (calcolo, ora) correct, right, exact; (preciso) accurate, precise; (puntuale) punctual.

esat'tore sm (di imposte etc) collector.

esau'dire vt to grant, fulfil.

esauri'ente ag exhaustive.

esauri'mento sm exhaustion; ~ nervoso nervous breakdown.

esau'rire vt (stancare) to exhaust, wear out; (provviste, miniera) to exhaust; ~rsi vr to exhaust o.s., wear o.s. out; (provviste) to run out; esau'rito, a ag exhausted; (merci) sold out; (libri) out of print; e'sausto, a ag exhausted.

'esca, pl esche sf bait; (sostanza infiammabile) tinder.

escande'scenza [eskandeʃ'ʃɛntsa] sf: dare in ~e to lose one's temper, fly into a rage.

'esce, 'esci ['ɛʃe,'ɛʃi] forme del vb uscire.

escla'mare vi to exclaim, cry out; esclamazi'one sf exclamation.

es'cludere vt to exclude; esclusi'one sf exclusion.

esclu'sivo, a ag exclusive // sf (DIR) exclusive o sole rights pl.

es'cluso, a pp di escludere.

'esco, 'escono forme del vb uscire.

'escono forma del vb uscire.

escre'menti smpl excrement sg, faeces.

escursi'one sf (gita) excursion, trip; (: a piedi) hike, walk; (METEOR) range.

ese'crare vt to loathe, abhor.

esecu'tivo, a ag, sm executive.

esecu'tore, 'trice sm/f (MUS) performer; (DIR) executor.

esecuzi'one [ezekut'tsjone] sf execution, carrying out; (MUS) performance; ~ capitale execution.

esegu'ire vt to carry out, execute; (MUS) to perform, execute.

e'sempio sm example; per ~ for example, for instance; esem'plare ag exemplary // sm example; (copia) copy; esemplifi'care vt to exemplify.

esen'tare vt: ~qd/qc da to exempt sb/sth from.

e'sente ag: ~ da (dispensato da) exempt from; (privo di) free from; esenzi'one sf exemption.

e'sequie sfpl funeral rites; funeral service sg.

eser'cente [ezer'tʃɛnte] sm/f trader, dealer; shopkeeper.

eserci'tare [ezertʃi'tare] vt (professione) to practise; (allenare: corpo, mente) to exercise, train; (diritto) to exercise; (influenza, pressione) to exert; ~rsi vr to practise; ~rsi alla lotta to practise fighting; esercitazi'one sf (scolastica, militare) exercise.

e'sercito [e'zertʃito] sm army.

eser'cizio [ezer'tʃittsjo] sm practise; exercising; (fisico, di matematica) exercise; (ECON) financial year; (azienda) business, concern; in ~ (medico etc) practising.

esi'bire vt to exhibit, display; (documenti) to produce, present; ~rsi vr (attore) to perform; (fig) to show off; esibizi'one sf exhibition; (di documento) presentation; (spettacolo) show, performance.

esi'gente [ezi'dʒɛnte] ag demanding; esi'genza sf demand, requirement.

e'sigere [e'zidʒere] vt (pretendere) to demand; (richiedere) to demand, require; (imposte) to collect.

e'siguo, a ag small, slight.

'esile ag slender, slim; (suono) faint.

esili'are vt to exile; e'silio sm exile.

e'simere vt: ~ qd/qc da to exempt sb/sth from.

esis'tenza [ezis'tɛntsa] sf existence.

e'sistere vi (2) to exist.

esis'tito, a pp di esistere.

esi'tare vi to hesitate; esitazi'one sf hesitation.

'esito sm result, outcome.

'esodo sm exodus.

esone'rare vt: ~ qd da to exempt sb from.

esorbi'tante ag exorbitant, excessive.

esorciz'zare [ezortʃid'dʒare] vt to exorcize.

e'sordio sm début.

esor'tare vt: ~ qd a fare to urge sb to do.

e'sotico, a, ci, che ag exotic.

es'pandere vt to expand; (confini) to extend; (influenza) to extend, spread; ~rsi vr to expand; **espansi'one** sf expansion; **espan'sivo, a** ag expansive, communicative.

espatri'are vi (2) to leave one's country.

espedi'ente sm expedient.

es'pellere vt to expel.

esperi'enza [espe'rjɛntsa] sf experience; (SCIENZA: prova) experiment; **parlare per ~** to speak from experience.

esperi'mento sm experiment.

es'perto, a ag, sm expert.

espi'are vt to atone for.

espi'rare vt, vi to breathe out.

espli'care vt (attività) to carry out, perform.

es'plicito, a [es'plitʃito] ag explicit.

es'plodere vi (anche fig) to explode; (fucile) to go off // vt to fire.

esplo'rare vt to explore; **esplora'tore, 'trice** sm/f explorer; **giovane esploratore** (boy) scout/(girl) guide // sm (NAUT) scout (ship); **esplorazi'one** sf exploration.

esplosi'one sf explosion; **esplo'sivo, a** ag, sm explosive; **es'ploso, a** pp di esplodere.

espo'nente sm/f (rappresentante) representative.

es'porre vt (merci) to display; (quadro) to exhibit, show; (fatti, idee) to explain, set out; (porre in pericolo, FOT) to expose.

espor'tare vt to export; **esporta'tore, 'trice** ag exporting // sm exporter; **esportazi'one** sf exportation; export.

esposizi'one [espozit'tsjone] sf displaying; exhibiting; setting out; (anche FOT) exposure; (mostra) exhibition; (narrazione) explanation, exposition.

es'posto, a pp di esporre // ag: ~ a nord facing north // sm (AMM) statement, account; (: petizione) petition.

espressi'one sf expression.

espres'sivo, a ag expressive.

es'presso, a pp di esprimere // ag express // sm (lettera) express letter; (anche: treno ~) express train; (anche: caffè ~) espresso.

es'primere vt to express; ~rsi vr to express o.s.

espulsi'one sf expulsion; **es'pulso, a** pp di espellere.

'essa pronome f, **'esse** pronome fpl vedi esso.

es'senza [es'sɛntsa] sf essence; **essenzi'ale** ag essential; **l'essenziale** the main o most important thing.

'essere sm being; ~ umano human being // vi, vb con attributo (2) to be // vb ausiliare (2) to have (o qualche volta be); **è giovane/professore** he is young/a teacher; **è l'una** it's one o'clock; **sono le otto** it's eight o'clock; **esserci: c'è/ci sono** there is/there are; **che c'è?** what's wrong?; **ci siamo!** here we are!; (fig) this

is it!; (: siamo alle solite) here we go again!; ~ **di** (appartenenza) to belong to; (origine) to be from; **è di mio fratello** it belongs to my brother, it's my brother's.

'esso, a pronome it; (fam: riferito a persona: soggetto) he/she; (: complemento) him/her; ~**i, e** pronome pl they; (complemento) them.

est sm east.

'estasi sf ecstasy.

es'tate sf summer.

es'tatico, a, ci, che ag ecstatic.

es'tendere vt to extend; ~**rsi** vr (diffondersi) to spread; (territorio, confini) to extend; **estensi'one** sf extension; (di superficie) expanse; (MUS) range.

esteri'ore ag outward, external.

es'terno, a ag (porta, muro) outer, outside; (scala) outside; (alunno, impressione) external // sm outside, exterior // sm/f (allievo) day pupil; **per uso ~** for external use only.

'estero, a ag foreign // sm: **all'~** abroad.

es'teso, a pp di estendere // ag extensive, large; **scrivere per ~** to write in full.

es'tetico, a, ci, che ag aesthetic // sf aesthetics sg; **este'tista** sf beautician.

'estimo sm valuation; (disciplina) surveying.

es'tinguere vt to extinguish, put out; (debito) to pay off; ~**rsi** vr to go out; (famiglia, animali) to become extinct; **es'tinto, a** pp di estinguere; **estin'tore** sm (fire) extinguisher; **estinzi'one** sf putting out; (di famiglia, animali) extinction.

es'tivo, a ag summer cpd.

es'torcere [es'tɔrtʃere] vt: ~ **qc (a qd)** to extort sth (from sb); **estorsi'one** sf extortion; **es'torto, a** pp di estorcere.

estradizi'one [estradit'tsjone] sf extradition.

es'traneo, a ag foreign; (discorso) extraneous, unrelated // sm/f stranger; **rimanere ~ a qc** to take no part in sth.

es'trarre vt to extract, pull out; (minerali) to mine; (sorteggiare) to draw; **es'tratto, a** pp di estrarre // ag extract; (di documento) abstract; **estratto conto** statement of account; **estrazi'one** sf extraction; mining; drawing q; draw.

estre'mista, i, e sm/f extremist.

estremità sf inv extremity, end // sfpl (ANAT) extremities.

es'tremo, a ag, sm extreme; **l'~ Oriente** the Far East.

'estro sm (capriccio) whim, fancy; (ispirazione creativa) inspiration; **es'troso, a** ag whimsical, capricious; inspired.

estro'verso, a ag, sm extrovert.

estu'ario sm estuary.

esube'rante ag exuberant.

'esule sm/f exile.

età sf inv age; **all'~ di 8 anni** at the age of 8, at 8 years of age; **raggiungere la maggiore ~** to come of age; **essere in ~ minore** to be under age.

'etere sm ether; **e'tereo, a** ag ethereal.

eternità *sf* eternity.
e'terno, a *ag* eternal.
etero'geneo, a [etero'dʒɛneo] *ag* heterogeneous.
'etica *sf vedi* **etico.**
eti'chetta [eti'ketta] *sf* label; (*cerimoniale*) etiquette.
'etico, a, ci, che *ag* ethical // *sf* ethics *sg.*
etimolo'gia, 'gie [etimolo'dʒia] *sf* etymology.
Eti'opia *sf*: l' ~ Ethiopia.
'Etna *sm*: l' ~ Etna.
'etnico, a, ci, che *ag* ethnic.
e'trusco, a, schi, sche *ag, sm/f* Etruscan.
'ettaro *sm* hectare (= *10,000 m²*).
'etto *sm abbr di* **ettogrammo.**
etto'grammo *sm* hectogram(me) (= *100 grams*).
Eucaris'tia *sf*: l' ~ the Eucharist.
eufe'mismo *sm* euphemism.
Eu'ropa *sf*: l' ~ Europe; **euro'peo, a** *ag, sm/f* European.
eutana'sia *sf* euthanasia.
evacu'are *vt* to evacuate; **evacuazi'one** *sf* evacuation.
e'vadere *vi* (*2*) (*fuggire*): ~ **da** to escape from // *vt* (*sbrigare*) to deal with, dispatch; (*tasse*) to evade.
evan'gelico, a, ci, che [evan'dʒɛliko] *ag* evangelical; **evange'lista, i** *sm* evangelist; **evan'gelo** *sm* = **vangelo.**
evapo'rare *vi* to evaporate; **evapora-zi'one** *sf* evaporation.
evasi'one *sf* escape; ~ **fiscale** tax evasion.
eva'sivo, a *ag* evasive.
e'vaso, a *pp di* **evadere** // *sm* escapee.
e'vento *sm* event.
eventu'ale *ag* possible.
evi'dente *ag* evident, obvious; **evi'denza** *sf* obviousness; **mettere in evidenza** to point out, highlight.
evi'tare *vt* to avoid; ~ **di fare** to avoid doing; ~ **qc a qd** to spare sb sth.
'evo *sm* age, epoch.
evo'care *vt* to evoke.
evo'luto, a *pp di* **evolvere.**
evoluzi'one [evolut'tsjone] *sf* evolution.
e'volversi *vr* to evolve.
ev'viva *escl* hurrah!; ~ **il re!** long live the king!, hurrah for the king!
ex *prefisso* ex-.
'extra *prep* outside, outwith // *ag inv* first-rate; top-quality // *sm inv* extra; **extraconiu'gale** *ag* extramarital.

F

fa *forma del vb* **fare** // *sm inv* (*MUS*) F; (: *solfeggiando la scala*) fa // *av*: **10 anni** ~ 10 years ago.
'fabbrica *sf* factory; **fabbri'cante** *sm* manufacturer, maker; **fabbri'care** *vt* to build; (*produrre*) to manufacture, make; (*fig*) to fabricate, invent.
'fabbro *sm* (black)smith.

fac'cenda [fat'tʃɛnda] *sf* matter, affair; (*cosa da fare*) task, chore.
fac'chino [fak'kino] *sm* porter.
'faccia, ce [fat'tʃa] *sf* face; (*di moneta, disco etc*) side; ~ **a** ~ face to face.
facci'ata [fat'tʃata] *sf* façade; (*di pagina*) side.
'faccio ['fattʃo] *forma del vb* **fare.**
fa'ceto, a [fa'tʃeto] *ag* witty, humorous.
'facile ['fatʃile] *ag* easy; (*affabile*) easy-going; (*disposto*): ~ **a** inclined to, prone to; (*probabile*): **è** ~ **che piova** it's likely to rain; **facilità** *sf* easiness; (*disposizione, dono*) aptitude; **facili'tare** *vt* to make easier.
facino'roso, a [fatʃino'roso] *ag* violent.
facoltà *sf inv* faculty; (*potere*) power.
facolta'tivo, a *ag* optional; (*fermata d'autobus*) request *cpd.*
'faggio ['faddʒo] *sm* beech.
fagi'ano [fa'dʒano] *sm* pheasant.
fagio'lino [fadʒo'lino] *sm* French bean.
fagi'olo [fa'dʒɔlo] *sm* bean.
fa'gotto *sm* bundle; (*MUS*) bassoon; **far** ~ (*fig*) to pack up and go.
'fai *forma del vb* **fare.**
'falce ['faltʃe] *sf* scythe; **fal'cetto** *sm* sickle; **falci'are** *vt* to cut; (*fig*) to mow down.
'falco, chi *sm* hawk.
fal'cone *sm* falcon.
'falda *sf* layer, stratum; (*di cappello*) brim; (*di monte*) lower slope; (*di tetto*) pitch; **nevica a larghe** ~**e** the snow is falling in large flakes; **abito a** ~**e** tails *pl.*
fale'gname [falen'ɲame] *sm* joiner.
fal'lace [fal'latʃe] *ag* misleading; deceptive.
falli'mento *sm* failure; bankruptcy.
fal'lire *vi* (*2: non riuscire*): ~ **(in)** to fail (in); (*DIR*) to go bankrupt // *vt* (*bersaglio, preda*) to miss; **fal'lito, a** *ag* unsuccessful; bankrupt // *sm* bankrupt.
'fallo *sm* error, mistake; (*imperfezione*) defect, flaw; (*SPORT*) foul; fault; **senza** ~ without fail.
falò *sm inv* bonfire.
fal'sare *vt* to distort, misrepresent; **fal-'sario** *sm* forger; counterfeiter; **falsifi-'care** *vt* to forge; (*monete*) to forge, counterfeit.
'falso, a *ag* false; (*errato*) wrong, incorrect; (*falsificato*) forged; fake // *sm* forgery; **giurare il** ~ to commit perjury.
'fama *sf* fame; (*reputazione*) reputation, name.
'fame *sf* hunger; **aver** ~ to be hungry; **fa-'melico, a, ci, che** *ag* ravenous.
fa'miglia [fa'miʎʎa] *sf* family.
famili'are *ag* (*della famiglia*) family *cpd*; (*ben noto*) familiar; (*tono*) friendly, informal; (*LING*) informal, colloquial // *sm* relative, relation; **familiarità** *sf* familiarity; informality.
fa'moso, a *ag* famous, well-known.
fa'nale *sm* (*AUT*) light, lamp; (*NAUT*) beacon; ~ **di coda** (*AUT*) tail-light.

fa'natico, a, ci, che *ag* fanatical; (*del teatro, calcio etc*): ~ di *o* per mad *o* wild about // *sm/f* fanatic; (*tifoso*) fan.

fanciul'lezza [fantʃul'lettsa] *sf* childhood.

fanci'ullo, a [fan'tʃullo] *sm/f* child.

fan'donia *sf* tall story; ~e *sfpl* nonsense *sg.*

fan'fara *sf* brass band; (*musica*) fanfare.

'fango, ghi *sm* mud; fan'goso, a *ag* muddy.

'fanno *forma del vb* fare.

fannul'lone, a *sm/f* idler, loafer.

fantasci'enza [fantaʃ'ʃɛntsa] *sf* science fiction.

fanta'sia *sf* fantasy, imagination; (*capriccio*) whim, caprice // *ag inv*: vestito ~ patterned dress.

fan'tasma, i *sm* ghost, phantom; (*immagine*) fantasy.

fantastiche'ria [fantastike'ria] *sf* daydream.

fan'tastico, a, ci, che *ag* fantastic; (*potenza, ingegno*) imaginative.

'fante *sm* infantryman; (*CARTE*) jack, knave; fante'ria *sf* infantry.

fan'toccio [fan'tɔttʃo] *sm* puppet.

far'dello *sm* bundle; (*fig*) burden.

'fare *vt* to make; (*operare, agire*) to do; (*TEATRO*) to act; ~ l'avvocato/il medico to be a lawyer/doctor; ~ del tennis to play tennis; ~ il morto/l'ignorante to act dead/the fool; non fa niente it doesn't matter; 2 più 2 fa 4 2 and 2 are *o* make 4; non ce la faccio più I can't go on any longer; farla a qd to get the better of sb; farla finita con qc to have done with sth // vi (*essere adatto*) to be suitable; (*stare per*): fece per parlare quando ... he was about to speak when ...; ~ in modo di to act in such a way that; faccia pure! go ahead!; ~ da (*far le funzioni di*) to act as // *vb impers*: vedi bello, freddo etc; ~ piangere/ridere qd to make sb cry/laugh; ~ venire qd to have sb come; fammi vedere let me see; ~rsi vr (*diventare*) to become; ~rsi la macchina to get a car for o.s.; ~rsi avanti to come forward; ~rsi notare to get o.s. noticed.

far'falla *sf* butterfly.

fa'rina *sf* flour.

fa'ringe [fa'rindʒe] *sf* (*ANAT*) pharynx.

farma'ceutico, a, ci, che [farma-'tʃeutiko] *ag* pharmaceutical.

farma'cia, 'cie [farma'tʃia] *sf* pharmacy; (*locale*) chemist's (shop), pharmacy; farma'cista, i, e *sm/f* chemist, pharmacist.

'farmaco, ci *o* chi *sm* drug, medicine.

'faro *sm* (*NAUT*) lighthouse; (*AER*) beacon; (*AUT*) headlight, headlamp.

'farsa *sf* farce.

'fascia, sce ['faʃʃa] *sf* band, strip; (*MED*) bandage; (*di carta*) wrapper; (*di sindaco, ufficiale*) sash; (*parte di territorio*) strip, belt.

fasci'are [faʃ'ʃare] *vt* to bandage.

fa'scicolo [faʃ'ʃikolo] *sm* (*di documenti*) file, dossier; (*di rivista*) issue, number; (*opuscolo*) booklet, pamphlet.

'fascino ['faʃʃino] *sm* charm, fascination.

'fascio ['faʃʃo] *sm* bundle, sheaf; (*di fiori*) bunch.

fa'scismo [faʃ'ʃizmo] *sm* fascism.

'fase *sf* phase.

fas'tidio *sm* (*molestia*) annoyance, bother, trouble; (*scomodo*) inconvenience; dare ~ a qd to bother *o* annoy sb; sento ~ allo stomaco my stomach's upset; fastidi'oso, a *ag* annoying, tiresome; (*schifiltoso*) fastidious.

'fasto *sm* pomp, splendour.

'fata *sf* fairy.

fa'tale *ag* fatal; (*inevitabile*) inevitable; (*fig*) irresistible; fatalità *sf* inevitability; (*avversità*) misfortune; (*fato*) fate, destiny.

fa'tica, che *sf* hard work, toil; (*sforzo*) effort; (*di metalli*) fatigue; a ~ with difficulty; fati'care *vi* to toil; faticare a fare qc to have difficulty doing sth; fati'coso, a *ag* tiring, exhausting; hard, difficult.

'fato *sm* fate, destiny.

'fatto, a *pp di* fare // *ag*: un uomo ~ a grown man; ~ a mano/in casa hand-/home-made // *sm* fact; (*azione*) deed; (*di romanzo, film*) action, story; (*affare, caso*) event; cogliere qd sul ~ to catch sb red-handed; il ~ sta *o* è che the fact remains *o* is that; in ~ di as for, as far as ... is concerned.

fat'tore *sm* (*AGR*) farm manager; (*elemento costitutivo*) factor.

fatto'ria *sf* farm; farmhouse.

fatto'rino *sm* errand-boy; office-boy.

fat'tura *sf* (*di abito, scarpa*) cut, design; (*lavorazione*) workmanship; (*COMM*) invoice; (*malia*) spell.

fattu'rare *vt* (*COMM*) to invoice; (*vino*) to adulterate.

'fatuo, a *ag* vain, fatuous.

'fauna *sf* fauna.

fau'tore *sm* advocate, supporter.

fa'vella *sf* speech.

fa'villa *sf* spark.

'favola *sf* (*fiaba*) fairy tale; (*d'intento morale*) fable; (*fandonia*) yarn; favo'loso, a *ag* fabulous.

fa'vore *sm* favour; per ~ please; favo'revole *ag* favourable.

favo'rire *vt* to favour; (*il commercio, l'industria, le arti*) to promote, encourage; vuole ~? won't you help yourself?; favorisca in salotto please come into the sitting room; favo'rito, a *ag*, *sm/f* favourite.

fazi'one [fat'tsjone] *sf* faction.

fazzo'letto [fattso'letto] *sm* handkerchief; (*per la testa*) (head)scarf.

feb'braio *sm* February.

'febbre *sf* fever; aver la ~ to have a high temperature; ~ da fieno hay fever; feb-'brile *ag* (*anche fig*) feverish.

'feccia, ce ['fettʃa] *sf* dregs *pl*.

'fecola *sf* potato flour.

fecon'dare vt to fertilize.

fe'condo, a ag fertile.

'fede sf (credenza) belief, faith; (REL) faith; (fiducia) faith, trust; (fedeltà) loyalty; (anello) wedding ring; (attestato) certificate; **aver ~ in qd** to have faith in sb; **fe'dele** ag: **fedele (a)** faithful (to) // sm/f follower; **i fedeli** (REL) the faithful; **fedeltà** sf faithfulness; (coniugale, RADIO) fidelity.

'federa sf pillowslip, pillowcase.

fede'rale ag federal.

federazi'one [federat'tsjone] sf federation.

'fegato sm liver; (fig) guts pl, nerve.

'felce ['feltʃe] sf fern.

fe'lice [fe'litʃe] ag happy; (fortunato) lucky; **felicità** sf happiness.

felici'tarsi [felitʃi'tarsi] vr (congratularsi): **~ con qd per qc** to congratulate sb on sth.

fe'lino, a ag feline.

'feltro sm felt; (cappello) felt hat.

'femmina sf (ZOOL, TECN) female; (figlia) girl, daughter; (spesso peg) woman; **femmi'nile** ag feminine; (sesso) female; (lavoro) woman's // sm (LING) feminine; **femmi'nismo** sm feminism.

'fendere vt to split, cleave; (attraversare) to force one's way through.

fe'nomeno sm phenomenon.

'feretro sm coffin.

feri'ale ag working cpd, work cpd, week cpd; **giorno ~** weekday.

'ferie sfpl holidays.

fe'rire vt to injure; (deliberatamente: MIL etc) to wound; (colpire) to hurt; **fe'rita** sf injury; wound.

'ferma sf (MIL) (period of) service; (CACCIA): **cane da ~** pointer.

fer'maglio [fer'maʎʎo] sm clasp; (gioiello) brooch.

fer'mare vt to stop, halt; (POLIZIA) to detain, hold; (bottone etc) to fasten, fix // vi to stop; **~rsi** vr to stop, halt; **~ l'attenzione su qc** to focus one's attention on sth.

fer'mata sf stop; **~ dell'autobus** bus stop.

fer'mento sm (anche fig) ferment; (lievito) yeast.

fer'mezza [fer'mettsa] sf (fig) firmness, steadfastness.

'fermo, a ag still, motionless; (veicolo) stationary; (orologio) not working; (saldo: anche fig) firm; (fissato: occhi) fixed // escl stop!; keep still! // sm (chiusura) catch, lock; (DIR) detention.

fe'roce [fe'rɔtʃe] ag (bestia) wild, fierce, ferocious; (persona) cruel, fierce; (fame, dolore) raging; **fe'rocia, cie** sf ferocity.

ferra'gosto sm (festa) feast of the Assumption; (periodo) August holidays pl.

ferra'menta sfpl ironmongery sg, hardware sg; **negozio di ~** ironmonger's, hardware shop.

fer'rare vt (cavallo) to shoe.

'ferreo, a ag iron.

'ferro sm iron; **una bistecca ai ~i** a grilled steak; **~ battuto** wrought iron; **~ di cavallo** horseshoe; **~ da stiro** iron.

ferro'via sf railway; **le ~e** the railways; **ferrovi'ario, a** ag railway cpd; **ferrovi'ere** sm railwayman.

'fertile ag fertile; **fertiliz'zante** sm fertilizer.

fer'vente ag fervent, ardent.

fer'vore sm fervour, ardour; (punto culminante) height.

'fesso, a pp di **fendere** // ag (fam: sciocco) crazy, cracked.

fes'sura sf crack, split; (per gettone, moneta) slot.

'festa sf (religiosa) feast; (pubblica) holiday; (compleanno) birthday; (onomastico) name day; (cerimonia) celebration, party; **far ~** to have a holiday; to live it up; **far ~ a qd** to give sb a warm welcome.

festeggi'are [fested'dʒare] vt to celebrate; (amici, sposi) to give a warm welcome to.

fes'tino sm party; (con balli) ball.

fes'tivo, a ag Sunday cpd; holiday cpd; **giorno ~** holiday.

fes'toso, a ag merry, joyful.

fe'ticcio [fe'tittʃo] sm fetish.

'feto sm foetus.

'fetta sf slice.

feu'dale ag feudal.

FF.SS. abbr di Ferrovie dello Stato.

fi'aba sf fairy tale.

fi'acca sf weariness; (svogliatezza) listlessness.

fiac'care vt to weaken.

fi'acco, a, chi, che ag (stanco) tired, weary; (svogliato) listless; (debole) weak; (mercato) slack.

fi'accola sf torch.

fi'ala sf phial.

fi'amma sf flame; (NAUT) pennant.

fiammeggi'are [fjammed'dʒare] vi to blaze.

fiam'mifero sm match.

fiam'mingo, a, ghi, ghe ag Flemish // sm/f Fleming // sm (LING) Flemish; (ZOOL) flamingo; **i F~ghi** the Flemish.

fiancheggi'are [fjanked'dʒare] vt to border; (fig) to support, back (up); (MIL) to flank.

fi'anco, chi sm side; (MIL) flank; **di ~** sideways, from the side; **a ~ a ~** side by side.

fi'asco, schi sm flask; (fig) fiasco; **fare ~** to be a fiasco.

fi'ato sm breath; (SPORT) stamina; **avere il ~ grosso** to be out of breath; **prendere ~** to catch one's breath.

'fibbia sf buckle.

'fibra sf fibre; (fig) constitution.

fic'care vt to push, thrust, drive.

'fico, chi sm (pianta) fig tree; (frutto) fig; **~ d'India** prickly pear; **~ secco** dried fig.

fidanza'mento [fidantsa'mento] sm engagement.

fidan'zarsi [fidan'tsarsi] vr to get engaged; **fidan'zato, a** sm/f fiancé/fiancée.

fi'darsi vr: ~ **di** to trust; **fi'dato, a** ag reliable, trustworthy.

'fido sm (seguace) loyal follower; (COMM) credit.

fi'ducia [fi'dutʃa] sf confidence, trust; **incarico di** ~ position of trust, responsible position; **persona di** ~ reliable person.

fi'ele sm (MED) bile; (fig) bitterness.

fie'nile sm barn; hayloft.

fi'eno sm hay.

fi'era sf fair.

fie'rezza [fje'rettsa] sf pride.

fi'ero, a ag proud; (crudele) fierce, cruel; (audace) bold.

'fifa sf (fam): **aver** ~ to have the jitters.

'figlia ['fiʎʎa] sf daughter.

figli'astro, a [fiʎ'ʎastro] sm/f stepson/daughter.

'figlio ['fiʎʎo] sm son; (senza distinzione di sesso) child; ~ **di papà** spoilt, wealthy young man; **figli'occio, a, ci, ce** sm/f godchild, godson/daughter.

fi'gura sf figure; (forma, aspetto esterno) form, shape; (illustrazione) picture, illustration; **far** ~ to look smart; **fare una brutta** ~ to make a bad impression.

figu'rare vt (plasmare) to model; (simboleggiare) to symbolize, stand for // vi to appear; ~**rsi** qc to imagine sth; **figurati!** imagine that!; **ti do noia? - ma figurati!** am I disturbing you? - not at all!

figura'tivo, a ag figurative.

'fila sf row, line; (coda) queue; (serie) series, string; **di** ~ in succession; **fare la** ~ to queue; **in** ~ **indiana** in single file.

fila'mento sm filament.

filantro'pia sf philanthropy.

fi'lare vt to spin; (NAUT) to pay out // vi (baco, ragno) to spin; (liquido) to trickle out; (discorso) to hang together; (fam: amoreggiare) to go steady; (4: muoversi a forte velocità) to go at full speed; (: andarsene lestamente) to make o.s. scarce; ~ **diritto** (fig) to toe the line.

filar'monico, a, ci, che ag philharmonic.

filas'trocca, che sf nursery rhyme.

fila'telia sf philately, stamp collecting.

fi'lato, a ag spun // sm yarn; **3 giorni** ~**i** 3 days running o on end; **fila'tura** sf spinning; (luogo) spinning mill.

fi'letto sm braid, trimming; (di vite) thread; (di carne) fillet.

fili'ale ag filial // sf (di impresa) branch.

fili'grana sf (in oreficeria) filigree; (su carta) watermark.

film sm inv film; **fil'mare** vt to film.

'filo sm (anche fig) thread; (filato) yarn; (metallico) wire; **per** ~ **e per segno** in detail; ~ **d'erba** blade of grass; ~ **di perle** string of pearls; ~ **spinato** barbed

wire; **con un** ~ **di voce** in a whisper.

'filobus sm inv trolley bus.

fi'lone sm (di minerali) seam, vein; (pane) Vienna loaf; (fig) trend.

filoso'fia sf philosophy; **fi'losofo, a** sm/f philosopher.

fil'trare vt, vi (2) to filter.

'filtro sm filter.

'filza ['filtsa] sf (anche fig) string.

fin av, prep = **fino.**

fi'nale ag final // sm (di opera) end, ending; (: MUS) finale // sf (SPORT) final; **finalità** sf (scopo) aim, purpose; **final-'mente** av finally, at last.

fi'nanza [fi'nantsa] sf finance; ~**e** sfpl (di individuo, Stato) finances; **finanzi'ario, a** ag financial; **finanzi'ere** sm financier; (guardia di finanza: doganale) customs officer; (: tributaria) inland revenue official.

finché [fin'ke] cong (per tutto il tempo che) as long as; (fino al momento in cui) until; **aspetta** ~ **io (non) sia ritornato** wait until I get back.

'fine ag (lamina, carta) thin; (capelli, polvere) fine; (vista, udito) keen, sharp; (persona: raffinata) refined, distinguished; (osservazione) subtle // sf end // sm aim, purpose; (esito) result, outcome; **secondo** ~ ulterior motive; **in o alla** ~ in the end, finally; ~ **settimana** sm o f inv weekend.

fi'nestra sf window; **fines'trino** sm (di treno, auto) window.

'fingere ['findʒere] vt to feign; (supporre) to imagine, suppose; ~**rsi** vr: ~**rsi ubriaco/pazzo** to pretend to be drunk/mad; ~ **di fare** to pretend to do.

fini'menti smpl (di cavallo etc) harness sg.

fini'mondo sm pandemonium.

fi'nire vt to finish // vi (2) to finish, end; ~ **di fare** (compiere) to finish doing; (smettere) to stop doing; ~ **ricco** to end up o finish up rich; **fini'tura** sf finish.

Fin'landia sf: la ~ Finland.

'fino, a ag (capelli, seta) fine; (oro) pure; (fig: acuto) shrewd // av (spesso troncato in fin: pure, anche) even // prep (spesso troncato in fin: tempo): **fin quando?** till when?; (: luogo): **fin qui** as far as here; ~ **a** (tempo) until, till; (luogo) as far as, (up) to; **fin da domani** from tomorrow onwards; **fin da ieri** since yesterday; **fin dalla nascita** from o since birth.

fi'nocchio [fi'nɔkkjo] sm fennel; (fam: pederasta) queer.

fi'nora av up till now.

'finto, a pp di **fingere** // sf pretence, sham; (SPORT) feint; **far** ~**a (di fare)** to pretend (to do).

finzi'one [fin'tsjone] sf pretence, sham.

fi'occo, chi sm (di nastro) bow; (di stoffa, lana) flock; (di neve) flake; (NAUT) jib; **coi** ~**chi** (fig) first-rate; ~**chi d'avena** oatflakes.

fi'ocina ['fjɔtʃina] sf harpoon.

fi'oco, a, chi, che ag faint, dim.

fi'onda sf catapult.

fio'raio, a sm/f florist.

fio'rami *smpl*: a ~ flowered, with a floral pattern.

fi'ordo *sm* fjord.

fio're *sm* flower; ~i *smpl* (*CARTE*) clubs; a **fior d'acqua/di pelle** on the surface of the water/skin.

fioren'tino, a *ag* Florentine.

fio'retto *sm* (*SCHERMA*) foil.

fio'rire *vi* (2) (*rosa*) to flower; (*albero*) to blossom; (*fig*) to flourish; (*ammuffire*) to become mouldy.

Fi'renze [fi'rentse] *sf* Florence.

'firma *sf* signature; (*reputazione*) name.

firma'mento *sm* firmament.

fir'mare *vt* to sign.

fisar'monica *sf* accordion.

fis'cale *ag* fiscal, tax *cpd*.

fischi'are [fis'kjare] *vi* to whistle // *vt* to whistle; (*attore*) to boo, hiss.

'fischio ['fiskjo] *sm* whistle.

'fisco *sm* tax authorities *pl*, ≈ Inland Revenue.

'fisico, a, ci, che *ag* physical // *sm/f* physicist // *sm* physique // *sf* physics *sg*.

fisiolo'gia [fizjolo'dʒia] *sf* physiology.

fisiono'mia *sf* face, physiognomy.

fisiotera'pia *sf* physiotherapy.

fis'sare *vt* to fix, fasten; (*guardare intensamente*) to stare at; (*data, condizioni*) to fix, establish, set; (*prenotare*) to book; ~rsi su (*sog: sguardo, attenzione*) to focus on; (*fig: idea*) to become obsessed with; **fissazi'one** *sf* (*PSIC*) fixation.

'fisso, a *ag* fixed; (*stipendio, impiego*) regular; (*occhi*) staring.

'fitta *sf* vedi **fitto**.

fit'tizio, a *ag* fictitious, imaginary.

'fitto, a *ag* thick, dense // *sm* depths *pl*, middle; (*affitto, pigione*) rent // *sf* sharp pain; a **capo** ~ head first.

fiu'mana *sf* swollen river; (*fig*) stream, flood.

fi'ume *sm* river.

fiu'tare *vt* to smell, sniff; (*sog: animale*) to scent; (*fig: inganno*) to get wind of, smell; **fi'uto** *sm* (sense of) smell; (*fig*) nose.

fla'gello [fla'dʒɛllo] *sm* scourge.

fla'grante *ag* flagrant; **cogliere qd in** ~ to catch sb red-handed.

fla'nella *sf* flannel.

flash [flaʃ] *sm inv* (*FOT*) flash; (*giornalistico*) newsflash.

'flauto *sm* flute.

'flebile *ag* faint, feeble.

'flemma *sf* (*calma*) coolness, phlegm; (*MED*) phlegm.

fles'sibile *ag* pliable; (*fig: che si adatta*) flexible.

'flesso, a *pp di* **flettere**

flessu'oso, a *ag* supple, lithe.

'flettere *vt* to bend.

F.lli (*abbr di fratelli*) Bros.

'flora *sf* flora.

'florido, a *ag* flourishing; (*fig*) glowing with health.

'floscio, a, sci, sce ['flɔʃʃo] *ag* floppy, soft; (*muscoli*) flabby.

'flotta *sf* fleet.

'fluido, a *ag, sm* fluid.

flu'ire *vi* (2) to flow.

fluore'scente [fluoreʃ'ʃɛnte] *ag* fluorescent.

flu'oro *sm* fluorine.

fluo'ruro *sm* fluoride.

'flusso *sm* flow; (*del mare*) flood tide; (*FISICA, MED*) flux; ~ **e riflusso** ebb and flow.

fluttu'are *vi* to rise and fall; (*ECON*) to fluctuate; (*fig*) to waver.

fluvi'ale *ag* river *cpd*, fluvial.

'foca, che *sf* (*ZOOL*) seal.

fo'caccia, ce [fo'kattʃa] *sf* kind of pizza; (*dolce*) bun.

'foce ['fotʃe] *sf* (*GEO*) mouth.

foco'laio *sm* (*MED*) centre of infection; (*fig*) hotbed.

foco'lare *sm* hearth, fireside; (*TECN*) furnace.

'fodera *sf* lining; (*di libro, poltrona*) cover; **fode'rare** *vt* to line; to cover.

'fodero *sm* sheath.

'foga *sf* enthusiasm, ardour.

'foggia, ge ['fɔddʒa] *sf* (*maniera*) style; (*aspetto*) form, shape; (*moda*) fashion, style.

'foglia ['fɔʎʎa] *sf* leaf; ~ **d'argento/d'oro** silver/gold leaf; **fogli'ame** *sm* foliage, leaves *pl*.

'foglio ['fɔʎʎo] *sm* (*di carta*) sheet (of paper); (*di metallo*) sheet; (*documento*) document; (*banconota*) (bank)note; ~ **rosa** (*AUT*) provisional licence; ~ **volante** pamphlet.

'fogna ['fɔɲɲa] *sf* drain, sewer; **fogna'tura** *sf* drainage, sewerage.

folgo'rare *vt* (*sog: fulmine*) to strike down; (: *alta tensione*) to electrocute.

'folla *sf* crowd, throng.

'folle *ag* mad, insane; (*TECN*) idle; **in** ~ (*AUT*) in neutral.

fol'lia *sf* folly, foolishness; foolish act; (*pazzia*) madness, lunacy.

'folto, a *ag* thick.

fomen'tare *vt* to stir up, foment.

fonda'mento *sm* foundation; ~a *sfpl* (*EDIL*) foundations.

fon'dare *vt* to found; (*edificio*) to lay the foundations for; (*fig: dar base*): ~ **qc su** to base sth on; **fondazi'one** *sf* founding; (*ente morale*) foundation; **fondazi'oni** *sfpl* (*EDIL*) foundations.

'fondere *vt* (*neve*) to melt; (*metallo*) to fuse, melt; (*fig: colori*) to merge, blend // *vi* to melt; ~rsi *vr* to melt; (*fig: partiti, correnti*) to unite, merge; **fonde'ria** *sf* foundry.

'fondo, a *ag* deep // *sm* (*di recipiente, pozzo*) bottom; (*di stanza*) back; (*quantità di liquido che resta, deposito*) dregs *pl*; (*sfondo*) background; (*unità immobiliare*) property, estate; (*somma di denaro*) fund; (*SPORT*) long-distance race; ~i *smpl* (*denaro*) funds; **in** ~ **a** at the bottom of; at the back of; **andare a** ~ (*nave*) to sink;

conoscere a ~ to know inside out; **in** ~ (*fig*) after all, all things considered; **andare fino in** ~ **a** (*fig*) to examine thoroughly; **a** ~ **perduto** (*COMM*) without security; ~**i di caffè** coffee grounds; ~**i di magazzino** old *o* unsold stock *sg*.

fo'netica *sf* phonetics *sg*.

fon'tana *sf* fountain.

'fonte *sf* spring, source; (*fig*) source.

fo'raggio [fo'raddʒo] *sm* fodder, forage.

fo'rare *vt* to pierce, make a hole in; (*biglietto*) to punch; ~ **una gomma** to burst a tyre.

'forbici ['fɔrbitʃi] *sfpl* scissors.

forbi'cina [forbi'tʃina] *sf* earwig.

'forca, che *sf* (*AGR*) fork, pitchfork; (*patibolo*) gallows *sg*.

for'cella [for'tʃɛlla] *sf* fork; (*di monte*) pass.

for'chetta [for'ketta] *sf* fork.

for'cina [for'tʃina] *sf* hairpin.

'forcipe ['fɔrtʃipe] *sm* forceps *pl*.

fo'resta *sf* forest.

foresti'ero, a *ag* foreign // *sm/f* foreigner.

'forfora *sf* dandruff.

'forgia, ge ['fɔrdʒa] *sf* forge; **forgi'are** *vt* to forge.

'forma *sf* form; (*aspetto esteriore*) form, shape; (*DIR: procedura*) procedure; (*per calzature*) last; (*stampo da cucina*) mould; ~**e** *sfpl* (*del corpo*) figure, shape; **le** ~**e** (*convenzioni*) appearances; **essere in** ~ to be in good shape.

formag'gino [formad'dʒino] *sm* processed cheese.

for'maggio [for'maddʒo] *sm* cheese.

for'male *ag* formal; **formalità** *sf inv* formality.

for'mare *vt* to form, shape, make; (*fig: carattere*) to form, mould; ~**rsi** *vr* to form, take shape; **for'mato** *sm* format, size; **formazi'one** *sf* formation; (*fig: educazione*) training.

for'mica, che *sf* ant; **formi'caio** *sm* anthill.

formico'lare *vi* (*2: gamba, braccio*) to tingle; (*brulicare: anche fig*): ~ **di** to be swarming with; **mi formicola la gamba** I've got pins and needles in my leg, my leg's tingling; **formico'lio** *sm* pins and needles *pl*; swarming.

formi'dabile *ag* powerful, formidable; (*straordinario*) remarkable.

'formula *sf* formula.

formu'lare *vt* to formulate; to express.

for'nace [for'natʃe] *sf* (*per laterizi etc*) kiln; (*per metalli*) furnace.

for'naio *sm* baker.

for'nello *sm* (*elettrico, a gas*) ring; (*di pipa*) bowl.

for'nire *vt*: ~ **qd di qc**, ~ **qc a qd** to provide *o* supply sb with sth, to supply sth to sb.

'forno *sm* (*di cucina*) oven; (*panetteria*) bakery; (*TECN: per calce etc*) kiln; (*: per metalli*) furnace.

'foro *sm* (*buco*) hole; (*STORIA*) forum; (*tribunale*) (law) court.

'forse *av* perhaps, maybe; (*circa*) about; **essere in** ~ to be in doubt.

forsen'nato, a *ag* mad, insane.

'forte *ag* strong; (*suono*) loud; (*spesa*) considerable, great; (*passione, dolore*) great, deep // *av* strongly; (*velocemente*) fast; (*a voce alta*) loud(ly) // *sm* (*edificio*) fort; (*specialità*) forte, strong point; **essere** ~ **in qc** to be good at sth.

for'tezza [for'tettsa] *sf* (*morale*) strength; (*luogo fortificato*) fortress.

fortifi'care *vt* to fortify, strengthen.

for'tuito, a *ag* fortuitous.

for'tuna *sf* (*destino*) fortune, luck; (*buona sorte*) success, fortune; (*eredità, averi*) fortune; **per** ~ luckily, fortunately; **di** ~ makeshift, improvised; **atterraggio di** ~ emergency landing; **fortu'nato, a** *ag* lucky, fortunate; (*impresa*) successful.

forvi'are *vt, vi* = **fuorviare**.

'forza ['fɔrtsa] *sf* strength; (*potere*) power; (*FISICA*) force; ~**e** *sfpl* (*fisiche*) strength *sg*; (*MIL*) forces // *escl* come on!; **per** ~ against one's will; (*naturalmente*) of course; **a viva** ~ by force; **a** ~ **di** by dint of; ~ **maggiore** circumstances beyond one's control; **la** ~ **pubblica** the police *pl*.

for'zare [for'tsare] *vt* to force; ~ **qd a fare** to force sb to do; **for'zato, a** *ag* forced // *sm* (*DIR*) prisoner sentenced to hard labour.

fos'chia [fos'kia] *sf* mist, haze.

'fosco, a, schi, sche *ag* dark, gloomy.

fos'fato *sm* phosphate.

'fosforo *sm* phosphorous.

'fossa *sf* pit; (*di cimitero*) grave; ~ **biologica** septic tank.

fos'sato *sm* ditch; (*di fortezza*) moat.

fos'setta *sf* dimple.

'fossile *ag, sm* fossil.

'fosso *sm* ditch; (*MIL*) trench.

'foto *sf* (*abbr di* **fotografia**) photo // *pref*: **foto'copia** *sf* photocopy; **fotocopi'are** *vt* to photocopy; **fotogra'fare** *vt* to photograph; **fotogra'fia** *sf* (*procedimento*) photography; (*immagine*) photograph; **fo'tografo, a** *sm/f* photographer; **foto-ro'manzo** *sm* romantic picture story.

fra *prep* = **tra**.

fracas'sare *vt* to shatter, smash; ~**rsi** *vr* to shatter, smash; (*veicolo*) to crash; **fra-'casso** *sm* smash; crash; (*baccano*) din, racket.

'fradicio, a, ci, ce ['fraditʃo] *ag* (*guasto*) rotten; (*molto bagnato*) soaking (wet); **ubriaco** ~ blind drunk.

'fragile ['fradʒile] *ag* fragile; (*fig: salute*) delicate.

'fragola *sf* strawberry.

frago'roso, a *ag* crashing, roaring.

fra'grante *ag* fragrant.

frain'tendere *vt* to misunderstand; **frain'teso, a** *pp di* **fraintendere**.

fram'mento *sm* fragment.

'**frana** *sf* landslide; **fra'nare** *vi* (2) to slip, slide down.

fran'cese [fran'tʃeze] *ag* French // *sm/f* Frenchman/woman // *sm* (*LING*) French; **i F—i** the French.

fran'chezza [fran'kettsa] *sf* frankness, openness.

'**Francia** ['frantʃa] *sf*: **la ~** France.

'**franco, a, chi, che** *ag* (*COMM*) free; (*sincero*) frank, open, sincere // *sm* (*moneta*) franc; **farla ~a** (*fig*) to get off scot-free; **~ di dogana** duty-free; **~ a domicilio** delivered free of charge; **prezzo ~ fabbrica** ex-works price; **~ tiratore** *sm* sniper.

franco'bollo *sm* (postage) stamp.

fran'gente [fran'dʒɛnte] *sm* breaker.

'**frangia, ge** ['frandʒa] *sf* fringe; (*fig: abbellimento*) frill, embellishment.

frantu'mare *vt*, **~rsi** *vr* to break into pieces, shatter; **fran'tumi** *smpl* pieces, bits; (*schegge*) splinters.

'**frasca, sche** *sf* (leafy) branch.

'**frase** *sf* (*LING*) sentence; (*locuzione, espressione, MUS*) phrase; **~ fatta** set phrase.

'**frassino** *sm* ash (tree).

frastu'ono *sm* hubbub, din.

'**frate** *sm* friar, monk.

fratel'lanza [fratel'lantsa] *sf* brotherhood; (*associazione*) fraternity.

fra'tello *sm* brother; **~i** *smpl* brothers; (*nel senso di fratelli e sorelle*) brothers and sisters.

fra'terno, a *ag* fraternal, brotherly.

frat'tanto *av* in the meantime, meanwhile.

frat'tempo *sm*: **nel ~** in the meantime, meanwhile.

frat'tura *sf* fracture.

fraudo'lento, a *ag* fraudulent.

frazi'one [frat'tsjone] *sf* fraction; (*borgata*): **~ di comune** hamlet.

'**freccia, ce** ['frettʃa] *sf* arrow; **~ di direzione** (*AUT*) indicator.

fred'dare *vt* to shoot dead.

fred'dezza [fred'dettsa] *sf* coldness.

'**freddo, a** *ag*, *sm* cold; **fa ~** it's cold; **aver ~** to be cold; **a ~** (*fig*) deliberately; **freddo'loso, a** *ag* sensitive to the cold.

fred'dura *sf* pun.

fre'gare *vt* to rub; (*fam: truffare*) to take in, cheat; (*: rubare*) to swipe, pinch; **fregarsene** (*fam!*): **chi se ne frega?** who gives a damn about it(?)

fre'gata *sf* rub; (*fam*) swindle; (*NAUT*) frigate.

'**fregio** ['fredʒo] *sm* (*ARCHIT*) frieze; (*ornamento*) decoration.

'**fremere** *vi*: **~ di** to tremble *o* quiver with; '**fremito** *sm* tremor, quiver.

fre'nare *vt* (*veicolo*) to slow down; (*cavallo*) to rein in; (*lacrime*) to restrain, hold back // *vi* to brake; **~rsi** (*fig*) to restrain o.s., control o.s.; **fre'nata** *sf*: **fare una frenata** to brake.

frene'sia *sf* frenzy; mania; **fre'netico, a, ci, che** *ag* frenzied.

'**freno** *sm* brake; (*morso*) bit; (*fig*) check; **~ a disco** disc brake; **~ a mano** handbrake.

frequen'tare *vt* (*luoghi*) to frequent; (*persone*) to see (often).

fre'quente *ag* frequent; **di ~** frequently; **fre'quenza** *sf* frequency; (*assiduità*) attendance.

fres'chezza [fres'kettsa] *sf* freshness.

'**fresco, a, schi, sche** *ag* fresh; (*temperatura*) cool; (*notizia*) recent, fresh // *sm*: **godere il ~** to enjoy the cool air; **stare ~** (*fig*) to be in for it; **mettere al ~** to put in a cool place.

'**fretta** *sf* hurry, haste; **in ~** in a hurry; **in ~ e furia** in a mad rush; **aver ~** to be in a hurry; **fretto'loso, a** *ag* hurried, rushed.

fri'abile *ag* (*terreno*) friable; (*pasta*) crumbly.

'**friggere** ['friddʒere] *vt* to fry // *vi* (*olio etc*) to sizzle.

fri'gido, a ['fridʒido] *ag* (*MED*) frigid.

'**frigo** *sm* fridge.

frigo'rifero, a *ag* refrigerating // *sm* refrigerator.

fringu'ello *sm* chaffinch.

frit'tata *sf* omelette; **fare una ~** (*fig*) to make a mess of things.

frit'tella *sf* (*CUC*) pancake; (*: ripiena*) fritter.

'**fritto, a** *pp di* **friggere** // *ag* fried // *sm* fried food; **~ misto** mixed fry.

'**frivolo, a** *ag* frivolous.

frizi'one [frit'tsjone] *sf* friction; (*di pelle*) rub, rub-down; (*AUT*) clutch.

friz'zante [frid'dzante] *ag* (*acqua*) fizzy, sparkling; (*vento, fig*) biting.

'**frizzo** ['friddzo] *sm* witticism.

fro'dare *vt* to defraud, cheat.

'**frode** *sf* fraud; **~ fiscale** tax evasion.

'**frollo, a** *ag* (*carne*) tender; (*: di selvaggina*) high; (*fig: persona*) soft; **pasta ~a** short(crust) pastry.

'**fronda** *sf* (leafy) branch; (*di partito politico*) internal opposition; **~e** *sfpl* foliage *sg*.

fron'tale *ag* frontal; (*scontro*) head-on.

'**fronte** *sf* (*ANAT*) forehead; (*di edificio*) front, façade // *sm* (*MIL, POL, METEOR*) front; **a ~, di ~** facing, opposite; **di ~ a** (*posizione*) opposite, facing, in front of; (*a paragone di*) compared with.

fronteggi'are [fronted'dʒare] *vt* (*avversari, difficoltà*) to face, stand up to; (*sog: edificio*) to face.

fronti'era *sf* border, frontier.

'**fronzolo** ['frondzolo] *sm* frill.

'**frottola** *sf* fib; **~e** *sfpl* nonsense *sg*.

fru'gale *ag* frugal.

fru'gare *vi* to rummage // *vt* to search.

frul'lare *vt* (*CUC*) to whisk // *vi* (*uccelli*) to flutter; **frulla'tore** *sm* electric mixer; **frul'lino** *sm* whisk.

fru'mento *sm* wheat.

fru'scio [fruʃʃjo] *sm* rustle; rustling; (*di acque*) murmur.

'frusta *sf* whip; (*cuc*) whisk.

frus'tare *vt* to whip.

frus'tino *sm* riding crop.

frus'trare *vt* to frustrate; **frustrazi'one** *sf* frustration.

'frutta *sf* fruit; (*portata*) dessert; **~ candita/secca** candied/dried fruit.

frut'teto *sm* orchard.

frutti'vendolo, a *sm/f* greengrocer.

'frutto *sm* fruit; (*fig: risultato*) result(s); (*ECON: interesse*) interest; (: *reddito*) income; **~ i di mare** seafood *sg*.

FS *abbr di Ferrovie dello Stato.*

fu *forma del vb* **essere** // *ag inv:* **il ~ Paolo Bianchi** the late Paolo Bianchi.

fuci'lare [futʃi'lare] *vt* to shoot; **fuci'lata** *sf* rifle shot.

fu'cile [fu'tʃile] *sm* rifle, gun; (*da caccia*) shotgun, gun.

fu'cina [fu'tʃina] *sf* forge.

'fuga *sf* flight; (*di gas, liquidi*) leak; (*MUS*) fugue; **prendere la ~** to take flight, flee.

fu'gace [fu'gatʃe] *ag* fleeting, transient.

fug'gevole [fud'dʒevole] *ag* fleeting.

fuggi'asco, a, schi, sche [fud'dʒasko] *ag, sm/f* fugitive.

fuggi'fuggi [fuddʒi'fuddʒi] *sm* scramble, stampede.

fug'gire [fud'dʒire] *vi* (*2*) to flee, run away; (*fig: passar veloce*) to fly // *vt* to avoid; **fuggi'tivo, a** *sm/f* fugitive, runaway.

'fulcro *sm* fulcrum.

ful'gore *sm* brilliance, splendour.

fu'liggine [fu'liddʒine] *sf* soot.

fulmi'nare *vt* to strike down; (*sog: alta tensione*) to electrocute.

'fulmine *sm* thunderbolt; lightning *q*.

fumai'olo *sm* (*di nave*) funnel; (*di fabbrica*) chimney-stack.

fu'mare *vi* to smoke; (*emettere vapore*) to steam // *vt* to smoke; **fu'mata** *sf* puff of smoke; (*segnale*) smoke signal; (*di tabacco*) smoke; **fare una fumata** to have a smoke; **fuma'tore, 'trice** *sm/f* smoker.

fu'metto *sm* comic strip; **~ i** *smpl* comics.

'fumo *sm* smoke; (*vapore*) steam; (*il fumare tabacco*) smoking; **~ i** *smpl* fumes; **vendere ~** to deceive, cheat; **fu'moso, a** *ag* smoky.

fu'nambolo, a *sm/f* tightrope walker.

'fune *sf* rope, cord; (*più grossa*) cable.

'funebre *ag* (*rito*) funeral; (*aspetto*) gloomy, funereal.

fune'rale *sm* funeral.

'fungere ['fundʒere] *vi:* **~ da** to act as.

'fungo, ghi *sm* fungus; (*commestibile*) mushroom; **~ velenoso** toadstool.

funico'lare *sf* funicular railway.

funi'via *sf* cable railway.

funzio'nare [funtsjo'nare] *vi* to work, function; (*fungere*): **~ da** to act as.

funzio'nario [funtsjo'narjo] *sm* official.

funzi'one [fun'tsjone] *sf* function; (*carica*) post, position; (*REL*) service; **entrare in**

~ to take up one's post; to take up office.

fu'oco, chi *sm* fire; (*fornello*) ring; (*FOT, FISICA*) focus; **dare ~ a qc** to set fire to sth; **far ~** (*sparare*) to fire; **~ d'artificio** firework.

fuorché [fwor'ke] *cong, prep* except.

fu'ori *av* outside; (*all'aperto*) outdoors, outside; (*fuori di casa, SPORT*) out; (*esclamativo*) get out! // *prep:* **~** (*di*) out of, outside // *sm* outside; **lasciar ~ qc/qd** to leave sth/sb out; **far ~ qd** (*fam*) to kill sb, do sb in; **essere ~ di sé** to be beside o.s.; **~ luogo** (*inopportuno*) out of place, uncalled for; **~ mano** out of the way, remote; **~ pericolo** out of danger; **~ uso** old-fashioned; obsolete.

fu'ori... *prefisso:* **fuori'bordo** *sm* speedboat (with outboard motor); outboard motor; **fuori'classe** *sm/f inv* (undisputed) champion; **fuorigi'oco** *sm* offside; **fuori'legge** *sm/f inv* outlaw; **fuori'serie** *ag inv* (*auto etc*) custom-built; **fuoru'scito, a, fuoriu'scito, a** *sm/f* exile; **fuorvi'are** *vt* to mislead, put on the wrong track; (*fig*) to lead astray // *vi* to go astray.

'furbo, a *ag* cunning, sly; (*astuto*) shrewd.

fu'rente *ag:* **~** (**contro**) furious (with).

fur'fante *sm* rascal, scoundrel.

fur'gone *sm* van.

'furia *sf* (*ira*) fury, rage; (*fig: impeto*) fury, violence; (*fretta*) rush; **a ~ di** by dint of; **montare in ~** to fly into a rage; **furi'bondo, a** *ag* furious.

furi'oso, a *ag* furious; (*mare, vento*) raging.

fu'rore *sm* fury; (*esaltazione*) frenzy; **far ~** to be all the rage.

fur'tivo, a *ag* furtive; (*merce*) stolen.

'furto *sm* theft; **~ con scasso** burglary.

'fusa *sfpl:* **fare le ~** to purr.

fu'sibile *sm* (*ELETTR*) fuse.

fusi'one *sf* (*di metalli*) fusion, melting; (*colata*) casting; (*COMM*) merger; (*fig*) merging.

'fuso, a *pp di* **fondere** // *sm* (*FILATURA*) spindle; **~ orario** time zone.

fus'tagno [fus'taɲɲo] *sm* corduroy.

'fusto *sm* stem; (*ANAT, di albero*) trunk; (*recipiente: in metallo*) drum, can; (: *in legno*) barrel, cask.

'futile *ag* vain, futile; **futilità** *sf inv* futility.

fu'turo, a *ag, sm* future.

G

gab'bare *vt* to take in, dupe; **~rsi** *vr:* **~rsi di qd** to make fun of sb.

'gabbia *sf* cage; (*DIR*) dock; (*da imballaggio*) crate; **~ dell'ascensore** lift shaft; **~ toracica** (*ANAT*) rib cage.

gabbi'ano *sm* (sea)gull.

gabi'netto *sm* (*MED etc*) consulting room; (*POL*) cabinet; (*di decenza*) toilet, lavatory; (*INS: di fisica etc*) laboratory.

gagli'ardo, a [gaʎ'ʎardo] *ag* strong, vigorous.

gai'ezza [ga'jettsa] *sf* gaiety, cheerfulness.

'gaio, a *ag* gay, cheerful.
'gala *sf* (*sfarzo*) pomp; (*festa*) ala.
ga'lante *ag* gallant, courteous; (*avventura, poesia*) amorous; **galante'ria** *sf* gallantry.
galantu'omo, *pl* **galantu'omini** *sm* gentleman.
ga'lassia *sf* galaxy.
gala'teo *sm* (good) manners *pl*.
gale'otto *sm* (*rematore*) galley slave; (*carcerato*) convict.
ga'lera *sf* prison.
'galla *sf* (*BOT*) gall; **a ~** afloat.
galleggi'ante [galled'dʒante] *ag* floating // *sm* (*natante*) barge; (*di pescatore, lenza, TECN*) float.
galleggi'are [galled'dʒare] *vi* to float.
galle'ria *sf* (*traforo*) tunnel; (*ARCHIT, d'arte*) gallery; (*TEATRO*) circle; (*strada coperta con negozi*) arcade; **~ del vento** *o* **aerodinamica** (*AER*) wind tunnel.
'Galles *sm*: **il ~** Wales.
gal'lina *sf* hen.
'gallo *sm* cock.
gal'lone *sm* piece of braid; (*MIL*) stripe; (*misura inglese e americana*) gallon.
galop'pare *vi* to gallop.
ga'loppo *sm* gallop; **al** *o* **di ~** at a gallop.
galvaniz'zare [galvanid'dzare] *vt* to galvanize.
'gamba *sf* leg; (*asta: di lettera*) stem; **in ~** (*in buona salute*) well; (*bravo*) bright, smart; **prendere qc sotto ~** (*fig*) to treat sth too lightly.
gambe'retto *sm* prawn; shrimp.
'gambero *sm* (*di acqua dolce*) crayfish; (*di mare*) lobster.
'gambo *sm* stem; (*di pianta*) stalk, stem; (*TECN*) shank.
'gamma *sf* (*MUS*) scale; (*di colori, fig*) range, gamut.
ga'nascia, sce [ga'naʃʃa] *sf* jaw; **~sce del freno** (*AUT*) brake shoes.
'gancio [ˈgantʃo] *sm* hook.
'ganghero [ˈgangero] *sm* (*arpione di ferro*) hinge; (*gancetto*) hook; **uscire dai ~i** (*fig*) to fly into a temper.
'gara *sf* competition; (*SPORT*) competition; contest; match; (: *corsa*) race; **fare a ~ to** compete, vie.
garan'tire *vt* to guarantee; (*dare per certo*) to assure.
garan'zia [garan'tsia] *sf* guarantee; (*pegno*) security.
gar'bato, a *ag* courteous, polite.
'garbo *sm* (*buone maniere*) politeness, courtesy; (*di vestito etc*) grace, style.
gareggi'are [gared'dʒare] *vi* to compete.
garga'rismo *sm* gargle; **fare i ~i to** gargle.
ga'rofano *sm* carnation; **chiodo di ~** clove.
'garza [ˈgardza] *sf* (*per bende*) gauze.
gar'zone [gar'dzone] *sm* boy; **~ di stalla** stableboy.
gas *sm inv* gas; **a tutto ~** at full speed; **dare ~** (*AUT*) to accelerate; **~ lacrimogeno** tear gas.

ga'solio *sm* diesel oil.
ga's(s)are *vt* to aerate, carbonate; (*asfissiare*) to gas.
gas'soso, a *ag* gaseous; gassy // *sf* lemonade.
'gastrico, a, ci, che *ag* gastric.
gastrono'mia *sf* gastronomy.
gat'tino *sm* kitten.
'gatto, a *sm/f* cat, tomcat/she-cat; **~ selvatico** wildcat.
gatto'pardo *sm*: **~ africano** serval; **~ americano** ocelot.
gat'tuccio [gat'tuttʃo] *sm* dogfish.
gau'dente *sm/f* pleasure-seeker.
ga'vetta *sf* (*MIL*) mess tin.
'gazza [ˈgaddza] *sf* magpie.
gaz'zella [gad'dzɛlla] *sf* gazelle.
gaz'zetta [gad'dzetta] *sf* news sheet; **G~ Ufficiale** official publication containing details of new laws.
gaz'zoso, a [gad'dzoso] *ag* = **gassoso.**
ge'lare [dʒe'lare] *vt, vi, vb impers* to freeze; **ge'lata** *sf* frost.
gelate'ria [dʒelate'ria] *sf* ice-cream shop.
gela'tina [dʒela'tina] *sf* gelatine; **~ esplosiva** dynamite; **~ di frutta** fruit jelly.
ge'lato, a [dʒe'lato] *ag* frozen // *sm* ice cream.
'gelido, a [ˈdʒɛlido] *ag* icy, ice-cold.
'gelo [ˈdʒɛlo] *sm* (*temperatura*) intense cold; (*brina*) frost; (*fig*) chill; **ge'lone** *sm* chilblain.
gelo'sia [dʒelo'sia] *sf* (*stato d'animo*) jealousy; (*persiana*) shutter.
ge'loso, a [dʒe'loso] *ag* jealous.
'gelso [ˈdʒɛlso] *sm* mulberry (tree).
gelso'mino [dʒelso'mino] *sm* jasmine.
ge'mello, a [dʒe'mɛllo] *ag, sm/f* twin; **~i** *smpl* (*di camicia*) cufflinks; (*dello zodiaco*) **G~i** Gemini *sg.*
'gemere [ˈdʒɛmere] *vi* to moan, groan; (*cigolare*) to creak; (*gocciolare*) to drip, ooze; **'gemito** *sm* moan, groan.
'gemma [ˈdʒɛmma] *sf* (*BOT*) bud; (*pietra preziosa*) gem.
gene'rale [dʒene'rale] *ag, sm* general; **in ~** (*per sommi capi*) in general terms; (*di solito*) usually, in general; **a ~ richiesta** by popular request; **generalità** *sfpl* (*dati d'identità*) particulars; **generaliz'zare** *vt, vi* to generalize.
gene'rare [dʒene'rare] *vt* (*dar vita*) to give birth to; (*produrre*) to produce; (*causare*) to arouse; (*TECN*) to produce, generate; **genera'tore** *sm* (*TECN*) generator; **generazi'one** *sf* generation.
'genere [ˈdʒɛnere] *sm* kind, type, sort; (*BIOL*) genus; (*merce*) article, product; (*LING*) gender; (*ARTE, LETTERATURA*) genre; **in ~** generally, as a rule; **il ~ umano** mankind; **~i alimentari** foodstuffs.
ge'nerico, a, ci, che [dʒe'nɛriko] *ag* generic; (*persona: non specializzata*) general, non-specialized.
'genero [ˈdʒɛnero] *sm* son-in-law.
generosità [dʒenerosi'ta] *sf* generosity.

gene'roso, a [dʒene'roso] *ag* generous.
'genesi ['dʒɛnesi] *sf* genesis.
ge'netico, a, ci, che [dʒe'nɛtiko] *ag*
genetic // *sf* genetics *sg*.
gen'giva [dʒen'dʒiva] *sf* (ANAT) gum.
geni'ale [dʒen'jale] *ag* (*persona*) of genius;
(*idea*) ingenious, brilliant.
'genio ['dʒɛnjo] *sm* genius; (*attitudine,
talento*) talent, flair, genius; **andare a ~
a qd** to be to sb's liking, appeal to sb.
geni'tale [dʒeni'tale] *ag* genital; **~i** *smpl*
genitals.
geni'tore [dʒeni'tore] *sm* parent, father *o*
mother; **~i** *smpl* parents.
gen'naio [dʒen'najo] *sm* January.
'Genova ['dʒɛnova] *sf* Genoa.
gen'taglia [dʒen'taʎʎa] *sf* (*peg*) rabble.
'gente ['dʒɛnte] *sf* people *pl*.
gen'tile [dʒen'tile] *ag* (*persona, atto*) kind;
(: *garbato*) courteous, polite; (*nelle lettere*):
G~ Signore Dear Sir; (: *sulla busta*): **G~
Signor Fernando Villa** Mr Fernando
Villa; **genti'lezza** *sf* kindness; courtesy,
politeness; **per gentilezza** (*per favore*)
please.
genuflessi'one [dʒenufles'sjone] *sf*
genuflection.
genu'ino, a [dʒenu'ino] *ag* genuine.
geogra'fia [dʒeogra'fia] *sf* geography;
geo'grafico, a, ci, che *ag* geographical.
geolo'gia [dʒeolo'dʒia] *sf* geology; **geo-
'logico, a, ci, che** *ag* geological.
ge'ometra, i, e [dʒe'ɔmetra] *sm/f*
(*professionista*) surveyor.
geome'tria [dʒeome'tria] *sf* geometry;
geo'metrico, a, ci, che *ag* geometric(al).
ge'ranio [dʒe'ranjo] *sm* geranium.
gerar'chia [dʒerar'kia] *sf* hierarchy.
ge'rente [dʒe'rɛnte] *sm/f*
manager/manageress.
'gergo, ghi ['dʒergo] *sm* jargon; slang.
geria'tria [dʒerja'tria] *sf* geriatrics *sg*.
Ger'mania [dʒer'manja] *sf*: **la ~**
Germany.
'germe ['dʒɛrme] *sm* germ.
germogli'are [dʒermoʎ'ʎare] *vi* to
sprout; to germinate; **ger'moglio** *sm*
shoot; bud.
gero'glifico, ci [dʒero'glifiko] *sm*
hieroglyphic.
'gesso ['dʒɛsso] *sm* chalk; (SCULTURA, MED,
EDIL) plaster; (*minerale*) gypsum.
gestazi'one [dʒestat'tsjone] *sf* gestation.
gestico'lare [dʒestiko'lare] *vi* to
gesticulate.
gesti'one [dʒes'tjone] *sf* management.
ges'tire [dʒes'tire] *vt* to run, manage.
'gesto ['dʒɛsto] *sm* gesture.
ges'tore [dʒes'tore] *sm* manager.
Gesù [dʒe'zu] *sm* Jesus.
gesu'ita, i [dʒezu'ita] *sm* Jesuit.
get'tare [dʒet'tare] *vt* to throw; (*anche: ~
via*) to throw away *o* out; (SCULTURA) to
cast; (EDIL) to lay; (*emettere*) to spout,
gush; **~rsi in** (*sog: fiume*) to flow into; **~
uno sguardo su** to take a quick look at;

get'tata *sf* (*di cemento, metalli*) cast;
(*diga*) jetty.
'getto ['dʒetto] *sm* (*di gas, liquido, AER*) jet;
(BOT) shoot; **a ~ continuo**
uninterruptedly; **di ~** (*fig*) straight off, in
one go.
get'tone [dʒet'tone] *sm* token; (*per giochi*)
counter; (: *roulette etc*) chip; **~
telefonico** telephone token.
'ghetto ['getto] *sm* ghetto.
ghiacci'aio [gjat'tʃajo] *sm* glacier.
ghiacci'are [gjat'tʃare] *vt* to freeze; (*fig*):
~ qd to make sb's blood run cold // *vi* to
freeze, ice over.
ghi'accio ['gjattʃo] *sm* ice.
ghiacci'olo [gjat'tʃɔlo] *sm* icicle; (*tipo di
gelato*) ice(d) lolly.
ghi'aia ['gjaja] *sf* gravel.
ghi'anda ['gjanda] *sf* (BOT) acorn.
ghi'andola ['gjandola] *sf* gland.
ghigliot'tina [giʎʎot'tina] *sf* guillotine.
ghi'gnare [gin'ɲare] *vi* to sneer.
ghi'otto, a ['gjotto] *ag* greedy; (*cibo*)
delicious, appetizing; **ghiot'tone, a** *sm/f*
glutton.
ghiri'bizzo [giri'biddzo] *sm* whim.
ghiri'goro [giri'gɔro] *sm* scribble,
squiggle.
ghir'landa [gir'landa] *sf* garland, wreath.
'ghiro ['giro] *sm* dormouse.
'ghisa ['giza] *sf* cast iron.
già [dʒa] *av* already; (*ex, in precedenza*)
formerly // *escl* of course!, yes indeed!
gi'acca, che ['dʒakka] *sf* jacket; **~ a
vento** windcheater.
giacché [dʒak'ke] *cong* since, as.
giac'chetta [dʒak'ketta] *sf* (light) jacket.
gia'cenza [dʒa'tʃɛntsa] *sf*: **merce in ~**
goods in stock; **capitale in ~** uninvested
capital; **~e di magazzino** unsold stock.
gia'cere [dʒa'tʃere] *vi* (2) to lie; **giaci-
'mento** *sm* deposit.
gia'cinto [dʒa'tʃinto] *sm* hyacinth.
gi'ada ['dʒada] *sf* jade.
giaggi'olo [dʒad'dʒɔlo] *sm* iris.
giagu'aro [dʒa'gwaro] *sm* jaguar.
gi'allo ['dʒallo] *ag* yellow; (*carnagione*)
sallow // *sm* yellow; (*anche:* **romanzo ~**)
detective novel; (*anche:* **film ~**) detective
film; **~ dell'uovo** yolk.
giam'mai [dʒam'mai] *av* never.
Giap'pone [dʒap'pone] *sm* Japan; **giappo-
'nese** *ag, sm/f, sm* Japanese.
gi'ara ['dʒara] *sf* jar.
giardi'naggio [dʒardi'naddʒo] *sm*
gardening.
giardini'ere, a [dʒardi'njere] *sm/f*
gardener // *sf* (*misto di sottaceti*) mixed
pickles *pl*; (*automobile*) estate car.
giar'dino [dʒar'dino] *sm* garden; **~
d'infanzia** nursery school; **~ pubblico**
public gardens *pl*, (public) park.
giarretti'era [dʒarret'tjera] *sf* garter.
giavel'lotto [dʒavel'lotto] *sm* javelin.
gi'gante, 'essa [dʒi'gante] *sm/f* giant //
ag giant, gigantic; **gigan'tesco, a, schi,
sche** *ag* gigantic.

'giglio ['dʒiʎʎo] sm lily.

gilè [dʒi'lɛ] sm inv waistcoat.

gin [dʒin] sm gin.

ginecolo'gia   [dʒinekolo'dʒia]   sf gynaecology.

gi'nepro [dʒi'nepro] sm juniper.

gi'nestra [dʒi'nɛstra] sf (BOT) broom.

Gi'nevra [dʒi'nevra] sf Geneva.

gingil'larsi [dʒindʒil'larsi] vr to fritter away one's time.

gin'gillo [dʒin'dʒillo] sm plaything.

gin'nasio [dʒin'nazjo] sm the 4th and 5th year of secondary school in Italy.

gin'nasta, i, e [dʒin'nasta] sm/f gymnast; **gin'nastica** sf gymnastics sg; keep-fit exercises.

gi'nocchio [dʒi'nɔkkjo], pl(m) **gi'nocchi** o pl(f) **gi'nocchia** sm knee; **stare in ~** to kneel, be on one's knees; **ginocchi'oni** av on one's knees.

gio'care [dʒo'kare] vt to play; (scommettere) to stake, wager, bet; (ingannare) to take in // vi to play; (a roulette etc) to gamble; (fig) to play a part, be important; (TECN: meccanismo) to be loose; **~ a** (gioco, sport) to play; (cavalli) to bet on; **gioca'tore, 'trice** sm/f player; gambler.

gio'cattolo [dʒo'kattolo] sm toy.

gio'chetto [dʒo'ketto] sm (fig): **è un ~** it's child's play.

gi'oco, chi ['dʒɔko] sm game; (divertimento, TECN) play; (al casinò) gambling; (CARTE) hand; (insieme di pezzi etc necessari per un gioco) set; **per ~** for fun; **fare il doppio ~ con qd** to double-cross sb; **~ d'azzardo** game of chance; **~ della palla** football; **~ degli scacchi** chess set; **i giochi olimpici** the Olympic Games.

gio'coso, a [dʒo'koso] ag playful, jesting.

gio'gaia [dʒo'gaja] sf (GEO) range of mountains.

gi'ogo, ghi ['dʒɔgo] sm yoke.

gi'oia ['dʒɔja] sf joy, delight; (pietra preziosa) jewel, precious stone.

gioiel'le'ria [dʒojelle'ria] sf jeweller's craft; jeweller's (shop).

gioielli'ere, a [dʒojel'ljere] sm/f jeweller.

gioi'ello [dʒo'jɛllo] sm jewel, piece of jewellery; **~i** smpl jewellery sg.

gioi'oso, a [dʒo'joso] ag joyful.

Gior'dania [dʒor'danja] sf: **la ~** Jordan.

giorna'laio, a   [dʒorna'lajo]   sm/f newsagent; news-vendor.

gior'nale [dʒor'nale] sm (news)paper; (diario) journal, diary; (COMM) journal; **~ di bordo** log; **~ radio** radio news sg.

giornali'ero, a [dʒorna'ljero] ag daily; (che varia: umore) changeable // sm/f day labourer.

giorna'lismo   [dʒorna'lizmo]   sm journalism.

giorna'lista, i, e [dʒorna'lista] sm/f journalist.

gior'nata [dʒor'nata] sf day; **~ lavorativa** working day.

gi'orno ['dʒorno] sm day; (opposto alla notte) day, daytime; (luce del ~) daylight; **al ~** per day; **di ~** by day; **al ~ d'oggi** nowadays.

gi'ostra ['dʒɔstra] sf merry-go-round; (torneo storico) joust.

gi'ovane ['dʒovane] ag young; (giovanile) youthful // sm/f youth/girl, young man/woman; **i ~i** young people; **giova'nile** ag youthful; **giova'notto** sm young man.

gio'vare [dʒo'vare] vi: **~ a** (essere utile) to be useful to; (far bene) to be good for // vb impers (essere bene, utile) to be useful; **~rsi di qc** to take advantage of sth.

giovedì [dʒove'di] sm Thursday; **di o il ~** on Thursdays.

gioventù [dʒoven'tu] sf youth; (i giovani) young people pl, youth.

giovi'ale [dʒo'vjale] ag jovial, jolly.

giovi'nezza [dʒovi'nettsa] sf youth.

gira'dischi [dʒira'diski] sm inv record player.

gi'raffa [dʒi'raffa] sf giraffe.

gi'randola [dʒi'randola]   sf   (fuoco d'artificio) Catherine wheel; (giocattolo) toy windmill; (banderuola) weather vane, weather cock.

gi'rare [dʒi'rare] vt (far ruotare) to turn; (percorrere, visitare) to go round; (CINEMA) to shoot; to make; (COMM) to endorse // vi to turn; (più veloce) to spin; (andare in giro) to wander, go around; **~rsi** vr to turn; **~ attorno a** qc to go round; to revolve round; **far ~ la testa a qd** to make sb dizzy; (fig) to turn sb's head.

girar'rosto [dʒirar'rɔsto] sm (CUC) spit.

gira'sole [dʒira'sole] sm sunflower.

gi'rata [dʒi'rata] sf (passeggiata) stroll; (con veicolo) drive; (COMM) endorsement.

gira'volta [dʒira'vɔlta] sf twirl, turn; (curva) sharp bend; (fig) about-turn.

gi'revole [dʒi'revole] ag revolving, turning.

gi'rino [dʒi'rino] sm tadpole.

'giro ['dʒiro] sm (cerchio) circle; (di manovella) turn; (viaggio) tour, excursion; (passeggiata) stroll, walk; (in macchina) drive; (in bicicletta) ride; (SPORT: della pista) lap; (di denaro) circulation; (CARTE) hand; (TECN) revolution; **prendere in ~ qd** (fig) to pull sb's leg; **fare un ~** to go for a walk (o a drive o a ride); **andare in ~** to go about, walk around; **a stretto ~ di posta** by return of post; **nel ~ di un mese** in a month's time; **~ d'affari** (COMM) turnover; **~ di parole** circumlocution; **~ di prova** (AUT) test drive; **giro'collo** sm: **a girocollo** crewneck cpd; **gi'rone** sm (SPORT) series of games; **girone di andata/ritorno** (CALCIO) first/second half of the season.

gironzo'lare [dʒirondzo'lare] vi to stroll about.

girova'gare [dʒirova'gare] vi to wander about.

'gita ['dʒita] sf excursion, trip.

gi'tano, a [dʒi'tano] sm/f gipsy.

giù [dʒu] av down; (dabbasso) downstairs; **in** ~ downwards, down; ~ **di lì** (pressappoco) thereabouts; **bambini dai 6 anni in** ~ children aged 6 and under; ~ **per: cadere** ~ **per le scale** to fall down the stairs; **portare i capelli** ~ **per le spalle** to… have shoulder-length hair; **essere** ~ (fig: di salute) to be run down; (: di spirito) to be depressed.

giub'botto [dʒub'bɔtto] sm jerkin.

giubi'lare [dʒubi'lare] vi to rejoice // vt to pension off.

gi'ubilo ['dʒubilo] sm rejoicing.

giudi'care [dʒudi'kare] vt to judge; ~ **qd/qc bello** to consider sb/sth (to be) beautiful.

gi'udice ['dʒuditʃe] sm judge; ~ **conciliatore** justice of the peace.

giu'dizio [dʒu'dittsjo] sm judgment; (opinione) opinion; (DIR) judgment, sentence; (: processo) trial; (: verdetto) verdict; **aver** ~ to be wise o prudent; **giudizi'oso, a** ag prudent, judicious.

gi'ugno ['dʒuɲɲo] sm June.

giul'lare [dʒul'lare] sm jester.

giu'menta [dʒu'menta] sf mare.

gi'unco, chi ['dʒunko] sm rush.

gi'ungere ['dʒundʒere] vi (2) to arrive // vt (mani etc) to join; ~ **a** to arrive at, reach.

gi'ungla ['dʒungla] sf jungle.

gi'unto, a ['dʒunto] pp di **giungere** // sm addition; (organo esecutivo, amministrativo) council, board; **per** ~**a** into the bargain, in addition; ~**a militare** military junta; **giun'tura** sf joint.

giuo'care [dʒwo'kare] vt, vi = **giocare; giu'oco** sm = **gioco**.

giura'mento [dʒura'mento] sm oath; ~ **falso** perjury.

giu'rare [dʒu'rare] vt to swear // vi to swear, take an oath; **giu'rato, a** ag: **nemico giurato** sworn enemy // sm/f juror, juryman/woman.

giu'ria [dʒu'ria] sf jury.

giu'ridico, a, ci, che [dʒu'ridiko] ag legal.

giurisdizi'one [dʒurizdit'tsjone] sf jurisdiction.

giurispru'denza [dʒurispru'dɛntsa] sf jurisprudence.

giustifi'care [dʒustifi'kare] vt to justify; **giustificazi'one** sf justification; (INS) (note of) excuse.

gius'tizia [dʒus'tittsja] sf justice; **giusti-zi'are** vt to execute, put to death; **giusti-zi'ere** sm executioner.

gi'usto, a ['dʒusto] ag (equo) fair, just; (vero) true, correct; (adatto) right, suitable; (preciso) exact, correct // av (esattamente) exactly, precisely; (per l'appunto, appena) just; **arrivare** ~ to arrive just in time; **ho** ~ **bisogno di te** you're just the person I need.

glaci'ale [gla'tʃale] ag glacial.

'glandola sf = **ghiandola**.

gli [ʎi] det mpl (dav V, s impura, gn, pn, ps, x, z) the // pronome (a lui) to him; (a esso) to

it; (in coppia con lo, la, li, le, ne: a lui, a lei, a loro etc): **gliele do** I'm giving them to him (o her o them).

glice'rina [glitʃe'rina] sf glycerine.

gli'ela ['ʎela] etc vedi **gli.**

glo'bale ag overall.

'globo sm globe.

'globulo sm globule; (ANAT) corpuscle.

'gloria sf glory; **glorifi'care** vt to exalt, glorify; **glori'oso, a** ag glorious.

glos'sario sm glossary.

glu'cosio sm glucose.

'gnocchi ['ɲɔkki] smpl (CUC) small dumplings made of semolina pasta or potato.

'gnomo ['ɲɔmo] sm gnome.

'gobba sf (ANAT) hump; (protuberanza) bump.

'gobbo, a ag hunchbacked; (ricurvo) round-shouldered // sm/f hunchback.

'goccia, ce ['gottʃa] sf drop; **goccio'lare** vi (2) to drip; **goccio'lio** sm dripping.

go'dere vi (compiacersi): ~ **(di)** to be delighted (at), rejoice (at); (trarre vantaggio): ~ **di** to enjoy, benefit from // vt to enjoy; ~**rsi la vita** to enjoy life; ~**sela** to have a good time, enjoy o.s.; **godi'mento** sm enjoyment.

'goffo, a ag clumsy, awkward.

'gola sf (ANAT) throat; (golosità) gluttony, greed; (di camino) flue; (di monte) gorge; **fare** ~ (anche fig) to tempt.

golf sm inv (SPORT) golf; (maglia) cardigan.

'golfo sm gulf.

go'loso, a ag greedy.

'gomito sm elbow; (di strada etc) sharp bend.

go'mitolo sm ball.

'gomma sf rubber; (colla) gum; (per cancellare) rubber, eraser; (di veicolo) tyre; ~ **a terra** flat tyre; **gommapi'uma** sf ® foam rubber.

'gondola sf gondola; **gondoli'ere** sm gondolier.

gonfa'lone sm banner.

gonfi'are vt (pallone) to blow up, inflate; (dilatare, ingrossare) to swell; (fig: persona) to flatter; (: notizia) to exaggerate; ~**rsi** vr to swell; (fiume) to rise; **'gonfio, a** ag swollen; (stomaco) bloated; **gonfi'ore** sm swelling.

gongo'lare vi to look pleased with o.s.; ~ **di gioia** to be overjoyed.

'gonna sf skirt.

'gonzo ['gondzo] sm simpleton, fool.

gorgheggi'are [gorged'dʒare] vi to warble; to trill.

'gorgo, ghi sm whirlpool.

gorgogli'are [gorgoʎ'ʎare] vi to gurgle.

go'rilla sm inv gorilla.

'gotico, a, ci, che ag, sm Gothic.

'gotta sf gout.

gover'nante sm/f ruler // sf (di bambini) governess; (donna di servizio) housekeeper.

gover'nare vt (Stato) to govern, rule; (azienda) to manage, run; (pilotare, guidare) to steer; (bestiame) to tend, look after; **governa'tivo, a** ag government cpd, state cpd; **governa'tore** sm governor.

go'verno sm government; management; running; steering; tending; ~ **della casa** housekeeping.

gozzo'viglia [gottso'viʎʎa] sf carousing.

gracchi'are [grak'kjare] vi to caw.

graci'dare [gratʃi'dare] vi to croak.

'gracile ['gratʃile] ag frail, delicate.

gra'dasso sm boaster.

gradazi'one [gradat'tsjone] sf (sfumatura) gradation; ~ **alcolica** alcoholic content, strength.

gra'devole ag pleasant, agreeable.

gradi'mento sm pleasure, satisfaction.

gradi'nata sf flight of steps; (in teatro, stadio) tiers pl.

gra'dino sm step; (ALPINISMO) foothold.

gra'dire vt (accettare con piacere) to accept; (desiderare) to wish, like; **gra'dito, a** ag pleasing; welcome.

'grado sm (MAT, FISICA etc) degree; (stadio) degree, level; (MIL, sociale) rank; **essere in ~ di fare** to be in a position to do.

gradu'ale ag gradual.

gradu'are vt to grade; **gradu'ato, a** ag (esercizi) graded; (scala, termometro) graduated // sm (MIL) non-commissioned officer; **graduazi'one** sf graduation.

'graffa sf (gancio) clip; (segno grafico) brace.

graffi'are vt to scratch.

'graffio sm scratch.

gra'fia sf spelling; (scrittura) handwriting.

'grafico, a, ci, che ag graphic // sm graph; (persona) graphic designer // sf graphic arts pl.

gra'migna [gra'miɲɲa] sf weed; couch grass.

gram'matica, che sf grammar; **grammati'cale** ag grammatical; **gram-'matico, a, ci, che** ag = **grammaticale**.

'grammo sm gram(me).

gram'mofono sm gramophone.

gran ag vedi **grande**.

'grana sf (granello, di minerali, corpi spezzati) grain; (fam: seccatura) trouble; (: soldi) cash // sm inv Parmesan (cheese).

gra'naio sm granary, barn.

gra'nata sf (scopa) broom; (frutto) pomegranate; (pietra preziosa) garnet; (proiettile) grenade.

Gran Bre'tagna [gran bre'taɲɲa] sf: **la ~** Great Britain.

'granchio ['grankjo] sm crab; (fig) blunder.

grandango'lare sm wide-angle lens sg.

'grande, qualche volta **gran** +C, **grand'** +V ag (grosso, largo, vasto) big, large; (alto) tall; (lungo) long; (in sensi astratti) great // sm/f (persona adulta) adult, grown-up; (chi ha ingegno e potenza) great man/woman; **fare le cose in ~** to do things in style; **una gran bella donna** a very beautiful woman; **non è una gran cosa** o **un gran che** it's nothing special; **non ne so gran che** I don't know very much about it.

grandeggi'are [granded'dʒare] vi (emergere per grandezza): ~ **su** to tower over; (darsi arie) to put on airs.

gran'dezza [gran'dettsa] sf (dimensione) size; magnitude; (fig) greatness; **in ~ naturale** lifesize.

grandi'nare vb impers to hail.

'grandine sf hail.

grandi'oso, a ag grand, grandiose.

gran'duca, chi sm grand duke.

gra'nello sm (di cereali, uva) seed; (di frutta) pip; (di sabbia etc) grain.

gra'nita sf kind of water ice.

gra'nito sm granite.

'grano sm (in quasi tutti i sensi) grain; (frumento) wheat; (di rosario, collana) bead; ~ **di pepe** peppercorn.

gran'turco sm maize.

'granulo sm granule; (MED) pellet.

'grappa sf (alcool) rough, strong brandy; (EDIL) cramp (iron).

'grappolo sm bunch, cluster.

'grasso, a ag fat; (cibo) fatty; (pelle) greasy; (terreno) rich; (fig: guadagno, annata) plentiful; (: volgare) coarse, lewd // sm (di persona, animale) fat; (sostanza che unge) grease; **gras'soccio, a, ci, ce** ag plump.

'grata sf grating.

gra'ticcio [gra'tittʃo] sm trellis; (stuoia) mat.

gra'ticola sf grill.

gra'tifica, che sf bonus.

'gratis av free, for nothing.

grati'tudine sf gratitude.

'grato, a ag grateful; (gradito) pleasant, agreeable.

gratta'capo sm worry, headache.

grattaci'elo [gratta'tʃɛlo] sm skyscraper.

grat'tare vt (pelle) to scratch; (raschiare) to scrape; (pane, formaggio, carote) to grate; (fam: rubare) to pinch // vi (stridere) to grate; (AUT) to grind; ~**rsi** vr to scratch o.s.

grat'tugia, gie [grat'tudʒa] sf grater; **grattugi'are** vt to grate.

gra'tuito, a ag free; (fig) gratuitous.

gra'vame sm (fig) burden, weight.

gra'vare vt to burden // vi (2): ~ **su** to weigh on.

'grave ag heavy; (fig: danno, pericolo, peccato etc) grave, serious; (: responsabilità) heavy, grave; (: contegno) grave, solemn; (voce, suono) deep, low-pitched; (LING): **accento ~** grave accent; **un malato ~** a person who is seriously ill.

gravi'danza [gravi'dantsa] sf pregnancy.

'gravido, a ag pregnant.

gravità sf seriousness; (anche FISICA) gravity.

gra'voso, a ag heavy, onerous.

'grazia ['grattsja] sf grace; (favore) favour; (DIR) pardon; **grazi'are** vt (DIR) to pardon.

'grazie ['grattsje] escl thank you!; ~

mille! o **tante!** o **infinite!** thank you very much!; ~ **a** thanks to.

grazi'oso, a [grat'tsjoso] ag charming, delightful; (gentile) gracious.

'Grecia ['grɛtʃa] sf: **la** ~ Greece; **'greco, a, ci, che** ag, sm/f Greek.

gre'gario sm (CICLISMO) supporting rider.

'gregge, pl(f) **i** ['greddʒe] sm flock.

'greggio, a, gi, ge ['greddʒo] ag raw, crude, rough; (fig) unrefined // sm (anche: **petrolio** ~) crude (oil).

grembi'ule sm apron; (sopravveste) overall.

'grembo sm lap; (ventre della madre) womb.

gre'mire vt to pack, cram; ~**rsi** vr: ~**rsi (di)** to become packed o crowded (with); **gre'mito, a** ag packed, crowded.

'gretto, a ag mean, stingy; (fig) narrow-minded.

'greve ag heavy.

'grezzo, a ['greddzo] ag = **greggio.**

gri'dare vi (per chiamare) to shout, cry (out); (strillare) to scream, yell // vt to shout (out), yell (out).

'grido, pl(m) **i** o pl(f) **a** sm shout, cry; scream, yell; (di animale) cry; **di** ~ famous.

'grigio, a, gi, gie ['gridʒo] ag grey.

'griglia ['griʎʎa] sf (per arrostire) grill; (ELETTR) grid; **alla** ~ (CUC) grilled.

gril'letto sm trigger.

'grillo sm (ZOOL) cricket; (fig) whim.

grimal'dello sm picklock.

'grinta sf grim expression; (SPORT) fighting spirit.

'grinza ['grintsa] sf crease, wrinkle; (ruga) wrinkle.

grip'pare vi (TECN) to seize.

gris'sino sm bread-stick.

'gronda sf eaves pl.

gron'daia sf gutter.

gron'dare vi (2) to pour; (essere bagnato): ~ **di** to be soaking o dripping with // vt to drip with.

'groppa sf (di animale) back, rump; (fam: dell'uomo) back, shoulders pl.

'groppo sm tangle; **avere un** ~ **alla gola** (fig) to have a lump in one's throat.

'grossa sf (unità di misura) gross.

gros'sezza [gros'settsa] sf size; thickness.

gros'sista, i, e sm/f (COMM) wholesaler.

'grosso, a ag big, large; (di spessore) thick; (grossolano: anche fig) coarse; (grave, insopportabile) serious, great; (tempo, mare) rough // sm: **il** ~ **di** the bulk of; **farla** ~**a** to do something very stupid; **dirle** ~**e** to tell tall stories; **sbagliarsi di** ~ to be completely wrong.

grosso'lano, a ag rough, coarse; (fig) coarse, crude.

grosso'modo av roughly.

'grotta sf cave; grotto.

grot'tesco, a, schi, sche ag grotesque.

grovi'era sm o f gruyère (cheese).

gro'viglio [gro'viʎʎo] sm tangle; (fig) muddle.

gru sf inv crane.

'gruccia, ce ['gruttʃa] sf (per camminare) crutch; (per abiti) coat-hanger.

gru'gnire [gruɲ'ɲire] vi to grunt; **gru-'gnito** sm grunt.

'grugno, [gruɲ'ɲo] sm snout.

'grullo, a ag silly, stupid.

'grumo sm (di sangue) clot; (di farina etc) lump.

'gruppo sm group; ~ **sanguigno** blood group.

gruvi'era sm o f = **groviera.**

guada'gnare [gwadaɲ'ɲare] vt (ottenere) to gain; (soldi, stipendio) to earn; (vincere) to win; (raggiungere) to reach.

gua'dagno [gwa'daɲɲo] sm earnings pl; (COMM) profit; (vantaggio, utile) advantage, gain; ~ **lordo/netto** gross/net earnings pl.

gu'ado sm ford; **passare a** ~ to ford.

gu'ai escl: ~**a te** (o lui etc)! woe betide you (o him etc)!

gua'ina sf (fodero) sheath; (indumento per donna) girdle.

gu'aio sm trouble, mishap; (inconveniente) trouble, snag.

gua'ire vi to whine, yelp.

gu'ancia, ce ['gwantʃa] sf cheek.

guanci'ale [gwan'tʃale] sm pillow.

gu'anto sm glove.

gu'arda... prefisso: ~**'boschi** sm inv forester; ~**'caccia** sm inv gamekeeper; ~**'coste** sm inv coastguard; (nave) coastguard patrol vessel; ~**'linee** sm inv (SPORT) linesman.

guar'dare vt (con lo sguardo: osservare) to look at; (film, televisione) to watch; (custodire) to look after, take care of // vi to look; (badare): ~ **a** to pay attention to; (luoghi: essere orientato): ~ **a** to face; ~**rsi** vr to look at o.s.; ~**rsi da** (astenersi) to refrain from; (stare in guardia) to beware of; ~**rsi da fare** to take care not to do; ~ **a vista** qd to keep a close watch on sb.

guarda'roba sm inv wardrobe; (locale) cloakroom; **guardarobi'ere, a** sm/f cloakroom attendant.

gu'ardia sf guard; (vigilanza, custodia) watch, guard; **fare la** ~ **a** qc/qd to guard sth/sb; **stare in** ~ (fig) to be on one's guard; ~ **di finanza** (corpo) customs pl; (persona) customs officer.

guardi'ano, a sm/f (di carcere) warder; (di villa etc) caretaker; (di museo) custodian; ~ **notturno** night watchman.

guar'dingo, a, ghi, ghe ag wary, cautious.

guardi'ola sf porter's lodge; (MIL) look-out tower.

guarigi'one [gwari'dʒone] sf recovery.

gua'rire vt (persona, malattia) to cure; (ferita) to heal // vi (2) to recover, be cured; to heal (up).

guarnigi'one [gwarni'dʒone] sf garrison.

guar'nire vt (ornare) to decorate, ornament; (: abiti) to trim; (CUC) to garnish; (MIL) to garrison; **guarnizi'one** sf decoration; trimming; garnish; (TECN) gasket.

guasta'feste sm/f inv spoilsport.

guas'tare vt to spoil, ruin; (meccanismo) to break; ~**rsi** vr (cibo) to go bad; (meccanismo) to break down; (tempo) to change for the worse; (fig) to be spoiled, be ruined; (: amici) to quarrel, fall out.

gu'asto, a ag (non funzionante) broken; (: telefono) out of order; (andato a male) bad, rotten; (: dente) decayed, bad; (fig: corrotto) depraved // sm breakdown, failure; (danno) damage; (fig) something rotten.

gu'azza ['gwattsa] sf heavy dew.

guazza'buglio [gwattsa'buʎʎo] sm muddle.

gu'azzo ['gwattso] sm puddle, pool; (PITTURA) gouache.

gu'ercio, a, ci, ce ['gwertʃo] ag cross-eyed.

gu'erra sf war; (tecnica: atomica, chimica etc) warfare; **fare la** ~ **(a)** to wage war (against); ~ **mondiale** world war; **guerreggi'are** vi to wage war; **guer-'resco, a, schi, sche** ag (di guerra) war cpd; (incline alla guerra) warlike; **guerri'ero, a** ag warlike // sm warrior; **guerrigli'ero** sm guerrilla.

'gufo sm owl.

gu'ida sf guide; (comando, direzione) guidance, direction; (AUT) driving; (: sterzo) steering; (tappeto, di tenda, cassetto) runner; ~ **a destra/sinistra** (AUT) right-/left-hand drive.

gui'dare vt to guide; (condurre a capo) to lead; (auto) to drive; (aereo, nave) to pilot; **sai** ~? can you drive?; **guida'tore** sm (conducente) driver.

guin'zaglio [gwin'tsaʎʎo] sm leash, lead.

gu'isa sf: **a** ~ **di** like, in the manner of.

guiz'zare [gwit'tsare] vi to dart; to flash; to flicker; to leap.

'guscio ['guʃʃo] sm shell.

gus'tare vt (cibi) to taste; (: assaporare con piacere) to enjoy, savour; (fig) to enjoy, appreciate // vi (2) to please; **non mi gusta affatto** I don't like it at all.

'gusto sm taste; (sapore) flavour; (godimento) enjoyment; **al** ~ **di fragola** strawberry-flavoured; **mangiare di** ~ to eat heartily; **prenderci** ~: **ci ha preso** ~ he's acquired a taste for it, he's got to like it; **gus'toso, a** ag tasty; (fig) agreeable.

guttu'rale ag guttural.

H

ha, 'hai [a, ai] forme del vb **avere**.

'handicap ['handikap] sm inv handicap.

'hanno ['anno] forma del vb **avere**.

'hascisc ['haʃiʃ] sm hashish.

ho [ɔ] forma del vb **avere**.

'hobby ['hɔbi] sm inv hobby.

'hockey ['hɔki] sm hockey; ~ **su ghiaccio** ice hockey.

I

i det mpl the.

i'ato sm hiatus.

ibernazi'one [ibernat'tsjone] sf hibernation.

'ibrido, a ag, sm hybrid.

i'cona sf icon.

Id'dio sm God.

i'dea sf idea; (opinione) opinion, view; (ideale) ideal; ~ **fissa** obsession; **neanche** o **neppure per** ~! not on your life!, certainly not!

ide'ale ag, sm ideal; **idea'lismo** sm idealism; **idea'lista, i, e** sm/f idealist; **idealiz'zare** vt to idealize.

ide'are vt (immaginare) to think up, conceive; (progettare) to plan.

i'dentico, a, ci, che ag identical.

identifi'care vt to identify; **identifica-zi'one** sf identification.

identità sf inv identity.

ideolo'gia, 'gie [ideolo'dʒia] sf ideology.

i'dillico, a, ci, che ag idyllic.

idi'oma, i sm idiom, language; **idio-'matico, a, ci, che** ag idiomatic.

idiosincra'sia sf idiosyncrasy.

idi'ota, i, e ag idiotic // sm/f idiot.

idio'tismo sm idiom, idiomatic phrase.

idola'trare vt to worship; (fig) to idolize.

'idolo sm idol.

idoneità sf suitability.

i'doneo, a ag: ~ **a** suitable for, fit for; (MIL) fit for; (qualificato) qualified for.

i'drante sm hydrant.

i'draulico, a, ci, che ag hydraulic // sm plumber // sf hydraulics sg.

idroe'lettrico, a, ci, che ag hydroelectric.

i'drofilo, a ag: vedi **cotone**.

idrofo'bia sf rabies sg.

i'drogeno [i'drɔdʒeno] sm hydrogen.

idros'calo sm seaplane base.

idrovo'lante sm seaplane.

i'ena sf hyena.

i'eri av yesterday; ~ **l'altro** the day before yesterday; ~ **sera** yesterday evening.

igi'ene [i'dʒene] sf hygiene; ~ **pubblica** public health; **igi'enico, a, ci, che** ag hygienic; (salubre) healthy.

i'gnaro, a [iɲ'ɲaro] ag: ~ **di** unaware of, ignorant of.

i'gnobile [iɲ'ɲɔbile] ag despicable, vile.

igno'minia [iɲɲo'minja] sf ignominy.

igno'rante [iɲɲo'rante] ag ignorant; **igno-'ranza** sf ignorance.

igno'rare [iɲɲo'rare] vt (non sapere, conoscere) to be ignorant o unaware of, not to know; (fingere di non vedere, sentire) to ignore.

i'gnoto, a [iɲ'ɲɔto] ag unknown.

il det m the.

'ilare ag cheerful; **ilarità** sf hilarity, mirth.

illangui'dire vi (2) to grow weak o feeble.

il'lecito, a [il'letʃito] *ag* illicit.
ille'gale *ag* illegal.
illeg'gibile [illed'dʒibile] *ag* illegible.
illegittimità [illedʒittimi'ta] *sf* illegitimacy.
ille'gittimo, a [ille'dʒittimo] *ag* illegitimate.
il'leso, a *ag* unhurt, unharmed.
illette'rato, a *ag* illiterate.
illimi'tato, a *ag* boundless; unlimited.
il'logico, a, ci, che [il'lɔdʒiko] *ag* illogical.
il'ludere *vt* to deceive, delude; ~**rsi** *vr* to deceive o.s., delude o.s.
illumi'nare *vt* to light up; (*con riflettori*) to illuminate, floodlight; (*fig*) to enlighten; ~**rsi** *vr* to light up; **illuminazi'one** *sf* lighting; illumination, floodlighting; (*fig*) flash of inspiration.
illusi'one *sf* illusion; **farsi delle** ~**i** to delude o.s.
illusio'nismo *sm* conjuring.
il'luso, a *pp di* **illudere**.
illus'trare *vt* to illustrate; **illustra'tivo, a** *ag* illustrative; **illustrazi'one** *sf* illustration.
il'lustre *ag* eminent, renowned.
imbacuc'care *vt, ~rsi* *vr* to wrap up.
imbal'laggio [imbal'laddʒo] *sm* packing q.
imbal'lare *vt* to pack; (*AUT*) to race; ~**rsi** *vr* (*AUT*) to race.
imbalsa'mare *vt* to embalm.
imbaraz'zare [imbarat'tsare] *vt* (*ostacolare*) to hamper; (*confondere*) to puzzle, perplex; (*mettere in imbarazzo*) to embarrass.
imba'razzo [imba'rattso] *sm* (*ostacolo*) hindrance, obstacle; (*perplessità*) bewilderment, puzzlement; (*disagio*) embarrassment; ~ **di stomaco** indigestion.
imbarca'dero *sm* landing stage.
imbar'care *vt* (*passeggeri*) to embark; (*merci*) to load; ~**rsi** *vr* to board; ~ **acqua** (*NAUT*) to ship water.
imbarcazi'one [imbarkat'tsjone] *sf* (*small*) boat, (*small*) craft *inv*; ~ **di salvataggio** lifeboat.
im'barco, chi *sm* embarkation; loading; boarding; (*banchina*) landing stage.
imbas'tire *vt* (*cucire*) to tack; (*fig: abbozzare*) to sketch, outline.
im'battersi *vr*: ~ **in** (*incontrare*) to bump *o* run into; (*avere la sorte*) to meet with.
imbat'tibile *ag* unbeatable, invincible.
imbavagli'are [imbavaʎ'ʎare] *vt* to gag.
imbec'cata *sf* (*TEATRO*) prompt.
imbe'cille [imbe'tʃille] *ag* idiotic // *sm/f* idiot; (*MED*) imbecile.
imbel'lire *vt* to adorn, embellish.
im'berbe *ag* beardless.
im'bevere *vt* to soak; ~**rsi** *vr*: ~**rsi di** to soak up, absorb.
imbian'care *vt* to whiten; (*muro*) to whitewash // *vi* (2) to become *o* turn white.

imbian'chino [imbjan'kino] *sm* (house) painter, painter and decorator.
imboc'care *vt* (*bambino*) to feed; (*fig: imbeccare*): ~ **qd** to prompt sb, put the words into sb's mouth; (*entrare: strada*) to enter, turn into; (*tromba*) to put to one's mouth // *vi*: ~ **in** (*sog: strada*) to lead into; (: *fiume*) to flow into.
imbocca'tura *sf* (*apertura*) opening; mouth; (*ingresso*) entrance; (*MUS*) mouthpiece.
im'bocco, chi *sm* entrance.
imbos'care *vt* to hide; ~**rsi** *vr* (*MIL*) to evade military service.
imbos'cata *sf* ambush.
imbottigli'are [imbottiʎ'ʎare] *vt* to bottle; (*NAUT*) to blockade; (*MIL*) to hem in; ~**rsi** *vr* to be stuck in a traffic jam.
imbot'tire *vt* to stuff; (*giacca*) to pad; **imbot'tita** *sf* quilt; **imbotti'tura** *sf* stuffing; padding.
imbrat'tare *vt* to dirty, smear, daub.
imbrigli'are [imbriʎ'ʎare] *vt* to bridle.
imbroc'care *vt* (*fig*) to guess correctly.
imbrogli'are [imbroʎ'ʎare] *vt* to mix up; (*CARTE*) to shuffle; (*fig: raggirare*) to deceive, cheat; (: *confondere*) to confuse, mix up; ~**rsi** *vr* to get tangled; (*fig*) to become confused; **im'broglio** *sm* (*groviglio*) tangle; (*situazione confusa*) mess; (*truffa*) swindle, trick; **imbrogli'one, a** *sm/f* cheat, swindler.
imbronci'are [imbron'tʃare] *vi* (2) (*anche:* ~**rsi**) to sulk.
imbru'nire *vi, vb impers* (2) to grow dark; **sull'** ~ at dusk.
imbrut'tire *vt* to make ugly // *vi* (2) to become ugly.
imbu'care *vt* to post.
imbur'rare *vt* to butter.
im'buto *sm* funnel.
imi'tare *vt* to imitate; (*riprodurre*) to copy; (*assomigliare*) to look like; **imitazi'one** *sf* imitation.
immaco'lato, a *ag* spotless; immaculate.
immagazzi'nare [immagaddzi'nare] *vt* to store.
immagi'nare [immadʒi'nare] *vt* to imagine; (*supporre*) to suppose; (*inventare*) to invent; **s'immagini!** don't mention it!, not at all!; **immagi'nario, a** *ag* imaginary; **immaginazi'one** *sf* imagination; (*cosa immaginata*) fancy.
im'magine [im'madʒine] *sf* image; (*rappresentazione grafica, mentale*) picture.
imman'cabile *ag* certain; unfailing.
immangi'abile [imman'dʒabile] *ag* inedible.
immatrico'lare *vt* to register; ~**rsi** *vr* (*INS*) to matriculate, enrol; **immatricolazi'one** *sf* registration; matriculation, enrolment.
imma'turo, a *ag* (*frutto*) unripe; (*persona*) immature; (*prematuro*) premature.
immedesi'marsi *vr*: ~ **in** to identify with.
immedi'ato, a *ag* immediate.
im'memore *ag*: ~ **di** forgetful of.

im'menso, a ag immense.
im'mergere [im'mɛrdʒere] vt to immerse, plunge; ~**rsi** vr to plunge; (sommergibile) to dive, submerge; (dedicarsi a): ~**rsi in** to immerse o.s. in.
immeri'tato, a ag undeserved.
immeri'tevole ag undeserving, unworthy.
immersi'one sf immersion; (di sommergibile) submersion, dive; (di palombaro) dive.
im'merso, a pp di **immergere**.
immi'grante ag, sm/f immigrant.
immi'grare vi (2) to immigrate; **immigrato, a** sm/f immigrant; **immigrazi'one** sf immigration.
immi'nente ag imminent.
immischi'are [immis'kjare] vt: ~ **qd in** to involve sb in; ~**rsi in** to interfere o meddle in.
im'mobile ag motionless, still; (beni) ~**i** smpl real estate sg; **immobili'are** ag (DIR) property cpd; **immobilità** sf stillness; immobility; **immobiliz'zare** vt to immobilize; (ECON) to lock up.
immode'rato, a ag excessive.
immo'desto, a ag immodest.
immo'lare vt to sacrifice, immolate.
immon'dizia [immon'dittsja] sf dirt, filth; (spesso al pl: spazzatura, rifiuti) rubbish q, refuse q.
im'mondo, a ag filthy, foul.
immo'rale ag immoral.
immorta'lare vt to immortalize.
immor'tale ag immortal.
im'mune (esente) exempt; (MED, DIR) immune; **immunità** sf immunity; **immunità parlamentare** parliamentary privilege; **immuniz'zare** vt (MED) to immunize.
immu'tabile ag immutable; unchanging.
impacchet'tare [impakket'tare] vt to pack up.
impacci'are [impat'tʃare] vt to hinder, hamper; **impacci'ato, a** ag awkward, clumsy; (imbarazzato) embarrassed; **im'paccio** sm obstacle; (imbarazzo) embarrassment; (situazione imbarazzante) awkward situation.
im'pacco, chi sm (MED) compress.
impadro'nirsi vr: ~ **di** to seize, take possession of; (fig: apprendere a fondo) to master.
impa'gabile ag priceless.
impagli'are [impaʎ'ʎare] vt to stuff (with straw).
impa'lato, a ag (fig) stiff as a poker.
impalca'tura sf scaffolding; (anche fig) framework.
impalli'dire vi (2) to turn pale; (fig) to fade.
impa'nare vt (CUC) to dip in breadcrumbs.
impanta'narsi vr to sink (in the mud); (fig) to get bogged down.
impappi'narsi vr to stammer, falter.
impa'rare vt to learn.

impareggi'abile [impared'dʒabile] ag incomparable.
imparen'tarsi vr: ~ **con** to marry into.
'impari ag inv (disuguale) unequal; (dispari) odd.
impar'tire vt to bestow, give.
imparzi'ale [impar'tsjale] ag impartial, unbiased.
impas'sibile ag impassive.
impas'tare vt (pasta) to knead; (colori) to mix.
im'pasto sm (anche fig) mixture; (di pane) dough.
im'patto sm impact.
impau'rire vt to scare, frighten // vi (2) (anche: ~**rsi**) to become scared o frightened.
impazi'ente [impat'tsjɛnte] ag impatient; **impazi'enza** sf impatience.
impaz'zire [impat'tsire] vi (2) to go mad; ~ **per qd/qc** to be crazy about sb/sth.
impec'cabile ag impeccable, flawless.
impedi'mento sm obstacle, hindrance.
impe'dire vt (vietare): ~ **a qd di fare** to prevent sb from doing; (ostruire) to obstruct; (impacciare) to hamper, hinder.
impe'gnare [impeɲ'ɲare] vt (dare in pegno) to pawn; (onore etc) to pledge; (prenotare) to book, reserve; (obbligare) to oblige; (occupare) to keep busy; (MIL: nemico) to engage; ~**rsi** vr (vincolarsi): ~**rsi a fare** to undertake to do; (mettersi risolutamente): ~**rsi in qc** to devote o.s. to sth; **impegna'tivo, a** ag binding; (lavoro) demanding, exacting; **impe'gnato, a** ag (occupato) busy; (fig: romanzo, autore) committed, engagé.
im'pegno [im'peɲɲo] sm (obbligo) obligation; (promessa) promise, pledge; (zelo) diligence, zeal; (compito, d'autore) commitment.
impel'lente ag pressing, urgent.
impene'trabile ag impenetrable.
impen'narsi vr (cavallo) to rear up; (AER) to nose up; (fig) to bridle.
impen'sato, a ag unforeseen, unexpected.
impensie'rire vt, ~**rsi** vr to worry.
impe'rare vi (anche fig) to reign, rule.
impera'tivo, a ag, sm imperative.
impera'tore, 'trice sm/f emperor/empress.
impercet'tibile [impertʃet'tibile] ag imperceptible.
imperdo'nabile ag unforgivable, unpardonable.
imper'fetto, a ag imperfect // sm (LING) imperfect (tense); **imperfezi'one** sf imperfection.
imperi'ale ag imperial.
imperi'oso, a ag (persona) imperious; (motivo, esigenza) urgent, pressing.
impe'rizia [impe'rittsja] sf lack of experience.
imperma'lirsi vr to take offence.
imperme'abile ag waterproof // sm raincoat.

im'pero *sm* empire; (*forza, autorità*) rule, control.

imperscru'tabile *ag* inscrutable.

imperso'nale *ag* impersonal.

imperso'nare *vt* to personify; (*TEATRO*) to play, act (the part of).

imperter'rito, a *ag* fearless, undaunted; impassive.

imperti'nente *ag* impertinent; **imperti-'nenza** *sf* impertinence.

impertur'babile *ag* imperturbable.

imperver'sare *vi* to rage.

'impeto *sm* (*moto, forza*) force, impetus; (*assalto*) onslaught; (*fig: impulso*) impulse; (: *slancio*) transport; **con** ~ energetically, vehemently.

impet'tito, a *ag* stiff, erect.

impetu'oso, a *ag* (*vento*) strong, raging; (*persona*) impetuous.

impian'tare *vt* (*motore*) to install; (*azienda, tempo*) to establish, start.

impi'anto *sm* (*installazione*) installation; (*apparecchiature*) plant; (*sistema*) system; ~ **elettrico** wiring; ~ **sportivo** sports complex.

impias'trare *vt* to smear, dirty.

impi'astro *sm* poultice.

impic'care *vt* to hang; ~**rsi** *vr* to hang o.s.

impicci'are [impit'tʃare] *vt* to hinder, hamper; ~**rsi** *vr* to meddle, interfere; **im-'piccio** *sm* (*ostacolo*) hindrance; (*seccatura*) trouble, bother; (*affare imbrogliato*) mess.

impie'gare *vt* (*usare*) to use, employ; (*assumere*) to employ, take on; (*spendere: denaro, tempo*) to spend; (*investire*) to invest; ~**rsi** *vr* to get a job, obtain employment; **impie'gato, a** *sm/f* employee.

impi'ego, ghi *sm* (*uso*) use; (*occupazione*) employment; (*posto*) (regular) job, post; (*ECON*) investment.

impieto'sire *vt* to move to pity; ~**rsi** *vr* to be moved to pity.

impigli'are [impiʎ'ʎare] *vt* to catch, entangle; ~**rsi** *vr* to get caught up *o* entangled.

impi'grire *vt* to make lazy // *vi* (2) (*anche*: ~**rsi**) to grow lazy.

impiom'bare *vt* (*pacco*) to seal (with lead); (*dente*) to fill.

impli'care *vt* to imply; (*coinvolgere*) to involve; ~**rsi** *vr* to become involved; **implicazi'one** *sf* implication.

im'plicito, a [im'plitʃito] *ag* implicit.

implo'rare *vt* to implore.

impoltro'nire *vt* to make lazy // *vi* (2) (*anche*: ~**rsi**) to grow lazy.

impolve'rare *vt* to cover with dust; ~**rsi** *vr* to get dusty.

impo'nente *ag* imposing, impressive.

impo'nibile *ag* taxable // *sm* taxable income.

impopo'lare *ag* unpopular; **impopolarità** *sf* unpopularity.

im'porre *vt* to impose; (*costringere*) to force, make; (*far valere*) to impose, enforce; **imporsi** *vr* (*persona*) to assert o.s.; (*cosa: rendersi necessario*) to become necessary; ~ **a qd di fare** to force sb to do, make sb do.

impor'tante *ag* important; **impor'tanza** *sf* importance; **dare importanza a qc** to attach importance to sth.

impor'tare *vt* (*introdurre dall'estero*) to import // *vi* (2) to matter, be important // *vb impers* (2) (*essere necessario*) to be necessary; (*interessare*) to matter; **non importa!** it doesn't matter!; **non me ne importa!** I don't care!; **importazi'one** *sf* importation; (*merci importate*) imports *pl*.

im'porto *sm* (total) amount.

importu'nare *vt* to bother.

impor'tuno, a *ag* irksome, annoying.

imposizi'one [impozit'tsjone] *sf* imposition; order, command; (*onere, imposta*) tax.

imposses'sarsi *vr*: ~ **di** to seize, take possession of.

impos'sibile *ag* impossible; **im-possibilità** *sf* impossibility; **essere nell'impossibilità di fare qc** to be unable to do sth.

im'posta *sf* (*di finestra*) shutter; (*tassa*) tax; ~ **sul reddito** income tax; ~ **sul valore aggiunto (I.V.A.)** value added tax (VAT).

impos'tare *vt* (*imbucare*) to post; (*preparare*) to plan, set up; (*avviare*) to begin, start off; (*voce*) to pitch.

im'posto, a *pp di* **imporre**.

impos'tore, a *sm/f* impostor.

impo'tente *ag* weak, powerless; (*anche MED*) impotent; **impo'tenza** *sf* weakness, powerlessness; impotence.

impove'rire *vt* to impoverish // *vi* (2) (*anche*: ~**rsi**) to become poor.

imprati'cabile *ag* (*strada*) impassable; (*campo da gioco*) unplayable.

imprati'chire [imprati'kire] *vt* to train; ~**rsi in qc** to practise sth.

impre'ciso, a [impre'tʃizo] *ag* imprecise, vague.

impre'gnare [impreɲ'ɲare] *vt*: ~ **(di)** (*imbevere*) to soak *o* impregnate (with); (*riempire: anche fig*) to fill (with).

imprendi'tore *sm* entrepreneur; (*appaltatore*) contractor; **piccolo** ~ small businessman.

im'presa *sf* (*iniziativa*) enterprise; (*azione*) exploit; (*azienda*) firm, concern.

impre'sario *sm* (*TEATRO*) manager, impresario; ~ **di pompe funebri** funeral director.

imprescin'dibile [impreʃʃin'dibile] *ag* not to be ignored.

impressio'nante *ag* impressive; upsetting.

impressio'nare *vt* to impress; (*turbare*) to upset; (*FOT*) to expose; ~**rsi** *vr* to be easily upset.

impressi'one *sf* impression; (*fig: sensazione*) sensation, feeling; (*stampa*) printing; **fare** ~ to impress; (*turbare*) to frighten, upset; **fare buona/cattiva ~ a** to make a good/bad impression on.

im'presso, a *pp di* **imprimere.**

impreve'dibile *ag* unforeseeable; *(persona)* unpredictable.

imprevi'dente *ag* lacking in foresight.

impre'visto, a *ag* unexpected, unforeseen // *sm* unforeseen event; **salvo ~i** unless anything unexpected happens.

imprigiona'mento [imprid3ona'mento] *sm* imprisonment.

imprigio'nare [imprid3o'nare] *vt* to imprison.

im'primere *vt (anche fig)* to impress, stamp; *(stampare)* to print; *(comunicare: movimento)* to transmit, give.

impro'babile *ag* improbable, unlikely.

im'pronta *sf* imprint, impression, sign; *(di piede, mano)* print; *(fig)* mark, stamp; **~ digitale** fingerprint.

impro'perio *sm* insult; **~i** *smpl* abuse sg.

im'proprio, a *ag* improper.

improvvisa'mente *av* suddenly; unexpectedly.

improvvi'sare *vt* to improvise; **~rsi** *vr:* **~rsi cuoco** (to decide to) act as cook; **improvvi'sata** *sf* (pleasant) surprise.

improv'viso, a *ag (improvviso)* unexpected; *(subitaneo)* sudden; **all'~** unexpectedly; suddenly.

impru'dente *ag* unwise, rash.

impu'dente *ag* impudent; **impu'denza** *sf* impudence.

impu'dico, a, chi, che *ag* immodest.

impu'gnare [impuɲ'ɲare] *vt* to grasp, grip; *(DIR)* to contest; **impugna'tura** *sf* grip, grasp; *(manico)* handle; *(: di spada)* hilt.

impul'sivo, a *ag* impulsive.

im'pulso *sm* impulse.

impu'nito, a *ag* unpunished.

impun'tarsi *vr* to stop dead, refuse to budge; *(fig)* to be obstinate.

impurità *sf inv* impurity.

im'puro, a *ag* impure.

impu'tare *vt (ascrivere):* **~ qc a** to attribute sth to; *(DIR: accusare):* **~ qd di** to charge sb with, accuse sb of; **impu'tato, a** *sm/f (DIR)* accused, defendant; **imputazi'one** *sf (DIR)* charge.

imputri'dire *vi (2)* to rot.

in *prep (in + il =* **nel,** *in + lo =* **nello,** *in + l' =* **nell',** *in + la =* **nella,** *in + i =* **nei,** *in + gli =* **negli,** *in + le =* **nelle)** in; *(moto a luogo)* to; *(: dentro)* into; *(mezzo):* **~ autobus/treno** by bus/train; *(composizione):* **~ marmo** made of marble, marble *cpd;* **essere ~ casa** to be at home; **andare ~ Austria** to go to Austria; **Maria Bianchi ~ Rossi** Maria Rossi née Bianchi; **siamo ~ quattro** there are four of us.

i'nabile *ag:* **~ a** incapable of; *(fisicamente, MIL)* unfit for; **inabilità** *sf* incapacity.

inabi'tabile *ag* uninhabitable.

inacces'sibile [inattʃes'sibile] *ag* inaccessible; *(persona)* unapproachable.

inaccet'tabile [inattʃet'tabile] *ag* unacceptable.

ina'datto, a *ag:* **~ (a)** unsuitable *o* unfit (for).

inadegu'ato, a *ag* inadequate.

inadempi'ente *sm/f* defaulter.

inaffer'rabile *ag* elusive; *(concetto, senso)* difficult to grasp.

ina'lare *vt* to inhale; **inala'tore** *sm* inhaler.

inalbe'rare *vt (NAUT)* to hoist, raise; **~rsi** *vr (impennarsi)* to rear up; *(fig)* to flare up, fly off the handle.

inalte'rabile *ag* unchangeable; *(colore)* fast, permanent; *(affetto)* constant.

inalte'rato, a *ag* unchanged.

inami'dare *vt* to starch; **inamidato, a** *ag* starched.

inammis'sibile *ag* inadmissible.

inani'mato, a *ag* inanimate; *(senza vita: corpo)* lifeless.

inappa'gabile *ag* insatiable.

inappel'labile *ag (DIR)* final, not open to appeal.

inappun'tabile *ag* irreproachable, flawless.

inar'care *vt (schiena)* to arch; *(sopracciglia)* to raise; **~rsi** *vr* to arch.

inari'dire *vt* to make arid, dry up // *vi (2) (anche:* **~rsi)** to dry up, become arid.

inaspet'tato, a *ag* unexpected.

inas'prire *vt* to embitter; to exacerbate; **~rsi** *vr* to grow bitter.

inattac'cabile *ag (MIL)* unassailable; *(fig: fama)* unimpeachable; **~ dalle tarme** moth-proof.

inatten'dibile *ag* unreliable.

inat'teso, a *ag* unexpected.

inat'tivo, a *ag* inactive, idle; *(CHIM)* inactive.

inattu'abile *ag* impracticable.

inau'dito, a *ag* unheard of.

inaugu'rale *ag* inaugural.

inaugu'rare *vt* to inaugurate, open; *(monumento)* to unveil; **inaugurazi'one** *sf* inauguration; unveiling.

inavve'duto, a *ag* careless, inadvertent.

inavver'tenza [inavver'tɛntsa] *sf* carelessness, inadvertence.

incagli'are [inkaʎ'ʎare] *vi (2) (NAUT: anche:* **~rsi)** to run aground // *vt (intralciare)* to hamper, hinder; **in'caglio** *sm (NAUT)* running aground; *(ostacolo)* obstacle, hindrance.

incalco'labile *ag* incalculable.

incal'lito, a *ag* calloused; *(fig)* hardened, inveterate; *(: insensibile)* hard.

incal'zare [inkal'tsare] *vt* to follow *o* pursue closely; *(fig)* to press // *vi (urgere)* to be pressing; *(essere imminente)* to be imminent.

incame'rare *vt (DIR)* to expropriate.

incammi'nare *vt (fig: avviare)* to start up; **~rsi** *vr* to set off.

incande'scente [inkandeʃ'ʃɛnte] *ag* incandescent, white-hot.

incan'tare *vt* to enchant, bewitch; **~rsi**

vr (rimanere intontito) to be spellbound; to be in a daze; *(meccanismo: bloccarsi)* to jam; **incanta'tore, 'trice** *ag* enchanting, bewitching // *sm/f* enchanter/enchantress; **incan'tesimo** *sm* spell, charm; **incan'tevole** *ag* charming, enchanting.

in'canto *sm* spell, charm, enchantment; *(asta)* auction; **come per ∼** as if by magic; **mettere all'∼** to put up for auction.

incanu'tire *vi (2)* to go white.

inca'pace [inka'patʃe] *ag* incapable; **incapacità** *sf* inability; *(DIR)* incapacity.

incapo'nirsi *vr* to be stubborn, be determined.

incap'pare *vi (2):* **∼ in qc/qd** *(anche fig)* to run into sth/sb.

incapricci'arsi [inkaprit'tʃarsi] *vr:* **∼ di** to take a fancy to *o* for.

incapsu'lare *vt (dente)* to crown.

incarce'rare [inkartʃe'rare] *vt* to imprison.

incari'care *vt:* **∼ qd di fare** to give sb the responsibility of doing; **∼rsi di** to take care *o* charge of; **incari'cato, a** *ag:* **incaricato (di)** in charge (of), responsible (for) // *sm/f* delegate, representative; **incaricato d'affari** *(POL)* chargé d'affaires.

in'carico, chi *sm* task, job.

incar'nare *vt* to embody; **∼rsi** *vr* to be embodied; *(REL)* to become incarnate; **incarnazi'one** *sf* incarnation.

incarta'mento *sm* dossier, file.

incar'tare *vt* to wrap (in paper).

incas'sare *vt (merce)* to pack (in cases); *(gemma: incastonare)* to set; *(ECON: riscuotere)* to collect; *(PUGILATO: colpi)* to take, stand up to; **in'casso** *sm* cashing, encashment; *(introito)* takings *pl.*

incasto'nare *vt* to set; **incastona'tura** *sf* setting.

incas'trare *vt* to fit in, insert; **∼rsi** *vr* to stick; **in'castro** *sm* slot, groove.

incate'nare *vt* to chain up; *(fig)* to tie.

incatra'mare *vt* to tar.

in'cauto, a *ag* imprudent, rash.

inca'vare *vt* to hollow out; **inca'vato, a** *ag* hollow; *(occhi)* sunken; **incava'tura** *sf* hollow; **in'cavo** *sm* hollow; *(solco)* groove.

incendi'are [intʃen'djare] *vt* to set fire to; **∼rsi** *vr* to catch fire, burst into flames.

incendi'ario, a [intʃen'djarjo] *ag* incendiary // *sm/f* arsonist.

in'cendio [in'tʃendjo] *sm* fire.

incene'rire [intʃene'rire] *vt* to burn to ashes, incinerate; *(cadavere)* to cremate; **∼rsi** *vr* to be burnt to ashes.

in'censo [in'tʃenso] *sm* incense.

incensu'rato, a [intʃensu'rato] *ag (DIR)*: **essere ∼** to have a clean record.

incen'tivo [intʃen'tivo] *sm* incentive.

incep'pare [intʃep'pare] *vt* to obstruct, hamper; **∼rsi** *vr* to jam.

ince'rata [intʃe'rata] *sf (tela)* tarpaulin; *(impermeabile)* oilskins *pl.*

incer'tezza [intʃer'tettsa] *sf* uncertainty.

in'certo, a [in'tʃerto] *ag* uncertain; *(irresoluto)* undecided, hesitating // *sm* uncertainty.

inces'sante [intʃes'sante] *ag* incessant.

in'cesto [in'tʃesto] *sm* incest.

in'cetta [in'tʃetta] *sf* buying up; **fare ∼ di qc** to buy up sth.

inchi'esta [in'kjɛsta] *sf* investigation, inquiry.

inchi'nare [inki'nare] *vt* to bow; **∼rsi** *vr* to bend down; *(per riverenza)* to bow; *(: donna)* to curtsy; **in'chino** *sm* bow; curtsy.

inchio'dare [inkjo'dare] *vt* to nail; *(chiudere con chiodi)* to nail down *(o up).*

inchi'ostro [in'kjɔstro] *sm* ink; **∼ simpatico** invisible ink.

inciam'pare [intʃam'pare] *vi* to trip, stumble.

inci'ampo [in'tʃampo] *sm* obstacle; **essere d'∼ a qd** *(fig)* to be in sb's way.

inciden'tale [intʃiden'tale] *ag* incidental.

inci'dente [intʃi'dɛnte] *sm* accident; **∼ d'auto** car accident.

inci'denza [intʃi'dɛntsa] *sf* incidence.

in'cidere [in'tʃidere] *vi:* **∼ su** to bear upon, affect // *vt (tagliare incavando)* to cut into; *(ARTE)* to engrave; to etch; *(canzone)* to record.

in'cinta [in'tʃinta] *ag f* pregnant.

incipi'ente [intʃi'pjɛnte] *ag* incipient.

incipri'are [intʃi'prjare] *vt* to powder.

in'circa [in'tʃirka] *av:* **all'∼** more or less, very nearly.

incisi'one [intʃi'zjone] *sf* cut; *(disegno)* engraving; etching; *(registrazione)* recording; *(MED)* incision.

inci'sivo, a [intʃi'zivo] *ag* incisive.

in'ciso [in'tʃizo] *sm:* **per ∼** incidentally, by the way.

inci'tare [intʃi'tare] *vt* to incite.

inci'vile [intʃi'vile] *ag* uncivilized; *(villano)* impolite.

incivi'lire [intʃivi'lire] *vt* to civilize.

incl. *(abbr di incluso)* encl.

incli'nare *vt* to tilt // *vi (fig):* **∼ a qc/a fare** to incline towards sth/doing; to tend towards sth/to do; **inclinato, a** *ag (anche fig)* inclined; **inclinazi'one** *sf (fig)* inclination, tendency; **in'cline** *ag:* **incline a** inclined to.

in'cludere *vt* to include; *(accludere)* to enclose; **inclusi'one** *sf* inclusion; **inclu'sivo, a** *ag:* **inclusivo di** inclusive of; **in'cluso, a** *pp di* **includere** // *ag* included; enclosed.

incoe'rente *ag* incoherent; *(contraddittorio)* inconsistent; **incoe'renza** *sf* incoherence; inconsistency.

in'cognito, a [in'kɔnnito] *ag* unknown // *sm:* **in ∼** incognito // *sf (MAT, fig)* unknown quantity.

incol'lare *vt* to glue, gum; *(unire con colla)* to stick together.

incolon'nare *vt* to draw up in columns.

inco'lore *ag* colourless.

incol'pare *vt:* **∼ qd di** to charge sb with.

in'colto, a *ag (terreno)* uncultivated;

(*trascurato: capelli*) neglected; (*persona*) uneducated.

in'colume *ag* safe and sound, unhurt.

in'combere *vi* (*sovrastare minacciando*): ~ **su** to threaten, hang over; (*spettare*) ~ **a** to rest *o* be incumbent upon.

incominci'are [inkomin'tʃare] *vi* (*2*), *vt* to begin, start.

in'comodo, a uncomfortable; (*inopportuno*) inconvenient // *sm* inconvenience, bother.

incompa'rabile *ag* incomparable.

incompa'tibile *ag* (*non ammissibile: negligenza*) intolerable; (*inconciliabile*) incompatible.

incompe'tente *ag* incompetent; **incompe'tenza** *sf* incompetence.

incompi'uto, a *ag* unfinished, incomplete.

incom'pleto, a *ag* incomplete.

incompren'sibile *ag* incomprehensible.

incomprensi'one *sf* incomprehension.

incom'preso, a *ag* not understood; misunderstood.

inconce'pibile [inkontʃe'pibile] *ag* inconceivable.

inconcili'abile [inkontʃi'ljabile] *ag* irreconcilable.

inconclu'dente *ag* inconclusive; (*persona*) ineffectual.

incondizio'nato, a [inkondittsjo'nato] *ag* unconditional.

inconfu'tabile *ag* irrefutable.

incongru'ente *ag* inconsistent.

in'congruo, a *ag* incongruous.

inconsa'pevole *ag*: ~ **di** unaware of, ignorant of.

in'conscio, a, sci, sce [in'kɔnʃo] *ag* unconscious // *sm* (*PSIC*): **l'**~ the unconscious.

inconsis'tente *ag* insubstantial; unfounded.

inconso'labile *ag* inconsolable.

inconsu'eto, a *ag* unusual.

incon'sulto, a *ag* rash.

inconti'nenza [inkonti'nɛntsa] *sf* incontinence.

incon'trare *vt* to meet; (*difficoltà*) to meet with; ~**rsi** *vr* to meet.

incontras'tabile *ag* incontrovertible, indisputable.

in'contro *av*: ~ **a** (*verso*) towards // *sm* meeting; (*SPORT*) match; meeting; ~ **di calcio** football match.

inconveni'ente *sm* drawback, snag.

incoraggia'mento [inkoraddʒa'mento] *sm* encouragement.

incoraggi'are [inkorad'dʒare] *vt* to encourage.

incornici'are [inkorni'tʃare] *vt* to frame.

incoro'nare *vt* to crown; **incoronazi'one** *sf* coronation.

incorpo'rare *vt* to incorporate; (*fig: annettere*) to annex.

incorreg'gibile [inkorred'dʒibile] *ag* incorrigible.

in'correre *vi* (*2*): ~ **in** to meet with, run into.

incorrut'tibile *ag* incorruptible.

incosci'ente [inkoʃ'ʃɛnte] *ag* (*inconscio*) unconscious; (*irresponsabile*) reckless, thoughtless; **incosci'enza** *sf* unconsciousness; recklessness, thoughtlessness.

incre'dibile *ag* incredible, unbelievable.

in'credulo, a *ag* incredulous, disbelieving.

incremen'tare *vt* to increase; (*dar sviluppo a*) to promote.

incre'mento *sm* (*sviluppo*) development; (*aumento numerico*) increase, growth.

incres'parsi *vr* (*acqua*) to ripple; (*capelli*) to go frizzy; (*pelle, tessuto*) to wrinkle.

incrimi'nare *vt* (*DIR*) to charge.

incri'nare *vt*, ~**rsi** *vr* to crack; **incrina'tura** *sf* crack.

incroci'are [inkro'tʃare] *vt* to cross; (*incontrare*) to meet // *vi* (*NAUT, AER*) to cruise; ~**rsi** *vr* (*strade*) to cross, intersect; (*persone, veicoli*) to pass each other; ~ **le braccia/le gambe** to fold one's arms/cross one's legs; **incrocia'tore** *sm* cruiser.

in'crocio [in'krotʃo] *sm* (*anche FERR*) crossing; (*di strade*) crossroads.

incros'tare *vt* to encrust.

incuba'trice [inkuba'tritʃe] *sf* incubator.

incubazi'one [inkubat'tsjone] *sf* incubation.

'incubo *sm* nightmare.

in'cudine *sf* anvil.

incul'care *vt*: ~ **qc in** to inculcate sth into, instill sth into.

incune'are *vt* to wedge.

incu'rabile *ag* incurable.

incu'rante *ag*: ~ (**di**) heedless (of), careless (of).

incurio'sire *vt* to make curious; ~**rsi** *vr* to become curious.

incursi'one *sf* raid.

incur'vare *vt*, ~**rsi** *vr* to bend, curve.

in'cusso, a *pp di* **incutere**.

incus'todito, a *ag* unguarded, unattended.

in'cutere *vt* to arouse; ~ **timore/rispetto a qd** to strike fear into sb/command sb's respect.

'indaco *sm* indigo.

indaffa'rato, a *ag* busy.

inda'gare *vt* to investigate.

in'dagine [in'dadʒine] *sf* investigation, inquiry; (*ricerca*) research, study.

indebi'tare *vt* to get into debt; ~**rsi** *vr* to run *o* get into debt.

in'debito, a *ag* undue; undeserved.

indebo'lire *vt*, *vi* (*2*) (*anche:* ~**rsi**) to weaken.

inde'cente [inde'tʃɛnte] *ag* indecent; **inde'cenza** *sf* indecency.

indeci'frabile [indetʃi'frabile] *ag* indecipherable.

indecisi'one [indetʃi'zjone] *sf* indecisiveness; indecision.

inde'ciso, a [inde'tʃizo] *ag* indecisive; (*irresoluto*) undecided.

inde'fesso, a *ag* untiring, indefatigable.

indefi'nibile *ag* indefinable.

indefi'nito, a ag (anche LING) indefinite; (impreciso, non determinato) undefined.

in'degno, a [in'deɲɲo] ag unworthy.

inde'lebile ag indelible.

indelica'tezza [indelika'tettsa] sf tactlessness.

indemoni'ato, a ag possessed (by the devil).

in'denne ag unhurt, uninjured; **indennità** sf inv (rimborso: di spese) allowance; (: di perdita) compensation, indemnity; **indennità di contingenza** cost-of-living allowance; **indennità di trasferta** travel expenses pl.

indenniz'zare [indennid'dzare] vt to compensate; **inden'nizzo** sm (somma) compensation, indemnity.

indero'gabile ag binding.

indeside'rabile ag undesirable.

indetermi'nato, a ag indefinite, indeterminate.

'India sf: **l'** ~ India; **indi'ano, a** ag Indian // sm/f (d'India) Indian; (d'America) Red Indian.

indiavo'lato, a ag possessed (by the devil); (vivace, violento) wild.

indi'care vt (mostrare) to show, indicate; (: col dito) to point to, point out; (consigliare) to suggest, recommend; **indica'tivo, a** ag indicative (/ sm (LING) indicative (mood); **indica'tore** sm (elenco) guide; directory; (TECN) gauge; indicator; **indicazi'one** sf indication; (notizia) information q; **indicazioni per l'uso** instructions for use.

'indice ['inditʃe] sm (ANAT: dito) index finger, forefinger; (lancetta) needle, pointer; (fig: indizio) sign; (TECN, MAT, nei libri) index.

indi'cibile [indi'tʃibile] ag inexpressible.

indietreggi'are [indietred'dʒare] vi to draw back, retreat.

indi'etro av back; (guardare) behind, back; (andare, cadere: anche: **all'** ~) backwards; **rimanere** ~ to be left behind; **essere** ~ (col lavoro) to be behind; (orologio) to be slow; **rimandare qc** ~ to send sth back.

indiffe'rente ag indifferent; **indiffe-'renza** sf indifference.

in'digeno, a [in'didʒeno] ag indigenous, native // sm/f native.

indi'gente [indi'dʒɛnte] ag poverty-stricken, destitute; **indi'genza** sf extreme poverty.

indigesti'one [indidʒes'tjone] sf indigestion.

indi'gesto, a [indi'dʒɛsto] ag indigestible.

indi'gnare [indiɲ'nare] vt to fill with indignation; ~**rsi** vr to be (o get) indignant; **indignazi'one** sf indignation.

indimenti'cabile ag unforgettable.

indipen'dente ag independent; **indipen-'denza** sf independence.

indi'retto, a ag indirect.

indiriz'zare [indirit'tsare] vt (dirigere) to direct; (mandare) to send; (lettera) to address; ~ **la parola a qd** to address sb.

indi'rizzo [indi'rittso] sm address; (direzione) direction; (avvio) trend, course.

indisci'plina [indiʃʃi'plina] sf indiscipline.

indis'creto, a ag indiscreet; **indiscre-zi'one** sf indiscretion.

indis'cusso, a ag unquestioned.

indispen'sabile ag indispensable, essential.

indispet'tire vt to irritate, annoy // vi (2) (anche: ~**rsi**) to get irritated o annoyed.

indis'posto, a pp di **indisporre** // ag indisposed, unwell.

indisso'lubile ag indissoluble.

indis'tinto, a ag indistinct.

indistrut'tibile ag indestructible.

in'divia sf endive.

individu'ale ag individual; **individualità** sf individuality.

individu'are vt (dar forma distinta a) to characterize; (determinare) to locate; (riconoscere) to single out.

indi'viduo sm individual.

indi'viso, a ag undivided.

indizi'are [indit'tsjare] vt: ~ **qd di qc** to cast suspicion on sb for sth; **indizi'ato, a** ag suspected // sm/f suspect.

in'dizio [in'dittsjo] sm (segno) sign, indication; (POLIZIA) clue; (DIR) piece of evidence.

'indole sf nature, character.

indo'lente ag indolent; **indo'lenza** sf indolence.

indolen'zito, a [indolen'tsito] ag stiff, aching; (intorpidito) numb.

indo'lore ag painless.

indo'mani sm: **l'** ~ the next day, the following day.

Indo'nesia sf: **l'** ~ Indonesia.

indos'sare vt (mettere indosso) to put on; (avere indosso) to have on; **indossa'tore, 'trice** sm/f model.

in'dotto, a pp di **indurre**.

indottri'nare vt to indoctrinate.

indovi'nare vt (scoprire) to guess; (immaginare) to imagine, guess; (il futuro) to foretell; **indovi'nato, a** ag successful; (scelta) inspired; **indovi'nello** sm riddle; **indo'vino, a** sm/f fortuneteller.

indubbia'mente av undoubtedly.

in'dubbio, a ag certain, undoubted.

indugi'are [indu'dʒare] vi to take one's time, delay; ~**rsi** vr (soffermarsi) to linger.

in'dugio [in'dudʒo] sm (ritardo) delay; **senza** ~ without delay.

indul'gente [indul'dʒɛnte] ag indulgent; (giudice) lenient; **indul'genza** sf indulgence; leniency.

in'dulgere [in'duldʒere] vi: ~ **a** (accondiscendere) to comply with; (abbandonarsi) to indulge in; **in'dulto, a** pp di **indulgere** // sm (DIR) pardon.

indu'mento sm article of clothing, garment; ~**i** smpl clothes.

indu'rire vt to harden // vi (2) (anche: ~**rsi**) to harden, become hard.

in'durre vt to induce, persuade, lead; ~ qd in errore to mislead sb.

in'dustria sf industry; **industri'ale** ag industrial // sm industrialist.

industrializ'zare [industrialid'dzare] vt to industrialize; **industrializzazi'one** sf industrialization.

industri'arsi vr to do one's best, try hard.

industri'oso, a ag industrious, hard-working.

induzi'one [indut'tsjone] sf induction.

inebe'tito, a ag dazed, stunned.

inebri'are vt (anche fig) to intoxicate; ~rsi vr to become intoxicated.

inecce'pibile [inettʃe'pibile] ag unexceptionable.

i'nedia sf starvation.

i'nedito, a ag unpublished.

ineffi'cace [ineffi'katʃe] ag ineffective.

ineffici'ente [ineffi'tʃɛnte] ag inefficient.

inegu'ale ag unequal; (irregolare) uneven.

ine'rente ag: ~ a concerning, regarding.

i'nerme ag unarmed; defenceless.

inerpi'carsi vr: ~ (su) to clamber (up).

i'nerte ag inert; (inattivo) indolent, sluggish; **i'nerzia** sf inertia; indolence, sluggishness.

ine'satto, a ag (impreciso) inexact; (erroneo) incorrect; (AMM: non riscosso) uncollected.

inesau'ribile ag inexhaustible.

inesis'tente ag non-existent.

ineso'rabile ag inexorable, relentless.

inesperi'enza [inespe'rjɛntsa] sf inexperience.

ines'perto, a ag inexperienced.

inespli'cabile ag inexplicable.

inesti'mabile ag inestimable.

i'netto, a ag (incapace) inept; (che non ha attitudine): ~ (a) unsuited (to).

inevi'tabile ag inevitable.

i'nezia [i'nɛttsja] sf trifle, thing of no importance.

infagot'tare vt to bundle up, wrap up; ~rsi vr to wrap up.

infal'libile ag infallible.

infa'mare vt to defame; **infama'torio, a** ag defamatory.

in'fame ag infamous; (fig: cosa, compito) awful, dreadful; **in'famia** sf infamy.

infan'tile ag child cpd; childlike; (adulto, azione) childish; **letteratura** ~ children's books pl.

in'fanzia [in'fantsja] sf childhood; (bambini) children pl; **prima** ~ babyhood, infancy.

infari'nare vt to cover with (o sprinkle with o dip in) flour; ~ **di zucchero** to sprinkle with sugar; **infarina'tura** sf (fig) smattering.

in'farto sm (MED): ~ (**cardiaco**) coronary.

infasti'dire vt to annoy, irritate; ~rsi vr to get annoyed o irritated.

infati'cabile ag tireless, untiring.

in'fatti cong as a matter of fact, in fact, actually.

infatu'arsi vr: ~ **di** o **per** to become infatuated with, fall for; **infatuazi'one** sf infatuation.

in'fausto, a ag unpropitious, unfavourable.

infe'condo, a ag infertile.

infe'dele ag unfaithful; **infedeltà** sf infidelity.

infe'lice [infe'litʃe] ag unhappy; (sfortunato) unlucky, unfortunate; (inopportuno) inopportune, ill-timed; (mal riuscito: lavoro) bad, poor; **infelicità** sf unhappiness.

inferi'ore ag lower; (per intelligenza, qualità) inferior // sm/f inferior; ~ a (numero, quantità) less o smaller than; (meno buono) inferior to; ~ **alla media** below average; **inferiorità** sf inferiority.

inferme'ria sf sick bay.

infermi'ere, a sm/f nurse.

infermità sf inv illness; infirmity.

in'fermo, a ag (ammalato) ill; (debole) infirm; ~ **di mente** mentally ill.

infer'nale ag infernal; (proposito, complotto) diabolical.

in'ferno sm hell.

inferri'ata sf grating.

infervo'rare vt to arouse enthusiasm in; ~rsi vr to get excited, get carried away.

infes'tare vt to infest.

infet'tare vt to infect; ~rsi vr to become infected; **infet'tivo, a** ag infectious; **in'fetto, a** ag infected; (acque) polluted, contaminated; **infezi'one** sf infection.

infiac'chire [infjak'kire] vt to weaken // vi (2) (anche: ~rsi) to grow weak.

infiam'mabile ag inflammable.

infiam'mare vt to set alight; (fig, MED) to inflame; ~rsi vr to catch fire; (MED) to become inflamed; (fig): ~rsi **di** to be fired with; **infiammazi'one** sf (MED) inflammation.

infias'care vt to bottle.

in'fido, a ag unreliable, treacherous.

in'figgere [in'fiddʒere] vt: ~ **qc in** to thrust o drive sth into; ~rsi **in** to penetrate, sink deeply into.

infi'lare vt (ago) to thread; (mettere: chiave) to insert; (: anello, vestito) to slip o put on; ~rsi vr: ~rsi **in/per** to slip into/through; ~ **l'uscio** to slip in; to slip out.

infil'trarsi vr to penetrate, seep through; (MIL) to infiltrate; **infiltrazi'one** sf infiltration.

infil'zare [infil'tsare] vt (infilare) to string together; (trafiggere) to pierce.

'infimo, a ag lowest.

in'fine av finally; (insomma) in short.

infinità sf infinity; (in quantità): **un'**~ **di** an infinite number of.

infi'nito, a ag infinite; (LING) infinitive // sm infinity; (LING) infinitive; **all'**~ (senza fine) endlessly.

infinocchi'are [infinok'kjare] vt (fam) to hoodwink.

infischi'arsi [infis'kjarsi] *vr*: ~ **di** not to care about.

in'fisso, a *pp di* **infiggere** // *sm* fixture; (*di porta, finestra*) frame.

infit'tire *vt, vi* (2) (*anche*: ~**rsi**) to thicken.

inflazi'one [inflat'tsjone] *sf* inflation.

infles'sibile *ag* inflexible; (*ferreo*) unyielding.

inflessi'one *sf* inflexion.

in'fliggere [in'fliddʒere] *vt* to inflict; **in-'flitto, a** *pp di* **infliggere**.

influ'ente *ag* influential; **influ'enza** *sf* influence; (*MED*) influenza, flu.

influ'ire *vi*: ~ **su** to influence.

in'flusso *sm* influence.

infol'tire *vt, vi* (2) to thicken.

infon'dato, a *ag* unfounded, groundless.

in'fondere *vt*: ~ **qc in qd** to instill sth in sb.

infor'care *vt* to fork (up); (*bicicletta, cavallo*) to get on; (*occhiali*) to put on.

infor'mare *vt* to inform, tell; ~**rsi** *vr*: ~**rsi (di)** to inquire (about); **infor-'matica** *sf* computer science; **informa-'tivo, a** *ag* informative; **informa'tore** *sm* informer; **informazi'one** *sf* piece of information; **informazioni** *sfpl* information *sg*.

in'forme *ag* shapeless.

infor'tunio *sm* accident; ~ **sul lavoro** industrial accident, accident at work.

infos'sarsi *vr* (*avvallarsi*) to sink; (*incavarsi*) to become hollow; **infos'sato, a** *ag* hollow; (*occhi*) deep-set; (: *per malattia*) sunken.

in'frangere [in'frandʒere] *vt* to smash; (*fig: patti*) to break; ~**rsi** *vr* to smash, break; **infran'gibile** *ag* unbreakable; **in-'franto, a** *pp di* **infrangere** // *ag* broken.

infra'rosso, a *ag, sm* infrared.

infrastrut'tura *sf* infrastructure.

infrazi'one [infrat'tsjone] *sf*: ~ **a** breaking of, violation of.

infredda'tura *sf* slight cold.

infred'dolito, a *ag* cold, chilled.

infre'quente *ag* infrequent, rare.

infruttu'oso, a *ag* fruitless.

infu'ori *av* out; **all'**~ outwards; **all'**~ **di** (*eccetto*) except, with the exception of.

infuri'are *vi* to rage; ~**rsi** *vr* to fly into a rage.

infusi'one *sf* infusion.

in'fuso, a *pp di* **infondere** // *sm* infusion; ~ **di camomilla** camomile tea.

Ing. *abbr di* **ingegnere**.

ingabbi'are *vt* to cage; **ingabbia'tura** *sf* (*EDIL*) supporting frame.

ingaggi'are [ingad'dʒare] *vt* (*assumere con compenso*) to take on, hire; (*SPORT*) to sign on; (*MIL*) to engage; **in'gaggio** *sm* hiring; signing on.

ingan'nare *vt* to deceive; (*coniuge*) to be unfaithful to; (*fisco*) to cheat; (*eludere*) to dodge, elude; (*fig: tempo*) to while away // *vi* (*apparenza*) to be deceptive; ~**rsi** *vr* to

be mistaken, be wrong; **ingan'nevole** *ag* deceptive.

in'ganno *sm* deceit, deception; (*azione*) trick; (*menzogna, frode*) cheat, swindle; (*illusione*) illusion.

ingarbugli'are [ingarbuʎ'ʎare] *vt* to tangle; (*fig*) to confuse, muddle; ~**rsi** *vr* to become confused o muddled.

inge'gnarsi [indʒeɲ'narsi] *vr* to do one's best, try hard; ~ **per vivere** to live by one's wits.

inge'gnere [indʒeɲ'ɲere] *sm* engineer; ~ **civile/navale** civil/naval engineer; **ingegne'ria** *sf* engineering.

in'gegno [in'dʒeɲɲo] *sm* (*intelligenza*) intelligence, brains *pl*; (*capacità creativa*) ingenuity; (*disposizione*) talent; **inge-'gnoso, a** *ag* ingenious, clever.

ingelo'sire [indʒelo'zire] *vt* to make jealous // *vi* (2) (*anche*: ~**rsi**) to become jealous.

in'gente [in'dʒente] *ag* huge, enormous.

ingenuità [indʒenui'ta] *sf* ingenuousness.

in'genuo, a [in'dʒɛnuo] *ag* ingenuous, naïve.

inge'rirsi [indʒe'rirsi] *vr* to interfere, meddle.

inges'sare [indʒes'sare] *vt* (*MED*) to put in plaster; **ingessa'tura** *sf* plaster.

Inghil'terra [ingil'tɛrra] *sf*: l'~ England.

inghiot'tire [ingjot'tire] *vt* to swallow.

ingial'lire [indʒal'lire] *vi* (2) to go yellow.

ingigan'tire [indʒigan'tire] *vt* to enlarge, magnify // *vi* (2) to become gigantic o enormous.

inginocchi'arsi [indʒinok'kjarsi] *vr* to kneel (down).

ingiù [in'dʒu] *av* down, downwards.

ingi'uria [in'dʒurja] *sf* insult; (*fig: danno*) damage; **ingiuri'are** *vt* to insult, abuse; **ingiuri'oso, a** *ag* insulting, abusive.

ingius'tizia [indʒus'tittsja] *sf* injustice.

ingi'usto, a [in'dʒusto] *ag* unjust, unfair.

in'glese *ag* English // *sm/f* Englishman/woman // *sm* (*LING*) English; **gli I~i** the English; **andarsene o filare all'**~ to take French leave.

ingoi'are *vt* to gulp (down); (*fig*) to swallow (up).

ingol'fare *vt*, ~**rsi** *vr* (*motore*) to flood.

ingom'brare *vt* (*strada*) to block; (*stanza*) to clutter up; **in'gombro** *sm* obstacle; (*di macchina*) **lunghezza/larghezza/al-tezza d'ingombro** maximum length/width/height.

in'gordo, a *ag*: ~ **di** greedy for; (*fig*) greedy o eager for.

ingor'garsi *vr* to be blocked up, be choked up.

in'gorgo, ghi *sm* blockage, obstruction; ~ **di traffico** traffic jam.

ingoz'zare [ingot'tsare] *vt* (*inghiottire*) to gulp down, gobble; (*costringere a mangiare: animali*) to fatten.

ingra'naggio [ingra'naddʒo] *sm* gear; (*fig*) mechanism; ~**i** *smpl* gears, gearing *sg*.

ingra'nare *vi* to mesh, engage // *vt* to

engage; **~ la marcia** to get into gear.

ingrandi'mento *sm* enlargement; extension.

ingran'dire *vt* (*anche* FOT) to enlarge; (*estendere*) to extend; (OTTICA, *fig*) to magnify // *vi* (2) (*anche:* ~**rsi**) to become larger *o* bigger; (*aumentare*) to grow, increase; (*espandersi*) to expand.

ingras'sare *vt* to make fat; (*animali*) to fatten; (AGR: *terreno*) to manure; (*lubrificare*) to oil, lubricate // *vi* (2) (*anche:* ~**rsi**) to get fat, put on weight; **in'grasso** *sm* (*di animali*) fattening; (*di terreno*) manuring *q*; manure.

ingrati'tudine *sf* ingratitude.

in'grato, a *ag* ungrateful; (*lavoro*) thankless, unrewarding.

ingrazi'are [ingrat'tsjare] *vt:* ~**rsi qd** to ingratiate o.s. with sb.

ingredi'ente *sm* ingredient.

in'gresso *sm* (*porta*) entrance; (*atrio*) hall; (*l'entrare*) entrance, entry; (*facoltà di entrare*) admission; **"~ libero"** "admission free".

ingros'sare *vt* to increase; (*folla, livello*) to swell // *vi* (2) (*anche:* ~**rsi**) to increase; to swell.

in'grosso *av:* **all'~** (COMM) wholesale; (*all'incirca*) roughly, about.

ingual'cibile [ingwal'tʃibile] *ag* crease-resistant.

ingua'ribile *ag* incurable.

'inguine *sm* (ANAT) groin.

ini'bire *vt* to forbid, prohibit; (PSIC) to inhibit; **inibizi'one** *sf* prohibition; inhibition.

iniet'tare *vt* to inject; ~**rsi di sangue** (*occhi*) to become bloodshot; **iniezi'one** *sf* injection.

inimi'carsi *vr:* ~ **con qd** to fall out with sb.

inimi'cizia [inimi'tʃittsja] *sf* animosity.

ininter'rotto, a *ag* unbroken; uninterrupted.

iniquità *sf inv* iniquity; (*atto*) wicked action.

i'niquo, a *ag* iniquitous.

inizi'ale [init'tsjale] *ag, sf* initial.

inizi'are [init'tsjare] *vi* (2), *vt* to begin, start; ~ **qd a** to initiate sb into; (*pittura etc*) to introduce sb to.

inizia'tiva [inittsja'tiva] *sf* initiative; ~ **privata** private enterprise.

i'nizio [i'nittsjo] *sm* beginning; **all'~** at the beginning, at the start; **dare ~ a qc** to start sth, get sth going.

innaffi'are *etc* = **annaffiare** *etc*.

innal'zare [innal'tsare] *vt* (*sollevare, alzare*) to raise; (*rizzare*) to erect; ~**rsi** *vr* to rise.

innamo'rare *vt* to enchant, charm; ~**rsi** *vr:* ~**rsi (di qd)** to fall in love (with sb); **innamo'rato, a** *ag* (*che nutre amore*): **innamorato (di)** in love (with); (*appassionato*): **innamorato di** very fond of.

in'nanzi [in'nantsi] *av* (*stato in luogo*) in front, ahead; (*moto a luogo*) forward, on;

(*tempo: prima*) before // *prep* (*prima*) before; ~ **a** in front of; **d'ora ~** from now on.

in'nato, a *ag* innate.

innatu'rale *ag* unnatural.

inne'gabile *ag* undeniable.

innervo'sire *vt:* ~ **qd** to get on sb's nerves; ~**rsi** *vr* to get irritated *o* upset.

innes'care *vt* to prime; **in'nesco, schi** *sm* primer.

innes'tare *vt* (BOT, MED) to graft; (TECN) to engage; (*inserire: presa*) to insert; **in'nesto** *sm* graft; grafting *q*; (TECN) clutch; (ELETTR) connection.

'inno *sm* hymn; ~ **nazionale** national anthem.

inno'cente [inno'tʃɛnte] *ag* innocent; **inno'cenza** *sf* innocence.

in'nocuo, a *ag* innocuous, harmless.

inno'vare *vt* to change, make innovations in; **innovazi'one** *sf* innovation.

innume'revole *ag* innumerable.

inocu'lare *vt* (MED) to inoculate.

ino'doro, a *ag* odourless.

inol'trare *vt* to pass on, forward; ~**rsi** *vr* (*addentrarsi*) to advance, go forward.

i'noltre *av* besides, moreover.

inon'dare *vt* to flood; **inondazi'one** *sf* flooding *q*; flood.

inope'roso, a *ag* inactive, idle.

inoppor'tuno, a *ag* untimely, ill-timed; inappropriate; (*momento*) inopportune.

inor'ganico, a, ci, che *ag* inorganic.

inorgo'glire [inorgoʎ'ʎire] *vt* to make proud // *vi* (2) (*anche:* ~**rsi**) to become proud; ~**rsi di qc** to pride o.s. on sth.

inorri'dire *vt* to horrify // *vi* (2) to be horrified.

inospi'tale *ag* inhospitable.

inosser'vato, a *ag* (*non notato*) unobserved; (*non rispettato*) not observed, not kept.

inossi'dabile *ag* stainless.

inqua'drare *vt* (*foto, immagine*) to frame; (*fig*) to situate, set.

inquie'tare *vt* (*turbare*) to disturb, worry; ~**rsi** *vr* to worry, become anxious; (*impazientirsi*) to get upset.

inqui'eto, a *ag* restless; (*preoccupato*) worried, anxious; **inquie'tudine** *sf* anxiety, worry.

inqui'lino, a *sm/f* tenant.

inquina'mento *sm* pollution.

inqui'nare *vt* to pollute.

inqui'sire *vt, vi* to investigate; **inquisi-'tore, 'trice** *ag* (*sguardo*) inquiring; (DIR) investigating; **inquisizi'one** *sf* (STORIA) inquisition.

insa'lata *sf* salad; **insalati'era** *sf* salad bowl.

insa'lubre *ag* unhealthy.

insa'nabile *ag* incurable; unhealable.

insangui'nare *vt* to stain with blood.

in'sania *sf* insanity.

insa'puta *sf:* **all'~ di qd** without sb knowing.

insazi'abile [insat'tsjabile] *ag* insatiable.
insce'nare [inʃe'nare] *vt* (*TEATRO*) to stage, put on; (*fig*) to stage.
in'segna [in'seɲɲa] *sf* sign; (*emblema*) sign, emblem; (*bandiera*) flag, banner; ~ **e** *sfpl* (*decorazioni*) insignia *pl*.
insegna'mento [inseɲɲa'mento] *sm* teaching.
inse'gnante [insen'ɲante] *ag* teaching // *sm/f* teacher.
inse'gnare [insen'ɲare] *vt*, *vi* to teach; ~ **a qd qc** to teach sb sth; ~ **qd a fare qc** to teach sb how to do sth.
insegui'mento *sm* pursuit, chase.
insegui're *vt* to pursue, chase; **insegui'tore, 'trice** *sm/f* pursuer.
inselvati'chire [inselvati'kire] *vi* (2) (*anche*: ~**rsi**) to grow wild.
insena'tura *sf* inlet, creek.
insen'sato, a *ag* senseless, stupid.
insen'sibile *ag* (*nervo*) insensible; (*movimento*) imperceptible; (*persona*) indifferent.
insepa'rabile *ag* inseparable.
inse'rire *vt* to insert; (*ELETTR*) to connect; ~**rsi** *vr* (*fig*): ~**rsi in** to become part of; **in'serto** *sm* (*pubblicazione*) insert.
inservi'ente *sm/f* attendant.
inserzi'one [inser'tsjone] *sf* insertion; (*avviso*) advertisement; **fare un'**~ (*sul giornale*) to put an advertisement in the paper.
insetti'cida, i [insetti'tʃida] *sm* insecticide.
in'setto *sm* insect.
in'sidia *sf* snare, trap; (*pericolo*) hidden danger; **insidi'are** *vt*, *vi*: **insidiare a** to lay a trap for; **insidi'oso, a** *ag* insidious.
insi'eme *av* together // *prep*: ~ **a** *o* **con** together with // *sm* whole; (*MAT, servizio, assortimento*) set; (*MODA*) ensemble, outfit; **tutti** ~ all together; **tutto** ~ at once go; (*in una volta*) at one go; **nell'**~ on the whole; **d'**~ (*veduta etc*) overall.
insignifi'cante [insiɲɲifi'kante] *ag* insignificant.
insi'gnire [insiɲ'ɲire] *vt* to decorate.
insin'cero, a [insin'tʃero] *ag* insincere.
insinda'cabile *ag* unquestionable.
insinu'are *vt* (*introdurre*): ~ **qc in** to slip *o* slide sth into; (*fig*) to insinuate, imply; ~**rsi** *vr*: ~**rsi in** to seep into; (*fig*) to creep into; to worm one's way into; **insinuazi'one** *sf* (*fig*) insinuation.
in'sipido, a *ag* insipid.
insis'tente *ag* insistent; persistent; **insis'tenza** *sf* insistence; persistence.
in'sistere *vi*: ~ **su qc** to insist on sth; ~ **in qc/a fare** (*perseverare*) to persist in sth/in doing; **insis'tito, a** *pp di* **insistere**.
insoddis'fatto, a *ag* dissatisfied.
insoffe'rente *ag* intolerant.
insolazi'one [insolat'tsjone] *sf* insolation; (*MED*) sunstroke.
inso'lente *ag* insolent; **insolen'tire** *vi* (2) to grow insolent // *vt* to insult, be rude to; **inso'lenza** *sf* insolence.

in'solito, a *ag* unusual, out of the ordinary.
inso'lubile *ag* insoluble.
inso'luto, a *ag* (*non risolto*) unsolved; (*non pagato*) unpaid, outstanding.
insol'vibile *ag* insolvent.
in'somma *av* (*in breve, in conclusione*) in short; (*dunque*) well // *escl* for heaven's sake!
in'sonne *ag* sleepless; **in'sonnia** *sf* insomnia, sleeplessness.
insonno'lito, a *ag* sleepy, drowsy.
insoppor'tabile *ag* unbearable.
in'sorgere [in'sordʒere] *vi* (2) (*ribellarsi*) to rise up, rebel; (*apparire*) (2) to come up, arise.
in'sorto, a *pp di* **insorgere** // *sm/f* rebel, insurgent.
insospet'tire *vt* to make suspicious // *vi* (2) (*anche*: ~**rsi**) to become suspicious.
inspi'rare *vt* to breathe in, inhale.
in'stabile *ag* (*carico, indole*) unstable; (*tempo*) unsettled; (*equilibrio*) unsteady.
instal'lare *vt* to install; ~**rsi** *vr* (*sistemarsi*): ~**rsi in** to settle in; **installazi'one** *sf* installation.
instan'cabile *ag* untiring, indefatigable.
instau'rare *vt* to introduce, institute; ~**rsi** *vr* to start, begin.
instra'dare *vt* to direct.
insubordinazi'one [insubordinat'tsjone] *sf* insubordination.
insuc'cesso [insut'tʃesso] *sm* failure, flop.
insudici'are [insudi'tʃare] *vt* to dirty; ~**rsi** *vr* to get dirty.
insuffici'ente [insuffi'tʃente] *ag* insufficient; (*compito, allievo*) inadequate; **insuffici'enza** *sf* insufficiency; inadequacy; (*INS*) fail.
insu'lare *ag* insular.
insu'lina *sf* insulin.
in'sulso, a *ag* (*sciocco*) inane, silly; (*persona*) dull, insipid.
insul'tare *vt* to insult, affront.
in'sulto *sm* insult, affront.
insurrezi'one [insurret'tsjone] *sf* revolt, insurrection.
insussis'tente *ag* non-existent.
intac'care *vt* (*fare tacche*) to cut into; (*corrodere*) *o* corrode; (*fig: cominciare ad usare: risparmi*) to break into; (*: ledere*) to damage.
intagli'are [intaʎ'ʎare] *vt* to carve; **in'taglio** *sm* carving.
intan'gibile [intan'dʒibile] *ag* untouchable; inviolable.
in'tanto *av* (*nel frattempo*) meanwhile, in the meantime; (*per cominciare*) just to begin with; ~ **che** *cong* while.
intarsi'are *vt* to inlay; **in'tarsio** *sm* inlaying *q*, marquetry *q*; inlay.
inta'sare *vt* to choke (up), block (up); (*AUT*) to obstruct, block; ~**rsi** *vr* to become choked *o* blocked.
intas'care *vt* to pocket.
in'tatto, a *ag* intact; (*puro*) unsullied.
intavo'lare *vt* to start, enter into.

inte'grale *ag* complete; (MAT): **calcolo ~** integral calculus.

inte'grante *ag*: **parte ~** integral part.

inte'grare *vt* to complete; (MAT) to integrate; **~rsi** *vr* (*persona*) to integrate; **integrazi'one** *sf* integration.

integrità *sf* integrity.

'integro, a *ag* (*intatto, intero*) complete, whole; (*retto*) upright.

intelaia'tura *sf* frame; (*fig*) structure, framework.

intel'letto *sm* intellect; **intellettu'ale** *ag, sm/f* intellectual.

intelli'gente [intelli'dʒɛnte] *ag* intelligent; **intelli'genza** *sf* intelligence; **intelli'gibile** *ag* intelligible.

intem'perie *sfpl* bad weather *sg*.

intempes'tivo, a *ag* untimely.

inten'dente *sm* principal administrator; **inten'denza** *sf*: **intendenza di finanza** finance office; **intendenza generale** (MIL) supplies office.

in'tendere *vt* (*avere intenzione*): **~ fare qc** to intend *o* mean to do sth; (*comprendere*) to understand; (*udire*) to hear; (*significare*) to mean; **~rsi** *vr* (*conoscere*): **~rsi di** to know a lot about, be a connoisseur of; (*accordarsi*) to get on (well); **intendersela con qd** (*avere una relazione amorosa*) to have an affair with sb; **intendi'mento** *sm* (*intelligenza*) understanding; (*proposito*) intention; **intendi'tore, 'trice** *sm/f* connoisseur, expert.

intene'rire *vt* (*fig*) to move (to pity); **~rsi** *vr* (*fig*) to be moved.

intensifi'care *vt*, **~rsi** *vr* to intensify.

intensità *sf* intensity.

inten'sivo, a *ag* intensive.

in'tenso, a *ag* intense.

in'tento, a *ag* (*teso, assorto*): **~ (a)** intent (on), absorbed (in) // *sm* aim, purpose.

intenzio'nale [intentsjo'nale] *ag* intentional.

intenzi'one [inten'tsjone] *sf* intention; (DIR) intent; **avere ~ di fare qc** to intend to do sth, have the intention of doing sth.

interca'lare *sm* pet phrase, stock phrase // *vt* to insert.

inter'cedere [inter'tʃedere] *vi* to intercede; **intercessi'one** *sf* intercession.

intercet'tare [intertʃet'tare] *vt* to intercept; (*telefono*) to tap.

inter'correre *vi* (2) (*esserci*) to exist; (*passare: tempo*) to elapse.

inter'detto, a *pp di* **interdire** // *ag* forbidden, prohibited; (*sconcertato*) dumbfounded // *sm* (REL) interdict.

inter'dire *vt* to forbid, prohibit, ban; (REL) to interdict; (DIR) to deprive of civil rights; **interdizi'one** *sf* prohibition, ban.

interessa'mento *sm* interest.

interes'sante *ag* interesting; **essere in stato ~** to be expecting (a baby).

interes'sare *vt* to interest; (*concernere*) to concern, be of interest to; (*far intervenire*): **~ qd a** to draw sb's attention to // *vi*: **~ a** to interest, matter to; **~rsi** *vr* (*mostrare interesse*): **~rsi a** to take an interest in, be interested in; (*occuparsi*): **~rsi di** to take care of.

inte'resse *sm* (*anche* COMM) interest.

interfe'renza [interfe'rɛntsa] *sf* interference.

interfe'rire *vi* to interfere.

interiezi'one [interjet'tsjone] *sf* exclamation, interjection.

interi'ora *sfpl* entrails.

interi'ore *ag* interior, inner, inside, internal; (*fig*) inner.

inter'ludio *sm* (MUS) interlude.

intermedi'ario, a *ag, sm/f* intermediary.

inter'medio, a *ag* intermediate.

inter'mezzo [inter'mɛddzo] *sm* (*intervallo*) interval; (*breve spettacolo*) intermezzo.

intermi'nabile *ag* interminable, endless.

inter'nare *vt* (*arrestare*) to intern; (MED) to commit (to a mental institution).

internazio'nale [internattsjo'nale] *ag* international.

in'terno, a *ag* (*di dentro*) internal, interior, inner; (: *mare*) inland; (*nazionale*) domestic, home *cpd*, internal; (*allievo*) boarding // *sm* inside, interior; (*di paese*) interior; (*fodera*) lining; (*di appartamento*) flat (number); (TEL) extension // *sm/f* (INS) boarder; **~i** *smpl* (CINEMA) interior shots; **all'~** inside; **ministro dell'I'~** Minister of the Interior, ≈ Home Secretary; **~ destro/sinistro** (CALCIO) inside right/left.

in'tero, a *ag* (*integro, intatto*) whole, entire; (*completo, totale*) complete; (*numero*) whole; (*non ridotto: biglietto*) full.

interpel'lare *vt* to consult.

inter'porre *vt* to interpose; **interporsi** *vr* to intervene; **inter'posto, a** *pp di* **interporre**.

interpre'tare *vt* to interpret; **interpretazi'one** *sf* interpretation; **in'terprete** *sm* interpreter; (TEATRO) actor, performer; (MUS) performer.

interro'gare *vt* to question; (INS) to test; **interroga'tivo, a** *ag* (*occhi, sguardo*) questioning, inquiring; (LING) interrogative // *sm* question; (*fig*) mystery; **interroga'torio** // *sm* (DIR) interrogatory, questioning // *sm* (DIR) questioning *q*; (INS) oral test.

inter'rompere *vt* to interrupt; (*studi, trattative*) to break off, interrupt; **~rsi** *vr* to break off, stop; **inter'rotto, a** *pp di* **interrompere**.

interrut'tore *sm* switch.

interruzi'one [interrut'tsjone] *sf* interruption; break.

interse'care *vt*, **~rsi** *vr* to intersect.

inter'stizio [inter'stittsjo] *sm* interstice, crack.

interur'bano, a *ag* inter-city; (TEL: *chiamata*) trunk *cpd*, long-distance; (: *telefono*) long-distance // *sf* trunk call, long-distance call.

inter'vallo *sm* interval; (*spazio*) space, gap.

interve'nire *vi* (2) (*partecipare*): ~ **a** to be present at, attend; (*intromettersi: anche POL*) to intervene; (*MED: operare*) to operate; **inter'vento** *sm* presence, attendance; (*inframmettenza*) intervention; (*MED*) operation.

inter'vista *sf* interview; **intervis'tare** *vt* to interview.

in'teso, a *pp di* intendere // *ag* agreed // *sf* (*fra amici, paesi*) understanding; (*accordo*) agreement, understanding; (*SPORT*) teamwork; **non darsi per** ~ **di qc** to take no notice of sth.

intes'tare *vt* to head; (*casa*): ~ **qc a** to put *o* register sth in the name of; **~rsi** *vr* (*ostinarsi*): **~rsi a fare** to take it into one's head to do; **intestazi'one** *sf* heading; (*su carta da lettere*) letterhead; (*registrazione*) registration.

intes'tino, a *ag* (*lotte*) internal, civil // *sm* (*ANAT*) intestine.

inti'mare *vt* to order, command; **intimazi'one** *sf* order, command.

intimidazi'one [intimidat'tsjone] *sf* intimidation.

intimi'dire *vt* to intimidate // *vi* (2) (*anche*: ~rsi) to grow shy.

intimità *sf* intimacy; privacy; (*familiarità*) familiarity.

'intimo, a *ag* intimate; (*affetti, vita*) private; (*fig: profondo*) inmost // *sm* (*persona*) intimate *o* close friend; (*dell'animo*) bottom, depths *pl*.

intimo'rire *vt* to frighten; **~rsi** *vr* to become frightened.

in'tingolo *sm* sauce; (*pietanza*) stew.

intiriz'zire [intirid'dzire] *vt* to numb // *vi* (2) (*anche*: ~rsi) to go numb.

intito'lare *vt* to give a title to; (*dedicare*) to dedicate.

intolle'rabile *ag* intolerable.

intolle'rante *ag* intolerant.

intona'care *vt* to plaster.

in'tonaco, ci *o* **chi** *sm* plaster.

into'nare *vt* (*canto*) to start to sing; (*strumenti*) to tune; (*armonizzare*) to match; **~rsi** *vr* to be in tune; to match; **intonazi'one** *sf* intonation.

inton'tire *vt* to stun, daze // *vi* (2) to be stunned *o* dazed.

in'toppo *sm* stumbling block, obstacle.

in'torno *av* around; ~ **a** *prep* (*attorno a*) around; (*riguardo, circa*) about.

intorpi'dire *vt* to numb; (*fig*) to make sluggish // *vi* (2) (*anche*: ~rsi) to grow numb; (*fig*) to become sluggish.

intossi'care *vt* to poison; **intossicazi'one** *sf* poisoning.

intralci'are [intral'tʃare] *vt* to hamper, hold up.

intransi'gente [intransi'dʒɛnte] *ag* intransigent, uncompromising.

intransi'tivo, a *ag, sm* intransitive.

intrapren'dente *ag* enterprising, go-ahead.

intra'prendere *vt* to undertake.

intrat'tabile *ag* intractable.

intratte'nere *vt* to entertain; to engage in conversation; **~rsi** *vr* to linger; **~rsi su qc** to dwell on sth.

intrave'dere *vt* to catch a glimpse of; (*fig*) to foresee.

intrecci'are [intret'tʃare] *vt* (*capelli*) to plait, braid; (*intessere: anche fig*) to weave, interweave, intertwine; **~rsi** *vr* to intertwine, become interwoven; ~ **le mani** to clasp one's hands; **in'treccio** *sm* (*fig: trama*) plot, story.

in'trepido, a *ag* fearless, dauntless.

intri'gare *vi* to manoeuvre, scheme; **~rsi** *vr* to interfere, meddle; **in'trigo, ghi** *sm* plot, intrigue.

in'trinseco, a, ci, che *ag* intrinsic; (*amico*) close, intimate.

in'triso, a *ag*: ~ (**di**) soaked (in).

intro'durre *vt* to introduce; (*chiave etc*): ~ **qc in** to insert sth into; (*persone: far entrare*) to show in; **introdursi** *vr* (*moda, tecniche*) to be introduced; **introdursi in** (*persona: penetrare*) to enter; (*: entrare furtivamente*) to steal *o* slip into; **introduzi'one** *sf* introduction.

in'troito *sm* income, revenue.

intro'mettersi *vr* to interfere, meddle; (*interporsi*) to intervene.

intro'verso, a *ag* introverted // *sm* introvert.

in'truglio [in'truʎʎo] *sm* concoction.

intrusi'one *sf* intrusion; interference.

in'truso, a *sm/f* intruder.

intu'ire *vt* to perceive by intuition; (*rendersi conto*) to realise; **in'tuito** *sm* intuition; (*perspicacia*) perspicacity; **intuizi'one** *sf* intuition.

inu'mano, a *ag* inhuman.

inumi'dire *vt* to dampen, moisten; **~rsi** *vr* to become damp *o* wet.

i'nutile *ag* useless; (*superfluo*) pointless, unnecessary; **inutilità** *sf* uselessness; pointlessness.

inva'dente *ag* (*fig*) interfering, nosey.

in'vadere *vt* to invade; (*affollare*) to swarm into, overrun; (*sog: acque*) to flood; **invadi'trice** *ag vedi* invasore.

invalidità *sf* infirmity; disability; (*DIR*) invalidity.

in'valido, a *ag* (*infermo*) infirm, invalid; (*al lavoro*) disabled; (*DIR*) invalid // *sm/f* invalid; disabled person.

in'vano *av* in vain.

invari'abile *ag* invariable.

invasi'one *sf* invasion.

in'vaso, a *pp di* invadere.

inva'sore, invadi'trice [invadi'tritʃe] *ag* invading // *sm* invader.

invecchi'are [invek'kjare] *vi* (2) (*persona*) to grow old; (*vino, popolazione*) to age; (*moda*) to become dated // *vt* to age; (*far apparire più vecchio*) to make look older.

in'vece [in'vetʃe] *av* instead; (*al contrario*) on the contrary; ~ **di** *prep* instead of.

inve'ire *vi*: ~ **contro** to rail against.

inven'tare vt to invent; (pericoli, pettegolezzi) to make up, invent.

inven'tario sm inventory; (COMM) stocktaking q.

inven'tivo, a ag inventive // sf inventiveness.

inven'tore sm inventor.

invenzi'one [inven'tsjone] sf invention; (bugia) lie, story.

inver'nale ag winter cpd; (simile all'inverno) wintry.

in'verno sm winter.

invero'simile ag unlikely.

inversi'one sf inversion; reversal; ~ di marcia (AUT) reversing; "divieto d'~" "no U-turns".

in'verso, a ag reverse; opposite; (MAT) inverse // sm contrary, opposite; in senso ~ in the opposite direction; nell'ordine ~ in the reverse order.

inverte'brato, a ag, sm invertebrate.

inver'tire vt to invert, reverse; ~ la marcia to reverse; **inver'tito, a** sm/f homosexual.

investi'gare vt, vi to investigate; investiga'tore sm investigator, detective; investigazi'one sf investigation, inquiry.

investi'mento sm (ECON) investment; (scontro, urto) crash, collision; (incidente stradale) road accident.

inves'tire vt (denaro) to invest; (sog: veicolo: pedone) to knock down; (: altro veicolo) to crash into; (sog: nave) to collide with; (apostrofare) to assail; (incaricare): ~ qd di to invest sb with; **investi'tura** sf investiture.

invete'rato, a ag inveterate.

invet'tiva sf invective.

invi'are vt to send; **invi'ato, a** sm/f envoy; (STAMPA) correspondent.

in'vidia sf envy; **invidi'are** vt to envy; **invidi'oso, a** ag envious.

invigo'rire vt to strengthen, invigorate // vi (2) (anche: ~rsi) to gain strength.

invin'cibile [invin'tʃibile] ag invincible.

in'vio, 'vii sm sending; (insieme di merci) consignment.

invio'labile ag inviolable.

invipe'rito, a ag furious.

invi'sibile ag invisible.

invi'tare vt to invite; ~ qd a fare to invite sb to do; (sog: cosa) to tempt sb to do; **invi'tato, a** sm/f guest; **in'vito** sm invitation.

invo'care vt (chiedere: aiuto, pace) to cry out for; (appellarsi: la legge, Dio) to appeal to, invoke.

invogli'are [invoʎ'ʎare] vt: ~ qd a fare to tempt sb to do, induce sb to do; ~rsi di to take a fancy to.

involon'tario, a ag (errore) unintentional; (gesto) involuntary.

invol'tino sm (CUC) roulade.

in'volto sm (pacco) parcel; (fagotto) bundle.

in'volucro sm cover, wrapping.

invo'luto, a ag involved, intricate.

invulne'rabile ag invulnerable.

inzacche'rare [intsakke'rare] vt to spatter with mud.

inzup'pare [intsup'pare] vt to soak; ~rsi vr to get soaked.

'io pronome I // sm inv: l'~ the ego, the self; ~ stesso(a) I myself.

i'odio sm iodine.

i'ogurt sm inv = yoghurt.

i'one sm ion.

l'onio sm: lo ~ the Ionian (Sea).

ipermer'cato sm hypermarket.

ipertensi'one sf high blood pressure, hypertension.

ip'nosi sf hypnosis; **ip'notico, a, ci, che** ag hypnotic; **ipno'tismo** sm hypnotism; **ipnotiz'zare** vt to hypnotize.

ipocri'sia sf hypocrisy.

i'pocrita, i, e ag hypocritical // sm/f hypocrite.

ipo'teca, che sf mortgage; **ipote'care** vt to mortgage.

i'potesi sf inv hypothesis; **ipo'tetico, a, ci, che** ag hypothetical.

'ippico, a, ci, che ag horse cpd // sf horseracing.

ippocas'tano sm horse chestnut.

ip'podromo sm racecourse.

ippo'potamo sm hippopotamus.

'ira sf anger, wrath.

I'ran sm: l'~ Iran.

I'raq sm: l'~ Iraq.

'iride sf (arcobaleno) rainbow; (ANAT, BOT) iris.

Ir'landa sf: l'~ Ireland; **irlan'dese** ag Irish // sm/f Irishman/woman; **gli Irlandesi** the Irish.

iro'nia sf irony; **i'ronico, a, ci, che** ag ironic(al).

irradi'are vt to radiate; (sog: raggi di luce: illuminare) to shine on, irradiate // vi (2) (diffondersi: anche: ~rsi) to radiate; **irradiazi'one** sf radiation; irradiation.

irragio'nevole [irradʒo'nevole] ag irrational; unreasonable.

irrazio'nale [irrattsjo'nale] ag irrational.

irre'ale ag unreal.

irrecu'sabile ag (offerta) not to be refused; (prova) irrefutable.

irrefu'tabile ag irrefutable.

irrego'lare ag irregular; (terreno) uneven; **irregolarità** sf inv irregularity; unevenness.

irremo'vibile ag (fig) unshakeable, unyielding.

irrepa'rabile ag irreparable; (fig) unavoidable.

irrepe'ribile ag nowhere to be found.

irrequi'eto, a ag restless.

irresis'tibile ag irresistible.

irreso'luto, a ag irresolute.

irrespon'sabile ag irresponsible.

irrevo'cabile ag irrevocable.

irridu'cibile [irridu'tʃibile] ag irreducible; (fig) indomitable.

irri'gare vt (annaffiare) to irrigate; (sog:

fiume etc) to flow through; **irrigazi'one** *sf* irrigation.

irrigi'dire [irridʒi'dire] *vt*, ~**rsi** *vr* to stiffen.

irri'sorio, a *ag* derisory.

irri'tabile *ag* irritable.

irri'tare *vt* (*mettere di malumore*) to irritate, annoy; (*MED*) to irritate; ~**rsi** *vr* (*stizzirsi*) to become irritated *o* annoyed; **irritazi'one** *sf* irritation; annoyance.

ir'rompere *vi*: ~ **in** to burst into.

irro'rare *vt* to sprinkle; (*AGR*) to spray.

irru'ente *ag* (*fig*) impetuous, violent.

irruzi'one [irrut'tsjone] *sf* irruption *q*; **fare** ~ **in** to burst into.

'irto, a *ag* bristly; ~ **di** bristling with.

is'critto, a *pp di* **iscrivere** // *sm/f* member; **per** *o* **in** ~ in writing.

is'crivere *vt* to register, enter; (*persona*) to register, enrol; ~**rsi** *vr*: ~**rsi (a)** (*club, partito*) to join; (*università*) to register *o* enrol (at); (*esame, concorso*) to register *o* enter (for); **iscrizi'one** *sf* (*epigrafe etc*) inscription; (*a scuola, società*) enrolment, registration; (*registrazione*) registration.

Is'landa *sf*: **l'** ~ Iceland.

'isola *sf* island; ~ **pedonale** (*AUT*) traffic island.

isola'mento *sm* isolation; (*TECN*) insulation.

iso'lano, a *ag* island *cpd* // *sm/f* islander.

iso'lante *ag* insulating // *sm* insulator.

iso'lare *vt* to isolate; (*TECN*) to insulate; (: *acusticamente*) to soundproof; **iso'lato, a** *ag* isolated; insulated // *sm* (*EDIL*) block.

ispetto'rato *sm* inspectorate.

ispet'tore *sm* inspector.

ispezio'nare [ispettsjo'nare] *vt* to inspect.

ispezi'one [ispet'tsjone] *sf* inspection.

'ispido, a *ag* bristly, shaggy.

ispi'rare *vt* to inspire; ~**rsi** *vr*: ~**rsi a** to draw one's inspiration from; **ispirazi'one** *sf* inspiration.

Isra'ele *sm*: **l'** ~ Israel; **israeli'ano, a** *ag, sm/f* Israeli.

is'sare *vt* to hoist.

istan'taneo, a *ag* instantaneous // *sf* (*FOT*) snapshot.

is'tante *sm* instant, moment; **all'**~, **sull'**~ instantly, immediately.

is'tanza [is'tantsa] *sf* petition, request.

is'terico, a, ci, che *ag* hysterical.

iste'rismo *sm* hysteria.

isti'gare *vt* to incite, instigate; **istiga-zi'one** *sf* instigation.

istin'tivo, a *ag* instinctive.

is'tinto *sm* instinct.

istitu'ire *vt* (*fondare*) to institute, found; (*porre: confronto*) to establish; (*intraprendere: inchiesta*) to set up.

isti'tuto *sm* institute; (*ente, DIR*) institution; ~ **di bellezza** beauty salon.

istituzi'one [istitut'tsjone] *sf* institution.

'istmo *sm* (*GEO*) isthmus.

'istrice ['istritʃe] *sm* porcupine.

istri'one *sm* (*peg*) ham actor.

istru'ire *vt* (*insegnare*) to teach;

(*ammaestrare*) to train; (*informare*) to instruct, inform; (*DIR*) to prepare; **istrut-'tivo, a** *ag* instructive; **istrut'tore, 'trice** *sm/f* instructor // *ag*: **giudice istruttore** examining magistrate; **istrut'toria** *sf* (*DIR*) (preliminary) investigation and hearing; **istruzi'one** *sf* education; training; (*direttiva*) instruction; (*DIR*) = **istruttoria**; **istruzioni** *sfpl* (*norme per l'uso*) instructions, directions.

I'talia *sf*: **l'** ~ Italy.

itali'ano, a *ag* Italian // *sm/f* Italian // *sm* (*LING*) Italian; **gli I** ~ **i** the Italians.

itine'rario *sm* itinerary.

itte'rizia [itte'rittsja] *sf* (*MED*) jaundice.

'ittico, a, ci, che *ag* fish *cpd*; fishing *cpd*.

Iugos'lavia *sf* = **Jugoslavia**.

iugos'lavo, a *ag, sm/f* = **jugoslavo, a**.

i'uta *sf* jute.

I.V.A. ['iva] *abbr f vedi* **imposta**.

J

jazz [dʒaz] *sm* jazz.

jeans [dʒinz] *smpl* jeans.

Jugos'lavia [jugoz'lavja] *sf*: **la** ~ Yugoslavia; **jugos'lavo, a** *ag, sm/f* Yugoslav(ian).

'juta ['juta] *sf* = **iuta**.

L

l' *det vedi* **la, lo.**

la *det f* (*dav V l'*) the // *pronome* (*dav V l'*) (*oggetto: persona*) her; (: *cosa*) it; (: *forma di cortesia*) you // *sm inv* (*MUS*) A; (: *solfeggiando la scala*) la.

là *av* there; **di** ~ (*da quel luogo*) from there; (*in quel luogo*) in there; (*dall'altra parte*) over there; **di** ~ **di** beyond; **per di** ~ that way; **andare in** ~ (*procedere*) to go on, proceed; **più in** ~ further on; (*tempo*) later on; *vedi* **quello.**

'labbro *sm* (*pl(f):* **labbra**: *solo nel senso ANAT*) lip.

labi'rinto *sm* labyrinth, maze.

labora'torio *sm* (*di ricerca*) laboratory; (*di arti, mestieri*) workshop; ~ **linguistico** language laboratory.

labori'oso, a *ag* (*faticoso*) laborious; (*attivo*) hard-working.

labu'rista, i, e *ag* Labour *cpd* // *sm/f* Labour Party member.

'lacca, che *sf* lacquer.

'laccio ['lattʃo] *sm* noose; (*lazo*) lasso; (*di scarpa*) lace; (*fig*) snare.

lace'rare [latʃe'rare] *vt* to tear to shreds, lacerate; ~**rsi** *vr* to tear; **'lacero, a** *ag* (*logoro*) torn, tattered.

la'conico, a, ci, che *ag* laconic, brief.

'lacrima *sf* tear; (*goccia*) drop; **in** ~**e in** tears; **lacri'mare** *vi* to weep, shed tears; **lacri'mogeno, a** *ag*: *vedi* **gas**; **lacri-'moso, a** *ag* tearful; (*commovente*) pitiful, pathetic.

la'cuna *sf* (*fig*) gap.

'ladro *sm* thief; **ladro'cinio** *sm* theft, larceny.

laggiù [lad'dʒu] *av* down there; (*di là*) over there.

la'gnarsi [laɲ'ɲarsi] *vr:* ~ **(di)** to complain (about).

'lago, ghi *sm* lake.

'lagrima *etc* = **lacrima** *etc*.

la'guna *sf* lagoon.

'laico, a, ci, che *ag* (*apostolato*) lay; (*vita*) secular; (*scuola*) non-denominational // *sm/f* layman/ woman // *sm* lay brother.

'lama *sf* blade // *sm inv* (ZOOL) llama; (REL) lama.

lambic'care *vt* to distil; ~rsi il cervello to rack one's brains.

lam'bire *vt* to lick; to lap.

la'mella *sf* (*di metallo etc*) thin sheet, thin strip; (*di fungo*) gill.

lamen'tare *vt* to lament; ~rsi *vr* (*emettere lamenti*) to moan, groan; (*rammaricarsi*): ~rsi **(di)** to complain (about); **lamen'tela** *sf* complaining *q*; **lamen'tevole** *ag* (*voce*) complaining, plaintive; (*destino*) pitiful; **la'mento** *sm* moan, groan; wail; **lamen'toso, a** *ag* plaintive.

la'metta *sf* razor blade.

lami'era *sf* sheet metal.

'lamina *sf* (*lastra sottile*) thin sheet (*o* layer *o* plate); ~ **d'oro** gold leaf; gold foil; **lami'nare** *vt* to laminate; **lami'nato, a** *ag* laminated; (*tessuto*) lamé // *sm* laminate; lamé.

'lampada *sf* lamp; ~ **da saldatore** blowlamp; ~ **da tavolo** table lamp.

lampa'dario *sm* chandelier.

lampa'dina *sf* light bulb; ~ **tascabile** pocket torch.

lam'pante *ag* (*fig: evidente*) crystal clear, evident.

lampeggi'are [lamped'dʒare] *vi* (*luce, fari*) to flash // *vb impers:* **lampeggia** there's lightning; **lampeggia'tore** *sm* (AUT) indicator.

lampi'one *sm* street light *o* lamp.

'lampo *sm* (METEOR) flash of lightning; (*di luce, fig*) flash; ~i *smpl* lightning *q* // *ag inv:* **cerniera** ~ zip (fastener); **guerra** ~ blitzkrieg.

lam'pone *sm* raspberry.

'lana *sf* wool; ~ **d'acciaio** steel wool; **pura** ~ **vergine** pure new wool; ~ **di vetro** glass wool.

lan'cetta [lan'tʃetta] *sf* (*indice*) pointer, needle; (*di orologio*) hand.

'lancia ['lantʃa] *sf* (*arma*) lance; (: *picca*) spear; (*imbarcazione*) launch.

lanciafi'amme [lantʃa'fjamme] *sm inv* flamethrower.

lanci'are [lan'tʃare] *vt* to throw, hurl, fling; (SPORT) to throw; (*far partire: automobile*) to get up to full speed; (*bombe*) to drop; (*razzo, prodotto, moda*) to launch; ~rsi *vr:* ~**rsi contro/su** to throw *o* hurl *o* fling o.s. against/on; ~**rsi in** (*fig*) to embark on.

lanci'nante [lantʃi'nante] *ag* (*dolore*) shooting, throbbing; (*grido*) piercing.

'lancio ['lantʃo] *sm* throwing *q*; throw; dropping *q*; drop; launching *q*; launch; ~ **del peso** putting the shot.

'landa *sf* (GEO) moor.

languido, a *ag* (*fiacco*) languid, weak; (*tenero, malinconico*) languishing.

langu'ire *vi* to languish; (*conversazione*) to flag.

langu'ore *sm* weakness, languor.

lani'ero, a *ag* wool *cpd*, woollen.

lani'ficio [lani'fitʃo] *sm* woollen mill.

la'noso, a *ag* woolly.

lan'terna *sf* lantern; (*faro*) lighthouse.

la'nugine [la'nudʒine] *sf* down.

lapi'dare *vt* to stone.

lapi'dario, a *ag* (*fig*) terse.

'lapide *sf* (*di sepolcro*) tombstone; (*commemorativa*) plaque.

'lapis *sm inv* pencil.

'lapsus *sm inv* slip.

'lardo *sm* bacon fat, lard.

largheggi'are [larged'dʒare] *vi:* ~ **di** *o* in to be generous *o* liberal with.

lar'ghezza [lar'gettsa] *sf* width; breadth; looseness; generosity; ~ **di vedute** broad-mindedness.

'largo, a, ghi, ghe *ag* wide; broad; (*maniche*) wide; (*abito: troppo ampio*) loose; (*fig*) generous // *sm* width; breadth; (*mare aperto*) il ~ the open sea; ~ **due metri** two metres wide; ~ **di spalle** broad-shouldered; ~ **di vedute** broad-minded; **su** ~**a scala** on a large scale; **al** ~ (NAUT) offshore; **farsi** ~ **tra la folla** to push one's way through the crowd.

'larice ['laritʃe] *sm* (BOT) larch.

la'ringe [la'rindʒe] *sf* larynx; **larin'gite** *sf* laryngitis.

'larva *sf* larva; (*fig*) shadow.

la'sagne [la'zaɲɲe] *sfpl* lasagna *sg*.

lasci'are [laʃ'ʃare] *vt* to leave; (*abbandonare*) to leave, abandon, give up; (*cessare di tenere*) to let go of // *vb ausiliare:* ~ **fare qd** to let sb do // *vi:* ~ **di fare** (*smettere*) to stop doing; ~rsi **andare/truffare** to let o.s. go/be cheated; ~ **andare** *o* **correre** *o* **perdere** to let things go their own way; ~ **stare** **qc/qd** to leave sth/sb alone.

'lascito ['laʃʃito] *sm* (DIR) legacy.

la'scivo, a [laʃ'ʃivo] *ag* lascivious.

'laser ['lazer] *ag, sm inv:* (**raggio**) ~ laser (beam).

lassa'tivo, a *ag, sm* laxative.

'lasso *sm:* ~ **di tempo** interval, lapse of time.

lassù *av* up there.

'lastra *sf* (*di pietra*) slab; (*di metallo, FOT*) plate; (*di ghiaccio, vetro*) sheet; (*radiografica*) X-ray (plate).

lastri'care *vt* to pave; **lastri'cato** *sm,* **'lastrico, ci** *o* **chi** *sm* pavement.

la'tente *ag* latent.

late'rale *ag* lateral, side *cpd* // *sm* (CALCIO) half-back.

late'rizi [late'rittsi] *smpl* bricks; tiles.

lati'fondo *sm* large estate.

la'tino, a *ag, sm* Latin; ~-ameri'cano a *ag* Latin-American.

lati'tante *sm/f* fugitive (from justice).

lati'tudine *sf* latitude.

'lato, a *ag (fig)* wide, broad // *sm* side; *(fig)* aspect, point of view; in senso ~ broadly speaking.

la'trare *vi* to bark.

la'trina *sf* latrine.

latro'cinio   [latro'tʃinjo]   *sm* = ladrocinio.

'latta *sf* tin; *(recipiente)* tin, can.

lat'taio, a *sm/f* milkman/ dairywoman.

lat'tante *ag* unweaned.

'latte *sm* milk; ~ detergente cleansing milk *o* lotion; ~ secco o in polvere dried *o* powdered milk; ~ scremato skimmed milk; 'latteo, a *ag* milky; *(dieta, prodotto)* milk *cpd*; latte'ria *sf* dairy; latti'cini *smpl* dairy products.

lat'tina *sf (di birra etc)* can.

lat'tuga *sf* lettuce.

'laurea *sf* degree; laure'ando, a *sm/f* final-year student; laure'are *vt* to confer a degree on; laurearsi *vr* to graduate; laure'ato, a, *ag, sm/f* graduate.

'lauro *sm* laurel.

'lava *sf* lava.

la'vabile *ag* washable.

la'vabo *sm* washbasin.

la'vaggio [la'vaddʒo] *sm* washing *q*; ~ del cervello brainwashing *q*.

la'vagna [la'vaɲɲa] *sf (GEO)* slate; *(di scuola)* blackboard.

la'vanda *sf (anche MED)* wash; *(BOT)* lavender; lavan'daia *sf* washerwoman; lavande'ria *sf* laundry; lavanderia automatica launderette; lavan'dino *sm* sink.

lavapi'atti *sm/f* dishwasher.

la'vare *vt* to wash; ~rsi *vr* to wash, have a wash; ~ a secco to dry-clean; ~rsi le mani/i denti to wash one's hands/clean one's teeth.

lava'secco *sm o f inv* drycleaner's.

lavasto'viglie [lavasto'viʎʎe] *sm o f inv (macchina)* dishwasher.

lava'toio *sm (public)* washhouse.

lava'trice [lava'tritʃe] *sf* washing machine.

lava'tura *sf* washing *q*; ~ di piatti dishwater.

lavo'rante *sm* workman.

lavo'rare *vi* to work; *(fig: bar, studio etc)* to do good business // *vt* to work; *(fig: persuadere)* to work on; ~ a to work on; ~ a maglia to knit; ~ la terra to till the land; lavora'tivo, a *ag* working; lavora'tore, 'trice *sm/f* worker // *ag* working; lavorazi'one *sf* manufacture; *(di materie prime)* processing; *(produzione)* production; lavo'rio *sm* intense activity.

la'voro *sm* work; *(occupazione)* job, work *q*; *(opera)* piece of work, job; *(ECON)* labour; ~i forzati hard labour *sg*;

ministro dei L~i pubblici Minister of Works.

le *det fpl* the // *pronome (oggetto)* them; *(: a lei, a essa)* to her; *(: forma di cortesia)* to you.

le'ale *ag* loyal; *(sincero)* sincere; *(onesto)* fair; lealtà *sf* loyalty; sincerity; fairness.

'lebbra *sf* leprosy.

'lecca 'lecca *sm inv* lollipop.

leccapi'edi *sm/f inv (peg)* toady, bootlicker.

lec'care *vt* to lick; *(sog: gatto: latte etc)* to lick *o* lap up; *(fig)* to flatter; ~rsi i baffi *o* le labbra to lick one's lips; lec'cata *sf* lick.

'leccio ['lettʃo] *sm* holm oak, ilex.

leccor'nia *sf* titbit, delicacy.

'lecito, a ['lɛtʃito] *ag* permitted, allowed.

'ledere *vt* to damage, injure; ~ gli interessi di qd to be prejudicial to sb's interests.

'lega, ghe *sf* league; *(di metalli)* alloy.

le'gaccio [le'gattʃo] *sm* string, lace.

le'gale *ag* legal // *sm* lawyer; legalità *sf* legality, lawfulness; legaliz'zare *vt* to authenticate; *(regolarizzare)* to legalize.

le'game *sm (corda, fig: affettivo)* tie, bond; *(nesso logico)* link, connection.

lega'mento *sm (ANAT)* ligament.

le'gare *vt (prigioniero, capelli, cane)* to tie (up); *(libro)* to bind; *(CHIM)* to alloy; *(fig: collegare)* to bind, join // *vi (far lega)* to unite; *(fig)* to get on well.

lega'tario, a *sm/f (DIR)* legatee.

le'gato *sm (REL)* legate; *(DIR)* legacy, bequest.

lega'tura *sf* tying *q*; binding *q*; *(di libro)* binding; *(MUS)* ligature.

legazi'one [legat'tsjone] *sf* legation.

'legge ['leddʒe] *sf* law.

leg'genda [led'dʒɛnda] *sf (narrazione)* legend; *(di carta geografica etc)* key, legend; *(di disegno)* caption, legend; leg-gen'dario, a *ag* legendary.

'leggere ['lɛddʒere] *vt, vi* to read.

legge'rezza [leddʒe'rettsa] *sf* lightness; thoughtlessness; fickleness.

leg'gero, a [led'dʒɛro] *ag* light; *(agile, snello)* nimble, agile, light; *(tè, caffè)* weak; *(fig: non grave, piccolo)* slight; *(: spensierato)* thoughtless; *(: incostante)* fickle; free and easy; alla ~a thoughtlessly.

leggi'adro, a [led'dʒadro] *ag* pretty, lovely; *(movimenti)* graceful.

leg'gibile [led'dʒibile] *ag* legible; *(libro)* readable, worth reading.

leg'gio, 'gii [led'dʒio] *sm* lectern; *(MUS)* music stand.

legio'nario [ledʒo'narjo] *sm (romano)* legionary; *(volontario)* legionnaire.

legi'one [le'dʒone] *sf* legion; ~ straniera foreign legion.

legisla'tivo, a [ledʒizla'tivo] *ag* legislative.

legisla'tore [ledʒizla'tore] *sm* legislator.

legisla'tura [ledʒizla'tura] sf legislature.
legislazi'one [ledʒizlat'tsjone] sf legislation.
legittimità [ledʒittimi'ta] sf legitimacy.
le'gittimo, a [le'dʒittimo] ag legitimate; (fig: giustificato, lecito) justified, legitimate; **~a difesa** (DIR) self-defence.
'legna ['leɲɲa] sf firewood; **le'gname** sm wood, timber.
'legno ['leɲɲo] sm wood; (pezzo di —) piece of wood; **di ~** wooden; **~ compensato** plywood; **le'gnoso, a** ag wooden; woody; (carne) tough.
le'gumi smpl (BOT) pulses.
'lei pronome (soggetto) she; (oggetto: per dare rilievo, con preposizione) her; (forma di cortesia: anche: **L~**) you // sm: **dare del ~ a qd** to address sb as 'lei'; **~ stessa** she herself; you yourself.
'lembo sm (di abito, strada) edge; (striscia sottile: di terra) strip.
'lemma, i sm headword.
'lemme 'lemme av (very) very slowly.
'lena sf (fig) energy, stamina.
le'nire vt to soothe.
'lente sf (OTTICA) lens sg; **~ d'ingrandimento** magnifying glass; **~i a contatto o corneali** contact lenses.
len'tezza [len'tettsa] sf slowness.
len'ticchia [len'tikkja] sf (BOT) lentil.
len'tiggine [len'tiddʒine] sf freckle.
'lento, a ag slow; (molle: fune) slack; (non stretto: vite, abito) loose.
'lenza ['lɛntsa] sf fishing-line.
lenzu'olo [len'tswɔlo] sm sheet; **~a** sfpl pair of sheets.
le'one sm lion; (dello zodiaco) **L~** Leo.
leo'pardo sm leopard.
'lepido, a ag witty.
lepo'rino, a ag: **labbro ~** harelip.
'lepre sf hare.
'lercio, a, ci, cie ['lɛrtʃo] ag filthy.
'lesbica, che sf lesbian.
lesi'nare vt to be stingy with // vi: **~ (su)** to skimp (on), be stingy (with).
lesi'one sf (MED) lesion; (DIR) injury, damage; (EDIL) crack.
le'sivo, a ag: **~ (di)** damaging (to), detrimental (to).
'leso, a pp di **ledere** // ag (offeso) injured.
les'sare vt (CUC) to boil.
'lessico, ci sm vocabulary; lexicon.
'lesso, a ag boiled // sm boiled meat.
'lesto, a ag quick; (agile) nimble; (cosa: sbrigativa) hasty, hurried; **~ di mano** (per rubare) light-fingered; (per picchiare) free with one's fists.
le'tale ag lethal; fatal.
leta'maio sm dunghill.
le'tame sm manure, dung.
le'targo, ghi sm lethargy; (ZOOL) hibernation.
le'tizia [le'tittsja] sf joy, happiness.
'lettera sf letter; **~e** sfpl (letteratura) literature // (studi umanistici) arts (subjects); **alla ~** literally; **in ~e** in words, in full; **lette'rale** ag literal.

lette'rario, a ag literary.
lette'rato, a ag well-read, scholarly.
lettera'tura sf literature.
let'tiga, ghe sf (portantina) litter; (barella) stretcher.
'letto, a pp di **leggere** // sm bed; **~ a castello** bunk beds pl; **~ a una piazza/a due piazze o matrimoniale** single/double bed.
let'tore, 'trice sm/f reader; (INS) (foreign language) assistant.
let'tura sf reading.
leuce'mia [leutʃe'mia] sf leukaemia.
'leva sf lever; (MIL) conscription; **far ~ su qd** to work on sb; **~ del cambio** (AUT) gear lever.
le'vante sm east; (vento) East wind; **il L~** the Levant.
le'vare vt (occhi, braccio) to raise; (sollevare, togliere: tassa, divieto) to lift; (indumenti) to take off, remove; (rimuovere) to take away; (: dal di sopra) to take off; (: dal di dentro) to take out; **~rsi** vr to get up; (sole) to rise; **le'vata** sf rising; (di posta) collection.
leva'toio, a ag: **ponte ~** drawbridge.
leva'tura sf intelligence, mental capacity.
levi'gare vt to smooth; (con carta vetrata) to sand.
levri'ero sm greyhound.
lezi'one [let'tsjone] sf lesson; (all'università, sgridata) lecture; **fare ~** to teach; to lecture.
lezi'oso, a [let'tsjoso] ag affected; simpering.
'lezzo ['leddzo] sm stench, stink.
li pronome pl (oggetto) them.
lì av there; **di o da ~** from there; **per di ~ that way**; **di ~ a pochi giorni** a few days later; **~ per ~** there and then; at first; **essere ~ (~) per fare** to be on the point of doing, be about to do; **~ dentro** in there; **~ sotto** under there; **~ sopra** on there; up there; **vedi quello**.
Li'bano sm: **il ~** the Lebanon.
'libbra sf (peso) pound.
li'beccio [li'bettʃo] sm south-west wind.
li'bello sm libel.
li'bellula sf dragonfly.
libe'rale ag, sm/f liberal.
liberaliz'zare [liberalid'dzare] vt to liberalize.
libe'rare vt to free, liberate; (prigioniero: sog: autorità, TECN) to release; (sottrarre a danni) to rescue; **libera'tore, 'trice** ag liberating // sm/f liberator; **liberazi'one** sf liberation, freeing; release; rescuing.
'libero, a ag free; (strada) clear; (non occupato: posto etc) vacant; not taken; empty; not engaged; **~ di fare qc** free to do sth; **~ da fronte**; **~ arbitrio** free will; **~ professionista** professional man; **~ scambio** free trade; **libertà** sf inv freedom; (tempo disponibile) free time // sfpl (licenza) liberties; **in libertà provvisoria/vigilata** on bail/probation; **libertà di riunione** right to hold meetings.

liber'tino, a *ag* libertine.

'Libia *sf*: **la** ~ Libya; **'libico, a, ci, che** *ag, sm/f* Libyan.

li'bidine *sf* lust; **libidi'noso, a** *ag* lustful, libidinous.

li'bido *sf* libido.

li'braio *sm* bookseller.

li'brarsi *vr* to hover.

li'brario, a *ag* book *cpd*.

libre'ria *sf* (*bottega*) bookshop; (*stanza*) library; (*mobile*) bookcase.

li'bretto *sm* booklet; (*taccuino*) notebook; (*MUS*) libretto; ~ **degli assegni** cheque book; ~ **di risparmio** (*savings*) bank-book, passbook; ~ **universitario** student's report book.

'libro *sm* book; ~ **di cassa** cash book; ~ **paga** payroll.

li'cenza [li'tʃɛntsa] *sf* (*permesso*) permission, leave; (*di pesca, caccia, circolazione*) permit, licence; (*MIL*) leave; (*INS*) leaving certificate, diploma; (*libertà*) liberty; licence; licentiousness; **andare in** ~ (*MIL*) to go on leave.

licenzia'mento [litʃentsja'mento] *sm* dismissal; **indennità di** ~ redundancy payment.

licenzi'are [litʃen'tsjare] *vt* (*impiegato*) to dismiss; (*INS*) to award a certificate to; ~**rsi** *vr* (*impiegato*) to resign, hand in one's notice; (*INS*) to obtain one's school-leaving certificate.

licenzi'oso, a [litʃen'tsjoso] *ag* licentious.

li'ceo [li'tʃɛo] *sm* (*INS*) secondary school (*for 14- to 19-year-olds*).

li'chene [li'kɛne] *sm* (*BOT*) lichen.

licitazi'one [litʃitat'tsjone] *sf* (*offerta*) bid.

'lido *sm* beach, shore.

li'eto, a *ag* happy, glad; **"molto** ~" (*nelle presentazioni*) "pleased to meet you".

li'eve *ag* light; (*di poco conto*) slight; (*sommesso: voce*) faint, soft.

lievi'tare *vi* (2) (*anche fig*) to rise // *vt* to leaven.

li'evito *sm* yeast; ~ **di birra** brewer's yeast.

'ligio, a, gi, gie ['lidʒo] *ag* faithful, loyal.

'lilla, lillà *sm inv* lilac.

'lima *sf* file.

limacci'oso, a [limat'tʃoso] *ag* slimy, muddy.

li'mare *vt* to file (down); (*fig*) to polish.

'limbo *sm* (*REL*) limbo.

li'metta *sf* nail file.

limi'tare *sm* (*anche fig*) threshold // *vt* to limit, restrict; (*circoscrivere*) to bound, surround; **limita'tivo, a** *ag* limiting, restricting; **limi'tato, a** *ag* limited, restricted; **limitazi'one** *sf* limitation, restriction.

'limite *sm* limit; (*confine*) border, boundary; ~ **di velocità** speed limit.

li'mitrofo, a *ag* neighbouring.

limo'nata *sf* lemonade; lemon squash.

li'mone *sm* (*pianta*) lemon tree; (*frutto*) lemon.

'limpido, a *ag* clear; (*acqua*) limpid, clear.

'lince ['lintʃe] *sf* lynx.

linci'are *vt* to lynch.

'lindo, a *ag* tidy, spick and span; (*biancheria*) clean.

'linea *sf* line; (*di mezzi pubblici di trasporto: itinerario*) route; (: *servizio*) service; **a grandi** ~**e** in outline; **mantenere la** ~ to look after one's figure; **di** ~: **aereo di** ~ airliner; **nave di** ~ liner; ~ **di partenza/d'arrivo** (*SPORT*) starting/finishing line; ~ **di tiro** line of fire.

linea'menti *smpl* features; (*fig*) outlines.

line'are *ag* linear; (*fig*) coherent, logical.

line'etta *sf* (*trattino*) dash; (*d'unione*) hyphen.

lin'gotto *sm* ingot, bar.

'lingua *sf* (*ANAT, CUC*) tongue; (*idioma*) language; **mostrare la** ~ to stick out one's tongue; **di** ~ **italiana** Italian-speaking; ~ **madre** mother tongue; **una** ~ **di terra** a spit of land; **linguacci'uto, a** *ag* gossipy.

lingu'aggio [lin'gwadd3o] *sm* language.

lingu'etta *sf* (*di strumento*) reed; (*di scarpa, strumento*) tongue; (*di busta*) flap.

lingu'ista, i, e *sm/f* linguist; **lingu'istico, a, ci, che** *ag* linguistic // *sf* linguistics *sg*.

lini'mento *sm* liniment.

'lino *sm* (*pianta*) flax; (*tessuto*) linen.

li'noleum *sm inv* linoleum, lino.

lio'corno *sm* unicorn.

lique'fare *vt* (*render liquido*) to liquefy; (*fondere*) to melt; ~**rsi** *vr* to liquefy; to melt.

liqui'dare *vt* (*società, beni; persona: uccidere*) to liquidate; (*persona: sbarazzarsene*) to get rid of; (*conto, problema*) to settle; (*COMM: merce*) to sell off, clear; **liquidazi'one** *sf* liquidation; settlement; clearance sale.

liquidità *sf* liquidity.

'liquido, a *ag, sm* liquid; ~ **per freni** brake fluid.

liqui'rizia [likwi'rittsja] *sf* (*BOT*) liquorice.

li'quore *sm* liqueur.

'lira *sf* (*unità monetaria*) lira; (*MUS*) lyre; ~ **sterlina** pound sterling.

'lirico, a, ci, che *ag* lyric(al); (*MUS*) lyric // *sf* (*poesia*) lyric poetry; (*componimento poetico*) lyric; (*MUS*) opera; **cantante/teatro** ~ opera singer/house.

Lis'bona *sf* Lisbon.

'lisca, sche *sf* (*di pesce*) fishbone.

lisci'are [liʃ'ʃare] *vt* to smooth; (*accarezzare*) to stroke; (*fig*) to flatter.

'liscio, a, sci, sce ['liʃʃo] *ag* smooth; (*capelli*) straight; (*mobile*) plain; (*bevanda alcolica*) neat; (*fig*) straightforward, simple // *av*: **andare** ~ to go smoothly; **passarla** ~**a** to get away with it.

'liso, a *ag* worn out, threadbare.

'lista *sf* (*striscia*) strip; (*elenco*) list; ~ **elettorale** electoral roll; ~ **delle vivande** menu; **lis'tare** *vt* to edge, border.

lis'tino *sm* list; ~ **dei cambi** (foreign) exchange rate; ~ **dei prezzi** price list.

litaʼnia *sf* litany.
ʼlite *sf* quarrel, argument; (*DIR*) lawsuit.
litiʼgare *vi* to quarrel; (*DIR*) to litigate.
liʼtigio [liʼtidʒo] *sm* quarrel; litigiʼoso, a *ag* quarrelsome; (*DIR*) litigious.
litograʼfia *sf* (*sistema*) lithography; (*stampa*) lithograph.
litoʼrale *ag* coastal, coast *cpd* // *sm* coast.
ʼlitro *sm* litre.
liturʼgia, ʼgie [liturʼdʒia] *sf* liturgy.
liʼuto *sm* lute.
liʼvella *sf* level; ~ a bolla dʼaria spirit level.
livelʼlare *vt* to level, make level; ~rsi *vr* to become level; (*fig*) to level out, balance out.
liʼvello *sm* level; (*fig*) level, standard; ad alto ~ (*fig*) high-level; ~ del mare sea level.
ʼlivido, a *ag* livid; (*per percosse*) bruised, black and blue; (*cielo*) leaden // *sm* bruise.
liʼvore *sm* malice, spite.
Liʼvorno *sf* Livorno, Leghorn.
liʼvrea *sf* livery.
ʼlizza [ʼlittsa] *sf* lists *pl*; scendere in ~ (*anche fig*) to enter the lists.
lo *det m* (*dav s impura, gn, pn, ps, x, z; dav V lʼ*) the // *pronome* (*dav V lʼ*) (*oggetto: persona*) him; (: *cosa*) it; ~ sapevo I knew it; ~ so I know; sii buono, anche se lui non ~ è be good, even if he isnʼt.
ʼlobo *sm* lobe; ~ dellʼorecchio ear lobe.
loʼcale *ag* local // *sm* room; (*luogo pubblico*) premises *pl*; ~ notturno nightclub; località *sf inv* locality; localizʼzare *vt* (*circoscrivere*) to confine, localize; (*accertare*) to locate, place.
loʼcanda *sf* inn; locandiʼere, a *sm/f* innkeeper.
locaʼtario, a *sm/f* tenant.
locaʼtore, ʼtrice *sm/f* landlord/lady.
locaziʼone [lokatˈtsjone] *sf* (*da parte del locatario*) renting *q*; (*da parte del proprietario*) renting out *q*, letting *q*; (*effetto*) rent(al).
locomoʼtiva *sf* locomotive.
locomoʼtore *sm* electric locomotive.
locomoziʼone [lokomotˈtsjone] *sf* locomotion; mezzi di ~ vehicles, means of transport.
loʼcusta *sf* locust.
locuziʼone [lokutˈtsjone] *sf* phrase, expression.
loʼdare *vt* to praise.
ʼlode *sf* praise; (*INS*): laurearsi con la ~ ≈ to graduate with a first-class honours degree; loʼdevole *ag* praiseworthy.
logaʼritmo *sm* logarithm.
ʼloggia, ge [ʼlɔddʒa] *sf* (*ARCHIT*) loggia; (*circolo massonico*) lodge; loggiʼone *sm* (*di teatro*): il loggione the Gods *sg*.
ʼlogico, a, ci, che [ʼlɔdʒiko] *ag* logical // *sf* logic.
logoʼrare *vt* to wear out; (*sciupare*) to waste; ~rsi *vr* to wear out; (*fig*) to wear o.s. out.
logoʼrio *sm* wear and tear; (*fig*) strain.

ʼlogoro, a *ag* (*stoffa*) worn out, threadbare; (*persona*) worn out.
lomʼbaggine [lomʼbaddʒine] *sf* lumbago.
Lombarʼdia *sf*: la ~ Lombardy.
lomʼbata *sf* (*taglio di carne*) loin.
ʼlombo *sm* (*ANAT*) loin.
lomʼbrico, chi *sm* earthworm.
ʼLondra *sf* London.
longevità [londʒeviˈta] *sf* longevity.
lonʼgevo, a [lonʼdʒevo] *ag* long-lived.
longiʼtudine [londʒiˈtudine] *sf* longitude.
lonʼtananza [lontaˈnantsa] *sf* distance; absence.
lonʼtano, a *ag* (*distante*) distant, faraway; (*assente*) absent; (*vago: sospetto*) slight, remote; (*tempo: remoto*) far-off, distant; (*parente*) distant, remote // *av* far; è ~a la casa? is it far to the house?, is the house far from here?; è ~ un chilometro itʼs a mile away *o* a mile from here; più ~ farther; da *o* di ~ from a distance; ~ da a long way from; alla ~a slightly, vaguely.
ʼlontra *sf* otter.
loʼquace [loʼkwatʃe] *ag* talkative, loquacious; (*fig: gesto etc*) eloquent.
ʼlordo, a *ag* dirty, filthy; (*peso, stipendio*) gross; lorʼdura *sf* filth.
ʼloro *pronome pl* (*oggetto, con preposizione*) them; (*complemento di termine*) to them; (*soggetto*) they; (*forma di cortesia: anche:* L~) you; to you; il(la) ~, i(le) ~ *det* their; (*forma di cortesia:* L~) your // *pronome* theirs; (*forma di cortesia: anche:* L~) yours; ~ stessi(e) they themselves, you yourselves.
ʼlosco, a, schi, sche *ag* (*fig*) shady, suspicious.
ʼloto *sm* lotus.
ʼlotta *sf* struggle, fight; (*SPORT*) wrestling; lotʼtare *vi* to fight, struggle; to wrestle; lotʼtatore *sm* wrestler.
lotteʼria *sf* lottery; (*di gara ippica*) sweepstake.
ʼlotto *sm* (*gioco*) (state) lottery; (*parte*) lot; (*EDIL*) site.
loziʼone [lotˈtsjone] *sf* lotion.
ʼlubrico, a, ci, che *ag* lewd, lascivious.
lubrifiʼcante *sm* lubricant.
lubrifiʼcare *vt* to lubricate.
lucʼchetto [lukʼketto] *sm* padlock.
lucciʼcare [luttʃiˈkare] *vi* to sparkle, glitter, twinkle.
ʼluccio [ʼluttʃo] *sm* (*ZOOL*) pike.
ʼlucciola [ʼluttʃola] *sf* (*ZOOL*) firefly; glowworm.
ʼluce [ʼlutʃe] *sf* light; (*finestra*) window; alla ~ di by the light of; fare ~ su qc (*fig*) to shed *o* throw light on sth; ~ del sole/della luna sun/moonlight; luʼcente *ag* shining.
luʼcerna [luʼtʃerna] *sf* oil-lamp.
lucerʼnario [lutʃerˈnarjo] *sm* skylight.
luʼcertola [luʼtʃertola] *sf* lizard.
luciʼdare [lutʃiˈdare] *vt* to polish; (*ricalcare*) to trace.
lucidità [lutʃidiˈta] *sf* lucidity.

'lucido, a ['lutʃido] *ag* shining, bright; (*lucidato*) polished; (*fig*) lucid // *sm* shine, lustre; (*per scarpe etc*) polish; (*disegno*) tracing.

lu'cignolo [lu'tʃiɲɲolo] *sm* wick.

lu'crare *vt* to earn, make.

'lucro *sm* profit, gain; **lu'croso, a** *ag* lucrative, profitable.

lu'dibrio *sm* mockery *q*; (*oggetto di scherno*) laughing-stock.

'luglio ['luʎʎo] *sm* July.

'lugubre *ag* gloomy.

'lui *pronome* (*soggetto*) he; (*oggetto: per dare rilievo, con preposizione*) him; ~ **stesso** he himself.

lu'maca, che *sf* slug; (*chiocciola*) snail.

'lume *sm* light; (*lampada*) lamp; (*fig*): **chiedere** ~**i a qd** to ask sb for advice.

lumi'naria *sf* (*per feste*) illuminations *pl*.

lumi'noso, a *ag* (*che emette luce*) luminous; (*cielo, colore, stanza*) bright; (*sorgente*) of light, light *cpd*; (*fig*) obvious, clear; **idea** ~**a** bright idea.

'luna *sf* moon; ~ **nuova/piena** new/full moon; ~ **di miele** honeymoon.

'luna park *sm inv* amusement park, funfair.

lu'nare *ag* lunar, moon *cpd*.

lu'nario *sm* almanac.

lu'natico, a, ci, che *ag* whimsical, temperamental.

lunedì *sm inv* Monday; **di** *o* **il** ~ on Mondays.

lun'gaggine [lun'gaddʒine] *sf* slowness; ~**i della burocrazia** red tape.

lun'ghezza [lun'gettsa] *sf* length; ~ **d'onda** (*FISICA*) wavelength.

'lungo, a, ghi, ghe *ag* long; (*lento: persona*) slow; (*diluito: caffè, brodo*) weak, watery, thin // *sm* length // *prep* along; ~ **3 metri** 3 metres long; **a** ~ for a long time; **a** ~ **andare** in the long run; **di gran** ~**a** (*molto*) by far; **andare in** ~ *o* **per le lunghe** to drag on; **saperla** ~**a** to know what's what; **in** ~ **e in largo** far and wide, all over; ~ **il corso dei secoli** throughout the centuries.

lungo'mare *sm* promenade.

lu'notto *sm* (*AUT*) rear *o* back window.

lu'ogo, ghi *sm* place; (*posto: di incidente etc*) scene, site; (*punto, passo di libro*) passage; **in** ~ **di** instead of; **in primo** ~ in the first place; **aver** ~ to take place; **dar** ~ **a** to give rise to; ~ **comune** commonplace; ~ **geometrico** locus.

luogote'nente *sm* (*MIL*) lieutenant.

lu'para *sf* sawn-off shotgun.

'lupo, a *sm/f* wolf.

'luppolo *sm* (*BOT*) hop.

'lurido, a *ag* filthy.

lu'singa, ghe *sf* (*spesso al pl*) flattery *q*.

lusin'gare *vt* to flatter; ~**rsi** *vr* (*sperare*) to deceive o.s.; **lusinghi'ero, a** *ag* flattering, gratifying.

lus'sare *vt* (*MED*) to dislocate.

Lussem'burgo *sm*: **il** ~ Luxembourg.

'lusso *sm* luxury; **di** ~ luxury *cpd*; **lus-su'oso, a** *ag* luxurious.

lussureggi'are [lussured'dʒare] *vi* to be luxuriant.

lus'suria *sf* lust.

lus'trare *vt* to polish, shine.

lustras'carpe *sm/f inv* shoeshine.

lus'trino *sm* sequin.

'lustro, a *ag* shiny; (*pelliccia*) glossy // *sm* shine, gloss; (*fig*) prestige, glory; (*quinquennio*) five-year period.

'lutto *sm* mourning; **essere in/portare il** ~ to be in/wear mourning; **luttu'oso, a** *ag* mournful, sad.

M

ma *cong* but; ~ **insomma!** for goodness sake!; ~ **no!** of course not!

'macabro, a *ag* gruesome, macabre.

macché [mak'ke] *escl* not at all!, certainly not!

macche'roni [makke'roni] *smpl* macaroni *sg*.

'macchia ['makkja] *sf* stain, spot; (*chiazza di diverso colore*) spot; splash, patch; (*tipo di boscaglia*) scrub; **macchi'are** *vt* (*sporcare*) to stain, mark; **macchiarsi** *vr* (*persona*) to get o.s. dirty; (*stoffa*) to stain; to get stained *o* marked.

'macchina ['makkina] *sf* machine; (*elettrica, a vapore*) engine; (*automobile*) car; (*fig: meccanismo*) machinery; **andare in** ~ (*AUT*) to go by car; (*STAMPA*) to go to press; ~ **da cucire** sewing machine; ~ **fotografica** camera; ~ **da scrivere** typewriter; ~ **a vapore** steam engine.

macchi'nare [makki'nare] *vt* to plot.

macchi'nario [makki'narjo] *sm* machinery.

macchi'netta [makki'netta] *sf* (*fam: caffettiera*) percolator; (*: accendino*) lighter.

macchi'nista, i [makki'nista] *sm* (*di treno*) engine-driver; (*di nave*) engineer; (*TEATRO, TV*) stagehand.

macchi'noso, a [makki'noso] *ag* complex, complicated.

mace'donia [matʃe'donja] *sf* fruit salad.

macel'laio [matʃel'lajo] *sm* butcher.

macel'lare [matʃel'lare] *vt* to slaughter, butcher; **macelle'ria** *sf* butcher's (shop); **ma'cello** *sm* (*mattatoio*) slaughterhouse, abattoir; (*fig*) slaughter, massacre; (*: disastro*) shambles *sg*.

mace'rare [matʃe'rare] *vt* to macerate; (*fig*) to mortify; ~**rsi** *vr* to waste away; (*fig*): ~**rsi in** to be consumed with.

ma'cerie [ma'tʃɛrje] *sfpl* rubble *sg*, debris *sg*.

ma'cigno [ma'tʃiɲɲo] *sm* (*masso*) rock, boulder.

maci'lento, a [matʃi'lɛnto] *ag* emaciated.

'macina ['matʃina] *sf* (*pietra*) millstone; (*macchina*) grinder; **macinacaffè** *sm inv* coffee grinder; **macina'pepe** *sm inv* peppermill.

maci'nare [matʃi'nare] *vt* to grind; **maci'nato** *sm* meal, flour; (*carne*) mince, minced meat.

maci'nino [matʃi'nino] *sm* coffee grinder; peppermill.

'madido, a *ag*: ~ (**di**) wet *o* moist (with).

Ma'donna *sf* (*REL*) Our Lady.

mador'nale *ag* enormous, huge.

'madre *sf* mother; (*matrice di bolletta*) counterfoil // *ag inv* mother *cpd*; **ragazza** ~ unmarried mother; **scena** ~ (*TEATRO*) principal scene.

madre'lingua *sf* mother tongue, native language.

madre'perla *sf* mother-of-pearl.

madri'gale *sm* madrigal.

ma'drina *sf* godmother.

maestà *sf inv* majesty; **maes'toso, a** *ag* majestic.

ma'estra *sf vedi* **maestro.**

maes'trale *sm* north-west wind, mistral.

maes'tranze [maes'trantse] *sfpl* workforce *sg.*

maes'tria *sf* mastery, skill.

ma'estro, a *sm/f* (*INS*: *anche*: ~ **elementare**) primary teacher; (*persona molto preparata*) expert // *sm* (*artigiano, fig: guida*) master; (*MUS*) maestro // *ag* (*principale*) main; (*di grande abilità*) masterly, skilful; ~ **di cerimonie** master of ceremonies; ~**a giardiniera** nursery teacher.

'mafia *sf* Mafia; **mafi'oso** *sm* member of the Mafia.

'maga *sf* sorceress.

ma'gagna [ma'gaɲɲa] *sf* defect, flaw, blemish.

ma'gari *escl* (*esprime desiderio*): ~ **fosse vero!** if only it were true!; **ti piacerebbe andare in Scozia?** — ~**!** would you like to go to Scotland? — and how! // *av* (*anche*) even; (*forse*) perhaps.

magaz'zino [magad'dzino] *sm* warehouse; (*grande emporio*) department store.

'maggio [ˈmaddʒo] *sm* May.

maggio'rana [maddʒo'rana] *sf* (*BOT*) (*sweet*) marjoram.

maggio'ranza [maddʒo'rantsa] *sf* majority.

maggio'rare [maddʒo'rare] *vt* to increase, raise.

maggior'domo [maddʒor'dɔmo] *sm* butler.

maggi'ore [mad'dʒore] *ag* (*comparativo: più grande*) bigger, larger; taller; greater; (: *più vecchio: sorella, fratello*) older, elder; (: *di grado superiore*) senior; (: *più importante, MIL, MUS*) major; (*superlativo*) biggest, largest; tallest; greatest; oldest, eldest // *sm/f* (*di grado*) superior; (*di età*) elder; (*MIL*) major; (: *AER*) squadron leader; **la maggior parte** the majority; **maggio'renne** *ag* of age // *sm/f* person who has come of age; **maggio'rente** *sm* notable; **maggior'mente** *av* much more; (*con senso superlativo*) most.

ma'gia [ma'dʒia] *sf* magic; **'magico, a, ci, che** *ag* magic; (*fig*) fascinating, charming, magical.

'magio [ˈmadʒo] *sm* (*REL*): **i re Magi** the Magi, the Three Wise Men.

magis'tero [madʒis'tero] *sm* (*INS*) teaching; (*fig: maestria*) skill; **magis'trale** *ag* primary teachers', primary teaching *cpd*; skilful.

magis'trato [madʒis'trato] *sm* magistrate; **magistra'tura** *sf* magistrature; (*magistrati*): **la magistratura** the Bench.

'maglia [ˈmaʎʎa] *sf* stitch; (*lavoro ai ferri*) knitting *q*; (*tessuto, SPORT*) jersey; (*maglione*) jersey, sweater; (*di catena*) link; (*di rete*) mesh; **avviare/diminuire le** ~**e** to cast on/cast off; ~ **diritta/rovescia** plain purl; **maglie'ria** *sf* knitwear; (*negozio*) knitwear shop; **magli'etta** *sf* (*canottiera*) vest; (*tipo camicia*) T-shirt; **magli'ficio** *sm* knitwear factory.

'maglio [ˈmaʎʎo] *sm* mallet; (*macchina*) power hammer.

ma'gnanimo, a [maɲ'ɲanimo] *ag* magnanimous.

ma'gnesia [maɲ'ɲezja] *sf* (*CHIM*) magnesia.

ma'gnesio [maɲ'ɲezjo] *sm* (*CHIM*) magnesium.

ma'gnete [maɲ'ɲete] *sm* magnet; **ma'gnetico, a, ci, che** *ag* magnetic; **magne'tismo** *sm* magnetism.

magne'tofono [maɲɲe'tɔfono] *sm* tape recorder.

magnifi'cenza [maɲɲifi'tʃentsa] *sf* magnificence, splendour.

ma'gnifico, a, ci, che [maɲ'ɲifiko] *ag* magnificent, splendid; (*ospite*) generous.

ma'gnolia [maɲ'ɲɔlja] *sf* magnolia.

'mago, ghi *sm* (*stregone*) magician, wizard; (*illusionista*) magician.

ma'grezza [ma'grettsa] *sf* thinness.

'magro, a *ag* (*very*) thin, skinny; (*carne*) lean; (*formaggio*) low-fat; (*fig: scarso, misero*) meagre, poor; (: *meschino: scusa*) poor, lame; **mangiare di** ~ not to eat meat.

'mai *av* (*nessuna volta*) never; (*talvolta*) ever; **non ...** ~ never; ~ **più** never again; **come** ~? why (*o* how) on earth?; **chi/dove/quando** ~? whoever/wherever/whenever?

mai'ale *sm* (*ZOOL*) pig; (*carne*) pork.

maio'nese *sf* mayonnaise.

'mais *sm inv* maize.

mai'uscolo, a *ag* (*lettera*) capital; (*fig*) enormous, huge // *sf* capital letter.

mal *av, sm vedi* **male.**

malac'corto, a *ag* rash, careless.

mala'copia *sf* rough copy.

malafede *sf* bad faith.

mala'mente *av* badly; dangerously.

malan'dato, a *ag* (*persona: di salute*) in poor health; (: *di condizioni finanziarie*) badly off; (*trascurato*) shabby.

ma'lanimo *sm* ill will, malevolence; **di** ~ unwillingly.

ma'lanno sm (disgrazia) misfortune; (malattia) ailment.

mala'pena sf: a ~ hardly, scarcely.

ma'laria sf (MED) malaria.

mala'sorte sf bad luck.

mala'ticcio, a [mala'tittʃo] ag sickly.

ma'lato, a ag ill, sick; (gamba) bad; (pianta) diseased // sm/f sick person; (in ospedale) patient; **malat'tia** sf (infettiva etc) illness, disease; (cattiva salute) illness, sickness.

malau'gurio sm bad o ill omen.

mala'vita sf underworld.

mala'voglia [mala'vɔʎʎa] sf reluctance, unwillingness; **di** ~ unwillingly, reluctantly.

mal'concio, a, ci, ce [mal'kontʃo] ag in a sorry state.

malcon'tento sm discontent.

malcos'tume sm immorality.

mal'destro, a ag (inabile) inexpert, inexperienced; (goffo) awkward.

maldi'cente [maldi'tʃɛnte] ag slanderous.

maldis'posto, a ag: ~ (verso) ill-disposed (towards).

'male av badly // sm (ciò che è ingiusto, disonesto) evil; (danno, svantaggio) harm; (sventura) misfortune; (dolore fisico, morale) pain, ache; **di** ~ **in peggio** from bad to worse; **sentirsi** ~ to feel ill; **far** ~ (dolere) to hurt; **far** ~ **alla salute** to be bad for one's health; **far del** ~ **a qd** to hurt o harm sb; **restare** o **rimanere** ~ to be sorry; to be disappointed; to be hurt; **andare a** ~ to go bad; **come va?** — **non c'è** ~ how are you? — not bad; **mal di mare** seasickness; **avere mal di gola/testa** to have a sore throat/a headache.

male'detto, a pp di **maledire** // ag cursed, damned; (fig: fastidioso) damned, wretched.

male'dire vt to curse; **maledizi'one** sf curse; **maledizione!** damn it!

maledu'cato, a ag rude, ill-mannered.

male'ficio [male'fitʃo] sm witchcraft.

ma'lefico, a, ci, che ag (aria, cibo) harmful, bad; (influsso, azione) evil.

ma'lessere sm indisposition, slight illness; (fig) uneasiness.

ma'levolo, a ag malevolent.

malfa'mato, a ag notorious.

mal'fatto, a ag (persona) deformed; (cosa) badly made.

malfat'tore, 'trice sm/f wrongdoer.

mal'fermo, a ag unsteady, shaky; (salute) poor, delicate.

malformazi'one [malformat'tsjone] sf malformation.

malgo'verno sm maladministration.

mal'grado prep in spite of, despite // cong although; **mio** (o tuo etc) ~ against my (o your etc) will.

ma'lia sf spell; (fig: fascino) charm.

mali'gnare [maliɲ'ɲare] vi: ~ **su** to malign, speak ill of.

ma'ligno, a [ma'liɲɲo] ag (malvagio) malicious, malignant; (MED) malignant.

malinco'nia sf melancholy, gloom; **malin'conico, a, ci, che** ag melancholy.

malincu'ore: a ~ av reluctantly, unwillingly.

malintenzio'nato, a [malintentsjo'nato] ag ill-intentioned.

malin'teso, a ag misunderstood; (riguardo, senso del dovere) mistaken, wrong // sm misunderstanding.

ma'lizia [ma'littsja] sf (malignità) malice; (furbizia) cunning; (espediente) trick; **malizi'oso, a** ag malicious; cunning; (vivace, birichino) mischievous.

malle'abile ag malleable.

malme'nare vt to beat up; (fig) to ill-treat.

mal'messo, a ag (persona) shabby, badly-dressed; (casa) badly-furnished.

malnu'trito, a ag undernourished; **malnutrizi'one** sf malnutrition.

ma'locchio [ma'lɔkkjo] sm evil eye.

ma'lora sf ruin; **andare in** ~ to go to the dogs; **va in** ~! go to hell!

ma'lore sm feeling of faintness; feeling of discomfort.

mal'sano, a ag unhealthy.

malsi'curo, a ag unsafe; (fig) uncertain; (: testimonianza) unreliable.

'malta sf (EDIL) mortar.

mal'tempo sm bad weather.

'malto sm malt.

maltrat'tare vt to ill-treat.

malu'more sm bad mood; (irritabilità) bad temper; (discordia) ill feeling; **di** ~ in a bad mood.

mal'vagio, a, gi, gie [mal'vadʒo] ag wicked, evil.

malversazi'one [malversat'tsjone] sf (DIR) embezzlement.

mal'visto, a ag: ~ **(da)** disliked (by), unpopular (with).

malvi'vente sm criminal.

malvolenti'eri av unwillingly, reluctantly.

malvo'lere vt: **farsi** ~ **da qd** to make o.s. unpopular with sb // sm (avversione) ill will; (scarsa volontà) unwillingness.

'mamma sf mummy, mum; ~ **mia!** my goodness!

mam'mario, a ag (ANAT) mammary.

mam'mella sf (ANAT) breast; (di vacca, capra etc) udder.

mam'mifero sm mammal.

'mammola sf (BOT) violet.

ma'nata sf (colpo) slap; (quantità) handful.

'manca sf vedi manco.

man'canza [man'kantsa] sf lack; (carenza) shortage, scarcity; (fallo) fault; (imperfezione) failing, shortcoming; **per** ~ **di tempo** through lack of time; **in** ~ **di meglio** for lack of anything better.

man'care vi (2: essere insufficiente) to be lacking; (: venir meno) to fail; (: non esserci) to be missing, not to be there; (: essere lontano): ~ **(da)** to be away (from) // vt to miss; ~ **di** to lack; ~ **a**

(*promessa*) to fail to keep; **tu mi manchi** I miss you; **mancò poco che morisse** he very nearly died; **mancano ancora 10 sterline** we're still £10 short; **manca un quarto alle 6** it's a quarter to 6; **man'cato, a** *ag* (*tentativo*) unsuccessful; (*artista*) failed.

'mancia, ce ['mantʃa] *sf* tip; ~ **competente** reward.

manci'ata [man'tʃata] *sf* handful.

man'cino, a [man'tʃino] *ag* (*braccio*) left; (*persona*) left-handed; (*fig*) underhand.

'manco, a, chi, che *ag* left // *sf* left hand // *av* (*nemmeno*) not even.

man'dare *vt* to send; (*far funzionare: macchina*) to drive; (*emettere*) to send out; (*: grido*) to give, utter, let out; ~ **a chiamare qd** to send for sb; ~ **giù** to send down; (*anche fig*) to swallow; ~ **via** to send away; (*licenziare*) to fire.

manda'rino *sm* mandarin (orange), tangerine; (*cinese*) mandarin.

man'data *sf* (*spedizione*) sending; (*quantità*) lot, batch; (*di chiave*) turn.

manda'tario *sm* (DIR) representative, agent.

man'dato *sm* (*incarico*) commission; (DIR: *provvedimento*) warrant; (*di deputato etc*) mandate; (*ordine di pagamento*) postal o money order; ~ **d'arresto** warrant for arrest.

man'dibola *sf* mandible, jaw.

'mandorla *sf* almond; **'mandorlo** *sm* almond tree.

'mandria *sf* herd.

maneggi'are [maned'dʒare] *vt* (*creta*) to mould, work, fashion; (*arnesi, utensili*) to handle; (*: adoperare*) to use; (*fig: persone*) to handle, deal with; **ma'neggio** *sm* moulding; handling; use; (*intrigo*) plot, scheme; (*per cavalli*) riding school.

ma'nesco, a, schi, sche *ag* free with one's fists.

ma'netta *sf* hand lever; ~**e** *sfpl* handcuffs.

manga'nello *sm* club.

manga'nese *sm* manganese.

'mangano *sm* mangle.

mange'reccio, a, ci, ce [mandʒe'rettʃo] *ag* edible.

mange'ria [mandʒe'ria] *sf* extortion.

mangia'dischi [mandʒa'diski] *sm inv* record player.

mangi'are [man'dʒare] *vt* to eat; (*intaccare*) to eat into o away; (CARTE, SCACCHI etc) to take // *vi* to eat // *sm* eating; (*cibo*) food; (*cucina*) cooking; ~**rsi le parole** to mumble; **mangia'toia** *sf* feeding-trough.

man'gime [man'dʒime] *sm* fodder.

'mango, ghi *sm* mango.

ma'nia *sf* (PSIC) mania; (*fig*) obsession, craze; **ma'niaco, a, ci, che** *ag* suffering from a mania; **maniaco (di)** obsessed (by), crazy (about).

'manica *sf* sleeve; (*fig: gruppo*) gang, bunch; (GEO): **la M**~ the (English) Channel; **essere di** ~ **larga/stretta** to be easy-going/strict; ~ **a vento** (AER) wind sock.

mani'chino [mani'kino] *sm* (*di sarto, vetrina*) dummy.

'manico, ci *sm* handle; (MUS) neck.

mani'comio *sm* mental hospital; (*fig*) madhouse.

mani'cotto *sm* muff; (TECN) coupling; sleeve.

mani'cure *sf inv* manicurist.

mani'era *sf* way, manner; (*stile*) style, manner; ~**e** *sfpl* manners; **in** ~ **che** so that; **in** ~ **da** so as to; **in tutte le** ~**e** at all costs.

manie'rato, a *ag* affected.

manifat'tura *sf* (*lavorazione*) manufacture; (*stabilimento*) factory.

manifes'tare *vt* to show, display; (*esprimere*) to express; (*rivelare*) to reveal, disclose // *vi* to demonstrate; ~**rsi** *vr* to show o.s.; ~**rsi amico** to prove o.s. (to be) a friend; **manifestazi'one** *sf* show, display; expression; (*sintomo*) sign, symptom; (*dimostrazione pubblica*) demonstration; (*cerimonia*) event.

mani'festo, a *ag* obvious, evident // *sm* poster, bill; (*scritto ideologico*) manifesto.

ma'niglia [ma'niʎʎa] *sf* handle; (*sostegno: negli autobus etc*) strap.

manipo'lare *vt* to manipulate; (*alterare: vino*) to adulterate; **manipolazi'one** *sf* manipulation; adulteration.

manis'calco, chi *sm* farrier.

'manna *sf* (REL) manna.

man'naia *sf* (*del boia*) (executioner's) axe; (*per carni*) cleaver.

man'naro: lupo ~ *sm* werewolf.

'mano, i *sf* hand; (*strato: di vernice etc*) coat; **di prima** ~ (*notizia*) first-hand; **di seconda** ~ second-hand; **man** ~ little by little, gradually; **man** ~ **che** as; **darsi o stringersi la** ~ to shake hands; **mettere le** ~**i avanti** (*fig*) to safeguard o.s.; **a** ~ by hand; ~**i in alto!** hands up!

mano'dopera *sf* labour.

ma'nometro *sm* gauge, manometer.

mano'mettere *vt* (*alterare*) to tamper with; (*frugare, aprire*) to break open illegally; (*ledere: diritti*) to violate, infringe; **mano'messo, a** *pp di* **manomettere**.

ma'nopola *sf* (*dell'armatura*) gauntlet; (*guanto*) mitt; (*di impugnatura*) hand-grip; (*pomello*) knob.

manos'critto, a *ag* handwritten // *sm* manuscript.

mano'vale *sm* labourer.

mano'vella *sf* handle; (TECN) crank; **albero a** ~ crankshaft.

ma'novra *sf* manoeuvre; (FERR) shunting; **mano'vrare** *vt* to manoeuvre; (*congegno*) to operate // *vi* to manoeuvre.

manro'vescio [manro'veʃʃo] *sm* slap (*with back of hand*).

man'sarda *sf* attic.

mansi'one *sf* task, duty, job.

mansu'eto, a *ag* gentle, docile.

man'tello *sm* cloak; (*fig: di neve etc*)

blanket, mantle; (TECN: involucro) casing, shell; (ZOOL) coat.

mante'nere vt to maintain; (adempiere: promesse) to keep, abide by; (provvedere a) to support, maintain; ~**rsi** vr: ~**rsi calmo/ giovane** to stay calm/young; **manteni'mento** sm maintenance.

'mantice ['mantitfe] sm bellows pl; (di carrozza, automobile) hood.

'manto sm cloak; ~ **stradale** road surface.

manu'ale ag manual // sm (testo) manual, handbook.

ma'nubrio sm handle; (di bicicletta etc) handlebars pl; (SPORT) dumbbell.

manu'fatto, a ag manufactured.

manutenzi'one [manuten'tsjone] sf maintenance, upkeep; (d'impianti) maintenance, servicing.

'manzo ['mandzo] sm (ZOOL) steer; (carne) beef.

'mappa sf (GEO) map; **mappa'mondo** sm map of the world; (globo girevole) globe.

ma'rasma, i sm (fig) decay, decline.

mara'tona sf marathon.

'marca, che sf mark; (bollo) stamp; (COMM: di prodotti) brand; (contrassegno, scontrino) ticket, check; ~ **da bollo** official stamp; ~ **di fabbrica** trademark.

mar'care vt (munire di contrassegno) to mark; (a fuoco) to brand; (SPORT: gol) to score; (: avversario) to mark; ~ **visita** (MIL) to report sick.

mar'chese, a [mar'keze] sm/f marquis o marquess/marchioness.

marchi'are [mar'kjare] vt to brand; **'marchio** sm (di bestiame, COMM, fig) brand; **marchio di fabbrica** trademark; **marchio depositato** registered trademark.

'marcia, ce ['martfa] sf (anche MUS, MIL) march; (funzionamento) running; (il camminare) walking; (AUT) gear; **mettere in** ~ to start; **mettersi in** ~ to get moving; **far** ~ **indietro** (AUT) to reverse; (fig) to back-pedal.

marciapi'ede [martfa'pjɛde] sm (di strada) pavement; (FERR) platform.

màrci'are [mar'tfare] vi to march; (andare: treno, macchina) to go; (funzionare) to run, work.

'marcio, a, ci, ce ['martfo] ag (frutta, legno) rotten, bad; (MED) festering; (fig) corrupt, rotten.

mar'cire [mar'tfire] vi (2) (andare a male) to go bad, rot; (suppurare) to fester; (fig) to rot, waste away.

'marco, chi sm (unità monetaria) mark.

'mare sm sea; **in** ~ at sea; **andare al** ~ (in vacanza etc) to go to the seaside; **il** ~ **del Nord** the North Sea.

ma'rea sf tide; **alta/bassa** ~ high/low tide.

mareggi'ata [mared'dʒata] sf heavy sea.

ma'remma sf (GEO) maremma, swampy coastal area.

mare'moto sm seaquake.

maresci'allo [mareʃ'ʃallo] sm (MIL)

marshal; (: sottufficiale) warrant officer.

marga'rina sf margarine.

marghe'rita [marge'rita] sf (ox-eye) daisy, marguerite; **margheri'tina** sf daisy.

margi'nale [mardʒi'nale] ag marginal.

'margine ['mardʒine] sm margin; (di bosco, via) edge, border.

ma'rina sf navy; (costa) coast; ~ **militare/mercantile** navy/merchant navy.

mari'naio sm sailor.

mari'nare vt (CUC) to marinate; ~ **la scuola** to play truant; **mari'nata** sf marinade.

ma'rino, a ag sea cpd, marine.

mario'netta sf puppet.

mari'tale ag marital.

mari'tare vt to marry; ~**rsi** vr: ~**rsi a** o **con qd** to marry sb, get married to sb.

ma'rito sm husband.

ma'rittimo, a ag maritime, sea cpd.

mar'maglia [mar'maʎʎa] sf mob, riff-raff.

marmel'lata sf jam; (di agrumi) marmalade.

mar'mitta sf (recipiente) pot; (AUT) silencer.

'marmo sm marble.

mar'mocchio [mar'mɔkkjo] sm (fam) tot, kid.

mar'motta sf (ZOOL) marmot.

Ma'rocco sm: **il** ~ Morocco.

'marra sf hoe.

mar'rone ag inv brown // sm (BOT) chestnut.

mar'sina sf tails pl, tail coat.

martedì sm inv Tuesday; **di** o **il** ~ on Tuesdays; ~ **grasso** Shrove Tuesday.

martel'lare vt to hammer // vi to hammer; (pulsare) to throb.

mar'tello sm hammer; (di uscio) knocker.

marti'netto sm (TECN) jack.

'martire sm/f martyr; **mar'tirio** sm martyrdom; (fig) agony, torture.

'martora sf marten.

martori'are vt to torment, torture.

marza'pane [martsa'pane] sm marzipan.

marzi'ale [mar'tsjale] ag martial.

'marzo ['martso] sm March.

mascal'zone [maskal'tsone] sm rascal, scoundrel.

ma'scella [maʃ'ʃella] sf (ANAT) jaw.

'maschera ['maskera] sf mask; (travestimento) disguise; (: per un ballo etc) fancy dress; (TEATRO, CINEMA) usher/usherette; (personaggio del teatro) stock character; **maschera'mento** sm disguise; (MIL) camouflage; **masche'rare** vt to mask; (travestire) to disguise; to dress up; (fig: celare) to hide, conceal; (MIL) to camouflage; ~**rsi da** to disguise o.s. as; to dress up as; (fig) to masquerade as.

mas'chile [mas'kile] ag masculine; (sesso, popolazione) male; (abiti) men's; (per ragazzi: scuola) boys'.

'maschio, a ['maskjo] ag (BIOL) male;

(*virile*) manly // *sm* male; (*ragazzo*) boy; (*figlio*) son.

masco'lino, a *ag* masculine.

mas'cotte *sf inv* mascot.

'massa *sf* mass; (*di errori etc*): **una ~ di** heaps of, masses of; (*di gente*) mass, multitude; (*ELETTR*) earth; **in ~** (*COMM*) in bulk; (*tutti insieme*) en masse; **adunata in ~** mass meeting; **la ~ dei popolo** the masses *pl*.

massa'crare *vt* to massacre, slaughter; **mas'sacro** *sm* massacre, slaughter; (*fig*) mess, disaster.

massaggi'are [massad'dʒare] *vt* to massage; **mas'saggio** *sm* massage.

mas'saia *sf* housewife.

masse'ria *sf* large farm.

masse'rizie [masse'rittsje] *sfpl* (*household*) furnishings.

mas'siccio, a, ci, ce [mas'sittʃo] *ag* (*oro, legno*) solid; (*palazzo*) massive; (*corporatura*) stout // *sm* (*GEO*) massif.

'massima *sf vedi* **massimo.**

massi'male *sm* maximum.

'massimo, a *ag*, *sm* maximum // *sf* (*sentenza, regola*) maxim; (*METEOR*) maximum temperature; **al ~** at (the) most; **in linea di ~a** generally speaking.

'masso *sm* rock, boulder.

mas'sone *sm* freemason; **massone'ria** *sf* freemasonry.

masti'care *vt* to chew.

'mastice [ˈmastitʃe] *sm* mastic; (*per vetri*) putty.

mas'tino *sm* mastiff.

masturbazi'one [masturbat'tsjone] *sf* masturbation.

ma'tassa *sf* skein; **trovare il bandolo della ~** (*fig*) to get to the bottom of a complicated matter.

mate'matico, a, ci, che *ag* mathematical // *sm/f* mathematician // *sf* mathematics *sg*.

mate'rasso *sm* mattress; **~ a molle** spring *o* interior-sprung mattress.

ma'teria *sf* (*FISICA*) matter; (*TECN, COMM*) material, matter *q*; (*disciplina*) subject; (*argomento*) subject matter, material; **~e prime** raw materials; **materi'ale** *ag* material; (*fig: grossolano*) rough, rude // *sm* material; (*insieme di strumenti etc*) equipment *q*, materials *pl*; **materia'lista, i, e** *ag* materialistic.

materni'tà *sf* motherhood, maternity; (*clinica*) maternity hospital.

ma'terno, a *ag* (*amore, cura etc*) maternal, motherly; (*nonno*) maternal; (*lingua, terra*) mother *cpd*.

ma'tita *sf* pencil.

ma'trice [ma'tritʃe] *sf* matrix; (*COMM*) counterfoil.

ma'tricola *sf* (*registro*) register; (*numero*) registration number; (*nell'università*) freshman, fresher.

ma'trigna [ma'triɲɲa] *sf* stepmother.

matrimoni'ale *ag* matrimonial, marriage *cpd*.

matri'monio *sm* marriage, matrimony;

(*durata*) marriage, married life; (*cerimonia*) wedding.

ma'trona *sf* (*fig*) matronly woman.

mat'tina *sf* morning; **matti'nata** *sf* morning; (*spettacolo*) matinée, afternoon performance; **mattini'ero, a** *ag*: **essere mattiniero** to be an early riser; **mat'tino** *sm* morning.

'matto, a *ag* mad, crazy; (*fig: falso*) false, imitation; (: *opaco*) matt, dull // *sm/f* madman/woman; **avere una voglia ~a di qc** to be dying for sth.

mat'tone *sm* brick.

matto'nella *sf* tile.

matu'rare *vi* (2) (*anche*: **~rsi**) (*frutta, grano*) to ripen; (*ascesso*) to come to a head; (*fig: persona, idea, ECON*) to mature // *vt* to ripen; to (make) mature.

maturi'tà *sf* maturity; (*di frutta*) ripeness, maturity; (*INS*) school-leaving examination, ≈ GCE A-levels.

ma'turo, a *ag* mature; (*frutto*) ripe, mature.

mauso'leo *sm* mausoleum.

'mazza [ˈmattsa] *sf* (*bastone*) club; (*martello*) sledge-hammer; (*SPORT: da golf*) club; (: *da baseball, cricket*) bat.

'mazzo [ˈmattso] *sm* (*di fiori, chiavi etc*) bunch; (*di carte da gioco*) pack.

me *pronome me*: **me'da λλ a**] of me; **sei bravo quanto ~** you are as clever as I (am) *o* as me.

me'andro *sm* meander.

M.E.C. [mɛk] *sm* (*abbr di* **Mercato Comune Europeo**) EEC.

mec'canico, a, ci, che *ag* mechanical // *sm* mechanic // *sf* mechanics *sg*; (*attività tecnologica*) mechanical engineering; (*meccanismo*) mechanism.

mecca'nismo *sm* mechanism.

me'daglia [me'daλλa] *sf* medal; **medagli'one** *sm* (*ARCHIT*) medallion; (*gioiello*) locket.

me'desimo, a *ag* same; (*in persona*): **io ~** I myself.

'media *sf vedi* **medio.**

medi'ano, a *ag* median; (*valore*) mean // *sm* (*CALCIO*) half-back.

medi'ante *prep* by means of.

medi'are *vt* (*fare da mediatore*) to act as mediator in; (*MAT*) to average.

media'tore, 'trice *sm/f* mediator; (*COMM*) middle man, agent.

mediazi'one [medjat'tsjone] *sf* mediation.

medica'mento *sm* medicine, drug.

medi'care *vt* to treat; (*ferita*) to dress; **medicazi'one** *sf* treatment, medication; dressing.

medi'cina [medi'tʃina] *sf* medicine; **~ legale** forensic medicine; **medici'nale** *ag* medicinal // *sm* drug, medicine.

'medico, a, ci, che *ag* medical // *sm* doctor; **~ generico** general practitioner, G.P.

medie'vale *ag* medieval.

'medio, a *ag* average; (*punto, ceto*) middle; (*altezza, statura*) medium // *sm* (*dito*) middle finger // *sf* average; (*MAT*) mean;

(*INS: voto*) end-of-term average.
medi'ocre *ag* mediocre, poor.
medioe'vale *ag* = **medievale.**
medio'evo *sm* Middle Ages *pl.*
medi'tare *vt* to ponder over, meditate on; (*progettare*) to plan, think out // *vi* to meditate; **meditazi'one** *sf* meditation.
mediter'raneo, a *ag* Mediterranean; **il (mare) M**~ the Mediterranean (Sea).
me'dusa *sf* (*ZOOL*) jellyfish.
me'gafono *sm* megaphone.
'**meglio** ['mεʎʎo] *av, ag inv* better; (*con senso superlativo*) best // *sm* (*la cosa migliore*): **il** ~ the best (thing); **alla** ~ as best one can; **andar di bene in** ~ to get better and better; **fare del proprio** ~ to do one's best; **per il** ~ for the best; **aver la** ~ **su qd** to get the better of sb.
'**mela** *sf* apple; ~ **cotogna** quince.
mela'grana *sf* pomegranate.
melan'zana [melan'dzana] *sf* aubergine.
me'lassa *sf* molasses *sg*, treacle.
me'lenso, a *ag* dull, stupid.
mel'lifluo, a *ag* (*peg*) sugary, honeyed.
'**melma** *sf* mud, mire.
'**melo** *sm* apple tree.
melo'dia *sf* melody; **me'lodico, a, ci, che** *ag* melodic; **melodi'oso, a** *ag* melodious.
melo'dramma, i *sm* melodrama.
me'lone *sm* (musk)melon.
'**membra** *sfpl vedi* **membro.**
mem'brana *sf* membrane.
'**membro** *sm* member; (*pl(f)* ~**a**: *arto*) limb.
memo'rabile *ag* memorable.
memo'randum *sm inv* memorandum.
me'moria *sf* memory; ~**e** *sfpl* (*opera autobiografica*) memoirs; **a** ~ (*imparare, sapere*) by heart; **a** ~ **d'uomo** within living memory; **memori'ale** *sm* (*raccolta di memorie*) memoirs *pl*; (*DIR*) memorial.
mena'dito: a ~ *av* perfectly, thoroughly; **sapere qc a** ~ to have sth at one's fingertips.
me'nare *vt* to lead; (*picchiare*) to hit, beat; (*dare: colpi*) to deal; ~ **la coda** (*cane*) to wag its tail.
mendi'cante *sm/f* beggar.
mendi'care *vt* to beg for // *vi* to beg.
'**meno** *av* less; (*in frasi comparative*): ~ **freddo che** not as cold as, less cold than; (: *seguito da nome, pronome*): ~ **alto di** not as tall as, less tall than; ~ **denaro di** less money than, not as much money as; (*in frasi superlative*): **il(la)** ~ **bravo(a)** the least clever; (*di temperatura*) below (zero), minus; (*MAT*) minus, less; (*l'ora*): **sono le 8** ~ **un quarto** it's a quarter to eight // *ag inv* (*tempo, denaro*) less; (*errori, persone*) fewer // *prep* except (for) // *sm inv* (*la parte minore*): **il** ~ the least; (*MAT*) minus; **i** ~ (*la minoranza*) the minority; **a** ~ **che** *cong* unless; **fare a** ~ **di qc** (*privarsene*) to do without sth; (*rinunciarvi*) to give up sth; **fare a** ~ **di fumare** to give up smoking; **non potevo fare a** ~ **di ridere** I couldn't help laughing; **mille lire in** ~

a thousand lire less; ~ **male** so much the better; thank goodness.
meno'mare *vt* (*danneggiare*) to maim, disable; (*diminuire: meriti*) to diminish, lessen.
meno'pausa *sf* menopause.
'**mensa** *sf* (*locale*) canteen; (: *MIL*) mess; (: *nelle università*) refectory.
men'sile *ag* monthly // *sm* (*periodico*) monthly (magazine); (*stipendio*) monthly salary.
'**mensola** *sf* bracket; (*ripiano*) shelf; (*ARCHIT*) corbel.
'**menta** *sf* mint; (*anche*: ~ **peperita**) peppermint.
men'tale *ag* mental; **mentalità** *sf inv* mentality.
'**mente** *sf* mind; **imparare/sapere qc a** ~ to learn/know sth by heart; **avere in** ~ **qc** to have sth in mind; **passare di** ~ **a qd** to slip sb's mind.
men'tire *vi* to lie.
'**mento** *sm* chin.
'**mentre** *cong* (*temporale*) while; (*avversativo*) whereas.
menzio'nare [mentsjo'nare] *vt* to mention.
menzi'one [men'tsjone] *sf* mention; **fare** ~ **di** to mention.
men'zogna [men'tsɔɲɲa] *sf* lie.
mera'viglia [mera'viʎʎa] *sf* amazement, wonder; (*persona, cosa*) marvel, wonder; **a** ~ perfectly, wonderfully; **meravigli'are** *vt* to amaze, astonish; **meravigliarsi (di)** to marvel (at); (*stupirsi*) to be amazed (at), be astonished (at); **meravigli'oso, a** *ag* wonderful, marvellous.
mer'cante *sm* merchant; ~ **di cavalli** horse dealer; **mercanteggi'are** *vt* (*onore, voto*) to sell // *vi* to bargain, haggle; **mercan'tile** *ag* commercial, mercantile, merchant *cpd* // *sm* (*nave*) merchantman; **mercan'zia** *sf* merchandise, goods *pl.*
mer'cato *sm* market; ~ **dei cambi** exchange market; **M**~ **Comune (Europeo)** Common Market; ~ **nero** black market.
'**merce** ['mεrtʃe] *sf* goods *pl*, merchandise; ~ **deperibile** perishable goods *pl.*
mercè [mer'tʃε] *sf* mercy.
merce'nario, a [mertʃe'narjo] *ag, sm* mercenary.
merce'ria [mertʃe'ria] *sf* (*bottega, articoli*) haberdashery.
mercoledì *sm inv* Wednesday; **di** *o* **il** ~ on Wednesdays; ~ **delle Ceneri** Ash Wednesday.
mer'curio *sm* mercury.
'**merda** *sf* (*fam!*) shit (!).
me'renda *sf* afternoon snack.
meridi'ano, a *ag* meridian; midday *cpd*, noonday // *sm* meridian // *sf* (*orologio*) sundial.
meridio'nale *ag* southern // *sm/f* southerner.
meridi'one *sm* south.
me'ringa, ghe *sf* (*CUC*) meringue.
meri'tare *vt* to deserve, merit.

meri'tevole *ag* worthy.

'merito *sm* merit; (*valore*) worth; **in ~ a** as regards, with regard to; **dare ~ a qd di** to give sb credit for; **meri'torio, a** *ag* praiseworthy.

mer'letto *sm* lace.

'merlo *sm* (*ZOOL*) blackbird; (*ARCHIT*) battlement.

mer'luzzo [mer'luttso] *sm* (*ZOOL*) cod.

mes'chino, a [mes'kino] *ag* wretched; (*scarso*) scanty, poor; (*persona: gretta*) mean; (*: limitata*) narrow-minded, petty.

'mescita [ˈmeʃʃita] *sf* public house.

mesco'lanza [mesko'lantsa] *sf* mixture.

mesco'lare *vt* to mix; (*colori*) to blend; (*mettere in disordine*) to mix up, muddle up; (*carte*) to shuffle; **~rsi** *vr* to mix; to blend; to get mixed up; (*fig*): **~rsi in** to get mixed up in, meddle in.

'mese *sm* month.

'messa *sf* (*REL*) mass; (*il mettere*): **~ in moto** starting; **~ in piega** set; **~ a punto** (*TECN*) adjustment; (*AUT*) tuning; (*fig*) clarification; **~ in scena** *vedi* **messinscena**.

messag'gero [messad'dʒero] *sm* messenger.

mes'saggio [mes'saddʒo] *sm* message.

mes'sale *sm* (*REL*) missal.

'messe *sf* harvest.

Mes'sia *sm inv* (*REL*): **il ~** the Messiah.

'Messico *sm*: **il ~** Mexico.

messin'scena [messin'ʃena] *sf* (*TEATRO*) production.

'messo, a *pp di* **mettere** // *sm* messenger.

mesti'ere *sm* (*professione*) job; (*: manuale*) trade; (*: artigianale*) craft; (*fig: abilità nel lavoro*) skill, technique; **essere del ~** to know the tricks of the trade.

'mesto, a *ag* sad, melancholy.

'mestola *sf* (*CUC*) ladle; (*EDIL*) trowel.

'mestolo *sm* (*CUC*) ladle.

mestruazi'one [mestruat'tsjone] *sf* menstruation.

'meta *sf* destination; (*fig*) aim, goal.

metà *sf inv* half; (*punto di mezzo*) middle; **dividere qc a ~ per ~** to divide sth in half, halve sth; **fare a ~ (di qc con qd)** to go halves (with sb in sth); **a ~ prezzo** at half price; **a ~ strada** halfway.

metabo'lismo *sm* metabolism.

meta'fisica *sf* metaphysics *sg*.

me'tafora *sf* metaphor.

me'tallico, a, ci, che *ag* (*di metallo*) metal *cpd*; (*splendore etc*) metallic.

me'tallo *sm* metal; **metallur'gia** *sf* metallurgy.

meta'morfosi *sf* metamorphosis.

me'tano *sm* methane.

me'teora *sf* meteor.

meteo'rite *sm* meteorite.

meteorolo'gia [meteorolo'dʒia] *sf* meteorology; **meteoro'logico, a, ci, che** *ag* meteorological, weather *cpd*.

me'ticcio, a, ci, ce [me'tittʃo] *sm/f* half-caste, half-breed.

metico'loso, a *ag* meticulous.

me'todico, a, ci, che *ag* methodical.

'metodo *sm* method; (*manuale*) tutor, manual.

'metrico, a, ci, che *ag* metric; (*POESIA*) metrical // *sf* metrics *sg*.

'metro *sm* metre; (*nastro*) tape measure; (*asta*) (metre) rule.

me'tropoli *sf* metropolis.

metropoli'tano, a *ag* metropolitan // *sm* (*city*) policeman // *sf* underground, subway.

'mettere *vt* to put; (*abito*) to put on; (*: portare*) to wear; (*installare: telefono*) to put in; (*fig: provocare*): **~ fame/allegria a qd** to make sb hungry/happy; (*supporre*): **mettiamo che ...** let's suppose *o* say that ... ; **~rsi** *vr* (*disporsi: faccenda*) to turn out; **~rsi a sedere** to sit down; **~rsi a letto** to get into bed; (*per malattia*) to take to one's bed; **~rsi il cappello** to put on one's hat; **~rsi a** (*cominciare*) to begin to, start to; **~rsi al lavoro** to set to work; **~rci**: **~rci molta cura/molto tempo** to take a lot of care/a lot of time; **ci ho messo 3 ore per venire** it's taken me 3 hours to get here; **~ a tacere qd/qc** to keep sb/sth quiet; **~ su casa** to set up house; **~ su un negozio** to start a shop; **~ via** to put away.

mez'zadro [med'dzadro] *sm* (*AGR*) sharecropper.

mezza'luna [meddza'luna] *sf* half-moon; (*dell'islamismo*) crescent; (*coltello*) (semicircular) chopping knife.

mezza'nino [meddza'nino] *sm* mezzanine (floor).

mez'zano, a [med'dzano] *ag* (*medio*) average, medium // *sm/f* (*intermediario*) go-between; (*ruffiano*) pimp.

mezza'notte [meddza'nɔtte] *sf* midnight.

'mezzo, a [ˈmɛddzo] *ag* half; **un ~ litro/panino** half a litre/roll // *av* half; **~ morto** half-dead // *sm* (*metà*) half; (*parte centrale: di strada etc*) middle; (*per raggiungere un fine*) means *sg*; (*veicolo*) vehicle; (*nell'indicare l'ora*): **le nove e ~** half past nine; **mezzogiorno e ~** half past twelve; **~i** *smpl* (*possibilità economiche*) means; **di ~a età** middle-aged; **di ~** middle, in the middle; **andarci di ~** (*patir danno*) to suffer; **levarsi** *o* **togliersi di ~** to get out of the way; **in ~ a** in the middle of; **per** *o* **a ~ di** by means of; **~i di comunicazione di massa** mass media *pl*; **~i pubblici** public transport *sg*; **~i di trasporto** means of transport.

mezzogi'orno [meddzo'dʒorno] *sm* midday, noon; (*GEO*) south; **a ~** at 12 (o'clock) *o* midday *o* noon; **il ~ d'Italia** southern Italy.

mez'z'ora, mez'zora [med'dzora] *sf* half-hour, half an hour.

mi *pronome* (*dav lo, la, li, le, ne diventa* **me**) (*oggetto*) me; (*complemento di termine*) to me; (*riflessivo*) myself // *sm* (*MUS*) E; (*: solfeggiando la scala*) mi.

'mia *vedi* **mio**.

miago'lare *vi* to miaow, mew.

'mica *sf* (CHIM) mica // *av* (*fam*): **non ... ~ non** ... at all; **non sono ~ stanco** I'm not a bit tired; **~ male** not bad.

'miccia, ce ['mittʃa] *sf* fuse.

micidi'ale [mitʃi'djale] *ag* fatal; (*dannosissimo*) deadly.

'microbo *sm* microbe.

mi'crofono *sm* microphone.

micros'copico, a, ci, che *ag* microscopic.

micros'copio *sm* microscope.

mi'dollo, *pl(f)* **~a** *sm* (ANAT) marrow.

'mie, mi'ei *vedi* **mio**.

'miele *sm* honey.

mi'etere *vt* (AGR) to reap, harvest; (*fig: vite*) to take, claim.

migli'aio [miʎ'ʎajo], *pl(f)* **~a** *sm* thousand; **un ~ (di)** about a thousand; **a ~a** by the thousand, in thousands.

'miglio ['miʎʎo] *sm* (BOT) millet; (*pl(f)* **~a**: *unità di misura*) mile; **~ marino** *o* **nautico** nautical mile.

miglio'rare [miʎʎo'rare] *vt, vi* to improve.

migli'ore [miʎ'ʎore] *ag* (*comparativo*) better; (*superlativo*) best // *sm*: **il ~** the best (thing) // *sm/f*: **il(la) ~** the best (person); **il miglior vino di questa regione** the best wine in this area.

'mignolo ['miɲɲolo] *sm* (ANAT) little finger, pinkie; (: *dito del piede*) little toe.

mi'grare *vi* to migrate; **migrazi'one** *sf* migration.

'mila *pl di* **mille**.

Mi'lano *sf* Milan.

miliar'dario, a *sm/f* millionaire.

mili'ardo *sm* milliard, thousand million.

mili'are *ag*: **pietra ~** milestone.

mili'one *sm* million; **un ~ di lire** a million lire.

mili'tante *ag, sm/f* militant.

mili'tare *vi* (MIL) to be a soldier, serve; (*fig: in un partito*) to be a militant // *ag* military // *sm* serviceman; **~ a favore di** (*sog: argomenti etc*) to militate in favour of; **fare il ~** to do one's military service.

'milite *sm* soldier.

mi'lizia [mi'littsja] *sf* (*corpo armato*) militia.

millan'ta'tore, 'trice *sm/f* boaster.

'mille *num* (*pl* **mila**) a *o* one thousand; **dieci mila** ten thousand.

mille'foglie [mille'fɔʎʎe] *sm inv* (CUC) cream *o* vanilla slice.

mil'lennio *sm* millennium.

millepi'edi *sm inv* centipede.

mil'lesimo, a *ag, sm* thousandth.

milli'grammo *sm* milligram(me).

mil'limetro *sm* millimetre.

'milza ['miltsa] *sf* (ANAT) spleen.

mimetiz'zare [mimetid'dzare] *vt* to camouflage; **~rsi** *vr* to camouflage o.s.

'mimica *sf* (*arte*) mime.

'mimo *sm* (*attore, componimento*) mime.

mi'mosa *sf* mimosa.

'mina *sf* (*esplosiva*) mine; (*di matita*) lead.

mi'naccia, ce [mi'nattʃa] *sf* threat; **minacci'are** *vt* to threaten; **minac-ci'oso, a** *ag* threatening.

mi'nare *vt* (MIL) to mine; (*fig*) to undermine.

mina'tore *sm* miner.

mina'torio, a *ag* threatening.

mine'rale *ag, sm* mineral; **mineralo'gia** *sf* mineralogy.

mine'rario, a *ag* (*delle miniere*) mining; (*dei minerali*) ore *cpd*.

mi'nestra *sf* soup; **~ in brodo** noodle soup; **mines'trone** *sm* thick vegetable and pasta soup.

mingher'lino, a [minger'lino] *ag* thin, slender.

minia'tura *sf* miniature.

mini'era *sf* mine.

'minimo, a *ag* minimum, least, slightest; (*piccolissimo*) very small, slight; (*il più basso*) lowest, minimum // *sm* minimum; **al ~** at least; **girare al ~** (AUT) to idle.

minis'tero *sm* (POL, REL) ministry; (*governo*) government; **~ delle Finanze** Ministry of Finance, ≈ Treasury.

mi'nistro *sm* (POL, REL) minister; **~ delle Finanze** Minister of Finance, ≈ Chancellor of the Exchequer.

mino'ranza [mino'rantsa] *sf* minority.

mino'rato, a *ag* handicapped // *sm/f* physically (*o* mentally) handicapped person.

mi'nore *ag* (*comparativo*) less; (*più piccolo*) smaller; (*numero*) lower; (*inferiore*) lower, inferior; (*meno importante*) minor; (*più giovane*) younger; (*superlativo*) least, smallest; lowest; youngest // *sm/f* (*minorenne*) minor, person under age.

mino'renne *ag* under age // *sm/f* minor, person under age.

mi'nuscolo, a *ag* (*scrittura, carattere*) small; (*piccolissimo*) tiny // *sf* small letter.

mi'nuta *sf* rough copy, draft.

mi'nuto, a *ag* tiny, minute; (*pioggia*) fine; (*corporatura*) delicate, fine; (*lavoro*) detailed // *sm* (*unità di misura*) minute; **al ~** (COMM) retail.

'mio, 'mia, mi'ei, 'mie *det*: **il ~, la mia** *etc* my // *pronome*: **il ~, la mia** *etc* mine; **i miei** my family; **un ~ amico** a friend of mine.

'miope *ag* short-sighted.

'mira *sf* (*anche fig*) aim; (*bersaglio*) target; (*congegno di mira*) sight; **prendere la ~** to take aim; **prendere di ~ qd** (*fig*) to pick on sb.

mi'rabile *ag* admirable, wonderful.

mi'racolo *sm* miracle; **miraco'loso, a** *ag* miraculous.

mi'raggio [mi'raddʒo] *sm* mirage.

mi'rare *vi*: **~ a** to aim at.

mi'rino *sm* (TECN) sight; (FOT) viewer, viewfinder.

mir'tillo *sm* bilberry, whortleberry.

'mirto *sm* myrtle.

mi'santropo, a *sm/f* misanthropist.

mi'scela [miʃ'ʃela] sf mixture; (di caffè) blend.

miscel'lanea [miʃʃel'lanea] sf miscellany.

'mischia ['miskja] sf scuffle.

mischi'are [mis'kjare] vt, **~rsi** vr to mix, blend.

mis'cuglio [mis'kuʎʎo] sm mixture, hotchpotch, jumble.

mise'rabile ag (infelice) miserable, wretched; (povero) poverty-stricken; (di scarso valore) miserable.

mi'seria sf extreme poverty; (infelicità) misery; **~e** sfpl (del mondo etc) misfortunes, troubles; **porca ~!** (fam), **~ ladra!** (fam) blast!, damn!

miseri'cordia sf mercy, pity.

'misero, a ag miserable, wretched; (povero) poverty-stricken; (insufficiente) miserable.

mis'fatto sm misdeed, crime.

mi'sogino [mi'zɔdʒino] sm misogynist.

'missile sm missile.

missio'nario, a ag, sm/f missionary.

missi'one sf mission.

misteri'oso, a ag mysterious.

mis'tero sm mystery.

'mistico, a, ci, che ag mystic(al) // sm mystic.

mistifi'care vt to fool, bamboozle.

'misto, a ag mixed; (scuola) mixed, coeducational // sm mixture.

mis'tura sf mixture.

mi'sura sf measure; (misurazione, dimensione) measurement; (taglia) size; (provvedimento) measure, step; (moderazione) moderation; (MUS) time; (: divisione) bar; (fig: limite) bounds pl, limit; **a ~ che** as; **su ~** made to measure.

misu'rare vt (ambiente, stoffa) to measure; (terreno) to survey; (abito) to try on; (pesare) to weigh; (fig: parole etc) to weigh up; (: spese, cibo) to limit; **~rsi** vr: **~rsi con qd** to have a confrontation with sb; to compete with sb; **misu'rato, a** ag (ponderato) measured; (prudente) cautious; (moderato) moderate; **misurazi'one** sf measuring; (di terreni) surveying.

'mite ag mild; (prezzo) moderate, reasonable.

miti'gare vt to mitigate, lessen; (lenire) to soothe, relieve; **~rsi** vr (odio) to subside; (tempo) to become milder.

'mito sm myth; **mitolo'gia, 'gie** sf mythology.

'mitra sf (REL) mitre // sm inv (arma) sub-machine gun.

mitraglia'trice [mitraʎʎa'tritʃe] sf machine gun.

mit'tente sm/f sender.

'mobile ag mobile; (parte di macchina) moving; (DIR: bene) movable, personal // sm (arredamento) piece of furniture; **~i** smpl furniture sg.

mo'bilia sf furniture.

mobili'are ag (DIR) personal, movable.

mo'bilio sm = **mobilia.**

mobilità sf mobility.

mobili'tare vt to mobilize; **mobilita-zi'one** sf mobilization.

mocas'sino sm moccasin.

'moccolo sm (di candela) candle-end; (fam: bestemmia) oath; (: moccio) snot; **reggere il ~** to play gooseberry.

'moda sf fashion; **alla ~, di ~** fashionable, in fashion.

modalità sf inv formality.

mo'della sf model.

model'lare vt (creta) to model, shape; **~rsi** vr: **~rsi su** to model o.s. on.

mo'dello sm model; (stampo) mould // ag inv model cpd; **~ di carta** (SARTORIA) (paper) pattern.

mode'rare vt to moderate; **~rsi** vr to restrain o.s.; **mode'rato, a** ag moderate.

modera'tore, 'trice sm/f moderator.

moderazi'one [moderat'tsjone] sf moderation.

mo'derno, a ag modern.

mo'destia sf modesty.

mo'desto, a ag modest.

'modico, a, ci, che ag reasonable, moderate.

mo'difica, che sf modification.

modifi'care vt to modify, alter; **~rsi** vr to alter, change.

'modo sm way, manner; (mezzo) means, way; (occasione) opportunity; (LING) mood; (MUS) mode; **~i** smpl manners; **a suo ~, a ~ suo** in his own way; **ad o in ogni ~** anyway; **di o in ~ che** so that; **in ~ da** so, as to; **in tutti i ~i** at all costs; (comunque sia) anyway; (in ogni caso) in any case; **in qualche ~** somehow or other; **~ di dire** turn of phrase; **per ~ di dire** so to speak.

modu'lare vt to modulate; **modulazi'one** sf modulation; **modulazione di frequenza** frequency modulation.

'modulo sm form; (lunare, di comando) module.

'mogano sm mahogany.

'mogio, a, gi, gie ['mɔdʒo] ag down in the dumps, dejected.

'moglie ['moʎʎe] sf wife.

mo'ine sfpl cajolery sg; (leziosità) affectation sg.

'mola sf millstone; (utensile abrasivo) grindstone.

mo'lare vt to grind // ag (pietra) mill cpd // sm (dente) molar.

'mole sf mass; (dimensioni) size; (edificio grandioso) massive structure.

mo'lecola sf molecule.

moles'tare vt to bother, annoy; **mo'lestia** sf annoyance, bother; **recar molestia a qd** to bother sb; **mo'lesto, a** ag annoying.

'molla sf spring; **~e** sfpl tongs.

mol'lare vt to release, let go; (NAUT) to ease; (fig: ceffone) to give // vi (cedere) to give in.

'molle ag soft; (peg) flabby, limp; (: fig) weak, feeble; (bagnato) wet.

mol'letta sf (per capelli) hairgrip; (per

panni stesi) clothes peg; ~**e** *sfpl* (*per zucchero*) tongs.

mol'lezza [mol'lettsa] *sf* softness; flabbiness, limpness; weakness, feebleness; ~**e** *sfpl*: **vivere nelle** ~**e to** live in the lap of luxury.

'**mollica, che** *sf* crumb, soft part; ~**che** *sfpl* (*briciole*) crumbs.

mol'lusco, schi *sm* mollusc.

'**molo** *sm* mole, breakwater; jetty.

mol'teplice [mol'teplitʃe] *ag* (*formato di più elementi*) complex; (*numeroso*) numerous; (: *interessi, attività*) many, manifold; **molteplicità** *sf* multiplicity.

moltipli'care *vt* to multiply; ~**rsi** *vr* to multiply; to increase in number; **moltiplica'tore** *sm* multiplier; **moltiplicazi'one** *sf* multiplication.

molti'tudine *sf* multitude; **una** ~ **di** a vast number *o* a multitude of.

'**molto, a** *det* much, a lot of; (*con sostantivi al plurale*): ~**i(e)** many, a lot of; (*lungo: tempo*) long // *av* a lot; (*in frasi negative*) much; (*intensivo*) very // *pronome* much, a lot; ~**i(e)** *pronome pl* many, a lot; ~ **meglio** much *o* a lot better; ~ **buono** very good; **per** ~ (**tempo**) for a long time.

momen'taneo, a *ag* momentary, fleeting.

mo'mento *sm* moment; **capitare nel** ~ **buono** to come at the right time; **da un** ~ **all'altro** at any moment; (*all'improvviso*) suddenly; **al** ~ **di fare** just as I was (*o* you were *o* he was *etc*) doing; **per il** ~ for the time being; **dal** ~ **che** ever since; (*dato che*) since.

'**monaca, che** *sf* nun.

'**monaco, ci** *sm* monk.

'**Monaco** *sf* Monaco; ~ (**di Baviera**) Munich.

mo'narca, chi *sm* monarch; **monar'chia** *sf* monarchy.

monas'tero *sm* (*di monaci*) monastery; (*di monache*) convent; **mo'nastico, a, ci, che** *ag* monastic.

'**monco, a, chi, che** *ag* maimed; (*fig*) incomplete; ~ **d'un braccio** one-armed.

mon'dana *sf* prostitute.

mon'dano, a *ag* (*anche fig*) worldly; (*dell'alta società*) society *cpd*; fashionable.

mon'dare *vt* (*frutta, patate*) to peel; (*piselli*) to shell; (*pulire*) to clean.

mondi'ale *ag* (*campionato, popolazione*) world *cpd*; (*influenza*) world-wide.

'**mondo** *sm* world; (*grande quantità*): **un** ~ **di** lots of, a host of; **il gran** *o* **bel** ~ high society.

mo'nello, a *sm/f* street urchin; (*ragazzo vivace*) scamp, imp.

mo'neta *sf* coin; (*ECON: valuta*) currency; (*denaro spicciolo*) (small) change; ~ **estera** foreign currency; ~ **legale** legal tender; **mone'tario, a** *ag* monetary.

mongo'loide *ag, sm/f* (*MED*) mongol.

'**monito** *sm* warning.

'**monitor** *sm inv* (*TECN, TV*) monitor.

mo'nocolo *sm* (*lente*) monocle, eyeglass.

monoco'lore *ag* (*POL*) one-party.

mono'gramma, i *sm* monogram.

mo'nologo, ghi *sm* monologue.

mono'plano *sm* monoplane.

mono'polio *sm* monopoly; **monopoliz'zare** *vt* to monopolize.

mono'sillabo, a *ag* monosyllabic // *sm* monosyllable.

monoto'nia *sf* monotony.

mo'notono, a *ag* monotonous.

monsi'gnore [monsin'ɲore] *sm* (*REL: titolo*) Your (*o* His) Grace.

mon'sone *sm* monsoon.

monta'carichi [monta'kariki] *sm inv* hoist, goods lift.

mon'taggio [mon'taddʒo] *sm* (*TECN*) assembly; (*CINEMA*) editing.

mon'tagna [mon'taɲɲa] *sf* mountain; (*zona montuosa*): **la** ~ **the** mountains *pl*; ~**e russe** roller coaster *sg*, big dipper *sg*; **monta'gnoso, a** *ag* mountainous.

monta'naro, a *ag* mountain *cpd* // *sm/f* mountain dweller.

mon'tano, a *ag* mountain *cpd*; alpine.

mon'tare *vt* to go (*o* come) up; (*apparecchiatura*) to set up, assemble; (*CUC*) to whip; (*ZOOL*) to cover; (*incastonare*) to mount, set; (*CINEMA*) to edit // *vi* (2) to go (*o* come) up; (*a cavallo*): ~ **bene/male** to ride well/badly; (*aumentare di livello, volume*) to rise; ~**rsi** *vr* to become big-headed; ~ **qc** to exaggerate sth; ~ **qd** *o* **la testa a qd** to turn sb's head; ~ **in bicicletta/treno** to get on a bicycle/train; ~ **a cavallo** to get on *o* mount a horse.

monta'tura *sf* assembling *q*; (*di occhiali*) frames *pl*; (*di gioiello*) mounting, setting; (*fig*): ~ **pubblicitaria** publicity stunt.

'**monte** *sm* mountain; (~ *upstream*); **mandare a** ~ **qc** to upset sth, cause sth to fail; **il M**— **Bianco** Mont Blanc; ~ **dei pegni** pawnshop.

mon'tone *sm* (*ZOOL*) ram.

montu'oso, a *ag* mountainous.

monu'mento *sm* monument.

'**mora** *sf* (*del rovo*) blackberry; (*del gelso*) mulberry; (*DIR*) delay; (: *somma*) arrears *pl*.

mo'rale *ag* moral // *sf* (*scienza*) ethics *sg*, moral philosophy; (*complesso di norme*) moral standards *pl*, morality; (*condotta*) morals *pl*; (*insegnamento morale*) moral // *sm* morale; **moralità** *sf* morality; (*condotta*) morals *pl*.

'**morbido, a** *ag* soft; (*pelle*) soft, smooth.

mor'billo *sm* (*MED*) measles *sg*.

'**morbo** *sm* disease.

mor'boso, a *ag* (*fig*) morbid.

'**morchia** ['mɔrkja] *sf* (*residuo grasso*) dregs *pl*; oily deposit.

mor'dace [mor'datʃe] *ag* biting, cutting.

mor'dente *sm* (*fig*) push, drive.

'**mordere** *vt* to bite; (*addentare*) to bite into; (*corrodere*) to eat into.

mor'fina *sf* morphine.

mori'bondo, a *ag* dying, moribund.

morige'rato, a [moridʒe'rato] *ag* of good morals.

mo'rire *vi (2)* to die; *(abitudine, civiltà)* to die out; ~ **di fame** to die of hunger; *(fig)* to be starving; ~ **di noia** to be bored to death; **fa un caldo da** ~ it's terribly hot.

mormo'rare *vi* to murmur; *(brontolare)* to grumble; **mormo'rio** *sm* murmuring; grumbling.

'moro, a *ag* dark(-haired); dark(-complexioned); **i M~i** *smpl (STORIA)* the Moors.

mo'roso, a *ag* in arrears // *sm/f (fam: innamorato)* sweetheart.

'morsa *sf* vice.

morsi'care *vt* to nibble (at), gnaw (at); *(sog: insetto)* to bite.

'morso, a *pp di* **mordere** // *sm* bite; *(di insetto)* sting; *(parte della briglia)* bit; ~**i della fame** pangs of hunger.

mor'taio *sm* mortar.

mor'tale *ag, sm* mortal; **mortalità** *sf* mortality, death rate.

'morte *sf* death.

mortifi'care *vt* to mortify.

'morto, a *pp di* **morire** // *ag* dead // *sm/f* dead man/woman; **i ~i** the dead; **fare il** ~ *(nell'acqua)* to float on one's back.

mor'torio *sm (anche fig)* funeral.

mo'saico, ci *sm* mosaic.

'mosca, sche *sf* fly; ~ **cieca** blind-man's-buff.

'Mosca *sf* Moscow.

mos'cato *sm* muscatel (wine).

mosce'rino [moʃʃe'rino] *sm* midge, gnat.

mos'chea [mos'kɛa] *sf* mosque.

mos'chetto [mos'ketto] *sm* musket.

'moscio, a, sci, sce ['moʃʃo] *ag (fig)* lifeless.

mos'cone *sm (ZOOL)* bluebottle; *(barca)* pedalo; *(:a remi)* kind of pedalo with oars.

'mossa *sf* movement; *(nel gioco)* move.

'mosso, a *pp di* **muovere** // *ag (mare)* rough; *(capelli)* wavy; *(FOT)* blurred; *(ritmo, prosa)* animated.

mos'tarda *sf* mustard.

'mostra *sf* exhibition, show; *(ostentazione)* show; **in** ~ on show; **far** ~ **di** *(fingere)* to pretend; **far** ~ **di sé** to show off.

mos'trare *vt* to show // *vi:* ~ **di fare** to pretend to do; ~**rsi** *vr* to appear.

'mostro *sm* monster; **mostru'oso, a** *ag* monstrous.

mo'tel *sm inv* motel.

moti'vare *vt (causare)* to cause; *(giustificare)* to justify, account for; **motivazi'one** *sf* justification; motive; *(PSIC)* motivation.

mo'tivo *sm (causa)* reason, cause; *(movente)* motive; *(letterario)* (central) theme; *(disegno)* motif, design, pattern; *(MUS)* motif; **per quale** ~? why?, for what reason?

'moto *sm (anche FISICA)* motion; *(movimento, gesto)* movement; *(esercizio fisico)* exercise; *(sommossa)* rising, revolt; *(commozione)* feeling, impulse // *sf inv (motocicletta)* motor-bike; **mettere in** ~

to set in motion; *(AUT)* to start up.

motoci'cletta [mototʃi'kletta] *sf* motorcycle; **motoci'clismo** *sm* motorcycling, motorcycle racing; **motoci'clista, i, e** *sm/f* motorcyclist.

mo'tore, 'trice *ag* motor; *(TECN)* driving // *sm* engine, motor; **a** ~ motor *cpd*, power-driven; ~ **a combustione interna/a reazione** internal combustion/jet engine; **moto'rino** *sm* moped; **motorino di avviamento** *(AUT)* starter; **motoriz'zato, a** *ag (truppe)* motorized; *(persona)* having a car *o* transport.

motos'cafo *sm* motorboat.

mot'teggio [mot'teddʒo] *sm* banter.

'motto *sm (battuta scherzosa)* witty remark; *(frase emblematica)* motto, maxim.

mo'vente *sm* motive.

movimen'tare *vt* to liven up.

movi'mento *sm* movement; *(fig)* activity, hustle and bustle; *(MUS)* tempo, movement.

mozi'one [mot'tsjone] *sf (POL)* motion.

moz'zare [mot'tsare] *vt* to cut off; *(coda)* to dock; ~ **il fiato** *o* **il respiro a qd** *(fig)* to take sb's breath away.

mozza'rella [mottsa'rɛlla] *sf* mozzarella *(a moist Neapolitan curd cheese).*

mozzi'cone [mottsi'kone] *sm* stub, butt, end; *(anche:* ~ **di sigaretta)** cigarette end.

'mozzo *sm* ['mɔddzo] *(MECCANICA)* hub; ['mottso] *(NAUT)* ship's boy; ~ **di stalla** stable boy.

'mucca, che *sf* cow.

'mucchio ['mukkjo] *sm* pile, heap; *(fig):* **un** ~ **di** lots of, heaps of.

'muco, chi *sm* mucus.

mu'cosa *sf* mucous membrane.

'muffa *sf* mould, mildew.

mug'gire [mud'dʒire] *vi (vacca)* to low, moo; *(toro)* to bellow; *(fig)* to roar; **mug'gito** *sm* low, moo; bellow; roar.

mu'ghetto [mu'getto] *sm* lily of the valley.

mu'gnaio, a [muɲ'ɲajo] *sm/f* miller.

mugo'lare *vi (cane)* to whimper, whine; *(fig: persona)* to moan.

muli'nare *vi* to whirl, spin (round and round).

muli'nello *sm (moto vorticoso)* eddy, whirl; *(per aria)* ventilating fan; *(di canna da pesca)* reel; *(NAUT)* windlass.

mu'lino *sm* mill; ~ **a vento** windmill.

'mulo *sm* mule.

'multa *sf* fine; **mul'tare** *vt* to fine.

multico'lore *ag* multicoloured.

'multiplo, a *ag, sm* multiple.

'mummia *sf* mummy.

'mungere ['mundʒere] *vt (anche fig)* to milk.

munici'pale [munitʃi'pale] *ag* municipal; town *cpd*.

muni'cipio [muni'tʃipjo] *sm* town council, corporation; *(edificio)* town hall.

mu'nire *vt:* ~ **qc/qd di** to equip sth/sb with.

munizi'oni [munit'tsjoni] *sfpl* (*MIL*) ammunition *sg*.

'munto, a *pp di* **mungere**.

mu'overe *vt* to move; (*ruota, macchina*) to drive; (*sollevare: questione, obiezione*) to raise, bring up; (*: accusa*) to make, bring forward; ~**rsi** *vr* to move; **muoviti!** hurry up!, get a move on!

'mura *sfpl vedi* **muro**.

mu'raglia [mu'raʎʎa] *sf* (high) wall.

mu'rale *ag* wall *cpd*; mural.

mu'rare *vt* (*persona, porta*) to wall up.

mura'tore *sm* mason; bricklayer.

'muro *sm* wall; ~**a** *sfpl* (*cinta cittadina*) walls; **a ~** wall *cpd*; (*armadio etc*) built-in; ~ **del suono** sound barrier.

'muschio ['muskjo] *sm* (*ZOOL*) musk; (*BOT*) moss.

musco'lare *ag* muscular, muscle *cpd*.

'muscolo *sm* (*ANAT*) muscle.

mu'seo *sm* museum.

museru'ola *sf* muzzle.

'musica *sf* music; **scrivere una ~** to write a piece of music; **~ da ballo/camera** dance/chamber music; **musi'cale** *ag* musical; **musi'cista, i, e** *sm/f* musician.

'muso *sm* muzzle; (*di auto, aereo*) nose; **tenere il ~** to sulk; **mu'sone, a** *sm/f* sulky person.

'mussola *sf* muslin.

'muta *sf* (*ZOOL*) moulting; (*: di serpenti*) sloughing; (*cambio*) change; (*di sentinella*) relief; (*per immersioni subacquee*) diving suit; (*gruppo di cani*) pack.

muta'mento *sm* change.

mu'tande *sfpl* (*da uomo*) (under)pants; **mutan'dine** *sfpl* (*da donna, bambino*) pants; **mutandine di plastica** plastic pants.

mu'tare *vt, vi* (*2*) to change, alter; **mutazi'one** *sf* change, alteration; (*BIOL*) mutation; **mu'tevole** *ag* changeable.

muti'lare *vt* to mutilate, maim; (*fig*) to mutilate, deface; **muti'lato, a** *sm/f* disabled person (*through loss of limbs*); **mutilazi'one** *sf* mutilation.

mu'tismo *sm* (*MED*) mutism; (*atteggiamento*) (stubborn) silence.

'muto, a *ag* (*MED*) dumb; (*emozione, dolore, CINEMA*) silent; (*LING*) silent, mute; (*carta geografica*) blank; ~ **per lo stupore** *etc* speechless with amazement *etc*.

'mutua *sf* (*anche:* **cassa ~**) health insurance scheme.

mutu'are *vt* (*fig*) to borrow.

mutu'ato, a *sm/f* member of a health insurance scheme.

'mutuo, a *ag* (*reciproco*) mutual // *sm* (*ECON*) (long-term) loan.

N

N. (*abbr di* **nord**) N.

'nacchere ['nakkere] *sfpl* castanets.

'nafta *sf* naphtha; (*per motori diesel*) diesel oil.

'naia *sf* (*ZOOL*) cobra; (*MIL*) *slang term for* national service.

'nailon *sm* nylon.

'nanna *sf* (*linguaggio infantile*): **andare a ~** to go bye-byes.

'nano, a *ag, sm/f* dwarf.

napole'tano, a *ag, sm/f* Neapolitan.

'Napoli *sf* Naples.

'nappa *sf* tassel.

nar'ciso [nar'tʃizo] *sm* narcissus.

nar'cosi *sf* narcosis.

nar'cotico, ci *sm* narcotic.

na'rice [na'ritʃe] *sf* nostril.

nar'rare *vt* to tell the story of, recount; **narra'tivo, a** *ag* narrative // *sf* (*branca letteraria*) fiction; **narra'tore, 'trice** *sm/f* narrator; **narrazi'one** *sf* narration; (*racconto*) story, tale.

na'sale *ag* nasal.

'nascere ['naʃʃere] *vi* (*2*) (*bambino*) to be born; (*pianta*) to come *o* spring up; (*fiume*) to rise, have its source; (*sole*) to rise; (*dente*) to come through; (*fig: derivare, conseguire*): ~ **da** to arise from, be born out of; **è nata nel 1952** she was born in 1952; **'nascita** *sf* birth.

nas'condere *vt* to hide, conceal; ~**rsi** *vr* to hide; **nascon'diglio** *sm* hiding place; **nascon'dino** *sm* (*gioco*) hide-and-seek; **nas'costo, a** *pp di* **nascondere** // *ag* hidden; **di nascosto** secretly.

na'sello *sm* (*ZOOL*) hake.

'naso *sm* nose.

'nastro *sm* ribbon; (*magnetico, isolante, SPORT*) tape; ~ **adesivo** adhesive tape; ~ **dattilografico** typewriter ribbon; ~ **trasportatore** conveyor belt.

nas'turzio [nas'turtsjo] *sm* nasturtium.

na'tale *ag* of one's birth // *sm* (*REL*): **N~** Christmas; (*giorno della nascita*) birthday; **natalità** *sf* birth rate; **nata'lizio, a** *ag* (*del Natale*) Christmas *cpd*; (*di nascita*) of one's birth.

na'tante *ag* floating // *sm* craft *inv*, boat.

'natica, che *sf* (*ANAT*) buttock.

na'tio, a, 'tii, 'tie *ag* native.

Natività *sf* (*REL*) Nativity.

na'tivo, a *ag, sm/f* native.

'nato, a *pp di* **nascere** // *ag*: **un attore ~** a born actor; ~**a Pieri** née Pieri.

na'tura *sf* nature; **pagare in ~** to pay in kind; ~ **morta** still life.

natu'rale *ag* natural; **natura'lezza** *sf* naturalness; **natura'lista, i, e** *sm/f* naturalist.

naturaliz'zare [naturalid'dzare] *vt* to naturalize.

natural'mente *av* naturally; (*certamente, sì*) of course.

naufra'gare *vi* (*nave*) to be wrecked;

(*persona*) to be shipwrecked; (*fig*) to fall through; **nau'fragio** *sm* shipwreck; (*fig*) ruin, failure; **'naufrago, ghi** *sm* castaway, shipwreck victim.

'nausea *sf* nausea; **nausea'bondo, a** *ag* nauseating, sickening; **nause'are** *vt* to nauseate, make (feel) sick.

'nautico, a, ci, che *ag* nautical // *sf* (art of) navigation.

na'vale *ag* naval.

/ **na'vata** *sf* (*anche:* ~ **centrale**) nave; (*anche:* ~ **laterale**) aisle.

'nave *sf* ship, vessel; ~ **cisterna** tanker; ~ **da guerra** warship; ~ **spaziale** spaceship.

na'vetta *sf* shuttle; (*servizio di collegamento*) shuttle (service).

navi'cella [navi'tʃɛlla] *sf* (*di aerostato*) gondola.

navi'gabile *ag* navigable.

navi'gare *vi* to sail; **navigazi'one** *sf* navigation.

na'viglio [na'viʎʎo] *sm* fleet, ships *pl*; (*canale artificiale*) canal; ~ **da pesca** fishing fleet.

nazio'nale [nattsjo'nale] *ag* national // *sf* (*SPORT*) national team; **naziona'lismo** *sm* nationalism; **nazionalità** *sf inv* nationality; **nazionaliz'zare** *vt* to nationalize.

nazi'one [nat'tsjone] *sf* nation.

ne *pronome* of him/her/it/them; about him/her/it/them; ~ **riconosco la voce** I recognize his (*o* her) voice; **non parliamone più!** let's not talk about him (*o* her *o* it *o* them) any more!; (*con valore partitivo*) **hai dei libri? — sì,** ~ **ho** have you any books? — yes, I have (some); **hai del pane? — no, non** ~ **ho** have you any bread? — no, I don't have any; **quanti anni hai?** — ~ **ho 17** how old are you? — I'm 17 // *av* (*moto da luogo*) from there.

né *cong:* ~ ... ~ neither ... nor; ~ **l'uno** ~ **l'altro lo vuole** neither of them wants it; **non parla** ~ **l'italiano** ~ **il tedesco** he speaks neither Italian nor German, he doesn't speak either Italian or German; **non piove** ~ **nevica** it isn't raining or snowing.

ne'anche [ne'anke] *av, cong* not even; **non ... ~** not even; ~ **se volesse potrebbe venire** he couldn't come even if he wanted to; **non l'ho visto** — ~ **io** I didn't see him — neither did I *o* I didn't either; ~ **per idea** *o* **sogno!** not on your life!

'nebbia *sf* fog; (*foschia*) mist; **nebbi'oso, a** *ag* foggy; misty.

necessaria'mente [netʃessarja'mente] *av* necessarily.

neces'sario, a [netʃes'sarjo] *ag* necessary.

necessità [netʃessi'ta] *sf inv* necessity; (*povertà*) need, poverty; **necessi'tare** *vt* to require // *vi (2)* (*aver bisogno*): **necessitare di** to need // *vb impers* to be necessary.

necro'logio [nekro'lɔdʒo] *sm* obituary notice; (*registro*) register of deaths.

necrosco'pia *sf* postmortem (examination).

ne'fando, a *ag* infamous, wicked.

ne'fasto, a *ag* inauspicious, ill-omened.

ne'gare *vt* to deny; (*rifiutare*) to deny, refuse; ~ **di aver fatto/che** to deny having done/that; **nega'tivo, a** *ag, sf* negative; **negazi'one** *sf* denial; (*contrario*) negation; (*LING*) negative.

neghit'toso, a [negit'toso] *ag* slothful.

ne'gletto, a [ne'ʎʎɛtto] *ag* (*trascurato*) neglected.

'negli ['neʎʎi] *prep + det vedi* **in**.

negli'gente [negli'dʒɛnte] *ag* negligent, careless; **negli'genza** *sf* negligence, carelessness.

negozi'ante [negot'tsjante] *sm/f* trader, dealer; (*bottegaio*) shopkeeper.

negozi'are [negot'tsjare] *vt* to negotiate // *vi:* ~ **in** to trade *o* deal in; **negozi'ato** *sm* negotiation.

ne'gozio [ne'gɔttsjo] *sm* (*locale*) shop; (*affare*) (piece of) business *q*.

'negro, a *ag, sm/f* Negro.

'nei, nel, nell', 'nella, 'nelle, 'nello *prep + det vedi* **in**.

'nembo *sm* (*METEOR*) nimbus.

ne'mico, a, ci, che *ag* hostile; (*MIL*) enemy *cpd* // *sm/f* enemy; **essere** ~ **di** to be strongly averse *o* opposed to.

nem'meno *av, cong* = **neanche**.

'nenia *sf* dirge; (*motivo monotono*) monotonous tune.

'neo *sm* mole; (*fig*) (slight) flaw.

neo... *prefisso* neo...; **neo'litico, a, ci, che** *ag* neolithic.

'neon *sm* (*CHIM*) neon.

neo'nato, a *ag* newborn // *sm/f* newborn baby.

neozelan'dese [neoddzelan'dese] *ag* New Zealand *cpd* // *sm/f* New Zealander.

nep'pure *av, cong* = **neanche**.

'nerbo *sm* lash; (*fig*) strength, backbone; **nerbo'ruto, a** *ag* muscular; robust.

ne'retto *sm* (*TIP*) bold type.

'nero, a *ag* black; (*scuro*) dark // *sm* black.

nerva'tura *sf* (*ANAT*) nervous system; (*BOT*) venation; (*ARCHIT, TECN*) rib.

'nervo *sm* (*ANAT*) nerve; (*BOT*) vein; **avere i ~i** to be on edge; **dare sui** ~**i a qd** to get on sb's nerves; **ner'voso, a** *ag* nervous; (*irritabile*) irritable // *sm* (*fam*): **far venire il nervoso a qd** to get on sb's nerves.

'nespola *sf* (*BOT*) medlar; (*fig*) blow, punch; **'nespolo** *sm* medlar tree.

'nesso *sm* connection, link.

nes'suno, a *det* (*dav sm* **nessun** + *C, V,* **nessuno** + *s impura, gn, pn, ps, x, z; dav sf* **nessuna** + *C,* **nessun'** + *V*) (*non uno*) no, *espressione negativa* + any; (*qualche*) any // *pronome* (*non uno*) no one, nobody, *espressione negativa* + any(one); (: *cosa*) none, *espressione negativa* + any; (*qualcuno*) someone, anybody; (*qualcosa*) anything; **non c'è nessun libro** there isn't any book, there is no book; **hai** ~ **a**

obiezione? do you have any objections?; **~ è venuto, non è venuto ~** nobody came; **nessun altro** no one else, nobody else; **nessun'altra cosa** nothing else; **in nessun luogo** nowhere.

net'tare *vt* to clean // *sm* ['nɛttare] nectar.

net'tezza [net'tettsa] *sf* cleanness, cleanliness; **~ urbana** cleansing department.

'netto, a *ag* (*pulito*) clean; (*chiaro*) clear, clear-cut; (*deciso*) definite; (*ECON*) net.

nettur'bino *sm* dustman.

neurolo'gia [neurolo'dʒia] *sf* neurology.

neu'rosi *sf* = **nevrosi.**

neu'trale *ag* neutral; **neutralità** *sf* neutrality; **neutraliz'zare** *vt* to neutralize.

'neutro, a *ag* neutral; (*LING*) neuter // *sm* (*LING*) neuter.

ne'vaio *sm* snowfield.

'neve *sf* snow; **nevi'care** *vb impers* to snow; **nevi'cata** *sf* snowfall.

ne'vischio [ne'viskjo] *sm* sleet.

ne'voso, a *ag* snowy; snow-covered.

nevral'gia [nevral'dʒia] *sf* neuralgia.

ne'vrosi *sf* neurosis.

'nibbio *sm* (*ZOOL*) kite.

'nicchia ['nikkja] *sf* niche.

nicchi'are [nik'kjare] *vi* to shilly-shally, hesitate.

'nichel ['nikel] *sm* nickel.

nico'tina *sf* nicotine.

'nido *sm* nest; **a ~ d'ape** (*tessuto etc*) honeycomb *cpd.*

ni'ente *pronome* (*nessuna cosa*) nothing; (*qualcosa*) anything; **non ... ~** nothing, espressione negativa + anything // *sm* nothing // *av* (*in nessuna misura*): **non è ~ buono** it's not good at all; **una cosa da ~** a trivial thing; **~ affatto** not at all, not in the least; **nient'altro** nothing else; **nient'altro che** nothing but; just, only; **~ di ~** absolutely nothing; **per ~** (*invano, gratuitamente*) for nothing; **non ... per ~** not ... at all.

nientedi'meno, niente'meno *av* actually, even // *escl* really!, I say!

'nimbo *sm* halo.

'ninfa *sf* nymph.

nin'fea *sf* water lily.

ninna-'nanna *sf* lullaby.

'ninnolo *sm* (*balocco*) plaything; (*gingillo*) knick-knack.

ni'pote *sm/f* (*di zii*) nephew/niece; (*di nonni*) grandson/daughter, grandchild.

'nitido, a *ag* clear; (*specchio*) bright.

ni'trato *sm* nitrate.

'nitrico, a, ci, che *ag* nitric.

ni'trire *vi* to neigh.

ni'trito *sm* (*di cavallo*) neighing *q*; neigh; (*CHIM*) nitrite.

nitroglice'rina [nitroglitʃe'rina] *sf* nitroglycerine.

'niveo, a *ag* snow-white.

no *av* (*risposta*) no; **vieni o ~?** are you coming or not?; **perché ~?** why not?

'nobile *ag* noble // *sm/f* noble, nobleman/woman; **nobili'are** *ag* noble; **nobiltà** *sf* nobility; (*di azione etc*) nobleness.

'nocca, che *sf* (*ANAT*) knuckle.

nocci'ola [not'tʃola] *sf* hazelnut.

'nocciolo ['nɔttʃolo] *sm* (*di frutto*) stone; (*fig*) heart, core; [not'tʃolo] (*albero*) hazel.

'noce ['notʃe] *sm* (*albero*) walnut tree // *sf* (*frutto*) walnut; **~ moscata** nutmeg.

no'civo, a [no'tʃivo] *ag* harmful, noxious.

'nodo *sm* (*di cravatta, legname, NAUT*) knot; (*AUT, FERR*) junction; (*MED, ASTR, BOT*) node; (*fig: legame*) bond, tie; (: *punto centrale*) heart, crux; **avere un ~ alla gola** to have a lump in one's throat; **no'doso, a** *ag* (*tronco*) gnarled.

'noi *pronome* (*soggetto*) we; (*oggetto: per dare rilievo, con preposizione*) us; **~ stessi(e)** we ourselves; (*oggetto*) ourselves.

'noia *sf* boredom; (*disturbo, impaccio*) bother *q*, trouble *q*; **avere qd/qc a ~** not to like sb/sth; **mi è venuto a ~** I'm tired of it; **dare ~ a** to annoy; **avere delle ~e con qd** to have trouble with sb.

noi'altri *pronome* we.

noi'oso, a *ag* boring; annoying, troublesome.

noleggi'are [noled'dʒare] *vt* (*prendere a noleggio*) to hire; (*dare a noleggio*) to hire out; (*aereo, nave*) to charter; **no'leggio** *sm* hire; charter.

'nolo *sm* hire; charter; (*per trasporto merci*) freight; **prendere/dare a ~ qc** to hire/hire out sth.

'nomade *ag* nomadic // *sm/f* nomad.

'nome *sm* name; (*LING*) noun; **in/a ~ di** in the name of; **di o per ~** (*chiamato*) called, named; **conoscere qd di ~** to know sb by name; **~ d'arte** stage name; **~ depositato** trade name; **~ di famiglia** surname.

no'mea *sf* notoriety.

no'mignolo [no'miɲɲolo] *sm* nickname.

'nomina *sf* appointment.

nomi'nale *ag* nominal; (*LING*) noun *cpd.*

nomi'nare *vt* to name; (*eleggere*) to appoint; (*citare*) to mention.

nomina'tivo, a *ag* (*LING*) nominative; (*ECON*) registered // *sm* (*LING: anche:* **caso ~**) nominative (case); (*AMM*) name.

non *av* not // *prefisso* non-; *vedi* **affatto, appena** *etc.*

nonché [non'ke] *cong* (*tanto più, tanto meno*) let alone; (*e inoltre*) as well as.

noncu'rante *ag*: **~ (di)** careless (of), indifferent (to); **noncu'ranza** *sf* carelessness, indifference.

nondi'meno *cong* (*tuttavia*) however; (*nonostante*) nevertheless.

'nonno, a *sm/f* grandfather/ mother; (*in senso più familiare*) grandma/grandpa; **~i** *smpl* grandparents.

non'nulla *sm inv*: **un ~** nothing, a trifle.

'nono, a *ag, sm* ninth.

nonos'tante *prep* in spite of,

notwithstanding // cong although, even though.

nontiscordardimé sm inv (BOT) forget-me-not.

nord sm North // ag inv north; northern; **nor'dest** sm North-East; **'nordico, a, ci, che** ag nordic, northern European; **nor'dovest** sm North-West.

'norma sf (criterio) norm; (regola) regulation, rule; (avvertenza) instruction; **a ~ di legge** according to law, as laid down by law.

nor'male ag normal; (che dà una norma: lettera) standard cpd; **normalità** sf normality; **normaliz'zare** vt to normalize, bring back to normal.

normal'mente av normally.

norve'gese [norve'dʒese] ag, sm/f, sm Norwegian.

Nor'vegia [nor'vedʒa] sf: **la ~** Norway.

nostal'gia [nostal'dʒia] sf (di casa, paese) homesickness; (del passato) nostalgia; **nos'talgico, a, ci, che** ag homesick; nostalgic.

nos'trano, a ag local; national; home-produced.

'nostro, a det: **il(la) ~(a)** etc our // pronome: **il(la) ~(a)** etc ours; **i ~i** (soldati etc) our own people.

'nota sf (segno) mark; (comunicazione scritta, MUS) note; (fattura) bill; (elenco) list; **degno di ~** noteworthy, worthy of note; **~e caratteristiche** distinguishing marks o features.

no'tabile ag notable; (persona) important // sm prominent citizen.

no'taio sm notary.

no'tare vt (segnare: errori) to mark; (registrare) to note (down), write down; (rilevare, osservare) to note, notice; **farsi ~** to get o.s. noticed.

notazi'one [notat'tsjone] sf marking; annotation; (MUS) notation.

no'tevole ag (talento) notable, remarkable; (peso) considerable.

no'tifica, che sf notification.

notifi'care vt (DIR): **~ qc a qd** to notify sb of sth, give sb notice of sth; **notifica-zi'one** sf notification.

no'tizia [no'tittsja] sf (piece of) news sg; (informazione) piece of information; **~e** sfpl news sg; information sg; **notizi'ario** sm (RADIO, TV, STAMPA) news sg.

'noto, a ag (well-)known.

notorietà sf fame; notoriety.

no'torio, a ag well-known; (peg) notorious.

not'tambulo sm night-bird.

not'tata sf night; **far ~** to sit up all night.

'notte sf night; **di ~** at night; (durante la notte) in the night, during the night; **peggio che andar di ~** worse than ever; **~ bianca** sleepless night; **notte'tempo** av at night; during the night.

not'turno, a ag nocturnal; (servizio, guardiano) night cpd.

no'vanta num ninety; **novan'tesimo, a** num ninetieth; **novan'tina** sf: **una novantina (di)** about ninety.

'nove num nine.

nove'cento [nove'tʃɛnto] num nine hundred // sm: **il N~** the twentieth century.

no'vella sf (LETTERATURA) short story.

novel'lino, a ag (pivello) green, inexperienced.

no'vello, a ag (piante, patate) new; (animale) young; (sposo) newly-married.

no'vembre sm November.

novi'lunio sm (ASTR) new moon.

novità sf inv novelty; (innovazione) innovation; (cosa originale, insolita) something new; (notizia) piece of) news sg; **le ~ della moda** the latest fashions.

novizi'ato [novit'tsjato] sm (REL) novitiate; (tirocinio) apprenticeship.

no'vizio, a [no'vittsjo] sm/f (REL) novice; (tirocinante) beginner, apprentice.

nozi'one [not'tsjone] sf notion, idea; **~i** sfpl basic knowledge sg, rudiments.

'nozze ['nɔttse] sfpl wedding sg, marriage sg; **~ d'argento/d'oro** silver/golden wedding sg.

ns. abbr commerciale di **nostro**.

'nube sf cloud; **nubi'fragio** sm cloudburst.

'nubile ag (donna) unmarried, single.

'nuca sf nape of the neck.

nucle'are ag nuclear.

'nucleo sm nucleus; (gruppo) team, unit, group; (MIL) squad.

nu'dista, i, e sm/f nudist.

nudità sf inv nudity, nakedness; (di paesaggio) bareness // sfpl (parti nude del corpo) nakedness sg.

'nudo, a ag (persona) bare, naked, nude; (membra) bare, naked; (montagna) bare // sm (ARTE) nude.

'nulla pronome, av = **niente** // sm: **il ~** nothing.

nulla'osta sm inv authorization.

nullità sf inv nullity; (persona) nonentity.

'nullo, a ag useless, worthless; (DIR) null (and void); (SPORT): **incontro ~** draw.

nume'rale ag, sm numeral.

nume'rare vt to number; **numerazi'one** sf numbering; (araba, decimale) notation.

nu'merico, a, ci, che ag numerical.

'numero sm number; (romano, arabo) numeral; (di spettacolo) act, turn; **~ civico** house number; **nume'roso, a** ag numerous, many; (con sostantivo sg: adunanza etc) large.

'nunzio ['nuntsjo] sm (REL) nuncio.

nu'ocere ['nwɔtʃere] vi: **~ a** to harm, damage; **nuoci'uto, a** pp di **nuocere**.

nu'ora sf daughter-in-law.

nuo'tare vi to swim; (galleggiare: oggetti) to float; **nuota'tore, 'trice** sm/f swimmer; **nu'oto** sm swimming; **nuoto sul dorso** backstroke.

nu'ova vedi **nuovo**.

nuova'mente av again.

nu'ovo, a ag, av // sf (notizia) (piece of) news sg; **di ~** again; **~ fiammante** o **di zecca** brand-new; **la N~a Zelanda** New Zealand.

nutri'ente *ag* nutritious, nourishing.
nutri'mento *sm* food, nourishment.
nu'trire *vt* to feed; (*fig: sentimenti*) to harbour, nurse; **nutri'tivo, a** *ag* nutritional; (*alimento*) nutritious; **nutri-zi'one** *sf* nutrition.
'nuvola *sf* cloud; **'nuvolo, a** *ag*, **nuvo-'loso, a** *ag* cloudy.
nuzi'ale [nut'tsjale] *ag* nuptial; wedding *cpd.*

O

o *cong* (*dav V spesso* **od**) or; ~ ... ~ either ... or; ~ **l'uno** ~ **l'altro** either (of them).
O. (*abbr di* **ovest**) W.
'oasi *sf inv* oasis.
obbedi'ente *etc vedi* **ubbidiente** *etc.*
obbli'gare *vt* (*costringere*): ~ **qd a fare** to force *o* oblige sb to do; (*DIR*) to bind; ~**rsi** *vr*: ~**rsi a fare** to undertake to do; **obbli'gato, a** *ag* (*costretto, grato*) obliged; **obbliga'torio, a** *ag* compulsory, obligatory; **obbligazi'one** *sf* obligation; (*COMM*) bond, debenture; **'obbligo, ghi** *sm* obligation; (*dovere*) duty; **avere l'obbligo di fare, essere nell'obbligo di fare** to be obliged to do.
ob'brobrio *sm* disgrace.
obesità *sf* obesity.
o'beso, a *ag* obese.
obiet'tare *vt* to object; ~ **su qc** to object to sth, raise objections concerning sth.
obiettività *sf* objectivity.
obiet'tivo, a *ag* objective; (*imparziale*) unbiased, impartial // *sm* (*OTTICA, FOT*) lens *sg*, objective; (*MIL, fig*) objective.
obiet'tore *sm* objector; ~ **di coscienza** conscientious objector.
obiezi'one [objet'tsjone] *sf* objection.
obi'torio *sm* morgue, mortuary.
o'bliquo, a *ag* oblique; (*inclinato*) slanting; (*fig*) devious, underhand; **sguardo** ~ sidelong glance.
oblite'rare *vt* to obliterate.
oblò *sm inv* porthole.
o'blungo, a, ghi, ghe *ag* oblong.
'oboe *sm* (*MUS*) oboe.
obsole'scenza [obsoleʃ'ʃɛntsa] *sf* (*ECON*) obsolescence.
'oca, pl 'oche *sf* goose.
occasi'one *sf* (*caso favorevole*) opportunity; (*causa, motivo, circostanza*) occasion; (*COMM*) bargain; **d'**~ (*a buon prezzo*) bargain *cpd*; (*usato*) secondhand.
occhi'aia [ok'kjaja] *sf* eye socket; ~**e** *sfpl* shadows (under the eyes).
occhi'ali [ok'kjali] *smpl* glasses, spectacles; ~ **da sole** sunglasses.
occhi'ata [ok'kjata] *sf* look, glance; **dare un'**~ **a** to have a look at.
occhieggi'are [okkjed'dʒare] *vt* to eye, ogle // *vi* (*apparire qua e là*) to peep (out).
occhi'ello [ok'kjɛllo] *sm* buttonhole; (*asola*) eyelet.
'occhio ['ɔkkjo] *sm* eye; ~**!** careful!, watch out!; **a** ~ **nudo** with the naked eye; **a**

quattr'~**i** privately, tête-à-tête; **dare all'**~ *o* **nell'**~ **a qd** to catch sb's eye; **fare l'**~ **a qc** to get used to sth; **tenere d'**~ **qd** to keep an eye on sb; **vedere di buon/mal** ~ **qc** to look favourably/unfavourably on sth.
occhio'lino [okkjo'lino] *sm*: **fare l'**~ **a qd** to wink at sb.
occiden'tale [ottʃiden'tale] *ag* western // *sm/f* Westerner.
occi'dente [ottʃi'dɛnte] *sm* west; (*POL*): **l'O**~ the West.
oc'cipite [ot'tʃipite] *sm* back of the head, occiput.
oc'cludere *vt* to block; **occlusi'one** *sf* blockage, obstruction; **oc'cluso, a** *pp di* **occludere**.
occor'rente *ag* necessary // *sm* all that is necessary.
occor'renza [okkor'rɛntsa] *sf* necessity, need; **all'**~ in case of need.
oc'correre (2) *vi* to be needed, be required // *vb impers*: **occorre farlo** it must be done; **occorre che tu parta** you must leave, you'll have to leave; **oc'corso, a** *pp di* **occorrere**.
occul'tare *vt* to hide, conceal.
oc'culto, a *ag* hidden, concealed; (*scienze, forze*) occult.
occu'pare *vt* to occupy; (*manodopera*) to employ; (*ingombrare*) to occupy, take up; ~**rsi** *vr* to occupy o.s., keep o.s. busy; (*impiegarsi*) to get a job; ~**rsi di** (*interessarsi*) to take an interest in; (*prendersi cura di*) to look after, take care of; **occu'pato, a** *ag* (*MIL, POL*) occupied; (*persona: affaccendato*) busy; (*posto, sedia*) taken; (*toilette, TEL*) engaged; **occu-pa'tore, 'trice** *sm/f* occupier; **occupa-zi'one** *sf* occupation; (*impiego, lavoro*) job; (*ECON*) employment.
o'ceano [o'tʃeano] *sm* ocean.
'ocra *sf* ochre.
ocu'lare *ag* ocular, eye *cpd*.
ocu'lato, a *ag* (*attento*) cautious, prudent; (*accorto*) shrewd.
ocu'lista, i, e *sm/f* eye specialist, oculist.
'ode *sf* ode.
odi'are *vt* to hate, detest.
odi'erno, a *ag* today's, of today; (*attuale*) present.
'odio *sm* hatred; **avere in** ~ **qc/qd** to hate *o* detest sth/sb; **odi'oso, a** *ag* hateful, odious.
odo'rare *vt* (*annusare*) to smell; (*profumare*) to perfume, scent // *vi*: ~ (**di**) to smell (of); **odo'rato** *sm* sense of smell.
o'dore *sm* smell; **gli** ~**i** *smpl* (*CUC*) (aromatic) herbs; **odo'roso, a** *ag* sweet-smelling.
of'fendere *vt* to offend; (*violare*) to break, violate; (*insultare*) to insult; (*ferire*) to injure; ~**rsi** *vr* (*con senso reciproco*) to insult one another; (*risentirsi*): ~**rsi (di)** to take offence (at), be offended (by); **offen'sivo, a** *ag, sf* offensive; **offen'sore,**

offendi'trice *sm/f* offender; (MIL) aggressor.

offe'rente *sm* (in aste): **al maggior ~** to the highest bidder.

of'ferto, a *pp di* **offrire** // *sf* offer; (donazione, anche REL) offering; (in gara d'appalto) tender; (in aste) bid; (ECON) supply.

of'feso, a *pp di* **offendere** // *ag* offended // *sm/f* offended party // *sf* insult, affront; (MIL) attack; (DIR) offence.

offi'cina [offi'tʃina] *sf* workshop.

of'frire *vt* to offer; **~rsi** *vr* (proporsi) to offer (o.s.), volunteer; (occasione) to present itself; (esporsi): **~rsi a** to expose o.s. to; **ti offro da bere** I'll buy you a drink.

offus'care *vt* to obscure, darken; (fig: intelletto) to dim, cloud; (: fama) to obscure, overshadow; **~rsi** *vr* to grow dark; to cloud, grow dim; to be obscured.

of'talmico, a, ci, che *ag* ophthalmic.

oggettività [oddʒettivi'ta] *sf* objectivity.

ogget'tivo, a [oddʒet'tivo] *ag* objective.

og'getto [od'dʒetto] *sm* object; (materia, argomento) subject (matter).

'oggi ['ɔddʒi] *av, sm* today; **~ a otto** a week today; **oggigi'orno** *av* nowadays.

o'giva [o'dʒiva] *sf* (ARCHIT) diagonal rib; (MIL) warhead; **arco a ~** lancet arch.

'ogni ['oɲɲi] *det* every, each; (tutti) all; **~ uomo è mortale** all men are mortal; (con valore distributivo) every; **viene ~ due giorni** he comes every two days; **~ cosa** everything; **in ~ luogo** everywhere; **~ tanto** every so often; **~ volta che** every time that.

Ognis'santi [oɲɲis'santi] *sm* All Saints' Day.

o'gnuno [oɲ'ɲuno] *pronome* everyone, everybody.

'ohi *escl* oh!; (esprimente dolore) ow!

ohimè *escl* oh dear!

O'landa *sf*: **l'~** Holland; **olan'dese** *ag* Dutch // *sm* (LING) Dutch // *sm/f* Dutchman/woman; **gli Olandesi** the Dutch.

oleo'dotto *sm* oil pipeline.

ole'oso, a *ag* oily; (che contiene olio) oil-yielding.

ol'fatto *sm* sense of smell.

oli'are *vt* to oil; **olia'tore** *sm* oil-can, oiler.

oli'era *sf* oil cruet.

olim'piadi *sfpl* Olympic games; **o'limpico, a, ci, che** *ag* Olympic.

'olio *sm* oil; **sott'~** (CUC) in oil; **~ d'oliva** olive oil; **~ di fegato di merluzzo** cod liver oil.

o'liva *sf* olive; **oli'vastro, a** *ag* olive(-coloured); (carnagione) sallow; **oli'veto** *sm* olive grove; **o'livo** *sm* olive tree.

'olmo *sm* elm.

oltraggi'are [oltrad'dʒare] *vt* to outrage; to offend gravely.

ol'traggio [ol'traddʒo] *sm* outrage; offence, insult; (LAW): **~ alla magistratura** contempt of court; **oltraggi'oso, a** *ag* offensive.

ol'tralpe *av* beyond the Alps.

ol'tranza [ol'trantsa] *sf*: **a ~** to the last, to the bitter end.

'oltre *av* (più in là) further; (di più: aspettare) longer, more // *prep* (di là da) beyond, over, on the other side of; (più di) more than, over; (in aggiunta a) besides; (eccetto): **~ a** except, apart from; **oltre-'mare** *av* overseas; **oltrepas'sare** *vt* to go beyond, exceed.

o'maggio [o'maddʒo] *sm* (dono) gift; (segno di rispetto) homage, tribute; **~i** *smpl* (complimenti) respects; **rendere ~ a** to pay homage o tribute to; **copia in ~** (STAMPA) complimentary copy.

ombeli'cale *ag* umbilical.

ombe'lico, chi *sm* navel.

'ombra *sf* (zona non assolata, fantasma) shade; (sagoma scura) shadow; **sedere all'~** to sit in the shade.

ombreggi'are [ombred'dʒare] *vt* to shade.

om'brello *sm* umbrella; **ombrel'lone** *sm* beach umbrella.

om'bretto *sm* eyeshadow.

om'broso, a *ag* shady, shaded; (cavallo) nervous, skittish; (persona) touchy, easily offended.

ome'lia *sf* (REL) homily, sermon.

omeopa'tia *sf* homoeopathy.

omertà *sf* conspiracy of silence.

o'messo, a *pp di* **omettere.**

o'mettere *vt* to omit, leave out; **~ di fare** to omit o fail to do.

omi'cida, i, e [omi'tʃida] *ag* homicidal, murderous // *sm/f* murderer/eress.

omi'cidio [omi'tʃidjo] *sm* murder; **~ colposo** culpable homicide.

omissi'one *sf* omission.

omogeneiz'zato [omodʒeneid'dzato] *sm* baby food.

omo'geneo, a [omo'dʒɛneo] *ag* homogeneous.

omolo'gare *vt* to approve, recognize; to ratify.

o'monimo, a *sm/f* namesake // *sm* (LING) homonym.

omosessu'ale *ag, sm/f* homosexual.

'oncia, ce ['ontʃa] *sf* ounce.

'onda *sf* wave; **mettere** *o* **mandare in ~** (RADIO, TV) to broadcast; **~e corte/medie/lunghe** short/medium/long wave; **on'data** *sf* wave, billow; (fig) wave, surge; **a ondate** in waves; **ondata di caldo** heatwave.

'onde *cong* (affinché: con il congiuntivo) so that, in order that; (: con l'infinito) so as to, in order to.

ondeggi'are [onded'dʒare] *vi* (acqua) to ripple; (muoversi sulle onde: barca) to rock, roll; (fig: muoversi come le onde, barcollare) to sway; (: essere incerto) to waver.

ondula'torio, a *ag* undulating; (FISICA) undulatory, wave cpd.

ondulazi'one [ondulat'tsjone] *sf* undulation; (acconciatura) wave; **~ permanente** permanent wave, perm.

'onere sm burden; ~**i fiscali** taxes; **one-'roso, a** ag (fig) heavy, onerous.

onestà sf honesty.

o'nesto, a ag (probo, retto) honest; (giusto) fair; (casto) chaste, virtuous.

'onice ['onitʃe] sf onyx.

onnipo'tente ag omnipotent.

onnisci'ente [onniʃ'ʃɛnte] ag omniscient.

onniveg'gente [onnived'dʒɛnte] ag all-seeing.

ono'mastico, ci sm name-day.

ono'ranze [ono'rantse] sfpl honours.

ono'rare vt to honour; (far onore a) to do credit to; ~**rsi** vr: ~**rsi di** to feel honoured at, be proud of.

ono'rario, a ag honorary // sm fee.

o'nore sm honour; **in** ~ **di** in honour of; **fare gli** ~**i di casa** to play host (o hostess); **fare** ~ **a** to honour; (pranzo) to do justice to; (famiglia) to be a credit to; **farsi** ~ to distinguish o.s.; **ono'revole** ag honourable // sm/f (POL) Member of Parliament; **onorifi'cenza** sf honour; decoration; **ono'rifico, a, ci, che** ag honorary.

'onta sf shame, disgrace.

'O.N.U. ['onu] sf (abbr di Organizzazione delle Nazioni Unite) UN, UNO.

o'paco, a, chi, che ag (vetro) opaque; (metallo) dull, matt.

o'pale sm o f opal.

'opera sf work; (azione rilevante) action, deed, work; (MUS) work; opus; (: melodramma) opera; (: teatro) opera house; (ente) institution, organization; ~ **d'arte** work of art; ~**e pubbliche** public works.

ope'raio, a ag working-class; workers' // sm/f worker; **classe** ~**a** working class.

ope'rare vt to carry out, make; (MED) to operate on // vi to operate, work; (rimedio) to act, work; (MED) to operate; ~**rsi** vr to occur, take place; **opera'tivo, a** ag operative, operating; **opera'tore, 'trice** sm/f operator; (MED) surgeon; (TV, CINEMA) cameraman; **operatore econo-mico** agent, broker; **opera'torio, a** ag (MED) operating; **operazi'one** sf operation.

ope'retta sf (MUS) operetta, light opera.

ope'roso, a ag busy, active, hard-working.

opi'ficio [opi'fitʃo] sm factory, works pl.

opini'one sf opinion.

'oppio sm opium.

oppo'nente ag opposing // sm/f opponent.

op'porre vt to oppose; **opporsi** vr: **opporsi (a qc)** to oppose (sth); to object (to sth); ~ **resistenza/un rifiuto** to offer resistance/refuse.

opportu'nista, i, e sm/f opportunist.

opportunità sf inv opportunity; (convenienza) opportuneness, timeliness.

oppor'tuno, a ag timely, opportune.

opposi'tore sm opposer, opponent.

opposizi'one [oppozit'tsjone] sf opposition; (DIR) objection.

op'posto, a pp di **opporre** // ag opposite;

(opinioni) conflicting // sm opposite, contrary; **all'**~ on the contrary.

oppressi'one sf oppression.

oppres'sivo, a ag oppressive.

op'presso, a pp di **opprimere**.

oppres'sore sm oppressor.

op'primere vt (premere, gravare) to weigh down; (estenuare: sog: caldo) to suffocate, oppress; (tiranneggiare: popolo) to oppress.

oppu'gnare [oppuɲ'ɲare] vt (fig) to refute.

op'pure cong or (else).

op'tare vi: ~ **per** to opt for.

opu'lento, a ag (ricco) rich, wealthy; (: arredamento etc) opulent.

o'puscolo sm booklet, pamphlet.

opzi'one [op'tsjone] sf option.

'ora sf (60 minuti) hour; (momento) time; **che** ~ **è?, che** ~**e sono?** what time is it?; **non veder l'**~ **di fare** to long to do, look forward to doing; **alla buon'**~! at last!; ~ **legale (estiva)** summer time; ~ **locale** local time; ~ **di punta** (AUT) rush hour // av (adesso) now; (poco fa) just now; (correlativo): ~ ... ~ now ... now; **d'**~ **in avanti** from now on; **or** ~ just now, a moment ago.

o'racolo sm oracle.

'orafo sm goldsmith.

o'rale ag, sm oral.

ora'mai av = **ormai**.

o'rario, a ag hourly; (velocità) per hour // sm timetable, schedule; (di ufficio, visite etc) hours pl, time(s pl).

ora'tore, 'trice sm/f speaker; orator.

ora'torio, a ag oratorical // sm (REL) oratory; (MUS) oratorio // sf (arte) oratory.

or'bene cong so, well (then).

'orbita sf (ASTR, FISICA) orbit; (ANAT) (eye-)socket.

or'chestra [or'kɛstra] sf orchestra; **orches'trale** ag orchestral // sm/f orchestra player; **orches'trare** vt to orchestrate; (fig) to mount, stage-manage.

orchi'dea [orki'dɛa] sf orchid.

'orcio ['ortʃo] sm jar.

'orco, chi sm ogre.

'orda sf horde.

or'digno [or'diɲɲo] sm (esplosivo) explosive device.

ordi'nale ag, sm ordinal.

ordina'mento sm order, arrangement; (regolamento) regulations pl, rules pl; ~ **scolastico/giuridico** education/legal system.

ordi'nanza [ordi'nantsa] sf (DIR, MIL) order; (persona: MIL) orderly, batman; **d'**~ (MIL) regulation cpd.

ordi'nare vt (mettere in ordine) to arrange, organize; (COMM) to order; (pres-crivere: medicina) to prescribe; (comandare): ~ **a qd di fare qc** to order o command sb to do sth; (REL) to ordain.

ordi'nario, a ag (comune) ordinary;

everyday; standard; (*grossolano*) coarse, common // *sm* ordinary; (*INS: di università*) full professor.

ordina'tivo, a *ag* regulating, regulative.

ordi'nato, a *ag* tidy, orderly.

ordinazi'one [ordinat'tsjone] *sf* (*COMM*) order; (*REL*) ordination.

'ordine *sm* order; (*carattere*): **d'~ pratico** of a practical nature; **all'~** (*COMM: assegno*) to order; **di prim'~** first-class; **fino a nuovo ~** until further notice; **mettere in ~** to put in order, tidy (up); **~ del giorno** (*di seduta*) agenda; (*MIL*) order of the day; **l'~ pubblico** law and order; **~i (sacri)** (*REL*) Holy orders.

or'dire *vt* (*fig*) to plot, scheme; **or'dito** *sm* (*fig*) plot.

orec'chino [orek'kino] *sm* earring.

o'recchio [o'rekkjo], *pl*(*f*) **o'recchie** *sm* (*ANAT*) ear.

orecchi'oni [orek'kjoni] *smpl* (*MED*) mumps *sg*.

o'refice [o'refitʃe] *sm* goldsmith; jeweller; **orefice'ria** *sf* (*arte*) goldsmith's art; (*negozio*) jeweller's (shop).

'orfano, a *ag* orphan(ed) // *sm/f* orphan; **~ di padre/madre** fatherless/motherless; **orfano'trofio** *sm* orphanage.

orga'netto *sm* barrel organ; (*armonica a bocca*) mouth organ; (*fisarmonica*) accordion.

or'ganico, a, ci, che *ag* organic // *sm* personnel, staff.

organi'gramma, i *sm* organization chart.

orga'nismo *sm* (*BIOL*) organism; (*corpo umano*) body; (*AMM*) body, organism.

orga'nista, i, e *sm/f* organist.

organiz'zare [organid'dzare] *vt* to organize; **~rsi** *vr* to get organized; **organizza'tore, 'trice** *ag* organizing // *sm/f* organizer; **organizzazi'one** *sf* organization.

'organo *sm* organ; (*di congegno*) part; (*portavoce*) spokesman, mouthpiece.

or'gasmo *sm* (*FISIOL*) orgasm; (*fig*) agitation, anxiety.

'orgia, ge ['ordʒa] *sf* orgy.

or'goglio [or'ɡɔʎʎo] *sm* pride; **orgogli'oso, a** *ag* proud.

orien'tale *ag* oriental; eastern; east.

orienta'mento *sm* positioning; orientation; direction; **senso di ~** sense of direction; **~ professionale** careers guidance.

orien'tare *vt* (*situare*) to position; (*fig*) to direct, orientate; **~rsi** *vr* to find one's bearings; (*fig: tendere*) to tend, lean; (*: indirizzarsi*): **~rsi verso** to take up, go in for.

ori'ente *sm* east; **l'O~** the East, the Orient.

o'rigano *sm* oregano.

origi'nale [oridʒi'nale] *ag* original; (*bizzarro*) eccentric // *sm* original; **originalità** *sf* originality; eccentricity.

origi'nare [oridʒi'nare] *vt* to bring about,

produce // *vi* (*2*): **~ da** to arise o spring from.

origi'nario, a [oridʒi'narjo] *ag* original; **essere ~ di** to be a native of; (*provenire da*) to originate from; to be native to.

o'rigine [o'ridʒine] *sf* origin; **all'~** originally; **d'~ inglese** of English origin; **dare ~ a** to give rise to.

origli'are [oriʎ'ʎare] *vi*: **~ (a)** to eavesdrop (on).

o'rina *sf* urine; **ori'nale** *sm* chamberpot.

ori'nare *vi* to urinate // *vt* to pass; **orina'toio** *sm* (public) urinal.

ori'undo, a *ag*: **~ (di)** native (of).

orizzon'tale [oriddzon'tale] *ag* horizontal.

oriz'zonte [orid'dzonte] *sm* horizon.

or'lare *vt* to hem; **orla'tura** *sf* hemming *q*; hem.

'orlo *sm* edge, border; (*di recipiente*) rim, brim; (*di vestito etc*) hem.

'orma *sf* (*di persona*) footprint; (*di animale*) track; (*impronta, traccia*) mark, trace.

or'mai *av* by now, by this time; (*adesso*) now; (*quasi*) almost, nearly.

ormeggi'are [ormed'dʒare] *vt* (*NAUT*) to moor; **or'meggio** *sm* (*atto*) mooring *q*; (*luogo*) moorings *pl*.

or'mone *sm* hormone.

ornamen'tale *ag* ornamental, decorative.

orna'mento *sm* ornament, decoration.

or'nare *vt* to adorn, decorate; **or'nato, a** *ag* ornate.

ornitolo'gia [ornitolo'dʒia] *sf* ornithology.

'oro *sm* gold; **d'~, in ~** gold *cpd*; **d'~** (*fig*) golden.

orologe'ria [orolodʒe'ria] *sf* watchmaking *q*; watchmaker's (shop); clockmaker's (shop); **bomba a ~** time bomb.

orologi'aio [orolo'dʒajo] *sm* watchmaker; clockmaker.

oro'logio [oro'lɔdʒo] *sm* clock; (*da tasca, da polso*) watch; **~ da polso** wristwatch; **~ a sveglia** alarm clock.

o'roscopo *sm* horoscope.

or'rendo, a *ag* (*spaventoso*) horrible, awful; (*bruttissimo*) hideous.

or'ribile *ag* horrible.

'orrido, a *ag* fearful, horrid.

orripi'lante *ag* hair-raising, horrifying.

or'rore *sm* horror; **avere in ~ qd/qc** to loathe o detest sb/sth.

orsacchi'otto [orsak'kjotto] *sm* teddy bear.

'orso *sm* bear; **~ bruno/bianco** brown/polar bear.

or'taggio [or'taddʒo] *sm* vegetable.

or'tica, che *sf* (stinging) nettle.

orti'caria *sf* nettle rash.

orticol'tura *sf* horticulture.

'orto *sm* vegetable garden, kitchen garden; **~ industriale** market garden.

orto'dosso, a *ag* orthodox.

ortogra'fia *sf* spelling.

orto'lano, a *sm/f* (*venditore*) greengrocer.

ortope'dia *sf* orthopaedics *sg*; **orto-**

'pedico, a, ci, che *ag* orthopaedic // *sm* orthopaedic specialist.

orzai'olo [ordza'jɔlo] *sm* (*MED*) stye.

or'zata [or'dzata] *sf* barley water.

'orzo ['ordzo] *sm* barley.

o'sare *vt, vi* to dare; ~ **fare** to dare (to) do.

oscenità [oʃʃeni'ta] *sf inv* obscenity.

o'sceno, a [oʃ'ʃeno] *ag* obscene; (*ripugnante*) ghastly.

oscil'lare [oʃʃil'lare] *vi* (*pendolo*) to swing; (*dondolare: al vento etc*) to rock; (*variare*) to fluctuate; (*TECN*) to oscillate; (*fig*): ~ **fra** to waver *o* hesitate between; **oscilla-zi'one** *sf* oscillation; (*di prezzi, temperatura*) fluctuation.

oscura'mento *sm* darkening; obscuring; (*in tempo di guerra*) blackout.

oscu'rare *vt* to darken, obscure; (*fig*) to obscure; ~**rsi** *vr* to grow dark.

os'curo, a *ag* dark; (*fig*) obscure; humble, lowly // *sm*: **all'**~ in the dark; **tenere qd all'**~ **di qc** to keep sb in the dark about sth.

ospe'dale *sm* hospital.

ospi'tale *ag* hospitable; **ospitalità** *sf* hospitality.

ospi'tare *vt* to give hospitality to; (*sog: albergo*) to accommodate.

'ospite *sm/f* (*persona che ospita*) host/hostess; (*persona ospitata*) guest.

os'pizio [os'pittsjo] *sm* (*per vecchi etc*) home.

'ossa *sfpl vedi* **osso.**

ossa'tura *sf* (*ANAT*) skeletal structure, frame; (*TECN, fig*) framework.

'osseo, a *ag* bony; (*tessuto etc*) bone *cpd.*

osse'quente *ag* respectful, deferential; ~ **alla legge** law-abiding.

os'sequio *sm* deference, respect; ~**i** *smpl* (*saluto*) respects, regards; **ossequi'oso, a** *ag* obsequious.

osser'vanza [osser'vantsa] *sf* observance.

osser'vare *vt* to observe, watch; (*esaminare*) to examine; (*notare, rilevare*) to notice, observe; (*DIR: la legge*) to observe, respect; (*mantenere: silenzio*) to keep, observe; **far** ~ **qc a qd** to point sth out to sb; **osserva'tore, 'trice** *ag* observant, perceptive // *sm/f* observer; **osserva'torio** *sm* (*ASTR*) observatory; (*MIL*) observation post; **osservazi'one** *sf* observation; (*di legge etc*) observance; (*considerazione critica*) observation, remark; (*rimprovero*) reproof; **in osservazione** under observation.

ossessio'nare *vt* to obsess, haunt; (*tormentare*) to torment, harass.

ossessi'one *sf* obsession.

os'sesso, a *ag* (*spiritato*) possessed.

os'sia *cong* that is, to be precise.

ossi'dare *vt*, ~**rsi** *vr* to oxidize.

os'sido *sm* oxide; ~ **di carbonio** carbon monoxide.

ossige'nare [ossidʒe'nare] *vt* to oxygenate; (*decolorare*) to bleach.

os'sigeno *sm* oxygen.

'osso *sm* (*pl(f)* **ossa** *nel senso ANAT*) bone; **d'**~ (*bottone etc*) of bone, bone *cpd.*

osso'buco, *pl* **ossi'buchi** *sm* (*CUC*) marrowbone; (: *piatto*) stew made with knuckle of veal in tomato sauce.

os'suto, a *ag* bony.

ostaco'lare *vt* to block, obstruct.

os'tacolo *sm* obstacle; (*EQUITAZIONE*) hurdle, jump.

os'taggio [os'taddʒo] *sm* hostage.

'oste, os'tessa *sm/f* innkeeper.

osteggi'are [osted'dʒare] *vt* to oppose, be opposed to.

os'tello *sm*: ~ **della gioventù** youth hostel.

osten'sorio *sm* (*REL*) monstrance.

osten'tare *vt* to make a show of, flaunt; **ostentazi'one** *sf* ostentation, show.

oste'ria *sf* inn.

os'tessa *sf vedi* **oste.**

os'tetrico, a, ci, che *ag* obstetric // *sm* obstetrician // *sf* midwife.

'ostia *sf* (*REL*) host; (*per medicinali*) wafer.

'ostico, a, ci, che *ag* (*fig*) harsh; hard, difficult; unpleasant.

os'tile *ag* hostile; **ostilità** *sf inv* hostility // *sfpl* (*MIL*) hostilities.

osti'narsi *vr* to insist, dig one's heels in; ~ **a fare** to persist (obstinately) in doing; **osti'nato, a** *ag* (*caparbio*) obstinate; (*tenace*) persistent, determined; **ostina-zi'one** *sf* obstinacy; persistence.

ostra'cismo [ostra'tʃizmo] *sm* ostracism.

'ostrica, che *sf* oyster.

ostru'ire *vt* to obstruct, block; **ostru-zi'one** *sf* obstruction, blockage.

'otre *sm* (*recipiente*) goatskin.

ottago'nale *ag* octagonal.

ot'tagono *sm* octagon.

ot'tanta *num* eighty; **ottan'tesimo, a** *num* eightieth; **ottan'tina** *sf*: **una ottantina (di)** about eighty.

ot'tavo, a *num* eighth // *sf* octave.

ottempe'rare *vi*: ~ **a** to comply with, obey.

ottene'brare *vt* to darken; (*fig*) to cloud.

otte'nere *vt* to obtain, get; (*risultato*) to achieve, obtain.

'ottico, a, ci, che *ag* (*della vista: nervo*) optic; (*dell'ottica*) optical // *sm* optician // *sf* (*scienza*) optics *sg*; (*FOT: lenti, prismi etc*) optics *pl.*

ottima'mente *av* excellently, very well.

otti'mismo *sm* optimism; **otti'mista, i, e** *sm/f* optimist.

'ottimo, a *ag* excellent, very good.

'otto *num* eight.

ot'tobre *sm* October.

otto'cento [otto'tʃɛnto] *num* eight hundred // *sm*: **l'O**~ the nineteenth century.

ot'tone *sm* brass; **gli** ~**i** (*MUS*) the brass.

ottuage'nario, a [ottuadʒe'narjo] *ag, sm/f* octogenarian.

ot'tundere *vt* (*fig*) to dull.

ottu'rare *vt* to close (up); (*dente*) to fill; **ottura'tore** *sm* (*FOT*) shutter; (*nelle armi*) breechblock; **otturazi'one** sf closing (up); (dentaria) filling.

ot'tuso, a pp di **ottundere** // ag (smussato) blunt, dull; (MAT, fig) obtuse; (suono) dull.

o'vaia sf, **o'vaio** sm (ANAT) ovary.

o'vale ag, sm oval.

o'vatta sf cotton wool; (per imbottire) padding, wadding.

ovazi'one [ovat'tsjone] sf ovation.

'ovest sm west.

o'vile sm pen, enclosure.

o'vino, a ag sheep cpd, ovine.

ovulazi'one [ovulat'tsjone] sf ovulation.

'ovulo sm (FISIOL) ovum.

ov'vero cong (ossia) that is, to be precise; (oppure) or (else).

ovvi'are vi: ~ a to obviate.

'ovvio, a ag obvious.

ozi'are [ot'tsjare] vi to laze, idle.

'ozio ['ɔttsjo] sm idleness; (tempo libero) leisure; **ore d'~** leisure time; **stare in ~** to be idle; **ozi'oso, a** ag idle.

o'zono [o'dzɔno] sm ozone.

P

pa'cato, a ag quiet, calm.

pac'chetto [pak'ketto] sm packet.

'pacco, chi sm parcel; (involto) bundle.

'pace ['patʃe] sf peace; **darsi ~** to resign o.s.

pacifi'care [patʃifi'kare] vt (riconciliare) to reconcile, make peace between; (mettere in pace) to pacify.

pa'cifico, a, ci, che [pa'tʃifiko] ag (persona) peaceable; (vita) peaceful; (fig: indiscusso) indisputable; (: ovvio) obvious, clear // sm: **il P~, l'Oceano P~** the Pacific (Ocean).

paci'fista, i, e [patʃi'fista] sm/f pacifist.

pa'della sf frying pan; (per infermi) bedpan.

padigli'one [padiʎ'ʎone] sm pavilion; (AUT) roof.

'Padova sf Padua.

'padre sm father; ~**i** smpl (antenati) forefathers; **pa'drino** sm godfather.

padro'nanza [padro'nantsa] sf command, mastery.

pa'drone, a sm/f master/mistress; (proprietario) owner; (datore di lavoro) employer; **essere ~ di sé** to be in control of o.s.; ~ **di casa** master/mistress of the house; (per gli inquilini) landlord/lady; **padroneggi'are** vt to rule, command; (fig: sentimenti) to master, control; (: materia) to master, know thoroughly.

pae'saggio [pae'zaddʒo] sm landscape.

pae'sano, a ag country cpd // sm/f villager; countryman.

pa'ese sm country; land; region; village; **i P~i Bassi** the Netherlands.

paf'futo, a ag chubby, plump.

'paga, ghe sf pay, wages pl.

paga'mento sm payment.

pa'gano, a ag, sm/f pagan.

pa'gare vt to pay; (acquisto, fig: colpa) to pay for; (contraccambiare) to repay, pay back // vi to pay; **quanto l'hai pagato?** how much did you pay for it?; ~ **un assegno a qd** (sog: banca) to cash sb a cheque.

pa'gella [pa'dʒella] sf (INS) report card.

'paggio ['paddʒo] sm page (boy).

pagherò [page'rɔ] sm inv acknowledgement of a debt, IOU.

'pagina ['padʒina] sf page.

'paglia ['paʎʎa] sf straw.

pagliac'cetto [paʎʎat'tʃetto] sm (per bambini) rompers pl.

pagli'accio [paʎ'ʎattʃo] sm clown.

pagli'etta [paʎ'ʎetta] sf (cappello per uomo) (straw) boater; (per tegami etc) steel wool.

pagli'uzza [paʎ'ʎuttsa] sf (blade of) straw; (d'oro etc) tiny particle, speck.

pa'gnotta [pan'nɔtta] sf round loaf.

pa'goda sf pagoda.

'paio, pl(f) 'paia sm pair; **un ~ di** (alcuni) a couple of.

pai'olo, paiu'olo sm (copper) pot.

'pala sf shovel; (di remo, ventilatore, elica) blade; (di ruota) paddle.

pa'lato sm palate.

pa'lazzo [pa'lattso] sm (reggia) palace; (edificio) building; ~ **di giustizia** courthouse; ~ **dello sport** sports stadium.

pal'chetto [pal'ketto] sm shelf.

'palco, chi sm (TEATRO) box; (tavolato) platform, stand; (ripiano) layer.

palco'scenico, ci [palkoʃ'ʃeniko] sm (TEATRO) stage.

pale'sare vt to reveal, disclose; ~**rsi** vr to reveal o show o.s.

pa'lese ag clear, evident.

Pales'tina sf: **la ~** Palestine.

pa'lestra sf gymnasium; (esercizio atletico) exercise, training; (fig) training ground, school.

pa'letta sf spade; (per il focolare) shovel; (del capostazione) signalling disc.

pa'letto sm stake, peg; (spranga) bolt.

'palio sm (gara): **il P~** horserace run at Siena; **mettere qc in ~** to offer sth as a prize.

paliz'zata [palit'tsata] sf palisade.

'palla sf ball; (pallottola) bullet; ~ **canestro** sm basketball; ~ **nuoto** sm water polo; ~ **volo** sm volleyball.

palleggi'are [palled'dʒare] vi (CALCIO) to practise with the ball; (TENNIS) to knock up.

pallia'tivo sm palliative; (fig) stopgap measure.

'pallido, a ag pale.

pal'lina sf (bilia) marble.

pallon'cino [pallon'tʃino] sm balloon; (lampioncino) chinese lantern.

pal'lone sm (palla) ball; (CALCIO) football; (aerostato) balloon; **gioco del ~** football.

pal'lore sm pallor, paleness.

pal'lottola sf pellet; (proiettile) bullet.

'**palma** sf (ANAT) = **palmo**; (BOT, simbolo) palm; ~ **da datteri** date palm.

'**palmo** sm (ANAT) palm; **restare con un ~ di naso** to be badly disappointed.

'**palo** sm (legno appuntito) stake; (sostegno) pole; **fare da o il ~** (fig) to act as lookout.

palom'baro sm diver.

pa'lombo sm (pesce) dogfish.

pal'pare vt to feel, finger.

'**palpebra** sf eyelid.

palpi'tare vi (cuore, polso) to beat; (: più forte) to pound, throb; (tremere) to quiver; **palpitazi'one** sf palpitation; '**palpito** sm (del cuore) beat; (fig: d'amore etc) throb.

paltò sm inv overcoat.

pa'lude sf marsh, swamp; **palu'doso, a** ag marshy, swampy.

pa'lustre ag marsh cpd, swamp cpd.

pam'pino sm vine leaf.

pana'cea [pana'tʃɛa] sf panacea.

'**panca, che** sf bench.

pan'cetta [pan'tʃetta] sf (CUC) bacon.

pan'chetto [pan'ketto] sm stool; footstool.

pan'china [pan'kina] sf garden seat; (di giardino pubblico) (park) bench.

'**pancia, ce** ['pantʃa] sf belly, stomach; **mettere o fare ~** to be getting a paunch; **avere mal di ~** to have stomach ache o a sore stomach.

panci'otto [pan'tʃɔtto] sm waistcoat.

pan'cone sm workbench.

'**pancreas** sm pancreas.

'**panda** sm inv panda.

pande'monio sm pandemonium.

'**pane** sm bread; (pagnotta) loaf (of bread); (forma): **un ~ di burro/cera** etc a pat of butter/bar of wax etc; **~ integrale** wholemeal bread; **~ tostato** toast.

panette'ria sf (forno) bakery; (negozio) baker's (shop), bakery.

panetti'ere, a sm/f baker.

panet'tone sm a kind of spiced brioche with sultanas, eaten at Christmas.

pangrat'tato sm breadcrumbs pl.

'**panico, a, ci, che** ag, sm panic.

pani'ere sm basket.

pani'ficio [pani'fitʃo] sm (forno) bakery; (negozio) baker's (shop), bakery.

pa'nino sm roll; **~ imbottito** filled roll; sandwich.

'**panna** sf (CUC) cream; (TECN) breakdown; **essere in ~** to have broken down; **~ montata** whipped cream.

pan'nello sm panel.

'**panno** sm cloth; **~i** smpl (abiti) clothes.

pan'nocchia [pan'nɔkkja] sf (di mais etc) ear.

panno'lino sm (per bambini) nappy.

pano'rama sm panorama; **pano'ramico, a, ci, che** ag panoramic.

panta'loni smpl trousers pl, pair of trousers.

pan'tano sm bog.

pan'tera sf panther.

pan'tofola sf slipper.

panto'mima sf pantomime.

pan'zana [pan'tsana] sf fib, tall story.

pao'nazzo, a [pao'nattso] ag purple.

'**papa, i** sm pope.

papà sm inv dad(dy).

pa'pale ag papal.

pa'pato sm papacy.

pa'pavero sm poppy.

'**papero, a** sm/f (ZOOL) gosling // sf (fig) slip of the tongue, blunder.

'**papiro** sm papyrus.

'**pappa** sf baby's cereal.

pappa'gallo sm parrot; (fig: uomo) Romeo, wolf.

pappa'gorgia, ge [pappa'gɔrdʒa] sf double chin.

'**para** sf: **suole di ~** crepe soles.

pa'rabola sf (MAT) parabola; (REL) parable.

para'brezza [para'breddza] sm inv (AUT) windscreen.

paraca'dute sm inv parachute; **paracadu'tista, i, e** sm/f parachutist.

para'carro sm kerbstone.

para'diso sm paradise.

parados'sale ag paradoxical.

para'dosso sm paradox.

para'fango, ghi sm mudguard.

paraf'fina sf paraffin, paraffin wax.

parafra'sare vt to paraphrase.

para'fulmine sm lightning conductor.

pa'raggi [pa'raddʒi] smpl: **nei ~** in the vicinity, in the neighbourhood.

parago'nare vt: **~ con/a** to compare with/to.

para'gone sm comparison; (esempio analogo) analogy, parallel; **reggere al ~** to stand comparison.

pa'ragrafo sm paragraph.

pa'ralisi sf paralysis; **para'litico, a, ci, che** ag, sm/f paralytic.

paraliz'zare [paralid'dzare] vt to paralyze.

paral'lelo, a ag parallel // sm (GEO) parallel; (comparazione): **fare un ~ tra** to draw a parallel between // sf parallel (line); **~e** sfpl (attrezzo ginnico) parallel bars.

para'lume sm lampshade.

pa'rametro sm parameter.

para'noia sf paranoia; **para'noico, a, ci, che** ag, sm/f paranoiac.

para'occhi [para'ɔkki] smpl blinkers.

para'petto sm parapet.

para'piglia [para'piʎʎa] sm commotion, uproar.

pa'rare vt (addobbare) to adorn, deck; (proteggere) to shield, protect; (scansare: colpo) to parry; (CALCIO) to save // vi: **dove vuole andare a ~?** what are you driving at?; **~rsi** vr (presentarsi) to appear, present o.s.

para'sole sm inv parasol, sunshade.

paras'sita, i sm parasite.

pa'rata sf (SPORT) save; (MIL) review, parade.

para'tia sf (di nave) bulkhead.

para'urti *sm inv* (*AUT*) bumper.

para'vento *sm* folding screen.

par'cella [par'tʃɛlla] *sf* account, fee (*of lawyer etc*).

parcheggi'are [parked'dʒare] *vt* to park; **par'cheggio** *sm* parking *q*; (*luogo*) car park.

par'chimetro [par'kimetro] *sm* parking meter.

'parco, chi *sm* park; (*spazio per deposito*) depot; (*complesso di veicoli*) fleet.

'parco, a, chi, che *ag*: ~ (in) (*sobrio*) moderate (in); (*avaro*) sparing (with).

pa'recchio, a [pa'rekkjo] *det* quite a lot of; (*tempo*) quite a lot of, a long; ~i(e) *det pl* quite a lot of, several // *pronome* quite a lot, quite a bit; (*tempo*) quite a while, a long time; ~i(e) *pronome pl* quite a lot, several // *av* (*con ag*) quite, rather; (*con vb*) quite a lot, quite a bit.

pareggi'are [pared'dʒare] *vt* to make equal; (*terreno*) to level, make level; (*bilancio, conti*) to balance // *vi* (*SPORT*) to draw; **pa'reggio** *sm* (*ECON*) balance; (*SPORT*) draw.

paren'tado *sm* relatives *pl*, relations *pl*.

pa'rente *sm/f* relative, relation.

paren'tela *sf* (*vincolo di sangue, fig*) relationship; (*insieme dei parenti*) relations *pl*, relatives *pl*.

pa'rentesi *sf* (*segno grafico*) bracket, parenthesis; (*frase incisa*) parenthesis; (*digressione*) parenthesis, digression.

pa'rere *sm* (*opinione*) opinion; (*consiglio*) advice, opinion; **a mio** ~ in my opinion // (*2*) *vi* to seem, appear // *vb impers*: **pare che** it seems *o* appears that, they say that; **mi pare che** it seems to me that; **fai come ti pare** do as you like; **che ti pare del mio libro?** what do you think of my book?

pa'rete *sf* wall.

'pari *ag inv* (*uguale*) equal, same; (*in giochi*) equal; drawn, tied; (*fig: adeguato*): ~ **a** equal to; (*MAT*) even // *sm* (*POL: di Gran Bretagna*) peer // *sm/f* peer, equal; **alla** ~ on the same level; **ragazza alla** ~ **au pair girl; mettersi alla** ~ **con** *o* to place o.s. on the same level as; **mettersi in** ~ **con** to catch up with; **andare di** ~ **passo con qd** to keep pace with sb.

Pa'rigi [pa'ridʒi] *sf* Paris.

pa'riglia [pa'riʎʎa] *sf* pair; **rendere la** ~ to give tit for tat.

parità *sf* parity, equality; (*SPORT*) draw, tie.

parlamen'tare *ag* parliamentary // *sm/f* member of parliament // *vi* to negotiate, parley.

parla'mento *sm* parliament.

parlan'tina *sf* (*fam*) talkativeness; **avere una buona** ~ to have the gift of the gab.

par'lare *vi* to speak, talk; (*confidare cose segrete*) to talk // *vt* to speak; ~ **(a qd) di** to speak *o* talk (to sb) about; **parla'tore, 'trice** *sm/f* speaker; **parla'torio** *sm* (*di carcere etc*) visiting room; (*REL*) parlour.

parmigi'ano [parmi'dʒano] *sm* (*grana*) Parmesan (cheese).

paro'dia *sf* parody.

pa'rola *sf* word; (*facoltà*) speech; ~**e** *sfpl* (*chiacchiere*) talk *sg*; **chiedere la** ~ to ask permission to speak; ~ **d'onore** word of honour; ~ **d'ordine** (*MIL*) password; ~**e incrociate** crossword (puzzle) *sg*; **paro'laccia, ce** *sf* bad word, swearword.

par'rocchia [par'rɔkkja] *sf* parish; parish church.

'parroco, ci *sm* parish priest.

par'rucca, che *sf* wig.

parrucchi'ere, a [parruk'kjere] *sm/f* hairdresser // *sm* barber.

parsi'monia *sf* frugality, thrift.

'parso, a *pp di* parere.

'parte *sf* part; (*lato*) side; (*quota spettante a ciascuno*) share; (*direzione*) direction; (*POL*) party; faction; (*DIR*) party; **a** ~ *ag* separate // *av* separately; **scherzi a** ~ joking aside; **a** ~ **ciò** apart from that; **da** ~ (*in disparte*) to one side, aside; **d'altra** ~ on the other hand; **da** ~ **mia** as far as I'm concerned, as for me; **da** ~ **a** ~ right through; **da ogni** ~ on all sides, everywhere; (*moto da luogo*) from all sides; **prendere** ~ **a qc** to take part in sth; **mettere qd a** ~ **di qc** to inform sb of sth.

parteci'pare [partetʃi'pare] *vi*: ~ **a** to take part in, participate in; (*utili etc*) to share in; (*spese etc*) to contribute to; (*dolore, successo di qd*) to share (in); **partecipazi'one** *sf* participation; sharing; (*ECON*) interest; **partecipazione agli utili** profit-sharing; **par'tecipe** *ag* participating; **essere partecipe di** to take part in, participate in; to share (in); (*consapevole*) to be aware of.

parteggi'are [parted'dʒare] *vi*: ~ **per** to side with, be on the side of.

par'tenza [par'tɛntsa] *sf* departure; (*SPORT*) start; **essere in** ~ to be about to leave, be leaving.

parti'cella [parti'tʃɛlla] *sf* particle.

parti'cipio [parti'tʃipjo] *sm* participle.

partico'lare *ag* (*specifico*) particular; (*proprio*) personal, private; (*speciale*) special, particular; (*caratteristico*) distinctive, characteristic; (*fuori dal comune*) peculiar // *sm* detail, particular; **in** ~ in particular, particularly; **particolareggi'are** *vt* to give full details of, detail; **particolarità** *sf inv* particularity; detail; characteristic, feature.

partigi'ano, a [parti'dʒano] *ag* partisan // *sm* (*fautore*) supporter, champion; (*MIL*) partisan.

par'tire *vi* (*2*) to go, leave; (*allontanarsi*) to go (*o drive etc*) away *o* off; (*petardo, colpo*) to go off; (*fig: avere inizio, SPORT*) to start; **sono partita da Roma alle 7** I left Rome at 7; **il volo parte da Ciampino** the flight leaves from Ciampino; **a** ~ **da** from.

par'tita *sf* (*COMM*) lot, consignment; (*ECON: registrazione*) entry, item; (*CARTE, SPORT:*

gioco) game; (: *competizione*) match, game; ~ **di caccia** hunting party.

par'tito *sm* (POL) party; (*decisione*) decision, resolution; (*persona da maritare*) match.

'parto *sm* (MED) delivery, (child)birth; labour; **parto'rire** *vt* to give birth to; (*fig*) to produce.

parzi'ale [par'tsjale] *ag* (*limitato*) partial; (*non obiettivo*) biased, partial.

'pascere ['paʃʃere] *vi* to graze // *vt* (*brucare*) to graze on; (*far pascolare*) to graze, pasture; (*nutrire: persone, animali*) to feed, nourish; **pasci'uto, a** *pp di* **pascere**.

pasco'lare *vt, vi* to graze.

'pascolo *sm* pasture.

'Pasqua *sf* Easter; **pas'quale** *ag* Easter *cpd*.

pas'sabile *ag* fairly good, passable.

pas'saggio ['paʃʃaddʒo] *sm* passing *q*, passage; (*traversata*) crossing *q*, passage; (*luogo, prezzo della traversata, brano di libro etc*) passage; (*su veicolo altrui*) lift; (SPORT) pass; **di** ~ (*persona*) passing through; ~ **pedonale/a livello** pedestrian/level crossing.

pas'sante *sm/f* passer-by // *sm* loop.

passa'porto *sm* passport.

pas'sare *vi* (2) (*andare*) to go; (*veicolo, pedone*) to pass (by), go by; (*fare una breve sosta: postino etc*) to come, call; (: *amico: per fare una visita*) to call *o* drop in; (*sole, aria, luce*) to get through; (*trascorrere: giorni, tempo*) to pass, go by; (*fig: proposta di legge*) to be passed; (: *dolore*) to pass, go away; (: *essere trasferito*) ~ **di ... in** to pass from ... to; (CARTE) to pass // *vt* (*attraversare*) to cross; (*trasmettere: messaggio*) ~ **qc a qd** to pass sth on to sb; (*dare*) ~ **qc a qd** to pass sth to sb, give sb sth; (*trascorrere: tempo*) to spend; (*superare: esame*) to pass; (*triturare: verdura*) to strain; (*approvare*) to pass, approve; (*oltrepassare, sorpassare: anche fig*) to go beyond, pass; (*fig: subire*) to go through; ~ **per** (*anche fig*) to go through; ~ **per stupido/un genio** to be taken for a fool/a genius; ~ **sopra** (*anche fig*) to pass over; ~ **attraverso** (*anche fig*) to go through; ~ **alla storia** to pass into history; ~ **a un esame** to go up (to the next class) after an exam; ~ **inosservato** to go unnoticed; ~ **di moda** to go out of fashion; **le passo il Signor X** (*al telefono*) here is Mr X; I'm putting you through to Mr X; **lasciar** ~ **qd/qc** to let sb/sth through; **passarsela: come te la passi?** how are you getting on *o* along?

pas'sata *sf*: **dare una** ~ **di vernice a qc** to give sth a coat of paint; **dare una** ~ **al giornale** to have a look at the paper, skim through the paper.

passa'tempo *sm* pastime, hobby.

pas'sato, a *ag* past; (*sfiorito*) faded // *sm* past; (LING) past (tense); ~ **prossimo** (LING) present perfect; ~ **remoto** (LING)

past historic; ~ **di verdura** (CUC) vegetable purée.

passaver'dura *sm inv* vegetable mill.

passeg'gero, a [passed'dʒero] *ag* passing // *sm/f* passenger.

passeggi'are [passed'dʒare] *vi* to go for a walk; (*in veicolo*) to go for a drive; **passeggi'ata** *sf* walk; drive; (*luogo*) promenade; **fare una passeggiata** to go for a walk (*o* drive); **passeg'gino** *sm* pushchair; **pas'seggio** *sm* walk, stroll; (*luogo*) promenade.

passe'rella *sf* footbridge; (*di nave, aereo*) gangway; (*pedana*) catwalk.

'passero *sm* sparrow.

pas'sibile *ag*: ~ **di** liable to.

passi'one *sf* passion.

pas'sivo, a *ag* passive // *sm* (LING) passive; (ECON) debit; (: *complesso dei debiti*) liabilities *pl*.

'passo *sm* step; (*andatura*) pace; (*rumore*) (foot)step; (*orma*) footprint; (*passaggio, fig: brano*) passage; (*valico*) pass; **a** ~ **d'uomo** at walking pace; ~ **(a)** ~ step by step; **fare due** *o* **quattro** ~**i** to go for a walk *o* a stroll; **'**~ **carraio'** 'vehicle entrance — keep clear'.

'pasta *sf* (CUC) dough; (: *impasto per dolce*) pastry; (: *anche*: ~ **alimentare**) pasta; (*massa molle di materia*) paste; (*fig: indole*) nature; ~**e** *sfpl* (*pasticcini*) pastries; ~ **di legno** wood pulp.

pastasci'utta [pastaʃ'ʃutta] *sf* pasta.

pas'tella *sf* batter.

pas'tello *sm* pastel.

pas'tetta *sf* (CUC) = **pastella.**

pas'ticca, che *sf* = **pastiglia.**

pasticce'ria [pastittʃe'ria] *sf* (*pasticcini*) pastries *pl*, cakes *pl*; (*negozio*) cake shop; (*arte*) confectionery.

pasticci'are [pastit'tʃare] *vt* to mess up, make a mess of // *vi* to make a mess.

pasticci'ere, a [pastit'tʃere] *sm/f* pastrycook; confectioner.

pas'ticcio [pas'tittʃo] *sm* (CUC) pie; (*lavoro disordinato, imbroglio*) mess; **trovarsi nei** ~**i** to get into trouble.

pasti'ficio [pasti'fitʃo] *sm* pasta factory.

pas'tiglia [pas'tiʎʎa] *sf* pastille, lozenge.

pas'tina *sf* small pasta shapes used in soup.

pasti'naca, che *sf* parsnip.

'pasto *sm* meal.

pasto'rale *ag* pastoral.

pas'tore *sm* shepherd; (REL) pastor, minister; (*anche*: **cane** ~) shepherd dog.

pastoriz'zare [pastorid'dzare] *vt* to pasteurize.

pas'toso, a *ag* doughy; pasty; (*fig: voce, colore*) mellow, soft.

pas'trano *sm* greatcoat.

pas'tura *sf* pasture.

pa'tata *sf* potato; ~**e fritte** chips, French fried potatoes; **pata'tine** *sfpl* (potato) crisps.

pata'trac *sm* (*crollo: anche fig*) crash.

pa'tella *sf* (ZOOL) limpet.

pa'tema, i *sm* anxiety, worry.

pa'tente sf licence; (anche: ~ **di guida**) driving licence.

paternità sf paternity, fatherhood.

pa'terno, a ag (affetto, consigli) fatherly; (casa, autorità) paternal.

pa'tetico, a, ci, che ag pathetic; (commovente) moving, touching.

'pathos ['patos] sm pathos.

pa'tibolo sm gallows sg, scaffold.

'patina sf (su rame etc) patina; (sulla lingua) fur, coating.

pa'tire vt, vi to suffer.

pa'tito, a sm/f enthusiast, fan, lover.

patolo'gia [patolo'dʒia] sf pathology; **pato'logico, a, ci, che** ag pathological.

'patria sf homeland.

patri'arca, chi sm patriarch.

pa'trigno [pa'trippo] sm stepfather.

patri'monio sm estate, property; (fig) heritage.

patri'ota, i, e sm/f patriot; **patri'ottico, a, ci, che** ag patriotic; **patriot'tismo** sm patriotism.

patroci'nare [patrotʃi'nare] vt (DIR: difendere) to defend; (sostenere) to sponsor, support; **patro'cinio** sm defence; support, sponsorship.

patro'nato sm patronage; (istituzione benefica) charitable institution o society.

pa'trono sm (REL) patron saint; (socio di patronato) patron; (DIR) counsel.

'patta sf flap; (dei pantaloni) fly.

patteggi'are [patted'dʒare] vt, vi to negotiate.

patti'naggio [patti'naddʒo] sm skating.

patti'nare vi to skate; **pattina'tore, 'trice** sm/f skater; **'pattino** sm skate; (di slitta) runner; (AER) skid; (TECN) sliding block; **pattini (da ghiaccio)** (ice) skates; **pattini a rotelle** roller skates; [pat'tino] (barca) kind of pedalo with oars.

'patto sm (accordo) pact, agreement; (condizione) term, condition; **a ~ che** on condition that.

pat'tuglia [pat'tuʎʎa] sf (MIL) patrol.

pattu'ire vt to reach an agreement on.

pattumi'era sf (dust)bin.

pa'ura sf fear; **aver ~ di/di fare/che** to be frightened o afraid of/of doing/that; **far ~ a** to frighten; **per ~ di/che** for fear of/that; **pau'roso, a** ag (che fa paura) frightening; (che ha paura) fearful, timorous.

'pausa sf (sosta) break; (nel parlare, MUS) pause.

pavi'mento sm floor.

pa'vone sm peacock; **pavoneggi'arsi** vr to strut about, show off.

pazien'tare [pattsjen'tare] vi to be patient.

pazi'ente [pat'tsjɛnte] ag, sm/f patient; **pazi'enza** sf patience.

paz'zesco, a, schi, sche [pat'tsesko] ag mad, crazy.

paz'zia [pat'tsia] sf (MED) madness, insanity; (azione) folly; (di azione, decisione) madness, folly.

'pazzo, a ['pattso] ag (MED) mad, insane; (strano) wild, mad // sm/f madman/woman; ~ **di** (gioia etc) mad o crazy with; ~ **per qc/qd** mad o crazy about sth/sb.

'pecca, che sf defect, flaw, fault.

peccami'noso, a ag sinful.

pec'care vi to sin; (fig) to err.

pec'cato sm sin; **è un ~ che** it's a pity that; **che ~!** what a shame o pity!

pecca'tore, 'trice sm/f sinner.

'pece ['petʃe] sf pitch.

'pecora sf sheep; **peco'raio** sm shepherd; **peco'rino** sm sheep's milk cheese.

peculi'are ag: ~ **di** peculiar to.

pecuni'ario, a ag financial, money cpd.

pe'daggio [pe'daddʒo] sm toll.

pedago'gia [pedago'dʒia] sf pedagogy, educational methods pl.

peda'lare vi to pedal; (andare in bicicletta) to cycle.

pe'dale sm pedal.

pe'dana sf (SPORT: nel salto) springboard; (: nella scherma) piste; (tappetino) rug.

pe'dante ag pedantic // sm/f pedant.

pe'data sf (impronta) footprint; (colpo) kick.

pede'rasta, i sm pederast; homosexual.

pe'destre ag prosaic, pedestrian.

pedi'atra, i, e sm/f paediatrician; **pedia'tria** sf paediatrics sg.

pedi'cure sm/f inv chiropodist.

pe'dina sf (della dama) draughtsman; (fig) pawn.

pedi'nare vt to shadow, tail.

pedo'nale ag pedestrian.

pe'done, a sm/f pedestrian // sm (SCACCHI) pawn.

'peggio ['peddʒo] av, ag inv worse // sm o f: **il o la ~** the worst; **alla ~** at worst, if the worst comes to the worst; **peggiora-'mento** sm worsening; **peggio'rare** vt to make worse, worsen // vi to grow worse, worsen; **peggiora'tivo, a** ag pejorative; **peggi'ore** ag (comparativo) worse; (superlativo) worst // sm/f: **il(la) peggiore** the worst (person).

'pegno ['peppo] sm (DIR) security, pledge; (nei giochi di società) forfeit; (fig) pledge, token; **dare in ~ qc** to pawn sth.

pe'lame sm (di animale) coat, fur.

pe'lare vt (spennare) to pluck; (spellare) to skin; (sbucciare) to peel; (fig) to make pay through the nose; ~**rsi** vr to go bald.

pel'lame sm skins pl, hides pl.

'pelle sf skin; (di animale) skin, hide; (cuoio) leather; **avere la ~ d'oca** to have goose pimples o goose flesh.

pellegri'naggio [pellegri'naddʒo] sm pilgrimage.

pelle'grino, a sm/f pilgrim.

pelle'rossa, pelli'rossa, pl pelli'rosse sm/f Red Indian.

pellette'ria sf leather goods pl; leather goods shop.

pelli'cano sm pelican.

pellicce'ria [pellittʃe'ria] sf (negozio)

furrier's (shop); (*quantità di pellicce*) furs *pl.*

pel'liccia, ce [pel'littʃa] *sf* (*mantello di animale*) coat, fur; (*indumento*) fur coat.

pel'licola *sf* (*membrana sottile*) film, layer; (*FOT, CINEMA*) film.

'pelo *sm* hair; (*pelame*) coat, hair; (*pelliccia*) fur; (*di tappeto*) pile; (*di liquido*) surface; **per un ~: per un ~ non ho perduto il treno** I very nearly missed the train; **c'è mancato un ~ che affogasse** he escaped drowning by the skin of his teeth; **pe'loso, a** *ag* hairy.

'peltro *sm* pewter.

pe'luria *sf* down.

'pena *sf* (*DIR*) sentence; (*punizione*) punishment; (*sofferenza*) sadness *q*, sorrow; (*fatica*) trouble *q*, effort; (*difficoltà*) difficulty; **far ~** to be pitiful; **mi fai ~** I feel sorry for you; **prendersi** *o* **darsi la ~ di fare** to go to the trouble of doing; **~ di morte** death sentence; **~ pecuniaria** fine; **pe'nale** *ag* penal; **penalità** *sf inv* penalty; **penaliz'zare** *vt* (*SPORT*) to penalize.

pe'nare *vi* (*patire*) to suffer; (*faticare*) to struggle.

pen'dente *ag* hanging; leaning // *sm* (*ciondolo*) pendant; (*orecchino*) drop earring; **pen'denza** *sf* slope, slant; (*grado d'inclinazione*) gradient; (*ECON*) outstanding account.

'pendere *vi* (*essere appeso*): **~ da** to hang from; (*essere inclinato*) to lean; (*fig: incombere*): **~ su** to hang over.

pen'dio, 'dii *sm* slope, slant; (*luogo in pendenza*) slope.

'pendola *sf* pendulum clock.

pendo'lare *ag* pendulum *cpd*, pendular // *sm/f* commuter.

'pendolo *sm* (*peso*) pendulum; (*anche: orologio a ~*) pendulum clock.

'pene *sm* penis.

pene'trante *ag* piercing, penetrating.

pene'trare *vi* to come *o* get in // *vt* to penetrate; **~ in** to enter; (*sog: proiettile*) to penetrate; (: *acqua, aria*) to go *o* come into.

penicil'lina [penitʃil'lina] *sf* penicillin.

pe'nisola *sf* peninsula.

peni'tente *ag, sm/f* penitent; **peni'tenza** *sf* penitence; (*punizione*) penance.

penitenzi'ario [peniten'tsjarjo] *sm* prison.

'penna *sf* (*di uccello*) feather; (*per scrivere*) pen; **~ a feltro/ stilografica/a sfera** felt-tip/ fountain/ballpoint pen.

pennel'lare *vi* to paint.

pen'nello *sm* brush; (*per dipingere*) (paint)brush; **a ~** (*perfettamente*) to perfection, perfectly; **~ per la barba** shaving brush.

pen'nino *sm* nib.

pen'none *sm* (*NAUT*) yard; (*stendardo*) banner, standard.

pe'nombra *sf* half-light, dim light.

pe'noso, a *ag* painful, distressing; (*faticoso*) tiring, laborious.

pen'sare *vi* to think // *vt* to think; (*inventare, escogitare*) to think out; **~ a** to think of; (*amico, vacanze*) to think of *o* about; (*problema*) to think about; **~ di fare qc** to think of doing sth.

pensi'ero *sm* thought; (*modo di pensare, dottrina*) thinking *q*; (*preoccupazione*) worry, care, trouble; **stare in ~ per qd** to be worried about sb; **pensie'roso, a** *ag* thoughtful.

'pensile *ag* hanging.

pensio'nante *sm/f* (*presso una famiglia*) lodger; (*di albergo*) guest.

pensio'nato, a *sm/f* pensioner.

pensi'one *sf* (*al prestatore di lavoro*) pension; (*vitto e alloggio*) board and lodging; (*albergo*) boarding house; **andare in ~** to retire.

pen'soso, a *ag* thoughtful, pensive, lost in thought.

pen'tagono *sm* pentagon.

Pente'coste *sf* Pentecost, Whit Sunday.

penti'mento *sm* repentance, contrition.

pen'tirsi *vr*: **~ di** to repent of; (*rammaricarsi*) to regret, be sorry for.

'pentola *sf* pot; **~ a pressione** pressure cooker.

pe'nultimo, a *ag* last but one, penultimate.

pe'nuria *sf* shortage.

penzo'lare [pendzo'lare] *vi* to dangle, hang loosely; **penzo'loni** *av* dangling, hanging down; **stare penzoloni** to dangle, hang down.

'pepe *sm* pepper; **~ macinato/in grani** ground/whole pepper.

pepe'rone *sm* pepper, capsicum; (*piccante*) chili.

pe'pita *sf* nugget.

per *prep* for; (*moto attraverso luogo*) through; (*mezzo, modo*) by; (*causa*) because of, owing to // *cong*: **~ fare** (so as) to do, in order to; **~ aver fatto** for having done; **partire ~ l'Inghilterra** to leave for England; **sedere ~ terra** to sit on the ground; **~ lettera/ferrovia** by letter/rail; **assentarsi ~ malattia** to be off because of *o* through *o* owing to illness; **uno ~ uno** one by one; **~ persona** per person; **moltiplicare/dividere 9 ~ 3** to multiply/divide 9 by 3; **~ cento** per cent; **~ poco che sia** however little it may be, little though it may be.

'pera *sf* pear.

pe'raltro *av* moreover, what's more.

per'bene *ag inv* respectable, decent // *av* (*con cura*) properly, well.

percentu'ale [pertʃentu'ale] *sf* percentage.

perce'pire [pertʃe'pire] *vt* (*sentire*) to perceive; (*ricevere*) to receive; **percet'tibile** *ag* perceptible; **percezi'one** *sf* perception.

perché [per'ke] *av* why // *cong* (*causale*) because; (*finale*) in order that, so that; (*consecutivo*): **è troppo forte ~ si possa batterlo** he's too strong to be beaten.

perciò [per'tʃɔ] *cong* so, for this (*o* that) reason.

per'correre *vt* (*luogo*) to go all over; (: *paese*) to travel up and down, go all over; (*distanza*) to cover.

per'corso, a *pp di* **percorrere** // *sm* (*tragitto*) journey; (*tratto*) route.

per'cosso, a *pp di* **percuotere** // *sf* blow.

percu'otere *vt* to hit, strike.

percussi'one *sf* percussion; **strumenti a ~ (MUS)** percussion instruments.

'perdere *vt* to lose; (*lasciarsi sfuggire*) to miss; (*sprecare: tempo, denaro*) to waste; (*mandare in rovina: persona*) to ruin // *vi* to lose; (*serbatoio etc*) to leak; **~rsi** *vr* (*smarrirsi*) to get lost; (*svanire*) to disappear, vanish; **saper ~** to be a good loser; **lascia ~!** forget it!, never mind!

perdigi'orno [perdi'dʒorno] *sm/f inv* idler, waster.

'perdita *sf* loss; (*spreco*) waste; (*fuoriuscita*) leak; **in ~** (*COMM*) at a loss; **a ~ d'occhio** as far as the eye can see.

perdi'tempo *sm* waste of time // *sm/f inv* waster, idler.

perdo'nare *vt* to pardon, forgive; (*scusare*) to excuse, pardon.

per'dono *sm* forgiveness; (*DIR*) pardon.

perdu'rare *vi* to go on, last; (*perseverare*) to persist.

perduta'mente *av* desperately, passionately.

per'duto, a *pp di* **perdere**.

peregri'nare *vi* to wander, roam.

pe'renne *ag* eternal, perpetual, perennial; (*BOT*) perennial.

peren'torio, a *ag* peremptory; (*decisivo*) final.

per'fetto, a *ag* perfect // *sm* (*LING*) perfect (tense).

perfezio'nare [perfettsjo'nare] *vt* to improve, perfect; **~rsi** *vr* to improve; (*INS*) to specialize.

perfezi'one [perfet'tsjone] *sf* perfection.

'perfido, a *ag* perfidious, treacherous.

per'fino *av* even.

perfo'rare *vt* to perforate; to punch a hole (*o* holes) in; (*banda, schede*) to punch; (*trivellare*) to drill; **perfora'tore, 'trice** *sm/f* punch-card operator // *sm* (*utensile*) punch; **perforatore di schede** card punch // *sf* (*TECN*) boring *o* drilling machine; (*INFORM*) card punch; **perforazi'one** *sf* perforation; punching; drilling; (*INFORM*) punch; (*MED*) perforation.

perga'mena *sf* parchment.

'pergamo *sm* pulpit.

perico'lante *ag* precarious.

pe'ricolo *sm* danger; **mettere in ~** to endanger, put in danger; **perico'loso, a** *ag* dangerous.

perife'ria *sf* periphery; (*di città*) outskirts *pl.*

pe'rifrasi *sf* circumlocution.

pe'rimetro *sm* perimeter.

peri'odico, a, ci, che *ag* periodic(al);

(*MAT*) recurring // *sm* periodical.

pe'riodo *sm* period.

peripe'zie [peripet'tsie] *sfpl* ups and downs, vicissitudes.

pe'rire *vi* (2) to perish, die.

peris'copio *sm* periscope.

pe'rito, a *ag* expert, skilled // *sm/f* expert; (*agronomo, navale*) surveyor; **un ~ chimico** a qualified chemist.

pe'rizia [pe'rittsja] *sf* (*abilità*) ability; (*consulenza*) expert opinion; expert's report; (*valutazione*) survey, appraisal.

'perla *sf* pearl; **per'lina** *sf* bead.

perlus'trare *vt* to patrol.

perma'loso, a *ag* touchy.

perma'nente *ag* permanent // *sf* permanent wave, perm; **perma'nenza** *sf* permanence; (*soggiorno*) stay.

perma'nere *vi* (2) to remain.

perme'are *vt* to permeate.

per'messo, a *pp di* **permettere** // *sm* (*autorizzazione*) permission, leave; (*dato a militare, impiegato*) leave; (*licenza*) licence, permit; (*MIL: foglio*) pass; **~?, è ~?** (*posso entrare?*) may I come in?; (*posso passare?*) excuse me; **~ di lavoro/pesca** work/fishing permit.

per'mettere *vt* to allow, permit; **~ a qd di fare/qc** to allow sb to do/sth.

permutazi'one [permutat'tsjone] *sf* (*baratto*) exchange, barter; (*MAT*) permutation.

per'nice [per'nitʃe] *sf* partridge.

pernici'oso, a [perni'tʃoso] *ag* pernicious.

'perno *sm* pivot.

pernot'tare *vi* to spend the night, stay overnight.

'pero *sm* pear tree.

però *cong* (*ma*) but; (*tuttavia*) however, nevertheless.

pero'rare *vt* to defend, support.

perpendico'lare *ag, sf* perpendicular.

perpen'dicolo *sm* plumbline; **a ~** perpendicularly.

perpe'trare *vt* to perpetrate.

perpetu'are *vt* to perpetuate.

per'petuo, a *ag* perpetual.

per'plesso, a *ag* perplexed; uncertain, undecided.

perqui'sire *vt* to search; **perquisizi'one** *sf* (police) search.

persecu'tore *sm* persecutor.

persecuzi'one [persekut'tsjone] *sf* persecution.

persegu'ire *vt* to pursue.

persegui'tare *vt* to persecute.

perseve'rante *ag* persevering; **perseve-'ranza** *sf* perseverance.

perseve'rare *vi* to persevere.

'Persia *sf*: **la ~** Persia.

persi'ano, a *ag, sm/f* Persian // *sf* shutter; **~a avvolgibile** Venetian blind.

'persico, a, ci, che *ag* (*GEO*) Persian; **il golfo P~** the Persian Gulf.

per'sino *av* = **perfino**.

persis'tente *ag* persistent.

per'sistere *vi* to persist; **~ a fare** to

persist in doing; **persis'tito, a** pp di **persistere.**

'perso, a pp di **perdere.**

per'sona sf person; (qualcuno): **una ~** someone, somebody, espressione interrogativa + anyone o anybody; **~e** sfpl people; **non c'è ~ che ...** there's nobody who ..., there isn't anybody who ... .

perso'naggio [perso'naddʒo] sm (persona ragguardevole) personality, figure; (tipo) character, individual; (LETTERATURA) character.

perso'nale ag personal // sm staff; personnel.

personalità sf inv personality.

personifi'care vt to personify; to embody.

perspi'cace [perspi'katʃe] ag shrewd, discerning.

persu'adere vt to persuade; **~ qd di qc/a fare** to persuade sb of sth/to do; **persuasi'one** sf persuasion; **persua'sivo, a** ag persuasive; **persu'aso, a** pp di **persuadere.**

per'tanto cong (quindi) so, therefore.

'pertica, che sf pole.

perti'nace [perti'natʃe] ag determined; persistent.

perti'nente ag: **~ (a)** relevant (to), pertinent (to).

per'tosse sf whooping cough.

per'tugio [per'tudʒo] sm hole, opening.

pertur'bare vt to disrupt; (persona) to disturb, perturb; **perturbazi'one** sf disruption; perturbation; **perturbazione atmosferica** atmospheric disturbance.

per'vadere vt to pervade; **per'vaso, a** pp di **pervadere.**

perve'nire vi (2): **~ a** to reach, arrive at, come to; (venire in possesso): **gli pervenne una fortuna** he inherited a fortune; **far ~ qc a** to have sth sent to; **perve'nuto, a** pp di **pervenire.**

perversi'one sf perversion.

per'verso, a ag depraved; perverse.

perver'tire vt to pervert.

p. es. (abbr di **per esempio**) e.g.

'pesa sf weighing q; weighbridge.

pe'sante ag heavy; (fig: noioso) dull, boring.

pe'sare vt to weigh // vi (avere un peso) to weigh; (essere pesante) to be heavy; (fig) to carry weight; **~ su** (fig) to lie heavy on; to influence; to hang over; **mi pesa sgridarlo** I find it hard to scold him.

'pesca sf (pl: **pesche**: frutto) peach; (il pescare) fishing; **andare a ~** to go fishing; **~ con la lenza** angling.

pes'care vt to fish for; (annegato) to fish out; (fig: trovare) to get hold of, find.

pesca'tore sm fisherman; angler.

'pesce [peʃe] sm fish (gen inv); **P~i** (dello zodiaco) Pisces; **~ d'aprile!** April Fool!; **~ spada** swordfish; **pesce'cane** sm shark.

pesche'reccio [peske'rettʃo] sm fishing boat.

pesche'ria [peske'ria] sf fishmonger's (shop).

peschi'era [pes'kjɛra] sf fishpond.

pesci'vendolo, a [peʃʃi'vɛndolo] sm/f fishmonger.

'pesco, schi sm peach tree.

pes'coso, a ag abounding in fish.

'peso sm weight; (SPORT) shot; **rubare sul ~** to give short weight; **~ lordo/netto** gross/net weight; **~ piuma/mosca/ gallo/medio/massimo** (PUGILATO) feather/fly/bantam/middle/heavyweight.

pessi'mismo sm pessimism; **pessi'mista, i, e** ag pessimistic // sm/f pessimist.

'pessimo, a ag very bad, awful.

pes'tare vt to tread on, trample on; (sale, pepe) to grind; (uva, aglio) to crush; **~ il muso a qd** to smash sb's face in.

'peste sf plague; (persona) nuisance, pest.

pes'tello sm pestle.

pesti'lenza [pesti'lɛntsa] sf pestilence; (fetore) stench.

'pesto, a ag (alimentari) ground; crushed // sm (CUC) sauce made with basil, garlic, cheese and oil; **c'è buio ~** it's pitch-dark; **occhio ~** black eye.

'petalo sm (BOT) petal.

pe'tardo sm banger, firecracker.

petizi'one [petit'tsjone] sf petition.

'peto sm (fam!) fart (!).

petrol'chimica [petrol'kimika] sf petrochemical industry.

petroli'era sf (nave) oil tanker.

petro'lifero, a ag oil-bearing; oil cpd.

pe'trolio sm oil, petroleum; (per lampada, fornello) paraffin.

pettego'lare vi to gossip.

pettego'lezzo [pettego'leddzo] sm gossip q; **fare ~i** to gossip.

pet'tegolo, a ag gossipy // sm/f gossip.

petti'nare vt to comb (the hair of); **~rsi** vr to comb one's hair; **pettina'tura** sf combing q; (acconciatura) hairstyle.

'pettine sm comb; (ZOOL) scallop.

petti'rosso sm robin.

'petto sm chest; (seno) breast, bust; (CUC: di carne bovina) brisket; (: di pollo etc) breast; **a doppio ~** (abito) double-breasted; **petto'ruto, a** ag broad-chested; full-breasted; (fig) haughty, puffed up with pride.

petu'lante ag insolent.

'pezza ['pɛttsa] sf piece of cloth; (toppa) patch; (cencio) rag, cloth.

pez'zato, a [pet'tsato] ag piebald.

pez'zente [pet'tsɛnte] sm/f beggar.

'pezzo ['pɛttso] sm (gen) piece; (brandello, frammento) piece, bit; (di macchina, arnese etc) part; (STAMPA) article; (di tempo): **aspettare un ~** to wait quite a while o some time; **in o a ~i** in o into pieces; **andare in ~i** to break into pieces; **un bel ~ d'uomo** a fine figure of a man; **abito a due ~i** two-piece suit; **~ di cronaca** (STAMPA) report; **~ grosso** (fig) bigwig; **~ di ricambio** spare part.

pia'cente [pja'tʃɛnte] *ag* attractive, pleasant.

pia'cere [pja'tʃere] *vi* (2) to please; **una ragazza che piace** a likeable girl; **un attractive girl; ~ a: mi piace** I like it; **quei ragazzi non mi piacciono** I don't like those boys; **gli piacerebbe andare al cinema** he would like to go to the cinema // *sm* pleasure; (*favore*) favour; '~l' (*nelle presentazioni*) 'pleased to meet you!'; **con ~** certainly, with pleasure; **per ~!** please; **fare un ~ a qd** to do sb a favour; **pia'cevole** *ag* pleasant, agreeable; **piaci'uto, a** *pp di* piacere.

pi'aga, ghe *sf* (*lesione*) sore; (*ferita: anche fig*) wound; (*fig: flagello*) scourge, curse; (: *persona*) pest, nuisance.

piagnis'teo [pjaɲɲis'tɛo] *sm* whining, whimpering.

piagnuco'lare [pjaɲɲuko'lare] *vi* to whimper.

pi'alla *sf* (*arnese*) plane; **pial'lare** *vt* to plane.

pi'ana *sf* stretch of level ground; (*più esteso*) plain.

pianeggi'ante [pjaned'dʒante] *ag* flat, level.

piane'rottolo *sm* landing.

pia'neta *sm* (ASTR) planet.

pi'angere ['pjandʒere] *vi* to cry, weep; (*occhi*) to water // *vt* to cry, weep; (*lamentare*) to bewail, lament; (: *morto*) to mourn (for).

pianifi'care *vt* to plan; **pianificazi'one** *sf* planning.

pia'nista, i, e *sm/f* pianist.

pi'ano, a *ag* (*piatto*) flat, level; (MAT) plane; (*facile*) straightforward, simple; (*chiaro*) clear, plain // *av* (*adagio*) slowly; (*a bassa voce*) softly; (*con cautela*) slowly, carefully // *sm* (MAT) plane; (GEO) plain; (*livello*) level, plane; (*di edificio*) floor; (*programma*) plan; (MUS) piano; **pian ~** very slowly; (*poco a poco*) little by little; **in primo/secondo ~** in the foreground/background; **di primo ~** (*fig*) prominent, high-ranking; **~ stradale** roadway.

piano'forte *sm* piano, pianoforte.

pi'anta *sf* (BOT) plant; (ANAT: *anche*: ~ **del piede**) sole (of the foot); (*grafico*) plan; (*topografica*) map; **in ~ stabile** on the permanent staff; **piantagi'one** *sf* plantation; **pian'tare** *vt* to plant; (*conficcare*) to drive *o* hammer in; (*tenda*) to put up, pitch; (*fig: lasciare*) to leave, desert; ~**rsi davanti a qd** to plant o.s. in front of sb; **piantala!** (*fam*) cut it out!

pianter'reno *sm* ground floor.

pi'anto, a *pp di* piangere // *sm* tears *pl*, crying.

pian'tone *sm* (*vigilante*) sentry, guard; (*soldato*) orderly; (AUT) steering column.

pia'nura *sf* plain.

pi'astra *sf* plate; (*di pietra*) slab.

pias'trella *sf* tile.

pias'trina *sf* (MIL) identity disc.

piatta'forma *sf* (*anche fig*) platform.

pi'atto, a *ag* flat; (*fig: scialbo*) dull // *sm* (*recipiente, vivanda*) dish; (*portata*) course; (*parte piana*) flat (part); ~**i** *smpl* (MUS) cymbals; ~ **fondo** soup dish; ~ **forte** main course; ~ **del giradischi** turntable.

pi'azza ['pjattsa] *sf* square; (COMM) market; **far ~ pulita** to make a clean sweep; **piazza'forte**, *pl* **piazze'forti** *sf* (MIL) stronghold; **piaz'zale** *sm* (large) square.

piaz'zare [pjat'tsare] *vt* to place; (COMM) to market, sell; ~**rsi** *vr* (SPORT) to be placed.

piaz'zista, i [pjat'tsista] *sm* (COMM) commercial traveller.

piaz'zola [pjat'tsɔla] *sf* (AUT) lay-by.

'picca, che *sf* pike; ~**che** *sfpl* (CARTE) spades.

pic'cante *ag* hot, pungent; (*fig*) racy; biting.

pic'carsi *vr*: ~ **di fare** to pride o.s. on one's ability to do; ~ **per qc** to take offence at sth.

pic'chetto [pik'ketto] *sm* (MIL, *di scioperanti*) picket.

picchi'are [pik'kjare] *vt* (*percuotere*) to thrash, beat; (*colpire*) to strike, hit // *vi* (*bussare*) to knock; (: *con forza*) to bang; (*colpire*) to hit, strike; **picchi'ata** *sf* knock; bang; blow; (*percosse*) beating, thrashing; (AER) dive.

picchiet'tare [pikkjet'tare] *vt* (*punteggiare*) to spot, dot; (*colpire*) to tap.

'picchio ['pikkjo] *sm* woodpecker.

pic'cino, a [pit'tʃino] *ag* tiny, very small.

piccio'naia [pittʃo'naja] *sf* pigeon-loft; (TEATRO): **la ~** the Gods *sg*.

picci'one [pit'tʃone] *sm* pigeon.

'picco, chi *sm* peak; **a ~** vertically.

'piccolo, a *ag* small; (*oggetto, mano, di età: bambino*) small, little; (*dav sostantivo*); (*di breve durata: viaggio*) short; (*fig*) mean, petty // *sm/f* child, little one; ~**i** *smpl* (*di animale*) young *pl*; **in ~** in miniature.

pic'cone *sm* pick-(axe).

pic'cozza [pik'kottsa] *sf* ice-axe.

pic'nic *sm inv* picnic.

pi'docchio [pi'dɔkkjo] *sm* louse.

pi'ede *sm* foot; (*di mobile*) leg; **in ~i** standing; **a ~i** on foot; **a ~i nudi** barefoot; **su due ~i** (*fig*) at once; **prendere ~** (*fig*) to gain ground, catch on; **sul ~ di guerra** (MIL) ready for action; ~ **di porco** crowbar.

piedis'tallo, piedes'tallo *sm* pedestal.

pi'ega, ghe *sf* (*piegatura*, GEO) fold; (*di gonna*) pleat; (*di pantaloni*) crease; (*grinza*) wrinkle, crease; (*fig: andamento*) turn.

pie'gare *vt* to fold; (*braccia, gambe, testa*) to bend // *vi* to bend; ~**rsi** *vr* to bend; (*fig*): ~**rsi (a)** to yield (to), submit (to); **piega'tura** *sf* folding *q*; bending *q*; fold; bend; **pieghet'tare** *vt* to pleat; **pie'ghevole** *ag* pliable, flexible; (*porta*) folding; (*fig*) yielding, docile.

Pie'monte *sm*: **il ~** Piedmont.

pi'ena *sf vedi* pieno.

pi'eno, a *ag* full; (*muro, mattone*) solid //

sm (colmo) height, peak; *(carico)* full load // *sf (di fiume)* flood, spate; *(gran folla)* crowd, throng; ~ **di** full of; **in** ~ **a notte** in the middle of the night; **fare il** ~ **(di benzina)** to fill up (with petrol).

pietà *sf* pity; *(REL)* piety; **senza** ~ pitiless, merciless; **avere** ~ **di** *(compassione)* to pity, feel sorry for; *(misericordia)* to have pity *o* mercy on.

pie'tanza [pje'tantsa] *sf* dish; (main) course.

pie'toso, a *ag (compassionevole)* pitying, compassionate; *(che desta pietà)* pitiful.

pi'etra *sf* stone; ~ **preziosa** precious stone, gem; **pie'traia** *sf (terreno)* stony ground; **pie'trame** *sm* stones *pl*; **pietrifi-'care** *vt* to petrify; *(fig)* to transfix, paralyze.

'piffero *sm (MUS)* pipe.

pigi'ama [pi'dʒama] *sm* pyjamas *pl*.

'pigia 'pigia ['pidʒa'pidʒa] *sm* crowd, press.

pigi'are [pi'dʒare] *vt* to press; **pigia'trice** *sf (macchina)* wine press.

pigi'one [pi'dʒone] *sf* rent; **dare/prendere a** ~ to let *o* rent out/rent.

pigli'are [piʎ'ʎare] *vt* to take, grab; *(afferrare)* to catch.

'piglio ['piʎʎo] *sm* look, expression.

pig'mento *sm* pigment.

pig'meo, a *sm/f* pygmy.

'pigna ['piɲɲa] *sf* pine cone.

pi'gnolo, a [piɲ'ɲɔlo] *ag* pernickety.

pigo'lare *vi* to cheep, chirp.

pi'grizia [pi'grittsja] *sf* laziness.

'pigro, a *ag* lazy; *(fig: ottuso)* slow, dull.

'pila *sf (catasta, di ponte)* pile; *(ELETTR)* battery; *(vasca)* basin.

pi'lastro *sm* pillar.

'pillola *sf* pill; **prendere la** ~ to be on the pill.

pi'lone *sm (di ponte)* pier; *(di linea elettrica)* pylon.

pi'lota, i, e *sm/f* pilot; *(AUT)* driver // *ag inv* pilot *cpd*; ~ **automatico** automatic pilot; **pilo'tare** *vt* to pilot, to drive.

piluc'care *vt (acini d'uva)* to pick off, pluck (one at a time); *(biscotto)* to nibble at.

pi'mento *sm* pimento, allspice.

pinaco'teca, che *sf* art gallery.

pi'neta *sf* pinewood.

ping-'pong [piŋ'pɔŋ] *sm* table tennis.

'pingue *ag* fat, corpulent; **pingu'edine** *sf* corpulence.

pingu'ino *sm (ZOOL)* penguin.

'pinna *sf* fin; *(di pinguino, spatola di gomma)* flipper.

pin'nacolo *sm* pinnacle.

'pino *sm* pine (tree); **pi'nolo** *sm* pine kernel.

'pinza ['pintsa] *sf* pliers *pl*; *(MED)* forceps *pl*; *(ZOOL)* pincer.

pin'zette [pin'tsette] *sfpl* tweezers.

'pio, a, 'pii, 'pie *ag* pious; *(opere, istituzione)* charitable, charity *cpd*.

pi'oggia, ge ['pjɔddʒa] *sf* rain.

pi'olo *sm* peg; *(di scala)* rung.

piom'bare *vi* to fall heavily; *(gettarsi con impeto)*: ~ **su** to fall upon, assail // *vt (dente)* to fill; **quel vestito piomba bene** that dress hangs well; **piomba'tura** *sf (di dente)* filling.

piom'bino *sm (sigillo)* (lead) seal; *(del filo a piombo)* plummet; *(PESCA)* sinker.

pi'ombo *sm (CHIM)* lead; *(sigillo)* (lead) seal; *(proiettile)* (lead) shot; **a** ~ *(cadere)* straight down.

pioni'ere, a *sm/f* pioneer.

pi'oppo *sm* poplar.

pi'overe (2) *vb impers* to rain // *vi (fig: scendere dall'alto)* to rain down; *(: affluire in gran numero)*: ~ **in** to pour into; **pioviggi'nare** *vb impers* to drizzle; **pio-'voso, a** *ag* rainy.

pi'ovra *sf* octopus.

'pipa *sf* pipe.

pipì *sf (fam)*: **fare** ~ to have a wee (wee).

pipis'trello *sm (ZOOL)* bat.

pi'ramide *sf* pyramid.

pi'rata, i *sm* pirate; ~ **della strada** hit-and-run driver.

Pire'nei *smpl*: **i** ~ the Pyrenees.

'pirico, a, ci, che *ag*: **polvere** ~**a** gunpowder.

pi'rite *sf* pyrite.

piro'etta *sf* pirouette.

pi'rofilo, a *ag* heat-resistant.

pi'roga, ghe *sf* dug-out canoe.

pi'romane *sm/f* pyromaniac; arsonist.

pi'roscafo *sm* steamer, steamship.

pisci'are [piʃ'ʃare] *vi (fam!)* to piss (!), pee (!).

pi'scina [piʃ'ʃina] *sf* (swimming) pool; *(stabilimento)* (swimming) baths *pl*.

pi'sello *sm* pea.

piso'lino *sm* nap.

'pista *sf (traccia)* track, trail; *(di stadio)* track; *(di pattinaggio)* rink; *(da sci)* run; *(AER)* runway; *(di circo)* ring; ~ **da ballo** dance floor.

pis'tacchio [pis'takkjo] *sm* pistachio (tree); pistachio (nut).

pis'tillo *sm (BOT)* pistil.

pis'tola *sf* pistol, gun; ~ **a spruzzo** spray gun.

pis'tone *sm* piston.

pi'tocco, chi *sm* skinflint, miser.

pi'tone *sm* python.

pit'tore, 'trice *sm/f* painter; **pitto'resco, a, schi, sche** *ag* picturesque; **pit'torico, a, ci, che** *ag* of painting, pictorial.

pit'tura *sf* painting; **pittu'rare** *vt* to paint.

più *av* more; *(in frasi comparative)* more, aggettivo corto + ...er; *(in frasi superlative)* most, aggettivo corto + ...est; *(negativo)*: **non ...** ~ no more, espressione negativa + any more; no longer; *(di temperatura)* above zero; *(MAT)* plus // *prep* plus, besides // *ag inv* more; *(parecchi)* several // *sm inv (la parte maggiore)*: **il** ~ the most; *(MAT)* plus (sign); **i** ~ the majority; ~ **che/di** more than; ~ **grande che**

bigger than; ~ **di 10 persone/te** more than 10 people/you; **il ~ intelligente/grande** the most intelligent/biggest; **di** ~ more; (*inoltre*) what's more, moreover; **3 ore/litri di** ~ **che** 3 hours/litres more than; **3 chili in** ~ 3 kilos more, 3 extra kilos; **a** ~ **non posso** as much as possible; **al** ~ **presto** as soon as possible; **al** ~ **tardi** at the latest; ~ **o meno** more or less; **né** ~ **né meno** no more, no less.

piucchepper'fetto [pjukkepper'fetto] *sm* (*LING*) pluperfect, past perfect.

pi'uma *sf* feather; ~**e** *sfpl* down *sg*; (*piumaggio*) plumage *sg*, feathers; **piu'maggio** *sm* plumage, feathers *pl*; **piu'mino** *sm* (*eider*)down; (*coperta*) eiderdown; (*per cipria*) powder puff; (*per spolverare*) feather duster.

piut'tosto *av* rather; ~ **che** (*anziché*) rather than.

pi'vello, a *sm/f* greenhorn.

'pizza *sf* pizza; **pizze'ria** *sf* place where pizzas are made, sold or eaten.

pizzi'cagnolo, a [pittsi'kaɲɲolo] *sm/f* specialist grocer.

pizzi'care [pittsi'kare] *vt* (*stringere*) to nip, pinch; (*pungere*) to sting; to bite; (*MUS*) to pluck // *vi* (*prudere*) to itch, be itchy; (*sentir pungere*) to sting, tingle; (*cibo*) to be hot *o* spicy.

pizziche'ria [pittsike'ria] *sf* delicatessen (shop).

'pizzico, chi [pittsiko] *sm*. (*pizzicotto*) pinch, nip; (*piccola quantità*) pinch, dash; (*d'insetto*) sting; bite.

pizzi'cotto [pittsi'kotto] *sm* pinch, nip.

'pizzo [pittso] *sm* (*merletto*) lace; (*barbetta*) goatee beard.

pla'care *vt* to placate, soothe; ~**rsi** *vr* to calm down.

'placca, che *sf* plate; (*con iscrizione*) plaque; (*d'eczema etc*) patch; **plac'care** *vt* to plate; **placcato in oro/argento** gold-/silver-plated.

pla'centa [pla'tʃɛnta] *sf* placenta.

'placido, a ['platʃido] *ag* placid, calm.

plagi'are [pla'dʒare] *vt* (*copiare*) to plagiarize; **'plagio** *sm* plagiarism.

pla'nare *vi* (*AER*) to glide.

'plancia, ce ['plantʃa] *sf* (*NAUT*) bridge.

'plancton *sm* plankton.

plane'tario, a *ag* planetary // *sm* (*locale*) planetarium.

'plasma *sm* plasma.

plas'mare *vt* to mould, shape.

'plastico, a, ci, che *ag* plastic // *sm* (*rappresentazione*) relief model; (*esplosivo*): **bomba al** ~ plastic bomb // *sf* (*arte*) plastic arts *pl*; (*MED*) plastic surgery; (*sostanza*) plastic.

plasti'lina *sf* " plasticine ".

'platano *sm* plane tree.

pla'tea *sf* (*TEATRO*) stalls *pl*.

'platino *sm* platinum.

pla'tonico, a, ci, che *ag* platonic.

plau'sibile *ag* plausible.

'plauso *sm* (*fig*) approval.

ple'baglia [ple'baʎʎa] *sf* (*peg*) rabble, mob.

'plebe *sf* common people; **ple'beo, a** *ag* plebeian; (*volgare*) coarse, common; **plebi'scito** *sm* plebiscite.

ple'nario, a *ag* plenary.

pleni'lunio *sm* full moon.

'plettro *sm* plectrum.

pleu'rite *sf* pleurisy.

'plico, chi *sm* bundle; (*pacco*) parcel; **in ~ a parte** (*COMM*) under separate cover.

plo'tone *sm* (*MIL*) platoon; ~ **d'esecuzione** firing squad.

'plumbeo, a *ag* leaden.

plu'rale *ag*, *sm* plural; **pluralità** *sf* plurality; (*di voti etc*) majority.

plusva'lore *sm* (*ECON*) surplus.

pluvi'ale *ag* rain *cpd*, pluvial.

pneu'matico, a, ci, che *ag* inflatable; pneumatic // *sm* (*AUT*) tyre.

po' *av*, *sm vedi* **poco**.

'poco, a, chi, che *ag* (*quantità*) little, negazione + (*very*) much; (*numero*) few, negazione + (*very*) many // *av* little, espressione negativa + much; (*con ag*) espressione negativa + very // pronome (*very*) little; ~**chi(che)** pronome *pl* few // *sm*: **il** ~ **che guadagna ...** what little he earns ...; **un po'** a little, a bit; **sono un po' stanco** I'm a bit tired; **un po' di soldi/pane** a little money/bread; **prima/dopo** shortly before/afterwards; ~ **fa** a short time ago; **a** ~ **a** ~ little by little; **fra** ~ **o un po'** in a little while.

po'dere *sm* (*AGR*) farm.

pode'roso, a *ag* powerful.

podestà *sm inv* (*nel fascismo*) podestà, mayor.

'podio *sm* dais, platform; (*MUS*) podium.

po'dismo *sm* (*SPORT*) track events *pl*.

po'ema, i *sm* poem.

poe'sia *sf* (*arte*) poetry; (*componimento*) poem.

po'eta, 'essa *sm/f* poet/poetess; **poe'tare** *vi* to write poetry; **po'etico, a, ci, che** *ag* poetic(al).

poggi'are [pod'dʒare] *vt* to lean, rest; (*posare*) to lay, place; **poggia'testa** *sm inv* (*AUT*) headrest.

'poggio ['poddʒo] *sm* hillock, knoll.

poi *av* then; (*avversativo*) but; (*alla fine*) finally, at last; **e** ~ and (then).

poiché [poi'ke] *cong* since, as.

'poker *sm* poker.

po'lacco, a, chi, che *ag* Polish // *sm/f* Pole.

po'lare *ag* polar.

'polca, che *sf* polka.

po'lemico, a, ci, che *ag* polemic(al), controversial // *sf* controversy.

po'lenta *sf* (*CUC*) sort of thick porridge made with maize flour.

'poli... *prefisso*: **poli'clinico, ci** *sm* polyclinic; **poliga'mia** *sf* polygamy; **po'ligono** *sm* polygon.

'polio(mie'lite) *sf* polio(myelitis).

'polipo *sm* polyp.

polisti'rolo *sm* polystyrene.
poli'tecnico, ci *sm* postgraduate technical college.
politiciz'zare [politit∫id'dzare] *vt* to politicize.
po'litico, a, ci, che *ag* political // *sm/f* politician // *sf* politics *sg*; (*linea di condotta*) policy.
poli'zia [polit'tsia] *sf* police; ~ **giudiziaria** ≈ Criminal Investigation Department, C.I.D.; ~ **stradale** traffic police; **polizi'esco, a schi, sche** *ag* police *cpd*; (*film, romanzo*) detective *cpd*; **poli-zi'otto** *sm* policeman; **cane poliziotto** police dog; **donna poliziotto** policewoman.
'polizza ['polittsa] *sf* (*COMM*) bill; ~ **di assicurazione** insurance policy; ~ **di carico** bill of lading.
pol'laio *sm* henhouse.
pollai'olo, a *sm/f* poulterer.
pol'lame *sm* poultry.
pol'lastro *sm* (*ZOOL*) cockerel.
'pollice ['pollit∫e] *sm* thumb.
'polline *sm* pollen.
'pollo *sm* chicken.
pol'mone *sm* lung; **polmo'nite** *sf* pneumonia.
'polo *sm* (*GEO, FISICA*) pole; (*gioco*) polo.
Po'lonia *sf*: **la** ~ Poland.
'polpa *sf* flesh, pulp; (*carne*) lean meat.
pol'paccio [pol'patt∫o] *sm* (*ANAT*) calf.
pol'petta *sf* (*CUC*) meatball; **polpet'tone** *sm* (*CUC*) meatloaf.
'polpo *sm* octopus.
pol'poso, a *ag* fleshy.
pol'sino *sm* cuff.
'polso *sm* (*ANAT*) wrist; (*pulsazione*) pulse; (*fig: forza*) drive, vigour.
pol'tiglia [pol'tiλλa] *sf* (*composto*) mash, mush; (*fango*) mire.
pol'trire *vi* to laze about.
pol'trona *sf* armchair; (*TEATRO: posto*) seat in the front stalls.
pol'trone *ag* lazy, slothful.
'polvere *sf* dust; (*anche:* ~ **da sparo**) (gun)powder; (*sostanza ridotta minutissima*) powder, dust; **latte in** ~ dried *o* powdered milk; **caffè in** ~ instant coffee; **sapone in** ~ soap powder; ~ **di carbone** coal dust; **polveri'era** *sf* powder magazine; **polveriz'zare** *vt* to pulverize; (*nebulizzare*) to atomize; (*fig*) to crush, pulverize; to smash; **polve'rone** *sm* thick cloud of dust; **polve'roso, a** *ag* dusty.
po'mata *sf* ointment, cream.
po'mello *sm* knob.
pomeridi'ano, a *ag* afternoon *cpd*; **nelle ore** ~ **e** in the afternoon.
pome'riggio [pome'riddʒo] *sm* afternoon.
'pomice ['pɔmit∫e] *sf* pumice.
'pomo *sm* (*mela*) apple; (*ornamentale*) knob; (*di sella*) pommel; ~ **d'Adamo** (*ANAT*) Adam's apple.
pomo'doro *sm* tomato.
'pompa *sf* pump; (*sfarzo*) pomp (and ceremony); ~ **e funebri** funeral parlour

sg, undertaker's *sg*; **pom'pare** *vt* to pump; (*trarre*) to pump out; (*gonfiare d'aria*) to pump up.
pom'pelmo *sm* grapefruit.
pompi'ere *sm* fireman.
pom'poso, a *ag* pompous.
ponde'rare *vt* to ponder over, consider carefully.
ponde'roso, a *ag* (*anche fig*) weighty.
po'nente *sm* west.
'ponte *sm* bridge; (*di nave*) deck; (*: anche:* ~ **di comando**) bridge; (*impalcatura*) scaffold; **fare il** ~ (*fig*) to take the extra day off (*between 2 public holidays*); **governo/soluzione** ~ interim government/solution; ~ **aereo** airlift; ~ **sospeso** suspension bridge; ~ **di volo** flight deck.
pon'tefice [pon'tɛfit∫e] *sm* (*REL*) pontiff.
pontifi'care *vi* (*anche fig*) to pontificate; **pontifi'cato** *sm* pontificate; **ponti'ficio, a, ci, cie** *ag* papal.
popo'lano, a *ag* popular, of the people.
popo'lare *ag* popular; (*quartiere, clientela*) working-class // *vt* (*rendere abitato*) to populate; (*abitare*) to inhabit; (*riempire di gente*) to fill with people; ~ **rsi** *vr* to fill with people, get crowded; **popolarità** *sf* popularity; **popolazi'one** *sf* population.
'popolo *sm* people; **popo'loso, a** *ag* densely populated.
po'pone *sm* melon.
'poppa *sf* (*di nave*) stern; (*mammella*) breast.
pop'pare *vt* to suck.
poppa'toio *sm* (feeding) bottle.
porcel'lana [port∫el'lana] *sf* porcelain, china; piece of china.
porcel'lino, a [port∫el'lino] *sm/f* piglet.
porche'ria [porke'ria] *sf* filth, muck; (*fig*) obscenity; (*: azione disonesta*) dirty trick; (*cosa mal fatta*) rubbish.
por'cile [por't∫ile] *sm* pigsty.
por'cino, a [por't∫ino] *ag* of pigs, pork *cpd* // *sm* (*fungo*) type of edible mushroom.
'porco, ci *sm* pig; (*carne*) pork.
porcos'pino *sm* porcupine.
'porgere ['pɔrdʒere] *vt* to hand, give; (*tendere*) to hold out.
pornogra'fia *sf* pornography; **porno-'grafico, a, ci, che** *ag* pornographic.
'poro *sm* pore; **po'roso, a** *ag* porous.
'porpora *sf* purple; **di** ~ purple.
'porre *vt* (*mettere*) to put; (*collocare*) to place; (*posare*) to lay (down), put (down); (*fig: supporre*): **poniamo che** ... let's suppose that ...; **porsi** *vr* (*mettersi*): **porsi a sedere/in cammino** to sit down/set off; ~ **una domanda a qd** to ask sb a question, put a question to sb; ~ **mente a qc** to turn one's mind to sth.
'porro *sm* (*BOT*) leek; (*MED*) wart.
'porta *sf* door; (*SPORT*) goal; ~ **e** *sfpl* (*di città*) gates; ~ **principale** main door; front door; **a** ~ **e chiuse** (*DIR*) in camera.
'porta... *prefisso*: **portaba'gagli** *sm inv* (*facchino*) porter; (*AUT, FERR*) luggage

rack; **portabandi'era** sm inv standard bearer; **porta'cenere** sm inv ashtray; **portachi'avi** sm inv keyring; **porta'cipria** sm inv powder compact; **porta'erei** sf inv (nave) aircraft carrier // sm inv (aereo) aircraft transporter; **portafi'nestra**, pl **portefi'nestre** sf French window; **porta'foglio** sm (busta) wallet; (borsa) briefcase; (POL, BORSA) portfolio; **portafor'tuna** sm inv lucky charm; mascot; **portagi'oie** sm inv, **portagioi'elli** sm inv jewellery box.

por'tale sm portal.

porta'lettere sm/f inv postman/woman.

porta'mento sm carriage, bearing; (fig) behaviour, conduct.

portamo'nete sm inv purse.

por'tante ag (muro etc) supporting, load-bearing.

portan'tina sf sedan chair; (per ammalati) stretcher.

por'tare vt (sostenere, sorreggere: peso, bambino, pacco) to carry; (indossare: abito, occhiali) to wear; (: capelli lunghi) to have; (avere: nome, titolo) to have, bear; (recare): ~ qc a qd to take (o bring) sth to sb; (fig: sentimenti) to bear; **~rsi** vr (trasferirsi) to go; (agire) to behave, act; ~ **i bambini a spasso** to take the children for a walk; ~ **fortuna** to bring good luck.

portasiga'rette sm inv cigarette case.

portas'pilli sm inv pincushion.

por'tata sf (vivanda) course; (AUT) carrying o loading capacity; (di arma) range; (volume d'acqua) (rate of) flow; (fig: limite) scope, capability; (: importanza) impact, import; **alla ~ di qd** at sb's level, within sb's capabilities; **a/fuori ~** (di) within/out of reach (of); **a ~ di mano** within (arm's) reach.

por'tatile ag portable.

por'tato, a ag (incline): ~ **a fare** inclined o apt to do.

porta'tore, 'trice sm/f (anche COMM) bearer; (MED) carrier.

portau'ovo sm inv eggcup.

porta'voce [porta'votʃe] sm/f inv spokesman/woman // sm inv loudhailer.

por'tento sm wonder, marvel.

'portico, ci sm portico.

porti'era sf door.

porti'ere sm (portinaio) doorman, commissionaire; (nel calcio) goalkeeper.

porti'naio, a sm/f porter, doorkeeper.

portine'ria sf porter's lodge.

'porto, a pp di **porgere** // sm (NAUT) harbour, port; (spesa di trasporto) carriage // sm inv port (wine); ~ **abusivo d'armi** unlawful carrying of arms.

Porto'gallo sm: **il ~** Portugal; **porto'ghese** ag, sm/f, sm Portuguese.

por'tone sm main entrance, main door.

portu'ale ag harbour cpd, port cpd // sm dock worker.

porzi'one [por'tsjone] sf portion, share; (di cibo) portion, helping.

'posa sf laying q; settling q; (riposo) rest,

peace; (FOT) exposure; (atteggiamento, di modello) pose.

po'sare vt to put (down), lay (down) // vi (fig: fondarsi): ~ **su** to be based on; (: atteggiarsi) to pose; (liquidi) to settle; **~rsi** vr (ape, aereo) to land.

po'sata sf piece of cutlery; ~**e** sfpl cutlery sg.

po'sato, a ag serious.

pos'critto sm postscript.

posi'tivo, a ag positive; (persona: pratica) down-to-earth, practical; **di ~** (certo) for sure.

posizi'one [pozit'tsjone] sf position; **prendere ~** (fig) to take a stand; **luci di ~** (AUT) sidelights.

posolo'gia, 'gie [pozolo'dʒia] sf dosage, directions pl for use.

pos'porre vt to place after; (differire) to postpone, defer; **pos'posto, a** pp di **posporre**.

posse'dere vt to own, possess; (qualità, virtù) to have, possess; (conoscere a fondo: lingua etc) to have a thorough knowledge of; (sog: ira etc) to possess; **possedi'mento** sm possession.

posses'sivo, a ag possessive.

pos'sesso sm ownership q; possession.

posses'sore sm owner.

pos'sibile ag possible // sm: **fare tutto il ~** to do everything possible; **nei limiti del ~** as far as possible; **al più tardi ~** as late as possible; **possibilità** sf inv possibility // sfpl (mezzi) means; **aver la possibilità di fare** to be in a position to do; to have the opportunity to do.

possi'dente sm/f landowner.

'posta sf (servizio) post, postal service; (corrispondenza) post, mail; (ufficio postale) post office; (nei giochi d'azzardo) stake; ~**e** sfpl (amministrazione) post office; ~ **aerea** airmail; **ministro delle P~e e Telecomunicazioni** Postmaster General; **posta'giro** sm postal giro; **pos'tale** ag postal, post office cpd.

post'bellico, a, ci, che ag postwar.

posteggi'are [posted'dʒare] vt, vi to park; **pos'teggio** sm car park; **posteggio per auto pubbliche** taxi rank.

postelegra'fonico, a, ci, che ag postal, telegraphic and telephonic.

posteri'ore ag (dietro) back; (dopo) later // sm (fam) behind.

posterità sf posterity.

pos'ticcio, a, ci, ce [pos'tittʃo] ag false // sm hairpiece.

postici'pare [postitʃi'pare] vt to defer, postpone.

pos'tilla sf marginal note.

pos'tino sm postman.

'posto, a pp di **porre** // sm (sito, posizione) place; (impiego) job; (spazio libero) room, space; (di parcheggio) space; (sedile: al teatro, in treno etc) seat; (MIL) post; **a ~** (in ordine) in place, tidy; (fig) settled; (: persona) reliable; **mettere a ~** qd (dargli un lavoro) to fix sb up with a job; **al ~ di**

in place of; **sul ~ on** the spot; **~ di blocco** roadblock.

pos'tribolo sm brothel.

'**postumo, a** ag (nascita) posthumous; (tardivo) belated; **~i** smpl (conseguenze) after-effects, consequences.

po'tabile ag drinkable; **acqua ~** drinking water.

po'tare vt to prune.

po'tassio sm potassium.

po'tente ag (nazione) strong, powerful; (veleno) potent, strong; **po'tenza** sf power; (forza) strength.

potenzi'ale [poten'tsjale] ag, sm potential.

po'tere vb + infinito can; (sog: persona) can, to be able to; (autorizzazione) can, may; (possibilità, ipotesi) may // vb impers: **può darsi** perhaps; **può darsi che** perhaps, it may be that // sm power; **avresti potuto dirmelo!** you could o might have told me!; **non ne posso più** I'm exhausted; I can't take any more; **~ d'acquisto** purchasing power.

potestà sf (potere) power; (DIR) authority.

'**povero, a** ag poor; (disadorno) plain, bare // sm/f poor man/woman; **i ~i** the poor; **~ di** lacking in, having little; **povertà** sf poverty.

pozi'one [pot'tsjone] sf potion.

'**pozza** ['pottsa] sf pool.

poz'zanghera [pot'tsangera] sf puddle.

'**pozzo** ['pottso] sm well; (cava: di carbone) pit; (di miniera) shaft; **~ petrolifero** oil well.

pran'zare [pran'dzare] vi to dine, have dinner; to lunch, have lunch.

'**pranzo** ['prandzo] sm dinner; (a mezzogiorno) lunch.

'**prassi** sf usual procedure.

'**pratica, che** sf practice; (esperienza) experience; (conoscenza) knowledge, familiarity; (tirocinio) training, practice; (AMM: affare) matter, case; (: incartamento) file, dossier; **~ che** sfpl dealings, negotiations; **in ~** (praticamente) in practice; **mettere in ~** to put into practice.

prati'cabile ag (progetto) practicable, feasible; (luogo) passable, practicable.

prati'cante sm/f apprentice, trainee; (REL) regular churchgoer.

prati'care vt to practise; (attuare) to put into practice; (frequentare: persona) to associate o mix with; (: luogo) to frequent; (eseguire) to carry out, perform; (: apertura, buco) to make.

'**pratico, a, ci, che** ag practical; **~ di** (esperto) experienced o skilled in; (familiare) familiar with.

'**prato** sm meadow; (di giardino) lawn.

preavvi'sare vt to forewarn; to inform in advance; **preav'viso** sm notice; **telefonata con preavviso telefonico** personal o person to person call.

pre'cario, a ag precarious.

precauzi'one [prekaut'tsjone] sf caution, care; (misura) precaution.

prece'dente [pretʃe'dɛnte] ag previous //

sm precedent; **il discorso/film ~** the previous o preceding speech/film; **prece-'denza** sf priority, precedence; (AUT) right of way.

pre'cedere [pre'tʃɛdere] vt to precede; (camminare, guidare innanzi) to be ahead of.

pre'cetto [pre'tʃɛtto] sm precept; (MIL) call-up notice.

precet'tore [pretʃet'tore] sm (private) tutor.

precipi'tare [pretʃipi'tare] vi (2) (cadere: anche fig) to fall headlong, plunge (down) // vt (gettare dall'alto in basso) to hurl, fling; (fig: affrettare) to rush; **~rsi** vr (gettarsi) to hurl o fling o.s.; (affrettarsi) to rush; **precipitazi'one** sf (METEOR) precipitation; (fig) haste; **precipi'toso, a** ag (caduta, fuga) headlong; (fig: avventato) rash, reckless; (: affrettato) hasty, rushed.

preci'pizio [pretʃi'pittsjo] sm precipice; **a ~** (fig: correre) headlong.

pre'cipuo, a [pre'tʃipuo] ag principal, main.

preci'sare [pretʃi'zare] vt to state, specify; (spiegare) to explain (in detail).

precisi'one [pretʃiz'jone] sf precision; accuracy.

pre'ciso, a [pre'tʃizo] ag (esatto) precise; (accurato) accurate, precise; (uguale): **2 vestiti ~i** 2 dresses exactly the same; **sono le 9 ~e** it's exactly 9 o'clock.

pre'cludere vt to block, obstruct; **pre-'cluso, a** pp di **precludere**.

pre'coce [pre'kɔtʃe] ag early; (bambino) precocious; (vecchiaia) premature.

precon'cetto, a [prekon'tʃetto] ag preconceived.

precur'sore sm forerunner, precursor.

'**preda** sf (bottino) booty; (animale, fig) prey; **essere ~ di** to fall prey to; **essere in ~ a** to be prey to; **preda'tore** sm predator.

predeces'sore, a [predetʃes'sore] sm/f predecessor.

pre'della sf platform, dais; altar-step.

predesti'nare vt to predestine.

pre'detto, a pp di **predire**.

'**predica, che** sf sermon; (fig) lecture, talking-to.

predi'care vt, vi to preach.

predi'cato sm (LING) predicate.

predi'letto pp di **prediligere** // ag, sm/f favourite.

predilezi'one [predilet'tsjone] sf fondness, partiality; **avere una ~ per qc/qd** to be partial to sth/fond of sb.

predi'ligere [predi'lidʒere] vt to prefer, have a preference for.

pre'dire vt to foretell, predict.

predis'porre vt to get ready, prepare; **~ qd a qc** to predispose sb to sth; **predis-'posto, a** pp di **predisporre**.

predizi'one [predit'tsjone] sf prediction.

predomi'nare vi to predominate; (prevalere) to prevail; **predo'minio** sm predominance; supremacy.

prefabbri'cato, a *ag* (EDIL) prefabricated.

prefazi'one [prefat'tsjone] *sf* preface, foreword.

prefe'renza [prefe'rɛntsa] *sf* preference; **preferenzi'ale** *ag* preferential.

prefe'rire *vt* to prefer, like better; ~ **il caffè al tè** to prefer coffee to tea, like coffee better than tea.

pre'fetto *sm* prefect; **prefet'tura** *sf* prefecture.

pre'figgere [pre'fiddʒere] *vt* to fix o arrange in advance; **~rsi uno scopo** to set o.s. a goal.

pre'fisso, a *pp di* **prefiggere** // *sm* (LING) prefix; (TEL) dialling code.

pre'gare *vi* to pray // *vt* (REL) to pray to; (*implorare*) to beg; (*chiedere*): ~ **qd di fare** to ask sb to do; **farsi ~** to need coaxing o persuading.

pre'gevole [pre'dʒevole] *ag* valuable.

preghi'era [pre'gjɛra] *sf* (REL) prayer; (*domanda*) request.

pregi'arsi [pre'dʒarsi] *vr*: **mi pregio di farle sapere che ...** I am pleased o honoured to inform you that ... .

'pregio ['prɛdʒo] *sm* (*stima*) esteem, regard; (*qualità*) (good) quality, merit; (*valore*) value, worth.

pregiudi'care [predʒudi'kare] *vt* to prejudice, harm, be detrimental to; **pregiudi'cato, a** *sm/f* (DIR) previous offender.

pregiu'dizio [predʒu'dittsjo] *sm* (*idea errata*) prejudice; (*danno*) harm q.

'pregno, a ['preɲɲo] *ag* (*gravido*) pregnant; (*saturo*): ~ **di** full of, saturated with.

'prego *escl* (*a chi ringrazia*) don't mention it!; (*invitando qd ad accomodarsi*) please sit down!; (*invitando qd ad andare prima*) after you!

pregus'tare *vt* to look forward to.

preis'torico, a, ci, che *ag* prehistoric.

pre'lato *sm* prelate.

prele'vare *vt* (*denaro*) to withdraw; (*campione*) to take; (*sog: polizia*) to take, capture.

preli'evo *sm* (MED): **fare un ~ (di)** to take a sample (of).

prelimi'nare *ag* preliminary; **~i** *smpl* preliminary talks; preliminaries.

pre'ludio *sm* prelude.

pre-ma'man [prema'mã] *sm inv* maternity dress.

prema'turo, a *ag* premature.

premeditazi'one [premeditat'tsjone] *sf* (DIR) premeditation; **con ~** *ag* premeditated // *av* with intent.

'premere *vt* to press // *vi*: ~ **su** to press down on; (*fig*) to put pressure on; ~ **a** (*fig: importare*) to matter to.

pre'messo, a *pp di* **premettere** // *sf* introductory statement, introduction.

pre'mettere *vt* to put before; (*dire prima*) to start by saying, state first.

premi'are *vt* to give a prize to; to reward.

premi'nente *ag* pre-eminent.

'premio *sm* prize, award; (*ricompensa*) reward; (COMM) premium; (AMM: *indennità*) bonus.

premu'nirsi *vr*: ~ **di** to provide o.s. with; ~ **contro** to protect o.s. from, guard o.s. against.

pre'mura *sf* (*fretta*) haste, hurry; (*riguardo*) attention, care; **premu'roso, a** *ag* thoughtful, considerate.

prena'tale *ag* antenatal.

'prendere *vt* to take; (*andare a prendere*) to get, fetch; (*ottenere*) to get; (*guadagnare*) to get, earn; (*catturare: ladro, pesce*) to catch; (*collaboratore, dipendente*) to take on; (*passeggero*) to pick up; (*chiedere: somma, prezzo*) to charge, ask; (*trattare: persona*) to handle // *vi* (*colla, cemento*) to set; (*pianta*) to take; (*fuoco: nel camino*) to catch; (: *incendio*) to start; (*voltare*): ~ **a destra** to turn (to the) right; **~rsi** *vr* (*azzuffarsi*): **~rsi a pugni** to come to blows; ~ **a fare qc** to start doing sth; ~ **qd/qc per** (*scambiare*) to take sb/sth for; ~ **le armi** to take up arms; ~ **fuoco** to catch fire; ~ **parte a** to take part in; **~rsi cura di qd/qc** to look after sb/sth; **prendersela** (*adirarsi*) to get annoyed; (*preoccuparsi*) to get upset, worry.

preno'tare *vt* to book, reserve; **prenotazi'one** *sf* booking, reservation.

preoccu'pare *vt* to worry; to preoccupy; **~rsi** *vr*: **~rsi di qd/qc** to worry about sb/sth; **~rsi per qd** to be anxious for sb; **preoccupazi'one** *sf* worry, anxiety.

prepa'rare *vt* to prepare; (*esame, concorso*) to prepare for; **~rsi** *vr*: **~rsi (a qc/a fare)** to get ready o prepare (o.s.) (for sth/to do); **prepara'tivi** *smpl* preparations; **prepa'rato** *sm* (*prodotto*) preparation; **prepara'torio, a** *ag* preparatory; **preparazi'one** *sf* preparation.

pre'porre *vt* to place before; (*fig*) to prefer.

preposizi'one [prepozit'tsjone] *sf* (LING) preposition.

pre'posto, a *pp di* **preporre**.

prepo'tente *ag* domineering, arrogant; (*bisogno, desiderio*) overwhelming, pressing // *sm/f* bully; **prepo'tenza** *sf* arrogance; arrogant behaviour.

pre'puzio [pre'puttsjo] *sm* (ANAT) foreskin.

preroga'tiva *sf* prerogative.

'presa *sf* taking q; catching q; (*di città*) capture; (*indurimento: di cemento*) setting; (*appiglio, SPORT*) hold; (ELETTR): ~ **di corrente**) socket; (: *al muro*) point; (*piccola quantità: di sale etc*) pinch; (CARTE) trick; **far ~** to catch, hold; (*cemento*) to set; (*pianta*) to take root; // ~ **d'acqua** water supply point; tap; ~ **d'aria** air inlet; ~ **di terra** (ELETTR) earth; **essere alle ~e con qc** (*fig*) to be struggling with sth.

pre'sagio [pre'zadʒo] *sm* omen.

presa'gire [preza'dʒire] vt to foresee.

'presbite ag long-sighted.

presbiteri'ano, a ag, sm/f Presbyterian.

presbi'terio sm presbytery.

pre'scindere [preʃʃindere] vi: ~ **da** to leave out of consideration; **a** ~ **da** apart from.

pres'critto, a pp di **prescrivere**.

pres'crivere vt to prescribe; **prescri- zi'one** sf (MED, DIR) prescription; (norma) rule, regulation.

presen'tare vt to present; (far conoscere): ~ **qd (a)** to introduce sb (to); (AMM: inoltrare) to submit; **~rsi** vr (in comune etc) to report, come; (in giudizio) to appear; (farsi conoscere) to introduce o.s.; (occasione) to arise; **~rsi candidato** (POL) to stand as a candidate; **~rsi bene/male** to look good/bad; **presentazi'one** sf presentation; introduction.

pre'sente ag present; (questo) this // sm present; **i ~i** those present; **aver** ~ **qc/qd** to remember sth/sb.

presenti'mento sm premonition.

pre'senza [pre'zɛntsa] sf presence; (aspetto esteriore) appearance; ~ **di spirito** presence of mind.

pre'sepio, pre'sepe sm crib.

preser'vare vt to protect; to save; **preserva'tivo** sm sheath, condom.

'preside sm/f (INS) headmaster/mistress; (di facoltà universitaria) dean.

presi'dente sm (POL) president; (di assemblea, COMM) chairman; **presiden- 'tessa** sf president; president's wife; chairwoman; **presi'denza** sf presidency; office of president; chairmanship; **presidenzi'ale** ag presidential.

presidi'are vt to garrison; **pre'sidio** sm garrison.

presi'edere vt to preside over // vi: ~ **a** to direct, be in charge of.

'preso, a pp di **prendere**.

'pressa sf crowd, throng; (TECN) press.

pressap'poco av roughly, approximately.

pres'sare vt to press.

pressi'one sf pressure; **far** ~ **su qd** to put pressure on sb; ~ **sanguigna** blood pressure.

'presso av (vicino) nearby, close at hand // prep (vicino a) near; (accanto a) beside, next to; (in casa di): ~ **qd** at sb's home; (nelle lettere) care of (abbr c/o); **lavora** ~ **di noi** he works for o with us.

pressuriz'zare [pressurid'dzare] vt to pressurize.

presta'nome sm/f inv (peg) figurehead.

pres'tante ag good-looking.

pres'tare vt to lend; **~rsi** vr (adoperarsi): **~rsi per qd/a fare** to help sb/to do; (essere adatto): **~rsi a** to lend itself to, be suitable for; ~ **aiuto** to lend a hand; ~ **orecchio** to listen; **prestazi'oni** sfpl (di macchina, atleta) performance sg; (di persona: servizi) services.

prestigia'tore, 'trice [prestidʒa'tore] sm/f conjurer.

pres'tigio [pres'tidʒo] sm (potere) prestige; (illusione): **gioco di** ~ conjuring trick.

'prestito sm lending q; loan; **dar in o a** ~ to lend; **prendere in** ~ to borrow.

'presto av (tra poco) soon; (in fretta) quickly; (di buon'ora) early; **a** ~ see you soon; **fare** ~ **a fare qc** to hurry up and do sth; (non costare fatica) to have no trouble doing sth; **si fa** ~ **a criticare** it's easy to criticize.

pre'sumere vt to presume, assume // vi: ~ **di** to overrate; **pre'sunto, a** pp di **presumere**.

presuntu'oso, a ag presumptuous.

presunzi'one [prezun'tsjone] sf presumption.

presup'porre vt to suppose; to presuppose.

'prete sm priest.

preten'dente sm/f pretender // sm (corteggiatore) suitor.

pre'tendere vt (esigere) to demand, require; (sostenere): ~ **che** to claim that // vi (presumere) to think, presume; **pretende di aver sempre ragione** he thinks he's always right; ~ **a** to lay claim to; **pretensi'one** sf claim; pretentiousness; **pretenzi'oso, a** ag pretentious.

pre'teso, a pp di **pretendere** // sf (esigenza) claim, demand; (presunzione, sfarzo) pretentiousness; **senza ~e** unpretentious.

pre'testo sm pretext, excuse.

pre'tore sm magistrate.

preva'lente ag prevailing; **preva'lenza** sf predominance.

preva'lere vi to prevail; **pre'valso, a** pp di **prevalere**.

preve'dere vt (indovinare) to foresee; (presagire) to foretell; (considerare) to make provision for.

preve'nire vt (anticipare) to forestall; to anticipate; (evitare) to avoid, prevent; (avvertire): ~ **qd (di)** to warn sb (of); to inform sb (of).

preventi'vare vt (COMM) to estimate.

preven'tivo, a ag preventive // sm (COMM) estimate.

prevenzi'one [preven'tsjone] sf prevention; (preconcetto) prejudice.

previ'dente ag showing foresight; prudent; **previ'denza** sf foresight; **istituto di previdenza** provident institution; **previdenza sociale** social security.

previsi'one sf forecast, prediction; **~i meteorologiche o del tempo** weather forecast sg.

pre'visto, a pp di **prevedere** // ag foreseen, expected; **più/meno del** ~ more/less than expected.

prezi'oso, a [pret'tsjoso] ag precious; invaluable // sm jewel; valuable.

prez'zemolo [pret'tsemolo] sm parsley.

'prezzo ['prɛttso] sm price; ~

d'acquisto/di vendita buying/ selling price.

prigi'one [pri'dʒone] *sf* prison; **prigio'nia** *sf* imprisonment; **prigioni'ero, a** *ag* captive // *sm/f* prisoner.

'**prima** *sf vedi* primo // *av* before; (*in anticipo*) in advance, beforehand; (*per l'addietro*) at one time, formerly; (*più presto*) sooner, earlier; (*in primo luogo*) first // *cong:* ~ **di fare/che parta** before doing/he leaves; ~ **di** *prep* before; ~ **o poi** sooner or later.

pri'mario, a *ag* primary; (*principale*) chief, leading, primary.

pri'mate *sm* (REL) primate.

pri'mato *sm* supremacy; (SPORT) record.

prima'vera *sf* spring; **primave'rile** *ag* spring *cpd.*

primeggi'are [primed'dʒare] *vi* to excel, be one of the best.

primi'tivo, a *ag* primitive; original.

pri'mizie [pri'mittsje] *sfpl* early produce *sg.*

'**primo, a** *ag* first; (*fig*) initial; basic; prime // *sf* (TEATRO) first night; (CINEMA) première; (AUT) first (gear); **le** ~**e ore del mattino** the early hours of the morning; **ai** ~**i di maggio** at the beginning of May; **viaggiare in** ~**a** to travel first-class; **in** ~ **luogo** first of all, in the first place; **di prim'ordine** *o* ~**a qualità** first-class, first-rate; **in un** ~ **tempo** at first; ~**a donna** leading lady; (*di opera lirica*) prima donna.

primo'genito, a [primo'dʒenito] *ag, sm/f* firstborn.

primordi'ale *ag* primordial.

'**primula** *sf* primrose.

princi'pale [printʃi'pale] *ag* main, principal // *sm* manager, boss.

princi'pato [printʃi'pato] *sm* principality.

'**principe** ['printʃipe] *sm* prince; ~ **ereditario** crown prince; **princi'pessa** *sf* princess.

principi'ante [printʃi'pjante] *sm/f* beginner.

principi'are [printʃi'pjare] *vt, vi* to start, begin.

prin'cipio [prin'tʃipjo] *sm* (*inizio*) beginning, start; (*origine*) origin, cause; (*concetto, norma*) principle; **al** *o* **in** ~ at first; **per** ~ on principle.

pri'ore *sm* (REL) prior.

priorità *sf* priority.

'**prisma, i** *sm* prism.

pri'vare *vt:* ~ **qd di** to deprive sb of; ~**rsi di** to go *o* do without.

priva'tiva *sf* (ECON) monopoly.

pri'vato, a *ag* private // *sm/f* private citizen; **in** ~ in private.

privazi'one [privat'tsjone] *sf* privation, hardship.

privilegi'are [privile'dʒare] *vt* to grant a privilege to.

privi'legio [privi'lɛdʒo] *sm* privilege.

'**privo, a** *ag:* ~ **di** without, lacking.

pro *prep* for, on behalf of // *sm inv* (*utilità*) advantage, benefit; **a che** ~? what's the use?; **il** ~ **e il contro** the pros and cons.

pro'babile *ag* probable, likely; **probabilità** *sf inv* probability.

pro'bante *ag* convincing.

probità *sf* integrity, probity.

pro'blema, i *sm* problem.

pro'boscide [pro'bɔʃʃide] *sf* (*di elefante*) trunk.

procacci'are [prokat'tʃare] *vt* to get, obtain.

pro'cedere [pro'tʃedere] *vi* to proceed; (*comportarsi*) to behave; (*iniziare*): ~ **a** to start; ~ **contro** (DIR) to start legal proceedings against; **procedi'mento** *sm* (*modo di condurre*) procedure; (*di avvenimenti*) course; (*comportamento*) behaviour; (TECN) process; **proce'dura** *sf* (DIR) procedure.

proces'sare [protʃes'sare] *vt* (DIR) to try.

processi'one [protʃes'sjone] *sf* procession.

pro'cesso [pro'tʃɛsso] *sm* (DIR) trial; proceedings *pl;* (*metodo*) process.

pro'cinto [pro'tʃinto] *sm:* **in** ~ **di fare** about to do, on the point of doing.

pro'clama, i *sm* proclamation.

procla'mare *vt* to proclaim; **proclamazi'one** *sf* proclamation, declaration.

procrastinazi'one [prokrastinat'tsjone] *sf* procrastination.

procre'are *vt* to procreate.

pro'cura *sf* (DIR) proxy; power of attorney; (*ufficio*) attorney's office.

procu'rare *vt:* ~ **qc a qd** (*provvedere*) to get *o* obtain sth for sb; (*causare*: *noie etc*) to bring *o* give sb sth.

procura'tore, 'trice *sm/f* (DIR) ≈ solicitor; (: *chi ha la procura*) attorney; proxy; ~ **generale** (*in corte d'appello*) public prosecutor; (*in corte di cassazione*) Attorney General; ~ **della Repubblica** (*in corte d'assise, tribunale*) public prosecutor.

prodi'gare *vt* to be lavish with; ~**rsi per qd** to do all one can for sb.

pro'digio [pro'didʒo] *sm* marvel, wonder; (*persona*) prodigy; **prodigi'oso, a** *ag* prodigious; phenomenal.

'**prodigo, a, ghi, ghe** *ag* lavish, extravagant.

pro'dotto, a *pp di* produrre // *sm* product; ~**i agricoli** farm produce *sg.*

pro'durre *vt* to produce; **prodursi** *vr* (*attore*) to perform, appear; **produttività** *sf* productivity; **produt'tivo, a** *ag* productive; **produt'tore, 'trice** *sm/f* producer; **produzi'one** *sf* production; (*rendimento*) output.

pro'emio *sm* introduction, preface.

Prof. (*abbr di* professore) Prof.

profa'nare *vt* to desecrate.

pro'fano, a *ag* (*mondano*) secular; profane; (*sacrilego*) profane.

profe'rire *vt* to utter.

profes'sare *vt* to profess; (*medicina etc*) to practise.

professio'nale *ag* professional.

professi'one sf profession; **professio-'nista, i, e** sm/f professional.

profes'sore, 'essa sm/f (INS) teacher; (: di università) lecturer; (: titolare di cattedra) professor.

pro'feta, i sm prophet; **profetiz'zare** vt to prophesy; **profe'zia** sf prophecy.

pro'ficuo, a ag useful, profitable.

profi'lare vt to outline; (ornare: vestito) to edge; (aereo) to streamline; ~**rsi** vr to stand out, be silhouetted; to loom up.

pro'filo sm profile; (contorno) contour, line; (breve descrizione) sketch, outline; **di ~** in profile.

profit'tare vi: ~ **in** to make progress in; ~ **di** (trarre profitto) to profit by; (approfittare) to take advantage of.

pro'fitto sm advantage, profit, benefit; (fig: progresso) progress; (COMM) profit.

pro'fondere vt (lodi) to lavish; (denaro) to squander; ~**rsi in** to be profuse in.

profondità sf inv depth.

pro'fondo, a ag deep; (rancore, meditazione) profound // sm depth(s pl), bottom; ~ **8 metri 8** metres deep.

'profugo, a, ghi, ghe sm/f refugee.

profu'mare vt to perfume // vi (2) to be fragrant; ~**rsi** vr to put on perfume o scent.

profume'ria sf perfumery; (negozio) perfume shop; ~**e** sfpl perfumes.

pro'fumo sm (prodotto) perfume, scent; (fragranza) scent, fragrance.

profusi'one sf profusion; a ~ in plenty.

pro'fuso, a pp di **profondere.**

proget'tare [prodʒet'tare] vt to plan; (TECN: edificio) to plan, design; **pro'getto** sm plan; (idea) plan, project; **progetto di legge** bill.

pro'gramma, i sm programme; (TV, RADIO) programmes pl; (INS) syllabus, curriculum; (INFORM) program; **program-'mare** vt (TV, RADIO) to put on; (INFORM) to program; (ECON) to plan; **programma-'tore, 'trice** sm/f (INFORM) computer programmer; (ECON) planner; **program-mazi'one** sf programming; planning.

progre'dire vi to progress, make progress.

progressi'one sf progression.

progres'sivo, a ag progressive.

pro'gresso sm progress q; **fare ~i** to make progress.

proi'bire vt to forbid, prohibit; **proibi-'tivo, a** ag prohibitive; **proibizi'one** sf prohibition.

proiet'tare vt (gettare) to throw out (o off o up); (CINEMA) to project; (: presentare) to show, screen; (luce, ombra) to throw, cast, project; **proiet'tile** sm projectile, bullet (o shell etc); **proiet'tore** sm (CINEMA) projector; (AUT) headlamp; (MIL) searchlight; **proiezi'one** sf (CINEMA) projection; showing.

'prole sf children pl, offspring.

proletari'ato sm proletariat.

prole'tario, a ag, sm proletarian.

prolife'rare vi (fig) to proliferate.

pro'lifico, a, ci, che ag prolific.

pro'lisso, a ag verbose.

'prologo, ghi sm prologue.

pro'lunga, ghe sf (di cavo elettrico etc) extension.

prolun'gare vt (discorso, attesa) to prolong; (linea, termine) to extend.

prome'moria sm inv memorandum.

pro'messa sf promise.

pro'messo, a pp di **promettere.**

pro'mettere vt to promise // vi to be o look promising; ~ **a qd di fare** to promise sb that one will do.

promi'nente ag prominent; **promi-'nenza** sf prominence.

promiscuità sf promiscuousness.

promon'torio sm promontory, headland.

pro'mosso, a pp di **promuovere.**

promo'tore sm promoter, organizer.

promozi'one [promot'tsjone] sf promotion.

promul'gare vt to promulgate.

promu'overe vt to promote.

proni'pote sm/f (di nonni) great-grandchild, great-grandson/grand-daughter; (di zii) great-nephew/ niece.

pro'nome sm (LING) pronoun.

pronosti'care vt to foretell, predict; to presage.

pron'tezza [pron'tettsa] sf readiness; quickness, promptness.

'pronto, a ag ready; (rapido) fast, quick, prompt; ~**!** (TEL) hello!; ~ **all'ira** quick-tempered; ~ **soccorso** first aid.

prontu'ario sm manual, handbook.

pro'nuncia [pro'nuntʃa] etc = **pronunzia** etc.

pro'nunzia [pro'nuntsja] sf pronunciation; **pronunzi'are** vt (parola, sentenza) to pronounce; (dire) to utter; (discorso) to deliver; **pronunziarsi** vr to declare one's opinion; **pronunzi'ato, a** ag (spiccato) pronounced, marked; (sporgente) prominent.

propa'ganda sf propaganda.

propa'gare vt (fig) to spread; (BIOL) to propagate; ~**rsi** vr to spread; to propagate; (FISICA) to be propagated.

pro'pendere vi: ~ **per** to favour, lean towards; **propensi'one** sf inclination, propensity; **pro'penso, a** pp di **propendere.**

propi'nare vt to administer.

pro'pizio, a [pro'pittsjo] ag favourable.

pro'porre vt (suggerire): ~ **qc (a qd)/di fare** to suggest sth (to sb)/doing, propose to do; (candidato) to put forward; (legge, brindisi) to propose; **proporsi di fare** to propose o intend to do; **proporsi una meta** to set o.s. a goal.

proporzio'nale [proportsjo'nale] ag proportional.

proporzio'nare [proportsjo'nare] vt: ~ **qc a** to proportion o adjust sth to.

proporzi'one [propor'tsjone] sf proportion; **in ~** in proportion to.

pro'posito sm (intenzione) intention, aim;

(*argomento*) subject, matter; **a ~ di** regarding, with regard to; **di ~** (*apposta*) deliberately, on purpose; **a ~** by the way; **capitare a ~** (*cosa, persona*) to turn up at the right time.

proposizi'one [propozit'tsjone] *sf* (*LING*) clause; (: *periodo*) sentence.

pro'posto, a *pp di* **proporre** // *sf* suggestion; proposal.

proprietà *sf inv* (*diritto*) ownership; (*ciò che si possiede*) property *gen q*, estate; (*caratteristica*) property; (*correttezza*) correctness; **proprie'tario, a** *sm/f* owner; (*di albergo etc*) proprietor, owner; (*per l'inquilino*) landlord/lady.

'proprio, a *ag* (*possessivo*) own; (: *impersonale*) one's; (*esatto*) exact, correct, proper; (*senso, significato*) literal; (*LING: nome*) proper; (*particolare*): **~ di** characteristic of, peculiar to // *av* (*precisamente*) just, exactly, precisely; (*davvero*) really; (*affatto*): **non ... ~** not ... at all.

propulsi'one *sf* propulsion.

'prora *sf* (*NAUT*) bow(s *pl*), prow.

'proroga, ghe *sf* extension; postponement; **proro'gare** *vt* to extend; (*differire*) to postpone, defer.

pro'rompere *vi* to burst out; **pro'rotto, a** *pp di* **prorompere**.

'prosa *sf* prose; **pro'saico, a, ci, che** *ag* (*fig*) prosaic, mundane.

pro'sciogliere [proʃ'ʃɔʎʎere] *vt* to release; (*DIR*) to acquit; **prosci'olto, a** *pp di* **prosciogliere**.

prosciu'gare [proʃʃu'gare] *vt* (*terreni*) to drain, reclaim; **~rsi** *vr* to dry up.

prosci'utto [proʃ'ʃutto] *sm* ham.

pros'critto, a *pp di* **proscrivere** // *sm* exile.

pros'crivere *vt* to exile, banish.

prosecuzi'one [prosekut'tsjone] *sf* continuation.

prosegui'mento *sm* continuation; **buon ~!** all the best!; (*a chi viaggia*) enjoy the rest of your journey!

prosegu'ire *vt* to carry on with, continue // *vi* to carry on, go on.

prospe'rare *vi* to thrive; **prosperità** *sf* prosperity; **'prospero, a** *ag* (*fiorente*) flourishing, thriving, prosperous; (*favorevole*) favourable; **prospe'roso, a** *ag* (*robusto*) hale and hearty; (: *ragazza*) buxom.

prospet'tare *vt* (*esporre*) to point out, show; **~rsi** *vr* to look, appear.

prospet'tiva *sf* (*ARTE*) perspective; (*veduta*) view; (*fig: previsione*) prospect.

pros'petto *sm* (*veduta*) view, prospect; (*facciata*) façade, front; (*tabella*) table.

prospici'ente [prospi'tʃɛnte] *ag*: **~ qc** facing *o* overlooking sth.

prossimità *sf* nearness, proximity; **in ~ di** near (to), close to.

'prossimo, a *ag* (*vicino*): **~ a** near (to), close to; (*che viene subito dopo*) next; (*parente*) close // *sm* neighbour, fellow man.

prosti'tuta *sf* prostitute; **prostituzi'one** *sf* prostitution.

pros'trare *vt* (*fig*) to exhaust, wear out; **~rsi** *vr* (*fig*) to humble o.s.

protago'nista, i, e *sm/f* protagonist.

pro'teggere [pro'tɛddʒere] *vt* to protect.

prote'ina *sf* protein.

pro'tendere *vt* to stretch out; **pro'teso, a** *pp di* **protendere**.

pro'testa *sf* protest; (*dichiarazione*) protestation, profession.

protes'tante *ag, sm/f* Protestant.

protes'tare *vt, vi* to protest; **~rsi** *vr*: **~ innocente** *etc* to protest one's innocence *o* that one is innocent *etc*.

protet'tivo, a *ag* protective.

pro'tetto, a *pp di* **proteggere**.

protetto'rato *sm* protectorate.

protet'tore, 'trice *sm/f* protector; (*sostenitore*) patron.

protezi'one [protet'tsjone] *sf* protection; (*patrocinio*) patronage.

protocol'lare *vt* to register // *ag* formal; of protocol.

proto'collo *sm* protocol; (*registro*) register of documents.

proto'tipo *sm* prototype.

pro'trarre *vt* (*prolungare*) to prolong; (*differire*) to put off; **pro'tratto, a** *pp di* **protrarre**.

protube'ranza [protube'rantsa] *sf* protuberance, bulge.

'prova *sf* (*esperimento, cimento*) test, trial; (*tentativo*) attempt, try; (*MAT, testimonianza, documento etc*) proof; (*DIR*) evidence *q*, proof; (*INS*) exam, test; (*TEATRO*) rehearsal; (*di abito*) fitting; **a ~ di** (*in testimonianza di*) as proof of; **a ~ di fuoco** fireproof; **mettere in ~** (*vestito*) to try on; **mettere alla ~** to put to the test; **viaggio** *o* **corsa di ~** test *o* trial run; **~ generale** (*TEATRO*) dress rehearsal.

pro'vare *vt* (*sperimentare*) to test; (*tentare*) to try, attempt; (*assaggiare*) to try, taste; (*sperimentare in sé*) to experience; (*sentire*) to feel; (*cimentare*) to put to the test; (*dimostrare*) to prove; (*abito*) to try on // *vi* to try; **~rsi** *vr*: **~rsi (a fare)** to try *o* attempt (to do); **~ a fare** to try *o* attempt to do.

proveni'enza [prove'njɛntsa] *sf* origin, source.

prove'nire *vi* (*2*): **~ da** to come from.

pro'venti *smpl* revenue *sg*.

prove'nuto, a *pp di* **provenire**.

pro'verbio *sm* proverb.

pro'vetta *sf* test tube.

pro'vetto, a *ag* skilled, experienced.

pro'vincia, ce *o* **cie** [pro'vintʃa] *sf* province; **provinci'ale** *ag* provincial.

pro'vino *sm* (*CINEMA*) screen test; (*campione*) specimen.

provo'cante *ag* (*attraente*) provocative.

provo'care *vt* (*causare*) to cause, bring about; (*eccitare: riso, pietà*) to arouse; (*irritare, sfidare*) to provoke; **provoca-**

'**torio, a** *ag* provocative; **provocazi'one** *sf* provocation.

provve'dere *vi* (*disporre*): ~ (**a**) to provide (for); (*prendere un provvedimento*) to take steps, act // *vt* to provide, supply; ~**rsi** *vr*: ~**rsi di** to provide o.s. with; **provvedi'mento** *sm* measure; (*di previdenza*) precaution.

provvi'denza [provvi'dɛntsa] *sf*: **la** ~ providence; **provvidenzi'ale** *ag* providential.

provvigi'one [provvi'dʒone] *sf* (*COMM*) commission.

provvi'sorio, a *ag* temporary; (*DIR*) provisional.

prov'vista *sf* provision, supply.

'**prua** *sf* (*NAUT*) = **prora**.

pru'dente *ag* cautious, careful, prudent; (*assennato*) sensible, wise; **pru'denza** *sf* prudence; (*cautela*) caution, care.

'**prudere** *vi* to itch, be itchy.

'**prugna** ['pruɲɲa] *sf* plum; ~ **secca** prune; '**prugno** *sm* plum tree.

prurigi'noso, a [pruridʒi'noso] *ag* itchy.

pru'rito *sm* itchiness *q*; itch.

P.S. (*abbr di postscriptum*) P.S.; *abbr di* **Pubblica Sicurezza**.

pseu'donimo *sm* pseudonym.

psica'nalisi *sf* psychoanalysis; **psicana-'lista, i, e** *sm/f* psychoanalyst; **psicana-liz'zare** *vt* to psychoanalyse.

'**psiche** ['psike] *sf* (*PSIC*) psyche.

psichi'atra, i, e [psi'kjatra] *sm/f* psychiatrist; **psichia'tria** *sf* psychiatry.

psico'logia [psikolo'dʒia] *sf* psychology; **psico'logico, a, ci, che** *ag* psychological; **psi'cologo, a, gi, ghe** *sm/f* psychologist.

psico'patico, a, ci, che *ag* psychopathic // *sm/f* psychopath.

P.T. (*abbr da Posta e Telegrafi*) P.O.

pubbli'care *vt* to publish.

pubblicazi'one [pubblikat'tsjone] *sf* publication; ~**i** (**matrimoniali**) *sfpl* (*marriage*) banns.

pubbli'cista, i, e [pubbli'tʃista] *sm/f* (*STAMPA*) occasional contributor.

pubblicità [pubbli'tʃita] *sf* (*diffusione*) publicity; (*attività*) advertising; (*annunci nei giornali*) advertisements *pl*; **pubblici-'tario, a** *ag* advertising *cpd*; (*trovata, film*) publicity *cpd*.

'**pubblico, a, ci, che** *ag* public; (*statale*: *scuola etc*) state *cpd* // *sm* public; (*spettatori*) audience; **in** ~ **in** public; ~ **funzionario** civil servant; **P**~ **Ministero** Public Prosecutor's Office; **la P**~**a Sicurezza** the Police.

'**pube** *sm* (*ANAT*) pubis.

pubertà *sf* puberty.

'**pudico, a, ci, che** *ag* modest.

pu'dore *sm* modesty.

puericul'tura *sf* paediatric nursing; infant care.

pue'rile *ag* childish.

pugi'lato [pudʒi'lato] *sm* boxing.

'**pugile** ['pudʒile] *sm* boxer.

pugna'lare [puɲɲa'lare] *vt* to stab.

pu'gnale [puɲ'ɲale] *sm* dagger.

'**pugno** ['puɲɲo] *sm* fist; (*colpo*) punch; (*quantità*) fistful.

'**pulce** ['pultʃe] *sf* flea.

pul'cino [pul'tʃino] *sm* chick.

pu'ledro, a *sm/f* colt/filly.

pu'leggia, ge [pu'leddʒa] *sf* pulley.

pu'lire *vt* to clean; (*lucidare*) to polish; **pu-'lito, a** *ag* (*anche fig*) clean; (*ordinato*) neat, tidy // *sf* quick clean; **pul'tura** *sf* cleaning; **puli'zia** *sf* cleaning; cleanness; **fare le pulizie** to do the cleaning, do the housework.

'**pullman** *sm inv* coach.

pul'lover *sm inv* pullover, jumper.

pullu'lare *vi* to swarm, teem.

pul'mino *sm* minibus.

'**pulpito** *sm* pulpit.

pul'sante *sm* (push-)button.

pul'sare *vi* to pulsate, beat; **pulsazi'one** *sf* beat.

pul'viscolo *sm* fine dust.

'**puma** *sm inv* puma.

pun'gente [pun'dʒente] *ag* prickly; stinging; (*anche fig*) biting.

'**pungere** ['pundʒere] *vt* to prick; (*sog*: *insetto, ortica*) to sting; (: *freddo*) to bite; (*fig*) to wound, offend.

pungigli'one [pundʒiʎ'ʎone] *sm* sting.

pungo'lare *vt* to goad.

pu'nire *vt* to punish; **puni'tivo, a** *ag* punitive; **punizi'one** *sf* punishment.

'**punta** *sf* point; (*parte terminale*) tip, end; (*di monte*) peak; (*di costa*) promontory; (*minima parte*) touch, trace; **in** ~ **di piedi** on tip-toe; **ore di** ~ peak hours; **uomo di** ~ front-rank *o* leading man.

pun'tare *vt* (*piedi a terra, gomiti sul tavolo*) to plant; (*dirigere*: *pistola*) to point; (*scommettere*) to bet // *vi* (*mirare*): ~ **a** to aim at; (*avviarsi*): ~ **su** to head *o* make for; (*fig: contare*): ~ **su** to count *o* rely on.

pun'tata *sf* (*gita*) short trip; (*scommessa*) bet; (*parte di opera*) instalment; **romanzo a** ~**e** serial.

punteggi'are [punted'dʒare] *vt* to dot; (*forare*) to make holes in; (*LING*) to punctuate; **punteggia'tura** *sf* (*LING*) punctuation.

pun'teggio [pun'teddʒo] *sm* score.

puntel'lare *vt* to support.

pun'tello *sm* prop, support.

pun'tiglio [pun'tiʎʎo] *sm* obstinacy, stubbornness.

pun'tina *sf*: ~ **da disegno** drawing pin.

pun'tino *sm* dot; **fare qc a** ~ to do sth properly.

'**punto, a** *pp di* **pungere** // *sm* (*segno, macchiolina*) dot; (*LING*) full stop; (*MAT, momento, di punteggio, fig: argomento*) point; (*posto*) spot; (*a scuola*) mark; (*nel cucire, nella maglia, MED*) stitch // *av*: **non** ... ~ not ... at all; **due** ~**i** *sm* (*LING*) colon; **sul** ~ **di fare** (just) about to do; **fare il** ~ (*NAUT*) to take a bearing; (*fig*): **fare il** ~ **su qc** to define sth; **alle 6 in** ~ at 6 o'clock sharp *o* on the dot; **essere a buon**

~ to have reached a satisfactory stage; **mettere a ~** to adjust; (*motore*) to tune; (*cannocchiale*) to focus; (*fig*) to settle; **di ~ in bianco** point-blank; **~ cardinale** point of the compass, cardinal point; **~ debole** weak point; **~ esclamativo/ interrogativo** exclamation/question mark; **~ di riferimento** landmark; (*fig*) point of reference; **~ di vendita** retail outlet; **~ e virgola** semicolon; **~ di vista** (*fig*) point of view; **~i di sospensione** suspension points.

puntu'ale *ag* punctual; precise, exact; **puntualità** *sf* punctuality; precision, exactness.

pun'tura *sf* (*di ago*) prick; (*di insetto*) sting, bite; (*MED*) puncture; (: *iniezione*) injection; (*dolore*) sharp pain.

punzecchi'are [puntsek'kjare] *vt* to prick; (*fig*) to tease.

pun'zone [pun'tsone] *sm* (*per metalli*) stamp, die.

'pupa *sf* doll.

pu'pazzo [pu'pattso] *sm* puppet.

pu'pillo, a *sm/f* (*DIR*) ward; (*prediletto*) favourite, pet // *sf* (*ANAT*) pupil.

purché [pur'ke] *cong* provided that, on condition that.

'pure *cong* (*tuttavia*) and yet, nevertheless; (*anche se*) even if // *av* (*anche*) too, also; **pur di** (*al fine di*) just to; **faccia ~!** go ahead!, please do!

purè *sm*, **pu'rea** *sf* (*CUC*) purée; (*di patate*) mashed potatoes.

pu'rezza [pu'rettsa] *sf* purity.

'purga, ghe *sf* (*MED*) purging *q*; purge; (*POL*) purge.

pur'gante *sm* (*MED*) purgative, purge.

pur'gare *vt* (*MED, POL*) to purge; (*pulire*) to clean.

purga'torio *sm* purgatory.

purifi'care *vt* to purify; (*metallo*) to refine.

puri'tano, a *ag, sm/f* Puritan.

'puro, a *ag* pure; (*acqua*) clear, limpid; (*vino*) undiluted; **puro'sangue** *sm/f inv* thoroughbred.

pur'troppo *av* unfortunately.

pus *sm* pus.

pusil'lanime *ag* fainthearted.

'pustola *sf* pimple.

puti'ferio *sm* rumpus, row.

putre'fare *vi* (2) to putrefy, rot; **putre-'fatto, a** *pp di* **putrefare**.

'putrido, a *ag* putrid, rotten.

put'tana *sf* (*fam!*) whore (!).

'puzza ['puttsa] *sf* = **puzzo**.

puz'zare [put'tsare] *vi* to stink.

'puzzo ['puttso] *sm* stink, foul smell.

'puzzola ['puttsola] *sf* polecat.

puzzo'lente [puttso'lɛnte] *ag* stinking.

Q

qua *av* here; **in ~** (*verso questa parte*) this way; **da un anno in ~** for a year now; **per di ~** (*passare*) this way; **al di ~ di**

(*fiume, strada*) on this side of; *vedi* **questo**.

qua'derno *sm* notebook; (*per scuola*) exercise book.

qua'drangolo *sm* quadrangle.

qua'drante *sm* quadrant; (*di orologio*) face.

qua'drare *vi* (*bilancio*) to balance, tally; (*descrizione*) to correspond; (*fig*): **~ a** to please, be to one's liking // *vt* (*MAT*) to square; **non mi quadra** I don't like it; **qua'drato, a** *ag* square; (*fig: equilibrato*) level-headed, sensible // *sm* (*MAT*) square; (*PUGILATO*) ring; **5 al quadrato** 5 squared.

qua'dretto *sm*: **a ~i** (*tessuto*) checked.

quadri'foglio [kwadri'fɔʎʎo] *sm* four-leaf clover.

'quadro *sm* (*pittura*) painting, picture; (*quadrato*) square; (*tabella*) table, chart; (*TECN*) board, panel; (*TEATRO*) scene; (*fig: scena, spettacolo*) sight; (: *descrizione*) outline, description; **~i** *smpl* (*POL*) party organizers; (*MIL*) cadres; (*CARTE*) diamonds.

qua'drupede *sm* quadruped.

quadrupli'care *vt* to quadruple.

'quadruplo, a *ag, sm* quadruple.

quaggiù [kwad'dʒu] *av* down here.

'quaglia ['kwaʎʎa] *sf* quail.

'qualche ['kwalke] *det* some; (*alcuni*) a few; (*in espressioni interrogative*) any; (*uno*): **c'è ~ medico?** is there a doctor?; **ho comprato ~ libro** I've bought some *o* a few books; **hai ~ sigaretta?** have you any cigarettes?; **una persona di ~ rilievo** a person of some importance; **~ cosa = qualcosa; in ~ modo** somehow; **~ volta** sometimes; **qualche'duno** *pronome* = **qualcuno.**

qual'cosa *pronome* something; (*in espressioni interrogative*) anything; **qual-cos'altro** something else; anything else; **~ di nuovo** something new; anything new.

qual'cuno *pronome* (*persona*) someone, somebody; (: *in espressioni interrogative*) anyone, anybody; (*alcuni*) some; **~ è favorevole a noi** some are on our side; **qualcun altro** someone *o* somebody else; anyone *o* anybody else.

'quale (*spesso troncato in* **qual**) *det* what; (*discriminativo*) which;- (*come*) as // *pronome* (*interrogativo*) what; which; (*relativo*): **il(la) ~** (*persona: soggetto*) who; (: *oggetto, con preposizione*) whom; (*cosa*) which; (*possessivo*): **la signora della ~ ammiriamo la bellezza** the lady whose beauty we admire // *av* (*in qualità di*) as; **~ disgrazia!** what a misfortune!

qua'lifica, che *sf* qualification; (*titolo*) title.

qualifi'care *vt* to qualify; (*definire*): **~ qd/qc come** to describe sb/sth as; **~rsi** *vr* (*anche SPORT*) to qualify; **qualifica-'tivo, a** *ag* qualifying; **qualificazi'one** *sf* qualification.

qualità *sf inv* quality; **in ~ di** in one's capacity as.

qua'lora *cong* in case, if.

qual'siasi, qua'lunque *det inv* any; (*quale che sia*) whatever; (*discriminativo*) whichever; (*posposto: mediocre*) poor, indifferent; ordinary; ~ **cosa accada** whatever happens; **a** ~ **costo** at any cost, whatever the cost; **l'uomo** ~ the man in the street; ~ **persona** anyone, anybody.

'quando *cong, av* when; ~ **sarò ricco** when I'm rich; **da** ~ (*dacché*) since; (*interrogativo*): **da** ~ **sei qui?** how long have you been here?; **quand'anche** even if.

quantità *sf inv* quantity; (*gran numero*): **una** ~ **di** a great deal of; a lot of; **in grande** ~ in large quantities.

'quanto, a *det* (*interrogativo: quantità*) how much; (: *numero*) how many; (*esclamativo*) what a lot of, how much (*o many*); (*relativo*) as much ... as; as many ... as; **ho** ~ **denaro mi occorre** I have as much money as I need // *pronome* (*interrogativo*) how much; how many; (: *tempo*) how long; (*relativo*) as much as; as many as; ~**i(e)** *pronome pl* (*persone*) all those who // *av* (*interrogativo: con ag, av*) how; (: *con vb*) how much; (*esclamativo: con ag, av*) how; (: *con vb*) how much, what a lot; (*con valore relativo*) as much as; **studierò** ~ **posso** I'll study as much as o all I can; ~**i ne abbiamo oggi?** what is the date today?; ~**i anni hai?** how old are you?; ~ **costa?, quant'è?** how much does it cost?, how much is it?; **in** ~ *av* (*in qualità di*) as; (*poiché*) since, as; **per** ~ **sia brava, fa degli errori** however good she may be, she makes mistakes; **per** ~ **io sappia** as far as I know; ~ **a** as regards, as for; ~ **prima** as soon as possible; ~ **tempo?** how long?, how much time?; ~ **più ... tanto meno** the more ... the less; ~ **più ... tanto più** the more ... the more.

quan'tunque *cong* although, though.

qua'ranta *num* forty.

quaran'tena *sf* quarantine.

quaran'tesimo, a *num* fortieth.

quaran'tina *sf*: **una** ~ (**di**) about forty.

qua'resima *sf*: **la** ~ Lent.

'quarta *sf vedi* **quarto.**

'quartetto *sm* quartet(te).

quarti'ere *sm* district, area; (*MIL*) quarters *pl*; ~ **generale** headquarters *pl*, HQ.

'quarto, a *ag* fourth // *sm* fourth; (*quarta parte*) quarter // *sf* (*AUT*) fourth (gear); ~ **d'ora** quarter of an hour; **le 6 e un** ~ **a** quarter past six.

'quarzo [ˈkwartso] *sm* quartz.

'quasi *av* almost, nearly // *cong* (*anche:* ~ **che**) as if; (*non*) ... ~ **mai** hardly ever; ~ ~ **me ne andrei** I've half a mind to leave.

quas'sù *av* up here.

'quatto, a *ag* crouched, squatting; (*silenzioso*) silent; ~ ~ very quietly; stealthily.

quat'tordici [kwatˈtorditʃi] *num* fourteen.

quat'trini *smpl* money *sg*, cash *sg*.

'quattro *num* four; **in** ~ **e quattr'otto** in less than no time; **quattro'cento** *num* four hundred // *sm*: **il Quattrocento** the fifteenth century; **quattro'mila** *num* four thousand.

'quello, a *det* (*dav sm* **quel** + *C*, **quell'** + *V*, **quello** + *s impura, gn, pn, ps, x, z; pl* **quei** + *C*, **quegli** + *V o s impura, gn, pn, ps, x, z; dav sf* **quella** + *C*, **quell'** + *V; pl* **quelle**) that; those *pl* // *pronome* that (one); those (ones) *pl*; (*ciò*) that; ~**(a) che** the one who; ~**i(e) che** those who; **ho fatto** ~ **che potevo** I did what I could; ~**(a) ... là** o **là** *det* that; **quell'uomo lì** that man; ~**(a) lì** o **là** *pronome* that one.

'quercia, ce [ˈkwertʃa] *sf* oak (tree); (*legno*) oak.

que'rela *sf* (*DIR*) (legal) action; **quere'lare** *vt* to bring an action against.

que'sito *sm* question, query; problem.

questio'nare *vi*: ~ **di/su qc** to argue about/over sth.

questio'nario *sm* questionnaire.

questi'one *sf* problem, question; (*affare*) matter; issue; (*litigio*) quarrel; **in** ~ in question; **fuor di** ~ out of the question; **è** ~ **di tempo** it's a matter o question of time.

'questo, a *det* this; these *pl* // *pronome* this (one); those (ones) *pl*; (*ciò*) this; ~**(a) ... qui** o **qua** *det* this; ~ **ragazzo qui** this boy; ~**(a) qui** o **qua** *pronome* this one; **io prendo** ~ **cappotto, tu prendi quello** I'll take this coat, you take that one; **preferisce** ~**i** o **quelli?** do you prefer these (ones) or those (ones)?; **vengono Paolo e Folco:** ~ **da Roma, quello da Palermo** Paolo and Folco are coming: the latter from Rome, the former from Palermo; **quest'oggi** today.

ques'tore *sm* ≈ chief constable.

'questua *sf* collection (of alms).

ques'tura *sf* police headquarters *pl*.

qui *av* here; **da** o **di** ~ from here; **di** ~ **in avanti** from now on; **di** ~ **a poco/una settimana** in a little while/a week's time; ~ **dentro/sopra/vicino** in/up/near here; *vedi* **questo.**

quie'tanza [kwjeˈtantsa] *sf* receipt.

quie'tare *vt* to calm, soothe.

qui'ete *sf* quiet, quietness; calmness; stillness; peace.

qui'eto, a *ag* quiet; (*calmo*) calm, still; (*tranquillo*) quiet, calm; (*pacifico*) peaceful; (: *persona*) peaceable.

'quindi *av* then // *cong* therefore, so.

'quindici [ˈkwinditʃi] *num* fifteen.

quindi'cina [kwindiˈtʃina] *sf* (*serie*): **una** ~ (**di**) about fifteen; **fra una** ~ **di giorni** in a fortnight.

quin'quennio *sm* period of five years.

quin'tale *sm* quintal (*100 kg*).

'quinte *sfpl* (*TEATRO*) wings.

quin'tetto *sm* quintet(te).

'quinto, a *num* fifth.

'quorum *sm* quorum.

'quota *sf* (*ripartizione*) quota, share; (*rata*) instalment; (*AER*) height, altitude; (*IPPICA*)

odds pl; **prendere/perdere** ∼ (AER) to
gain/lose height o altitude.

quo'tare vt (BORSA) to quote; **quotazi'one**
sf quotation.

quotidi'ano, a ag daily; (banale) everyday
// sm (giornale) daily (paper).

quozi'ente [kwot'tsjɛnte] sm (MAT)
quotient; ∼ **d'intelligenza** intelligence
quotient, IQ.

R

ra'barbaro sm rhubarb.

'rabbia sf (ira) anger, rage; (accanimento,
furia) fury; (MED: idrofobia) rabies sg.

rab'bino sm rabbi.

rabbi'oso, a ag angry, furious; (facile
all'ira) quick-tempered; (forze, acqua etc)
furious, raging; (MED) rabid, mad.

rabbo'nire vt, ∼**rsi** vr to calm down.

rabbrivi'dire vi (2) to shudder, shiver.

rabbui'arsi vr to grow dark.

raccapez'zare [rakkapet'tsare] vt
(denaro) to scrape together; (senso) to
make out, understand; ∼**rsi** vr: **non** ∼**rsi**
to be at a loss.

raccapricci'ante [rakkaprit'tʃante] ag
horrifying.

raccatta'palle sm inv (SPORT) ballboy.

raccat'tare vt to pick up.

rac'chetta [rak'ketta] sf (per tennis)
racket; (per ping-pong) bat; ∼ **da neve**
snowshoe; ∼ **da sci** ski stick.

racchi'udere [rak'kjudere] vt to contain;
racchi'uso, a pp di **racchiudere**.

rac'cogliere [rak'kɔʎʎere] vt to collect;
(raccattare) to pick up; (frutti, fiori) to
pick, pluck; (AGR) to harvest;
(approvazione, voti) to win; (profughi) to
take in; ∼**rsi** vr to gather; (fig) to gather
one's thoughts; to meditate; **raccogli-
'mento** sm meditation; **raccogli'tore,
'trice** sm/f collector // sm (cartella)
folder, binder; **raccoglitore a fogli
mobili** loose-leaf binder.

rac'colto, a pp di **raccogliere** // ag
(rannicchiato) curled up; (pensoso)
thoughtful; (assorto) absorbed, engrossed
// sm (AGR) crop, harvest // sf collecting
q; collection; (AGR) harvesting
q, gathering q; harvest, crop; (adunata)
gathering.

raccoman'dare vt to recommend;
(affidare) to entrust; (lettera) to register;
∼**rsi a qd** to commend o.s. to sb; **mi
raccomando!** don't forget!; **raccoman-
'data** sf (anche: **lettera raccomandata**)
registered letter; **raccomandazi'one** sf
recommendation.

raccomo'dare vt (rassettare) to put in
order; (riparare) to repair, mend.

raccon'tare vt: ∼ **(a qd)** (dire) to tell
(sb); (narrare) to relate (to sb), tell (sb)
about; **rac'conto** sm telling q, relating q;
(fatto raccontato) story, tale.

raccorci'are [rakkor'tʃare] vt to shorten.

raccor'dare vt to link up, join; **rac'cordo**
sm (TECN: giunzione) connection, joint;

(AUT: di autostrada) slip road; **raccordo
anulare** (AUT) ring road.

ra'chitico, a, ci, che [ra'kitiko] ag
suffering from rickets; (fig) scraggy,
scrawny.

rachi'tismo [raki'tizmo] sm (MED) rickets
sg.

racimo'lare [ratʃimo'lare] vt (fig) to
scrape together, glean.

'rada sf (natural) harbour.

'radar sm radar.

raddol'cire [raddol'tʃire] vt to sweeten;
(fig: lenire) to ease, soothe; (: voce, colori)
to soften; ∼**rsi** vr (tempo) to grow milder.

raddoppi'are vt to double; (accrescere:
anche fig) to redouble, increase // vi to
double.

raddriz'zare [raddrit'tsare] vt to
straighten; (fig: correggere) to put straight,
correct.

'radere vt (barba) to shave off; (mento) to
shave; (fig: rasentare) to graze; to skim;
∼**rsi** vr to shave (o.s.); ∼ **al suolo** to
raze to the ground.

radi'ale ag radial.

radi'are vt to strike off.

radia'tore sm radiator.

radiazi'one [radjat'tsjone] sf (FISICA)
radiation; (cancellazione) striking off.

radi'cale ag radical // sm (LING) root.

ra'dicchio [ra'dikkjo] sm chicory.

ra'dice [ra'ditʃe] sf root.

'radio sf inv radio // sm (CHIM) radium;
radioattività sf radioactivity; **radioat-
'tivo, a** ag radioactive; **radiodiffusi'one**
sf (radio) broadcasting; **radiogra'fia** sf
radiography; (foto) X-ray photograph;
radiogra'fare vt to X-ray; **radi'ologo, a,
gi, ghe** sm/f radiologist.

radi'oso, a ag radiant.

radiostazi'one [radjostat'tsjone] sf radio
station.

'rado, a ag (capelli) sparse, thin; (visite)
infrequent; **di** ∼ rarely.

radu'nare vt, ∼**rsi** vr to gather,
assemble.

ra'dura sf clearing.

'rafano sm radish.

raffazzo'nare [raffattso'nare] vt to patch
up.

raf'fermo, a ag stale.

'raffica, che sf (METEOR) gust (of wind);
(di colpi: scarica) burst of gunfire.

raffigu'rare vt to represent.

raffi'nare vt to refine; **raffina'tezza** sf
refinement; **raffi'nato, a** ag refined;
raffine'ria sf refinery.

raffor'zare [raffor'tsare] vt to reinforce.

raffredda'mento sm cooling.

raffred'dare vt to cool; (fig) to dampen,
have a cooling effect on; ∼**rsi** vr to grow
cool o cold; (prendere raffreddore) to catch
a cold; (fig) to cool (off).

raffred'dore sm (MED) cold.

raf'fronto sm comparison.

'rafia sf (fibra) raffia.

ra'gazzo, a [ra'gattso] sm/f boy/girl; (fam:

fidanzato) boyfriend/girlfriend.

raggi'ante [rad'dʒante] *ag* radiant, shining.

'raggio ['raddʒo] *sm* (*di sole etc*) ray; (*MAT, distanza*) radius; (*di ruota etc*) spoke; ~ **d'azione** range; ~**i X** X-rays.

raggi'rare [raddʒi'rare] *vt* to take in, trick; **rag'giro** *sm* trick.

raggi'ungere [rad'dʒundʒere] *vt* to reach; (*persona: riprendere*) to catch up (with); (*bersaglio*) to hit; (*fig: meta*) to achieve; **raggi'unto, a** *pp di* **raggiungere**.

raggomito'larsi *vr* to curl up.

raggranel'lare *vt* to scrape together.

raggrin'zare [raggrin'tsare] *vt, vi* (2) (*anche:* ~**rsi**) to wrinkle.

raggrup'pare *vt* to group (together).

ragguagli'are [raggwaʎ'ʎare] *vt* (*paragonare*) to compare; (*informare*) to inform; **raggu'aglio** *sm* comparison; piece of information.

ragguar'devole *ag* (*degno di riguardo*) distinguished, notable; (*notevole: somma*) considerable.

'ragia ['radʒa] *sf* resin; **acqua** ~ turpentine.

ragiona'mento [radʒona'mento] *sm* reasoning *q*; arguing *q*; argument.

ragio'nare [radʒo'nare] *vi* (*usare la ragione*) to reason; (*discorrere*) ~ (**di**) to argue (about).

ragi'one [ra'dʒone] *sf* reason; (*dimostrazione, prova*) argument, reason; (*diritto*) right; **aver** ~ to be right; **aver** ~ **di qd** to get the better of sb; **in** ~ **di** at the rate of; to the amount of; according to; **a** *o* **con** ~ rightly, justly; **perdere la** ~ to become insane; (*fig*) to take leave of one's senses; **a ragion veduta** after due consideration.

ragione'ria [radʒone'ria] *sf* accountancy; accounts department.

ragio'nevole [radʒo'nevole] *ag* reasonable.

ragioni'ere, a [radʒo'njɛre] *sm/f* accountant.

ragli'are [raʎ'ʎare] *vi* to bray.

ragna'tela [raɲɲa'tela] *sf* cobweb, spider's web.

'ragno ['raɲɲo] *sm* spider.

ragù *sm inv* (*CUC*) meat sauce; stew.

RAI-TV [raiti'vu] *abbr f di Radio televisione italiana.*

rallegra'menti *smpl* congratulations.

ralle'grare *vt* to cheer up; ~**rsi** *vr* to cheer up; (*provare allegrezza*) to rejoice; ~**rsi con qd** to congratulate sb.

rallenta'mento *sm* slowing down; lessening, slackening.

rallen'tare *vt* to slow down; (*fig*) to lessen, slack // *vi* to slow down; ~**rsi** *vr* (*fig*) to lessen, slacken (off).

raman'zina [raman'dzina] *sf* lecture, telling-off.

'rame *sm* (*CHIM*) copper.

ramificazi'one [ramifikat'tsjone] *sf* ~~ramification~~

rammari'carsi *vr:* ~ (**di**) (*rincrescersi*) to be sorry (about), regret; (*lamentarsi*) to complain (about); **ram'marico, chi** *sm* regret.

rammen'dare *vt* to mend; (*calza*) to darn; **ram'mendo** *sm* mending *q*; darning *q*; mend; darn.

rammen'tare *vt* to remember, recall; (*richiamare alla memoria*): ~ **qc a qd** to remind sb of sth; ~**rsi** *vr:* ~**rsi (di qc)** to remember (sth).

rammol'lire *vt* to soften // *vi* (2) (*anche:* ~**rsi**) to go soft.

'ramo *sm* branch.

ramo'scello [ramoʃ'ʃɛllo] *sm* twig.

'rampa *sf* flight (of stairs); ~ **di lancio** launching pad.

rampi'cante *ag* (*BOT*) climbing.

ram'pino *sm* (*gancio*) hook; (*NAUT*) grapnel; (*fig*) pretext, excuse.

ram'pone *sm* harpoon; (*ALPINISMO*) crampon.

'rana *sf* frog.

'rancido, a ['rantʃido] *ag* rancid.

ran'core *sm* rancour, resentment.

ran'dagio, a, gi, gie *o* **ge** [ran'dadʒo] *ag* (*gatto, cane*) stray.

ran'dello *sm* club, cudgel.

'rango, ghi *sm* (*condizione sociale, MIL: riga*) rank.

rannicchi'arsi [rannik'kjarsi] *vr* to crouch, huddle.

rannuvo'larsi *vr* to cloud over, become overcast.

ra'nocchio [ra'nɔkkjo] *sm* (*edible*) frog.

'rantolo *sm* wheeze; (*di agonizzanti*) death rattle.

'rapa *sf* (*BOT*) turnip.

ra'pace [ra'patʃe] *ag* (*animale*) predatory; (*fig*) rapacious, grasping // *sm* bird of prey.

ra'pare *vt* (*capelli*) to crop, cut very short.

'rapida *sf vedi* **rapido**.

rapidità *sf* speed.

'rapido, a *ag* fast; (*esame, occhiata*) quick, rapid // *sm* (*FERR*) express (train) // *sf* (*di fiume*) rapid.

rapi'mento *sm* kidnapping; (*fig*) rapture.

ra'pina *sf* robbery; (*bottino*) loot; ~ **a mano armata** armed robbery; **rapi'nare** *vt* to rob; **rapina'tore, 'trice** *sm/f* robber.

ra'pire *vt* (*cose*) to steal; (*persone*) to kidnap; (*fig*) to enrapture, delight; **rapi-'tore, 'trice** *sm/f* kidnapper.

rappez'zare [rappet'tsare] *vt* to patch.

rappor'tare *vt* (*riferire*) to report; (*confrontare*) to compare; (*riprodurre*) to reproduce.

rap'porto *sm* (*resoconto*) report; (*legame*) relationship; (*MAT, TECN*) ratio; ~**i** *smpl* (*fra persone, paesi*) relations; ~**i sessuali** sexual intercourse *sg*.

rap'prendersi *vr* to coagulate, clot; (*latte*) to curdle.

rappre'saglia [rappre'saʎʎa] *sf* reprisal, retaliation.

rappresen'tante *sm/f* representative;

rappresen'tanza *sf* delegation, deputation; (*COMM: ufficio, sede*) agency.

rappresen'tare *vt* to represent; (*TEATRO*) to perform; **rappresenta'tivo, a** *ag* representative; **rappresentazi'one** *sf* representation; performing *q*; (*spettacolo*) performance.

rap'preso, a *pp di* **rapprendere**.

rapso'dia *sf* rhapsody.

rare'fare *vt*, **~rsi** *vr* to rarefy; **rare-'fatto, a** *pp di* **rarefare**.

rarità *sf inv* rarity.

'raro, a *ag* rare.

ra'sare *vt* (*barba etc*) to shave off; (*siepi, erba*) to trim, cut; **~rsi** *vr* to shave (o.s.).

raschi'are [ras'kjare] *vt* to scrape; (*macchia, fango*) to scrape off // *vi* to clear one's throat.

rasen'tare *vt* (*andar rasente*) to keep close to; (*sfiorare*) to skim along (*o* over); (*fig*) to border on.

ra'sente *prep*: **~ (a)** close to, very near.

'raso, a *pp di* **radere** // *ag* (*barba*) shaved; (*capelli*) cropped; (*con misure di capacità*) level; (*pieno: bicchiere*) full to the brim // *sm* (*tessuto*) satin; **~ terra** close to the ground; **un cucchiaio ~** a level spoonful.

ra'soio *sm* razor; **~ elettrico** electric shaver *o* razor.

ras'segna [ras'seɲɲa] *sf* (*MIL*) inspection, review; (*esame*) inspection; (*resoconto*) review, survey; (*pubblicazione letteraria etc*) review; (*mostra*) exhibition, show; **passare in ~** (*MIL*) to inspect, review.

rasse'gnare [rasseɲ'ɲare] *vt* to resign, relinquish; **~rsi** *vr* (*accettare*) to resign o.s.; **rassegnazi'one** *sf* resignation.

rassere'narsi *vr* (*tempo*) to clear up.

rasset'tare *vt* to tidy, put in order; (*aggiustare*) to repair, mend.

rassicu'rare *vt* to reassure.

rasso'dare *vt* to harden, stiffen; (*fig*) to strengthen, consolidate.

rassomigli'anza [rassomiʎ'ʎantsa] *sf* resemblance.

rassomigli'are [rassomiʎ'ʎare] *vi*: **~ a** to resemble, look like.

rastrel'lare *vt* to rake; (*fig: perlustrare*) to comb.

rastrelli'era *sf* rack; (*per piatti*) dishrack.

ras'trello *sm* rake.

'rata *sf* (*quota*) instalment; **pagare a ~e** to pay by instalments *o* on hire purchase; **rate'are, rateiz'zare** *vt* to divide into instalments.

ratifi'care *vt* (*DIR*) to ratify.

'ratto *sm* (*DIR*) abduction; (*ZOOL*) rat.

rattop'pare *vt* to patch; **rat'toppo** *sm* patching *q*; patch.

rattrap'pire *vt* to make stiff; **~rsi** *vr* to be stiff.

rattris'tare *vt* to sadden; **~rsi** *vr* to become sad.

'rauco, a, chi, che *ag* hoarse.

rava'nello *sm* radish.

ravi'oli *smpl* ravioli *sg*.

ravve'dersi *vr* to mend one's ways.

ravvici'nare [ravvitʃi'nare] *vt* (*avvicinare*): **~ qc a** to bring sth nearer to; (*: due tubi*) to bring closer together; (*riconciliare*) to reconcile, bring together.

ravvi'sare *vt* to recognize.

ravvi'vare *vt* to revive; (*fig*) to brighten up, enliven; **~rsi** *vr* to revive; to brighten up.

razio'cinio [ratsjo'tʃinjo] *sm* reasoning *q*; reason; (*buon senso*) common sense.

razio'nale [rattsjo'nale] *ag* rational.

razio'nare [rattsjo'nare] *vt* to ration.

razi'one [rat'tsjone] *sf* ration; (*porzione*) portion, share.

'razza ['rattsa] *sf* race; (*ZOOL*) breed; (*discendenza, stirpe*) stock, race; (*sorta*) sort, kind.

raz'zia [rat'tsia] *sf* raid, foray.

razzi'ale [rat'tsjale] *ag* racial.

raz'zismo [rat'tsizmo] *sm* racism, racialism.

raz'zista, i, e [rat'tsista] *ag, sm/f* racist, racialist.

'razzo ['raddzo] *sm* rocket.

razzo'lare [rattso'lare] *vi* (*galline*) to scratch about.

re *sm inv* (*sovrano*) king; (*MUS*) D; (*: solfeggiando la scala*) re.

rea'gire [rea'dʒire] *vi* to react.

re'ale *ag* real; (*di, da re*) royal // *sm*: **il ~** reality; **rea'lismo** *sm* realism; **rea'lista, i, e** *sm/f* realist; (*POL*) royalist.

realiz'zare [realid'dzare] *vt* (*progetto etc*) to realize, carry out; (*sogno, desiderio*) to realize, fulfil; (*scopo*) to achieve; (*COMM: titoli etc*) to realize; (*CALCIO etc*) to score; **~rsi** *vr* to be realized; **realizzazi'one** *sf* realization; fulfilment; achievement; **realizzazione scenica** stage production.

real'mente *av* really, actually.

realtà *sf inv* reality.

re'ato *sm* offence.

reat'tore *sm* (*FISICA*) reactor; (*AER: aereo*) jet; (*: motore*) jet engine.

reazio'nario, a [reattsjo'narjo] *ag* (*POL*) reactionary.

reazi'one [reat'tsjone] *sf* reaction.

'rebbio *sm* prong.

recapi'tare *vt* to deliver.

re'capito *sm* (*indirizzo*) address; (*consegna*) delivery.

re'care *vt* (*portare*) to bring; (*avere su di sé*) to carry, bear; (*cagionare*) to cause, bring; **~rsi** *vr* to go.

re'cedere [re'tʃedere] *vi* to withdraw.

recensi'one [retʃen'sjone] *sf* review; **recen'sire** *vt* to review; **recen'sore, e** *sm/f* reviewer.

re'cente [re'tʃɛnte] *ag* recent; **di ~** recently.

recessi'one [retʃes'sjone] *sf* (*ECON*) recession.

re'cidere [re'tʃidere] *vt* to cut off, chop off.

reci'divo, a [retʃi'divo] *sm/f* (*DIR*) second (*o* habitual) offender, recidivist.

re'cinto [re'tʃinto] *sm* enclosure; (*ciò che*

recinge) fence; surrounding wall.
recipi'ente [retʃi'pjɛnte] *sm* container.
re'ciproco, a, ci, che [re'tʃiproko] *ag* reciprocal.
re'ciso, a [re'tʃizo] *pp di* recidere.
'recita ['rɛtʃita] *sf* performance.
'recital ['rɛtʃital] *sm inv* recital.
reci'tare [retʃi'tare] *vt* (*poesia, lezione*) to recite; (*dramma*) to perform; (*ruolo*) to play *o* act (the part of); **recitazi'one** *sf* recitation; (*di attore*) acting.
recla'mare *vi* to complain // *vt* (*richiedere*) to demand, claim; (*necessitare*) to need, require.
ré'clame [re'klam] *sf inv* advertising *q*; advert(isement).
re'clamo *sm* complaint.
reclusi'one *sf* (*DIR*) imprisonment.
re'cluso, a *sm/f* prisoner.
'recluta *sf* recruit; **recluta'mento** *sm* recruitment; **reclu'tare** *vt* to recruit.
re'condito, a *ag* secluded; (*fig*) secret, hidden.
recriminazi'one [rekriminat'tsjone] *sf* recrimination.
recrude'scenza [rekrudeʃ'ʃɛntsa] *sf* fresh outbreak.
redargu'ire *vt* to rebuke.
re'datto, a *pp di* redigere; **redat'tore, 'trice** *sm/f* (*giornalista*) writer; sub-editor; (*di casa editrice*) editor; **redazi'one** *sf* writing; editing; (*sede*) editorial office(s); (*personale*) editorial staff; (*versione*) version.
reddi'tizio, a [reddi'tittsjo] *ag* profitable.
'reddito *sm* income; (*dello Stato*) revenue; (*di un capitale*) yield.
re'dento, a *pp di* redimere.
redenzi'one [reden'tsjone] *sf* redemption.
re'digere [re'didʒere] *vt* to write; (*contratto*) to draw up.
re'dimere *vt* to deliver; (*REL*) to redeem.
'redini *sfpl* reins.
redi'vivo, a *ag* returned to life, reborn.
'reduce ['rɛdutʃe] *ag:* ~ **da** returning from, back from // *sm/f* survivor.
'refe *sm* thread.
refe'rendum *sm inv* referendum.
refe'renza [refe'rɛntsa] *sf* reference.
re'ferto *sm* medical report.
refet'torio *sm* refectory.
refrat'tario, a *ag* refractory; (*fig*): **essere ~ alla matematica** to have no aptitude for mathematics.
refrige'rare [refridʒe'rare] *vt* to refrigerate; (*rinfrescare*) to cool, refresh; **refrigerazi'one** *sf* refrigeration.
rega'lare *vt* to give (as a present), make a present of.
re'gale *ag* regal.
re'galo *sm* gift, present.
re'gata *sf* regatta.
reg'gente [red'dʒɛnte] *sm/f* regent; **reg'genza** *sf* regency.
'reggere ['rɛddʒere] *vt* (*tenere*) to hold; (*sostenere*) to support, bear, hold up; (*portare*) to carry; bear; (*resistere*) to

withstand; (*dirigere: impresa*) to manage, run; (*governare*) to rule, govern; (*LING*) to take, be followed by // *vi* (*resistere*): ~ **a** to stand up to, hold out against; (*sopportare*): ~ **a** to stand; (*durare*) to last; ~**rsi** *vr* (*stare ritto*) to stand; (*fig: dominarsi*) to control o.s.; ~**rsi sulle gambe** *o* **in piedi** to stand up.
'reggia, ge ['rɛddʒa] *sf* royal palace.
reggi'calze [reddʒi'kaltse] *sm inv* suspender belt.
reggi'mento [reddʒi'mento] *sm* (*MIL*) regiment.
reggi'petto [reddʒi'pɛtto] *sm,* **reggi-'seno** [reddʒi'seno] *sm* bra.
re'gia, 'gie [re'dʒia] *sf* (*TV, CINEMA etc*) direction.
re'gime [re'dʒime] *sm* (*POL*) regime; (*DIR: aureo, patrimoniale etc*) system; (*MED*) diet; (*TECN*) (engine) speed; **essere a ~** to be on a diet.
re'gina [re'dʒina] *sf* queen.
'regio, a, gi, gie ['rɛdʒo] *ag* royal.
regio'nale [redʒo'nale] *ag* regional.
regi'one [re'dʒone] *sf* region; (*territorio*) region, district, area.
re'gista, i, e [re'dʒista] *sm/f* (*TV, CINEMA etc*) director.
regis'trare [redʒis'trare] *vt* (*AMM*) to register; (*COMM*) to enter; (*notare*) to note, take note of; (*canzone, conversazione, sog: strumento di misura*) to record; (*mettere a punto*) to adjust, regulate; **registra'tore** *sm* (*strumento di misura*) recorder, register; (*magnetofono*) tape recorder; (*classificatore*) folder; **registratore di cassa** cash register; **registrazi'one** *sf* recording; (*AMM*) registration; (*COMM*) entry.
re'gistro [re'dʒistro] *sm* (*libro*) register; ledger; logbook; (*DIR*) registry; (*MUS, TECN*) register.
re'gnare [reɲ'ɲare] *vi* to reign, rule; (*fig*) to reign.
'regno ['reɲɲo] *sm* kingdom; (*periodo*) reign; (*fig*) realm; **il ~ animale/vegetale** the animal/ vegetable kingdom; **il R~ Unito** the United Kingdom.
'regola *sf* rule; **a ~ d'arte** duly; perfectly; **in ~** in order.
regola'mento *sm* (*complesso di norme*) regulations *pl*; (*di debito*) settlement; ~ **di conti** (*fig*) settling of scores.
rego'lare *ag* regular; (*in regola: domanda*) in order, lawful // *vt* to regulate, control; (*apparecchio*) to adjust, regulate; (*questione, conto, debito*) to settle; ~**rsi** *vr* (*moderarsi*): ~**rsi nel bere/nello spendere** to control one's drinking/spending; (*comportarsi*) to behave, act; **regolarità** *sf inv* regularity.
'regolo *sm* ruler; ~ **calcolatore** slide rule.
reinte'grare *vt* to restore; (*in una carica*) to reinstate.
relatività *sf* relativity.
rela'tivo, a *ag* relative.

relazi'one [relat'tsjone] *sf* (*fra cose, persone*) relation(ship); (*resoconto*) report, account; **~i** *sfpl* (*conoscenze*) connections.

rele'gare *vt* to banish; (*fig*) to relegate.

religi'one [reli'dʒone] *sf* religion; (*rispetto*) veneration, reverence; **reli-gi'oso, a** *ag* religious // *sm/f* monk/nun.

re'liquia *sf* relic.

re'litto *sm* wreck; (*fig*) down-and-out.

re'mare *vi* to row.

remini'scenze [reminiʃ'ʃɛntse] *sfpl* reminiscences.

remissi'one *sf* remission; (*deferenza*) submissiveness, compliance.

remis'sivo, a *ag* submissive, compliant.

'remo *sm* oar.

re'moto, a *ag* remote.

'rendere *vt* (*ridare*) to return, give back; (*: saluto etc*) to return; (*produrre*) to yield, bring in; (*esprimere, tradurre*) to render; (*far diventare*): **~ qc possibile** to make sth possible; **~ la vista a qd** to restore sb's sight; **~ grazie a qd** to thank sb; **~rsi utile** to make o.s. useful; **~rsi conto di qc** to realize sth.

rendi'conto *sm* (*rapporto*) report, account; (*COMM*) statement of account.

rendi'mento *sm* (*reddito*) yield; (*di manodopera, TECN*) efficiency; (*capacità di produrre*) output; (*di studenti*) performance.

'rendita *sf* (*di individuo*) private o unearned income; (*COMM*) revenue; **~ annua** annuity.

'rene *sm* kidney.

'reni *sfpl* back *sg*.

reni'tente *ag* reluctant, unwilling; **~ ai consigli di qd** unwilling to follow sb's advice; **essere ~ alla leva** (*MIL*) to fail to report for military service.

'renna *sf* reindeer *inv*.

'Reno *sm*: **il ~** the Rhine.

'reo, a *sm/f* (*DIR*) offender.

re'parto *sm* department, section; (*MIL*) detachment.

repel'lente *ag* repulsive.

repen'taglio [repen'taʎʎo] *sm*: **mettere a ~** to jeopardize, risk.

repen'tino, a *ag* sudden, unexpected.

repe'ribile *ag* to be found, available.

re'perto *sm* (*ARCHEOLOGIA*) find; (*MED*) report.

reper'torio *sm* (*TEATRO*) repertory; (*elenco*) index, (alphabetical) list.

'replica, che *sf* repetition; reply, answer; (*obiezione*) objection; (*TEATRO, CINEMA*) repeat performance; (*copia*) replica.

repli'care *vt* (*ripetere*) to repeat; (*rispondere*) to answer, reply.

repressi'one *sf* repression.

re'presso, a *pp di* **reprimere**.

re'primere *vt* to suppress, repress.

re'pubblica, che *sf* republic; **repub-bli'cano, a** *ag, sm/f* republican.

repu'tare *vt* to consider, judge.

reputazi'one [reputat'tsjone] *sf* reputation.

'requie *sf* rest.

requi'sire *vt* to requisition.

requi'sito *sm* requirement.

requisizi'one [rekwizit'tsjone] *sf* requisition.

'resa *sf* (*l'arrendersi*) surrender; (*restituzione, rendimento*) return; **~ dei conti** rendering of accounts; (*fig*) day of reckoning.

resi'dente *ag* resident; **resi'denza** *sf* residence; **residenzi'ale** *ag* residential.

re'siduo, a *ag* residual, remaining // *sm* remainder; (*CHIM*) residue.

'resina *sf* resin.

resis'tente *ag* (*che resiste*): **~ a** resistant to; (*forte*) strong; (*duraturo*) long-lasting, durable; **~ al caldo** heat-resistant; **resis'tenza** *sf* resistance; (*di persona*) endurance, resistance.

re'sistere *vi* to resist; **~ a** (*assalto, tentazioni*) to resist; (*dolore, sog: pianta*) to withstand; (*non patir danno*) to be resistant to; **resis'tito, a** *pp di* **resistere**.

'reso, a *pp di* **rendere**.

reso'conto *sm* report, account.

respin'gente [respin'dʒɛnte] *sm* (*FERR*) buffer.

res'pingere [res'pindʒere] *vt* to drive back, repel; (*rifiutare*) to reject; (*INS: bocciare*) to fail; **res'pinto, a** *pp di* **respingere**.

respi'rare *vi* to breathe; (*fig*) to get one's breath; to breathe again // *vt* to breathe (in), inhale; **respira'tore** *sm* respirator; **respira'torio, a** *ag* respiratory; **respirazi'one** *sf* breathing; **respirazione artificiale** artificial respiration; **res'piro** *sm* breathing *q*; (*singolo atto*) breath; (*fig*) respite, rest; **mandare un respiro di sollievo** to give a sigh of relief.

respon'sabile *ag* responsible // *sm/f* person responsible; (*capo*) person in charge; **~ di** responsible for; (*DIR*) liable for; **responsabilità** *sf inv* responsibility; (*legale*) liability.

res'ponso *sm* answer.

'ressa *sf* crowd, throng.

res'tare *vi* (2) (*rimanere*) to remain, stay; (*diventare*): **~ orfano/cieco** to become o be left an orphan/become blind; (*trovarsi*): **~ sorpreso** to be surprised; (*avanzare*) to be left, remain; **~ d'accordo** to agree; **non resta più niente** there's nothing left; **restano pochi giorni** there are only a few days left.

restau'rare *vt* to restore; **restaura-zi'one** *sf* (*POL*) restoration; **res'tauro** *sm* (*di edifici etc*) restoration.

res'tio, a, 'tii, 'tie *ag* restive; (*persona*): **~ a** reluctant to.

restitu'ire *vt* to return, give back; (*energie, forze*) to restore.

'resto *sm* remainder, rest; (*denaro*) change; (*MAT*) remainder; **~i** *smpl* leftovers; (*di città, mortali*) remains; **del ~** moreover, besides.

res'tringere [res'trindʒere] *vt* to reduce; (*vestito*) to take in; (*stoffa*) to shrink; (*fig*) to restrict, limit; ~**rsi** *vr* (*strada*) to narrow; (*stoffa*) to shrink; (*persone*) to draw closer together; **restrizi'one** *sf* restriction.

'**rete** *sf* net; (*fig*) trap, snare; (*di recinzione*) wire netting; (*AUT, FERR, di spionaggio etc*) network; **segnare una** ~ (*CALCIO*) to score a goal.

reti'cente [reti'tʃɛnte] *ag* reticent.

retico'lato *sm* grid; (*rete metallica*) wire netting.

'**retina** *sf* (*ANAT*) retina.

re'torico, a, ci, che *ag* rhetorical // *sf* rhetoric.

retribu'ire *vt* to pay; (*premiare*) to reward; **retribuzi'one** *sf* payment; reward.

re'trivo, a *ag* (*fig*) reactionary.

'**retro** *sm inv* back // *av* (*dietro*): **vedi** ~ see over(leaf).

retro'cedere [retro'tʃɛdere] *vi* (2) to withdraw // *vt* (*CALCIO*) to relegate; (*MIL*) to degrade.

retroda'tare *vt* (*AMM*) to backdate.

re'trogrado, a *ag* (*fig*) reactionary, backward-looking.

retrogu'ardia *sf* (*MIL*) rearguard.

retro'marcia [retro'martʃa] *sf* (*AUT*) reverse; (: *dispositivo*) reverse gear.

retrospet'tivo, a *ag* retrospective.

retrovi'sore *sm* (*AUT*) driving mirror.

'**retta** *sf* (*MAT*) straight line; (*di convitto*) charge for bed and board; (*fig: ascolto*): **dar** ~ **a** to listen to, pay attention to.

rettango'lare *ag* rectangular.

ret'tangolo, a *ag* right-angled // *sm* rectangle.

ret'tifica, che *sf* rectification, correction.

rettifi'care *vt* (*curva*) to straighten; (*fig*) to rectify, correct.

'**rettile** *sm* reptile.

retti'lineo, a *ag* rectilinear; (*fig: condotta*) upright, honest.

retti'tudine *sf* rectitude, uprightness.

'**retto, a** *pp di* **reggere** // *ag* straight; (*MAT*): **angolo** ~ right angle; (*onesto*) honest, upright; (*giusto, esatto*) correct, proper, right.

ret'tore *sm* (*REL*) rector; (*di università*) ≈ chancellor.

reuma'tismo *sm* rheumatism.

reve'rendo, a *ag*: **il** ~ **padre Belli** the Reverend Father Belli.

rever'sibile *ag* reversible.

revisio'nare *vt* (*componimento*) to revise; (*conti*) to audit; (*TECN*) to overhaul, service; (*DIR: processo*) to review.

revisi'one *sf* revision; auditing *q*; audit; servicing *q*; overhaul; review.

revi'sore *sm*: ~ **di conti/bozze** auditor/proofreader.

'**revoca** *sf* revocation.

revo'care *vt* to revoke.

re'volver *sm inv* revolver.

riabili'tare *vt* to rehabilitate; (*fig*) to restore to favour; **riabilitazi'one** *sf* rehabilitation.

rial'zare [rial'tsare] *vt* to raise, lift; (*alzare di più*) to heighten, raise; (*aumentare: prezzi*) to increase, raise // *vi* (2) (*prezzi*) to rise, increase; **ri'alzo** *sm* (*di prezzi*) increase, rise; (*sporgenza*) rise.

ria'prire *vt*, ~**rsi** *vr* to reopen, open again.

ri'armo *sm* (*MIL*) rearmament.

rias'setto *sm* (*di stanza etc*) rearrangement; (*ordinamento*) reorganization.

rias'sumere *vt* (*riprendere*) to resume; (*impiegare di nuovo*) to re-employ; (*sintetizzare*) to summarize; **rias'sunto, a** *pp di* **riassumere** // *sm* summary.

ria'vere *vt* to have again; (*avere indietro*) to get back; (*riacquistare*) to recover; ~**rsi** *vr* to recover.

riba'dire *vt* (*fig*) to confirm.

ri'balta *sf* flap; (*TEATRO: proscenio*) front of the stage; (: *apparecchio d'illuminazione*) footlights *pl*; (*fig*) limelight.

ribal'tabile *ag* (*sedile*) tip-up.

ribal'tare *vt*, *vi* (2) (*anche*: ~**rsi**) to turn over, tip over.

ribas'sare *vt* to lower, bring down // *vi* (2) to come down, fall; **ri'basso** *sm* reduction, fall.

ri'battere *vt* to return, hit back; (*confutare*) to refute // *vi* to retort; ~ **su qc** (*fig*) to harp on about sth.

ribel'larsi *vr*: ~ (**a**) to rebel (against); **ri'belle** *ag* (*soldati*) rebel; (*ragazzo*) rebellious // *sm/f* rebel; **ribelli'one** *sf* rebellion.

'**ribes** *sm inv* currant; redcurrant; ~ **nero** blackcurrant.

ribol'lire *vi* (*fermentare*) to ferment; (*fare bolle*) to bubble, boil; (*fig*) to seethe.

ri'brezzo [ri'breddzo] *sm* disgust, loathing; **far** ~ **a** to disgust.

ribut'tante *ag* disgusting, revolting.

rica'dere *vi* (2) to fall again; (*scendere a terra, fig: nel peccato etc*) to fall back; (*vestiti, capelli etc*) to hang (down); (*riversarsi: fatiche, colpe*): ~ **su** to fall on; **rica'duta** *sf* (*MED*) relapse.

rical'care *vt* (*disegni*) to trace; (*fig*) to follow faithfully.

rica'mare *vt* to embroider.

ricambi'are *vt* to change again; (*contraccambiare*) to repay, return; **ri'cambio** *sm* exchange, return; (*FISIOL*) metabolism; **ricambi** *smpl*, **pezzi di ricambio** spare parts.

ri'camo *sm* embroidery.

ricapito'lare *vt* to recapitulate, sum up.

ricat'tare *vt* to blackmail; **ricat'tore, 'trice** *sm/f* blackmailer; **ri'catto** *sm* blackmail.

rica'vare *vt* (*estrarre*) to draw out, extract; (*ottenere*) to obtain, gain; **ri'cavo** *sm* proceeds *pl*.

ric'chezza [rik'kettsa] *sf* wealth; (*fig*) richness; ~**e** *sfpl* (*beni*) wealth *sg*, riches.

'**riccio, a** ['rittʃo] *ag* curly // *sm* (*ZOOL*) hedgehog; (: *anche*: ~ **di mare**) sea

urchin; **'ricciolo** sm curl; **ricci'uto, a** ag
curly.

'ricco, a, chi, che ag rich; (persona,
paese) rich, wealthy // sm/f rich
man/woman; **i ~chi** the rich; **~ di** full
of; rich in.

ri'cerca, che [ri'tʃerka] sf search;
(indagine) investigation, inquiry; (studio):
la ~ research; **una ~** piece of research.

ricer'care [ritʃer'kare] vt (cercare con
cura) to look for, search for; (indagare) to
investigate; (tentare di scoprire: verità etc)
to try to find; **ricer'cato, a** ag
(apprezzato) much sought-after; (affettato)
studied, affected // sm (POLIZIA) wanted
man.

ri'cetta [ri'tʃetta] sf (MED) prescription;
(CUC) recipe.

ricettazi'one [ritʃettat'tsjone] sf (DIR)
receiving (stolen goods).

ri'cevere [ri'tʃevere] vt to receive;
(stipendio, lettera) to get, receive;
(accogliere: ospite) to welcome; (vedere:
cliente, rappresentante etc) to see // vi to
receive visitors; to see clients etc; **ricevi-
'mento** sm receiving q; (accoglienza)
welcome, reception; (trattenimento) reception; **ricevi'tore** sm (TECN) receiver;
ricevitore delle imposte tax collector;
rice'vuta sf receipt; **ricezi'one** sf (RADIO,
TV) reception.

richia'mare [rikja'mare] vt (chiamare
indietro, ritelefonare) to call back; (ambasciatore, truppe) to recall; (rimproverare)
to reprimand; (attirare) to attract, draw;
(riportare) to cite; **~rsi a** (riferirsi a) to
refer to; **~ qc alla mente** to recall sth;
richi'amo sm call; (MIL, di ambasciatore)
recall; (attrazione) attraction, call, appeal.

richi'edere [ri'kjedere] vt to ask again
for; (chiedere indietro): **~ qc** to ask for sth
back; (chiedere: per sapere) to ask; (: per
avere) to ask for; (AMM: documenti) to
apply for; (esigere) to need, require; **richi'esto, a** pp di **richiedere** // sf (domanda) request; (AMM) application, request;
(esigenza) demand, request; **a richiesta**
on request.

'ricino ['ritʃino] sm: **olio di ~** castor oil.

ricognizi'one [rikoɲɲit'tsjone] sf (MIL)
reconnaissance; (DIR) recognition,
acknowledgement.

ricominci'are [rikomin'tʃare] vt, vi to
start again, begin again.

ricom'pensa sf reward.

ricompen'sare vt to reward.

riconcili'are [rikontʃi'ljare] vt to
reconcile; **~rsi** vr to be reconciled;
riconciliazi'one sf reconciliation.

ricono'scente [rikonoʃ'ʃente] ag grateful;
ricono'scenza sf gratitude.

rico'noscere [riko'noʃʃere] vt to
recognize; (DIR: figlio, debito) to
acknowledge; (ammettere: errore) to
admit, acknowledge; (MIL) to reconnoitre;
riconosci'mento sm recognition,
acknowledgement; (identificazione)

identification; **riconosci'uto, a** pp di
riconoscere.

rico'prire vt to re-cover; (coprire) to
cover; (occupare: carica) to hold.

ricor'dare vt to remember, recall;
(richiamare alla memoria): **~ qc a qd** to
remind sb of sth; **~rsi** vr: **~rsi (di)** to
remember; **~rsi di qc/di aver fatto** to
remember sth/having done.

ri'cordo sm memory; (regalo) keepsake,
souvenir; (di viaggio) souvenir; **~i** smpl
(memorie) memoirs.

ricor'rente ag recurrent, recurring;
ricor'renza sf recurrence; (festività)
anniversary.

ri'correre vi (2) (ripetersi) to recur; **~ a**
(rivolgersi) to turn to; (: DIR) to appeal to;
(servirsi di) to have recourse to; **ri'corso,
a** pp di **ricorrere** // sm recurrence; (DIR)
appeal; **far ricorso a = ricorrere a**.

ricostitu'ire vt to re-establish,
reconstitute; (MED) to restore.

ricostru'ire vt (casa) to rebuild; (fatti) to
reconstruct; **ricostruzi'one** sf rebuilding
q; reconstruction.

ri'cotta sf soft white unsalted cheese made
from sheep's milk.

ricove'rare vt to give shelter to; **~ qd in
ospedale** to admit sb to hospital.

ri'covero sm shelter, refuge; admission
(to hospital); (per vecchi, indigenti) home.

ricre'are vt to recreate; (rinvigorire) to
restore; (fig: distrarre) to amuse.

ricreazi'one [rikreat'tsjone] sf
recreation, entertainment; (INS) break.

ri'credersi vr to change one's mind.

ricupe'rare vt (rientrare in possesso di) to
recover, get back; (tempo perduto) to
make up for; (NAUT) to salvage; (:
naufraghi) to rescue; (delinquente) to
rehabilitate.

ricu'sare vt to refuse.

ridacchi'are [ridak'kjare] vi to snigger.

ri'dare vt to return, give back.

'ridere vi to laugh; (deridere, beffare): **~
di** to laugh at, make fun of.

ri'detto, a pp di **ridire**.

ri'dicolo, a ag ridiculous, absurd.

ridimensio'nare vt to reorganize; (fig) to
see in the right perspective.

ri'dire vt to repeat; (criticare) to find fault
with; to object to; **trova sempre
qualcosa da ~** he always manages to
find fault.

ridon'dante ag redundant.

ri'dotto, a pp di **ridurre**.

ri'durre vt (anche CHIM, MAT) to reduce;
(prezzo, spese) to cut, reduce; (accorciare:
vestito) to shorten; (: opera letteraria) to
abridge; (: RADIO, TV) to adapt; **ridursi** vr
(diminuirsi) to be reduced, shrink; **ridursi
a** to be reduced to; **ridursi pelle e ossa**
to be reduced to skin and bone; **ridu-
zi'one** sf reduction; abridgement;
adaptation.

riempi'mento sm filling.

riem'pire vt to fill (up); (modulo) to fill in
o out; **~rsi** vr to fill (up); (mangiare

troppo) to stuff o.s.; ~ **qc di** to fill sth (up) with; **riempi'tivo, a** *ag* filling // *sm* (*anche fig*) filler.

rien'tranza [rien'trantsa] *sf* recess; indentation.

rien'trare *vi* (2) (*entrare di nuovo*) to go (*o* come) back in; (*tornare*) to return; (*fare una rientranza*) to go in, curve inwards; to be indented; (*riguardare*) ~ **in** to be included among, form part of; **ri'entro** *sm* (*ritorno*) return; (*anche ASTR*) re-entry.

riepilo'gare *vt* to summarize // *vi* to recapitulate.

ri'fare *vt* to do again; (*riparare*) to repair; (*imitare*) to imitate, copy; ~**rsi** *vr* (*ristabilirsi: malato*) to recover; (: *tempo*) to clear up; (*ricominciare*) to start again; (*vendicarsi*) to get even; (*risarcirsi*): ~**rsi di** to make up for; ~ **il letto** to make the bed; ~**rsi una vita** to make a new life for o.s.; **ri'fatto, a** *pp di* **rifare**.

riferi'mento *sm* reference; **in** *o* **con** ~ **a** with reference to.

rife'rire *vt* (*riportare*) to report; (*ascrivere*): ~ **qc a** to attribute sth to // *vi* to make a report; ~**rsi** *vr*: ~**rsi a** to refer to.

rifi'nire *vt* to finish off, put the finishing touches to; **rifini'tura** *sf* finish; finishing touches *pl*.

rifiu'tare *vt* to refuse; ~ **di fare** to refuse to do; **rifi'uto** *sm* refusal; **rifiuti** *smpl* (*spazzatura*) rubbish *sg*, refuse *sg*.

riflessi'one *sf* (*FISICA, meditazione*) reflection; (*il pensare*) thought, reflection; (*osservazione*) remark.

rifles'sivo, a *ag* (*persona*) thoughtful, reflective; (*LING*) reflexive.

ri'flesso, a *pp di* **riflettere** // *sm* (*di luce, rispecchiamento*) reflection; (*FISIOL*) reflex; **di** *o* **per** ~ indirectly.

ri'flettere *vt* to reflect // *vi* to think; ~**rsi** *vr* to be reflected; ~ **su** to think about.

riflet'tore *sm* reflector; (*proiettore*) floodlight; searchlight.

ri'flusso *sm* flowing back; (*della marea*) ebb.

ri'fondere *vt* (*rimborsare*) to refund, repay.

ri'forma *sf* reform; (*MIL*) declaration of unfitness for service; discharge (*on health grounds*); **la R**~ (*REL*) the Reformation.

rifor'mare *vt* to re-form; (*cambiare, innovare*) to reform; (*MIL: recluta*) to declare unfit for service; (: *soldato*) to invalid out, discharge; **riforma'torio** *sm* (*DIR*) approved school.

riforni'mento *sm* supplying; providing; restocking; ~**i** *smpl* supplies, provisions.

rifor'nire *vt* (*provvedere*): ~ **di** to supply *o* provide with; (*fornire di nuovo: casa etc*) to restock.

ri'frangere [ri'frandʒere] *vt* to refract; **ri'fratto, a** *pp di* **rifrangere**; **rifrazi'one** *sf* refraction.

rifug'gire [rifud'dʒire] *vi* (2) to escape again; (*fig*): ~ **da** to shun.

rifugi'arsi [rifu'dʒarsi] *vr* to take refuge; **rifugi'ato, a** *sm/f* refugee.

ri'fugio [ri'fudʒo] *sm* refuge, shelter; ~ **antiaereo** air-raid shelter.

'riga, ghe *sf* line; (*striscia*) stripe; (*di persone, cose*) line, row; (*regolo*) ruler; (*scriminatura*) parting; **mettersi in** ~ to line up; **a** ~**ghe** (*foglio*) lined; (*vestito*) striped.

ri'gagnolo [ri'gaɲɲolo] *sm* rivulet.

ri'gare *vt* (*foglio*) to rule // *vi*: ~ **diritto** (*fig*) to toe the line.

rigatti'ere *sm* junk dealer.

riget'tare [ridʒet'tare] *vt* (*gettare indietro*) to throw back; (*fig: respingere*) to reject; (*vomitare*) to bring *o* throw up; **ri'getto** *sm* (*anche MED*) rejection.

rigidità [ridʒidi'ta] *sf* rigidity; stiffness; severity, rigours *pl*; strictness; ~ **cadaverica** rigor mortis.

'rigido, a [ˈridʒido] *ag* rigid, stiff; (*membro etc: indurito*) stiff; (*METEOR*) harsh, severe; (*fig*) strict.

rigi'rare [ridʒi'rare] *vt* to turn; (*ripercorrere*) to go round; (*fig: persona*) to get round; ~**rsi** *vr* to turn round; (*nel letto*) to turn over; ~ **il discorso** to change the subject; **ri'giri** *smpl* (*fig*) tricks.

'rigo, ghi *sm* line; (*MUS*) staff, stave.

rigogli'oso, a [rigoʎ'ʎoso] *ag* (*anche fig*) exuberant.

ri'gonfio, a [ri'gonfjo] *ag* swollen.

ri'gore *sm* (*METEOR*) harshness, rigours *pl*; (*fig*) severity, strictness; (*anche*: **calcio di** ~) penalty; **di** ~ compulsory; **a rigor di termini** strictly speaking; **rigo'roso, a** *ag* (*severo: persona*) strict, stern; (: *disciplina*) rigorous, strict; (*preciso*) rigorous.

rigover'nare *vt* to wash (up).

riguar'dare *vt* to look at again; (*considerare*) to regard, consider; (*concernere*) to regard, concern; ~**rsi** *vr* (*aver cura di sé*) to look after o.s.; ~**rsi da** to beware of, keep away from.

rigu'ardo *sm* (*attenzione*) care; (*considerazione*) regard, respect; ~ **a** concerning, with regard to; **non aver** ~**i nell'agire/nel parlare** to act/speak freely.

rilasci'are [rilaʃ'ʃare] *vt* (*rimettere in libertà*) to release; (*AMM: documenti*) to issue; **ri'lascio** *sm* release; issue.

rilas'sare *vt* to relax; ~**rsi** *vr* to relax; (*moralità*) to become slack.

rile'gare *vt* (*libro*) to bind; **rilega'tura** *sf* binding.

ri'leggere [ri'leddʒere] *vt* to reread, read again; (*rivedere*) to read over.

ri'lento: a ~ *av* slowly.

rileva'mento *sm* (*topografico, statistico*) survey; (*NAUT*) bearing.

rile'vante *ag* considerable; important.

rile'vare *vt* (*ricavare*) to find; (*notare*) to notice; (*mettere in evidenza*) to point out; (*venire a conoscere: notizia*) to learn; (*raccogliere: dati*) to gather, collect; (*TOPO-*

GRAFIA) to survey; (MIL) to relieve; (COMM) to take over.

rili'evo *sm* (ARTE, GEO) relief; (fig: rilevanza) importance; (osservazione) point, remark; (TOPOGRAFIA) survey; **dar** ~ **a** o **mettere in** ~ **qc** (fig) to bring sth out, highlight sth.

rilut'tante *ag* reluctant; **rilut'tanza** *sf* reluctance.

'rima *sf* rhyme.

riman'dare *vt* to send again; (restituire, rinviare) to send back, return; (differire): ~ **qc (a)** to postpone sth o put sth off (till); (fare riferimento): ~ **qd a** to refer sb to; **essere rimandato** (INS) to have to repeat one's exams; **ri'mando** *sm* (rinvio) return; (dilazione) postponement; (riferimento) cross-reference.

rima'nente *ag* remaining // *sm* rest, remainder; **i** ~**i** (persone) the rest of them, the others; **rima'nenza** *sf* rest, remainder; **rimanenze** *sfpl* (COMM) unsold stock *sg*.

rima'nere *vi* (2) (restare) to remain, stay; (avanzare) to be left, remain; (restare stupito) to be amazed; (restare, mancare): **rimangono poche settimane a Pasqua** there are only a few weeks left till Easter; **rimane da vedere se** it remains to be seen whether; (diventare): ~ **vedovo** to be left a widower; (trovarsi): ~ **confuso/sorpreso** to be confused/surprised.

rimar'chevole [rimar'kevole] *ag* remarkable.

ri'mare *vt, vi* to rhyme.

rimargi'nare [rimardʒi'nare] *vt, vi* (anche: ~**rsi**) to heal.

ri'masto, a *pp di* **rimanere**.

rima'sugli [rima'suʎʎi] *smpl* leftovers.

rimbal'zare [rimbal'tsare] *vi* to bounce back, rebound; (proiettile) to ricochet; **rim'balzo** *sm* rebound; ricochet.

rimbam'bire *vi* (2) to be in one's dotage; (rincretinire) to grow foolish.

rimboc'care *vt* (orlo) to turn up; (coperta) to tuck in; (maniche, pantaloni) to turn o roll up.

rimbom'bare *vi* to resound.

rimbor'sare *vt* to pay back, repay; **rim'borso** *sm* repayment.

rimedi'are *vi* (2): ~ **a** to remedy // *vt* (fam: procurarsi) to get o scrape together.

ri'medio *sm* (medicina) medicine; (cura, fig) remedy, cure.

rimesco'lare *vt* to mix well, stir well; (carte) to shuffle; **sentirsi** ~ **il sangue** (per paura) to feel one's blood run cold; (per rabbia) to feel one's blood boil.

ri'messa *sf* (locale: per veicoli) garage; (: per aerei) hangar; (COMM: di merce) consignment; (: di denaro) remittance; (CALCIO: anche: ~ **in gioco**) throw-in; **vendere a** ~ (COMM) to sell at a loss.

ri'messo, a *pp di* **rimettere**.

ri'mettere *vt* (mettere di nuovo) to put back; (indossare di nuovo): ~ **qc** to put sth back on, put sth on again; (restituire) to

return, give back; (affidare) to entrust; (: decisione) to refer; (condonare) to remit; (COMM: merci) to deliver; (: denaro) to remit; (vomitare) to bring up; (rimandare): ~ **qc (a)** to postpone sth o put sth off (until); ~**rsi al bello** (tempo) to clear up; ~**rsi in salute** to get better, recover one's health.

'rimmel *sm inv* ® mascara.

rimoder'nare *vt* to modernize.

rimon'tare *vt* (meccanismo) to reassemble; (scale) to go up again; (SPORT) to overtake // *vi* (2) to go back up; ~ **a** (risalire a) to date o go back to; ~ **a cavallo** to remount.

rimorchi'are [rimor'kjare] *vt* to tow; **rimorchia'tore** *sm* (NAUT) tug(boat).

ri'morchio [ri'mɔrkjo] *sm* tow; (traino) trailer.

ri'morso *sm* remorse.

rimozi'one [rimot'tsjone] *sf* removal; (da un impiego) dismissal; (PSIC) repression.

rim'pasto *sm* (POL) reshuffle.

rimpatri'are *vi* (2) to return home // *vt* to repatriate; **rim'patrio** *sm* repatriation.

rimpi'angere [rim'pjandʒere] *vt* to regret; (persona) to miss; **rimpi'anto, a** *pp di* **rimpiangere** // *sm* regret.

rimpiat'tino *sm* hide-and-seek.

rimpiaz'zare [rimpjat'tsare] *vt* to replace.

rimpicco'lire *vt* to make smaller // *vi* (2) (anche: ~**rsi**) to become smaller.

rimpin'zare [rimpin'tsare] *vt*: ~ **di** to cram o stuff with.

rimprove'rare *vt* to rebuke, reprimand; **rim'provero** *sm* rebuke, reprimand.

rimugi'nare [rimudʒi'nare] *vt* (fig) to turn over in one's mind.

rimunerazi'one [rimunerat'tsjone] *sf* remuneration; (premio) reward.

rimu'overe *vt* to remove; (destituire) to dismiss; (fig: distogliere) to dissuade.

Rinasci'mento [rinaʃʃi'mento] *sm*: **il** ~ the Renaissance.

ri'nascita [ri'naʃʃita] *sf* rebirth, revival.

rincal'zare [rinkal'tsare] *vt* (sostenere) to support, prop up; (lenzuola) to tuck in; **rin'calzo** *sm* support, prop; (rinforzo) reinforcement; (SPORT) reserve (player); **rincalzi** *smpl* (MIL) reserves.

rinca'rare *vt* to increase the price of // *vi* (2) to go up, become more expensive.

rinca'sare *vi* (2) to go home.

rinchi'udere [rin'kjudere] *vt* to shut (o lock) up; ~**rsi** *vr*: ~**rsi in** to shut o.s. up in; ~**rsi in se stesso** to withdraw into o.s.; **rinchi'uso, a** *pp di* **rinchiudere**.

rin'correre *vt* to chase, run after; **rin'corso, a** *pp di* **rincorrere** // *sf* short run.

rin'crescere [rin'kreʃʃere] *vb impers* (2): **mi rincresce che/di non poter fare** I'm sorry that/I can't do, I regret that/being unable to do; **rincresci'mento** *sm* regret; **rincresci'uto, a** *pp di* **rincrescere**.

rincu'lare *vi* (2) to draw back; (arma) to recoil.

rinfacci'are [rinfat'tʃare] vt (fig): ~ qc a qd to throw sth in sb's face.

rinfor'zare [rinfor'tsare] vt to reinforce, strengthen // vi (2) (anche: ~rsi) to grow stronger; **rin'forzo** sm reinforcement; (appoggio: anche fig) support; **rinforzi** smpl (MIL) reinforcements.

rinfran'care vt to encourage, reassure.

rinfres'care vt (atmosfera, temperatura) to cool (down); (abito, pareti) to freshen up // vi (2) (tempo) to grow cooler; ~**rsi** vr (ristorarsi) to refresh o.s.; (lavarsi) to freshen up; **rin'fresco, schi** sm (festa) party; **rinfreschi** smpl refreshments.

rin'fusa sf: **alla** ~ in confusion, higgledy-piggledy.

ringhi'are [rin'gjare] vi to growl, snarl.

ringhi'era [rin'gjɛra] sf railing; (delle scale) banister(s pl).

ringiova'nire [rindʒova'nire] vt (sog: vestito, acconciatura etc): ~ qd to make sb look younger; (: vacanze etc) te rejuvenate // vi (2) (anche: ~rsi) to become (o look) younger.

ringrazia'menti [ringrattsja'menti] smpl thanks.

ringrazi'are [ringrat'tsjare] vt to thank; ~ qd di qc to thank sb for sth.

rinne'gare vt (fede) to renounce; (figlio) to disown, repudiate; **rinne'gato, a** sm/f renegade.

rinno'vare vt to renew; (ripetere) to repeat, renew; ~**rsi** vr (fenomeno) to be repeated, recur; **rin'novo** sm renewal; recurrence.

rinnova'mento sm renewal.

rinoce'ronte [rinotʃe'ronte] sm rhinoceros.

rino'mato, a ag renowned, celebrated.

rinsal'dare vt to strengthen.

rinsa'vire vi (2) to come to one's senses.

rintoc'care vi (campana) to toll; (orologio) to strike.

rintracci'are [rintrat'tʃare] vt to track down.

rintro'nare vi to boom, roar // vt (assordare) to deafen; (stordire) to stun.

rintuz'zare [rintut'tsare] vt (fig: sentimento) to check, repress; (: accusa) to refute.

ri'nuncia [ri'nuntʃa] etc = **rinunzia** etc.

ri'nunzia [ri'nuntsja] sf renunciation.

rinunzi'are [rinun'tsjare] vi: ~ a to give up, renounce.

rinve'nire vt to find, recover; (scoprire) to discover, find out // vi (2) (riprendere i sensi) to come round; (riprendere l'aspetto naturale) to revive.

rinvi'are vt (rimandare indietro) to send back, return; (differire): ~ qc (a) to postpone sth o put sth off (till); to adjourn sth (till); (fare un rimando): ~ qd a to refer sb to.

rinvigo'rire vt to strengthen.

rin'vio, 'vii sm (rimando) return; (differimento) postponement; (: di seduta) adjournment; (in un testo) cross-reference.

ri'one sm district, quarter.

riordi'nare vt (rimettere in ordine) to tidy; (riorganizzare) to reorganize.

riorganiz'zare [riorganid'dzare] vt to reorganize.

ripa'gare vt to repay.

ripa'rare vt (proteggere) to protect, defend; (correggere: male, torto) to make up for; (: errore) to put right; (aggiustare) to repair // vi (mettere rimedio): ~ a to make up for; ~**rsi** vr (rifugiarsi) to take refuge o shelter; **riparazi'one** sf (di un torto) reparation; (di guasto, scarpe) repairing q; repair; (risarcimento) compensation.

ri'paro sm (protezione) shelter, protection; (rimedio) remedy.

ripar'tire vt (dividere) to divide up; (distribuire) to share out // vi (2) to set off again; to leave again.

ripas'sare vi (2) to come (o go) back // vt (scritto, lezione) to go over (again).

ripen'sare vi to think; (cambiare pensiero) to change one's mind; (tornare col pensiero): ~ a to recall.

ripercu'otere vt (luce) to reflect, throw back; (suono) to throw back; ~**rsi** vr (luce) to be reflected; (suoni) to reverberate; (fig): ~**rsi su** to have repercussions on.

ripercussi'one sf reflection; reverberation; ~**i** sfpl (fig) repercussions.

ri'petere vt to repeat; (ripassare) to go over; **ripetizi'one** sf repetition; (di lezione) revision; **ripetizioni** sfpl (INS) private tutoring o coaching sg.

ripi'ano sm (GEO) terrace; (di mobile) shelf.

'ripido, a ag steep.

ripie'gare vt to refold; (piegare più volte) to fold (up) // vi (MIL) to retreat, fall back; ~**rsi** vr to bend; **ripi'ego, ghi** sm expedient; **vivere di ripieghi** to live by one's wits.

ripi'eno, a ag full; (CUC) stuffed; (: panino) filled // sm (CUC) stuffing.

ri'porre vt (porre al suo posto) to put back, replace; (mettere via) to put away; (fiducia, speranza): ~ qc in qd to place o put sth in sb.

ripor'tare vt (portare indietro) to bring (o take) back; (riferire) to report; (citare) to quote; (ricevere) to receive, get; (MAT) to carry; (COMM) to carry forward; ~**rsi a** (anche fig) to go back to; (riferirsi a) to refer to; ~ **danni** to suffer damage.

ripo'sare vt (bicchiere, valigia) to put down; (dare sollievo) to rest // vi to rest; ~**rsi** vr to rest; **ri'poso** sm rest; (MIL): **riposo!** at ease!; **a riposo** (in pensione) retired; **giorno di riposo** day off.

ripos'tiglio [ripos'tiλλo] sm lumber-room; hiding-place.

ri'posto, a pp di **riporre**.

ri'prendere vt (prigioniero, fortezza) to recapture; (prendere indietro) to take back; (ricominciare: lavoro) to resume; (andare a prendere) to fetch, come back for; (assumere di nuovo: impiegati) to take on again, re-employ; (*rimproverare*) to tell off; (*restringere: abito*) to take in; (*CINEMA*) to shoot // *vi* to revive; **~rsi** *vr* to recover; (*correggersi*) to correct o.s.; **ri'preso, a** *pp di* **riprendere** // *sf* recapture; resumption; (*economica, da malattia, emozione*) recovery; (*AUT*) acceleration *q*; (*TEATRO, CINEMA*) rerun; (*CINEMA: presa*) shooting *q*; shot; (*SPORT*) second half; (: *PUGILATO*) round; **a più riprese** on several occasions, several times.

ripristi'nare *vt* to restore.

ripro'durre *vt* to reproduce; **riprodursi** *vr* (*BIOL*) to reproduce; (*riformarsi*) to form again; **riprodut'tivo, a** *ag* reproductive; **riproduzi'one** *sf* reproduction; **riproduzione vietata** all rights reserved.

ripudi'are *vt* to repudiate, disown.

ripu'gnante [ripun'ɲante] *ag* disgusting, repulsive.

ripu'gnare [ripun'ɲare] *vi*: ~ **a qd** to repel *o* disgust sb.

ripu'lire *vt* to clean up; (*sog: ladri*) to clean out; (*perfezionare*) to polish, refine.

ri'quadro *sm* square; (*ARCHIT*) panel.

ri'saia *sf* paddy field.

risa'lire *vi* (2) (*ritornare in su*) to go back up; ~ **a** (*ritornare con la mente*) to go back to; (*datare da*) to date back to, go back to.

risal'tare *vi* (*fig: distinguersi*) to stand out; (*ARCHIT*) to project, jut out; **ri'salto** *sm* prominence; (*sporgenza*) projection; **mettere** *o* **porre in risalto qc** to make sth stand out.

risa'nare *vt* (*guarire*) to heal, cure; (*rendere salubre, bonificare*) to reclaim; (*fig: emendare*) to improve.

risa'pere *vt*: ~ **qc** to come to know of sth.

risarci'mento [risartʃi'mento] *sm* compensation.

risar'cire [risar'tʃire] *vt* (*cose*) to pay compensation for; (*persona*): ~ **qd di qc** to compensate sb for sth.

ri'sata *sf* laugh.

riscalda'mento *sm* heating; ~ **centrale** central heating.

riscal'dare *vt* (*scaldare*) to heat; (: *mani, persona*) to warm; (*minestra*) to reheat; **~rsi** *vr* to warm up.

riscat'tare *vt* (*prigioniero*) to ransom, pay a ransom for; (*DIR*) to redeem; **~rsi** *vr* (*da disonore*) to redeem o.s.; **ris'catto** *sm* ransom; redemption.

rischia'rare [riskja'rare] *vt* (*illuminare*) to light up; (*colore*) to make lighter; **~rsi** *vr* (*tempo*) to clear up; (*cielo*) to clear; (*fig: volto*) to brighten up; **~rsi la voce** to clear one's throat.

rischi'are [ris'kjare] *vt* to risk // *vi*: ~ **di fare qc** to run the risk of doing sth.

'rischio ['riskjo] *sm* risk; **rischi'oso, a** *ag* risky, dangerous.

riscia'cquare [riʃʃa'kware] *vt* to rinse.

riscon'trare *vt* (*confrontare: due cose*) to compare; (*esaminare*) to check, verify; (*rilevare*) to find; **ris'contro** *sm* comparison; check, verification; (*AMM:*

lettera di risposta) reply; **mettere a riscontro** to compare.

ris'cosso, a *pp di* **riscuotere** // *sf* (*riconquista*) recovery, reconquest.

riscossi'one *sf* collection.

ris'cuotere *vt* (*anche fig*) to shake, rouse, stir; (*ritirare una somma dovuta*) to collect; (: *stipendio*) to draw, collect; (*fig: successo etc*) to win, earn; **~rsi** *vr*: **~rsi (da)** to shake o.s. (out of), rouse o.s. (from).

risenti'mento *sm* resentment.

risen'tire *vt* to hear again; (*provare*) to feel // *vi*: ~ **di** to feel (*o* show) the effects of; **~rsi** *vr*: **~rsi per** to take offence at, resent; **risen'tito, a** *ag* resentful.

ri'serbo *sm* reserve.

ri'serva *sf* reserve; (*di caccia, pesca*) preserve; (*restrizione, di indigeni*) reservation; **di** ~ (*provviste etc*) in reserve.

riser'vare *vt* (*tenere in serbo*) to keep, put aside; (*prenotare*) to book, reserve; **riser'vato, a** *ag* (*prenotato, fig: persona*) reserved; (*confidenziale*) confidential!; **riserva'tezza** *sf* reserve.

risi'edere *vi*: ~ **a/in** to reside in.

'risma *sf* (*di carta*) ream; (*fig*) kind, sort.

'riso, a *pp di* **ridere** // *sm* (*pl(f*) ~ **a**: *il ridere*): **un** ~ a laugh; **il** ~ laughter; (*pianta*) rice.

riso'lino *sm* snigger.

ri'solto, a *pp di* **risolvere**.

risolu'tezza [risolu'tettsa] *sf* determination.

riso'luto, a *ag* determined, resolute.

risoluzi'one [risolut'tsjone] *sf* solving *q*; (*MAT*) solution; (*decisione*) resolution.

ri'solvere *vt* (*difficoltà, controversia*) to resolve; (*problema*) to solve; (*decidere*): ~ **di fare** to resolve to do; **~rsi** *vr* (*decidersi*): **~rsi a fare** to make up one's mind to do; (*andare a finire*): **~rsi in** to end up, turn out; **~rsi in nulla** to come to nothing.

riso'nanza [riso'nantsa] *sf* resonance; **aver vasta** ~ (*fig: fatto etc*) to be known far and wide.

riso'nare *vt, vi* = **risuonare**.

ri'sorgere [ri'sordʒere] *vi* (2) to rise again; **risorgi'mento** *sm* revival; **il Risorgimento** (*STORIA*) the Risorgimento.

ri'sorsa *sf* expedient, resort; **~e** *sfpl* (*naturali, finanziarie etc*) resources; **persona piena di** ~**e** resourceful person.

ri'sorto, a *pp di* **risorgere**.

ri'sotto *sm* (*CUC*) risotto.

risparmi'are *vt* to save; (*evitare di consumare, non uccidere*) to spare // *vi* to save; ~ **qc a qd** to spare sb sth.

ris'parmio *sm* saving *q*; (*denaro*) savings *pl*.

rispet'tabile *ag* respectable.

rispet'tare *vt* to respect; **farsi** ~ to command respect.

rispet'tivo, a *ag* respective.

ris'petto *sm* respect; **~i** *smpl* (*saluti*) respects, regards; ~ **a** (*in paragone a*) compared to; (*in relazione a*) as regards, as for; **rispet'toso, a** *ag* respectful.

ris'plendere *vi* to shine.

rispon'dente *ag*: ~ **a** in keeping *o* conformity with; **rispon'denza** *sf* correspondence; harmony; agreement.

ris'pondere *vi* to answer, reply; (*freni*) to respond; ~ **a** (*domanda*) to answer, reply to; (*persona*) to answer; (*invito*) to reply to; (*provocazione, sog: veicolo, apparecchio*) to respond to; (*corrispondere a*) to correspond to; (: *speranze, bisogno*) to answer; ~ **di** to answer for; **ris'posto, a** *pp di* **rispondere** // *sf* answer, reply; **in** *o* **per risposta a** in reply to.

'rissa *sf* brawl.

ristabi'lire *vt* to re-establish, restore; (*persona: sog: riposo etc*) to restore to health; ~**rsi** *vr* to recover.

rista'gnare [ristaɲˈɲare] *vi* (*acqua*) to become stagnant; (*sangue*) to cease flowing; (*fig: industria*) to stagnate; **ris'tagno** *sm* stagnation.

ris'tampa *sf* reprinting *q*; reprint.

ristam'pare *vt* to reprint.

risto'rante *sm* restaurant.

risto'rarsi *vr* to have something to eat and drink; (*riposarsi*) to rest, have a rest; **ris'toro** *sm* (*bevanda, cibo*) refreshment; (*sollievo*) relief.

ristret'tezza [ristretˈtettsa] *sf* (*strettezza*) narrowness; (*fig: scarsezza*) scarcity, lack; (: *meschinità*) meanness; ~**e** *sfpl* (*povertà*) financial straits.

ris'tretto, a *pp di* **restringere** // *ag* (*racchiuso*) enclosed, hemmed in; (*angusto*) narrow; (*limitato*): ~ (**a**) restricted *o* limited (to); (*riassunto, condensato*) condensed; ~ **di mente** narrow-minded.

risucchi'are [risukˈkjare] *vt* to suck in.

risul'tare *vi* (2) (*conseguire*) to result, ensue; (*dimostrarsi*) to prove (to be), turn out (to be); (*riuscire*) to be, come out; ~ **da** (*provenire*) to result from, be the result of; **risul'tato** *sm* result.

risuo'nare *vi* (*rimbombare*) to resound, reverberate; (: *stanza*) to be resonant.

risurrezi'one [risurretˈtsjone] *sf* (REL) resurrection.

risusci'tare [risuʃʃiˈtare] *vt* to resuscitate, restore to life; (*fig*) to revive, bring back // *vi* (2) to rise (from the dead).

ris'veglio [rizˈveʎʎo] *sm* waking up; (*fig*) revival.

ris'volto *sm* (*di giacca*) lapel; (*di pantaloni*) turn-up; (*di manica*) cuff; (*di tasca*) flap; (*di libro*) inside flap; (*fig*) implication.

ritagli'are [ritaʎˈʎare] *vt* (*tagliar via*) to cut out; **ri'taglio** *sm* (*di giornale*) cutting, clipping; (*di stoffa etc*) scrap.

ritar'dare *vi* (*persona, treno*) to be late; (*orologio*) to be slow // *vt* (*rallentare*) to slow down; (*impedire*) to delay, hold up; (*differire*) to postpone, delay; **ritarda-'tario, a** *sm/f* latecomer.

ri'tardo *sm* delay; (*di persona aspettata*) lateness *q*; (*fig: mentale*) backwardness; **in** ~ late.

ri'tegno [riˈteɲɲo] *sm* restraint.

rite'nere *vt* (*trattenere*) to hold back; (: *somma*) to deduct; (*giudicare*) to consider, believe; ~ **qc a memoria** to know sth by heart; **rite'nuta** *sf* (*sul salario*) deduction.

riti'rare *vt* to withdraw; (POL: *richiamare*) to recall; (*andare a prendere: pacco etc*) to collect, pick up; ~**rsi** *vr* to withdraw; (*da un'attività*) to retire; (*stoffa*) to shrink; (*marea*) to recede; **riti'rata** *sf* (MIL) retreat; (*latrina*) lavatory; **ri'tiro** *sm* withdrawal; recall; collection; retirement; shrinking; (*luogo appartato*) retreat.

'ritmico, a, ci, che *ag* rhythmic(al).

'ritmo *sm* rhythm; (*fig*) rate; (: *della vita*) pace, tempo.

'rito *sm* rite; **di** ~ usual, customary.

ritoc'care *vt* (*disegno, fotografia*) to touch up; (*testo*) to alter; **ri'tocco, chi** *sm* touching up *q*; alteration.

ritor'nare *vi* (2) to return, go (*o* come) back; (*ripresentarsi*) to recur; (*ridiventare*): ~ **ricco** to become rich again // *vt* (*restituire*) to return, give back.

ritor'nello *sm* refrain.

ri'torno *sm* return; **essere di** ~ to be back; **far** ~ **di fiamma** (AUT) to backfire.

ri'trarre *vt* (*trarre indietro, via*) to withdraw; (*distogliere: sguardo*) to turn away; (*rappresentare*) to portray, depict; (*ricavare*) to get, obtain.

ritrat'tare *vt* (*disdire*) to retract, take back.

ri'tratto, a *pp di* **ritrarre** // *sm* portrait.

ri'troso, a *ag* (*restio*): ~ **(a)** reluctant (to); (*schivo*) shy; **andare a** ~ to go backwards.

ritro'vare *vt* to find; (*salute*) to regain; (*persona*) to find; to meet again; ~**rsi** *vr* (*essere, capitare*) to find o.s.; (*raccapezzarsi*) to find one's way; (*con senso reciproco*) to meet (again); **ri'trovo** *sm* meeting place; **ritrovo notturno** night club.

'ritto, a *ag* (*in piedi*) standing, on one's feet; (*levato in alto*) erect, raised; (: *capelli*) standing on end; (*posto verticalmente*) upright.

ritu'ale *ag, sm* ritual.

riuni'one *sf* (*adunanza*) meeting; (*riconciliazione*) reunion.

riu'nire *vt* (*ricongiungere*) to join (together); (*riconciliare*) to reunite, bring together (again); ~**rsi** *vr* (*adunarsi*) to meet; (*tornare a stare insieme*) to be reunited.

riu'scire [riuʃˈʃire] *vi* (2) (*uscire di nuovo*) to go out again, go back out; (*aver esito: fatti, azioni*) to go, turn out; (*aver successo*) to succeed, be successful; (*essere, apparire*) to be, prove; (*raggiungere il fine*) to manage, succeed; ~ **a fare qc** to manage to do *o* succeed in doing *o* be able to do sth; **questo mi riesce nuovo** this is new to me; **riu'scita** *sf* (*esito*) result, outcome; (buon esito) success; **cattiva riuscita** failure.

'**riva** sf (di fiume) bank; (di lago, mare) shore.

ri'**vale** sm/f rival; **rivalità** sf rivalry.

ri'**valsa** sf (rivincita) revenge; (risarcimento) compensation.

rivalu'**tare** vt (ECON) to revalue.

rive'**dere** vt to see again; (ripassare) to revise; (verificare) to check.

rive'**lare** vt to reveal; (divulgare) to reveal, disclose; (dare indizio) to reveal, show; ~**rsi** vr (manifestarsi) to be revealed; ~**rsi onesto** etc to prove to be honest etc; **rivela'tore**, '**trice** ag revealing // sm (TECN) detector; (FOT) developer; **rivelazi'one** sf revelation.

rivendi'**care** vt to claim, demand.

ri'**vendita** sf (bottega) retailer's (shop).

rivendi'**tore**, '**trice** sm/f retailer.

riverbe'**rare** vt to reflect; **ri'verbero** sm (di luce, calore) reflection; (di suono) reverberation.

rive'**renza** [rive'rɛntsa] sf reverence; (inchino) bow; curtsey.

rive'**rire** vt (rispettare) to revere; (salutare) to pay one's respects to.

river'**sare** vt (anche fig) to pour; ~**rsi** vr (fig: persone) to pour out.

rivesti'**mento** sm (materiale) covering; coating.

rives'**tire** vt (provvedere di abiti) to dress; (indossare) to put on; (fig: carica) to hold; (ricoprire) to cover; to coat; ~**rsi** vr to get dressed again; to change (one's clothes); ~ **con isolante termico** to lag, insulate.

rivi'**era** sf coast; **la** ~ **italiana** the Italian Riviera.

ri'**vincita** [ri'vintʃita] sf (SPORT) return match; (fig) revenge.

rivis'**suto**, **a** pp di **rivivere**.

ri'**vista** sf review; (periodico) magazine, review; (TEATRO) revue; variety show.

ri'**vivere** vi (2) (riacquistare forza) to come alive again; (tornare in uso) to be revived // vt to relive.

'**rivo** sm stream.

ri'**volgere** [ri'vɔldʒere] vt (attenzione, sguardo) to turn, direct; (parole) to address; (distogliere): ~ **da** to turn away from; ~**rsi** vr to turn round; (fig: dirigersi per informazioni): ~**rsi a** to go and see, go and speak to; (: ufficio) to enquire at; **rivolgi'mento** sm upheaval.

ri'**volta** sf revolt, rebellion.

rivol'**tare** vt to turn over; (con l'interno all'esterno) to turn inside out; (provocare disgusto: stomaco) to upset, turn; (: fig) to revolt; to outrage; ~**rsi** vr (ribellarsi): ~**rsi (a)** to rebel (against).

rivol'**tella** sf revolver.

ri'**volto**, **a** pp di **rivolgere**.

rivoluzio'**nare** [rivoluttsjo'nare] vt to revolutionize.

rivoluzio'**nario**, **a** [rivoluttsjo'narjo] ag, sm/f revolutionary.

rivoluzi'**one** [rivolut'tsjone] sf revolution.

riz'**zare** [rit'tsare] vt to raise, erect; ~**rsi**

vr to stand up; (capelli) to stand on end.

'**roba** sf stuff, things pl; (possessi, beni) belongings pl, things pl, possessions pl; ~ **da mangiare** things pl to eat, food; ~ **da matti** sheer madness o lunacy.

'**robot** sm inv robot.

ro'**busto**, **a** ag robust, sturdy; (solido: catena) strong.

'**rocca**, **che** sf fortress.

rocca'**forte** sf stronghold.

roc'**chetto** [rok'ketto] sm reel, spool.

'**roccia**, **ce** ['rɔttʃa] sf rock.

ro'**daggio** [ro'daddʒo] sm running in; **in** ~ running in.

ro'**dare** vt (AUT, TECN) to run in.

'**rodere** vt to gnaw (at); (distruggere poco a poco) to eat into.

'**Rodi** sf Rhodes.

rodi'**tore** sm (ZOOL) rodent.

rodo'**dendro** sm rhododendron.

'**rogna** ['rɔɲɲa] sf (MED) scabies sg; (fig) bother, nuisance.

ro'**gnone** [roɲ'ɲone] sm (CUC) kidney.

'**rogo**, **ghi** sm (per cadaveri) (funeral) pyre; (supplizio): **il** ~ the stake.

rol'**lio** sm rolling.

'**Roma** sf Rome.

Roma'**nia** sf: **la** ~ Romania.

ro'**manico**, **a**, **ci**, **che** ag Romanesque.

ro'**mano**, **a** ag, sm/f Roman.

romanti'**cismo** [romanti'tʃizmo] sm romanticism.

ro'**mantico**, **a**, **ci**, **che** ag romantic.

ro'**manza** [ro'mandza] sf (MUS, LETTERATURA) romance.

roman'**zesco**, **a**, **schi**, **sche** [roman-'dzesko] ag (cavalleresco) romance cpd; (del romanzo) of the novel; (fig) storybook cpd.

romanzi'**ere** [roman'dzjere] sm novelist.

ro'**manzo**, **a** [ro'mandzo] ag (LING) romance cpd // sm (medievale) romance; (moderno) novel; ~ **d'appendice** serial (story).

rom'**bare** vi to rumble, thunder, roar.

'**rombo** sm rumble, thunder, roar; (MAT) rhombus; (ZOOL) turbot; brill.

ro'**meno**, **a** ag, sm/f, sm = **rumeno**, **a**.

'**rompere** vt to break; (conversazione, fidanzamento) to break off // vi to break; ~**rsi** vr to break; ~ **in pianto** to burst into tears; ~**rsi un braccio** to break an arm; **rompi'capo** sm worry, headache; (indovinello) puzzle; (in enigmistica) brain-teaser; **rompi'collo** sm daredevil; **a rompicollo** av at breakneck speed; **rompighi'accio** sm (NAUT) icebreaker; **rompis'catole** sm/f inv (fam) pest, pain in the neck.

'**ronda** sf (MIL) rounds pl, patrol.

ron'**della** sf (TECN) washer.

'**rondine** sf (ZOOL) swallow.

ron'**done** sm (ZOOL) swift.

ron'**zare** [ron'dzare] vi to buzz, hum.

ron'**zino** [ron'dzino] sm (peg: cavallo) nag.

'**rosa** sf rose // ag inv, sm pink; **ro'saio** (pianta) rosebush, rose tree; (giardino) rose garden; **ro'sario** sm (REL) rosary; **ro'sato, a** ag pink, rosy // sm (vino) rosé (wine); **ro'seo, a** ag (anche fig) rosy; **ro'setta** sf (diamante) rose diamond; (rondella) washer.

rosicchi'are [rosik'kjare] vt to gnaw (at); (mangiucchiare) to nibble (at).

rosma'rino sm rosemary.

'roso, a pp di **rodere**.

roso'lare vt (CUC) to brown.

roso'lia sf (MED) German measles sg, rubella.

ro'sone sm rosette; (vetrata) rose window.

'rospo sm (ZOOL) toad.

ros'setto sm (per labbra) lipstick; (per guance) rouge.

'rosso, a ag, sm, sm/f red; **il mar R~** the Red Sea; **~ d'uovo** egg yolk; **ros'sore** sm flush, blush; (fig) shame.

rosticce'ria [rostittʃe'ria] sf shop selling roast meat and other cooked food.

'rostro sm rostrum; (becco) beak.

ro'tabile ag (percorribile): **strada ~** carriageway; (FERR): **materiale** m **~** rolling stock.

ro'taia sf rut, track; (FERR) rail; **le ~e** (FERR) the rails, the track sg.

ro'tare vt, vi to rotate; **rotazi'one** sf rotation.

rote'are vt, vi to whirl; **~ gli occhi** to roll one's eyes.

ro'tella sf small wheel; (di mobile) castor.

roto'lare vt, vi (2) to roll; **~rsi** vr to roll (about).

'rotolo sm roll; **andare a ~i** (fig) to go to rack and ruin.

ro'tondo, a ag round // sf rotunda.

ro'tore sm rotor.

'rotta sf (AER, NAUT) course, route; (MIL) rout; **a ~ di collo** at breakneck speed; **essere in ~ con qd** to be on bad terms with sb.

rot'tame sm fragment, scrap, broken bit; (relitto: anche fig) wreck; **~i di ferro** scrap iron.

'rotto, a pp di **rompere** // ag broken; (calzoni) torn, split; (persona: pratico, resistente): **~ a** accustomed o inured to; **per il ~ della cuffia** by the skin of one's teeth.

rot'tura sf breaking q; break; breaking off; (MED) fracture, break.

ro'vente ag red-hot.

'rovere sm oak.

rovesci'are [rovej'ʃare] vt (versare in giù) to pour; (: accidentalmente) to spill; (capovolgere) to turn upside down; (gettare a terra) to knock down; (: fig: governo) to overthrow; (piegare all'indietro: testa) to throw back; **~rsi** vr to pour down; to spill; (fig: persone) to pour (out).

ro'vescio, sci [ro'veʃʃo] sm other side, wrong side; (della mano) back; (di moneta) reverse; (pioggia) sudden downpour; (fig) setback; (MAGLIA: anche: **punto ~**) purl (stitch); (TENNIS) backhand (stroke); **a ~** upside-down; inside-out; **capire qc a ~** to misunderstand sth.

ro'vina sf ruin; **~e** sfpl ruins; **andare in ~** (andare a pezzi) to collapse; (fig) to go to rack and ruin.

rovi'nare vi (2) to collapse, fall down // vt (far cadere giù: casa) to demolish; (danneggiare, fig) to ruin; **rovi'noso, a** ag disastrous; damaging; violent.

rovis'tare vt (casa) to ransack; (tasche) to rummage in (o through).

'rovo sm (BOT) blackberry bush, bramble bush.

'rozzo, a ['roddzo] ag rough, coarse.

'ruba sf: **andare a ~** to sell like hot cakes.

ru'bare vt to steal; **~ qc a qd** to steal sth from sb.

rubi'netto sm tap.

ru'bino sm ruby.

ru'brica, che sf (STAMPA) column; (quadernetto) index book; address book.

'rude ag tough, rough.

'ruderi smpl ruins.

rudimen'tale ag rudimentary, basic.

rudi'menti smpl rudiments; basic principles; basic knowledge sg.

ruffi'ano sm pimp.

'ruga, ghe sf wrinkle.

'ruggine ['ruddʒine] sf rust.

rug'gire [rud'dʒire] vi to roar.

rugi'ada [ru'dʒada] sf dew.

ru'goso, a ag wrinkled.

rul'lare vi (tamburo, nave) to roll; (aereo) to taxi.

'rullo sm (di tamburi) roll; (arnese cilindrico, TIP) roller; **~ compressore** steam roller; **~ di pellicola** roll of film.

rum sm rum.

ru'meno, a ag, sm/f, sm Romanian.

rumi'nare vt (ZOOL) to ruminate; (fig) to ruminate on o over, chew over.

ru'more sm: **un ~** a noise, a sound; (fig) a rumour; **il ~** noise; **rumoreggi'are** vi to make a noise; **rumo'roso, a** ag noisy.

ru'olo sm (elenco) roll, register, list; (TEATRO, fig) role, part; **di ~** permanent, on the permanent staff.

ru'ota sf wheel; **a ~** (forma) circular; **~ anteriore/posteriore** front/back wheel; **~ di scorta** spare wheel.

'rupe sf cliff.

ru'rale ag rural, country cpd.

ru'scello [ruʃ'ʃello] sm stream.

'ruspa sf excavator.

rus'sare vi to snore.

'Russia sf: **la ~** Russia; **'russo, a** ag, sm/f, sm Russian.

'rustico, a, ci, che ag rustic; (fig) rough, unrefined.

rut'tare vi to belch; **'rutto** sm belch.

'ruvido, a ag rough, coarse.

ruzzo'lare [ruttso'lare] vi (2) to tumble down; **ruzzo'loni** av: **cadere ruzzoloni** to tumble down; **fare le scale ruzzoloni** to tumble down the stairs.

S

S. (*abbr di* **sud**) S.

sa *forma del vb* **sapere**.

'sabato *sm* Saturday; **di** *o* **il** ~ **on** Saturdays.

'sabbia *sf* sand; ~**e mobili** quicksand(s); **sabbi'oso, a** *ag* sandy.

sabo'taggio [sabo'taddʒo] *sm* sabotage.

sabo'tare *vt* to sabotage.

'sacca, che *sf* bag; (*bisaccia*) haversack; (*insenatura*) inlet; ~ **da viaggio** travelling bag.

sacca'rina *sf* saccharin(e).

sac'cente [sat'tʃɛnte] *sm/f* know-all.

saccheggi'are [sakked'dʒare] *vt* to sack, plunder; **sac'cheggio** *sm* sack(ing).

sac'chetto [sak'ketto] *sm* (small) bag; (small) sack.

'sacco, chi *sm* bag; (*per carbone etc*) sack; (ANAT, BIOL) sac; (*tela*) sacking; (*saccheggio*) sack(ing); (*fig*: *grande quantità*): **un** ~ **di** lots of, heaps of; ~ **a pelo** sleeping bag.

sacer'dote [satʃer'dote] *sm* priest; **sacer'dozio** *sm* priesthood.

sacra'mento *sm* sacrament.

sacrifi'care *vt* to sacrifice; ~**rsi** *vr* to sacrifice o.s.; (*privarsi di qc*) to make sacrifices.

sacri'ficio [sakri'fitʃo] *sm* sacrifice.

sacri'legio [sakri'lɛdʒo] *sm* sacrilege.

'sacro, a *ag* sacred.

sacro'santo, a *ag* sacrosanct.

'sadico, a, ci, che *ag* sadistic // *sm/f* sadist.

sa'dismo *sm* sadism.

sa'etta *sf* arrow; (*fulmine: anche fig*) thunderbolt; flash of lightning.

sa'fari *sm inv* safari.

sa'gace [sa'gatʃe] *ag* shrewd, sagacious.

sag'gezza [sad'dʒettsa] *sf* wisdom.

saggi'are [sad'dʒare] *vt* (*metalli*) to assay; (*fig*) to test.

'saggio, a, gi, ge ['saddʒo] *ag* wise // *sm* (*persona*) sage; (*operazione sperimentale*) test; (: *dell'oro*) assay; (*fig*: *prova*) proof; (*campione indicativo*) sample; (*ricerca, esame critico*) essay.

Sagit'tario [sad'ʒit'tarjo] *sm* Sagittarius.

'sagoma *sf* (*profilo*) outline, profile; (*forma*) form, shape; (TECN) template.

'sagra *sf* festival.

sagres'tano *sm* sacristan; sexton.

sagres'tia *sf* sacristy; (*culto protestante*) vestry.

'sai *forma del vb* **sapere**.

'sala *sf* hall; (*stanza*) room; ~ **d'aspetto** waiting room; ~ **da ballo** ballroom; ~ **operatoria** operating theatre; ~ **da pranzo** dining room; ~ **per concerti** concert hall.

sala'mandra *sf* salamander.

sa'lame *sm* salami *q*, salami sausage.

sala'moia *sf* (CUC) brine.

sa'lare *vt* to salt.

salari'ato, a *sm/f* wage-earner.

sa'lario *sm* pay, wages *pl*.

sa'lato, a *ag* (*sapore*) salty; (CUC) salted, salt *cpd*; (*fig*: *discorso etc*) biting, sharp; (: *prezzi*) steep, stiff.

sal'dare *vt* (*congiungere*) to join, bind; (*parti metalliche*) to solder; (: *con saldatura autogena*) to weld; (*conto*) to settle, pay; **salda'tura** *sf* soldering; welding; (*punto saldato*) soldered joint; weld.

sal'dezza [sal'dettsa] *sf* firmness; strength.

'saldo, a *ag* (*resistente, forte*) strong, firm; (*fermo*) firm, steady, stable; (*fig*) firm, steadfast // *sm* (*svendita*) sale; (*di conto*) settlement; (ECON) balance.

'sale *sm* salt; (*fig*) wit.

'salice ['salitʃe] *sm* willow; ~ **piangente** weeping willow.

sali'ente *ag* (*fig*) salient, main.

sali'era *sf* salt cellar.

sa'lino, a *ag* saline // *sf* saltworks *sg*.

sa'lire *vi* (2) to go (*o* come) up; (*aereo etc*) to climb, go up; (*passeggero*) to get on; (*sentiero, prezzi, livello*) to go up, rise // *vt* (*scale, gradini*) to go (*o* come) up; ~ **su** to climb up onto; ~ **sul treno/sull'autobus** to board the train/the bus; ~ **in macchina** to get into the car; **sa'lita** *sf* climb, ascent; (*erta*) hill, slope; **in salita** *ag, av* uphill.

sa'liva *sf* saliva.

'salma *sf* corpse.

'salmo *sm* psalm.

sal'mone *sm* salmon.

sa'lotto *sm* lounge, sitting room; (*mobilio*) lounge suite.

sal'pare *vi* (2) (NAUT) to set sail; (*anche*: ~ **l'ancora**) to weigh anchor.

'salsa *sf* (CUC) sauce; ~ **di pomodoro** tomato sauce.

sal'siccia, ce [sal'sittʃa] *sf* pork sausage.

sal'tare *vi* to jump, leap; (*esplodere*) to blow up, explode; (: *valvola*) to blow; (*rompersi*) to snap, burst; (*venir via*) to pop off // *vt* to jump (over), leap (over); (*fig*: *pranzo, capitolo*) to skip, miss (out); (CUC) to sauté; **far** ~ to blow up; to burst open.

saltel'lare *vi* to skip; to hop.

saltim'banco *sm* acrobat.

'salto *sm* jump; (SPORT) jumping; **fare un** ~ to jump, leap; **fare un** ~ **da qd** to pop over to sb's (place); ~ **in alto/lungo** high/long jump; ~ **con l'asta** pole vaulting; ~ **mortale** somersault.

saltu'ario, a *ag* occasional, irregular.

sa'lubre *ag* healthy, salubrious.

salume'ria *sf* delicatessen.

sa'lumi *smpl* salted pork meats.

salu'tare *ag* healthy; (*fig*) salutary, beneficial // *vt* (*per dire buon giorno, fig*) to greet; (*per dire addio*) to say goodbye to; (MIL) to salute.

sa'lute *sf* health; ~**!** (*a chi starnutisce*) bless you!; (*nei brindisi*) cheers!; **bere alla** ~ **di qd** to drink (to) sb's health.

sa'luto *sm* (*gesto*) wave; (*parola*) greeting;

(MIL) salute; ~**i** smpl greetings; **cari** ~**i** best regards; **vogliate gradire i nostri più distinti** ~**i** Yours faithfully.

'salva sf salvo.

salvacon'dotto sm (MIL) safe-conduct.

salva'gente [salva'dʒɛnte] sm (NAUT) lifebuoy; (stradale) traffic island; ~ **a ciambella;** ~ **a giubbotto** lifejacket.

salvaguar'dare vt to safeguard.

sal'vare vt to save; (trarre da un pericolo) to rescue; (proteggere) to protect; ~**rsi** vr to save o.s.; to escape; **salva'taggio** sm rescue; **salva'tore, 'trice** sm/f saviour; **salvazi'one** sf (REL) salvation.

'salve escl (fam) hi!

sal'vezza [sal'vettsa] sf salvation; (sicurezza) safety.

'salvia sf (BOT) sage.

'salvo, a ag safe, unhurt, unharmed; (fuori pericolo) safe, out of danger // prep (eccetto) except; ~ **che** cong (a meno che) unless; (eccetto che) except (that); ~ **imprevisti** barring accidents.

sam'buco sm elder (tree).

sa'nare vt to heal, cure; (fig) to put right.

sana'torio sm sanatorium.

san'cire [san'tʃire] vt to sanction.

'sandalo sm (BOT) sandalwood; (calzatura) sandal.

'sangue sm blood; **farsi cattivo** ~ to fret, get in a state; ~ **freddo** (fig) sangfroid, calm; **a** ~ **freddo** in cold blood; **sangu'igno, a** ag blood cpd; (colore) blood-red; **sangui'nare** vi to bleed; **sangui'noso, a** ag bloody; (cruento) bitter, mortal; **sangui'suga** sf leech.

sanità sf health; (salubrità) healthiness; **Ministro della S**~ Minister of Health; ~ **mentale** sanity.

sani'tario, a ag health cpd; (condizioni) sanitary // sm (AMM) doctor.

'sanno forma del vb sapere.

'sano, a ag healthy; (denti, costituzione) healthy, sound; (integro) whole, unbroken; (fig: politica, consigli) sound; ~ **di mente** sane; **di** ~ **a pianta** completely, entirely; ~ **e salvo** safe and sound.

santifi'care vt to sanctify; (canonizzare) to canonize; (venerare) to honour.

santità sf sanctity; holiness; **Sua/Vostra** ~ (titolo di Papa) His/Your Holiness.

'santo, a ag holy; (fig) saintly; (seguito da nome proprio: dav sm **san** + C, **sant'** + V, **santo** + s impura, gn, pn, ps, x, z; dav sf **santa** + C, **sant'** + V) saint // sm/f saint; **la S**~**a Sede** the Holy See; **il S**~ **Spirito** the Holy Spirit o Ghost.

santu'ario sm sanctuary.

sanzio'nare [santsjo'nare] vt to sanction.

sanzi'one [san'tsjone] sf sanction; (penale, civile) sanction, penalty.

sa'pere vt to know; (essere capace di): **so nuotare** I know how to swim, I can swim // vi: ~ **di** (aver sapore) to taste of; (aver odore) to smell of; **sa di muffa** it smells of mould, it smells mouldy // sm knowledge; **far** ~ **qc a qd** to inform sb about sth, let sb know sth.

sapi'enza [sa'pjɛntsa] sf wisdom.

sa'pone sm soap; ~ **da bucato** washing soap; **sapo'netta** sf cake o bar o tablet of soap.

sa'pore sm taste, flavour; **sapo'rito, a** ag tasty; (fig: arguto) witty; (: piccante) racy.

sappi'amo forma del vb sapere.

saraci'nesca [saratʃi'neska] sf (serranda) rolling shutter.

sar'casmo sm sarcasm q; sarcastic remark; **sar'castico, a, ci, che** ag sarcastic.

Sar'degna [sar'deɲɲa] sf: **la** ~ Sardinia.

sar'dina sf sardine.

'sardo, a ag, sm/f Sardinian.

sar'donico, a, ci, che ag sardonic.

'sarto, a sm/f tailor/dressmaker; **sarto'ria** sf tailor's (shop); dressmaker's (shop); (più grande) fashion house; (arte) couture.

'sasso sm stone; (ciottolo) pebble; (masso) rock.

sas'sofono sm saxophone.

sas'soso, a ag stony; pebbly.

'Satana sm Satan; **sa'tanico, a, ci, che** ag satanic, fiendish.

sa'tellite sm, ag satellite.

'satira sf satire; **sa'tirico, a, ci, che** ag satiric(al).

satu'rare vt to saturate; **saturazi'one** sf saturation; **'saturo, a** ag saturated; (fig): **saturo di** full of.

'sauna sf sauna.

Sa'voia sf: **la** ~ Savoy.

savoi'ardo, a ag of Savoy, Savoyard // sm (biscotto) sponge finger.

sazi'are [sat'tsjare] vt to satisfy, satiate; ~**rsi** vr (riempirsi di cibo): ~**rsi (di)** to eat one's fill (of); (fig): ~**rsi di** to grow tired o weary of.

'sazio, a ['sattsjo] ag: ~ **(di)** sated (with), full (of); (fig: stufo) fed up (with), sick (of).

sba'dato, a ag careless, inattentive.

sbadigli'are [zbadiʎ'ʎare] vi to yawn; **sba'diglio** sm yawn.

sbagli'are [zbaʎ'ʎare] vt to make a mistake in, get wrong // vi to make a mistake, to be mistaken; to be wrong; (operare in modo non giusto) to err; ~**rsi** vr to make a mistake, to be mistaken; to be wrong; ~ **la mira/strada** to miss one's aim/take the wrong road; ~ **qd con qd altro** to mistake sb for sb else; **'sbaglio** sm mistake, error; (morale) error.

sbal'lare vt (merce) to unpack.

sballot'tare vt to toss (about).

sbalor'dire vt to stun, amaze // vi to be stunned, be amazed; **sbalordi'tivo, a** ag amazing; (prezzo) incredible, absurd.

sbal'zare [zbal'tsare] vt to throw, hurl; (fig: da una carica) to remove, dismiss // vi (2) (balzare) to bounce; (saltare) to leap, bound; **'sbalzo** sm bounce; leap; (spostamento improvviso) jolt, jerk; **a sbalzi** jerkily; (fig) in fits and starts.

sban'dare vi (NAUT) to list; (AER) to bank; (AUT) to skid; ~**rsi** vr (folla) to disperse;

(*truppe*) to disband; (*fig: famiglia*) to break up.

sbandie'rare *vt* (*bandiera*) to wave; (*fig*) to parade, show off.

sbaragli'are [zbara*ʎ'ʎ*are] *vt* (*MIL*) to rout; (*in gare sportive etc*) to beat, defeat.

sba'raglio [zba'ra*ʎʎ*o] *sm* rout; defeat; **gettarsi allo ~** to risk everything.

sbaraz'zarsi [zbarat'tsarsi] *vr*: **~ di** to get rid of, rid o.s. of.

sbar'care *vt* (*passeggeri*) to disembark; (*merci*) to unload // *vi* (2) to disembark; **~ il lunario** (*fig*) to make ends meet; **'sbarco** *sm* disembarkation; unloading; (*MIL*) landing.

'sbarra *sf* bar; (*di passaggio a livello*) barrier; (*DIR*): **presentarsi alla ~** to appear before the court.

sbarra'mento *sm* (*stradale*) roadblock, barricade; (*diga*) dam, barrage; (*MIL*) barrage.

sbar'rare *vt* (*strada etc*) to block, bar; (*assegno*) to cross; **~ il passo** to bar the way; **~ gli occhi** to open one's eyes wide.

'sbattere *vt* (*porta*) to slam, bang; (*tappeti, ali, cuc*) to beat; (*urtare*) to knock, hit // *vi* (*porta*) to slam, bang; (*agitarsi: ali, vele etc*) to flap; **sbat'tuto, a** *ag* (*viso, aria*) dejected, worn out; (*uovo*) beaten.

sba'vare *vi* to dribble; (*colore*) to smear, smudge.

sbia'dire *vi* (2) (*anche*: **~rsi**), *vt* to fade; **sbia'dito, a** *ag* faded; (*fig*) colourless, dull.

sbian'care *vt* to whiten; (*tessuto*) to bleach // *vi* (2) (*impallidire*) to grow pale *o* white.

sbi'eco, a, chi, che *ag* (*storto*) squint, askew; **di ~**: **guardare qd di ~** (*fig*) to look askance at sb; **tagliare una stoffa di ~** to cut a material on the bias.

sbigot'tire *vt* to dismay, stun // *vi* (2) (*anche*: **~rsi**) to be dismayed.

sbilanci'are [zbilan'tʃare] *vt* to throw off balance // *vi* (*perdere l'equilibrio*) to overbalance; (*pendere da una parte*) to be unbalanced; **~rsi** *vr* (*fig*): **non si sbilancia mai** (*nel parlare*) he always weighs his words; (*nello spendere*) he never spends beyond his means.

sbirci'are [zbir'tʃare] *vt* to cast sidelong glances at, eye.

'sbirro *sm* (*peg*) cop.

sbizzar'rirsi [zbiddzar'rirsi] *vr* to indulge one's whims.

sbloc'care *vt* to unblock, free; (*freno*) to release; (*prezzi, affitti*) to decontrol.

sboc'care *vi* (2): **~ in** (*fiume*) to flow into; (*strada*) to lead into; (*persona*) to come (out) into; (*fig: concludersi*) to end (up) in.

sboc'cato, a *ag* (*persona*) foul-mouthed; (*linguaggio*) foul.

sbocci'are [zbot'tʃare] *vi* (2) (*fiore*) to bloom, open (out).

'sbocco, chi *sm* (*apertura*) opening; (*uscita*) way out; (*di fiume*) mouth; (*COMM*) outlet; (: *mercato*) market.

sbol'lire *vi* (2) (*fig*) to cool down, calm down.

'sbornia *sf* (*fam*): **prendere una ~** to get plastered.

sbor'sare *vt* (*denaro*) to pay out.

sbot'tare *vi* (2) to burst out; **~ a ridere/per la collera** to burst out laughing/explode with anger.

sbotto'nare *vt* to unbutton, undo.

sbracci'ato, a [zbrat'tʃato] *ag* (*camicia*) sleeveless; (*persona*) bare-armed.

sbrai'tare *vi* to yell, bawl.

sbra'nare *vt* to tear to pieces.

sbricio'lare [zbritʃo'lare] *vt*, **~rsi** *vr* to crumble.

sbri'gare *vt* to deal with, get through; (*cliente*) to attend to, deal with; **~rsi** *vr* to hurry (up); **sbriga'tivo, a** *ag* (*persona, modo*) quick, expeditious; (*giudizio*) hasty.

sbrindel'lato, a *ag* tattered, in tatters.

sbrodo'lare *vt* to stain, dirty.

'sbronzo, a ['zbrontso] *ag* (*fam*) tight // *sf*: **prendere una ~a** to get tight *o* plastered.

sbu'care *vi* (2) to come out, emerge; (*apparire improvvisamente*) to pop out (*o* up).

sbucci'are [zbut'tʃare] *vt* (*arancia, patata*) to peel; (*piselli*) to shell; (*braccio*) to graze.

sbudel'larsi *vr*: **~ dalle risa** to split one's sides laughing.

sbuf'fare *vi* (*persona, cavallo*) to snort; (: *ansimare*) to puff, pant; (*treno*) to puff; **'sbuffo** *sm* snort; puff, pant; (*di aria, fumo, vapore*) puff.

'scabbia *sf* (*MED*) scabies *sg*.

'scabro, a *ag* rough, harsh.

sca'broso, a *ag* (*fig: delicato*) delicate, awkward; (: *difficile*) difficult.

scacchi'era [skak'kjera] *sf* chessboard.

scacci'are [skat'tʃare] *vt* to chase away *o* out, drive away *o* out.

'scacco, chi *sm* (*pezzo del gioco*) chessman; (*quadretto di scacchiera*) square; (*fig*) setback, reverse; **~ chi** *smpl* (*gioco*) chess *sg*; **a ~chi** (*tessuto*) check(ed); **scacco'matto** *sm* checkmate.

sca'dente *ag* shoddy, of poor quality.

sca'denza [ska'dentsa] *sf* (*di cambiale, contratto*) maturity; (*di passaporto*) expiry date; **a breve/lunga ~** short-/long-term; **lo farò a breve ~** I'll do it in the near future.

sca'dere *vi* (2) (*contratto etc*) to expire; (*debito*) to fall due; (*valore, forze, peso*) to decline, go down.

sca'fandro *sm* (*di palombaro*) diving suit; (*di astronauta*) space-suit.

scaf'fale *sm* shelf; (*mobile*) set of shelves.

'scafo *sm* (*NAUT, AER*) hull.

scagio'nare [skadʒo'nare] *vt* to exonerate, free from blame.

'scaglia ['ska*ʎʎ*a] *sf* (*ZOOL*) scale; (*scheggia*) chip, flake.

scagli'are [ska*ʎ'ʎ*are] *vt* (*lanciare: anche fig*) to hurl, fling; **~rsi** *vr*: **~rsi su** *o* **contro** to hurl *o* fling o.s. at; (*fig*) to rail at.

scaglio'nare [skaλλo'nare] *vt* (*pagamenti*) to space out, spread out; (MIL) to echelon; **scagli'one** *sm* echelon; (GEO) terrace.

'scala *sf* (*a gradini etc*) staircase, stairs *pl*; (*a pioli, di corda*) ladder; (MUS, GEO, *di colori, valori, fig*) scale; ~**e** *sfpl* (*scalinata*) stairs; **su vasta** ~/~ **ridotta** on a large/small scale; ~ **a libretto** stepladder; ~ **mobile** escalator; (ECON) sliding scale; ~ **mobile dei salari** index-linked pay scale.

sca'lare *vt* (ALPINISMO, *muro*) to climb, scale; (*debito*) to scale down, reduce; **sca-'lata** *sf* scaling *q*, climbing *q*; climb; **scala'tore, 'trice** *sm/f* climber.

scalda'bagno [skalda'baɲɲo] *sm* waterheater.

scal'dare *vt* to heat; ~**rsi** *vr* to warm up, heat up; (*al sole*) to warm o.s.; (*fig*) to get excited.

scal'fire *vt* to scratch.

scali'nata *sf* staircase.

sca'lino *sm* (*anche fig*) step; (*di scala a pioli*) rung.

'scalo *sm* (NAUT) slipway; (: *porto d'approdo*) port of call; (AER) stopover; **fare** ~ **(a)** (NAUT) to call (at), put in (at); (AER) to land (at), make a stop (at); ~ **merci** (FERR) goods yard.

scalop'pina *sf* (CUC) escalope.

scal'pello *sm* chisel.

scal'pore *sm* noise, row; **far** ~ to make a noise; (*fig*) to cause a sensation o a stir.

scal'tro, a *ag* cunning, shrewd.

scal'zare [skal'tsare] *vt* (*albero*) to bare the roots of; (*muro, fig*: *autorità*) to undermine; (: *escludere: collega*) to oust; ~ **i piedi** to take off one's socks and shoes.

'scalzo, a ['skaltso] *ag* barefoot.

scambi'are *vt* to exchange; (*confondere*): ~ **qd/qc per** to take o mistake sb/sth for; **mi hanno scambiato il cappello** they've given me the wrong hat.

scambi'evole *ag* mutual, reciprocal.

'scambio *sm* exchange; (FERR) points *pl*; ~ **di persona** case of mistaken identity.

scampa'gnata [skampaɲ'ɲata] *sf* trip to the country.

scampa'nare *vi* to peal.

scam'pare *vt* (*salvare*) to rescue, save; (*evitare: morte, prigione*) to escape // *vi* (2): ~ **(a qc)** to survive (sth), escape (sth); **scamparla bella** to have a narrow escape; **'scampo** *sm* escape; **cercare scampo nella fuga** to seek safety in flight.

'scampolo *sm* scrap; (*di tessuto*) remnant.

scanala'tura *sf* (*incavo*) channel, groove.

scandagli'are [skandaʎ'ʎare] *vt* (NAUT) to sound; (*fig*) to sound out; to probe.

scandaliz'zare [skandalid'dzare] *vt* to shock, scandalize; ~**rsi** *vr* to be shocked.

'scandalo *sm* scandal; **scanda'loso, a** *ag* scandalous, shocking.

Scandi'navia *sf*: **la** ~ Scandinavia; **scandi'navo, a** *ag, sm/f* Scandinavian.

scan'dire *vt* (*versi*) to scan; (*parole*) to articulate, pronounce distinctly; ~ **il tempo** (MUS) to beat time.

scan'nare *vt* (*animale*) to butcher, slaughter; (*persona*) to cut o slit the throat of.

'scanno *sm* seat, bench.

scansafa'tiche [skansafa'tike] *sm/f inv* idler, loafer.

scan'sare *vt* (*rimuovere*) to move (aside), shift; (*schivare: schiaffo*) to dodge; (*sfuggire*) to avoid; ~**rsi** *vr* to move aside.

scan'sia *sf* shelves *pl*; (*per libri*) bookcase.

'scanso *sm*: **a** ~ **di** in order to avoid, as a precaution against.

scanti'nato *sm* basement.

scanto'nare *vi* to turn the corner; (*svignarsela*) to sneak off.

scapes'trato, a *ag* dissolute.

'scapito *sm* (*perdita*) loss; (*danno*) damage, detriment; **a** ~ **di** to the detriment of.

'scapola *sf* shoulder blade.

'scapolo *sm* bachelor.

scappa'mento *sm* (AUT) exhaust.

scap'pare *vi* (2) (*fuggire*) to escape; (*andare via in fretta*) to rush off; **lasciarsi** ~ **un'occasione** to let an opportunity go by; ~ **di prigione** to escape from prison; ~ **di mano** (*oggetto*) to slip out of one's hands; ~ **di mente** a qd to slip sb's mind; **mi scappò detto** I let it slip; **scap'pata** *sf* quick visit o call; (*scappatella*) escapade; **scappa'tella** *sf* escapade; **scappa'toia** *sf* way out.

scara'beo *sm* beetle.

scarabocchi'are [skarabok'kjare] *vt* to scribble, scrawl; **scara'bocchio** *sm* scribble, scrawl.

scara'faggio [skara'faddʒo] *sm* cockroach.

scaraven'tare *vt* to fling, hurl; (*fig: impiegato*) to shift.

scarce'rare [skartʃe'rare] *vt* to release (from prison).

'scarica, che *sf* (*di arma da fuoco, ELETTR, FISIOL*) discharge; (*di piùarmi*) volley of shots; (*di sassi, pugni*) hail, shower.

scari'care *vt* (*merci, camion etc*) to unload; (*passeggeri*) to set down, put off; (*arma*) to unload; (: *sparare, ELETTR*) to discharge; (*sog: corso d'acqua*) to empty, pour; (*fig: liberare da un peso*) to unburden, relieve; ~**rsi** *vr* (*orologio*) to run o wind down; (*accumulatore*) to go flat o dead; (*fig: rilassarsi*) to unwind; **scarica'tore** *sm* loader; (*di porto*) docker.

'scarico, a, chi, che *ag* unloaded; (*orologio*) run down; (*accumulatore*) dead, flat; (*fig: libero*): ~ **di** free from // *sm* (*di merci, materiali*) unloading; (*di immondizie*) dumping, tipping; (: *luogo*) rubbish dump; (TECN: *deflusso*) draining; (: *dispositivo*) drain; (AUT) exhaust.

scarlat'tina *sf* scarlet fever.

scar'latto, a *ag* scarlet.

'scarno, a *ag* thin, bony.

'scarpa *sf* shoe; ~**e da tennis** tennis shoes.

scar'pata *sf* escarpment.

scarseggi'are [skarsed'dʒare] *vi* to be scarce; ~ **di** to be short of, lack.

scar'sezza [skar'settsa] *sf* scarcity, lack.

'scarso, a *ag* (*insufficiente*) insufficient, meagre; (*povero: annata*) poor, lean; (*INS: nota*) poor; ~ **di** lacking in; **3 chili** ~ **i** just under 3 kilos, barely 3 kilos.

scarta'mento *sm* (*FERR*) gauge; ~ **normale/ridotto** standard/ narrow gauge.

scar'tare *vt* (*pacco*) to unwrap; (*idea*) to reject; (*MIL*) to declare unfit for military service; (*carte da gioco*) to discard; (*CALCIO*) to dodge (past) // *vi* to swerve.

'scarto *sm* (*cosa scartata, anche COMM*) reject; (*di veicolo*) swerve; (*differenza*) gap, difference.

scassi'nare *vt* to break, force.

'scasso *sm vedi* **furto.**

scate'nare *vt* (*fig*) to incite, stir up; ~**rsi** *vr* (*fig*) to break out; to rage.

scatola *sf* box; (*di latta*) tin, can; **cibi in** ~ tinned *o* canned foods; ~ **cranica** cranium.

scat'tare *vt* (*fotografia*) to take // *vi* (*2*) (*congegno, molla etc*) to be released; (*balzare*) to spring up; (*SPORT*) to put on a spurt; (*fig: per l'ira*) to fly into a rage; ~ **in piedi** to spring to one's feet.

'scatto *sm* (*dispositivo*) release; (: *di arma da fuoco*) trigger mechanism; (*rumore*) click; (*balzo*) jump, start; (*SPORT*) spurt; (*fig: di ira etc*) fit; (: *di stipendio*) increment; **di** ~ suddenly.

scatu'rire *vi* (*2*) to gush, spring.

scaval'care *vt* (*ostacolo*) to pass (*o* climb) over; (*fig*) to get ahead of, overtake.

sca'vare *vt* (*terreno*) to dig; (*legno*) to hollow out; (*tesoro*) to dig up; (*città*) to excavate.

'scavo *sm* excavating *q*; excavation.

'scegliere ['ʃeʎʎere] *vt* to choose, select.

sce'icco, chi [ʃe'ikko] *sm* sheik.

scelle'rato, a [ʃelle'rato] *ag* wicked, evil.

scel'lino [ʃel'lino] *sm* shilling.

'scelto, a ['ʃelto] *pp di* **scegliere** // *ag* (*di prima scelta*) carefully chosen; select; (*di ottima qualità: merce*) choice, top quality; (*MIL: specializzato*) crack *cpd*, highly skilled // *sf* choice; selection; **frutta o formaggi a** ~**a** choice of fruit or cheese.

sce'mare [ʃe'mare] *vt* to diminish, reduce.

'scemo, a ['ʃemo] *ag* stupid, silly.

'scempio ['ʃempjo] *sm* slaughter, massacre; (*fig*) ruin; **far** ~ **di** (*fig*) to play havoc with, ruin.

'scena ['ʃena] *sf* (*gen*) scene; (*palcoscenico*) stage; **le** ~**e** (*fig: teatro*) the stage; **fare una** ~ to make a scene; **andare in** ~ to be staged *o* put on *o* performed; **mettere in** ~ to stage.

sce'nario [ʃe'narjo] *sm* scenery; (*di film*) scenario.

sce'nata [ʃe'nata] *sf* row, scene.

'scendere ['ʃendere] *vi* (*2*) to go (*o* come) down; (*strada, sole*) to go down; (*passeggero: fermarsi*) to get out, alight;

(*fig: temperatura, prezzi*) to go *o* come down, fall, drop // *vt* (*scale, pendio*) to go (*o* come) down; ~ **dal treno** to get off *o* out of the train; ~ **da cavallo** to dismount, get off one's horse.

'scenico, a, ci, che ['ʃeniko] *ag* stage *cpd*, scenic.

scervel'lato, a [ʃervel'lato] *ag* feather-brained, scatterbrained.

'sceso, a ['ʃeso] *pp di* **scendere.**

scetti'cismo [ʃetti'tʃizmo] *sm* scepticism; **'scettico, a, ci, che** *ag* sceptical.

'scettro ['ʃettro] *sm* sceptre.

'scheda ['skɛda] *sf* (index) card; ~ **elettorale** ballot paper; ~ **perforata** punch card; **sche'dare** *vt* (*dati*) to file; (*libri*) to catalogue; (*registrare: anche POLIZIA*) to put on one's files; **sche'dario** *sm* file; (*mobile*) filing cabinet.

'scheggia, ge ['skeddʒa] *sf* splinter, sliver.

'scheletro ['skɛletro] *sm* skeleton.

'schema, i ['skɛma] *sm* (*diagramma*) diagram, sketch; (*progetto, abbozzo*) outline, plan.

'scherma ['skerma] *sf* fencing.

scher'maglia [sker'maʎʎa] *sf* (*fig*) skirmish.

'schermo ['skermo] *sm* shield, screen; (*CINEMA, TV*) screen.

scher'nire [sker'nire] *vt* to mock, sneer at; **'scherno** *sm* mockery, derision.

scher'zare [sker'tsare] *vi* to joke.

'scherzo ['skertso] *sm* joke; (*tiro*) trick; (*MUS*) scherzo; **è uno** ~**!** (*una cosa facile*) it's child's play!, it's easy!; **per** ~ in jest; **for a joke** *o* **a laugh; fare un brutto** ~ **a qd** to play a nasty trick on sb; **scher'zoso, a** *ag* joking, jesting; (*cagnolino etc*) playful.

schiaccia'noci [skjattʃa'notʃi] *sm inv* nutcracker.

schiacci'are [skjat'tʃare] *vt* (*dito*) to crush; (*noci*) to crack; ~ **un pisolino** to have a nap.

schiaffeggi'are [skjaffed'dʒare] *vt* to slap.

schi'affo ['skjaffo] *sm* slap.

schiamaz'zare [skjamat'tsare] *vi* to squawk, cackle.

schian'tare [skjan'tare] *vt* to break, tear apart; ~**rsi** *vr* to break (up), shatter; **schi'anto** *sm* (*rumore*) crash; tearing sound; (*fig: tormento*) torment; **provare uno schianto al cuore** to feel a wrench at one's heart; **è uno schianto!** (*fam*) it's (*o* he's *o* she's) terrific!

schia'rire [skja'rire] *vt* to lighten, make lighter // *vi* (*2*) (*anche:* ~**rsi**) to grow lighter; (*tornar sereno*) to clear, brighten up; ~**rsi la voce** to clear one's throat.

schiavitù [skjavi'tu] *sf* slavery.

schi'avo, a ['skjavo] *sm/f* slave.

schi'ena ['skjena] *sf* (*ANAT*) back; **schie-'nale** *sm* (*di sedia*) back.

schi'era ['skjera] *sf* (*MIL*) rank; (*gruppo*) group, band.

schiera'mento [skjera'mento] *sm* lining up, drawing up; (*SPORT*) formation; line-up.

schie'rare [skje'rare] vt (esercito) to line
up, draw up, marshal; ~rsi vr to line up;
(fig) to take sides.

schi'etto, a ['skjɛtto] ag (puro) pure; (fig)
frank, straightforward; sincere.

'schifo ['skifo] sm disgust; fare ~ (essere
fatto male, dare pessimi risultati) to be
awful; mi fa ~ it makes me sick, it's
disgusting; quel libro è uno ~ that
book's rotten; schi'foso, a ag disgusting,
revolting; (molto scadente) rotten, lousy.

schioc'care [skjɔk'kare] vt (frusta) to
crack; (dita) to snap; (lingua) to click; ~
le labbra to smack one's lips.

schi'udere ['skjudere] vt, ~rsi vr to
open.

schi'uma ['skjuma] sf foam; (di sapone)
lather; (fig: feccia) scum; schiu'mare vt
to skim // vi to foam.

schi'uso, a ['skjuso] pp di schiudere.

schi'vare [ski'vare] vt to dodge, avoid.

'schivo, a ['skivo] ag (ritroso) stand-offish,
reserved; (timido) shy; ~ a fare loath to
do, reluctant to do.

schizo'frenico, a, ci, che [skidzo-
'frɛniko] ag schizophrenic.

schiz'zare [skit'tsare] vt (spruzzare) to
spurt, squirt; (sporcare) to splash, spatter;
(fig: abbozzare) to sketch // vi to spurt,
squirt; (saltar fuori) to dart up (o off etc).

schizzi'noso, a [skittsi'noso] ag fussy,
finicky.

'schizzo ['skittso] sm (di liquido) spurt;
splash, spatter; (abbozzo) sketch.

sci [ʃi] sm (attrezzo) ski; (attività) skiing; ~
nautico water-skiing.

'scia, pl 'scie ['ʃia] sf (di imbarcazione)
wake; (di profumo) trail.

scià [ʃa] sm inv shah.

sci'abola ['ʃabola] sf sabre.

scia'callo [ʃa'kallo] sm jackal.

sciac'quare [ʃa'kware] vt to rinse.

scia'gura [ʃa'gura] sf disaster, calamity;
misfortune; sciagu'rato, a ag
unfortunate; (malvagio) wicked.

scialac'quare [ʃalak'kware] vt to
squander.

scia'lare [ʃa'lare] vi to lead a life of
luxury.

sci'albo, a [ʃa'albo] ag pale, dull; (fig) dull,
colourless.

sci'alle ['ʃalle] sm shawl.

scia'luppa [ʃa'luppa] sf (anche: ~ di
salvataggio) lifeboat.

sci'ame ['ʃame] sm swarm.

scian'cato, a [ʃan'kato] ag lame; (mobile)
rickety.

sci'are [ʃi'are] vi to ski.

sci'arpa ['ʃarpa] sf scarf; (fascia) sash.

scia'tore, 'trice [ʃa'tore] sm/f skier.

sci'atto, a [ʃatto] ag (persona, aspetto)
slovenly, unkempt; (lavoro) sloppy,
careless.

scien'tifico, a, ci, che [ʃen'tifiko] ag
scientific.

sci'enza ['ʃɛntsa] sf science; (sapere)
knowledge; ~e sfpl (INS) science sg; ~e

naturali natural sciences; scienzi'ato, a
sm/f scientist.

'scimmia ['ʃimmja] sf monkey;
scimmiot'tare vt to ape, mimic.

scimpanzé [ʃimpan'tse] sm inv
chimpanzee.

scimu'nito, a [ʃimu'nito] ag silly, idiotic.

'scindere ['ʃindere] vt, ~rsi vr to split
(up).

scin'tilla [ʃin'tilla] sf spark; scintil'lare
vi to spark; (acqua, occhi) to sparkle.

scioc'chezza [ʃok'kettsa] sf stupidity q;
stupid o foolish thing; dire ~e to talk
nonsense.

sci'occo, a, chi, che ['ʃɔkko] ag stupid,
foolish.

sci'ogliere ['ʃɔʎʎere] vt (nodo) to untie;
(animale) to untie, release; (fig: persona):
~ da to release from; (neve) to melt;
(nell'acqua: zucchero etc) to dissolve; (fig:
problema) to resolve; (: muscoli) to loosen
up; (fig: porre fine a: contratto) to cancel; (:
società, matrimonio) to dissolve;
(adempiere: voto etc) to fulfil; ~rsi vr to
loosen, come untied; to melt; to dissolve.

sciol'tezza [ʃol'tettsa] sf agility;
suppleness; ease.

sci'olto, a ['ʃɔlto] pp di sciogliere // ag
loose; (agile) agile, nimble; supple;
(disinvolto) free and easy; versi ~i
(POESIA) blank verse.

sciope'rante [ʃope'rante] sm/f striker.

sciope'rare [ʃope'rare] vi to strike, go on
strike.

sci'opero ['ʃɔpero] sm strike; fare ~ to
strike; ~ bianco work-to-rule; ~
selvaggio wildcat strike; ~ a
singhiozzo on-off strike.

sci'rocco [ʃi'rɔkko] sm sirocco.

sci'roppo [ʃi'rɔppo] sm syrup.

'scisma, i ['ʃizma] sm (REL) schism.

scissi'one [ʃis'sjone] sf (anche fig) split,
division; (FISICA) fission.

'scisso, a ['ʃisso] pp di scindere.

sciu'pare [ʃu'pare] vt (abito, libro,
appetito) to spoil, ruin; (tempo, denaro) to
waste; ~rsi vr to get spoilt o ruined;
(rovinarsi la salute) to ruin one's health.

scivo'lare [ʃivo'lare] vi (2) to slide o glide
along; (involontariamente) to slip, slide;
'scivolo sm slide; (TECN) chute.

scle'rosi sf sclerosis.

scoc'care vt (freccia) to shoot // vi (2)
(guizzare) to shoot up; (battere: ora) to
strike.

scocci'are [skot'tʃare] (fam) vt to bother,
annoy; ~rsi vr to be bothered o annoyed.

sco'della sf bowl.

scodinzo'lare [skodintso'lare] vi to wag
its tail.

scogli'era [skoʎ'ʎɛra] sf reef; cliff.

'scoglio ['skoʎʎo] sm (al mare) rock.

scoi'attolo sm squirrel.

sco'lare: età ~ school age // vt to
drain // vi (2) to drip.

scola'resca sf schoolchildren pl, pupils pl.

sco'laro, a sm/f pupil, schoolboy/girl.

sco'lastico, a, ci, che *ag* school *cpd*; scholastic.

scol'lare *vt* (*staccare*) to unstick; **~rsi** *vr* to come unstuck; **scolla'tura** *sf* neckline.

'scolo *sm* drainage.

scolo'rire *vt* to fade; to discolour // *vi* (*2*) (*anche*: **~rsi**) to fade; to become discoloured; (*impallidire*) to turn pale.

scol'pire *vt* to carve, sculpt.

scombi'nare *vt* to mess up, upset.

scombusso'lare *vt* to upset.

scom'messo, a *pp di* **scommettere** // *sf* bet, wager.

scom'mettere *vt, vi* to bet.

scomo'dare *vt* to trouble, bother; to disturb; **~rsi** *vr* to put o.s. out; **~rsi a fare** to go to the bother *o* trouble of doing.

'scomodo, a *ag* uncomfortable; (*sistemazione, posto*) awkward, inconvenient.

scompagi'nare [skompadʒi'nare] *vt* to upset, disarrange; (*TIP*) to break up.

scompa'rire *vi* (*2*) to disappear, vanish; (*fig*) to be insignificant; **scom'parso, a** *pp di* **scomparire** // *sf* disappearance.

scomparti'mento *sm* (*FERR*) compartment.

scom'parto *sm* compartment, division.

scompigli'are [skompiʎ'ʎare] *vt* (*cassetto, capelli*) to mess up, disarrange; (*fig: piani*) to upset; **scom'piglio** *sm* mess, confusion.

scom'porre *vt* (*disfare*) to break up, take to pieces; (*scompigliare*) to disarrange, mess up; **scomporsi** *vr* (*fig*) to get upset, lose one's composure; **scom'posto, a** *pp di* **scomporre** // *ag* (*gesto*) unseemly; (*capelli*) ruffled, dishevelled.

sco'munica *sf* excommunication.

scomuni'care *vt* to excommunicate.

sconcer'tare [skontʃer'tare] *vt* to disconcert, bewilder.

'sconcio, a, ci, ce ['skontʃo] *ag* (*osceno*) indecent, obscene // *sm* (*cosa riprovevole, mal fatta*) disgrace.

sconfes'sare *vt* to renounce, disavow; to repudiate.

scon'figgere [skon'fiddʒere] *vt* to defeat, overcome.

sconfi'nare *vi* to cross the border; (*in proprietà privata*) to trespass; (*fig*): **~ da** to stray *o* digress from; **sconfi'nato, a** *ag* boundless, unlimited.

scon'fitto, a *pp di* **sconfiggere** // *sf* defeat.

scon'forto *sm* despondency.

scongiu'rare [skondʒu'rare] *vt* (*implorare*) to entreat, beseech, implore; (*eludere: pericolo*) to ward off, avert; **scongi'uro** *sm* entreaty; (*esorcismo*) exorcism; **fare gli scongiuri** to touch wood.

scon'nesso, a *pp di* **sconnettere** // *ag* (*fig: discorso*) incoherent, rambling.

sconosci'uto, a [skonoʃ'ʃuto] *ag* unknown; new, strange // *sm/f* stranger; unknown person.

sconquas'sare *vt* to shatter, smash; (*scombussolare*) to upset.

sconside'rato, a *ag* thoughtless, rash.

sconsigli'are [skonsiʎ'ʎare] *vt*: **~ qc a qd** to advise sb against sth; **~ qd da fare qc** to advise sb not to do *o* against doing sth.

sconso'lato, a *ag* inconsolable; desolate.

scon'tare *vt* (*detrarre*) to deduct; (*debito*) to pay off; (*COMM*) to discount; (*pena*) to serve; (*colpa, errori*) to pay for, suffer for.

scon'tato, a *ag* (*previsto*) foreseen, taken for granted; **dare per ~ che** to take it for granted that.

scon'tento, a *ag*: **~ (di)** discontented *o* dissatisfied (with) // *sm* discontent, dissatisfaction.

'sconto *sm* discount.

scon'trarsi *vr* (*treni etc*) to crash, collide; (*venire a combattimento, fig*) to clash; **~ con** to crash into, collide with.

scon'trino *sm* ticket.

'scontro *sm* clash, encounter; crash, collision.

scon'troso, a *ag* sullen, surly; (*permaloso*) touchy.

sconveni'ente *ag* unseemly, improper.

scon'volgere [skon'vɔldʒere] *vt* to throw into confusion, upset; (*turbare*) to shake, disturb, upset; **scon'volto, a** *pp di* **sconvolgere**.

'scopa *sf* broom; (*CARTE*) Italian card game; **sco'pare** *vt* to sweep.

sco'perto, a *pp di* **scoprire** // *ag* uncovered; (*capo*) uncovered, bare; (*luogo*) open, exposed; (*MIL*) exposed, without cover; (*conto*) overdrawn // *sf* discovery.

'scopo *sm* aim, purpose; **a che ~?** what for?

scoppi'are *vi* (*2*) (*spaccarsi*) to burst; (*esplodere*) to explode; (*fig*) to break out; **~ in pianto** *o* **a piangere** to burst out crying; **~ dalle risa** *o* **dal ridere** to split one's sides laughing; **'scoppio** *sm* explosion; (*di tuono, arma etc*) crash, bang; (*fig: di risa, ira*) fit, outburst; (*: di guerra*) outbreak; **a scoppio ritardato** delayed-action.

scoppiet'tare *vi* to crackle.

sco'prire *vt* to discover; (*liberare da ciò che copre*) to uncover; (*: monumento*) to unveil; **~rsi** *vr* to put on lighter clothes; (*fig*) to give o.s. away.

scoraggi'are [skorad'dʒare] *vt* to discourage; **~rsi** *vr* to become discouraged, lose heart.

scorcia'toia [skortʃa'toja] *sf* short cut.

'scorcio ['skortʃo] *sm* (*ARTE*) foreshortening; (*di secolo, periodo*) end, close.

scor'dare *vt* to forget; **~rsi** *vr*: **~rsi di qc/di fare** to forget sth/to do.

'scorgere ['skɔrdʒere] *vt* to make out, distinguish, see.

'scorno *sm* ignominy, disgrace.

scorpacci'ata [skorpat'tʃata] *sf*: **fare**

una ~ **(di)** to stuff o.s. (with), eat one's fill (of).

scorpi'one sm scorpion; (dello zodiaco): S~ Scorpio.

scorraz'zare [skorrat'tsare] vi to run about.

'**scorrere** vt (giornale, lettera) to run o skim through // vi (2) (scivolare) to glide, slide; (colare, fluire) to run, flow; (trascorrere) to pass (by).

scor'retto, a ag incorrect; (sgarbato) impolite; (sconveniente) improper.

scor'revole ag (porta) sliding; (fig: stile) fluent, flowing.

scorri'banda sf (MIL) raid; (escursione) trip, excursion.

'**scorso, a** pp di **scorrere** // ag last // sf quick look, glance.

scor'soio, a ag: **nodo** ~ noose.

'**scorta** sf (di personalità, convoglio) escort; (provvista) supply, stock; **scor'tare** vt to escort.

scor'tese ag discourteous, rude; **scorte- 'sia** sf lack of courtesy, rudeness.

scorti'care vt to skin.

'**scorto, a** pp di **scorgere**.

'**scorza** ['skɔrdza] sf (di albero) bark; (di agrumi) peel, skin; (di pesce, serpente) skin.

sco'sceso, a [skoʃ'ʃeso] ag steep.

'**scosso, a** pp di **scuotere** // ag (turbato) shaken, upset // sf jerk, jolt, shake; (ELETTR, fig) shock.

scos'tante ag (fig) off-putting, unpleasant.

scos'tare vt to move (away), shift; ~**rsi** vr to move away.

scostu'mato, a ag immoral, dissolute.

scot'tare vt (ustionare) to burn; (: con liquido bollente) to scald; (sog: offesa) to hurt, offend // vi to burn; (caffè) to be too hot; **scotta'tura** sf burn; scald.

'**scotto, a** ag overcooked // sm (fig): **pagare lo** ~ **(di)** to pay the penalty (for).

sco'vare vt to drive out, flush out; (fig) to discover.

'**Scozia** ['skɔttsia] sf: **la** ~ Scotland; **scoz- 'zese** ag Scottish // sm/f Scot.

scredi'tare vt to discredit.

screpo'lare vt, ~**rsi** vr to crack; **screpola'tura** sf cracking q; crack.

screzi'ato, a [skret'tsjato] ag streaked, speckled.

'**screzio** ['skrɛttsjo] sm disagreement.

scricchio'lare [skrikkjo'lare] vi to creak, squeak.

scric'ciolo ['skrittʃolo] sm wren.

'**scrigno** ['skriɲɲo] sm casket.

scrimina'tura sf parting.

'**scritto, a** pp di **scrivere** // ag written // sm writing; (lettera) letter, note // sf inscription; ~**i** smpl (letterari etc) writing sg; **per o in** ~ in writing.

scrit'toio sm writing desk.

scrit'tore, 'trice sm/f writer.

scrit'tura sf writing; (COMM) entry; (contratto) contract; (REL): **la Sacra S**~ the Scriptures pl; ~**e** sfpl (COMM) accounts, books.

scrittu'rare vt (TEATRO, CINEMA) to sign up, engage; (COMM) to enter.

scriva'nia sf desk.

scri'vente sm/f writer.

'**scrivere** vt to write; **come si si scrive?** how is it spelt?, how do you write it?

scroc'cone, a sm/f scrounger.

'**scrofa** sf (ZOOL) sow.

scrol'lare vt to shake; ~**rsi** vr (anche fig) to give o.s. a shake; ~ **le spalle/il capo** to shrug one's shoulders/shake one's head.

scrosci'are [skroʃ'ʃare] vi (2) (pioggia) to pour down, pelt down; (torrente, fig: applausi) to thunder, roar; '**scroscio** sm pelting; thunder, roar; (di applausi) burst.

scros'tare vt (intonaco) to scrape off, strip; ~**rsi** vr to peel off, flake off.

'**scrupolo** sm scruple; (meticolosità) care, conscientiousness; **scrupo'loso, a** ag scrupulous; conscientious, thorough.

scru'tare vt to search, scrutinize; (intenzioni, causa) to examine, scrutinize.

scruti'nare vt (voti) to count; **scru'tinio** sm (votazione) ballot; (insieme delle operazioni) poll; (INS) (meeting for) assignment of marks at end of a term or year.

scu'cire [sku'tʃire] vt (orlo etc) to unpick, undo.

scude'ria sf stable.

scu'detto sm (SPORT) (championship) shield; (distintivo) badge.

'**scudo** sm shield.

scul'tore, 'trice sm/f sculptor.

scul'tura sf sculpture.

scu'ola sf school; ~ **elemen- tare/materna/media** primary/nur- sery/secondary school; ~ **guida** driving school.

scu'otere vt to shake; ~**rsi** vr to jump, be startled; (fig: muoversi) to rouse o.s., stir o.s.; (: commuoversi) to be shaken.

'**scure** sf axe.

'**scuro, a** ag dark; (fig: espressione) grim // sm darkness; dark colour; (imposta) (window) shutter; **verde/rosso** etc ~ dark green/red etc.

scur'rile ag scurrilous.

'**scusa** sf excuse; ~**e** sfpl apology sg, apologies; **chiedere** ~ **a qd (per)** to apologize to sb (for); **chiedo** ~ I'm sorry; (disturbando etc) excuse me.

scu'sare vt to excuse; ~**rsi** vr: ~**rsi (di)** to apologize (for); **(mi) scusi** I'm sorry; (per richiamare l'attenzione) excuse me.

sde'gnare [zdeɲ'ɲare] vt to scorn, despise; ~**rsi** vr (adirarsi) to get angry.

'**sdegno** ['zdeɲɲo] sm scorn, disdain; **sde- 'gnoso, a** ag scornful, disdainful.

sdolci'nato, a [zdoltʃi'nato] ag mawkish, oversentimental.

sdoppi'are vt (dividere) to divide o split in two.

sdrai'arsi vr to stretch out, lie down.

'**sdraio** sm: **sedia a** ~ deck chair.

sdruccio'lare [zdruttʃo'lare] vi (2) to slip, slide.

se pronome vedi **si** // cong if; (in frasi

interrogative indirette) if, whether; **non so** ~ **scrivere o telefonare** I don't know whether *o* if I should write or phone; ~ **mai** if, if ever; *(caso mai)* in case; ~ **solo** *o* **solamente** if only.

sé *pronome (gen)* oneself; *(esso, essa, lui, lei, loro)* itself; himself; herself; themselves; ~ **stesso(a)** *pronome* oneself; itself; himself; herself; ~ **stessi(e)** *pronome pl* themselves.

seb'bene *cong* although, though.

sec. *(abbr di* **secolo)** c.

'secca *sf vedi* **secco.**

sec'care *vt* to dry; *(prosciugare)* to dry up; *(fig: importunare)* to annoy, bother; ~ *(annoiare)* to bore // *vi (2)* to dry; to dry up; ~**rsi** *vr* to dry; to dry up; *(fig)* to grow annoyed; to grow bored; **secca'tura** *sf (fig)* bother *q,* trouble *q.*

'secchia ['sekkja] *sf* bucket, pail.

'secco, a, chi, che *ag* dry; *(fichi, pesce)* dried; *(foglie, ramo)* withered; *(magro: persona)* thin, skinny; *(fig: risposta, modo di fare)* curt, abrupt; *(: colpo)* clean, sharp // *sm (siccità)* drought // *sf (del mare)* shallows *pl;* **restarci** ~ *(fig: morire sul colpo)* to drop dead; **mettere in** ~ *(barca)* to beach; **rimanere in** *o* **a** ~ *(NAUT)* to run aground; *(fig)* to be left in the lurch.

seco'lare *ag* age-old, centuries-old; *(laico, mondano)* secular.

'secolo *sm* century; *(epoca)* age.

se'conda *sf vedi* **secondo.**

secon'dario, a *ag* secondary.

se'condo, a *ag* second // *sm* second; *(di pranzo)* main course // *sf (AUT)* second (gear) // *prep* according to; *(nel modo prescritto)* in accordance with; ~ **me** in my opinion, to my mind; **di** ~ **a classe** second-class; **di** ~**a mano** second-hand; **viaggiare in** ~**a** to travel second-class; **a** ~**a di** *prep* according to; in accordance with.

secrezi'one [sekret'tsjone] *sf* secretion.

'sedano *sm* celery.

seda'tivo, a *ag, sm* sedative.

'sede *sf* seat; *(di ditta)* head office; *(di organizzazione)* headquarters *pl;* **in** ~ **di** *(in occasione di)* during; ~ **sociale** registered office.

seden'tario, a *ag* sedentary.

se'dere *vi (2)* to sit, be seated; ~**rsi** *vr* to sit down // *sm (deretano)* behind, bottom.

'sedia *sf* chair.

sedi'cente [sedi'tʃɛnte] *ag* self-styled.

'sedici ['seditʃi] *num* sixteen.

se'dile *sm* seat; *(nei giardini)* bench.

sedi'mento *sm* sediment.

sedizi'one [sedit'tsjone] *sf* revolt, rebellion; **sedizi'oso, a** *ag* seditious; rebellious.

se'dotto, a *pp di* **sedurre.**

sedu'cente [sedu'tʃɛnte] *ag* seductive; *(proposta)* very attractive.

se'durre *vt* to seduce.

se'duta *sf* session, sitting; *(riunione)*

meeting; *(di modello)* sitting; ~ **stante** *(fig)* immediately.

seduzi'one [sedut'tsjone] *sf* seduction; *(fascino)* charm, appeal.

'sega, ghe *sf* saw.

'segale *sf* rye.

se'gare *vt* to saw; *(recidere)* to saw off; **sega'tura** *sf (residuo)* sawdust.

'seggio ['sɛddʒo] *sm* seat; ~ **elettorale** polling station.

'seggiola ['sɛddʒola] *sf* chair; **seggio'lone** *sm (per bambini)* highchair.

seggio'via [sɛddʒo'via] *sf* chairlift.

seghe'ria [sege'ria] *sf* sawmill.

seg'mento *sm* segment.

segna'lare [seɲɲa'lare] *vt (manovra etc)* to signal; to indicate; *(annunciare)* to announce; to report; *(fig: far conoscere)* to point out; *(: persona)* to single out; ~**rsi** *vr (distinguersi)* to distinguish o.s.

se'gnale [seɲ'ɲale] *sm* signal; *(cartello)* sign; ~ **d'allarme** alarm signal; *(FERR)* communication chord; ~ **orario** time signal; **segna'letica** *sf* signalling, signposting; **segnaletica stradale** roadsigns *pl.*

se'gnare [seɲ'ɲare] *vt* to mark; *(prendere nota)* to note; *(indicare)* to indicate, mark; *(SPORT: goal)* to score; ~**rsi** *vr (REL)* to make the sign of the cross, cross o.s.

'segno ['seɲɲo] *sm* sign; *(impronta, contrassegno)* mark; *(limite)* limit, bounds *pl;* *(bersaglio)* target; **fare** ~ **di sì/no** to nod (one's head)/shake one's head; **fare** ~ **a qd di fermarsi** to motion (to) sb to stop; **cogliere** *o* **colpire nel** ~ *(fig)* to hit the mark.

segre'gare *vt* to segregate, isolate; **segregazi'one** *sf* segregation.

segre'tario, a *sm/f* secretary; ~ **comunale** town clerk; ~ **di Stato** Secretary of State.

segrete'ria *sf (di ditta, scuola)* (secretary's) office; *(d'organizzazione internazionale)* secretariat; *(POL etc: carica)* office of Secretary.

segre'tezza [segre'tettsa] *sf* secrecy.

se'greto, a *ag* secret // *sm* secret; secrecy *q;* **in** ~ in secret, secretly.

segu'ace [se'gwatʃe] *sm/f* follower, disciple.

segu'ente *ag* following, next.

segu'ire *vt* to follow; *(frequentare: corso)* to attend // *vi (2)* to follow; *(continuare: testo)* to continue.

segui'tare *vt* to continue, carry on with // *vi* to continue, carry on.

'seguito *sm (scorta)* suite, retinue; *(discepoli)* followers *pl;* *(favore)* following; *(serie)* sequence, series *sg;* *(continuazione)* continuation; *(conseguenza)* result; **di** ~ at a stretch, on end; **in** ~ later on; **in** ~ **a, a** ~ **di** following; *(a causa di)* as a result of, owing to.

'sei *forma del vb* **essere** // *num* six.

sei'cento [sei'tʃɛnto] *num* six hundred // *sm:* **il S**~ the seventeenth century.

selci'ato [sel'tʃato] *sm* pavement.

selezio'nare [selettsjo'nare] *vt* to select.
selezi'one [selet'tsjone] *sf* selection.
'sella *sf* saddle; **sel'lare** *vt* to saddle.
selvag'gina [selvad'dʒina] *sf* (*animali*) game.
sel'vaggio, a, gi, ge [sel'vaddʒo] *ag* wild; (*tribù*) savage, uncivilized; (*fig*) savage, fierce; unsociable // *sm* savage.
sel'vatico, a, ci, che *ag* wild.
se'maforo *sm* (*AUT*) traffic lights *pl*.
sem'brare (2) *vi* to seem // *vb impers:* **sembra che** it seems that; **mi sembra che** it seems to me that; I think (that); ~ **di essere** to seem to be.
'seme *sm* seed; (*sperma*) semen; (*CARTE*) suit.
se'mestre *sm* half-year; (*INS*) semester.
'semi... *prefisso* semi...; **semi'cerchio** *sm* semicircle; **semifi'nale** *sf* semifinal; **semi'freddo, a** *ag* (*CUC*) chilled // *sm* ice-cream cake.
'semina *sf* (*AGR*) sowing.
semi'nare *vt* to sow.
semi'nario *sm* seminar; (*REL*) seminary.
se'mitico, a, ci, che *ag* semitic.
sem'mai = se mai; *vedi* **se**.
'semola *sf* bran.
semo'lino *sm* semolina.
'semplice ['semplitʃe] *ag* simple; (*di un solo elemento*) single; **semplice'mente** *av* simply; **semplicità** *sf* simplicity; **semplifi'care** *vt* to simplify.
'sempre *av* always; (*ancora*) still; **posso ~ tentare** I can always try, anyway, I can try; **per ~** forever; **una volta per ~** once and for all; ~ **che** *cong* provided (that); ~ **più** more and more; ~ **meno** less and less.
sempre'verde *ag, sm o f* (*BOT*) evergreen.
'senape *sf* (*CUC*) mustard.
se'nato *sm* senate; **sena'tore, 'trice** *sm/f* senator.
se'nile *ag* senile.
'senno *sm* judgment, (common) sense.
'seno *sm* (*petto*) breast; (*ventre materno, fig*) womb; (*GEO*) inlet, creek; (*ANAT*) sinus; (*MAT*) sine.
sen'sato, a *ag* sensible.
sensazio'nale [sensattsjo'nale] *ag* sensational.
sensazi'one [sensat'tsjone] *sf* sensation; **fare ~** to cause a sensation, create a stir.
sen'sibile *ag* sensitive; (*ai sensi*) perceptible; (*rilevante, notevole*) appreciable, noticeable; ~ **a** sensitive to; **sensibilità** *sf* sensitivity.
'senso *sm* (*FISIOL, istinto*) sense; (*impressione, sensazione*) feeling, sensation; (*significato*) meaning, sense; (*direzione*) direction; ~**i** *smpl* (*coscienza*) consciousness *sg*; (*sensualità*) senses; **ciò non ha ~** that doesn't make sense; **fare ~ a** (*ripugnare*) to disgust, repel; ~ **comune** common sense; **in ~ orario/antiorario** clockwise/anticlockwise; ~ **unico, ~ vietato** (*AUT*) one-way street.

sensu'ale *ag* sensual; sensuous; **sensualità** *sf* sensuality; sensuousness.
sen'tenza [sen'tɛntsa] *sf* (*DIR*) sentence; (*massima*) maxim; **sentenzi'are** *vi* (*DIR*) to pass judgment.
senti'ero *sm* path.
sentimen'tale *ag* sentimental; (*vita, avventura*) love *cpd*.
senti'mento *sm* feeling.
senti'nella *sf* sentry.
sen'tire *vt* (*percepire al tatto, fig*) to feel; (*udire*) to hear; (*ascoltare*) to listen to; (*odore*) to smell; (*avvertire con il gusto, assaggiare*) to taste // *vi:* ~ **di** (*avere sapore*) to taste of; (*avere odore*) to smell of; ~**rsi bene/male** to feel well/unwell *o* ill; ~**rsi di fare qc** (*essere disposto*) to feel like doing sth.
sen'tito, a *ag* (*sincero*) sincere, warm; **per ~ dire** by hearsay.
'senza ['sɛntsa] *prep, cong* without; ~ **dir nulla** without saying a word; **fare ~ qc** to do without sth; ~ **di me** without me; ~ **che io lo sapessi** without me *o* my knowing; **senz'altro** of course, certainly; ~ **dubbio** no doubt; ~ **scrupoli** unscrupulous; ~ **amici** friendless.
sepa'rare *vt* to separate; (*dividere*) to divide; (*tenere distinto*) to distinguish; ~**rsi** *vr* (*coniugi*) to separate, part; (*amici*) to part, leave each other; ~**rsi da** (*coniuge*) to separate *o* part from; (*amico, socio*) to part company with; (*oggetto*) to part with; **separazi'one** *sf* separation.
se'polcro *sm* sepulchre.
se'polto, a *pp di* **seppellire**.
seppel'lire *vt* to bury.
'seppia *sf* cuttlefish // *ag inv* sepia.
se'quenza [se'kwɛntsa] *sf* sequence.
seques'trare *vt* (*DIR*) to impound; (*rapire*) to kidnap; (*costringere in un luogo*) to keep, confine; **se'questro** *sm* (*DIR*) impoundment; **sequestro di persona** kidnapping; illegal confinement.
'sera *sf* evening; **di ~** in the evening; **domani ~** tomorrow evening, tomorrow night; **se'rale** *ag* evening *cpd*; **se'rata** *sf* evening; (*ricevimento*) party.
ser'bare *vt* to keep; (*mettere da parte*) to put aside; ~ **rancore/odio verso qd** to bear sb a grudge/hate sb.
serba'toio *sm* tank; (*di apparecchio igienico*) cistern; (*TECN*) reservoir.
'serbo *sm:* **mettere** (*o tenere o avere*) **in ~ qc** to put (*o* keep) sth aside.
sere'nata *sf* (*MUS*) serenade.
serenità *sf* serenity.
se'reno, a *ag* (*tempo, cielo*) clear; (*fig*) serene, calm.
ser'gente [ser'dʒɛnte] *sm* (*MIL*) sergeant.
'serie *sf inv* (*successione*) series *inv*; (*gruppo, collezione: di chiavi etc*) set; (*SPORT*) division; league; (*COMM*): **modello di ~/fuori ~** standard/custom-built model; **in ~** in quick succession; (*COMM*) mass *cpd*.
serietà *sf* seriousness; reliability.
'serio, a *ag* serious; (*impiegato*)

responsible, reliable; (ditta, cliente) reliable, dependable; sul ~ (davvero) really, truly; (seriamente) seriously, in earnest.

ser'mone sm sermon.

serpeggi'are [serped'dʒare] vi to wind; (fig) to spread.

ser'pente sm snake; ~ a sonagli rattlesnake.

'serra sf greenhouse; hothouse.

ser'randa sf roller shutter.

ser'rare vt to close, shut; (a chiave) to lock; (stringere) to tighten; (premere: nemico) to close in on; ~ i pugni/i denti to clench one's fists/teeth; ~ le file to close ranks.

serra'tura sf lock.

'serva sf vedi servo.

ser'vire vt to serve; (clienti: al ristorante) to wait on; (: al negozio) to serve, attend to; (fig: giovare) to aid, help // vi (TENNIS) to serve; (2) (essere utile): ~ a qd to be of use to sb; ~ a qc/a fare (utensile etc) to be used for sth/for doing; ~ (a qd) di to serve as (for sb); ~rsi vr (usare): ~rsi di to use; (prendere: cibo): ~rsi (di) to help o.s. (to); (essere cliente abituale): ~rsi da to be a regular customer at, go to.

servitù sf servitude; slavery; captivity; (personale di servizio) servants pl, domestic staff.

servizi'evole [servit'tsjevole] ag obliging, willing to help.

ser'vizio [ser'vittsjo] sm service; (compenso: al ristorante) service (charge); (STAMPA, TV, RADIO) report; (da tè, caffè etc) set, service; ~i smpl (di casa) kitchen and bathroom; (ECON) services; essere di ~ to be on duty; fare ~ to operate; (essere aperto) to be open; (essere di turno) to be on duty; ~ militare military service; ~i segreti secret service sg.

'servo, a sm/f servant.

ses'santa num sixty.

sessan'tina sf: una ~ (di) about sixty.

sessi'one sf session.

'sesso sm sex; sessu'ale ag sexual, sex cpd.

ses'tante sm sextant.

'sesto, a ag, sm sixth.

'seta sf silk.

'sete sf thirst; avere ~ to be thirsty.

'setola sf bristle.

'setta sf sect.

set'tanta num seventy.

settan'tina sf: una ~ (di) about seventy.

'sette num seven.

sette'cento [sette'tʃento] num seven hundred // sm: il S~ the eighteenth century.

set'tembre sm September.

settentrio'nale ag northern.

settentri'one sm north.

'settico, a, ci, che ag (MED) septic.

setti'mana sf week; settima'nale ag, sm weekly.

'settimo, a ag, sm seventh.

set'tore sm sector.

severità sf severity.

se'vero, a ag severe.

se'vizie [se'vittsje] sfpl torture sg; sevi'zi'are vt to torture.

sezio'nare [settsjo'nare] vt to divide into sections; (MED) to dissect.

sezi'one [set'tsjone] sf section; (MED) dissection.

sfaccen'dato, a [sfattʃen'dato] ag idle.

sfacci'ato, a [sfat'tʃato] ag (maleducato) cheeky, impudent; (vistoso) gaudy.

sfa'celo [sfa'tʃelo] sm (fig) ruin, collapse.

sfal'darsi vr to flake (off).

'sfarzo ['sfartso] sm pomp, splendour.

sfasci'are [sfaʃ'ʃare] vt (ferita) to unbandage; (distruggere: porta) to smash, shatter; ~rsi vr (rompersi) to smash, shatter; (fig) to collapse.

sfa'tare vt (leggenda) to explode.

sfavil'lare vi to spark, send out sparks; (risplendere) to sparkle.

sfavo'revole ag unfavourable.

'sfera sf sphere; 'sferico, a, ci, che ag spherical.

sfer'rare vt (fig: colpo) to land, deal; (: attacco) to launch.

sfer'zare [sfer'tsare] vt to whip; (fig) to lash out at.

sfiata'toio sm blowhole.

sfi'brare vt (indebolire) to exhaust, enervate.

'sfida sf challenge; sfi'dare vt to challenge; (fig) to defy, brave.

sfi'ducia [sfi'dutʃa] sf distrust, mistrust.

sfigu'rare vt (persona) to disfigure; (quadro, statua) to deface // vi (far cattiva figura) to make a bad impression.

sfi'lare vt to unthread; (abito, scarpe) to slip off // vi (truppe) to march past; (atleti) to parade; ~rsi vr (perle etc) to come unstrung; (calza) to run, ladder; sfi'lata sf march past; parade; sfilata di moda fashion show.

'sfinge ['sfindʒe] sf sphinx.

sfi'nito, a ag exhausted.

sfio'rare vt to brush (against); (argomento) to touch upon.

sfio'rire vi (2) to wither, fade.

sfo'cato, a ag (FOT) out of focus.

sfoci'are [sfo'tʃare] vi (2): ~ in to flow into.

sfo'gare vt to vent, pour out; ~rsi vr (sfogare la propria rabbia) to give vent to one's anger; (confidarsi): ~rsi (con) to pour out one's feelings (to); non sfogarti su di me! don't take your bad temper out on me!

sfoggi'are [sfod'dʒare] vt, vi to show off.

'sfoglia ['sfoʎʎa] sf sheet of pasta dough; pasta ~ (CUC) puff pastry.

sfogli'are [sfoʎ'ʎare] vt (libro) to leaf through.

'sfogo, ghi sm outlet; (eruzione cutanea) rash; (fig) outburst; dare ~ a (fig) to give vent to.

sfolgo'rare *vi* to blaze.

sfol'lare *vt* to empty, clear // *vi* (2) to disperse; (*in tempo di guerra*): ~ **(da)** to evacuate.

sfon'dare *vt* (*porta*) to break down; (*scarpe*) to wear a hole in; (*cesto, scatola*) to burst, knock the bottom out of; (*MIL*) to break through // *vi* (*riuscire*) to make a name for o.s.

'sfondo *sm* background.

sfor'mato *sm* (*CUC*) type of soufflé.

sfor'nire *vt*: ~ **di** to deprive of.

sfor'tuna *sf* misfortune, ill luck *q*; **sfortu'nato, a** *ag* unlucky; (*impresa, film*) unsuccessful.

sfor'zare [sfor'tsare] *vt* to force; ~**rsi** *vr*: ~**rsi di** *o a o per* **fare** to try hard to do.

'sforzo ['sfortso] *sm* effort; (*tensione eccessiva, TECN*) strain.

sfrat'tare *vt* to evict; **'sfratto** *sm* eviction.

sfrec'ciare [sfret'tʃare] *vi* (2) to shoot *o* flash past.

sfregi'are [sfre'dʒare] *vt* to slash, gash; (*persona*) to disfigure; (*quadro*) to deface; **'sfregio** *sm* gash; scar; (*fig*) insult.

sfre'nato, a *ag* (*fig*) unrestrained, unbridled.

sfron'tato, a *ag* shameless.

sfrutta'mento *sm* exploitation.

sfrut'tare *vt* (*terreno*) to overwork, exhaust; (*miniera*) to exploit, work; (*fig: operai, occasione, potere*) to exploit.

sfug'gire [sfud'dʒire] *vi* (2) to escape; ~ **a** (*custode*) to escape (from); (*morte*) to escape; ~ **a qd** (*dettaglio, nome*) to escape sb; ~ **di mano a qd** to slip out of sb's hand (*o* hands); **sfug'gita: di sfuggita** *ad* (*rapidamente, in fretta*) in passing.

sfu'mare *vt* (*colori, contorni*) to soften, shade off // *vi* (2) to shade (off), fade; (*svanire*) to vanish, disappear; (*fig: speranze*) to come to nothing; **sfuma'tura** *sf* shading off *q*; (*tonalità*) shade, tone; (*fig*) touch, hint.

sfuri'ata *sf* (*scatto di collera*) fit of anger; (*rimprovero*) sharp rebuke.

sga'bello *sm* stool.

sgabuz'zino [sgabud'dzino] *sm* lumber room.

sgambet'tare *vi* to kick one's legs about; to scurry along.

sgam'betto *sm*: **far lo** ~ **a qd** to trip sb up.

sganasci'arsi [zganaʃ'ʃarsi] *vr*: ~ **dalle risa** to roar with laughter.

sganci'are [zgan'tʃare] *vt* to unhook; (*FERR*) to uncouple; (*bombe: da aereo*) to release, drop; (*fig: fam: soldi*) to fork out.

sganghe'rato, a [zgange'rato] *ag* (*porta*) off its hinges; (*auto*) ramshackle; (*riso*) wild, boisterous.

sgar'bato, a *ag* rude, impolite.

'sgarbo *sm*: **fare uno** ~ **a qd** to be rude to sb.

sgattaio'lare *vi* to sneak away *o* off.

sge'lare [zdʒe'lare] *vi* (2), *vt* to thaw.

'sghembo, a ['zgembo] *ag* (*obliquo*) slanting; (*storto*) crooked.

sghignaz'zare [zgiɲɲat'tsare] *vi* to laugh scornfully.

sgob'bare *vi* (*fam: scolaro*) to swot; (*: operaio*) to slog.

sgoccio'lare [zgottʃo'lare] *vt* (*vuotare*) to drain (to the last drop) // *vi* (*acqua*) to drip; (*recipiente*) to drain.

sgo'larsi *vr* to talk (*o* shout *o* sing) o.s. hoarse.

sgomb(e)'rare *vt* to clear; (*andarsene da: stanza*) to vacate; (*evacuare*) to evacuate.

'sgombro, a *ag*: ~ **(di)** clear (of), free (from) // *sm* (*trasloco*) removal; (*ZOOL*) mackerel.

sgomen'tare *vt* to dismay; ~**rsi** *vr* to be dismayed; **sgo'mento, a** *ag* dismayed // *sm* dismay, consternation.

sgonfi'are *vt* to let down, deflate; ~**rsi** *vr* to go down.

'sgorbio *sm* blot; scribble.

sgor'gare *vi* (2) to gush (out).

sgoz'zare [zgot'tsare] *vt* to cut the throat of.

sgra'devole *ag* unpleasant, disagreeable.

sgra'dito, a *ag* unpleasant, unwelcome.

sgra'nare *vt* (*piselli*) to shell; ~ **gli occhi** to open one's eyes wide.

sgran'chirsi [zgran'kirsi] *vr* to stretch; ~ **le gambe** to stretch one's legs.

sgranocchi'are [zgranok'kjare] *vt* to munch.

'sgravio *sm*: ~ **fiscale** tax relief.

sgrazi'ato, a [zgrat'tsjato] *ag* clumsy, ungainly.

sgreto'lare *vt* to cause to crumble; ~**rsi** *vr* to crumble.

sgri'dare *vt* to scold; **sgri'data** *sf* scolding.

sguai'ato, a *ag* coarse, vulgar.

sgual'cire [zgwal'tʃire] *vt* to crumple (up), crease.

sgual'drina *sf* (*peg*) slut.

sgu'ardo *sm* (*occhiata*) look, glance; (*espressione*) look (in one's eye).

sguaz'zare [zgwat'tsare] *vi* (*nell'acqua*) to splash about; (*nella melma*) to wallow; ~ **nella ricchezza** to be rolling in money.

sguinzagli'are [zgwintsaʎ'ʎare] *vt* to let off the leash.

sgusci'are [zguʃ'ʃare] *vt* to shell // *vi* (*uccelli*) to hatch; (*sfuggire di mano*) to slip; (*fig*) to slip *o* slink away.

'shampoo ['ʃampo] *sm inv* shampoo.

shock [ʃɔk] *sm inv* shock.

si *pronome* (*dav* **lo, la, li, le, ne** diventa **se**) (*riflessivo*) oneself, *m* himself, *f* herself, itself; *pl* themselves; (*soggetto non umano*) itself; *pl* themselves; (*reciproco*) one another, each other; (*passivante*): **lo** ~ **ripara facilmente** it is easily repaired; (*possessivo*): **lavarsi le mani** to wash one's hands; (*impersonale*): ~ **vede che è felice** one *o* you can see that he's happy; (*noi*): **tra poco** ~ **parte** we're leaving soon; (*la gente*): ~ **dice che**

they *o* people say that // *sm* (MUS) B; (: *solfeggiando la scala*) ti.

sì *av* yes.

'sia *cong*: ~ ... ~ (*o* ... *o*): ~ **che lavori,** ~ **che non lavori** whether he works or not; (*tanto ... quanto*): **verranno ~ Luigi** ~ **suo fratello** both Luigi and his brother will be coming.

sia'mese *ag* siamese.

si'amo *forma del vb* **essere.**

Si'beria *sf*: la ~ Siberia.

sibi'lare *vi* to hiss; (*fischiare*) to whistle; '**sibilo** *sm* hiss; whistle.

si'cario *sm* hired killer.

sicché [sik'ke] *cong* (*perciò*) so (that), therefore; (*e quindi*) (and) so.

siccità [sitʃi'ta] *sf* drought.

sic'come *cong* since, as.

Si'cilia [si'tʃilja] *sf*: la ~ Sicily; **sicili'ano, a** *ag, sm/f* Sicilian.

sico'moro *sm* sycamore.

sicu'rezza [siku'rettsa] *sf* safety; security; (*fiducia*) confidence; (*certezza*) certainty; **di** ~ safety *cpd*; **la** ~ **stradale** road safety.

si'curo, a *ag* safe; (*ben difeso*) secure; (*fiducioso*) confident; (*certo*) sure, certain; (*notizia, amico*) reliable; (*esperto*) skilled // *av* (*anche*: **di** ~) certainly; **essere/mettere al** ~ to be safe/put in a safe place; **sentirsi** ~ to feel safe *o* secure.

siderur'gia [siderur'dʒia] *sf* iron and steel industry.

'**sidro** *sm* cider.

si'epe *sf* hedge.

si'ero *sm* (MED) serum.

si'esta *sf* siesta, (afternoon) nap.

si'ete *forma del vb* **essere.**

si'filide *sf* syphilis.

si'fone *sm* siphon.

Sig. (*abbr di* **signore**) Mr.

siga'retta *sf* cigarette.

'**sigaro** *sm* cigar.

Sigg. (*abbr di* **signori**) Messrs.

sigil'lare [sidʒil'lare] *vt* to seal.

si'gillo [si'dʒillo] *sm* seal.

'**sigla** *sf* initials *pl*; acronym, abbreviation; ~ **musicale** signature tune.

si'glare *vt* to initial.

Sig.na *abbr di* **signorina.**

signifi'care [siɲɲifi'kare] *vt* to mean; **significa'tivo, a** *ag* significant; **signifi'cato** *sm* meaning.

si'gnora [siɲ'ɲora] *sf* lady; **la** ~ **X** Mrs ['mɪsɪz] X; **buon giorno S~/Signore/Signorina** good morning; (*deferente*) good morning Madam/ Sir/Madam; (*quando si conosce il nome*) good morning Mrs/Mr/Miss X; **Gentile S~/Signore/Signorina** (*in una lettera*) Dear Madam/Sir/Madam; **il signor Rossi e** ~ Mr Rossi and his wife; ~**e e signori** ladies and gentlemen.

si'gnore [siɲ'ɲore] *sm* gentleman; (*padrone*) lord, master; (REL) **il S~** the Lord; **il signor X** Mr ['mɪstə°] X; **i** ~**i**

Bianchi (*coniugi*) Mr and Mrs Bianchi; *vedi anche* **signora.**

signo'rile [siɲɲo'rile] *ag* refined.

signo'rina [siɲɲo'rina] *sf* young lady; **la** ~ **X** Miss X; *vedi anche* **signora.**

Sig.ra (*abbr di* **signora**) Mrs.

silenzia'tore [silentsja'tore] *sm* silencer.

si'lenzio [si'lɛntsjo] *sm* silence; **silenzi'oso, a** *ag* silent, quiet.

'**sillaba** *sf* syllable.

silu'rare *vt* to torpedo; (*fig: privare del comando*) to oust.

si'luro *sm* torpedo.

simboleggi'are [simboled'dʒare] *vt* to symbolize.

sim'bolico, a, ci, che *ag* symbolic(al).

simbo'lismo *sm* symbolism.

'**simbolo** *sm* symbol.

'**simile** *ag* (*analogo*) similar; (*di questo tipo*): **un uomo** ~ such a man, a man like this; **libri** ~**i** such books; ~ **a** similar to; **i suoi** ~**i** one's fellow men; one's peers.

simme'tria *sf* symmetry; **sim'metrico, a, ci, che** *ag* symmetrical.

simpa'tia *sf* (*inclinazione*) liking; (*partecipazione ai sentimenti di qd*) sympathy; **avere** ~ **per qd** to like sb, have a liking for sb; **sim'patico, a, ci, che** *ag* nice, friendly; pleasant; likeable.

simpatiz'zare [simpatid'dzare] *vi*: ~ **con** to take a liking to.

sim'posio *sm* symposium.

simu'lare *vt* to sham, simulate; (TECN) to simulate; **simulazi'one** *sf* shamming; simulation.

simul'taneo, a *ag* simultaneous.

sina'goga, ghe *sf* synagogue.

sincerità [sintʃeri'ta] *sf* sincerity.

sin'cero, a [sin'tʃero] *ag* sincere; genuine; heartfelt.

'**sincope** *sf* syncopation; (MED) blackout.

sincroniz'zare [sinkronid'dzare] *vt* to synchronize.

sinda'cale *ag* (trade-)union *cpd*; **sindaca'lista, i, e** *sm/f* trade unionist.

sinda'cato *sm* (*di lavoratori*) (trade) union; (AMM, ECON, DIR) syndicate, trust, pool; ~ **dei datori di lavoro** employers' association, employers' federation.

'**sindaco, ci** *sm* mayor.

'**sindrome** *sf* (MED) syndrome.

sinfo'nia *sf* (MUS) symphony.

singhioz'zare [singjot'tsare] *vi* to sob; to hiccup.

singhi'ozzo [sin'gjottso] *sm* sob; (MED) hiccup; **avere il** ~ to have the hiccups; **a** ~ (*fig*) by fits and starts.

singo'lare *ag* (*insolito*) remarkable, singular; (LING) singular // *sm* (LING) singular; (TENNIS): ~ **maschile/femminile** men's/women's singles.

'**singolo, a** *ag* single, individual // *sm* (*persona*) individual; (TENNIS) = **singolare.**

si'nistro, a *ag* left, left-hand; (*fig*) sinister // *sm* (*incidente*) accident // *sf* (POL) left (wing); **a ~a** on the left; (*direzione*) to the left.

'sino *prep* = **fino**.

si'nonimo, a *ag* synonymous // *sm* synonym; **~ di** synonymous with.

sin'tassi *sf* syntax.

'sintesi *sf* synthesis; (*riassunto*) summary, résumé.

sin'tetico, a, ci, che *ag* synthetic.

sintetiz'zare [sintetid'dzare] *vt* to synthesize; (*riassumere*) to summarize.

sinto'matico, a, ci, che *ag* symptomatic.

'sintomo *sm* symptom.

sinu'oso, a *ag* (*strada*) winding.

si'pario *sm* (TEATRO) curtain.

si'rena *sf* (*apparecchio*) siren; (*nella mitologia, fig*) siren, mermaid.

'Siria *sf*: **la ~** Syria; **siri'ano, a** *ag, sm/f* Syrian.

si'ringa, ghe *sf* syringe.

'sismico, a, ci, che *ag* seismic.

sis'mografo *sm* seismograph.

sis'tema, i *sm* system; method, way; **cambiare ~** to change one's way of life.

siste'mare *vt* (*mettere a posto*) to tidy, put in order; (*risolvere: questione*) to sort out, settle; (*procurare un lavoro a*) to find a job for; (*dare un alloggio a*) to settle, find accommodation for; **~rsi** *vr* to settle down; (*trovarsi un lavoro*) to get fixed up with a job; **ti sistemo io!** I'll soon sort you out!

siste'matico, a, ci, che *ag* systematic.

sistemazi'one [sistemat'tsjone] *sf* arrangement; order; settlement; employment; accommodation.

situ'are *vt* to site, situate; **situ'ato, a** *ag*: **situato a/su** situated at/on.

situazi'one [situat'tsjone] *sf* situation.

slacci'are [zlat'tʃare] *vt* to undo, unfasten.

slanci'arsi [zlan'tʃarsi] *vr* to dash, fling o.s.; **slanci'ato, a** *ag* slender; **'slancio** *sm* dash, leap; (*fig*) surge.

sla'vato, a *ag* faded, washed out; (*fig: viso, occhi*) pale, colourless.

'slavo, a *ag* Slav(onic), Slavic.

sle'ale *ag* disloyal; (*concorrenza etc*) unfair.

sle'gare *vt* to untie.

'slitta *sf* sledge; (*trainata*) sleigh.

slit'tare *vi* (2) to slide; (AUT) to skid.

slo'gare *vt* (MED) to dislocate.

sloggi'are [zlod'dʒare] *vt* (*inquilino*) to turn out; (*nemico*) to drive out, dislodge // *vi* to move out.

smacchi'are [zmak'kjare] *vt* to remove stains from.

'smacco, chi *sm* humiliating defeat.

smagli'ante [zmaʎ'ʎante] *ag* brilliant, dazzling.

smagli'are [zmaʎ'ʎare] *vt*, **~rsi** *vr* (*calza*) to ladder.

smalizi'ato, a [smalit'tsjato] *ag* shrewd, cunning.

smal'tare *vt* to enamel; (*a vetro*) to glaze; (*unghie*) to varnish.

smal'tire *vt* (*merce*) to sell; (: *svendere*) to sell off; (*rifiuti*) to dispose of; (*cibo*) to digest; **~ la sbornia** to sober up.

'smalto *sm* (*anche: di denti*) enamel; (*per ceramica*) glaze; **~ per unghie** nail varnish.

'smania *sf* agitation, restlessness; (*fig*) longing, desire; **avere la ~ addosso** to have the fidgets; **smani'are** *vi* (*agitarsi*) to be restless o agitated; (*fig*): **smaniare di fare** to long o yearn to do.

smantel'lare *vt* to dismantle.

smarri'mento *sm* loss; (*fig*) bewilderment; dismay.

smar'rire *vt* to lose; (*non riuscire a trovare*) to mislay; **~rsi** *vr* (*perdersi*) to lose one's way, get lost; (: *oggetto*) to go astray; (*fig: turbarsi*) to be bewildered; (*essere sbigottito*) to be dismayed.

smasche'rare [zmaske'rare] *vt* to unmask.

smemo'rato, a *ag* forgetful.

smen'tire *vt* (*negare*) to deny; (*sbugiardare*) to give the lie to; (*sconfessare*) to retract, take back; **~rsi** *vr* to be inconsistent (in one's behaviour); **smen'tita** *sf* denial; retraction.

sme'raldo *sm* emerald.

smerci'are [zmer'tʃare] *vt* (COMM) to sell; (: *svendere*) to sell off.

sme'riglio [zme'riʎʎo] *sm* emery.

'smesso, a *pp di* **smettere**.

'smettere *vt* to stop; (*vestiti*) to stop wearing // *vi* to stop, cease; **~ di fare** to stop doing.

'smilzo, a ['zmiltso] *ag* thin, lean.

sminu'ire *vt* to diminish, lessen; (*fig*) to belittle.

sminuz'zare [zminut'tsare] *vt* to break into small pieces; to crumble.

smis'tare *vt* (*pacchi etc*) to sort; (FERR) to shunt.

smisu'rato, a *ag* boundless, immeasurable; (*grandissimo*) immense, enormous.

smobili'tare *vt* to demobilize, demob (*col*).

smo'dato, a *ag* immoderate.

smoking ['zmɔukiŋ] *sm inv* dinner jacket.

smon'tare *vt* (*mobile, macchina etc*) to take to pieces, dismantle; (*far scendere: da veicolo*) to let off, drop (off); (*fig: scoraggiare*) to dishearten // *vi* (2) (*scendere: da cavallo*) to dismount; (: *da treno*) to get off; (*terminare il lavoro*) to stop (work); **~rsi** *vr* to lose heart; to lose one's enthusiasm.

'smorfia *sf* grimace; (*atteggiamento lezioso*) simpering; **fare ~e** to make faces; to simper; **smorfi'oso, a** *ag* simpering.

'smorto, a *ag* (*viso*) pale, wan; (*colore*) dull.

smor'zare [zmor'tsare] *vt* (*suoni*) to deaden; (*colori*) to tone down; (*luce*) to dim; (*sete*) to quench; (*entusiasmo*) to dampen; **~rsi** *vr* (*attutirsi*) to fade away.

'smosso, a *pp di* **smuovere**.

smotta'mento *sm* landslide.

'smunto, a *ag* haggard, pinched.

smu'overe *vt* to move, shift; (*fig: commuovere*) to move; (*: dall'inerzia*) to rouse, stir; ~**rsi** *vr* to move, shift.

smus'sare *vt* (*angolo*) to round off, smooth; (*lama etc*) to blunt; ~**rsi** *vr* to become blunt.

snatu'rato, a *ag* inhuman, heartless.

'snello, a *ag* (*agile*) agile; (*svelto*) slender, slim.

sner'vare *vt* to enervate, wear out; ~**rsi** *vr* to become enervated.

sni'dare *vt* to drive out, flush out.

snob'bare *vt* to snub.

sno'bismo *sm* snobbery.

snoccio'lare [znɔttʃo'lare] *vt* (*frutta*) to stone; (*fig: orazioni*) to rattle off; (*: verità*) to blab; (*: fam: soldi*) to shell out.

sno'dare *vt* to untie, undo; (*rendere agile, mobile*) to loosen; ~**rsi** *vr* to come loose; (*articolarsi*) to bend; (*strada, fiume*) to wind.

so *forma del vb* **sapere**.

so'ave *ag* sweet, gentle, soft.

sobbal'zare [sobbal'tsare] *vi* to jolt, jerk; (*trasalire*) to jump, start; **sob'balzo** *sm* jerk, jolt; jump, start.

sobbar'carsi *vr:* ~ **a** to take on, undertake.

sob'borgo, ghi *sm* suburb.

sobil'lare *vt* to stir up, incite.

'sobrio, a *ag* temperate; sober.

socchi'udere [sok'kjudere] *vt* (*porta*) to leave ajar; (*occhi*) to half-close; **socchi'uso, a** *pp di* **socchiudere**.

soc'correre *vt* to help, assist; **soc'corso, a** *pp di* **soccorrere** // *sm* help, aid, assistance; **soccorsi** *smpl* (*MIL*) reinforcements.

socialdemo'cratico, a, ci, che [sotʃaldemo'kratiko] *sm/f* Social Democrat.

soci'ale [so'tʃale] *ag* social; (*di associazione*) club *cpd*, association *cpd*.

socia'lismo [sotʃa'lizmo] *sm* socialism; **socia'lista, i, e** *ag, sm/f* socialist.

società [sotʃe'ta] *sf inv* society; (*sportiva*) club; (*COMM*) company; ~ **per azioni** (**S.p.A.**) limited company.

soci'evole [so'tʃevole] *ag* sociable.

'socio ['sɔtʃo] *sm* (*DIR, COMM*) partner; (*membro di associazione*) member.

'soda *sf* (*CHIM*) soda; (*acqua gassata*) soda (water).

soda'lizio [soda'littsjo] *sm* association, society.

soddis'fare *vt, vi:* ~ **a** to satisfy; (*impegno*) to fulfil; (*debito*) to pay off; (*richiesta*) to meet, comply with; (*offesa*) to make amends for; **soddis'fatto, a** *pp di* **soddisfare** // *ag* satisfied; **soddisfatto di** happy *o* satisfied with; pleased with; **soddisfazi'one** *sf* satisfaction.

'sodo, a *ag* firm, hard; (*fig*) sound // *av* (*picchiare, lavorare*) hard; **dormire** ~ to sleep soundly.

sofà *sm inv* sofa.

soffe'renza [soffe'rɛntsa] *sf* suffering.

sof'ferto, a *pp di* **soffrire**.

soffi'are *vt* to blow; (*notizia, segreto*) to whisper // *vi* to blow; ~**rsi il naso** to blow one's nose; ~ **qc/qd a qd** (*fig*) to pinch *o* steal sth/sb from sb; ~ **via qc** to blow sth away.

'soffice ['soffitʃe] *ag* soft.

'soffio *sm* (*di vento*) breath; (*di fumo*) puff; (*MED*) murmur.

sof'fitta *sf* attic.

sof'fitto *sm* ceiling.

soffo'care *vi* (*anche:* ~**rsi**) to suffocate, choke // *vt* to suffocate, choke; (*fig*) to stifle, suppress; **soffocazi'one** *sf* suffocation.

sof'friggere [sof'friddʒere] *vt* to fry lightly.

sof'frire *vt* to suffer, endure; (*sopportare*) to bear, stand // *vi* to suffer; to be in pain; ~ (**di**) **qc** (*MED*) to suffer from sth.

sof'fritto, a *pp di* **soffriggere**.

sofisti'care *vt* (*vino, cibo*) to adulterate // *vi* to split hairs, quibble; **sofisti'cato, a** *ag* sophisticated.

sogget'tivo, a [soddʒet'tivo] *ag* subjective.

sog'getto, a [sod'dʒɛtto] *ag:* ~ **a** (*sottomesso*) subject to; (*esposto: a variazioni, danni etc*) subject *o* liable to // *sm* subject.

soggezi'one [soddʒet'tsjone] *sf* subjection; (*timidezza*) awe; **avere** ~ **di qd** to stand in awe of sb; to be ill at ease in sb's presence.

sogghi'gnare [soggiŋ'ɲare] *vi* to sneer.

soggior'nare [soddʒor'nare] *vi* to stay; **soggi'orno** *sm* (*invernale, marino*) stay; (*stanza*) living room.

'soglia ['sɔʎʎa] *sf* doorstep; (*anche fig*) threshold.

'sogliola ['sɔʎʎola] *sf* (*ZOOL*) sole.

so'gnare [soɲ'ɲare] *vt, vi* to dream; ~ **a occhi aperti** to daydream; **sogna'tore, 'trice** *sm/f* dreamer.

'sogno ['soɲɲo] *sm* dream.

'soia *sf* (*BOT*) soya.

sol *sm* (*MUS*) G; (*: solfeggiando la scala*) so(h).

so'laio *sm* (*soffitta*) attic.

sola'mente *av* only, just.

so'lare *ag* solar, sun *cpd*.

'solco, chi *sm* (*scavo, fig: ruga*) furrow; (*incavo*) rut, track; (*di disco*) groove; (*scia*) wake.

sol'dato *sm* soldier; ~ **semplice** private.

'soldo *sm* (*fig*): **non avere un** ~ to be penniless; **non vale un** ~ it's not worth a penny; ~**i** *smpl* (*denaro*) money *sg*.

'sole *sm* sun; (*luce*) sun(light); (*tempo assolato*) sun(shine); **prendere il** ~ to sunbathe.

so'lenne *ag* solemn; **solennità** *sf* solemnity; grand occasion.

sol'fato *sm* (*CHIM*) sulphate.

sol'furo *sm* (*CHIM*) sulphur.

soli'dale *ag* (*DIR*) joint and several.

solidarietà *sf* solidarity.

solidifi'care *vt, vi* (2) (*anche:* ~**rsi**) to solidify.

solidità *sf* solidity.

'solido, a *ag* solid; (*forte, robusto*) sturdy, solid; (*fig: ditta*) sound, solid // *sm* (*MAT*) solid.

soli'loquio *sm* soliloquy.

so'lista, i, e *ag* solo // *sm/f* soloist.

solita'mente *av* usually, as a rule.

soli'tario, a *ag* (*senza compagnia*) solitary, lonely; (*solo, isolato*) solitary, lone; (*deserto*) lonely // *sm* (*gioiello, gioco*) solitaire.

'solito, a *ag* usual; **essere** ~ **fare** to be in the habit of doing; **di** ~ usually; **più tardi del** ~ later than usual; **come al** ~ as usual.

soli'tudine *sf* solitude.

solleci'tare [solletʃi'tare] *vt* (*lavoro*) to speed up; (*persona*) to urge on; (*chiedere con insistenza*) to press for, request urgently; (*stimolare*) : ~ **qd a fare** to urge sb to do; (*TECN*) to stress; **sollecitazi'one** *sf* entreaty, request; (*fig*) incentive; (*TECN*) stress.

sol'lecito, a [sol'letʃito] *ag* prompt, quick // *sm* (*lettera*) reminder; **solleci'tudine** *sf* promptness, speed.

solleti'care *vt* to tickle.

solle'vare *vt* to lift, raise; (*fig: persona: alleggerire*) : ~ (**da**) to relieve (of); (*: dar conforto*) to comfort, relieve; (*: questione*) to raise; (*: far insorgere*) to stir (to revolt); ~**rsi** *vr* to rise; (*fig: riprendersi*) to recover; (*: ribellarsi*) to rise up.

solli'evo *sm* relief; (*conforto*) comfort.

'solo, a *ag* alone; (*in senso spirituale: isolato*) lonely; (*unico*) : **un** ~ **libro** only one book, a single book; (*con ag numerale*) : **veniamo noi tre** ~**i** just *o* only the three of us are coming // *av* (*soltanto*) only, just; **non** ~ **... ma anche** not only ... but also; **fare qc da** ~ to do sth (all) by oneself; **da me** ~ single-handed, on my own.

sol'stizio [sol'stittsjo] *sm* solstice.

sol'tanto *av* only.

so'lubile *ag* (*sostanza*) soluble.

soluzi'one [solut'tsjone] *sf* solution.

sol'vente *ag, sm* solvent.

'soma *sf* load, burden; **bestia da** ~ beast of burden.

so'maro *sm* ass, donkey.

somigli'anza [somiʎ'ʎantsa] *sf* resemblance.

somigli'are [somiʎ'ʎare] *vi* (2) : ~ **a** to be like, resemble; (*nell'aspetto fisico*) to look like; ~**rsi** *vr* to be (*o* look) alike.

'somma *sf* (*MAT*) sum; (*di denaro*) sum (of money); (*complesso di varie cose*) whole amount, sum total.

som'mare *vt* to add up; (*aggiungere*) to add; **tutto sommato** all things considered.

som'mario, a *ag* (*racconto, indagine*) brief; (*giustizia*) summary // *sm* summary.

som'mergere [som'mɛrdʒere] *vt* to submerge.

sommer'gibile [sommer'dʒibile] *sm* submarine.

som'merso, a *pp di* **sommergere**.

som'messo, a *ag* (*voce*) soft, subdued.

somminis'trare *vt* to give, administer.

sommità *sf inv* top; (*di monte*) summit, top; (*fig*) height.

'sommo, a *ag* highest, topmost; (*fig*) supreme; (*the*) greatest // *sm* (*fig*) height; **per** ~**i capi** briefly, covering the main points.

som'mossa *sf* uprising.

so'naglio [so'naʎʎo] *sm* bell.

so'nare *etc* = **suonare** *etc*.

son'daggio [son'daddʒo] *sm* sounding; probe; boring, drilling; (*indagine*) survey; ~ (**d'opinioni**) (opinion) poll.

son'dare *vt* (*NAUT*) to sound; (*atmosfera, piaga*) to probe; (*MINERALOGIA*) to bore, drill; (*fig*) to sound out; to probe.

so'netto *sm* sonnet.

son'nambulo, a *sm/f* sleepwalker.

sonnecchi'are [sonnek'kjare] *vi* to doze, nod.

son'nifero *sm* sleeping drug (*o* pill).

'sonno *sm* sleep; **prendere** ~ to fall asleep; **aver** ~ to be sleepy.

'sono *forma del vb* **essere**.

so'noro, a *ag* (*ambiente*) resonant; (*voce*) sonorous, ringing; (*onde, film*) sound *cpd*.

sontu'oso, a *ag* sumptuous; lavish.

sopo'rifero, a *ag* soporific.

soppe'sare *vt* to weigh in one's hand(s), feel the weight of; (*fig*) to weigh up.

soppi'atto: di ~ *av* secretly; furtively.

soppor'tare *vt* (*reggere*) to support; (*subire: perdita, spese*) to bear, sustain; (*soffrire: dolore*) to bear, endure; (*sog: cosa: freddo*) to withstand; (*sog: persona: freddo, vino*) to take; (*tollerare*) to put up with, tolerate.

soppressi'one *sf* suppression; deletion.

sop'presso, a *pp di* **sopprimere**.

sop'primere *vt* (*carica, privilegi, testimone*) to do away with; (*pubblicazione*) to suppress; (*parola, frase*) to delete.

'sopra *prep* (*gen*) on; (*al di sopra di, più in alto di*) above; over; (*riguardo a*) on, about // *av* on top; (*attaccato, scritto*) on it; (*al di sopra*) above; (*al piano superiore*) upstairs; **donne** ~ **i 30 anni** women over 30 (years of age); **dormirci** ~ (*fig*) to sleep on it.

so'prabito *sm* overcoat.

soprac'ciglio [soprat'tʃiʎʎo] *pl(f)* **soprac'ciglia** *sm* eyebrow.

sopracco'perta *sf* (*di letto*) bedspread; (*di libro*) jacket.

soprad'detto, a *ag* aforesaid.

sopraf'fare *vt* to overcome, overwhelm; **sopraf'fatto, a** *pp di* **sopraffare**.

sopraf'fino, a *ag* excellent; (*fig*) consummate, supreme.

sopraggi'ungere [soprad'dʒundʒere] *vi* (2) (*giungere all'improvviso*) to arrive (unexpectedly); (*accadere*) to occur (unexpectedly).

soprannatu'rale *ag* supernatural.

sopran'nome *sm* nickname.

so'prano, a *sm/f* (*persona*) soprano // *sm* (*voce*) soprano.

soprappensi'ero *av* lost in thought.

sopras'salto *sm*: **di ~** with a start; suddenly.

soprasse'dere *vi*: **~ a** to delay, put off.

soprat'tutto *av* (*anzitutto*) above all; (*specialmente*) especially.

sopravve'nire *vi* (2) to arrive, appear; (*fatto*) to occur.

sopravvis'suto, a *pp di* **sopravvivere.**

soprav'vivere *vi* (2) to survive; (*continuare a vivere*): **~ (in)** to live on (in); **~ a** (*incidente etc*) to survive; (*persona*) to outlive.

soprinten'dente *sm/f* supervisor; (*statale*: *di belle arti etc*) keeper; **soprinten'denza** *sf* (*ente*): **soprintendenza alle Antichità e ai Monumenti** ≈ National Trust.

so'pruso *sm* abuse of power; **fare un ~ a qd** to treat sb unjustly.

soq'quadro *sm*: **mettere a ~** to turn upside-down.

sor'betto *sm* sorbet, water ice.

sor'bire *vt* to sip; (*fig*) to put up with.

'sordido, a *ag* sordid; (*fig*: *gretto*) stingy.

sor'dina *sf*: **in ~** softly; (*fig*) on the sly.

sordità *sf* deafness.

'sordo, a *ag* deaf; (*rumore*) muffled; (*dolore*) dull; (*lotta*) silent, hidden // *sm/f* deaf person; **sordo'muto, a** *ag* deaf-and-dumb // *sm/f* deaf-mute.

so'rella *sf* sister; **sorel'lastra** *sf* stepsister.

sor'gente [sor'dʒɛnte] *sf* (*acqua che sgorga*) spring; (*di fiume*, FISICA, *fig*) source.

'sorgere ['sordʒere] *vi* (2) to rise; (*scaturire*) to spring, rise; (*fig*: *difficoltà*) to arise.

sormon'tare *vt* (*fig*) to overcome, surmount.

sorni'one, a *ag* sly.

sorpas'sare *vt* (AUT) to overtake; (*fig*) to surpass; (: *eccedere*) to exceed, go beyond; **~ in altezza** to be higher than; (*persona*) to be taller than.

sor'prendere *vt* (*cogliere*: *in flagrante etc*) to catch; (*stupire*, *prendere a un tratto*) to surprise; **~rsi** *vr*: **~rsi (di)** to be surprised (at); **sor'preso, a** *pp di* **sorprendere** // *sf* surprise.

sor'reggere [sor'rɛddʒere] *vt* to support, hold up; (*fig*) to sustain; **sor'retto, a** *pp di* **sorreggere.**

sor'ridere *vi* to smile; **sor'riso, a** *pp di* **sorridere** // *sm* smile.

'sorso *sm* sip.

'sorta *sf* sort, kind; **di ~** whatever, of any kind, at all.

'sorte *sf* (*fato*) fate, destiny; (*evento fortuito*) chance; **tirare a ~** to draw lots.

sor'teggio [sor'teddʒo] *sm* draw.

sorti'legio [sorti'ledʒo] *sm* witchcraft *q*; (*incantesimo*) spell; **fare un ~ a qd** to cast a spell on sb.

sor'tire *vi* (2) (*uscire a sorte*) to come out, be drawn.

sor'tita *sf* (MIL) sortie.

'sorto, a *pp di* **sorgere.**

sorvegli'anza [sorveʎ'ʎantsa] *sf* watch; supervision; (POLIZIA, MIL) surveillance.

sorvegli'are [sorveʎ'ʎare] *vt* (*bambino, bagagli, prigioniero*) to watch, keep an eye on; (*malato*) to watch over; (*territorio, casa*) to watch o keep watch over; (*lavori*) to supervise.

sorvo'lare *vt* (*territorio*) to fly over // *vi*: **~ su** (*fig*) to skim over.

'sosia *sm inv* double.

sos'pendere *vt* (*appendere*) to hang (up); (*interrompere, privare di una carica*) to suspend; (*rimandare*) to defer; **~ un quadro al muro/un lampadario al soffitto** to hang a picture on the wall/a chandelier from the ceiling; **sospensi'one** *sf* (*anche* CHIM, AUT) suspension; deferment; **sos'peso, a** *pp di* **sospendere** // *ag* (*appeso*): **sospeso a** hanging on (o from); (*fig*) anxious; **in sospeso** in abeyance; (*conto*) outstanding; **tenere in sospeso** (*fig*) to keep in suspense.

sospet'tare *vt* to suspect // *vi*: **~ di** to suspect; (*diffidare*) to be suspicious of.

sos'petto, a *ag* suspicious // *sm* suspicion; **sospet'toso, a** *ag* suspicious.

sos'pingere [sos'pindʒere] *vt* to drive, push; **sos'pinto, a** *pp di* **sospingere.**

sospi'rare *vi* to sigh // *vt* to long for, yearn for; **sos'piro** *sm* sigh.

'sosta *sf* (*fermata*) stop, halt; (*pausa*) pause, break; **senza ~** non-stop, without a break.

sostan'tivo *sm* noun, substantive.

sos'tanza [sos'tantsa] *sf* substance; **~e** *sfpl* (*ricchezze*) wealth *sg*, possessions; **in ~** in short, to sum up; **sostanzi'oso, a** *ag* (*cibo*) nourishing, substantial.

sos'tare *vi* (*fermarsi*) to stop (for a while), stay; (*fare una pausa*) to take a break.

sos'tegno [sos'teɲɲo] *sm* support.

soste'nere *vt* to support; (*prendere su di sé*) to take on, bear; (*resistere*) to withstand, stand up to; (*affermare*): **~ che** to maintain that; **~rsi** *vt* to hold o.s. up, support o.s.; (*fig*) to keep up one's strength; **~ gli esami** to sit exams; **sosteni'tore, 'trice** *sm/f* supporter.

sostenta'mento *sm* maintenance.

soste'nuto, a *ag* (*riservato*) reserved, aloof; (*stile*) elevated; (*prezzo*) continuing high.

sostitu'ire *vt* (*mettere al posto di*): **~ qd/qc a** to substitute sb/sth for; (*prendere il posto di*: *persona*) to substitute for; (: *cosa*) to take the place of.

sosti'tuto, a *sm/f* substitute.

sostituzi'one [sostitut'tsjone] *sf* substitution; **in ~ di** as a substitute for, in place of.

sotta'ceti [sotta'tʃeti] *smpl* pickles.

sot'tana sf (sottoveste) underskirt; (gonna) skirt; (REL) soutane, cassock.

sotter'fugio [sotter'fudʒo] sm subterfuge.

sotter'raneo, a ag underground // sm cellar // sf (FERR) underground.

sotter'rare vt to bury.

sottigli'ezza [sottiʎ'ʎettsa] sf thinness; slimness; (fig: acutezza) subtlety; shrewdness; ~e sfpl (pedanteria) quibbles.

sot'tile ag thin; (figura, caviglia) thin, slim, slender; (fine: polvere, capelli) fine; (fig: leggero) light; (: vista) sharp, keen; (: olfatto) fine, discriminating; (: mente) subtle; shrewd.

sottin'tendere vt (intendere qc non espresso) to understand; (implicare) to imply; **sottin'teso, a** pp di **sottintendere** // sm allusion; **parlare senza sottintesi** to speak plainly.

'sotto prep (gen) under; (più in basso di) below // av underneath, beneath; below; (al piano inferiore) downstairs; ~ il monte at the foot of the mountain; ~ la pioggia/il sole in the rain/sun(shine); ~ terra underground; ~ voce in a low voice; chiuso ~ vuoto vacuum packed.

sottoline'are vt to underline; (fig) to emphasize, stress.

sottoma'rino, a ag (flora) submarine; (cavo, navigazione) underwater // sm (NAUT) submarine.

sotto'messo, a pp di **sottomettere**.

sotto'mettere vt to subdue, subjugate; ~rsi vr to submit.

sottopas'saggio [sottopas'saddʒo] sm (AUT) underpass; (pedonale) subway, underpass.

sotto'porre vt (costringere) to subject; (fig: presentare) to submit; **sottoporsi** vr to submit; **sottoporsi a** (subire) to undergo; **sotto'posto, a** pp di **sottoporre**.

sottos'critto, a pp di **sottoscrivere**.

sottos'crivere vt to sign // vi: ~ a to subscribe to; **sottoscrizi'one** sf signing; subscription.

sottosegre'tario sm: ~ di Stato Under-Secretary of State.

sotto'sopra av upside-down.

sotto'terra av underground.

sotto'titolo sm subtitle.

sotto'veste sf underskirt.

sotto'voce [sotto'votʃe] av in a low voice.

sot'trarre vt (MAT) to subtract, take away; ~ qd/qc a (togliere) to remove sb/sth from; (salvare) to save o rescue sb/sth from; ~ qc a qd (rubare) to steal sth from sb; **sottrarsi vr: sottrarsi a** (sfuggire) to escape; (evitare) to avoid; **sot'tratto, a** pp di **sottrarre**; **sottrazi'one** sf subtraction; removal.

sovi'etico, a, ci, che ag Soviet // sm/f Soviet citizen.

sovraccari'care vt to overload.

sovrac'carico, a, chi, che ag: ~ (di) overloaded (with) // sm excess load; ~ di lavoro extra work.

sovrannatu'rale ag = **sopran-naturale**.

so'vrano, a ag sovereign; (fig: sommo) supreme // sm/f sovereign, monarch.

sovras'tare vi (2): ~ a, vt (vallata, fiume) to overhang; (fig) to hang over, threaten.

sovrinten'dente sm/f = **soprintendente**; **sovrinten'denza** sf = **soprintendenza**.

sovru'mano, a ag superhuman.

sovvenzi'one [sovven'tsjone] sf subsidy, grant.

sovver'sivo, a ag subversive.

'sozzo, a ['sottso] ag filthy, dirty.

S.p.A. abbr vedi **società**.

spac'care vt to split, break; (legna) to chop; ~rsi vr to split, break; **spacca'tura** sf split.

spacci'are [spat'tʃare] vt (vendere) to sell (off); (mettere in circolazione) to circulate; ~rsi vr: ~rsi per (farsi credere) to pass o.s. off as, pretend to be; **spaccia'tore, 'trice** sm/f (di droga) pusher; (di denaro falso) dealer; **'spaccio** sm sale; (bottega) shop.

'spacco, chi sm (fenditura) split, crack; (strappo) tear; (di gonna) slit.

spac'cone sm/f boaster, braggart.

'spada sf sword.

spae'sato, a ag disorientated, lost.

spa'ghetti [spa'getti] smpl (CUC) spaghetti sg.

'Spagna ['spaɲɲa] sf: la ~ Spain; **spa'gnolo, a** ag Spanish // sm/f Spaniard // sm (LING) Spanish; **gli Spagnoli** the Spanish.

'spago, ghi sm string, twine.

spai'ato, a ag (calza, guanto) odd.

spalan'care vt, ~rsi vr to open wide.

spa'lare vt to shovel.

'spalla sf shoulder; (fig: TEATRO) stooge; ~e sfpl (dorso) back; **spalleggi'are** vt to back up, support.

spal'letta sf (parapetto) parapet.

spalli'era sf (di sedia etc) back; (di letto: da capo) head(board); (: da piedi) foot(board); (GINNASTICA) wall bars pl.

spal'mare vt to spread.

'spandere vt to spread; (versare) to pour (out); ~rsi vr to spread; ~ lacrime to shed tears; **'spanto, a** pp di **spandere**.

spa'rare vt to fire // vi (far fuoco) to fire; (tirare) to shoot; **spara'tore** sm gunman; **spara'toria** sf exchange of shots.

sparecchi'are [sparek'kjare] vt: ~ (la tavola) to clear the table.

spa'reggio [spa'reddʒo] sm (SPORT) play-off.

'spargere ['spardʒere] vt (gettare all'intorno) to scatter, strew; (versare: vino) to spill; (: lacrime, sangue) to shed; (diffondere) to spread; (emanare) to give off (o out); ~rsi vr to spread; **spargi'mento** sm scattering, strewing; spilling; shedding; **spargimento di sangue** bloodshed.

spa'rire vi (2) to disappear, vanish.

spar'lare vi: ~ di to run down, speak ill of.

'sparo *sm* shot.

sparpagli'are [sparpaʎ'ʎare] *vt*, **~rsi** *vr* to scatter.

'sparso, a *pp di* **spargere** // *ag* scattered; (*sciolto*) loose.

spar'tire *vt* (*eredità, bottino*) to share out; (*avversari*) to separate.

sparti'traffico *sm inv* (*AUT*) central reservation.

spa'ruto, a *ag* (*viso etc*) haggard.

sparvi'ero *sm* (*ZOOL*) sparrowhawk.

spasi'mare *vi* to be in agony; **~ di fare** (*fig*) to yearn to do; **~ per qd** to be madly in love with sb.

'spasimo *sm* pang; **'spasmo** *sm* (*MED*) spasm; **spas'modico, a, ci, che** *ag* (*angoscioso*) agonizing; (*MED*) spasmodic.

spassio'nato, a *ag* dispassionate, impartial.

'spasso *sm* (*divertimento*) amusement, enjoyment; **andare a ~** to go out for a walk; **essere a ~** (*fig*) to be out of work; **mandare qd a ~** to send sb packing.

'spatola *sf* spatula.

spau'racchio [spau'rakkjo] *sm* scarecrow.

spau'rire *vt* to frighten, terrify.

spa'valdo, a *ag* arrogant, bold.

spaventa'passeri *sm inv* scarecrow.

spaven'tare *vt* to frighten, scare; **~rsi** *vr* to be frightened, be scared; to get a fright; **spa'vento** *sm* fear, fright; **far spavento a qd** to give sb a fright; **spaven'toso, a** *ag* frightening, terrible; (*fig: fam*) tremendous, fantastic.

spazien'tire [spattsjen'tire] *vi* (2) (*anche:* **~rsi**) to lose one's patience.

'spazio ['spattsjo] *sm* space; **spazi'oso, a** *ag* spacious.

spazzaca'mino [spattsaka'mino] *sm* chimney sweep.

spaz'zare [spat'tsare] *vt* to sweep; (*foglie etc*) to sweep up; (*cacciare*) to sweep away; **spazza'tura** *sf* sweepings *pl*; (*immondizia*) rubbish; **spaz'zino** *sm* street sweeper.

'spazzola ['spattsola] *sf* brush; **~ per abiti** clothesbrush; **~ da capelli** hairbrush; **spazzo'lare** *vt* to brush; **spazzo-'lino** *sm* (small) brush; **spazzolino da denti** toothbrush.

specchi'arsi [spek'kjarsi] *vr* to look at o.s. in a mirror; (*riflettersi*) to be mirrored, be reflected; (*fig*): **~ in qd** to model o.s. on sb.

'specchio ['spekkjo] *sm* mirror.

speci'ale [spe'tʃale] *ag* special; **specia-'lista, i, e** *sm/f* specialist; **specialità** *sf inv* speciality; (*branca di studio*) special field, speciality; **specializ'zarsi** *vr*: **specializzarsi (in)** to specialize (in); **special'mente** *av* especially, particularly.

'specie ['spetʃe] *sf inv* (*BIOL, BOT, ZOOL*) species *inv*; (*tipo*) kind, sort // *av* especially, particularly; **fare ~ a qd** to surprise sb; **la ~ umana** mankind.

specifi'care [spetʃifi'kare] *vt* to specify, state.

spe'cifico, a, ci, che [spe'tʃifiko] *ag* specific.

specu'lare *vi* to speculate; **~ su** (*COMM*) to speculate in; (*meditare*) to speculate on; (*sfruttare*) to exploit; **speculazi'one** *sf* speculation.

spe'dire *vt* to send; **spedizi'one** *sf* sending; (*collo*) parcel, consignment; (*scientifica etc*) expedition.

'spegnere ['speɲɲere] *vt* (*fuoco, sigaretta*) to put out, extinguish; (*apparecchio elettrico*) to turn o switch off; (*fig: suoni, passioni*) to stifle; (*debito*) to extinguish; **~rsi** *vr* to go out; to go off; (*morire*) to pass away.

spel'lare *vt* (*scuoiare*) to skin; (*scorticare*) to graze; **~rsi** *vr* to peel.

'spendere *vt* to spend.

spen'nare *vt* to pluck.

spensie'rato, a *ag* carefree.

'spento, a *pp di* **spegnere** // *ag* (*suono*) muffled; (*colore*) dull; (*civiltà, vulcano*) extinct.

spe'ranza [spe'rantsa] *sf* hope.

spe'rare *vt* to hope for // *vi*: **~ in** to trust in; **~ che/di fare** to hope that/to do; **lo spero, spero di sì** I hope so.

sper'duto, a *ag* (*isolato*) out-of-the-way; (*persona: smarrita, a disagio*) lost.

spergi'uro, a [sper'dʒuro] *sm/f* perjurer // *sm* perjury.

sperimen'tale *ag* experimental.

sperimen'tare *vt* to experiment with, test; (*fig*) to test, put to the test.

'sperma, i *sm* (*BIOL*) sperm.

spe'rone *sm* spur.

sperpe'rare *vt* to squander.

'spesa *sf* (*somma di denaro*) expense; (*costo*) cost; (*acquisto*) purchase; (*fam: acquisto del cibo quotidiano*) shopping; **~e** *sfpl* expenses; (*COMM*) costs; charges; **fare la ~** to do the shopping; **a ~ di** (*a carico di*) at the expense of; **~e generali** overheads; **~e postali** postage *sg*; **~e di viaggio** travelling expenses.

'speso, a *pp di* **spendere**.

'spesso, a *ag* (*fitto*) thick; (*frequente*) frequent // *av* often; **~e volte** frequently, often.

spes'sore *sm* thickness.

spet'tabile *ag* (*abbr*: **Spett.**: *in lettere*): **~ ditta X** Messrs X and Co.

spet'tacolo *sm* (*rappresentazione*) performance, show; (*vista, scena*) sight; **dare ~ di sé** to make an exhibition o a spectacle of o.s.; **spettaco'loso, a** *ag* spectacular.

spet'tanza [spet'tantsa] *sf* (*competenza*) concern; **non è di mia ~** it's no concern of mine.

spet'tare *vi* (2): **~ a** (*decisione*) to be up to; (*stipendio*) to be due to; **spetta a te decidere** it's up to you to decide.

spetta'tore, 'trice *sm/f* (*CINEMA, TEATRO*) member of the audience; (*di avvenimento*) onlooker, witness.

spetti'nare vt: ~ qd to ruffle sb's hair; ~**rsi** vr to get one's hair in a mess.

'spettro sm (fantasma) spectre; (FISICA) spectrum.

'spezie ['spɛttsje] sfpl (CUC) spices.

spez'zare [spet'tsare] vt (rompere) to break; (fig: interrompere) to break up; ~**rsi** vr to break.

spezza'tino [spettsa'tino] sm (CUC) stew.

spezzet'tare [spettset'tare] vt to break up (o chop) into small pieces.

'spia sf spy; (confidente della polizia) informer; (ELETTR) indicating light; warning light; (fessura) spy hole, peephole; (fig: sintomo) sign, indication.

spia'cente [spja'tʃɛnte] ag sorry; essere ~ **di qc/di fare qc** to be sorry about sth/for doing sth.

spia'cevole [spja'tʃevole] ag unpleasant, disagreeable.

spi'aggia, ge ['spjaddʒa] sf beach.

spia'nare vt (terreno) to level, make level; (edificio) to raze to the ground; (pasta) to roll out; (rendere liscio) to smooth (out).

spi'ano sm: a tutto ~ (lavorare) non-stop, without a break; (spendere) lavishly.

spian'tato, a ag penniless, ruined.

spi'are vt to spy on; (occasione etc) to watch o wait for.

spi'azzo ['spjattso] sm open space; (radura) clearing.

spic'care vt (staccare) to detach, cut off; (foglia, fiore) to pick, pluck; (parole) to pronounce distinctly; (assegno, mandato di cattura) to issue // vi (risaltare) to stand out; ~ **il volo** to fly up; (fig) to take flight; ~ **un balzo** to take a leap; **spic'cato, a** ag (marcato) marked, strong; (notevole) remarkable.

'spicchio ['spikkjo] sm (di agrumi) segment; (di aglio) clove; (parte) piece, slice.

spicci'arsi [spit'tʃarsi] vr to hurry up.

'spicciolo, a ['spittʃolo] ag: **moneta ~a, ~i** smpl (small) change.

'spicco, chi sm prominence; **fare ~** to stand out.

spi'edo sm (CUC) spit.

spie'gare vt (far capire) to explain; (tovaglia) to unfold; (vele) to unfurl; ~**rsi** vr to explain o.s., make o.s. clear; **il problema si spiega** one can understand the problem; **spiegazi'one** sf explanation; **avere una spiegazione con qd** to have it out with sb.

spiegaz'zare [spjegat'tsare] vt to crease, crumple.

spie'tato, a ag ruthless, pitiless.

spiffe'rare vt (fam) to blurt out, blab // vi to whistle.

'spiga, ghe sf (BOT) ear.

spigli'ato, a [spiʎ'ʎato] ag self-possessed, self-confident.

spigo'lare vt (anche fig) to glean.

'spigolo sm corner; (MAT) edge.

'spilla sf brooch; (da cravatta, cappello) pin.

spil'lare vt (vino, fig) to tap; ~ **denaro/notizie a qd** to tap sb for money/information.

'spillo sm pin; (spilla) brooch; ~ **di sicurezza** o **da balia** safety pin; ~ **di sicurezza** (MIL) safety pin.

spi'lorcio, a, ci, ce [spi'lortʃo] ag mean, stingy.

'spina sf (BOT) thorn; (ZOOL) spine, prickle; (di pesce) bone; (ELETTR) plug; (di botte) bunghole; **birra alla** ~ draught beer; ~ **dorsale** (ANAT) backbone.

spi'nacio [spi'natʃo] sm spinach q.

spi'nale ag (ANAT) spinal.

'spingere ['spindʒere] vt to push; (condurre: anche fig) to drive; (stimolare): ~ **qd a fare** to urge o press sb to do; ~**rsi** vr (inoltrarsi) to push on, carry on; ~**rsi troppo lontano** (anche fig) to go too far; **fin dove spinge lo sguardo** as far as the eye can see.

spi'noso, a ag thorny, prickly.

'spinto, a pp di **spingere** // sf (urto) push; (FISICA) thrust; (fig: stimolo) incentive, spur; (: appoggio) string-pulling q; **dare una ~a a qd** (fig) to pull strings for sb.

spio'naggio [spio'naddʒo] sm espionage, spying.

spi'overe vi (2) (scorrere) to flow down; (ricadere) to hang down, fall.

'spira sf coil.

spi'raglio [spi'raʎʎo] sm (fessura) chink, narrow opening; (raggio di luce, fig) glimmer, gleam; **uno ~ d'aria** a breath of air.

spi'rale sf spiral; (contraccettivo) coil; **a ~** spiral(-shaped).

spi'rare vi (vento) to blow; (2: morire) to expire, pass away.

spiri'tato, a ag possessed; (fig: persona, espressione) wild.

spiri'tismo sm spiritualism.

'spirito sm (REL, CHIM, disposizione d'animo, di legge etc, fantasma) spirit; (pensieri, intelletto) mind; (arguzia) wit; (umorismo) humour, wit; **lo S**~ **Santo** the Holy Spirit o Ghost.

spirito'saggine [spirito'saddʒine] sf witticism; (peg) wisecrack.

spiri'toso, a ag witty.

spiritu'ale ag spiritual.

'splendere vi to shine.

'splendido, a ag splendid; (splendente) shining; (sfarzoso) magnificent, splendid.

splen'dore sm splendour; (luce intensa) brilliance, brightness.

spodes'tare vt to deprive of power; (sovrano) to depose.

'spoglia ['spoʎʎa] sf vedi **spoglio**.

spogli'are [spoʎ'ʎare] vt (svestire) to undress; (privare, fig: depredare): ~ **qd di qc** to deprive sb of sth; (togliere ornamenti: anche fig): ~ **qd/qc di** to strip sb/sth of; (fare lo spoglio di) to go through, peruse; ~**rsi** vr to undress, strip; ~**rsi di** (ricchezze etc) to deprive o.s. of, give up; (pregiudizi) to rid o.s. of; **spoglia'toio** sm dressing room; (di scuola etc) cloakroom;

(SPORT) changing room; **'spoglio, a** ag (pianta, terreno) bare; (privo): ~ **di** stripped of; lacking in, without // sm going through, perusal // sf (ZOOL) skin, hide; (: di rettile) slough; **spoglie** sfpl (preda) spoils, booty sg.

'spola sf shuttle; (bobina di filo) cop; **fare la ~ (fra)** to go to and fro o shuttle (between).

spol'pare vt to strip the flesh off.

spolve'rare vt (anche CUC) to dust; (con spazzola) to brush; (con battipanni) to beat; (fig) to polish off // vi to dust.

'sponda sf (di fiume) bank; (di mare, lago) shore; (bordo) edge.

spon'taneo, a ag spontaneous; (persona) unaffected, natural.

spopo'lare vt to depopulate // vi (attirare folla) to draw the crowds; ~**rsi** vr to become depopulated.

spo'radico, a, ci, che ag sporadic.

spor'care vt to dirty, make dirty; (fig) to sully, soil; ~**rsi** vr to get dirty.

spor'cizia [spor'tʃittsja] sf (stato) dirtiness; (sudiciume) dirt, filth; (: cosa sporca) dirt q, something dirty; (fig: cosa oscena) obscenity.

'sporco, a, chi, che ag dirty, filthy.

spor'genza [spor'dʒɛntsa] sf projection.

'sporgere ['spɔrdʒere] vt to put out, stretch out // vi (2) (venire in fuori) to stick out; (protendersi) to jut out; ~**rsi** vr to lean out; ~ **querela contro qd** (DIR) to take legal action against sb.

sport inv sm sport.

'sporta sf shopping bag.

spor'tello sm (di treno, auto etc) door; (di banca, ufficio) window, counter.

spor'tivo, a ag (gara, giornale) sports cpd; (persona) sporty; (abito) casual; (spirito, atteggiamento) sporting.

'sporto, a pp di **sporgere**.

'sposa sf bride; (moglie) wife.

sposa'lizio [spoza'littsjo] sm wedding.

spo'sare vt to marry; (fig: idea, fede) to espouse; ~**rsi** vr to get married, marry; ~**rsi con qd** to marry sb, get married to sb.

'sposo sm (bride)groom; (marito) husband; **gli ~ i** smpl the newlyweds.

spos'sato, a ag exhausted, weary.

spos'tare vt to move, shift; (cambiare: orario) to change; ~**rsi** vr to move.

'spranga, ghe sf (sbarra) bar; (catenaccio) bolt.

'sprazzo ['sprattso] sm (di sole etc) flash; (fig: di gioia etc) burst.

spre'care vt to waste; ~**rsi** vr (persona) to waste one's energy; **'spreco** sm waste.

spre'gevole [spre'dʒevole] ag contemptible, despicable.

spregiudi'cato, a [spredʒudi'kato] ag unprejudiced, unbiased; (peg) unscrupulous.

'spremere vt to squeeze.

spre'muta sf fresh juice; ~ **d'arancia** fresh orange juice.

sprez'zante [spret'tsante] ag scornful, contemptuous.

sprigio'nare [spridʒo'nare] vt to give off, emit; ~**rsi** vr to emanate; (uscire con impeto) to burst out.

spriz'zare [sprit'tsare] vt, vi (2) to spurt; ~ **gioia/salute** to be bursting with joy/health.

sprofon'dare vi (2) to sink; (casa) to collapse; (suolo) to give way, subside; ~**rsi** vr: ~**rsi in** (poltrona) to sink into; (fig) to become immersed o absorbed in.

spro'nare vt to spur (on).

'sprone sm (sperone, fig) spur.

sproporzio'nato, a [sproportsjo'nato] ag disproportionate, out of all proportion.

sproporzi'one [sɛpropor'tsjone] sf disproportion.

sproposi'tato, a ag (lettera, discorso) full of mistakes; (fig: costo) excessive, enormous.

spro'posito sm blunder; **a ~** at the wrong time; (rispondere, parlare) irrelevantly.

sprovve'duto, a ag (privo): ~ **di** lacking in, without; (impreparato) unprepared.

sprov'visto, a ag (mancante): ~ **di** lacking in, without; **alla ~ a** unawares.

spruz'zare [sprut'tsare] vt (a nebulizzazione) to spray; (aspergere) to sprinkle; (inzaccherare) to splash; **'spruzzo** sm spray; splash.

'spugna ['spuɲɲa] sf (ZOOL) sponge; (tessuto) towelling; **spu'gnoso, a** ag spongy.

'spuma sf (schiuma) foam; (bibita) mineral water.

spu'mante sm sparkling wine.

spu'mare vi to foam.

spumeggi'ante [spumed'dʒante] ag (vino, fig) sparkling.

spu'mone sm (CUC) mousse.

spun'tare vt (coltello) to break the point of; (capelli) to trim // vi (2) (uscire: germogli) to sprout; (: capelli) to begin to grow; (: denti) to come through; (apparire) to appear (suddenly); ~**rsi** vr to become blunt, lose its point; **spuntarla** (fig) to make it, win through.

spun'tino sm snack.

'spunto sm (TEATRO, MUS) cue; (fig) starting point; (di vino) sour taste; **dare lo ~ a** (fig) to give rise to.

spur'gare vt (fogna) to clean, clear; ~**rsi** vr (MED) to expectorate.

spu'tare vt to spit out; (fig) to belch (out) // vi to spit; **'sputo** sm spittle q, spit q.

'squadra sf (strumento) (set) square; (gruppo) team, squad; (di operai) gang, squad; (MIL) squad; (: AER, NAUT) squadron; (SPORT) team; **a o in ~** straight; ~ **doppia o a T** T-square.

squa'drare vt to square, make square; (osservare) to look at closely.

squa'driglia [skwa'driʎʎa] sf (AER) flight; (NAUT) squadron.

squa'drone sm squadron.

squagli'arsi [skwaʎ'ʎarsi] vr to melt; (fig) to sneak off.

squa'lifica sf disqualification.
squalifi'care vt to disqualify.
'squallido, a ag wretched, bleak.
squal'lore sm wretchedness, bleakness.
'squalo sm shark.
'squama sf scale; **squa'mare** vt to scale; **squamarsi** vr to flake o peel (off).
squarcia'gola [skwartʃa'gola]: **a ~** av at the top of one's voice.
squar'tare vt to quarter, cut up.
squattri'nato, a ag penniless.
squili'brare vt to unbalance; **squili-'brato, a** ag (PSIC) unbalanced; **squi'li-brio** sm (differenza, sbilancio) imbalance; (PSIC) unbalance.
squil'lante ag shrill, sharp.
squil'lare vi (campanello, telefono) to ring (out); (tromba) to blare; **'squillo** sm ring, ringing q; blare; **ragazza** f **squillo** inv call girl.
squi'sito, a ag exquisite; (cibo) delicious.
squit'tire vi (uccello) to squawk; (topo) to squeak.
sradi'care vt to uproot; (fig) to eradicate.
sragio'nare [zradʒo'nare] vi to talk nonsense, rave.
srego'lato, a ag (senza ordine: vita) disorderly; (smodato) immoderate; (dissoluto) dissolute.
'stabile ag stable, steady; (tempo: non variabile) settled; (TEATRO: compagnia) resident // sm (edificio) building.
stabili'mento sm establishing q; (edificio) establishment; (fabbrica) plant, factory; **~ carcerario** prison.
stabi'lire vt to establish; (fissare: prezzi, data) to fix; (decidere) to decide; **~rsi** vr (prendere dimora) to settle.
stabilità sf stability.
stabiliz'zare [stabilid'dzare] vt to stabilize; **stabilizza'tore** sm stabilizer.
stac'care vt (levare) to detach, remove; (separare: anche fig) to separate, divide; (strappare) to tear off (o out); (scandire: parole) to pronounce clearly; (SPORT) to leave behind; **~rsi** vr (bottone etc) to come off (scostarsi): **~rsi (da)** to move away (from); (fig: separarsi): **~rsi da** to leave; **non ~ gli occhi da qd** not to take one's eyes off sb.
'stadio sm (SPORT) stadium; (periodo, fase) phase, stage.
'staffa sf (di sella) štirrup.
staf'fetta sf (messo) dispatch rider; (SPORT) relay race.
stagio'nale [stadʒo'nale] ag seasonal.
stagio'nare [stadʒo'nare] vt (legno) to season; (formaggi, vino) to mature.
stagi'one [sta'dʒone] sf season; **alta/bassa ~** high/low season.
stagli'arsi [staʎ'ʎarsi] vr to stand out, be silhouetted.
sta'gnante [stan'nante] ag stagnant.
sta'gnare [stan'nare] vt (vaso, tegame) to tin-plate; (barca, botte) to make watertight; (sangue) to stop // vi to stagnate.

'stagno, a ['stanno] ag watertight; (a tenuta d'aria) airtight // sm (acquitrino) pond; (CHIM) tin.
sta'gnola [stan'nola] sf tinfoil.
stalag'mite sf stalagmite.
stalat'tite sf stalactite.
'stalla sf (per bovini) cowshed; (per cavalli) stable.
stal'lone sm stallion.
sta'mani, stamat'tina av this morning.
'stampa sf (TIP, FOT: tecnica) printing; (impressione, copia fotografica) print; (insieme di quotidiani, giornalisti etc) press; **~e** sfpl printed matter.
stam'pare vt to print; (pubblicare) to publish; (coniare) to strike, coin; (imprimere: anche fig) to impress.
stampa'tello sm block letters pl.
stam'pella sf crutch.
'stampo sm mould; (fig: indole) type, kind, sort.
sta'nare vt to drive out.
stan'care vt to tire, make tired; (annoiare) to bore; (infastidire) to annoy; **~rsi** vr to get tired, tire o.s. out; **~rsi (di)** to grow weary (of), grow tired (of).
stan'chezza [stan'kettsa] sf tiredness, fatigue.
'stanco, a, chi, che ag tired; **~ di** tired of, fed up with.
standardiz'zare [standardid'dzare] vt to standardize.
'stanga, ghe sm bar; (di carro) shaft.
stan'gata sf (colpo: anche fig) blow; (INS) poor result; (CALCIO) shot.
sta'notte av tonight; (notte passata) last night.
'stante prep owing to, because of; **a sé ~** (appartamento, casa) independent, separate.
stan'tio, a, 'tii, 'tie ag stale; (burro) rancid; (fig) old.
stan'tuffo sm piston.
'stanza ['stantsa] sf room; (POESIA) stanza; **~ da letto** bedroom.
stanzi'are [stan'tsjare] vt to allocate.
stap'pare vt to uncork; to uncap.
'stare vi (2) (restare in un luogo) to stay, remain; (abitare) to stay, live; (essere situato) to be, be situated; (anche: **~ in piedi**) to be, stand; (essere, trovarsi) to be; (dipendere): **se stesse in me** if it were up to me, if it depended on me; (seguito da gerundio): **sta studiando** he's studying; **starci** (esserci spazio): **nel baule non ci sta più niente** there's no more room in the boot; (accettare) to accept; **ci stai?** is that okay with you?; **~ a** (attenersi a) to follow, stick to; (seguito dall'infinito): **stiamo a discutere** we're talking; (toccare a) to be up to: **sta a te giocare** it's your turn to play; **~ per fare qc** to be about to do sth; **come sta?** how are you?; **io sto bene/male** I'm very well/not very well; **~ a qd** (abiti etc) to fit sb; **queste scarpe mi stanno strette** these shoes are tight for me; **il rosso ti sta bene** red suits you.

starnu'tire *vi* to sneeze; **star'nuto** *sm* sneeze.

sta'sera *av* this evening, tonight.

sta'tale *ag* state *cpd*; government *cpd // sm/f* state employee, local authority employee; (*nell'amministrazione*) ≈ civil servant.

sta'tista, i *sm* statesman.

sta'tistico, a, ci, che *ag* statistical *// sf* statistics *sg*.

'stato, a *pp di* **essere, stare** *// sm* (*condizione*) state, condition; (*POL*) state; (*DIR*) status; **essere in ~ d'accusa** (*DIR*) to be committed for trial; **~ d'assedio/d'emergenza** state of siege/emergency; **~ maggiore** (*MIL*) staff; **gli S~i Uniti (d'America)** the United States (of America).

'statua *sf* statue.

statuni'tense *ag* United States *cpd*, of the United States.

sta'tura *sf* (*ANAT*) height, stature; (*fig*) stature.

sta'tuto *sm* (*DIR*) statute; constitution.

sta'volta *av* this time.

stazio'nario, a [stattsjo'narjo] *ag* stationary; (*fig*) unchanged.

stazi'one [stat'tsjone] *sf* station; (*balneare, termale*) resort; **~ degli autobus** bus station; **~ balneare** seaside resort; **~ invernale** winter sports resort; **~ di polizia** police station (*in small town*); **~ di servizio** service *o* petrol *o* filling station; **~ trasmittente** (*RADIO, TV*) transmitting station.

'stecca, che *sf* stick; (*di ombrello*) rib; (*di sigarette*) carton; (*MED*) splint; (*stonatura*): **fare una ~** to sing (*o* play) a wrong note.

stec'cato *sm* fence.

stec'chito, a [stek'kito] *ag* dried up; (*persona*) skinny; **lasciar ~ qd** (*fig*) to leave sb flabbergasted.

'stella *sf* star; **~ alpina** (*BOT*) edelweiss; **~ di mare** (*ZOOL*) starfish.

'stelo *sm* stem; (*asta*) rod; **lampada a ~** standard lamp.

'stemma, i *sm* coat of arms.

stempe'rare *vt* to dilute; to dissolve, melt; (*colori*) to mix.

sten'dardo *sm* standard.

'stendere *vt* (*braccia, gambe*) to stretch (out); (*tovaglia*) to spread (out); (*bucato*) to hang out; (*mettere a giacere*) to lay (down); (*spalmare: colore*) to spread; (*mettere per iscritto*) to draw up; **~rsi** *vr* (*coricarsi*) to stretch out, lie down; (*estendersi*) to extend, stretch.

stenodatti'lografo, a *sm/f* shorthand typist.

stenogra'fare *vt* to take down in shorthand; **stenogra'fia** *sf* shorthand.

sten'tare *vi*: **~ a fare** to find it hard to do, have difficulty doing.

'stento, a (*fatica*) difficulty; **~i** *smpl* (*privazioni*) hardship *sg*, privation *sg*; **a ~** *av* with difficulty, barely.

'sterco *sm* dung.

'stereo('fonico, a, ci, che) *ag* stereo(phonic).

stereoti'pato, a *ag* stereotyped.

'sterile *ag* sterile; (*terra*) barren; (*fig*) futile, fruitless; **sterilità** *sf* sterility.

steriliz'zare [sterilid'dzare] *vt* to sterilize; **sterilizzazi'one** *sf* sterilization.

ster'lina *sf* pound (sterling).

stermi'nare *vt* to exterminate, wipe out.

stermi'nato, a *ag* immense; endless.

ster'minio *sm* extermination, destruction.

'sterno *sm* (*ANAT*) breastbone.

ster'zare [ster'tsare] *vt, vi* (*AUT*) to steer; **'sterzo** *sm* steering; (*volante*) steering wheel.

'steso, a *pp di* **stendere**.

'stesso, a *ag* same; (*rafforzativo: in persona, proprio*): **il re ~** the king himself *o* in person *// pronome*: **lo(la) ~(a)** the same (one); **i suoi ~i avversari lo ammirano** even his enemies admire him; **fa lo ~** it doesn't matter; **per me è lo ~** it's all the same to me, it doesn't matter to me; *vedi* **io, tu** etc.

ste'sura *sf* drafting *q*, drawing up *q*; draft.

stetos'copio *sm* stethoscope.

'stigma, i *sm* stigma.

'stigmate *sfpl* (*REL*) stigmata.

sti'lare *vt* to draw up, draft.

'stile *sm* style; **sti'lista, i** *sm* stylist; designer; **stiliz'zato, a** *ag* stylized.

stil'lare *vi* (2) (*trasudare*) to ooze; (*gocciolare*) to drip; **~rsi il cervello** (*fig*) to rack one's brains; **stilli'cidio** *sm* drip, dripping.

stilo'grafica, che *sf* (*anche*: **penna ~**) fountain pen.

'stima *sf* esteem; valuation; assessment, estimate.

sti'mare *vt* (*persona*) to esteem, hold in high regard; (*terreno, casa etc*) to value; (*stabilire in misura approssimativa*) to estimate, assess; (*ritenere*): **~ che** to consider that; **~rsi fortunato** to consider o.s. (to be) lucky.

stimo'lante *ag* stimulating *// sm* (*MED*) stimulant.

stimo'lare *vt* to stimulate; (*incitare*): **~ qd (a fare)** to spur sb on (to do).

'stimolo *sm* (*sollecitazione*) stimulus, spur; (*FISIOL, PSIC*) stimulus; **lo ~ della fame/del rimorso** the pangs of hunger/remorse.

'stinco, chi *sm* shin; shinbone.

'stingere ['stindʒere] *vt, vi* (2) (*anche*: **~rsi**) to fade; **'stinto, a** *pp di* **stingere**.

sti'pare *vt* to cram, pack; **~rsi** *vr* (*accalcarsi*) to crowd, throng.

sti'pendio *sm* salary.

'stipite *sm* (*di porta, finestra*) jamb.

stipu'lare *vt* (*redigere*) to draw up.

sti'rare *vt* (*abito*) to iron; (*distendere*) to stretch; **~rsi** *vr* (*fam*) to stretch (o.s.); **stira'tura** *sf* ironing.

'stirpe *sf* birth, stock; descendants *pl*.

stiti'chezza [stiti'kettsa] *sf* constipation.

'stitico, a, ci, che *ag* constipated.

'stiva *sf (di nave)* hold.
sti'vale *sm* boot.
'stizza ['stittsa] *sf* anger, vexation; **stiz'zirsi** *vr* to lose one's temper; **stiz'zoso, a** *ag (persona)* quick-tempered, irascible; *(risposta)* angry.
stocca'fisso *sm* stockfish, dried cod.
stoc'cata *sf (colpo)* stab, thrust; *(fig)* gibe, cutting remark.
'stoffa *sf* material, fabric; *(fig)*: **aver la ~ di** to have the makings of.
'stoico, a, ci, che *ag* stoic(al).
'stola *sf* stole.
'stolto, a *ag* stupid, foolish.
'stomaco, a *chi sm* stomach; **dare di ~** to vomit, be sick.
sto'nare *vt* to sing *(o play)* out of tune // *vi* to be out of tune, sing *(o play)* out of tune; *(fig)* to be out of place, jar; *(: colori)* to clash; **stona'tura** *sf (suono)* false note.
stop *sm inv (TEL)* stop; *(AUT: cartello)* stop sign; *(: fanalino d'arresto)* brake-light.
'stoppa *sf* tow.
'stoppia *sf (AGR)* stubble.
stop'pino *sm* wick; *(miccia)* fuse.
'storcere ['stortʃere] *vt* to twist; **~rsi** *vr* to writhe, twist; **~ il naso** *(fig)* to turn up one's nose; **~rsi la caviglia** to twist one's ankle.
stor'dire *(intontire)* to stun, daze; **~rsi** *vr*: **~rsi col bere** to drown one's sorrows; **stor'dito, a** *ag* stunned; *(sbadato)* scatterbrained, heedless.
'storia *sf (scienza, avvenimenti)* history; *(racconto, bugia)* story; *(faccenda, questione)* business *q; (pretesto)* excuse, pretext; **~e** *sfpl (smancerie)* fuss *sg*; **'storico, a, ci, che** *ag* historic(al) // *sm* historian.
stori'one *sm (ZOOL)* sturgeon.
stor'mire *vi* to rustle.
'stormo *sm (di uccelli)* flock.
stor'nare *vt (COMM)* to transfer.
'storno *sm* starling.
storpi'are *vt* to cripple, maim; *(fig: parole)* to mangle.
'storpio, a *ag* crippled, maimed.
'storto, a *pp di* **storcere** // *ag (chiodo)* twisted, bent; *(gamba, quadro)* crooked; *(fig: ragionamento)* false, wrong // *sf (distorsione)* sprain, twist; *(recipiente)* retort.
sto'viglie [sto'viʎʎe] *sfpl* dishes *pl*, crockery.
'strabico, a, ci, che *ag* squint-eyed; *(occhi)* squint.
stra'bismo *sm* squinting.
stra'carico, a, chi, che *ag* overloaded.
stracci'are [strat'tʃare] *vt* to tear.
'straccio, a, ci, ce ['strattʃo] *ag* torn // *sm* rag; *(per pulire)* cloth, duster; **carta ~a** waste paper; **stracci'vendolo** *sm* ragman.
stra'cotto, a *ag* overcooked // *sm (cuc)* beef stew.
'strada *sf* road; *(di città)* street; *(cammino, via, fig)* way; **farsi ~** *(fig)* to do well for

o.s.; **essere fuori ~** *(fig)* to be on the wrong track; **~ facendo** on the way; **~ senza uscita** dead end; **stra'dale** *ag* road *cpd*.
strafalci'one [strafal'tʃone] *sm* blunder, howler.
stra'fare *vi* to overdo it; **stra'fatto, a** *pp di* **strafare**.
strafot'tente *ag*: **è ~** he doesn't give a damn, he couldn't care less.
'strage ['stradʒe] *sf* massacre, slaughter.
stralu'nare *vt*: **~ gli occhi** to roll one's eyes; **stralu'nato, a** *ag (occhi)* rolling; *(persona)* beside o.s., very upset.
stramaz'zare [stramat'tsare] *vi (2)* to fall heavily.
'strambo, a *ag* strange, queer.
strampa'lato, a *ag* odd, eccentric.
stra'nezza [stra'nettsa] *sf* strangeness.
strango'lare *vt* to strangle; **~rsi** *vr* to choke.
strani'ero, a *ag* foreign // *sm/f* foreigner.
'strano, a *ag* strange, odd.
straordi'nario, a *ag* extraordinary; *(treno etc)* special // *sm (lavoro)* overtime.
strapaz'zare [strapat'tsare] *vt* to ill-treat; **~rsi** *vr* to tire o.s. out, overdo things; **stra'pazzo** *sm* strain, fatigue; **da strapazzo** *(fig)* third-rate.
strapi'ombo *sm* overhanging rock; **a ~** overhanging.
strapo'tere *sm* excessive power.
strap'pare *vt* to pull out; *(pagina etc)* to tear off, tear out; *(fazzoletto, lenzuolo, foglio)* to tear, rip; *(sradicare)* to pull up; **~ qc a qd** to snatch sth from sb; *(fig)* to wrest sth from sb; **~rsi** *vr (lacerarsi)* to rip, tear; *(rompersi)* to break; **'strappo** *sm* pull, tug; tear, rip; **fare uno strappo alla regola** to make an exception to the rule; **strappo muscolare** torn muscle.
strapun'tino *sm* jump *o* foldaway seat.
strari'pare *vi* to overflow.
strasci'care [straʃʃi'kare] *vt* to trail; *(piedi)* to drag; *(parole)* to drawl.
'strascico, chi ['straʃʃiko] *sm (di abito)* train; *(consequenza)* after-effect.
strata'gemma, i [strata'dʒemma] *sm* stratagem.
strate'gia, 'gie [strate'dʒia] *sf* strategy; **stra'tegico, a, ci, che** *ag* strategic.
'strato *sm* layer; *(rivestimento)* coat, coating; *(GEO, fig)* stratum; *(METEOR)* stratus.
stratos'fera *sf* stratosphere.
strava'gante *ag* odd, eccentric; **strava'ganza** *sf* eccentricity.
stra'vecchio, a [stra'vekkjo] *ag* very old.
stra'vizio [stra'vittsjo] *sm* excess.
stra'volgere [stra'voldʒere] *vt (volto)* to contort; *(fig: animo)* to trouble deeply; *(: verità)* to twist, distort; **stra'volto, a** *pp di* **stravolgere**.
strazi'are [strat'tsjare] *vt* to torture, torment; **'strazio** *sm* torture; *(fam: persona, libro)* bore.

'strega, ghe sf witch.

stre'gare vt to bewitch.

stre'gone sm (mago) wizard; (di tribù) witch doctor.

'stregua sf: **alla ~ di** by the same standard as.

stre'mare vt to exhaust.

'stremo sm very end; **essere allo ~** to be at the end of one's tether.

'strenna sf Christmas present.

'strenuo, a ag brave, courageous.

strepi'toso, a ag clamorous, deafening; (fig: successo) resounding.

'stretta sf vedi **stretto**.

stretta'mente av tightly; (rigorosamente) strictly.

stret'tezza [stret'tettsa] sf narrowness; **~e** sfpl poverty sg, straitened circumstances.

'stretto, a pp di **stringere** // ag (non largo) narrow; (: gonna, serrato: nodo) tight; (intimo: parente, amico) close; (rigoroso: osservanza) strict; (preciso: significato) precise, exact // sm (braccio di mare) strait // sm (di mano) grasp; (finanziaria) squeeze; (fig: dolore, turbamento) pang; **a denti ~i** with clenched teeth; **lo ~ necessario** the bare minimum; **essere alle ~e** to have one's back to the wall; **stret'toia** sf bottleneck; (fig) tricky situation.

stri'ato, a ag streaked.

stri'dente ag strident.

'stridere vi (porta) to squeak; (animale) to screech, shriek; (colori) to clash; **'strido**, pl(f) **strida** sm screech, shriek; **stri'dore** sm screeching, shrieking; **'stridulo, a** ag shrill.

stril'lare vt, vi to scream, shriek; **'strillo** sm scream, shriek.

stril'lone sm newspaper seller.

strimin'zito, a [strimin'tsito] ag (misero) shabby; (molto magro) skinny.

strimpel'lare vt (MUS) to strum.

'stringa, ghe sf lace.

strin'gato, a ag (fig) concise.

'stringere ['strindʒere] vt (avvicinare due cose) to press (together), squeeze (together); (tenere stretto) to hold tight, clasp, clutch; (avvitare) to tighten; (abito) to take in; (sog: scarpe) to pinch, be tight for; (fig: concludere: patto) to make; (: accelerare: passo, tempo) to quicken // vi (incalzare) to be pressing; **~rsi** vr (accostarsi) to ~**rsi (a)** to draw close (to), press o.s. (to); (restringersi) to squeeze up; **~ la mano a qd** to shake sb's hand; **~ le labbra/gli occhi** to tighten one's lips/screw up one's eyes.

'striscia, sce ['striʃʃa] sf (di carta, tessuto etc) strip; (riga) stripe; **~sce (pedonali)** zebra crossing sg.

strisci'are [striʃ'ʃare] vt (piedi) to drag; (muro, macchina) to graze // vi to crawl, creep; **~rsi** vr: **~rsi a** (sfregarsi) to rub against; (fig) to grovel before o in front of.

'striscio ['striʃʃo] sm graze; (MED) smear; **colpire di ~** to graze.

strito'lare vt to grind.

striz'zare [strit'tsare] vt (arancia) to squeeze; (panni) to wring (out); **~ l'occhio** to wink.

'strofe sf inv, **'strofa** sf strophe.

strofi'naccio [strofi'nattʃo] sm duster, cloth.

strofi'nare vt to rub.

stron'care vt to break off; (fig: ribellione) to suppress, put down; (: film, libro) to tear to pieces.

stropicci'are [stropit'tʃare] vt to rub.

stroz'zare [strot'tsare] vt (soffocare) to choke, strangle; **~rsi** vr to choke; **strozza'tura** sf (restringimento) narrowing; (di strada etc) bottleneck.

'struggere ['struddʒere] vt (sciogliere) to melt; (fig) to consume; **~rsi** vr to melt; (fig): **~rsi di** to be consumed with.

strumen'tale ag (MUS) instrumental.

strumentaliz'zare [strumentalid'dzare] vt to exploit, use to one's own ends.

stru'mento sm (arnese, fig) instrument, tool; (MUS) instrument; **~ a corda/fiato** stringed/wind instrument.

'strutto sm lard.

strut'tura sf structure; **struttu'rare** vt to structure.

'struzzo ['struttso] sm ostrich.

stuc'care vt (muro) to plaster; (vetro) to putty; (decorare con stucchi) to stucco.

stuc'chevole [stuk'kevole] ag nauseating; (fig) tedious, boring.

'stucco, chi sm plaster; (da vetri) putty; (ornamentale) stucco; **rimanere di ~** (fig) to be dumbfounded.

stu'dente, essa sm/f student; (scolaro) pupil, schoolboy/girl; **studen'tesco, a, schi, sche** ag student cpd; school cpd.

studi'are vt to study; **~rsi** vr (sforzarsi): **~rsi di fare** to try o endeavour to do.

'studio sm studying; (: ricerca, saggio, stanza) study; (di professionista) office; (di artista, CINEMA, TV, RADIO) studio; **~i** smpl (INS) studies.

studi'oso, a ag studious, hardworking // sm/f scholar.

'stufa sf stove; **~ elettrica** electric fire o heater.

stu'fare vt (CUC) to stew; (fig: fam) to bore; **stu'fato** sm (CUC) stew; **'stufo, a** ag (fam): **essere stufo di** to be fed up with, be sick and tired of.

stu'oia sf mat.

stupefa'cente [stupefa'tʃente] ag stunning, astounding // sm drug, narcotic.

stu'pendo, a ag marvellous, wonderful.

stupi'daggine [stupi'daddʒine] sf stupid thing (to do o say).

stupidità sf stupidity.

'stupido, a ag stupid.

stu'pire vt to amaze, stun // vi (2) (anche: **~rsi**) to be amazed, be stunned.

stu'pore sm amazement, astonishment.

'stupro sm rape.

'stura sf: **dare la ~ a** (bottiglia) to uncork; (sentimenti) to give vent to.

stu'rare vt (lavandino) to clear.

stuzzica'denti [stuttsika'denti] sm toothpick.

stuzzi'care [stuttsi'kare] vt (ferita etc) to poke (at), prod (at); (fig) to tease; ~ **i denti** to pick one's teeth.

su prep (su + il = **sul**, su + lo = **sullo**, su + l' = **sull'**, su + la = **sulla**, su + i = **sui**, su + gli = **sugli**, su + le = **sulle**) on; (moto a luogo) on, on to; (intorno a, riguardo a) about, on; (approssimazione: circa) about, around // av up; (sopra) (up) above // escl come on!; **in** ~ av up(wards); **prezzi dalle mille lire in** ~ prices from 1000 lire (upwards); **una ragazza sui 17 anni** a girl of about 17 (years of age); **in 3 casi** ~ **10** in 3 cases out of 10.

'sua vedi **suo**.

su'bacqueo, a ag underwater // sm skindiver.

sub'buglio [sub'buʎʎo] sm confusion, turmoil.

subcosci'ente [subkoʃ'ʃɛnte] ag, sm subconscious.

'subdolo, a ag underhand, sneaky.

suben'trare vi (2): ~ **a qd in qc** to take over sth from sb.

su'bire vt to suffer, endure.

subis'sare vt (fig): ~ **di** to overwhelm with, load with.

subi'taneo, a ag sudden.

'subito av immediately, at once, straight away.

su'blime ag sublime.

subodo'rare vt (insidia etc) to smell, suspect.

subordi'nato, a ag subordinate; (dipendente): ~ **a** dependent on, subject to // sm/f subordinate.

subur'bano, a ag suburban.

succe'daneo [suttʃe'daneo] sm substitute.

suc'cedere [sut'tʃedere] vi (2) (prendere il posto di qd): ~ **a** to succeed; (venire dopo): ~ **a** to follow; (accadere) to happen; ~**rsi** vr to follow each other; ~ **al trono** to succeed to the throne; **successi'one** sf succession; **succes'sivo, a** ag successive; **suc'cesso, a** pp di **succedere** // sm (esito) outcome; (buona riuscita) success; **succes'sore** sm successor.

succhi'are [suk'kjare] vt to suck (up).

suc'cinto, a [sut'tʃinto] ag (discorso) succinct; (abito) brief.

'succo, chi sm juice; (fig) essence, gist; **suc'coso, a** ag juicy; (fig) pithy; **succu'lento, a** ag succulent.

succur'sale sf branch (office).

sud sm south // ag inv south; (lato) south, southern.

su'dare vi to perspire, sweat; ~ **freddo** to come out in a cold sweat; **su'data** sf sweat; **ho fatto una bella sudata per finirlo in tempo** it was a real sweat to get it finished in time.

sud'detto, a ag above-mentioned.

sud'dito, a sm/f subject.

suddi'videre vt to subdivide; **suddivi-si'one** sf subdivision.

su'dest sm south-east.

'sudicio, a, ci, ce ['sudit'ʃo] ag dirty, filthy; **sudici'ume** sm dirt, filth.

su'dore sm perspiration, sweat.

su'dovest sm south-west.

'sue vedi **suo**.

suffici'ente [suffi'tʃɛnte] ag enough, sufficient; (borioso) self-important; (INS) satisfactory; **suffici'enza** sf self-importance; pass mark; **aver sufficienza di qc** to have enough of sth; **a sufficienza** av enough.

suf'fisso sm (LING) suffix.

suf'fragio [suf'fradʒo] sm (voto) vote; ~ **universale** universal suffrage.

sugel'lare [suddʒel'lare] vt (fig) to seal.

sugeri'mento [suddʒeri'mento] sm suggestion; (consiglio) piece of advice, advice q.

sugge'rire [suddʒe'rire] vt (risposta) to tell; (consigliare) to advise; (proporre) to suggest; (TEATRO) to prompt; **suggeri-'tore, 'trice** sm/f (TEATRO) prompter.

suggestio'nare [suddʒestjo'nare] vt to influence.

suggesti'one [suddʒes'tjone] sf (PSIC) suggestion; (istigazione) instigation.

sugges'tivo, a [suddʒes'tivo] ag (paesaggio) evocative; (teoria) interesting, attractive.

'sughero ['sugero] sm cork.

'sugli ['suʎʎi] prep + det vedi **su**.

'sugna ['suɲɲa] sf suet.

'sugo, ghi sm (succo) juice; (di carne) gravy; (condimento) sauce; (fig) gist, essence.

'sui prep + det vedi **su**.

sui'cida, i, e [sui'tʃida] ag suicidal // sm/f suicide.

suici'darsi [suitʃi'darsi] vr to commit suicide.

sui'cidio [sui'tʃidjo] sm suicide.

su'ino, a ag: **carne** ~**a** pork // sm pig; ~**i** smpl swine pl.

sul, sui', sulla, 'sulle, 'sullo prep + det vedi **su**.

sulta'nina ag f: (uva) ~ sultana.

sul'tano, a sm/f sultan/sultana.

'sunto sm summary.

'suo, 'sua, 'sue, su'oi det: **il** ~, **la sua** etc (di lui) his; (di lei) her; (di esso) its; (con valore indefinito) one's, his/her; (forma di cortesia: anche: **S**~) your // pronome: **il** ~, **la sua** etc his; hers; yours; **i suoi** (parenti) one's family.

su'ocero, a ['swɔtʃero] sm/f father/mother-in-law; **i** ~**i** smpl father-and mother-in-law.

su'oi vedi **suo**.

su'ola sf (di scarpa) sole.

su'olo sm (terreno) ground; (terra) soil.

suo'nare vt (MUS) to play; (campana) to ring; (ore) to strike; (clacson, allarme) to sound // vi to play; (telefono, campana) to ring; (ore) to strike; (clacson, fig: parole) to sound.

su'ono sm sound.

su'ora *sf* (REL) sister.

supe'rare *vt* (*oltrepassare: limite*) to exceed, surpass; (*percorrere*) to cover; (*attraversare: fiume*) to cross; (*sorpassare: veicolo*) to overtake; (*fig: essere più bravo di*) to surpass, outdo; (: *difficoltà*) to overcome; (: *esame*) to get through; ~ **qd in altezza/peso** to be taller/heavier than sb; **ha superato la cinquantina** he's over fifty.

su'perbia *sf* pride.

su'perbo, a *ag* proud; (*fig*) magnificent, superb.

superfici'ale [superfi'tʃale] *ag* superficial.

super'ficie, ci [super'fitʃe] *sf* surface.

su'perfluo, a *ag* superfluous.

superi'ore *ag* (*piano, arto, classi*) upper; (*più elevato: temperatura, livello*): ~ **(a)** higher (than); (*migliore*): ~ **(a)** superior (to); ~, **a** *sm/f* (*anche* REL) superior; **superiorità** *sf* superiority.

superla'tivo, a *ag, sm* superlative.

supermer'cato *sm* supermarket.

su'perstite *ag* surviving // *sm/f* survivor.

superstizi'one [superstit'tsjone] *sf* superstition; **superstizi'oso, a** *ag* superstitious.

su'pino, a *ag* supine.

suppel'lettile *sf* furnishings *pl*.

suppergiù [supper'dʒu] *av* more or less, roughly.

supple'mento *sm* supplement.

sup'plente *ag* temporary; (*insegnante*) supply *cpd* // *sm/f* temporary member of staff; supply teacher.

'supplica, che *sf* (*preghiera*) plea; (*domanda scritta*) petition, request.

suppli'care *vt* to implore, beseech.

sup'plire *vi*: ~ **a** to make up for, compensate for.

sup'plizio [sup'plittsjo] *sm* torture.

sup'porre *vt* to suppose.

sup'porto *sm* (*sostegno*) support.

supposizi'one [suppozit'tsjone] *sf* supposition.

sup'posta *sf* (MED) suppository.

sup'posto, a *pp di* **supporre**.

suppu'rare *vi* to suppurate.

suprema'zia [supremat'tsia] *sf* supremacy.

su'premo, a *ag* supreme.

surge'lare [surdʒe'lare] *vt* to (deep-)freeze.

sur'plus *sm inv* (ECON) surplus.

surriscal'dare *vt* to overheat.

surro'gato *sm* substitute.

suscet'tibile [suʃʃet'tibile] *ag* (*sensibile*) touchy, sensitive; (*soggetto*): ~ **di miglioramento** that can be improved, open to improvement.

susci'tare [suʃʃi'tare] *vt* to provoke, arouse.

su'sina *sf* plum; **su'sino** *sm* plum (tree).

sussegu'ire *vt* to follow; ~**rsi** *vr* to follow one another.

sussidi'ario, a *ag* subsidiary; auxiliary.

sus'sidio *sm* subsidy.

sussis'tenza [sussis'tɛntsa] *sf* subsistence.

sus'sistere *vi* (2) to exist; to be valid *o* sound.

sussul'tare *vi* to shudder.

sussur'rare *vt, vi* to whisper, murmur; **sus'surro** *sm* whisper, murmur.

su'tura *sf* (MED) suture; **sutu'rare** *vt* to stitch up, suture.

sva'gare *vt* (*distrarre*) to distract; (*divertire*) to amuse; ~**rsi** *vr* to amuse o.s.; to enjoy o.s.

'svago, ghi *sm* (*riposo*) relaxation; (*ricreazione*) amusement; (*passatempo*) pastime.

svaligi'are [zvali'dʒare] *vt* to rob, burgle.

svalu'tare *vt* (ECON) to devalue; (*fig*) to belittle; **svalutazi'one** *sf* devaluation.

sva'nire *vi* (2) to disappear, vanish.

svan'taggio [zvan'taddʒo] *sm* disadvantage; (*inconveniente*) drawback, disadvantage.

svapo'rare *vi* (2) to evaporate.

svari'ato, a *ag* varied; various.

'svastica *sf* swastika.

sve'dese *ag* Swedish // *sm/f* Swede // *sm* (LING) Swedish.

'sveglia ['zveʎʎa] *sf* waking up; (*orologio*) alarm (clock); **suonare la** ~ (MIL) to sound the reveille.

svegli'are [zveʎ'ʎare] *vt* to wake up; (*fig*) to awaken, arouse; ~**rsi** *vr* to wake up; (*fig*) to be revived, reawaken.

'sveglio, a ['zveʎʎo] *ag* awake; (*fig*) alert, quick-witted.

sve'lare *vt* to reveal.

'svelto, a *ag* (*passo*) quick; (*mente*) quick, alert; (*linea*) slim, slender; **alla** ~**a** *av* quickly.

sven'dita *sf* (COMM) (clearance) sale.

sveni'mento *sm* fainting fit, faint.

sve'nire *vi* (2) to faint.

sven'tare *vt* to foil, thwart.

sven'tato, a *ag* (*distratto*) scatterbrained; (*imprudente*) rash.

svento'lare *vt, vi* to wave, flutter.

sven'trare *vt* to disembowel.

sven'tura *sf* misfortune; **sventu'rato, a** *ag* unlucky, unfortunate.

sve'nuto, a *pp di* **svenire**.

svergo'gnato, a [zvergoɲ'ɲato] *ag* shameless.

sver'nare *vi* to spend the winter.

sves'tire *vt* to undress; ~**rsi** *vr* to get undressed.

'Svezia ['zvettsja] *sf*: **la** ~ Sweden.

svez'zare [zvet'tsare] *vt* to wean.

svi'are *vt* to divert; (*fig*) to lead astray; ~**rsi** *vr* to go astray.

svi'gnarsela [zviɲ'ɲarsela] *vr* to slip away, sneak off.

svilup'pare *vt*, ~**rsi** *vr* to develop.

svi'luppo *sm* development.

svinco'lare *vt* to free, release; (*merce*) to clear; **'svincolo** *sm* clearance; (*stradale*) link road.

svi'sare *vt* to distort.

svisce'rare [zviʃʃe'rare] vt (fig: argomento) to examine in depth; **svisce-'rato, a** ag (amore) passionate; (lodi) obsequious.

'svista sf oversight.

svi'tare vt to unscrew.

'Svizzera ['zvittsera] sf: **la ~** Switzerland.

'svizzero, a ['zvittsero] ag, sm/f Swiss.

svogli'ato, a [zvoʎ'ʎato] ag listless; (pigro) lazy.

svolaz'zare [zvolat'tsare] vi to flutter.

'svolgere ['zvɔldʒere] vt to unwind; (srotolare) to unroll; (fig: argomento) to develop; (: piano, programma) to carry out; **~rsi** vr to unwind; to unroll; (fig: aver luogo) to take place; (: procedere) to go on; **svolgi'mento** sm development; (andamento) course.

'svolta sf (atto) turning q; (curva) turn, bend; (fig) turning-point.

svol'tare vi to turn.

'svolto, a pp di **svolgere**.

svuo'tare vt to empty (out).

T

tabac'caio, a sm/f tobacconist.

tabacche'ria [tabakke'ria] sf tobacconist's (shop).

ta'bacco, tm sm tobacco.

ta'bella sf (tavola) table; (elenco) list.

taber'nacolo sm tabernacle.

tabù ag, sm inv taboo.

tabula'tore sm tabulator.

'tacca, che sf notch, nick; **di mezza ~** (fig) mediocre.

tac'cagno, a [tak'kaɲɲo] ag mean, stingy.

tac'cheggio [tak'keddʒo] sm shoplifting.

tac'chino [tak'kino] sm turkey.

'taccia, ce ['tattʃa] sf bad reputation.

'tacco, chi sm heel.

taccu'ino sm notebook.

ta'cere [ta'tʃere] vi to be silent o quiet; (smettere di parlare) to fall silent // vt to keep to oneself, say nothing about; **far ~ qd** to make sb be quiet; (fig) to silence sb.

ta'chimetro [ta'kimetro] sm speedometer.

'tacito, a ['tatʃito] ag silent; (sottinteso) tacit, unspoken.

taci'turno, a [tatʃi'turno] ag taciturn.

ta'fano sm horsefly.

taffe'ruglio [taffe'ruʎʎo] sm brawl, scuffle.

taffettà sm taffeta.

'taglia ['taʎʎa] sf (statura) height; (misura) size; (riscatto) ransom; (ricompensa) reward.

taglia'carte [taʎʎa'karte] sm inv paperknife.

tagli'ando [taʎ'ʎando] sm coupon.

tagli'are [taʎ'ʎare] vt to cut; (recidere, interrompere) to cut off; (intersecare) to cut across, intersect; (carne) to carve; (vini) to blend // vi to cut; (prendere una scorciatoia) to take a short-cut; **~ corto** (fig) to cut short.

taglia'telle [taʎʎa'tɛlle] sfpl tagliatelle pl.

tagli'ente [taʎ'ʎɛnte] ag sharp.

'taglio ['taʎʎo] sm cutting q; cut; (parte tagliente) cutting edge; (di abito) cut, style; (di stoffa: lunghezza) length; (di vini) blending; **di ~** on edge, edgeways; **banconote di piccolo/grosso ~** notes of small/large denomination.

tagli'ola [taʎ'ʎola] sf trap, snare.

tagliuz'zare [taʎʎut'tsare] vt to cut into small pieces.

'talco sm talcum powder.

'tale det such; (intensivo): **un ~/~i ...** such (a)/such ... // pronome (questa, quella persona già menzionata) the one, the person; (indefinito): **un(una) ~** someone; **il ~ giorno alla ~ ora** on such and such a day at such and such a time; **~: quale: il tuo vestito è ~ quale il mio** your dress is just o exactly like mine; **quel/quella ~** that person, that man/woman.

ta'lento sm talent.

talis'mano sm talisman.

tallon'cino [tallon'tʃino] sm counterfoil.

tal'lone sm heel.

tal'mente av so.

ta'lora av = **talvolta**.

'talpa sf (ZOOL) mole.

tal'volta av sometimes, at times.

tambu'rello sm tambourine.

tambu'rino sm drummer.

tam'buro sm drum.

Ta'migi [ta'midʒi] sm: **il ~** the Thames.

tampo'nare vt (otturare) to plug; (urtare: macchina) to crash o ram into.

tam'pone sm (MED) wad, pad; (per timbri) ink-pad; (respingente) buffer; **~ assorbente** tampon.

'tana sf lair, den.

'tanfo sm stench; musty smell.

tan'gente [tan'dʒɛnte] ag (MAT): **~ a** tangential to // sf tangent; (quota) share.

tan'gibile [tan'dʒibile] ag tangible.

'tango, ghi sm tango.

tan'nino sm tannin.

tan'tino: un ~ av a little, a bit.

'tanto, a det (pane, acqua, soldi) so much; (persone, libri) so many // pronome so much (o many) // av (con ag, av) so; (con vb) so much, such a lot; (: così a lungo) so long; **due volte ~** twice as much; **~ ... quanto: ho ~i libri quanti (ne hanno) loro** I have as many books as they have o as them; **conosco ~ Carlo quanto suo padre** I know both Carlo and his father; **è ~ bella quanto buona** she is as beautiful as she is good; **più ... ~ più** the more ... the more; **~ ... ~: costa un ~ al metro** it costs so much per metre; **guardare con ~ d'occhi** to gaze wide-eyed at; **~ per cambiare** just for a change; **una volta ~** just once; **~ è inutile** in any case it's useless; **di ~ in ~, ogni ~** every so often.

tapi'oca sf tapioca.

'tappa sf (luogo di sosta, fermata) stop, halt;

(*parte di un percorso*) stage, leg; (*SPORT*) lap; **a ~ e** in stages.

tap'pare *vt* to plug, stop up; (*bottiglia*) to cork.

tap'peto *sm* carpet; (*anche: tappetino*) rug; (*di tavolo*) cloth; (*SPORT*): **andare al ~** to go down for the count; **mettere sul ~** (*fig*) to bring up for discussion.

tappez'zare [tappet'tsare] *vt* (*con carta*) to paper; (*rivestire*): **~ qc (di)** to cover sth (with); **tappezze'ria** *sf* (*tessuto*) tapestry; (*carta da parato*) wallpaper; (*arte*) upholstery; **far da tappezzeria** (*fig*) to be a wallflower; **tappezzi'ere** *sm* upholsterer.

'tappo *sm* stopper; (*in sughero*) cork.

ta'rantola *sf* tarantula.

tarchi'ato, a [tar'kjato] *ag* stocky, thickset.

tar'dare *vi* to be late // *vt* to delay; **~ a fare** to delay doing.

'tardi *av* late; **più ~** later (on); **al più ~** at the latest; **far ~** to be late; (*restare alzato*) to stay up late.

tar'divo, a *ag* (*primavera*) late; (*rimedio*) belated, tardy; (*fig: bambino*) retarded.

'tardo, a *ag* (*lento, fig: ottuso*) slow; (*tempo: avanzato*) late.

'targa, ghe *sf* plate; (*AUT*) number plate.

ta'riffa *sf* rates *pl*; fares *pl*; tariff; (*prezzo*) rate; fare; (*elenco*) price list; tariff.

'tarlo *sm* woodworm.

'tarma *sf* moth.

ta'rocco, chi *sm* tarot card; **~ chi** *smpl* (*gioco*) tarot *sg*.

tartagli'are [tarta/'/are] *vi* to stutter, stammer.

'tartaro, a *ag, sm* (*in tutti i sensi*) tartar.

tarta'ruga, ghe *sf* tortoise; (*di mare*) turtle; (*materiale*) tortoiseshell.

tar'tina *sf* canapé.

tar'tufo *sm* (*BOT*) truffle.

'tasca, sche *sf* pocket; **tas'cabile** *ag* (*libro*) pocket *cpd*; **tasca'pane** *sm* haversack; **tas'chino** *sm* breast pocket.

'tassa *sf* (*imposta*) tax; (*doganale*) duty; (*per iscrizione: a scuola etc*) fee; **~ di circolazione/di soggiorno** road/tourist tax.

tas'sametro *sm* taximeter.

tas'sare *vt* to tax; to levy a duty on.

tassa'tivo, a *ag* peremptory.

tassazi'one [tassat'tsjone] *sf* taxation.

tas'sello *sm* plug; wedge.

tassì *sm inv* = **taxi**; **tas'sista, i, e** *sm/f* taxi driver.

'tasso *sm* (*di natalità, d'interesse etc*) rate; (*BOT*) yew; (*ZOOL*) badger; **~ di cambio/d'interesse** rate of exchange/interest.

tas'tare *vt* to feel; **~ il terreno** (*fig*) to see how the land lies.

tasti'era *sf* keyboard.

'tasto *sm* key; (*tatto*) touch, feel.

tas'toni *av*: **procedere (a) ~** to grope one's way forward.

'tattico, a, ci, che *ag* tactical // *sf* tactics *pl*.

'tatto *sm* (*senso*) touch; (*fig*) tact; **duro al ~** hard to the touch; **aver ~** to be tactful, have tact.

tatu'aggio [tatu'add3o] *sm* tattooing; (*disegno*) tattoo.

tatu'are *vt* to tattoo.

'tavola *sf* table; (*asse*) plank, board; (*lastra*) tablet; (*quadro*) panel (painting); (*illustrazione*) plate; **~ calda** snack bar.

tavo'lato *sm* boarding; (*pavimento*) wooden floor.

tavo'letta *sf* tablet, bar.

'tavolo *sm* table.

tavo'lozza [tavo'lɔttsa] *sf* (*ARTE*) palette.

'taxi *sm inv* taxi.

'tazza ['tattsa] *sf* cup; **~ da caffè/tè** coffee/tea cup.

te *pronome* (*soggetto: in forme comparative, oggetto*) you.

tè *sm inv* tea; (*trattenimento*) tea party.

tea'trale *ag* theatrical.

te'atro *sm* theatre.

'tecnico, a, ci, che *ag* technical // *sm/f* technician // *sf* technique; (*tecnologia*) technology.

tecnolo'gia [teknolo'dʒia] *sf* technology.

te'desco, a, schi, sche *ag, sm/f, sm* German.

'tedio *sm* tedium, boredom.

te'game *sm* (*CUC*) pan.

'tegola *sf* tile.

tei'era *sf* teapot.

'tela *sf* (*tessuto*) cloth; (*per vele, quadri*) canvas; (*dipinto*) canvas, painting; (*TEATRO*) curtain; **~ cerata** oilcloth; (*copertone*) tarpaulin.

te'laio *sm* (*apparecchio*) loom; (*struttura*) frame.

tele'camera *sf* television camera.

telecomunicazi'oni [telekomunikat-'tsjoni] *sfpl* telecommunications.

tele'cronaca *sf* television report.

tele'ferica, che *sf* cableway.

telefo'nare *vi* to telephone, ring; to make a phone call // *vt* to telephone; **~ a** to phone up, ring up, call up.

telefo'nata *sf* (*telephone*) call; **~ a carico del destinatario** reverse charge call.

tele'fonico, a, ci, che *ag* (tele)phone *cpd*.

telefo'nista, i, e *sm/f* telephonist; (*d'impresa*) switchboard operator.

te'lefono *sm* telephone; **~ a gettoni** ≈ pay phone.

telegior'nale [teledʒor'nale] *sm* television news (programme).

telegra'fare *vt, vi* to telegraph, cable.

telegra'fia *sf* telegraphy; **tele'grafico, a, ci, che** *ag* telegraph *cpd*, telegraphic; **te'legrafo** *sm* telegraph; (*ufficio*) telegraph office.

tele'gramma, i *sm* telegram.

telepa'tia *sf* telepathy.

teles'copio *sm* telescope.

teleselezi'one [teleselet'tsjone] *sf* ≈ subscriber trunk dialling.

telespetta'tore, 'trice sm/f (television) viewer.

televisi'one sf television.

televi'sore sm television set.

'telex sm inv telex.

'tema, i sm theme; (INS) essay, composition.

teme'rario, a ag rash, reckless.

te'mere vt to fear, be afraid of; (essere sensibile a: freddo, calore) to suffer from; (sog: cose) to be easily damaged by // vi to fear; (essere preoccupato): ~ **per** to worry about, fear for; ~ **di/che** to be afraid of/that.

temperama'tite sm inv pencil sharpener.

tempera'mento sm temperament.

tempe'rare vt (aguzzare) to sharpen; (fig) to moderate, control, temper.

tempe'rato, a ag moderate, temperate; (clima) temperate.

tempera'tura sf temperature.

tempe'rino sm penknife.

tem'pesta sf storm; ~ **di sabbia/neve** sand/snowstorm.

tempes'tivo, a ag timely.

tempes'toso, a ag stormy.

'tempia sf (ANAT) temple.

'tempio sm (edificio) temple.

'tempo sm (METEOR) weather; (cronologico) time; (epoca) time, times pl; (di film, gioco: parte) part; (MUS) time; (: battuta) beat; (LING) tense; **un** ~ once; ~ **fa** some time ago; **al** ~ **stesso o a un** ~ at the same time; **per** ~ early; **aver fatto il suo** ~ to have had its (o his etc) day; **primo/secondo** ~ (TEATRO) first/second part; (SPORT) first/second half; **in** ~ **utile** in due time o course.

tempo'rale ag temporal // sm (METEOR) (thunder)storm.

tempo'raneo, a ag temporary.

temporeggi'are [tempored'dʒare] vi to play for time, temporize.

tem'prare vt to temper.

te'nace [te'natʃe] ag strong, tough; (fig) tenacious; **te'nacia** sf tenacity.

te'naglie [te'naʎʎe] sfpl pincers pl.

'tenda sf (riparo) awning; (di finestra) curtain; (per campeggio etc) tent.

ten'denza [ten'dɛntsa] sf tendency; (orientamento) trend; **avere** ~ **a qc** to have a bent for sth.

'tendere vt (allungare al massimo) to stretch, draw tight; (porgere: mano) to hold out; (fig: trappola) to lay, set // vi: ~ **a qc/a fare** to tend towards sth/to do; ~ **l'orecchio** to prick up one's ears; **il tempo tende al caldo** the weather is getting hot.

ten'dina sf curtain.

'tendine sm tendon, sinew.

ten'done sm (da circo) tent.

'tenebre sfpl darkness sg; **tene'broso, a** ag dark, gloomy.

te'nente sm lieutenant.

te'nere vt to hold; (conservare, mantenere) to keep; (ritenere, considerare) to consider; (spazio: occupare) to take up, occupy; (seguire: strada) to keep to // vi to hold; (colori) to be fast; (dare importanza): ~ **a** to care about; ~ **a fare** to want to do, be keen to do; ~ **rsi** vr (stare in una determinata posizione) to stand; (stimarsi) to consider o.s.; (aggrapparsi): ~ **rsi a** to hold on to; (attenersi): ~ **rsi a** to stick to; ~ **una conferenza** to give a lecture; ~ **conto di qc** to take sth into consideration; ~ **presente qc** to bear sth in mind.

tene'rezza [tene'rettsa] sf tenderness.

'tenero, a ag tender; (pietra, cera, colore) soft; (fig) tender, loving.

'tenia sf tapeworm.

'tennis sm tennis.

te'nore sm tenor, way; (contenuto) content; (MUS) tenor; ~ **di vita** way of life; (livello) standard of living.

tensi'one sf tension.

ten'tacolo sm (ZOOL) tentacle.

ten'tare vt (indurre) to tempt; (provare): ~ **qc/di fare** to attempt o try sth/to do; **tenta'tivo** sm attempt; **tentazi'one** sf temptation.

tenten'nare vi to shake, be unsteady; (fig) to hesitate, waver // vt: ~ **il capo** to shake one's head.

ten'toni av: **andare (a)** ~ to grope one's way.

te'nue ag (sottile) fine; (colore) soft; (fig) slender, slight.

te'nuta sf (capacità) capacity; (divisa) uniform; (abito) dress; (AGR) estate; **a** ~ **d'aria** airtight; ~ **di strada** roadholding power.

teolo'gia [teolo'dʒia] sf theology; **teo-'logico, a, ci, che** ag theological; **te'ologo, gi** sm theologian.

teo'rema, i sm theorem.

teo'ria sf theory; **te'orico, a, ci, che** ag theoretic(al).

'tepido, a ag = **tiepido**.

te'pore sm warmth.

'teppa sf mob, hooligans pl; **tep'pismo** sm hooliganism; **tep'pista, i** sm hooligan.

tera'pia sf therapy.

tergicris'tallo [terdʒikris'tallo] sm windscreen wiper.

tergiver'sare [terdʒiver'sare] vi to shilly-shally.

'tergo sm: **a** ~ behind; **vedi a** ~ please turn over.

ter'male ag thermal; **stazione** f ~ spa.

'terme sfpl thermal baths.

'termico, a, ci, che ag thermic; (unità) thermal.

termi'nale ag, sm terminal.

termi'nare vt to end; (lavoro) to finish // vi to end.

'termine sm term; (fine, estremità) end; (di territorio) boundary, limit; **contratto a** ~ (COMM) forward contract; **a breve/lungo** ~ short-/long-term; **parlare senza mezzi** ~**i** to talk frankly, not to mince one's words.

terminolo'gia [terminolo'dʒia] sf terminology.

'ter'mite *sf* termite.
ter'mometro *sm* thermometer.
'termos *sm inv* = **thermos.**
termosi'fone *sm* radiator; (riscaldamento a) ~ central heating.
ter'mostato *sm* thermostat.
'terra *sf* (*gen*, ELETTR) earth; (*sostanza*) soil, earth; (*opposto al mare*) land *q*; (*regione, paese*) land; (*argilla*) clay; ~e *sfpl* (*possedimento*) lands, land *sg*; a *o* per ~ (*stato*) on the ground (*o floor*); (*moto*) to the ground, down; **mettere a** ~ (ELETTR) to earth.
terra'cotta *sf* terracotta; **vasellame** *m* di ~ earthenware.
terra'ferma *sf* dry land, terra firma; (*continente*) mainland.
terrapi'eno *sm* embankment, bank.
ter'razza [ter'rattsa] *sf,* **ter'razzo** [ter'rattso] *sm* terrace.
terre'moto *sm* earthquake.
ter'reno, a *ag* (*vita, beni*) earthly // *sm* (*suolo, fig*) ground; (COMM) land *q*, plot (*of land*); site; (SPORT, MIL) field.
ter'restre *ag* (*superficie*) of the earth, earth's; (*di terra: battaglia, animale*) land *cpd*; (REL) earthly, worldly.
ter'ribile *ag* terrible, dreadful.
terrifi'cante *ag* terrifying.
territori'ale *ag* territorial.
terri'torio *sm* territory.
ter'rore *sm* terror; **terro'rismo** *sm* terrorism; **terro'rista, i, e** *sm/f* terrorist; **terroriz'zare** *vt* to terrorize.
'terso, a *ag* clear.
'terzo, a ['tɛrtso] *ag* third // *sm* (*frazione*) third; (DIR) third party; ~i *smpl* (*altri*) others, other people.
'tesa *sf* brim.
'teschio ['tɛskjo] *sm* skull.
'tesi *sf* thesis.
'teso, a *pp di* **tendere** // *ag* (*tirato*) taut, tight; (*fig*) tense.
tesore'ria *sf* treasury.
tesori'ere *sm* treasurer.
te'soro *sm* treasure; **il Ministero del T~** the Treasury.
'tessera *sf* (*documento*) card.
'tessere *vt* to weave; **'tessile** *ag, sm* textile; **tessili** *smpl* (*operai*) textile workers; **tessi'tore, 'trice** *sm/f* weaver; **tessi'tura** *sf* weaving.
tes'suto *sm* fabric, material; (BIOL) tissue; (*fig*) web.
'testa *sf* head; (*di cose: estremità, parte anteriore*) head, front; **di** ~ *ag* (*vettura etc*) front; **fare** ~ **a qd** (*nemico etc*) to face sb; **fare di** ~ **propria** to go one's own way; **in** ~ (SPORT) in the lead; ~ **o croce?** heads or tails?; **avere la** ~ **dura** to be stubborn; ~ **di serie** (TENNIS) seed, seeded player.
testa'mento *sm* (*atto*) will; (REL): T~ Testament.
tes'tardo, a *ag* stubborn, pig-headed.
tes'tata *sf* (*parte anteriore*) head; (*intestazione*) heading.

'teste *sm/f* witness.
tes'ticolo *sm* testicle.
testi'mone *sm/f* (DIR) witness.
testimoni'anza [testimo'njantsa] *sf* testimony.
testimoni'are *vt* to testify; (*fig*) to bear witness to, testify to // *vi* to give evidence, testify.
'testo *sm* text; **fare** ~ (*fig: persona*) to be an authority; (: *opera*) to be the standard work; **testu'ale** *ag* textual; literal, word for word.
tes'tuggine [tes'tuddʒine] *sf* tortoise; (*di mare*) turtle.
'tetano *sm* (MED) tetanus.
'tetro, a *ag* gloomy.
'tetto *sm* roof; **tet'toia** *sf* shed; (*di piattaforma etc*) roofing.
'Tevere *sm*: **il** ~ the Tiber.
'thermos ® ['tɛrmos] *sm inv* vacuum *o* Thermos ® flask.
ti *pronome* (*dav lo, la, li, le, ne diventa* **te**) (*oggetto*) you; (*complemento di termine*) (to) you; (*riflessivo*) yourself.
ti'ara *sf* (REL) tiara.
'tibia *sf* tibia, shinbone.
tic *sm inv* tic, (*nervous*) twitch; (*fig*) mannerism.
ticchet'tio [tikket'tio] *sm* clicking; (*di orologio*) ticking; (*della pioggia*) patter.
'ticchio ['tikkjo] *sm* (*ghiribizzo*) whim; (*tic*) tic, (*nervous*) twitch.
ti'epido, a *ag* lukewarm, tepid.
ti'fare *vi*: ~ **per** to be a fan of; (*parteggiare*) to side with.
'tifo *sm* (MED) typhus; (*fig*): **fare il** ~ **per** to be a fan of.
tifoi'dea *sf* typhoid.
ti'fone *sm* typhoon.
ti'foso, a *sm/f* (SPORT etc) fan.
'tiglio ['tiʎʎo] *sm* lime (*tree*), linden (*tree*).
'tigre *sf* tiger.
tim'ballo *sm* (*strumento*) kettle drum; (CUC) timbale.
'timbro *sm* stamp; (MUS) timbre, tone.
'timido, a *ag* shy; timid.
'timo *sm* thyme.
ti'mone *sm* (NAUT) rudder; **timoni'ere** *sm* helmsman.
ti'more *sm* (*paura*) fear; (*rispetto*) awe; **timo'roso, a** *ag* timid, timorous.
'timpano *sm* (ANAT) eardrum; (MUS): ~i *smpl* kettledrums, timpani.
'tingere ['tindʒere] *vt* to dye.
'tino *sm* vat.
ti'nozza [ti'nɔttsa] *sf* tub.
'tinta *sf* (*materia colorante*) dye; (*colore*) colour, shade; **tinta'rella** *sf* (*fam*) (sun)tan.
tintin'nare *vi* to tinkle.
'tinto, a *pp di* **tingere.**
tinto'ria *sf* (*officina*) dyeworks *sg*; (*lavasecco*) dry cleaner's (shop).
tin'tura *sf* (*operazione*) dyeing; (*colorante*) dye; ~ **di iodio** tincture of iodine.
'tipico, a, ci, che *ag* typical.

'tipo sm type; (genere) kind, type; (fam) chap, fellow.

tipogra'fia sf typography; (procedimento) letterpress (printing); (officina) printing house; **tipo'grafico, a, ci, che** ag typographic(al); letterpress cpd; **ti'pografo** sm typographer.

ti'raggio [ti'raddʒo] sm (di camino etc) draught.

tiranneggi'are [tiranned'dʒare] vt to tyrannize.

tiran'nia sf tyranny.

ti'ranno, a ag tyrannical // sm tyrant.

ti'rare vt (gen) to pull; (estrarre): ~ **qc da** to take o pull sth out of; to get sth out of; to extract sth from; (chiudere: tenda etc) to draw, pull; (tracciare, disegnare) to draw, trace; (lanciare: sasso, palla) to throw; (stampare) to print; (pistola, freccia) to fire // vi (pipa, camino) to draw; (vento) to blow; (abito) to be tight; (fare fuoco) to fire; (fare del tiro, CALCIO) to shoot; ~ **avanti** vi to struggle on // vt to keep going; ~ **fuori** vt (estrarre) to take out, pull out; ~ **giù** vt (abbassare) to bring down; ~ **su** vt to pull up; (capelli) to put up; (fig: bambino) to bring up; ~**rsi indietro** to move back.

tira'tore sm gunman; **un buon** ~ a good shot; ~ **scelto** marksman.

tira'tura sf (azione) printing; (di libro) (print) run; (di giornale) circulation.

'tirchio, a ['tirkjo] ag mean, stingy.

'tiro sm shooting q, firing q; (colpo, sparo) shot; (di palla: lancio) throwing q; throw; (fig) trick; **cavallo da** ~ draught horse; ~ **a segno** target shooting; (luogo) shooting range.

tiro'cinio [tiro'tʃinjo] sm apprenticeship; (professionale) training.

ti'roide sf thyroid (gland).

Tir'reno sm: **il (mar)** ~ the Tyrrhenian Sea.

ti'sana sf herb tea.

tito'lare ag appointed; (sovrano) titular // sm/f incumbent; (proprietario) owner; (CALCIO) regular player.

'titolo sm title; (di giornale) headline; (diploma) qualification; (COMM) security; (: azione) share; **a che** ~? for what reason?; **a** ~ **di amicizia** out of friendship; **a** ~ **di premio** as a prize; ~ **di credito** share; ~ **di proprietà** title deed.

titu'bante ag hesitant, irresolute.

'tizio, a ['tittsjo] sm/f fellow, chap.

tiz'zone [tit'tsone] sm brand.

toc'cante ag touching.

toc'care vt to touch; (tastare) to feel; (fig: riguardare) to concern; (: commuovere) to touch, move; (: pungere) to hurt, wound; (: far cenno a: argomento) to touch on, mention // vi (2): ~ **a** (accadere) to happen to; (spettare) to be up to; **tocca a te difenderci** it's up to you to defend us; **a chi tocca?** whose turn is it?; **mi toccò pagare** I had to pay.

'tocco, chi sm touch; (ARTE) stroke, touch; **il** ~ (l'una) one o'clock, one p.m.

'toga, ghe sf toga; (di magistrato, professore) gown.

'togliere ['tɔʎʎere] vt (rimuovere) to take away (o off), remove; (riprendere, non concedere più) to take away, remove; (MAT) to take away, subtract; (liberare) to free; ~ **qc a qd** to take sth (away) from sb; **ciò non toglie che** nevertheless, be that as it may; ~**rsi il cappello** to take off one's hat.

to'letta sf toilet; (mobile) dressing table.

tolle'ranza [tolle'rantsa] sf tolerance.

tolle'rare vt to tolerate.

'tolto, a pp di **togliere**.

to'maia sf (di scarpa) upper.

'tomba sf tomb.

tom'bino sm manhole cover.

'tombola sf (gioco) tombola; (ruzzolone) tumble.

tombo'lare vi (2) to tumble.

'tomo sm volume.

'tonaca, che sf (REL) habit.

to'nare vi = **tuonare**.

'tondo, a ag round.

'tonfo sm splash; (rumore sordo) thud.

'tonico, a, ci, che ag, sm tonic.

tonifi'care vt (muscoli, pelle) to tone up; (irrobustire) to invigorate, brace.

tonnel'laggio [tonnel'laddʒo] sm (NAUT) tonnage.

tonnel'lata sf ton.

'tonno sm tuna (fish).

'tono sm (gen) tone; (MUS: di pezzo) key; (di colore) shade, tone.

ton'silla sf tonsil; **tonsil'lite** sf tonsillitis.

ton'sura sf tonsure.

'tonto, a ag dull, stupid.

to'pazio [to'pattsjo] sm topaz.

'topo sm mouse.

topogra'fia sf topography.

'toppa sf (serratura) keyhole; (pezza) patch.

to'race [to'ratʃe] sm chest.

'torba sf peat.

'torbido, a ag (liquido) cloudy; (: fiume) muddy; (fig) dark; troubled; **pescare nel** ~ (fig) to fish in troubled water.

'torcere ['tɔrtʃere] vt to twist; (biancheria) to wring (out); ~**rsi** vr to twist, writhe.

torchi'are [tor'kjare] vt to press; **'torchio** sm press; **torchio tipografico/per uva** printing/wine press.

'torcia, ce ['tɔrtʃa] sf torch.

torci'collo [tortʃi'kɔllo] sm stiff neck.

'tordo sm thrush.

To'rino sf Turin.

tor'menta sf snowstorm.

tormen'tare vt to torment; ~**rsi** vr to fret, worry o.s.; **tor'mento** sm torment.

torna'conto sm advantage, benefit.

tor'nado sm tornado.

tor'nante sm hairpin bend.

tor'nare vi (2) to return, go (o come) back; (ridiventare: anche fig) to become (again); (riuscire giusto, esatto: conto) to work out; (risultare) to turn out (to be), prove (to be); ~ **utile** to prove o turn out (to be) useful.

torna'sole sm inv litmus.

tor'neo sm tournament.

'tornio sm lathe.

'toro sm bull; (dello zodiaco): **T**~ Taurus.

tor'pedine sf torpedo; **torpedini'era** sf torpedo boat.

tor'pore sm torpor, drowsiness; (pigrizia) torpor, sluggishness.

'torre sf tower; (SCACCHI) rook, castle.

torrefazi'one [torrefat'sjone] sf roasting.

tor'rente sm torrent; **torrenzi'ale** ag torrential.

tor'retta sf turret.

'torrido, a ag torrid.

torri'one sm keep.

tor'rone sm nougat.

torsi'one sf twisting; torsion.

'torso sm torso, trunk; (ARTE) torso.

'torsolo sm (di cavolo etc) stump; (di frutta) core.

'torta sf cake.

torti'era sf cake tin.

'torto, a pp di **torcere** // ag (ritorto) twisted; (storto) twisted, crooked // sm (ingiustizia) wrong; (colpa) fault; **a** ~ wrongly; **aver** ~ to be wrong.

'tortora sf turtle dove.

tortu'oso, a ag (strada) twisting; (fig) tortuous.

tor'tura sf torture; **tortu'rare** vt to torture.

'torvo, a ag menacing, grim.

tosa'erba sm o f inv (lawn)mower.

to'sare vt (pecora) to shear; (siepe) to clip, trim.

Tos'cana sf: **la** ~ Tuscany.

'tosse sf cough; ~ **convulsa** o **canina** whooping cough.

'tossico, a, ci, che ag toxic.

tossi'comane sm/f drug addict.

tos'sire vi to cough.

tosta'pane sm inv toaster.

tos'tare vt to toast; (caffè) to roast.

'tosto, a ag: **faccia** ~a cheek.

to'tale ag, sm total; **totalità** sf: **la totalità di** all of, the total amount (o number) of; **the whole** + sg; **totali'tario, a** ag totalitarian; **totaliz'zare** vt to total; (SPORT: punti) to score.

toto'calcio [toto'kaltʃo] sm football pools pl.

to'vaglia [to'vaʎʎa] sf tablecloth; **tova-gli'olo** sm napkin.

'tozzo, a ['tɔttso] ag squat // sm: ~ **di pane** crust of bread.

tra prep (di due persone, cose) between; (di più persone, cose) among(st); (tempo: entro) within, in; ~ **5 giorni** in 5 days' time; **litigano** ~ **(di) loro** they're fighting amongst themselves; ~ **breve** soon; ~ **sé e sé** (parlare etc) to oneself.

trabal'lare vi to stagger, totter.

traboc'care vi (2) to overflow.

traboc'cnetto [trabok'ketto] sm (fig) trap.

tracan'nare vt to gulp down.

'traccia, ce ['trattʃa] sf (segno, striscia) trail, track; (orma) tracks pl; (residuo, testimonianza) trace, sign; (abbozzo) outline.

tracci'are [trat'tʃare] vt to trace, mark (out); (disegnare) to draw; (fig: abbozzare) to outline; **tracci'ato** sm (grafico) layout, plan.

tra'chea [tra'kɛa] sf windpipe, trachea.

tra'colla sf shoulder strap; **borsa a** ~ shoulder bag.

tra'collo sm (fig) collapse, crash.

traco'tante ag overbearing, arrogant.

tradi'mento sm betrayal; (DIR, MIL) treason.

tra'dire vt to betray; (coniuge) to be unfaithful to; (doveri: mancare) to fail in; (rivelare) to give away, reveal; **tradi'tore, 'trice** sm/f traitor.

tradizio'nale [tradittsjo'nale] ag traditional.

tradizi'one [tradit'tsjone] sf tradition.

tra'dotto, a pp di **tradurre**.

tra'durre vt to translate; (spiegare) to render, convey; **tradut'tore, 'trice** sm/f translator; **traduzi'one** sf translation.

tra'ente sm/f (ECON) drawer.

trafe'lato, a ag out of breath.

traffi'cante sm/f dealer; (peg) trafficker.

traffi'care vi (commerciare): ~ **(in)** to trade (in), deal (in); (affaccendarsi) to busy o.s. // vt (peg) to traffic in.

'traffico, ci sm traffic; (commercio) trade, traffic.

tra'figgere [tra'fiddʒere] vt to run through, stab; (fig) to pierce; **tra'fitto, a** pp di **trafiggere**.

trafo'rare vt to bore, drill; **tra'foro** sm (azione) boring, drilling; (galleria) tunnel.

tra'gedia [tra'dʒɛdja] sf tragedy.

tra'ghetto [tra'getto] sm crossing; (barca) ferry(boat).

'tragico, a, ci, che ['tradʒiko] ag tragic // sm (autore) tragedian.

tra'gitto [tra'dʒitto] sm (passaggio) crossing; (viaggio) journey.

tragu'ardo sm (SPORT) finishing line; (fig) goal, aim.

traiet'toria sf trajectory.

trai'nare vt to drag, haul; (rimorchiare) to tow; **'traino** sm (carro) wagon, v (slitta) sledge; (carico) load.

tralasci'are [tralaʃ'ʃare] vt (studi) to interrupt; (dettagli) to leave out, omit.

'tralcio ['traltʃo] sm (BOT) shoot.

tra'liccio [tra'littʃo] sm (tela) ticking; (struttura) trellis; (ELETTR) pylon.

tram sm inv tram.

'trama sf (filo) weft, woof; (fig: argomento, maneggio) plot.

traman'dare vt to pass on, hand down.

tra'mare vt (fig) to scheme, plot.

tram'busto sm turmoil.

trames'tio sm bustle.

tramez'zino [tramed'dzino] sm sandwich.

tra'mezzo [tra'mɛddzo] *sm* (*EDIL*) partition.

'**tramite** *prep* through.

tramon'tare *vi* (2) to set, go down; **tra-'monto** *sm* setting; (*del sole*) sunset.

tramor'tire *vi* (2) to faint // *vt* to stun.

trampo'lino *sm* (*per tuffi*) springboard, diving board; (*per lo sci*) ski-jump.

'**trampolo** *sm* stilt.

tramu'tare *vt* (*trasferire*) to transfer; (*mutare*) to change, transform.

'**trancia, ce** ['trantʃa] *sf* slice; (*cesoia*) shearing machine.

tra'nello *sm* trap.

trangugi'are [trangu'dʒare] *vt* to gulp down.

'**tranne** *prep* except (for), but (for).

tranquil'lante *sm* (*MED*) tranquillizer.

tranquil'lità *sf* calm, stillness; quietness; peace of mind.

tranquilliz'zare [trankwillid'dzare] *vt* to reassure.

tran'quillo, a *ag* calm, quiet; (*bambino, scolaro*) quiet; (*sereno*) with one's mind at rest; **sta' ~** don't worry.

transat'lantico, a, ci, che *ag* transatlantic // *sm* transatlantic liner.

tran'satto, a *pp di* **transigere**.

transazi'one [transat'tsjone] *sf* compromise; (*DIR*) settlement; (*COMM*) transaction, deal.

tran'senna *sf* barrier.

tran'setto *sm* transept.

tran'sigere [tran'sidʒere] *vi* (*DIR*) to reach a settlement; (*venire a patti*) to compromise, come to an agreement.

tran'sistor *sm*, **transis'tore** *sm* transistor.

transi'tabile *ag* passable.

transi'tare *vi* (2) to pass.

transi'tivo, a *ag* transitive.

'**transito** *sm* transit; **di ~** (*merci*) in transit; (*stazione*) transit *cpd*; **divieto di ~** no thoroughfare.

transi'torio, a *ag* transitory, transient; (*provvisorio*) provisional.

transizi'one [transit'tsjone] *sf* transition.

tran'via *sf* tramway.

'**trapano** *sm* (*utensile*) drill; (: *MED*) trepan.

trapas'sare *vt* to pierce.

tra'passo *sm* passage.

trape'lare *vi* (2) to leak, drip; (*fig*) to leak out.

tra'pezio [tra'pɛttsjo] *sm* (*MAT*) trapezium; (*attrezzo ginnico*) trapeze.

trapian'tare *vt* to transplant; **trapi'anto** *sm* transplanting; (*MED*) transplant.

'**trappola** *sf* trap.

tra'punta *sf* quilt.

'**trarre** *vt* to draw, pull; (*portare*) to take; (*prendere, tirare fuori*) to take (out), draw; (*derivare*) to obtain; **~ origine da qc** to have its origins *o* originate in sth.

trasa'lire *vi* to start, jump.

trasan'dato, a *ag* shabby.

trasbor'dare *vt* to transfer; (*NAUT*) to tran(s)ship // *vi* to change.

trascenden'tale [traʃʃenden'tale] *ag* transcendental.

trasci'nare [traʃʃi'nare] *vt* to drag; **~rsi** *vr* to drag o.s. along; (*fig*) to drag on.

tras'correre *vt* (*tempo*) to spend, pass; (*libro*) to skim (through) // *vi* (2) to pass; **tras'corso, a** *pp di* **trascorrere**.

tras'critto, a *pp di* **trascrivere**.

tras'crivere *vt* to transcribe; **trascri-zi'one** *sf* transcription.

trascu'rare *vt* to neglect; (*non considerare*) to disregard; **trascura'tezza** *sf* carelessness, negligence; **trascu'rato, a** *ag* (*casa*) neglected; (*persona*) careless, negligent.

traseco'lato, a *ag* astounded, amazed.

trasferi'mento *sm* transfer; (*trasloco*) removal, move.

trasfe'rire *vt* to transfer; **~rsi** *vr* to move; **tras'ferta** *sf* transfer; (*indennità*) travelling expenses *pl*; (*SPORT*) away game.

trasfigu'rare *vt* to transfigure.

trasfor'mare *vt* to transform, change; **trasforma'tore** *sm* transformer; **trasformazi'one** *sf* transformation.

trasfusi'one *sf* (*MED*) transfusion.

trasgre'dire *vt* to disobey, contravene.

tras'lato, a *ag* metaphorical, figurative.

traslo'care *vt* to move, transfer; **~rsi** *vr* to move; **tras'loco, chi** *sm* removal.

tras'messo, a *pp di* **trasmettere**.

tras'mettere *vt* (*passare*): **~ qc a qd** to pass sth on to sb; (*mandare*) to send; (*TECN, TEL, MED*) to transmit; (*TV, RADIO*) to broadcast; **trasmetti'tore** *sm* transmitter; **trasmissi'one** *sf* (*gen, FISICA, TECN*) transmission; (*passaggio*) transmission, passing on; (*TV, RADIO*) broadcast; **trasmit'tente** *sf* transmitting *o* broadcasting station.

traso'gnato, a [trasoɲ'ɲato] *ag* dreamy.

traspa'rente *ag* transparent; **traspa-'renza** *sf* transparency.

traspa'rire *vi* (2) to show (through).

traspi'rare *vi* (2) to perspire; (*fig*) to come to light, leak out; **traspirazi'one** *sf* perspiration.

traspor'tare *vt* to carry, move; (*merce*) to transport, convey; **lasciarsi ~ (da qc)** to let o.s. be carried away (by sth); **tras-'porto** *sm* transport.

trastul'lare *vt* to amuse; **~rsi** *vr* to amuse o.s.

trasu'dare *vi* (2) (*filtrare*) to ooze; (*sudare*) to sweat // *vt* to ooze with.

trasver'sale *ag* transverse, cross(-); running at right angles.

trasvo'lare *vt* to fly over // *vi* (*fig*): **~ su** to barely touch on.

'**tratta** *sf* (*ECON*) draft; (*di persone*): **la ~ delle bianche** the white slave trade.

tratta'mento *sm* treatment; (*servizio*) service.

trat'tare *vt* (*gen*) to treat; (*commerciare*) to deal in; (*svolgere: argomento*) to discuss, deal with; (*negoziare*) to negotiate // vi: ~ **di** to deal with; ~ **con** (*persona*) to deal with; **si tratta di ...** it's about ...; **tratta-'tive** *sfpl* negotiations; **trat'tato** *sm* (*testo*) treatise; (*accordo*) treaty; **trattazi'one** *sf* treatment.

tratteggi'are [tratted'dʒare] *vt* (*disegnare: a tratti*) to sketch, outline; (: *col tratteggio*) to hatch.

tratte'nere *vt* (*far rimanere: persona*) to detain; (*intrattenere: ospiti*) to entertain; (*tenere, frenare, reprimere*) to hold back, keep back; (*astenersi dal consegnare*) to hold, keep; (*detrarre: somma*) to deduct; ~**rsi** *vr* (*astenersi*) to restrain o.s., stop o.s.; (*soffermarsi*) to stay, remain.

tratteni'mento *sm* entertainment; (*festa*) party.

tratte'nuta *sf* deduction.

trat'tino *sm* dash; (*in parole composte*) hyphen.

'tratto, a *pp di* **trarre** // *sm* (*di penna, matita*) stroke; (*parte*) part, piece; (*di strada*) stretch; (*di mare, cielo*) expanse; (*di tempo*) period (of time); (*modo di comportarsi*) ways *pl*, manners *pl*; ~**i** *smpl* (*lineamenti, caratteristiche*) features; **a un** ~, **d'un** ~ suddenly.

trat'tore *sm* tractor.

tratto'ria *sf* restaurant.

'trauma, i *sm* trauma; **trau'matico, a, ci, che** *ag* traumatic.

tra'vaglio [tra'vaʎʎo] *sm* (*angoscia*) pain, suffering; (*MED*) pains *pl*; ~ **di parto** labour pains.

trava'sare *vt* to decant.

trava'tura *sf* beams *pl*.

tra'versa *sf* (*trave*) crosspiece; (*via*) sidestreet; (*FERR*) sleeper; (*CALCIO*) crossbar.

traver'sare *vt* to cross; **traver'sata** *sf* crossing; (*AER*) flight, trip.

traver'sie *sfpl* mishaps, misfortunes.

traver'sina *sf* (*FERR*) sleeper.

tra'verso, a *ag* oblique; **di** ~ *ag* askew // *av* sideways; **andare di** ~ (*cibo*) to go down the wrong way; **guardare di** ~ to look askance at.

travesti'mento *sm* disguise.

traves'tire *vt* to disguise; ~**rsi** *vr* to disguise o.s.; **traves'tito, a** *ag* disguised, in disguise // *sm* (*PSIC*) transvestite.

travi'are *vt* (*fig*) to lead astray.

travi'sare *vt* (*fig*) to distort, misrepresent.

tra'volgere [tra'vɔldʒere] *vt* to sweep away, carry away; (*fig*) to overwhelm; **tra'volto, a** *pp di* **travolgere**.

trazi'one [trat'tsjone] *sf* traction.

tre *num* three.

trebbi'are *vt* to thresh; **trebbia'trice** *sf* threshing machine.

'treccia, ce ['trettʃa] *sf* plait, braid.

tre'cento [tre'tʃɛnto] *num* three hundred // *sm*: **il T** ~ the fourteenth century.

'tredici ['treditʃi] *num* thirteen.

'tregua *sf* truce; (*fig*) respite.

tre'mare *vi* to tremble, shake; ~ **di**

(*freddo etc*) to shiver o tremble with; (*paura*) to shake o tremble with.

tre'mendo, a *ag* terrible, awful.

tremen'tina *sf* turpentine.

tre'mila *num* three thousand.

'tremito *sm* trembling *q*; shaking *q*; shivering *q*.

tremo'lare *vi* to tremble; (*luce*) to flicker; (*foglie*) to quiver.

tre'more *sm* tremor.

'treno *sm* train; ~ **di gomme** set of tyres; ~ **merci** goods train; ~ **viaggiatori** passenger train.

'trenta *num* thirty; **tren'tesimo, a** *ag* thirtieth; **tren'tina** *sf*: **una trentina (di)** thirty or so, about thirty.

'trepido, a *ag* anxious.

treppi'ede *sm* tripod; (*CUC*) trivet.

'tresca, sche *sf* (*fig*) intrigue; (: *relazione amorosa*) affair.

'trespolo *sm* trestle.

tri'angolo *sm* triangle.

tribolazi'one [tribolat'tsjone] *sf* suffering, tribulation.

tribù *sf inv* tribe.

tri'buna *sf* (*podio*) platform; (*in aule etc*) gallery; (*di stadio*) stand.

tribu'nale *sm* court.

tribu'tare *vt* to bestow.

tribu'tario, a *ag* (*imposta*) fiscal, tax *cpd*; (*GEO*): **essere** ~ **di** to be a tributary of.

tri'buto *sm* tax; (*fig*) tribute.

tri'checo, chi [tri'kɛko] *sm* (*ZOOL*) walrus.

tri'ciclo [tri'tʃiklo] *sm* tricycle.

trico'lore *ag* three-coloured // *sm* tricolour; (*bandiera italiana*) Italian flag.

tri'dente *sm* trident.

tri'foglio [tri'fɔʎʎo] *sm* clover.

'triglia ['triʎʎa] *sf* red mullet.

trigonome'tria *sf* trigonometry.

tril'lare *vi* (*MUS*) to trill.

tri'mestre *sm* period of three months; (*INS*) term; (*COMM*) quarter.

'trina *sf* lace.

trin'cea [trin'tʃea] *sf* trench; **trince'rare** *vt* to entrench.

trinci'are [trin'tʃare] *vt* to cut up.

Trinità *sf* (*REL*) Trinity.

'trio, pl 'trii *sm* trio.

trion'fale *ag* triumphal, triumphant.

trion'fante *ag* triumphant.

trion'fare *vi* to triumph, win; ~ **su** to triumph over, overcome; **tri'onfo** *sm* triumph.

tripli'care *vt* to triple.

'triplice ['triplitʃe] *ag* triple; **in** ~ **copia** in triplicate.

'triplo, a *ag* triple; treble // *sm*: **il** ~ **(di)** three times as much (as); **una somma** ~**a** a sum three times as great, three times as much money.

'tripode *sm* tripod.

'trippa *sf* (*CUC*) tripe.

'triste *ag* sad; (*luogo*) dreary, gloomy; **tris'tezza** *sf* sadness; gloominess.

'tristo, a *ag* (*cattivo*) wicked, evil;

(*meschino*) sorry, poor; **fare una ~a figura** to cut a poor figure.

trita'carne *sm inv* mincer.

tri'tare *vt* to mince.

'trito, a *ag* (*tritato*) minced.

'trittico, ci *sm* (ARTE) triptych.

tri'vella *sf* drill; **trivel'lare** *vt* to drill.

trivi'ale *ag* vulgar, low.

tro'feo *sm* trophy.

'trogolo *sm* (*per maiali*) trough.

'troia *sf* (ZOOL) sow.

'tromba *sf* (MUS) trumpet; (AUT) horn; **~ d'aria** whirlwind; **~ delle scale** stairwell.

trom'bone *sm* trombone.

trom'bosi *sf* thrombosis.

tron'care *vt* to cut off; (*spezzare*) to break off.

'tronco, a, chi, che *ag* cut off; broken off; (LING) truncated; (*fig*) cut short // *sm* (BOT, ANAT) trunk; (*fig: tratto*) section; (: *pezzo: di lancia*) stump.

troneggi'are [troned'dʒare] *vi:* **~ (su)** to tower (over).

'tronfio, a *ag* conceited.

'trono *sm* throne.

tropi'cale *ag* tropical.

'tropico, ci *sm* tropic; **~ci** *smpl* tropics.

'troppo, a *det, pronome* (*quantità*) too much; (*numero*) too many // *av* (*con vb*) too much; (*con ag, av*) too; **di ~:** qualche tazza di **~** a few cups too many, a few extra cups; **3000 lire di ~** 3000 lire too much.

'trota *sf* trout.

trot'tare *vi* to trot; **trotterel'lare** *vi* to trot along; (*bambino*) to toddle; **'trotto** *sm* trot.

'trottola *sf* spinning top.

tro'vare *vt* to find; (*giudicare*): **trovo che** I find *o* think that; **~rsi** *vr* (*incontrarsi*) to meet; (*essere, stare*) to be; (*arrivare, capitare*) to find *o.s.;* **andare a ~ qd** to go and see sb; **~ qd colpevole** to find sb guilty; **~rsi bene** to feel well; **tro'vata** *sf* good idea.

truc'care *vt* (*falsare*) to fake; (*attore etc*) to make up; (*travestire*) to disguise; (SPORT) to fix; (AUT) to soup up; **~rsi** *vr* to make up (one's face); **trucca'tore, 'trice** *sm/f* (CINEMA, TEATRO) make-up artist.

'trucco, chi *sm* trick; (*cosmesi*) make-up.

'truce ['trutʃe] *ag* fierce.

truci'dare [trutʃi'dare] *vt* to slaughter.

truciolo ['trutʃolo] *sm* shaving.

'truffa *sf* fraud, swindle; **truf'fare** *vt* to swindle, cheat.

'truppa *sf* troop.

tu *pronome* you; **dare del ~ a qd** to address sb as 'tu'.

'tua *vedi* tuo.

'tuba *sf* (MUS) tuba; (*cappello*) top hat.

tu'bare *vi* to coo.

tuba'tura *sf*, **tubazi'one** [tubat'tsjone] *sf* piping *q*, pipes *pl*.

tuberco'losi *sf* tuberculosis.

tu'betto *sm* tube.

'tubo *sm* tube; pipe; **~ digerente** (ANAT) alimentary canal, digestive tract; **~ di scappamento** (AUT) exhaust pipe.

'tue *vedi* tuo.

tuf'fare *vt* to plunge, dip; **~rsi** *vr* to plunge, dive; **'tuffo** *sm* dive; (*breve bagno*) dip.

tu'gurio *sm* hovel.

tuli'pano *sm* tulip.

tumefazi'one [tumefat'tsjone] *sf* (MED) swelling.

'tumido, a *ag* swollen.

tu'more *sm* (MED) tumour.

tu'multo *sm* uproar, commotion; (*sommossa*) riot; (*fig*) turmoil; **tumul-tu'oso, a** *ag* rowdy, unruly; (*fig*) turbulent, stormy.

'tunica, che *sf* tunic.

Tuni'sia *sf:* **la ~** Tunisia.

'tuo, 'tua, tu'oi, 'tue *det:* **il ~, la tua** *etc* your // *pronome:* **il ~, la tua** *etc* yours.

tuo'nare *vi* to thunder; **tuona** it is thundering, there's some thunder.

tu'ono *sm* thunder.

tu'orlo *sm* yolk.

tu'racciolo [tu'rattʃolo] *sm* cap, top; (*di sughero*) cork.

tu'rare *vt* to stop, plug; (*con sughero*) to cork; **~rsi il naso** to hold one's nose.

turba'mento *sm* disturbance; (*di animo*) anxiety, agitation.

tur'bante *sm* turban.

tur'bare *vt* to disturb, trouble.

tur'bina *sf* turbine.

turbi'nare *vi* to whirl.

'turbine *sm* whirlwind; **~ di polvere/sabbia** dust/sandstorm.

turbo'lento, a *ag* turbulent; (*ragazzo*) boisterous, unruly.

turbo'lenza [turbo'lɛntsa] *sf* turbulence.

turboreat'tore *sm* turbojet engine.

tur'chese [tur'kese] *sf* turquoise.

Tur'chia [tur'kia] *sf:* **la ~** Turkey.

tur'chino, a [tur'kino] *ag* deep blue.

'turco, a, chi, che *ag* Turkish // *sm/f* Turk/Turkish woman // *sm* (LING) Turkish.

tu'rismo *sm* tourism; tourist industry; **tu'rista, i, e** *sm/f* tourist; **tu'ristico, a, ci, che** *ag* tourist *cpd*.

'turno *sm* turn; (*di lavoro*) shift; **di ~** (*soldato, medico, custode*) on duty; **a ~** (*rispondere*) in turn; (*lavorare*) in shifts; **fare a ~ a fare qc** to take turns to do sth; **è il suo ~** it's your (*o his etc*) turn.

'turpe *ag* filthy, vile; **turpi'loquio** *sm* obscene language.

'tuta *sf* overalls *pl*; (SPORT) tracksuit.

tu'tela *sf* (DIR: *di minore*) guardianship; (: *protezione*) protection; (*difesa*) defence; **tute'lare** *vt* to protect, defend.

tu'tore, 'trice *sm/f* (DIR) guardian.

tutta'via *cong* nevertheless, yet.

'tutto, a *det* all; **~ il latte** all the milk, the whole of the milk; **~a la sera** all evening, the whole evening; **~a una bottiglia** a whole bottle; **~i i ragazzi** all the boys; ∼ **e le sere** every evening // *pronome* everything, all; ∼**i(e)** *pronome pl* all (of them); (*ognuno*) everyone // *av* (*completamente*) completely, quite // *sm* whole; (*l'intero*): **il** ∼ all of it, the whole lot; ∼**i e due** both *o* each of us (*o* them); ∼**i e cinque** all five of us (*o* them); **a** ∼ **a velocità** at full *o* top speed; **del** ∼ completely; **in** ∼ in all; **tutt'altro** on the contrary; (*affatto*) not at all; **tutt'altro che felice** anything but happy; ∼ **considerato** all things considered; **a tutt'oggi** so far, up till now; **tutt'al più** at (the) most; (*al più tardi*) at the latest; ∼**e le volte che** every time (that).

tutto'fare *ag inv*: **domestica** ∼ general maid; **ragazzo** ∼ office boy // *sm inv* handyman.

tut'tora *av* still.

U

ubbidi'ente *ag* obedient; **ubbidi'enza** *sf* obedience.

ubbi'dire *vi* to obey; ∼ **a** to obey; (*sog: veicolo, macchina*) to respond to.

ubiquità *sf*: **non ho il dono dell'**∼ I can't be everywhere at once.

ubria'care *vt*: ∼ **qd** to get sb drunk; (*sog: alcool*) to make sb drunk; (*fig*) to make sb's head spin *o* reel; ∼**rsi** *vr* to get drunk; ∼**rsi di** (*fig*) to become intoxicated with.

ubria'chezza [ubria'kettsa] *sf* drunkenness.

ubri'aco, a, chi, che *ag, sm/f* drunk.

uccelli'era [uttʃel'ljɛra] *sf* aviary.

uc'cello [ut'tʃɛllo] *sm* bird.

uc'cidere [ut'tʃidere] *vt* to kill; ∼**rsi** *vr* (*suicidarsi*) to kill o.s.; (*perdere la vita*) to be killed; **uccisi'one** *sf* killing; **uc'ciso,** a *pp di* **uccidere**; **ucci'sore, uccidi'trice** *sm/f* killer.

u'dibile *ag* audible.

udi'enza [u'djɛntsa] *sf* audience; (*DIR*) hearing, sitting.

u'dire *vt* to hear; **udi'tivo, a** *ag* auditory; **u'dito** *sm* (sense of) hearing; **udi'tore, 'trice** *sm/f* listener; (*INS*) unregistered student (*attending lectures*); **udi'torio** *sm* (*persone*) audience.

uffici'ale [uffi'tʃale] *ag* official // *sm* (*AMM*) official, officer; (*MIL*) officer; ∼ **di stato civile** registrar.

uf'ficio [uf'fitʃo] *sm* (*gen*) office; (*dovere*) duty; (*mansione*) task, function, job; (*agenzia*) agency, bureau; (*REL*) service; **d'**∼ *ag* office *cpd*; official // *av* officially; ∼ **di collocamento** employment office; ∼ **postale** post office.

uffici'oso, a [uffi'tʃoso] *ag* unofficial.

'ufo: a ∼ *av* free, for nothing.

uggi'oso, a [ud'dʒoso] *ag* tiresome; (*tempo*) dull.

uguagli'anza [ugwaʎ'ʎantsa] *sf* equality.

uguagli'are [ugwaʎ'ʎare] *vt* to make equal; (*essere uguale*) to equal, be equal to; (*livellare*) to level; ∼**rsi a** *o* **con qd** (*paragonarsi*) to compare o.s. to sb.

ugu'ale *ag* equal; (*identico*) identical, the same; (*uniforme*) level, even; **ugual'mente** *av* equally; (*lo stesso*) all the same.

'ulcera ['ultʃera] *sf* ulcer.

u'liva *etc* = **oliva** *etc*.

ulteri'ore *ag* further.

ulti'mare *vt* to finish, complete.

ulti'matum *sm inv* ultimatum.

'ultimo, a *ag* (*finale*) last; (*estremo*) farthest, utmost; (*recente: notizia, moda*) latest; (*fig: sommo, fondamentale*) ultimate // *sm/f* last (one); **fino all'**∼ to the last, until the end; **da** ∼, **in** ∼ in the end; **abitare all'**∼ **piano** to live on the top floor.

ultravio'letto, a *ag* ultraviolet.

ulu'lare *vi* to howl; **ulu'lato** *sm* howling *q*; howl.

umanità *sf* humanity; **umani'tario, a** *ag* humanitarian.

u'mano, a *ag* human; (*comprensivo*) humane.

umbi'lico *sm* = **ombelico**.

umet'tare *vt* to dampen, moisten.

umidità *sf* dampness; humidity.

'umido, a *ag* damp; (*mano, occhi*) moist; (*clima*) humid // *sm* dampness, damp; **carne in** ∼ stew.

'umile *ag* humble.

umili'are *vt* to humiliate; ∼**rsi** *vr* to humble o.s.; **umiliazi'one** *sf* humiliation.

umiltà *sf* humility, humbleness.

u'more *sm* (*disposizione d'animo*) mood; (*carattere*) temper; **di buon/cattivo** ∼ in a good/bad mood.

umo'rismo *sm* humour; **avere il senso dell'**∼ to have a sense of humour; **umo'rista, i, e** *sm/f* humorist; **umo'ristico, a, ci, che** *ag* humorous, funny.

un, un', una *vedi* **uno**.

u'nanime *ag* unanimous; **unanimità** *sf* unanimity; **all'unanimità** unanimously.

unci'netto [untʃi'netto] *sm* crochet hook.

un'cino [un'tʃino] *sm* hook.

'undici ['unditʃi] *num* eleven.

'ungere ['undʒere] *vt* to grease, oil; (*REL*) to anoint; (*fig*) to flatter, butter up; ∼**rsi** *vr* (*sporcarsi*) to get covered in grease; ∼**rsi con la crema** to put on cream.

unghe'rese [unge'rese] *ag, sm/f, sm* Hungarian.

Unghe'ria [unge'ria] *sf*: **l'**∼ Hungary.

'unghia ['ungja] *sf* (*ANAT*) nail; (*di animale*) claw; (*di rapace*) talon; (*di cavallo*) hoof; **unghi'ata** *sf* (*graffio*) scratch.

ungu'ento *sm* ointment.

'unico, a, ci, che *ag* (*solo*) only; (*ineguagliabile*) unique; (*singolo: binario*) single.

uni'corno *sm* unicorn.

unifi'care *vt* to unite, unify; (*sistemi*) to standardize; **unificazi'one** *sf* uniting; unification; standardization.

uni'forme *ag* uniform; (*superficie*) even // *sf* (*divisa*) uniform; **uniformità** *sf* uniformity; evenness.

unilate'rale *ag* one-sided; *(DIR)* unilateral.

uni'one *sf* union; *(fig: concordia)* unity, harmony; **l'U~ Sovietica** the Soviet Union.

u'nire *vt* to unite; *(congiungere)* to join, connect; *(: ingredienti, colori)* to combine; *(in matrimonio)* to unite, join together; **~rsi** *vr* to unite; *(in matrimonio)* to be joined together; **~ qc a** to unite sth with; to join *o* connect sth with; to combine sth with; **~rsi a** *(gruppo, società)* to join.

u'nisono *sm*: **all'~** in unison.

unità *sf inv (unione, concordia)* unity; *(MAT, MIL, COMM, di misura)* unit; **uni'tario, a** *ag* unitary; **prezzo unitario** price per unit.

u'nito, a *ag (paese)* united; *(famiglia)* close; *(tinta)* solid.

univer'sale *ag* universal; general.

università *sf inv* university; **universi-'tario, a** *ag* university *cpd* // *sm/f (studente)* university student; *(insegnante)* academic, university lecturer.

uni'verso *sm* universe.

'uno, a *det, num (dav sm un* + *C, V, uno* + *s impura, gn, pn, ps, x, z; dav sf un'* + *V, una* + *C) det* a, an + *vocale* // *num* one // *pronome (un tale)* someone, somebody; *(con valore impersonale)* one, you // *sf*: **è l'~a** it's one o'clock.

'unto, a *pp di* **ungere** // *ag* greasy, oily // *sm* grease; **untu'oso, a** *ag* greasy, oily.

u'omo, *pl* **u'omini** *sm* man; **da ~** *(abito, scarpe)* men's, for men; **~ d'affari** businessman; **~ di paglia** stooge; **~ rana** frogman.

u'opo *sm*: **all'~** if necessary.

u'ovo, *pl(f)* **u'ova** *sm* egg; **~ affogato** poached egg; **~ bazzotto/sodo** soft-/hard-boiled egg; **~ alla coque** boiled egg; **~ di Pasqua** Easter egg; **uova strapazzate** scrambled eggs.

ura'gano *sm* hurricane.

u'ranio *sm (CHIM)* uranium.

urba'nesimo *sm* urbanization.

urba'nistica *sf* town planning.

ur'bano, a *ag* urban, city *cpd*, town *cpd*; *(fig)* urbane.

ur'gente [ur'dʒɛnte] *ag* urgent; **ur'genza** *sf* urgency; **in caso d'urgenza** in (case of) an emergency; **d'urgenza** *ag* emergency // *av* urgently, as a matter of urgency.

'urgere ['urdʒere] *vi* to be urgent; to be needed urgently.

u'rina *sf* = **orina**.

ur'lare *vi (persona)* to scream, yell; *(animale, vento)* to howl // *vt* to scream, yell.

'urlo, *pl(m)* **'urli,** *pl(f)* **'urla** *sm* scream, yell; howl.

'urna *sf* urn; *(elettorale)* ballot-box; **andare alle ~e** to go to the polls.

urrà *escl* hurrah!

U.R.S.S. *abbr f*: **l'~** the USSR.

ur'tare *vt* to bump into, knock against; *(fig: irritare)* to annoy // *vi*: **~ contro** *o* **in** to bump into, knock against, crash into; *(fig: imbattersi)* to come up against; **~rsi**

vr (reciproco: scontrarsi) to collide; *(: fig)* to clash; *(irritarsi)* to get annoyed; **'urto** *sm (colpo)* knock, bump; *(scontro)* crash, collision; *(fig)* clash.

U.S.A. ['uza] *abbr mpl*: **gli ~** the U.S.A.

u'sanza [u'zantsa] *sf* custom; *(moda)* fashion.

u'sare *vt* to use, employ // *vi (servirsi)*: **~ di** to use; *(: diritto)* to exercise; *(essere di moda)* to be fashionable; *(essere solito)*: **~ fare** to be in the habit of doing, be accustomed to doing; **u'sato, a** *ag* used; *(consumato)* worn; *(di seconda mano)* used, second-hand; **secondo l'usato** as usual; **fuori dell'usato** unusual.

usci'ere [uʃ'ʃɛre] *sm* usher.

'uscio ['uʃʃo] *sm* door.

u'scire [uʃ'ʃire] *vi (2) (gen)* to come out; *(partire, andare a passeggio, a uno spettacolo etc)* to go out; *(essere sorteggiato: numero)* to come up; **~ da** *(gen)* to leave; *(posto)* to go *(o* come) out of, leave; *(solco, vasca etc)* to come out of; *(muro)* to stick out of; *(competenza etc)* to be outside; *(infanzia, adolescenza)* to leave behind; *(famiglia nobile etc)* to come from; **~ da** *o* **di casa** to go out; *(fig)* to leave home; **~ in automobile** to go out in the car, go for a drive; **~ di strada** *(AUT)* to go off *o* leave the road.

u'scita [uʃ'ʃita] *sf (passaggio, varco)* exit, way out; *(per divertimento)* outing; *(ECON: somma)* expenditure; *(TEATRO)* entrance; *(fig: battuta)* witty remark; **~ di sicurezza** emergency exit.

usi'gnolo [uzin'ɲɔlo] *sm* nightingale.

'uso *sm (utilizzazione)* use; *(esercizio)* practice; *(abitudine)* custom; **a ~ di** for (the use of); **d'~** *(corrente)* in use; **fuori ~** out of use.

usti'one *sf* burn.

usu'ale *ag* common, everyday.

u'sura *sf* usury; *(logoramento)* wear (and tear); **usu'raio** *sm* usurer.

usur'pare *vt* to usurp.

uten'sile *sm* tool, implement; **~i da cucina** kitchen utensils.

u'tente *sm/f* user.

u'tero *sm* uterus.

'utile *ag* useful // *sm (vantaggio)* advantage, benefit; *(ECON: profitto)* profit; **utilità** *sf* usefulness *q*; use; *(vantaggio)* benefit; **utili'tario, a** *ag* utilitarian // *sf (AUT)* economy car.

utiliz'zare [utilid'dzare] *vt* to use, make use of, utilize; **utilizzazi'one** *sf* utilization, use.

'uva *sf* grapes *pl*; **~ passa** raisins *pl*; **~ spina** gooseberry.

V

v. *(abbr di* vedi*)* v.

va'cante *ag* vacant.

va'canza [va'kantsa] *sf (l'essere vacante)* vacancy; *(riposo, ferie)* holiday(s *pl)*; *(giorno di permesso)* day off, holiday; **~e** *sfpl (periodo di ferie)* holidays, vacation *sg*;

essere/andare in ~ to be/go on holiday; ~ **e estive** summer holiday(s).

'vacca, che sf cow.

vacci'nare [vatt∫i'nare] vt to vaccinate; **vaccinazi'one** sf vaccination.

vac'cino [vat't∫ino] sm (MED) vaccine.

vacil'lare [vat∫il'lare] vi to sway, wobble; (luce) to flicker; (fig: memoria, coraggio) to be failing, falter.

'vacuo, a ag (fig) empty, vacuous // sm vacuum.

vaga'bondo, a sm/f tramp, vagrant; (fannullone) idler, loafer.

va'gare vi to wander.

vagheggi'are [vaged'dʒare] vt to long for, dream of.

va'gina [va'dʒina] sf vagina.

va'gire [va'dʒire] vi to whimper.

'vaglia ['vaʎʎa] sm inv money order; ~ **postale** postal order.

vagli'are [vaʎ'ʎare] vt to sift; (fig) to weigh up; **'vaglio** sm sieve.

'vago, a, ghi, ghe ag vague.

va'gone sm (FERR: per passeggeri) coach; (: per merci) truck, wagon; ~ **letto** sleeper, sleeping car; ~ **ristorante** dining o restaurant car.

vai'olo sm smallpox.

va'langa, ghe sf avalanche.

va'lente ag able, talented.

va'lere vi (2) (avere forza, potenza) to have influence; (essere valido) to be valid; (avere vigore, autorità) to hold, apply; (essere capace: poeta, studente) to be good, be able // vt (prezzo, sforzo) to be worth; (corrispondere) to correspond to; (procurare): ~ **qc a qd** to earn sb sth; ~**rsi di** to make use of, take advantage of; **far** ~ (autorità etc) to assert; **vale a dire** that is to say; ~ **la pena** to be worth the effort o worth it.

va'levole ag valid.

vali'care vt to cross.

'valico, chi sm (passo) pass.

validità sf validity.

'valido, a ag valid; (in buona salute) fit; (efficace) effective; (forte) strong.

valige'ria [validʒe'ria] sf leather goods pl; leather goods factory; leather goods shop.

va'ligia, gie o **ge** [va'lidʒa] sf (suit)case; **fare le** ~**gie** to pack (up); ~ **diplomatica** diplomatic bag.

val'letto sm valet.

va'lle sf valley; **a** ~ (di fiume) downstream; **scendere a** ~ to go downhill.

val'letto sm valet.

va'lore sm (gen) value; (merito) merit, worth; (coraggio) valour, courage; (COMM: titolo) security; ~**i** smpl (oggetti preziosi) valuables; **mettere in** ~ (bene) to exploit; (fig) to highlight, show off to advantage.

valoriz'zare [valorid'dzare] vt (terreno) to develop; (fig) to make the most of.

valo'roso, a ag valorous.

'valso, a pp di **valere**.

va'luta sf currency, money; (BANCA): ~ **15 gennaio** interest to run from January 15th.

valu'tare vt (casa, gioiello, fig) to value; (stabilire: peso, entrate, fig) to estimate; **valutazi'one** sf valuation; estimate.

'valva sf (ZOOL, BOT) valve.

'valvola sf (TECN, ANAT) valve; (ELETTR) fuse.

'valzer ['valtser] sm inv waltz.

vam'pata sf (di fiamma) blaze; (di calore) blast; (: al viso) flush.

vam'piro sm vampire.

vanda'lismo sm vandalism.

'vandalo sm vandal.

vaneggi'are [vaned'dʒare] vi to rave.

'vanga, ghe sf spade; **van'gare** vt to dig.

van'gelo [van'dʒɛlo] sm gospel.

va'niglia [va'niʎʎa] sf vanilla.

vanità sf vanity; **vani'toso, a** ag vain, conceited.

'vano, a ag vain // sm (spazio) space; (apertura) opening; (stanza) room.

van'taggio [van'taddʒo] sm advantage; **portarsi in** ~ (SPORT) to take the lead; **vantaggi'oso, a** ag advantageous; favourable.

van'tare vt to praise, speak highly of; ~**rsi** vr to boast; **vante'ria** sf boasting; **'vanto** sm boasting; (merito) virtue, merit; (gloria) pride.

'vanvera sf: **a** ~ haphazardly; **parlare a** ~ to talk nonsense.

va'pore sm vapour; (anche: ~ **acqueo**) steam; (nave) steamer; **a** ~ (turbina etc) steam cpd; **al** ~ (CUC) steamed; **vapo-'retto** sm steamer; **vapori'era** sf (FERR) steam engine; **vaporiz'zare** vt to vaporize.

va'rare vt (NAUT, fig) to launch; (DIR) to pass.

var'care vt to cross.

'varco, chi sm passage; **aprirsi un** ~ **tra la folla** to push one's way through the crowd.

vari'abile ag variable; (tempo, umore) changeable, variable // sf (MAT) variable.

vari'ante sf variant.

vari'are vt to vary // vi to vary; (subire variazioni) to vary, change; ~ **di camera/opinione** to change rooms/one's mind; **variazi'one** sf variation; change.

va'rice [va'rit∫e] sf varicose vein.

vari'cella [vari't∫ɛlla] sf chickenpox.

vari'coso, a ag varicose.

varie'gato, a ag variegated.

varietà sf inv variety // sm inv variety show.

'vario, a ag varied; (parecchi: col sostantivo al pl) various; (mutevole: umore) changeable; **vario'pinto, a** ag multicoloured.

'varo sm (NAUT, fig) launch; (di leggi) passing.

va'saio sm potter.

'vasca, sche sf basin; (anche: ~ da bagno) bathtub, bath.

va'scello [vaʃ'ʃello] sm (NAUT) vessel, ship.

vase'lina sf vaseline.

vasel'lame sm china; ~ d'oro/d'argento gold/silver plate.

'vaso sm (recipiente) pot; (: barattolo) jar; (: decorativo) vase; (ANAT) vessel; ~ da fiori vase; (per piante) flowerpot.

vas'soio sm tray.

'vasto, a ag vast, immense.

Vati'cano sm: il ~ the Vatican.

ve pronome, av vedi vi.

vecchi'aia [vek'kjaja] sf old age.

'vecchio, a ['vɛkkjo] ag old // sm/f old man/woman; i ~i the old.

'vece ['vetʃe] sf: in ~ di in the place of, for; fare le ~ di qd to take sb's place.

ve'dere vt, vi to see; ~rsi vr to meet, see one another; avere a che ~ con to have sth to do with; far ~ qc a qd to show sb sth; farsi ~ to show o.s.; (farsi vivo) to show one's face.

ve'detta sf (sentinella, posto) look-out; (NAUT) patrol boat.

'vedovo, a sm/f widower/widow.

ve'duta sf view.

vee'mente ag vehement; violent.

vege'tale [vedʒe'tale] ag, sm vegetable.

vege'tare [vedʒe'tare] vi to vegetate; vegetari'ano, a ag, sm/f vegetarian; vegetazi'one sf vegetation.

ve'geto, a ['vɛdʒeto] ag (pianta) thriving; (persona) strong, vigorous.

'veglia ['veʎʎa] sf wakefulness; (sorveglianza) watch; (trattenimento) evening gathering; stare a ~ to keep watch; fare la ~ a un malato to watch over a sick person.

vegli'are [veʎ'ʎare] vi to be awake; to stay o sit up; (stare vigile) to watch; to keep watch // vt (malato, morto) to watch over, sit up with.

ve'icolo sm vehicle.

'vela sf (NAUT: tela) sail; (sport) sailing.

ve'lare vt to veil; ~rsi vr (occhi, luna) to mist over; (voce) to become husky; ~rsi il viso to cover one's face (with a veil); ve'lato, a ag veiled.

veleggi'are [veled'dʒare] vi to sail; (AER) to glide.

ve'leno sm poison; vele'noso, a ag poisonous.

veli'ero sm sailing ship.

ve'lina sf (anche: carta ~: per imballare) tissue paper; (: per copie) flimsy paper; (copia) carbon copy.

ve'livolo sm aircraft.

velleità sf inv vain ambition, vain desire.

'vello sm fleece.

vel'luto sm velvet; ~ a coste cord.

'velo sm veil; (tessuto) voile.

ve'loce [ve'lotʃe] ag fast, quick // av fast, quickly; velo'cista, i, e sm/f (SPORT) sprinter; velocità sf speed; (AUT: marcia) gear; velocità di crociera cruising

speed; velocità del suono speed of sound.

ve'lodromo sm velodrome.

'vena sf (gen) vein; (filone) vein, seam; (fig: ispirazione) inspiration; (: umore) mood; essere in ~ di qc to be in the mood for sth.

ve'nale ag (prezzo, valore) market cpd; (fig) venal; mercenary.

ven'demmia sf (raccolta) grape harvest; (quantità d'uva) grape crop, grapes pl; (vino ottenuto) vintage; vendemmi'are vt to harvest // vi to harvest the grapes.

'vendere vt to sell; 'vendesi' 'for sale'.

ven'detta sf revenge.

vendi'care vt to avenge; ~rsi vr: ~rsi (di) to avenge o.s. (for); (per rancore) to take one's revenge (for); vendica'tivo, a ag vindictive.

'vendita sf sale; la ~ (attività) selling; (smercio) sales pl; in ~ on sale; ~ all'asta sale by auction; vendi'tore sm seller, vendor; (gestore di negozio) trader, dealer.

ve'nefico, a, ci, che ag poisonous.

vene'rabile ag, vene'rando, a ag venerable.

vene'rare vt to venerate.

venerdì sm inv Friday; di o il ~ on Fridays; V~ Santo Good Friday.

ve'nereo, a ag venereal.

Ve'nezia [ve'nɛttsja] sf Venice; vene-zi'ano, a ag, sm/f Venetian.

veni'ale ag venial.

ve'nire vi (2) to come; (riuscire: dolce, fotografia) to turn out; (come ausiliare: essere): viene ammirato da tutti he is admired by everyone; ~ da to come from; quanto viene? how much does it cost?; far ~ (mandare a chiamare) to send for; ~ giù to come down; ~ meno (svenire) to faint; ~ meno a qc to fail in sth; ~ su to come up; ~ via to come away.

ven'taglio [ven'taʎʎo] sm fan.

ven'tata sf gust (of wind).

ven'tenne ag: una ragazza ~ a twenty-year-old girl, a girl of twenty.

ven'tesimo, a ag, sm twentieth.

'venti num twenty.

venti'lare vt to ventilate; (fig: esaminare) to discuss; ventila'tore sm ventilator, fan; ventilazi'one sf ventilation.

ven'tina sf: una ~ (di) around twenty, twenty or so.

'vento sm wind.

ven'tosa sf (ZOOL) sucker; (di gomma) suction pad.

ven'toso, a ag windy.

'ventre sm stomach.

ven'triloquo sm ventriloquist.

ven'tura sf (good) fortune.

ven'turo, a ag next, coming.

ve'nuto, a pp di venire // sf coming, arrival.

vera'mente av really.

ve'randa sf veranda(h).

ver'bale *ag* verbal // *sm* (*di riunione*) minutes *pl.*
'verbo *sm* (*LING*) verb; (*parola*) word; (*REL*): **il V~** the Word.
ver'boso, a *ag* verbose, wordy.
'verde *ag, sm* green; **essere al ~** to be broke; **~ bottiglia/oliva** *ag inv* bottle/olive green.
verde'rame *sm* verdigris.
ver'detto *sm* verdict.
ver'dura *sf* vegetables *pl.*
'verga, ghe *sf* rod.
ver'gato a *ag* (*foglio*) ruled.
vergi'nale [verdʒi'nale] *ag* virginal.
'vergine ['verdʒine] *sf* virgin; (*dello zodiaco*): **V~** Virgo // *ag* virgin; (*ragazza*): **essere ~** to be a virgin; **verginità** *sf* virginity.
ver'gogna [ver'goɲɲa] *sf* shame; (*timidezza*) shyness, embarrassment; **vergo'gnarsi** *vr*: **vergognarsi (di)** to be *o* feel ashamed (of); to be shy (about), be embarrassed (about); **vergo'gnoso, a** *ag* ashamed; (*timido*) shy, embarrassed; (*causa di vergogna: azione*) shameful.
ve'ridico, a, ci, che *ag* truthful.
ve'rifica, che *sf* checking *q*, check.
verifi'care *vt* (*controllare*) to check; (*confermare*) to confirm, bear out.
verità *sf inv* truth.
veriti'ero, a *ag* (*che dice la verità*) truthful; (*conforme a verità*) true.
'verme *sm* worm.
vermi'celli [vermi'tʃelli] *smpl* vermicelli *sg.*
ver'miglio [ver'miʎʎo] *sm* vermilion, scarlet.
'vermut *sm inv* vermouth.
ver'nacolo *sm* vernacular.
ver'nice [ver'nitʃe] *sf* (*colorazione*) paint; (*trasparente*) varnish; (*pelle*) patent leather; (*fig*) veneer; **vernici'are** *vt* to paint; to varnish; **vernicia'tura** *sf* painting; varnishing.
'vero, a *ag* (*veridico: fatti, testimonianza*) true; (*autentico*) real // *sm* (*verità*) truth; (*realtà*) (real) life; **un ~ e proprio delinquente** a real criminal, an out and out criminal.
vero'simile *ag* likely, probable.
ver'ruca, che *sf* wart.
versa'mento *sm* (*pagamento*) payment; (*deposito di denaro*) deposit.
ver'sante *sm* slopes *pl*, side.
ver'sare *vt* (*fare uscire: vino, farina*) to pour (out); (*spargere: lacrime, sangue*) to shed; (*rovesciare*) to spill; (*ECON*) to pay; (*: depositare*) to deposit, pay in; **~rsi** *vr* (*rovesciarsi*) to spill; (*fiume, folla*): **~rsi (in)** to pour (into).
versa'tile *ag* versatile.
ver'sato, a *ag*: **~ in** to be (well-) versed in.
ver'setto *sm* (*REL*) verse.
versi'one *sf* version; (*traduzione*) translation.

'verso *sm* (*di poesia*) verse, line; (*di animale, uccello, venditore ambulante*) cry; (*direzione*) direction; (*modo*) way; (*di foglio di carta*) verso; (*di moneta*) reverse; **~i** *smpl* (*poesia*) verse *sg*; **non c'è ~ di persuaderlo** there's no way of persuading him, he can't be persuaded // *prep* (*in direzione di*) toward(s); (*nei pressi di*) near, around (about); (*in senso temporale*) about, around; **~ di me** towards me; **~ pagamento** (*COMM*) upon payment.
'vertebra *sf* vertebra.
verti'cale *ag, sf* vertical.
'vertice ['vertitʃe] *sm* summit, top; (*MAT*) vertex; **conferenza al ~** (*POL*) summit conference.
ver'tigine [ver'tidʒine] *sf* dizziness *q*; dizzy spell; (*MED*) vertigo; **avere le ~i** to feel dizzy; **vertigi'noso, a** *ag* (*altezza*) dizzy; (*fig*) breathtakingly high (*o* deep *etc*).
ve'scica, che [veʃ'ʃika] *sf* (*ANAT*) bladder; (*MED*) blister.
'vescovo *sm* bishop.
'vespa *sf* wasp.
'vespro *sm* (*REL*) vespers *pl.*
ves'sillo *sm* standard; (*bandiera*) flag.
ves'taglia [ves'taʎʎa] *sf* dressing gown.
'veste *sf* garment; (*rivestimento*) covering; (*qualità, facoltà*) capacity; **~i** *sfpl* clothes, clothing *sg*; **in ~ ufficiale** (*fig*) in an official capacity; **in ~ di** in the guise of, as; **vesti'ario** *sm* wardrobe, clothes *pl.*
ves'tibolo *sm* (*entrance*) hall.
ves'tigio, pl(m) gi o pl(f) gia [ves'tidʒo] *sm* trace.
ves'tire *vt* (*bambino, malato*) to dress; (*avere indosso*) to have on, wear; **~rsi** *vr* to dress, get dressed; **ves'tito, a** *ag* dressed // *sm* garment; (*da donna*) dress; (*da uomo*) suit; **vestiti** *smpl* clothes; **vestito di bianco** dressed in white.
Ve'suvio *sm*: **il ~** Vesuvius.
vete'rano, a *ag, sm/f* veteran.
veteri'nario, a *ag* veterinary // *sm* veterinary surgeon, vet // *sf* veterinary medicine.
'veto *sm inv* veto.
ve'traio *sm* glassmaker; glazier.
ve'trato, a *ag* (*porta, finestra*) glazed; (*che contiene vetro*) glass *cpd* // *sf* glass door (*o* window); (*di chiesa*) stained glass window.
vetre'ria *sf* (*stabilimento*) glassworks *sg*; (*oggetti di vetro*) glassware.
ve'trina *sf* (*di negozio*) (shop) window; (*armadio*) display cabinet; **vetri'nista, i, e** *sm/f* window dresser.
vetri'olo *sm* vitriol.
'vetro *sm* glass; (*per finestra, porta*) pane (of glass); **ve'troso, a** *ag* vitreous.
'vetta *sf* peak, summit, top.
vet'tore *sm* (*MAT, FISICA*) vector; (*DIR*) carrier.
vetto'vaglie [vetto'vaʎʎe] *sfpl* supplies.
vet'tura *sf* (*carrozza, FERR*) carriage; (*autovettura*) (motor) car.
vezzeggi'are [vettsed'dʒare] *vt* to fondle,

caress; **vezzeggia'tivo** *sm* (*LING*) term of endearment.

'vezzo ['vettso] *sm* habit; ~**i** *smpl* (*smancerie*) affected ways; (*leggiadria*) charms; **vez'zoso, a** *ag* (*grazioso*) charming, pretty; (*lezioso*) affected.

vi, *dav lo, la, li, le, ne diventa* **ve** *pronome* (*oggetto*) you; (*complemento di termine*) (to) you; (*riflessivo*) yourselves; (*reciproco*) each other // *av* (*lì*) there; (*qui*) here; ~ **è/sono** there is/are.

'via *sf* (*gen*) way; (*strada*) street; (*sentiero, pista*) path, track; (*AMM: procedimento*) channels *pl* // *prep* (*passando per*) via, by way of // *av* away // *escl* go away!; (*suvvia*) come on!; (*SPORT*) go! // *sm* (*SPORT*) starting signal; **per ~ di** (*a causa di*) because of, on account of; **per ~ d'esempio** by way of example; **in** *o* **per ~** on the way; **per ~ aerea** by air; (*lettere*) by airmail; ~ ~ **che** (*a mano a mano*) as; **dare il ~** (*SPORT*) to give the starting signal; **dare il ~ a** (*fig*) to start; **V~ lattea** (*ASTR*) Milky Way; ~ **di mezzo** middle course; **in ~ provvisoria** provisionally.

viabilità *sf* (*di strada*) practicability; (*rete stradale*) roads *pl*, road network.

via'dotto *sm* viaduct.

viaggi'are [viad'dʒare] *vi* to travel; **viaggia'tore, 'trice** *ag* travelling // *sm* traveller; (*passeggero*) passenger.

vi'aggio [vi'jaddʒo] *sm* travel(ling); (*tragitto*) journey, trip; ~ **di nozze** honeymoon.

vi'ale *sm* avenue.

via'vai *sm* coming and going, bustle.

vi'brare *vi* to vibrate; (*agitarsi*): ~ **(di)** to quiver (with); **vibrazi'one** *sf* vibration.

vi'cario *sm* (*apostolico etc*) vicar.

'vice ['vitʃe] *sm/f* deputy // *prefisso*: ~**'console** *sm* vice-consul; ~**diret'tore** *sm* assistant manager.

vi'cenda [vi'tʃɛnda] *sf* event; **a ~** in turn; **vicen'devole** *ag* mutual, reciprocal.

vice'versa [vitʃe'vɛrsa] *av* vice versa; **da Roma a Pisa e ~** from Rome to Pisa and back.

vici'nanza [vitʃi'nantsa] *sf* nearness, closeness; ~**e** *sfpl* neighbourhood, vicinity.

vici'nato [vitʃi'nato] *sm* neighbourhood; (*vicini*) neighbours *pl*.

vi'cino, a [vi'tʃino] *ag* (*gen*) near; (*nello spazio*) near, nearby; (*accanto*) next; (*nel tempo*) near, close at hand // *sm/f* neighbour // *av* near, close by; ~ **a** (*guardare*) close up; (*esaminare, seguire*) closely; (*conoscere*) well, intimately; ~ **a** *prep* near (to), close to; (*accanto a*) beside; ~ **di casa** neighbour.

vicissi'tudini [vitʃissi'tudini] *sfpl* trials and tribulations.

'vicolo *sm* alley; ~ **cieco** blind alley.

vie'tare *vt* to forbid; (*AMM*) to prohibit; ~ **a qd di fare** to forbid sb to do; to prohibit sb from doing; **'vietato**

fumare/l'ingresso 'no smoking/admittance'.

vi'gente [vi'dʒɛnte] *ag* in force.

vigi'lante [vidʒi'lante] *ag* vigilant, watchful; **vigi'lanza** *sf* vigilance.

vigi'lare [vidʒi'lare] *vt* to watch over, keep an eye on // *vi*: ~ **a** to attend to, see to; ~ **che** to make sure that, see to it that.

'vigile ['vidʒile] *ag* watchful // *sm* (*anche*: ~ **urbano**) policeman (*in towns*); ~ **del fuoco** fireman.

vi'gilia [vi'dʒilja] *sf* (*giorno antecedente*) eve; **la ~ di Natale** Christmas Eve.

vigli'acco, a, chi, che [viʎ'ʎakko] *ag* cowardly // *sm/f* coward.

'vigna ['viɲɲa] *sf*, **vi'gneto** [viɲ'ɲeto] *sm* vineyard.

vi'gnetta [viɲ'ɲetta] *sf* cartoon.

vi'gore *sm* vigour; (*DIR*): **essere/entrare in** ~ to be in/come into force; **vigo'roso, a** *ag* vigorous.

'vile *ag* (*spregevole*) low, mean, base; (*codardo*) cowardly.

vili'pendio *sm* contempt, scorn; public insult.

'villa *sf* villa.

vil'laggio [vil'laddʒo] *sm* village.

villa'nia *sf* rudeness, lack of manners; **fare/dire una ~ a qd** to be rude to sb.

vil'lano, a *ag* rude, ill-mannered // *sm* boor.

villeggi'are [villed'dʒare] *vi* to holiday, spend one's holidays; **villeggia'tura** *sf* holiday(s *pl*).

vil'lino *sm* small house (with a garden), cottage.

vil'loso, a *ag* hairy.

viltà *sf* cowardice *q*; cowardly act.

'vimine *sm* wicker; **mobili di ~i** wicker furniture *sg*.

'vincere ['vintʃere] *vt* (*in guerra, al gioco, a una gara*) to defeat, beat; (*premio, guerra, partita*) to win; (*fig*) to overcome, conquer // *vi* to win; ~ **qd in bellezza** to be better-looking than sb; **'vincita** *sf* win; (*denaro vinto*) winnings *pl*; **vinci'tore** *sm* winner; (*MIL*) victor.

vinco'lare *vt* to bind; (*COMM: denaro*) to tie up; **'vincolo** *sm* (*fig*) bond, tie; (*DIR: servitù*) obligation.

vi'nicolo, a *ag* wine *cpd*.

'vino *sm* wine; ~ **bianco/rosso** white/red wine.

'vinto, a *pp di* **vincere**.

vi'ola *sf* (*BOT*) violet; (*MUS*) viola // *ag, sm inv* (*colore*) purple.

vio'lare *vt* (*chiesa*) to desecrate, violate; (*giuramento, legge*) to violate; **violazi'one** *sf* desecration; violation.

violen'tare *vt* to use violence on; (*donna*) to rape.

vio'lento, a *ag* violent; **vio'lenza** *sf* violence; **violenza carnale** rape.

vio'letto, a *ag, sm* (*colore*) violet // *sf* violet.

violi'nista, i, e *sm/f* violinist.

vio'lino *sm* violin.

violon'cello [violon'tʃɛllo] *sm* cello.
vi'ottolo *sm* path, track.
'vipera *sf* viper, adder.
vi'raggio [vi'raddʒo] *sm* (NAUT, AER) turn; (FOT) toning.
vi'rare *vt* (NAUT) to haul (in), heave (in) // *vi* (NAUT, AER) to turn; (FOT) to tone; ~ **di bordo** (NAUT) to tack.
virginità [virdʒini'ta] *sf* = **verginità**.
'virgola *sf* (LING) comma; (MAT) point; **virgo'lette** *sfpl* inverted commas, quotation marks.
vi'rile *ag* (*proprio dell'uomo*) masculine; (*non puerile, da uomo*) manly, virile; **virilità** *sf* masculinity; manliness; (*sessuale*) virility.
virtù *sf inv* virtue; **in o per** ~ **di** by virtue of, by.
virtu'ale *ag* virtual.
virtu'oso, a *ag* virtuous // *sm/f* (MUS etc) virtuoso.
viru'lento, a *ag* virulent.
'virus *sm inv* virus.
'viscere ['viʃʃere] *sm* (ANAT) internal organ // *sfpl* (*di animale*) entrails *pl*; (fig) bowels *pl*.
'vischio ['viskjo] *sm* (BOT) mistletoe; (*pania*) birdlime; **vischi'oso, a** *ag* sticky.
'viscido, a ['viʃʃido] *ag* slimy.
vis'conte, 'essa *sm/f* viscount/ viscountess.
vis'coso, a *ag* viscous.
vi'sibile *ag* visible.
visi'bilio *sm* profusion; **andare in** ~ to go into raptures.
visibilità *sf* visibility.
visi'era *sf* (*di elmo*) visor; (*di berretto*) peak.
visi'one *sf* vision; **prendere** ~ **di qc** to examine sth, look sth over; **prima/seconda** ~ (CINEMA) first/second showing.
'visita *sf* visit; (MED) visit, call; (: *esame*) examination; **visi'tare** *vt* to visit; (MED) to visit, call on; (: *esaminare*) to examine; **visita'tore, 'trice** *sm/f* visitor.
vi'sivo, a *ag* visual.
'viso *sm* face.
vi'sone *sm* mink.
'vispo, a *ag* quick, lively.
vis'suto, a *pp di* **vivere**.
'vista *sf* (*facoltà*) (eye)sight; (*fatto di vedere*): **la** ~ **di** the sight of; (*veduta*) view; **sparare a** ~ to shoot on sight; **in** ~ in sight; **perdere qd di** ~ to lose sight of sb; (fig) to lose touch with sb; **a** ~ **d'occhio** as far as the eye can see; (fig) before one's very eyes; **far** ~ **di fare** to pretend to do.
'visto, a *pp di* **vedere** // *sm* visa.
vis'toso, a *ag* gaudy, garish; (*ingente*) considerable.
visu'ale *ag* visual.
'vita *sf* life; (ANAT) waist; **a** ~ for life.
vi'tale *ag* vital; **vitalità** *sf* vitality; **vita-'lizio, a** *ag* life *cpd* // *sm* life annuity.
vita'mina *sf* vitamin.

'vite *sf* (BOT) vine; (TECN) screw.
vi'tello *sm* (ZOOL) calf; (*carne*) veal; (*pelle*) calfskin.
vi'ticcio [vi'tittʃo] *sm* (BOT) tendril.
viticol'tore *sm* wine grower; **viticol'tura** *sf* wine growing.
'vitreo, a *ag* vitreous; (*occhio, sguardo*) glassy.
'vittima *sf* victim.
'vitto *sm* food; (*in un albergo etc*) board; ~ **e alloggio** board and lodging.
vit'toria *sf* victory; **vittori'oso, a** *ag* victorious.
vitupe'rare *vt* to rail at *o* against.
'viva *escl*: ~ **il re!** long live the king!
vi'vace [vi'vatʃe] *ag* (*vivo, animato*) lively; (: *mente*) lively, sharp; (*colore*) bright; **vivacità** *sf* vivacity; liveliness; brightness.
vi'vaio *sm* (*di pesci*) hatchery; (AGR) nursery.
vi'vanda *sf* food; (*piatto*) dish.
vi'vente *ag* living, alive; **i** ~ **i** the living.
'vivere *vi* (2) to live // *vt* to live; (*passare: brutto momento*) to live through, go through; (*sentire: gioie, pene di qd*) to share // *sm* life; (*anche: modo di* ~) way of life; ~ **i** *smpl* food *sg*, provisions; ~ **di** to live on.
'vivido, a *ag* (*colore*) vivid, bright.
vivifi'care *vt* to enliven, give life to; (*piante etc*) to revive.
vivisezi'one [viviset'tsjone] *sf* vivisection.
'vivo, a *ag* (*vivente*) alive, living; (: *animale*) live; (fig) lively; (: *colore*) bright, brilliant; **i** ~ **i** the living; ~ **e vegeto** hale and hearty; **farsi** ~ to show one's face; to be heard from; **ritrarre al** ~ to paint from life; **pungere qd nel** ~ (fig) to cut sb to the quick.
vizi'are [vit'tsjare] *vt* (*bambino*) to spoil; (*corrompere moralmente*) to corrupt; **vi-zi'ato, a** *ag* spoilt; (*aria, acqua*) polluted.
'vizio ['vittsjo] *sm* vice; (*cattiva abitudine*) bad habit; (*imperfezione*) flaw, defect; (*errore*) fault, mistake; **vizi'oso, a** *ag* depraved; defective; (*inesatto*) incorrect, wrong.
vocabo'lario *sm* (*dizionario*) dictionary; (*lessico*) vocabulary.
vo'cabolo *sm* word.
vo'cale *ag* vocal // *sf* vowel.
vocazi'one [vokat'tsjone] *sf* vocation; (fig) natural bent.
'voce ['votʃe] *sf* voice; (*diceria*) rumour; (*di un elenco, in bilancio*) item; **aver** ~ **in capitolo** (fig) to have a say in the matter.
voci'are [vo'tʃare] *vi* to shout, yell.
'voga *sf* (NAUT) rowing; (*usanza*): **essere in** ~ to be in fashion *o* in vogue.
vo'gare *vi* to row.
'voglia ['vɔʎʎa] *sf* desire, wish; (*macchia*) birthmark; **aver** ~ **di qc/di fare** to feel like sth/like doing; (*più forte*) to want sth/to do.
'voi *pronome* you; **voi'altri** *pronome* you (lot).

vo'lano sm (SPORT) shuttlecock; (TECN) flywheel.

vo'lante ag flying // sm (steering) wheel.

volan'tino sm leaflet.

vo'lare vi (uccello, aereo, fig) to fly; (cappello) to blow away o off, to fly away o off; ~ **via** to fly away o off.

vo'lata sf flight; (d'uccelli) flock, flight; (corsa) rush; (SPORT) final sprint.

vo'latile ag (CHIM) volatile // sm (ZOOL) bird.

volenti'eri av willingly; '~' 'with pleasure', 'I'd be glad to'.

vo'lere sm will; ~**i** smpl wishes // vt to want; (esigere, richiedere) to demand, require; **vuole un po' di formaggio?** would you like some cheese?; ~ **che faccia** to want sb to do; **vorrei questo** I would like this; ~**rci** (essere necessario): **quanto ci vuole per andare da Roma a Firenze?** how long does it take to go from Rome to Florence?; **ci vogliono 4 metri di stoffa** 4 metres of material are required, you will need 4 metres of material; ~ **bene a qd** to love sb; ~ **male a qd** to dislike sb; **volerne a qd** to bear sb a grudge; ~ **dire (che)** to mean (that); **senza** ~ without meaning to, unintentionally.

vol'gare ag vulgar; **l'opinione** ~ common opinion; **volgarità** sf vulgarity; **volgariz'zare** vt to popularize.

'volgere ['vɔldʒere] vt to turn // vi to turn; (tendere): ~ **a**: **il tempo volge al brutto** the weather is breaking; **un rosso che volge al viola** a red verging on purple; ~**rsi** vr to turn; ~ **al peggio** to take a turn for the worse.

'volgo sm (REL) common people.

voli'era sf aviary.

voli'tivo, a ag strong-willed.

'volo sm flight; **al** ~: **colpire qc al** ~ to hit sth as it flies past; **capire al** ~ to understand straight away.

volontà sf will; **a** ~ (mangiare, bere) as much as one likes; **buona/cattiva** ~ goodwill/lack of goodwill.

volon'tario, a ag voluntary // sm (MIL) volunteer.

volonte'roso, a ag willing.

'volpe sf fox.

'volta sf (momento, circostanza) time; (turno, giro) turn; (curva) turn, bend; (ARCHIT) vault; **a mia** (o **tua** etc) ~ in turn; **una** ~ once; **due** ~**e** twice; **una cosa per** ~ one thing at a time; **una** ~ **per tutte** once and for all; **a** ~**e** at times, sometimes; **una** ~ **che** (temporale) once; (causale) since; **3** ~**e 4 3** times 4.

volta'faccia [volta'fattʃa] sm inv (fig) volte-face.

vol'taggio [vol'taddʒo] sm (ELETTR) voltage.

vol'tare vt to turn; (girare: moneta) to turn over; (rigirare) to turn round // vi to turn; ~**rsi** vr to turn; to turn over; to turn round.

volteggi'are [volted'dʒare] vi (volare) to circle; (in equitazione) to do trick riding; (in ginnastica) to vault; to perform acrobatics.

'volto, a pp di **volgere** // sm face.

vo'lubile ag changeable, fickle.

vo'lume sm volume; **volumi'noso, a** ag voluminous, bulky.

voluttà sf sensual pleasure o delight; **voluttu'oso, a** ag voluptuous.

vomi'tare vt, vi to vomit; **'vomito** sm vomiting q; vomit.

'vongola sf clam.

vo'race [vo'ratʃe] ag voracious, greedy.

vo'ragine [vo'radʒine] sf abyss, chasm.

'vortice ['vortitʃe] sm whirlwind; whirlpool; (fig) whirl.

'vostro, a det: **il(la)** ~**(a)** etc your // pronome: **il(la)** ~**(a)** etc yours.

vo'tante sm/f voter.

vo'tare vi to vote // vt (sottoporre a votazione) to take a vote on; (approvare) to vote for; (REL): ~ **qc** a to dedicate sth to; **votazi'one** sf vote, voting; **votazioni** sfpl (POL) votes; (INS) marks.

vo'tivo, a ag (REL) votive.

'voto sm (POL) vote; (INS) mark; (REL) vow; (: offerta) votive offering.

vs. abbr commerciale di **vostro**.

vul'canico, a, ci, che ag volcanic.

vul'cano sm volcano.

vulne'rabile ag vulnerable.

vuo'tare vt, ~**rsi** vr to empty.

vu'oto, a ag empty // (fig: privo): ~ **di** (senso etc) devoid of // sm empty space, gap; (spazio in bianco) blank; (FISICA) vacuum; (fig: mancanza) gap, void; **a mani** ~**e** empty-handed; ~ **d'aria** air pocket; ~ **a rendere** returnable bottle.

W X Y

watt [vat] sm inv watt.

'whisky ['wiski] sm inv whisky.

'xeres ['kseres] sm inv sherry.

xero'copia [ksero'kɔpja] sf xerox, photocopy.

xi'lofono [ksi'lɔfono] sm xylophone.

yacht [jɔt] sm inv yacht.

'yoghurt ['jɔgurt] sm inv yoghourt.

Z

zabai'one [dzaba'jone] sm dessert made of egg yolks, sugar and marsala.

'zacchera ['tsakkera] sf splash of mud.

zaf'fata [tsaf'fata] sf (tanfo) stench.

zaffe'rano [dzaffe'rano] sm saffron.

zaf'firo [dzaf'firo] sm sapphire.

'zagara ['dzagara] sf orange blossom.

'zaino ['dzaino] sm rucksack.

'zampa ['tsampa] sf (di animale: gamba) leg; (: piede) paw; **a quattro** ~**e** on all fours.

zampil'lare [tsampil'lare] vi to gush, spurt; **zam'pillo** sm gush, spurt.

zam'pogna [tsam'poɲɲa] sf instrument similar to bagpipes.

'**zanna** ['tsanna] *sf* (*di elefante*) tusk; (*di carnivori*) fang.

zan'zara [dzan'dzara] *sf* mosquito; **zanzari'era** *sf* mosquito net.

'**zappa** ['tsappa] *sf* hoe; **zap'pare** *vt* to hoe.

zar, za'rina [tsar, tsa'rina] *sm/f* tsar/tsarina.

'**zattera** ['dzattera] *sf* raft.

za'vorra [dza'vɔrra] *sf* ballast.

'**zazzera** ['tsattsera] *sf* shock of hair.

'**zebra** ['dzɛbra] *sf* zebra; **~e** *sfpl* (AUT) zebra crossing *sg*.

'**zecca, che** ['tsekka] *sf* (ZOOL) tick; (*officina di monete*) mint.

ze'lante [dze'lante] *ag* zealous.

'**zelo** ['dzɛlo] *sm* zeal.

'**zenit** ['dzɛnit] *sm* zenith.

'**zenzero** ['dzendzero] *sm* ginger.

'**zeppa** ['tseppa] *sf* wedge.

'**zeppo, a** ['tseppo] *ag:* **~ di** crammed *o* packed with.

zer'bino [dzer'bino] *sm* doormat.

'**zero** ['dzɛro] *sm* zero, nought; **vincere per tre a ~** (SPORT) to win three-nil.

'**zeta** ['dzɛta] *sm o f* zed, (the letter) z.

'**zia** ['tsia] *sf* aunt.

zibel'lino [dzibel'lino] *sm* sable.

'**zigomo** ['dzigomo] *sm* cheekbone.

zig'zag [dzig'dzag] *sm inv* zigzag; **andare a ~** to zigzag.

zim'bello [dzim'bɛllo] *sm* (*oggetto di burle*) laughing-stock.

'**zinco** ['dzinko] *sm* zinc.

'**zingaro, a** ['dzingaro] *sm/f* gipsy.

'**zio** ['tsio], *pl* '**zii** *sm* uncle; **zii** *smpl* (*zio e zia*) uncle and aunt.

zi'tella [dzi'tɛlla] *sf* spinster; (*peg*) old maid.

'**zitto, a** ['tsitto] *ag* quiet, silent; **sta' ~!** be quiet!

'**zoccolo** ['tsɔkkolo] *sm* (*calzatura*) clog; (*di cavallo etc*) hoof; (*basamento*) base; plinth.

zo'diaco [dzo'diako] *sm* zodiac.

'**zolfo** ['tsolfo] *sm* sulphur.

'**zolla** ['dzɔlla] *sf* clod (of earth).

zol'letta [dzol'letta] *sf* sugar lump.

'**zona** ['dzɔna] *sf* zone, area; **~ di depressione** (METEOR) trough of low pressure; **~ verde** (*di abitato*) green area.

'**zonzo** ['dzondzo] **a ~** *av:* **andare a ~** to wander about, stroll about.

zoo ['dzɔo] *sm inv* zoo.

zoolo'gia [dzoolo'dʒia] *sf* zoology; **zoo'logico, a, ci, che** *ag* zoological; **zo'ologo, a, gi, ghe** *sm/f* zoologist.

zoppi'care [tsoppi'kare] *vi* to limp; to be shaky, rickety.

'**zoppo, a** ['tsɔppo] *ag* lame; (*fig: mobile*) shaky, rickety.

zoti'cone [dzoti'kone] *sm* lout.

'**zucca, che** ['tsukka] *sf* marrow; pumpkin.

zucche'rare [tsukke'rare] *vt* to put sugar in.

zuccheri'era [tsukke'rjɛra] *sf* sugar bowl.

zuccheri'ficio [tsukkeri'fitʃo] *sm* sugar refinery.

zucche'rino, a [tsukke'rino] *ag* sugary, sweet.

'**zucchero** ['tsukkero] *sm* sugar; **zucche'roso, a** *ag* sugary.

zuc'chino [tsuk'kino] *sm* courgette, zucchini.

'**zuffa** ['tsuffa] *sf* brawl.

zufo'lare [tsufo'lare] *vt, vi* to whistle.

'**zuppa** ['tsuppa] *sf* soup; (*fig*) mixture, muddle; **~ inglese** (CUC) ≈ trifle; **zup-pi'era** *sf* soup tureen.

'**zuppo, a** ['tsuppo] *ag:* **~ (di)** drenched (with), soaked (with).

ENGLISH - ITALIAN
INGLESE - ITALIANO

A

a, an [eɪ, ə, æn, ən, n] det un (uno + s impure, gn, pn, ps, x, z), f una (un' + vowel); **3 a day/week** 3 al giorno/la or alla settimana; **10 km an hour** 10 km all'ora.

A [eɪ] n (MUS) la m.

A.A. n (abbr of Automobile Association) ≈ A.C.I.; abbr of Alcoholics Anonymous.

aback [ə'bæk] ad: **to be taken** ~ essere sbalordito(a).

abandon [ə'bændən] vt abbandonare // n abbandono.

abashed [ə'bæʃt] a imbarazzato(a).

abate [ə'beɪt] vi calmarsi.

abattoir ['æbətwɑ:*] n mattatoio.

abbey ['æbɪ] n abbazia, badia.

abbot ['æbət] n abate m.

abbreviate [ə'bri:vɪeɪt] vt abbreviare; **abbreviation** [-'eɪʃən] n abbreviazione f.

abdicate ['æbdɪkeɪt] vt abdicare a // vi abdicare; **abdication** [-'keɪʃən] n abdicazione f.

abdomen ['æbdəmən] n addome m.

abduct [æb'dʌkt] vt rapire; **abduction** [-ʃən] n rapimento.

abet [ə'bet] vt see **aid.**

abeyance [ə'beɪəns] n: **in** ~ in sospeso.

abhor [əb'hɔ:*] vt aborrire; ~**rent** a odioso(a).

abide [ə'baɪd] vt sopportare; **to** ~ **by** vt fus conformarsi a.

ability [ə'bɪlɪtɪ] n abilità f inv.

ablaze [ə'bleɪz] a in fiamme; ~ **with light** risplendente di luce.

able ['eɪbl] a capace; **to be** ~ **to do sth** essere capace di fare qc, poter fare qc; ~**bodied** a robusto(a); **ably** ad abilmente.

abnormal [æb'nɔːməl] a anormale.

aboard [ə'bɔːd] ad a bordo // prep a bordo di.

abolish [ə'bɔlɪʃ] vt abolire.

abolition [æbəu'lɪʃən] n abolizione f.

abominable [ə'bɔmɪnəbl] a abominevole.

aborigine [æbə'rɪdʒɪnɪ] n aborigeno/a.

abort [ə'bɔːt] vt abortire; ~**ion** [ə'bɔːʃən] n aborto; ~**ive** a abortivo(a).

abound [ə'baund] vi abbondare; **to** ~ **in** abbondare di.

about [ə'baut] prep intorno a, riguardo a // ad circa; (here and there) qua e là; **it takes** ~ **10 hours** ci vogliono circa 10 ore; **at** ~ **2 o'clock** verso le due; **it's** ~ **here** è qui dintorno; **to walk** ~ **the town** camminare per la città; **to be** ~ **to**: **he was** ~ **to cry** lui stava per piangere; **what** or **how** ~ **doing this?** che ne pensa di fare questo?; ~ **turn** n dietro front m inv.

above [ə'bʌv] ad, prep sopra; **mentioned** ~ suddetto; **costing** ~ **£10** che costa più di 10 sterline; ~ **all** soprattutto; ~**board** a aperto(a); onesto(a).

abrasive [ə'breɪzɪv] a abrasivo(a).

abreast [ə'brest] ad di fianco; **3** ~ per 3 di fronte; **to keep** ~ **of** tenersi aggiornato su.

abridge [ə'brɪdʒ] vt ridurre.

abroad [ə'brɔːd] ad all'estero.

abrupt [ə'brʌpt] a (steep) erto(a); (sudden) improvviso(a); (gruff, blunt) brusco(a).

abscess ['æbsɪs] n ascesso.

abscond [əb'skɔnd] vi scappare.

absence ['æbsəns] n assenza.

absent ['æbsənt] a assente; ~**ee** [-'tiː] n assente m/f; ~**eeism** [-'tiːɪzəm] n assenteismo; ~-**minded** a distratto(a).

absolute ['æbsəluːt] a assoluto(a); ~**ly** [-'luːtlɪ] ad assolutamente.

absolve [əb'zɔlv] vt: **to** ~ **sb (from)** assolvere qd (da).

absorb [əb'zɔːb] vt assorbire; **to be** ~**ed in a book** essere immerso in un libro; ~**ent** a assorbente; ~**ent cotton** n (US) cotone m idrofilo.

abstain [əb'steɪn] vi: **to** ~ **(from)** astenersi (da).

abstemious [əb'stiːmɪəs] a astemio(a).

abstention [əb'stenʃən] n astensione f.

abstinence ['æbstɪnəns] n astinenza.

abstract ['æbstrækt] a astratto(a) // n (summary) riassunto.

absurd [əb'sɜːd] a assurdo(a); ~**ity** n assurdità f inv.

abundance [ə'bʌndəns] n abbondanza; **abundant** a abbondante.

abuse n [ə'bjuːs] abuso; (insults) ingiurie fpl // vt [ə'bjuːz] abusare di; **abusive** a ingiurioso(a).

abysmal [ə'bɪzməl] a spaventoso(a).

abyss [ə'bɪs] n abisso.

academic [ækə'demɪk] a accademico(a); (pej: issue) puramente formale // n universitario/a.

academy [ə'kædəmɪ] n (learned body) accademia; (school) scuola privata; **military/naval** ~ scuola militare/navale; ~ **of music** conservatorio.

accede [æk'siːd] vi: **to** ~ **to** (request) accedere a; (throne) ascendere a.

accelerate [æk'seləreɪt] vt,vi accelerare; **acceleration** [-'reɪʃən] n accelerazione f; **accelerator** n acceleratore m.

accent ['æksɛnt] n accento.

accept [ək'sept] vt accettare; ~**able** a accettabile; ~**ance** n accettazione f.

access ['æksɛs] n accesso; **to have** ~ **to**

accessory [æk'sɛsəri] *n* accessorio; **toilet accessories** *npl* articoli *mpl* da toilette.

accident ['æksɪdənt] *n* incidente *m*; (*chance*) caso; **by** ~ per caso; ~**al** [-'dɛntl] *a* accidentale; ~**ally** [-'dɛntəli] *ad* per caso; ~**-prone** *a*: **he's very** ~**-prone** è un vero passaguai.

acclaim [ə'kleɪm] *vt* acclamare // *n* acclamazione *f*.

acclimatize [ə'klaɪmətaɪz] *vt*: **to become** ~**d** acclimatarsi.

accommodate [ə'kɔmədeɪt] *vt* alloggiare; (*oblige, help*) favorire.

accommodating [ə'kɔmədeɪtɪŋ] *a* compiacente.

accommodation [əkɔmə'deɪʃən] *n* alloggio.

accompaniment [ə'kʌmpənɪmənt] *n* accompagnamento.

accompany [ə'kʌmpənɪ] *vt* accompagnare.

accomplice [ə'kʌmplɪs] *n* complice *m/f*.

accomplish [ə'kʌmplɪʃ] *vt* compiere; ~**ed** *a* (*person*) esperto(a); ~**ment** *n* compimento; realizzazione *f*; ~**ments** *npl* doti *fpl*.

accord [ə'kɔːd] *n* accordo // *vt* accordare; **of his own** ~ di propria iniziativa; ~**ance** *n*: **in** ~**ance with** in conformità con; ~**ing** *to prep* secondo; ~**ingly** *ad* in conformità.

accordion [ə'kɔːdiən] *n* fisarmonica.

accost [ə'kɔst] *vt* avvicinare.

account [ə'kaunt] *n* (*COMM*) conto; (*report*) descrizione *f*, resoconto // *a* quanto si dice; **of little** ~ di poca importanza; **on** ~ in acconto; **on no** ~ per nessun motivo; **on** ~ **of** a causa di; **to take into** ~, **take** ~ **of** tener conto di; **to** ~ **for** spiegare; giustificare; ~**able** *a* responsabile.

accountancy [ə'kauntənsɪ] *n* ragioneria.

accountant [ə'kauntənt] *n* ragioniere/a.

accumulate [ə'kjuːmjuleɪt] *vt* accumulare // *vi* accumularsi; **accumulation** [-'leɪʃən] *n* accumulazione *f*.

accuracy ['ækjurəsɪ] *n* precisione *f*.

accurate ['ækjurɪt] *a* preciso(a); ~**ly** *ad* precisamente.

accusation [ækju'zeɪʃən] *n* accusa.

accuse [ə'kjuːz] *vt* accusare; ~**d** *n* accusato/a.

accustom [ə'kʌstəm] *vt* abituare; ~**ed** *a* (*usual*) abituale; ~**ed to** abituato(a) a.

ace [eɪs] *n* asso; **within an** ~ **of** a un pelo da.

ache [eɪk] *n* male *m*, dolore *m* // *vi* (*be sore*) far male, dolere; **my head** ~**s** mi fa male la testa; **I'm aching all over** mi duole dappertutto.

achieve [ə'tʃiːv] *vt* (*aim*) raggiungere; (*victory, success*) ottenere; (*task*) compiere; ~**ment** *n* compimento; successo.

acid ['æsɪd] *a* acido(a) // *n* acido; ~**ity** [ə'sɪdɪtɪ] *n* acidità.

acknowledge [ək'nɔlɪdʒ] *vt* (*letter*) confermare la ricevuta di; (*fact*) riconoscere; ~**ment** *n* conferma; riconoscimento.

acne ['æknɪ] *n* acne *f*.

acorn ['eɪkɔːn] *n* ghianda.

acoustic [ə'kuːstɪk] *a* acustico(a); ~**s** *n,npl* acustica.

acquaint [ə'kweɪnt] *vt*: **to** ~ **sb with sth** far sapere qc a qd; **to be** ~**ed with** (*person*) conoscere; ~**ance** *n* conoscenza; (*person*) conoscente *m/f*.

acquire [ə'kwaɪə*] *vt* acquistare.

acquisition [ækwɪ'zɪʃən] *n* acquisto.

acquisitive [ə'kwɪzɪtɪv] *a* a cui piace accumulare le cose.

acquit [ə'kwɪt] *vt* assolvere; **to** ~ **o.s. well** comportarsi bene; ~**tal** *n* assoluzione *f*.

acre ['eɪkə*] *n* acro (= 4047 m²).

acrimonious [ækrɪ'məunɪəs] *a* astioso(a).

acrobat ['ækrəbæt] *n* acrobata *m/f*.

acrobatics [ækrəu'bætɪks] *n* acrobatica // *npl* acrobazie *fpl*.

across [ə'krɔs] *prep* (*on the other side*) dall'altra parte di; (*crosswise*) attraverso // *ad* dall'altra parte; in larghezza; **to walk** ~ **(the road)** attraversare (la strada); ~ **from** di fronte a.

act [ækt] *n* atto; (*in music-hall etc*) numero; (*LAW*) decreto // *vi* agire; (*THEATRE*) recitare; (*pretend*) fingere // *vt* (*part*) recitare; **to** ~ **Hamlet** recitare la parte di Amleto; **to** ~ **the fool** fare lo stupido; **to** ~ **as** agire da; ~**ing** *a* che fa le funzioni di // *n* (*of actor*) recitazione *f*; (*activity*): **to do some** ~**ing** fare del teatro (*or* del cinema).

action ['ækʃən] *n* azione *f*; (*MIL*) combattimento; (*LAW*) processo; **out of** ~ fuori combattimento; fuori servizio; **to take** ~ agire.

activate ['æktɪveɪt] *vt* (*mechanism*) fare funzionare; (*CHEM, PHYSICS*) rendere attivo(a).

active ['æktɪv] *a* attivo(a).

activity [æk'tɪvɪtɪ] *n* attività *f inv*.

actor ['æktə*] *n* attore *m*.

actress ['æktrɪs] *n* attrice *f*.

actual ['æktjuəl] *a* reale, vero(a); ~**ly** *ad* realmente; infatti.

acumen ['ækjumən] *n* acume *m*.

acupuncture ['ækjupʌŋktʃə*] *n* agopuntura.

acute [ə'kjuːt] *a* acuto(a).

ad [æd] *n abbr of* **advertisement**.

A.D. *ad* (*abbr of Anno Domini*) d.C.

Adam ['ædəm] *n* Adamo; ~**'s apple** *n* pomo di Adamo.

adamant ['ædəmənt] *a* adamantino(a).

adapt [ə'dæpt] *vt* adattare // *vi*: **to** ~ **(to)** adattarsi (a); ~**able** *a* (*device*) adattabile; (*person*) che sa adattarsi; ~**ation** [ædæp'teɪʃən] *n* adattamento; ~**er** *n* (*ELEC*) adattatore *m*.

add [æd] *vt* aggiungere; (*figures: also*: **to** ~

up) addizionare // vi: **to ~ to** (increase) aumentare.

adder ['ædə*] n vipera.

addict ['ædɪkt] n tossicomane m/f; (fig) fanatico/a; **~ed** [ə'dɪktɪd] a: **to be ~ed to** (drink etc) essere dedito a; (fig: football etc) essere tifoso di; **~ion** [ə'dɪkʃən] n (MED) tossicomania.

addition [ə'dɪʃən] n addizione f; **in ~** inoltre; **~ in ~ to** oltre; **~al** a supplementare.

additive ['ædɪtɪv] n additivo.

address [ə'drɛs] n indirizzo; (talk) discorso // vt indirizzare; (speak to) fare un discorso a.

adenoids ['ædɪnɔɪdz] npl adenoidi fpl.

adept ['ædɛpt] a: **~ at** esperto(a) in.

adequate ['ædɪkwɪt] a adeguato(a); sufficiente.

adhere [əd'hɪə*] vi: **to ~ to** aderire a; (fig: rule, decision) seguire.

adhesion [əd'hiːʒən] n adesione f.

adhesive [əd'hiːzɪv] a adesivo(a) // n adesivo.

adjacent [ə'dʒeɪsənt] a adiacente; **~ to** accanto a.

adjective ['ædʒɛktɪv] n aggettivo.

adjoining [ə'dʒɔɪnɪŋ] a accanto inv, adiacente // prep accanto a.

adjourn [ə'dʒəːn] vt rimandare // vi aggiornare; (go) spostarsi.

adjust [ə'dʒʌst] vt aggiustare; (COMM) rettificare // vi: **to ~ (to)** adattarsi (a); **~able** a regolabile; **~ment** n adattamento; (of prices, wages) aggiustamento.

adjutant ['ædʒətənt] n aiutante m.

ad-lib [æd'lɪb] vt,vi improvvisare // n improvvisazione f.

administer [əd'mɪnɪstə*] vt amministrare; (justice) somministrare.

administration [ədmɪnɪs'treɪʃən] n amministrazione f.

administrative [əd'mɪnɪstrətɪv] a amministrativo(a).

administrator [əd'mɪnɪstreɪtə*] n amministratore/trice.

admiral ['ædmərəl] n ammiraglio; **A~ty** n Ammiragliato; Ministero della Marina.

admiration [ædmə'reɪʃən] n ammirazione f.

admire [əd'maɪə*] vt ammirare; **~r** n ammiratore/trice.

admission [əd'mɪʃən] n ammissione f; (to exhibition, night club etc) ingresso; (confession) confessione f.

admit [əd'mɪt] vt ammettere; far entrare; (agree) riconoscere; **to ~ of** lasciare adito a; **to ~ to** riconoscere; **~tance** n ingresso; **~tedly** ad bisogna pur riconoscere (che).

admonish [əd'mɒnɪʃ] vt ammonire.

ado [ə'duː] n: **without (any) more ~** senza più indugi.

adolescence [ædəu'lɛsns] n adolescenza.

adolescent [ædəu'lɛsnt] a,n adolescente (m/f).

adopt [ə'dɒpt] vt adottare; **~ed** a adottivo(a); **~ion** [ə'dɒpʃən] n adozione f.

adore [ə'dɔː*] vt adorare.

adorn [ə'dɔːn] vt adornare.

adrenalin [ə'drɛnəlɪn] n adrenalina.

Adriatic (Sea) [eɪdrɪ'ætɪk(siː)] n Adriatico.

adrift [ə'drɪft] ad alla deriva.

adroit [ə'drɔɪt] a abile, destro(a).

adult ['ædʌlt] n adulto/a.

adulterate [ə'dʌltəreɪt] vt adulterare.

adultery [ə'dʌltərɪ] n adulterio.

advance [əd'vɑːns] n avanzamento; (money) anticipo // vt avanzare; (date, money) anticipare // vi avanzare; **in ~** in anticipo; **~d** a avanzato(a); (SCOL: studies) superiore; **~ment** n avanzamento.

advantage [əd'vɑːntɪdʒ] n (also TENNIS) vantaggio; **to take ~ of** approfittarsi di; **~ous** [ædvən'teɪdʒəs] a vantaggioso(a).

advent ['ædvənt] n avvento; **A~** Avvento.

adventure [əd'vɛntʃə*] n avventura; **adventurous** a avventuroso(a).

adverb ['ædvəːb] n avverbio.

adversary ['ædvəsərɪ] n avversario/a.

adverse ['ædvəs] a avverso(a); **in ~ circumstances** nelle avversità; **~ to** contrario(a) a.

adversity [əd'vəsɪtɪ] n avversità.

advert ['ædvəːt] n abbr of **advertisement**.

advertise ['ædvətaɪz] vi(vt) fare pubblicità or réclame // fare un'inserzione (per vendere).

advertisement [əd'vəːtɪsmənt] n (COMM) réclame f inv, pubblicità f inv; (in classified ads) inserzione f.

advertising ['ædvətaɪzɪŋ] n pubblicità.

advice [əd'vaɪs] n consigli mpl; (notification) avviso; **piece of ~** consiglio.

advisable [əd'vaɪzəbl] a consigliabile.

advise [əd'vaɪz] vt consigliare; **to ~ sb of sth** informare qd di qc; **~r** n consigliere/a; **advisory** [-ərɪ] a consultivo(a).

advocate ['ædvəkeɪt] vt propugnare.

aegis ['iːdʒɪs] n: **under the ~ of** sotto gli auspici di.

aerial ['ɛərɪəl] n antenna // a aereo(a).

aeroplane ['ɛərəpleɪn] n aeroplano.

aerosol ['ɛərəsɒl] n aerosol m inv.

aesthetic [ɪs'θɛtɪk] a estetico(a).

affable ['æfəbl] a affabile.

affair [ə'fɛə*] n affare m; (also: love ~) relazione f amorosa.

affect [ə'fɛkt] vt toccare; (feign) fingere; **~ation** [æfɛk'teɪʃən] n affettazione f; **~ed** a affettato(a).

affection [ə'fɛkʃən] n affezione f; **~ate** a affettuoso(a).

affiliated [ə'fɪlɪeɪtɪd] a affiliato(a).

affinity [ə'fɪnɪtɪ] n affinità f inv.

affirmation [æfə'meɪʃən] n affermazione f.

affirmative [ə'fəːmətɪv] a affermativo(a) // n: **in the ~** affermativamente.

affix [ə'fɪks] vt apporre; attaccare.

afflict [ə'flıkt] *vt* affliggere; ~**ion** [ə'flıkʃən] *n* afflizione *f*.

affluence ['æfluəns] *n* abbondanza; opulenza.

affluent ['æfluənt] *a* abbondante; opulente; (*person*) ricco(a).

afford [ə'fɔːd] *vt* permettersi; (*provide*) fornire; **I can't** ~ **the time** non ho veramente il tempo.

affront [ə'frʌnt] *n* affronto; ~**ed** *a* insultato(a).

afield [ə'fiːld] *ad*: **far** ~ lontano.

afloat [ə'fləut] *a*, *ad* a galla.

afoot [ə'fut] *ad*: **there is something** ~ si sta preparando qualcosa.

aforesaid [ə'fɔːsɛd] *a* suddetto(a), predetto(a).

afraid [ə'freɪd] *a* impaurito(a); **to be** ~ **of** aver paura di; **to be** ~ **of doing** *or* **to do** aver paura di fare; **I am** ~ **that I'll be late** mi dispiace, ma farò tardi.

afresh [ə'frɛʃ] *ad* di nuovo.

Africa ['æfrɪkə] *n* Africa; ~**n** *a*, *n* africano(a).

aft [ɑːft] *ad* a poppa, verso poppa.

after ['ɑːftə*] *prep*,*ad* dopo; **what/who are you** ~? che/chi cerca?; ~ **all** dopo tutto; ~-**effects** *npl* conseguenze *fpl*; (*of illness*) postumi *mpl*; ~**life** *n* vita dell'al di là; ~**math** *n* conseguenze *fpl*; **in the** ~**math of** nel periodo dopo; ~**noon** *n* pomeriggio; ~-**shave** (**lotion**) *n* dopobarba *m inv*; ~**thought** *n*: **as an** ~**thought** come aggiunta; ~**wards** *ad* dopo.

again [ə'gɛn] *ad* di nuovo; **to begin/see** ~ ricominciare/rivedere; **not ...** ~ non ... più; ~ **and** ~ ripetutamente.

against [ə'gɛnst] *prep* contro; ~ **a blue background** su uno sfondo azzurro.

age [eɪdʒ] *n* età *f inv* // *vt*,*vi* invecchiare; **it's been** ~**s since** sono secoli che; **to come of** ~ diventare maggiorenne; ~**d** *a* (*elderly*: ['eɪdʒɪd]) anziano(a); ~**d 10** di 10 anni; **the** ~**d** ['eɪdʒɪd] gli anziani; ~ **group** *n* generazione *f*; ~-**less** *a* senza età; ~ **limit** *n* limite *m* d'età.

agency ['eɪdʒənsɪ] *n* agenzia; **through** *or* **by the** ~ **of** grazie a.

agenda [ə'dʒɛndə] *n* ordine *m* del giorno.

agent ['eɪdʒənt] *n* agente *m*.

aggravate ['ægrəveɪt] *vt* aggravare; (*annoy*) esasperare.

aggregate ['ægrɪgeɪt] *n* aggregato; **on** ~ (*SPORT*) con punteggio complessivo.

aggression [ə'grɛʃən] *n* aggressione *f*.

aggressive [ə'grɛsɪv] *a* aggressivo(a); ~**ness** *n* aggressività.

aggrieved [ə'griːvd] *a* addolorato(a).

aghast [ə'gɑːst] *a* sbigottito(a).

agile ['ædʒaɪl] *a* agile.

agitate ['ædʒɪteɪt] *vt* turbare; agitare // *vi*: **to** ~ **for** agitarsi per; **agitator** *n* agitatore/trice.

ago [ə'gəu] *ad*: **2 days** ~ 2 giorni fa; **not long** ~ poco tempo fa.

agonizing ['ægənaɪzɪŋ] *a* straziante.

agony ['ægənɪ] *n* agonia.

agree [ə'griː] *vi*: **to** ~ (**with**) essere d'accordo (con); (*LING*) concordare (con); **to** ~ **to sth/to do sth** accettare qc/di fare qc; **to** ~ **that** (*admit*) ammettere che; **to** ~ **on sth** accordarsi su qc; **garlic doesn't** ~ **with me** l'aglio non mi va; ~**able** *a* gradevole; (*willing*) disposto(a); **are you** ~**able to this?** sei d'accordo con questo?; ~**d** *a* (*time*, *place*) stabilito(a); **to be** ~**d** essere d'accordo; ~**ment** *n* accordo; **in** ~**ment** d'accordo.

agricultural [ægrɪ'kʌltʃərəl] *a* agricolo(a).

agriculture ['ægrɪkʌltʃə*] *n* agricoltura.

aground [ə'graund] *ad*: **to run** ~ arenarsi.

ahead [ə'hɛd] *ad* avanti; davanti; ~ **of** davanti a; (*fig*: *schedule etc*) in anticipo su; ~ **of time** in anticipo; **go** ~**!** avanti!; **go right** *or* **straight** ~ tiri dritto; **they were (right)** ~ **of us** erano (proprio) davanti a noi.

aid [eɪd] *n* aiuto // *vt* aiutare; **to** ~ **and abet** (*LAW*) essere complice di.

aide [eɪd] *n* (*person*) aiutante *m*.

ailment ['eɪlmənt] *n* indisposizione *f*.

aim [eɪm] *vt*: **to** ~ **sth at** (*such as gun*) mirare qc a, puntare qc a; (*camera*, *remark*) rivolgere qc a; (*missile*) lanciare qc contro; (*blow etc*) tirare qc a // *vi* (*also*: **to take** ~) prendere la mira // *n* mira; **to** ~ **at** mirare; **to** ~ **to do** aver l'intenzione di fare; ~**less** *a*, ~**lessly** *ad* senza scopo.

air [ɛə*] *n* aria // *vt* aerare; (*grievances*, *ideas*) esprimere pubblicamente // *cpd* (*currents*) d'aria; (*attack*) aereo(a); ~**bed** *n* materassino gonfiabile; ~**borne** *a* in volo; aerotrasportato(a); ~ **conditioning** *n* condizionamento d'aria; ~-**cooled** *a* raffreddato(a) ad aria; ~**craft** *n*, *pl inv* apparecchio; ~**craft carrier** *n* portaerei *f inv*; **A** ~ **Force** *n* aviazione *f* militare; ~**gun** *n* fucile *m* ad aria compressa; ~ **hostess** *n* hostess *f inv*; ~**ily** *ad* con disinvoltura; ~ **letter** *n* aerogramma *m*; ~**line** *n* linea aerea; ~**liner** *n* aereo di linea; ~**lock** *n* cassa d'aria; **by** ~**mail** per via aerea; ~**plane** *n* (*US*) aeroplano; ~**port** *n* aeroporto; ~ **raid** *n* incursione *f* aerea; ~**sick** *a* che ha il mal d'aereo; ~**strip** *n* pista d'atterraggio; ~**tight** *a* ermetico(a); ~**y** *a* arioso(a); (*manners*) non curante.

aisle [aɪl] *n* (*of church*) navata laterale; navata centrale.

ajar [ə'dʒɑː*] *a* socchiuso(a).

alarm [ə'lɑːm] *n* allarme *m* // *vt* allarmare; ~ **clock** *n* sveglia; ~**ist** *n* allarmista *m*.

Albania [æl'beɪnɪə] *n* Albania.

album ['ælbəm] *n* album *m inv*; (*L.P.*) 33 giri *m inv*, L.P. *m inv*.

alchemy ['ælkɪmɪ] *n* alchimia.

alcohol ['ælkəhɔl] *n* alcool *m*; ~**ic** [-'hɔlɪk] *a* alcolico(a) // *n* alcolizzato/a; ~**ism** *n* alcolismo.

alcove ['ælkəuv] *n* alcova.

alderman ['ɔ:ldəmən] *n* consigliere *m* comunale.

ale [eil] *n* birra.

alert [ə'lɔ:t] *a* vivo(a); (*watchful*) vigile // in allarme *m*; **on the** ~ all'erta.

algebra ['ældʒibrə] *n* algebra.

Algeria [æl'dʒiəriə] *n* Algeria; ~**n** *a*, *n* algerino(a).

alias ['eiliæs] *ad* alias // *n* pseudonimo, falso nome *m*.

alibi ['ælibai] *n* alibi *m inv*.

alien ['eiliən] *n* straniero/a // *a*: ~ **with** estraneo(a) a; ~**ate** *vt* alienare; ~**ation** [-'neiʃən] *n* alienazione *f*.

alight [ə'lait] *a* acceso(a) // *vi* scendere; (*bird*) posarsi.

align [ə'lain] *vt* allineare; ~**ment** *n* allineamento.

alike [ə'laik] *a* simile // *ad* sia ... sia; **to look** ~ assomigliarsi.

alimony ['æliməni] *n* (*payment*) alimenti *mpl*.

alive [ə'laiv] *a* vivo(a); (*active*) attivo(a); ~ **with** pieno(a) di; ~ **to** conscio(a) di.

alkali ['ælkəlai] *n* alcali *m inv*.

all [ɔ:l] *a* tutto(a), tutti(e) *pl* // *pronoun* tutto *m*; (*pl*) tutti(e) // *ad* tutto; ~ **wrong/alone** tutto sbagliato/solo; ~ **the time/his life** tutto il tempo/tutta la sua vita; ~ **five** tutti e cinque; ~ **of them** tutti(e); ~ **of it** tutto; ~ **of us went** ci siamo andati tutti; **it's not as hard** *etc* **as** ~ **that** non è mica così duro *etc*; ~ **in** ~ tutto sommato.

allay [ə'lei] *vt* (*fears*) dissipare.

allegation [æli'geiʃən] *n* asserzione *f*.

allege [ə'ledʒ] *vt* asserire; ~**dly** [ə'ledʒidli] *ad* secondo che si asserisce.

allegiance [ə'li:dʒəns] *n* fedeltà.

allegory ['æligəri] *n* allegoria.

allergic [ə'lə:dʒik] *a*: ~ **to** allergico(a) a.

allergy ['ælədʒi] *n* allergia.

alley ['æli] *n* vicolo; (*in garden*) vialetto.

alliance [ə'laiəns] *n* alleanza.

allied ['ælaid] *a* alleato(a).

alligator ['æligeitə*] *n* alligatore *m*.

all-important ['ɔ:lim'pɔ:tənt] *a* importantissimo(a).

all-in ['ɔ:lin] *a* (*also ad: charge*) tutto compreso; ~ **wrestling** *n* lotta americana.

all-night ['ɔ:l'nait] *a* aperto(a) (*or che* dura) tutta la notte.

allocate ['æləkeit] *vt* (*share out*) distribuire; (*duties, sum, time*): **to** ~ **sth to** assegnare qc a; **to** ~ **sth for** stanziare qc per.

allocation [æləu'keiʃən] *n*: ~ (**of money**) stanziamento.

allot [ə'lɔt] *vt* (*share out*) spartire; (*time*): **to** ~ **sth to** dare qc a; (*duties*): **to** ~ **sth to** assegnare qc a; ~**ment** *n* (*share*) spartizione *f*; (*garden*) lotto di terra.

all-out ['ɔ:laut] *a* (*effort etc*) totale // *ad*: **to go all out for** mettercela tutta per.

allow [ə'lau] *vt* (*practice, behaviour*) permettere; (*sum to spend etc*) accordare; (*sum, time estimated*) dare; (*concede*): **to** ~ **that** ammettere che; **to** ~ **sb to do** permettere a qd di fare; **to** ~ **for** *vt fus* tener conto di; ~**ance** *n* (*money received*) assegno; indennità *f inv*; (*TAX*) detrazione *f* di imposta; **to make** ~**ances for** tener conto di.

alloy ['ælɔi] *n* lega.

all right ['ɔ:l'rait] *ad* (*feel, work*) bene; (*as answer*) va bene.

all-round ['ɔ:l'raund] *a* completo(a).

all-time ['ɔ:l'taim] *a* (*record*) assoluto(a).

allude [ə'lu:d] *vi*: **to** ~ **to** alludere a.

alluring [ə'ljuəriŋ] *a* seducente.

allusion [ə'lu:ʒən] *n* allusione *f*.

ally ['ælai] *n* alleato.

almighty [ɔ:l'maiti] *a* onnipotente.

almond ['ɑ:mənd] *n* mandorla.

almost ['ɔ:lməust] *ad* quasi.

alms [ɑ:mz] *n* elemosina.

alone [ə'ləun] *a* solo(a); **to leave sb** ~ lasciare qd in pace; **to leave sth** ~ lasciare stare qc.

along [ə'lɔŋ] *prep* lungo // *ad*: **is he coming** ~? viene con noi?; **he was hopping/limping** ~ lui veniva saltellando/zoppicando; ~ **with** insieme con; ~**side** *prep* accanto a; lungo // *ad* accanto.

aloof [ə'lu:f] *a* distaccato(a) // *ad* a distanza, a disparte.

aloud [ə'laud] *ad* ad alta voce.

alphabet ['ælfəbet] *n* alfabeto.

alpine ['ælpain] *a* alpino(a).

Alps [ælps] *npl*: **the** ~ le Alpi.

already [ɔ:l'redi] *ad* già.

alright ['ɔ:l'rait] *ad* = **all right**.

also ['ɔ:lsəu] *ad* anche.

altar ['ɔltə*] *n* altare *m*.

alter ['ɔltə*] *vt*, *vi* alterare; ~**ation** [ɔltə'reiʃən] *n* modificazione *f*, alterazione *f*.

alternate *a* [ɔl'tɔ:nit] alterno(a) // *vi* ['ɔltɔ:neit] alternare; **on** ~ **days** ogni due giorni; **alternating** *a* (*current*) alternato(a).

alternative [ɔl'tɔ:nətiv] *a* (*solutions*) alternativo(a); (*solution*) altro(a) // *n* (*choice*) alternativa; (*other possibility*) altra possibilità; ~**ly** *ad* alternativamente.

alternator ['ɔltɔ:neitə*] *n* (*AUT*) alternatore *m*.

although [ɔ:l'ðəu] *cj* benché + *sub*, sebbene + *sub*.

altitude ['æltitju:d] *n* altitudine *f*.

alto ['æltəu] *n* contralto.

altogether [ɔ:ltə'geðə*] *ad* del tutto, completamente; (*on the whole*) tutto considerato; (*in all*) in tutto.

altruistic [æltru'istik] *a* altruistico(a).

aluminium [ælju'miniəm] *n* alluminio.

always ['ɔ:lweiz] *ad* sempre.

am [æm] *vb see* **be**.

a.m. ad (abbr of ante meridiem) della mattina.

amalgamate [ə'mælgəmeɪt] vt amalgamare // vi amalgamarsi; **amalgamation** [-'meɪʃən] n amalgamazione f; (COMM) fusione f.

amass [ə'mæs] vt ammassare.

amateur ['æmətə*] n dilettante m/f // a (SPORT) dilettante; ~**ish** a (pej) da dilettante.

amaze [ə'meɪz] vt stupire; ~**ment** n stupore m.

ambassador [æm'bæsədə*] n ambasciatore/trice.

amber ['æmbə*] n ambra; at ~ (AUT) giallo.

ambiguity [æmbɪ'gjuɪtɪ] n ambiguità f inv.

ambiguous [æm'bɪgjuəs] a ambiguo(a).

ambition [æm'bɪʃən] n ambizione f.

ambitious [æm'bɪʃəs] a ambizioso(a).

ambivalent [æm'bɪvələnt] a (attitude) ambivalente.

amble ['æmbl] vi (gen: to ~ along) camminare tranquillamente.

ambulance ['æmbjuləns] n ambulanza.

ambush ['æmbuʃ] n imboscata // vt fare un'imboscata a.

amenable [ə'miːnəbl] a: ~ to (advice etc) ben disposto(a) a.

amend [ə'mɛnd] vt (law) emendare; (text) correggere // vi emendarsi; to make ~s fare ammenda; ~**ment** n emendamento; correzione f.

amenity [ə'miːnɪtɪ] n amenità f inv.

America [ə'mɛrɪkə] n America; ~**n** a, n americano(a).

amethyst ['æmɪθɪst] n ametista.

amiable ['eɪmɪəbl] a amabile, gentile.

amicable ['æmɪkəbl] a amichevole.

amid(st) [ə'mɪd(st)] prep fra, tra, in mezzo a.

amiss [ə'mɪs] a,ad: there's something ~ c'è qualcosa che non va bene; to take sth ~ aversene a male.

ammunition [æmju'nɪʃən] n munizioni fpl.

amnesia [æm'niːzɪə] n amnesia.

amnesty ['æmnɪstɪ] n amnistia.

amok [ə'mɔk] ad: to run ~ diventare pazzo(a) furioso(a).

among(st) [ə'mʌŋ(st)] prep fra, tra, in mezzo a.

amoral [æ'mɔrəl] a amorale.

amorous ['æmərəs] a amoroso(a).

amorphous [ə'mɔːfəs] a amorfo(a).

amount [ə'maunt] n somma; ammontare m; quantità f inv // vi: to ~ to (total) ammontare a; (be same as) essere come.

amp(ère) ['æmp(ɛə*)] n ampère m inv.

amphibious [æm'fɪbɪəs] a anfibio(a).

amphitheatre ['æmfɪθɪətə*] n anfiteatro.

ample ['æmpl] a ampio(a); spazioso(a); (enough): this is ~ questo è più che sufficiente; to have ~ time/room avere assai tempo/posto.

amplifier ['æmplɪfaɪə*] n amplificatore m.

amplify ['æmplɪfaɪ] vt amplificare.

amply ['æmplɪ] ad ampiamente.

amputate ['æmpjuteɪt] vt amputare.

amuck [ə'mʌk] ad = amok.

amuse [ə'mjuːz] vt divertire; ~**ment** n divertimento.

an [æn, ən, n] det see a.

anaemia [ə'niːmɪə] n anemia.

anaemic [ə'niːmɪk] a anemico(a).

anaesthetic [ænɪs'θetɪk] a anestetico(a) // n anestetico.

anaesthetist [æ'niːsθɪtɪst] n anestesista m/f.

analogy [ə'nælədʒɪ] n analogia.

analyse ['ænəlaɪz] vt analizzare.

analysis, pl **analyses** [ə'næləsɪs, -siːz] n analisi f inv.

analyst ['ænəlɪst] n analista m/f.

analytic(al) [ænə'lɪtɪk(əl)] a analitico(a).

anarchist ['ænəkɪst] a anarchico(a) // n anarchista m/f.

anarchy ['ænəkɪ] n anarchia.

anathema [ə'næθɪmə] n anatema m.

anatomical [ænə'tɔmɪkəl] a anatomico(a).

anatomy [ə'nætəmɪ] n anatomia.

ancestor ['ænsɪstə*] n antenato/a.

ancestral [æn'sɛstrəl] a avito(a).

ancestry ['ænsɪstrɪ] n antenati mpl; ascendenza.

anchor ['æŋkə*] n ancora // vi (also: to drop ~) gettar l'ancora // vt ancorare; ~**age** n ancoraggio.

anchovy ['æntʃəvɪ] n acciuga.

ancient ['eɪnʃənt] a antico(a); (fig) anziano(a).

and [ænd] cj e (often ed before vowel); ~ so on e così via; come ~ sit here vieni a sedere qui; better ~ better sempre meglio.

Andes ['ændiːz] npl: the ~ le Ande.

anecdote ['ænɪkdəut] n aneddoto.

anemia [ə'niːmɪə] etc = **anaemia** etc.

anesthetic [ænɪs'θetɪk] etc = **anaesthetic** etc.

anew [ə'njuː] ad di nuovo.

angel ['eɪndʒəl] n angelo.

anger ['æŋgə*] n rabbia // vt arrabbiare.

angina [æn'dʒaɪnə] n angina pectoris.

angle ['æŋgl] n angolo; from their ~ dal loro punto di vista // vi: to ~ for (fig) cercare di farsi fare; ~**r** n pescatore m con la lenza.

Anglican ['æŋglɪkən] a,n anglicano(a).

anglicize ['æŋglɪsaɪz] vt anglicizzare.

angling ['æŋglɪŋ] n pesca con la lenza.

Anglo- ['æŋgləu] prefix anglo...; ~**Saxon** a,n anglosassone (m/f).

angrily ['æŋgrɪlɪ] ad con rabbia.

angry ['æŋgrɪ] a arrabbiato(a), furioso(a); to be ~ with sb/at sth essere in collera con qd/per qc; to get ~ arrabbiarsi; to make sb ~ fare arrabbiare qd.

anguish ['æŋgwɪʃ] n angoscia.

angular ['æŋgjulə*] a angolare.

animal ['ænɪməl] a, n animale (m).

animate vt ['ænɪmeɪt] animare // a ['ænɪmɪt] animato(a); ~**d** a animato(a).

animosity [ænɪ'mɔsɪtɪ] n animosità.

aniseed ['ænɪsiːd] n semi mpl di anice.

ankle ['æŋkl] n caviglia.

annex n ['ænɛks] (also: **annexe**) edificio annesso // vt [ə'nɛks] annettere; **~ation** ['eɪʃən] n annessione f.

annihilate [ə'naɪəleɪt] vt annientare.

anniversary [ænɪ'vəːsərɪ] n anniversario.

annotate ['ænəuteɪt] vt annotare.

announce [ə'nauns] vt annunciare; **~ment** n annuncio; (letter, card) partecipazione f; **~r** n (RADIO, TV: between programmes) annunciatore/trice; (in a programme) presentatore/trice.

annoy [ə'nɔɪ] vt dare fastidio a; **don't get ~ed!** non irritarti!; **~ance** n noia; **~ing** a noioso(a).

annual ['ænjuəl] a annuale // n (BOT) pianta annua; (book) annuario; **~ly** ad annualmente.

annuity [ə'njuːɪtɪ] n annualità f inv; **life ~** vitalizio.

annul [ə'nʌl] vt annullare; (law) rescindere; **~ment** n annullamento; rescissione f.

annum ['ænəm] n see **per**.

anoint [ə'nɔɪnt] vt ungere.

anomaly [ə'nɔmǝlɪ] n anomalia.

anonymous [ə'nɔnɪməs] a anonimo(a).

anorak ['ænəræk] n giacca a vento.

another [ə'nʌðə*] a: **~ book** (one more) un altro libro, ancora un libro; (a different one) un altro libro // pronoun un altro(un'altra), ancora uno(a); see also **one.**

answer ['ɑːnsə*] n risposta; soluzione f // vi rispondere // vt (reply to) rispondere a; (problem) risolvere; (prayer) esaudire; **to ~ the phone** rispondere (al telefono); **in ~ to your letter** in risposta alla sua lettera; **to ~ the bell** rispondere al campanello; **to ~ the door** aprire la porta; **to ~ back** vi ribattere; **to ~ for** vt fus essere responsabile di; **to ~ to** vt fus (description) corrispondere a; **~able** a: **~able (to sb/for sth)** responsabile (verso qd/di qc).

ant [ænt] n formica.

antagonism [æn'tægənɪzəm] n antagonismo.

antagonist [æn'tægənɪst] n antagonista m/f; **~ic** [æntægə'nɪstɪk] a antagonistico(a).

antagonize [æn'tægənaɪz] vt provocare l'ostilità di.

Antarctic [ænt'ɑːktɪk] n Antartide f // a antartico(a).

antelope ['æntɪləup] n antilope f.

antenatal ['æntɪ'neɪtl] a prenatale; **~ clinic** n assistenza medica preparto.

antenna, pl **~e** [æn'tɛnə, -niː] n antenna.

anthem ['ænθəm] n antifona; **national ~** inno nazionale.

ant-hill ['ænthɪl] n formicaio.

anthology [æn'θɔlədʒɪ] n antologia.

anthropology [ænθrə'pɔlədʒɪ] n antropologia.

anti- ['æntɪ] prefix anti... .

anti-aircraft ['æntɪ'ɛəkrɑːft] a antiaereo(a).

antibiotic ['æntɪbaɪ'ɔtɪk] a antibiotico(a) // n antibiotico.

anticipate [æn'tɪsɪpeɪt] vt prevedere; pregustare; (wishes, request) prevenire.

anticipation [æntɪsɪ'peɪʃən] n anticipazione f; (expectation) aspettative fpl; **thanking you in ~** vi ringrazio in anticipo.

anticlimax ['æntɪ'klaɪmæks] n: **it was an ~** fu una completa delusione.

anticlockwise ['æntɪ'klɔkwaɪz] a in senso antiorario.

antics ['æntɪks] npl buffonerie fpl.

anticyclone ['æntɪ'saɪkləun] n anticiclone m.

antidote ['æntɪdəut] n antidoto.

antifreeze ['æntɪ'friːz] n anticongelante m.

antipathy [æn'tɪpəθɪ] n antipatia.

antiquated ['æntɪkweɪtɪd] a antiquato(a).

antique [æn'tiːk] n antichità f inv // a antico(a); (old-fashioned) antiquato/a; **~ shop** n negozio d'antichità.

antiquity [æn'tɪkwɪtɪ] n antichità f inv.

antiseptic ['æntɪ'sɛptɪk] a antisettico(a) // n antisettico.

antisocial ['æntɪ'səuʃəl] a antisociale.

antlers ['æntləz] npl palchi mpl.

anus ['eɪnəs] n ano.

anvil ['ænvɪl] n incudine f.

anxiety [æŋ'zaɪətɪ] n ansia; (keenness): **~ to do** smania di fare.

anxious ['æŋkʃəs] a ansioso(a), inquieto(a); (keen): **~ to do/that** impaziente di fare/che + sub.

any ['ɛnɪ] det (in negative and interrogative sentences = some) del, dell', dello, dei, degli, della, delle; alcuno(a); qualche; nessuno(a); (no matter which) non importa che; (each and every) tutto(a), ogni; **I haven't ~ bread/books** non ho pane/libri; **come (at) ~ time** vieni a qualsiasi ora; **at ~ moment** da un momento all'altro; **in ~ case** in ogni caso; **at ~ rate** ad ogni modo // pronoun uno(a) qualsiasi; (anybody) chiunque; (in negative and interrogative sentences): **I haven't ~** non ne ho; **have you got ~?** ne hai?; **can ~ of you sing?** c'è qualcuno che sa cantare? // ad (in negative sentences) per niente; (in interrogative and conditional constructions) un po'; **I can't hear him ~ more** non lo sento più; **are you feeling ~ better?** ti senti un po' meglio?; **do you want ~ more soup?** vuoi ancora della minestra?; **~body** pronoun qualsiasi persona; (in interrogative sentences) qualcuno; (in negative sentences): **I don't see ~body** non vedo nessuno; **~how** ad in qualsiasi modo; **~one = ~body; ~thing** pronoun (see anybody) qualsiasi cosa; qualcosa; non ... niente, non ... nulla; **~time** ad in qualunque momento; quando vuoi; **~way** ad in qualsiasi modo; in or ad ogni modo; **~where** ad (see anybody) da qualsiasi parte; da qualche parte; **I don't see him** ~**where** non lo vedo da nessuna parte.

apart [ə'pɑːt] *ad* (*to one side*) a parte; (*separately*) separatamente; **10 miles/a long way** ~ a 10 miglia di distanza/molto lontani l'uno dall'altro; **they are living** ~ sono separati; ~ **from** *prep* a parte, eccetto.

apartheid [ə'pɑːteit] *n* apartheid *f*.

apartment [ə'pɑːtmənt] *n* (*US*) appartamento; ~**s** *npl* appartamento ammobiliato.

apathetic [æpə'θɛtik] *a* apatico(a).

apathy ['æpəθi] *n* apatia.

ape [eip] *n* scimmia // *vt* scimmiottare.

aperitif [ə'peritiv] *n* aperitivo.

aperture ['æpətʃjuə*] *n* apertura.

apex ['eipɛks] *n* apice *m*.

aphrodisiac [æfrəu'diziæk] *a* afrodisiaco(a) // *n* afrodisiaco.

apiece [ə'piːs] *ad* ciascuno(a).

aplomb [ə'plɔm] *n* disinvoltura.

apologetic [əpɔlə'dʒɛtik] *a* (*tone, letter*) di scusa; **to be very** ~ **about** scusarsi moltissimo di.

apologize [ə'pɔlədʒaiz] *vi*: **to** ~ (**for sth to sb**) scusarsi (di qc a qd), chiedere scusa (a qd per qc).

apology [ə'pɔlədʒi] *n* scuse *fpl*.

apoplexy ['æpəplɛksi] *n* apoplessia.

apostle [ə'pɔsl] *n* apostolo.

apostrophe [ə'pɔstrəfi] *n* (*segno*) apostrofo.

appal [ə'pɔːl] *vt* atterrire; sgomentare; ~**ling** a spaventoso(a).

apparatus [æpə'reitəs] *n* apparato.

apparent [ə'pærənt] *a* evidente; ~**ly** *ad* evidentemente.

apparition [æpə'riʃən] *n* apparizione *f*.

appeal [ə'piːl] *vi* (*LAW*) appellarsi alla legge // *n* (*LAW*) appello; (*request*) richiesta; (*charm*) attrattiva; **to** ~ **for** chiedere (con insistenza); **to** ~ **to** (*subj: person*) appellarsi a; (*subj: thing*) piacere a; **to** ~ **to sb for mercy** chiedere pietà a qd; **it doesn't** ~ **to me** mi dice poco.

appear [ə'piə*] *vi* apparire; (*LAW*) comparire; (*publication*) essere pubblicato(a); (*seem*) sembrare; **it would** ~ **that** sembra che; **to** ~ **in Hamlet** recitare nell'Amleto; **to** ~ **on TV** presentarsi in televisione; ~**ance** *n* apparizione *f*; apparenza; (*look, aspect*) aspetto; **to put in** *or* **make an** ~**ance** fare atto di presenza.

appease [ə'piːz] *vt* calmare, appagare.

appendage [ə'pendidʒ] *n* aggiunta.

appendicitis [əpendi'saitis] *n* appendicite *f*.

appendix, *pl* **appendices** [ə'pendiks, -siːz] *n* appendice *f*.

appetite ['æpitait] *n* appetito.

appetizing ['æpitaiziŋ] *a* appetitoso(a).

applaud [ə'plɔːd] *vt,vi* applaudire.

applause [ə'plɔːz] *n* applauso.

apple ['æpl] *n* mela; ~ **tree** *n* melo.

appliance [ə'plaiəns] *n* apparecchio.

applicable [ə'plikəbl] *a* applicabile.

applicant ['æplikənt] *n* candidato.

application [æpli'keiʃən] *n* applicazione *f*; (*for a job, a grant etc*) domanda.

applied [ə'plaid] *a* applicato(a).

apply [ə'plai] *vt* (*paint, ointment*): **to** ~ (**to**) dare (a); (*theory, technique*): **to** ~ (**to**) applicare (a) // *vi*: **to** ~ **to** (*ask*) rivolgersi a; (*be suitable for, relevant to*) riguardare, riferirsi a; **to** ~ (**for**) (*permit, grant, job*) fare domanda (per); **to** ~ **the brakes** frenare; **to** ~ **o.s.** to dedicarsi a.

appoint [ə'pɔint] *vt* nominare; ~**ment** *n* nomina; (*arrangement to meet*) appuntamento.

appraisal [ə'preizl] *n* valutazione *f*.

appreciable [ə'priːʃəbl] *a* apprezzabile.

appreciate [ə'priːʃieit] *vt* (*like*) apprezzare; (*be grateful for*) essere riconoscente di; (*be aware of*) rendersi conto di // *vi* (*COMM*) aumentare.

appreciation [əpriːʃi'eiʃən] *n* apprezzamento; (*COMM*) aumento del valore.

appreciative [ə'priːʃiətiv] *a* (*person*) sensibile; (*comment*) elogiativo(a).

apprehend [æpri'hend] *vt* arrestare; (*understand*) comprendere.

apprehension [æpri'henʃən] *n* inquietudine *f*.

apprehensive [æpri'hensiv] *a* apprensivo(a).

apprentice [ə'prentis] *n* apprendista *m/f*; ~**ship** *n* apprendistato.

approach [ə'prəutʃ] *vi* avvicinarsi // *vt* (*come near*) avvicinarsi a; (*ask, apply to*) rivolgersi a; (*subject, passer-by*) avvicinare // *n* approccio; accesso; (*to problem*) modo di affrontare; ~**able** a accessibile.

appropriate *vt* [ə'prəuprieit] (*take*) appropriarsi // *a* [ə'prəupriit] appropriato(a); adatto(a); ~**ly** *ad* in modo appropriato.

approval [ə'pruːvəl] *n* approvazione *f*; **on** ~ (*COMM*) in prova, in esame.

approve [ə'pruːv] *vt, vi* approvare; **to** ~ **of** *vt fus* approvare; ~**d school** *n* riformatorio; **approvingly** *ad* in approvazione.

approximate [ə'prɔksimit] *a* approssimativo(a); ~**ly** *ad* circa; **approximation** [-'meiʃən] *n* approssimazione *f*.

apricot ['eiprikɔt] *n* albicocca.

April ['eiprəl] *n* aprile *m*; ~ **fool!** pesce d'aprile!

apron ['eiprən] *n* grembiule *m*.

apt [æpt] *a* (*suitable*) adatto(a); (*able*) capace; (*likely*): **to be** ~ **to do** avere tendenza a fare.

aptitude ['æptitjuːd] *n* abilità *f inv*.

aqualung ['ækwəlʌŋ] *n* autorespiratore *m*.

aquarium [ə'kwɛəriəm] *n* acquario.

Aquarius [ə'kwɛəriəs] *n* Acquario.

aquatic [ə'kwætik] *a* acquatico(a).

aqueduct ['ækwidʌkt] *n* acquedotto.

Arab ['ærəb] n arabo/a.
Arabia [ə'reɪbɪə] n Arabia; ~**n** a arabo(a).
Arabic ['ærəbɪk] a arabico(a) // n arabo.
arable ['ærəbl] a arabile.
arbitrary ['ɑːbɪtrərɪ] a arbitrario(a).
arbitrate ['ɑːbɪtreɪt] vi arbitrare; **arbitration** [-'treɪʃən] n (LAW) arbitrato; (INDUSTRY) arbitraggio.
arbitrator ['ɑːbɪtreɪtə*] n arbitro.
arc [ɑːk] n arco.
arcade [ɑː'keɪd] n portico; (passage with shops) galleria.
arch [ɑːtʃ] n arco; (of foot) arco plantare // vt inarcare // a malizioso(a).
archaeologist [ɑːkɪ'ɔlədʒɪst] n archeologo/a.
archaeology [ɑːkɪ'ɔlədʒɪ] n archeologia.
archaic [ɑː'keɪɪk] a arcaico(a).
archbishop [ɑːtʃ'bɪʃəp] n arcivescovo.
arch-enemy ['ɑːtʃ'enɪmɪ] n arcinemico/a.
archer ['ɑːtʃə*] n arciere m; ~**y** n tiro all'arco.
archetype ['ɑːkɪtaɪp] n archetipo.
archipelago [ɑːkɪ'pelɪɡəu] n arcipelago.
architect ['ɑːkɪtekt] n architetto; ~**ural** [ɑːkɪ'tektʃərəl] a architettonico(a); ~**ure** ['ɑːkɪtektʃə*] n architettura.
archives ['ɑːkaɪvz] npl archivi mpl.
archway ['ɑːtʃweɪ] n arco.
Arctic ['ɑːktɪk] a artico(a) // n: **the** ~ l'Artico.
ardent ['ɑːdənt] a ardente.
arduous ['ɑːdjuəs] a arduo(a).
are [ɑː*] vb see **be**.
area ['ɛərɪə] n (GEOM) area; (zone) zona; (: smaller) settore m; **dining** ~ n zona pranzo.
arena [ə'riːnə] n arena.
aren't [ɑːnt] = **are not**.
Argentina [ɑːdʒən'tiːnə] n Argentina; **Argentinian** [-'tɪnɪən] a, n argentino(a).
arguable ['ɑːɡjuəbl] a discutibile.
argue ['ɑːɡjuː] vi (quarrel) litigare; (reason) ragionare; **to** ~ **that** sostenere che.
argument ['ɑːɡjumənt] n (reasons) argomento; (quarrel) lite f; (debate) discussione f; ~**ative** [ɑːɡjuː'mentətɪv] a litigioso(a).
arid ['ærɪd] a arido(a).
Aries ['ɛərɪz] n Ariete m.
arise, pt **arose**, pp **arisen** [ə'raɪz, -'rəuz, -'rɪzn] vi alzarsi; (opportunity, problem) presentarsi; **to** ~ **from** risultare da.
aristocracy [ærɪs'tɔkrəsɪ] n aristocrazia.
aristocrat ['ærɪstəkræt] n aristocratico/a; ~**ic** [-'krætɪk] a aristocratico(a).
arithmetic [ə'rɪθmətɪk] n aritmetica.
ark [ɑːk] n: **Noah's A**~ l'arca di Noè.
arm [ɑːm] n braccio; (MIL: branch) arma // vt armare; ~**s** npl (weapons) armi fpl; ~ **in** ~ a braccetto; ~**band** n bracciale m; ~**chair** n poltrona; ~**ed** a armato(a); ~**ed robbery** n rapina a mano armata; ~**ful** n bracciata.
armistice ['ɑːmɪstɪs] n armistizio.
armour ['ɑːmə*] n armatura; (also:

~-**plating**) corazza, blindatura; (MIL: tanks) mezzi mpl blindati; ~**ed car** n autoblinda f inv; ~**y** n arsenale m.
armpit ['ɑːmpɪt] n ascella.
army ['ɑːmɪ] n esercito.
aroma [ə'rəumə] n aroma; ~**tic** [ærə'mætɪk] a aromatico(a).
arose [ə'rəuz] pt of **arise**.
around [ə'raund] ad attorno, intorno // prep intorno a; (fig: about): ~ **£5/3 o'clock** circa 5 sterline/le 3; **is he** ~? è in giro?
arouse [ə'rauz] vt (sleeper) svegliare; (curiosity, passions) suscitare.
arrange [ə'reɪndʒ] vt sistemare; (programme) preparare; ~**ment** n sistemazione f; (plans etc): ~**ments** progetti mpl, piani mpl.
array [ə'reɪ] n: ~ **of** fila di.
arrears [ə'rɪəz] npl arretrati mpl; **to be in** ~ **with one's rent** essere in arretrato con l'affitto.
arrest [ə'rest] vt arrestare; (sb's attention) attirare // n arresto; **under** ~ in arresto.
arrival [ə'raɪvəl] n arrivo; (person) arrivato/a.
arrive [ə'raɪv] vi arrivare; **to** ~ **at** vt fus (fig) raggiungere.
arrogance ['ærəɡəns] n arroganza.
arrogant ['ærəɡənt] a arrogante.
arrow ['ærəu] n freccia.
arsenal ['ɑːsɪnl] n arsenale m.
arsenic ['ɑːsnɪk] n arsenico.
arson ['ɑːsn] n incendio doloso.
art [ɑːt] n arte f; (craft) mestiere m; **A**~**s** npl (SCOL) Lettere fpl; ~ **gallery** n galleria d'arte.
artefact ['ɑːtɪfækt] n manufatto.
artery ['ɑːtərɪ] n arteria.
artful ['ɑːtful] a furbo(a).
arthritis [ɑː'θraɪtɪs] n artrite f.
artichoke ['ɑːtɪtʃəuk] n carciofo.
article ['ɑːtɪkl] n articolo.
articulate a [ɑː'tɪkjulɪt] (person) che si esprime forbitamente; (speech) articolato(a) // vi [ɑː'tɪkjuleɪt] articolare; ~**d lorry** n autotreno.
artificial [ɑːtɪ'fɪʃəl] a artificiale; ~ **respiration** n respirazione f artificiale.
artillery [ɑː'tɪlərɪ] n artiglieria.
artisan ['ɑːtɪzæn] n artigiano/a.
artist ['ɑːtɪst] n artista m/f; ~**ic** [ɑː'tɪstɪk] a artistico(a); ~**ry** n arte f.
artless ['ɑːtlɪs] a semplice, ingenuo(a).
as [æz, əz] cj (cause) siccome, poiché; (time: moment) come, quando; (: duration) mentre; (manner) come; (in the capacity of) da; ~ **big** ~ tanto grande quanto; **twice** ~ **big** ~ due volte più grande che; **big** ~ **it is** grande com'è; ~ **she said** come lei ha detto; ~ **if** or **though** come se + sub; ~ **for** or **to** quanto a; ~ or **so long** ~ cj finché; purché; ~ **much** (~) tanto(a) (... quanto(a)); ~ **many** (~) tanti(e) (... quanti(e)); ~ **soon** ~ cj appena; ~ **such** ad come tale; ~ **well** ad

anche; ~ **well** ~ *cj* come pure; *see also* **so, such.**

asbestos [æz'bɛstɔs] *n* asbesto, amianto.

ascend [ə'sɛnd] *vt* salire; ~**ancy** *n* ascendente *m.*

ascent [ə'sɛnt] *n* salita.

ascertain [æsə'tein] *vt* accertare.

ascetic [ə'sɛtik] *a* ascetico(a).

ascribe [ə'skraib] *vt*: **to ~ sth to** attribuire qc a.

ash [æʃ] *n* (*dust*) cenere *f*; ~ (**tree**) frassino.

ashamed [ə'feimd] *a* vergognoso(a); **to be ~ of** vergognarsi di; **to be ~ (of o.s.) for having done** vergognarsi di aver fatto.

ashen ['æʃn] *a* (*pale*) livido(a).

ashore [ə'ʃɔː] *ad* a terra; **to go ~** sbarcare.

ashtray ['æʃtrei] *n* portacenere *m.*

Asia ['eiʃə] *n* Asia; ~ **Minor** *n* Asia minore; ~**n** *a*, *n* asiatico(a); ~**tic** [eisi'ætik] *a* asiatico(a).

aside [ə'said] *ad* da parte // *n* a parte *m*; **to take sb ~** prendere qd a parte.

ask [ɑːsk] *vt* (*request*) chiedere; (*question*) domandare; (*invite*) invitare; **to ~ sb sth/sb to do sth** chiedere qc a qd/a qd di fare qc; **to ~ sb about sth** chiedere a qd di qc; **to ~ (sb) a question** fare una domanda (a qd); **to ~ sb out to dinner** invitare qd a mangiare fuori; **to ~ after** *vt fus* chiedere di; **to ~ for** *vt fus* chiedere.

askance [ə'skɑːns] *ad*: **to look ~ at sb** guardare qd di traverso.

askew [ə'skjuː] *ad* di traverso, storto.

asleep [ə'sliːp] *a* addormentato(a); **to be ~** dormire; **to fall ~** addormentarsi.

asparagus [əs'pærəgəs] *n* asparagi *mpl.*

aspect ['æspɛkt] *n* aspetto.

aspersions [əs'pəːʃənz] *npl*: **to cast ~ on** diffamare.

asphalt ['æsfælt] *n* asfalto.

asphyxiate [æs'fiksieit] *vt* asfissiare; **asphyxiation** [-'eiʃən] *n* asfissia.

aspiration [æspə'reiʃən] *n* aspirazione *f.*

aspire [əs'paiə] *vi*: **to ~ to** aspirare a.

aspirin ['æsprin] *n* aspirina.

ass [æs] *n* asino.

assail [ə'seil] *vt* assalire; ~**ant** *n* assalitore *m.*

assassin [ə'sæsin] *n* assassino; ~**ate** *vt* assassinare; ~**ation** [əsæsi'neiʃən] *n* assassinio.

assault [ə'sɔːlt] *n* (*MIL*) assalto; (*gen: attack*) aggressione *f*; (*LAW*): ~ (**and battery**) minacce *fpl* e vie di fatto *fpl* // *vt* assaltare; aggredire; (*sexually*) violentare.

assemble [ə'sɛmbl] *vt* riunire; (*TECH*) montare // *vi* riunirsi.

assembly [ə'sɛmbli] *n* (*meeting*) assemblea; (*construction*) montaggio; ~ **line** *n* catena di montaggio.

assent [ə'sɛnt] *n* assenso, consenso // *vi* assentire.

assert [ə'səːt] *vt* asserire; (*insist on*) far valere; ~**ion** [ə'səːʃən] *n* asserzione *f*; ~**ive** *a* assertivo(a).

assess [ə'sɛs] *vt* valutare; ~**ment** *n* valutazione *f.*

asset ['æsɛt] *n* vantaggio; ~**s** *npl* beni *mpl*; disponibilità *fpl*; attivo.

assign [ə'sain] *vt* (*date*) fissare; (*task*): **to ~ sth to** assegnare qc a; (*resources*): **to ~ sth to** riservare qc a; (*cause, meaning*): **to ~ sth to** attribuire qc a; ~**ment** *n* compito.

assimilate [ə'simileit] *vt* assimilare; **assimilation** [-'leiʃən] *n* assimilazione *f.*

assist [ə'sist] *vt* assistere, aiutare; ~**ance** *n* assistenza, aiuto; ~**ant** *n* assistente *m/f*; (*also*: **shop ~ant**) commesso/a.

assizes [ə'saiziz] *npl* assise *fpl.*

associate *a* [ə'səuʃiit] associato(a); (*member*) aggiunto(a) // *n* collega *m/f*; (*in business*) socio/a // *vb* [ə'səuʃieit] *vt* associare // *vi*: **to ~ with sb** frequentare qd.

association [əsəusi'eiʃən] *n* associazione *f*; ~ **football** *n* (gioco del) calcio.

assorted [ə'sɔːtid] *a* assortito(a).

assortment [ə'sɔːtmənt] *n* assortimento.

assume [ə'sjuːm] *vt* supporre; (*responsibilities etc*) assumere; (*attitude, name*) prendere; ~**d name** *n* nome *m* falso.

assumption [ə'sʌmpʃən] *n* supposizione *f*, ipotesi *f inv.*

assurance [ə'fuərəns] *n* assicurazione *f*; (*self-confidence*) fiducia in se stesso.

assure [ə'fuə] *vt* assicurare.

asterisk ['æstərisk] *n* asterisco.

astern [ə'stəːn] *ad* a poppa.

asthma ['æsmə] *n* asma; ~**tic** [æs'mætik] *a,n* asmatico(a).

astir [ə'stəː*] *ad* in piedi; (*excited*) in fermento.

astonish [ə'stɔniʃ] *vt* stupire; ~**ment** *n* stupore *m.*

astound [ə'staund] *vt* sbalordire.

astray [ə'strei] *ad*: **to go ~** smarrirsi; (*fig*) traviarsi.

astride [ə'straid] *prep* a cavalcioni di.

astrologer [əs'trɔlədʒə*] *n* astrologo/a.

astrology [əs'trɔlədʒi] *n* astrologia.

astronaut ['æstrənɔːt] *n* astronauta *m/f.*

astronomer [əs'trɔnəmə*] *n* astronomo/a.

astronomical [æstrə'nɔmikəl] *a* astronomico(a).

astronomy [əs'trɔnəmi] *n* astronomia.

astute [əs'tjuːt] *a* astuto(a).

asylum [ə'sailəm] *n* asilo; (*building*) manicomio.

at [æt] *prep* a; (*because of: following surprised, annoyed etc*) di; con; ~ **Paolo's da** Paolo; ~ **the baker's** dal panettiere; ~ **times** talvolta.

ate [eit] *pt of* **eat.**

atheism ['eiθiizəm] *n* ateismo.

atheist ['eiθiist] *n* ateo/a.

Athens ['æθnz] *n* Atene *f.*

athlete ['æθliːt] *n* atleta *m/f.*

athletic [æθ'lɛtik] *a* atletico(a); ~**s** *n* atletica.

Atlantic [ət'læntik] *a* atlantico(a) // *n*: **the**

~ **(Ocean)** l'Atlantico, l'Oceano Atlantico.
atlas ['ætləs] n atlante m.
atmosphere ['ætməsfɪə*] n atmosfera.
atmospheric [ætməs'ferɪk] a atmosferico(a); ~s n (RADIO) scariche fpl.
atom ['ætəm] n atomo; ~ic [ə'tɒmɪk] a atomico(a); ~**(ic) bomb** n bomba atomica; ~**izer** ['ætəmaɪzə*] n atomizzatore m.
atone [ə'təun] vi: to ~ for espiare.
atrocious [ə'trəuʃəs] a (very bad) pessimo(a).
atrocity [ə'trɒsɪtɪ] n atrocità f inv.
attach [ə'tætʃ] vt attaccare; (document, letter) allegare; (MIL: troops) assegnare; to be ~ed to sb/sth (to like) essere affezionato(a) a qd/qc; ~é [ə'tæʃeɪ] n addetto; ~é case n valigetta per documenti; ~ment n (tool) accessorio; (love): ~ment (to) affetto (per).
attack [ə'tæk] vt attaccare; (task etc) iniziare; (problem) affrontare // n attacco; (also: heart ~) infarto.
attain [ə'teɪn] vt (also: to ~ to) arrivare a, raggiungere; ~ments npl cognizioni fpl.
attempt [ə'tempt] n tentativo // vt tentare; ~ed murder (LAW) tentato omicidio; to make an ~ on sb's life attentare alla vita di qd.
attend [ə'tend] vt frequentare; (meeting, talk) andare a; (patient) assistere; to ~ to vt fus (needs, affairs etc) prendersi cura di; (customer) occuparsi di; ~ance n (being present) presenza; (people present) gente f presente; ~ant n custode m/f; persona di servizio // a concomitante.
attention [ə'tenʃən] n attenzione f; ~s premure fpl, attenzioni fpl; ~! (MIL) attenti!; at ~ (MIL) sull'attenti; for the ~ of (ADMIN) per l'attenzione di.
attentive [ə'tentɪv] a attento(a); (kind) premuroso(a); ~ly ad attentamente.
attest [ə'test] vi: to ~ to attestare.
attic ['ætɪk] n soffitta.
attire [ə'taɪə*] n abbigliamento; posa.
attitude ['ætɪtjuːd] n atteggiamento.
attorney [ə'tɜːnɪ] n (lawyer) avvocato; (having proxy) mandatario; A~ General n (Brit) Procuratore m Generale; (US) Ministro della Giustizia; power of ~ n procura.
attract [ə'trækt] vt attirare; ~ion [ə'trækʃən] n (gen pl: pleasant things) attrattiva; (PHYSICS, fig: towards sth) attrazione f; ~ive a attraente.
attribute n ['ætrɪbjuːt] attributo // vt [ə'trɪbjuːt]: to ~ sth to attribuire qc a.
attrition [ə'trɪʃən] n: war of ~ guerra di logoramento.
aubergine ['əubəʒiːn] n melanzana.
auburn ['ɔːbən] a tizianesco(a).
auction ['ɔːkʃən] n (also: sale by ~) asta // vt (also: to sell by ~) vendere all'asta; (also: to put up for ~) mettere all'asta; ~eer [-'nɪə*] n banditore m.
audacity [ɔː'dæsɪtɪ] n audacia.

audible ['ɔːdɪbl] a udibile.
audience ['ɔːdɪəns] n (people) pubblico; spettatori mpl; ascoltatori mpl; (interview) udienza.
audio-visual [ɔːdɪəu'vɪzjuəl] a audiovisivo(a).
audit ['ɔːdɪt] n revisione f, verifica // vt rivedere, verificare.
audition [ɔː'dɪʃən] n audizione f.
auditor ['ɔːdɪtə*] n revisore m.
auditorium [ɔːdɪ'tɔːrɪəm] n sala, auditorio.
augment [ɔːg'ment] vt,vi aumentare.
augur ['ɔːgə*] vt (be a sign of) predire // vi: it ~s well promette bene.
August ['ɔːgəst] n agosto.
august [ɔː'gʌst] a augusto(a).
aunt [ɑːnt] n zia; ~ie, ~y n zietta.
au pair ['əu'peə*] n (also: ~ girl) (ragazza f) alla pari inv.
aura ['ɔːrə] n aura.
auspices ['ɔːspɪsɪz] npl: under the ~ of sotto gli auspici di.
auspicious [ɔːs'pɪʃəs] a propizio(a).
austere [ɒs'tɪə*] a austero(a).
Australia [ɒs'treɪlɪə] n Australia; ~n a, n australiano(a).
Austria ['ɒstrɪə] n Austria; ~n a, n austriaco(a).
authentic [ɔː'θentɪk] a autentico(a).
author ['ɔːθə*] n autore/trice.
authoritarian [ɔːθɒrɪ'teərɪən] a autoritario(a).
authoritative [ɔː'θɒrɪtətɪv] a (account etc) autorevole; (manner) autoritario(a).
authority [ɔː'θɒrɪtɪ] n autorità f inv; (permission) autorizzazione f; the authorities npl le autorità.
authorize ['ɔːθəraɪz] vt autorizzare.
auto ['ɔːtəu] n (US) auto f inv.
autobiography [ɔːtəbaɪ'ɒgrəfɪ] n autobiografia.
autocratic [ɔːtə'krætɪk] a autocratico(a).
autograph ['ɔːtəgrɑːf] n autografo // vt firmare.
automatic [ɔːtə'mætɪk] a automatico(a) // n (gun) arma automatica; (car) automobile f con cambio automatico; ~ally ad automaticamente.
automation [ɔːtə'meɪʃən] n automazione f.
automaton, pl **automata** [ɔː'tɒmətən, -tə] n automa m.
automobile [ˈɔːtəməbiːl] n (US) automobile f.
autonomy [ɔː'tɒnəmɪ] n autonomia.
autopsy ['ɔːtɒpsɪ] n autopsia.
autumn ['ɔːtəm] n autunno.
auxiliary [ɔːg'zɪlɪərɪ] a ausiliario(a) // n ausiliare m/f.
avail [ə'veɪl] vt: to ~ o.s. of servirsi di; approfittarsi di // n: to no ~ inutilmente.
availability [əveɪlə'bɪlɪtɪ] n disponibilità.
available [ə'veɪləbl] a disponibile; every ~ means tutti i mezzi disponibili.
avalanche ['ævəlɑːnʃ] n valanga.
avant-garde ['ævãŋ'gɑːd] a d'avanguardia.
avarice ['ævərɪs] n avarizia.

Ave. *abbr of* **avenue**.
avenge [ə'vɛndʒ] *vt* vendicare.
avenue ['ævənjuː] *n* viale *m*.
average ['ævərɪdʒ] *n* media *f // a* medio(a) // *vt (a certain figure)* fare di *or* in media; **on ~** in media; **above/below (the) ~** sopra/sotto la media.
averse [ə'vɜːs] *a*: **to be ~ to sth/doing** essere avverso(a) a qc/a fare.
aversion [ə'vɜːʃən] *n* avversione *f.*
avert [ə'vɜːt] *vt* evitare, prevenire; *(one's eyes)* distogliere.
aviation [eɪvɪ'eɪʃən] *n* aviazione *f.*
avid ['ævɪd] *a* avido(a).
avocado [ævə'kɑːdəu] *n (also:* **~ pear)** avocado *m inv.*
avoid [ə'vɔɪd] *vt* evitare; **~able** *a* evitabile; **~ance** *n* l'evitare *m.*
await [ə'weɪt] *vt* aspettare; **~ing attention** *(COMM: letter)* in attesa di risposta; *(: order)* in attesa di essere evaso.
awake [ə'weɪk] *a* sveglio(a) // *vb (pt* **awoke** [ə'wəuk], *pp* **awoken** [ə'wəukən] *or* **awaked)** *vt* svegliare // *vi* svegliarsi; **~ to** consapevole di; **~ning** [ə'weɪknɪŋ] *n* risveglio.
award [ə'wɔːd] *n* premio; *(LAW)* decreto // *vt* assegnare; *(LAW: damages)* decretare.
aware [ə'wɛə*] *a*: **~ of** *(conscious)* conscio(a) di; *(informed)* informato(a) di; **to become ~ of** accorgersi di; **politically/socially ~** politicamente/socialmente preparato; **~ness** *n* consapevolezza.
awash [ə'wɒʃ] *a*: **~ (with)** inondato(a) (da).
away [ə'weɪ] *a,ad* via; lontano(a); **two kilometres ~** a due chilometri di distanza; **two hours ~ by car** a due ore di distanza in macchina; **the holiday was two weeks ~** ci mancavano due settimane alle vacanze; **~ from** lontano da; **he's ~ for a week** è andato via per una settimana; **he was working/pedalling** *etc* **~** *la particella indica la continuità e l'energia dell'azione:* lui lavorava/pedalava *etc* più che poteva; **to fade/wither** *etc* **~** *la particella rinforza l'idea della diminuzione;* **~ match** *n (SPORT)* partita fuori casa.
awe [ɔː] *n* timore *m;* **~-inspiring, ~some** *a* imponente.
awful ['ɔːfəl] *a* terribile; **~ly** *ad (very)* terribilmente.
awhile [ə'waɪl] *ad* (per) un po'.
awkward ['ɔːkwəd] *a (clumsy)* goffo(a); *(inconvenient)* scomodo(a); *(embarrassing)* imbarazzante.
awning ['ɔːnɪŋ] *n (of tent)* veranda; *(of shop, hotel etc)* tenda.
awoke, awoken [ə'wəuk, -kən] *pt,pp of* **awake**.
awry [ə'raɪ] *ad* di traverso // *a* storto(a); **to go ~** andare a monte.
axe [æks] *n* scure *f // vt (project etc)* abolire; *(jobs)* sopprimere.
axiom ['æksɪəm] *n* assioma *m.*
axis, *pl* **axes** ['æksɪs, -siːz] *n* asse *m.*

axle ['æksl] *n (also:* **~-tree)** asse *m.*
ay(e) [aɪ] *excl (yes)* sì.

B

B [biː] *n (MUS)* si *m.*
B.A. *abbr see* **bachelor**.
babble ['bæbl] *vi* cianciare; mormorare // *n* ciance *fpl;* mormorio.
baby ['beɪbɪ] *n* bambino/a; **~ carriage** *n (US)* carrozzina; **~hood** *n* prima infanzia; **~ish** *a* infantile; **~-sit** *vi* fare il *(or* la) babysitter.
bachelor ['bætʃələ*] *n* scapolo; **B~ of Arts/Science (B.A./B.Sc.)** ≈ laureato/a in lettere/scienze; **~hood** *n* celibato.
back [bæk] *n (of person, horse)* dorso, schiena; *(of hand)* dorso; *(of house, car)* didietro; *(of train)* coda; *(of chair)* schienale *m; (of page)* rovescio; *(FOOTBALL)* difensore *m // vt (candidate: also:* **~ up)** appoggiare; *(horse: at races)* puntare su; *(car)* guidare a marcia indietro // *vi* indietreggiare; *(car etc)* fare marcia indietro // *a (in compounds)* posteriore, di dietro; arretrato(a); **~ seats/wheels** *(AUT)* sedili *mpl/*ruote *fpl* posteriori; **~ payments/rent** arretrati *mpl // ad (not forward)* indietro; *(returned):* **he's ~** lui è tornato; **he ran ~** tornò indietro di corsa; *(restitution):* **throw the ball ~** ritira la palla; **can I have it ~?** posso riaverlo?; *(again):* **he called ~** ha richiamato; **to ~ down** *vi* fare marcia indietro; **to ~ out** *vi (of promise)* tirarsi indietro; **~ache** *n* mal *m* di schiena; **~bencher** *n* membro del Parlamento senza potere amministrativo; **~biting** *n* maldicenza; **~bone** *n* spina dorsale; **~-cloth** *n* scena di sfondo; **~date** *vt (letter)* retrodatare; **~dated pay rise** aumento retroattivo; **~er** *n* sostenitore/trice; *(COMM)* fautore *m;* **~fire** *vi (AUT)* far ritorno di fiamma; *(plans)* fallire; **~gammon** *n* tavola reale; **~ground** *n* sfondo; *(of events)* background *m inv; (basic knowledge)* base *f; (experience)* esperienza; **family ~ground** ambiente *m* familiare; **~ground noise** *n* rumore *m* di fondo; **~hand** *n (TENNIS: also:* **~hand stroke)** rovescio; **~handed** *a (fig)* ambiguo(a); **~hander** *n (bribe)* bustarella; **~ing** *n (fig)* appoggio; **~lash** *n* contraccolpo, ripercussione *f;* **~log** *n:* **~log of work** lavoro arretrato; **~ number** *n (of magazine etc)* numero arretrato; **~ pay** *n* arretrato di paga; **~side** *n (col)* sedere *m;* **~stroke** *n* nuoto sul dorso; **~ward** *a (movement)* indietro *inv; (person)* tardivo(a); *(country)* arretrato(a); **~ward and forward movement** movimento avanti e indietro; **~wards** *ad* indietro; *(fall, walk)* all'indietro; **~water** *n (fig)* posto morto; **~yard** *n* cortile *m* dietro la casa.
bacon ['beɪkən] *n* pancetta.
bacteria [bæk'tɪərɪə] *npl* batteri *mpl.*

bad [bæd] *a* cattivo(a); (*child*) cattivello(a); (*meat, food*) andato(a) a male; **his ~ leg** la sua gamba malata.

bade [bæd] *pt of* **bid.**

badge [bædʒ] *n* insegna; (*of policemen*) stemma *m.*

badger ['bædʒə*] *n* tasso // *vt* tormentare.

badly ['bædli] *ad* (*work, dress etc*) male; **~ wounded** gravemente ferito; **he needs it ~** ne ha gran bisogno; **~ off** a povero(a).

badminton ['bædmɪntən] *n* badminton *m.*

bad-tempered ['bæd'tɛmpəd] *a* irritabile; di malumore.

baffle ['bæfl] *vt* (*puzzle*) confondere.

bag [bæg] *n* sacco; (*handbag etc*) borsa; (*of hunter*) carniere *m*; bottino // *vt* (*col: take*) mettersi in tasca; prendersi; **~s under the eyes** borse sotto gli occhi.

baggage ['bægɪdʒ] *n* bagagli *mpl.*

baggy ['bægɪ] *a* largo(a) largo(a).

bagpipes ['bægpaɪps] *npl* cornamusa.

Bahamas [bə'hɑːməz] *npl:* **the ~** le isole Bahama.

bail [beɪl] *n* cauzione *f* // *vt* (*prisoner: gen:* **to grant ~ to**) concedere la libertà provvisoria su cauzione a; (*boat: also:* **~ out**) aggottare; *see* **bale**; **to ~ out** *vt* (*prisoner*) ottenere la libertà provvisoria su cauzione di.

bailiff ['beɪlɪf] *n* usciere *m*; fattore *m.*

bait [beɪt] *n* esca.

bake [beɪk] *vt* cuocere al forno // *vi* cuocersi al forno; **~d beans** *npl* fagioli *mpl* all'uccelletto; **~r** *n* fornaio/a; panettiere/a; **~ry** *n* panetteria; **baking powder** *n* lievito in polvere.

balaclava [bælə'klɑːvə] *n* (*also: ~ helmet*) passamontagna *m inv.*

balance ['bæləns] *n* equilibrio; (*COMM: sum*) bilancio; (*scales*) bilancia // *vt* tenere in equilibrio; (*pros and cons*) soppesare; (*budget*) far quadrare; (*account*) pareggiare; (*compensate*) contrappesare; **~ of trade/payments** bilancia commerciale/dei pagamenti; **~d** *a* (*personality, diet*) equilibrato(a); **~ sheet** *n* bilancio.

balcony ['bælkənɪ] *n* balcone *m.*

bald [bɔːld] *a* calvo(a); **~ness** *n* calvizie *f.*

bale [beɪl] *n* balla; **to ~ out** *vi* (*of a plane*) gettarsi col paracadute.

baleful ['beɪlful] *a* funesto(a).

balk [bɔːk] *vi:* **to ~ (at)** tirarsi indietro (davanti a); (*horse*) recalcitrare (davanti a).

ball [bɔːl] *n* palla; (*football*) pallone *m*; (*for golf*) pallina; (*dance*) ballo.

ballad ['bæləd] *n* ballata.

ballast ['bæləst] *n* zavorra.

ballerina [bælə'riːnə] *n* ballerina.

ballet ['bæleɪ] *n* balletto.

ballistics [bə'lɪstɪks] *n* balistica.

balloon [bə'luːn] *n* pallone *m.*

ballot ['bælət] *n* scrutinio; **~ box** *n* urna (per le schede); **~ paper** *n* scheda.

ball-point pen ['bɔːlpɔɪnt'pɛn] *n* penna a sfera.

ballroom ['bɔːlrum] *n* sala da ballo.

balsam ['bɔːlsəm] *n* balsamo.

Baltic [bɔːltɪk] *a,n:* **the ~ (Sea)** il (mare) Baltico.

bamboo [bæm'buː] *n* bambù *m.*

bamboozle [bæm'buːzl] *vt* (*col*) corbellare.

ban [bæn] *n* interdizione *f* // *vt* interdire.

banal [bə'nɑːl] *a* banale.

banana [bə'nɑːnə] *n* banana.

band [bænd] *n* banda; (*at a dance*) orchestra; (*MIL*) fanfara; **to ~ together** *vi* collegarsi.

bandage ['bændɪdʒ] *n* benda.

bandit ['bændɪt] *n* bandito.

bandwagon ['bændwægən] *n:* **to jump on the ~** (*fig*) seguire la corrente.

bandy ['bændɪ] *vt* (*jokes, insults*) scambiare; **to ~ about** *vt* far circolare.

bandy-legged ['bændɪ'lɛgɪd] *a* dalle gambe storte.

bang [bæŋ] *n* botta; (*of door*) lo sbattere; (*blow*) colpo // *vt* battere (violentemente); (*door*) sbattere // *vi* scoppiare; sbattere; **to ~ at the door** picchiare alla porta.

bangle ['bæŋgl] *n* braccialetto.

banish ['bænɪʃ] *vt* bandire.

banister(s) ['bænɪstə(z)] *n(pl)* ringhiera.

banjo, ~es *or* **~s** ['bændʒəu] *n* banjo *m inv.*

bank [bæŋk] *n* (*for money*) banca, banco; (*of river, lake*) riva, sponda; (*of earth*) banco // *vi* (*AVIAT*) inclinarsi in virata; (*COMM*): **they ~ with Pitt's** sono clienti di Pitt's; **to ~ on** *vt fus* contare su; **~ account** *n* conto di banca; **~er** *n* banchiere *m*; **B~ holiday** *n* giorno di festa (*in cui le banche sono chiuse*); **~ing** *n* attività bancaria; professione *f* di banchiere; **~ing hours** *npl* orario di sportello; **~note** *n* banconota; **~ rate** *n* tasso bancario.

bankrupt ['bæŋkrʌpt] *a, n* fallito(a); **to go ~** fallire; **~cy** *n* fallimento.

banner ['bænə*] *n* bandiera.

bannister(s) ['bænɪstə(z)] *n(pl)* = **banister(s).**

banns [bænz] *npl* pubblicazioni *fpl* di matrimonio.

banquet ['bæŋkwɪt] *n* banchetto.

banter ['bæntə*] *n* scherzi *mpl* bonari.

baptism ['bæptɪzəm] *n* battesimo.

baptize [bæp'taɪz] *vt* battezzare.

bar [bɑː*] *n* barra; (*of window etc*) sbarra; (*of chocolate*) tavoletta; (*fig*) ostacolo; restrizione *f*; (*pub*) bar *m inv*; (*counter: in pub*) banco; (*MUS*) battuta // *vt* (*road, window*) sbarrare; (*person*) escludere; (*activity*) interdire; **~ of soap** saponetta; **the B~** (*LAW*) l'Ordine *m* degli avvocati; **~ none** senza eccezione.

barbaric [bɑː'bærɪk] *a* barbarico(a).

barbecue ['bɑːbɪkjuː] *n* barbecue *m inv.*

barbed wire ['bɑːbd'waɪə*] *n* filo spinato.

barber ['bɑːbə*] *n* barbiere *m.*

barbiturate [bɑː'bɪtjurɪt] *n* barbiturico.

bare [bɛə*] *a* nudo(a) // *vt* scoprire,

denudare; (*teeth*) mostrare; **the ~ essentials** lo stretto necessario; **~back** ad senza sella; **~faced** a sfacciato(a); **~foot** a,ad scalzo(a); **~headed** a,ad a capo scoperto; **~ly** ad appena.

bargain ['bɑ:gin] n (*transaction*) contratto; (*good buy*) affare m // vi trattare; **into the ~** per giunta.

barge [bɑ:dʒ] n chiatta; **to ~ in** vi (*walk in*) piombare dentro; (*interrupt talk*) intromettersi a sproposito; **to ~ into** vt fus urtare contro.

baritone ['bærɪtəun] n baritono.

bark [bɑ:k] n (*of tree*) corteccia; (*of dog*) abbaio // vi abbaiare.

barley ['bɑ:lɪ] n orzo.

barmaid ['bɑ:meɪd] n cameriera al banco.

barman ['bɑ:mən] n barista m.

barmy ['bɑ:mɪ] a (col) tocco(a).

barn [bɑ:n] n granaio.

barnacle ['bɑ:nəkl] n cirripede m.

barometer [bə'rɔmɪtə*] n barometro.

baron ['bærən] n barone m; **~ess** n baronessa.

barracks ['bæroks] npl caserma.

barrage ['bærɑ:ʒ] n (MIL) sbarramento.

barrel ['bærəl] n barile m; (*of gun*) canna; **~ organ** n organetto a cilindro.

barren ['bærən] a sterile; (*hills*) arido(a).

barricade [bærɪ'keɪd] n barricata // vt barricare.

barrier ['bærɪə*] n barriera.

barring ['bɑ:rɪŋ] prep salvo.

barrister ['bærɪstə*] n avvocato/essa (*in diritto di parlare davanti a tutte le corti*).

barrow ['bærəu] n (*cart*) carriola.

bartender ['bɑ:tɛndə*] n (US) barista m.

barter ['bɑ:tə*] n baratto // vt: **to ~ sth for** barattare qc con.

base [beɪs] n base f // vt: **to ~ sth on** basare qc su // a vile; **coffee-~d** a base di caffè; **a Paris-~d firm** una ditta con sede centrale a Parigi; **~ball** n baseball m; **~ment** n seminterrato; (*of shop*) interrato.

bases ['beɪsi:z] npl of **basis**; ['beɪsɪz] npl of **base**.

bash [bæʃ] vt (col) picchiare; **~ed in** a sfondato(a).

bashful ['bæʃful] a timido(a).

basic ['beɪsɪk] a rudimentale; essenziale; **~ally** [-lɪ] ad fondamentalmente; sostanzialmente.

basil ['bæzl] n basilico.

basin ['beɪsn] n (*vessel, also* GEO) bacino; (*also*: **wash~**) lavabo.

basis, pl bases ['beɪsɪs, -si:z] n base f.

bask [bɑ:sk] vi: **to ~ in the sun** crogiolarsi al sole.

basket ['bɑ:skɪt] n cesta; (*smaller*) cestino; (*with handle*) paniere m; **~ball** n pallacanestro f.

bass [beɪs] n (MUS) basso; **~ clef** n chiave f di basso.

bassoon [bə'su:n] n fagotto.

bastard ['bɑ:stəd] n bastardo/a; (col!) stronzo (!).

baste [beɪst] vt (CULIN) ungere con grasso; (SEWING) imbastire.

bat [bæt] n pipistrello; (*for baseball etc*) mazza; (*for table tennis*) racchetta; **off one's own ~** di propria iniziativa; **he didn't ~ an eyelid** non battè ciglio.

batch [bætʃ] n (*of bread*) infornata; (*of papers*) cumulo.

bated ['beɪtɪd] a: **with ~ breath** col fiato sospeso.

bath [bɑ:θ, pl bɑ:ðz] n (*see also* **baths**) bagno; (*bathtub*) vasca da bagno // vt far fare il bagno a; **to have a ~** fare un bagno; **~chair** n poltrona a rotelle.

bathe [beɪð] vi fare il bagno // vt bagnare; **~r** n bagnante m/f.

bathing ['beɪðɪŋ] n bagni mpl; **~ cap** n cuffia da bagno; **~ costume** n costume m da bagno.

bath: ~room n stanza da bagno; **~s** npl bagni mpl pubblici; **~ towel** n asciugamano da bagno.

batman ['bætmən] n (MIL) attendente m.

baton ['bætən] n bastone m; (MUS) bacchetta.

battalion [bə'tælɪən] n battaglione m.

batter ['bætə*] vt battere // n pastetta; **~ed** a (*hat*) sformato(a); (*pan*) ammaccato(a); **~ed wife/baby** consorte f/bambino(a) maltrattato(a); **~ing ram** n ariete m.

battery ['bætərɪ] n batteria; (*of torch*) pila.

battle ['bætl] n battaglia // vi battagliare, lottare; **~field** n campo di battaglia; **~ments** npl bastioni mpl; **~ship** n nave f da guerra.

baulk [bɔ:lk] vi = **balk**.

bawdy ['bɔ:dɪ] a piccante.

bawl [bɔ:l] vi urlare.

bay [beɪ] n (*of sea*) baia; **to hold sb at ~** tenere qd a bada.

bayonet ['beɪənɪt] n baionetta.

bay window ['beɪ'wɪndəu] n bovindo.

bazaar [bə'zɑ:*] n bazar m inv; vendita di beneficenza.

b. & b., B. & B. abbr see **bed.**

BBC n abbr of British Broadcasting Corporation.

B.C. ad (abbr of before Christ) a.C.

be, pt **was, were,** pp **been** [bi:, wɔz, wɔ:*, bi:n] vi essere; **how are you?** come sta?; **I am warm** ho caldo; **it is cold** fa freddo; **how much is it?** quanto costa?; **he is four (years old)** ha quattro anni; **2 and 2 are 4** 2 più 2 fa 4; **where have you been?** dov'è stato?; dov'è andato?

beach [bi:tʃ] n spiaggia // vt tirare in secco; **~wear** n articoli mpl da spiaggia.

beacon ['bi:kən] n (*lighthouse*) faro; (*marker*) segnale m.

bead [bi:d] n perlina.

beak [bi:k] n becco.

beaker ['bi:kə*] n coppa.

beam [bi:m] n trave f; (*of light*) raggio // vi brillare; **~ing** a (*sun, smile*) raggiante.

bean [bi:n] n fagiolo; (*of coffee*) chicco.

bear [bɛə*] n orso // vb (pt **bore**, pp **borne**

[bɔː*, bɔːn]) vt portare; (endure) sopportare // vi: to ~ right/left piegare a destra/sinistra; to ~ the responsibility of assumersi la responsabilità di; ~able a sopportabile.

beard [biːd] n barba; ~ed a barbuto(a).

bearer ['beərə*] n portatore m.

bearing ['beəriŋ] n portamento; (behaviour) condotta; (connection) rapporto; (ball) ~s npl cuscinetti mpl a sfere; to take a ~ fare un rilevamento; to find one's ~s orientarsi.

beast [biːst] n bestia; ~ly a meschino(a); (weather) da cani.

beat [biːt] n battimento; (of policeman) giro // vt (pt beat, pp beaten) battere ~ off the ~en track fuori mano; to ~ about the bush menare il can per l'aia; to ~ time battere il tempo; to ~ off vt respingere; to ~ up vt (col: person) picchiare; (eggs) sbattere; ~er n (for eggs, cream) frullino; ~ing n bastonata.

beautician [bjuː'tiʃən] n estetista m/f.

beautiful ['bjuːtiful] a bello(a); ~ly ad splendidamente.

beauty ['bjuːti] n bellezza; ~ salon o istituto di bellezza; ~ spot n neo; (TOURISM) luogo pittoresco.

beaver ['biːvə*] n castoro.

becalmed [bi'kɑːmd] a in bonaccia.

became [bi'keim] pt of **become**.

because [bi'kɔz] cj perché; ~ of prep a causa di.

beckon ['bekən] vt (also: ~ to) chiamare con un cenno.

become [bi'kʌm] vt (irg: like **come**) diventare; to ~ fat/thin ingrassare/dimagrire; what has ~ of him? che gli è successo?

becoming [bi'kʌmiŋ] a (behaviour) che si conviene; (clothes) grazioso(a).

bed [bed] n letto; (of flowers) aiuola; (of coal, clay) strato; ~ and breakfast (b. & b.) n (terms) camera con colazione; ~clothes npl biancheria e coperte fpl da letto.

bedlam ['bedləm] n manicomio (fig).

bedraggled [bi'drægld] a fradicio(a).

bed: ~ridden a costretto(a) a letto; ~room n camera da letto; ~side n: at sb's ~side al capezzale di qd; ~sit(ter) n monolocale m; ~spread n copriletto.

bee [biː] n ape f.

beech [biːtʃ] n faggio.

beef [biːf] n manzo.

beehive ['biːhaiv] n alveare m.

beeline ['biːlain] n: to make a ~ for buttarsi a capo fitto verso.

been [biːn] pp of **be**.

beer [biə*] n birra.

beetle ['biːtl] n scarafaggio; coleottero.

beetroot ['biːtruːt] n barbabietola.

befall [bi'fɔːl] vi(vt) (irg: like **fall**) accadere (a).

before [bi'fɔː*] prep (in time) prima di; (in space) davanti a // cj prima che + sub; prima di // ad prima; the week ~ la

settimana prima; I've seen it ~ l'ho già visto; I've never seen it ~ è la prima volta che lo vedo; ~hand ad in anticipo.

befriend [bi'frend] vt assistere; mostrarsi amico a.

beg [beg] vi chiedere l'elemosina // vt chiedere in elemosina; (favour) chiedere; (entreat) pregare.

began [bi'gæn] pt of **begin**.

beggar ['begə*] n (also: ~man, ~woman) mendicante m/f.

begin [bi'gin], pt **began**, pp **begun** [bi'gin, -'gæn, -'gʌn] vt, vi cominciare; ~ner n principiante m/f; ~ning n inizio, principio.

begrudge [bi'grʌdʒ] vt: to ~ sb sth dare qc a qd a malincuore; invidiare qd per qc.

begun [bi'gʌn] pp of **begin**.

behalf [bi'hɑːf] n: on ~ of per conto di; a nome di.

behave [bi'heiv] vi comportarsi; (well: also: ~ o.s.) comportarsi bene.

behaviour [bi'heivjə*] n comportamento, condotta.

beheld [bi'held] pt,pp of **behold**.

behind [bi'haind] prep dietro; (followed by pronoun) dietro di; (time) in ritardo con // ad dietro; in ritardo // n didietro.

behold [bi'həuld] vt (irg: like **hold**) vedere, scorgere.

beige [beiʒ] a beige inv.

being ['biːiŋ] n essere m; to come into ~ cominciare ad esistere.

belated [bi'leitid] a tardo(a).

belch [beltʃ] vi ruttare // vt (gen: ~ out: smoke etc) eruttare.

belfry ['belfri] n campanile m.

Belgian ['beldʒən] a,n belga (m/f).

Belgium ['beldʒəm] n Belgio.

belie [bi'lai] vt smentire.

belief [bi'liːf] n (opinion) opinione f, convinzione f; (trust, faith) fede f; (acceptance as true) credenza.

believe [bi'liːv] vt,vi credere; ~r n credente m/f.

belittle [bi'litl] vt sminuire.

bell [bel] n campana; (small, on door, electric) campanello.

belligerent [bi'lidʒərənt] a (at war) belligerante; (fig) bellicoso(a).

bellow ['beləu] vi muggire.

bellows ['beləuz] npl soffietto.

belly ['beli] n pancia.

belong [bi'lɔŋ] vi: to ~ to appartenere a; (club etc) essere socio di; this book ~s here questo libro va qui; ~ings npl cose fpl, roba.

beloved [bi'lʌvid] a adorato(a).

below [bi'ləu] prep sotto, al di sotto di // ad sotto, di sotto; giù; see ~ vedi sotto oltre.

belt [belt] n cintura; (TECH) cinghia // vt (thrash) picchiare // vi (col) filarsela.

bench [bentʃ] n panca; (in workshop) banco; the B~ (LAW) la Corte.

bend [bend] vb (pt,pp **bent** [bent]) vt curvare; (leg, arm) piegare // vi curvarsi;

piegarsi // *n* (*in road*) curva; (*in pipe, river*) gomito; **to ~ down** *vi* chinarsi; **to ~ over** *vi* piegarsi.

beneath [bɪ'niːθ] *prep* sotto, al di sotto di; (*unworthy of*) indegno(a) di // *ad* sotto, di sotto.

benefactor ['bɛnɪfæktə*] *n* benefattore *m*.

beneficial [bɛnɪ'fɪʃəl] *a* che fa bene; vantaggioso(a).

benefit ['bɛnɪfɪt] *n* beneficio, vantaggio; (*allowance of money*) indennità *f inv* // *vt* far bene a // *vi*: **he'll ~ from it** ne trarrà beneficio *or* profitto.

Benelux ['bɛnɪlʌks] *n* Benelux *m*.

benevolent [bɪ'nɛvələnt] *a* benevolo(a).

bent [bɛnt] *pt,pp of* **bend** // *n* inclinazione *f* // *a* (*col: dishonest*) losco(a); **to be ~ on** essere deciso(a) a.

bequeath [bɪ'kwiːð] *vt* lasciare in eredità.

bequest [bɪ'kwɛst] *n* lascito.

bereavement [bɪ'riːvmənt] *n* lutto.

beret ['bɛreɪ] *n* berretto.

Bermuda [bəː'mjuːdə] *n* le Bermude.

berry ['bɛrɪ] *n* bacca.

berserk [bə'səːk] *a*: **to go ~** montare su tutte le furie.

berth [bəːθ] *n* (*bed*) cuccetta; (*for ship*) ormeggio // *vi* (*in harbour*) entrare in porto; (*at anchor*) gettare l'ancora.

beseech, *pt,pp* **besought** [bɪ'siːtʃ, -'sɔːt] *vt* implorare.

beset, *pt,pp* **beset** [bɪ'sɛt] *vt* assalire.

beside [bɪ'saɪd] *prep* accanto a; **to be ~ o.s.** (**with anger**) essere fuori di sé.

besides [bɪ'saɪdz] *ad* inoltre, per di più // *prep* oltre a; a parte.

besiege [bɪ'siːdʒ] *vt* (*town*) assediare; (*fig*) tempestare.

besought [bɪ'sɔːt] *pt,pp of* **beseech**.

best [bɛst] *a* migliore // *ad* meglio; **the ~ part of** (*quantity*) la maggior parte di; **at ~** tutt'al più; **to make the ~ of sth** cavare il meglio possibile da qc; **to the ~ of my knowledge** per quel che ne so; **to the ~ of my ability** al massimo delle mie capacità; **~ man** *n* testimone *m* dello sposo.

bestow [bɪ'stəʊ] *vt* accordare; (*title*) conferire.

bestseller ['bɛst'sɛlə*] *n* bestseller *m inv*.

bet [bɛt] *n* scommessa // *vt,vi* (*pt,pp* **bet** *or* **betted**) scommettere.

betray [bɪ'treɪ] *vt* tradire; **~al** *n* tradimento.

better ['bɛtə*] *a* migliore // *ad* meglio // *vt* migliorare // *n*: **to get the ~ of** avere la meglio su; **you had ~ do it** è meglio che lo faccia; **he thought ~ of it** cambiò idea; **to get ~** migliorare; **~ off** *a* più ricco(a); (*fig*): **you'd be ~ off this way** starebbe meglio così.

betting ['bɛtɪŋ] *n* scommesse *fpl*; **~ shop** *n* ufficio del'allibratore.

between [bɪ'twiːn] *prep* tra // *ad* in mezzo, nel mezzo.

beverage ['bɛvərɪdʒ] *n* bevanda.

beware [bɪ'wɛə*] *vt,vi*: **to ~ (of)** stare attento(a) (a).

bewildered [bɪ'wɪldəd] *a* sconcertato(a), confuso(a).

bewitching [bɪ'wɪtʃɪŋ] *a* affascinante.

beyond [bɪ'jɔnd] *prep* (*in space*) oltre; (*exceeding*) al di sopra di // *ad* di là; **~ doubt** senza dubbio; **~ repair** irreparabile.

bias ['baɪəs] *n* (*prejudice*) pregiudizio; (*preference*) preferenza; **~(s)ed** *a* parziale.

bib [bɪb] *n* bavaglino.

Bible ['baɪbl] *n* Bibbia.

bicker ['bɪkə*] *vi* bisticciare.

bicycle ['baɪsɪkl] *n* bicicletta.

bid [bɪd] *n* offerta; (*attempt*) tentativo // *vb* (*pt* **bade** [bæd] *or* **bid**, *pp* **bidden** [bɪdn] *or* **bid**) *vi* fare un'offerta // *vt* fare un'offerta di; **to ~ sb good day** dire buon giorno a qd; **~der** *n*: **the highest ~der** il maggior offerente; **~ding** *n* offerte *fpl*.

bide [baɪd] *vt*: **to ~ one's time** aspettare il momento giusto.

bier [bɪə*] *n* bara.

big [bɪg] *a* grande; grosso(a).

bigamy ['bɪgəmɪ] *n* bigamia.

bigheaded ['bɪg'hɛdɪd] *a* presuntuoso(a).

bigot ['bɪgət] *n* persona gretta; **~ed** *a* gretto(a); **~ry** *n* grettezza.

bigwig ['bɪgwɪg] *n* (*col*) pezzo grosso.

bike [baɪk] *n* bici *f inv*.

bikini [bɪ'kiːnɪ] *n* bikini *m inv*.

bile [baɪl] *n* bile *f*.

bilingual [baɪ'lɪŋgwəl] *a* bilingue.

bilious ['bɪlɪəs] *a* biliare; (*fig*) bilioso(a).

bill [bɪl] *n* conto; (*POL*) atto; (*US: banknote*) banconota; (*of bird*) becco; **to fit** *or* **fill the ~** (*fig*) fare al caso.

billet ['bɪlɪt] *n* alloggio.

billfold ['bɪlfəʊld] *n* (*US*) portafoglio.

billiards ['bɪlɪədz] *n* biliardo.

billion ['bɪlɪən] *n* (*Brit*) bilione *m*; (*US*) miliardo.

bin [bɪn] *n* bidone *m*; **bread~** *n* cassetta *f* portapane *inv*.

bind, *pt,pp* **bound** [baɪnd, baʊnd] *vt* legare; (*oblige*) obbligare; **~ing** *n* (*of book*) legatura // *a* (*contract*) vincolante.

bingo ['bɪŋgəʊ] *n* gioco simile alla tombola.

binoculars [bɪ'nɔkjʊləz] *npl* binocolo.

bio... [baɪə'...] *prefix*: **~chemistry** *n* biochimica; **~graphy** [baɪ'ɔgrəfɪ] *n* biografia; **~logical** *a* biologico(a); **~logist** [baɪ'ɔlədʒɪst] *n* biologo/a; **~logy** [baɪ'ɔlədʒɪ] *n* biologia.

birch [bəːtʃ] *n* betulla.

bird [bəːd] *n* uccello; (*col: girl*) bambola; **~ watcher** *n* ornitologo/a dilettante.

birth [bəːθ] *n* nascita; **~ certificate** *n* certificato di nascita; **~ control** *n* controllo delle nascite; contraccezione *f*; **~day** *n* compleanno; **~place** *n* luogo di nascita; **~ rate** *n* indice *m* di natalità.

biscuit ['bɪskɪt] *n* biscotto.

bishop ['bɪʃəp] *n* vescovo.

bit [bɪt] *pt of* **bite** // *n* pezzo; (*of tool*) punta;

(*of horse*) morso; **a ~ of** un po' di; **a ~ mad/dangerous** un po' matto/pericoloso.

bitch [bɪtʃ] *n* (*dog*) cagna; (*col!*) vacca.

bite [baɪt] *vt,vi* (*pt bit* [bɪt], *pp bitten* [ˈbɪtn]) mordere // *n* morso; (*insect ~*) puntura; (*mouthful*) boccone *m*; **let's have a ~ (to eat)** mangiamo un boccone; **to ~ one's nails** mangiarsi le unghie.

biting [ˈbaɪtɪŋ] *a* pungente.

bitten [ˈbɪtn] *pp of* **bite**.

bitter [ˈbɪtə*] *a* amaro(a); (*wind, criticism*) pungente // *n* (*beer*) birra amara; **to the ~ end** a oltranza; **~ness** *n* amarezza; gusto amaro; **~sweet** *a* agrodolce.

bivouac [ˈbɪvuæk] *n* bivacco.

bizarre [bɪˈzɑː*] *a* bizzarro(a).

blab [blæb] *vi* parlare troppo.

black [blæk] *a* nero(a) // *n* nero // *vt* (*INDUSTRY*) boicottare; **to give sb a ~ eye** dare un occhio nero a qd; **~ and blue** a tutto(a) pesto(a); **~berry** *n* mora; **~bird** *n* merlo; **~board** *n* lavagna; **~currant** *n* ribes *m inv*; **~en** *vt* annerire; **~leg** *n* crumiro; **~list** *n* lista nera; **~mail** *n* ricatto // *vt* ricattare; **~mailer** *n* ricattatore/trice; **~market** *n* mercato nero; **~out** *n* oscuramento; (*fainting*) svenimento; **the B~ Sea** il Mar Nero; **~ sheep** *n* pecora nera; **~smith** *n* fabbro ferraio.

bladder [ˈblædə*] *n* vescica.

blade [bleɪd] *n* lama; (*of oar*) pala; **~ of grass** filo d'erba.

blame [bleɪm] *n* colpa // *vt*: **to ~ sb/sth for sth** dare la colpa di qc a qd/qc; **who's to ~?** chi è colpevole?; **~less** *a* irreprensibile.

bland [blænd] *a* mite; (*taste*) blando(a).

blank [blæŋk] *a* bianco(a); (*look*) distratto(a) // *n* spazio vuoto; (*cartridge*) cartuccia a salve.

blanket [ˈblæŋkɪt] *n* coperta.

blare [blɛə*] *vi* strombettare.

blasé [ˈblɑːzeɪ] *a* blasé *inv*.

blasphemy [ˈblæsfɪmɪ] *n* bestemmia.

blast [blɑːst] *n* raffica di vento; esplosione *f* // *vt* far saltare; **~-off** *n* (*SPACE*) lancio.

blatant [ˈbleɪtənt] *a* flagrante.

blaze [bleɪz] *n* (*fire*) incendio; (*fig*) vampata // *vi* (*fire*) ardere, fiammeggiare; (*fig*) infiammarsi // *vt*: **to ~ a trail** (*fig*) tracciare una via nuova.

blazer [ˈbleɪzə*] *n* blazer *m inv*.

bleach [bliːtʃ] *n* (*also*: **household ~**) varechina // *vt* (*linen*) sbiancare; **~ed** *a* (*hair*) decolorato(a).

bleak [bliːk] *a* tetro(a).

bleary-eyed [ˈblɪərɪˈaɪd] *a* dagli occhi offuscati.

bleat [bliːt] *vi* belare.

bleed, *pt,pp* **bled** [bliːd, blɛd] *vt* dissanguare // *vi* sanguinare; **my nose is ~ing** mi viene fuori sangue dal naso.

blemish [ˈblɛmɪʃ] *n* macchia.

blend [blɛnd] *n* miscela // *vt* mescolare // *vi* (*colours etc*) armonizzare.

bless, *pt,pp* **blessed** *or* **blest** [blɛs, blɛst]

vt benedire; **~ you!** (*sneezing*) salute!; **to be ~ed with** godere di; **~ing** *n* benedizione *f*; fortuna.

blew [bluː] *pt of* **blow**.

blight [blaɪt] *n* (*of plants*) golpe *f* // *vt* (*hopes etc*) deludere.

blimey [ˈblaɪmɪ] *excl* (*col*) accidenti!

blind [blaɪnd] *a* cieco(a) // *n* (*for window*) cortina // *vt* accecare; **to turn a ~ eye (on** *or* **to)** chiudere gli occhi (di fronte a); **~ alley** *n* vicolo cieco; **~ corner** *n* svolta cieca; **~fold** *n* benda // *a,ad* bendato(a) // *vt* bendare gli occhi a; **~ness** *n* cecità; **~ spot** *n* (*AUT etc*) punto cieco; (*fig*) punto debole.

blink [blɪŋk] *vi* battere gli occhi; (*light*) lampeggiare; **~ers** *npl* paraocchi *mpl*.

bliss [blɪs] *n* estasi *f*.

blister [ˈblɪstə*] *n* (*on skin*) vescica; (*on paintwork*) bolla // *vi* (*paint*) coprirsi di bolle.

blithe [blaɪð] *a* gioioso(a), allegro(a).

blitz [blɪts] *n* blitz *m*.

blizzard [ˈblɪzəd] *n* bufera di neve.

bloated [ˈbləutɪd] *a* gonfio(a).

blob [blɔb] *n* (*drop*) goccia; (*stain, spot*) macchia.

block [blɔk] *n* blocco; (*in pipes*) ingombro; (*toy*) cubo; (*of buildings*) isolato // *vt* bloccare; **~ade** [-ˈkeɪd] *n* blocco // *vt* assediare; **~age** *n* ostacolo; **~head** *n* testa di legno; **~ of flats** *n* caseggiato; **in ~ letters** in stampatello.

bloke [bləuk] *n* (*col*) tizio.

blonde [blɔnd] *a,n* biondo(a).

blood [blʌd] *n* sangue *m*; **~ donor** *n* donatore/trice di sangue; **~ group** *n* gruppo sanguigno; **~less** *a* (*coup*) senza sangue; **~ poisoning** *n* setticemia; **~ pressure** *n* pressione *f* sanguigna; **~shed** *n* spargimento di sangue; **~shot** *a*: **~shot eyes** occhi iniettati di sangue; **~stained** *a* macchiato(a) di sangue; **~stream** *n* flusso del sangue; **~thirsty** *a* assetato(a) di sangue; **~ transfusion** *n* trasfusione *f* di sangue; **~y** *a* sanguinoso(a); (*col!*): **this ~y ...** questo maledetto ...; **~y awful/good** (*col!*) veramente terribile/forte; **~y-minded** *a* perverso(a), ostinato(a).

bloom [bluːm] *n* fiore *m* // *vi* essere in fiore; **~ing** *a* (*col*): **this ~ing ...** questo dannato ... .

blossom [ˈblɔsəm] *n* fiore *m*; (*with pl sense*) fiori *mpl* // *vi* essere in fiore.

blot [blɔt] *n* macchia // *vt* macchiare; **to ~ out** *vt* (*memories*) cancellare; (*view*) nascondere; (*nation, city*) annientare.

blotchy [ˈblɔtʃɪ] *a* (*complexion*) coperto(a) di macchie.

blotting paper [ˈblɔtɪŋpeɪpə*] *n* carta assorbente.

blouse [blauz] *n* (*feminine garment*) camicetta.

blow [bləu] *n* colpo // *vb* (*pt* **blew**, *pp* **blown** [bluː, bləun]) *vi* soffiare // *vt* (*fuse*) far saltare; **to ~ one's nose** soffiarsi il naso; **to ~ a whistle** fischiare; **to ~**

away vt portare via; **to ~ down** vt
abbattere; **to ~ off** vt far volare via; **to
~ off course** far uscire di rotta; **to ~
out** vi scoppiare; **to ~ over** vi calmarsi;
to ~ up vi saltare in aria // vt far saltare
in aria; (tyre) gonfiare; (PHOT) ingrandire;
~lamp n lampada a benzina per saldare;
~-out n (of tyre) scoppio.

blubber ['blʌbə*] n grasso di balena // vi
(pej) piangere forte.

bludgeon ['blʌdʒən] vt prendere a
randellate.

blue [blu:] a azzurro(a); **~ film/joke**
film/barzelletta pornografico(a); **to have
the ~s** essere depresso(a); **~bell** n
giacinto di bosco; **~bottle** n moscone m;
~ jeans npl blue-jeans mpl; **~print** n
(fig) progetto.

bluff [blʌf] vi bluffare // n bluff m inv // a
(person) brusco(a); **to call sb's ~**
mettere alla prova il bluff di qd.

blunder ['blʌndə*] n abbaglio // vi
prendere un abbaglio.

blunt [blʌnt] a smussato(a); spuntato(a);
(person) brusco(a) // vt smussare;
spuntare; **~ly** a chiaro; bruscamente.

blur [blə:*] n cosa offuscata // vt offuscare.

blurt [blə:t]: **to ~ out** vt lasciarsi sfuggire.

blush [blʌʃ] vi arrossire // n rossore m.

blustery ['blʌstərɪ] a (weather)
burrascoso(a).

B.O. n (abbr of body odour) odori mpl del
corpo.

boar [bɔ:*] n cinghiale m.

board [bɔ:d] n tavola; (on wall) tabellone
m; (committee) consiglio, comitato; (in
firm) consiglio d'amministrazione // (in
ship) salire a bordo di; (train) salire su;
~ and lodging n vitto e alloggio; **full ~**
pensione f completa; **with ~ and
lodging** (job) inclusivo di vitto e alloggio;
to go by the ~ (fig): **which goes by the
~** che viene abbandonato; **to ~ up** vt
(door) chiudere con assi; **~er** n
pensionante m/f; (SCOL) convittore/trice;
~ing house n pensione f; **~ing school** n
collegio; **~ room** n sala del consiglio.

boast [bəust] vi vantare // vt vantarsi di //
n vanteria; vanto; **~ful** a vanaglorioso(a).

boat [bəut] n nave f; (small) barca; **~er** n
(hat) paglietta; **~ing** n canottaggio.

bob [bɔb] vi (boat, cork on water: also: **~ up
and down**) andare su e giù // n (col) =
shilling; to ~ up vi saltare fuori.

bobbin ['bɔbɪn] n bobina; (of sewing
machine) rocchetto.

bobby ['bɔbɪ] n (col) ≈ poliziotto.

bobsleigh ['bɔbsleɪ] n bob m inv.

bodice ['bɔdɪs] n corsetto.

bodily ['bɔdɪlɪ] a fisico(a), corporale // ad
corporalmente; interamente; in persona.

body ['bɔdɪ] n corpo; (of car) carrozzeria;
(of plane) fusoliera; (fig: quantity) quantità
f inv; **a wine with ~** un vino corposo;
~guard n guardia del corpo; **~work** n
carrozzeria.

bog [bɔg] n palude f // vt: **to get ~ged
down** (fig) impantanarsi.

boggle ['bɔgl] vi: **the mind ~s** è
incredibile.

bogus ['bəugəs] a falso(a); finto(a).

boil [bɔɪl] vt, vi bollire // n (MED)
foruncolo; **to ~ down to** vi (fig): **to ~
down to** ridursi a; **~er** n caldaia; **~er
suit** n tuta; **~ing hot** a bollente.

boisterous ['bɔɪstərəs] a chiassoso(a).

bold [bəuld] a audace; (child) impudente;
(outline) chiaro(a); (colour) deciso(a);
~ness n audacia; impudenza.

Bolivia [bə'lɪvɪə] n Bolivia.

bollard ['bɔləd] n (NAUT) bitta; (AUT)
colonnina luminosa.

bolster ['bəulstə*] n capezzale m; **to ~ up**
vt sostenere.

bolt [bəult] n chiavistello; (with nut) bullone
m // vt serrare; (food) mangiare in fretta
// vi scappare via; **a ~ from the blue**
(fig) un fulmine a ciel sereno.

bomb [bɔm] n bomba // vt bombardare;
~ard [bɔm'bɑ:d] vt bombardare.

bombastic [bɔm'bæstɪk] a ampolloso(a).

bomb disposal ['bɔmdɪspəuzl] n: **~ unit**
corpo degli artificieri.

bomber ['bɔmə*] n bombardiere m.

bombshell ['bɔmʃɛl] n (fig) notizia bomba.

bona fide ['bəunə'faɪdɪ] a sincero(a);
(offer) onesto(a).

bond [bɔnd] n legame m; (binding promise,
FINANCE) obbligazione f.

bone [bəun] n osso; (of fish) spina, lisca //
vt disossare; togliere le spine a; **~-dry** a
asciuttissimo(a).

bonfire ['bɔnfaɪə*] n falò m inv.

bonnet ['bɔnɪt] n cuffia; (Brit: of car)
cofano.

bonus ['bəunəs] n premio.

bony ['bəunɪ] a (arm, face, MED: tissue)
osseo(a); (meat) pieno di ossi; (fish)
pieno(a) di spine.

boo [bu:] excl ba! // vt fischiare // n fischio.

booby trap ['bu:bɪtræp] n trappola.

book [buk] n libro; (of stamps etc)
blocchetto; (COMM): **~s** conti mpl // vt
(ticket, seat, room) prenotare; (driver)
multare; (football player) ammonire;
~able a: **seats are ~able** si possono
prenotare i posti; **~case** n scaffale m;
~ing office n biglietteria; **~-keeping** n
contabilità; **~let** n libricino; **~maker** n
allibratore m; **~seller** n libraio; **~shop**
n libreria; **~stall** n bancarella di libri;
~store n = **~shop**.

boom [bu:m] n (noise) rimbombo; (busy
period) boom m inv // vi rimbombare;
andare a gonfie vele.

boomerang ['bu:məræŋ] n boomerang m
inv.

boon [bu:n] n vantaggio.

boorish ['buərɪʃ] a maleducato(a).

boost [bu:st] n spinta // vt spingere.

boot [bu:t] n stivale m; (for hiking)
scarpone m da montagna; (for football etc)
scarpa; (Brit: of car) portabagagli m inv;
to ~ (in addition) per giunta, in più.

booth [bu:ð] n (at fair) baraccone m; (of

cinema, telephone etc) cabina.
booty ['buːtɪ] *n* bottino.
booze [buːz] (*col*) *n* alcool *m* // *vi* trincare.
border ['bɔːdə*] *n* orlo; margine *m*; (*of a country*) frontiera; **to ~ on** *vt fus* confinare con; **~line** *n* (*fig*) linea di demarcazione; **~line case** *n* caso limite.
bore [bɔː*] *pt of* **bear** // *vt* (*hole*) perforare; (*person*) annoiare // *n* (*person*) seccatore/trice; (*of gun*) calibro; **~dom** *n* noia.
boring ['bɔːrɪŋ] *a* noioso(a).
born [bɔːn] *a*: **to be ~** nascere; **I was ~ in 1960** sono nato nel 1960; **~ blind** nato(a) cieco(a); **a ~ comedian** un comico nato.
borne [bɔːn] *pp of* **bear**.
borough ['bʌrə] *n* municipio.
borrow ['bɔrəu] *vt*: **to ~ sth (from sb)** prendere in prestito qc (da qd).
borstal ['bɔːstl] *n* riformatorio.
bosom ['buzəm] *n* petto; (*fig*) seno; **~ friend** *n* amico/a del cuore.
boss [bɔs] *n* capo // *vt* comandare; **~y** *a* prepotente.
bosun ['bəusn] *n* nostromo.
botanical [bə'tænɪkl] *a* botanico(a).
botanist ['bɔtənɪst] *n* botanico/a.
botany ['bɔtənɪ] *n* botanica.
botch [bɔtʃ] *vt* (*also*: **~ up**) fare un pasticcio di.
both [bəuθ] *a* entrambi, tutt'e due // *pronoun*: **~ (of them)** entrambi; **~ of us went, we ~ went** ci siamo andati tutt'e due // *ad*: **they sell ~ meat and poultry** vendono insieme la carne e il pollame.
bother ['bɔðə*] *vt* (*worry*) preoccupare; (*annoy*) infastidire // *vi* (*gen*: **~ o.s.**) preoccuparsi; **can you be ~ed doing it?** ti va di farlo? // *n*: **it is a ~ to have to do** è una seccatura dover fare; **it was no ~ finding** non c'era problema nel trovare.
bottle ['bɔtl] *n* bottiglia; (*baby's*) biberon *m inv* // *vt* imbottigliare; **to ~ up** *vt* contenere; **~neck** *n* ingorgo; **~-opener** *n* apribottiglie *m inv*.
bottom ['bɔtəm] *n* fondo; (*buttocks*) sedere *m* // *a* più basso(a); ultimo(a); **at the ~ of** in fondo a; **~less** *a* senza fondo.
bough [bau] *n* ramo.
bought [bɔːt] *pt,pp of* **buy**.
boulder ['bəuldə*] *n* masso (tondeggiante).
bounce [bauns] *vi* (*ball*) rimbalzare; (*cheque*) essere restituito(a) // *vt* far rimbalzare // *n* (*rebound*) rimbalzo; **~r** *n* buttafuori *m inv*.
bound [baund] *pt,pp of* **bind** // *n* (*gen pl*) limite *m*; (*leap*) salto // *vt* (*leap*) saltare; (*limit*) delimitare // *a*: **to be ~ to do sth** (*obliged*) essere costretto a fare qc; out of **~s** il cui accesso è vietato; **he's ~ to fail** (*likely*) è certo di fallire; **~ for** diretto(a) a.
boundary ['baundrɪ] *n* confine *m*.
boundless ['baundlɪs] *a* illimitato(a).

bout [baut] *n* periodo; (*of malaria etc*) attacco; (*BOXING etc*) incontro.
bow *n* [bəu] nodo; (*weapon*) arco; (*MUS*) archetto; [bau] inchino // *vi* [bau] inchinarsi; (*yield*): **to ~ to or before** sottomettersi a.
bowels [bauəlz] *npl* intestini *mpl*; (*fig*) viscere *fpl*.
bowl [bəul] *n* (*for eating*) scodella; (*for washing*) bacino; (*ball*) boccia; (*of pipe*) fornello // *vi* (*CRICKET*) servire (la palla); **~s** *n* gioco delle bocce; **to ~ over** *vt* (*fig*) sconcertare.
bow-legged ['bəulɛgɪd] *a* dalle gambe storte.
bowler ['bəulə*] *n* giocatore *m* di bocce; (*CRICKET*) giocatore che serve la palla; (*also*: **~ hat**) bombetta.
bowling ['bəulɪŋ] *n* (*game*) gioco delle bocce; **~ alley** *n* pista da bowling; **~ green** *n* campo di bocce.
bow tie ['bəu'taɪ] *n* cravatta a farfalla.
box [bɔks] *n* scatola; (*THEATRE*) palco // *vt* fare del pugilato; **~er** *n* (*person*) pugile *m*; (*dog*) boxer *m inv*; **~ing** *n* (*SPORT*) pugilato; **B~ing Day** *n* Santo Stefano; **~ing gloves** *npl* guantoni *mpl* da pugile; **~ office** *n* biglietteria; **~ room** *n* ripostiglio.
boy [bɔɪ] *n* ragazzo; (*servant*) servo.
boycott ['bɔɪkɔt] *n* boicottaggio // *vt* boicottare.
boyfriend ['bɔɪfrɛnd] *n* ragazzo.
boyish ['bɔɪɪʃ] *a* di *or* da ragazzo.
B.R. *abbr of* British Rail.
bra [braː] *n* reggipetto, reggiseno.
brace [breɪs] *n* sostegno; (*on teeth*) apparecchio correttore; (*tool*) trapano // *vt* rinforzare, sostenere; **~s** *npl* bretelle *fpl*; **to ~ o.s.** (*fig*) farsi coraggio.
bracelet ['breɪslɪt] *n* braccialetto.
bracing ['breɪsɪŋ] *a* invigorente.
bracken ['brækən] *n* felce *f*.
bracket ['brækɪt] *n* (*TECH*) mensola; (*group*) gruppo; (*TYP*) parentesi *f inv* // *vt* mettere fra parentesi.
brag [bræg] *vi* vantarsi.
braid [breɪd] *n* (*trimming*) passamano; (*of hair*) treccia.
brain [breɪn] *n* cervello; **~s** *npl* cervella *fpl*; **he's got ~s** è intelligente; **~wash** *vt* fare un lavaggio di cervello a; **~wave** *n* lampo di genio; **~y** *a* intelligente.
braise [breɪz] *vt* brasare.
brake [breɪk] *n* (*on vehicle*) freno // *vt, vi* frenare.
bramble ['bræmbl] *n* rovo.
bran [bræn] *n* crusca.
branch [brɑːntʃ] *n* ramo; (*COMM*) succursale *f* // *vi* diramarsi.
brand [brænd] *n* marca // *vt* (*cattle*) marcare (a ferro rovente); (*fig: pej*): **to ~ sb a communist** *etc* definire qd come comunista *etc*.
brandish ['brændɪʃ] *vt* brandire.
brand-new ['brænd'njuː] *a* nuovo(a) di zecca.

brandy ['brændɪ] *n* brandy *m inv*.

brash [bræʃ] *a* sfacciato(a).

brass [brɑːs] *n* ottone *m*; **the ~** (*MUS*) gli ottoni; **~ band** *n* fanfara.

brassière ['bræsɪə*] *n* reggipetto, reggiseno.

brat [bræt] *n* (*pej*) marmocchio, monello/a.

bravado [brə'vɑːdəu] *n* spavalderia.

brave [breɪv] *a* coraggioso(a) // *n* guerriero *m* pelle rossa *inv* // *vt* affrontare; **~ry** *n* coraggio.

brawl [brɔːl] *n* rissa.

brawn [brɔːn] *n* muscolo; (*meat*) carne *f* di testa di maiale; **~y** *a* muscoloso(a).

bray [breɪ] *vi* ragliare.

brazen ['breɪzn] *a* svergognato(a) // *vt*: **to ~ it out** fare lo sfacciato.

brazier ['breɪzɪə*] *n* braciere *m*.

Brazil [brə'zɪl] *n* Brasile *m*; **~ian** *a* brasiliano(a); **~ nut** *n* noce *f* del Brasile.

breach [briːtʃ] *vt* aprire una breccia in // *n* (*gap*) breccia, varco; (*breaking*): **~ of contract** rottura di contratto; **~ of the peace** violazione *f* dell'ordine pubblico.

bread [brɛd] *n* pane *m*; **~ and butter** *n* pane e burro; (*fig*) mezzi *mpl* di sussistenza; **~bin** *n* cassetta *f* portapane *inv*; **~crumbs** *npl* briciole *fpl*; (*CULIN*) pangrattato; **~ line** *n*: **to be on the ~ line** avere appena denaro per vivere.

breadth [brɛtθ] *n* larghezza.

breadwinner ['brɛdwɪnə*] *n* chi guadagna il pane per tutta la famiglia.

break [breɪk] *vb* (*pt* **broke** [brəuk], *pp* **broken** ['brəukən]) *vt* rompere; (*law*) violare // *vi* rompersi; (*weather*) cambiare // *n* (*gap*) breccia; (*fracture*) rottura; (*rest, also SCOL*) intervallo; (: *short*) pausa; (*chance*) possibilità *f inv*; **to ~ one's leg** *etc* rompersi la gamba *etc*; **to ~ a record** battere un primato; **to ~ the news to sb** comunicare per primo la notizia a qd; **to ~ down** *vt* (*figures, data*) analizzare // *vi* crollare; (*MED*) avere un esaurimento (nervoso); (*AUT*) guastarsi; **to ~ even** *vi* coprire le spese; **to ~ free** *or* **loose** *vi* spezzare i legami; **to ~ in** *vt* (*horse etc*) domare // *vi* (*burglar*) fare irruzione; **to ~ into** *vt fus* (*house*) fare irruzione in; **to ~ off** *vi* (*speaker*) interrompersi; (*branch*) troncarsi; **to ~ open** *vt* (*door etc*) sfondare; **to ~ out** *vi* evadere; **to ~ out in spots** coprirsi di macchie; **to ~ up** *vi* (*partnership*) sciogliersi; (*friends*) separarsi // *vt* fare in pezzi, spaccare; (*fight etc*) interrompere, far cessare; **~able** *a* fragile; **~age** *n* rottura; **~down** *n* (*AUT*) guasto, panna; (*in communications*) interruzione *f*; (*MED*) esaurimento nervoso; **~down service** *n* servizio riparazioni; **~er** *n* frangente *m*.

breakfast ['brɛkfəst] *n* colazione *f*.

breakthrough ['breɪkθruː] *n* (*MIL*) breccia; (*fig*) passo avanti.

breakwater ['breɪkwɔːtə*] *n* frangiflutti *m inv*.

breast [brɛst] *n* (*of woman*) seno; (*chest*) petto; **~-stroke** *n* nuoto a rana.

breath [brɛθ] *n* fiato; **out of ~** senza fiato; **~alyser** *n* test di verifica per la sobrietà.

breathe [briːð] *vt,vi* respirare; **~r** *n* attimo di respiro.

breathless ['brɛθlɪs] *a* senza fiato.

breath-taking ['brɛθteɪkɪŋ] *a* sbalorditivo(a).

breed [briːd] *vb* (*pt,pp* **bred** [brɛd]) *vt* allevare // *vi* riprodursi // *n* razza, varietà *f inv*; **~ing** *n* riproduzione *f*; allevamento.

breeze [briːz] *n* brezza.

breezy ['briːzɪ] *a* arioso(a); allegro(a).

brevity ['brɛvɪtɪ] *n* brevità.

brew [bruː] *vt* (*tea*) fare un infuso di; (*beer*) fare; (*plot*) tramare // *vi* (*tea*) essere in infusione; (*beer*) essere in fermentazione; (*fig*) bollire in pentola; **~er** *n* birraio; **~ery** *n* fabbrica di birra.

bribe [braɪb] *n* bustarella // *vt* comprare; **~ry** *n* corruzione *f*.

brick [brɪk] *n* mattone *m*; **~layer** *n* muratore *m*.

bridal ['braɪdl] *a* nuziale.

bride [braɪd] *n* sposa; **~groom** *n* sposo; **~smaid** *n* damigella d'onore.

bridge [brɪdʒ] *n* ponte *m*; (*NAUT*) ponte di comando; (*of nose*) dorso; (*CARDS, DENTISTRY*) bridge *m inv* // *vt* (*river*) fare un ponte sopra; (*gap*) colmare.

bridle ['braɪdl] *n* briglia // *vt* tenere a freno; (*horse*) mettere la briglia a; **~ path** *n* pista per traffico animale.

brief [briːf] *a* breve // *n* (*LAW*) comparsa // *vt* dare istruzioni a; **~s** *npl* mutande *fpl*; **~case** *n* cartella; **~ing** *n* istruzioni *fpl*.

brigade [brɪ'geɪd] *n* (*MIL*) brigata.

brigadier [brɪgə'dɪə*] *n* generale *m* di brigata.

bright [braɪt] *a* luminoso(a); (*person*) sveglio(a); (*colour*) vivace; **~en** *vt* (*room*) rendere luminoso; ornare // *vi* schiarirsi; (*person: gen*: **~en up**) rallegrarsi.

brilliance ['brɪljəns] *n* splendore *m*.

brilliant ['brɪljənt] *a* splendente.

brim [brɪm] *n* orlo; **~ful** *a* pieno(a) or colmo(a) fino all'orlo; (*fig*) pieno(a).

brine [braɪn] *n* acqua salmastra; (*CULIN*) salamoia.

bring, *pt,pp* **brought** [brɪŋ, 'brɔːt] *vt* portare; **to ~ about** *vt* causare; **to ~ back** *vt* riportare; **to ~ down** *vt* portare giù; abbattere; **to ~ forward** *vt* portare avanti; (*in time*) anticipare; **to ~ off** *vt* (*task, plan*) portare a compimento; **to ~ out** *vt* (*meaning*) mettere in evidenza; **to ~ round** *or* **to** *vt* (*unconscious person*) far rinvenire; **to ~ up** *vt* allevare; (*question*) introdurre.

brink [brɪŋk] *n* orlo.

brisk [brɪsk] *a* vivace.

bristle ['brɪsl] *n* setola // *vi* rizzarsi; **bristling with** irto(a) di.

Britain ['brɪtən] *n* Gran Bretagna.

British ['brɪtɪʃ] *a* britannico(a); **the ~** *npl* i Britannici; **the ~ Isles** *npl* le Isole Britanniche.

Briton ['brɪtən] n britannico/a.
brittle ['brɪtl] a fragile.
broach [brəutʃ] vt (subject) affrontare.
broad [brɔːd] a largo(a); (distinction)
generale; (accent) spiccato(a); in ~
daylight in pieno giorno; ~ hint n
allusione f esplicita; ~cast n trasmissione
f // vb (pt,pp broadcast) vt trasmettere
per radio (or per televisione) // vi fare
una trasmissione; ~casting n radio f inv;
televisione f; ~en vt allargare // vi
allargarsi; ~ly ad (fig) in generale;
~-minded a di mente aperta.
brochure ['brəuʃjuə*] n dépliant m inv.
broil [brɔɪl] vt cuocere a fuoco vivo.
broke [brəuk] pt of break // a (col)
squattrinato(a); ~n pp of break // a: ~n
leg etc gamba etc rotta; in ~n
French/English in un francese/inglese
stentato; ~n-hearted a: to be ~n-
hearted avere il cuore spezzato.
broker ['brəukə*] n agente m.
bronchitis [brɔŋ'kaɪtɪs] n bronchite f.
bronze [brɔnz] n bronzo; ~d a
abbronzato(a).
brooch [brəutʃ] n spilla.
brood [bruːd] n covata // vi (hen) covare;
(person) rimuginare.
brook [bruk] n ruscello.
broom [brum] n scopa; ~stick n manico
di scopa.
Bros. abbr of Brothers.
broth [brɔθ] n brodo.
brothel ['brɔθl] n bordello.
brother ['brʌðə*] n fratello; ~hood n
fratellanza; confraternità f inv; ~-in-law
n cognato; ~ly a fraterno(a).
brought [brɔːt] pt,pp of bring.
brow [brau] n fronte f; (rare, gen: eye~)
sopracciglio; (of hill) cima; ~beat vt
intimidire.
brown [braun] a bruno(a), marrone // n
(colour) color m bruno or marrone // vt
(CULIN) rosolare; ~ie n giovane
esploratrice f.
browse [brauz] vi (among books) curiosare
fra i libri.
bruise [bruːz] n ammaccatura // vt
ammaccare // vi (fruit) ammaccarsi.
brunette [bruː'nɛt] n bruna.
brunt [brʌnt] n: the ~ of (attack, criticism
etc) il peso maggiore di.
brush [brʌʃ] n spazzola; (quarrel)
schermaglia // vt spazzolare; (gen: ~
past, ~ against) sfiorare; to ~ aside vt
scostare; to ~ up vt (knowledge)
rinfrescare; ~-off n: to give sb the
~-off dare il ben servito a qd; ~wood n
macchia.
Brussels ['brʌslz] n Bruxelles; ~ sprout
n cavolo di Bruxelles.
brutal ['bruːtl] a brutale; ~ity [bruː'tælɪtɪ]
n brutalità.
brute [bruːt] n bestia.
B.Sc. abbr see bachelor.
bubble ['bʌbl] n bolla // vi ribollire;
(sparkle, fig) essere effervescente.

buck [bʌk] n maschio (di camoscio, caprone,
coniglio etc); (US: col) dollaro // vi
sgroppare; to pass the ~ (to sb)
scaricare (su di qd) la propria
responsabilità; to ~ up vi (cheer up)
rianimarsi.
bucket ['bʌkɪt] n secchio.
buckle ['bʌkl] n fibbia // vt affibbiare;
(warp) deformare.
bud [bʌd] n gemma; (of flower) boccio // vi
germogliare; (flower) sbocciare.
Buddha ['budə] n Budda m.
budding ['bʌdɪŋ] a (flower) in boccio; (poet
etc) in erba.
buddy ['bʌdɪ] n (US) compagno.
budge [bʌdʒ] vt scostare // vi spostarsi.
budgerigar ['bʌdʒərɪgɑː*] n pappagallino.
budget ['bʌdʒɪt] n bilancio preventivo //
vi: to ~ for sth fare il bilancio per qc.
budgie ['bʌdʒɪ] n = budgerigar.
buff [bʌf] a color camoscio // n (enthusiast)
appassionato/a.
buffalo, pl ~ or ~es ['bʌfələu] n bufalo;
(US) bisonte m.
buffer ['bʌfə*] n respingente m; ~ state n
stato cuscinetto.
buffet n ['bufeɪ] (bar, food) buffet m inv //
vt ['bʌfɪt] schiaffeggiare; scuotere; urtare.
buffoon [bə'fuːn] n buffone m.
bug [bʌg] n (insect) cimice f; (: gen)
insetto; (fig: germ) virus m inv; (spy device)
microfono spia // vt mettere sotto
controllo; ~bear n spauracchio.
bugle ['bjuːgl] n tromba.
build [bɪld] n (of person) corporatura // vt
(pt,pp built [bɪlt]) costruire; ~er n
costruttore m; ~ing n costruzione f;
edificio; (also: ~ing trade) edilizia;
~ing society n società di credito edilizio;
to ~ up vt accumulare; aumentare;
~-up n (of gas etc) accumulo.
built [bɪlt] pt,pp of build; well-~ a
(person) robusto(a); ~-in a (cupboard) a
muro; (device) incorporato(a); ~-up
area n abitato.
bulb [bʌlb] n (BOT) bulbo; (ELEC)
lampadina; ~ous a bulboso(a).
Bulgaria [bʌl'gɛərɪə] n Bulgaria.
bulge [bʌldʒ] n rigonfiamento // vi essere
protuberante or rigonfio(a); to be
bulging with essere pieno(a) or zeppo(a)
di.
bulk [bʌlk] n massa, volume m; in ~ a
pacchi (or cassette etc); (COMM)
all'ingrosso; the ~ of il grosso di; ~head
n paratia; ~y a grosso(a); voluminoso(a).
bull [bul] n toro; ~dog n bulldog m inv.
bulldozer ['buldəuzə*] n bulldozer m inv.
bullet ['bulɪt] n pallottola.
bulletin ['bulɪtɪn] n bollettino.
bullfight ['bulfaɪt] n corrida; ~er n
torero; ~ing n tauromachia.
bullion ['buljən] n oro or argento in
lingotti.
bullock ['bulək] n giovenco.
bull's-eye ['bulzaɪ] n centro del bersaglio.
bully ['bulɪ] n prepotente m // vt

angariare; (frighten) intimidire; ~ing n prepotenze fpl.

bum [bʌm] n (col: backside) culo; (tramp) vagabondo/a; **to ~ around** vi fare il vagabondo.

bumblebee ['bʌmblbi:] n (ZOOL) bombo.

bump [bʌmp] n (blow) colpo; (jolt) scossa; (on road etc) protuberanza; (on head) bernoccolo // vt battere; **to ~ along** vi procedere sobbalzando; **to ~ into** vt fus scontrarsi con; **~er** n (Brit) paraurti m inv // a: **~er harvest** raccolto eccezionale.

bumptious ['bʌmpʃəs] a presuntuoso(a).

bumpy ['bʌmpɪ] a dissestato(a).

bun [bʌn] n focaccia; (of hair) crocchia.

bunch [bʌntʃ] n (of flowers, keys) mazzo; (of bananas) ciuffo; (of people) gruppo; ~ **of grapes** grappolo d'uva.

bundle ['bʌndl] n fascio // vt (also: ~ up) legare in un fascio; (put): **to ~ sth/sb into** spingere qc/qd in; **to ~ off** vt (person) mandare via in gran fretta.

bung [bʌŋ] n tappo // vt (throw) buttare.

bungalow ['bʌŋgələʊ] n bungalow m inv.

bungle ['bʌŋgl] vt abborracciare.

bunion ['bʌnjən] n callo (al piede).

bunk [bʌŋk] n cuccetta; ~ **beds** npl letti mpl a castello.

bunker ['bʌŋkə*] n (coal store) ripostiglio per il carbone; (MIL, GOLF) bunker m inv.

bunny ['bʌnɪ] n (also: ~ **rabbit**) coniglietto; ~ **girl** n coniglietta.

bunting ['bʌntɪŋ] n pavesi mpl, bandierine fpl.

buoy [bɔɪ] n boa; **to ~ up** vt tenere a galla; (fig) sostenere; ~**ancy** n (of ship) galleggiabilità; ~**ant** a galleggiante; (fig) vivace.

burden ['bə:dn] n carico, fardello // vt caricare; (oppress) opprimere.

bureau, pl ~**x** [bjuə'rəu, -z] n (furniture) scrivania; (office) ufficio, agenzia.

bureaucracy [bjuə'rɔkrəsɪ] n burocrazia.

bureaucrat ['bjuərəkræt] n burocrate m/f; ~**ic** [-'krætɪk] a burocratico(a).

burglar ['bə:glə*] n scassinatore m; ~ **alarm** n campanello antifurto; ~**ize** n (US) svaligiare; ~**y** n furto con scasso.

burgle ['bə:gl] vt svaligiare.

burial ['berɪəl] n sepoltura; ~ **ground** n cimitero.

burly ['bə:lɪ] a robusto(a).

Burma ['bə:mə] n Birmania.

burn [bə:n] vt,vi (pt,pp **burned** or **burnt** [bə:nt]) bruciare // n bruciatura, scottatura; **to ~ down** vt distruggere col fuoco; ~**ing question** n questione f scottante.

burnish ['bə:nɪʃ] vt brunire.

burnt [bə:nt] pt,pp of **burn**.

burp [bə:p] (col) n rutto // vi ruttare.

burrow ['bʌrəʊ] n tana // vt scavare.

bursar ['bə:sə*] n economo/a; ~**y** n borsa di studio.

burst [bə:st] vb (pt,pp **burst**) vt far scoppiare (or esplodere) // vi esplodere;

(tyre) scoppiare // n scoppio; (also: ~ **pipe**) rottura nel tubo, perdita; ~ **of energy** scoppio d'energia; ~ **of laughter** scoppio di risa; ~ **blood vessel** rottura di un vaso sanguigno; **to ~ into flames/tears** scoppiare in fiamme/lacrime; **to be ~ing with** essere pronto a scoppiare di; **to ~ into** vt fus (room etc) irrompere in; **to ~ open** vi aprirsi improvvisamente; (door) spalancarsi; **to ~ out laughing** scoppiare a ridere; **to ~ out of** vt fus precipitarsi fuori da.

bury ['berɪ] vt seppellire; **to ~ one's face in one's hands** nascondere la faccia tra le mani.

bus, ~**es** [bʌs, 'bʌsɪz] n autobus m inv.

bush [buʃ] n cespuglio; (scrub land) macchia.

bushel ['buʃl] n staio.

bushy ['buʃɪ] a cespuglioso(a).

business ['bɪznɪs] n (matter) affare m; (trading) affari mpl; (firm) azienda; (job, duty) lavoro; **to be away on ~** essere andato via per affari; **it's none of my ~** questo non mi riguarda; **he means ~** non scherza; ~**like** a serio(a); efficiente; ~**man** n uomo d'affari.

bus-stop ['bʌsstɔp] n fermata d'autobus.

bust [bʌst] n busto; (ANAT) seno // a (broken) rotto(a); **to go ~** fallire.

bustle ['bʌsl] n movimento, attività // vi darsi da fare; **bustling** a (person) indaffarato(a); (town) animato(a).

busy ['bɪzɪ] a occupato(a); (shop, street) molto frequentato(a) // vt: **to ~ o.s.** darsi da fare; ~**body** n ficcanaso.

but [bʌt] cj ma // prep eccetto, tranne; **nothing ~** null'altro che; ~ **for** senza, se non fosse per; **all ~ finished** quasi finito; **anything ~ finished** tutt'altro che finito.

butane ['bju:teɪn] n butano.

butcher ['butʃə*] n macellaio // vt macellare.

butler ['bʌtlə*] n maggiordomo.

butt [bʌt] n (cask) grossa botte f; (thick end) estremità f inv più grossa; (of gun) calcio; (of cigarette) mozzicone m; (fig: target) oggetto // vt cozzare.

butter ['bʌtə*] n burro // vt imburrare.

butterfly ['bʌtəflaɪ] n farfalla.

buttocks ['bʌtəks] npl natiche fpl.

button ['bʌtn] n bottone m // vt abbottonare; ~**hole** n asola, occhiello // vt attaccare un bottone a.

buttress ['bʌtrɪs] n contrafforte f.

buxom ['bʌksəm] a formoso(a).

buy [baɪ] vt (pt,pp **bought** [bɔ:t]) comprare; **to ~ sb sth/sth from sb** comprare qc per qd/qc da qd; **to ~ sb a drink** offrire da bere a qd; **to ~ up** vt accaparrare; ~**er** n compratore/trice.

buzz [bʌz] n ronzio; (col: phone call) colpo di telefono // vi ronzare.

buzzard ['bʌzəd] n poiana.

buzzer ['bʌzə*] n cicalino.

by [baɪ] prep da; (beside) accanto a; vicino

a, presso; (*before*): ~ 4 o'clock entro le 4 // *ad see* pass, go *etc*; ~ bus/car in autobus/macchina; paid ~ the hour pagato(a) a ore; to increase *etc* ~ the hour aumentare di ora in ora; (all) ~ oneself tutto(a) solo(a); ~ the way a proposito; ~ and large nell'insieme; ~ and ~ di qui a poco or presto.

bye(-bye) ['baɪ('baɪ)] *excl* ciao!, arrivederci!

by(e)-law ['baɪlɔː] *n* legge *f* locale.

by-election ['baɪlɛkʃən] *n* elezione *f* straordinaria.

bygone ['baɪgɔn] *a* passato(a) // *n*: let ~s be ~s mettiamo una pietra sopra.

bypass ['baɪpɑːs] *n* circonvallazione *f* // *vt* fare una deviazione intorno a.

by-product ['baɪprɔdʌkt] *n* sottoprodotto; (*fig*) conseguenza secondaria.

bystander ['baɪstændə*] *n* spettatore/trice.

byword ['baɪwəːd] *n*: to be a ~ for essere sinonimo di.

C

C [siː] *n* (*MUS*) do.

C. *abbr of* centigrade.

cab [kæb] *n* taxi *m inv*; (*of train, truck*) cabina; (*horse-drawn*) carrozza.

cabaret ['kæbəreɪ] *n* cabaret *m inv*.

cabbage ['kæbɪdʒ] *n* cavolo.

cabin ['kæbɪn] *n* capanna; (*on ship*) cabina; ~ cruiser *n* cabinato.

cabinet ['kæbɪnɪt] *n* (*POL*) gabinetto; (*furniture*) armadietto; (*also*: display ~) vetrinetta; cocktail ~ *n* mobile *m* bar *inv*; ~-maker *n* stipettaio.

cable ['keɪbl] *n* cavo; fune *f*; (*TEL*) cablogramma *m* // *vt* telegrafare; ~-car *n* funivia; ~gram *n* cablogramma *m*; ~ railway *n* funicolare *f*.

cache [kæʃ] *n* nascondiglio; a ~ of food *etc* un deposito segreto di viveri *etc*.

cackle ['kækl] *vi* schiamazzare.

cactus, *pl* cacti ['kæktəs, -taɪ] *n* cacto.

caddie ['kædɪ] *n* caddie *m inv*.

cadet [kə'dɛt] *n* (*MIL*) cadetto.

cadge [kædʒ] *vt* accattare; to ~ a meal (off sb) scroccare un pranzo (a qd).

Caesarean [siː'zɛərɪən] *a*: ~ (section) operazione *f* cesarea.

café ['kæfeɪ] *n* caffè *m inv*; cafeteria [kæfɪ'tɪərɪə] *n* self-service *m inv*.

caffein(e) ['kæfiːn] *n* caffeina.

cage [keɪdʒ] *n* gabbia.

cagey ['keɪdʒɪ] *a* (*col*) chiuso(a); guardingo(a).

cajole [kə'dʒəul] *vt* allettare.

cake [keɪk] *n* torta; ~ of soap saponetta; ~d a: ~d with incrostato(a) di.

calamity [kə'læmɪtɪ] *n* calamità *f inv*.

calcium ['kælsɪəm] *n* calcio.

calculate ['kælkjuleɪt] *vt* calcolare; calculating *a* calcolatore(trice); calculation [-'leɪʃən] *n* calcolo; calculator *n* calcolatrice *f*.

calculus ['kælkjuləs] *n* calcolo.

calendar ['kæləndə*] *n* calendario; ~ month *n* mese *m* (secondo il calendario); ~ year *n* anno civile.

calf, calves [kɑːf, kɑːvz] *n* (*of cow*) vitello; (*of other animals*) piccolo; (*also*: ~skin) (pelle *f* di) vitello; (*ANAT*) polpaccio.

calibre ['kælɪbə*] *n* calibro.

call [kɔːl] *vt* (*gen, also TEL*) chiamare // *vi* chiamare; (*visit*: *also*: ~ in, ~ round): to ~ (for) passare (a prendere) // *n* (*shout*) grido, urlata; visita; (telephone) ~ telefonata; to be on ~ essere disponibile; to ~ for *vt fus* richiedere; to ~ off *vt* disdire; to ~ on *vt fus* (*visit*) passare da; (*request*): to ~ on sb to do chiedere a qd di fare; to ~ up *vt* (*MIL*) richiamare; ~box *n* cabina telefonica; ~er *n* persona che chiama; visitatore/trice; ~ girl *n* ragazza *f* squillo *inv*; ~ing *n* vocazione *f*; ~ing card *n* (*US*) biglietto da visita.

callous ['kæləs] *a* indurito(a), insensibile.

calm [kɑːm] *n* calma // *vt* calmare // *a* calmo(a); ~ly *ad* con calma; ~ness *n* calma; to ~ down *vi* calmarsi // *vt* calmare.

calorie ['kælərɪ] *n* caloria.

calve [kɑːv] *vi* figliare.

calves [kɑːvz] *npl of* calf.

camber ['kæmbə*] *n* (*of road*) bombatura.

Cambodia [kæm'bəudjə] *n* Cambogia.

came [keɪm] *pt of* come.

camel ['kæməl] *n* cammello.

cameo ['kæmɪəu] *n* cammeo.

camera ['kæmərə] *n* macchina fotografica; (*also*: cine-~, movie ~) cinepresa; in ~ a porte chiuse; ~man *n* cameraman *m inv*.

camouflage ['kæməflɑːʒ] *n* camuffamento; (*MIL*) mimetizzazione *f* // *vt* camuffare; mimetizzare.

camp [kæmp] *n* campeggio; (*MIL*) campo // *vi* campeggiare; accamparsi.

campaign [kæm'peɪn] *n* (*MIL*, *POL etc*) campagna // *vi* (*also fig*) fare una campagna.

campbed ['kæmp'bɛd] *n* brandina.

camper ['kæmpə*] *n* campeggiatore/trice.

camping ['kæmpɪŋ] *n* campeggio.

campsite ['kæmpsaɪt] *n* campeggio.

campus ['kæmpəs] *n* campus *m inv*.

can [kæn] *auxiliary vb* potere; (*know how to*) sapere; I ~ swim *etc* so nuotare *etc*; I ~ speak French so parlare francese // *n* (*of milk*) scatola; (*of oil*) bidone *m*; (*of water*) tanica; (*tin*) scatola // *vt* mettere in scatola.

Canada ['kænədə] *n* Canada *m*.

Canadian [kə'neɪdɪən] *a*, *n* canadese (*m/f*).

canal [kə'næl] *n* canale *m*.

canary [kə'nɛərɪ] *n* canarino.

cancel ['kænsəl] *vt* annullare; (*train*) sopprimere; (*cross out*) cancellare; ~lation [-'leɪʃən] *n* annullamento; soppressione *f*; cancellazione *f*; (*TOURISM*) prenotazione *f* annullata.

cancer ['kænsə*] n cancro; **C~** (sign) Cancro.

candid ['kændɪd] a onesto(a).

candidate ['kændɪdeɪt] n candidato.

candle ['kændl] n candela; **by ~ light** a lume di candela; **~stick** n (also: **~ holder**) bugia; (bigger, ornate) candeliere m.

candour ['kændə*] n sincerità.

candy ['kændɪ] n zucchero candito; (US) caramella; **~floss** n zucchero filato.

cane [keɪn] n canna; (SCOL) verga // vt punire a colpi di verga.

canine ['kænaɪn] a canino(a).

canister ['kænɪstə*] n scatola metallica.

cannabis ['kænəbɪs] n (drug) hascisc m.

canned ['kænd] a (food) in scatola.

cannibal ['kænɪbəl] n cannibale m/f; **~ism** n cannibalismo.

cannon, pl **~** or **~s** ['kænən] n (gun) cannone m; **~ball** n palla di cannone.

cannot ['kænɔt] = **can not**.

canny ['kænɪ] a furbo(a).

canoe [kə'nuː] n canoa; (SPORT) canotto; **~ing** n (SPORT) canottaggio; **~ist** n canottiere m.

canon ['kænən] n (clergyman) canonico; (standard) canone m.

canonize ['kænənaɪz] vt canonizzare.

can opener ['kænəupnə*] n apriscatole m inv.

canopy ['kænəpɪ] n baldacchino.

cant [kænt] n gergo.

can't [kænt] = **can not**.

cantankerous [kæn'tæŋkərəs] a stizzoso(a).

canteen [kæn'tiːn] n mensa; (of cutlery) portaposate m inv.

canter ['kæntə*] n piccolo galoppo.

cantilever ['kæntɪliːvə*] n trave f a sbalzo.

canvas ['kænvəs] n tela; **under ~** (camping) sotto la tenda; (NAUT) sotto la vela.

canvass ['kænvəs] vt: **~ing** sollecitazione f.

canyon ['kænjən] n canyon m inv.

cap [kæp] n (also FOOTBALL) berretto; (of pen) coperchio; (of bottle) tappo // vt tappare; (outdo) superare; **~ped with** ricoperto(a) di.

capability [keɪpə'bɪlɪtɪ] n capacità f inv, abilità f inv.

capable ['keɪpəbl] a capace; **~ of** capace di; suscettibile di.

capacity [kə'pæsɪtɪ] n capacità f inv; (of lift etc) capienza; **in his ~** as nella sua qualità di; **to work at full ~** lavorare al massimo delle proprie capacità.

cape [keɪp] n (garment) cappa; (GEO) capo.

capital ['kæpɪtl] n (also: **~ city**) capitale f; (money) capitale m; (also: **~ letter**) (lettera) maiuscola; **~ gains** npl utili mpl di capitale; **~ism** n capitalismo; **~ist** a capitalista; **~ punishment** n pena capitale.

capitulate [kə'pɪtjuleɪt] vi capitolare.

capricious [kə'prɪʃəs] a capriccioso(a).

Capricorn ['kæprɪkɔːn] n Capricorno.

capsize [kæp'saɪz] vt capovolgere // vi capovolgersi.

capstan ['kæpstən] n argano.

capsule ['kæpsjuːl] n capsula.

captain ['kæptɪn] n capitano // vt capitanare.

caption ['kæpʃən] n leggenda.

captivate ['kæptɪveɪt] vt avvincere.

captive ['kæptɪv] a, n prigioniero(a).

captivity [kæp'tɪvɪtɪ] n prigionia; **in ~** (animal) in servitù.

capture ['kæptʃə*] vt catturare, prendere; (attention) attirare // n cattura.

car [kɑː*] n macchina, automobile f.

carafe [kə'ræf] n caraffa.

caramel ['kærəməl] n caramello.

carat ['kærət] n carato.

caravan ['kærəvæn] n roulotte f inv.

caraway ['kærəweɪ] n: **~ seed** seme m di cumino.

carbohydrates [kɑːbəu'haɪdreɪts] npl (foods) carboidrati mpl.

carbon ['kɑːbən] n carbonio; **~ copy** n copia f carbone inv; **~ paper** n carta carbone.

carburettor [kɑːbjuˈrɛtə*] n carburatore m.

carcass ['kɑːkəs] n carcassa.

card [kɑːd] n carta; (visiting **~** etc) biglietto; (Christmas **~** etc) cartolina; **~board** n cartone m; **~ game** n gioco di carte.

cardiac ['kɑːdɪæk] a cardiaco(a).

cardigan ['kɑːdɪgən] n cardigan m inv.

cardinal ['kɑːdɪnl] a, n cardinale (m).

card index ['kɑːdɪndɛks] n schedario.

care [kɛə*] n cura, attenzione f; (worry) preoccupazione f // vi: **to ~ about** interessarsi di; **would you ~ to/for ...?** ti piacerebbe ...?; **I wouldn't ~ to do it** non lo vorrei fare; **in sb's ~** alle cure di qd; **to take ~** fare attenzione; **to take ~ of** vt curarsi di; **to ~ for** vt fus aver cura di; (like) volere bene a; **I don't ~** non me ne importa; **I couldn't ~ less** non me ne importa un bel niente.

career [kə'rɪə*] n carriera // vi (also: **~ along**) andare di (gran) carriera.

carefree ['kɛəfriː] a sgombro(a) di preoccupazione.

careful ['kɛəful] a attento(a); (cautious) cauto(a); **(be) ~!** attenzione!; **~ly** ad con cura; cautamente.

careless ['kɛəlɪs] a negligente; (heedless) spensierato(a); **~ly** ad trascuratamente, senza cura; **~ness** n negligenza, spensieratezza.

caress [kə'rɛs] n carezza // vt accarezzare.

caretaker ['kɛəteɪkə*] n custode m.

car-ferry ['kɑːfɛrɪ] n traghetto.

cargo, **~es** ['kɑːgəu] n carico.

Caribbean [kærɪ'biːən] a: **the ~ (Sea)** il Mar dei Caraibi.

caricature ['kærɪkətjuə*] n caricatura.

carnal ['kɑːnl] a carnale.

carnation [kɑːˈneɪʃən] n garofano.
carnival [ˈkɑːnɪvəl] n (public celebration) carnevale m.
carol [ˈkærəl] n: (Christmas) ~ canto di Natale.
carp [kɑːp] n (fish) carpa; **to** ~ **at** vt fus trovare a ridire su.
car park [ˈkɑːpɑːk] n parcheggio.
carpenter [ˈkɑːpɪntə*] n carpentiere m.
carpentry [ˈkɑːpɪntrɪ] n carpenteria.
carpet [ˈkɑːpɪt] n tappeto // vt coprire con tappeto.
carriage [ˈkærɪdʒ] n vettura; trasporto; (of typewriter) carrello; (bearing) portamento; ~**way** n (part of road) strada rotabile.
carrier [ˈkærɪə*] n (of disease) portatore/trice; (COMM) impresa di trasporti; (NAUT) portaerei m inv; (on car, bicycle) portabagagli m inv; ~ **bag** n sacchetto.
carrot [ˈkærət] n carota.
carry [ˈkærɪ] vt (subj: person) portare; (: vehicle) trasportare; (a motion, bill) far passare; (involve: responsibilities etc) comportare // vi (sound) farsi sentire; **to be carried away** (fig) farsi trascinare; **to** ~ **on** vi: **to** ~ **on with sth/doing** continuare qc/a fare // vt mandare avanti; **to** ~ **out** vt (orders) eseguire; (investigation) svolgere; ~**cot** n culla portabile.
cart [kɑːt] n carro // vt trasportare con carro.
cartilage [ˈkɑːtɪlɪdʒ] n cartilagine f.
carton [ˈkɑːtən] n (box) scatola di cartone; (of yogurt) cartone m; (of cigarettes) stecca.
cartoon [kɑːˈtuːn] n (PRESS) disegno umoristico; (satirical) caricatura; (comic strip) fumetto; (CINEMA) disegno animato; ~**ist** n disegnatore/trice, caricaturista m/f; fumettista m/f.
cartridge [ˈkɑːtrɪdʒ] n (for gun, pen) cartuccia; (for camera) caricatore m; (music tape) cassetta; (of record player) testina.
carve [kɑːv] vt (meat) trinciare; (wood, stone) intagliare; **carving** n (in wood etc) scultura; **carving knife** n trinciante m.
car wash [ˈkɑːwɒʃ] n lavaggio auto.
cascade [kæsˈkeɪd] n cascata // vi scendere a cascata.
case [keɪs] n caso; (LAW) causa, processo; (box) scatola; (also: **suit**~) valigia; **he hasn't put forward his** ~ **very well** non ha dimostrato bene il suo caso; **in** ~ **of** in caso di; **in** ~ **he** caso mai lui; **just in** ~ in caso di bisogno.
cash [kæʃ] n denaro; (COMM) denaro liquido; (COMM: in payment) pagamento in contanti // vt incassare; **to pay (in)** ~ pagare in contanti; ~ **with order/on delivery** (COMM) pagamento all'ordinazione/contro assegno; ~**book** n giornale m di cassa; ~**desk** n cassa.
cashew [kæˈʃuː] n (also: ~ **nut**) anacardio.
cashier [kæˈʃɪə*] n cassiere(a).

cashmere [kæʃˈmɪə*] n cachemire m.
cash register [ˈkæʃredʒɪstə*] n registratore m di cassa.
casing [ˈkeɪsɪŋ] n rivestimento.
casino [kəˈsiːnəu] n casinò m inv.
cask [kɑːsk] n botte f.
casket [ˈkɑːskɪt] n cofanetto; (US: coffin) bara.
casserole [ˈkæsərəul] n casseruola; (food) stufato (nella casseruola).
cast [kɑːst] vt (pt, pp cast) (throw) gettare; (shed) perdere; spogliarsi di; (metal) gettare, fondere // n (THEATRE) complesso di attori; (mould) forma; (also: **plaster** ~) ingessatura; (THEATRE): **to** ~ **sb as Hamlet** scegliere qd per la parte di Amleto; **to** ~ **one's vote** votare, dare il voto; **to** ~ **off** vi (NAUT) salpare.
castanets [kæstəˈnɛts] npl castagnette fpl.
castaway [ˈkɑːstəwəɪ] n naufrago/a.
caste [kɑːst] n casta.
casting [ˈkɑːstɪŋ] a: ~ **vote** voto decisivo.
cast iron [ˈkɑːstˈaɪən] n ferro battuto.
castle [ˈkɑːsl] n castello; (fortified) rocca.
castor [ˈkɑːstə*] n (wheel) rotella; ~ **oil** n olio di ricino; ~ **sugar** n zucchero semolato.
castrate [kæsˈtreɪt] vt castrare.
casual [ˈkæʒjul] a (by chance) casuale, fortuito(a); (irregular: work etc) avventizio(a); (unconcerned) noncurante, indifferente; ~ **wear** n casual m; ~ **labour** n manodopera avventizia; ~**ly** ad con disinvoltura; casualmente.
casualty [ˈkæʒjultɪ] n ferito/a; (dead) morto/a, vittima; **heavy casualties** npl grosse perdite fpl.
cat [kæt] n gatto.
catalogue [ˈkætəlɒg] n catalogo.
catalyst [ˈkætəlɪst] n catalizzatore m.
catapult [ˈkætəpʌlt] n catapulta, fionda.
cataract [ˈkætərækt] n (also MED) cateratta.
catarrh [kəˈtɑː*] n catarro.
catastrophe [kəˈtæstrəfɪ] n catastrofe f; **catastrophic** [kætəˈstrɒfɪk] a catastrofico(a).
catch [kætʃ] vb (pt, pp caught [cɔːt]) vt (train, thief, cold) acchiappare; (ball) chiappare; (person: by surprise) sorprendere; (understand) comprendere; (get entangled) impigliare // vi (fire) prendere // n (fish etc caught) retata, presa; (trick) inganno; (TECH) gancio; **to** ~ **sb's attention or eye** attirare l'attenzione di qd; **to** ~ **fire** prendere fuoco; **to** ~ **sight of** scorgere; **to** ~ **up** vi mettersi in pari // vt (also: ~ **up with**) raggiungere.
catching [ˈkætʃɪŋ] a (MED) contagioso(a).
catchment area [ˈkætʃməntˈeərɪə] n (SCOL) circoscrizione f scolare; (GEO) bacino pluviale.
catch phrase [ˈkætʃfreɪz] n slogan m inv; frase f fatta.
catchy [ˈkætʃɪ] a orecchiabile.

catechism ['kætɪkɪzəm] *n* (*REL*) catechismo.

categoric(al) [kætɪ'gɔrɪk(əl)] *a* categorico(a).

categorize ['kætɪgəraɪz] *vt* categorizzare.

category ['kætɪgərɪ] *n* categoria.

cater ['keɪtə*] *vi* (*gen*: ~ **for**) provvedere da mangiare (per); **to ~ for** *vt fus* (*needs*) provvedere a; (*readers*, *consumers*) incontrare i gusti di; ~**er** *n* fornitore *m*; ~**ing** *n* approvvigionamento; ~**ing trade** *n* settore *m* ristoranti.

caterpillar ['kætəpɪlə*] *n* bruco; ~ **track/vehicle** *n* catena/trattore *m* a cingoli.

cathedral [kə'θi:drəl] *n* cattedrale *f*, duomo.

catholic ['kæθəlɪk] *a* universale; aperto(a); eclettico(a); **C~** *a,n* (*REL*) cattolico(a).

cattle ['kætl] *npl* bestiame *m*, bestie *fpl*.

caught [kɔ:t] *pt,pp* of **catch**.

cauliflower ['kɔlɪflauə*] *n* cavolfiore *m*.

cause [kɔ:z] *n* causa // *vt* causare; **there is no ~ for concern** non c'è ragione di preoccuparsi.

causeway ['kɔ:zweɪ] *n* strada rialzata.

caustic ['kɔ:stɪk] *a* caustico(a).

caution ['kɔ:ʃən] *n* prudenza; (*warning*) avvertimento // *vt* avvertire; ammonire.

cautious ['kɔ:ʃəs] *a* cauto(a); ~**ly** *ad* prudentemente; ~**ness** *n* cautela.

cavalry ['kævəlrɪ] *n* cavalleria.

cave [keɪv] *n* caverna, grotta; **to ~ in** *vi* (*roof etc*) crollare; ~**man** *n* uomo delle caverne.

cavern ['kævən] *n* caverna.

caviar(e) ['kævɪɑ:*] *n* caviale *m*.

cavity ['kævɪtɪ] *n* cavità *f inv*.

cavort [kə'vɔ:t] *vi* far capriole.

CBI *n* (*abbr of Confederation of British Industries*) ≈ Confindustria.

cc *abbr of cubic centimetres; carbon copy.*

cease [si:s] *vt,vi* cessare; ~**fire** *n* cessate il fuoco *m inv*; ~**less** *a* incessante, continuo(a).

cedar ['si:də*] *n* cedro.

cede [si:d] *vt* cedere.

ceiling ['si:lɪŋ] *n* soffitto.

celebrate ['sɛlɪbreɪt] *vt,vi* celebrare; ~**d** *a* celebre; **celebration** [-'breɪʃən] *n* celebrazione *f*.

celebrity [sɪ'lɛbrɪtɪ] *n* celebrità *f inv*.

celery ['sɛlərɪ] *n* sedano.

celestial [sɪ'lɛstɪəl] *a* celeste.

celibacy ['sɛlɪbəsɪ] *n* celibato.

cell [sɛl] *n* cella; (*ELEC*) elemento (di batteria).

cellar ['sɛlə*] *n* sottosuolo, cantina.

'cello ['tʃɛləu] *n* violoncello.

cellophane ['sɛləfeɪn] *n* cellophane *m*.

cellulose ['sɛljuləus] *n* cellulosa.

Celtic ['kɛltɪk, 'sɛltɪk] *a* celtico(a).

cement [sə'mɛnt] *n* cemento // *vt* cementare.

cemetery ['sɛmɪtrɪ] *n* cimitero.

cenotaph ['sɛnətɑ:f] *n* cenotafio.

censor ['sɛnsə*] *n* censore *m*; ~**ship** *n* censura.

censure ['sɛnʃə*] *vt* riprovare, censurare.

census ['sɛnsəs] *n* censimento.

cent [sɛnt] *n* (*US: coin*) centesimo, = *1:100* di un dollaro; see also **per**.

centenary [sɛn'ti:nərɪ] *n* centenario.

centi... ['sɛntɪ] *prefix:* ~**grade** *a* centigrado(a); ~**metre** *n* centimetro.

centipede ['sɛntɪpi:d] *n* centopiedi *m inv*.

central ['sɛntrəl] *a* centrale; ~ **heating** *n* riscaldamento centrale; ~**ize** *vt* accentrare.

centre ['sɛntə*] *n* centro; ~**-forward** *n* (*SPORT*) centroavanti *m inv*; ~**-half** *n* (*SPORT*) centromediano.

centrifugal [sɛn'trɪfjugəl] *a* centrifugo(a).

century ['sɛntjurɪ] *n* secolo.

ceramic [sɪ'ræmɪk] *a* ceramico(a).

cereal ['si:rɪəl] *n* cereale *m*.

ceremony ['sɛrɪmənɪ] *n* cerimonia; **to stand on ~** fare complimenti.

certain ['sə:tən] *a* certo(a); **to make ~ of** assicurarsi di; **for ~** per certo, di sicuro; ~**ly** *ad* certamente, certo; ~**ty** *n* certezza.

certificate [sə'tɪfɪkɪt] *n* certificato; diploma *m*.

certify ['sə:tɪfaɪ] *vt* certificare // *vi*: **to ~ to** attestare a.

cervix ['sə:vɪks] *n* cervice *f*.

cessation [sə'seɪʃən] *n* cessazione *f*; arresto.

cesspool ['sɛspu:l] *n* pozzo nero.

cf. (*abbr = compare*) cfr., confronta.

chafe [tʃeɪf] *vt* fregare, irritare.

chaffinch ['tʃæfɪntʃ] *n* fringuello.

chain [tʃeɪn] *n* catena // *vt* (*also:* ~ **up**) incatenare; ~ **reaction** *n* reazione *f* a catena; **to ~ smoke** vi fumare una sigaretta dopo l'altra; ~ **store** *n* negozio a catena.

chair [tʃɛə*] *n* sedia; (*armchair*) poltrona; (*of university*) cattedra // *vt* (*meeting*) presiedere; ~**lift** *n* seggiovia; ~**man** *n* presidente *m*.

chalet ['ʃæleɪ] *n* chalet *m inv*.

chalice ['tʃælɪs] *n* calice *m*.

chalk [tʃɔ:k] *n* gesso.

challenge ['tʃælɪndʒ] *n* sfida // *vt* sfidare; (*statement*, *right*) mettere in dubbio; **to ~ sb to a fight/game** sfidare qd a battersi/ad una partita; **to ~ sb to do** sfidare qd a fare; ~**r** *n* (*SPORT*) sfidante *m/f*; **challenging** *a* sfidante; provocatorio(a).

chamber ['tʃeɪmbə*] *n* camera; ~ **of commerce** camera di commercio; ~**maid** *n* cameriera; ~ **music** *n* musica da camera.

chamois ['ʃæmwɑ:] *n* camoscio; ~ **leather** ['ʃæmɪleðə*] *n* pelle *f* di camoscio.

champagne [ʃæm'peɪn] *n* champagne *m inv*.

champion ['tʃæmpɪən] *n* campione/essa; ~**ship** *n* campionato.

chance [tʃɑ:ns] *n* caso; (*opportunity*)

occasione f; (*likelihood*) possibilità f *inv* // *vt*: **to ~ it** rischiarlo // *a* fortuito(a); **there is little ~ of his coming** è molto improbabile che venga; **to take a ~** arrischiarlo; **by ~** per caso.

chancel ['tʃɑːnsəl] *n* coro.

chancellor ['tʃɑːnsələ*] *n* cancelliere *m*; **C~ of the Exchequer** *n* Cancelliere dello Scacchiere.

chandelier [ʃændə'liə*] *n* lampadario.

change [tʃeɪndʒ] *vt* cambiare; (*transform*): **to ~ sb into** trasformare qd in // *vi* cambiarsi; (*be transformed*): **to ~ into** trasformarsi in // *n* cambiamento; (*money*) resto; **to ~ one's mind** cambiare idea; **a ~ of clothes** una cambiata; **for a ~** tanto per cambiare; **small ~** spiccioli *mpl*, moneta; **~able** *a* (*weather*) variabile; **~over** *n* cambiamento, passaggio.

changing ['tʃeɪndʒɪŋ] *a* che cambia; (*colours*) cangiante; **~ room** *n* (*in shop*) camerino; (*SPORT*) spogliatoio.

channel ['tʃænl] *n* canale *m*; (*of river, sea*) alveo // *vt* canalizzare; **through the usual ~s** per le solite vie; **the (English) C~** la Manica; **the C~ Islands** le Isole Normanne.

chant [tʃɑːnt] *n* canto; salmodia // *vt* cantare; salmodiare.

chaos ['keɪɔs] *n* caos *m*.

chaotic [keɪ'ɔtɪk] *a* caotico(a).

chap [tʃæp] *n* (*col: man*) tipo // *vt* (*skin*) screpolare.

chapel ['tʃæpəl] *n* cappella.

chaperon ['ʃæpərəun] *n* accompagnatrice f // *vt* accompagnare.

chaplain ['tʃæplɪn] *n* cappellano.

chapter ['tʃæptə*] *n* capitolo.

char [tʃɑː*] *vt* (*burn*) carbonizzare // *vi* (*cleaner*) lavorare come domestica (a ore) // *n* = **charlady**.

character ['kærɪktə*] *n* carattere *m*; (*in novel, film*) personaggio; (*eccentric*) originale *m*; **~istic** [-'rɪstɪk] *a* caratteristico(a) // *n* caratteristica; **~ize** *vt* caratterizzare.

charade [ʃə'rɑːd] *n* sciarada.

charcoal ['tʃɑːkəul] *n* carbone *m* di legna.

charge [tʃɑːdʒ] *n* accusa; (*cost*) prezzo; (*of gun, battery,* MIL: *attack*) carica // *vt* (*LAW*): **to ~ sb (with)** accusare qd (di); (*gun, battery,* MIL: *enemy*) caricare; (*customer*) fare pagare a; (*sum*) fare pagare // *vi* (*gen with: up, along etc*) lanciarsi; **~s** *npl*: **bank ~s** commissioni *fpl* bancarie; **labour ~s** costi *mpl* del lavoro; **to ~ in/out** precipitarsi dentro/fuori; **is there a ~?** c'è da pagare?; **there's no ~** non c'è niente da pagare; **to take ~ of** incaricarsi di; **to be in ~ of** essere responsabile per; **to have ~ of** sb aver cura di qd; **to ~ an expense (up) to sb** addebitare una spesa a qd.

chariot ['tʃærɪət] *n* carro.

charitable ['tʃærɪtəbl] *a* caritatevole.

charity ['tʃærɪtɪ] *n* carità; opera pia.

charlady ['tʃɑːleɪdɪ] *n* domestica a ore.

charm [tʃɑːm] *n* fascino; amuleto // *vt* affascinare, incantare; **~ing** *a* affascinante.

chart [tʃɑːt] *n* tabella; grafico; (*map*) carta nautica // *vt* fare una carta nautica di.

charter ['tʃɑːtə*] *vt* (*plane*) noleggiare // *n* (*document*) carta; **~ed accountant** *n* ragioniere/a professionista; **~ flight** *n* volo *m* charter *inv*.

chase [tʃeɪs] *vt* inseguire; (*away*) cacciare // *n* caccia.

chasm ['kæzm] *n* abisso.

chassis ['ʃæsɪ] *n* telaio.

chastity ['tʃæstɪtɪ] *n* castità.

chat [tʃæt] *vi* (*also*: **have a ~**) chiacchierare // *n* chiacchierata.

chatter ['tʃætə*] *vi* (*person*) ciarlare // *n* ciarle *fpl*; **~box** *n* chiacchierone/a.

chatty ['tʃætɪ] *a* (*style*) familiare; (*person*) chiacchierino(a).

chauffeur ['ʃəufə*] *n* autista *m*.

cheap [tʃiːp] *a* a buon mercato; (*joke*) grossolano(a); (*poor quality*) di cattiva qualità // *ad* a buon mercato; **~en** *vt* ribassare; (*fig*) avvilire.

cheat [tʃiːt] *vi* imbrogliare; (*at school*) copiare // *vt* ingannare; (*rob*) defraudare // *n* imbroglione *m*; copione *m*; (*trick*) inganno.

check [tʃɛk] *vt* verificare; (*passport, ticket*) controllare; (*halt*) fermare; (*restrain*) contenere // *n* verifica; controllo; (*curb*) freno; (*bill*) conto; (*pattern: gen pl*) quadretti *mpl*; (*US*) = **cheque**; **to ~ in** *vi* (*in hotel*) registrare; (*at airport*) presentarsi all'accettazione // *vt* (*luggage*) depositare; **to ~ off** *vt* segnare; **to ~ out** *vi* (*in hotel*) saldare il conto // *vt* (*luggage*) ritirare; **to ~ up** *vi*: **to ~ up (on sth)** investigare (qc); **to ~ up on sb** informarsi sul conto di qd; **~ers** *n* (*US*) dama; **~mate** *n* scaccomatto; **~up** *n* (*MED*) controllo medico.

cheek [tʃiːk] *n* guancia; (*impudence*) faccia tosta; **~bone** *n* zigomo; **~y** *a* sfacciato(a).

cheer [tʃɪə*] *vt* applaudire; (*gladden*) rallegrare // *vi* applaudire // *n* (*gen pl*) applausi *mpl*; evviva *mpl*; **~s!** salute!; **to ~ up** *vi* rallegrarsi, farsi animo // *vt* rallegrare; **~ful** *a* allegro(a); **~io** *excl* ciao!

cheese [tʃiːz] *n* formaggio; **~board** *n* piatto da formaggio.

chef [ʃɛf] *n* capocuoco.

chemical ['kɛmɪkəl] *a* chimico(a) // *n* prodotto chimico.

chemist ['kɛmɪst] *n* farmacista *m/f*; (*scientist*) chimico/a; **~ry** *n* chimica; **~'s (shop)** *n* farmacia.

cheque [tʃɛk] *n* assegno; **~book** *n* libretto degli assegni.

chequered ['tʃɛkəd] *a* (*fig*) eclettico(a).

cherish ['tʃɛrɪʃ] *vt* aver caro; (*hope etc*) nutrire.

cherry ['tʃɛrɪ] *n* ciliegia.

chess [tʃɛs] *n* scacchi *mpl*; **~board** *n* scacchiera; **~man** *n* pezzo degli scacchi.

chest [tʃest] n petto; (box) cassa; ~ of drawers n cassettone m.

chestnut ['tʃesnʌt] n castagna; ~ (tree) n castagno.

chew [tʃu:] vt masticare; ~ing gum n chewing gum m.

chic [ʃi:k] a elegante.

chick [tʃik] n pulcino.

chicken ['tʃikɪn] n pollo; ~ feed n (fig) miseria; ~ pox n varicella.

chicory ['tʃikərɪ] n cicoria.

chief [tʃi:f] n capo // a principale; ~ly ad per lo più, soprattutto.

chiffon ['ʃifɔn] n chiffon m inv.

chilblain ['tʃilbleɪn] n gelone m.

child, pl ~ren [tʃaild, 'tʃildrən] n bambino/a; ~birth n parto; ~hood n infanzia; ~ish a puerile; ~like a fanciullesco(a); ~ minder n bambinaia.

Chile ['tʃili] n Cile m; ~an a, n cileno(a).

chill [tʃil] n freddo; (MED) infreddatura // a freddo(a), gelido(a) // vt raffreddare; ~y a freddo(a), fresco(a); (sensitive to cold) freddoloso(a); to feel ~y sentirsi infreddolito(a).

chime [tʃaim] n carillon m inv // vi suonare, scampanare.

chimney ['tʃimni] n camino.

chimpanzee [tʃimpæn'zi:] n scimpanzé m inv.

chin [tʃin] n mento.

china ['tʃainə] n porcellana.

China ['tʃainə] n Cina.

Chinese [tʃai'ni:z] a cinese // n cinese m/f; (LING) cinese m.

chink [tʃiŋk] n (opening) fessura; (noise) tintinnio.

chip [tʃip] n (gen pl: CULIN) patatina fritta; (of wood, glass, stone) scheggia // vt (cup, plate) scheggiare; ~pings npl: loose ~pings brecciame m.

chiropodist [ki'rɔpədist] n pedicure m/f inv.

chirp [tʃə:p] n cinguettio // vi cinguettare.

chisel ['tʃizl] n cesello.

chit [tʃit] n biglietto.

chivalrous ['ʃivəlrəs] a cavalleresco(a).

chivalry ['ʃivəlrɪ] n cavalleria; cortesia.

chives [tʃaivz] npl erba cipollina.

chloride ['klɔ:raɪd] n cloruro.

chlorine ['klɔ:ri:n] n cloro.

chock [tʃɔk] n zeppa; ~-a-block, ~-full a pieno(a) zeppo(a).

chocolate ['tʃɔklit] n (substance) cioccolato, cioccolata; (drink) cioccolata; (a sweet) cioccolatino.

choice [tʃɔis] n scelta // a scelto(a).

choir ['kwaiə*] n coro; ~boy n corista m fanciullo.

choke [tʃəuk] vi soffocare // vt soffocare; (block) ingombrare // n (AUT) valvola dell'aria.

cholera ['kɔlərə] n colera m.

choose, pt chose, pp chosen [tʃu:z, tʃəuz, 'tʃəuzn] vt scegliere; to ~ to do decidere di fare; preferire fare.

chop [tʃɔp] vt (wood) spaccare; (CULIN: also:

~ up) tritare // n colpo netto; (CULIN) braciola; to ~ down vt (tree) abbattere; ~py a (sea) mosso(a); ~sticks npl bastoncini mpl cinesi.

choral ['kɔ:rəl] a corale.

chord [kɔ:d] n (MUS) accordo.

chore [tʃɔ:*] n faccenda; household ~s faccende fpl domestiche.

choreographer [kɔri'ɔgrəfə*] n coreografo/a.

chorister ['kɔristə*] n corista m/f.

chortle ['tʃɔ:tl] vi ridacchiare.

chorus ['kɔ:rəs] n coro; (repeated part of song, also fig) ritornello.

chose [tʃəuz] pt of choose.

chosen ['tʃəuzn] pp of choose.

Christ [kraist] n Cristo.

christen ['krisn] vt battezzare; ~ing n battesimo.

Christian ['kristiən] a,n cristiano(a); ~ity [-'æniti] n cristianesimo; cristianità; ~ name n prenome m.

Christmas ['krisməs] n Natale m; ~ card n cartolina di Natale; ~ Eve n la vigilia di Natale; ~ tree n albero di Natale.

chrome [krəum] n = chromium plating.

chromium ['krəumiəm] n cromo; ~ plating n cromatura.

chromosome ['krəuməsoum] n cromosoma m.

chronic ['krɔnik] a cronico(a).

chronicle ['krɔnikl] n cronaca.

chronological [krɔnə'lɔdʒikəl] a cronologico(a).

chrysanthemum [kri'sænθəməm] n crisantemo.

chubby ['tʃʌbi] a paffuto(a).

chuck [tʃʌk] vt buttare, gettare; to ~ out vt buttar fuori; to ~ (up) vt piantare.

chuckle ['tʃʌkl] vi ridere sommessamente.

chum [tʃʌm] n compagno/a.

chunk [tʃʌŋk] n pezzo; (of bread) tocco.

church [tʃə:tʃ] n chiesa; ~yard n sagrato.

churn [tʃə:n] n (for butter) zangola; (also: milk ~) bidone m.

chute [ʃu:t] n cascata; (also: rubbish ~) canale m di scarico; (children's slide) scivolo.

CID n (abbr of Criminal Investigation Department) ≈ polizia giudiziaria.

cider ['saidə*] n sidro.

cigar [si'ga:*] n sigaro.

cigarette [sigə'ret] n sigaretta; ~ case n portasigarette m inv; ~ end n mozzicone m; ~ holder n bocchino.

cinch [sintʃ] n (col): it's a ~ è presto fatto.

cinder ['sində*] n cenere f.

cine ['sini]: ~-camera n cinepresa; ~-film n pellicola.

cinema ['sinəmə] n cinema m inv.

cine-projector [siniprə'dʒektə*] n proiettore m.

cinnamon ['sinəmən] n cannella.

cipher ['saifə*] n cifra; (fig: faceless

employee etc) persona di nessun conto.
circle ['sɜːkl] *n* cerchio; (*of friends etc*) circolo; (*in cinema*) galleria // *vi* girare in circolo // *vt* (*surround*) circondare; (*move round*) girare intorno a.
circuit ['sɜːkɪt] *n* circuito; ~**ous** [sɜː'kjuːtəs] *a* indiretto(a).
circular ['sɜːkjulə*] *a*, *n* circolare (*f*).
circulate ['sɜːkjuleɪt] *vi* circolare // *vt* far circolare; **circulation** [-'leɪʃən] *n* circolazione *f*; (*of newspaper*) tiratura.
circumcise ['sɜːkəmsaɪz] *vt* circoncidere.
circumference [sə'kʌmfərəns] *n* circonferenza.
circumstances ['sɜːkəmstənsɪz] *npl* circostanze *fpl*; (*financial condition*) condizioni *fpl* finanziarie.
circus ['sɜːkəs] *n* circo.
cistern ['sɪstən] *n* cisterna; (*in toilet*) serbatoio d'acqua.
cite [saɪt] *vt* citare.
citizen ['sɪtɪzn] *n* (*POL*) cittadino/a; (*resident*): **the ~s of this town** gli abitanti di questa città; ~**ship** *n* cittadinanza.
citrus fruit ['sɪtrəs'fruːt] *n* agrume *m*.
city ['sɪtɪ] *n* città *f inv*; **the C~** la Città di Londra (*centro commerciale*).
civic ['sɪvɪk] *a* civico(a).
civil ['sɪvɪl] *a* civile; ~ **engineer** *n* ingegnere *m* civile; ~**ian** [sɪ'vɪlɪən] *a*, *n* borghese (*m/f*).
civilization [sɪvɪlaɪ'zeɪʃən] *n* civiltà *f inv*.
civilized ['sɪvɪlaɪzd] *a* civilizzato(a); (*fig*) cortese.
civil: ~ **law** *n* codice *m* civile; (*study*) diritto civile; ~ **servant** *n* impiegato/a statale; **C~ Service** *n* amministrazione *f* statale; ~ **war** *n* guerra civile.
claim [kleɪm] *vt* rivendicare; sostenere, pretendere; (*damages*) richiedere // *vi* (*for insurance*) richiedere // *n* rivendicazione *f*; pretesa; (*right*) diritto; (*insurance*) ~ richiesta; ~**ant** *n* (*ADMIN, LAW*) rivendicatore/trice.
clam [klæm] *n* vongola.
clamber ['klæmbə*] *vi* arrampicarsi.
clammy ['klæmɪ] *a* (*weather*) caldo(a) umido(a); (*hands*) viscido(a).
clamp [klæmp] *n* grappa; pinza; morsa // *vt* ammorsare.
clan [klæn] *n* clan *m inv*.
clang [klæŋ] *n* fragore *m*, suono metallico.
clap [klæp] *vi* applaudire; ~**ping** *n* applausi *mpl*.
claret ['klærət] *n* vino di Bordeaux.
clarification [klærɪfɪ'keɪʃən] *n* (*fig*) chiarificazione *f*, schiarimento.
clarify ['klærɪfaɪ] *vt* chiarificare, schiarire.
clarinet [klærɪ'nɛt] *n* clarinetto.
clarity ['klærɪtɪ] *n* chiarità.
clash [klæʃ] *n* frastuono; (*fig*) scontro // *vi* scontrarsi; cozzare.
clasp [klɑːsp] *n* fermaglio, fibbia // *vt* stringere.
class [klɑːs] *n* classe *f* // *vt* classificare.

classic ['klæsɪk] *a* classico(a) // *n* classico; ~**al** *a* classico(a).
classification [klæsɪfɪ'keɪʃən] *n* classificazione *f*.
classify ['klæsɪfaɪ] *vt* classificare.
classmate ['klɑːsmeɪt] *n* compagno/a di classe.
classroom ['klɑːsrum] *n* aula.
clatter ['klætə*] *n* acciottolio; scalpitio // *vi* acciottolare; scalpitare.
clause [klɔːz] *n* clausola; (*LING*) proposizione *f*.
claustrophobia [klɔːstrə'fəubɪə] *n* claustrofobia.
claw [klɔː] *n* tenaglia; (*of bird of prey*) artiglio; (*of lobster*) pinza // *vt* graffiare; afferrare.
clay [kleɪ] *n* argilla.
clean [kliːn] *a* pulito(a); (*clear, smooth*) liscio(a) // *vt* pulire; **to ~ out** *vt* far piazza pulita di; **to ~ up** *vi* far pulizia // *vt* (*also fig*) ripulire; ~**er** *n* (*person*) donna delle pulizie; (*also:* **dry ~er**) tintore/a; (*product*) smacchiatore *m*; ~**ing** *n* pulizia; ~**liness** ['klɛnlɪnɪs] *n* pulizia.
cleanse [klɛnz] *vt* pulire; purificare; ~**r** *n* detergente *m*.
clean-shaven ['kliːn'ʃeɪvn] *a* sbarbato(a).
clean-up ['kliːn'ʌp] *n* pulizia.
clear [klɪə*] *a* chiaro(a); (*road, way*) libero(a) // *vt* sgombrare; liberare; (*table*) sparecchiare; (*COMM: goods*) liquidare; (*LAW: suspect*) discolpare; (*obstacle*) superare // *vi* (*weather*) rasserenarsi; (*fog*) andarsene // *ad:* ~ **of** distante da; **to ~ up** *vi* schiarirsi // *vt* mettere in ordine; (*mystery*) risolvere; ~**ance** *n* (*removal*) sgombro; (*free space*) spazio; (*permission*) autorizzazione *f*, permesso; ~**ance sale** *n* vendita di liquidazione; ~**-cut** *a* ben delineato(a), distinto(a); ~**ing** *n* radura; (*BANKING*) clearing *m*; ~**ly** *ad* chiaramente; ~**way** *n* (*Brit*) strada con divieto di sosta.
clef [klɛf] *n* (*MUS*) chiave *f*.
clench [klɛntʃ] *vt* stringere.
clergy ['klɜːdʒɪ] *n* clero; ~**man** *n* ecclesiastico.
clerical ['klɛrɪkəl] *a* d'impiegato; (*REL*) clericale.
clerk [klɑːk, (*US*) klɜːrk] *n* impiegato/a; (*US: salesman/ woman*) commesso/a.
clever ['klɛvə*] *a* (*mentally*) intelligente; (*deft, skilful*) abile; (*device, arrangement*) ingegnoso(a).
cliché ['kliːʃeɪ] *n* cliché *m inv*.
click [klɪk] *vi* scattare.
client ['klaɪənt] *n* cliente *m/f*; ~**ele** [kliːɑ̃:n'tɛl] *n* clientela.
cliff [klɪf] *n* scogliera scoscesa, rupe *f*.
climate ['klaɪmɪt] *n* clima *m*.
climax ['klaɪmæks] *n* culmine *m*.
climb [klaɪm] *vi* salire; (*clamber*) arrampicarsi // *vt* salire; (*CLIMBING*) scalare // *n* salita; arrampicata; scalata; **to ~ down** *vi* scendere; ~**er** *n* (*also:* **rock ~er**) rocciatore/trice; alpinista

m/f; ~ing n (also: rock ~ing) alpinismo.

clinch [klɪntʃ] vt (deal) concludere.

cling, pt, pp clung [klɪŋ, klʌŋ] vi: to ~ (to) tenersi stretto (a); (of clothes) aderire strettamente (a).

clinic ['klɪnɪk] n clinica; ~al a clinico(a).

clink [klɪŋk] vi tintinnare.

clip [klɪp] n (for hair) forcina; (also: paper ~) graffetta; (holding hose etc) anello d'attacco // vt (also: ~ together: papers) attaccare insieme; (hair, nails) tagliare; (hedge) tosare; ~pers npl macchinetta per capelli; (also: nail ~pers) forbicine fpl per le unghie.

clique [kli:k] n cricca.

cloak [kləʊk] n mantello; ~room n (for coats etc) guardaroba m inv; (W.C.) gabinetti mpl.

clock [klɔk] n orologio; ~wise ad in senso orario; ~work n movimento or meccanismo a orologeria.

clog [klɔg] n zoccolo // vt intasare.

cloister ['klɔɪstə*] n chiostro.

close a, ad and derivatives [kləʊs] a vicino(a); (writing, texture) fitto(a); (watch) stretto(a); (examination) attento(a); (weather) afoso(a) // ad vicino, dappresso; a ~ friend un amico intimo; to have a ~ shave (fig) scamparla bella // vb and derivatives [kləʊz] vt chiudere // vi (shop etc) chiudere; (lid, door etc) chiudersi; (end) finire // n (end) fine f; to ~ down vt chiudere (definitivamente) // vi cessare (definitivamente); ~d a chiuso(a); ~d shop n azienda o fabbrica che impiega solo aderenti ai sindacati; ~ly ad (examine, watch) da vicino.

closet ['klɔzɪt] n (cupboard) armadio.

close-up ['kləʊsʌp] n primo piano.

closure ['kləʊʒə*] n chiusura.

clot [klɔt] n (also: blood ~) coagulo; (col: idiot) scemo/a // vi coagularsi; ~ted cream n panna rappresa.

cloth [klɔθ] n (material) tessuto, stoffa; (also: tea ~) strofinaccio.

clothe [kləʊð] vt vestire; ~s npl abiti mpl, vestiti mpl; ~s line n corda (per stendere il bucato); ~s peg n molletta.

clothing ['kləʊðɪŋ] n = clothes.

cloud [klaʊd] n nuvola; ~burst n acquazzone m; ~y a nuvoloso(a); (liquid) torbido(a).

clout [klaʊt] n (blow) colpo // vt dare un colpo a.

clove [kləʊv] n chiodo di garofano; ~ of garlic spicchio d'aglio.

clover ['kləʊvə*] n trifoglio.

clown [klaʊn] n pagliaccio // vi (also: ~ about, ~ around) fare il pagliaccio.

club [klʌb] n (society) club m inv, circolo; (weapon, GOLF) mazza // vt bastonare // vi: to ~ together associarsi; ~s npl (CARDS) fiori mpl; ~house n sede f del circolo.

cluck [klʌk] vi chiocciare.

clue [klu:] n indizio; (in crosswords)

definizione f; I haven't a ~ non ho la minima idea.

clump [klʌmp] n: ~ of trees folto d'alberi.

clumsy ['klʌmzɪ] a (person) goffo(a), maldestro(a); (object) malfatto(a), mal costruito(a).

clung [klʌŋ] pt, pp of cling.

cluster ['klʌstə*] n gruppo // vi raggrupparsi.

clutch [klʌtʃ] n (grip, grasp) presa, stretta; (AUT) frizione f // vt afferrare, stringere forte; to ~ at aggrapparsi a.

clutter ['klʌtə*] vt ingombrare.

Co. abbr of county; company.

c/o (abbr of care of) presso.

coach [kəʊtʃ] n (bus) pullman m inv; (horse-drawn, of train) carrozza; (SPORT) allenatore/trice // vt allenare.

coagulate [kəʊ'ægjʊleɪt] vi coagularsi.

coal [kəʊl] n carbone m; ~ face n fronte f; ~field n bacino carbonifero.

coalition [kəʊə'lɪʃən] n coalizione f.

coalman, coal merchant ['kəʊlmən, 'kəʊlmɑ:tʃənt] n negoziante m di carbone.

coalmine ['kəʊlmaɪn] n miniera di carbone.

coarse [kɔ:s] a (salt, sand etc) grosso(a); (cloth, person) rozzo(a).

coast [kəʊst] n costa // vi (with cycle etc) scendere a ruota libera; ~al a costiero(a); ~guard n guardia costiera; ~line n linea costiera.

coat [kəʊt] n cappotto; (of animal) pelo; (of paint) mano f // vt coprire; ~ of arms n stemma m; ~ hanger n attaccapanni m inv; ~ing n rivestimento.

coax [kəʊks] vt indurre (con moine).

cobbles, cobblestones ['kɔblz, 'kɔblstəʊnz] npl ciottoli mpl.

cobra ['kəʊbrə] n cobra.

cobweb ['kɔbwɛb] n ragnatela.

cocaine [kə'keɪn] n cocaina.

cock [kɔk] n (rooster) gallo; (male bird) maschio // vt (gun) armare; to ~ one's ears (fig) drizzare le orecchie; ~erel n galletto; ~-eyed a (fig) storto(a); strampalato(a).

cockle ['kɔkl] n cardio.

cockney ['kɔknɪ] n cockney m/f inv (abitante dei quartieri popolari dell'East End di Londra).

cockpit ['kɔkpɪt] n (in aircraft) abitacolo.

cockroach ['kɔkrəʊtʃ] n blatta.

cocktail ['kɔkteɪl] n cocktail m inv; ~ shaker n shaker m inv.

cocoa ['kəʊkəʊ] n cacao.

coconut ['kəʊkənʌt] n noce f di cocco.

cocoon [kə'ku:n] n bozzolo.

cod [kɔd] n merluzzo.

code [kəʊd] n codice m.

codify ['kəʊdɪfaɪ] vt codificare.

coeducational ['kəʊɛdju'keɪʃənl] a misto(a).

coerce [kəʊ'ə:s] vt costringere; coercion [-'ə:ʃən] n coercizione f.

coexistence [ˈkəuɪgˈzɪstəns] *n* coesistenza.

coffee [ˈkɔfɪ] *n* caffè *m inv*; ~ **grounds** *npl* fondi *mpl* di caffè; ~**pot** *n* caffettiera; ~ **table** *n* tavolino da tè.

coffin [ˈkɔfɪn] *n* bara.

cog [kɔg] *n* dente *m*; ~**wheel** *n* ruota dentata.

cogent [ˈkəudʒənt] *a* convincente.

coherent [kəuˈhɪərənt] *a* coerente.

coil [kɔɪl] *n* rotolo; (*one loop*) anello; (*contraceptive*) spirale *f* // *vt* avvolgere.

coin [kɔɪn] *n* moneta // *vt* (*word*) coniare; ~**age** *n* sistema *m* monetario.

coincide [kəuɪnˈsaɪd] *vi* coincidere; ~**nce** [kəuˈɪnsɪdəns] *n* combinazione *f*.

coke [kəuk] *n* coke *m*.

colander [ˈkɔləndəʳ] *n* colino.

cold [kəuld] *a* freddo(a) // *n* freddo; (*MED*) raffreddore *m*; **it's** ~ fa freddo; **to be** ~ aver freddo; **to have** ~ **feet** avere i piedi freddi; (*fig*) aver la fifa; **to give sb the** ~ **shoulder** ignorare qd; ~**ly** *ad* freddamente; ~ **sore** *n* erpete *m*.

coleslaw [ˈkəulslɔ:] *n* insalata di cavolo e di salsa maionese.

collaborate [kəˈlæbəreɪt] *vi* collaborare; **collaboration** [-ˈreɪʃən] *n* collaborazione *f*; **collaborator** *n* collaboratore/trice.

collage [kɔˈlɑ:ʒ] *n* collage *m inv*.

collapse [kəˈlæps] *vi* crollare // *n* crollo; (*MED*) collasso.

collapsible [kəˈlæpsəbl] *a* pieghevole.

collar [ˈkɔləʳ] *n* (*of coat, shirt*) colletto; ~ **bone** *n* clavicola.

colleague [ˈkɔli:g] *n* collega *m/f*.

collect [kəˈlekt] *vt* adunare; raccogliere; (*as a hobby*) fare collezione di; (*call and pick up*) prendere; (*mail*) raccogliere; (*money owed, pension*) riscuotere; (*donations, subscriptions*) fare una colletta di // *vi* adunarsi, riunirsi; ammucchiarsi; ~**ed** *a*: ~**ed works** opere *fpl* raccolte; ~**ion** [kəˈlekʃən] *n* collezione *f*; raccolta; (*for money*) colletta.

collector [kəˈlektəʳ] *n* collezionista *m/f*; (*of taxes*) esattore *m*.

college [ˈkɔlɪdʒ] *n* collegio.

collide [kəˈlaɪd] *vi*: **to** ~ (**with**) scontrarsi (con).

colliery [ˈkɔlɪərɪ] *n* miniera di carbone.

collision [kəˈlɪʒən] *n* collisione *f*, scontro.

colloquial [kəˈləukwɪəl] *a* familiare.

colon [ˈkəulɔn] *n* (*sign*) due punti *mpl*; (*MED*) colon *m inv*.

colonel [ˈkə:nl] *n* colonnello.

colonial [kəˈləunɪəl] *a* coloniale.

colonize [ˈkɔlənaɪz] *vt* colonizzare.

colony [ˈkɔlənɪ] *n* colonia.

colossal [kəˈlɔsl] *a* colossale.

colour [ˈkʌləʳ] *n* colore *m* // *vt* colorare; dipingere; (*news*) svisare; ~**s** *npl* (*of party, club*) emblemi *mpl*; ~ **bar** *n* discriminazione *f* razziale (*in locali etc*); ~-**blind** *a* daltonico(a); ~**ed** *a* colorato(a); (*photo*) a colori // *n*: ~**eds** gente *f* di colore; ~ **film** *n* (*for camera*)

pellicola a colori; ~**ful** *a* pieno(a) di colore, a vivaci colori; (*personality*) colorato(a); ~ **television** *n* televisione *f* a colori.

colt [kəult] *n* puledro.

column [ˈkɔləm] *n* colonna; ~**ist** [ˈkɔləmnɪst] *n* articolista *m/f*.

coma [ˈkəumə] *n* coma *m inv*.

comb [kəum] *n* pettine *m* // *vt* (*hair*) pettinare; (*area*) battere a tappeto.

combat [ˈkɔmbæt] *n* combattimento // *vt* combattere, lottare contro.

combination [kɔmbɪˈneɪʃən] *n* combinazione *f*.

combine *vb* [kəmˈbaɪn] *vt* combinare; (*one quality with another*) unire (a) // *vi* unirsi; (*CHEM*) combinarsi // *n* [ˈkɔmbaɪn] lega; (*ECON*) associazione *f*; ~ (**harvester**) *n* mietitrebbia.

combustible [kəmˈbʌstɪbl] *a* combustibile.

combustion [kəmˈbʌstʃən] *n* combustione *f*.

come, *pt* **came**, *pp* **come** [kʌm, keɪm] *vi* venire; arrivare; **to** ~ **to** (*decision etc*) raggiungere; **to** ~ **about** *vi* succedere; **to** ~ **across** *vt fus* trovare per caso; **to** ~ **along** *vi* = **to come on**; **to** ~ **apart** *vi* andare in pezzi; staccarsi; **to** ~ **away** *vi* venire via; staccarsi; **to** ~ **back** *vi* ritornare; **to** ~ **by** *vt fus* (*acquire*) ottenere; procurarsi; **to** ~ **down** *vi* discendere; (*prices*) calare; (*buildings*) essere demolito(a); **to** ~ **forward** *vi* farsi avanti; presentarsi; **to** ~ **from** *vt* venire da; provenire da; **to** ~ **in** *vi* entrare; **to** ~ **in for** *vt fus* (*criticism etc*) ricevere; **to** ~ **into** *vt fus* (*money*) ereditare; **to** ~ **off** *vi* (*button*) staccarsi; (*stain*) andar via; (*attempt*) riuscire; **to** ~ **on** *vi* (*pupil, undertaking*) fare progressi; ~ **on!** avanti!, andiamo!, forza!; **to** ~ **out** *vi* uscire; (*strike*) entrare in sciopero; **to** ~ **to** *vi* rinvenire; **to** ~ **up** *vi* venire su; **to** ~ **up against** *vt fus* (*resistance, difficulties*) urtare contro; **to** ~ **up with** *vt fus*: **he came up with an idea** venne fuori con un'idea; **to** ~ **upon** *vt fus* trovare per caso; ~**back** *n* (*THEATRE etc*) ritorno.

comedian [kəˈmi:dɪən] *n* comico.

comedown [ˈkʌmdaun] *n* rovescio.

comedy [ˈkɔmɪdɪ] *n* commedia.

comet [ˈkɔmɪt] *n* cometa.

comfort [ˈkʌmfət] *n* comodità *f inv*, benessere *m*; (*solace*) consolazione *f*, conforto // *vt* consolare, confortare; ~**s** *npl* comodi *mpl*; ~**able** *a* comodo(a); ~ **station** *n* (*US*) gabinetti *mpl*.

comic [ˈkɔmɪk] *a* (*also*: ~**al**) comico(a) // *n* comico; (*magazine*) giornaletto; ~ **strip** *n* fumetto.

coming [ˈkʌmɪŋ] *n* arrivo; ~(**s**) **and going(s)** *n(pl)* andirivieni *m inv*.

comma [ˈkɔmə] *n* virgola.

command [kəˈmɑ:nd] *n* ordine *m*, comando; (*MIL: authority*) comando; (*mastery*) padronanza // *vt* comandare; **to** ~ **sb to do** ordinare a qd di fare; ~**eer**

[kɔmən'diɔ*] vt requisire; ~er n capo; (MIL) comandante m; ~ing officer n comandante m.

commando [kə'mɑːndəu] n commando m inv; membro di un commando.

commemorate [kə'mɛmɔreit] vt commemorare; commemoration [-'reiʃən] n commemorazione f.

commence [kə'mɛns] vt,vi cominciare.

commend [kə'mɛnd] vt lodare; raccomandare; ~able a lodevole; ~ation [kɔmɛn'deiʃən] n lode f; raccomandazione f.

commensurate [kə'mɛnʃərit] a: ~ with proporzionato(a) a.

comment ['kɔmɛnt] n commento // vi fare commenti; ~ary ['kɔmɛntəri] n commentario; (SPORT) radiocronaca; telecronaca; ~ator ['kɔmɛnteitə*] n commentatore/trice; radiocronista m/f; telecronista m/f.

commerce ['kɔmɔːs] n commercio.

commercial [kə'mɔːʃəl] a commerciale // n (TV: also: ~ break) pubblicità f inv; ~ize vt commercializzare; ~ television n televisione f commerciale; ~ traveller n commesso viaggiatore; ~ vehicle n veicolo commerciale.

commiserate [kə'mizəreit] vi: to ~ with condolersi con.

commission [kə'miʃən] n commissione f // vt (MIL) nominare (al comando); (work of art) commissionare; out of ~ (NAUT) in disarmo; ~aire [kəmiʃə'nɛə*] n (at shop, cinema etc) portiere m in livrea; ~er n commissionario; (POLICE) questore m.

commit [kə'mit] vt (act) commettere; (to sb's care) affidare; to ~ o.s. (to do) impegnarsi (a fare); to ~ suicide suicidarsi; ~ment n impegno; promessa.

committee [kə'miti] n comitato.

commodity [kə'mɔditi] n prodotto, articolo; (food) derrata.

common ['kɔmən] a comune; (pej) volgare; (usual) normale // n terreno comune; the C~s npl la Camera dei Comuni; ~ in ~ in comune; it's ~ knowledge that è di dominio pubblico che; ~er n cittadino/a (non nobile); ~ ground n (fig) terreno comune; ~ law n diritto consuetudinario; ~ly ad comunemente, usualmente; C~ Market n Mercato Comune; ~place a banale, ordinario(a); ~room n sala di riunione; (SCOL) sala dei professori; ~ sense n buon senso; the C~wealth n il Commonwealth.

commotion [kə'məuʃən] n confusione f, tumulto.

communal ['kɔmjuːnl] a (life) comunale; (for common use) pubblico(a).

commune n ['kɔmjuːn] (group) comune m // vi [kə'mjuːn]: to ~ with mettersi in comunione con.

communicate [kə'mjuːnikeit] vt comunicare, trasmettere // vi: to ~ (with) comunicare (con).

communication [kɔmjuːni'keiʃən] n

comunicazione f; ~ cord n segnale m d'allarme.

communion [kə'mjuːniən] n comunione f.

communiqué [kə'mjuːnikei] n comunicato.

communism ['kɔmjunizəm] n comunismo; communist a,n comunista (m/f).

community [kə'mjuːniti] n comunità f inv; ~ centre n circolo ricreativo; ~ chest n (US) fondo di beneficenza.

commutation ticket [kɔmjuː'teiʃəntikit] n (US) biglietto di abbonamento.

commute [kə'mjuːt] vi fare il pendolare // vt (LAW) commutare; ~r n pendolare m/f.

compact a [kəm'pækt] compatto(a) // n ['kɔmpækt] (also: powder ~) portacipria.

companion [kəm'pæniən] n compagno/a; ~ship n compagnia.

company ['kʌmpəni] n (also COMM, MIL, THEATRE) compagnia; he's good ~ è di buona compagnia; we have ~ abbiamo ospiti; to keep sb ~ tenere compagnia a qd; to part ~ with separarsi da.

comparable ['kɔmpərəbl] a comparabile.

comparative [kəm'pærətiv] a comparativo(a); (LING) comparato(a); ~ly ad relativamente.

compare [kəm'pɛə*] vt: to ~ sth/sb with/to confrontare qc/qd con/a // vi: to ~ (with) reggere il confronto (con); comparison [-'pærisn] n confronto; in comparison (with) a confronto di.

compartment [kəm'pɑːtmənt] n compartimento; (RAIL) scompartimento.

compass ['kʌmpəs] n bussola; ~es npl compassi mpl.

compassion [kəm'pæʃən] n compassione f; ~ate a compassionevole.

compatible [kəm'pætibl] a compatibile.

compel [kəm'pɛl] vt costringere, obbligare; ~ling a (fig: argument) irresistibile.

compendium [kəm'pɛndiəm] n compendio.

compensate ['kɔmpənseit] vt risarcire // vi: to ~ for compensare; compensation [-'seiʃən] n compensazione f; (money) risarcimento.

compère ['kɔmpɛə*] n presentatore/trice.

compete [kəm'piːt] vi (take part) concorrere; (vie): to ~ (with) fare concorrenza (a).

competence ['kɔmpitəns] n competenza.

competent ['kɔmpitənt] a competente.

competition [kɔmpi'tiʃən] n gara; concorso; (ECON) concorrenza.

competitive [kəm'pɛtitiv] a di concorso; di concorrenza.

competitor [kəm'pɛtitə*] n concorrente m/f.

compile [kəm'pail] vt compilare.

complacency [kəm'pleisnsi] n compiacenza di sé.

complacent [kəm'pleisənt] a compiaciuto(a) di sé.

complain [kəm'plein] vi: to ~ (about) lagnarsi (di); (in shop etc) reclamare (per); **to ~ of** vt fus (MED) accusare; **~t** n lamento; reclamo; (MED) malattia.

complement ['komplɪmənt] n complemento; (especially of ship's crew etc) effettivo; **~ary** [komplɪ'mentəri] a complementare.

complete [kəm'pli:t] a completo(a) // vt completare, compire; (a form) riempire; **~ly** ad completamente; **completion** n completamento.

complex ['kompleks] a complesso(a) // n (PSYCH, buildings etc) complesso.

complexion [kəm'plekʃən] n (of face) carnagione f; (of event etc) aspetto.

complexity [kəm'pleksɪtɪ] n complessità f inv.

compliance [kəm'plaɪəns] n acquiescenza; **in ~ with** (orders, wishes etc) in conformità con.

compliant [kəm'plaɪənt] a acquiescente, arrendevole.

complicate ['komplɪkeɪt] vt complicare; **~d** a complicato(a); **complication** [-'keɪʃən] n complicazione f.

compliment n ['komplɪmənt] complimento // vt ['komplɪmənt] fare un complimento a; **~s** npl complimenti mpl; rispetti mpl; **~ary** [-'mentəri] a complimentoso(a), elogiativo(a); (free) in omaggio; **~ary ticket** n biglietto d'omaggio.

comply [kəm'plaɪ] vi: **to ~ with** assentire a; conformarsi a.

component [kəm'pəunənt] n componente m.

compose [kəm'pəuz] vt comporre; **to ~ o.s.** ricomporsi; **~d** a calmo(a); **~d of** composto(a) di; **~r** n (MUS) compositore/trice.

composition [kompə'zɪʃən] n composizione f.

compost ['kompəst] n composta, concime m.

composure [kəm'pəuʒə*] n calma.

compound ['kompaund] n (CHEM, LING) composto; (enclosure) recinto // a composto(a); **~ fracture** n frattura composta; **~ interest** n interesse m composto.

comprehend [komprɪ'hend] vt comprendere, capire; **comprehension** [-'henʃən] n comprensione f.

comprehensive [komprɪ'hensɪv] a comprensivo(a); **~ policy** n (INSURANCE) polizza che copre tutti i rischi; **~ (school)** n scuola secondaria aperta a tutti.

compress vt [kəm'pres] comprimere // n ['kompres] (MED) compressa; **~ion** [-'preʃən] n compressione f.

comprise [kəm'praɪz] vt (also: **be ~d of**) comprendere.

compromise ['komprəmaɪz] n compromesso // vt compromettere // vi venire a un compromesso.

compulsion [kəm'pʌlʃən] n costrizione f.

compulsive [kəm'pʌlsɪv] a (reason, demand) stringente; (PSYCH) inguaribile.

compulsory [kəm'pʌlsərɪ] a obbligatorio(a).

computer [kəm'pju:tə*] n computer m inv; **~ize** vt computerizzare; **~ programming** n programmazione f di computer.

comrade ['komrɪd] n compagno/a; **~ship** n cameratismo.

con [kon] vt (col) truffare.

concave ['konkeɪv] a concavo(a).

conceal [kən'si:l] vt nascondere.

concede [kən'si:d] vt concedere // vi fare una concessione.

conceit [kən'si:t] n presunzione f, vanità; **~ed** a presuntuoso(a), vanitoso(a).

conceivable [kən'si:vəbl] a concepibile.

conceive [kən'si:v] vt concepire // vi concepire un bambino.

concentrate ['konsəntreɪt] vi concentrarsi // vt concentrare.

concentration [konsən'treɪʃən] n concentrazione f; **~ camp** n campo di concentramento.

concept ['konsept] n concetto.

conception [kən'sepʃən] n concezione f.

concern [kən'sə:n] n (COMM) azienda, ditta; (anxiety) preoccupazione f // vt riguardare; **to be ~ed (about)** preoccuparsi (di); **~ing** prep riguardo a, circa.

concert ['konsət] n concerto; **in ~** di concerto; **~ed** [kən'sə:tɪd] a concertato(a); **~ hall** n sala da concerti.

concertina [konsə'ti:nə] n piccola fisarmonica // vi ridursi come una fisarmonica.

concerto [kən'tʃə:təu] n concerto.

concession [kən'seʃən] n concessione f.

conciliation [kənsɪlɪ'eɪʃən] n conciliazione f.

conciliatory [kən'sɪlɪətrɪ] a conciliativo(a).

concise [kən'saɪs] a conciso(a).

conclave ['konkleɪv] n riunione f segreta; (REL) conclave m.

conclude [kən'klu:d] vt concludere; **conclusion** [-'klu:ʒən] n conclusione f; **conclusive** [-'klu:sɪv] a conclusivo(a).

concoct [kən'kokt] vt inventare.

concourse ['konkɔ:s] n (hall) atrio.

concrete ['konkri:t] n conglomerato (di cemento) // a concreto(a); di cemento.

concur [kən'kə:*] vi concordare.

concurrently [kən'kʌrntlɪ] ad simultaneamente.

concussion [kən'kʌʃən] n commozione f cerebrale.

condemn [kən'dem] vt condannare; **~ation** [kondem'neɪʃən] n condanna.

condensation [konden'seɪʃən] n condensazione f.

condense [kən'dens] vi condensarsi // vt condensare; **~d milk** n latte m condensato.

condescend [kondɪ'send] vi condiscendere; **~ing** a condiscendente.

condition [kən'dɪʃən] n condizione f // vt condizionare, regolare; **on ~ that** a condizione che + *sub*, a condizione di; ~**al** a condizionale.

condolences [kən'dəulənsız] *npl* condoglianze *fpl*.

condone [kən'dəun] *vt* condonare.

conducive [kən'dju:sıv] *a*: ~ **to** favorevole a.

conduct *n* ['kɔndʌkt] condotta // *vt* [kən'dʌkt] condurre; (*manage*) dirigere; amministrare; (*MUS*) dirigere; **to** ~ **o.s.** comportarsi; ~**ed tour** *n* gita accompagnata; ~**or** *n* (*of orchestra*) direttore *m* d'orchestra; (*on bus*) bigliettaio; (*ELEC*) conduttore *m*; ~**ress** *n* (*on bus*) bigliettaia.

conduit ['kɔndıt] *n* condotto; tubo.

cone [kəun] *n* cono; (*BOT*) pigna.

confectionery [kən'fɛkʃənərı] *n* dolciumi *mpl*.

confederation [kənfedə'reıʃən] *n* confederazione *f*.

confer [kən'fə:*] *vt*: **to** ~ **sth on** conferire qc a // *vi* conferire.

conference ['kɔnfərns] *n* congresso.

confess [kən'fɛs] *vt* confessare, ammettere // *vi* confessarsi; ~**ion** [-'fɛʃən] *n* confessione *f*; ~**ional** [-'fɛʃənl] *n* confessionale *m*; ~**or** *n* confessore *m*.

confetti [kən'fɛtı] *n* coriandoli *mpl*.

confide [kən'faıd] *vi*: **to** ~ **in** confidarsi con.

confidence ['kɔnfıdns] *n* confidenza; (*trust*) fiducia; (*also*: **self~**) sicurezza di sé; ~ **trick** *n* truffa; **confident** *a* confidente; sicuro(a) di sé; **confidential** [kɔnfı'dɛnʃəl] *a* riservato(a).

confine [kən'faın] *vt* limitare; (*shut up*) rinchiudere; ~**s** ['kɔnfaınz] *npl* confini *mpl*; ~**d** *a* (*space*) ristretto(a); ~**ment** *n* prigionia; (*MED*) consegna; (*MED*) parto.

confirm [kən'fə:m] *vt* confermare; (*REL*) cresimare; ~**ation** [kɔnfə'meıʃən] *n* conferma; cresima; ~**ed** *a* inveterato(a).

confiscate ['kɔnfıskeıt] *vt* confiscare; **confiscation** [-'keıʃən] *n* confisca.

conflict *n* ['kɔnflıkt] conflitto // *vi* [kən-'flıkt] essere in conflitto; ~**ing** *a* contrastante.

conform [kən'fɔ:m] *vi*: **to** ~ **(to)** conformarsi (a); ~**ist** *n* conformista *m/f*.

confound [kən'faund] *vt* confondere; ~**ed** *a* maledetto(a).

confront [kən'frʌnt] *vt* confrontare; (*enemy*, *danger*) affrontare; ~**ation** [kɔnfrən'teıʃən] *n* confronto.

confuse [kən'fju:z] *vt* imbrogliare; (*one thing with another*) confondere; **confusing** *a* che fa confondere; **confusion** [-'fju:ʒən] *n* confusione *f*.

congeal [kən'dʒi:l] *vi* (*blood*) congelarsi.

congenial [kən'dʒi:nıəl] *a* (*person*) simpatico(a); (*thing*) congeniale.

congenital [kən'dʒɛnıtl] *a* congenito(a).

conger eel ['kɔngəri:l] *n* grongo.

congested [kən'dʒɛstıd] *a* congestionato(a).

congestion [kən'dʒɛstʃən] *n* congestione *f*.

conglomeration [kənglɔmə'reıʃən] *n* conglomerazione *f*.

congratulate [kən'grætjuleıt] *vt*: **to** ~ **sb (on)** congratularsi con qd (per *or* di); **congratulations** [-'leıʃənz] *npl* auguri *mpl*; (*on success*) complimenti *mpl*.

congregate [kɔŋgrıgeıt] *vi* congregarsi, riunirsi.

congregation [kɔŋgrı'geıʃən] *n* congregazione *f*.

congress ['kɔŋgrɛs] *n* congresso; ~**man** *n* (*US*) membro del Congresso.

conical ['kɔnıkl] *a* conico(a).

conifer ['kɔnıfə*] *n* conifero.

conjecture [kən'dʒɛktʃə*] *n* congettura // *vt*, *vi* congetturare.

conjugal ['kɔndʒugl] *a* coniugale.

conjunction [kən'dʒʌŋkʃən] *n* congiunzione *f*.

conjunctivitis [kəndʒʌŋktı'vaıtıs] *n* congiuntivite *f*.

conjure ['kʌndʒə*] *vt* prestigiare; **to** ~ **up** *vt* (*ghost*, *spirit*) evocare; (*memories*) rievocare; ~**r** *n* prestidigitatore/trice; **conjuring trick** *n* gioco di prestigio.

conk [kɔŋk]: **to** ~ **out** *vi* (*col*) andare in panne.

conman ['kɔnmæn] *n* truffatore *m*.

connect [kə'nɛkt] *vt* connettere, collegare; (*ELEC*) collegare; (*fig*) associare // *vi* (*train*): **to** ~ **with** essere in coincidenza con; **to be** ~**ed with** aver rapporti con; essere imparentato con; ~**ion** [-ʃən] *n* relazione *f*, rapporto; (*ELEC*) connessione *f*; (*TEL*) collegamento; **in** ~**ion with** con riferimento a.

connexion [kə'nɛkʃən] *n* = **connection**.

conning tower ['kɔnıŋtauə*] *n* torretta di comando.

connive [kə'naıv] *vi*: **to** ~ **at** essere connivente n.

connoisseur [kɔnı'sə*] *n* conoscitore/trice.

connotation [kɔnə'teıʃən] *n* connotazione *f*.

conquer ['kɔŋkə*] *vt* conquistare; (*feelings*) vincere; ~**or** *n* conquistatore *m*.

conquest ['kɔŋkwɛst] *n* conquista.

cons [kɔnz] *npl see* **pro, convenience**.

conscience ['kɔnʃəns] *n* coscienza.

conscientious [kɔnʃı'ɛnʃəs] *a* coscienzioso(a); ~ **objector** *n* obiettore *m* di coscienza.

conscious ['kɔnʃəs] *a* consapevole; (*MED*) conscio(a); ~**ness** *n* consapevolezza; coscienza; **to lose/regain** ~**ness** perdere/ riprendere coscienza.

conscript ['kɔnskrıpt] *n* coscritto; ~**ion** [kən'skrıpʃən] *n* coscrizione *f*.

consecrate ['kɔnsıkreıt] *vt* consacrare.

consecutive [kən'sɛkjutıv] *a* consecutivo(a).

consensus [kən'sɛnsəs] *n* consenso.

consent [kən'sɛnt] *n* consenso // *vi*: **to** ~ **(to)** acconsentire (a).

consequence ['kɔnsıkwəns] *n* conseguenza, risultato; importanza.

consequently ['kɒnsɪkwəntlɪ] *ad* di conseguenza, dunque.
conservation [kɒnsə'veɪʃən] *n* conservazione *f*.
conservative [kən'sɔːvətɪv] *a* conservativo(a); (*cautious*) cauto(a); **C~** *a*, *n* conservatore(trice).
conservatory [kən'sɔːvətrɪ] *n* (*greenhouse*) serra.
conserve [kən'sɔːv] *vt* conservare.
consider [kən'sɪdə*] *vt* considerare; (*take into account*) tener conto di.
considerable [kən'sɪdərəbl] *a* considerevole, notevole.
considerate [kən'sɪdərɪt] *a* premuroso(a).
consideration [kənsɪdə'reɪʃən] *n* considerazione *f*; (*reward*) rimunerazione *f*; **out of ~ for** per riguardo a; **under ~** in esame.
considering [kən'sɪdərɪŋ] *prep* in considerazione di.
consign [kən'saɪn] *vt* consegnare; (*send: goods*) spedire; **~ment** *n* consegna; spedizione *f*.
consist [kən'sɪst] *vi*: **to ~ of** constare di, essere composto(a) di.
consistency [kən'sɪstənsɪ] *n* consistenza; (*fig*) concordanza; coerenza.
consistent [kən'sɪstənt] *a* coerente; (*constant*) costante; **~ with** compatibile con.
consolation [kɒnsə'leɪʃən] *n* consolazione *f*.
console *vt* [kən'səʊl] consolare // *n* ['kɒnsəʊl] mensola.
consolidate [kən'sɒlɪdeɪt] *vt* consolidare.
consonant ['kɒnsənənt] *n* consonante *f*.
consortium [kən'sɔːtɪəm] *n* consorzio.
conspicuous [kən'spɪkjʊəs] *a* cospicuo(a).
conspiracy [kən'spɪrəsɪ] *n* congiura, cospirazione *f*.
conspire [kən'spaɪə*] *vi* congiurare, cospirare.
constable ['kʌnstəbl] *n* ≈ poliziotto, agente *m* di polizia; **chief ~** *n* capo della polizia.
constant ['kɒnstənt] *a* costante; continuo(a); **~ly** *ad* costantemente; continuamente.
constellation [kɒnstə'leɪʃən] *n* costellazione *f*.
consternation [kɒnstə'neɪʃən] *n* costernazione *f*.
constipated ['kɒnstɪpeɪtəd] *a* stitico(a).
constipation [kɒnstɪ'peɪʃən] *n* stitichezza.
constituency [kən'stɪtjuənsɪ] *n* collegio elettorale.
constituent [kən'stɪtjuənt] *n* elettore/trice; (*part*) elemento componente.
constitute ['kɒnstɪtjuːt] *vt* costituire.
constitution [kɒnstɪ'tjuːʃən] *n* costituzione *f*; **~al** *a* costituzionale.
constrain [kən'streɪn] *vt* costringere; **~ed** *a* costretto(a); **~t** *n* costrizione *f*.
constrict [kən'strɪkt] *vt* comprimere; opprimere.

construct [kən'strʌkt] *vt* costruire; **~ion** [-ʃən] *n* costruzione *f*; **~ive** *a* costruttivo(a).
construe [kən'struː] *vt* interpretare.
consul ['kɒnsl] *n* console *m*; **~ate** ['kɒnsjuːlɪt] *n* consolato.
consult [kən'sʌlt] *vt* consultare; **~ancy** *n*: **~ancy fee** spese *fpl* di consultazione; **~ant** *n* (*MED*) consulente *m* medico; (*other specialist*) consulente; **~ation** [kɒnsəl'teɪʃən] *n* consultazione *f*; (*MED, LAW*) consulto; **~ing room** *n* ambulatorio.
consume [kən'sjuːm] *vt* consumare; **~r** *n* consumatore/trice; **~r society** *n* società dei consumi.
consummate ['kɒnsʌmeɪt] *vt* consumare.
consumption [kən'sʌmpʃən] *n* consumo; (*MED*) consunzione *f*.
contact ['kɒntækt] *n* contatto; (*person*) conoscenza // *vt* mettersi in contatto con; **~ lenses** *npl* lenti *fpl* a contatto.
contagious [kən'teɪdʒəs] *a* contagioso(a).
contain [kən'teɪn] *vt* contenere; **to ~ o.s.** contenersi; **~er** *n* recipiente *m*; (*for shipping etc*) container *m*.
contaminate [kən'tæmɪneɪt] *vt* contaminare; **contamination** [-'neɪʃən] *n* contaminazione *f*.
cont'd *abbr of* continued.
contemplate ['kɒntəmpleɪt] *vt* contemplare; (*consider*) pensare a (or di); **contemplation** [-'pleɪʃən] *n* contemplazione *f*.
contemporary [kən'tempərərɪ] *a* contemporaneo(a); (*design*) moderno(a) // *n* contemporaneo/a.
contempt [kən'tempt] *n* disprezzo; **~ible** *a* spregevole; **~uous** *a* sdegnoso(a).
contend [kən'tend] *vt*: **to ~ that** sostenere che // *vi*: **to ~ with** lottare contro; **~er** *n* contendente *m/f*; concorrente *m/f*.
content [kən'tent] *a* contento(a), soddisfatto(a) // *vt* contentare, soddisfare // *n* ['kɒntent] contenuto; **~s** *npl* contenuto; (*of barrel etc: capacity*) capacità *f inv*; (**table of**) **~s** indice *m*; **to be ~ with** essere contento di; **~ed** *a* contento(a), soddisfatto(a).
contention [kən'tenʃən] *n* contesa; (*argument*) affermazione *f*.
contentment [kən'tentmənt] *n* contentezza.
contest *n* ['kɒntest] lotta; (*competition*) gara, concorso // *vt* [kən'test] contestare; impugnare; (*compete for*) contendere; **~ant** [kən'testənt] *n* concorrente *m/f*; (*in fight*) avversario/a.
context ['kɒntekst] *n* contesto.
continent ['kɒntɪnənt] *n* continente *m*; **the C~** l'Europa continentale; **~al** [-'nentl] *a* continentale // *n* abitante *m/f* dell'Europa continentale.
contingency [kən'tɪndʒənsɪ] *n* eventualità *f inv*; **~ plan** *n* misura d'emergenza.
contingent [kən'tɪndʒənt] *n* contingenza; **to be ~ upon** dipendere da.

continual [kən'tınjuəl] a continuo(a); ~**ly**
ad di continuo.
continuation [kəntınju'eıʃən] n
continuazione f; (after interruption)
ripresa; (of story) seguito.
continue [kən'tınjuː] vi continuare // vt
continuare; (start again) riprendere.
continuity [kəntı'njuıtı] n continuità.
continuous [kən'tınjuəs] a continuo(a),
ininterrotto(a).
contort [kən'tɔːt] vt contorcere; ~**ion**
[-'tɔːʃən] n contorcimento; (of acrobat)
contorsione f; ~**ionist** [-'tɔːʃənıst] n
contorsionista m/f.
contour ['kɔntuə*] n contorno, profilo;
(also: ~ **line**) curva di livello.
contraband ['kɔntrəbænd] n
contrabbando.
contraception [kɔntrə'sɛpʃən] n
contraccezione f.
contraceptive [kɔntrə'sɛptıv] a
contraccettivo(a) // n contraccettivo.
contract n ['kɔntrækt] contratto // vb
[kən'trækt] vi (COMM) to ~ to do sth fare
un contratto per fare qc; (become smaller)
contrarre; ~**ion** [-ʃən] n contrazione f;
~**or** n imprenditore m.
contradict [kɔntrə'dıkt] vt contraddire;
~**ion** [-ʃən] n contraddizione f.
contralto [kən'træltəu] n contralto.
contraption [kən'træpʃən] n (pej)
aggeggio.
contrary ['kɔntrərı] a contrario(a);
(unfavourable) avverso(a), contrario(a);
[kən'trɛərı] (perverse) bisbetico(a) // n
contrario; on the ~ al contrario; unless
you hear to the ~ a meno che non si
disdica.
contrast n ['kɔntrɑːst] contrasto // vt
[kən'trɑːst] mettere in contrasto; ~**ing** a
contrastante, di contrasto.
contravene [kɔntrə'viːn] vt
contravvenire.
contribute [kən'trıbjuːt] vi contribuire //
vt: to ~ £10/an article to dare 10
sterline/un articolo a; to ~ to contribuire
a; (newspaper) scrivere per; **contribution**
[kɔntrı'bjuːʃən] n contribuzione f;
contributor n (to newspaper)
collaboratore/trice.
contrite ['kɔntraıt] a contrito(a).
contrivance [kən'traıvəns] n congegno;
espediente m.
contrive [kən'traıv] vt inventare;
escogitare // vi: to ~ to do fare in modo
di fare.
control [kən'trəul] vt dominare; (firm,
operation etc) dirigere; (check) controllare
// n autorità; controllo; ~**s** npl comandi
mpl; to be in ~ of aver autorità su;
essere responsabile di; controllare;
circumstances beyond our ~
circostanze fpl che non dipendono da noi;
~ **point** n punto di controllo; ~ **tower** n
(AVIAT) torre f di controllo.
controversial [kɔntrə'vəːʃl] a
controverso(a), polemico(a).

controversy ['kɔntrəvəːsı] n controversia,
polemica.
convalesce [kɔnvə'lɛs] vi rimettersi in
salute.
convalescence [kɔnvə'lɛsns] n
convalescenza.
convalescent [kɔnvə'lɛsnt] a, n
convalescente (m/f).
convector [kən'vɛktə*] n convettore m.
convene [kən'viːn] vt convocare // vi
convenire, adunarsi.
convenience [kən'viːnıəns] n
convenienza; at your ~ a suo còmodo;
all modern ~**s, all mod cons** tutte le
comodità moderne.
convenient [kən'viːnıənt] a conveniente,
comodo(a).
convent ['kɔnvənt] n convento.
convention [kən'vɛnʃən] n convenzione f;
(meeting) convegno; ~**al** a convenzionale.
converge [kən'vəːdʒ] vi convergere.
conversant [kən'vəːsnt] a: to be ~ with
essere al corrente di; essere pratico(a) di.
conversation [kɔnvə'seıʃən] n
conversazione f; ~**al** a non formale; ~**al**
Italian l'italiano parlato.
converse [kən'vəːs] n contrario, opposto;
~**ly** [-'vəːslı] ad al contrario, per contro.
conversion [kən'vəːʃən] n conversione f;
~ **table** n tavola di equivalenza.
convert vt [kən'vəːt] (REL, COMM)
convertire; (alter) trasformare // n
['kɔnvəːt] convertito/a; ~**ible** n macchina
decappottabile.
convex ['kɔn'vɛks] a convesso(a).
convey [kən'veı] vt trasportare; (thanks)
comunicare; (idea) dare; ~**or belt** n
nastro trasportatore.
convict vt [kən'vıkt] dichiarare colpevole
// n ['kɔnvıkt] condannato; ~**ion** [-ʃən] n
condanna; (belief) convinzione f.
convince [kən'vıns] vt convincere,
persuadere; **convincing** a convincente.
convivial [kən'vıvıəl] a allegro(a).
convoy ['kɔnvɔı] n convoglio.
convulse [kən'vʌls] vt sconvolgere; to be
~**d with laughter** contorcersi dalle risa.
convulsion [kən'vʌlʃən] n convulsione f.
coo [kuː] vi tubare.
cook [kuk] vt cucinare, cuocere // vi
cuocere; (person) cucinare // n cuoco/a;
~**book** n = ~**ery book**; ~**er** n fornello,
cucina; ~**ery** n cucina; ~**ery book** n
libro di cucina; ~**ie** n (US) biscotto; ~**ing**
n cucina.
cool [kuːl] a fresco(a); (not afraid)
calmo(a); (unfriendly) freddo(a);
(impertinent) sfacciato(a) // vt
raffreddare, rinfrescare // vi raffreddarsi,
rinfrescarsi; ~**ing tower** n torre f di
raffreddamento; ~**ness** n freschezza;
sangue m freddo, calma.
coop [kuːp] n stia // vt: to ~ up (fig)
stipare.
cooperate [kəu'ɔpəreıt] vi cooperare,
collaborare; **cooperation** [-'reıʃən] n
cooperazione f, collaborazione f.
cooperative [kəu'ɔpərətıv] a

cooperativo(a) // n cooperativa.
coordinate [kəʊ'ɔːdɪneɪt] vt coordinare; **coordination** [-'neɪʃən] n coordinazione f.
coot [kuːt] n folaga.
cop [kɔp] n (col) sbirro.
cope [kəʊp] vi farcela; **to ~ with** (problems) far fronte a.
co-pilot ['kəʊ'paɪlət] n secondo pilota m.
copious ['kəʊpɪəs] a copioso(a), abbondante.
copper ['kɔpə*] n rame m; (col: policeman) sbirro; **~s** npl spiccioli mpl.
copse [kɔps] n bosco ceduo.
copulate ['kɔpjuleɪt] vi accoppiarsi.
copy ['kɔpɪ] n copia; (book etc) esemplare m // vt copiare; **~cat** a (pej) copione m; **~right** n diritto d'autore; **~writer** n redattore m pubblicitario.
coral ['kɔrəl] n corallo; **~ reef** n barriera corallina.
cord [kɔːd] n corda; (fabric) velluto a coste.
cordial ['kɔːdɪəl] a, n cordiale (m).
cordon ['kɔːdn] n cordone m; **to ~ off** vt fare cordone a.
corduroy ['kɔːdərɔɪ] n fustagno.
core [kɔː*] n (of fruit) torsolo; (TECH) centro // vt estrarre il torsolo da.
cork [kɔːk] n sughero; (of bottle) tappo; **~age** n somma da pagare se il cliente porta il proprio vino; **~screw** n cavatappi m inv.
cormorant ['kɔːmərənt] n cormorano.
corn [kɔːn] n grano; (US: maize) granturco; (on foot) callo; **~ on the cob** (CULIN) pannocchia cotta.
cornea ['kɔːnɪə] n cornea.
corned beef ['kɔːnd'biːf] n carne f di manzo in scatola.
corner ['kɔːnə*] n angolo; (AUT) curva // vt mettere in un angolo; mettere con le spalle al muro; (COMM: market) accaparrare // vi prendere una curva; **~flag** n (FOOTBALL) bandierina d'angolo; **~kick** n calcio d'angolo; **~stone** n pietra angolare.
cornet ['kɔːnɪt] n (MUS) cornetta; (of ice-cream) cono.
cornflour ['kɔːnflaʊə*] n farina finissima di granturco.
cornice ['kɔːnɪs] n cornicione m; cornice f.
Cornwall ['kɔːnwəl] n Cornovaglia.
corny ['kɔːnɪ] a (col) trito(a).
corollary [kə'rɔlərɪ] n corollario.
coronary ['kɔrənərɪ] n trombosi f coronaria.
coronation [kɔrə'neɪʃən] n incoronazione f.
coroner ['kɔrənə*] n magistrato incaricato di indagare la causa di morte in circostanze sospettose.
coronet ['kɔrənɪt] n diadema m.
corporal ['kɔːpərl] n caporalmaggiore m // a: **~ punishment** pena corporale.
corporate ['kɔːpərɪt] a costituito(a) (in corporazione); comune.
corporation [kɔːpə'reɪʃən] n (of town) consiglio comunale; (COMM) ente m; **~tax** n imposta societaria.

corps [kɔː*], pl **corps** [kɔːz] n corpo.
corpse [kɔːps] n cadavere m.
corpuscle ['kɔːpʌsl] n corpuscolo.
corral [kə'rɑːl] n recinto.
correct [kə'rekt] a (accurate) corretto(a), esatto(a); (proper) corretto(a) // vt correggere; **~ion** [-ʃən] n correzione f.
correlate ['kɔrɪleɪt] vt mettere in correlazione.
correspond [kɔrɪs'pɔnd] vi corrispondere; **~ence** n corrispondenza; **~ence course** n corso per corrispondenza; **~ent** n corrispondente m/f.
corridor ['kɔrɪdɔː*] n corridoio.
corroborate [kə'rɔbəreɪt] vt corroborare, confermare.
corrode [kə'rəʊd] vt corrodere // vi corrodersi; **corrosion** [-'rəʊʒən] n corrosione f.
corrugated ['kɔrəgeɪtɪd] a increspato(a); ondulato(a); **~ iron** n lamiera di ferro ondulata.
corrupt [kə'rʌpt] a corrotto(a) // vt corrompere; **~ion** [-ʃən] n corruzione f.
corset ['kɔːsɪt] n busto.
Corsica ['kɔːsɪkə] n Corsica.
cortège [kɔː'teːʒ] n corteo.
cosh [kɔʃ] n randello (corto).
cosmetic [kɔz'metɪk] n cosmetico.
cosmonaut ['kɔzmənɔːt] n cosmonauta m/f.
cosmopolitan [kɔzmə'pɔlɪtn] a cosmopolita.
cosmos ['kɔzmɔs] n cosmo.
cosset ['kɔsɪt] vt vezzeggiare.
cost [kɔst] n costo // vb (pt, pp cost) vi costare // vt stabilire il prezzo di; **it ~s £5/too much** costa 5 sterline/troppo; **it ~ him his life/job** gli costò la vita/il suo lavoro; **at all ~s** a ogni costo.
co-star ['kəʊstɑː*] n attore/trice della stessa importanza del protagonista.
costly ['kɔstlɪ] a costoso(a), caro(a).
cost price ['kɔst'praɪs] n prezzo all'ingrosso.
costume ['kɔstjuːm] n costume m; (lady's suit) tailleur m inv; (also: **swimming ~**) costume da bagno; **~ jewellery** n bigiotteria.
cosy ['kəʊzɪ] a intimo(a).
cot [kɔt] n (child's) lettino.
cottage ['kɔtɪdʒ] n cottage m inv; **~ cheese** n fiocchi mpl di latte magro.
cotton ['kɔtn] n cotone m; **~ dress** etc vestito etc di cotone; **~ wool** n cotone idrofilo.
couch [kautʃ] n sofà m inv // vt esprimere.
cough [kɔf] vi tossire // n tosse f; **~ drop** n pasticca per la tosse.
could [kud] pt of **can**.
council ['kaunsl] n concilio; **city or town ~** concilio comunale; **~ estate** n quartiere m di case popolari; **~ house** n casa popolare; **~lor** n consigliere/a.
counsel ['kaunsl] n avvocato; consultazione f; **~lor** n consigliere/a.
count [kaunt] vt, vi contare // n conto;

(*nobleman*) conte *m*; **to ~ on** *vt fus* contare su; **to ~ up** *vt* addizionare; **~down** *n* conto alla rovescia.

countenance ['kauntɪnəns] *n* volto, aspetto // *vt* approvare.

counter ['kauntə*] *n* banco // *vt* opporsi a; (*blow*) parare // *ad:* **~ to** contro; in opposizione a; **~act** *vt* agire in opposizione a; (*poison etc*) annullare gli effetti di; **~attack** *n* contrattacco // *vi* contrattaccare; **~balance** *vt* contrappesare; **~-espionage** *n* controspionaggio.

counterfeit ['kauntəfɪt] *n* contraffazione *f*, falso // *vt* contraffare, falsificare // *a* falso(a).

counterfoil ['kauntəfɔɪl] *n* matrice *f*.

counterpart ['kauntəpɑ:t] *n* (*of document etc*) copia; (*of person*) corrispondente *m/f*.

countess ['kauntɪs] *n* contessa.

countless ['kauntlɪs] *a* innumerevole.

country ['kʌntrɪ] *n* paese *m*; (*native land*) patria; (*as opposed to town*) campagna; (*region*) regione *f*; **~ dancing** *n* danza popolare; **~ house** *n* villa in campagna; **~man** *n* (*national*) compatriota *m*; (*rural*) contadino; **~side** *n* campagna.

county ['kauntɪ] *n* contea.

coup, **~s** [ku:, -z] *n* colpo; (*also:* **~ d'état**) colpo di Stato.

coupé [ku:'peɪ] *n* coupé *m inv*.

couple ['kʌpl] *n* coppia // *vt* (*carriages*) agganciare; (*TECH*) accoppiare; (*ideas, names*) associare; **a ~ of** un paio di.

couplet ['kʌplɪt] *n* distico.

coupling ['kʌplɪŋ] *n* (*RAIL*) agganciamento.

coupon ['ku:pɔn] *n* buono; (*COMM*) coupon *m inv*.

courage ['kʌrɪdʒ] *n* coraggio; **~ous** [kə'reɪdʒəs] *a* coraggioso(a).

courier ['kurɪə*] *n* corriere *m*; (*for tourists*) guida.

course [kɔ:s] *n* corso; (*of ship*) rotta; (*for golf*) campo; (*part of meal*) piatto; **first ~** primo piatto; **of ~** *ad* senz'altro, naturalmente; **~ of action** modo d'agire; **~ of lectures** corso di lezioni.

court [kɔ:t] *n* corte *f*; (*TENNIS*) campo // *vt* (*woman*) fare la corte a; **out of ~** (*LAW: settle*) in via amichevole; **to take to ~** sottoporre alla magistratura.

courteous ['kə:tɪəs] *a* cortese.

courtesan [kɔ:tɪ'zæn] *n* cortigiana.

courtesy ['kə:təsɪ] *n* cortesia.

court-house ['kɔ:thaus] *n* (*US*) palazzo di giustizia.

courtier ['kɔ:tɪə*] *n* cortigiano/a.

court-martial, *pl* **courts-martial** ['kɔ:t-'mɑ:ʃəl] *n* corte *f* marziale.

courtroom ['kɔ:trum] *n* tribunale *m*.

courtyard ['kɔ:tjɑ:d] *n* cortile *m*.

cousin ['kʌzn] *n* cugino/a.

cove [kəuv] *n* piccola baia.

covenant ['kʌvənənt] *n* accordo.

cover ['kʌvə*] *vt* coprire // *n* (*of pan*) coperchio; (*over furniture*) fodera; (*of

book) copertina; (*shelter*) riparo; (*COMM*) copertura; **under ~** al riparo; **~age** *n* reportage *m*; (*INSURANCE*) copertura; **~ charge** *n* coperto; **~ing** *n* copertura; **~ing letter** *n* lettera d'accompagnamento.

covet ['kʌvɪt] *vt* bramare.

cow [kau] *n* vacca.

coward ['kauəd] *n* vigliacco/a; **~ice** [-ɪs] *n* vigliaccheria; **~ly** *a* vigliacco(a).

cowboy ['kaubɔɪ] *n* cow-boy *m inv*.

cower ['kauə*] *vi* acquattarsi.

cowshed ['kauʃed] *n* stalla.

coxswain ['kɔksn] *n* (*abbr:* **cox**) timoniere *m*; (*of ship*) nocchiere *m*.

coy [kɔɪ] *a* falsamente timido(a).

crab [kræb] *n* granchio; **~ apple** *n* mela selvatica.

crack [kræk] *n* fessura, crepa; incrinatura; (*noise*) schiocco; (: *of gun*) scoppio // *vt* spaccare; incrinare; (*whip*) schioccare; (*nut*) schiacciare // *a* (*troops*) fuori classe; **to ~ up** *vi* crollare; **~ed** *a* (*col*) matto(a); **~er** *n* cracker *m inv*; petardo.

crackle ['krækl] *vi* crepitare; **crackling** *n* crepitio; (*of pork*) cotenna croccante (del maiale).

cradle ['kreɪdl] *n* culla.

craft [krɑːft] *n* mestiere *m*; (*cunning*) astuzia; (*boat*) naviglio; **~sman** *n* artigiano; **~smanship** *n* abilità; **~y** *a* furbo(a), astuto(a).

crag [kræg] *n* roccia.

cram [kræm] *vt* (*fill*): **to ~ sth with** riempire qc di; (*put*): **to ~ sth into** stipare qc in; **~ming** *n* (*fig: pej*) sgobbare *m*.

cramp [kræmp] *n* crampo; **~ed** *a* ristretto(a).

crampon [kræmpɔn] *n* (*CLIMBING*) rampone *m*.

cranberry ['krænbərɪ] *n* mirtillo.

crane [kreɪn] *n* gru *f inv*.

cranium, *pl* **crania** ['kreɪnɪəm, 'kreɪnɪə] *n* cranio.

crank [kræŋk] *n* manovella; (*person*) persona stramba; **~shaft** *n* albero a manovelle.

cranny ['krænɪ] *n see* **nook**.

crash [kræʃ] *n* fragore *m*; (*of car*) incidente *m*; (*of plane*) caduta // *vt* (*car*) fracassare // *vi* (*plane*) fracassarsi; (*two cars*) scontrarsi, (*fig*) fallire, andare in rovina; **to ~ into** scontrarsi con; **~ course** *n* corso intensivo; **~ helmet** *n* casco; **~ landing** *n* atterraggio di fortuna.

crate [kreɪt] *n* gabbia.

crater ['kreɪtə*] *n* cratere *m*.

cravat(e) [krə'væt] *n* fazzoletto da collo.

crave [kreɪv] *vi:* **to ~ for** desiderare ardentemente.

crawl [krɔ:l] *vi* strisciare carponi; (*vehicle*) avanzare lentamente // *n* (*SWIMMING*) crawl *m*.

crayfish ['kreɪfɪʃ] *n*, *pl inv* gambero (d'acqua dolce).

crayon ['kreɪən] *n* matita colorata.

craze [kreɪz] n mania.

crazy ['kreɪzɪ] a matto(a); ~ **paving** n lastricato m a mosaico irregolare.

creak [kri:k] vi cigolare, scricchiolare.

cream [kri:m] n crema; (fresh) panna // a (colour) color crema inv; ~ **cake** n torta alla crema; ~ **cheese** n mascarpone m; ~**y** a cremoso(a).

crease [kri:s] n grinza; (deliberate) piega // vt sgualcire.

create [kri:'eɪt] vt creare; **creation** [-ʃən] n creazione f; **creative** a creativo(a); **creator** n creatore/trice.

creature ['kri:tʃə*] n creatura.

crèche, creche [kreʃ] n asilo infantile.

credence n credenza, fede f.

credentials [krɪ'denʃlz] npl (papers) credenziali fpl.

credibility [kredɪ'bɪlɪtɪ] n credibilità.

credible ['kredɪbl] a credibile.

credit ['kredɪt] n credito; onore m // vt (COMM) accreditare; (believe: also: **give** ~ **to**) credere, prestar fede a; ~**s** npl (CINEMA) titoli mpl; **to** ~ **sb with** (fig) attribuire a qd; **to one's** ~ a proprio onore; **to take the** ~ **for** farsi il merito di; ~**able** a che fa onore, degno(a) di lode; ~ **card** n carta di credito; ~**or** n creditore/trice.

credulity [krɪ'dju:lɪtɪ] n credulità.

creed [kri:d] n credo; dottrina.

creek [kri:k] n insenatura; (US) piccolo fiume m.

creep, pt, pp **crept** [kri:p, krept] vi avanzare furtivamente (or pian piano); (plant) arrampicarsi; ~**er** n pianta rampicante; ~**y** a (frightening) che fa accapponare la pelle.

cremate [krɪ'meɪt] vt cremare; **cremation** [-ʃən] n cremazione f.

crematorium, pl **crematoria** [kremə'tɔ:rɪəm, -'tɔ:rɪə] n forno crematorio.

creosote ['krɪəsəut] n creosoto.

crêpe [kreɪp] n crespo; ~ **bandage** n fascia elastica.

crept [krept] pt, pp of **creep**.

crescendo [krɪ'ʃendəu] n crescendo.

crescent ['kresnt] n forma di luna crescente; strada semicircolare.

cress [kres] n crescione m.

crest [krest] n cresta; (of helmet) pennacchiera; (of coat of arms) cimiero; ~**fallen** a mortificato(a).

Crete ['kri:t] n Creta.

crevasse [krɪ'væs] n crepaccio.

crevice ['krevɪs] n fessura, crepa.

crew [kru:] n equipaggio; **to have a** ~**-cut** avere i capelli a spazzola; ~**-neck** n girocollo.

crib [krɪb] n culla; (REL) presepio // vt (col) copiare.

crick [krɪk] n crampo.

cricket ['krɪkɪt] n (insect) grillo; (game) cricket m; ~**er** n giocatore m di cricket.

crime [kraɪm] n crimine m; **criminal** ['krɪmɪnl] a, n criminale (m/f).

crimson ['krɪmzn] a color cremisi inv.

cringe [krɪndʒ] vi acquattarsi; (fig) essere servile.

crinkle ['krɪŋkl] vt arricciare, increspare.

cripple ['krɪpl] n zoppo/a // vt azzoppare.

crisis, pl **crises** ['kraɪsɪs, -si:z] n crisi f inv.

crisp [krɪsp] a croccante; (fig) frizzante; vivace; deciso(a); ~**s** npl patatine fpl fritte.

criss-cross ['krɪskrɔs] a incrociato(a).

criterion, pl **criteria** [kraɪ'tɪərɪən, -'tɪərɪə] n criterio.

critic ['krɪtɪk] n critico; ~**al** a critico(a); ~**ally** ad criticamente; ~**ally ill** gravemente malato; ~**ism** ['krɪtɪsɪzm] n critica; ~**ize** ['krɪtɪsaɪz] vt criticare.

croak [krəuk] vi gracchiare.

crochet ['krəuʃeɪ] n lavoro all'uncinetto.

crockery ['krɔkərɪ] n vasellame m.

crocodile ['krɔkədaɪl] n coccodrillo.

crocus ['krəukəs] n croco.

croft [krɔft] n piccolo podere m; ~**er** n affittuario di un piccolo podere.

crony ['krəunɪ] n (col) amicone/a.

crook [kruk] n truffatore m; (of shepherd) bastone m; ~**ed** ['krukɪd] a curvo(a), storto(a); (action) disonesto(a).

crop [krɔp] n raccolto; **to** ~ **up** vi presentarsi.

cropper ['krɔpə*] n: **to come a** ~ (col) fare fiasco.

croquet ['krəukeɪ] n croquet m.

croquette [krə'ket] n crocchetta.

cross [krɔs] n croce f; (BIOL) incrocio // vt (street etc) attraversare; (arms, legs, BIOL) incrociare; (cheque) sbarrare // a di cattivo umore; **to** ~ **out** vt cancellare; **to** ~ **over** vi attraversare; ~**bar** n traversa; ~**breed** n incrocio; ~**-country** (race) n cross-country m inv; ~**-examination** n interrogatorio in contraddittorio; ~**-examine** vt (LAW) interrogare in contraddittorio; ~**-eyed** a strabico(a); ~**ing** n incrocio; (sea-passage) traversata; (also: **pedestrian** ~**ing**) passaggio pedonale; ~**-roads** n incrocio; ~ **section** n (BIOL) sezione f trasversale; (in population) settore m rappresentativo; ~**wind** n vento di traverso; ~**word** n cruciverba m inv.

crotch [krɔtʃ] n (of garment) pattina.

crotchet ['krɔtʃɪt] n (MUS) semiminima.

crotchety ['krɔtʃɪtɪ] a (person) burbero(a).

crouch [krautʃ] vi acquattarsi; rannicchiarsi.

crouton ['kru:tɔn] n crostino.

crow [krəu] n (bird) cornacchia; (of cock) canto del gallo // vi (cock) cantare; (fig) vantarsi; cantar vittoria.

crowbar ['krəuba:*] n piede m di porco.

crowd [kraud] n folla // vt affollare, stipare // vi affollarsi; ~**ed** a affollato(a); ~**ed with** stipato(a) di.

crown [kraun] n corona; (of head) calotta cranica; (of hat) cocuzzolo; (of hill) cima // vt incoronare; ~ **jewels** npl gioielli mpl della Corona; ~ **prince** n principe m ereditario.

crow's-nest ['krəuznɛst] n (on sailing-ship) coffa.

crucial ['kru:ʃl] a cruciale, decisivo(a).

crucifix ['kru:sɪfɪks] n crocifisso; ~**ion** [-'fɪkʃən] n crocifissione f.

crucify ['kru:sɪfaɪ] vt crocifiggere, mettere in croce.

crude [kru:d] a (materials) greggio(a); non raffinato(a); (fig: basic) crudo(a), primitivo(a); (: vulgar) rozzo(a), grossolano(a); ~ **(oil)** n (petrolio) greggio.

cruel ['kruəl] a crudele; ~**ty** n crudeltà f inv.

cruet ['kru:ɪt] n ampolla.

cruise [kru:z] n crociera // vi andare a velocità di crociera; (taxi) circolare; ~**r** n incrociatore m; **cruising speed** n velocità f inv di crociera.

crumb [krʌm] n briciola.

crumble ['krʌmbl] vt sbriciolare // vi sbriciolarsi; (plaster etc) sgretolarsi; (land, earth) franare; (building, fig) crollare; **crumbly** a friabile.

crumpet ['krʌmpɪt] n crostino da tè.

crumple ['krʌmpl] vt raggrinzare, spiegazzare.

crunch [krʌntʃ] vt sgranocchiare; (underfoot) scricchiolare // n (fig) punto or momento cruciale; ~**y** a croccante.

crusade [kru:'seɪd] n crociata; ~**r** n crociato.

crush [krʌʃ] n folla // vt schiacciare; (crumple) sgualcire; ~**ing** a schiacciante.

crust [krʌst] n crosta.

crutch [krʌtʃ] n gruccia.

crux [krʌks] n nodo.

cry [kraɪ] vi piangere; (shout) urlare // n urlo, grido; to ~ **off** vi ritirarsi; ~**ing** a (fig) palese; urgente.

crypt [krɪpt] n cripta.

cryptic ['krɪptɪk] a ermetico(a).

crystal ['krɪstl] n cristallo; ~**-clear** a cristallino(a); **crystallize** vi cristallizzarsi.

cu. abbr: ~ **ft.** = cubic feet; ~ **in.** = cubic inches.

cub [kʌb] n cucciolo.

Cuba ['kju:bə] n Cuba; ~**n** a, n cubano(a).

cubbyhole ['kʌbɪhəul] n angolino.

cube [kju:b] n cubo // vt (MATH) elevare al cubo; ~ **root** n radice f cubica; **cubic** a cubico(a).

cubicle ['kju:bɪkl] n scompartimento separato; cabina.

cuckoo ['kuku:] n cucù m inv; ~ **clock** n orologio a cucù.

cucumber ['kju:kʌmbə*] n cetriolo.

cud [kʌd] n: to chew the ~ ruminare.

cuddle ['kʌdl] vt abbracciare, coccolare // vi abbracciarsi; **cuddly** a da coccolare.

cudgel ['kʌdʒl] n randello.

cue [kju:] n stecca; (THEATRE etc) segnale m.

cuff [kʌf] n (of shirt, coat etc) polsino; (US)

= turn-up; off the ~ ad a braccio; ~**link** n gemello.

cuisine [kwɪ'zi:n] n cucina.

cul-de-sac ['kʌldəsæk] n vicolo cieco.

culinary ['kʌlɪnərɪ] a culinario(a).

culminate ['kʌlmɪneɪt] vi culminare; **culmination** [-'neɪʃən] n culmine m.

culpable ['kʌlpəbl] a colpevole.

culprit ['kʌlprɪt] n colpevole m/f.

cult [kʌlt] n culto.

cultivate ['kʌltɪveɪt] vt (also fig) coltivare; **cultivation** [-'veɪʃən] n coltivazione f.

cultural ['kʌltʃərəl] a culturale.

culture ['kʌltʃə*] n (also fig) cultura; ~**d** a colto(a).

cumbersome ['kʌmbəsəm] a ingombrante.

cumulative ['kju:mjulətɪv] a cumulativo(a).

cunning ['kʌnɪŋ] n astuzia, furberia // a astuto(a), furbo(a).

cup [kʌp] n tazza; (prize) coppa.

cupboard ['kʌbəd] n armadio.

cupola ['kju:pələ] n cupola.

cup-tie ['kʌptaɪ] n partita di coppa.

curable ['kjuərəbl] a curabile.

curate ['kju:rɪt] n cappellano.

curator [kju'reɪtə*] n direttore m (di museo etc).

curb [kə:b] vt tenere a freno // n freno; (US) = **kerb**.

curdle ['kə:dl] vi cagliare.

curds [kə:ds] npl latte m cagliato.

cure [kjuə*] vt guarire; (CULIN) trattare; affumicare; essiccare // n rimedio.

curfew ['kə:fju:] n coprifuoco.

curio ['kjuərɪəu] n curiosità f inv.

curiosity [kjuərɪ'ɔsɪtɪ] n curiosità.

curious ['kjuərɪəs] a curioso(a).

curl [kə:l] n riccio // vt ondulare; (tightly) arricciare // vi arricciarsi; to ~ **up** vi avvolgersi a spirale; rannicchiarsi; ~**er** n bigodino.

curling ['kə:lɪŋ] n (SPORT) curling m.

curly ['kə:lɪ] a ricciuto(a).

currant ['kʌrnt] n sultanina.

currency ['kʌrnsɪ] n moneta; **foreign** ~ divisa estera; to gain ~ (fig) acquistare larga diffusione.

current ['kʌrnt] a, n corrente (f); ~ **account** n conto corrente; ~ **affairs** npl attualità pl; ~**ly** ad attualmente.

curriculum, pl ~**s** or **curricula** [kə'rɪkjuləm, -lə] n curriculum m inv; ~ **vitae** n curriculum vitae m inv.

curry ['kʌrɪ] n curry m inv // vt: to ~ **favour with** cercare di attirarsi i favori di; **chicken** ~ pollo al curry.

curse [kə:s] vt maledire // vi bestemmiare // n maledizione f; bestemmia.

cursory ['kə:sərɪ] a superficiale.

curt [kə:t] a secco(a).

curtail [kə:'teɪl] vt (visit etc) accorciare; (expenses etc) ridurre, decurtare.

curtain ['kə:tn] n tenda.

curts(e)y ['kə:tsɪ] n inchino, riverenza // vi fare un inchino or una riverenza.

curve [kə:v] n curva // vi curvarsi.

cushion ['kuʃən] n cuscino // vt (shock) fare da cuscinetto a.

custard ['kʌstəd] n (for pouring) crema.

custodian [kʌs'təudiən] n custode m/f.

custody ['kʌstədi] n (of child) tutela; (for offenders) arresto.

custom ['kʌstəm] n costume m, usanza; (LAW) consuetudine f; (COMM) clientela; ~ary a consueto(a).

customer ['kʌstəmə*] n cliente m/f.

custom-made ['kʌstəm'meid] a (clothes) fatto(a) su misura; (other goods) fatto(a) su ordinazione.

customs ['kʌstəmz] npl dogana; ~ **duty** n dazio doganale; ~ **officer** n doganiere m.

cut [kʌt] vb (pt, pp **cut**) vt tagliare; (shape, make) intagliare; (reduce) ridurre f; vi tagliare; (intersect) tagliarsi // n taglio; (in salary etc) riduzione f; **power** ~ mancanza di corrente elettrica; **to** ~ **a tooth** mettere un dente; **to** ~ **down (on)** vt fus ridurre; **to** ~ **off** vt tagliare; (fig) isolare; **to** ~ **out** vt tagliare fuori; eliminare; ritagliare; ~**back** n riduzione f.

cute [kju:t] a grazioso(a); (clever) astuto(a).

cut glass [kʌt'glɑ:s] n cristallo.

cuticle ['kju:tikl] n (on nail) cuticola.

cutlery ['kʌtləri] n posate fpl.

cutlet ['kʌtlit] n costoletta.

cut: ~**out** n interruttore m; ~-**price** a a prezzo ridotto; ~-**throat** n assassino.

cutting ['kʌtiŋ] a tagliente; (fig) pungente // n (PRESS) ritaglio (di giornale); (RAIL) trincea.

cuttlefish ['kʌtlfiʃ] n seppia.

cut-up ['kʌtʌp] a stravolto(a).

cwt abbr of **hundredweight(s)**.

cyanide ['saiənaid] n cianuro.

cyclamen ['sikləmən] n ciclamino.

cycle ['saikl] n ciclo; bicicletta // vi andare in bicicletta.

cycling ['saikliŋ] n ciclismo.

cyclist ['saiklist] n ciclista m/f.

cyclone ['saikloun] n ciclone m.

cygnet ['signit] n cigno giovane.

cylinder ['silində*] n cilindro; ~ **capacity** n cilindrata; ~-**head gasket** n guarnizione f della testata del cilindro.

cymbals ['simblz] npl cembali mpl.

cynic ['sinik] n cinico/a; ~**al** a cinico(a); ~**ism** ['sinisizəm] n cinismo.

cypress ['saipris] n cipresso.

Cypriot ['sipriət] a, n cipriota (m/f).

Cyprus ['saiprəs] n Cipro.

cyst [sist] n cisti f inv.

czar [zɑ:*] n zar m inv.

Czech [tʃek] a ceco(a) // n ceco/a; (LING) ceco.

Czechoslovakia [tʃekəslə'vækiə] n Cecoslovacchia; ~**n** a, n cecoslovacco(a).

D

D [di:] n (MUS) re m; ~-**day** n giorno dello sbarco degli alleati in Normandia.

dab [dæb] vt (eyes, wound) tamponare; (paint, cream) applicare (con leggeri colpetti); **a** ~ **of paint** un colpetto di vernice.

dabble ['dæbl] vi: **to** ~ **in** occuparsi (da dilettante) di.

dad, daddy [dæd, 'dædi] n babbo, papà m inv; **daddy-long-legs** n tipula.

daffodil ['dæfədil] n giunchiglia.

daft [dɑ:ft] a sciocco(a).

dagger ['dægə*] n pugnale m.

daily ['deili] a quotidiano(a), giornaliero(a) // n quotidiano // ad tutti i giorni.

dainty ['deinti] a delicato(a), grazioso(a).

dairy ['dɛəri] n (shop) latteria; (on farm) caseificio // a caseario(a).

daisy ['deizi] n margherita.

dale [deil] n valle f.

dally ['dæli] vi trastullarsi.

dam [dæm] n diga // vt sbarrare; costruire dighe su.

damage ['dæmidʒ] n danno; danni mpl; (fig) danno // vt danneggiare; (fig) recar danno a; ~**s** npl (LAW) danni.

damn [dæm] vt condannare; (curse) maledire // n (col): **I don't give a** ~ non me ne importa un fico // a (col): **this** ~ ... questo maledetto ...; ~ **(it)!** accidenti!; ~**ing** a (evidence) schiacciante.

damp [dæmp] a umido(a) // n umidità, umido // vt (also: ~**en**) (cloth, rag) inumidire, bagnare; (enthusiasm etc) spegnere; ~**ness** n umidità, umido.

damson ['dæmzən] n susina damaschina.

dance [dɑ:ns] n danza, ballo; (ball) ballo // vi ballare; ~ **hall** n dancing m inv, sala da ballo; ~**r** n danzatore/trice; (professional) ballerino/a.

dancing ['dɑ:nsiŋ] n danza, ballo.

dandelion ['dændilaiən] n dente m di leone.

dandruff ['dændrəf] n forfora.

Dane [dein] n danese m/f.

danger ['deindʒə*] n pericolo; **there is a** ~ **of fire** c'è pericolo di fuoco; **in** ~ **in** pericolo; **he was in** ~ **of falling** rischiava di cadere; ~**ous** a pericoloso(a).

dangle ['dæŋgl] vt dondolare; (fig) far balenare // vi pendolare.

Danish ['deiniʃ] a danese // n (LING) danese m.

dapper ['dæpə*] a lindo(a).

dare [dɛə*] vt: **to** ~ **sb to do** sfidare qd a fare // vi: **to** ~ **(to) do sth** osare fare qc; ~**devil** n scavezzacollo m/f; **daring** a audace, ardito(a).

dark [dɑ:k] a (night, room) buio(a), scuro(a); (colour, complexion) scuro(a); (fig) cupo(a), tetro(a), nero(a) // n: **in the** ~ al buio; **in the** ~ **about** (fig) all'oscuro di; **after** ~ a notte fatta; ~**en** vt (room) oscurare; (photo, painting) far scuro(a) // vi oscurarsi; imbrunirsi; ~ **glasses** npl occhiali mpl scuri; ~**ness** n oscurità, buio; ~ **room** n camera oscura.

darling ['dɑ:lɪŋ] a caro(a) // n tesoro.

darn [dɑ:n] vt rammendare.

dart [dɑ:t] n freccetta // vi: **to** ~ **towards** precipitarsi verso; **to** ~ **away** guizzare via; ~**s** n tiro al bersaglio (con freccette); ~**board** n bersaglio (per freccette).

dash [dæʃ] n (sign) lineetta // vt (missile) gettare; (hopes) infrangere // vi: **to** ~ **towards** precipitarsi verso; **to** ~ **away** vi scappare via; ~**board** n cruscotto; ~**ing** a ardito(a).

data ['deɪtə] npl dati mpl; ~ **processing** n elaborazione f (elettronica) dei dati.

date [deɪt] n data; appuntamento; (fruit) dattero // vt datare; **to** ~ ad fino a oggi; **out of** ~ scaduto(a); (old-fashioned) passato(a) di moda; ~**d the 13th** datato il 13; ~**d** a passato(a) di moda; ~**line** n linea del cambiamento di data.

daub [dɔ:b] vt imbrattare.

daughter ['dɔ:tə*] n figlia; ~**-in-law** n nuora.

daunt [dɔ:nt] vt intimidire; ~**less** a intrepido(a).

dawdle ['dɔ:dl] vi bighellonare.

dawn [dɔ:n] n alba // vi (day) spuntare; (fig) venire in mente.

day [deɪ] n giorno; (as duration) giornata; (period of time, age) tempo, epoca; **the** ~ **before** il giorno avanti or prima; **by** ~ di giorno; ~**break** n spuntar m del giorno; ~**dream** n sogno a occhi aperti // vi sognare a occhi aperti; ~**light** n luce f del giorno; ~**time** n giorno.

daze [deɪz] vt (subject: drug) inebetire; (: blow) stordire // vi: **in a** ~ inebetito(a); stordito(a).

dazzle ['dæzl] vt abbagliare.

dead [dɛd] a morto(a); (numb) intirizzito(a) // ad assolutamente, perfettamente; **he was shot** ~ fu colpito a morte; ~ **on time** in perfetto orario; ~ **tired** stanco(a) morto(a); **to stop** ~ fermarsi in tronco; **the** ~ i morti; ~**en** vt (blow, sound) ammortire; (make numb) intirizzire; ~ **end** n vicolo cieco; ~ **heat** n (SPORT): **to finish in a** ~ **heat** finire alla pari; ~**line** n scadenza; ~**lock** n punto morto; ~**ly** a mortale; (weapon, poison) micidiale; ~**pan** a a faccia impassibile.

deaf [dɛf] a sordo(a); ~**-aid** n apparecchio per la sordità; ~**en** vt assordare; ~**ening** a fragoroso(a), assordante; ~**ness** n sordità; ~**-mute** n sordomuto/a.

deal [di:l] n accordo; affare m // vt (pt, pp dealt [dɛlt]) (blow, cards) dare; **a great** ~ **(of)** molto(a); **to** ~ **with** vt fus (COMM) fare affari con, trattare con; (handle) occuparsi di; (be about: book etc) trattarsi di; ~**er** n commerciante m/f; ~**ings** npl (COMM) relazioni fpl; (relations) rapporti mpl.

dean [di:n] n (SCOL) preside m di facoltà (or di collegio).

dear [dɪə*] a caro(a) // n: **my** ~ caro mio/cara mia; ~ **me!** Dio mio!; **D~ Sir/Madam** (in letter) Egregio(a) Signore(a); **D~ Mr/Mrs X** Gentile Signor/Signora X; ~**ly** ad (love) moltissimo; (pay) a caro prezzo.

dearth [də:θ] n scarsità, carestia.

death [dɛθ] n morte f; (ADMIN) decesso; ~**bed** n letto di morte; ~ **certificate** n atto di decesso; ~ **duties** npl (Brit) imposta or tassa di successione; ~**ly** a di morte; ~ **penalty** n pena di morte; ~ **rate** n indice m di mortalità.

debar [dɪ'bɑ:*] vt: **to** ~ **sb from doing** impedire a qd di fare.

debase [dɪ'beɪs] vt (currency) adulterare; (person) degradare.

debatable [dɪ'beɪtəbl] a discutibile.

debate [dɪ'beɪt] n dibattito // vt dibattere; discutere // vi (consider): **to** ~ **whether** riflettere se.

debauchery [dɪ'bɔ:tʃərɪ] n dissolutezza.

debit ['dɛbɪt] n debito // vt: **to** ~ **a sum to sb** addebitare una somma a qd.

debris ['dɛbri:] n detriti mpl.

debt [dɛt] n debito; **to be in** ~ essere indebitato(a); ~**or** n debitore/trice.

début ['deɪbju:] n debutto.

decade ['dɛkeɪd] n decennio.

decadence ['dɛkədəns] n decadenza.

decanter [dɪ'kæntə*] n caraffa.

decay [dɪ'keɪ] n decadimento; imputridimento; (fig) rovina; (also: **tooth** ~) carie f // vi (rot) imputridire; (fig) andare in rovina.

decease [dɪ'si:s] n decesso; ~**d** n defunto/a.

deceit [dɪ'si:t] n inganno; ~**ful** a ingannevole, perfido(a).

deceive [dɪ'si:v] vt ingannare.

decelerate [di:'sɛləreɪt] vt,vi rallentare.

December [dɪ'sɛmbə*] n dicembre m.

decency ['di:sənsɪ] n decenza.

decent ['di:sənt] a decente; **they were very** ~ **about it** si sono comportati da signori riguardo a ciò.

decentralize [di:'sɛntrəlaɪz] vt decentrare.

deception [dɪ'sɛpʃən] n inganno.

deceptive [dɪ'sɛptɪv] a ingannevole.

decibel ['dɛsɪbɛl] n decibel m inv.

decide [dɪ'saɪd] vt (person) far prendere una decisione a; (question, argument) risolvere, decidere // vi decidere, decidersi; **to** ~ **to do/that** decidere di fare/che; **to** ~ **on** decidere per; ~**d** a (resolute) deciso(a); (clear, definite) netto(a), chiaro(a); ~**dly** [-dɪdlɪ] ad indubbiamente; decisamente.

deciduous [dɪ'sɪdjuəs] a deciduo(a).

decimal ['dɛsɪməl] a, n decimale (m); ~ **point** n ≃ virgola.

decimate ['dɛsɪmeɪt] vt decimare.

decipher [dɪ'saɪfə*] vt decifrare.

decision [dɪ'sɪʒən] n decisione f.

decisive [dɪ'saɪsɪv] a decisivo(a).

deck [dɛk] n (NAUT) ponte m; (of bus): **top ~** imperiale m; (of cards) mazzo; **~chair** n sedia a sdraio; **~ hand** n marinaio.

declaration [dɛklə'reɪʃən] n dichiarazione f.

declare [dɪ'klɛə*] vt dichiarare.

decline [dɪ'klaɪn] n (decay) declino; (lessening) ribasso // vt declinare; rifiutare // vi declinare; diminuire.

decode ['di:'kəʊd] vt decifrare.

decompose [di:kəm'pəʊz] vi decomporre; **decomposition** [di:kɔmpə'zɪʃən] n decomposizione f.

decontaminate [di:kən'tæmɪneɪt] vt decontaminare.

décor ['deɪkɔ:*] n decorazione f.

decorate ['dɛkəreɪt] vt (adorn, give a medal to) decorare; (paint and paper) tinteggiare e tappezzare; **decoration** [-'reɪʃən] n (medal etc, adornment) decorazione f; **decorative** ['dɛkərətɪv] a decorativo(a); **decorator** n decoratore m.

decoy ['di:kɔɪ] n zimbello.

decrease [di:'kri:s] diminuzione f // vt, vi [di:'kri:s] diminuire.

decree [dɪ'kri:] n decreto; **~ nisi** n sentenza provvisoria di divorzio.

decrepit [dɪ'krɛpɪt] a decrepito(a).

dedicate ['dɛdɪkeɪt] vt consacrare; (book etc) dedicare.

dedication [dɛdɪ'keɪʃən] n (devotion) dedizione f.

deduce [dɪ'dju:s] vt dedurre.

deduct [dɪ'dʌkt] vt: **to ~ sth (from)** dedurre qc (da); (from wage etc) trattenere qc (da); **~ion** [dɪ'dʌkʃən] n (deducting) deduzione f; (from wage etc) trattenuta; (deducing) deduzione f, conclusione f.

deed [di:d] n azione f, atto; (LAW) atto.

deep [di:p] a profondo(a); **4 metres ~** profondo(a) 4 metri // ad: **~ in snow** affondato(a) nella neve; **spectators stood 20 ~** c'erano 20 file di spettatori; **knee-~ in water** in acqua fino alle ginocchia; **~en** vt (hole) approfondire // vi approfondirsi; (darkness) farsi più buio; **~-freeze** n congelatore m // vt congelare; **~-sea** a: **~-sea diving** n immersione f in alto mare; **~-sea fishing** n pesca d'alto mare; **~-seated** a (beliefs) radicato(a); **~-set** a (eyes) infossato(a).

deer [dɪə*] n, pl inv: **the ~** i cervidi; **(red) ~** cervo; **(fallow) ~** daino; **(roe) ~** capriolo; **~skin** n pelle f di daino.

deface [dɪ'feɪs] vt imbrattare.

defamation [dɛfə'meɪʃən] n diffamazione f.

default [dɪ'fɔ:lt] vi (LAW) essere contumace; (gen) essere inadempiente // n: **by ~** (LAW) in contumacia; (SPORT) per abbandono; **~er** n (in debt) inadempiente m/f.

defeat [dɪ'fi:t] n sconfitta // vt (team, opponents) sconfiggere; (fig: plans, efforts) frustrare; **~ist** a,n disfattista (m/f).

defect n ['di:fɛkt] difetto // vi [dɪ'fɛkt]: **to**

~ to the enemy/the West passare al nemico/all'Ovest; **~ive** [dɪ'fɛktɪv] a difettoso(a).

defence [dɪ'fɛns] n difesa; **in ~ of** in difesa di; **~less** a senza difesa.

defend [dɪ'fɛnd] vt difendere; **~ant** n imputato/a; **~er** n difensore/a.

defensive [dɪ'fɛnsɪv] a difensivo(a).

defer [dɪ'fə:*] vt (postpone) differire, rinviare.

deference ['dɛfərəns] n deferenza; riguardo.

defiance [dɪ'faɪəns] n sfida; **in ~ of** a dispetto di.

defiant [dɪ'faɪənt] a di sfida.

deficiency [dɪ'fɪʃənsɪ] n deficienza; carenza.

deficient [dɪ'fɪʃənt] a deficiente; insufficiente; **to be ~ in** mancare di.

deficit ['dɛfɪsɪt] n disavanzo.

defile vb [dɪ'faɪl] vt contaminare // vi sfilare // n ['di:faɪl] gola, stretta.

define [dɪ'faɪn] vt definire.

definite ['dɛfɪnɪt] a (fixed) definito(a), preciso(a); (clear, obvious) ben definito(a), esatto(a); (LING) determinativo(a); **he was ~ about it** ne era sicuro; **~ly** ad indubbiamente.

definition [dɛfɪ'nɪʃən] n definizione f.

definitive [dɪ'fɪnɪtɪv] a definitivo(a).

deflate [di:'fleɪt] vt sgonfiare.

deflation [di:'fleɪʃən] n (ECON) deflazione f.

deflect [dɪ'flɛkt] vt deflettere, deviare.

deform [dɪ'fɔ:m] vt deformare; **~ed** a deforme; **~ity** n deformità f inv.

defraud [dɪ'frɔ:d] vt defraudare.

defray [dɪ'freɪ] vt: **to ~ sb's expenses** sostenere le spese di qd.

defrost [di:'frɔst] vt (fridge) disgelare.

deft [dɛft] a svelto(a), destro(a).

defunct [dɪ'fʌŋkt] a defunto(a).

defuse [di:'fju:z] vt disarmare.

defy [dɪ'faɪ] vt sfidare; (efforts etc) resistere a.

degenerate vi [dɪ'dʒɛnəreɪt] degenerare // a [dɪ'dʒɛnərɪt] degenere.

degradation [dɛgrə'deɪʃən] n degradazione f.

degrading [dɪ'greɪdɪŋ] a degradante.

degree [dɪ'gri:] n grado; laurea (universitaria); **a (first) ~ in maths** una laurea in matematica.

dehydrated [di:haɪ'dreɪtɪd] a disidratato(a); (milk, eggs) in polvere.

de-ice [di:'aɪs] vt (windscreen) disgelare.

deign [deɪn] vi: **to ~ to do** degnarsi di fare.

deity ['di:ɪtɪ] n deità f inv; dio/dea.

dejected [dɪ'dʒɛktɪd] a abbattuto(a), avvilito(a).

dejection [dɪ'dʒɛkʃən] n abbattimento, avvilimento.

delay [dɪ'leɪ] vt (journey, operation) ritardare, rinviare; (travellers, trains) ritardare // n ritardo; **without ~** senza ritardo; **~ed-action** a a azione ritardata.

delegate n ['dɛlɪgɪt] delegato/a // vt ['dɛlɪgeɪt] delegare.
delegation [dɛlɪ'geɪʃən] n delegazione f.
delete [dɪ'liːt] vt cancellare.
deliberate a [dɪ'lɪbərɪt] (intentional) intenzionale; (slow) misurato(a) // vi [dɪ'lɪbəreɪt] deliberare, riflettere; ~ly ad (on purpose) deliberatamente.
delicacy ['dɛlɪkəsɪ] n delicatezza.
delicate ['dɛlɪkɪt] a delicato(a).
delicatessen [dɛlɪkə'tɛsn] n salumeria.
delicious [dɪ'lɪʃəs] a delizioso(a), squisito(a).
delight [dɪ'laɪt] n delizia, gran piacere m // vt dilettare; **to take ~ in** divertirsi a; ~**ful** a delizioso(a); incantevole.
delinquency [dɪ'lɪŋkwənsɪ] n delinquenza.
delinquent [dɪ'lɪŋkwənt] a,n delinquente (m/f).
delirium [dɪ'lɪrɪəm] n delirio.
deliver [dɪ'lɪvə*] vt (mail) distribuire; (goods) consegnare; (speech) pronunciare; (free) liberare; (MED) far partorire; **to ~ a message** fare un'ambasciata; **to ~ the goods** (fig) partorire; ~y n consegna; distribuzione f; (of speaker) modo di proporre; (MED) parto; **to take ~y of** prendere in consegna.
delta ['dɛltə] n delta m.
delude [dɪ'luːd] vt deludere, illudere.
deluge ['dɛljuːdʒ] n diluvio.
delusion [dɪ'luːʒən] n illusione f.
delve [dɛlv] vi: **to ~ into** frugare in; (subject) far ricerche in.
demagogue ['dɛməgɒg] n demagogo.
demand [dɪ'mɑːnd] vt richiedere // n domanda; (ECON, claim) richiesta; **in ~** ricercato(a), richiesto(a); **on ~** a richiesta; ~**ing** a (boss) esigente; (work) impegnativo(a).
demarcation [diːmɑː'keɪʃən] n demarcazione f.
demean [dɪ'miːn] vt: **to ~ o.s.** umiliarsi.
demeanour [dɪ'miːnə*] n comportamento; contegno.
demented [dɪ'mɛntɪd] a demente, impazzito(a).
demise [dɪ'maɪz] n decesso.
demobilize [diː'məubɪlaɪz] vt smobilitare.
democracy [dɪ'mɒkrəsɪ] n democrazia.
democrat ['dɛməkræt] n democratico/a; ~**ic** [dɛmə'krætɪk] a democratico(a).
demolish [dɪ'mɒlɪʃ] vt demolire.
demolition [dɛmə'lɪʃən] n demolizione f.
demonstrate ['dɛmənstreɪt] vt dimostrare, provare.
demonstration [dɛmən'streɪʃən] n dimostrazione f; (POL) manifestazione f, dimostrazione.
demonstrative [dɪ'mɒnstrətɪv] a dimostrativo(a).
demonstrator ['dɛmənstreɪtə*] n (POL) dimostrante m/f.
demoralize [dɪ'mɒrəlaɪz] vt demoralizzare.
demote [dɪ'məut] vt far retrocedere.
demure [dɪ'mjuə*] a contegnoso(a).

den [dɛn] n tana, covo.
denial [dɪ'naɪəl] n diniego; rifiuto.
denigrate ['dɛnɪgreɪt] vt denigrare.
denim ['dɛnɪm] n tessuto di cotone ritorto; ~**s** npl blue jeans mpl.
Denmark ['dɛnmɑːk] n Danimarca.
denomination [dɪnɒmɪ'neɪʃən] n (money) valore m; (REL) confessione f.
denominator [dɪ'nɒmɪneɪtə*] n denominatore m.
denote [dɪ'nəut] vt denotare.
denounce [dɪ'nauns] vt denunciare.
dense [dɛns] a fitto(a); (stupid) ottuso(a), duro(a); ~**ly** ad: ~**ly wooded** fittamente boscoso; ~**ly populated** densamente popolato(a).
density ['dɛnsɪtɪ] n densità f inv.
dent [dɛnt] n ammaccatura // vt (also: **make a ~ in**) ammaccare.
dental ['dɛntl] a dentale; ~ **surgeon** n medico/a dentista.
dentifrice ['dɛntɪfrɪs] n dentifricio.
dentist ['dɛntɪst] n dentista m/f; ~**ry** n odontoiatria.
denture ['dɛntʃə*] n dentiera.
deny [dɪ'naɪ] vt negare; (refuse) rifiutare.
deodorant [diː'əudərənt] n deodorante m.
depart [dɪ'pɑːt] vi partire; **to ~ from** (leave) allontanarsi da, partire da.
department [dɪ'pɑːtmənt] n (COMM) reparto; (SCOL) sezione f, dipartimento; (POL) ministero; ~ **store** n grande magazzino.
departure [dɪ'pɑːtʃə*] n partenza; (fig): ~ **from** allontanamento da.
depend [dɪ'pɛnd] vi: **to ~ on** dipendere da; (rely on) contare su; **it ~s** dipende; ~**able** a fidato(a); (car etc) affidabile; ~**ence** n dipendenza; ~**ant, ~ent** n persona a carico.
depict [dɪ'pɪkt] vt (in picture) dipingere; (in words) descrivere.
depleted [dɪ'pliːtɪd] a diminuito(a).
deplorable [dɪ'plɔːrəbl] a deplorabile, lamentevole.
deplore [dɪ'plɔː*] vt deplorare.
deploy [dɪ'plɔɪ] vt dispiegare.
depopulation ['diːpɒpju'leɪʃən] n spopolamento.
deport [dɪ'pɔːt] vt deportare; espellere; ~**ation** [diːpɔː'teɪʃən] n deportazione f; ~**ment** n portamento.
depose [dɪ'pəuz] vt deporre.
deposit [dɪ'pɒzɪt] n (COMM, GEO) deposito; (of ore, oil) giacimento; (CHEM) sedimento; (part payment) acconto; (for hired goods etc) cauzione f // vt depositare; dare in acconto; mettere o lasciare in deposito; ~ **account** n conto vincolato; ~**or** n depositante m/f.
depot ['dɛpəu] n deposito.
deprave [dɪ'preɪv] vt depravare, corrompere, pervertire.
depravity [dɪ'prævɪtɪ] n depravazione f.
depreciate [dɪ'priːʃɪeɪt] vt svalutare // vi svalutarsi; **depreciation** [-'eɪʃən] n svalutazione f.

depress [dɪ'prɛs] vt deprimere; (press down) premere; ~ed a (person) depresso(a), abbattuto(a); (area) depresso(a); ~ing a deprimente; ~ion [dɪ'prɛʃən] n depressione f.

deprivation [dɛprɪ'veɪʃən] n privazione f; (loss) perdita.

deprive [dɪ'praɪv] vt: to ~ sb of privare qd di; ~d a disgraziato(a).

depth [dɛpθ] n profondità f inv; in the ~s of nel profondo di; nel cuore di; in the ~s of winter in pieno inverno; ~ charge n carica di profondità.

deputation [dɛpju'teɪʃən] n deputazione f, delegazione f.

deputize ['dɛpjʊtaɪz] vi: to ~ for svolgere le funzioni di.

deputy ['dɛpjʊtɪ] a: ~ head vicepresidente m/f; (SCOL) vicepreside m/f // n (replacement) supplente m/f; (second in command) vice m/f.

derail [dɪ'reɪl] vt far deragliare; to be ~ed essere deragliato; ~ment n deragliamento.

deranged [dɪ'reɪndʒd] a: to be (mentally) ~ essere pazzo(a).

derelict ['dɛrɪlɪkt] a abbandonato(a).

deride [dɪ'raɪd] vt deridere.

derision [dɪ'rɪʒən] n derisione f.

derisive [dɪ'raɪsɪv] a di derisione.

derisory [dɪ'raɪsərɪ] a (sum) irrisorio(a).

derivation [dɛrɪ'veɪʃən] n derivazione f.

derivative [dɪ'rɪvətɪv] n derivato // a derivato(a).

derive [dɪ'raɪv] vt: to ~ sth from derivare qc da; trarre qc da // vi: to ~ from derivare da.

derogatory [dɪ'rɔgətərɪ] a denigratorio(a).

derrick ['dɛrɪk] n gru f inv; (for oil) derrick m inv.

descend [dɪ'sɛnd] vt, vi discendere, scendere; to ~ from discendere da; ~ant n discendente m/f.

descent [dɪ'sɛnt] n discesa; (origin) discendenza, famiglia.

describe [dɪs'kraɪb] vt descrivere; **description** [-'krɪpʃən] n descrizione f; (sort) genere m, specie f; **descriptive** [-'krɪptɪv] a descrittivo(a).

desecrate ['dɛsɪkreɪt] vt profanare.

desert n ['dɛzət] deserto // vb [dɪ'zɜːt] vt lasciare, abbandonare // vi (MIL) disertare; ~er n disertore m; ~ion [dɪ'zɜːʃən] n diserzione f.

deserve [dɪ'zɜːv] vt meritare; **deserving** a (person) meritevole, degno(a); (cause) meritorio(a).

design [dɪ'zaɪn] n (sketch) disegno; (layout, shape) linea; (pattern) fantasia; (COMM) disegno tecnico; (intention) intenzione f // vt disegnare; progettare; to have ~s on aver mire su.

designate vt ['dɛzɪgneɪt] designare // a ['dɛzɪgnɪt] designato(a); **designation** [-'neɪʃən] n designazione f.

designer [dɪ'zaɪnə*] n (ART, TECH)

disegnatore/trice; (of fashion) modellista m/f.

desirability [dɪzaɪərə'bɪlɪtɪ] n desiderabilità; vantaggio.

desirable [dɪ'zaɪərəbl] a desiderabile.

desire [dɪ'zaɪə*] n desiderio, voglia // vt desiderare, volere.

desk [dɛsk] n (in office) scrivania; (for pupil) banco; (in shop, restaurant) cassa; (in hotel) ricevimento; (at airport) accettazione f.

desolate ['dɛsəlɪt] a desolato(a).

desolation [dɛsə'leɪʃən] n desolazione f.

despair [dɪs'pɛə*] n disperazione f // vi: to ~ of disperare di.

despatch [dɪs'pætʃ] n, vt = **dispatch**.

desperate ['dɛspərɪt] a disperato(a); (fugitive) capace di tutto; ~ly ad disperatamente; (very) terribilmente, estremamente.

desperation [dɛspə'reɪʃən] n disperazione f.

despicable [dɪs'pɪkəbl] a disprezzabile.

despise [dɪs'paɪz] vt disprezzare, sdegnare.

despite [dɪs'paɪt] prep malgrado, a dispetto di, nonostante.

despondent [dɪs'pɔndənt] a abbattuto(a), scoraggiato(a).

dessert [dɪ'zɜːt] n dolce m; frutta; ~spoon n cucchiaio da dolci.

destination [dɛstɪ'neɪʃən] n destinazione f.

destine ['dɛstɪn] vt destinare.

destiny ['dɛstɪnɪ] n destino.

destitute ['dɛstɪtjuːt] a indigente, bisognoso(a).

destroy [dɪs'trɔɪ] vt distruggere; ~er n (NAUT) cacciatorpediniere m inv.

destruction [dɪs'trʌkʃən] n distruzione f.

destructive [dɪs'trʌktɪv] a distruttivo(a).

detach [dɪ'tætʃ] vt staccare, distaccare; ~able a staccabile; ~ed a (attitude) distante; ~ed house n villa; ~ment n (MIL) distaccamento; (fig) distacco.

detail ['diːteɪl] n particolare m, dettaglio // vt dettagliare, particolareggiare; in ~ nei particolari; ~ed a particolareggiato(a).

detain [dɪ'teɪn] vt trattenere; (in captivity) detenere.

detect [dɪ'tɛkt] vt scoprire, scorgere; (MED, POLICE, RADAR etc) individuare; ~ion [dɪ'tɛkʃən] n scoperta; individuazione f; ~ive n agente m investigativo; **private** ~ive investigatore m privato; ~ive story n giallo; ~or n rivelatore m.

detention [dɪ'tɛnʃən] n detenzione f; (SCOL) permanenza forzata per punizione.

deter [dɪ'tɜː*] vt distogliere.

detergent [dɪ'tɜːdʒənt] n detersivo.

deteriorate [dɪ'tɪərɪəreɪt] vi deteriorarsi; **deterioration** [-'reɪʃən] n deterioramento.

determination [dɪtɜːmɪ'neɪʃən] n determinazione f.

determine [dɪ'tɜːmɪn] vt determinare; ~d a (person) risoluto(a), deciso(a).

deterrent [dɪ'tɛrənt] n deterrente m.

detest [dɪ'tɛst] vt detestare; ~**able** a detestabile, abominevole.

detonate ['dɛtəneɪt] vi detonare; esplodere // vt far detonare or esplodere; **detonator** n detonatore m.

detour ['di:tuə*] n deviazione f.

detract [dɪ'trækt] vt: to ~ **from** detrarre da.

detriment ['dɛtrɪmənt] n: to the ~ of a detrimento di; ~**al** [dɛtrɪ'mɛntl] a: ~**al to** dannoso(a) a, nocivo(a) a.

devaluation [dɪvælju'eɪʃən] n svalutazione f.

devalue ['di:'vælju:] vt svalutare.

devastate ['dɛvəsteɪt] vt devastare.

devastating ['dɛvəsteɪtɪŋ] a devastatore(trice).

develop [dɪ'vɛləp] vt sviluppare; (habit) prendere (gradualmente) // vi svilupparsi; (facts, symptoms: appear) manifestarsi, rivelarsi; ~**er** n (PHOT) sviluppatore m; (of land) imprenditore/trice; ~**ing country** paese m in via di sviluppo; ~**ment** n sviluppo.

deviate ['di:vɪeɪt] vi deviare.

deviation [di:vɪ'eɪʃən] n deviazione f.

device [dɪ'vaɪs] n (apparatus) congegno.

devil ['dɛvl] n diavolo; demonio; ~**ish** a diabolico(a).

devious ['di:vɪəs] a: ~ (means) indiretto(a), tortuoso(a); (person) subdolo(a).

devise [dɪ'vaɪz] vt escogitare, concepire.

devoid [dɪ'vɔɪd] a: ~ **of** privo(a) di.

devote [dɪ'vəut] vt: to ~ **sth** to dedicare qc a; ~**d** a devoto(a); **to be** ~**d to** essere affezionato(a) a; ~**e** [dɛvəu'ti:] n (MUS, SPORT) appassionato/a.

devotion [dɪ'vəuʃən] n devozione f, attaccamento, (REL) atto di devozione, preghiera.

devour [dɪ'vauə*] vt divorare.

devout [dɪ'vaut] a pio(a), devoto(a).

dew [dju:] n rugiada.

dexterity [dɛks'tɛrɪtɪ] n destrezza.

diabetes [daɪə'bi:ti:z] n diabete m; **diabetic** [-'bɛtɪk] a diabetico(a) // n diabetico.

diagnose [daɪəg'nəuz] vt diagnosticare.

diagnosis, pl **diagnoses** [daɪəg'nəusɪs, -si:z] n diagnosi f inv.

diagonal [daɪ'ægənl] a, n diagonale (f).

diagram ['daɪəgræm] n diagramma m.

dial ['daɪəl] n quadrante m; (on telephone) disco combinatore // vt (number) fare; ~ **ling tone** n segnale m di linea libera.

dialect ['daɪəlɛkt] n dialetto.

dialogue ['daɪəlɔg] n dialogo.

diameter [daɪ'æmɪtə*] n diametro.

diamond ['daɪəmənd] n diamante m; (shape) rombo; ~**s** npl (CARDS) quadri mpl.

diaper ['daɪəpə*] n (US) pannolino.

diaphragm ['daɪəfræm] n diaframma m.

diarrhoea [daɪə'ri:ə] n diarrea.

diary ['daɪərɪ] n (daily account) diario; (book) agenda.

dice [daɪs] n, pl inv dado // vt (CULIN) tagliare a dadini.

dictate vt [dɪk'teɪt] dettare // n ['dɪkteɪt] dettame m.

dictation [dɪk'teɪʃən] n dettato.

dictator [dɪk'teɪtə*] n dittatore m; ~**ship** n dittatura.

diction ['dɪkʃən] n dizione f.

dictionary ['dɪkʃənrɪ] n dizionario.

did [dɪd] pt of **do**.

die [daɪ] n (pl: **dies**) conio; matrice f; stampo // vi morire; to ~ **away** vi spegnersi a poco a poco; to ~ **down** vi abbassarsi; to ~ **out** vi estinguersi.

Diesel ['di:zəl]: ~ **engine** n motore m diesel inv.

diet ['daɪət] n alimentazione f; (restricted food) dieta // vi (also: **be on a** ~) stare a dieta.

differ ['dɪfə*] vi: to ~ **from** sth differire da qc; essere diverso(a) da qc; to ~ **from** **sb over** sth essere in disaccordo con qd su qc; ~**ence** n differenza; (quarrel) screzio; ~**ent** a diverso(a); ~**ential** [-'rɛnʃəl] n (AUT, wages) differenziale m; ~**entiate** [-'rɛnʃieɪt] vi differenziarsi; to ~**entiate between** discriminare or fare differenza fra; ~**ently** ad diversamente.

difficult ['dɪfɪkəlt] a difficile; ~**y** n difficoltà f inv.

diffident ['dɪfɪdənt] a sfiduciato(a).

diffuse a [dɪ'fju:s] diffuso(a) // vt [dɪ'fju:z] diffondere, emanare.

dig [dɪg] vt (pt, pp **dug** [dʌg]) (hole) scavare; (garden) vangare // n (prod) gomitata; (fig) frecciata; to ~ **into** (snow, soil) scavare; to ~ **up** vt scavare; (tree etc) sradicare.

digest vt [daɪ'dʒɛst] vt digerire; ~**ible** [dɪ'dʒɛstəbl] a digeribile; ~**ion** [dɪ'dʒɛstʃən] n digestione f.

digit ['dɪdʒɪt] n cifra; (finger) dito; ~**al** a digitale.

dignified ['dɪgnɪfaɪd] a dignitoso(a).

dignitary ['dɪgnɪtərɪ] n dignitario.

dignity ['dɪgnɪtɪ] n dignità.

digress [daɪ'grɛs] vi: to ~ **from** divagare da; ~**ion** [daɪ'grɛʃən] n digressione f.

digs [dɪgz] npl (Brit: col) camera ammobiliata.

dilapidated [dɪ'læpɪdeɪtɪd] a cadente.

dilate [daɪ'leɪt] vt dilatare // vi dilatarsi.

dilatory ['dɪlətərɪ] a dilatorio(a).

dilemma [daɪ'lɛmə] n dilemma m.

diligent ['dɪlɪdʒənt] a diligente.

dilute [daɪ'lu:t] vt diluire; (with water) annacquare.

dim [dɪm] a (light, eyesight) debole; (memory, outline) vago(a); (stupid) lento(a) d'ingegno // vt (light) abbassare.

dime [daɪm] n (US) = 10 cents.

dimension [dɪ'mɛnʃən] n dimensione f.

diminish [dɪ'mɪnɪʃ] vt, vi diminuire.

diminutive [dɪ'mɪnjutɪv] a minuscolo(a) // n (LING) diminutivo.

dimly ['dɪmlɪ] ad debolmente; indistintamente.

dimple ['dɪmpl] n fossetta.

din [dɪn] n chiasso, fracasso.

dine [daɪn] vi pranzare.
dinghy ['dɪŋgɪ] n battello pneumatico; (also: **sailing** ~) dinghy m inv.
dingy ['dɪndʒɪ] a grigio(a).
dining ['daɪnɪŋ] cpd: ~ **car** n vagone m ristorante; ~ **room** n sala da pranzo.
dinner ['dɪnə*] n pranzo; (public) banchetto; ~ **jacket** n smoking m inv; ~ **party** n cena.
diocese ['daɪəsɪs] n diocesi f inv.
dip [dɪp] n discesa; (in sea) bagno // vt immergere; bagnare; (AUT: lights) abbassare // vi abbassarsi.
diphtheria [dɪf'θɪərɪə] n difterite f.
diphthong ['dɪfθɒŋ] n dittongo.
diploma [dɪ'pləumə] n diploma m.
diplomacy [dɪ'pləuməsɪ] n diplomazia.
diplomat ['dɪpləmæt] n diplomatico; ~**ic** [dɪplə'mætɪk] a diplomatico(a); ~**ic corps** n corpo diplomatico.
dipstick ['dɪpstɪk] n (AUT) indicatore m di livello dell'olio.
dire [daɪə*] a terribile; estremo(a).
direct [daɪ'rɛkt] a diretto(a) // vt dirigere; **can you** ~ **me to ...?** mi può indicare la strada per ...?; ~ **current** n corrente f continua.
direction [dɪ'rɛkʃən] n direzione f; ~**s** npl (advice) chiarimenti mpl; ~**s for use** istruzioni fpl.
directly [dɪ'rɛktlɪ] ad (in straight line) direttamente; (at once) subito.
director [dɪ'rɛktə*] n direttore/trice; amministratore/trice; (THEATRE, CINEMA) regista m/f.
directory [dɪ'rɛktərɪ] n elenco.
dirt [dɜːt] n sporcizia; immondizia; ~-**cheap** a da due soldi; ~**y** a sporco(a) // vt sporcare; ~**y trick** n brutto scherzo.
disability [dɪsə'bɪlɪtɪ] n invalidità f inv; (LAW) incapacità f inv.
disabled [dɪs'eɪbld] a invalido(a); (maimed) mutilato(a); (through illness, old age) inabile.
disadvantage [dɪsəd'vɑːntɪdʒ] n svantaggio; ~**ous** [dɪsædvɑːn'teɪdʒəs] a svantaggioso(a).
disagree [dɪsə'griː] vi (differ) discordare; (be against, think otherwise): **to** ~ (**with**) essere in disaccordo (con), dissentire (da); **garlic** ~**s with me** l'aglio non mi va; ~**able** a sgradevole; (person) antipatico(a); ~**ment** n disaccordo.
disallow ['dɪsə'lau] vt respingere.
disappear [dɪsə'pɪə*] vi scomparire; ~**ance** n scomparsa.
disappoint [dɪsə'pɔɪnt] vt deludere; ~**ment** n delusione f.
disapproval [dɪsə'pruːvəl] n disapprovazione f.
disapprove [dɪsə'pruːv] vi: **to** ~ **of** disapprovare.
disarm [dɪs'ɑːm] vt disarmare; ~**ament** n disarmo.
disaster [dɪ'zɑːstə*] n disastro; **disastrous** a disastroso(a).

disband [dɪs'bænd] vt sbandare; (MIL) congedare.
disbelief ['dɪsbə'liːf] n incredulità.
disc [dɪsk] n disco.
discard [dɪs'kɑːd] vt (old things) scartare; (fig) abbandonare.
disc brake ['dɪskbreɪk] n freno a disco.
discern [dɪ'sɜːn] vt discernere, distinguere; ~**ing** a perspicace.
discharge vt [dɪs'tʃɑːdʒ] (duties) compiere; (ELEC, waste etc) scaricare; (MED) emettere; (patient) dimettere; (employee) licenziare; (soldier) congedare; (defendant) liberare // n ['dɪstʃɑːdʒ] (ELEC) scarica; (MED) emissione f; (dismissal) licenziamento; congedo; liberazione f.
disciple [dɪ'saɪpl] n discepolo.
disciplinary ['dɪsɪplɪnərɪ] a disciplinare.
discipline ['dɪsɪplɪn] n disciplina // vt disciplinare; (punish) punire.
disc jockey ['dɪskdʒɒkɪ] n disc jockey m inv.
disclaim [dɪs'kleɪm] vt ripudiare.
disclose [dɪs'kləuz] vt rivelare, svelare; **disclosure** [-'kləuʒə*] n rivelazione f.
disco ['dɪskəu] n abbr of **discothèque**.
discoloured [dɪs'kʌləd] a scolorito(a); ingiallito(a).
discomfort [dɪs'kʌmfət] n disagio; (lack of comfort) scomodità f inv.
disconcert [dɪskən'sɜːt] vt sconcertare.
disconnect [dɪskə'nɛkt] vt sconnettere, staccare; (ELEC, RADIO) staccare; (gas, water) chiudere; ~**ed** a (speech, thought) sconnesso(a).
disconsolate [dɪs'kɒnsəlɪt] a sconsolato(a).
discontent [dɪskən'tɛnt] n scontentezza; ~**ed** a scontento(a).
discontinue [dɪskən'tɪnjuː] vt smettere, cessare; '~**d**' (COMM) 'sospeso'.
discord ['dɪskɔːd] n disaccordo; (MUS) dissonanza; ~**ant** [dɪs'kɔːdənt] a discordante; dissonante.
discothèque ['dɪskəutɛk] n discoteca.
discount n ['dɪskaunt] sconto // vt [dɪs'kaunt] scontare.
discourage [dɪs'kʌrɪdʒ] vt scoraggiare; **discouraging** a scoraggiante.
discourteous [dɪs'kɜːtɪəs] a scortese.
discover [dɪs'kʌvə*] vt scoprire; ~**y** n scoperta.
discredit [dɪs'krɛdɪt] vt screditare; mettere in dubbio.
discreet [dɪ'skriːt] a discreto(a).
discrepancy [dɪ'skrɛpənsɪ] n discrepanza.
discretion [dɪ'skrɛʃən] n discrezione f.
discriminate [dɪ'skrɪmɪneɪt] vi: **to** ~ **between** distinguere tra; **to** ~ **against** discriminare contro; **discriminating** a fine, giudizioso(a); **discrimination** [-'neɪʃən] n discriminazione f; (judgment) discernimento.
discus ['dɪskəs] n disco.
discuss [dɪ'skʌs] vt discutere; (debate) dibattere; ~**ion** [dɪ'skʌʃən] n discussione f.
disdain [dɪs'deɪn] n disdegno.

disease [dɪ'ziːz] n malattia.
disembark [dɪsɪm'bɑːk] vt,vi sbarcare.
disembodied [dɪsɪm'bɔdɪd] a disincarnato(a).
disembowel [dɪsɪm'bauəl] vt sbudellare, sventrare.
disenchanted [dɪsɪn'tʃɑːntɪd] a disincantato(a), disilluso(a).
disengage [dɪsɪn'geɪdʒ] vt disimpegnare; (TECH) distaccare; (AUT) disinnestare.
disentangle [dɪsɪn'tæŋgl] vt sbrogliare.
disfavour [dɪs'feɪvə*] n sfavore m; disgrazia.
disfigure [dɪs'fɪgə*] vt sfigurare.
disgrace [dɪs'greɪs] n vergogna; (disfavour) disgrazia // vt disonorare, far cadere in disgrazia; ~ful a scandaloso(a), vergognoso(a).
disgruntled [dɪs'grʌntld] a scontento(a), di cattivo umore.
disguise [dɪs'gaɪz] n travestimento // vt travestire; **in** ~ travestito(a).
disgust [dɪs'gʌst] n disgusto, nausea // vt disgustare, far schifo a; ~**ing** a disgustoso(a); ripugnante.
dish [dɪʃ] n piatto; **to do** or **wash the** ~**es** fare i piatti; **to** ~ **up** servire; (facts, statistics) presentare; ~**cloth** n (for drying) asciugatoio; (for washing) strofinaccio.
dishearten [dɪs'hɑːtn] vt scoraggiare.
dishevelled [dɪ'ʃevəld] a arruffato(a); scapigliato(a).
dishonest [dɪs'ɔnɪst] a disonesto(a); ~**y** n disonestà.
dishonour [dɪs'ɔnə*] n disonore m; ~**able** a disonorevole.
dishwasher ['dɪʃwɔʃə*] n lavastoviglie f inv; (person) sguattero/a.
disillusion [dɪsɪ'luːʒən] vt disilludere; disingannare // n disillusione f.
disinfect [dɪsɪn'fekt] vt disinfettare; ~**ant** n disinfettante m.
disintegrate [dɪs'ɪntɪgreɪt] vi disintegrarsi.
disinterested [dɪs'ɪntrəstɪd] a disinteressato(a).
disjointed [dɪs'dʒɔɪntɪd] a sconnesso(a).
disk [dɪsk] n = **disc**.
dislike [dɪs'laɪk] n antipatia, avversione f // vt: **he** ~**s it** non gli piace.
dislocate ['dɪsləkeɪt] vt slogare; disorganizzare.
dislodge [dɪs'lɔdʒ] vt rimuovere, staccare; (enemy) sloggiare.
disloyal [dɪs'lɔɪəl] a sleale.
dismal ['dɪzml] a triste, cupo(a).
dismantle [dɪs'mæntl] vt smantellare, smontare; (fort, warship) disarmare.
dismay [dɪs'meɪ] n costernazione f // vt sgomentare.
dismiss [dɪs'mɪs] vt congedare; (employee) licenziare; (idea) scacciare; (LAW) respingere; ~**al** n congedo; licenziamento.
dismount [dɪs'maunt] vi scendere.

disobedience [dɪsə'biːdɪəns] n disubbidienza.
disobedient [dɪsə'biːdɪənt] a disubbidiente.
disobey [dɪsə'beɪ] vt disubbidire.
disorder [dɪs'ɔːdə*] n disordine m; (rioting) tumulto; (MED) disturbo; ~**ly** a disordinato(a); tumultuoso(a).
disorganize [dɪs'ɔːgənaɪz] vt disorganizzare.
disown [dɪs'əun] vt ripudiare.
disparaging [dɪs'pærɪdʒɪŋ] a spregiativo(a), sprezzante.
disparity [dɪs'pærɪtɪ] n disparità f inv.
dispassionate [dɪs'pæʃənət] a calmo(a), freddo(a); imparziale.
dispatch [dɪs'pætʃ] vt spedire, inviare // n spedizione f, invio; (MIL, PRESS) dispaccio.
dispel [dɪs'pel] vt dissipare, scacciare.
dispensary [dɪs'pensərɪ] n farmacia; (in chemist's) dispensario.
dispense [dɪs'pens] vt distribuire, amministrare; **to** ~ **with** vt fus fare a meno di; ~**r** n (container) distributore m; **dispensing chemist** n farmacista m/f.
dispersal [dɪs'pəːsl] n dispersione f.
disperse [dɪs'pəːs] vt disperdere; (knowledge) disseminare // vi disperdersi.
dispirited [dɪs'pɪrɪtɪd] a scoraggiato(a), abbattuto(a).
displace [dɪs'pleɪs] vt spostare; ~**d person** n (POL) profugo/a.
display [dɪs'pleɪ] n mostra; esposizione f; (of feeling etc) manifestazione f; (screen) schermo; (pej) ostentazione f // vt mostrare; (goods) esporre; (results) affiggere; (departure times) indicare.
displease [dɪs'pliːz] vt dispiacere a, scontentare; **displeasure** [-'pleʒə*] n dispiacere m.
disposable [dɪs'pəuzəbl] a (pack etc) a perdere; (income) disponibile.
disposal [dɪs'pəuzl] n (of rubbish) evacuazione f; distruzione f; **at one's** ~ alla sua disposizione.
dispose [dɪs'pəuz] vt disporre; **to** ~ **of** (time, money) disporre di; (unwanted goods) sbarazzarsi di; (problem) sbrigarsi; ~**d a: to** ~**d to do** disposto(a) a fare; **disposition** [-'zɪʃən] n disposizione f; (temperament) carattere m.
disproportionate [dɪsprə'pɔːʃənət] a sproporzionato(a).
disprove [dɪs'pruːv] vt confutare.
dispute [dɪs'pjuːt] n disputa; (also: **industrial** ~) controversia (sindacale) // vt contestare; (matter) discutere; (victory) disputare.
disqualification [dɪskwɔlɪfɪ'keɪʃən] n squalifica; ~ (**from driving**) ritiro della patente.
disqualify [dɪs'kwɔlɪfaɪ] vt (SPORT) squalificare; **to** ~ **sb from sth/from doing** rendere qd incapace a qc/a fare; squalificare qd da qc/da fare.
disquiet [dɪs'kwaɪət] n inquietudine f.
disregard [dɪsrɪ'gɑːd] vt non far caso a, non badare a.

disrepair [dɪsrɪ'pɛə*] n cattivo stato.

disreputable [dɪs'rɛpjutəbl] a (person) di cattiva fama.

disrespectful [dɪsrɪ'spɛktful] a che manca di rispetto.

disrupt [dɪs'rʌpt] vt mettere in disordine; ~ion [-'rʌpʃən] n disordine m; interruzione f.

dissatisfaction [dɪssætɪs'fækʃən] n scontentezza, insoddisfazione f.

dissatisfied [dɪs'sætɪsfaɪd] a: ~ (with) scontento(a) or insoddisfatto(a) (di).

dissect [dɪ'sɛkt] vt sezionare.

disseminate [dɪ'sɛmɪneɪt] vt disseminare.

dissent [dɪ'sɛnt] n dissenso.

disservice [dɪs'sɜːvɪs] n: to do sb a ~ fare un cattivo servizio a qd.

dissident [dɪ'sɪdnt] a dissidente.

dissimilar [dɪ'sɪmɪlə*] a: ~ (to) dissimile or diverso(a) (da).

dissipate ['dɪsɪpeɪt] vt dissipare; ~d a dissipato(a).

dissociate [dɪ'səuʃɪeɪt] vt dissociare.

dissolute ['dɪsəluːt] a dissoluto(a), licenzioso(a).

dissolve [dɪ'zɔlv] vt dissolvere, sciogliere // vi dissolversi, sciogliersi; (fig) svanire.

dissuade [dɪ'sweɪd] vt: to ~ sb (from) dissuadere qd da.

distance ['dɪstns] n distanza; in the ~ in lontananza.

distant ['dɪstnt] a lontano(a), distante; (manner) riservato(a), freddo(a).

distaste [dɪs'teɪst] n ripugnanza; ~ful a ripugnante, sgradevole.

distemper [dɪs'tɛmpə*] n (paint) tempera.

distend [dɪs'tɛnd] vt dilatare // vi dilatarsi.

distil [dɪs'tɪl] vt distillare; ~lery n distilleria.

distinct [dɪs'tɪŋkt] a distinto(a); (preference, progress) netto(a); ~ion [dɪs'tɪŋkʃən] n distinzione f; (in exam) lode f; ~ive a distintivo(a); ~ly ad chiaramente; manifestamente.

distinguish [dɪs'tɪŋgwɪʃ] vt distinguere; discernere; ~ed a (eminent) eminente; ~ing a (feature) distinto(a), caratteristico(a).

distort [dɪs'tɔːt] vt distorcere; (TECH) deformare; ~ion [dɪs'tɔːʃən] n distorsione f; deformazione f.

distract [dɪs'trækt] vt distrarre; ~ed a distratto(a); ~ion [dɪs'trækʃən] n distrazione f; to drive sb to ~ion spingere qd alla pazzia.

distraught [dɪs'trɔːt] a stravolto(a).

distress [dɪs'trɛs] n angoscia; (pain) dolore m // vt affliggere; ~ing a doloroso(a); ~ signal n segnale m di pericolo.

distribute [dɪs'trɪbjuːt] vt distribuire; distribution [-'bjuːʃən] n distribuzione f; distributor n distributore m.

district ['dɪstrɪkt] n (of country) regione f; (of town) quartiere m; (ADMIN) distretto; ~ attorney n (US) ≈ sostituto

procuratore m della Repubblica; ~ nurse n (Brit) infermiera di quartiere.

distrust [dɪs'trʌst] n diffidenza, sfiducia // vt non aver fiducia in.

disturb [dɪs'tɜːb] vt disturbare; (inconvenience) scomodare; ~ance n disturbo; (political etc) tumulto; (by drunks etc) disordini mpl; ~ing a sconvolgente.

disuse [dɪs'juːs] n: to fall into ~ cadere in disuso.

disused [dɪs'juːzd] a abbandonato(a).

ditch [dɪtʃ] n fossa // vt (col) piantare in asso.

dither ['dɪðə*] vi vacillare.

ditto ['dɪtəu] ad idem.

divan [dɪ'væn] n divano.

dive [daɪv] n tuffo; (of submarine) immersione f; (AVIAT) picchiata; (pej) buco // vi tuffarsi; ~r n tuffatore/trice; palombaro.

diverge [daɪ'vɜːdʒ] vi divergere.

diverse [daɪ'vɜːs] a vario(a).

diversify [daɪ'vɜːsɪfaɪ] vt diversificare.

diversion [daɪ'vɜːʃən] n (AUT) deviazione f; (distraction) divertimento; (MIL) diversione f.

diversity [daɪ'vɜːsɪtɪ] n diversità f inv, varietà f inv.

divert [daɪ'vɔːt] vt deviare; (amuse) divertire.

divide [dɪ'vaɪd] vt dividere; (separate) separare // vi dividersi.

dividend ['dɪvɪdɛnd] n dividendo.

divine [dɪ'vaɪn] a divino(a).

diving ['daɪvɪŋ] n tuffo; ~ board n trampolino.

divinity [dɪ'vɪnɪtɪ] n divinità f inv; teologia.

division [dɪ'vɪʒən] n divisione f; separazione f.

divorce [dɪ'vɔːs] n divorzio // vt divorziare da; ~d a divorziato(a); ~e [-'siː] n divorziato/a.

divulge [daɪ'vʌldʒ] vt divulgare, rivelare.

D.I.Y. a,n abbr of do-it-yourself.

dizziness ['dɪzɪnɪs] n vertigini fpl.

dizzy ['dɪzɪ] a (height) vertiginoso(a); to feel ~ avere il capogiro.

DJ n abbr of disc jockey.

do, pt did, pp done [duː, dɪd, dʌn] vt, vi fare; he didn't laugh non ha riso; ~ you want any? ne vuole?; he laughed, didn't he? lui ha riso, vero?; ~ they? ah sì?, vero?; who broke it? - I did chi l'ha rotto? - sono stato io; ~ you agree? - I ~ è d'accordo? - sì; to ~ one's nails farsi le unghie; to ~ one's teeth pulirsi i denti; will it ~? andrà bene?; to ~ without sth fare a meno di qc; to ~ away with vt fus abolire; to ~ up vt abbottonare; allacciare; (house etc) rimettere a nuovo.

docile ['dəusaɪl] a docile.

dock [dɔk] n bacino; (LAW) banco degli imputati // vi entrare in bacino; ~er n scaricatore m.

dockyard ['dɔkjɑːd] n cantiere m navale.

doctor ['dɔktə*] n medico/a; (Ph.D. etc) dottore/essa.

doctrine ['dɔktrɪn] n dottrina.
document ['dɔkjumənt] n documento;
~ary [-'mɛntərɪ] a documentario(a) // n
documentario; ~ation [-'teɪʃən] n
documentazione f.
doddering ['dɔdərɪŋ] a traballante.
dodge [dɔdʒ] n trucco; schivata // vt
schivare, eludere.
dodgems ['dɔdʒəmz] npl autoscontro.
dog [dɔg] n cane m; ~ collar n collare m
di cane; (fig) collarino; ~-eared a (book)
con orecchie.
dogged ['dɔgɪd] a ostinato(a), tenace.
dogma ['dɔgmə] n dogma m; ~tic
[-'mætɪk] a dogmatico(a).
doings ['duɪŋz] npl attività fpl.
do-it-yourself [du:ɪtjɔ:'sɛlf] n il far da sé.
doldrums ['dɔldrəmz] npl: **to be in the ~**
essere giù.
dole [dəul] n (Brit) sussidio di
disoccupazione; **to be on the ~** vivere
del sussidio; **to ~ out** vt distribuire.
doleful ['dəulful] a triste, doloroso(a).
doll [dɔl] n bambola; **to ~ o.s. up** farsi
bello(a).
dollar ['dɔlə*] n dollaro.
dolphin ['dɔlfɪn] n delfino.
domain [də'meɪn] n dominio.
dome [dəum] n cupola.
domestic [də'mɛstɪk] a (duty, happiness,
animal) domestico(a); (policy, affairs,
flights) nazionale; ~ated a
addomesticato(a).
domicile ['dɔmɪsaɪl] n domicilio.
dominant ['dɔmɪnənt] a dominante.
dominate ['dɔmɪneɪt] vt dominare;
domination [-'neɪʃən] n dominazione f;
domineering [-'nɪərɪŋ] a despotico(a), au-
toritario(a).
dominion [də'mɪnɪən] n dominio,
sovranità; dominion m inv.
domino, ~es ['dɔmɪnəu] n domino; ~es
n (game) gioco del domino.
don [dɔn] n docente m/f universitario(a) //
vt indossare.
donate [də'neɪt] vt donare; **donation**
[də'neɪʃən] n donazione f.
done [dʌn] pp of **do**.
donkey ['dɔŋkɪ] n asino.
donor ['dəunə*] n donatore/trice.
don't [dəunt] vb = **do not**.
doom [du:m] n destino; rovina // vt: **to**
~ed (**to failure**) essere predestinato(a)
a fallire; ~sday n il giorno del Giudizio.
door [dɔ:*] n porta; ~bell n campanello;
~ handle n maniglia; ~man n (in hotel)
portiere m in livrea; (in block of flats)
portinaio; ~mat n stuoia della porta;
~step n gradino della porta.
dope [dəup] n (col: drugs) roba // vt (horse
etc) drogare.
dopey ['dəupɪ] a (col) inebetito(a).
dormant ['dɔ:mənt] a inattivo(a); (fig)
latente.
dormitory ['dɔ:mɪtrɪ] n dormitorio.
dormouse, pl dormice ['dɔ:maus, -maɪs]
n ghiro.

dose [dəus] n dose f; (bout) attacco.
doss house ['dɔshaus] n asilo notturno.
dot [dɔt] n punto; macchiolina; **on the ~** in
punto.
dote [dəut]: **to ~ on** vt fus essere
infatuato(a) di.
dotted line [dɔtɪd'laɪn] n linea puntata.
double ['dʌbl] a doppio(a) // ad (fold) in
due, doppio; (twice): **to cost ~ (sth)**
costare il doppio (di qc) // n sosia m inv;
(CINEMA) controfigura // vt raddoppiare;
(fold) piegare doppio or in due // vi
raddoppiarsi; **at the ~** a passo di corsa;
~s n (TENNIS) doppio; ~ bass n
contrabbasso; ~ bed n letto
matrimoniale; ~ bend n doppia curva;
~-breasted a a doppio petto; ~cross vt
fare il doppio gioco con; ~decker n
autobus m inv a due piani; ~ parking n
parcheggio in doppia fila; ~ room n
camera per due; **doubly** ad doppiamente.
doubt [daut] n dubbio // vt dubitare di; **to**
~ **that** dubitare che + sub; ~ful a
dubbioso(a), incerto(a); (person)
equivoco(a); ~less ad indubbiamente.
dough [dəu] n pasta, impasto; ~nut n
bombolone m.
dove [dʌv] n colombo/a.
dovetail ['dʌvteɪl] n: ~ **joint** n incastro a
coda di rondine // vi (fig) combaciare.
dowdy ['daudɪ] a trasandato(a);
malvestito(a).
down [daun] n (fluff) piumino // ad giù, di
sotto // prep giù per // vt (col: drink)
scolarsi; ~ **with X!** abbasso X!; ~-at-
heel a scalcagnato(a); (fig) trasandato(a);
~cast a abbattuto(a); ~fall n caduta,
rovina; ~hearted a scoraggiato(a);
~hill ad: **to go ~hill** andare in discesa;
~ **payment** n acconto; ~pour n scroscio
di pioggia; ~right a onesto(a), franco(a);
(refusal) assoluto(a); ~stairs ad di sotto;
al piano inferiore; ~stream ad a valle;
~-to-earth a pratico(a); ~town ad in
città // a (US): ~town Chicago il centro
di Chicago; ~ward a downwəd] a,ad,
~wards ['daunwədz] ad in giù, in discesa.
dowry ['daurɪ] n dote f.
doz. abbr of **dozen**.
doze [dəuz] vi sonnecchiare; **to ~ off** vi
appisolarsi.
dozen ['dʌzn] n dozzina; **a ~ books** una
dozzina di libri.
Dr. abbr of **doctor**; **drive** (n).
drab [dræb] a tetro(a), grigio(a).
draft [dra:ft] n abbozzo; (COMM) tratta; (US:
MIL) contingente m; (: call-up) leva // vt
abbozzare; see also **draught**.
drag [dræg] vt trascinare; (river) dragare
// vi trascinarsi // n (col) noioso/a; noia,
fatica; **to ~ on** vi tirar avanti lentamente.
dragonfly ['drægənflaɪ] n libellula.
drain [dreɪn] n canale m di scolo; (for
sewage) fogna; (on resources) salasso // vt
(land, marshes) prosciugare; (vegetables)
scolare; (reservoir etc) vuotare // vi
(water) defluire (via); ~age n prosciuga-
mento; fognatura; ~ing board, ~board

(US) n asciugapiatti m inv; ~**pipe** n tubo di scarico.

drama ['drɑːmə] n (art) dramma m, teatro; (play) commedia; (event) dramma; ~**tic** [drə'mætɪk] a drammatico(a); ~**tist** ['dræmətɪst] n drammaturgo/a.

drank [dræŋk] pt of **drink**.

drape [dreɪp] vt drappeggiare; ~**s** npl (US) tende fpl; ~**r** n negoziante m/f di stoffe.

drastic ['dræstɪk] a drastico(a).

draught [drɑːft] n corrente f d'aria; (NAUT) pescaggio; ~**s** n (gioco della) dama; **on** ~ (beer) alla spina; ~**board** n scacchiera.

draughtsman ['drɑːftsmən] n disegnatore m.

draw [drɔː] vb (pt **drew**, pp **drawn** [druː, drɔːn]) vt tirare; (attract) attirare; (picture) disegnare; (line, circle) tracciare; (money) ritirare // vi (SPORT) pareggiare // n pareggio; estrazione f; attrazione f; **to** ~ **to a close** avvicinarsi alla conclusione; **to** ~ **near** vi avvicinarsi; **to** ~ **out** vi (lengthen) allungarsi // vt (money) ritirare; **to** ~ **up** vi (stop) arrestarsi, fermarsi // vt (document) compilare; ~**back** n svantaggio, inconveniente m; ~**bridge** n ponte m levatoio.

drawer [drɔː*] n cassetto.

drawing ['drɔːɪŋ] n disegno; ~ **board** n tavola da disegno; ~ **pin** n puntina da disegno; ~ **room** n salotto.

drawl [drɔːl] n pronuncia strascicata.

drawn [drɔːn] pp of **draw**.

dread [drɛd] n terrore m // vt tremare all'idea di; ~**ful** a terribile.

dream [driːm] n sogno // vt, vi (pt, pp **dreamed** or **dreamt** [drɛmt]) sognare; ~**er** n sognatore/trice; ~**y** a sognante.

dreary ['drɪərɪ] a tetro(a); monotono(a).

dredge [drɛdʒ] vt dragare; ~**r** n draga; (also: **sugar** ~**r**) spargizucchero m inv.

dregs [drɛgz] npl feccia.

drench [drɛntʃ] vt inzuppare.

dress [drɛs] n vestito; (clothing) abbigliamento // vt vestire; (wound) fasciare; (food) condire; preparare // vi vestirsi; **to** ~ **up** vi vestirsi a festa; (in fancy dress) vestirsi in costume; ~ **circle** n prima galleria; ~**er** n (THEATRE) assistente m/f del camerino; (furniture) credenza; ~**ing** n (MED) benda; (CULIN) condimento; ~**ing gown** n vestaglia; ~**ing room** n (THEATRE) camerino; (SPORT) spogliatoio; ~**ing table** n toilette f inv; ~**maker** n sarta; ~**making** n sartoria; confezioni fpl per donna; ~ **rehearsal** n prova generale; ~ **shirt** n camicia da sera.

drew [druː] pt of **draw**.

dribble ['drɪbl] vi gocciolare; (baby) sbavare.

dried [draɪd] a (fruit, beans) secco(a); (eggs, milk) in polvere.

drift [drɪft] n (of current etc) direzione f; forza; (of sand etc) turbine m; (of snow) cumulo; turbine; (general meaning) senso

// vi (boat) essere trasportato(a) dalla corrente; (sand, snow) ammucchiarsi; ~**wood** n resti mpl della mareggiata.

drill [drɪl] n trapano; (MIL) esercitazione f // vt trapanare // vi (for oil) fare perforazioni.

drink [drɪŋk] n bevanda, bibita // vt, vi (pt **drank**, pp **drunk** [dræŋk, drʌŋk]) bere; **to have a** ~ bere qualcosa; ~**er** n bevitore/trice; ~**ing water** n acqua potabile.

drip [drɪp] n goccia; gocciolamento; (MED) apparecchio per fleboclisi // vi gocciolare; (washing) sgocciolare; (wall) trasudare; ~**-dry** a (shirt) che non si stira; ~**ping** n grasso d'arrosto; ~**ping wet** a fradicio(a).

drive [draɪv] n passeggiata or giro in macchina; (also: ~**way**) viale m d'accesso; (energy) energia; (PSYCH) impulso; bisogno; (push) sforzo eccezionale; campagna; (SPORT) drive m inv; (TECH) trasmissione f; propulsione f; presa // vb (pt **drove**, pp **driven** [drəuv, 'drɪvn]) vt guidare; (nail) piantare; (push) cacciare, spingere; (TECH: motor) azionare; far funzionare // vi (AUT: at controls) guidare; (: travel) andare in macchina; **left-/right-hand** ~ guida a sinistra/destra.

driver ['draɪvə*] n conducente m/f; (of taxi) tassista m; (of bus) autista m.

driving ['draɪvɪŋ] a: ~ **rain** n pioggia sferzante // n guida; ~ **instructor** n istruttore/trice di scuola guida; ~ **lesson** n lezione f di guida; ~ **licence** n (Brit) patente f di guida; ~ **school** n scuola f guida inv; ~ **test** n esame m di guida.

drizzle ['drɪzl] n pioggerella // vi piovigginare.

droll [drəul] a buffo(a).

dromedary ['drɒmədərɪ] n dromedario.

drone [drəun] n ronzio; (male bee) fuco.

drool [druːl] vi sbavare.

droop [druːp] vi abbassarsi; languire.

drop [drɒp] n goccia; (fall) caduta; (also: **parachute** ~) lancio; (of cliff) discesa // vt lasciare cadere; (voice, eyes, price) abbassare; (set down from car) far scendere // vi cascare; **to** ~ **off** vi (sleep) addormentarsi; **to** ~ **out** vi (withdraw) ritirarsi; (student etc) smettere di studiare; ~**pings** npl sterco.

dross [drɒs] n scoria; scarto.

drought [draut] n siccità f inv.

drove [drəuv] pt of **drive** // n: ~**s of people** una moltitudine di persone.

drown [draun] vt affogare // vi affogarsi.

drowsy ['drauzɪ] a sonnolento(a), assonnato(a).

drudge [drʌdʒ] n bestia da fatica; ~**ry** ['drʌdʒərɪ] n lavoro faticoso.

drug [drʌg] n farmaco; (narcotic) droga // vt drogare; ~ **addict** n tossicomane m/f; ~**gist** n (US) persona che gestisce un drugstore; ~**store** n (US) drugstore m inv.

drum [drʌm] n tamburo; (for oil, petrol) fusto; ~**mer** n batterista m/f.

drunk [drʌŋk] *pp of* **drink** // *a* ubriaco(a); ebbro(a) // *n* ubriacone/a; ~**ard** ['drʌŋkəd] *n* ubriacone/a; ~**en** *a* ubriaco(a); da ubriaco; ~**enness** *n* ubriachezza; ebbrezza.

dry [draɪ] *a* secco(a); (*day, clothes*) asciutto(a) // *vt* seccare; (*clothes*) asciugare // *vi* asciugarsi; **to** ~ **up** *vi* seccarsi; ~-**cleaner's** *n* lavasecco *m inv*; ~**er** *n* essiccatore *m*; ~ **rot** *n* fungo del legno.

dual ['djuəl] *a* doppio(a); ~ **carriageway** *n* strada a doppia carreggiata; ~ **nationality** *n* doppia nazionalità; ~-**purpose** *a* a doppio uso.

dubbed [dʌbd] *a* (*CINEMA*) doppiato(a); (*nicknamed*) soprannominato(a).

dubious ['dju:bɪəs] *a* dubbio(a).

duchess ['dʌtʃɪs] *n* duchessa.

duck [dʌk] *n* anatra // *vi* abbassare la testa; ~**ling** *n* anatroccolo.

duct [dʌkt] *n* condotto; (*ANAT*) canale *m*.

dud [dʌd] *n* (*shell*) proiettile *m* che fa cilecca; (*object, tool*): **it's a** ~ è inutile, non funziona // *a* (*cheque*) a vuoto; (*note, coin*) falso(a).

due [dju:] *a* dovuto(a); (*expected*) atteso(a); (*fitting*) giusto(a) // *n* dovuto // *ad*: ~ **north** diritto verso nord; ~**s** *npl* (*for club, union*) quota; (*in harbour*) diritti *mpl* di porto; **in** ~ **course** a tempo debito; finalmente; ~ **to** dovuto a; a causa di.

duel ['djuəl] *n* duello.

duet [dju:'et] *n* duetto.

dug [dʌg] *pt, pp of* **dig**.

duke [dju:k] *n* duca *m*.

dull [dʌl] *a* noioso(a); ottuso(a); (*sound, pain*) sordo(a); (*weather, day*) fosco(a), scuro(a); (*blade*) smussato(a) // *vt* (*pain, grief*) attutire; (*mind, senses*) intorpidire.

duly ['dju:lɪ] *ad* (*on time*) a tempo debito; (*as expected*) debitamente.

dumb [dʌm] *a* muto(a); (*stupid*) stupido(a); **dumbfounded** [dʌm'faʊndɪd] *a* stupito(a), stordito(a).

dummy ['dʌmɪ] *n* (*tailor's model*) manichino; (*SPORT*) finto; (*for baby*) tettarella // *a* falso(a), finto(a).

dump [dʌmp] *n* mucchio di rifiuti; (*place*) luogo di scarico; (*MIL*) deposito // *vt* (*put down*) scaricare; mettere giù; (*get rid of*) buttar via; ~**ing** *n* (*ECON*) dumping *m*; (*of rubbish*): 'no ~**ing**' 'vietato lo scarico'.

dumpling ['dʌmplɪŋ] *n* specie di gnocco.

dunce [dʌns] *n* asino.

dune [dju:n] *n* duna.

dung [dʌŋ] *n* concime *m*.

dungarees [dʌŋgə'ri:z] *npl* tuta.

dungeon ['dʌndʒən] *n* prigione *f* sotterranea.

dupe [dju:p] *vt* gabbare, ingannare.

duplicate *n* ['dju:plɪkət] doppio // *vt* ['dju:plɪkeɪt] raddoppiare; (*on machine*) ciclostilare; **in** ~ in duplice copia.

durable ['djuərəbl] *a* durevole; (*clothes, metal*) resistente.

duration [djuə'reɪʃən] *n* durata.

duress [djuə'rɛs] *n*: **under** ~ sotto costrizione.

during ['djuərɪŋ] *prep* durante, nel corso di.

dusk [dʌsk] *n* crepuscolo; ~**y** *a* scuro(a).

dust [dʌst] *n* polvere *f* // *vt* (*furniture*) spolverare; (*cake etc*): **to** ~ **with** cospargere con; ~**bin** *n* (*Brit*) pattumiera; ~**er** *n* straccio per la polvere; ~ **jacket** *n* sopraccoperta; ~**man** *n* (*Brit*) netturbino; ~**y** *a* polveroso(a).

Dutch [dʌtʃ] *a* olandese // *n* (*LING*) olandese *m*; **the** ~ gli Olandesi; ~**man/woman** *n* olandese *m/f*.

duty ['dju:tɪ] *n* dovere *m*; (*tax*) dazio, tassa; **duties** *npl* mansioni *fpl*; **on** ~ di servizio; **off** ~ libero(a), fuori servizio; ~-**free** *a* esente da dazio.

dwarf [dwɔ:f] *n* nano/a // *vt* far apparire piccolo.

dwell, *pt, pp* **dwelt** [dwɛl, dwɛlt] *vi* dimorare; **to** ~ **on** *vt fus* indugiare su; ~**ing** *n* dimora.

dwindle ['dwɪndl] *vi* diminuire, decrescere.

dye [daɪ] *n* tinta // *vt* tingere.

dying ['daɪɪŋ] *a* morente, moribondo(a).

dyke [daɪk] *n* diga.

dynamic [daɪ'næmɪk] *a* dinamico(a); ~**s** *n or npl* dinamica.

dynamite ['daɪnəmaɪt] *n* dinamite *f*.

dynamo ['daɪnəməu] *n* dinamo *f inv*.

dynasty ['dɪnəstɪ] *n* dinastia.

dysentery ['dɪsntrɪ] *n* dissenteria.

E

E [i:] *n* (*MUS*) mi *m*.

each [i:tʃ] *det* ogni, ciascuno(a) // *pronoun* ciascuno(a), ognuno(a); ~ **one** ognuno(a); ~ **other** si (*or* ci *etc*); **they hate** ~ **other** si odiano (l'un l'altro); **you are jealous of** ~ **other** siete gelosi l'uno dell'altro.

eager ['i:gə*] *a* impaziente; desideroso(a); ardente; **to be** ~ **to do sth** non veder l'ora di fare qc; essere desideroso di fare qc; **to be** ~ **for** essere desideroso di, aver gran voglia di.

eagle ['i:gl] *n* aquila.

ear [ɪə*] *n* orecchio; (*of corn*) pannocchia; ~**ache** *n* mal *m* d'orecchi; ~**drum** *n* timpano.

earl [ə:l] *n* conte *m*.

early ['ə:lɪ] *ad* presto, di buon'ora; (*ahead of time*) in anticipo // *a* precoce; anticipato(a); che si fa vedere di buon'ora; **have an** ~ **night/start** vada a letto/parta presto; **in the** ~ *or* ~ **in the spring/19th century** all'inizio della primavera/dell'Ottocento; ~ **retirement** *n* ritiro anticipato.

earmark ['ɪəmɑ:k] *vt*: **to** ~ **sth for** destinare qc a.

earn [ə:n] *vt* guadagnare; (*rest, reward*) meritare; **this** ~**ed him much praise, he** ~**ed much praise for this** si è attirato grandi lodi per questo.

earnest ['ɔːnɪst] *a* serio(a); **in ~** *ad* sul serio.

earnings ['ɔːnɪŋz] *npl* guadagni *mpl*; (*salary*) stipendio.

earphones ['ɪəfəʊnz] *npl* cuffia.

earring ['ɪərɪŋ] *n* orecchino.

earshot ['ɪəʃɔt] *n*: **out of/within ~** fuori portata/a portata d'orecchio.

earth [ɔːθ] *n* (*gen, also* ELEC) terra; (*of fox etc*) tana // *vt* (ELEC) mettere a terra; **~enware** *n* terracotta; stoviglie *fpl* di terracotta // *a* di terracotta; **~quake** *n* terremoto; **~ tremor** *n* scossa sismica; **~y** *a* (*fig*) grossolano(a).

earwig ['ɪəwɪg] *n* forbicina.

ease [iːz] *n* agio, comodo // *vt* (*soothe*) calmare; (*loosen*) allentare; **to ~ sth out/in** tirare fuori/infilare qc con delicatezza; facilitare l'uscita/l'entrata di qc; **life of ~** vita comoda; **at ~** all'agio; (MIL) a riposo; **to ~ off** *or* **up** *vi* diminuire; (*slow down*) rallentarsi; (*fig*) rilassarsi.

easel ['iːzl] *n* cavalletto.

easily ['iːzɪlɪ] *ad* facilmente.

east [iːst] *n* est *m* // *a* dell'est // *ad a* oriente; **the E~** l'Oriente *m*.

Easter ['iːstə*] *n* Pasqua.

easterly ['iːstəlɪ] *a* dall'est, d'oriente.

eastern ['iːstən] *a* orientale, d'oriente.

East Germany [iːst'dʒɜːmənɪ] *n* Germania dell'Est.

eastward(s) ['iːstwəd(z)] *ad* verso est, verso levante.

easy ['iːzɪ] *a* facile; (*manner*) disinvolto(a) // *ad*: **to take it** *or* **things ~** prendersela con calma; **~ chair** *n* poltrona; **~ going** *a* accomodante.

eat, *pt* **ate**, *pp* **eaten** [iːt, eɪt, 'iːtn] *vt* mangiare; **to ~ into** *vt fus* rodere; **~able** *a* mangiabile; (*safe to eat*) commestibile.

eaves [iːvz] *npl* gronda.

eavesdrop ['iːvzdrɔp] *vi*: **to ~ (on a conversation)** origliare (una conversazione).

ebb [eb] *n* riflusso // *vi* rifluire; (*fig: also*: **~ away**) declinare.

ebony ['ebənɪ] *n* ebano.

ebullient [ɪ'bʌlɪənt] *a* esuberante.

eccentric [ɪk'sentrɪk] *a,n* eccentrico(a).

ecclesiastic [ɪkliːzɪ'æstɪk] *n* ecclesiastico; **~al** *a* ecclesiastico(a).

echo, ~es ['ekəʊ] *n* eco *m or f* // *vt* ripetere; fare eco a // *vi* echeggiare; dare un eco.

eclipse [ɪ'klɪps] *n* eclissi *f inv* // *vt* eclissare.

ecology [ɪ'kɔlədʒɪ] *n* ecologia.

economic [iːkə'nɔmɪk] *a* economico(a); **~al** *a* economico(a); (*person*) economo(a); **~s** *n* economia.

economist [ɪ'kɔnəmɪst] *n* economo/a.

economize [ɪ'kɔnəmaɪz] *vi* risparmiare, fare economia.

economy [ɪ'kɔnəmɪ] *n* economia.

ecstasy ['ekstəsɪ] *n* estasi *f inv*; **to go into**

ecstasies over andare in estasi davanti a; **ecstatic** [-'tætɪk] *a* estatico(a), in estasi.

ecumenical [iːkjuː'menɪkl] *a* ecumenico(a).

eczema ['eksɪmə] *n* eczema *m*.

eddy ['edɪ] *n* mulinello.

edge [edʒ] *n* margine *m*; (*of table, plate, cup*) orlo; (*of knife etc*) taglio // *vt* bordare; **on ~** (*fig*) = **edgy**; **to have the ~ on** essere in vantaggio su; **to ~ away from** scattaiolare da; **~ways** *ad* di fianco; **he couldn't get a word in ~ways** non riuscì a dire una parola.

edgy ['edʒɪ] *a* nervoso(a).

edible ['edɪbl] *a* commestibile; (*meal*) mangiabile.

edict ['iːdɪkt] *n* editto.

edifice ['edɪfɪs] *n* edificio.

edit ['edɪt] *vt* curare; **~ion** [ɪ'dɪʃən] *n* edizione *f*; **~or** *n* (*in newspaper*) redattore/trice; redattore/trice capo; (*of sb's work*) curatore/trice; **~orial** [-'tɔːrɪəl] *a* redazionale, editoriale // *n* editoriale *m*.

educate ['edjukeɪt] *vt* istruire; educare.

education [edju'keɪʃən] *n* educazione *f*; (*schooling*) istruzione *f*; **~al** *a* pedagogico(a); scolastico(a); istruttivo(a).

EEC *n* (*abbr of European Economic Community*) C.E.E. *f* (*Comunità Economica Europea*).

eel [iːl] *n* anguilla.

eerie ['ɪərɪ] *a* che fa accapponare la pelle.

effect [ɪ'fekt] *n* effetto // *vt* effettuare; **~s** *npl* (THEATRE) effetti *mpl* scenici; **to take ~** (*law*) entrare in vigore; (*drug*) fare effetto; **in ~** effettivamente; **~ive** *a* efficace; **~iveness** *n* efficacia.

effeminate [ɪ'femɪnɪt] *a* effeminato(a).

effervescent [efə'vesnt] *a* effervescente.

efficacy ['efɪkəsɪ] *n* efficacia.

efficiency [ɪ'fɪʃənsɪ] *n* efficienza; rendimento effettivo.

efficient [ɪ'fɪʃənt] *a* efficiente.

effigy ['efɪdʒɪ] *n* effigie *f*.

effort ['efət] *n* sforzo; **~less** *a* senza sforzo, facile.

effrontery [ɪ'frʌntərɪ] *n* sfrontatezza.

e.g. *ad* (*abbr of exempli gratia*) per esempio, p.es.

egalitarian [ɪgælɪ'tɛərɪən] *a* egualitario(a).

egg [eg] *n* uovo; **to ~ on** *vt* incitare; **~cup** *n* portauovo *m inv*; **~plant** *n* melanzana; **~shell** *n* guscio d'uovo.

ego ['iːgəu] *n* ego *m inv*.

egotist ['egəutɪst] *n* egotista *m/f*.

Egypt ['iːdʒɪpt] *n* Egitto; **~ian** [ɪ'dʒɪpʃən] *a, n* egiziano(a).

eiderdown ['aɪdədaun] *n* piumino.

eight [eɪt] *num* otto; **~een** *num* diciotto; **eighth** [eɪtθ] *num* ottavo(a); **~y** *num* ottanta.

Eire ['ɛərə] *n* Repubblica d'Irlanda.

either ['aɪðə*] *det* l'uno(a) o l'altro(a); (*both, each*) ciascuno(a); **on ~ side** su ciascun lato // *pronoun*: **~ (of them)** (o) l'uno(a) o l'altro(a); **I don't like ~** non

mi piace né l'uno né l'altro // ad neanche;
no, I don't ~ no, neanch'io // cj: ~ **good
or bad** o buono o cattivo.
ejaculation [ɪdʒækjuˈleɪʃən] n (PHYSIOL)
eiaculazione f.
eject [ɪˈdʒɛkt] vt espellere; lanciare; ~**or
seat** n sedile m eiettabile.
eke [iːk]: **to** ~ **out** vt far durare;
aumentare.
elaborate a [ɪˈlæbərɪt] elaborato(a),
minuzioso(a) // vb [ɪˈlæbəreɪt] vt
elaborare // vi fornire i particolari.
elapse [ɪˈlæps] vi trascorrere, passare.
elastic [ɪˈlæstɪk] a elastico(a) // n elastico;
~ **band** n elastico.
elated [ɪˈleɪtɪd] a pieno(a) di gioia.
elation [ɪˈleɪʃən] n gioia.
elbow [ˈɛlbəu] n gomito.
elder [ˈɛldə*] a maggiore, più vecchio(a)
// n (tree) sambuco; **one's** ~**s** i più
anziani; ~**ly** a anziano(a).
eldest [ˈɛldɪst] a,n: **the** ~ **(child)** il(la) più
vecchio(a) (dei bambini).
elect [ɪˈlɛkt] vt eleggere; **to** ~ **to do**
decidere di fare // a: **the president** ~ il
presidente designato; ~**ion** [ɪˈlɛkʃən] n
elezione f; ~**ioneering** [ɪlɛkʃəˈnɪərɪŋ] n
propaganda elettorale; ~**or** n
elettore/trice; ~**oral** a elettorale;
~**orate** n elettorato.
electric [ɪˈlɛktrɪk] a elettrico(a); ~**al** a
elettrico(a); ~ **blanket** n coperta
elettrica; ~ **chair** n sedia elettrica; ~
cooker n cucina elettrica; ~ **current** n
corrente f elettrica; ~ **fire** n stufa
elettrica.
electrician [ɪlɛkˈtrɪʃən] n elettricista m.
electricity [ɪlɛkˈtrɪsɪtɪ] n elettricità f.
electrify [ɪˈlɛktrɪfaɪ] vt (RAIL)
elettrificare; (audience) elettrizzare.
electro... [ɪˈlɛktrəu] prefix: **electrocute**
[-kjuːt] vt fulminare; **electrode** [ɪˈlɛktrəud]
n elettrodo.
electron [ɪˈlɛktrɔn] n elettrone m.
electronic [ɪlɛkˈtrɔnɪk] a elettronico(a);
~**s** n elettronica.
elegance [ˈɛlɪgəns] n eleganza.
elegant [ˈɛlɪgənt] a elegante.
element [ˈɛlɪmənt] n elemento; (of heater,
kettle etc) resistenza; ~**ary** [-ˈmɛntərɪ] a
elementare.
elephant [ˈɛlɪfənt] n elefante/essa.
elevate [ˈɛlɪveɪt] vt elevare.
elevation [ɛlɪˈveɪʃən] n elevazione f;
(height) altitudine f.
elevator [ˈɛlɪveɪtə*] n elevatore m; (US:
lift) ascensore m.
eleven [ɪˈlɛvn] num undici; ~**ses** npl caffè
m a metà mattina; ~**th** a undicesimo(a).
elf, elves [ɛlf, ɛlvz] n elfo.
elicit [ɪˈlɪsɪt] vt: **to** ~ **(from)** trarre (da),
cavare fuori (da).
eligible [ˈɛlɪdʒəbl] a eleggibile; (for
membership) che ha i requisiti.
eliminate [ɪˈlɪmɪneɪt] vt eliminare;
elimination n eliminazione f.
élite [eɪˈliːt] n élite f inv.

ellipse [ɪˈlɪps] n ellisse f.
elm [ɛlm] n olmo.
elocution [ɛləˈkjuːʃən] n elocuzione f.
elongated [ˈiːlɔŋgeɪtɪd] a allungato(a).
elope [ɪˈləup] vi (lovers) scappare; ~**ment**
n fuga romantica.
eloquence [ˈɛləkwəns] n eloquenza.
eloquent [ˈɛləkwənt] a eloquente.
else [ɛls] ad altro; **something** ~
qualcos'altro; **somewhere** ~ altrove;
everywhere ~ in qualsiasi altro luogo;
where ~? in quale altro luogo?; **little** ~
poco altro; ~**where** ad altrove.
elucidate [ɪˈluːsɪdeɪt] vt delucidare.
elude [ɪˈluːd] vt eludere.
elusive [ɪˈluːsɪv] a elusivo(a); (answer)
evasivo(a).
elves [ɛlvz] npl of **elf**.
emaciated [ɪˈmeɪsɪeɪtɪd] a emaciato(a).
emanate [ˈɛməneɪt] vi: **to** ~ **from**
emanare da.
emancipate [ɪˈmænsɪpeɪt] vt emancipare;
emancipation [-ˈpeɪʃən] n emancipazione
f.
embalm [ɪmˈbɑːm] vt imbalsamare.
embankment [ɪmˈbæŋkmənt] n (of road,
railway) terrapieno; (riverside) argine m;
(dyke) diga.
embargo, ~es [ɪmˈbɑːgəu] n embargo.
embark [ɪmˈbɑːk] vi: **to** ~ **(on)**
imbarcarsi (su) // vt imbarcare; **to** ~ **on**
(fig) imbarcarsi in; ~**ation** [ɛmbɑːˈkeɪʃən]
n imbarco.
embarrass [ɪmˈbærəs] vt imbarazzare;
~**ing** a imbarazzante; ~**ment** n
imbarazzo.
embassy [ˈɛmbəsɪ] n ambasciata.
embed [ɪmˈbɛd] vt conficcare, incastrare.
embellish [ɪmˈbɛlɪʃ] vt abbellire.
embers [ˈɛmbəz] npl braci fpl.
embezzle [ɪmˈbɛzl] vt appropriarsi
indebitamente di; ~**ment** n
appropriazione f indebita, malversazione f.
embitter [ɪmˈbɪtə*] vt amareggiare,
inasprire.
emblem [ˈɛmbləm] n emblema m.
embodiment [ɪmˈbɔdɪmənt] n
personificazione f, incarnazione f.
embody [ɪmˈbɔdɪ] vt (features)
racchiudere, comprendere; (ideas) dare
forma concreta a, esprimere.
embossed [ɪmˈbɔst] a in rilievo;
goffrato(a).
embrace [ɪmˈbreɪs] vt abbracciare // n
abbraccio.
embroider [ɪmˈbrɔɪdə*] vt ricamare; (fig:
story) abbellire; ~**y** n ricamo.
embryo [ˈɛmbrɪəu] n (also fig) embrione
m.
emerald [ˈɛmərəld] n smeraldo.
emerge [ɪˈmɜːdʒ] vi apparire, sorgere.
emergence [ɪˈmɜːdʒəns] n apparizione f.
emergency [ɪˈmɜːdʒənsɪ] n emergenza; **in
an** ~ in caso di emergenza; ~ **exit** n
uscita di sicurezza.
emergent [ɪˈmɜːdʒənt] a: ~ **nation** paese
m in via di sviluppo.

emery ['ɛmərɪ] n: ~ **board** n limetta di carta smerigliata; ~ **paper** n carta smerigliata.

emetic [ɪ'mɛtɪk] n emetico.

emigrant ['ɛmɪgrənt] n emigrante m/f.

emigrate ['ɛmɪgreɪt] vi emigrare; **emigration** [-'greɪʃən] n emigrazione f.

eminence ['ɛmɪnəns] n eminenza.

eminent ['ɛmɪnənt] a eminente.

emission [ɪ'mɪʃən] n emissione f.

emit [ɪ'mɪt] vt emettere.

emotion [ɪ'məʊʃən] n emozione f; ~**al** a (person) emotivo(a); (scene) commovente; (tone, speech) carico(a) d'emozione; ~**ally** ad: ~**ally disturbed** con turbe emotive.

emotive [ɪ'məʊtɪv] a emotivo(a).

emperor ['ɛmpərə*] n imperatore m.

emphasis, pl **ases** ['ɛmfəsɪs, -siːz] n enfasi f inv; importanza.

emphasize ['ɛmfəsaɪz] vt (word, point) sottolineare; (feature) mettere in evidenza.

emphatic [ɛm'fætɪk] a (strong) vigoroso(a); (unambiguous, clear) netto(a); ~**ally** ad vigorosamente; nettamente.

empire ['ɛmpaɪə*] n impero.

empirical [ɛm'pɪrɪkl] a empirico(a).

employ [ɪm'plɔɪ] vt impiegare; ~**ee** [-'iː] n impiegato/a; ~**er** n principale m/f, datore m di lavoro; ~**ment** n impiego; ~**ment agency** n agenzia di collocamento.

empower [ɪm'paʊə*] vt: **to** ~ **sb to do** concedere autorità a qd di fare.

empress ['ɛmprɪs] n imperatrice f.

emptiness ['ɛmptɪnɪs] n vuoto.

empty ['ɛmptɪ] a vuoto(a); (threat, promise) vano(a) // vt vuotare // vi vuotarsi; (liquid) scaricarsi; **on an** ~ **stomach** a stomaco vuoto; ~**-handed** a a mani vuote.

emulate ['ɛmjʊleɪt] vt emulare.

emulsion [ɪ'mʌlʃən] n emulsione f; ~ (paint) n colore m a tempera.

enable [ɪ'neɪbl] vt: **to** ~ **sb to do** permettere a qd di fare.

enamel [ɪ'næməl] n smalto.

enamoured [ɪ'næməd] a: ~ **of** innamorato(a) di.

enchant [ɪn'tʃɑːnt] vt incantare; (subj: magic spell) catturare; ~**ing** a incantevole, affascinante.

encircle [ɪn'sɜːkl] vt accerchiare.

encl. (abbr of enclosed) all.

enclose [ɪn'kləʊz] vt (land) circondare, recingere; (letter etc): **to** ~ **(with)** allegare (con); **please find** ~**d** trovi qui accluso.

enclosure [ɪn'kləʊʒə*] n recinto; (COMM) allegato.

encore [ɔŋ'kɔː*] excl, n bis (m inv).

encounter [ɪn'kaʊntə*] n incontro // vt incontrare.

encourage [ɪn'kʌrɪdʒ] vt incoraggiare; ~**ment** n incoraggiamento.

encroach [ɪn'krəʊtʃ] vi: **to** ~ **(up)on**

(rights) usurpare; (time) abusare di; (land) oltrepassare i limiti di.

encyclop(a)edia [ɛnsaɪkləʊ'piːdɪə] n enciclopedia.

end [ɛnd] n fine f; (aim) fine m; (of table) bordo estremo // vt finire; (also: **bring to an** ~, **put an** ~ **to**) mettere fine a // vi finire; **to come to an** ~ arrivare alla fine, finire; **in the** ~ alla fine; **at the** ~ **of the street** in fondo alla strada; **on** ~ (object) ritto(a); **for 5 hours on** ~ per 5 ore di fila; **to** ~ **up** vi: **to** ~ **up in** finire in.

endanger [ɪn'deɪndʒə*] vt mettere in pericolo.

endearing [ɪn'dɪərɪŋ] a accattivante.

endeavour [ɪn'dɛvə*] n sforzo, tentativo // vi: **to** ~ **to do** cercare or sforzarsi di fare.

ending ['ɛndɪŋ] n fine f, conclusione f; (LING) desinenza.

endless ['ɛndlɪs] a senza fine; (patience, resources) infinito(a).

endorse [ɪn'dɔːs] vt (cheque) girare; (approve) approvare, appoggiare; ~**ment** n (on driving licence) contravvenzione registrata sulla patente.

endow [ɪn'daʊ] vt (provide with money) devolvere denaro a; (equip): **to** ~ **with** fornire di, dotare di.

end product ['ɛndprɒdəkt] n prodotto finito; (fig) risultato.

endurance [ɪn'djʊərəns] n resistenza; pazienza.

endure [ɪn'djʊə*] vt sopportare, resistere a // vi durare.

enemy ['ɛnəmɪ] a,n nemico(a).

energetic [ɛnə'dʒɛtɪk] a energico(a); attivo(a).

energy ['ɛnədʒɪ] n energia.

enervating ['ɛnɔːveɪtɪŋ] a debilitante.

enforce [ɪn'fɔːs] vt (LAW) applicare, far osservare; ~**d** a forzato(a).

engage [ɪn'geɪdʒ] vt assumere; (subj: activity, MIL) impegnare; (attention) occupare // vi (TECH) ingranare; **to** ~ **in** impegnarsi in; ~**d** a (busy, in use) occupato(a); (betrothed) fidanzato(a); **to get** ~**d** fidanzarsi; ~**ment** n impegno, obbligo; appuntamento; (to marry) fidanzamento; (MIL) combattimento; ~**ment ring** n anello di fidanzamento.

engaging [ɪn'geɪdʒɪŋ] a attraente.

engender [ɪn'dʒɛndə*] vt produrre, causare.

engine ['ɛndʒɪn] n (AUT) motore m; (RAIL) locomotiva; ~ **failure** n guasto al motore; ~ **trouble** n panne f.

engineer [ɛndʒɪ'nɪə*] n ingegnere m; (US: RAIL) macchinista m; ~**ing** n ingegneria; (of bridges, ships, machine) tecnica di costruzione.

England ['ɪŋglənd] n Inghilterra.

English ['ɪŋglɪʃ] a inglese // n (LING) inglese m; **the** ~ gli Inglesi; ~**man/woman** n inglese m/f.

engrave [ɪn'greɪv] vt incidere.

engraving [ɪn'greɪvɪŋ] n incisione f.

engrossed [ɪn'grəʊst] a: ~ **in** assorbito(a) da, preso(a) da.

engulf [ɪn'gʌlf] vt inghiottire.

enhance [ɪn'hɑːns] vt accrescere.

enigma [ɪ'nɪgmə] n enigma m; ~**tic** [ɛnɪg'mætɪk] a enigmatico(a).

enjoy [ɪn'dʒɔɪ] vt godere; (have: success, fortune) avere; **I** ~ **dancing** mi piace ballare; **to** ~ **oneself** godersela, divertirsi; ~**able** a piacevole; ~**ment** n piacere m, godimento.

enlarge [ɪn'lɑːdʒ] vt ingrandire // vi: **to** ~ **on** (subject) dilungarsi su; ~**ment** n (PHOT) ingrandimento.

enlighten [ɪn'laɪtn] vt illuminare; dare schiarimenti a; ~**ed** a illuminato(a); ~**ment** n progresso culturale; schiarimenti mpl; (HISTORY): **the E**~**ment** l'Illuminismo.

enlist [ɪn'lɪst] vt arruolare; (support) procurare // vi arruolarsi.

enmity ['ɛnmɪtɪ] n inimicizia.

enormity [ɪ'nɔːmɪtɪ] n enormità f inv.

enormous [ɪ'nɔːməs] a enorme.

enough [ɪ'nʌf] a, n: ~ **time/books** assai tempo/libri; **have you got** ~? ne ha abbastanza or a sufficienza? // ad: **big** ~ abbastanza grande; **he has not worked** ~ non ha lavorato abbastanza; ~! basta!; **it's hot** ~ **(as it is)!** fa caldo assai così!; ... **which, funnily** ~ ... che, strano a dirsi.

enquire [ɪn'kwaɪə*] vt,vi = **inquire.**

enrich [ɪn'rɪtʃ] vt arricchire.

enrol [ɪn'rəʊl] vt iscrivere // vi iscriversi; ~**ment** n iscrizione f.

ensign n (NAUT) ['ɛnsən] bandiera; (MIL) ['ɛnsaɪn] portabandiera m inv.

enslave [ɪn'sleɪv] vt fare schiavo.

ensue [ɪn'sjuː] vi seguire, risultare.

ensure [ɪn'ʃʊə*] vt assicurare; garantire; **to** ~ **that** assicurarsi che.

entail [ɪn'teɪl] vt comportare.

enter ['ɛntə*] vt (room) entrare in; (club) associarsi a; (army) arruolarsi in; (competition) partecipare a; (sb for a competition) iscrivere; (write down) registrare; **to** ~ **into** vt fus (explanation) cominciare a dare; (debate) partecipare a; (agreement) concludere; **to** ~ **(up)on** vt fus cominciare.

enterprise ['ɛntəpraɪz] n (undertaking, company) impresa; (spirit) iniziativa.

enterprising ['ɛntəpraɪzɪŋ] a intraprendente.

entertain [ɛntə'teɪn] vt divertire; (invite) ricevere; (idea, plan) nutrire; ~**er** n comico/a; ~**ing** a divertente; ~**ment** n (amusement) divertimento; (show) spettacolo.

enthralled [ɪn'θrɔːld] a affascinato(a).

enthusiasm [ɪn'θuːzɪæzəm] n entusiasmo.

enthusiast [ɪn'θuːzɪæst] n entusiasta m/f; ~**ic** [-'æstɪk] a entusiasta, entusiastico(a).

entice [ɪn'taɪs] vt allettare, sedurre.

entire [ɪn'taɪə*] a intero(a); ~**ly** ad completamente, interamente; ~**ty** [ɪn'taɪərətɪ] n: **in its** ~**ty** nel suo complesso.

entitle [ɪn'taɪtl] vt (allow): **to** ~ **sb to do** dare il diritto a qd di fare; ~**d** a (book) che si intitola; **to be** ~**d to do** avere il diritto di fare.

entrance n ['ɛntrns] entrata, ingresso; (of person) entrata // vt [ɪn'trɑːns] incantare, rapire; ~ **fee** n tassa d'iscrizione; (to museum etc) prezzo d'ingresso.

entrant ['ɛntrnt] n partecipante m/f; concorrente m/f.

entreat [ɛn'triːt] vt supplicare; ~**y** n supplica, preghiera.

entrenched [ɛn'trɛntʃd] a radicato(a).

entrust [ɪn'trʌst] vt: **to** ~ **sth to** affidare qc a.

entry ['ɛntrɪ] n entrata; (way in) entrata, ingresso; (item: on list) iscrizione f; (in dictionary) voce f; **'no** ~' 'vietato l'ingresso'; (AUT) 'divieto di accesso'; ~ **form** n modulo d'iscrizione.

entwine [ɪn'twaɪn] vt intrecciare.

enumerate [ɪ'njuːməreɪt] vt enumerare.

enunciate [ɪ'nʌnsɪeɪt] vt enunciare; pronunciare.

envelop [ɪn'vɛləp] vt avvolgere, avviluppare.

envelope ['ɛnvələʊp] n busta.

envious ['ɛnvɪəs] a invidioso(a).

environment [ɪn'vaɪərnmənt] n ambiente m; ~**al** [-'mɛntl] a ecologico(a); ambientale.

envisage [ɪn'vɪzɪdʒ] vt immaginare; prevedere.

envoy ['ɛnvɔɪ] n inviato/a.

envy ['ɛnvɪ] n invidia // vt invidiare.

enzyme ['ɛnzaɪm] n enzima m.

ephemeral [ɪ'fɛmərl] a effimero(a).

epic ['ɛpɪk] n poema m epico // a epico(a).

epidemic [ɛpɪ'dɛmɪk] n epidemia.

epilepsy ['ɛpɪlɛpsɪ] n epilessia; **epileptic** [-'lɛptɪk] a,n epilettico(a).

epilogue ['ɛpɪlɔg] n epilogo.

Epiphany [ɪ'pɪfənɪ] n Epifania.

episode ['ɛpɪsəʊd] n episodio.

epistle [ɪ'pɪsl] n epistola.

epitaph ['ɛpɪtɑːf] n epitaffio.

epitome [ɪ'pɪtəmɪ] n epitome f; quintessenza; **epitomize** vt compendiare; essere l'emblema di.

epoch ['iːpɔk] n epoca.

equable ['ɛkwəbl] a uniforme; equanime.

equal ['iːkwl] a, n uguale (m/f) // vt uguagliare; ~ **to** (task) all'altezza di; ~**ity** [iː'kwɔlɪtɪ] n uguaglianza; ~**ize** vt,vi pareggiare; ~**izer** n pareggio; ~**ly** ad ugualmente; ~**(s) sign** n segno d'uguaglianza.

equanimity [ɛkwə'nɪmɪtɪ] n equanimità.

equate [ɪ'kweɪt] vt: **to** ~ **sth with** considerare qc uguale a; (compare) paragonare qc con; **equation** [ɪ'kweɪʃən] n (MATH) equazione f.

equator [ɪ'kweɪtə*] n equatore m.

equilibrium [iːkwɪ'lɪbrɪəm] n equilibrio.

equinox ['iːkwɪnɔks] n equinozio.

equip [ɪ'kwɪp] vt equipaggiare, attrezzare; **to** ~ **sb/sth with** fornire qd/qc di;

~**ment** *n* attrezzatura; (*electrical etc*) apparecchiatura.

equitable ['ɛkwɪtəbl] *a* equo(a), giusto(a).

equity ['ɛkwɪtɪ] *n* equità; **equities** *npl* (COMM) azioni *fpl* ordinarie.

equivalent [ɪ'kwɪvəlnt] *a, n* equivalente (*m*).

equivocal [ɪ'kwɪvəkl] *a* equivoco(a); (*open to suspicion*) dubbio(a).

era ['ɪərə] *n* era, età *f inv.*

eradicate [ɪ'rædɪkeɪt] *vt* sradicare.

erase [ɪ'reɪz] *vt* cancellare; ~**r** *n* gomma.

erect [ɪ'rɛkt] *a* eretto(a) // *vt* costruire; (*monument, tent*) alzare.

erection [ɪ'rɛkʃən] *n* erezione *f.*

ermine ['ɜ:mɪn] *n* ermellino.

erode [ɪ'rəud] *vt* erodere; (*metal*) corrodere; **erosion** [ɪ'rəuʒən] *n* erosione *f.*

erotic [ɪ'rɒtɪk] *a* erotico(a); ~**ism** [ɪ'rɒtɪsɪzm] *n* erotismo.

err [ɜ:*] *vi* errare; (REL) peccare.

errand ['ɛrnd] *n* commissione *f.*

erratic [ɪ'rætɪk] *a* imprevedibile; (*person, mood*) incostante.

erroneous [ɪ'rəunɪəs] *a* erroneo(a).

error ['ɛrə*] *n* errore *m.*

erudite ['ɛrjudaɪt] *a* erudito(a).

erupt [ɪ'rʌpt] *vi* erompere; (*volcano*) mettersi (*or* essere) in eruzione; ~**ion** [ɪ'rʌpʃən] *n* eruzione *f.*

escalate ['ɛskəleɪt] *vi* intensificarsi; **escalation** [-'leɪʃən] *n* escalation *f;* (*of prices*) aumento.

escalator ['ɛskəleɪtə*] *n* scala mobile.

escapade [ɛskə'peɪd] *n* scappatella; avventura.

escape [ɪ'skeɪp] *n* evasione *f;* fuga; (*of gas etc*) fuga, fuoriuscita // *vi* fuggire; (*from jail*) evadere, scappare; (*fig*) sfuggire; (*leak*) uscire // *vt* sfuggire a; **to ~ from** *sb* sfuggire a qd; **escapism** *n* evasione *f* (dalla realtà).

escort *n* ['ɛskɔ:t] scorta; (*male companion*) cavaliere *m* // *vt* [ɪ'skɔ:t] scortare; accompagnare.

Eskimo ['ɛskɪməu] *n* esquimese *m/f.*

especially [ɪ'spɛʃlɪ] *ad* specialmente; soprattutto; espressamente.

espionage ['ɛspɪɒnɑ:ʒ] *n* spionaggio.

Esquire [ɪ'skwaɪə*] *n* (*abbr* Esq.): **J. Brown, ~** = Signor J. Brown.

essay ['ɛseɪ] *n* (SCOL) composizione *f;* (LITERATURE) saggio.

essence ['ɛsns] *n* essenza.

essential [ɪ'sɛnʃl] *a* essenziale; (*basic*) fondamentale; ~**ly** *ad* essenzialmente.

establish [ɪ'stæblɪʃ] *vt* stabilire; (*business*) mettere su; (*one's power etc*) confermare; ~**ment** *n* stabilimento; **the E**~**ment** le autorità; l'Establishment *m.*

estate [ɪ'steɪt] *n* proprietà *f inv;* beni *mpl,* patrimonio; ~ **agent** *n* agente *m* immobiliare; ~ **car** *n* (*Brit*) giardiniera.

esteem [ɪ'sti:m] *n* stima.

esthetic [ɪs'θɛtɪk] *a* (US) = **aesthetic**.

estimate *n* ['ɛstɪmət] stima; (COMM) preventivo // *vt* ['ɛstɪmeɪt] stimare,

valutare; **estimation** [-'meɪʃən] *n* stima; opinione *f.*

estuary ['ɛstjuərɪ] *n* estuario.

etching ['ɛtʃɪŋ] *n* acquaforte *f.*

eternal [ɪ'tɜ:nl] *a* eterno(a).

eternity [ɪ'tɜ:nɪtɪ] *n* eternità.

ether ['i:θə*] *n* etere *m.*

ethical ['ɛθɪkl] *a* etico(a), morale.

ethics ['ɛθɪks] *n* etica // *npl* morale *f.*

ethnic ['ɛθnɪk] *a* etnico(a).

etiquette ['ɛtɪkɛt] *n* etichetta.

eulogy ['ju:lədʒɪ] *n* elogio.

euphemism ['ju:fəmɪzm] *n* eufemismo.

euphoria [ju:'fɔ:rɪə] *n* euforia.

Europe ['juərəp] *n* Europa; ~**an** [-'pi:ən] *a, n* europeo(a).

euthanasia [ju:θə'neɪzɪə] *n* eutanasia.

evacuate [ɪ'vækjueɪt] *vt* evacuare; **evacuation** [-'eɪʃən] *n* evacuazione *f.*

evade [ɪ'veɪd] *vt* eludere; (*question, duties etc*) evadere.

evaluate [ɪ'væljueɪt] *vt* valutare.

evangelist [ɪ'vændʒəlɪst] *n* evangelista *m.*

evaporate [ɪ'væpəreɪt] *vi* evaporare // *vt* far evaporare; ~**d milk** *n* latte *m* evaporato; **evaporation** [-'reɪʃən] *n* evaporazione *f.*

evasion [ɪ'veɪʒən] *n* evasione *f;* scappatoia.

evasive [ɪ'veɪsɪv] *a* evasivo(a).

eve [i:v] *n*: **on the ~ of** alla vigilia di.

even ['i:vn] *a* regolare; (*number*) pari *inv* // *ad* anche, perfino; ~ **more** anche più; **he loves her ~ more** la ama anche di più; ~ **so** ciò nonostante; **to ~ out** *vi* pareggiare; **to get ~ with** *sb* dare la pari a qd.

evening ['i:vnɪŋ] *n* sera; (*as duration, event*) serata; **in the ~** la sera; ~ **class** *n* corso serale; ~ **dress** *n* (*man's*) frac *m,* smoking *m;* (*woman's*) vestito da sera.

event [ɪ'vɛnt] *n* avvenimento; (SPORT) gara; **in the ~ of** in caso di; ~**ful** *a* denso(a) di eventi.

eventual [ɪ'vɛntʃuəl] *a* finale; ~**ity** [-'ælɪtɪ] *n* possibilità *f inv,* eventualità *f inv;* ~**ly** *ad* finalmente.

ever ['ɛvə*] *ad* mai; (*at all times*) sempre; **the best ~** il migliore che ci sia mai stato; **have you ~ seen it?** l'ha mai visto?; **hardly ~** non ... quasi mai; ~ **since** *ad* da allora // *cj* sin da quando; ~ **so pretty** così bello(a); ~**green** *n* sempreverde *m;* ~**lasting** *a* eterno(a).

every ['ɛvrɪ] *det* ogni; ~ **day** tutti i giorni, ogni giorno; ~ **other/third day** ogni due/tre giorni; ~ **other car** una macchina su due; ~ **now and then** ogni tanto, di quando in quando; ~**body** *pronoun* ognuno, tutti *pl;* ~**day** *a* quotidiano(a); di ogni giorno; ~**one** = ~**body**; ~**thing** *pronoun* tutto, ogni cosa; ~**where** *ad* in ogni luogo, dappertutto.

evict [ɪ'vɪkt] *vt* sfrattare; ~**ion** [ɪ'vɪkʃən] *n* sfratto.

evidence ['ɛvɪdns] *n* (*proof*) prova; (*of witness*) testimonianza; (*sign*): **to show ~ of** dare segni di; **to give ~** deporre; **in ~**

(*obvious*) in evidenza; in vista.
evident ['ɛvɪdnt] *a* evidente; ~**ly** *ad* evidentemente.
evil ['iːvl] *a* cattivo(a), maligno(a) // *n* male *m*.
evocative [ɪ'vɔkətɪv] *a* evocativo(a).
evoke [ɪ'vəuk] *vt* evocare.
evolution [iːvə'luːʃən] *n* evoluzione *f*.
evolve [ɪ'vɔlv] *vt* elaborare // *vi* svilupparsi, evolversi.
ewe [juː] *n* pecora.
ex- [ɛks] *prefix* ex.
exact [ɪg'zækt] *a* esatto(a) // *vt*: **to ~ sth (from)** estorcere qc (da); esigere qc (da); ~**ing** *a* esigente; (*work*) faticoso(a); ~**itude** *n* esattezza, precisione *f*; ~**ly** *ad* esattamente.
exaggerate [ɪg'zædʒəreɪt] *vt,vi* esagerare; **exaggeration** [-'reɪʃən] *n* esagerazione *f*.
exalt [ɪg'zɔːlt] *vt* esaltare; elevare.
exam [ɪg'zæm] *n* (*SCOL*) *abbr of* **examination.**
examination [ɪgzæmɪ'neɪʃən] *n* (*SCOL*) esame *m*; (*MED*) controllo.
examine [ɪg'zæmɪn] *vt* esaminare; (*LAW: person*) interrogare; ~**r** *n* esaminatore/trice.
example [ɪg'zɑːspəreɪt] *n* esempio; **for ~** *ad* or per esempio.
exasperate [ɪg'zɑːspəreɪt] *vt* esasperare.
excavate ['ɛkskəveɪt] *vt* scavare; **excavation** [-'veɪʃən] *n* escavazione *f*; **excavator** *n* scavatore *m*, scavatrice *f*.
exceed [ɪk'siːd] *vt* superare; (*one's powers, time limit*) oltrepassare; ~**ingly** *ad* eccessivamente.
excel [ɪk'sɛl] *vi* eccellere // *vt* sorpassare.
excellence ['ɛksələns] *n* eccellenza.
Excellency ['ɛksələnsɪ] *n*: **His ~** Sua Eccellenza.
excellent ['ɛksələnt] *a* eccellente.
except [ɪk'sɛpt] *prep* (*also*: ~ **for**, ~**ing**) salvo, all'infuori di, eccetto // *vt* escludere; ~ **if/when** salvo se/quando; ~ **that** salvo che; ~**ion** [ɪk'sɛpʃən] *n* eccezione *f*; **to take** ~**ion to** trovare a ridire su; ~**ional** [ɪk'sɛpʃənl] *a* eccezionale.
excerpt ['ɛksəːpt] *n* estratto.
excess [ɪk'sɛs] *n* eccesso; ~ **fare** *n* supplemento; ~ **baggage** *n* bagaglio in eccedenza; ~**ive** *a* eccessivo(a).
exchange [ɪks'tʃeɪndʒ] *n* scambio; (*also*: **telephone** ~) centralino // *vt* scambiare; ~ **market** *n* mercato dei cambi.
exchequer [ɪks'tʃɛkə*] *n* Scacchiere *m*, ≈ ministero delle Finanze.
excisable [ɪk'saɪzəbl] *a* soggetto(a) a dazio.
excise *n* ['ɛksaɪz] imposta, dazio // *vt* [ɛk-'saɪz] recidere; ~ **duties** *npl* dazi *mpl*.
excite [ɪk'saɪt] *vt* eccitare; **to get** ~**d** eccitarsi; ~**ment** *n* eccitazione *f*; agitazione *f*; **exciting** *a* avventuroso(a); (*film, book*) appassionante.
exclaim [ɪk'skleɪm] *vi* esclamare; **exclamation** [ɛksklə'meɪʃən] *n*

esclamazione *f*; **exclamation mark** *n* punto esclamativo.
exclude [ɪk'skluːd] *vt* escludere; **exclusion** [ɪk'skluːʒən] *n* esclusione *f*.
exclusive [ɪk'skluːsɪv] *a* esclusivo(a); (*club*) selettivo(a); (*district*) snob *inv* // *ad* (*COMM*) non compreso; ~ **of VAT** I.V.A. esclusa; ~**ly** *ad* esclusivamente; ~ **rights** *npl* (*COMM*) diritti *mpl* esclusivi.
excommunicate [ɛkskə'mjuːnɪkeɪt] *vt* scomunicare.
excrement ['ɛkskrəmənt] *n* escremento.
excruciating [ɪk'skruːʃɪeɪtɪŋ] *a* straziante, atroce.
excursion [ɪk'skəːʃən] *n* escursione *f*, gita.
excuse *n* [ɪk'skjuːs] scusa // *vt* [ɪk'skjuːz] scusare; **to ~ sb from** (*activity*) dispensare qd da; ~ **me!** mi scusi!
execute ['ɛksɪkjuːt] *vt* (*prisoner*) giustiziare; (*plan etc*) eseguire.
execution [ɛksɪ'kjuːʃən] *n* esecuzione *f*; ~**er** *n* boia *m inv*.
executive [ɪg'zɛkjutɪv] *n* (*COMM*) dirigente *m*; (*POL*) esecutivo // *a* esecutivo(a).
executor [ɪg'zɛkjutə*] *n* esecutore(trice) testamentario(a).
exemplary [ɪg'zɛmplərɪ] *a* esemplare.
exemplify [ɪg'zɛmplɪfaɪ] *vt* esemplificare.
exempt [ɪg'zɛmpt] *a* esentato(a) // *vt*: **to ~ sb from** esentare qd da; ~**ion** [ɪg-'zɛmpʃən] *n* esenzione *f*.
exercise ['ɛksəsaɪz] *n* esercizio // *vt* esercitare; (*dog*) portar fuori; **to take ~** fare del movimento; ~ **book** *n* quaderno.
exert [ɪg'zəːt] *vt* esercitare; **to ~ o.s.** sforzarsi.
exhaust [ɪg'zɔːst] *n* (*also*: ~ **fumes**) scappamento; (*also*: ~ **pipe**) tubo di scappamento // *vt* esaurire; ~**ed** *a* esaurito(a); ~**ion** [ɪg'zɔːstʃən] *n* esaurimento; ~**ive** *a* esauriente.
exhibit [ɪg'zɪbɪt] *n* (*ART*) oggetto esposto; (*LAW*) documento or oggetto esibito // *vt* esporre; (*courage, skill*) dimostrare; ~**ion** [ɛksɪ'bɪʃən] *n* mostra, esposizione *f*; ~**ionist** [ɛksɪ'bɪʃənɪst] *n* esibizionista *m/f*; ~**or** *n* espositore/trice.
exhilarating [ɪg'zɪləreɪtɪŋ] *a* esilarante, stimolante.
exhort [ɪg'zɔːt] *vt* esortare.
exile ['ɛksaɪl] *n* esilio; esiliato/a // *vt* esiliare; **in ~** in esilio.
exist [ɪg'zɪst] *vi* esistere; ~**ence** *n* esistenza; **to be in ~ence** esistere.
exit ['ɛksɪt] *n* uscita.
exonerate [ɪg'zɔnəreɪt] *vt*: **to ~ from** discolpare da.
exorcize ['ɛksɔːsaɪz] *vt* esorcizzare.
exotic [ɪg'zɔtɪk] *a* esotico(a).
expand [ɪk'spænd] *vt* espandere; estendere; allargare // *vi* (*trade etc*) svilupparsi, ampliarsi; espandersi; (*gas*) espandersi; (*metal*) dilatarsi.
expanse [ɪk'spæns] *n* distesa, estensione *f*.
expansion [ɪk'spænʃən] *n* sviluppo; espansione *f*; dilatazione *f*.
expatriate *n* [ɛks'pætrɪət] espatriato/a // *vt* [ɛks'pætrɪeɪt] espatriare.

expect [ɪk'spɛkt] *vt* (*anticipate*) prevedere, aspettarsi, prevedere *or* aspettarsi che + *sub*; (*count on*) contare su; (*hope for*) sperare; (*require*) richiedere, esigere; (*suppose*) supporre; (*await, also baby*) aspettare // *vi*: **to be ~ing** essere in stato interessante; **to ~ sb to do** aspettarsi che qd faccia; **~ant** *a* pieno(a) di aspettative; **~ant mother** *n* gestante *f*; **~ation** [ɛkspɛk'teɪʃən] *n* aspettativa; speranza.

expedience, expediency [ɛk'spiːdɪəns, ɛk'spiːdɪənsɪ] *n* convenienza.

expedient [ɪk'spiːdɪənt] *a* conveniente; vantaggioso(a) // *n* espediente *m*.

expedite ['ɛkspədaɪt] *vt* sbrigare; facilitare.

expedition [ɛkspə'dɪʃən] *n* spedizione *f*.

expel [ɪk'spɛl] *vt* espellere.

expend [ɪk'spɛnd] *vt* spendere; (*use up*) consumare; **~able** *a* sacrificabile; **~iture** [ɪk'spɛndɪtʃə*] *n* spesa; spese *fpl*.

expense [ɪk'spɛns] *n* spesa; spese *fpl*; (*high cost*) costo; **~s** *npl* (*COMM*) spese *fpl*, indennità *fpl*; **at the ~ of** a spese di; **~ account** *n* nota *f* spese *inv*.

expensive [ɪk'spɛnsɪv] *a* caro(a), costoso(a).

experience [ɪk'spɪərɪəns] *n* esperienza // *vt* (*pleasure*) provare; (*hardship*) soffrire; **~d** *a* esperto(a).

experiment [ɪk'spɛrɪmənt] *n* esperimento, esperienza // *vi* fare esperimenti; **~al** [-'mɛntl] *a* sperimentale.

expert ['ɛkspəːt] *a,* ° *n* esperto(a); **~ise** [-'tiːz] *n* competenza.

expire [ɪk'spaɪə*] *vi* (*period of time, licence*) scadere; **expiry** *n* scadenza.

explain [ɪk'spleɪn] *vt* spiegare; **explanation** [ɛksplə'neɪʃən] *n* spiegazione *f*; **explanatory** [ɪk'splænətrɪ] *a* esplicativo(a).

explicit [ɪk'splɪsɪt] *a* esplicito(a); (*definite*) netto(a).

explode [ɪk'spləud] *vi* esplodere.

exploit *n* ['ɛksplɔɪt] impresa // *vt* [ɪk-'splɔɪt] sfruttare; **~ation** [-'teɪʃən] *n* sfruttamento.

exploration [ɛksplə'reɪʃən] *n* esplorazione *f*.

exploratory [ɪk'splɔrətrɪ] *a* (*fig: talks*) esplorativo(a).

explore [ɪk'splɔː*] *vt* esplorare; (*possibilities*) esaminare; **~r** ˌ *n* esploratore/trice.

explosion [ɪk'spləuʒən] *n* esplosione *f*.

explosive [ɪk'spləusɪv] *a* esplosivo(a) // *n* esplosivo.

exponent [ɪk'spəunənt] *n* esponente *m/f*.

export *vt* [ɛk'spɔːt] esportare // *n* ['ɛkspɔːt] esportazione *f*; articolo di esportazione // *cpd* d'esportazione; **~ation** [-'teɪʃən] *n* esportazione *f*; **~er** *n* esportatore *m*.

expose [ɪk'spəuz] *vt* esporre; (*unmask*) smascherare; **to ~ o.s.** (*LAW*) oltraggiare il pudore.

exposure [ɪk'spəuʒə*] *n* esposizione *f*; (*PHOT*) posa; (*MED*) assideramento; **~ meter** *n* esposimetro.

expound [ɪk'spaund] *vt* esporre.

express [ɪk'sprɛs] *a* (*definite*) chiaro(a), espresso(a); (*letter etc*) espresso *inv* // *n* (*train*) espresso // *ad* (*send*) espresso // *vt* esprimere; **~ion** [ɪk'sprɛʃən] *n* espressione *f*; **~ive** *a* espressivo(a); **~ly** *ad* espressamente.

expulsion [ɪk'spʌlʃən] *n* espulsione *f*.

exquisite [ɛk'skwɪzɪt] *a* squisito(a).

extend [ɪk'stɛnd] *vt* (*visit*) protrarre; (*street*) prolungare; (*building*) ampliare; (*offer*) offrire, porgere // *vi* (*land*) estendersi.

extension [ɪk'stɛnʃən] *n* prolungamento; estensione *f*; (*building*) annesso; (*to wire, table*) prolunga; (*telephone*) interno; (: *in private house*) apparecchio addizionale.

extensive [ɪk'stɛnsɪv] *a* esteso(a), ampio(a); (*damage*) su larga scala; (*alterations*) notevole; (*inquiries*) esauriente; (*use*) grande; **he's travelled ~ly** ha viaggiato molto.

extent [ɪk'stɛnt] *n* estensione *f*; **to some ~** fino a un certo punto; **to what ~?** fino a che punto?

exterior [ɛk'stɪərɪə*] *a* esteriore, esterno(a) // *n* esteriore *m*, esterno; aspetto (esteriore).

exterminate [ɪk'stəːmɪneɪt] *vt* sterminare; **extermination** [-'neɪʃən] *n* sterminio.

external [ɛk'stəːnl] *a* esterno(a), esteriore.

extinct [ɪk'stɪŋkt] *a* estinto(a); **~ion** [ɪk-'stɪŋkʃən] *n* estinzione *f*.

extinguish [ɪk'stɪŋgwɪʃ] *vt* estinguere; **~er** *n* estintore *m*.

extort [ɪk'stɔːt] *vt*: **to ~ sth (from)** estorcere qc (da); **~ion** [ɪk'stɔːʃən] *n* estorsione *f*; **~ionate** [ɪk'stɔːʃnət] *a* esorbitante.

extra ['ɛkstrə] *a* extra *inv*, supplementare // *ad* (*in addition*) di più // *n* supplemento; (*THEATRE*) comparso.

extra... ['ɛkstrə] *prefix* extra... .

extract *vt* [ɪk'strækt] estrarre; (*money, promise*) strappare // *n* ['ɛkstrækt] estratto; (*passage*) brano; **~ion** [ɪk-'strækʃən] *n* estrazione *f*; (*descent*) origine *f*.

extradite ['ɛkstrədaɪt] *vt* estradare; **extradition** [-'dɪʃən] *n* estradizione *f*.

extramarital [ɛkstrə'mærɪtl] *a* extraconiugale.

extramural [ɛkstrə'mjuərl] *a* fuori dell'università.

extraneous [ɛk'streɪnɪəs] *a*: **~ to** estraneo(a) a.

extraordinary [ɪk'strɔːdnrɪ] *a* straordinario(a).

extra time [ɛkstrə'taɪm] *n* (*FOOTBALL*) tempo supplementare.

extravagant [ɪk'strævəgənt] *a* stravagante; (*in spending*) dispendioso(a).

extreme [ɪk'striːm] *a* estremo(a) // *n* estremo; **~ly** *ad* estremamente;

extremist *a,n* estremista (*m/f*).
extremity [ɪk'strɛmɪtɪ] *n* estremità *f inv*.
extricate ['ɛkstrɪkeɪt] *vt*: **to ~ sth (from)** districare qc (da).
extrovert ['ɛkstrəvɜːt] *n* estroverso/a.
exuberant [ɪg'zjuːbərnt] *a* esuberante.
exude [ɪg'zjuːd] *vt* trasudare; (*fig*) emanare.
exult [ɪg'zʌlt] *vi* esultare, gioire.
eye [aɪ] *n* occhio; (*of needle*) cruna // *vt* osservare; **to keep an ~ on** tenere d'occhio; **in the public ~** esposto(a) al pubblico; **~ball** *n* globo dell'occhio; **~brow** *n* sopracciglio; **~-catching** *a* che colpisce l'occhio; **~drops** *npl* gocce *fpl* oculari, collirio; **~lash** *n* ciglio; **~lid** *n* palpebra; **~-opener** *n* rivelazione *f*; **~shadow** *n* ombretto; **~sight** *n* vista; **~ sore** *n* pugno nell'occhio; **~ witness** *n* testimone *m/f* oculare.
eyrie ['ɪərɪ] *n* nido (d'aquila).

F

F [ɛf] *n* (MUS) fa *m*.
F. *abbr of* Fahrenheit.
fable ['feɪbl] *n* favola.
fabric ['fæbrɪk] *n* stoffa, tessuto.
fabrication [fæbrɪ'keɪʃən] *n* fabbricazione *f*; falsificazione *f*.
fabulous ['fæbjuləs] *a* favoloso(a); (*col: super*) favoloso(a), fantastico(a).
façade [fə'sɑːd] *n* facciata.
face [feɪs] *n* faccia, viso, volto; (*expression*) faccia; (*grimace*) smorfia; (*of clock*) quadrante *m*; (*of building*) facciata; (*side, surface*) faccia // *vt* fronteggiare; (*fig*) affrontare; **to lose ~** perdere la faccia; **in the ~ of** (*difficulties etc*) di fronte a; **on the ~ of it** a prima vista; **to ~ up to** *vt fus* affrontare, far fronte a; **~ cloth** *n* guanto di spugna; **~ cream** *n* crema per il viso; **~ lift** *n* lifting *m inv*; (*of façade etc*) ripulita.
facet ['fæsɪt] *n* faccetta, sfaccettatura; (*fig*) sfaccettatura.
facetious [fə'siːʃəs] *a* faceto(a).
face-to-face ['feɪstə'feɪs] *ad* a faccia a faccia.
face value ['feɪs'væljuː] *n* (*of coin*) valore *m* facciale *or* nominale; **to take sth at ~** (*fig*) giudicare qc dalle apparenze.
facial ['feɪʃəl] *a* facciale.
facile ['fæsaɪl] *a* facile.
facilitate [fə'sɪlɪteɪt] *vt* facilitare.
facility [fə'sɪlɪtɪ] *n* facilità; **facilities** *npl* attrezzature *fpl*.
facsimile [fæk'sɪmɪlɪ] *n* facsimile *m inv*.
fact [fækt] *n* fatto; **in ~** infatti.
faction ['fækʃən] *n* fazione *f*.
factor ['fæktə*] *n* fattore *m*.
factory ['fæktərɪ] *n* fabbrica, stabilimento.
factual ['fæktjuəl] *a* che si attiene ai fatti.
faculty ['fækəltɪ] *n* facoltà *f inv*.
fad [fæd] *n* mania; capriccio.
fade [feɪd] *vi* sbiadire, sbiadirsi; (*light,*

sound, hope) attenuarsi, affievolirsi; (*flower*) appassire.
fag [fæg] *n* (*col: cigarette*) cicca; **~ end** *n* mozzicone *m*; **~ged out** *a* (*col*) stanco(a) morto(a).
fail [feɪl] *vt* (*exam*) non superare; (*candidate*) bocciare; (*subj: courage, memory*) mancare a // *vi* fallire; (*student*) essere respinto(a); (*supplies*) mancare; (*eyesight, health, light*) venire a mancare; **to ~ to do sth** (*neglect*) mancare di fare qc; (*be unable*) non riuscire a fare qc; **without ~** senza fallo; certamente; **~ing** *n* difetto // *prep* in mancanza di; **~ure** ['feɪljə*] *n* fallimento; (*person*) fallito/a; (*mechanical etc*) guasto.
faint [feɪnt] *a* debole; (*recollection*) vago(a); (*mark*) indistinto(a) // *vi* svenire; **to feel ~** sentirsi svenire; **~-hearted** *a* pusillanime; **~ly** *ad* debolmente; vagamente; **~ness** *n* debolezza.
fair [fɛə*] *a* (*person, decision*) giusto(a), equo(a); (*hair etc*) biondo(a); (*skin, complexion*) bianco(a); (*weather*) bello(a), clemente; (*good enough*) assai buono(a); (*sizeable*) bello(a) // *ad* (*play*) lealmente // *n* fiera; **~ copy** *n* bella copia; **~ly** *ad* equamente; (*quite*) abbastanza; **~ness** *n* equità, giustizia.
fairy ['fɛərɪ] *n* fata; **~ tale** *n* fiaba.
faith [feɪθ] *n* fede *f*; (*trust*) fiducia; (*sect*) religione *f*, fede *f*; **~ful** *a* fedele; **~fully** *ad* fedelmente.
fake [feɪk] *n* (*painting etc*) contraffazione *f*; (*photo*) trucco; (*person*) impostore/a // *a* falso(a) // *vt* simulàre, falsare; (*painting*) contraffare; (*photo*) truccare; (*story*) falsificare.
falcon ['fɔːlkən] *n* falco, falcone *m*.
fall [fɔːl] *n* caduta; (*in temperature*) abbassamento; (*in price*) ribasso; (*US: autumn*) autunno // *vi* (*pt fell, pp fallen* [fɛl, 'fɔːlən]) cadere; (*temperature, price*) abbassare; **~s** *npl* (*waterfall*) cascate *fpl*; **to ~ flat** *vi* (*on one's face*) cadere bocconi; (*joke*) fare cilecca; (*plan*) fallire; **to ~ behind** *vi* rimanere indietro; **to ~ down** *vi* (*person*) cadere; (*building, hopes*) crollare; **to ~ for** *vt fus* (*trick*) cascarci dentro; (*person*) prendere una cotta per; **to ~ in** *vi* crollare; (*MIL*) mettersi in riga; **to ~ off** *vi* cadere; (*diminish*) diminuire, abbassarsi; **to ~ out** *vi* (*friends etc*) litigare; **to ~ through** *vi* (*plan, project*) fallire.
fallacy ['fæləsɪ] *n* errore *m*; falso ragionamento.
fallen ['fɔːlən] *pp of* **fall**.
fallible ['fæləbl] *a* fallibile.
fallout ['fɔːlaut] *n* fall-out *m*.
fallow ['fæləu] *a* incolto(a); a maggese.
false [fɔːls] *a* falso(a); **~ alarm** *n* falso allarme *m*; **~hood** *n* menzogna; **~ly** *ad* (*accuse*) a torto; **~ teeth** *npl* denti *mpl* finti.
falter ['fɔːltə*] *vi* esitare, vacillare.
fame [feɪm] *n* fama, celebrità.
familiar [fə'mɪlɪə*] *a* familiare; (*common*

comune; (*close*) intimo(a); **to be ~ with** (*subject*) conoscere; **~ity** [fəmɪlɪ'ærɪtɪ] *n* familiarità; intimità; **~ize** [fə'mɪlɪəraɪz] *vt*: **to ~ize sb with sth** far conoscere qc a qd.

family ['fæmɪlɪ] *n* famiglia; **~ allowance** *n* assegni *mpl* familiari; **~ doctor** *n* medico di famiglia; **~ life** *n* vita familiare.

famine ['fæmɪn] *n* carestia.

famished ['fæmɪʃt] *a* affamato(a).

famous ['feɪməs] *a* famoso(a); **~ly** *ad* (*get on*) a meraviglia.

fan [fæn] *n* (*folding*) ventaglio; (ELEC) ventilatore *m*; (*person*) ammiratore/trice; tifoso/a // *vt* far vento a; (*fire, quarrel*) alimentare; **to ~ out** *vi* spargersi (a ventaglio).

fanatic [fə'nætɪk] *n* fanatico/a; **~al** *a* fanatico(a).

fan belt ['fænbɛlt] *n* cinghia del ventilatore.

fancied ['fænsɪd] *a* immaginario(a).

fanciful ['fænsɪful] *a* fantasioso(a); (*object*) di fantasia.

fancy ['fænsɪ] *n* desiderio; immaginazione *f*, fantasia; (*whim*) capriccio *m* // *cpd* (di) fantasia *inv* // *vt* (*feel like, want*) aver voglia di; **to take a ~** to incapricciarsi di; **~ dress** *n* costume *m* (per maschera); **~-dress ball** *n* ballo in maschera.

fang [fæŋ] *n* zanna; (*of snake*) dente *m*.

fanlight ['fænlaɪt] *n* lunetta.

fantastic [fæn'tæstɪk] *a* fantastico(a).

fantasy ['fæntəzɪ] *n* fantasia, immaginazione *f*; fantasticheria; chimera.

far [fɑː*] *a*: **the ~ side/end** l'altra parte/l'altro capo // *ad* lontano; **~ away, ~ off** lontano, distante; **~ better** assai migliore; **~ from** lontano da; **by ~** di gran lunga; **go as ~ as the farm** vada fino alla fattoria; **as ~ as I know** per quel che so; **~away** *a* lontano(a).

farce [fɑːs] *n* farsa.

farcical ['fɑːsɪkəl] *a* farsesco(a).

fare [fɛə*] *n* (*on trains, buses*) tariffa; (*in taxi*) prezzo della corsa; (*food*) vitto, cibo // *vi* passarsela.

Far East [fɑːr'iːst] *n*: **the ~** l'Estremo Oriente *m*.

farewell [fɛə'wɛl] *excl, n* addio; **~ party** *n* festa d'addio.

far-fetched ['fɑː'fɛtʃt] *a* gonfiato(a).

farm [fɑːm] *n* fattoria, podere *m* // *vt* coltivare; **~er** *n* coltivatore/trice; agricoltore/trice; **~hand** *n* bracciante *m* agricolo; **~house** *n* fattoria; **~ing** *n* agricoltura; **~land** *n* terreno da coltivare; **~yard** *n* aia.

far-reaching ['fɑː'riːtʃɪŋ] *a* di vasta portata.

far-sighted ['fɑː'saɪtɪd] *a* presbite; (*fig*) lungimirante.

fart [fɑːt] (*col!*) *n* scoreggia(!) // *vi* scoreggiare (!).

farther ['fɑːðə*] *ad* più lontano.

farthest ['fɑːðɪst] *superlative of* **far**.

fascia ['feɪʃə] *n* (AUT) cruscotto.

fascinate ['fæsɪneɪt] *vt* affascinare; **fascination** [-'neɪʃən] *n* fascino.

fascism ['fæʃɪzəm] *n* fascismo.

fascist ['fæʃɪst] *a,n* fascista (*m/f*).

fashion ['fæʃən] *n* moda; (*manner*) maniera, modo // *vt* foggiare, formare; **in ~** alla moda; **out of ~** passato(a) di moda; **~able** *a* alla moda, di moda; **~ show** *n* sfilata di modelli.

fast [fɑːst] *a* rapido(a), svelto(a), veloce; (*clock*): **to be ~** andare avanti; (*dye, colour*) solido(a) // *ad* rapidamente; (*stuck, held*) saldamente // *n* digiuno // *vi* digiunare; **~ asleep** profondamente addormentato.

fasten ['fɑːsn] *vt* chiudere, fissare; (*coat*) abbottonare, allacciare // *vi* chiudersi, fissarsi; **~er, ~ing** *n* fermaglio, chiusura.

fastidious [fæs'tɪdɪəs] *a* esigente, difficile.

fat [fæt] *a* grasso(a) // *n* grasso.

fatal ['feɪtl] *a* fatale; mortale; disastroso(a); **~ism** *n* fatalismo; **~ity** [fə'tælɪtɪ] *n* (*road death etc*) morto/a, vittima; **~ly** *ad* a morte.

fate [feɪt] *n* destino; (*of person*) sorte *f*; **~ful** *a* fatidico(a).

father ['fɑːðə*] *n* padre *m*; **~-in-law** *n* suocero; **~ly** *a* paterno(a).

fathom ['fæðəm] *n* braccio (= *1828 mm*) // *vt* (*mystery*) penetrare, sondare.

fatigue [fə'tiːg] *n* stanchezza; (MIL) corvé *f*.

fatten ['fætn] *vt,vi* ingrassare.

fatty ['fætɪ] *a* (*food*) grasso(a).

fatuous ['fætjuəs] *a* fatuo(a).

faucet ['fɔːsɪt] *n* (US) rubinetto.

fault [fɔːlt] *n* colpa; (TENNIS) fallo; (*defect*) difetto; (GEO) faglia // *vt* criticare; **it's my ~** è colpa mia; **to find ~ with** trovare da ridire su; **at ~** in fallo; **to a ~** eccessivamente; **~less** *a* perfetto(a); senza difetto; impeccabile; **~y** *a* difettoso(a).

fauna ['fɔːnə] *n* fauna.

favour ['feɪvə*] *n* favore *m*, cortesia, piacere *m* // *vt* (*proposition*) favorire, essere favorevole a; (*pupil etc*) favorire; (*team, horse*) dare per vincente; **to do sb a ~** fare un favore *or* una cortesia a qd; **in ~ of** in favore di; **~able** *a* favorevole; (*price*) di favore; **~ably** *ad* favorevolmente; **~ite** [-rɪt] *a,n* favorito(a); **~itism** *n* favoritismo.

fawn [fɔːn] *n* daino // *a* marrone chiaro *inv* // *vi*: **to ~ (up)on** adulare servilmente.

fear [fɪə*] *n* paura, timore *m* // *vt* aver paura di, temere; **for ~ of** per paura di; **~ful** *a* pauroso(a); (*sight, noise*) terribile, spaventoso(a); **~less** *a* intrepido(a), senza paura.

feasibility [fiːzə'bɪlɪtɪ] *n* praticabilità.

feasible ['fiːzəbl] *a* possibile, realizzabile.

feast [fiːst] *n* festa, banchetto; (REL: *also*: **~ day**) festa // *vi* banchettare; **to ~ on** godersi, gustare.

feat [fiːt] *n* impresa, fatto insigne.

feather ['fɛðə*] *n* penna.

feature ['fiːtʃə*] *n* caratteristica; (*article*)

articolo // vt (subj: film) avere come protagonista // vi figurare; **~s** npl (of face) fisionomia; **~ film** n film m inv principale; **~less** a anonimo(a), senza caratteri distinti.

February ['februəri] n febbraio.

fed [fɛd] pt,pp of **feed**; **to be ~ up** essere stufo(a).

federal ['fɛdərəl] a federale.

federation [fɛdə'reiʃən] n federazione f.

fee [fi:] n pagamento; (of doctor, lawyer) onorario; (of school, college etc) tasse fpl scolastiche; (for examination) tassa d'esame.

feeble ['fi:bl] a debole; **~-minded** a deficiente.

feed [fi:d] n (of baby) pappa // vt (pt, pp fed [fɛd]) nutrire; (horse etc) dare da mangiare a; (fuel) alimentare; **to ~ material into sth** imboccare qc con materiali; **to ~ data/information into sth** nutrire qc di data/informazioni; **to ~ on** vt fus nutrirsi di; **~back** n feed-back m; **~ing bottle** n biberon m inv.

feel [fi:l] n sensazione f; (of substance) tatto // vt (pt, pp felt [fɛlt]) toccare; palpare; tastare; (cold, pain, anger) sentire; (grief) provare; (think, believe): **to ~ (that)** pensare che; **to ~ hungry/cold** aver fame/freddo; **to ~ lonely/better** sentirsi solo/meglio; **it ~s soft** è morbido al tatto; **to ~ like** (want) aver voglia di; **to ~ about** or **around** for cercare a tastoni; **to ~ about** or **around in one's pocket for** frugarsi in tasca per cercare; **~er** n (of insect) antenna; **to put out a ~er** fare un sondaggio; **~ing** n sensazione f; sentimento; **my ~ing is that...** ho l'impressione che... .

feet [fi:t] npl of **foot**.

feign [fein] vt fingere, simulare.

fell [fɛl] pt of **fall** // vt (tree) abbattere; (person) atterrare.

fellow ['fɛləu] n individuo, tipo; compagno; (of learned society) membro; **their ~ prisoners/students** i loro compagni di prigione/studio; **~ citizen** n concittadino/a; **~ countryman** n compatriota m; **~ men** npl simili mpl; **~ship** n associazione f; compagnia; specie di borsa di studio universitaria.

felony ['fɛləni] n reato, crimine m.

felt [fɛlt] pt, pp of **feel** // n feltro; **~-tip pen** n pennarello.

female ['fi:meil] n femmina // a femminile; (BIOL, ELEC) femmina inv; **male and ~ students** studenti e studentesse; **~ impersonator** n travestito.

feminine ['fɛminin] a, n femminile (m).

feminist ['fɛminist] n femminista m/f.

fence [fɛns] n recinto; (col: person) ricettatore/trice // vt (also: **~ in**) recingere // vi schermire; **fencing** n (SPORT) scherma.

fend [fɛnd] vi: **to ~ for o.s.** arrangiarsi.

fender ['fɛndə*] n parafuoco; (US) parafango; paraurti m inv.

ferment vi [fə'mɛnt] fermentare // n ['fə:mɛnt] agitazione f, eccitazione f; **~ation** [-'teiʃən] n fermentazione f.

fern [fə:n] n felce f.

ferocious [fə'rəuʃəs] a feroce.

ferocity [fə'rɔsiti] n ferocità.

ferry ['fɛri] n (small) traghetto; (large: also: **~boat**) nave f traghetto inv // vt traghettare.

fertile ['fə:tail] a fertile; (BIOL) fecondo(a); **fertility** [fə'tiliti] n fertilità; fecondità; **fertilize** ['fə:tilaiz] vt fertilizzare; fecondare; **fertilizer** n fertilizzante m.

fervent ['fə:vənt] a ardente, fervente.

fester ['fɛstə*] vi suppurare.

festival ['fɛstivəl] n (REL) festa; (ART, MUS) festival m inv.

festive ['fɛstiv] a di festa; **the ~ season** la stagione delle feste.

festivities [fɛs'tivitiz] npl festeggiamenti mpl.

fetch [fɛtʃ] vt andare a prendere; (sell for) essere venduto(a) per.

fetching ['fɛtʃiŋ] a attraente.

fête [feit] n festa.

fetish ['fɛtiʃ] n feticcio.

fetters ['fɛtəz] npl catene fpl.

fetus ['fi:təs] n (US) = **foetus**.

feud [fju:d] n contesa, lotta // vi essere in lotta.

feudal ['fju:dl] a feudale; **~ism** n feudalesimo.

fever ['fi:və*] n febbre f; **~ish** a febbrile.

few [fju:] a pochi(e); **they were ~** erano pochi; **a ~** a qualche inv // pronoun alcuni(e); **~er** a meno inv; meno numerosi(e); **~est** a il minor numero di.

fiancé [fi'ɑ̃:ŋsei] n fidanzato; **~e** n fidanzata.

fiasco [fi'æskəu] n fiasco.

fib [fib] n piccola bugia.

fibre ['faibə*] n fibra; **~glass** n fibra di vetro.

fickle ['fikl] a incostante, capriccioso(a).

fiction ['fikʃən] n narrativa, romanzi mpl; finzione f; **~al** a immaginario(a).

fictitious [fik'tiʃəs] a fittizio(a).

fiddle ['fidl] n (MUS) violino; (cheating) imbroglio; truffa // vt (accounts) falsificare, falsare; **to ~ with** vt fus gingillarsi con; **~r** n violinista m/f.

fidelity [fi'dɛliti] n fedeltà; (accuracy) esattezza.

fidget ['fidʒit] vi agitarsi; **~y** a agitato(a).

field [fi:ld] n campo; **~ glasses** npl binocolo (da campagna); **~ marshal** n feldmaresciallo; **~work** n ricerche fpl esterne.

fiend [fi:nd] n demonio; **~ish** a demoniaco(a).

fierce [fiəs] a (look, fighting) fiero(a); (wind) furioso(a); (attack) feroce; (enemy) acerrimo(a).

fiery ['faiəri] a ardente; infocato(a).

fifteen [fif'ti:n] num quindici.

fifth [fifθ] num quinto(a).

fiftieth ['fiftiiθ] num cinquantesimo(a).

fifty ['fıftı] *num* cinquanta.

fig [fıg] *n* fico.

fight [faıt] *n* zuffa, rissa; (*MIL*) battaglia, combattimento; (*against cancer etc*) lotta // *vb* (*pt, pp* **fought** [fɔːt]) *vt* picchiare; combattere; (*cancer, alcoholism*) lottare contro, combattere // *vi* battersi, combattere; ~**er** *n* combattente *m*; (*plane*) aeroplano da caccia; ~**ing** *n* combattimento.

figment ['fıgmənt] *n*: **a** ~ **of the imagination** un parto della fantasia.

figurative ['fıgjurətıv] *a* figurato(a).

figure ['fıgə*] *n* (*DRAWING, GEOM*) figura; (*number, cipher*) cifra; (*body, outline*) forma // *vi* (*appear*) figurare; (*US: make sense*) spiegarsi; **to** ~ **out** *vt* riuscire a capire; calcolare; ~**head** *n* (*NAUT*) polena; (*pej*) prestanome *m/f inv*.

filament ['fıləmənt] *n* filamento.

file [faıl] *n* (*tool*) lima; (*dossier*) incartamento; (*folder*) cartellina; (*for loose leaf*) raccoglitore *m*; (*row*) fila // *vt* (*nails, wood*) limare; (*papers*) archiviare; (*LAW: claim*) presentare; passare agli atti; **to** ~ **in/out** *vi* entrare/uscire in fila; **to** ~ **past** *vt fus* marciare in fila davanti a.

filing ['faılıŋ] *n* archiviare *m*; ~**s** *npl* limatura; ~ **cabinet** *n* casellario.

fill [fıl] *vt* riempire; (*tooth*) otturare; (*job*) coprire // *n*: **to eat one's** ~ mangiare a sazietà; **to** ~ **in** *vt* (*hole*) riempire; (*form*) compilare; **to** ~ **up** *vt* riempire // *vi* (*AUT*) fare il pieno; ~ **it up, please** (*AUT*) mi faccia il pieno, per piacere.

fillet ['fılıt] *n* filetto.

filling ['fılıŋ] *n* (*CULIN*) impasto, ripieno; (*for tooth*) otturazione *f*; ~ **station** *n* stazione *f* di rifornimento.

fillip ['fılıp] *n* incentivo, stimolo.

film [fılm] *n* (*CINEMA*) film *m inv*; (*PHOT*) pellicola; (*thin layer*) velo // *vt* (*scene*) filmare; ~ **star** *n* divo/a dello schermo.

filter ['fıltə*] *n* filtro // *vt* filtrare; ~ **lane** *n* (*AUT*) corsia di svincolo; ~ **tip** *n* filtro.

filth [fılθ] *n* sporcizia; (*fig*) oscenità; ~**y** *a* lordo(a), sozzo(a); (*language*) osceno(a).

fin [fın] *n* (*of fish*) pinna.

final ['faınl] *a* finale, ultimo(a); definitivo(a) // *n* (*SPORT*) finale *f*; ~**s** *npl* (*SCOL*) esami *mpl* finali; ~**e** [fı'nɑːlı] *n* finale *m*; ~**ist** *n* (*SPORT*) finalista *m/f*; ~**ize** *vt* mettere a punto; ~**ly** *ad* (*lastly*) alla fine; (*eventually*) finalmente.

finance [faı'næns] *n* finanza; ~**s** *npl* finanze *fpl* // *vt* finanziare.

financial [faı'nænʃəl] *a* finanziario(a).

financier [faı'nænsıə*] *n* finanziatore *m*.

find [faınd] *vt* (*pt, pp* **found** [faund]) trovare; (*lost object*) ritrovare // *n* trovata, scoperta; **to** ~ **sb guilty** (*LAW*) giudicare qd colpevole; **to** ~ **out** *vt* informarsi di; (*truth, secret*) scoprire; (*person*) cogliere in fallo; ~**ings** *npl* (*LAW*) sentenza, conclusioni *pl*; (*of report*) conclusioni.

fine [faın] *a* bello(a); ottimo(a); fine // *ad* (*well*) molto bene; (*small*) finemente // *n* (*LAW*) contravvenzione *f*, ammenda; multa

// *vt* (*LAW*) fare una contravvenzione a; multare; ~ **arts** *npl* belle arti *fpl*.

finery ['faınərı] *n* abiti *mpl* eleganti.

finesse [fı'nɛs] *n* finezza.

finger ['fıŋgə*] *n* dito // *vt* toccare, tastare; ~**nail** *n* unghia; ~**print** *n* impronta digitale; ~**tip** *n* punta del dito.

finicky ['fınıkı] *a* esigente, pignolo(a); minuzioso(a).

finish ['fınıʃ] *n* fine *f*; (*polish etc*) finitura // *vt* finire; (*use up*) esaurire // *vi* finire; (*session*) terminare; **to** ~ **off** *vt* compiere; (*kill*) uccidere; **to** ~ **up** *vi, vt* finire; ~**ing line** *n* linea d'arrivo; ~**ing school** *n* scuola privata di perfezionamento (*per signorine*).

finite ['faınaıt] *a* limitato(a); (*verb*) finito(a).

Finland ['fınlənd] *n* Finlandia.

Finn [fın] *n* finlandese *m/f*; ~**ish** *a* finlandese // *n* (*LING*) finlandese *m*.

fiord [fjɔːd] *n* fiordo.

fir [fəː*] *n* abete *m*.

fire [faıə*] *n* fuoco; incendio // *vt* (*discharge*): **to** ~ **a gun** scaricare un fucile; (*fig*) infiammare; (*dismiss*) licenziare // *vi* sparare, far fuoco; **on** ~ in fiamme; ~ **alarm** *n* allarme *m* d'incendio; ~**arm** *n* arma da fuoco; ~ **brigade** *n* (*corpo dei*) pompieri *mpl*; ~ **engine** *n* autopompa; ~ **escape** *n* scala di sicurezza; ~ **extinguisher** *n* estintore *m*; ~**man** *n* pompiere *m*; ~**place** *n* focolare *m*; ~**side** *n* angolo del focolare; ~ **station** *n* caserma dei pompieri; ~**wood** *n* legna; ~**work** *n* fuoco d'artificio.

firing ['faıərıŋ] *n* (*MIL*) spari *mpl*, tiro; ~ **squad** *n* plotone *m* d'esecuzione.

firm [fəːm] *a* fermo(a) // *n* ditta, azienda.

first [fəːst] *a* primo(a) // *ad* (*before others*) il primo, la prima; (*before other things*) per primo; (*when listing reasons etc*) per prima cosa // *n* (*person: in race*) primo/a; (*SCOL*) laurea con lode; (*AUT*) prima; **at** ~ dapprima, all'inizio; ~ **of all** prima di tutto; ~-**aid kit** *n* cassetta pronto soccorso; ~-**class** *a* di prima classe; ~-**hand** *a* di prima mano; ~ **lady** *n* (*US*) moglie *f* del presidente; ~**ly** *ad* in primo luogo; ~ **name** *n* prenome *m*; ~ **night** *n* (*THEATRE*) prima; ~-**rate** *a* di prima qualità, ottimo(a).

fiscal ['fıskəl] *a* fiscale.

fish [fıʃ] *n,pl inv* pesce *m* // *vi* pescare; **to go** ~**ing** andare a pesca; ~**erman** *n* pescatore *m*; ~**ery** *n* zona da pesca; ~ **fingers** *npl* bastoncini *mpl* di pesce (*surgelati*); ~**ing boat** *n* barca da pesca; ~**ing line** *n* lenza; ~**ing rod** *n* canna da pesca; ~**monger** *n* pescivendolo; ~**y** *a* (*fig*) sospetto(a).

fission ['fıʃən] *n* fissione *f*.

fissure ['fıʃə*] *n* fessura.

fist [fıst] *n* pugno.

fit [fıt] *a* (*MED, SPORT*) in forma; (*proper*) adatto(a), appropriato(a); conveniente // *vt* (*subj: clothes*) stare bene a; (*adjust*) aggiustare; (*put in, attach*) mettere; installare; (*equip*) fornire, equipaggiare // *vi* (*clothes*) stare bene; (*parts*) andare bene, adattarsi; (*in space, gap*) entrare // *n* (*MED*) accesso, attacco; ~ **to** in grado di; ~ **for** adatto(a) a; degno(a) di; **this dress is a tight/good** ~ questo vestito è stretto/sta bene; **by** ~**s and starts** a sbalzi; **to** ~ **in** *vi* accordarsi; adattarsi; **to** ~ **out** (*also:* ~ **up**) *vt* equipaggiare; ~**ful** saltuario(a); ~**ment** *n* componibile *m*; ~**ness** *n* (*MED*) forma fisica; (*of remark*) appropriatezza; ~**ter** *n* aggiustatore *m or* montatore *m* meccanico; (*DRESSMAKING*) sarto/a; ~**ting** *a* appropriato(a) // *n* (*of dress*) prova; (*of piece of equipment*) montaggio, aggiustaggio; ~**tings** *npl* impianti *mpl*.

five [faɪv] *num* cinque; ~**r** *n* (*Brit: col*) biglietto da cinque sterline.

fix [fɪks] *vt* fissare; mettere in ordine; (*mend*) riparare // *n*: **to be in a** ~ essere nei guai; ~**ed** [fɪkst] *a* (*prices etc*) fisso(a); ~**ture** [ˈfɪkstʃə*] *n* impianto (fisso); (*SPORT*) incontro (del calendario sportivo).

fizz [fɪz] *vi* frizzare.

fizzle [ˈfɪzl] *vi* frizzare; **to** ~ **out** *vi* finire in nulla.

fizzy [ˈfɪzɪ] *a* frizzante; gassato(a).

fjord [fjɔːd] *n* = **fiord**.

flabbergasted [ˈflæbəgɑːstɪd] *a* sbalordito(a).

flabby [ˈflæbɪ] *a* flaccido(a).

flag [flæg] *n* bandiera; (*also:* ~**stone**) pietra da lastricare // *vi* avvizzire; affievolirsi; **to** ~ **down** *vt* fare segno (di fermarsi) a.

flagon [ˈflægən] *n* bottiglione *m*.

flagpole [ˈflægpəul] *n* albero.

flagrant [ˈfleigrənt] *a* flagrante.

flair [flɛə*] *n* (*for business etc*) fiuto; (*for languages etc*) facilità.

flake [fleik] *n* (*of rust, paint*) scaglia; (*of snow, soap powder*) fiocco // *vi* (*also:* ~ **off**) sfaldarsi.

flamboyant [flæmˈbɔɪənt] *a* sgargiante.

flame [fleim] *n* fiamma.

flamingo [fləˈmɪŋgəu] \ *n* fenicottero, fiammingo.

flammable [ˈflæməbl] *a* infiammabile.

flan [flæn] *n* flan *m inv*.

flange [flændʒ] *n* flangia; (*on wheel*) suola.

flank [flæŋk] *n* fianco.

flannel [ˈflænl] *n* (*also:* **face** ~) guanto di spugna; (*fabric*) flanella; ~**s** *npl* pantaloni *mpl* di flanella.

flap [flæp] *n* (*of pocket*) patta; (*of envelope*) lembo // *vt* (*wings*) battere // *vi* (*sail, flag*) sbattere; (*col: also:* **be in a** ~) essere in agitazione.

flare [flɛə*] *n* razzo; (*in skirt etc*) svasatura; **to** ~ **up** *vi* andare in fiamma; (*fig: person*) infiammarsi di rabbia; (*: revolt*) scoppiare; ~**d** *a* (*trousers*) svasato(a).

flash [flæʃ] *n* vampata; (*also:* **news** ~) notizia *f* lampo *inv*; (*PHOT*) flash *m inv* // *vt* accendere e spegnere; (*send: message*) trasmettere // *vi* brillare; (*light on* ambulance, eyes etc) lampeggiare; **in a** ~ in un lampo; **to** ~ **one's headlights** lampeggiare; **he** ~**ed by** *or* **past** ci passò davanti come un lampo; ~**back** *n* flashback *m inv*; ~**bulb** *n* cubo *m* flash *inv*; ~**er** *n* (*AUT*) lampeggiatore *m*.

flashy [ˈflæʃɪ] *a* (*pej*) vistoso(a).

flask [flɑːsk] *n* fiasco; (*CHEM*) beuta; (*also:* **vacuum** ~) thermos *m inv* (*.*.

flat [flæt] *a* piatto(a); (*tyre*) sgonfio(a), a terra; (*denial*) netto(a); (*MUS*) bemolle *inv*; (*: voice*) stonato(a) // *n* (*Brit: rooms*) appartamento; (*MUS*) bemolle *m*; (*AUT*) pneumatico sgonfio; ~**ly** *ad* recisamente; ~**ten** *vt* (*also:* ~**ten out**) appiattare.

flatter [ˈflætə*] *vt* lusingare; ~**er** *n* adulatore/trice; ~**ing** *a* lusinghiero(a); ~**y** *n* adulazione *f*.

flaunt [flɔːnt] *vt* fare mostra di.

flavour [ˈfleɪvə*] *n* gusto, sapore *m* // *vt* insaporire, aggiungere sapore a; **vanilla-**~**ed** al gusto di vaniglia; ~**ing** *n* essenza (artificiale).

flaw [flɔː] *n* difetto; ~**less** *a* senza difetti.

flax [flæks] *n* lino; ~**en** *a* biondo(a).

flea [fliː] *n* pulce *f*.

fledg(e)ling [ˈfledʒlɪŋ] *n* uccellino.

flee, *pt, pp* **fled** [fliː, fled] *vt* fuggire da // *vi* fuggire, scappare.

fleece [fliːs] *n* vello // *vt* (*col*) pelare.

fleet [fliːt] *n* flotta; (*of lorries etc*) convoglio; parco.

fleeting [ˈfliːtɪŋ] *a* fugace, fuggitivo(a); (*visit*) volante.

Flemish [ˈflɛmɪʃ] *a* fiammingo(a) // *n* (*LING*) fiammingo.

flesh [flɛʃ] *n* carne *f*.

flew [fluː] *pt of* **fly**.

flex [flɛks] *n* filo (flessibile) // *vt* flettere; (*muscles*) contrarre; ~**ibility** [-ˈbɪlɪtɪ] *n* flessibilità; ~**ible** *a* flessibile.

flick [flɪk] *n* colpetto; scarto; **to** ~ **through** *vt fus* sfogliare.

flicker [ˈflɪkə*] *vi* tremolare // *n* tremolio.

flier [ˈflaɪə*] *n* aviatore *m*.

flight [flaɪt] *n* volo; (*escape*) fuga; (*also:* ~ **of steps**) scalinata; **to take** ~ darsi alla fuga; **to put to** ~ mettere in fuga; ~ **deck** *n* (*AVIAT*) cabina di controllo; (*NAUT*) ponte *m* di comando.

flimsy [ˈflɪmzɪ] *a* (*fabric*) inconsistente; (*excuse*) meschino(a).

flinch [flɪntʃ] *vi* ritirarsi; **to** ~ **from** tirarsi indietro di fronte a.

fling, *pt, pp* **flung** [flɪŋ, flʌŋ] *vt* lanciare, gettare.

flint [flɪnt] *n* selce *f*; (*in lighter*) pietrina.

flip [flɪp] *n* colpetto.

flippant [ˈflɪpənt] *a* senza rispetto, irriverente.

flirt [flɜːt] *vi* flirtare // *n* civetta; ~**ation** [-ˈteɪʃən] *n* flirt *m inv*.

flit [flɪt] *vi* svolazzare.

float [fləut] *n* galleggiante *m*; (*in procession*) carro // *vi* galleggiare // *vt* far galleggiare; (*loan, business*) lanciare; ~**ing** *a* a galla.

flock [flɔk] *n* gregge *m*; (*of people*) folla.

flog [flɔg] *vt* flagellare.

flood [flʌd] *n* alluvione *m*; (*of words, tears etc*) diluvio // *vt* allagare; **in** ~ in pieno; ~**ing** *n* alluvionamento; ~**light** *n* riflettore *m* // *vt* illuminare a giorno.

floor [flɔ:*] *n* pavimento; (*storey*) piano; (*fig: at meeting*): **the** ~ il pubblico // *vt* pavimentare; (*knock down*) atterrare; **first** ~ (*Brit*), **second** ~ (*US*) primo piano; ~**board** *n* tavellone *m* di legno; ~ **show** *n* spettacolo di varietà.

flop [flɔp] *n* fiasco // *vi* (*fail*) fare fiasco.

floppy ['flɔpi] *a* floscio(a), molle.

flora ['flɔːrə] *n* flora.

floral ['flɔːrl] *a* floreale.

Florence ['flɔrəns] *n* Firenze *f*; **Florentine** ['flɔrəntaɪn] *a* fiorentino(a).

florid ['flɔrɪd] *a* (*complexion*) florido(a); (*style*) fiorito(a).

florist ['flɔrɪst] *n* fioraio/a.

flounce [flauns] *n* balzo; **to** ~ **out** *vi* uscire stizzito(a).

flounder ['flaundə*] *vi* annaspare // *n* (*zool*) passera di mare.

flour ['flauə*] *n* farina.

flourish ['flʌrɪʃ] *vi* fiorire // *vt* brandire // *n* abbellimento; svolazzo; (*of trumpets*) fanfara; ~**ing** *a* prosperoso(a), fiorente.

flout [flaut] *vt* disprezzare.

flow [fləu] *n* flusso; circolazione *f* // *vi* fluire; (*traffic, blood in veins*) circolare; (*hair*) scendere; ~ **chart** *n* schema *m* di flusso.

flower ['flauə*] *n* fiore *m* // *vi* fiorire; ~**bed** *n* aiuola; ~**pot** *n* vaso da fiori; ~**y** *a* fiorito(a).

flown [fləun] *pp* *of* **fly**.

flu [fluː] *n* influenza.

fluctuate ['flʌktjueɪt] *vi* fluttuare, oscillare; **fluctuation** [-'eɪʃən] *n* fluttuazione *f*, oscillazione *f*.

fluency ['fluːənsɪ] *n* facilità, scioltezza; (*in foreign language*) buona conoscenza della lingua parlata.

fluent ['fluːənt] *a* (*speech*) facile, sciolto(a); corrente; **he speaks** ~ **Italian** parla l'italiano correntemente; ~**ly** *ad* con facilità; correntemente.

fluff [flʌf] *n* lanugine *f*; ~**y** *a* lanuginoso(a); (*toy*) di peluche.

fluid ['fluːɪd] *a* fluido(a) // *n* fluido; ~ **ounce** *n* = 0.028 l; 0.05 pints.

fluke [fluːk] *n* (*col*) colpo di fortuna.

flung [flʌŋ] *pt*,*pp* *of* **fling**.

fluorescent [fluə'rɛsnt] *a* fluorescente.

fluoride ['fluəraɪd] *n* fluoruro.

flurry ['flʌrɪ] *n* (*of snow*) tempesta; **a** ~ **of activity/excitement** una febbre di attività/improvvisa agitazione.

flush [flʌʃ] *n* rossore *m*; (*fig*) ebbrezza // *vt* ripulire con un getto d'acqua // *vi* arrossire // *a*: ~ **with** a livello di, pari a; ~ **against** aderente a; **to** ~ **the toilet** tirare la catena, tirare la scarica; ~**ed** *a* tutto(a) rosso(a).

fluster ['flʌstə*] *n* agitazione *f*; ~**ed** *a* sconvolto(a).

flute [fluːt] *n* flauto.

flutter ['flʌtə*] *n* agitazione *f*; (*of wings*) frullio // *vi* (*bird*) battere le ali.

flux [flʌks] *n*: **in a state of** ~ in continuo mutamento.

fly [flaɪ] *n* (*insect*) mosca; (*on trousers: also*: **flies**) bracchetta // *vb* (*pt* **flew**, *pp* **flown** [fluː, fləun]) *vt* pilotare; (*passengers, cargo*) trasportare (in aereo); (*distances*) percorrere // *vi* volare; (*passengers*) andare in aereo; (*escape*) fuggire; (*flag*) sventolare; **to** ~ **open** *vi* spalancarsi all'improvviso; ~**ing** *n* (*activity*) aviazione *f*; (*action*) volo // *a*: ~**ing visit** visita volante; **with** ~**ing colours** con risultati brillanti; ~**ing saucer** *n* disco volante; ~**ing start** *n*: **to get off to a** ~**ing start** partire come un razzo; ~**over** *n* (*Brit: bridge*) cavalcavia *m inv*; ~**past** *n* parata aerea; ~**sheet** *n* (*for tent*) sopratetto; ~**wheel** *n* volano.

foal [fəul] *n* puledro.

foam [fəum] *n* schiuma // *vi* schiumare; ~ **rubber** *n* gommapiuma Ⓡ.

fob [fɔb] *vt*: **to** ~ **sb off with** appioppare qd con; sbarazzarsi di qd con.

focal ['fəukəl] *a* focale.

focus ['fəukəs] *n* (*pl*: ~**es**) fuoco; (*of interest*) centro // *vt* (*field glasses etc*) mettere a fuoco; **in** ~ a fuoco; **out of** ~ sfocato(a).

fodder ['fɔdə*] *n* foraggio.

foe [fəu] *n* nemico.

foetus ['fiːtəs] *n* feto.

fog [fɔg] *n* nebbia; ~**gy** *a* nebbioso(a); **it's** ~**gy** c'è nebbia.

foible ['fɔɪbl] *n* debolezza, punto debole.

foil [fɔɪl] *vt* confondere, frustrare // *n* lamina di metallo; (*also*: **kitchen** ~) foglio di alluminio; (*FENCING*) fioretto.

fold [fəuld] *n* (*bend, crease*) piega; (*AGR*) ovile *m*; (*fig*) gregge *m* // *vt* piegare; **to** ~ **up** *vi* (*map etc*) piegarsi; (*business*) crollare // *vt* (*map etc*) piegare, ripiegare; ~**er** *n* (*for papers*) cartella, cartellina; (*brochure*) dépliant *m inv*; ~**ing** *a* (*chair, bed*) pieghevole.

foliage ['fəulɪdʒ] *n* fogliame *m*.

folk [fəuk] *npl* gente *f* // *a* popolare; ~**s** *npl* famiglia; ~**lore** ['fəuklɔ:*] *n* folclore *m*; ~**song** *n* canto popolare.

follow ['fɔləu] *vt* seguire // *vi* seguire; (*result*) conseguire, risultare; **he** ~**ed suit** lui ha fatto lo stesso; **to** ~ **up** *vt* (*victory*) sfruttare; (*letter, offer*) fare seguito a; (*case*) seguire; ~**er** *n* seguace *m/f*, discepolo/a; ~**ing** *a* seguente, successivo(a) // *n* seguito, discepoli *mpl*.

folly ['fɔlɪ] *n* pazzia, follia.

fond [fɔnd] *a* (*memory, look*) tenero(a), affettuoso(a); **to be** ~ **of** volere bene a.

fondle ['fɔndl] *vt* accarezzare.

fondness ['fɔndnɪs] *n* affetto.

font [fɔnt] *n* fonte *m* (battesimale).

food [fuːd] *n* cibo; ~ **poisoning** *n*

intossicazione f; ~**stuffs** npl generi fpl alimentari.

fool [fu:l] n sciocco/a; (HISTORY: of king) buffone m; (CULIN) frullato // vt ingannare // vi (gen: ~ **around**) fare lo sciocco; ~**hardy** a avventato(a); ~**ish** a scemo(a), stupido(a); imprudente; ~**proof** a (plan etc) sicurissimo(a).

foot [fut] n (pl: **feet** [fi:t]) piede m; (measure) piede (= 304 mm; 12 inches); (of animal) zampa // vt (bill) pagare; **on** ~ a piedi; ~ **and mouth (disease)** n afta epizootica; ~**ball** n pallone m; (sport) calcio; ~**baller** n calciatore m; ~**brake** n freno a pedale; ~**bridge** n passerella; ~**hills** npl contrafforti fpl; ~**hold** n punto d'appoggio; ~**ing** n (fig) posizione f; **to lose one's** ~**ing** mettere un piede in fallo; **on an equal** ~**ing** in condizioni di parità; ~**lights** npl luci fpl della ribalta; ~**man** n lacchè m inv; ~**note** n nota (a piè di pagina); ~**path** n sentiero m; (in street) marciapiede m; ~**sore** a coi piedi doloranti or dolenti; ~**step** n passo; ~**wear** n calzatura.

for [fɔ:*] prep per // cj poiché; ~ **all his money/he says ...** nonostante or malgrado tutto il suo denaro/quel che dice ...; **I haven't seen him** ~ **a week** è una settimana che non lo vedo, non lo vedo da una settimana; **he went down** ~ **the paper** è sceso a prendere il giornale; ~ **sale** da vendere.

forage ['fɔrɪdʒ] vi foraggiare.

foray ['fɔreɪ] n incursione f.

forbad(e) [fə'bæd] pt of **forbid**.

forbearing [fɔ:'bɛərɪŋ] a paziente, tollerante.

forbid, pt **forbad(e)**, pp **forbidden** [fə'bɪd, -'bæd, -'bɪdn] vt vietare, interdire; ~**den** a vietato(a); ~**ding** a arcigno(a), d'aspetto minaccioso.

force [fɔ:s] n forza // vt forzare; **the F~s** npl le forze armate; **in** ~ (in large numbers) in gran numero; (law) in vigore; **to come into** ~ entrare in vigore; ~**d** [fɔ:st] a forzato(a); ~**ful** a forte, vigoroso(a).

forceps ['fɔ:sɛps] npl forcipe m.

forcibly ['fɔ:səblɪ] ad con la forza; (vigorously) vigorosamente.

ford [fɔ:d] n guado // vt guadare.

fore [fɔ:*] n: **to the** ~ in prima linea; **to come to the** ~ mettersi in evidenza.

forearm ['fɔ:rɑ:m] n avambraccio.

foreboding [fɔ:'bəudɪŋ] n presagio di male.

forecast ['fɔ:kɑ:st] n previsione f // vt (irg: like **cast**) prevedere.

forecourt ['fɔ:kɔ:t] n (of garage) corte f esterna.

forefathers ['fɔ:fɑ:ðəz] npl antenati mpl, avi mpl.

forefinger ['fɔ:fɪŋgə*] n (dito) indice m.

forego [fɔ:'gəu] vt = **forgo**.

foregone ['fɔ:gɔn] a: **it's a** ~ **conclusion** è una conclusione scontata.

foreground ['fɔ:graund] n primo piano.

forehead ['fɔrɪd] n fronte f.

foreign ['fɔrɪn] a straniero(a); (trade) estero(a); ~ **body** n corpo estraneo; ~**er** n straniero/a; ~ **exchange market** n mercato delle valute; ~ **exchange rate** n cambio; ~ **minister** n ministro degli Affari esteri.

foreman ['fɔ:mən] n caposquadra m.

foremost ['fɔ:məust] a principale; più in vista.

forensic [fə'rɛnsɪk] a: ~ **medicine** medicina legale.

forerunner ['fɔ:rʌnə*] n precursore m.

foresee, pt **foresaw**, pp **foreseen** [fɔ:'si:, -'sɔ:, -'si:n] vt prevedere; ~**able** a prevedibile.

foresight ['fɔ:saɪt] n previdenza.

forest ['fɔrɪst] n foresta.

forestall [fɔ:'stɔ:l] vt prevenire.

forestry ['fɔrɪstrɪ] n silvicoltura.

foretaste ['fɔ:teɪst] n pregustazione f.

foretell, pt,pp **foretold** [fɔ:'tɛl, -'təuld] vt predire.

forever [fə'rɛvə*] ad per sempre; (fig) sempre, di continuo.

forewent [fɔ:'wɛnt] pt of **forego**.

foreword ['fɔ:wəd] n prefazione f.

forfeit ['fɔ:fɪt] n ammenda, pena // vt perdere; (one's happiness, health) giocarsi.

forgave [fə'geɪv] pt of **forgive**.

forge [fɔ:dʒ] n fucina // vt (signature, money) contraffare, falsificare; (wrought iron) fucinare, foggiare; **to** ~ **ahead** vi tirare avanti; ~**r** n contraffattore m; ~**ry** n falso; (activity) contraffazione f.

forget, pt **forgot**, pp **forgotten** [fə'gɛt, -'gɔt, -'gɔtn] vt,vi dimenticare; ~**ful** a di corta memoria; ~**ful of** dimentico(a) di.

forgive, pt **forgave**, pp **forgiven** [fə'gɪv, -'geɪv, -'gɪvn] vt perdonare; ~**ness** n perdono.

forgo, pt **forwent**, pp **forgone** [fɔ:'gəu, -'wɛnt, -'gɔn] vt rinunciare a.

forgot [fə'gɔt] pt of **forget**.

forgotten [fə'gɔtn] pp of **forget**.

fork [fɔ:k] n (for eating) forchetta; (for gardening) forca; (of roads) bivio; (of railways) inforcazione f // vi (road) biforcarsi; **to** ~ **out** (col: pay) vt sborsare // vi pagare; ~**ed** [fɔ:kt] a (lightning) a zigzag; ~**lift truck** n carrello elevatore.

form [fɔ:m] n forma; (SCOL) classe f; (questionnaire) scheda // vt formare; **in top** ~ in gran forma.

formal ['fɔ:məl] a (offer, receipt) vero(a) e proprio(a); (person) cerimonioso(a); (occasion, dinner) formale, ufficiale; (ART, PHILOSOPHY) formale; ~**ly** ad ufficialmente; formalmente; cerimoniosamente.

format ['fɔ:mæt] n formato.

formation [fɔ:'meɪʃən] n formazione f.

formative ['fɔ:mətɪv] a: ~ **years** anni mpl formativi.

former ['fɔ:mə*] a vecchio(a) (before n), ex inv (before n); **the** ~ ... **the latter** quello ... questo; ~**ly** ad in passato.

formidable ['fɔ:mɪdəbl] a formidabile.

formula ['fɔ:mjulə] n formula.
formulate ['fɔ:mjuleit] vt formulare.
forsake, pt **forsook**, pp **forsaken** [fə'seik, -'suk, -'seikən] vt abbandonare.
fort [fɔ:t] n forte m.
forte ['fɔ:ti] n forte m.
forth [fɔ:θ] ad in avanti; **to go back and ~** andare avanti e indietro; **and so ~** e così via; **~coming** a prossimo(a); (character) aperto(a), comunicativo(a); **~right** a franco(a), schietto(a).
fortieth ['fɔ:tiiθ] num quarantesimo(a).
fortification [fɔ:tifi'keiʃən] n fortificazione f.
fortify ['fɔ:tifai] vt fortificare.
fortitude ['fɔ:titju:d] n forza d'animo.
fortnight ['fɔ:tnait] n quindici giorni mpl, due settimane fpl; **~ly** a bimensile // ad ogni quindici giorni.
fortress ['fɔ:tris] n fortezza, rocca.
fortuitous [fɔ:'tju:itəs] a fortuito(a).
fortunate ['fɔ:tʃənit] a fortunato(a); **it is ~ that** è una fortuna che; **~ly** ad fortunatamente.
fortune ['fɔ:tʃən] n fortuna; **~teller** n indovino/a.
forty ['fɔ:ti] num quaranta.
forum ['fɔ:rəm] n foro.
forward ['fɔ:wəd] a (ahead of schedule) in anticipo; (movement, position) in avanti; (not shy) aperto(a); diretto(a); sfacciato(a) // ad avanti // n (SPORT) avanti m inv // vt (letter) inoltrare; (parcel, goods) spedire; (fig) promuovere, appoggiare; **to move ~** avanzare; **~(s)** ad avanti.
forwent [fɔ:'went] pt of **forgo**.
fossil ['fɔsl] a,n fossile (m).
foster ['fɔstə*] vt incoraggiare, nutrire; (child) adottare; **~ brother** n fratello adottivo; fratello di latte; **~ child** n bambino(a) adottato(a); **~ mother** n madre f adottiva; nutrice f.
fought [fɔ:t] pt, pp of **fight**.
foul [faul] a (smell, food) cattivo(a); (weather) sporco(a); (language) osceno(a); (deed) infame // n (FOOTBALL) fallo // vt sporcare; (football player) commettere un fallo su.
found [faund] pt, pp of **find** // vt (establish) fondare; **~ation** [-'deiʃən] n (act) fondazione f; (base) base f; (also: **~ation cream**) fondo tinta; **~ations** npl (of building) fondamenta fpl.
founder ['faundə*] n fondatore/ trice // vi affondare.
foundry ['faundri] n fonderia.
fount [faunt] n fonte f; **~ain** ['fauntin] n fontana; **~ain pen** n penna stilografica.
four [fɔ:*] num quattro; **on all ~s** a carponi; **~some** ['fɔ:səm] n partita a quattro; uscita in quattro; **~teen** num quattordici; **~th** num quarto(a).
fowl [faul] n pollame m; volatile m.
fox [fɔks] n volpe f // vt confondere.
foyer ['fɔiei] n atrio; (THEATRE) ridotto.
fraction ['frækʃən] n frazione f.

fracture ['fræktʃə*] n frattura // vt fratturare.
fragile ['frædʒail] a fragile.
fragment ['frægmənt] n frammento; **~ary** a frammentario(a).
fragrance ['freigrəns] n fragranza, profumo.
fragrant ['freigrənt] a fragrante, profumato(a).
frail [freil] a debole, delicato(a).
frame [freim] n (of building) armatura; (of human, animal) ossatura, corpo; (of picture) cornice f; (of door, window) telaio; (of spectacles: also: **~s**) montatura; **~ of mind** n stato d'animo; **~work** n struttura.
France [frɑ:ns] n Francia.
franchise ['fræntʃaiz] n (POL) diritto di voto.
frank [fræŋk] a franco(a), aperto(a) // vt (letter) affrancare; **~ly** ad francamente, sinceramente; **~ness** n franchezza.
frantic ['fræntik] a frenetico(a).
fraternal [frə'tə:nl] a fraterno(a).
fraternity [frə'tə:niti] n (club) associazione f; (spirit) fratellanza.
fraternize ['frætənaiz] vi fraternizzare.
fraud [frɔ:d] n frode f, inganno, truffa; impostore/a.
fraudulent ['frɔ:djulənt] a fraudolento(a).
fraught [frɔ:t] a: **~ with** pieno(a) di, intriso(a) da.
fray [frei] n baruffa // vt logorare // vi logorarsi; **her nerves were ~ed** aveva i nervi a pezzi.
freak [fri:k] n fenomeno, mostro // cpd fenomenale.
freckle ['frekl] n lentiggine f.
free [fri:] a libero(a); (gratis) gratuito(a); (liberal) generoso(a) // vt (prisoner, jammed person) liberare; (jammed object) districare; **~ (of charge), for free** ad gratuitamente; **~dom** ['fri:dəm] n libertà; **~-for-all** n parapiglia m generale; **~ kick** n calcio libero; **~lance** a indipendente; **~ly** ad liberamente; (liberally) liberalmente; **~mason** n massone m; **~ trade** n libero scambio; **~way** n (US) superstrada; **~wheel** vi andare a ruota libera; **~ will** n libero arbitrio; **of one's own ~ will** di spontanea volontà.
freeze [fri:z] vb (pt **froze**, pp **frozen** [frəuz, 'frəuzn]) vi gelare // vt gelare; (food) congelare; (prices, salaries) bloccare // n gelo; blocco; **~r** n congelatore m.
freezing ['fri:ziŋ] a: **~ cold** a gelido(a); **~ point** n punto di congelamento; **3 degrees below ~** 3 gradi sotto zero.
freight [freit] n (goods) merce f, merci fpl; (money charged) spese fpl di trasporto; **~ car** n (US) carro m merci inv; **~er** n (NAUT) nave f da carico.
French [frentʃ] a francese // n (LING) francese m; **the ~** i Francesi; **~ fried potatoes** npl patate fpl fritte; **~man** n francese m; **~ window** n portafinestra; **~woman** n francese f.
frenzy ['frenzi] n frenesia.

frequency ['fri:kwənsɪ] n frequenza.
frequent a ['fri:kwənt] frequente // vt [frɪ'kwent] frequentare; **~ly** ad frequentemente, spesso.
fresco ['freskəu] n affresco.
fresh [freʃ] a fresco(a); (new) nuovo(a); (cheeky) sfacciato(a); **~en** vi (wind, air) rinfrescare; **to ~en up** vi rinfrescarsi; **~ly** ad di recente, di fresco; **~ness** n freschezza; **~water** a (fish) d'acqua dolce.
fret [fret] vi agitarsi, affliggersi.
friar ['fraɪə*] n frate m.
friction ['frɪkʃən] n frizione f, attrito.
Friday ['fraɪdɪ] n venerdì m inv.
fridge [frɪdʒ] n frigo, frigorifero.
fried [fraɪd] pt, pp of **fry** // a fritto(a).
friend [frend] n amico/a; **~liness** n amichevolezza; **~ly** a amichevole; **~ship** n amicizia.
frieze [fri:z] n fregio.
frigate ['frɪgɪt] n (NAUT: modern) fregata.
fright [fraɪt] n paura, spavento; **~en** vt spaventare, far paura a; **~ening** a spaventoso(a), pauroso(a); **~ful** a orribile; **~fully** ad terribilmente.
frigid ['frɪdʒɪd] a (woman) frigido(a).
frill [frɪl] n balza.
fringe [frɪndʒ] n frangia; (edge: of forest etc) margine m; (fig): **on the ~** al margine.
frisk [frɪsk] vt perquisire.
frisky ['frɪskɪ] a vivace, vispo(a).
fritter ['frɪtə*] n frittella; **to ~ away** vt sprecare.
frivolity [frɪ'vɔlɪtɪ] n frivolezza.
frivolous ['frɪvələs] a frivolo(a).
frizzy ['frɪzɪ] a crespo(a).
fro [frəu] see **to**.
frock [frɔk] n vestito.
frog [frɔg] n rana; **~man** n uomo m rana inv.
frolic ['frɔlɪk] vi sgambettare.
from [frɔm] prep da; **~ a pound/January** da una sterlina in su/gennaio in poi; **~ what he says** a quanto dice.
front [frʌnt] n (of house, dress) davanti m inv; (of train) testa; (of book) copertina; (promenade: also: **sea ~**) lungomare m; (MIL, POL, METEOR) fronte m; (fig: appearances) fronte f // a primo(a); anteriore, davanti inv; **~al** a frontale; **~door** n porta d'entrata; (of car) sportello anteriore; **~ier** ['frʌntɪə*] n frontiera; **~ page** n prima pagina; **~ room** n (Brit) salotto; **~-wheel drive** n trasmissione f anteriore.
frost [frɔst] n gelo; (also: **hoar ~**) brina; **~bite** n congelamento; **~ed** a (glass) smerigliato(a); **~y** a (window) coperto(a) di ghiaccio; (welcome) gelido(a).
froth ['frɔθ] n spuma; schiuma.
frown [fraun] n cipiglio // vi accigliarsi.
froze [frəuz] pt of **freeze**; **~n** pp of **freeze** // a (food) congelato(a).
frugal ['fru:gəl] a frugale.
fruit [fru:t] n, pl inv frutto; (collectively)

frutta; **~ful** a fruttuoso(a); (plant) fruttifero(a); (soil) fertile; **~ion** [fru:'ɪʃən] n: **to come to ~ion** realizzarsi; **~ machine** n macchina f mangiasoldi inv; **~ salad** n macedonia.
frustrate [frʌs'treɪt] vt frustrare; **~d** a frustrato(a); **frustration** [-'treɪʃən] n frustrazione f.
fry, pt, pp **fried** [fraɪ, -d] vt friggere; **the small ~** i pesci piccoli; **~ing pan** n padella.
ft. abbr of **foot**, **feet**.
fuchsia ['fju:ʃə] n fucsia.
fudge [fʌdʒ] n (CULIN) specie di caramella a base di latte, burro e zucchero.
fuel [fjuəl] n (for heating) combustibile m; (for propelling) carburante m; **~ oil** n nafta; **~ tank** n deposito m nafta inv; (on vehicle) serbatoio (della benzina).
fugitive ['fju:dʒɪtɪv] n fugitivo/a, profugo/a.
fulfil [ful'fɪl] vt (function) compiere; (order) eseguire; (wish, desire) soddisfare, appagare; **~ment** n (of wishes) soddisfazione f, appagamento.
full [ful] a pieno(a); (details, skirt) ampio(a) // ad: **to know ~ well that** sapere benissimo che; **~ employment** piena occupazione; **~ fare** tariffa completa; **a ~ two hours** due ore intere; **at ~ speed** a tutta velocità; **in ~** per intero; **~back** n (RUGBY, FOOTBALL) terzino; **~-length** a (portrait) in piedi; **~ moon** n luna piena; **~-sized** a (portrait etc) a grandezza naturale; **~ stop** n punto; **~-time** a (work) a tempo pieno // n (SPORT) fine f partita; **~y** ad interamente, pienamente, completamente.
fumble ['fʌmbl] vi brancolare, andare a tentoni // vt (ball) lasciarsi sfuggire; **to ~ with** vt fus trafficare.
fume [fju:m] vi essere furioso(a); **~s** npl esalazioni fpl, vapori mpl.
fumigate ['fju:mɪgeɪt] vt suffumicare.
fun [fʌn] n divertimento, spasso; **to have ~** divertirsi; **for ~** per scherzo; **it's not much ~** non è molto divertente; **to make ~ of** vt fus prendersi gioco di.
function ['fʌŋkʃən] n funzione f; cerimonia, ricevimento // vi funzionare; **~al** a funzionale.
fund [fʌnd] n fondo, cassa; (source) fondo; (store) riserva; **~s** npl fondi mpl.
fundamental [fʌndə'mentl] a fondamentale; **~s** npl basi fpl; **~ly** ad essenzialmente, fondamentalmente.
funeral ['fju:nərəl] n funerale m; **~ service** n ufficio funebre.
fun fair ['fʌnfɛə*] n luna park m inv.
fungus, pl **fungi** ['fʌŋgəs, -gaɪ] n fungo; (mould) muffa.
funnel ['fʌnl] n imbuto; (of ship) ciminiera.
funny ['fʌnɪ] a divertente, buffo(a); (strange) strano(a), bizzarro(a).
fur [fə:*] n pelo; pelliccia; (in kettle etc) deposito calcare; **~ coat** n pelliccia.
furious ['fjuərɪəs] a furioso(a); (effort)

accanito(a); ~**ly** *ad* furiosamente; accanitamente.

furlong ['fɔːlɒŋ] *n* = 201.17 *m* (*termine ippico*).

furlough ['fɔːləu] *n* (*US*) congedo, permesso.

furnace ['fɔːnɪs] *n* fornace *f*.

furnish ['fɔːnɪʃ] *vt* ammobiliare; (*supply*) fornire; ~**ings** *npl* mobili *mpl*, mobilia.

furniture ['fɔːnɪtʃə*] *n* mobili *mpl*; **piece of** ~ mobile *m*.

furrow ['fʌrəu] *n* solco.

furry ['fɔːrɪ] *a* (*animal*) peloso(a).

further ['fɔːðə*] *a* supplementare, altro(a); nuovo(a); più lontano(a) // *ad* più lontano; (*more*) di più; (*moreover*) inoltre // *vt* favorire, promuovere; **until** ~ **notice** fino a nuovo avviso; **college of** ~ **education** *n* istituto statale con corsi specializzati (*di formazione professionale, aggiornamento professionale etc*); ~**more** [fɔːðə'mɔː*] *ad* inoltre, per di più.

furthest ['fɔːðɪst] *superlative of* **far**.

furtive ['fɔːtɪv] *a* furtivo(a).

fury ['fjuərɪ] *n* furore *m*.

fuse [fjuːz] *n* fusibile *m*; (*for bomb etc*) miccia, spoletta // *vt* fondere; (*ELEC*) **to** ~ **the lights** far saltare i fusibili // *vi* fondersi; ~ **box** *n* cassetta dei fusibili.

fuselage ['fjuːzəlɑːʒ] *n* fusoliera.

fusion ['fjuːʒən] *n* fusione *f*.

fuss [fʌs] *n* chiasso, trambusto, confusione *f*; (*complaining*) storie *fpl*; **to make a** ~ fare delle storie; ~**y** *a* (*person*) puntiglioso(a), esigente; che fa le storie; (*dress*) carico(a) di fronzoli; (*style*) elaborato(a).

futile ['fjuːtaɪl] *a* futile.

futility [fjuː'tɪlɪtɪ] *n* futilità.

future ['fjuːtʃə*] *a* futuro(a) // *n* futuro, avvenire *m*; (*LING*) futuro; **in** ~ in futuro; **futuristic** [-'rɪstɪk] *a* futuristico(a).

fuzzy ['fʌzɪ] *a* (*PHOT*) indistinto(a), sfocato(a); (*hair*) crespo(a).

G

g. *abbr of* **gram(s)**.

G [dʒiː] *n* (*MUS*) sol *m*.

gabble ['gæbl] *vi* borbottare; farfugliare.

gable ['geɪbl] *n* timpano.

gadget ['gædʒɪt] *n* aggeggio.

gag [gæg] *n* bavaglio; (*joke*) facezia, scherzo // *vt* imbavagliare.

gaiety ['geɪɪtɪ] *n* gaiezza.

gaily ['geɪlɪ] *ad* allegramente.

gain [geɪn] *n* guadagno, profitto // *vt* guadagnare // *vi* (*watch*) andare avanti; **to** ~ **in/by** aumentare di/con; **to** ~ **3lbs (in weight)** crescere di 3 libbre; ~**ful** *a* profittevole, lucrativo(a).

gainsay [geɪn'seɪ] *vt irg* (*like* **say**) contraddire; negare.

gait [geɪt] *n* andatura.

gal. *abbr of* **gallon**.

gala ['gɑːlə] *n* gala.

galaxy ['gæləksɪ] *n* galassia.

gale [geɪl] *n* vento forte; burrasca.

gallant ['gælənt] *a* valoroso(a); (*towards ladies*) galante, cortese.

gall-bladder ['gɔːlblædə*] *n* cistifellea.

gallery ['gælərɪ] *n* galleria.

galley ['gælɪ] *n* (*ship's kitchen*) cambusa; (*ship*) galea.

gallon ['gælən] *n* gallone *m* (= 4.543 *l*; 8 *pints*).

gallop ['gæləp] *n* galoppo // *vi* galoppare.

gallows ['gæləuz] *n* forca.

gallstone ['gɔːlstəun] *n* calcolo biliare.

gambit ['gæmbɪt] *n* (*fig*): (**opening**) ~ prima mossa.

gamble ['gæmbl] *n* azzardo, rischio calcolato // *vi*, *vt* giocare; **to** ~ **on** (*fig*) giocare su; ~**r** *n* giocatore/trice d'azzardo; **gambling** *n* gioco d'azzardo.

game [geɪm] *n* gioco; (*event*) partita; (*HUNTING*) selvaggina // *a* coraggioso(a); (*ready*): **to be** ~ (**for sth/to do**) essere pronto(a) (a qc/a fare); **big** ~ *n* selvaggina grossa; ~**keeper** *n* guardacaccia *m inv*.

gammon ['gæmən] *n* (*bacon*) prosciutto praga; (*ham*) prosciutto affumicato.

gang [gæŋ] *n* banda, squadra // *vi*: **to** ~ **up on sb** far combutta contro qd.

gangrene ['gæŋgriːn] *n* cancrena.

gangster ['gæŋstə*] *n* gangster *m inv*.

gangway ['gæŋweɪ] *n* passerella; (*of bus*) passaggio.

gaol [dʒeɪl] *n*, *vt* = **jail**.

gap [gæp] *n* buco; (*in time*) intervallo; (*fig*) lacuna; vuoto.

gape [geɪp] *vi* restare a bocca aperta; **gaping** *a* (*hole*) squarciato(a).

garage ['gærɑːʒ] *n* garage *m inv*.

garbage ['gɑːbɪdʒ] *n* immondizie *fpl*, rifiuti *mpl*; ~ **can** *n* (*US*) bidone *m* della spazzatura.

garbled ['gɑːbld] *a* deformato(a); ingarbugliato(a).

garden ['gɑːdn] *n* giardino // *vi* lavorare nel giardino; ~**er** *n* giardiniere/a; ~**ing** *n* giardinaggio.

gargle ['gɑːgl] *vi* fare gargarismi // *n* gargarismo.

gargoyle ['gɑːgɔɪl] *n* gargouille *f inv*.

garish ['gɛərɪʃ] *a* vistoso(a).

garland ['gɑːlənd] *n* ghirlanda; corona.

garlic ['gɑːlɪk] *n* aglio.

garment ['gɑːmənt] *n* indumento.

garnish ['gɑːnɪʃ] *vt* guarnire.

garret ['gærɪt] *n* soffitta.

garrison ['gærɪsn] *n* guarnigione *f* // *vt* guarnire.

garrulous ['gærjuləs] *a* ciarliero(a), loquace.

garter ['gɑːtə*] *n* giarrettiera.

gas [gæs] *n* gas *m inv*; (*US: gasoline*) benzina // *vt* asfissiare con il gas; (*MIL*) gasare; ~ **cooker** *n* cucina a gas; ~ **fire** *n* radiatore *m* a gas.

gash [gæʃ] *n* sfregio // *vt* sfregiare.

gasket ['gæskɪt] *n* (*AUT*) guarnizione *f*.

gasmask ['gæsmɑːsk] n maschera f antigas inv.

gas meter ['gæsmiːtə*] n contatore m del gas.

gasoline ['gæsəliːn] n (US) benzina.

gasp [gɑːsp] vi ansare, boccheggiare; (fig) tirare il fiato.

gas ring ['gæsrɪŋ] n fornello a gas.

gas stove ['gæsstəuv] n cucina a gas.

gassy ['gæsɪ] a gassoso(a).

gastric ['gæstrɪk] a gastrico(a).

gastronomy [gæs'trɔnəmɪ] n gastronomia.

gate [geɪt] n cancello; ~**crash** vt partecipare senza invito a; ~**way** n porta.

gather ['gæðə*] vt (flowers, fruit) cogliere; (pick up) raccogliere; (assemble) radunare; raccogliere; (understand) capire // vi (assemble) radunarsi; to ~ **speed** acquistare velocità; ~**ing** n adunanza.

gauche [gəuʃ] a goffo(a), maldestro(a).

gaudy ['gɔːdɪ] a vistoso(a).

gauge [geɪdʒ] n (standard measure) calibro; (RAIL) scartamento; (instrument) indicatore m // vt misurare.

gaunt [gɔːnt] a scarno(a); (grim, desolate) desolato(a).

gauntlet ['gɔːntlɪt] n (fig): to run the ~ **through an angry crowd** passare sotto il fuoco di una folla ostile.

gauze [gɔːz] n garza.

gave [geɪv] pt of give.

gawp [gɔːp] vi: to ~ at guardare a bocca aperta.

gay [geɪ] a (person) gaio(a), allegro(a); (colour) vivace, vivo(a); (col) omosessuale.

gaze [geɪz] n sguardo fisso; to ~ at vt fus guardare fisso.

gazelle [gə'zɛl] n gazzella.

gazumping [gə'zʌmpɪŋ] n il fatto di non mantenere una promessa di vendita per accettare un prezzo più alto.

G.B. abbr see great.

G.C.E. n (abbr of General Certificate of Education) ≈ maturità.

gear [gɪə*] n attrezzi mpl, equipaggiamento; roba; (TECH) ingranaggio; (AUT) marcia; in top/low/bottom ~ in quarta (or quinta)/seconda/prima; in ~ in marcia; out of ~ in folle; ~ box n scatola del cambio; ~ **lever**, ~ **shift** (US) n leva del cambio.

geese [giːs] npl of goose.

gelatin(e) ['dʒɛlətiːn] n gelatina.

gelignite ['dʒɛlɪgnaɪt] n nitroglicerina.

gem [dʒɛm] n gemma.

Gemini ['dʒɛmɪnaɪ] n Gemelli mpl.

gender ['dʒɛndə*] n genere m.

general ['dʒɛnərl] n generale m // a generale; in ~ in genere; ~ **election** n elezioni fpl generali; ~**ization** [-'zeɪʃən] n generalizzazione f; ~**ize** vi generalizzare; ~**ly** ad generalmente; ~ **practitioner** (G.P.) n medico generico.

generate ['dʒɛnəreɪt] vt generare.

generation [dʒɛnə'reɪʃən] n generazione f.

generator ['dʒɛnəreɪtə*] n generatore m.

generosity [dʒɛnə'rɔsɪtɪ] n generosità.

generous ['dʒɛnərəs] a generoso(a); (copious) abbondante.

genetics [dʒɪ'nɛtɪks] n genetica.

Geneva [dʒɪ'niːvə] n Ginevra.

genial ['dʒiːnɪəl] a geniale, cordiale.

genitals ['dʒɛnɪtlz] npl genitali mpl.

genitive ['dʒɛnɪtɪv] n genitivo.

genius ['dʒiːnɪəs] n genio.

gent [dʒɛnt] n abbr of **gentleman**.

genteel [dʒɛn'tiːl] a raffinato(a), distinto(a).

gentle ['dʒɛntl] a delicato(a); (persona) dolce.

gentleman ['dʒɛntlmən] n signore m; (well-bred man) gentiluomo.

gentleness ['dʒɛntlnɪs] n delicatezza; dolcezza.

gently ['dʒɛntlɪ] ad delicatamente.

gentry ['dʒɛntrɪ] n nobiltà minore.

gents [dʒɛnts] n W.C. m (per signori).

genuine ['dʒɛnjuɪn] a autentico(a); sincero(a).

geographic(al) [dʒɪə'græfɪk(l)] a geografico(a).

geography [dʒɪ'ɔgrəfɪ] n geografia.

geological [dʒɪə'lɔdʒɪkl] a geologico(a).

geologist [dʒɪ'ɔlədʒɪst] n geologo/a.

geology [dʒɪ'ɔlədʒɪ] n geologia.

geometric(al) [dʒɪə'mɛtrɪk(l)] a geometrico(a).

geometry [dʒɪ'ɔmətrɪ] n geometria.

geranium [dʒɪ'reɪnjəm] n geranio.

germ [dʒəːm] n (MED) microbo; (BIOL, fig) germe m.

German ['dʒəːmən] a tedesco(a) // n tedesco/a; (LING) tedesco; ~ **measles** n rosolia.

Germany ['dʒəːmənɪ] n Germania.

germination [dʒəːmɪ'neɪʃən] n germinazione f.

gestation [dʒɛs'teɪʃən] n gestazione f.

gesticulate [dʒɛs'tɪkjuleɪt] vi gesticolare.

gesture ['dʒɛstjə*] n gesto.

get, pt, pp **got**, pp **gotten** (US) [gɛt, gɔt, 'gɔtn] vt (obtain) avere, ottenere; (receive) ricevere; (find) trovare; (buy) comprare; (catch) chiappare; (fetch) andare a prendere; (understand) comprendere, capire; (have): to **have got** avere; (become) to ~ **rich/old** arricchirsi/invecchiarsi // vi: to ~ **to** (place) andare a; arrivare a; pervenire a; **he got across the bridge/under the fence** lui ha attraversato il ponte/è passato sotto il recinto; to ~ **ready/washed/shaved** etc prepararsi/lavarsi/farsi la barba etc; to ~ **sb to do sth** far fare qc a qd; to ~ **sth through/out of** far passare qc per/uscire qc da; to ~ **about/in** muoversi; (news) diffondersi; to ~ **along** vi (agree) andare d'accordo; (depart) andarsene; (manage) = to **get by**; to ~ **at** vt fus (attack) prendersela con; (reach) raggiungere, arrivare a; to ~ **away** vi partire, andarsene; (*escape*) scappare; **to ~ away with** *vt fus* cavarsela; farla franca; **to ~ back** *vi* (*return*) ritornare, tornare // *vt* riottenere, riavere; **to ~ by** *vi* (*pass*) passare; (*manage*) farcela; **to ~ down** *vi*, *vt fus* scendere // *vt* far scendere; (*depress*) buttare giù; **to ~ down to** *vt fus* (*work*) mettersi a ~ (fare); **to ~ in** *vi* entrare; (*train*) arrivare; (*arrive home*) ritornare, tornare; **to ~ into** *vt fus* entrare in; (*into a rage*) incavolarsi; **to ~ off** *vi* (*from train etc*) scendere; (*depart: person, car*) andare via; (*escape*) cavarsela // *vt* (*remove: clothes, stain*) levare // *vt fus* (*train, bus*) scendere da; **to ~ on** *vi* (*at exam etc*) andare; (*agree*): **to ~ on (with)** andare d'accordo (con) // *vt fus* montare in; (*horse*) montare su; **to ~ out** *vi* uscire; (*of vehicle*) scendere // *vt* tirar fuori, far uscire; **to ~ out of** *vt fus* uscire da; (*duty etc*) evitare; **to ~ over** *vt fus* (*illness*) riaversi da; **to ~ round** *vt fus* aggirare; (*fig: person*) rigirare; **to ~ through** *vi* (*TEL*) avere la linea; **to ~ through to** *vt fus* (*TEL*) parlare a; **to ~ together** *vi* riunirsi // *vt* raccogliere; (*people*) adunare; **to ~ up** *vi* (*rise*) alzarsi // *vt fus* far alzare; **to ~ up to** *vt fus* (*reach*) raggiungere; (*prank etc*) fare; **~ away** *n* fuga.

geyser ['giːzə*] *n* scaldabagno; (*GEO*) geyser *m inv*.

Ghana ['gɑːnə] *n* Ghana *m*; **~ian** [-'neɪən] *a*, *n* ganaense (*m/f*).

ghastly ['gɑːstlɪ] *a* orribile, orrendo(a).

gherkin ['gɜːkɪn] *n* cetriolino.

ghetto ['gɛtəʊ] *n* ghetto.

ghost [gəʊst] *n* fantasma *m*, spettro; **~ly** *a* spettrale.

giant ['dʒaɪənt] *n* gigante/essa // *a* gigante, enorme.

gibberish ['dʒɪbərɪʃ] *n* farfuglìare *m*.

gibe [dʒaɪb] *n* frecciata.

giblets ['dʒɪblɪts] *npl* frattaglie *fpl*.

giddiness ['gɪdɪnɪs] *n* vertigine *f*.

giddy ['gɪdɪ] *a* (*dizzy*): **to be ~** aver le vertigini; (*height*) vertiginoso(a).

gift [gɪft] *n* regalo; (*donation, ability*) dono; **~ed** *a* dotato(a).

gigantic [dʒaɪ'gæntɪk] *a* gigantesco(a).

giggle ['gɪgl] *vi* ridere scioccamente.

gild [gɪld] *vt* dorare.

gill [dʒɪl] *n* (*measure*) = 0.14 *l*; 0.25 *pints*; **~s** [gɪlz] *npl* (*of fish*) branchie *fpl*.

gilt [gɪlt] *n* doratura // *a* dorato(a).

gimlet ['gɪmlɪt] *n* succhiello.

gimmick ['gɪmɪk] *n* trucco.

gin [dʒɪn] *n* (*liquor*) gin *m*.

ginger ['dʒɪndʒə*] *n* zenzero; **~ ale, ~ beer** *n* bibita gassosa allo zenzero; **~bread** *n* pan *m* di zenzero; **~-haired** *a* rossiccio(a).

gingerly ['dʒɪndʒəlɪ] *ad* cautamente.

gingham ['gɪŋəm] *n* percalle *m* a righe *or* quadretti.

gipsy ['dʒɪpsɪ] *n* zingaro/a.

giraffe [dʒɪ'rɑːf] *n* giraffa.

girder ['gɜːdə*] *n* trave *f*.

girdle ['gɜːdl] *n* (*corset*) guaina.

girl [gɜːl] *n* ragazza; (*young unmarried woman*) signorina; (*daughter*) figlia, figliola; **~friend** *n* (*of girl*) amica; (*of boy*) ragazza; **~ish** *a* da ragazza.

girth [gɜːθ] *n* circonferenza; (*of horse*) cinghia.

gist [dʒɪst] *n* succo.

give [gɪv] *n* (*of fabric*) elasticità // *vb* (*pt* **gave**, *pp* **given** [geɪv, 'gɪvn]) *vt* dare // *vi* cedere; **to ~ sb sth, ~ sth to sb** dare qc a qd; **to ~ a cry/sigh** emettere un grido/sospiro; **to ~ away** *vt* dare via; (*give free*) fare dono di; (*betray*) tradire; (*disclose*) rivelare; (*bride*) condurre all'altare; **to ~ back** *vt* rendere; **to ~ in** *vi* cedere // *vt* consegnare; **to ~ off** *vt* emettere; **to ~ out** *vt* distribuire; annunciare; **to ~ up** *vi* rinunciare // *vt* rinunciare a; **to ~ up smoking** smettere di fumare; **to ~ o.s. up** rendersi; **to ~ way** *vi* cedere; (*AUT*) dare la precedenza.

glacier ['glæsɪə*] *n* ghiacciaio.

glad [glæd] *a* lieto(a), contento(a); **~den** *vt* rallegrare, allietare.

gladly ['glædlɪ] *ad* volentieri.

glamorous ['glæmərəs] *a* attraente, seducente.

glamour ['glæmə*] *n* attrattiva.

glance [glɑːns] *n* occhiata, sguardo // *vi*: **to ~ at** dare un'occhiata a; **to ~ off** (*bullet*) rimbalzare su; **glancing** *a* (*blow*) che colpisce di striscio.

gland [glænd] *n* ghiandola.

glare [glɛə*] *n* riverbero, luce *f* abbagliante; (*look*) sguardo furioso // *vi* abbagliare; **to ~ at** guardare male; **glaring** *a* (*mistake*) madornale.

glass [glɑːs] *n* (*substance*) vetro; (*tumbler*) bicchiere *m*; (*also*: **looking ~**) specchio; **~es** *npl* occhiali *mpl*; **~house** *n* serra; **~ware** *n* vetrame *m*; **~y** *a* (*eyes*) vitreo(a).

glaze [gleɪz] *vt* (*door*) fornire di vetri; (*pottery*) smaltare // *n* vetrina; **~d** *a* (*eye*) vitreo(a); (*tiles, pottery*) smaltato(a).

glazier ['gleɪzɪə*] *n* vetraio.

gleam [gliːm] *n* barlume *m*; raggio // *vi* luccicare; **~ing** *a* lucente.

glee [gliː] *n* allegrezza, gioia; **~ful** *a* allegro(a), gioioso(a).

glen [glɛn] *n* valletta.

glib [glɪb] *a* dalla parola facile; facile.

glide [glaɪd] *vi* scivolare; (*AVIAT, birds*) planare // *n* scivolata; planata; **~r** *n* (*AVIAT*) aliante *m*; **gliding** *n* (*AVIAT*) volo a vela.

glimmer ['glɪmə*] *vi* luccicare // *n* barlume *m*.

glimpse [glɪmps] *n* impressione *f* fugace // *vt* vedere al volo.

glint [glɪnt] *n* luccichio // *vi* luccicare.

glisten ['glɪsn] *vi* luccicare.

glitter ['glɪtə*] *vi* scintillare // *n* scintillio.

gloat [gləʊt] *vi*: **to ~ (over)** gongolare di piacere (per).

global ['gləʊbl] *a* globale.

globe [gləʊb] *n* globo, sfera.

gloom [glu:m] *n* oscurità, buio; (*sadness*) tristezza, malinconia; **~y** *a* fosco(a), triste.

glorify ['glɔ:rɪfaɪ] *vt* glorificare.

glorious ['glɔ:rɪəs] *a* glorioso(a); magnifico(a).

glory ['glɔ:rɪ] *n* gloria; splendore *m* // *vi*: **to ~ in** gloriarsi di *or* in.

gloss [glɔs] *n* (*shine*) lucentezza; **to ~ over** *vt fus* scivolare su.

glossary ['glɔsərɪ] *n* glossario.

glossy ['glɔsɪ] *a* lucente; **~ (magazine)** *n* rivista di lusso.

glove [glʌv] *n* guanto.

glow [gləu] *vi* ardere; (*face*) essere luminoso(a) // *n* bagliore *m*; (*of face*) rossore *m*.

glower ['glauə*] *vi*: **to ~ (at sb)** guardare (qd) in cagnesco.

glucose ['glu:kəus] *n* glucosio.

glue [glu:] *n* colla // *vt* incollare.

glum [glʌm] *a* abbattuto(a).

glut [glʌt] *n* eccesso // *vt* saziare; (*market*) saturare.

glutton ['glʌtn] *n* ghiottone/a; **a ~ for work** un(a) patito(a) del lavoro; **~ous** *a* ghiotto(a), goloso(a); **~y** *n* ghiottoneria; (*sin*) gola.

glycerin(e) ['glɪsəri:n] *n* glicerina.

gm, gms *abbr of* **gram(s)**.

gnarled [nɑ:ld] *a* nodoso(a).

gnat [næt] *n* moscerino.

gnaw [nɔ:] *vt* rodere.

gnome [nəum] *n* gnomo.

go [gəu] *vb* (*pt* **went**, *pp* **gone** [wɛnt, gɔn]) *vi* andare; (*depart*) partire, andarsene; (*work*) funzionare; (*be sold*): **to ~ for £10** essere venduto per 10 sterline; (*fit, suit*): **to ~ with** andare bene con; (*become*): **to ~ pale** diventare pallido(a); **to ~ mouldy** ammuffire; (*break etc*) cedere // *n* (*pl*: **~es**): **to have a ~ (at)** provare; **to be on the ~** essere in moto; **whose ~ is it?** a chi tocca?; **he's going to do sta per fare; to ~ for a walk** andare a fare una passeggiata; **to ~ dancing/shopping** andare a ballare/fare la spesa; **how did it ~?** com'è andato?; **to ~ about** *vi* (*rumour*) correre, circolare // *vt fus*: **how do I ~ about this?** qual'è la prassi per questo?; **to ~ ahead** *vi* andare avanti; **~ ahead!** faccia pure!; **to ~ along** *vi* andare, avanzare // *vt fus* percorrere; **to ~ away** *vi* partire, andarsene; **to ~ back** *vi* tornare, ritornare; **to ~ back on** *vt fus* (*go again*) andare di nuovo; **to ~ back on** *vt fus* (*promise*) non mantenere; **to ~ by** *vi* (*years, time*) scorrere // *vt fus* attenersi a, seguire (alla lettera); prestar fede a; **to ~ down** *vi* scendere; (*ship*) affondare; (*sun*) tramontare // *vt fus* scendere; **to ~ for** *vt fus* (*fetch*) andare a prendere; (*like*) andar matto(a) per; (*attack*) attaccare; saltare addosso a; **to ~ in** *vi* entrare; **to ~ in for** *vt fus* (*competition*) iscriversi a; (*like*) interessarsi di; **to ~ into** *vt fus* entrare in; (*investigate*) indagare, esaminare; (*embark on*) lanciarsi in; **to ~ off** *vi* partire, andar

via; (*food*) guastarsi; (*explode*) esplodere, scoppiare; (*event*) passare // *vt fus*: **I've gone off chocolate** la cioccolata non mi piace più; **the gun went off** il fucile si scaricò; **to ~ on** *vi* continuare; (*happen*) succedere; **to ~ on doing** continuare a fare; **to ~ on with** *vt fus* continuare, proseguire; **to ~ out** *vi* uscire; (*fire, light*) spegnersi; **to ~ over** *vi* (*ship*) ribaltarsi // *vt fus* (*town etc*) attraversare; **to ~ up** *vi*, *vt fus* salire; **to ~ without** *vt fus* fare a meno di.

goad [gəud] *vt* spronare.

go-ahead ['gəuəhɛd] *a* intraprendente // *n* via *m*.

goal [gəul] *n* (*SPORT*) gol *m*, rete *f*; (: *place*) porta; (*fig: aim*) fine *m*, scopo; **~keeper** *n* portiere *m*; **~-post** *n* palo (della porta).

goat [gəut] *n* capra.

gobble ['gɔbl] *vt* (*also*: **~ down**, **~ up**) ingoiare.

go-between ['gəubɪtwi:n] *n* intermediario/a.

goblet ['gɔblɪt] *n* calice *m*, coppa.

goblin ['gɔblɪn] *n* folletto.

god [gɔd] *n* dio; **G~** *n* Dio; **~child** *n* figlioccio/a; **~dess** *n* dea; **~father** *n* padrino; **~forsaken** *a* desolato(a), sperduto(a); **~mother** *n* madrina; **~send** *n* dono del cielo; **~son** *n* figlioccio.

goggles ['gɔglz] *npl* occhiali *mpl* (di protezione).

going ['gəuɪŋ] *n* (*conditions*) andare *m*, stato del terreno // *a*: **the ~ rate** la tariffa in vigore; **a ~ concern** un'azienda avviata.

gold [gəuld] *n* oro // *a* d'oro; **~en** *a* (*made of gold*) d'oro; (*gold in colour*) dorato(a); **~en rule** regola prima; **~en age** età d'oro; **~fish** *n* pesce *m* dorato *or* rosso; **~mine** *n* miniera d'oro.

golf [gɔlf] *n* golf *m*; **~ club** *n* circolo di golf; (*stick*) bastone *m* *or* mazza da golf; **~ course** *n* campo di golf; **~er** *n* giocatore/trice di golf.

gondola ['gɔndələ] *n* gondola.

gone [gɔn] *pp of* **go** // *a* partito(a).

gong [gɔŋ] *n* gong *m inv*.

good [gud] *a* buono(a); (*kind*) buono(a), gentile; (*child*) bravo(a) // *n* bene *m*; **~s** *npl* beni *mpl*; merci *fpl*; **she is ~ with children/her hands** lei sa fare coi bambini/è abile nei lavori manuali; **would you be ~ enough to ...?** avrebbe la gentilezza di ...?; **a ~ deal (of)** molto(a), una buona quantità (di); **a ~ many** molti(e); **~ morning!** buon giorno!; **~ afternoon/evening!** buona sera!; **~ night!** buona notte!; **~bye!** arrivederci!; **G~ Friday** *n* Venerdì Santo; **~-looking** *a* bello(a); **~ness** *n* (*of person*) bontà; **for ~ness sake!** per amor di Dio!; **~-will** *n* amicizia, benevolenza; (*COMM*) avviamento.

goose, *pl* **geese** [gu:s, gi:s] *n* oca.

gooseberry ['guzbərɪ] *n* uva spina.

gooseflesh ['gu:sfleʃ] *n* pelle *f* d'oca.
gore [gɔ:*] *vt* incornare // *n* sangue *m* (coagulato).
gorge [gɔ:dʒ] *n* gola // *vt*: **to ~ o.s. (on)** ingozzarsi (di).
gorgeous ['gɔ:dʒəs] *a* magnifico(a).
gorilla [gə'rɪlə] *n* gorilla *m inv*.
gorse [gɔ:s] *n* ginestrone *m*.
gory ['gɔ:rɪ] *a* sanguinoso(a).
go-slow ['gəu'sləu] *n* rallentamento dei lavori (*per agitazione sindacale*).
gospel ['gɔspl] *n* vangelo.
gossamer ['gɔsəmə*] *n* (*cobweb*) fili *mpl* della Madonna *or* di ragnatela; (*light fabric*) stoffa sottilissima.
gossip ['gɔsɪp] *n* chiacchiere *fpl*; pettegolezzi *mpl*; (*person*) pettegolo/a // *vi* chiacchierare; (*maliciously*) pettegolare.
got [gɔt] *pt,pp of* **get**; **~ten** (*US*) *pp of* **get**.
gout [gaut] *n* gotta.
govern ['gʌvən] *vt* governare; (*LING*) reggere.
governess ['gʌvənɪs] *n* governante *f*.
government ['gʌvnmənt] *n* governo; (*ministers*) ministero // *cpd* statale; **~al** [-'mentl] *a* governativo(a).
governor ['gʌvənə*] *n* (*of state, bank*) governatore *m*; (*of school, hospital*) amministratore *m*.
Govt *abbr of* **government**.
gown [gaun] *n* vestito lungo; (*of teacher, judge*) toga.
G.P. *n abbr see* **general**.
grab [græb] *vt* afferrare, arraffare; (*property, power*) impadronirsi di.
grace [greɪs] *n* grazia // *vt* onorare; **5 days' ~** dilazione *f* di 5 giorni; **to say ~** dire il benedicite; **~ful** *a* elegante, aggraziato(a); **gracious** ['greɪʃəs] *a* grazioso(a); misericordioso(a).
gradation [grə'deɪʃən] *n* gradazione *f*.
grade [greɪd] *n* (*COMM*) qualità *f inv*; classe *f*; categoria; (*in hierarchy*) grado; (*US: SCOL*) voto; classe *f* // *vt* classificare; ordinare; graduare; **~ crossing** *n* (*US*) passaggio a livello.
gradient ['greɪdɪənt] *n* pendenza, inclinazione *f*.
gradual ['grædjuəl] *a* graduale; **~ly** *ad* man mano, a poco a poco.
graduate *n* ['grædjuɪt] laureato/a // *vi* ['grædjueɪt] laurearsi; **graduation** [-'eɪʃən] *n* cerimonia del conferimento della laurea.
graft [grɑ:ft] *n* (*AGR, MED*) innesto // *vt* innestare; **hard ~** *n* (*col*): **by sheer hard ~** lavorando da matti.
grain [greɪn] *n* grano; (*of sand*) granello; (*of wood*) venatura; **it goes against the ~** va contro la propria natura.
gram [græm] *n* grammo.
grammar ['græmə*] *n* grammatica.
grammatical [grə'mætɪkl] *a* grammaticale.
gramme [græm] *n* = **gram**.

gramophone ['græməfəun] *n* grammofono.
granary ['grænərɪ] *n* granaio.
grand [grænd] *a* grande, magnifico(a); grandioso(a); **~children** *npl* nipoti *mpl*; **~dad** *n* nonno; **~daughter** *n* nipote *f*; **~father** *n* nonno; **~iose** ['grændɪəuz] *a* grandioso(a); (*pej*) pomposo(a); **~ma** *n* nonna; **~mother** *n* nonna; **~pa** *n* = **~dad**; **~ piano** *n* pianoforte *m* a coda; **~son** *n* nipote *m*; **~stand** *n* (*SPORT*) tribuna.
granite ['grænɪt] *n* granito.
granny ['grænɪ] *n* nonna.
grant [grɑ:nt] *vt* accordare; (*a request*) accogliere; (*admit*) ammettere, concedere // *n* (*SCOL*) borsa; (*ADMIN*) sussidio, sovvenzione *f*; **to take sth for ~ed** dare qc per scontato.
granulated ['grænjuleɪtɪd] *a*: **~ sugar** *n* zucchero cristallizzato.
granule ['grænju:l] *n* granello.
grape [greɪp] *n* chicco d'uva, acino.
grapefruit ['greɪpfru:t] *n* pompelmo.
graph [grɑ:f] *n* grafico; **~ic** *a* grafico(a); (*vivid*) vivido(a).
grapple ['græpl] *vi*: **to ~ with** essere alle prese con.
grasp [grɑ:sp] *vt* afferrare // *n* (*grip*) presa; (*fig*) potere *m*; comprensione *f*; **~ing** *a* avido(a).
grass [grɑ:s] *n* erba; **~hopper** *n* cavalletta; **~land** *n* prateria; **~y** *a* erboso(a).
grate [greɪt] *n* graticola (del focolare) // *vi* cigolare, stridere // *vt* (*CULIN*) grattugiare.
grateful ['greɪtful] *a* grato(a), riconoscente; **~ly** *ad* con gratitudine.
grater ['greɪtə*] *n* grattugia.
gratify ['grætɪfaɪ] *vt* appagare; (*whim*) soddisfare; **~ing** *a* gradito(a); soddisfacente.
grating ['greɪtɪŋ] *n* (*iron bars*) grata // *a* (*noise*) stridente, stridulo(a).
gratitude ['grætɪtju:d] *n* gratitudine *f*.
gratuity [grə'tju:ɪtɪ] *n* mancia.
grave [greɪv] *n* tomba // *a* grave, serio(a).
gravel ['grævl] *n* ghiaia.
gravestone ['greɪvstəun] *n* pietra tombale.
graveyard ['greɪvjɑ:d] *n* cimitero.
gravitate ['grævɪteɪt] *vi* gravitare.
gravity ['grævɪtɪ] *n* (*PHYSICS*) gravità; pesantezza; (*seriousness*) gravità, serietà.
gravy ['greɪvɪ] *n* intingolo della carne; salsa.
gray [greɪ] *a* = **grey**.
graze [greɪz] *vi* pascolare, pascere // *vt* (*touch lightly*) sfiorare; (*scrape*) escoriare // *n* (*MED*) escoriazione *f*.
grease [gri:s] *n* (*fat*) grasso; (*lubricant*) lubrificante *m* // *vt* ingrassare; lubrificare; **~proof paper** *n* carta oleata; **greasy** *a* grasso(a), untuoso(a).
great [greɪt] *a* grande; (*col*) magnifico(a), meraviglioso(a); **G~ Britain** *n* Gran

Bretagna; **~-grandfather** n bisnonno; **~-grandmother** n bisnonna; **~ly** ad molto; **~ness** n grandezza.

Grecian ['griːʃən] a greco(a).

Greece [griːs] n Grecia.

greed [griːd] n (also: **~iness**) avarizia; (for food) golosità, ghiottoneria; **~ily** ad avidamente; golosamente; **~y** a avido(a); goloso(a), ghiotto(a).

Greek [griːk] a greco(a) // n greco/a; (LING) greco.

green [griːn] a verde; (inexperienced) inesperto(a), ingenuo(a) // n verde m; (stretch of grass) prato; (also: **village ~**) ≈ piazza del paese; **~s** npl verdura; **~grocer** n fruttivendolo/a, erbivendolo/a; **~house** n serra.

Greenland ['griːnlənd] n Groenlandia.

greet [griːt] vt salutare; **~ing** n saluto; Christmas/birthday **~ings** auguri mpl di Natale/di compleanno.

gregarious [grə'gɛərɪəs] a gregario(a); socievole.

grenade [grə'neɪd] n granata.

grew [gruː] pt of **grow**.

grey [greɪ] a grigio(a); **~-haired** a dai capelli grigi; **~hound** n levriere m.

grid [grɪd] n grata; (ELEC) rete f; **~iron** n graticola.

grief [griːf] n dolore m.

grievance ['griːvəns] n doglianza, lagnanza.

grieve [griːv] vi addolorarsi; rattristarsi // vt addolorare.

grill [grɪl] n (on cooker) griglia // vt cuocere ai ferri; (question) interrogare senza sosta.

grille [grɪl] n grata; (AUT) griglia.

grill(room) ['grɪl(rum)] n rosticceria.

grim [grɪm] a sinistro(a), brutto(a).

grimace [grɪ'meɪs] n smorfia // vi fare smorfie; fare boccacce.

grime [graɪm] n sudiciume m.

grimy ['graɪmɪ] a sudicio(a).

grin [grɪn] n sorriso smagliante // vi sorridere.

grind [graɪnd] vt (pt, pp ground [graund]) macinare; (make sharp) arrotare // n (work) sgobbata; **to ~ one's teeth** digrignare i denti.

grip [grɪp] n impugnatura; presa; (holdall) borsa da viaggio // vt impugnare; afferrare; **to come to ~s with** affrontare; cercare di risolvere.

gripe(s) [graɪp(s)] n(pl) colica.

gripping ['grɪpɪŋ] a avvincente.

grisly ['grɪzlɪ] a macabro(a), orrido(a).

gristle ['grɪsl] n cartilagine f.

grit [grɪt] n ghiaia; (courage) fegato // vt (road) coprire di sabbia; **to ~ one's teeth** stringere i denti.

groan [grəun] n gemito // vi gemere.

grocer ['grəusə*] n negoziante m di generi alimentari; **~ies** npl provviste fpl.

groggy ['grɔgɪ] a barcollante.

groin [grɔɪn] n inguine m.

groom [gruːm] n palafreniere m; (also:

bride~) sposo // vt (horse) strigliare; (fig): **to ~ sb for** avviare qd a.

groove [gruːv] n scanalatura, solco.

grope [grəup] vi andar tentoni; **to ~ for** vt fus cercare a tastoni.

gross [grəus] a grossolano(a); (COMM) lordo(a) // n, pl inv (twelve dozen) grossa; **~ly** ad (greatly) molto.

grotesque [grə'tɛsk] a grottesco(a).

grotto ['grɔtəu] n grotta.

ground [graund] pt, pp of **grind** // n suolo, terra; (land) terreno; (SPORT) campo; (reason: gen pl) ragione f // vt (plane) tenere a terra // vi (ship) arenarsi; **~s** npl (of coffee etc) fondi mpl; (gardens etc) terreno, giardini mpl; **on/to the ~** per/a terra; **~ floor** n pianterreno; **~ing** n (in education) basi fpl; **~sheet** n pavimento a catino per tenda; **~ staff** n personale m di terra; **~work** n preparazione f.

group [gruːp] n gruppo // vt raggruppare // vi raggrupparsi.

grouse [graus] n, pl inv (bird) tetraone m // vi (complain) brontolare.

grove [grəuv] n boschetto.

grovel ['grɔvl] vi (fig): **to ~ (before)** avvilirsi (ai piedi di).

grow, pt **grew,** pp **grown** [grəu, gruː, grəun] vi crescere; (increase) aumentare; (become): **to ~ rich/weak** arricchirsi/indebolirsi // vt coltivare, far crescere; **to ~ up** vi farsi grande, crescere; **~er** n coltivatore/trice; **~ing** a (fear, amount) crescente.

growl [graul] vi ringhiare.

grown [grəun] pp of **grow** // a adulto(a), maturo(a); **~-up** n adulto/a, grande m/f.

growth [grəuθ] n crescita, sviluppo; (what has grown) crescita; (MED) escrescenza, tumore m.

grub [grʌb] n larva; (col: food) roba (da mangiare).

grubby ['grʌbɪ] a sporco(a).

grudge [grʌdʒ] n rancore m // vt: **to ~ sb sth** dare qc a qd di malavoglia; invidiare qc a qd; **to bear sb a ~ (for)** serbar rancore a qd (per); **grudgingly** ad di malavoglia, di malincuore.

gruelling ['gruəlɪŋ] a strapazzoso(a).

gruesome ['gruːsəm] a orribile.

gruff [grʌf] a rozzo(a).

grumble ['grʌmbl] vi brontolare, lagnarsi.

grumpy ['grʌmpɪ] a stizzito(a).

grunt [grʌnt] vi grugnire // n grugnito.

guarantee [gærən'tiː] n garanzia // vt garantire.

guarantor [gærən'tɔː*] n garante m/f.

guard [gɑːd] n guardia, custodia; (squad, FENCING) guardia; (BOXING) difesa; (one man) guardia, sentinella; (RAIL) capotreno // vt fare la guardia a; **~ed** a (fig) cauto(a), guardingo(a); **~ian** n custode m; (of minor) tutore/trice; **~'s van** n (RAIL) vagone m di servizio.

guerrilla [gə'rɪlə] n guerrigliero; **~ warfare** n guerriglia.

guess [gɛs] vi indovinare // vt indovinare; (US) credere, pensare // n congettura; **to**

have a ~ cercare di indovinare.

guest [gɛst] *n* ospite *m/f*; (*in hotel*) cliente *m/f*; **~-house** *n* pensione *f*; **~ room** *n* camera degli ospiti.

guffaw [gʌ'fɔː] *n* risata sonora // *vi* scoppiare di una risata sonora.

guidance ['gaɪdəns] *n* guida, direzione *f*.

guide [gaɪd] *n* (*person, book etc*) guida // *vt* guidare; (**girl**) ~ *n* giovane esploratrice *f*; **~book** *n* guida; **~d missile** *n* missile *m* telecomandato; ~ **dog** *n* cane *m* guida *inv*; **~lines** *npl* (*fig*) indicazioni *fpl*, linee *fpl* direttive.

guild [gɪld] *n* arte *f*, corporazione *f*; associazione *f*; **~hall** *n* (*Brit*) palazzo municipale.

guile [gaɪl] *n* astuzia.

guillotine ['gɪlətiːn] *n* ghigliottina.

guilt [gɪlt] *n* colpevolezza; **~y** *a* colpevole.

guinea ['gɪnɪ] *n* (*Brit*) ghinea (= *21 shillings: valuta ora fuori uso*).

guinea pig ['gɪnɪpɪg] *n* cavia.

guise [gaɪz] *n* maschera.

guitar [gɪ'tɑː*] *n* chitarra; **~ist** *n* chitarrista *m/f*.

gulf [gʌlf] *n* golfo; (*abyss*) abisso.

gull [gʌl] *n* gabbiano.

gullet ['gʌlɪt] *n* gola.

gullible ['gʌlɪbl] *a* credulo(a).

gully ['gʌlɪ] *n* burrone *m*; gola; canale *m*.

gulp [gʌlp] *vi* deglutire; (*from emotion*) avere il nodo in gola // *vt* (*also*: ~ **down**) tracannare, inghiottire.

gum [gʌm] *n* (ANAT) gengiva; (*glue*) colla; (*sweet*) gelatina di frutta; (*also*: **chewing-~**) chewing-gum *m* // *vt* incollare; **~boots** *npl* stivali *mpl* di gomma.

gumption ['gʌmpʃən] *n* buon senso, senso pratico.

gun [gʌn] *n* fucile *m*; (*small*) pistola, rivoltella; (*rifle*) carabina; (*shotgun*) fucile da caccia; (*cannon*) cannone *m*; **~boat** *n* cannoniera; **~fire** *n* spari *mpl*; **~man** *n* bandito armato; **~ner** *n* artigliere *m*; **at ~point** sotto minaccia di fucile; **~powder** *n* polvere *f* da sparo; **~shot** *n* sparo; **within ~shot** a portata di fucile.

gurgle ['gəːgl] *n* gorgoglio // *vi* gorgogliare.

gush [gʌʃ] *n* fiotto, getto // *vi* sgorgare; (*fig*) abbandonarsi ad effusioni.

gusset ['gʌsɪt] *n* gherone *m*.

gust [gʌst] *n* (*of wind*) raffica; (*of smoke*) buffata.

gusto ['gʌstəu] *n* entusiasmo.

gut [gʌt] *n* intestino, budello; (MUS *etc*) minugia; **~s** *npl* (*courage*) fegato.

gutter ['gʌtə*] *n* (*of roof*) grondaia; (*in street*) cunetta.

guttural ['gʌtərl] *a* gutturale.

guy [gaɪ] *n* (*also*: ~ **rope**) cavo *or* corda di fissaggio; (*col: man*) tipo, elemento.

guzzle ['gʌzl] *vi* gozzovigliare // *vt* tranguggiare.

gym [dʒɪm] *n* (*also*: **gymnasium**) palestra; (*also*: **gymnastics**) ginnastica; ~ **slip** *n*

grembiule *m* da scuola (*per ragazze*).

gymnast ['dʒɪmnæst] *n* ginnasta *m/f*; **~ics** [-'næstɪks] *n*, *npl* ginnastica.

gynaecology [gaɪnə'kɔlədʒɪ] *n* ginecologia.

gypsy ['dʒɪpsɪ] *n* = **gipsy**.

gyrate [dʒaɪ'reɪt] *vi* girare.

H

haberdashery ['hæbə'dæʃərɪ] *n* merceria.

habit ['hæbɪt] *n* abitudine *f*; (*costume*) abito; (REL) tonaca.

habitation [hæbɪ'teɪʃən] *n* abitazione *f*.

habitual [hə'bɪtjuəl] *a* abituale; (*drinker, liar*) inveterato(a); **~ly** *ad* abitualmente, di solito.

hack [hæk] *vt* tagliare, fare a pezzi // *n* (*cut*) taglio; (*blow*) colpo; (*pej: writer*) negro.

hackney cab ['hæknɪ'kæb] *n* carrozza a nolo.

hackneyed ['hæknɪd] *a* comune, trito(a).

had [hæd] *pt, pp* of **have**.

haddock ['hædək] *n* eglefino.

haemorrhage ['hɛmərɪdʒ] *n* emorragia.

haemorrhoids ['hɛmərɔɪdz] *npl* emorroidi *fpl*.

haggard ['hægəd] *a* smunto(a).

haggle ['hægl] *vi* mercanteggiare.

Hague [heɪg] *n*: **The** ~ L'Aia.

hail [heɪl] *n* grandine *f* // *vt* (*call*) chiamare; (*greet*) salutare // *vi* grandinare; **~stone** *n* chicco di grandine.

hair [hɛə*] *n* capelli *mpl*; (*single hair: on head*) capello; (: *on body*) pelo; **to do one's ~** pettinarsi; **~brush** *n* spazzola per capelli; **~cut** *n* taglio di capelli; **I need a ~cut** ho bisogno di farmi i capelli; **~do** ['hɛəduː] *n* acconciatura, pettinatura; **~-dresser** *n* parrucchiere/a; **~-drier** *n* asciugacapelli *m inv*; **~net** *n* retina (per capelli); ~ **oil** *n* brillantina; **~piece** *n* toupet *m inv*; **~pin** *n* forcina; **~pin bend** *n* tornante *m*; **~raising** *a* orripilante; **~style** *n* pettinatura, acconciatura; **~y** *a* irsuto(a); peloso(a); (*fig*) spaventoso(a).

hake [heɪk] *n* nasello.

half [hɑːf] *n* (*pl*: **halves** [hɑːvz]) mezzo, metà *f inv* // *a* mezzo(a) // *ad* a mezzo, a metà; **~-an-hour** mezz'ora; **two and a ~** due e mezzo; **a week and a ~** una settimana e mezza; ~ (**of it**) la metà; ~ (**of**) la metà di; ~ **the amount of** la metà di; **to cut sth in ~** tagliare qc in due; **~-back** *n* (SPORT) mediano; **~-breed**, **~-caste** *n* meticcio/a; **~-hearted** *a* tiepido(a); **~-hour** *n* mezz'ora; **~-penny** ['heɪpnɪ] *n* mezzo penny *m inv*; (**at**) **~-price** a metà prezzo; **~-time** *n* intervallo; **~-way** *ad* a metà strada.

halibut ['hælɪbət] *n, pl inv* ippoglosso.

hall [hɔːl] *n* sala, salone *m*; (*entrance way*) entrata; (*corridor*) corridoio; (*mansion*) grande villa, maniero; ~ **of residence** *n* casa dello studente.

hallmark ['hɔːlmɑːk] *n* marchio di garanzia; (*fig*) caratteristica.

hallo [hə'ləu] *excl* = **hello**.
hallucination [həluːsɪ'neɪʃən] *n* allucinazione *f*.
halo ['heɪləu] *n* (*of saint etc*) aureola; (*of sun*) alone *m*.
halt [hɔːlt] *n* fermata // *vt* fermare // *vi* fermarsi.
halve [hɑːv] *vt* (*apple etc*) dividere a metà; (*expense*) ridurre di metà.
halves [hɑːvz] *npl of* **half**.
ham [hæm] *n* prosciutto.
hamburger ['hæmbəgə*] *n* hamburger *m inv*.
hamlet ['hæmlɪt] *n* paesetto.
hammer ['hæmə*] *n* martello // *vt* martellare; (*fig*) sconfiggere duramente.
hammock ['hæmək] *n* amaca.
hamper ['hæmpə*] *vt* impedire // *n* cesta.
hand [hænd] *n* mano *f*; (*of clock*) lancetta; (*handwriting*) scrittura; (*at cards*) carte *fpl*; (*: game*) partita; (*worker*) operaio/a // *vt* dare, passare; **to give sb a ~** dare una mano a qd; **at ~** a portata di mano; **in ~** a disposizione; (*work*) in corso; **on the one ~ ..., on the other ~** da un lato ..., dall'altro; **to ~ in** *vt* consegnare; **to ~ out** *vt* distribuire; **to ~ over** *vt* passare; cedere; **~bag** *n* borsetta; **~ball** *n* pallamano *f*; **~basin** *n* lavandino; **~book** *n* manuale *m*; **~brake** *n* freno a mano; **~cuffs** *npl* manette *fpl*; **~ful** *n* manata; pugno.
handicap ['hændɪkæp] *n* handicap *m inv* // *vt* andicappare.
handicraft ['hændɪkrɑːft] *n* lavoro d'artigiano.
handkerchief ['hæŋkətʃɪf] *n* fazzoletto.
handle ['hændl] *n* (*of door etc*) maniglia; (*of cup etc*) ansa; (*of knife etc*) impugnatura; (*of saucepan*) manico; (*for winding*) manovella // *vt* toccare, maneggiare; (*deal with*) occuparsi di; (*treat: people*) trattare; '~ **with care**' 'fragile'; **~bar(s)** *n(pl)* manubrio.
hand-luggage ['hændlʌgɪdʒ] *n* bagagli *mpl* a mano.
handmade ['hændmeɪd] *a* fatto(a) a mano.
handsome ['hænsəm] *a* bello(a); generoso(a); considerevole.
handwriting ['hændraɪtɪŋ] *n* scrittura.
handwritten ['hændrɪtn] *a* scritto(a) a mano, manoscritto(a).
handy ['hændɪ] *a* (*person*) destro(a); (*close at hand*) a portata di mano; (*convenient*) comodo(a); **tools for the ~man** arnesi per il fatelo-da-voi.
hang, *pt, pp* **hung** [hæŋ, hʌŋ] *vt* appendere; (*criminal: pt, pp* **hanged**) impiccare // *vi* pendere; (*hair*) scendere; (*drapery*) cadere; **to ~ about** *vi* bighellonare, ciondolare; **to ~ on** *vi* (*wait*) aspettare; **to ~ up** *vi* (*TEL*) riattaccare // *vt* appendere.
hangar ['hæŋə*] *n* hangar *m inv*.
hanger ['hæŋə*] *n* gruccia.
hanger-on [hæŋər'ɔn] *n* parassita *m*.

hang-gliding ['hæŋglaɪdɪŋ] *n* volo col deltaplano.
hangover ['hæŋəuvə*] *n* (*after drinking*) postumi *mpl* di sbornia.
hang-up ['hæŋʌp] *n* complesso.
hank [hæŋk] *n* matassa.
hanker ['hæŋkə*] *vi*: **to ~ after** bramare.
hankie, hanky ['hæŋkɪ] *n abbr of* **handkerchief**.
haphazard [hæp'hæzəd] *a* a casaccio, alla carlona.
happen ['hæpən] *vi* accadere, succedere; **I ~ed to be out** mi capitò di essere fuori; **as it ~s** guarda caso; **~ing** *n* avvenimento.
happily ['hæpɪlɪ] *ad* felicemente; fortunatamente.
happiness ['hæpɪnɪs] *n* felicità, contentezza.
happy ['hæpɪ] *a* felice, contento(a); **~ with** (*arrangements etc*) soddisfatto(a) di; **~-go-lucky** *a* spensierato(a).
harass ['hærəs] *vt* molestare; **~ment** *n* molestia.
harbour ['hɑːbə*] *n* porto // *vt* dare rifugio a; **~ master** *n* capitano di porto.
hard [hɑːd] *a* duro(a) // *ad* (*work*) sodo; (*think, try*) bene; **to drink ~** bere forte; **~ luck!** peccato!; **no ~ feelings!** senza rancore!; **to be ~ of hearing** essere duro(a) d'orecchio; **to be ~ done by** essere trattato(a) ingiustamente; **~back** *n* libro rilegato; **~board** *n* legno precompresso; **~-boiled egg** *n* uovo sodo; **~ cash** *n* denaro in contanti; **~en** *vt*, *vi* indurire; **~ labour** *n* lavori forzati *mpl*.
hardly ['hɑːdlɪ] *ad* (*scarcely*) appena; **it's ~ the case** non è proprio il caso; **~ anyone/ anywhere** quasi nessuno/da nessuna parte.
hardness ['hɑːdnɪs] *n* durezza.
hard sell ['hɑːd'sɛl] *n* (*COMM*) intensa campagna promozionale.
hardship ['hɑːdʃɪp] *n* avversità *f inv*; privazioni *fpl*.
hard-up [hɑːd'ʌp] *a* (*col*) al verde.
hardware ['hɑːdwɛə*] *n* ferramenta *fpl*; (*COMPUTERS*) hardware *m*; **~ shop** *n* (negozio di) ferramenta *fpl*.
hardy ['hɑːdɪ] *a* robusto(a); (*plant*) resistente al gelo.
hare [hɛə*] *n* lepre *f*; **~-brained** *a* folle; scervellato(a); **~lip** *n* (*MED*) labbro leporino.
harem [hɑː'riːm] *n* harem *m inv*.
harm [hɑːm] *n* male *m*; (*wrong*) danno // *vt* (*person*) fare male a; (*thing*) danneggiare; **to mean no ~** non avere l'intenzione di offendere; **out of ~'s way** al sicuro; **~ful** *a* dannoso(a); **~less** *a* innocuo(a); inoffensivo(a).
harmonica [hɑː'mɔnɪkə] *n* armonica.
harmonics [hɑː'mɔnɪks] *npl* armonia.
harmonious [hɑː'məunɪəs] *a* armonioso(a).
harmonium [hɑː'məunɪəm] *n* armonium *m inv*.

harmonize ['hɑːmənaɪz] *vt, vi* armonizzare.

harmony ['hɑːmənɪ] *n* armonia.

harness ['hɑːnɪs] *n* bardatura, finimenti *mpl* // *vt* (*horse*) bardare; (*resources*) sfruttare.

harp [hɑːp] *n* arpa // *vi*: to ~ on about insistere tediosamente su; ~ist *n* arpista *m/f*.

harpoon [hɑːˈpuːn] *n* arpione *m*.

harpsichord ['hɑːpsɪkɔːd] *n* clavicembalo.

harrow ['hærəu] *n* (*AGR*) erpice *m*.

harrowing ['hærəuɪŋ] *a* straziante.

harsh [hɑːʃ] *a* (*hard*) duro(a); (*severe*) severo(a); (*unpleasant: sound*) rauco(a); (: *colour*) chiassoso(a); violento(a); ~ly *ad* duramente; severamente; ~ness *n* durezza; severità.

harvest ['hɑːvɪst] *n* raccolto; (*of grapes*) vendemmia // *vt* fare il raccolto di, raccogliere; vendemmiare; ~er *n* (*machine*) mietitrice *f*.

has [hæz] *see* have.

hash [hæʃ] *n* (*CULIN*) specie di spezzatino fatto con carne già cotta; (*fig: mess*) pasticcio; *also abbr of* **hashish**.

hashish ['hæʃɪʃ] *n* hascisc *m*.

haste [heɪst] *n* fretta; precipitazione *f*; ~n ['heɪsn] *vt* affrettare // *vi* affrettarsi; **hastily** *ad* in fretta; precipitosamente; **hasty** *a* affrettato(a); precipitoso(a).

hat [hæt] *n* cappello; ~ box *n* cappelliera.

hatch [hætʃ] *n* (*NAUT: also*: ~way) boccaporto; (*also*: **service** ~) portello di servizio // *vi* schiudersi // *vt* covare.

hatchback ['hætʃbæk] *n* (*AUT*) tre (*or* cinque) porte *f inv*.

hatchet ['hætʃɪt] *n* accetta.

hate [heɪt] *vt* odiare, detestare // *n* odio; to ~ to do *or* doing detestare fare; ~ful *a* odioso(a), detestabile.

hatred ['heɪtrɪd] *n* odio.

hat trick ['hættrɪk] *n* (*SPORT, also fig*) tris *m inv* (3 *reti segnate durante una partita etc*).

haughty ['hɔːtɪ] *a* altero(a), arrogante.

haul [hɔːl] *vt* trascinare, tirare // *n* (*of fish*) pescata; (*of stolen goods etc*) bottino; ~age *n* trasporto; autotrasporto; ~ier *n* trasportatore *m*.

haunch [hɔːntʃ] *n* anca.

haunt [hɔːnt] *vt* (*subj: fear*) pervadere; (: *person*) frequentare // *n* rifugio; a ghost ~s this house questa casa è abitata da un fantasma.

have *pt,pp* had [hæv, hæd] *vt* avere; (*meal, shower*) fare; to ~ sth done far fare qc; he had a suit made si fece fare un abito; she has to do it lo deve fare; I had better leave è meglio che io vada; to ~ it out with sb metterlo in chiaro con qd; I won't ~ it questo non mi va affatto; he's been had (*col*) c'è cascato dentro.

haven ['heɪvn] *n* porto; (*fig*) rifugio.

haversack ['hævəsæk] *n* zaino.

havoc ['hævək] *n* caos *m*.

hawk [hɔːk] *n* falco.

hawker ['hɔːkə*] *n* venditore *m* ambulante.

hay [heɪ] *n* fieno; ~ fever *n* febbre *f* da fieno; ~stack *n* mucchio di fieno.

haywire ['heɪwaɪə*] *a* (*col*): to go ~ perdere la testa; impazzire.

hazard ['hæzəd] *n* azzardo, ventura; pericolo, rischio; ~ous *a* pericoloso(a), rischioso(a).

haze [heɪz] *n* foschia.

hazelnut ['heɪzlnʌt] *n* nocciola.

hazy ['heɪzɪ] *a* fosco(a); (*idea*) vago(a); (*photograph*) indistinto(a).

he [hiː] *pronoun* lui, egli; it is ~ who ... è lui che ...; here ~ is eccolo; ~-bear *n* orso maschio.

head [hɛd] *n* testa, capo; (*leader*) capo // *vt* (*list*) essere in testa a; (*group*) essere a capo di; ~s (*or* tails) testa (*o* croce), pari (*o* gaffo); to ~ the ball dare di testa alla palla; to ~ for *vt fus* dirigersi verso; ~ache *n* mal *m* di testa; ~ing *n* titolo; intestazione *f*; ~lamp *n* fanale *m*; ~land *n* promontorio; ~light = ~lamp; ~line *n* titolo; ~long *ad* (*fall*) a capofitto; (*rush*) precipitosamente; ~master *n* preside *m*; ~mistress *n* preside *f*; ~office *n* sede *f* (centrale); ~-on (*a collision*) frontale; ~quarters (HQ) *npl* ufficio centrale; (*MIL*) quartiere *m* generale; ~-rest *n* poggiacapo; ~room *n* (*in car*) altezza dell'abitacolo; (*under bridge*) altezza limite; ~scarf *n* foulard *m inv*; ~strong *a* testardo(a); ~waiter *n* capocameriere *m*; ~way *n* progresso, cammino; ~wind *n* controvento; ~y *a* che dà alla testa; inebriante.

heal [hiːl] *vt, vi* guarire.

health [hɛlθ] *n* salute *f*; the H~ Service ≈ il Servizio Sanitario Statale; ~y *a* (*person*) in buona salute; (*climate*) salubre; (*food*) salutare; (*attitude etc*) sano(a).

heap [hiːp] *n* mucchio // *vt* ammucchiare.

hear, *pt, pp* heard [hɪə*, hɜːd] *vt* sentire; (*news*) ascoltare; (*lecture*) assistere a // *vi* sentire; to ~ about avere notizie di; sentire parlare di; to ~ from sb ricevere notizie da qd; ~ing *n* (*sense*) udito; (*of witnesses*) audizione *f*; (*of a case*) udienza; ~ing aid *n* apparecchio acustico; by ~say *ad* per sentito dire.

hearse [hɜːs] *n* carro funebre.

heart [hɑːt] *n* cuore *m*; ~s *npl* (*CARDS*) cuori *mpl*; at ~ in fondo; by ~ (*learn, know*) a memoria; to lose ~ perdere coraggio, scoraggiarsi; ~ attack *n* attacco di cuore; ~beat *n* battito del cuore; ~breaking *a* straziante; to be ~broken avere il cuore spezzato; ~burn *n* bruciore *m* di stomaco; ~felt *a* sincero(a).

hearth [hɑːθ] *n* focolare *m*.

heartily ['hɑːtɪlɪ] *ad* (*laugh*) di cuore; (*eat*) di buon appetito.

heartless ['hɑːtlɪs] *a* senza cuore, insensibile; crudele.

heartwarming ['hɑːtwɔːmɪŋ] *a* confortante, che scalda il cuore.

hearty ['hɑ:tɪ] a caloroso(a); robusto(a), sano(a); vigoroso(a).

heat [hi:t] n calore m; (fig) ardore m; fuoco; (SPORT: also: **qualifying ~**) prova eliminatoria // vt scaldare; **to ~ up** vi (liquids) scaldarsi; (room) riscaldarsi // vt riscaldare; **~ed** a riscaldato(a); (fig) appassionato(a); acceso(a), eccitato(a); **~er** n stufa; radiatore m.

heath [hi:θ] n (Brit) landa.

heathen ['hi:ðn] a, n pagano(a).

heather ['hɛðə*] n erica.

heating ['hi:tɪŋ] n riscaldamento.

heatstroke ['hi:tstrəuk] n colpo di sole.

heatwave ['hi:tweɪv] n ondata di caldo.

heave [hi:v] vt sollevare (con sforzo) // vi sollevarsi // n conato di vomito; (push) grande spinta.

heaven ['hɛvn] n paradiso, cielo; **~ forbid!** Dio ce ne guardi!; **~ly** a divino(a), celeste.

heavily ['hɛvɪlɪ] ad pesantemente; (drink, smoke) molto.

heavy ['hɛvɪ] a pesante; (sea) grosso(a); (rain) forte; (drinker, smoker) gran (before noun); **it's ~ going** è una gran fatica; **~weight** n (SPORT) peso massimo.

Hebrew ['hi:bru:] a ebreo(a) // n (LING) ebraico.

heckle ['hɛkl] vt interpellare e dare noia a (un oratore).

hectic ['hɛktɪk] a movimentato(a).

he'd [hi:d] = he would, he had.

hedge [hɛdʒ] n siepe f // vi essere elusivo(a); **to ~ one's bets** (fig) coprirsi dai rischi.

hedgehog ['hɛdʒhɔg] n riccio.

heed [hi:d] vt (also: **take ~ of**) badare a, far conto di; **~less** a sbadato(a).

heel [hi:l] n (ANAT) calcagno; (of shoe) tacco // vt (shoe) rifare i tacchi a.

hefty ['hɛftɪ] a (person) solido(a); (parcel) pesante; (piece, price) grosso(a).

heifer ['hɛfə*] n giovenca.

height [haɪt] n altezza; (high ground) altura; (fig: of glory) apice m; (: of stupidity) colmo; **~en** vt innalzare; (fig) accrescere.

heir [ɛə*] n erede m; **~ess** n erede f; **~loom** n mobile m (or gioiello or quadro) di famiglia.

held [hɛld] pt, pp of hold.

helicopter ['hɛlɪkɔptə*] n elicottero.

hell [hɛl] n inferno; **a ~ of a ...** (col) un(a) maledetto(a) ... .

he'll [hi:l] = he will, he shall.

hellish ['hɛlɪʃ] a infernale.

hello [hə'ləu] excl buon giorno!; ciao! (to sb one addresses as 'tu'); (surprise) ma guarda!

helm [hɛlm] n (NAUT) timone m.

helmet ['hɛlmɪt] n casco.

helmsman ['hɛlmzmən] n timoniere m.

help [hɛlp] n aiuto; (charwoman) donna di servizio; (assistant etc) impiegato/a // vt aiutare; **~!** aiuto!; **~ yourself** (to bread) si serva (del pane); **I can't ~ saying** non posso evitare di dire; **he can't ~ it** non ci

può far niente; **~er** n aiutante m/f, assistente m/f; **~ful** a di grande aiuto; (useful) utile; **~ing** n porzione f; **~less** a impotente; debole.

hem [hɛm] n orlo // vt fare l'orlo a; **to ~ in** vt cingere.

hemisphere ['hɛmɪsfɪə*] n emisfero.

hemp [hɛmp] n canapa.

hen [hɛn] n gallina.

hence [hɛns] ad (therefore) dunque; **2 years ~** di qui a 2 anni; **~forth** ad d'ora in poi.

henchman ['hɛntʃmən] n (pej) caudatario.

henpecked ['hɛnpɛkt] a dominato dalla moglie.

her [hə:*] pronoun (direct) la, l' + vowel; (indirect) le; (stressed, after prep) lei; see note at she // a il(la) suo(a), i(le) suoi(sue); **I see ~** la vedo; **give ~ a book** le dia un libro; **after ~** dopo (di) lei.

herald ['hɛrəld] n araldo // vt annunciare.

heraldry ['hɛrəldrɪ] n araldica.

herb [hə:b] n erba; **~s** npl (CULIN) erbette fpl.

herd [hə:d] n mandria.

here [hɪə*] ad qui, qua // excl ehi!; **~!** presente!; **~'s my sister** ecco mia sorella; **~ she is** eccola; **~ she comes** eccola che viene; **~after** ad in futuro; dopo questo // n: the **~after** l'al di là m; **~by** ad (in letter) con la presente.

hereditary [hɪ'rɛdɪtrɪ] a ereditario(a).

heredity [hɪ'rɛdɪtɪ] n eredità.

heresy ['hɛrəsɪ] n eresia.

heretic ['hɛrətɪk] n eretico/a; **~al** [hɪ'rɛtɪkl] a eretico(a).

herewith [hɪə'wɪð] ad qui accluso.

heritage ['hɛrɪtɪdʒ] n eredità; (fig) retaggio.

hermetically [hə:'mɛtɪklɪ] ad ermeticamente.

hermit ['hə:mɪt] n eremita m.

hernia ['hə:nɪə] n ernia.

hero, ~es ['hɪərəu] n eroe m; **~ic** [hɪ'rəuɪk] a eroico(a).

heroin ['hɛrəuɪn] n eroina.

heroine ['hɛrəuɪn] n eroina.

heroism ['hɛrəuɪzm] n eroismo.

heron ['hɛrən] n airone m.

herring ['hɛrɪŋ] n aringa.

hers [hə:z] pronoun il(la) suo(a), i(le) suoi(sue).

herself [hə:'sɛlf] pronoun (reflexive) si; (emphatic) lei stessa; (after prep) se stessa, sé.

he's [hi:z] = he is, he has.

hesitant ['hɛzɪtənt] a esitante, indeciso(a).

hesitate ['hɛzɪteɪt] vi: **to ~ (about/to do)** esitare (su/a fare); **hesitation** [-'teɪʃən] n esitazione f.

het up [hɛt'ʌp] a agitato(a).

hew [hju:] vt tagliare (con l'accetta).

hexagon ['hɛksəgən] n esagono; **~al** [-'sægənl] a esagonale.

heyday ['heɪdeɪ] n: the **~ of** i bei giorni di, l'età d'oro di.

hi [haɪ] excl ciao!

hibernate ['haɪbəneɪt] *vi* svernare.

hiccough, hiccup ['hɪkʌp] *vi* singhiozzare // *n* singhiozzo; **to have (the)** ~**s** avere il singhiozzo.

hid [hɪd] *pt of* **hide**.

hidden ['hɪdn] *pp of* **hide**.

hide [haɪd] *n* (*skin*) pelle *f* // *vb* (*pt* **hid**, *pp* **hidden** [hɪd, 'hɪdn]) *vt*: **to** ~ **sth (from sb)** nascondere qc (a qd) // *vi*: **to** ~ **(from sb)** nascondersi (da qd); ~**-and-seek** *n* rimpiattino; ~**away** *n* nascondiglio.

hideous ['hɪdɪəs] *a* laido(a); orribile.

hiding ['haɪdɪŋ] *n* (*beating*) bastonata; **to be in** ~ (*concealed*) tenersi nascosto(a); ~ **place** *n* nascondiglio.

hierarchy ['haɪərɑːkɪ] *n* gerarchia.

high [haɪ] *a* alto(a); (*speed, respect, number*) grande; (*wind*) forte // *ad* alto, in alto; **20m** ~ alto(a) 20m; ~**brow** *a, n* intellettuale (*m/f*); ~**chair** *n* seggiolone *m*; ~**-flying** *a* (*fig*) ambizioso(a); ~**-handed** *a* prepotente; ~**-heeled** *a* a tacchi alti; ~**jack** = **hijack**; ~ **jump** *n* (*SPORT*) salto in alto; ~**light** *n* (*fig: of event*) momento culminante // *vt* lumeggiare; ~**ly** *ad* molto; ~**ly strung** *a* teso(a) di nervi, eccitabile; **H**~ **Mass** *n* messa cantata *or* solenne; ~**ness** *n* altezza; **Her H**~**ness** Sua Altezza; ~**-pitched** *a* acuto(a); ~**-rise block** *n* palazzone *m*.

high school ['haɪskuːl] *n* scuola secondaria; (*US*) istituto superiore d'istruzione.

high street ['haɪstriːt] *n* strada principale.

highway ['haɪweɪ] *n* strada maestra.

hijack ['haɪdʒæk] *vt* dirottare; ~**er** *n* dirottatore/trice.

hike [haɪk] *vi* fare un'escursione a piedi // *n* escursione *f* a piedi; ~**r** *n* escursionista *m/f*.

hilarious [hɪ'lɛərɪəs] *a* (*behaviour, event*) che fa schiantare dal ridere.

hilarity [hɪ'lærɪtɪ] *n* ilarità.

hill [hɪl] *n* collina, colle *m*; (*fairly high*) montagna; (*on road*) salita; ~**side** *n* fianco della collina; ~**y** *a* collinoso(a); montagnoso(a).

hilt [hɪlt] *n* (*of sword*) elsa.

him [hɪm] *pronoun* (*direct*) lo, l' + *vowel*; (*indirect*) gli; (*stressed, after prep*) lui; **I see** ~ lo vedo; **give** ~ **a book** gli dia un libro; **after** ~ dopo (di) lui; ~**self** *pronoun* (*reflexive*) si; (*emphatic*) lui stesso; (*after prep*) se stesso, sé.

hind [haɪnd] *a* posteriore // *n* cerva.

hinder ['hɪndə*] *vt* ostacolare; (*delay*) tardare; (*prevent*): **to** ~ **sb from doing** impedire a qd di fare; **hindrance** ['hɪndrəns] *n* ostacolo, impedimento.

Hindu ['hɪnduː] *n* indù *m/f inv*.

hinge [hɪndʒ] *n* cardine *m* // *vi* (*fig*): **to** ~ **on** dipendere da.

hint [hɪnt] *n* accenno, allusione *f*; (*advice*) consiglio // *vt*: **to** ~ **that** lasciar capire che // *vi*: **to** ~ **at** accennare a.

hip [hɪp] *n* anca, fianco.

hippopotamus [hɪpə'pɒtəməs] *n* ippopotamo.

hire ['haɪə*] *vt* (*car, equipment*) noleggiare; (*worker*) assumere, dare lavoro a // *n* nolo, noleggio; **for** ~ da nolo; (*taxi*) libero(a); ~ **purchase (H.P.)** *n* acquisto (*or* vendita) rateale.

his [hɪz] *a, pronoun* il(la) suo(sua), i(le) suoi(sue).

hiss [hɪs] *vi* fischiare; (*cat, snake*) sibilare // *n* fischio; sibilo.

historian [hɪ'stɔːrɪən] *n* storico/a.

historic(al) [hɪ'stɔrɪk(l)] *a* storico(a).

history ['hɪstərɪ] *n* storia.

hit [hɪt] *vt* (*pt, pp* **hit**) colpire, picchiare; (*knock against*) battere; (*reach: target*) raggiungere; (*collide with: car*) urtare contro; (*fig: affect*) colpire; (*find*) incontrare // *n* colpo; (*success, song*) successo; **to** ~ **it off with sb** andare molto d'accordo con qd; ~**-and-run driver** *n* pirata *m* della strada.

hitch [hɪtʃ] *vt* (*fasten*) attaccare; (*also:* ~ **up**) tirare su // *n* (*difficulty*) intoppo, difficoltà *f inv*; **to** ~ **a lift** fare l'autostop.

hitch-hike ['hɪtʃhaɪk] *vi* fare l'autostop; ~**r** *n* autostoppista *m/f*.

hive [haɪv] *n* alveare *m*.

H.M.S. *abbr of* His(Her) Majesty's Ship.

hoard [hɔːd] *n* (*of food*) provviste *fpl*; (*of money*) gruzzolo // *vt* ammassare.

hoarding ['hɔːdɪŋ] *n* tabellone *m* per affissioni.

hoarse [hɔːs] *a* rauco(a).

hoax [həʊks] *n* scherzo; falso allarme.

hob [hɒb] *n* piastra (con fornelli).

hobble ['hɒbl] *vi* zoppicare.

hobby ['hɒbɪ] *n* hobby *m inv*, passatempo.

hobo ['həʊbəʊ] *n* (*US*) vagabondo.

hock [hɒk] *n* vino del Reno.

hockey ['hɒkɪ] *n* hockey *m*.

hoe [həʊ] *n* zappa.

hog [hɒg] *n* maiale *m* // *vt* (*fig*) arraffare; **to go the whole** ~ farlo fino in fondo.

hoist [hɔɪst] *n* paranco // *vt* issare.

hold [həʊld] *vb* (*pt, pp* **held** [hɛld]) *vt* tenere; (*contain*) contenere; (*keep back*) trattenere; (*believe*) mantenere; considerare; (*possess*) avere, possedere; detenere // *vi* (*withstand pressure*) tenere; (*be valid*) essere valido(a) // *n* presa; (*fig*) potere *m*; (*NAUT*) stiva; ~ **the line!** (*TEL*) resti in linea!; **to** ~ **one's own** (*fig*) difendersi bene; **to catch** *or* **get** (**a**) ~ **of** afferrare; **to get** ~ **of** (*fig*) trovare; **to** ~ **back** *vt* trattenere; (*secret*) tenere celato(a); **to** ~ **down** *vt* (*person*) tenere a terra; (*job*) tenere; **to** ~ **off** *vt* tener lontano; **to** ~ **on** *vi* tener fermo; (*wait*) aspettare; **to** ~ **on to** *vt fus* tenersi stretto(a) a; (*keep*) conservare; **to** ~ **out** *vt* offrire // *vi* (*resist*) resistere; **to** ~ **up** *vt* (*raise*) alzare; (*support*) sostenere; (*delay*) ritardare; ~**all** *n* borsone *m*; ~**er** *n* (*of ticket, title*) possessore/posseditrice; (*of office etc*) incaricato/a; (*of record*) detentore/trice; ~**ing** *n* (*share*) azioni *fpl*, titoli *mpl*; (*farm*) podere *m*, tenuta; ~**ing**

company n holding f inv; ~**up** n (robbery) rapina a mano armata; (delay) ritardo; (in traffic) blocco.

hole [həʊl] n buco, buca // vt bucare.

holiday ['hɔlədɪ] n vacanza; (day off) giorno di vacanza; (public) giorno festivo; ~-**maker** n villeggiante m/f; ~ **resort** n luogo di villeggiatura.

holiness ['həʊlɪnɪs] n santità.

Holland ['hɔlənd] n Olanda.

hollow ['hɔləʊ] a cavo(a), vuoto(a); (fig) falso(a); vano(a) // n cavità f inv; (in land) valletta, depressione f // vt: **to ~ out** scavare.

holly ['hɔlɪ] n agrifoglio.

holster ['həʊlstə*] n fondina (di pistola).

holy ['həʊlɪ] a santo(a); (bread) benedetto(a), consacrato(a); (ground) consacrato(a); H~ **Ghost** or **Spirit** n Spirito Santo; ~ **orders** npl ordini mpl (sacri).

homage ['hɔmɪdʒ] n omaggio; **to pay ~ to** rendere omaggio a.

home [həʊm] n casa; (country) patria; (institution) casa, ricovero // a familiare; (cooking etc) casalingo(a); (ECON, POL) nazionale, interno(a) // ad a casa; in patria; (right in: nail etc) fino in fondo; at ~ a casa; **to go** (or **come**) ~ tornare a casa (or in patria); **make yourself at ~** si metta a suo agio; ~ **address** n indirizzo di casa; ~**land** n patria; ~**less** a senza tetto; spatriato(a); ~**ly** a semplice, alla buona; accogliente; ~-**made** a casalingo(a); ~ **rule** n autogoverno; H~ **Secretary** n (Brit) ministro dell'Interno; ~**sick** a: **to be** ~**sick** avere la nostalgia; ~ **town** n città f inv natale; ~**ward** ['həʊmwəd] a (journey) di ritorno; ~**work** n compiti mpl (per casa).

homicide ['hɔmɪsaɪd] n (US) omicidio.

homoeopathy [həʊmɪ'ɔpəθɪ] n omeopatia.

homogeneous [hɔməʊ'dʒiːnɪəs] a omogeneo(a).

homosexual [hɔməʊ'sɛksjuəl] a,n omosessuale (m/f).

honest ['ɔnɪst] a onesto(a); ~**ly** ad sinceramente; onestamente; ~**y** n onestà.

honey ['hʌnɪ] n miele m; ~**comb** n favo; ~**moon** n luna di miele; (trip) viaggio di nozze.

honk [hɔŋk] n (AUT) colpo di clacson // vi suonare il clacson.

honorary ['ɔnərərɪ] a onorario(a); (duty, title) onorifico(a).

honour ['ɔnə*] vt onorare // n onore m; ~**able** a onorevole; ~**s degree** n (SCOL) laurea specializzata.

hood [hud] n cappuccio; (Brit: AUT) capote f; (US: AUT) cofano; ~**wink** vt infinocchiare.

hoof, ~**s** or **hooves** [huːf, huːvz] n zoccolo.

hook [huk] n gancio; (for fishing) amo // vt uncinare; (dress) agganciare.

hooligan ['huːlɪgən] n giovinastro, teppista m.

hoop [huːp] n cerchio.

hoot [huːt] vi (AUT) suonare il clacson // n colpo di clacson; ~**er** n (AUT) clacson m inv; (NAUT) sirena.

hooves [huːvz] npl of **hoof**.

hop [hɔp] vi saltellare, saltare; (on one foot) saltare su una gamba // n salto.

hope [həʊp] vt,vi sperare // n speranza; **I** ~ **so/not** spero di sì/no; ~**ful** a (person) pieno(a) di speranza; (situation) promettente; ~**fully** ad con speranza; ~**less** a senza speranza, disperato(a); (useless) inutile.

hops [hɔps] npl luppoli mpl.

horde [hɔːd] n orda.

horizon [hə'raɪzn] n orizzonte m; ~**tal** [hɔrɪ'zɔntl] a orizzontale.

hormone ['hɔːməʊn] n ormone m.

horn [hɔːn] n corno; (AUT) clacson m inv; ~**ed** a (animal) cornuto(a).

hornet ['hɔːnɪt] n calabrone m.

horny ['hɔːnɪ] a corneo(a); (hands) calloso(a).

horoscope ['hɔrəskəʊp] n oroscopo.

horrible ['hɔrɪbl] a orribile, tremendo(a).

horrid ['hɔrɪd] a orrido(a); (person) antipatico(a).

horrify ['hɔrɪfaɪ] vt scandalizzare.

horror ['hɔrə*] n orrore m; ~ **film** n film m inv dell'orrore.

hors d'œuvre [ɔː'dəːvrə] n antipasto.

horse [hɔːs] n cavallo; **on ~back** a cavallo; ~ **chestnut** n ippocastano; ~-**drawn** a tirato(a) da cavallo; ~**man** n cavaliere m; ~**power** (h.p.) n cavallo (vapore); ~-**racing** n ippica; ~**radish** n barbaforte m; ~**shoe** n ferro di cavallo.

horticulture ['hɔːtɪkʌltʃə*] n orticoltura.

hose [həʊz] n (also: ~**pipe**) tubo; (also: **garden** ~) tubo per annaffiare.

hosiery ['həʊzɪərɪ] n (in shop) (reparto di) calze fpl e calzini mpl.

hospitable [hɔs'pɪtəbl] a ospitale.

hospital ['hɔspɪtl] n ospedale m.

hospitality [hɔspɪ'tælɪtɪ] n ospitalità.

host [həʊst] n ospite m; (large number): **a** ~ **of** una schiera di; (REL) ostia.

hostage ['hɔstɪdʒ] n ostaggio/a.

hostel ['hɔstl] n ostello; (youth) ~ n ostello della gioventù.

hostess ['həʊstɪs] n ospite f.

hostile ['hɔstaɪl] a ostile.

hostility [hɔ'stɪlɪtɪ] n ostilità.

hot [hɔt] a caldo(a); (as opposed to only warm) molto caldo(a); (spicy) piccante; (fig) accanito(a); ardente; violento(a), focoso(a); ~ **dog** n hot dog m inv.

hotel [həʊ'tɛl] n albergo; ~**ier** n albergatore/trice.

hot: ~-**headed** a focoso(a), eccitabile; ~**house** n serra; ~**ly** ad violentemente; ~**plate** n fornello; piastra riscaldante; ~-**water bottle** n borsa dell'acqua calda.

hound [haund] vt perseguitare // n segugio.

hour ['auə*] n ora; ~**ly** a ogni ora.

house n [haus] (pl: ~**s** ['hauzɪz]) (also:

firm) casa; (*POL*) camera; (*THEATRE*) sala; pubblico; spettacolo // *vt* [hauz] (*person*) ospitare, alloggiare; **the H~ (of Commons)** la Camera dei Comuni; **on the ~** (*fig*) offerto(a) dalla casa; **~ arrest** *n* confino (a casa); **~boat** *n* house boat *f inv*; **~breaking** *n* furto con scasso; **~hold** *n* famiglia; casa; **~keeper** *n* governante *f*; **~keeping** *n* (*work*) governo della casa; **~-warming party** *n* festa per inaugurare la casa nuova; **~wife** *n* massaia; **~work** *n* faccende *fpl* domestiche.

housing ['hauzɪŋ] *n* alloggio; **~ estate** *n* zona residenziale con case popolari e/o private.

hovel ['hɔvl] *n* casupola.

hover ['hɔvə*] *vi* librarsi a volo; **to ~ round sb** aggirarsi intorno a qd; **~craft** *n* hovercraft *m inv*.

how [hau] *ad* come; **~ are you?** come sta?; **~ long have you been here?** da quanto tempo sta qui?; **~ lovely!** che bello!; **~ many?** quanti(e)?; **~ much?** quanto(a)?; **~ many people/much milk?** quante persone/quanto latte?; **~ is it that ...?** com'è che ...? + *sub*; **~ever** *ad* in qualsiasi modo or maniera che; (+ *adjective*) per quanto + *sub*; (*in questions*) come // *cj* comunque, però.

howl [haul] *n* ululato // *vi* ululare.

howler ['haulə*] *n* marronata.

h.p., H.P. *see* hire; horse.

HQ *abbr of* headquarters.

hub [hʌb] *n* (*of wheel*) mozzo; (*fig*) fulcro.

hubbub ['hʌbʌb] *n* baccano.

huddle ['hʌdl] *vi*: **to ~ together** rannicchiarsi l'uno contro l'altro.

hue [hju:] *n* tinta; **~ and cry** *n* clamore *m*.

huff [hʌf] *n*: **in a ~** stizzito(a).

hug [hʌg] *vt* abbracciare; (*shore, kerb*) stringere // *n* abbraccio, stretta.

huge [hju:dʒ] *a* enorme, immenso(a).

hulk [hʌlk] *n* carcassa; **~ing** *a*: **~ing (great)** grosso(a) e goffo(a).

hull [hʌl] *n* (*of ship*) scafo.

hullo [hə'ləu] *excl* = **hello.**

hum [hʌm] *vt* (*tune*) canticchiare // *vi* canticchiare; (*insect, plane, tool*) ronzare.

human ['hju:mən] *a* umano(a) // *n* essere *m* umano.

humane [hju:'meɪn] *a* umanitario(a).

humanity [hju:'mænɪtɪ] *n* umanità; **the humanities** gli studi umanistici.

humble ['hʌmbl] *a* umile, modesto(a) // *vt* umiliare; **humbly** *ad* umilmente, modestamente.

humbug ['hʌmbʌg] *n* inganno; sciocchezze *fpl*.

humdrum ['hʌmdrʌm] *a* monotono(a), tedioso(a).

humid ['hju:mɪd] *a* umido(a); **~ity** [-'mɪdɪtɪ] *n* umidità.

humiliate [hju:'mɪlɪeɪt] *vt* umiliare; **humiliation** [-'eɪʃən] *n* umiliazione *f*.

humility [hju:'mɪlɪtɪ] *n* umiltà.

humorist ['hju:mərɪst] *n* umorista *m/f*.

humorous ['hju:mərəs] *a* umoristico(a); (*person*) buffo(a).

humour ['hju:mə*] *n* umore *m* // *vt* (*person*) compiacere; (*sb's whims*) assecondare.

hump [hʌmp] *n* gobba; **~back** *n* schiena d'asino.

hunch [hʌntʃ] *n* gobba; (*premonition*) intuizione *f*; **~back** *n* gobbo/a; **~ed** *a* incurvato(a).

hundred ['hʌndrəd] *num* cento; **~weight** *n* (*Brit*) = 50.8 *kg*; 112 *lb*; (*US*) = 45.3 *kg*; 100 *lb*.

hung [hʌŋ] *pt, pp of* hang.

Hungarian [hʌŋ'gɛərɪən] *a* ungherese // *n* ungherese *m/f*; (*LING*) ungherese *m*.

Hungary ['hʌŋgərɪ] *n* Ungheria.

hunger ['hʌŋgə*] *n* fame *f* // *vi*: **to ~ for** desiderare ardentemente.

hungrily ['hʌŋgrəlɪ] *ad* voracemente; (*fig*) avidamente.

hungry ['hʌŋgrɪ] *a* affamato(a); **to be ~** aver fame.

hunt [hʌnt] *vt* (*seek*) cercare; (*SPORT*) cacciare // *vi* andare a caccia // *n* caccia; **~er** *n* cacciatore *m*; **~ing** *n* caccia.

hurdle ['hə:dl] *n* (*SPORT, fig*) ostacolo.

hurl [hə:l] *vt* lanciare con violenza.

hurrah, hurray [hu'ra:, hu'reɪ] *excl* urra!, evviva!

hurricane ['hʌrɪkən] *n* uragano.

hurried ['hʌrɪd] *a* affrettato(a); (*work*) fatto(a) in fretta; **~ly** *ad* in fretta.

hurry ['hʌrɪ] *n* fretta // *vi* affrettarsi // *vt* (*person*) affrettare; (*work*) far in fretta; **to be in a ~** aver fretta; **to do sth in a ~** fare qc in fretta; **to ~ in/out** entrare/uscire in fretta.

hurt [hə:t] *vb* (*pt, pp* hurt) *vt* (*cause pain to*) far male a; (*injure, fig*) ferire // *vi* far male // *a* ferito(a); **~ful** *a* (*remark*) che ferisce.

hurtle ['hə:tl] *vt* scagliare // *vi*: **to ~ past/down** passare/scendere a razzo.

husband ['hʌzbənd] *n* marito.

hush [hʌʃ] *n* silenzio, calma // *vt* zittire; **~!** zitto(a)!

husk [hʌsk] *n* (*of wheat*) cartoccio; (*of rice, maize*) buccia.

husky ['hʌskɪ] *a* roco(a) // *n* cane *m* esquimese.

hustle ['hʌsl] *vt* spingere, incalzare // *n* pigia pigia *m inv*; **~ and bustle** *n* trambusto.

hut [hʌt] *n* rifugio; (*shed*) ripostiglio.

hutch [hʌtʃ] *n* gabbia.

hyacinth ['haɪəsɪnθ] *n* giacinto.

hybrid ['haɪbrɪd] *a* ibrido(a) // *n* ibrido.

hydrant ['haɪdrənt] *n* idrante *m*.

hydraulic [haɪ'drɔ:lɪk] *a* idraulico(a).

hydroelectric [haɪdrəuɪ'lɛktrɪk] *a* idroelettrico(a).

hydrogen ['haɪdrədʒən] *n* idrogeno.

hyena [haɪ'i:nə] *n* iena.

hygiene ['haɪdʒi:n] *n* igiene *f*.

hygienic [haɪ'dʒi:nɪk] *a* igienico(a).

hymn [hɪm] *n* inno; cantica.

hyphen ['haɪfn] *n* trattino.
hypnosis [hɪp'nəʊsɪs] *n* ipnosi *f*.
hypnotism ['hɪpnətɪzm] *n* ipnotismo.
hypnotist ['hɪpnətɪst] *n* ipnotiz-zatore/trice.
hypnotize ['hɪpnətaɪz] *vt* ipnotizzare.
hypocrisy [hɪ'pɒkrɪsɪ] *n* ipocrisia.
hypocrite ['hɪpəkrɪt] *n* ipocrita *m/f*; **hypocritical** [-'krɪtɪkl] *a* ipocrita.
hypothesis, *pl* **hypotheses** [haɪ'pɒθɪsɪs, -siːz] *n* ipotesi *f inv*.
hypothetical [haɪpəʊ'θetɪkl] *a* ipotetico(a).
hysteria [hɪ'stɪərɪə] *n* isteria.
hysterical [hɪ'sterɪkl] *a* isterico(a).
hysterics [hɪ'sterɪks] *npl* accesso di isteria; (*laughter*) attacco di riso.

I

I [aɪ] *pronoun* io.
ice [aɪs] *n* ghiaccio; (*on road*) gelo // *vt* (*cake*) glassare; (*drink*) mettere in fresco // *vi* (*also*: ~ **over**) ghiacciare; (*also*: ~ **up**) gelare; ~ **axe** *n* picozza da ghiaccio; ~**berg** *n* iceberg *m inv*; ~**box** *n* (*US*) frigorifero; (*Brit*) reparto ghiaccio; (*insulated box*) frigo portatile; ~**cold** *a* gelato(a); ~ **cream** *n* gelato; ~ **hockey** *n* hockey *m* su ghiaccio.
Iceland ['aɪslənd] *n* Islanda; ~**er** *n* islandese *m/f*; ~**ic** [-'lændɪk] *a* islandese // *n* (*LING*) islandese *m*.
ice rink ['aɪsrɪŋk] *n* pista di pattinaggio.
icicle ['aɪsɪkl] *n* ghiacciolo.
icing ['aɪsɪŋ] *n* (*AVIAT etc*) patina di ghiaccio; (*CULIN*) glassa; ~ **sugar** *n* zucchero a velo.
icon ['aɪkɒn] *n* icona.
icy ['aɪsɪ] *a* ghiacciato(a); (*weather, temperature*) gelido(a).
I'd [aɪd] = **I would, I had**.
idea [aɪ'dɪə] *n* idea.
ideal [aɪ'dɪəl] *a, n* ideale (*m*); ~**ist** *n* idealista *m/f*.
identical [aɪ'dentɪkl] *a* identico(a).
identification [aɪdentɪfɪ'keɪʃən] *n* identificazione *f*; **means of** ~ carta d'identità.
identify [aɪ'dentɪfaɪ] *vt* identificare.
identity [aɪ'dentɪtɪ] *n* identità *f inv*.
ideology [aɪdɪ'ɒlədʒɪ] *n* ideologia.
idiocy ['ɪdɪəsɪ] *n* idiozia.
idiom ['ɪdɪəm] *n* idioma *m*; (*phrase*) espressione *f* idiomatica.
idiosyncrasy [ɪdɪəʊ'sɪŋkrəsɪ] *n* idiosincrasia.
idiot ['ɪdɪət] *n* idiota *m/f*; ~**ic** [-'ɒtɪk] *a* idiota.
idle ['aɪdl] *a* inattivo(a); (*lazy*) pigro(a), ozioso(a); (*unemployed*) disoccupato(a); (*question, pleasures*) inutile, vano(a); **to lie** ~ stare fermo, non funzionare; ~**ness** *n* ozio; pigrizia; ~**r** *n* ozioso/a; fannullone/a.
idol ['aɪdl] *n* idolo; ~**ize** *vt* idoleggiare.
idyllic [ɪ'dɪlɪk] *a* idillico(a).

i.e. *ad* (*abbr of id est*) cioè.
if [ɪf] *cj* se.
igloo ['ɪgluː] *n* igloo *m inv*.
ignite [ɪg'naɪt] *vt* accendere // *vi* accendersi.
ignition [ɪg'nɪʃən] *n* (*AUT*) accensione *f*; **to switch on/off the** ~ accendere/spegnere il motore; ~ **key** *n* (*AUT*) chiave *f* dell'accensione.
ignorance ['ɪgnərəns] *n* ignoranza.
ignorant ['ɪgnərənt] *a* ignorante.
ignore [ɪg'nɔː*] *vt* non tener conto di; (*person, fact*) ignorare.
I'll [aɪl] = **I will, I shall**.
ill [ɪl] *a* (*sick*) malato(a); (*bad*) cattivo(a) // *n* male *m*; **to take** *or* **be taken** ~ ammalarsi; ~**advised** *a* (*decision*) poco giudizioso(a); (*person*) mal consigliato(a); ~**at-ease** *a* a disagio.
illegal [ɪ'liːgl] *a* illegale.
illegible [ɪ'ledʒɪbl] *a* illeggibile.
illegitimate [ɪlɪ'dʒɪtɪmət] *a* illegittimo(a).
ill-fated [ɪl'feɪtɪd] *a* nefasto(a).
ill feeling [ɪl'fiːlɪŋ] *n* rancore *m*.
illicit [ɪ'lɪsɪt] *a* illecito(a).
illiterate [ɪ'lɪtərət] *a* illetterato(a); (*letter*) scorretto(a).
ill-mannered [ɪl'mænəd] *a* maleducato(a), sgarbato(a).
illness ['ɪlnɪs] *n* malattia.
illogical [ɪ'lɒdʒɪkl] *a* illogico(a).
ill-treat [ɪl'triːt] *vt* maltrattare.
illuminate [ɪ'luːmɪneɪt] *vt* illuminare; **illumination** [-'neɪʃən] *n* illuminazione *f*.
illusion [ɪ'luːʒən] *n* illusione *f*.
illusive, illusory [ɪ'luːsɪv, ɪ'luːsərɪ] *a* illusorio(a).
illustrate ['ɪləstreɪt] *vt* illustrare; **illustration** [-'streɪʃən] *n* illustrazione *f*.
illustrious [ɪ'lʌstrɪəs] *a* illustre.
ill will [ɪl'wɪl] *n* cattiva volontà.
I'm [aɪm] = **I am**.
image ['ɪmɪdʒ] *n* immagine *f*; (*public face*) immagine (pubblica); ~**ry** *n* immagini *fpl*.
imaginary [ɪ'mædʒɪnərɪ] *a* immaginario(a).
imagination [ɪmædʒɪ'neɪʃən] *n* immaginazione *f*, fantasia.
imaginative [ɪ'mædʒɪnətɪv] *a* immaginoso(a).
imagine [ɪ'mædʒɪn] *vt* immaginare.
imbalance [ɪm'bæləns] *n* sbilancio.
imbecile ['ɪmbəsiːl] *n* imbecille *m/f*.
imitate ['ɪmɪteɪt] *vt* imitare; **imitation** [-'teɪʃən] *n* imitazione *f*; **imitator** *n* imitatore/trice.
immaculate [ɪ'mækjulət] *a* immacolato(a); (*dress, appearance*) impeccabile.
immaterial [ɪmə'tɪərɪəl] *a* immateriale, indifferente.
immature [ɪmə'tjʊə*] *a* immaturo(a).
immediate [ɪ'miːdɪət] *a* immediato(a); ~**ly** *ad* (*at once*) subito, immediatamente; ~**ly next to** proprio accanto a.
immense [ɪ'mens] *a* immenso(a); enorme.
immerse [ɪ'məːs] *vt* immergere.

immersion heater [ɪˈmɜːʃnhiːtə*] *n* riscaldatore *m* a immersione.

immigrant [ˈɪmɪɡrənt] *n* immigrante *m/f*; immigrato/a.

immigration [ɪmɪˈɡreɪʃən] *n* immigrazione *f*.

imminent [ˈɪmɪnənt] *a* imminente.

immobilize [ɪˈməubɪlaɪz] *vt* immobilizzare.

immoral [ɪˈmɔrl] *a* immorale; ~ity [-ˈrælɪtɪ] *n* immoralità.

immortal [ɪˈmɔːtl] *a, n* immortale (*m/f*); ~ize *vt* rendere immortale.

immune [ɪˈmjuːn] *a*: ~ (to) immune (da).

immunize [ˈɪmjunaɪz] *vt* immunizzare.

impact [ˈɪmpækt] *n* impatto.

impair [ɪmˈpɛə*] *vt* danneggiare.

impale [ɪmˈpeɪl] *vt* impalare.

impartial [ɪmˈpɑːʃl] *a* imparziale; ~ity [ɪmpɑːʃɪˈælɪtɪ] *n* imparzialità.

impassable [ɪmˈpɑːsəbl] *a* insuperabile; (*road*) impraticabile.

impatience [ɪmˈpeɪʃəns] *n* impazienza.

impatient [ɪmˈpeɪʃənt] *a* impaziente.

impeach [ɪmˈpiːtʃ] *vt* accusare, attaccare; (*public official*) incriminare.

impeccable [ɪmˈpɛkəbl] *a* impeccabile.

impede [ɪmˈpiːd] *vt* impedire.

impediment [ɪmˈpedɪmənt] *n* impedimento; (*also:* **speech** ~) difetto di pronuncia.

impending [ɪmˈpendɪŋ] *a* imminente.

imperative [ɪmˈperətɪv] *a* imperativo(a); necessario(a), urgente; (*voice*) imperioso(a) // *n* (*LING*) imperativo.

imperceptible [ɪmpəˈsɛptɪbl] *a* impercettibile.

imperfect [ɪmˈpɜːfɪkt] *a* imperfetto(a); (*goods etc*) difettoso(a) // *n* (*LING*: *also:* ~ **tense**) imperfetto; ~ion [-ˈfekʃən] *n* imperfezione *f*.

imperial [ɪmˈpɪərɪəl] *a* imperiale; (*measure*) legale.

impersonal [ɪmˈpɜːsənl] *a* impersonale.

impersonate [ɪmˈpɜːsəneɪt] *vt* impersonare; (*THEATRE*) fare la mimica di; **impersonation** [-ˈneɪʃən] *n* (*LAW*) usurpazione *f* d'identità; (*THEATRE*) mimica.

impertinent [ɪmˈpɜːtɪnənt] *a* insolente, impertinente.

impervious [ɪmˈpɜːvɪəs] *a* impermeabile; (*fig*): ~ **to** insensibile a; impassibile di fronte a.

impetuous [ɪmˈpetjuəs] *a* impetuoso(a), precipitoso(a).

impetus [ˈɪmpətəs] *n* impeto.

impinge [ɪmˈpɪndʒ]: **to** ~ **on** *vt fus* (*person*) colpire; (*rights*) ledere.

implausible [ɪmˈplɔːzɪbl] *a* non plausibile.

implement *n* [ˈɪmplɪmənt] attrezzo; (*for cooking*) utensile *m* // *vt* [ˈɪmplɪment] effettuare.

implicate [ˈɪmplɪkeɪt] *vt* implicare; **implication** [-ˈkeɪʃən] *n* implicazione *f*.

implicit [ɪmˈplɪsɪt] *a* implicito(a); (*complete*) completo(a).

implore [ɪmˈplɔː*] *vt* implorare.

imply [ɪmˈplaɪ] *vt* insinuare; suggerire.

impolite [ɪmpəˈlaɪt] *a* scortese.

imponderable [ɪmˈpɒndərəbl] *a* imponderabile.

import *vt* [ɪmˈpɔːt] importare // *n* [ˈɪmpɔːt] (*COMM*) importazione *f*; (*meaning*) significato, senso.

importance [ɪmˈpɔːtns] *n* importanza.

important [ɪmˈpɔːtnt] *a* importante.

imported [ɪmˈpɔːtɪd] *a* importato(a).

importer [ɪmˈpɔːtə*] *n* importatore/trice.

impose [ɪmˈpəuz] *vt* imporre // *vi*: **to** ~ **on sb** sfruttare la bontà di qd.

imposing [ɪmˈpəuzɪŋ] *a* imponente.

impossibility [ɪmpɒsəˈbɪlɪtɪ] *n* impossibilità.

impossible [ɪmˈpɒsɪbl] *a* impossibile.

impostor [ɪmˈpɒstə*] *n* impostore/a.

impotence [ˈɪmpətns] *n* impotenza.

impotent [ˈɪmpətnt] *a* impotente.

impound [ɪmˈpaund] *vt* confiscare.

impoverished [ɪmˈpɒvərɪʃt] *a* impoverito(a).

impracticable [ɪmˈpræktɪkəbl] *a* impraticabile.

impractical [ɪmˈpræktɪkl] *a* non pratico(a).

imprecise [ɪmprɪˈsaɪs] *a* impreciso(a).

impregnable [ɪmˈpreɡnəbl] *a* (*fortress*) inespugnabile; (*fig*) inoppugnabile; irrefutabile.

impregnate [ˈɪmpreɡneɪt] *vt* impregnare; (*fertilize*) fecondare.

impresario [ɪmprɪˈsɑːrɪəu] *n* impresario/a.

impress [ɪmˈpres] *vt* impressionare; (*mark*) imprimere, stampare; **to** ~ **sth on sb** far capire qc a qd.

impression [ɪmˈpreʃən] *n* impressione *f*; **to be under the** ~ **that** avere l'impressione che; ~**able** *a* impressionabile; ~**ist** *n* impressionista *m/f*.

impressive [ɪmˈpresɪv] *a* impressionante.

imprison [ɪmˈprɪzn] *vt* imprigionare; ~**ment** *n* imprigionamento.

improbable [ɪmˈprɒbəbl] *a* improbabile; (*excuse*) inverosimile.

impromptu [ɪmˈprɒmptjuː] *a* improvvisato(a).

improper [ɪmˈprɒpə*] *a* scorretto(a); (*unsuitable*) inadatto(a), improprio(a); sconveniente, indecente; **impropriety** [ɪmprəˈpraɪətɪ] *n* sconvenienza; (*of expression*) improprietà.

improve [ɪmˈpruːv] *vt* migliorare // *vi* migliorare; (*pupil etc*) fare progressi; ~**ment** *n* miglioramento; progresso.

improvisation [ɪmprəvaɪˈzeɪʃən] *n* improvvisazione *f*.

improvise [ˈɪmprəvaɪz] *vt,vi* improvvisare.

impudent [ˈɪmpjudnt] *a* impudente, sfacciato(a).

impulse [ˈɪmpʌls] *n* impulso.

impulsive [ɪmˈpʌlsɪv] *a* impulsivo(a).

impunity [ɪm'pju:nɪtɪ] n impunità.
impure [ɪm'pjuə*] a impuro(a).
impurity [ɪm'pjuərɪtɪ] n impurità f inv.
in [ɪn] prep in; (with time: during, within): ~
  May/2 days in maggio/2 giorni; (: after):
  ~ **2 weeks** entro 2 settimane; (with town)
  a; (with country): **it's ~ France** è in
  Francia // ad entro, dentro; (fashionable)
  alla moda; **is he ~?** lui c'è?; ~ **town/the**
  country in città/campagna; ~ **the sun**
  al sole; ~ **the rain** sotto la pioggia; ~
  French in francese; **a man ~ 10** un
  uomo su 10; ~ **hundreds** a centinaia; **the**
  best pupil ~ the class il migliore
  alunno della classe; ~ **saying this** nel
  dire questo; **their party is ~** il loro
  partito è al potere; **to run/limp** etc ~
  entrare correndo/zoppicando; **the ~s**
  and outs of i dettagli di.
in., ins abbr of **inch(es)**.
inability [ɪnə'bɪlɪtɪ] n inabilità, incapacità.
inaccessible [ɪnək'sɛsɪbl] a inaccessibile.
inaccuracy [ɪn'ækjurəsɪ] n inaccuratezza;
  imprecisione f.
inaccurate [ɪn'ækjurət] a inesatto(a),
  impreciso(a).
inactivity [ɪnæk'tɪvɪtɪ] n inattività.
inadequacy [ɪn'ædɪkwəsɪ] n insufficienza.
inadequate [ɪn'ædɪkwət] a insufficiente.
inadvertently [ɪnəd'və:tntlɪ] ad senza
  volerlo.
inadvisable [ɪnəd'vaɪzəbl] a
  sconsigliabile.
inane [ɪ'neɪn] a vacuo(a), stupido(a).
inanimate [ɪn'ænɪmət] a inanimato(a).
inappropriate [ɪnə'prəuprɪət] a
  disadatto(a); (word, expression) impro-
  prio(a).
inapt [ɪn'æpt] a maldestro(a); fuori luogo;
  ~**itude** n improprietà.
inarticulate [ɪnɑː'tɪkjulət] a (person) che
  si esprime male; (speech) inarticolato(a).
inasmuch as [ɪnəz'mʌtʃæz] ad in quanto
  che; (seeing that) poiché.
inattention [ɪnə'tɛnʃən] n mancanza di
  attenzione.
inattentive [ɪnə'tɛntɪv] a disattento(a),
  distratto(a); negligente.
inaudible [ɪn'ɔːdɪbl] a impercettibile.
inaugural [ɪ'nɔːgjurəl] a inaugurale.
inaugurate [ɪ'nɔːgjureɪt] vt inaugurare;
  (president, official) insediare;
  inauguration [-'reɪʃən] n inaugurazione f;
  insediamento in carica.
in-between [ɪnbɪ'twiːn] a fra i (or le) due.
inborn [ɪn'bɔːn] a (feeling) innato(a);
  (defect) congenito(a).
inbred [ɪn'brɛd] a innato(a); (family)
  connaturato(a).
inbreeding [ɪn'briːdɪŋ] n incrocio ripetuto
  di animali consanguinei; unioni fpl fra
  consanguinei.
Inc. abbr see **incorporated**.
incapability [ɪnkeɪpə'bɪlɪtɪ] n incapacità.
incapable [ɪn'keɪpəbl] a incapace.
incapacitate [ɪnkə'pæsɪteɪt] vt: **to ~ sb**
  from doing rendere qd incapace di fare.

incarnate [ɪn'kɑːnɪt] a incarnato(a);
  incarnation [-'neɪʃən] n incarnazione f.
incendiary [ɪn'sɛndɪərɪ] a incendiario(a).
incense n ['ɪnsɛns] incenso // vt [ɪn'sɛns]
  (anger) infuriare.
incentive [ɪn'sɛntɪv] n incentivo.
incessant [ɪn'sɛsnt] a incessante; ~**ly** ad
  di continuo, senza sosta.
incest ['ɪnsɛst] n incesto.
inch [ɪntʃ] n pollice m (= 25 mm; 12 in a
  foot); **within an ~ of** a un pelo da.
incidence ['ɪnsɪdns] n (of crime, disease)
  incidenza.
incident ['ɪnsɪdnt] n incidente m; (in book)
  episodio.
incidental [ɪnsɪ'dɛntl] a accessorio(a),
  d'accompagnamento; (unplanned)
  incidentale; ~ **to** marginale a; ~
  expenses npl spese fpl accessorie; ~**ly**
  [-'dɛntəlɪ] ad (by the way) a proposito.
incinerator [ɪn'sɪnəreɪtə*] n inceneritore
  m.
incipient [ɪn'sɪpɪənt] a incipiente.
incision [ɪn'sɪʒən] n incisione f.
incisive [ɪn'saɪsɪv] a incisivo(a); tagliente;
  acuto(a).
incite [ɪn'saɪt] vt incitare.
inclination [ɪnklɪ'neɪʃən] n inclinazione f.
incline n ['ɪnklaɪn] pendenza, pendio // vb
  [ɪn'klaɪn] vt inclinare // vi: **to ~ to**
  tendere a; **to be ~d to** do tendere a fare;
  essere propenso(a) a fare; **to be well ~d**
  towards sb essere ben disposto(a) verso
  qd.
include [ɪn'kluːd] vt includere,
  comprendere; **including** prep
  compreso(a), incluso(a).
inclusion [ɪn'kluːʒən] n inclusione f.
inclusive [ɪn'kluːsɪv] a incluso(a),
  compreso(a).
incognito [ɪnkɔg'niːtəu] ad in incognito.
incoherent [ɪnkəu'hɪərənt] a incoerente.
income ['ɪnkʌm] n reddito; ~ **tax** n
  imposta sul reddito; ~ **tax return** n
  dichiarazione f annuale dei redditi.
incoming ['ɪnkʌmɪŋ] a: ~ **tide** n marea
  montante.
incompatible [ɪnkəm'pætɪbl] a
  incompatibile.
incompetence [ɪn'kɔmpɪtns] n
  incompetenza, incapacità.
incompetent [ɪn'kɔmpɪtnt] a
  incompetente, incapace.
incomplete [ɪnkəm'pliːt] a incompleto(a).
incomprehensible [ɪnkɔmprɪ'hɛnsɪbl] a
  incomprensibile.
inconclusive [ɪnkən'kluːsɪv] a
  improduttivo(a); (argument) poco
  convincente.
incongruous [ɪn'kɔŋgruəs] a poco
  appropriato(a); (remark, act)
  incongruo(a).
inconsequential [ɪnkɔnsɪ'kwɛnʃl] a senza
  importanza.
inconsiderate [ɪnkən'sɪdərət] a
  sconsiderato(a).
inconsistent [ɪnkən'sɪstnt] a incoerente;

poco logico(a); contraddittorio(a).

inconspicuous [ɪnkən'spɪkjuəs] *a* incospicuo(a); (*colour*) poco appariscente; (*dress*) dimesso(a).

inconstant [ɪn'kɔnstnt] *a* incostante; mutevole.

incontinent [ɪn'kɔntɪnənt] *a* incontinente.

inconvenience [ɪnkən'viːnjəns] *n* inconveniente *m*; (*trouble*) disturbo // *vt* disturbare.

inconvenient [ɪnkən'viːnjənt] *a* scomodo(a).

incorporate [ɪn'kɔːpəreɪt] *vt* incorporare; (*contain*) contenere; ~ **d** *a*: ~**d company** (*US, abbr* **Inc.**) società *f inv* anonima (S.A.).

incorrect [ɪnkə'rɛkt] *a* scorretto(a); (*opinion, statement*) impreciso(a).

incorruptible [ɪnkə'rʌptɪbl] *a* incorruttibile.

increase *n* ['ɪnkriːs] aumento // *vi* [ɪn'kriːs] aumentare.

increasing [ɪn'kriːsɪŋ] *a* (*number*) crescente; ~**ly** *ad* sempre più.

incredible [ɪn'krɛdɪbl] *a* incredibile.

incredulous [ɪn'krɛdjuləs] *a* incredulo(a).

increment ['ɪnkrɪmənt] *n* aumento, incremento.

incriminate [ɪn'krɪmɪneɪt] *vt* compromettere.

incubation [ɪnkju'beɪʃən] *n* incubazione *f*.

incubator ['ɪnkjubeɪtə*] *n* incubatrice *f*.

incur [ɪn'kɔː*] *vt* (*expenses*) incorrere; (*anger, risk*) esporsi a; (*debt*) contrarre; (*loss*) subire.

incurable [ɪn'kjuərəbl] *a* incurabile.

incursion [ɪn'kɔːʃən] *n* incursione *f*.

indebted [ɪn'dɛtɪd] *a*: **to be ~ to sb** (**for**) essere obbligato(a) verso qd (per).

indecent [ɪn'diːsnt] *a* indecente.

indecision [ɪndɪ'sɪʒən] *n* indecisione *f*.

indecisive [ɪndɪ'saɪsɪv] *a* indeciso(a); (*discussion*) non decisivo(a).

indeed [ɪn'diːd] *ad* infatti; veramente; **yes** ~! certamente!

indefinable [ɪndɪ'faɪnəbl] *a* indefinibile.

indefinite [ɪn'dɛfɪnɪt] *a* indefinito(a); (*answer*) vago(a); (*period, number*) indeterminato(a); ~**ly** *ad* (*wait*) indefinitamente.

indelible [ɪn'dɛlɪbl] *a* indelebile.

indemnify [ɪn'dɛmnɪfaɪ] *vt* indennizzare.

indentation [ɪndɛn'teɪʃən] *n* intaccatura.

independence [ɪndɪ'pɛndns] *n* indipendenza.

independent [ɪndɪ'pɛndnt] *a* indipendente.

indescribable [ɪndɪ'skraɪbəbl] *a* indescrivibile.

index ['ɪndɛks] *n* (*pl*: ~**es**: *in book*) indice *m*; (: *in library etc*) catalogo; (*pl*: **indices** ['ɪndɪsiːz]: *ratio, sign*) indice *m*; ~ **card** *n* scheda; ~ **finger** *n* (dito) indice *m*; ~-**linked** *a* legato(a) al costo della vita.

India ['ɪndɪə] *n* India; ~**n** *a*, *n* indiano(a); ~**n ink** *n* inchiostro di china; ~**n Ocean** *n* Oceano Indiano.

indicate ['ɪndɪkeɪt] *vt* indicare;

indication [-'keɪʃən] *n* indicazione *f*, segno.

indicative [ɪn'dɪkətɪv] *a* indicativo(a) // *n* (*LING*) indicativo.

indicator ['ɪndɪkeɪtə*] *n* indicatore *m*.

indices ['ɪndɪsiːz] *npl of* **index**.

indict [ɪn'daɪt] *vt* accusare; ~**able** *a* passibile di pena; ~**ment** *n* accusa.

indifference [ɪn'dɪfrəns] *n* indifferenza.

indifferent [ɪn'dɪfrənt] *a* indifferente; (*poor*) mediocre.

indigenous [ɪn'dɪdʒɪnəs] *a* indigeno(a).

indigestible [ɪndɪ'dʒɛstɪbl] *a* indigeribile.

indigestion [ɪndɪ'dʒɛstʃən] *n* indigestione *f*.

indignant [ɪn'dɪgnənt] *a*: ~ (**at sth/with sb**) indignato(a) (per qc/contro qd).

indignation [ɪndɪg'neɪʃən] *n* indignazione *f*.

indignity [ɪn'dɪgnɪtɪ] *n* affronto.

indirect [ɪndɪ'rɛkt] *a* indiretto(a).

indiscreet [ɪndɪ'skriːt] *a* indiscreto(a); (*rash*) imprudente.

indiscretion [ɪndɪ'skrɛʃən] *n* indiscrezione *f*; imprudenza.

indiscriminate [ɪndɪ'skrɪmɪnət] *a* (*person*) che non sa discernere; (*admiration*) cieco(a); (*killings*) indiscriminato(a).

indispensable [ɪndɪ'spɛnsəbl] *a* indispensabile.

indisposed [ɪndɪ'spəuzd] *a* (*unwell*) indisposto(a).

indisputable [ɪndɪ'spjuːtəbl] *a* incontestabile, indiscutibile.

indistinct [ɪndɪ'stɪŋkt] *a* indistinto(a); (*memory, noise*) vago(a).

individual [ɪndɪ'vɪdjuəl] *n* individuo // *a* individuale; (*characteristic*) particolare, originale; ~**ist** *n* individualista *m/f*; ~**ity** [-'ælɪtɪ] *n* individualità.

indoctrinate [ɪn'dɔktrɪneɪt] *vt* indottrinare; **indoctrination** [-'neɪʃən] *n* indottrinamento.

indolent ['ɪndələnt] *a* indolente.

indoor ['ɪndɔː*] *a* da interno; (*plant*) d'appartamento; (*swimming-pool*) coperto(a); (*sport, games*) fatto(a) al coperto; ~**s** [ɪn'dɔːz] *ad* all'interno; (*at home*) in casa.

indubitable [ɪn'djuːbɪtəbl] *a* indubitabile.

induce [ɪn'djuːs] *vt* persuadere; (*bring about*) provocare; ~**ment** *n* incitamento; (*incentive*) stimolo, incentivo.

induction [ɪn'dʌkʃən] *n* (*MED*: *of birth*) parto indotto; ~ **course** *n* corso di avviamento.

indulge [ɪn'dʌldʒ] *vt* (*whim*) compiacere, soddisfare; (*child*) viziare // *vi*: **to ~ in sth** concedersi qc; abbandonarsi a qc; ~**nce** *n* lusso (che uno si permette); (*leniency*) indulgenza; ~**nt** *a* indulgente.

industrial [ɪn'dʌstrɪəl] *a* industriale; (*injury*) sul lavoro; (*dispute*) di lavoro; ~ **action** *n* azione *f* rivendicativa; ~ **estate** *n* zona industriale; ~**ist** *n* industriale *m*; ~**ize** *vt* industrializzare.

industrious [ɪnˈdʌstrɪəs] a industrioso(a), assiduo(a).

industry [ˈɪndəstrɪ] n industria; (*diligence*) operosità.

inebriated [ɪˈniːbrɪeɪtɪd] a ubriaco(a).

inedible [ɪnˈɛdɪbl] a immangiabile.

ineffective [ɪnɪˈfɛktɪv] a inefficace.

ineffectual [ɪnɪˈfɛktʃuəl] a inefficace; incompetente.

inefficiency [ɪnɪˈfɪʃənsɪ] n inefficienza.

inefficient [ɪnɪˈfɪʃənt] a inefficiente.

ineligible [ɪnˈɛlɪdʒɪbl] a (*candidate*) ineleggibile; **to be ~ for sth** non avere il diritto a qc.

inept [ɪˈnɛpt] a inetto(a).

inequality [ɪnɪˈkwɔlɪtɪ] n ineguaglianza.

inert [ɪˈnɜːt] a inerte.

inertia [ɪˈnɜːʃə] n inerzia.

inescapable [ɪnɪˈskeɪpəbl] a inevitabile.

inestimable [ɪnˈɛstɪməbl] a inestimabile, incalcolabile.

inevitable [ɪnˈɛvɪtəbl] a inevitabile.

inexact [ɪnɪɡˈzækt] a inesatto(a).

inexhaustible [ɪnɪɡˈzɔːstɪbl] a inesauribile; (*person*) instancabile.

inexorable [ɪnˈɛksɔrəbl] a inesorabile.

inexpensive [ɪnɪkˈspɛnsɪv] a poco costoso(a).

inexperience [ɪnɪkˈspɪərɪəns] n inesperienza; **~d** a inesperto(a), senza esperienza.

inexplicable [ɪnɪkˈsplɪkəbl] a inesplicabile.

inextricable [ɪnɪkˈstrɪkəbl] a inestricabile.

infallibility [ɪnfæləˈbɪlɪtɪ] n infallibilità.

infallible [ɪnˈfælɪbl] a infallibile.

infamous [ˈɪnfəməs] a infame.

infamy [ˈɪnfəmɪ] n infamia.

infancy [ˈɪnfənsɪ] n infanzia.

infant [ˈɪnfənt] n (*baby*) infante m/f; (*young child*) bambino/a; **~ile** a infantile; **~ school** n scuola elementare (*per bambini dall'età di 5 a 7 anni*).

infantry [ˈɪnfəntrɪ] n fanteria; **~man** n fante m.

infatuated [ɪnˈfætjueɪtɪd] a: **~ with** infatuato(a) di.

infatuation [ɪnfætjuˈeɪʃən] n infatuazione f.

infect [ɪnˈfɛkt] vt infettare; **~ed with** (*illness*) affetto(a) da; **~ion** [ɪnˈfɛkʃən] n infezione f; contagio; **~ious** [ɪnˈfɛkʃəs] a infettivo(a); (*also: fig*) contagioso(a).

infer [ɪnˈfɜː*] vt inferire, dedurre; **~ence** [ˈɪnfərəns] n deduzione f, conclusione f.

inferior [ɪnˈfɪərɪə*] a inferiore; (*goods*) di qualità scadente // n inferiore m/f; (*in rank*) subalterno/a; **~ity** [ɪnfɪərɪˈɔrətɪ] n inferiorità; **~ity complex** n complesso di inferiorità.

infernal [ɪnˈfɜːnl] a infernale.

inferno [ɪnˈfɜːnəu] n inferno.

infertile [ɪnˈfɜːtaɪl] a sterile; **infertility** [-ˈtɪlɪtɪ] n sterilità.

infested [ɪnˈfɛstɪd] a: **~ (with)** infestato(a) (di).

infidelity [ɪnfɪˈdɛlɪtɪ] n infedeltà.

in-fighting [ˈɪnfaɪtɪŋ] n lotte fpl intestine.

infiltrate [ˈɪnfɪltreɪt] vt (*troops etc*) far penetrare; (*enemy line etc*) infiltrare // vi infiltrarsi.

infinite [ˈɪnfɪnɪt] a infinito(a).

infinitive [ɪnˈfɪnɪtɪv] n infinito.

infinity [ɪnˈfɪnɪtɪ] n infinità; (*also MATH*) infinito.

infirmary [ɪnˈfɜːmərɪ] n ospedale m; (*in school, factory*) infermeria.

infirmity [ɪnˈfɜːmɪtɪ] n infermità f inv.

inflame [ɪnˈfleɪm] vt infiammare.

inflammable [ɪnˈflæməbl] a infiammabile.

inflammation [ɪnfləˈmeɪʃən] n infiammazione f.

inflate [ɪnˈfleɪt] vt (*tyre, balloon*) gonfiare; (*fig*) esagerare; gonfiare; **to ~ the currency** far ricorso all'inflazione; **~d** a (*style*) gonfio(a); (*value*) esagerato(a); **inflation** [ɪnˈfleɪʃən] n (*ECON*) inflazione f.

inflexible [ɪnˈflɛksɪbl] a inflessibile, rigido(a).

inflict [ɪnˈflɪkt] vt: **to ~ on** infliggere a; **~ion** [ɪnˈflɪkʃən] n infliggere m; inflizione f; afflizione f.

inflow [ˈɪnfləu] n afflusso.

influence [ˈɪnfluəns] n influenza // vt influenzare; **under the ~ of** sotto l'influenza di.

influential [ɪnfluˈɛnʃl] a influente.

influenza [ɪnfluˈɛnzə] n (*MED*) influenza.

influx [ˈɪnflʌks] n afflusso.

inform [ɪnˈfɔːm] vt: **to ~ sb (of)** informare qd (di); **to ~ sb about** mettere qd al corrente di.

informal [ɪnˈfɔːml] a (*person, manner*) alla buona, semplice; (*visit, discussion*) informale; (*announcement, invitation*) non ufficiale; **'dress ~'** 'non è richiesto l'abito scuro'; **~ity** [-ˈmælɪtɪ] n semplicità, informalità; carattere m non ufficiale.

information [ɪnfəˈmeɪʃən] n informazioni fpl; notizie fpl; (*knowledge*) particolari mpl; **a piece of ~** un'informazione.

informative [ɪnˈfɔːmətɪv] a istruttivo(a).

informer [ɪnˈfɔːmə*] n informatore/trice.

infra-red [ɪnfrəˈrɛd] a infrarosso(a).

infrequent [ɪnˈfriːkwənt] a infrequente, raro(a).

infringe [ɪnˈfrɪndʒ] vt infrangere // vi: **to ~ on** calpestare; **~ment** n: **~ment (of)** infrazione f (di).

infuriating [ɪnˈfjuərɪeɪtɪŋ] a molto irritante.

ingenious [ɪnˈdʒiːnjəs] a ingegnoso(a).

ingenuity [ɪndʒɪˈnjuːɪtɪ] n ingegnosità.

ingot [ˈɪŋɡət] n lingotto.

ingrained [ɪnˈɡreɪnd] a radicato(a).

ingratiate [ɪnˈɡreɪʃɪeɪt] vt: **to ~ o.s. with** ingraziarsi.

ingratitude [ɪnˈɡrætɪtjuːd] n ingratitudine f.

ingredient [ɪnˈɡriːdɪənt] n ingrediente m; elemento.

inhabit [ɪnˈhæbɪt] vt abitare.

inhabitant [ɪn'hæbɪtnt] n abitante m/f.
inhale [ɪn'heɪl] vt inalare // vi (in smoking) aspirare.
inherent [ɪn'hɪərənt] a: ~ (in or to) inerente (a).
inherit [ɪn'hɛrɪt] vt ereditare; ~ance n eredità.
inhibit [ɪn'hɪbɪt] vt (PSYCH) inibire; **to ~ sb from doing** impedire a qd di fare; ~**ion** [-'bɪʃən] n inibizione f.
inhospitable [ɪnhɔs'pɪtəbl] a inospitale.
inhuman [ɪn'hjuːmən] a inumano(a).
inimitable [ɪ'nɪmɪtəbl] a inimitabile.
iniquity [ɪ'nɪkwɪtɪ] n iniquità f inv.
initial [ɪ'nɪʃl] a iniziale // n iniziale f // vt siglare; ~**s** npl iniziali fpl; (as signature) sigla; ~**ly** ad inizialmente, all'inizio.
initiate [ɪ'nɪʃɪeɪt] vt (start) avviare; intraprendere; iniziare; (person) iniziare; **initiation** [-'eɪʃən] n (into secret etc) iniziazione f.
initiative [ɪ'nɪʃətɪv] n iniziativa.
inject [ɪn'dʒɛkt] vt (liquid) iniettare; (person) fare una puntura a; ~**ion** [ɪn-'dʒɛkʃən] n iniezione f, puntura.
injure [ˈɪndʒə*] vt ferire; (wrong) fare male or torto a; (damage: reputation etc) nuocere a.
injury [ˈɪndʒərɪ] n ferita; (wrong) torto; ~**time** n (SPORT) tempo di recupero.
injustice [ɪn'dʒʌstɪs] n ingiustizia.
ink [ɪŋk] n inchiostro.
inkling [ˈɪŋklɪŋ] n sentore m, vaga idea.
inlaid [ˈɪnleɪd] a incrostato(a); (table etc) intarsiato(a).
inland a [ˈɪnlənd] interno(a) // ad [ɪn-ˈlænd] all'interno; **I~ Revenue** n (Brit) fisco, entrate fpl fiscali.
in-laws [ˈɪnlɔːz] npl suoceri mpl; cognati mpl.
inlet [ˈɪnlɛt] n (GEO) insenatura, baia; ~**pipe** n (TECH) tubo d'immissione.
inmate [ˈɪnmeɪt] n (in prison) carcerato/a; (in asylum) ricoverato/a.
inn [ɪn] n locanda.
innate [ɪ'neɪt] a innato(a).
inner [ˈɪnə*] a interno(a), interiore; ~**tube** n camera d'aria.
innocence [ˈɪnəsns] n innocenza.
innocent [ˈɪnəsnt] a innocente.
innocuous [ɪ'nɔkjuəs] a innocuo(a).
innovation [ɪnəu'veɪʃən] n innovazione f.
innuendo, ~**es** [ɪnjuˈɛndəu] n insinuazione f.
innumerable [ɪ'njuːmrəbl] a innumerevole.
inoculation [ɪnɔkjuˈleɪʃən] n inoculazione f.
inopportune [ɪn'ɔpɔtjuːn] a inopportuno(a).
inordinately [ɪ'nɔːdɪnətlɪ] ad smoderatamente.
inorganic [ɪnɔː'gænɪk] a inorganico(a).
in-patient [ˈɪnpeɪʃənt] n ricoverato/a.
input [ˈɪnput] n (ELEC) energia, potenza; (of machine) alimentazione f; (of computer) input m.

inquest [ˈɪnkwɛst] n inchiesta.
inquire [ɪn'kwaɪə*] vi informarsi // vt domandare, informarsi di; **to ~ about** vt fus informarsi di; **to ~ into** vt fus fare indagini su; **inquiring** a (mind) inquisitivo(a); **inquiry** n domanda; (LAW) indagine f, investigazione f.
inquisitive [ɪn'kwɪzɪtɪv] a curioso(a).
inroad [ˈɪnrəud] n incursione f.
insane [ɪn'seɪn] a matto(a), pazzo(a); (MED) alienato(a).
insanitary [ɪn'sænɪtərɪ] a insalubre.
insanity [ɪn'sænɪtɪ] n follia; (MED) alienazione f mentale.
insatiable [ɪn'seɪʃəbl] a insaziabile.
inscribe [ɪn'skraɪb] vt iscrivere.
inscription [ɪn'skrɪpʃən] n iscrizione f; dedica.
inscrutable [ɪn'skruːtəbl] a imperscrutabile.
insect [ˈɪnsɛkt] n insetto; ~**icide** [ɪn-ˈsɛktɪsaɪd] n insetticida m.
insecure [ɪnsɪ'kjuə*] a malfermo(a); malsicuro(a); (person) ansioso(a); **insecurity** n mancanza di sicurezza.
insensible [ɪn'sɛnsɪbl] a insensibile; (unconscious) privo(a) di sensi.
insensitive [ɪn'sɛnsɪtɪv] a insensibile.
inseparable [ɪn'sɛprəbl] a inseparabile.
insert vt [ɪn'sɔːt] inserire, introdurre // n [ˈɪnsɔːt] inserto; ~**ion** [ɪn'sɔːʃən] n inserzione f.
inshore [ɪn'ʃɔː*] a costiero(a) // ad presso la riva; verso la riva.
inside [ˈɪn'saɪd] n interno, parte f interiore // a interno(a), interiore // ad dentro, all'interno // prep dentro, all'interno di; (of time): ~ **10 minutes** entro 10 minuti; ~**s** npl (col) ventre m; ~ **lane** n (AUT) corsia di marcia; ~ **out** ad (turn) a rovescio; (know) in fondo.
insidious [ɪn'sɪdɪəs] a insidioso(a).
insight [ˈɪnsaɪt] n acume m, perspicacia; (glimpse, idea) percezione f.
insignificant [ɪnsɪg'nɪfɪknt] a insignificante.
insincere [ɪnsɪn'sɪə*] a insincero(a).
insinuate [ɪn'sɪnjueɪt] vt insinuare; **insinuation** [-'eɪʃən] n insinuazione f.
insipid [ɪn'sɪpɪd] a insipido(a), insulso(a).
insist [ɪn'sɪst] vi insistere; **to ~ on doing** insistere per fare; **to ~ that** insistere perché + sub; (claim) sostenere che; ~**ence** n insistenza; ~**ent** a insistente.
insolence [ˈɪnsələns] n insolenza.
insolent [ˈɪnsələnt] a insolente.
insoluble [ɪn'sɔljubl] a insolubile.
insolvent [ɪn'sɔlvənt] a insolvente.
insomnia [ɪn'sɔmnɪə] n insonnia.
inspect [ɪn'spɛkt] vt ispezionare; (ticket) controllare; ~**ion** [ɪn'spɛkʃən] n ispezione f; controllo; ~**or** n ispettore/trice; controllore m.
inspiration [ɪnspə'reɪʃən] n ispirazione f.
inspire [ɪn'spaɪə*] vt ispirare; **inspiring** a stimolante.
instability [ɪnstə'bɪlɪtɪ] n instabilità.

install [ɪn'stɔːl] vt installare; **~ation** [ɪnstə'leɪʃən] n installazione f.

instalment [ɪn'stɔːlmənt] n rata; (of TV serial etc) puntata.

instance ['ɪnstəns] n esempio, caso; **for ~** per or ad esempio.

instant ['ɪnstənt] n istante m, attimo // a immediato(a); urgente; (coffee, food) in polvere; **the 10th ~** il 10 corrente; **~ly** ad immediatamente, subito.

instead [ɪn'sted] ad invece; **~ of** invece di.

instep ['ɪnstep] n collo del piede; (of shoe) collo della scarpa.

instigation [ɪnstɪ'geɪʃən] n istigazione f.

instil [ɪn'stɪl] vt: **to ~ (into)** inculcare (in).

instinct ['ɪnstɪŋkt] n istinto.

instinctive [ɪn'stɪŋktɪv] a istintivo(a); **~ly** ad per istinto.

institute ['ɪnstɪtjuːt] n istituto // vt istituire, stabilire; (inquiry) avviare; (proceedings) iniziare.

institution [ɪnstɪ'tjuːʃən] n istituzione f; istituto (d'istruzione); istituto (psichiatrico).

instruct [ɪn'strʌkt] vt istruire; **to ~ sb in sth** insegnare qc a qd; **to ~ sb to do sth** dare ordini a qd di fare; **~ion** [ɪn'strʌkʃən] n istruzione f; **~ive** a istruttivo(a); **~or** n istruttore/trice; (for skiing) maestro/a.

instrument ['ɪnstrəmənt] n strumento; **~al** [-'mentl] a (MUS) strumentale; **to be ~al in** essere d'aiuto in; **~alist** [-'mentəlɪst] n strumentista m/f; **~ panel** n quadro m portastrumenti inv.

insubordinate [ɪnsə'bɔːdənɪt] a insubordinato(a); **insubordination** [-'neɪʃən] n insubordinazione f.

insufferable [ɪn'sʌfrəbl] a insopportabile.

insufficient [ɪnsə'fɪʃənt] a insufficiente.

insular ['ɪnsjulə*] a insulare; (person) di mente ristretta.

insulate ['ɪnsjuleɪt] vt isolare; **insulating tape** n nastro isolante; **insulation** [-'leɪʃən] n isolamento.

insulin ['ɪnsjulɪn] n insulina.

insult n ['ɪnsʌlt] insulto, affronto // vt [ɪn'sʌlt] insultare; **~ing** a offensivo(a), ingiurioso(a).

insuperable [ɪn'sjuːprəbl] a insormontabile, insuperabile.

insurance [ɪn'ʃuərəns] n assicurazione f; **fire/life ~** assicurazione contro gli incendi/sulla vita; **~ policy** n polizza d'assicurazione.

insure [ɪn'ʃuə*] vt assicurare.

insurrection [ɪnsə'rekʃən] n insurrezione f.

intact [ɪn'tækt] a intatto(a).

intake ['ɪnteɪk] n (TECH) immissione f; (of food) consumo; (of pupils etc) afflusso.

intangible [ɪn'tændʒɪbl] a intangibile.

integral ['ɪntɪgrəl] a integrale; (part) integrante.

integrate ['ɪntɪgreɪt] vt integrare.

integrity [ɪn'tegrɪtɪ] n integrità.

intellect ['ɪntəlekt] n intelletto; **~ual** [-'lektjuəl] a, n intellettuale (m/f).

intelligence [ɪn'telɪdʒəns] n intelligenza; (MIL etc) informazioni fpl.

intelligent [ɪn'telɪdʒənt] a intelligente.

intelligible [ɪn'telɪdʒɪbl] a intelligibile.

intemperate [ɪn'tempərət] a immoderato(a); (drinking too much) intemperante nel bere.

intend [ɪn'tend] vt (gift etc): **to ~ sth for** destinare qc a; **to ~ to do** aver l'intenzione di fare.

intense [ɪn'tens] a intenso(a); (person) di forti sentimenti; **~ly** ad intensamente; profondamente.

intensify [ɪn'tensɪfaɪ] vt intensificare.

intensity [ɪn'tensɪtɪ] n intensità.

intensive [ɪn'tensɪv] a intensivo(a); **~ care unit** n reparto terapia intensiva.

intent [ɪn'tent] n intenzione f // a: **~ (on)** intento(a) (a), immerso(a) (in); **to all ~s and purposes** a tutti gli effetti; **to be ~ on doing sth** essere deciso a fare qc.

intention [ɪn'tenʃən] n intenzione f; **~al** a intenzionale, deliberato(a); **~ally** ad apposta.

intently [ɪn'tentlɪ] ad attentamente.

inter [ɪn'tɜː*] vt sotterrare.

interact [ɪntər'ækt] vi agire reciprocamente; **~ion** [-'ækʃən] n azione f reciproca.

intercede [ɪntə'siːd] vi: **to ~ (with)** intercedere (presso).

intercept [ɪntə'sept] vt intercettare; (person) fermare; **~ion** [-'sepʃən] n intercettamento.

interchange n ['ɪntətʃeɪndʒ] (exchange) scambio; (on motorway) incrocio pluridirezionale // vt [ɪntə'tʃeɪndʒ] scambiare; sostituire l'uno/a per l'altro(a); **~able** a intercambiabile.

intercom ['ɪntəkɔm] n interfono.

interconnect [ɪntəkə'nekt] vi (rooms) essere in comunicazione.

intercourse ['ɪntəkɔːs] n rapporti mpl.

interest ['ɪntrɪst] n interesse m; (COMM: stake, share) interessi mpl // vt interessare; **~ed** a interessato(a); **to be ~ed in** interessarsi di; **~ing** a interessante.

interfere [ɪntə'fɪə*] vi: **to ~ in** (quarrel, other people's business) immischiarsi in; **to ~ with** (object) toccare; (plans) ostacolare; (duty) interferire con.

interference [ɪntə'fɪərəns] n interferenza.

interim ['ɪntərɪm] a provvisorio(a) // n: **in the ~** nel frattempo.

interior [ɪn'tɪərɪə*] n interno; (of country) entroterra // a interiore, interno(a).

interjection [ɪntə'dʒekʃən] n interiezione f.

interlock [ɪntə'lɔk] vi ingranarsi // vt ingranare.

interloper ['ɪntələupə*] n intruso/a.

interlude ['ɪntəluːd] n intervallo; (THEATRE) intermezzo.

intermarry [ɪntə'mærɪ] vi imparentarsi

per mezzo di matrimonio; sposarsi tra parenti.

intermediary [ɪntə'miːdɪərɪ] n intermediario/a.

intermediate [ɪntə'miːdɪət] a intermedio(a); (SCOL: course, level) medio(a).

intermission [ɪntə'mɪʃən] n pausa; (THEATRE, CINEMA) intermissione f, intervallo.

intermittent [ɪntə'mɪtnt] a intermittente.

intern vt [ɪn'təːn] internare // n ['ɪntəːn] (US) medico interno.

internal [ɪn'təːnl] a interno(a); ~ly ad all'interno; I~ Revenue n (US) fisco.

international [ɪntə'næʃənl] a internazionale // n (SPORT) partita internazionale.

internment [ɪn'təːnmənt] n internamento.

interplay ['ɪntəpleɪ] n azione e reazione f.

interpret [ɪn'təːprɪt] vt interpretare // fare da interprete; ~ation [-'teɪʃən] n interpretazione f; ~er n interprete m/f.

interrelated [ɪntərɪ'leɪtɪd] a correlato(a).

interrogate [ɪn'tɛrəugeɪt] vt interrogare; **interrogation** [-'geɪʃən] n interrogazione f; (of suspect etc) interrogatorio; **interrogative** [ɪntə'rɔgətɪv] a interrogativo(a) // n (LING) interrogativo; **interrogator** n interrogante m/f.

interrupt [ɪntə'rʌpt] vt interrompere; ~ion [-'rʌpʃən] n interruzione f.

intersect [ɪntə'sɛkt] vt intersecare // vi (roads) intersecarsi; ~ion [-'sɛkʃən] n intersezione f; (of roads) incrocio.

intersperse [ɪntə'spəːs] vt: to ~ with costellare di.

intertwine [ɪntə'twaɪn] vt intrecciare // vi intrecciarsi.

interval ['ɪntəvl] n intervallo; at ~s a intervalli.

intervene [ɪntə'viːn] vi (time) intercorrere; (event, person) intervenire; **intervention** [-'vɛnʃən] n intervento.

interview ['ɪntəvjuː] n (RADIO, TV etc) intervista; (for job) colloquio // vt intervistare; avere un colloquio con; ~er n intervistatore/trice.

intestate [ɪn'tɛsteɪt] a intestato(a).

intestine [ɪn'tɛstɪn] n intestino.

intimacy ['ɪntɪməsɪ] n intimità.

intimate a ['ɪntɪmət] intimo(a); (knowledge) profondo(a) // vt ['ɪntɪmeɪt] sottintendere, suggerire; ~ly ad intimamente.

intimation [ɪntɪ'meɪʃən] n annuncio.

intimidate [ɪn'tɪmɪdeɪt] vt intimidire, intimorire; **intimidation** [-'deɪʃən] n intimidazione f.

into ['ɪntu] prep dentro, in; come ~ the house vieni dentro la casa.

intolerable [ɪn'tɔlərəbl] a intollerabile.

intolerance [ɪn'tɔlərns] n intolleranza.

intolerant [ɪn'tɔlərnt] a intollerante.

intonation [ɪntəu'neɪʃən] n intonazione f.

intoxicate [ɪn'tɔksɪkeɪt] vt inebriare; ~d

a inebriato(a); **intoxication** [-'keɪʃən] n ebbrezza.

intractable [ɪn'træktəbl] a intrattabile.

intransigent [ɪn'trænsɪdʒənt] a intransigente.

intransitive [ɪn'trænsɪtɪv] a intransitivo(a).

intravenous [ɪntrə'viːnəs] a endovenoso(a).

intrepid [ɪn'trɛpɪd] a intrepido(a).

intricacy ['ɪntrɪkəsɪ] n complessità f inv.

intricate ['ɪntrɪkət] a intricato(a), complicato(a).

intrigue [ɪn'triːg] n intrigo // vt affascinare; **intriguing** a affascinante.

intrinsic [ɪn'trɪnsɪk] a intrinseco(a).

introduce [ɪntrə'djuːs] vt introdurre; to ~ sb (to sb) presentare qd (a qd); to ~ sb to (pastime, technique) iniziare qd a; **introduction** [-'dʌkʃən] n introduzione f; (of person) presentazione f; **introductory** a introduttivo(a).

introspective [ɪntrəu'spɛktɪv] a introspettivo(a).

introvert ['ɪntrəuvəːt] a introverso(a) // n introverso.

intrude [ɪn'truːd] vi (person) intrudersi; to ~ on or into intrudersi in; am I intruding? disturbo?; ~r n intruso(a); **intrusion** [-ʒən] n intrusione f.

intuition [ɪntjuː'ɪʃən] n intuizione f.

intuitive [ɪn'tjuːɪtɪv] a intuitivo(a); dotato(a) di intuito.

inundate [ɪn'ʌndeɪt] vt: to ~ with inondare di.

invade [ɪn'veɪd] vt invadere; ~r n invasore m.

invalid n ['ɪnvəlɪd] malato/a; (with disability) invalido/a // a [ɪn'vælɪd] (not valid) invalido(a), non valido(a); ~ate [ɪn-'vælɪdeɪt] vt invalidare.

invaluable [ɪn'væljuəbl] a inapprezzabile, inestimabile.

invariable [ɪn'vɛərɪəbl] a invariabile; (fig) scontato(a).

invasion [ɪn'veɪʒən] n invasione f.

invective [ɪn'vɛktɪv] n invettiva.

invent [ɪn'vɛnt] vt inventare; ~ion [ɪn-'vɛnʃən] n invenzione f; ~ive a inventivo(a); ~or n inventore m.

inventory ['ɪnvəntrɪ] n inventario.

inverse [ɪn'vəːs] a inverso(a) // n inverso, contrario.

invert [ɪn'vəːt] vt invertire; (cup, object) rovesciare; ~ed commas npl virgolette fpl.

invertebrate [ɪn'vəːtɪbrət] n invertebrato.

invest [ɪn'vɛst] vt investire // vi fare investimenti.

investigate [ɪn'vɛstɪgeɪt] vt investigare, indagare; (crime) fare indagini su; **investigation** [-'geɪʃən] n investigazione f; (of crime) indagine f; **investigator** n investigatore/trice.

investiture [ɪn'vɛstɪtʃə*] n investitura.

investment [ɪn'vɛstmənt] n investimento.

investor [ɪn'vɛstə*] n investitore/trice; azionista m/f.

inveterate [ɪn'vɛtərət] a inveterato(a).

invidious [ɪn'vɪdɪəs] a odioso(a); (task) spiacevole.

invigorating [ɪn'vɪgəreɪtɪŋ] a stimolante; vivificante.

invincible [ɪn'vɪnsɪbl] a invincibile.

inviolate [ɪn'vaɪələt] a inviolato(a).

invisible [ɪn'vɪzɪbl] a invisibile.

invitation [ɪnvɪ'teɪʃən] n invito.

invite [ɪn'vaɪt] vt invitare; (opinions etc) sollecitare; (trouble) provocare; **inviting** a invitante, attraente.

invoice ['ɪnvɔɪs] n fattura // vt fatturare.

invoke [ɪn'vəuk] vt invocare.

involuntary [ɪn'vɔləntrɪ] a involontario(a).

involve [ɪn'vɔlv] vt (entail) richiedere, comportare; (associate): **to ~ sb (in)** implicare qd (in); coinvolgere qd (in); **~d** a involuto(a), complesso(a); **to feel ~d** sentirsi coinvolto(a); **~ment** n implicazione f; coinvolgimento f; **~ment (in)** impegno (in); partecipazione f (in).

invulnerable [ɪn'vʌlnərəbl] a invulnerabile.

inward ['ɪnwəd] a (movement) verso l'interno; (thought, feeling) interiore, intimo(a); **~ly** ad (feel, think etc) nell'intimo, entro di sé; **~(s)** ad verso l'interno.

iodine ['aɪəudi:n] n iodio.

iota [aɪ'əutə] n (fig) ette m, briciolo.

IOU n (abbr of I owe you) pagherò m inv.

IQ n (abbr of intelligence quotient) quoziente m d'intelligenza.

Iran [ɪ'rɑːn] n Iran m; **~ian** [ɪ'reɪnɪən] a iraniano(a) // n iraniano/a; (LING) iranico.

Iraq [ɪ'rɑːk] n Iraq m; **~i** a iracheno(a) // n iracheno/a; (LING) iracheno.

irascible [ɪ'ræsɪbl] a irascibile.

irate [aɪ'reɪt] a irato(a).

Ireland ['aɪlənd] n Irlanda.

iris, **~es** ['aɪrɪs, -ɪz] n iride f; (BOT) giaggiolo, iride.

Irish ['aɪrɪʃ] a irlandese // n gli Irlandesi; **~man** n irlandese m; **~ sea** n Mar m d'Irlanda; **~woman** n irlandese f.

irk [əːk] vt seccare; **~some** a seccante.

iron ['aɪən] n ferro; (for clothes) ferro da stiro // a di or in ferro // vt (clothes) stirare; **~s** npl (chains) catene fpl; **to ~ out** vt (crease) appianare; (fig) spianare; far sparire; **the ~ curtain** la cortina di ferro.

ironic(al) [aɪ'rɔnɪk(l)] a ironico(a).

ironing ['aɪənɪŋ] n stiratura; **~ board** n cavalletto da stiro.

ironmonger ['aɪənmʌngə*] n negoziante m in ferramenta; **~'s (shop)** n (negozio di) ferramenta.

ironworks ['aɪənwəːks] n ferriera.

irony ['aɪrənɪ] n ironia.

irrational [ɪ'ræʃənl] a irrazionale; irragionevole; illogico(a).

irreconcilable [ɪrɛkən'saɪləbl] a irreconciliabile; (opinion): **~ with** inconciliabile con.

irredeemable [ɪrɪ'diːməbl] a (COMM) irredimibile.

irrefutable [ɪrɪ'fjuːtəbl] a irrefutabile.

irregular [ɪ'rɛgjulə*] a irregolare; **~ity** [-'lærɪtɪ] n irregolarità f inv.

irrelevance [ɪ'rɛləvəns] n inappropriatezza.

irrelevant [ɪ'rɛləvənt] a non appropriato(a).

irreparable [ɪ'rɛprəbl] a irreparabile.

irreplaceable [ɪrɪ'pleɪsəbl] a insostituibile.

irrepressible [ɪrɪ'prɛsəbl] a irrefrenabile.

irreproachable [ɪrɪ'prəutʃəbl] a irreprensibile.

irresistible [ɪrɪ'zɪstɪbl] a irresistibile.

irresolute [ɪ'rɛzəluːt] a irresoluto(a), indeciso(a).

irrespective [ɪrɪ'spɛktɪv]: **~ of** prep senza riguardo a.

irresponsible [ɪrɪ'spɔnsɪbl] a irresponsabile.

irreverent [ɪ'rɛvərnt] a irriverente.

irrevocable [ɪ'rɛvəkəbl] a irrevocabile.

irrigate ['ɪrɪgeɪt] vt irrigare; **irrigation** [-'geɪʃən] n irrigazione f.

irritable ['ɪrɪtəbl] a irritabile.

irritate ['ɪrɪteɪt] vt irritare; **irritation** [-'teɪʃən] n irritazione f.

is [ɪz] vb see **be**.

Islam ['ɪzlɑːm] n Islam m.

island ['aɪlənd] n isola; (also: **traffic ~**) salvagente m inv; **~er** n isolano/a.

isle [aɪl] n isola.

isn't ['ɪznt] = **is not**.

isolate ['aɪsəleɪt] vt isolare; **~d** a isolato(a); **isolation** [-'leɪʃən] n isolamento.

isotope ['aɪsəutəup] n isotopo.

Israel ['ɪzreɪl] n Israele m; **~i** [ɪz'reɪlɪ] a, n israeliano(a).

issue ['ɪsjuː] n questione f, problema m; (outcome) esito, risultato; (of banknotes etc) emissione f; (of newspaper etc) numero; (offspring) discendenza // vt (rations, equipment) distribuire; (orders) dare; (book) pubblicare; (banknotes, cheques, stamps) emettere; **at ~** in gioco, in discussione.

isthmus ['ɪsməs] n istmo.

it [ɪt] pronoun (subject) esso(a); (direct object) lo(la), l'; (indirect object) gli(le); **~'s raining** piove; **it's on ~** è lì sopra; **he's proud of ~** ne è fiero; **he agreed to ~** ha acconsentito.

Italian [ɪ'tæljən] a italiano(a) // n italiano/a; (LING) italiano; **the ~s** gli Italiani.

italic [ɪ'tælɪk] a corsivo(a); **~s** npl corsivo.

Italy ['ɪtəlɪ] n Italia.

itch [ɪtʃ] n prurito // vi (person) avere il prurito; (part of body) prudere; **I'm ~ing to do** non vedo l'ora di fare; **~y** a che prude.

it'd ['ɪtd] = **it would**; **it had**.

item ['aɪtəm] n articolo; (on agenda) punto; (in programme) numero; (also: **news** ~) notizia; ~**ize** vt specificare, dettagliare.

itinerant [ɪ'tɪnərənt] a ambulante.

itinerary [aɪ'tɪnərərɪ] n itinerario.

it'll ['ɪtl] = **it will, it shall**.

its [ɪts] a, pronoun il(la) suo(a), i(le) suoi(sue).

it's [ɪts] = **it is; it has**.

itself [ɪt'sɛlf] pronoun (emphatic) esso(a) stesso(a); (reflexive) si.

ITV n abbr of Independent Television (canale televisivo in concorrenza con la BBC).

I've [aɪv] = **I have**.

ivory ['aɪvərɪ] n avorio.

ivy ['aɪvɪ] n edera.

J

jab [dʒæb] vt: **to** ~ **sth into** affondare or piantare qc dentro // n colpo; (MED: col) puntura.

jabber ['dʒæbə*] vt, vi borbottare.

jack [dʒæk] n (AUT) cricco; (CARDS) fante m; **to** ~ **up** vt sollevare sul cricco.

jacket ['dʒækɪt] n giacca; (of book) copertura; **potatoes in their** ~**s** patate fpl con la buccia.

jack-knife ['dʒæknaɪf] vi: **the lorry** ~**d** l'autotreno si è piegato su se stesso.

jackpot ['dʒækpɔt] n bottino.

jade [dʒeɪd] n (stone) giada.

jaded ['dʒeɪdɪd] a sfinito(a), spossato(a).

jagged ['dʒægɪd] a sboccencellato(a); (cliffs etc) frastagliato(a).

jail [dʒeɪl] n prigione f; ~**break** n evasione f; ~**er** n custode m del carcere.

jam [dʒæm] n marmellata; (of shoppers etc) ressa; (also: **traffic** ~) ingorgo // vt (passage etc) ingombrare, ostacolare; (mechanism, drawer etc) bloccare; (RADIO) disturbare con interferenze // vi (mechanism, sliding part) incepparsi, bloccarsi; (gun) incepparsi; **to** ~ **sth into** forzare qc dentro; infilare qc a forza dentro.

Jamaica [dʒə'meɪkə] n Giamaica.

jangle ['dʒæŋgl] vi risuonare; (bracelet) tintinnare.

janitor ['dʒænɪtə*] n (caretaker) portiere m; (: SCOL) bidello.

January ['dʒænjuərɪ] n gennaio.

Japan [dʒə'pæn] n Giappone m; ~**ese** [dʒæpə'niːz] a giapponese // n, pl inv giapponese m/f; (LING) giapponese m.

jar [dʒɑː*] n (glass) barattolo, vasetto // vi (sound) stridere; (colours etc) stonare.

jargon ['dʒɑːgən] n gergo.

jasmin(e) ['dʒæzmɪn] n gelsomino.

jaundice ['dʒɔːndɪs] n itterizia; ~**d** a (fig) invidioso(a) e critico(a).

jaunt [dʒɔːnt] n gita; ~**y** a vivace, disinvolto(a).

javelin ['dʒævlɪn] n giavellotto.

jaw [dʒɔː] n mascella.

jaywalker ['dʒeɪwɔːkə*] n pedone(a) indisciplinato(a).

jazz [dʒæz] n jazz m; **to** ~ **up** vt rendere

vivace; ~**y** a vistoso(a), chiassoso(a).

jealous ['dʒɛləs] a geloso(a); ~**y** n gelosia.

jeans [dʒiːnz] npl (blue-)jeans mpl.

jeep [dʒiːp] n jeep m inv.

jeer [dʒɪə*] vi: **to** ~ **(at)** fischiare; beffeggiare.

jelly ['dʒɛlɪ] n gelatina; ~**fish** n medusa.

jeopardize ['dʒɛpədaɪz] vt mettere in pericolo.

jeopardy ['dʒɛpədɪ] n: **in** ~ in pericolo.

jerk [dʒɜːk] n scossa; strappo; contrazione f, spasimo // vt dare una scossa a // vi (vehicles) sobbalzare.

jerkin ['dʒɜːkɪn] n giubbotto.

jerky ['dʒɜːkɪ] a a scatti; a sobbalzi.

jersey ['dʒɜːzɪ] n maglia.

jest [dʒɛst] n scherzo; **in** ~ per scherzo.

jet [dʒɛt] n (of gas, liquid) getto; (AVIAT) avioigetto; ~**-black** a nero(a) come l'ebano, corvino(a); ~ **engine** n motore m a reazione.

jetsam ['dʒɛtsəm] n relitti mpl di mare.

jettison ['dʒɛtɪsn] vt gettare in mare.

jetty ['dʒɛtɪ] n molo.

Jew [dʒuː] n ebreo.

jewel ['dʒuːəl] n gioiello; ~**ler** n orefice m, gioielliere/a; ~**ler's (shop)** n oreficeria, gioielleria; ~**lery** n gioielli mpl.

Jewess ['dʒuːɪs] n ebrea.

Jewish ['dʒuːɪʃ] a ebreo(a); giudaico(a).

jib [dʒɪb] n (NAUT) fiocco; (of crane) braccio.

jibe [dʒaɪb] n beffa.

jiffy ['dʒɪfɪ] n (col): **in a** ~ in un batter d'occhio.

jigsaw ['dʒɪgsɔː] n (also: ~ **puzzle**) puzzle m inv.

jilt [dʒɪlt] vt piantare in asso.

jingle ['dʒɪŋgl] n (advert) sigla pubblicitaria // vi tintinnare, scampanellare.

jinx [dʒɪŋks] n (col) iettatura; (person) iettatore/trice.

jitters ['dʒɪtəz] npl (col): **to get the** ~ aver fifa.

job [dʒɔb] n lavoro; (employment) impiego, posto; ~**less** a senza lavoro, disoccupato(a).

jockey ['dʒɔkɪ] n fantino, jockey m inv // vi: **to** ~ **for position** manovrare per una posizione di vantaggio.

jocular ['dʒɔkjulə*] a gioviale, scherzoso(a); faceto(a).

jog [dʒɔg] vt scuotere // vi (SPORT) fare il footing; **to** ~ **along** trottare; (fig) andare avanti piano piano; **to** ~ **sb's memory** stimolare la memoria di qd; ~**ging** n footing m.

join [dʒɔɪn] vt unire, congiungere; (become member of) iscriversi a; (meet) raggiungere; riunirsi a // vi (roads, rivers) confluire // n giuntura; **to** ~ **up** vi arruolarsi.

joiner ['dʒɔɪnə*] n falegname m; ~**y** n falegnameria.

joint [dʒɔɪnt] n (TECH) giuntura; giunto; (ANAT) articolazione f, giuntura; (CULIN)

arrosto; (col: place) locale m // a comune;
~ly ad in comune, insieme.
joist [dʒɔɪst] n trave f.
joke [dʒəuk] n scherzo; (funny story)
barzelletta; (also: **practical** ~) beffa // vi
scherzare; ~r n buffone/a, burlone/a;
(CARDS) matta, jolly m inv.
jolly [dʒɔlɪ] a allegro(a), gioioso(a) / / ad
(col) veramente, proprio.
jolt [dʒəult] n scossa, sobbalzo // vt
scossare.
Jordan [dʒɔːdən] n Giordania.
jostle [dʒɔsl] vt spingere coi gomiti // vi
farsi spazio coi gomiti.
jot [dʒɔt] n: **not one** ~ nemmeno un po';
to ~ **down** vt annotare in fretta, gettare
giù; ~**ter** n quaderno; blocco.
journal [dʒɔːnl] n giornale m; rivista;
diario; ~**ese** [-liːz] n (pej) stile m
giornalistico; ~**ism** n giornalismo; ~**ist**
n giornalista m/f.
journey [dʒɔːnɪ] n viaggio; (distance
covered) tragitto.
jowl [dʒaul] n mandibola; guancia.
joy [dʒɔɪ] n gioia; ~**ful**, ~**ous** a gioioso(a),
allegro(a); ~ **ride** n gita in automobile
(specialmente rubata).
J.P. n abbr see **justice.**
Jr, Jun., Junr abbr of **junior.**
jubilant [dʒuːbɪlnt] a giubilante;
trionfante.
jubilation [dʒuːbɪleɪʃən] n giubilo.
jubilee [dʒuːbɪliː] n giubileo.
judge [dʒʌdʒ] n giudice m/f // vt giudicare;
judg(e)ment n giudizio; (punishment)
punizione f.
judicial [dʒuːdɪʃl] a giudiziale,
giudiziario(a).
judicious [dʒuːdɪʃəs] a giudizioso(a).
judo [dʒuːdəu] n judo m.
jug [dʒʌg] n brocca, bricco.
juggernaut [dʒʌgənɔːt] n (huge truck)
bestione m.
juggle [dʒʌgl] vi fare giochi di destrezza;
~**r** n giocoliere/a.
Jugoslav [juːgəuˈslɑːv] a,n = **Yugoslav.**
juice [dʒuːs] n succo.
juicy [dʒuːsɪ] a succoso(a).
jukebox [dʒuːkbɔks] n juke-box m inv.
July [dʒuːˈlaɪ] n luglio.
jumble [dʒʌmbl] n miscuglio // vt (also:
~ **up**) mischiare; ~ **sale** n (Brit) vendita
di oggetti per beneficenza.
jumbo [dʒʌmbəu] a: ~ **jet** jumbo-jet m
inv.
jump [dʒʌmp] vi saltare, balzare; (start)
sobbalzare; (increase) rincarare // vt
saltare // n salto, balzo; sobbalzo.
jumper [dʒʌmpə*] n maglia.
jumpy [dʒʌmpɪ] a nervoso(a), agitato(a).
junction [dʒʌŋkʃən] n (of roads) incrocio;
(of rails) nodo ferroviario.
juncture [dʒʌŋktʃə*] n: **at this** ~ in
questa congiuntura.
June [dʒuːn] n giugno.
jungle [dʒʌŋgl] n giungla.
junior [dʒuːnɪə*] a, n: **he's** ~ **to me (by 2**

years), he's my ~ **(by 2 years)** è più
giovane di me (di 2 anni); **he's** ~ **to me**
(seniority) è al di sotto di me, ho più
anzianità di lui; ~ **school** n scuola
elementare (da 8 a 11 anni).
juniper [dʒuːnɪpə*] n: ~ **berry** bacca di
ginepro.
junk [dʒʌŋk] n (rubbish) chincaglia; (ship)
giunca; ~**shop** n chincaglieria.
junta [dʒʌntə] n giunta.
jurisdiction [dʒuərɪsˈdɪkʃən] n
giurisdizione f.
jurisprudence [dʒuərɪsˈpruːdəns] n
giurisprudenza.
juror [dʒuərə*] n giurato.
jury [dʒuərɪ] n giuria.
just [dʒʌst] a giusto(a) // ad: **he's** ~ **done
it/left** lui lo ha appena fatto/è appena
partito; ~ **as I expected** proprio come
me lo aspettavo; ~ **right** proprio giusto;
~ **2 o'clock** le 2 precise; **it was** ~
before/enough/here era poco
prima/appena assai/proprio qui; **it's** ~
me sono solo io; **it's** ~ **a mistake** non è
che uno sbaglio; ~ **missed/caught**
appena perso/preso; ~ **listen to this!**
senta un po' questo!
justice [dʒʌstɪs] n giustizia; **J**~ **of the
Peace (J.P.)** n giudice m conciliatore.
justification [dʒʌstɪfɪˈkeɪʃən] n
giustificazione f.
justify [dʒʌstɪfaɪ] vt giustificare.
justly [dʒʌstlɪ] ad giustamente.
justness [dʒʌstnɪs] n giustezza.
jut [dʒʌt] vi (also: ~ **out**) sporgersi.
juvenile [dʒuːvənaɪl] a giovane, giovanile;
(court) dei minorenni; (books) per ragazzi
// n giovane m/f, minorenne m/f.
juxtapose [dʒʌkstəpəuz] vt giustapporre.

K

kaleidoscope [kəˈlaɪdəskəup] n
caleidoscopio.
kangaroo [kæŋgəˈruː] n canguro.
keel [kiːl] n chiglia; **on an even** ~ (fig) in
uno stato normale.
keen [kiːn] a (interest, desire) vivo(a); (eye,
intelligence) acuto(a); (competition)
serrato(a); (edge) affilato(a); (eager)
entusiastico(a); **to be** ~ **to do** or **on
doing sth** avere una gran voglia di fare
qc; **to be** ~ **on sth** essere
appassionato(a) di qc; **to be** ~ **on sb**
avere un debole per qd; ~**ness** n
(eagerness) entusiasmo.
keep [kiːp] vb (pt,pp **kept** [kɛpt]) vt tenere;
(hold back) trattenere; (feed: one's family
etc) mantenere, sostentare; (a promise)
mantenere; (chickens, bees, pigs etc)
allevare // vi (food) mantenersi; (remain:
in a certain state or place) restare // n (of
castle) maschio; (food etc): **enough for
his** ~ abbastanza per vitto e alloggio; **to**
~ **doing sth** continuare a fare qc; fare qc
di continuo; **to** ~ **sb from doing/sth
from happening** impedire a qd di
fare/che qc succeda; **to** ~ **sb happy/a**

place tidy tenere qd occupato(a)/un luogo in ordine; **to ~ sth to o.s.** tenere qc per sé; **to ~ sth (back) from sb** celare qc a qd; **to ~ time** (clock) andar bene; **to ~ on** vi continuare; **to ~ on doing** continuare a fare; **to ~ out** vt tener fuori; '**~ out**' 'vietato l'accesso'; **to ~ up** vi mantenersi // vt continuare, mantenere; **to ~ up with** tener dietro a, andare di pari passo con; (work etc) farcela a seguire; **~er** n custode m/f, guardiano/a; **~ing** n (care) custodia; **in ~ing with** in armonia con; in accordo con; **~sake** n ricordo.

keg [kɛg] n barilotto.
kennel ['kɛnl] n canile m.
Kenya ['kɛnjə] n Kenia m.
kept [kɛpt] pt,pp of **keep**.
kerb [kə:b] n orlo del marciapiede.
kernel ['kə:nl] n nocciolo.
kerosene ['kɛrəsi:n] n cherosene m.
ketchup ['kɛtʃəp] n ketchup m inv.
kettle ['kɛtl] n bollitore m; **~ drum** n timpano.
key [ki:] n (gen, MUS) chiave f; (of piano, typewriter) tasto // cpd chiave inv; **~board** n tastiera; **~hole** n buco della serratura; **~note** n (MUS) tonica; (fig) nota dominante; **~ ring** n portachiavi m inv.
khaki ['kɑ:kɪ] a,n cachi (m).
kick [kɪk] vt calciare, dare calci a // vi (horse) tirar calci // n calcio; (of rifle) contraccolpo; (thrill): **he does it for ~s** lo fa giusto per il piacere di farlo; **to ~ off** vi (SPORT) dare il primo calcio; **~-off** n (SPORT) calcio d'inizio.
kid [kɪd] n ragazzino/a; (animal, leather) capretto // vi (col) scherzare // vt (col) prendere in giro.
kidnap ['kɪdnæp] vt rapire; **~per** n rapitore/trice; **~ping** n rapimento.
kidney ['kɪdnɪ] n (ANAT) rene m; (CULIN) rognone m.
kill [kɪl] vt uccidere, ammazzare; (fig) sopprimere; sopraffare; ammazzare // n uccisione f; **~er** n uccisore m, killer m inv; assassino/a; **~ing** n assassinio; (massacre) strage f.
kiln [kɪln] n forno.
kilo ['ki:ləu] n chilo; **~gram(me)** ['kɪləugræm] n chilogrammo; **~metre** ['kɪləmi:tə*] n chilometro; **~watt** ['kɪləuwɔt] n chilowatt m inv.
kilt [kɪlt] n gonnellino scozzese.
kimono [kɪ'məunəu] n chimono.
kin [kɪn] n see **next, kith**.
kind [kaɪnd] a gentile, buono(a) // n sorta, specie f; (species) genere m; **in ~** (COMM) in natura; (fig): **to repay sb in ~** ripagare qd della stessa moneta.
kindergarten ['kɪndəgɑ:tn] n giardino d'infanzia.
kind-hearted [kaɪnd'hɑ:tɪd] a di buon cuore.
kindle ['kɪndl] vt accendere, infiammare.
kindly ['kaɪndlɪ] a pieno(a) di bontà, benevolo(a) // ad con bontà, gentilmente;

will you ~... vuole... per favore; **he didn't take it ~** se l'è presa a male.
kindness ['kaɪndnɪs] n bontà, gentilezza.
kindred ['kɪndrɪd] a imparentato(a); **~ spirit** n spirito affino.
kinetic [kɪ'nɛtɪk] a cinetico(a).
king [kɪŋ] n re m inv; **~dom** n regno, reame m; **~fisher** n martin m inv pescatore; **~-size** a super inv; gigante.
kink [kɪŋk] n (of rope) storta.
kinky ['kɪŋkɪ] a (fig) eccentrico(a); dai gusti particolari.
kiosk ['ki:ɔsk] n edicola, chiosco; cabina (telefonica).
kipper ['kɪpə*] n aringa affumicata.
kiss [kɪs] n bacio // vt baciare; **to ~ (each other)** baciarsi.
kit [kɪt] n equipaggiamento, corredo; (set of tools etc) attrezzi mpl; (for assembly) scatola di montaggio; **~bag** n zaino; sacco militare.
kitchen ['kɪtʃɪn] n cucina; **~ sink** n acquaio.
kite [kaɪt] n (toy) aquilone m; (ZOOL) nibbio.
kith [kɪθ] n: **~ and kin** amici e parenti mpl.
kitten ['kɪtn] n gattino/a, micino/a.
kitty ['kɪtɪ] n (money) fondo comune.
kleptomaniac [klɛptəu'meɪnɪæk] n cleptomane m/f.
knack [næk] n: **to have a ~ (for doing)** avere una pratica (per fare); **to have the ~ of** avere l'abitudine di; **there's a ~** c'è un modo.
knapsack ['næpsæk] n zaino, sacco da montagna.
knave [neɪv] n (CARDS) fante m.
knead [ni:d] vt impastare.
knee [ni:] n ginocchio; **~cap** n rotula.
kneel [ni:l] vi (pt,pp knelt [nɛlt]) inginocchiarsi.
knell [nɛl] n intocco.
knew [nju:] pt of **know**.
knickers ['nɪkəz] npl mutandine fpl.
knife, knives [naɪf, naɪvz] n coltello // vt accoltellare, dare una coltellata a.
knight [naɪt] n cavaliere m; (CHESS) cavallo; **~hood** n cavalleria; (title): **to get a ~hood** essere fatto cavaliere.
knit [nɪt] vt fare a maglia; (fig): **to ~ together** unire // vi lavorare a maglia; (broken bones) saldarsi; **~ting** n lavoro a maglia; **~ting needle** n ferro; **~wear** n maglieria.
knives [naɪvz] npl of **knife**.
knob [nɔb] n bottone m; manopola; (fig): **a ~ of butter** una noce di burro.
knock [nɔk] vt colpire; urtare; (fig: col) criticare // vi (engine) battere; (at door etc): **to ~ at/on** bussare a // n bussata; colpo, botta; **to ~ down** vt abbattere; **to ~ off** vi (col: finish) smettere (di lavorare); **to ~ out** vt stendere; (BOXING) mettere K.O.; **~er** n (on door) battente m; **~-kneed** a che ha le gambe ad x; **~out** n (BOXING) knock out m inv.

knot [nɔt] *n* nodo // *vt* annodare; ~**ty** *a* (*fig*) spinoso(a).

know [nəu] *vt* (*pt* **knew,** *pp* **known** [njuː, nəun]) sapere; (*person, author, place*) conoscere; **to ~ that...** sapere che...; **to ~ how to do** sapere fare; ~**how** *n* tecnica; pratica; ~**ing** *a* (*look etc*) d'intesa; ~**ingly** *ad* consapevolmente; di complicità.

knowledge ['nɔlidʒ] *n* consapevolezza; (*learning*) conoscenza, sapere *m*; ~**able** *a* ben informato(a).

known [nəun] *pp of* **know.**

knuckle ['nʌkl] *n* nocca.

K.O. *n* (*abbr of* knockout) K.O. *m* // *vt* mettere K.O.

Koran [kɔ'rɑːn] *n* Corano.

kw *abbr of* **kilowatt(s)**.

L

l. *abbr of* **litre**.

lab [læb] *n* (*abbr of* **laboratory**) laboratorio.

label ['leibl] *n* etichetta, cartellino; (*brand: of record*) casa // *vt* etichettare.

laboratory [lə'bɔrətəri] *n* laboratorio.

laborious [lə'bɔːriəs] *a* laborioso(a).

labour ['leibə*] *n* (*task*) lavoro; (*workmen*) manodopera; (*MED*) travaglio del parto, doglie *fpl* // *vi:* **to ~ (at)** lavorare duro (a); **in ~** (*MED*) in travaglio; **L~, the L~ party** il partito laburista, i laburisti; ~ **camp** *n* campo dei lavori forzati; ~**er** *n* manovale *m*; (*on farm*) lavoratore *m* agricolo; ~ **force** *n* manodopera; ~**pains** *npl* doglie *fpl*.

labyrinth ['læbirinθ] *n* labirinto.

lace [leis] *n* merletto, pizzo; (*of shoe etc*) laccio // *vt* (*shoe*) allacciare.

lack [læk] *n* mancanza // *vt* mancare di; **through** *or* **for ~ of** per mancanza di; **to be ~ing** mancare; **to be ~ing in** mancare di.

lackadaisical [lækə'deizikl] *a* disinteressato(a), noncurante.

laconic [lə'kɔnik] *a* laconico(a) (di).

lacquer ['lækə*] *n* lacca.

lad [læd] *n* ragazzo, giovanotto.

ladder ['lædə*] *n* scala; (*in tights*) smagliatura // *vt* (*tights*) smagliare // *vi* smagliarsi.

laden ['leidn] *a:* ~ **(with)** carico(a) *or* caricato(a) (di).

ladle ['leidl] *n* mestolo.

lady ['leidi] *n* signora; dama; **L~ Smith** lady Smith; **the ladies' (toilets)** gabinetti *mpl* per signore; ~**bird,** ~**bug** (*US*) *n* coccinella; ~**-in-waiting** *n* dama di compagnia; ~**like** *a* da signora, distinto(a).

lag [læg] *n* = **time ~** // *vi* (*also:* ~ **behind**) trascinarsi // *vt* (*pipes*) rivestire di materiale isolante.

lager ['lɑːgə*] *n* lager *m inv*.

lagging ['lægiŋ] *n* rivestimento di materiale isolante.

lagoon [lə'guːn] *n* laguna.

laid [leid] *pt, pp of* **lay.**

lain [lein] *pp of* **lie.**

lair [leə*] *n* covo, tana.

laity ['leiəti] *n* laici *mpl*.

lake [leik] *n* lago.

lamb [læm] *n* agnello; ~ **chop** *n* cotoletta d'agnello; ~**swool** *n* lamb's wool *m*.

lame [leim] *a* zoppo(a).

lament [lə'mɛnt] *n* lamento // *vt* lamentare, piangere; ~**able** ['læməntəbl] *a* doloroso(a); deplorevole.

laminated ['læmineitid] *a* laminato(a).

lamp [læmp] *n* lampada.

lampoon [læm'puːn] *n* pasquinata.

lamp: ~**post** *n* lampione *m*; ~**shade** *n* paralume *m*.

lance [lɑːns] *n* lancia // *vt* (*MED*) incidere; ~ **corporal** *n* caporale *m*.

land [lænd] *n* (*as opposed to sea*) terra (ferma); (*country*) paese *m*; (*soil*) terreno; suolo; (*estate*) terreni *mpl*, terre *fpl* // *vi* (*from ship*) sbarcare; (*AVIAT*) atterrare; (*fig: fall*) cadere // *vt* (*obtain*) acchiappare; (*passengers*) sbarcare; (*goods*) scaricare; **to ~ up** *vi* andare a finire; ~**ing** *n* sbarco; atterraggio; (*of staircase*) pianerottolo; ~**ing stage** *n* pontile *m* da sbarco; ~**ing strip** *n* pista d'atterraggio; ~**lady** *n* padrona *or* proprietaria di casa; ~**locked** *a* senza sbocco sul mare; ~**lord** *n* padrone *m or* proprietario di casa; (*of pub etc*) oste *m*; ~**lubber** *n* marinaio d'acqua dolce; ~**mark** *n* punto di riferimento; ~**owner** *n* proprietario(a) terriero(a).

landscape ['lænskeip] *n* paesaggio.

landslide ['lændslaid] *n* (*GEO*) frana; (*fig: POL*) valanga.

lane [lein] *n* (*in country*) viottolo; (*in town*) stradetta; (*AUT, in race*) corsia.

language ['læŋgwidʒ] *n* lingua; (*way one speaks*) linguaggio; **bad ~** linguaggio volgare.

languid ['læŋgwid] *a* languente; languido(a).

languish ['læŋgwiʃ] *vi* languire.

lank [læŋk] *a* (*hair*) liscio(a) e opaco(a).

lanky ['læŋki] *a* allampanato(a).

lantern ['læntn] *n* lanterna.

lap [læp] *n* (*of track*) giro; (*of body*): **in** *or* **on one's ~** in grembo // *vt* (*also:* ~ **up**) papparsi, leccare // *vi* (*waves*) sciabordare.

lapel [lə'pɛl] *n* risvolto.

Lapland ['læplænd] *n* Lapponia.

Lapp [læp] *a* lappone // *n* lappone *m/f*; (*LING*) lappone *m*.

lapse [læps] *n* lapsus *m inv*; (*longer*) caduta // *vi* (*law, act*) passare; (*ticket, passport*) scadere; **to ~ into bad habits** pigliare cattive abitudini; ~ **of time** spazio di tempo.

larceny ['lɑːsəni] *n* furto.

lard [lɑːd] *n* lardo.

larder ['lɑːdə*] *n* dispensa.

large [lɑːdʒ] *a* grande; (*person, animal*)

grosso(a); **at ~** (free) in libertà; (generally) in generale; nell'insieme; **~ly** ad in gran parte.

lark [lɑːk] n (bird) allodola; (joke) scherzo, gioco; **to ~ about** vi fare lo stupido.

larva, pl **larvae** ['lɑːvə, -iː] n larva.

laryngitis [lærɪn'dʒaɪtɪs] n laringite f.

larynx ['lærɪŋks] n laringe f.

lascivious [lə'sɪvɪəs] a lascivo(a).

laser ['leɪzə*] n laser m.

lash [læʃ] n frustata; (gen: eyelash) ciglio // vt frustare; (tie) assicurare con una corda; **to ~ out** vi: **to ~ out** (at or against sb/sth) attaccare violentemente (qd/qc); **to ~ out** (on sth) (col: spend) spendere un sacco di soldi (per qc).

lass [læs] n ragazza.

lasso [læ'suː] n laccio // vt acchiappare con il laccio.

last [lɑːst] a ultimo(a); (week, month, year) scorso(a), passato(a) // ad per ultimo // vi durare; **~ week** la settimana scorsa; **~ night** ieri sera, la notte scorsa; **at ~** finalmente, alla fine; **~ing** a durevole; **~-minute** a fatto(a) (or preso(a) etc) all'ultimo momento.

latch [lætʃ] n serratura a scatto; **~key** n chiave f di casa.

late [leɪt] a (not on time) in ritardo; (far on in day etc) tardi inv; tardo(a); (recent) recente, ultimo(a); (former) ex; (dead) defunto(a) // ad tardi; (behind time, schedule) in ritardo; **of ~** di recente; **in ~** May verso la fine di maggio; **~comer** n ritardatario/a; **~ly** ad recentemente; **~ness** n (of person) ritardo; (of event) tardezza, ora tarda.

latent ['leɪtnt] a latente.

later ['leɪtə*] a (date etc) posteriore; (version etc) successivo(a) // ad più tardi.

lateral ['lætərl] a laterale.

latest ['leɪtɪst] a ultimo(a), più recente; **at the ~** al più tardi.

lath, **~s** [læθ, læðz] n assicella.

lathe [leɪð] n tornio.

lather ['lɑːðə*] n schiuma di sapone // vt insaponare.

Latin ['lætɪn] n latino // a latino(a); **~ America** n America Latina; **~-American** a sudamericano(a).

latitude ['lætɪtjuːd] n latitudine f.

latrine [lə'triːn] n latrina.

latter ['lætə*] a secondo(a); più recente // n: **the ~** quest'ultimo, il secondo; **~ly** ad recentemente, negli ultimi tempi.

lattice ['lætɪs] n traliccio; graticolato.

laudable ['lɔːdəbl] a lodevole.

laugh [lɑːf] n risata // vi ridere; **to ~ at** vi fus (misfortune etc) ridere di; **I ~ed at his joke** la sua barzelletta mi fece ridere; **to ~ off** vt prendere alla leggera; **~able** a ridicolo(a); **~ing** a (face) ridente; **the ~ing stock of** lo zimbello di; **~ter** n riso; risate fpl.

launch [lɔːntʃ] n (of rocket etc) lancio; (of new ship) varo; (boat) scialuppa; (also: **motor ~**) lancia // vt (rocket) lanciare; (ship, plan) varare; **~ing** n lancio; varo;

~(ing) pad n rampa di lancio.

launder ['lɔːndə*] vt lavare e stirare.

launderette [lɔːn'drɛt] n lavanderia (automatica).

laundry ['lɔːndrɪ] n lavanderia; (clothes) biancheria; **to do the ~** fare il bucato.

laureate ['lɔːrɪət] a see **poet**.

laurel ['lɔrl] n lauro.

lava ['lɑːvə] n lava.

lavatory ['lævətərɪ] n gabinetto.

lavender ['lævəndə*] n lavanda.

lavish ['lævɪʃ] a copioso(a); abbondante; (giving freely): **~ with** prodigo(a) di, largo(a) in // vt: **to ~ on sb/sth** (care) profondere a qd/qc.

law [lɔː] n legge f; **~-abiding** a ubbidiente alla legge; **~ and order** n l'ordine m pubblico; **~-breaker** n violatore/trice della legge; **~ court** n tribunale m, corte f di giustizia; **~ful** a legale; lecito(a); **~less** a senza legge; illegale.

lawn [lɔːn] n tappeto erboso; **~mower** n tosaerba m or f inv; **~ tennis** ['tɛnɪs] n tennis m su prato.

law: ~ school n facoltà di legge; **~ student** n studente/essa di legge.

lawsuit ['lɔːsuːt] n processo, causa.

lawyer ['lɔːjə*] n (consultant, with company) giurista m/f; (for sales, wills etc) ≈ notaio; (partner, in court) ≈ avvocato/essa.

lax [læks] a rilassato(a).

laxative ['læksətɪv] n lassativo.

laxity ['læksɪtɪ] n rilassamento.

lay [leɪ] pt of **lie** // a laico(a); secolare // vt (pt, pp **laid** [leɪd]) posare, mettere; (eggs) fare; (trap) tendere; (plans) fare, elaborare; **to ~ the table** apparecchiare la tavola; **to ~ aside** or **by** vt mettere da parte; **to ~ down** vt mettere giù; **to ~ off** vt (workers) licenziare; **to ~ on** vt (water, gas) installare, mettere; (provide) fornire; (paint) applicare; **to ~ out** vt (design) progettare; (display) presentare; (spend) sborsare; **to ~ up** vt (to store) accumulare; (ship) mettere in disarmo; (subj: illness) costringere a letto; **~about** n sfaccendato/a, fannullone/a; **~-by** n piazzola (di sosta).

layer ['leɪə*] n strato.

layman ['leɪmən] n laico; profano.

layout ['leɪaut] n lay-out m inv, disposizione f; (PRESS) impaginazione f.

laze [leɪz] vi oziare.

laziness ['leɪzɪnɪs] n pigrizia.

lazy ['leɪzɪ] a pigro(a).

lb. abbr of **pound** (weight).

lead [liːd] (see also next headword; n (front position) posizione f di testa; (distance, time ahead) vantaggio; (clue) indizio; (to battery) filo conduttore; (ELEC) conduttore m isolato; (for dog) guinzaglio; (THEATRE) parte f principale // vb (pt,pp **led** [lɛd]) vt menare, guidare, condurre; (induce) indurre; (be leader of) essere a capo di; (SPORT) essere in testa a // vi condurre, essere in testa; **to ~ to** menare a; condurre a; portare a; **to ~ astray** vt sviare; **to ~ away** vt condurre via; **to ~ back** to ricondurre a; **to ~ on** vt (tease) tenere sulla corda; **to ~ on** to vt (induce) portare a; **to ~ up** to portare a; (fig) preparare la strada per.

lead [lɛd] see also previous headword; n piombo; (in pencil) mina; **~en** a di piombo.

leader ['liːdə*] n capo; direttore/trice, leader m inv; (in newspaper) articolo di fondo; **~ship** n direzione f; capacità di comando.

leading ['liːdɪŋ] a primo(a); principale; **~ man/lady** n (THEATRE) primo attore/prima attrice.

leaf, leaves [liːf, liːvz] n foglia; (of table) ribalta.

leaflet ['liːflɪt] n dépliant m inv; (POL, REL) volantino.

league [liːg] n lega; (FOOTBALL) campionato; **to be in ~ with** essere in lega con.

leak [liːk] n (out, also fig) fuga; (in) infiltrazione f // vi (pipe, liquid etc) perdere; (shoes) lasciar passare l'acqua // vt (liquid) spandere; (information) divulgare; **to ~ out** vi perdere; (information) trapelare.

lean [liːn] a magro(a) // n (of meat) carne f magra // vb (pt,pp **leaned** or **leant** [lɛnt]) vt: **to ~ sth on** appoggiare qc su // vi (slope) pendere; (rest): **to ~ against** appoggiarsi contro; essere appoggiato(a) a; **to ~ on** appoggiarsi a; **to ~ back/forward** vi sporgersi in avanti/indietro; **to ~ over** vi inclinarsi; **~ing** n: **~ing (towards)** propensione f (per).

leap [liːp] n salto, balzo // vi (pt,pp **leaped** or **leapt** [lɛpt]) saltare, balzare; **~frog** n gioco di saltamontone; **~ year** n anno bisestile.

learn, pt,pp learned or **learnt** [lɜːn, -t] vt,vi imparare; **~ed** ['lɜːnɪd] a erudito(a), dotto(a); **~er** n principiante m/f; apprendista m/f; **~ing** n erudizione f, sapienza.

lease [liːs] n contratto d'affitto // vt affittare.

leash [liːʃ] n guinzaglio.

least [liːst] a: **the ~ +** noun il(la) più piccolo(a), il(la) minimo(a); (smallest amount of) il(la) meno; **the ~ +** adjective: **the ~ beautiful girl** la ragazza meno bella; **the ~ expensive** il(la) meno caro(a); **the ~ money** il meno denaro; **at ~** almeno; **not in the ~** affatto, per nulla.

leather ['lɛðə*] n cuoio // cpd di cuoio.

leave [liːv] vb (pt,pp **left** [lɛft]) vt lasciare; (go away from) partire da // vi partire, andarsene // n (time off) congedo; (MIL, also: consent) licenza; **to be left** rimanere; **there's some milk left over** c'è rimasto del latte; **on ~** in congedo; **to take one's ~ of** congedarsi di; **to ~ out** vt omettere, tralasciare.

leaves [liːvz] npl of **leaf**.

Lebanon ['lɛbənən] n Libano.

lecherous ['lɛtʃərəs] a lascivo(a), lubrico(a).

lectern ['lɛktɜːn] n leggio.

lecture ['lɛktʃə*] n conferenza; (SCOL) lezione f // vi fare conferenze; fare lezioni; **to ~ on** fare una conferenza su.

lecturer ['lɛktʃərə*] n (speaker) conferenziere/a; (at university) professore/essa, docente m/f.

led [lɛd] pt,pp of **lead**.

ledge [lɛdʒ] n (of window) davanzale m; (on wall etc) sporgenza; (of mountain) cornice f, cengia.

ledger ['lɛdʒə*] n libro maestro, registro.

lee [liː] n lato sottovento.

leech [liːtʃ] n sanguisuga.

leek [liːk] n porro.

leer [lɪə*] vi: **to ~ at sb** gettare uno sguardo voglioso or maligno su qd.

leeway ['liːweɪ] n (fig): **to have some ~** avere una certa libertà di agire.

left [lɛft] pt,pp of **leave** // a sinistra(a) // ad a sinistra // n sinistra; **the L~** (POL) la sinistra; **~-handed** a mancino(a); **~-hand side** n lato or fianco sinistro; **~-luggage (office)** n deposito m bagagli inv; **~-overs** npl avanzi mpl, resti mpl; **~wing** n (MIL, SPORT) ala sinistra; (POL) sinistra; **~-wing** a (POL) di sinistra.

leg [lɛg] n gamba; (of animal) zampa; (of furniture) piede m; (CULIN: of chicken) coscia; (of journey) tappa; **lst/2nd ~** (SPORT) partita di andata/ritorno.

legacy ['lɛgəsɪ] n eredità f inv.

legal ['liːgl] a legale; **~ize** vt legalizzare.

legation [lɪ'geɪʃən] n legazione f.

legend ['lɛdʒənd] n leggenda; **~ary** a leggendario(a).

leggings ['lɛgɪŋz] npl ghette fpl.

legible ['lɛdʒəbl] a leggibile.

legion ['liːdʒən] n legione f.

legislate ['lɛdʒɪsleɪt] vi legiferare; **legislation** [-'leɪʃən] n legislazione f; **legislative** ['lɛdʒɪslətɪv] a legislativo(a); **legislator** n legislatore/trice; **legislature** ['lɛdʒɪslətʃə*] n corpo legislativo.

legitimacy [lɪ'dʒɪtɪməsɪ] n legittimità.

legitimate [lɪ'dʒɪtɪmət] a legittimo(a).

leg-room ['lɛgruːm] n spazio per le gambe.

leisure ['lɛʒə*] n agio, tempo libero; ricreazioni fpl; **at ~** all'agio; a proprio comodo; **~ centre** n centro di ricreazione; **~ly** a tranquillo(a); fatto(a) con comodo or senza fretta.

lemon ['lɛmən] n limone m; **~ade** n [-'neɪd] limonata.

lend, pt,pp lent [lɛnd, lɛnt] vt: **to ~ sth (to sb)** prestare qc (a qd); **~er** n prestatore/trice; **~ing library** n biblioteca circolante.

length [lɛŋθ] n lunghezza; (section: of road, pipe etc) pezzo, tratto; **at ~** (at last) finalmente, alla fine; (lengthily) a lungo; **~en** vt allungare, prolungare // vi allungarsi; ~**ways** ad per il lungo; ~**y** a molto lungo(a).

leniency ['liːnɪənsɪ] n indulgenza, clemenza.

lenient ['liːnɪənt] a indulgente, clemente.

lens [lɛnz] n lente f; (of camera) obiettivo.

lent [lɛnt] pt,pp of **lend**.

Lent [lɛnt] n Quaresima.

lentil ['lɛntl] n lenticchia.

Leo ['liːəu] n Leone m.

leopard ['lɛpəd] n leopardo.

leotard ['liːətɑːd] n calzamaglia.

leper ['lɛpə*] n lebbroso/a.

leprosy ['lɛprəsɪ] n lebbra.

lesbian ['lɛzbɪən] n lesbica.

less [lɛs] det, pronoun, ad meno; ~ **than you/ever** meno di Lei/che mai; ~ **and** ~ sempre meno; **the** ~ **he works ...** meno lui lavora ... .

lessen ['lɛsn] vi diminuire, attenuarsi // vt diminuire, ridurre.

lesson ['lɛsn] n lezione f.

lest [lɛst] cj per paura di + infinitive, per paura che + sub.

let, pt,pp **let** [lɛt] vt lasciare; (lease) dare in affitto; **he** ~ **me go** mi ha lasciato andare; ~**'s go** andiamo; ~ **him come** lo lasci venire; **'to** ~' 'affittasi'; **to** ~ **down** vt (lower) abbassare; (dress) allungare; (hair) sciogliere; (disappoint) deludere; **to** ~ **go** vi mollare // vt lasciare andare; **to** ~ **in** vt lasciare entrare; (visitor etc) far entrare; **to** ~ **off** vt lasciare andare; (firework etc) far partire; (smell etc) emettere; **to** ~ **out** vt lasciare uscire; (dress) allargare; (scream) emettere; **to** ~ **up** vi diminuire.

lethal ['liːθl] a letale, mortale.

lethargic [lɛ'θɑːdʒɪk] a letargico(a).

lethargy ['lɛθədʒɪ] n letargia.

letter ['lɛtə*] n lettera; ~**s** npl (LITERATURE) lettere; ~ **bomb** n lettera esplosiva; ~**box** n buca delle lettere; ~**ing** n iscrizione f; caratteri mpl.

lettuce ['lɛtɪs] n lattuga, insalata.

leukaemia [luː'kiːmɪə] n leucemia.

level ['lɛvl] a piatto(a), piano(a); orizzontale // n livello // vt livellare, spianare; **to be** ~ **with** essere alla pari di; **'A'** ~**s** npl ≈ esami mpl di maturità; **'O'** ~ **s** npl esami fatti in Inghilterra all'età di 16 anni; **on the** ~ piatto(a); (fig) onesto(a); **to** ~ **off** or **out** vi (prices etc) stabilizzarsi; ~ **crossing** n passaggio a livello; ~**-headed** a equilibrato(a).

lever ['liːvə*] n leva // vt: **to** ~ **up/out** sollevare/estrarre con una leva; ~**age** n: ~**age (on** or **with)** ascendente m (su).

levity ['lɛvɪtɪ] n leggerezza, frivolità.

levy ['lɛvɪ] n tassa, imposta // vt imporre; percepire.

lewd [luːd] a osceno(a), lascivo(a).

liability [laɪə'bɪlɪtɪ] n responsabilità f inv; (handicap) peso; **liabilities** npl debiti mpl; (on balance sheet) passivo.

liable ['laɪəbl] a (subject): ~ **to** soggetto(a) a; passibile di; (responsible):

~ **(for)** responsabile di; (likely): ~ **to do** propenso(a) a fare.

liaison [liː'eɪzɔn] n relazione f; (MIL) collegamento.

liar ['laɪə*] n bugiardo/a.

libel ['laɪbl] n libello; diffamazione f // vt diffamare.

liberal ['lɪbərl] a liberale; (generous): **to be** ~ **with** distribuire liberalmente.

liberate ['lɪbəreɪt] vt liberare; **liberation** [-'reɪʃən] n liberazione f.

liberty ['lɪbətɪ] n libertà f inv; **at** ~ **to do** libero(a) di fare; **to take the** ~ **of** prendersi la libertà di, permettersi di.

Libra ['liːbrə] n Bilancia.

librarian [laɪ'brɛərɪən] n bibliotecario/a.

library ['laɪbrərɪ] n biblioteca.

libretto [lɪ'brɛtəu] n libretto.

Libya ['lɪbɪə] n Libia; ~**n** a, n libico(a).

lice [laɪs] npl of **louse**.

licence ['laɪsns] n autorizzazione f, permesso; (COMM) licenza; (RADIO, TV) canone m, abbonamento; (also: **driving** ~) patente f di guida; (excessive freedom) licenza; ~ **plate** n targa.

license ['laɪsns] n (US) = **licence** // vt dare una licenza a; ~**d** a (for alcohol) che ha la licenza di vendere bibite alcoliche.

licentious [laɪ'sɛnʃəs] a licenzioso(a).

lichen ['laɪkən] n lichene m.

lick [lɪk] vt leccare // n leccata; **a** ~ **of paint** una passata di vernice.

licorice ['lɪkərɪs] n = **liquorice**.

lid [lɪd] n coperchio.

lido ['laɪdəu] n piscina all'aperto.

lie [laɪ] n bugia, menzogna // vi mentire, dire bugie; (pt **lay**, pp **lain** [leɪ, leɪn]) (rest) giacere, star disteso(a); (in grave) giacere, riposare; (of object: be situated) trovarsi, essere; **to** ~ **low** (fig) latitare; **to have a** ~**-down** sdraiarsi, riposarsi; **to have a** ~**-in** rimanere a letto.

lieutenant [lɛf'tɛnənt] n tenente m.

life, **lives** [laɪf, laɪvz] n vita // cpd di vita; della vita; **a** ~ vita; ~ **assurance** n assicurazione f sulla vita; ~**belt** n cintura di salvataggio; ~**boat** n scialuppa di salvataggio; ~**expectancy** n durata media della vita; ~**guard** n bagnino; ~ **jacket** n salvagente m, cintura di salvataggio; ~**less** a senza vita; ~**like** a verosimile; rassomigliante; ~**line** n cavo di salvataggio; ~**long** a per tutta la vita; ~ **preserver** n (US) salvagente m, cintura di salvataggio; (Brit: col) sfollagente m inv; ~**-raft** n zattera di salvataggio; ~**-saver** n bagnino; ~**-sized** a a grandezza naturale; ~**time** n: **in his** ~**time** durante la sua vita; **in a** ~**time** nell'arco della vita; in tutta la vita.

lift [lɪft] vt sollevare, levare; (steal) prendere, rubare // vi (fog) alzarsi // n (elevator) ascensore m; **to give sb a** ~ dare un passaggio a qd; ~**-off** n decollo.

ligament ['lɪgəmənt] n legamento.

light [laɪt] n luce f, lume m; (daylight) luce f, giorno; (lamp) lampada; (AUT: rear ~) luce f di posizione; (: headlamp) fanale m;

(for cigarette etc): **have you got a ~?** ha del fuoco?; **~s** *npl (AUT: traffic ~s)* semaforo // *vt (pt, pp* **lighted** *or* **lit** [lɪt]) *(candle, cigarette, fire)* accendere; *(room)* illuminare // *a (room, colour)* chiaro(a); *(not heavy, also fig)* leggero(a); **to ~ up** *vi* illuminarsi // *vt (illuminate)* illuminare; **~ bulb** *n* lampadina; **~ en** *vi* schiarirsi // *vt (give light to)* illuminare; *(make lighter)* schiarire; *(make less heavy)* alleggerire; **~er** *n (also:* **cigarette ~)** accendino; *(boat)* chiatta; **~-headed** *a* stordito(a); **~-hearted** *a* gioioso(a), gaio(a); **~house** *n* faro; **~ing** *n* illuminazione *f;* **~ing-up time** *n* orario per l'accensione delle luci; **~ly** *ad* leggermente; **~ meter** *n (PHOT)* esposimetro; **~ness** *n* chiarezza; *(in weight)* leggerezza.

lightning ['laɪtnɪŋ] *n* lampo, fulmine *m;* **~ conductor** *n* parafulmine *m.*

lightweight ['laɪtweɪt] *a (suit)* leggero(a); *(boxer)* peso leggero *inv.*

light year ['laɪtjɪə*] *n* anno *m* luce *inv.*

like [laɪk] *vt (person)* volere bene a; *(activity, object, food):* **I ~ swimming/that book/chocolate** mi piace nuotare/quel libro/il cioccolato // *prep* come // *a* simile, uguale // *n:* the ~ un(a) simile; uno(a) uguale; *(pej)* una cosa simile; uno(a) uguale; **his ~s and dislikes** i suoi gusti; **I would ~, I'd ~** mi piacerebbe, vorrei; **to be/look ~ sb/sth** somigliare a qd/qc; **that's just ~ him** è proprio da lui; **~able** *a* simpatico(a).

likelihood ['laɪklɪhud] *n* probabilità.

likely ['laɪklɪ] *a* probabile; plausibile; **he's ~ to leave** probabilmente partirà, è probabile che parta.

like-minded [laɪk'maɪndɪd] *a* che pensa allo stesso modo.

liken ['laɪkən] *vt:* **to ~ sth to** paragonare qc a.

likewise ['laɪkwaɪz] *ad* similmente, nello stesso modo.

liking ['laɪkɪŋ] *n:* **~ (for)** simpatia (per); debole *m* (per).

lilac ['laɪlək] *n* lilla *m inv* // *a* lilla *inv.*

lilting ['lɪltɪŋ] *a* melodioso(a).

lily ['lɪlɪ] *n* giglio; **~ of the valley** *n* mughetto.

limb [lɪm] *n* membro.

limber ['lɪmbə*]: **to ~ up** *vi* riscaldarsi i muscoli.

limbo ['lɪmbəu] *n:* **to be in ~** *(fig)* essere in sospeso.

lime [laɪm] *n (tree)* tiglio; *(fruit)* limetta; *(GEO)* calce *f.*

limelight ['laɪmlaɪt] *n:* **in the ~** *(fig)* alla ribalta, in vista.

limerick ['lɪmərɪk] *n* poesiola umoristica di 5 versi.

limestone ['laɪmstəun] *n* pietra calcarea; *(GEO)* calcare *m.*

limit ['lɪmɪt] *n* limite *m* // *vt* limitare; **~ation** [-'teɪʃən] *n* limitazione *f*, limite *m;* **~ed** *a* limitato(a), ristretto(a); **~ed (liability) company (Ltd)** *n* ≈ società *f*

inv a responsabilità limitata (S.r.l.).

limousine ['lɪməziːn] *n* limousine *f inv.*

limp [lɪmp] *vi* zoppicare // *a* floscio(a), flaccido(a).

limpet ['lɪmpɪt] *n* patella.

line [laɪn] *n* linea; *(rope)* corda; *(wire)* filo; *(of poem)* verso; *(row, series)* fila, riga; coda // *vt (clothes):* **to ~ (with)** foderare (di); *(box):* **to ~ (with)** rivestire or foderare (di); *(subj: trees, crowd)* fiancheggiare; **in ~ with** d'accordo con; **to ~ up** *vi* allinearsi, mettersi in fila // *vt* mettere in fila.

linear ['lɪnɪə*] *a* lineare.

linen ['lɪnɪn] *n* biancheria, panni *mpl; (cloth)* tela di lino.

liner ['laɪnə*] *n* nave *f* di linea.

linesman ['laɪnzmən] *n* guardalinee *m inv.*

line-up ['laɪnʌp] *n* allineamento, fila; *(SPORT)* formazione *f* di gioco.

linger ['lɪŋgə*] *vi* attardarsi; indugiare; *(smell, tradition)* persistere; **~ing** *a* lungo(a); persistente; *(death)* lento(a).

lingo, ~es ['lɪŋgəu] *n (pej)* gergo.

linguist ['lɪŋgwɪst] *n* linguista *m/f;* poliglotta *m/f;* **~ic** [lɪŋ'gwɪstɪk] *a* linguistico(a); **~ics** *n* linguistica.

lining ['laɪnɪŋ] *n* fodera.

link [lɪŋk] *n (of a chain)* anello; *(connection)* legame *m*, collegamento // *vt* collegare, unire, congiungere; **~s** *npl* pista or terreno da golf; **to ~ up** *vt* collegare, unire // *vi* riunirsi; associarsi.

linoleum [lɪ'nəuliəm] *n* linoleum *m inv.*

lint [lɪnt] *n* garza.

lintel ['lɪntl] *n* architrave *f.*

lion ['laɪən] *n* leone *m;* **~ cub** leoncino; **~ess** *n* leonessa.

lip [lɪp] *n* labbro; *(of cup etc)* orlo; *(insolence)* sfacciataggine *f;* **~-read** *vi* leggere sulle labbra; **to pay ~ service to sth** essere favorevole a qc solo a parole; **~stick** *n* rossetto.

liqueur [lɪ'kjuə*] *n* liquore *m.*

liquid ['lɪkwɪd] *n* liquido // *a* liquido(a); **~ assets** *npl* attività *fpl* liquide, crediti *mpl* liquidi.

liquidate ['lɪkwɪdeɪt] *vt* liquidare; **liquidation** [-'deɪʃən] *n* liquidazione *f;* **liquidator** *n* liquidatore *m.*

liquidize ['lɪkwɪdaɪz] *vt (CULIN)* passare al frullatore.

liquor ['lɪkə*] *n* alcool *m.*

liquorice ['lɪkərɪs] *n* liquirizia.

lisp [lɪsp] *n* difetto nel pronunciare le sibilanti.

list [lɪst] *n* lista, elenco; *(of ship)* sbandamento // *vt (write down)* mettere in lista; fare una lista di; *(enumerate)* elencare // *vi (ship)* sbandare.

listen ['lɪsn] *vi* ascoltare; **to ~ to** ascoltare; **~er** *n* ascoltatore/trice.

listless ['lɪstlɪs] *a* apatico(a).

lit [lɪt] *pt,pp of* **light.**

litany ['lɪtənɪ] *n* litania.

literacy ['lɪtərəsɪ] *n* fatto di sapere leggere e scrivere; cultura.

literal ['lɪtərl] *a* letterale; **~ly** *ad* alla lettera, letteralmente.

literary ['lɪtərərɪ] *a* letterario(a).

literate ['lɪtərət] *a* che sa leggere e scrivere, istruito(a).

literature ['lɪtərɪtʃə*] *n* letteratura; *(brochures etc)* materiale *m*.

lithe [laɪð] *a* agile, snello(a).

litigate ['lɪtɪgeɪt] *vt* muovere causa a // *vi* litigare; **litigation** [-'geɪʃən] *n* causa.

litre ['liːtə*] *n* litro.

litter ['lɪtə*] *n* *(rubbish)* rifiuti *mpl*; *(young animals)* figliata // *vt* sparpagliare; lasciare rifiuti in; **~ bin** *n* cestino per rifiuti; **~ed** *with* coperto(a) di.

little ['lɪtl] *a* *(small)* piccolo(a); *(not much)* poco(a) // *ad* poco; **a ~** un po' (di); **a ~ milk** un po' di latte; **~ by ~** a poco a poco; **to make ~ of** dare poca importanza a.

liturgy ['lɪtədʒɪ] *n* liturgia.

live *vi* [lɪv] vivere; *(reside)* vivere, abitare // *a* [laɪv] *(animal)* vivo(a); *(wire)* sotto tensione; *(broadcast)* diretto(a); **to ~ down** *vt* far dimenticare (alla gente); **to ~ in** *vi* essere interno(a); avere vitto e alloggio; **to ~ on** *vt fus (food)* vivere di // *vi* sopravvivere, continuare a vivere; **to ~ up to** *vt fus* tener fede a, non venir meno a.

livelihood ['laɪvlɪhud] *n* vita, mezzi *mpl* di sussistenza.

liveliness ['laɪvlɪnəs] *n* vivacità.

lively ['laɪvlɪ] *a* vivace, vivo(a).

liver ['lɪvə*] *n* fegato.

livery ['lɪvərɪ] *n* livrea.

lives [laɪvz] *npl of* **life**.

livestock ['laɪvstɔk] *n* bestiame *m*.

livid ['lɪvɪd] *a* livido(a); *(furious)* livido(a) di rabbia, furibondo(a).

living ['lɪvɪŋ] *a* vivo(a), vivente // *n*: **to earn** *o* **make a ~** guadagnarsi la vita; **~ room** *n* soggiorno; **~ standards** *npl* tenore *m* di vita; **~ wage** *n* salario sufficiente per vivere.

lizard ['lɪzəd] *n* lucertola.

llama ['lɑːmə] *n* lama *m inv*.

load [ləud] *n* *(weight)* peso; *(ELEC, TECH, thing carried)* carico // *vt*: **to ~ (with)** *(lorry, ship)* caricare (di); *(gun, camera)* caricare (con); **a ~ of, ~s of** *(fig)* un sacco di; **~ed** *a* *(dice)* falsato(a); *(question, word)* capzioso(a).

loaf, loaves [ləuf, ləuvz] *n* pane *m*, pagnotta // *vi* *(also:* **~ about, ~ around)** bighellonare.

loam [ləum] *n* terra di marna.

loan [ləun] *n* prestito // *vt* dare in prestito; **on ~** in prestito.

loath [ləuθ] *a*: **to be ~ to do** essere restio(a) a fare.

loathe [ləuð] *vt* detestare, aborrire; **loathing** *n* aborrimento, disgusto.

loaves [ləuvz] *npl of* **loaf**.

lobby ['lɔbɪ] *n* atrio, vestibolo; *(POL: pressure group)* gruppo di pressione // *vt* fare pressione su.

lobe [ləub] *n* lobo.

lobster ['lɔbstə*] *n* aragosta.

local ['ləukl] *a* locale // *n* *(pub)* bar *m inv* or caffè *m inv* vicino; **the ~s** *npl* la gente della zona; **~ call** *n* telefonata urbana; **~ government** *n* amministrazione *f* locale.

locality [ləu'kælɪtɪ] *n* località *f inv*; *(position)* posto, luogo.

locally ['ləukəlɪ] *ad* da queste parti; nel vicinato.

locate [ləu'keɪt] *vt* *(find)* trovare; *(situate)* collocare.

location [ləu'keɪʃən] *n* posizione *f*; **on ~** *(CINEMA)* all'esterno.

loch [lɔx] *n* lago.

lock [lɔk] *n* *(of door, box)* serratura; *(of canal)* chiusa; *(of hair)* ciocca, riccio // *vt* *(with key)* chiudere a chiave; *(immobilize)* bloccare // *vi* *(door etc)* chiudersi a chiave; *(wheels)* bloccarsi, incepparsi.

locker ['lɔkə*] *n* armadietto.

locket ['lɔkɪt] *n* medaglione *m*.

lockjaw ['lɔkdʒɔː] *n* tetano.

locomotive [ləukə'məutɪv] *n* locomotiva.

locust ['ləukəst] *n* locusta.

lodge [lɔdʒ] *n* casetta, portineria // *vi* *(person)*: **to ~ (with)** essere a pensione *(presso or da)* // *vt* *(appeal etc)* presentare, fare; **to ~ a complaint** presentare un reclamo; **to ~ (itself) in/between** piantarsi dentro/fra; **~r** *n* affittuario/a; *(with room and meals)* pensionante *m/f*.

lodgings ['lɔdʒɪŋz] *npl* camera d'affitto; camera ammobiliata.

loft [lɔft] *n* soffitto; *(AGR)* granaio.

lofty ['lɔftɪ] *a* alto(a); *(haughty)* altezzoso(a).

log [lɔg] *n* *(of wood)* ceppo; *(book)* = **logbook**.

logbook ['lɔgbuk] *n* *(NAUT, AVIAT)* diario di bordo; *(of lorry-driver)* registro di viaggio; *(of events, movement of goods etc)* registro; *(of car)* libretto di circolazione.

loggerheads ['lɔgəhɛdz] *npl*: **at ~ (with)** ai ferri corti (con).

logic ['lɔdʒɪk] *n* logica; **~al** *a* logico(a); **~ally** *ad* logicamente.

logistics [lɔ'dʒɪstɪks] *n* logistica.

loin [lɔɪn] *n* *(CULIN)* lombata; **~s** *npl* reni *fpl*.

loiter ['lɔɪtə*] *vi* attardarsi; **to ~ (about)** indugiare, bighellonare.

loll [lɔl] *vi* *(also:* **~ about)** essere stravaccato(a).

lollipop ['lɔlɪpɔp] *n* lecca lecca *m inv*; **~ man/lady** *n* impiegato/a che aiuta i bambini ad attraversare la strada in vicinanza di scuole.

London ['lʌndən] *n* Londra; **~er** *n* londinese *m/f*.

lone [ləun] *a* solitario(a).

loneliness ['ləunlɪnɪs] *n* solitudine *f*, isolamento.

lonely ['ləunlɪ] *a* solo(a); solitario(a), isolato(a); **to feel ~** sentirsi solo.

loner ['ləunə*] *n* solitario/a.

long [lɔŋ] a lungo(a) // ad a lungo, per
molto tempo // vi: **to ~ for sth/to do**
desiderare qc/di fare; non veder l'ora di
aver qc/di fare; **he had ~ understood
that...** aveva capito da molto tempo che...;
how ~ is this river/course? quanto è
lungo questo fiume/corso?; **6 metres ~**
lungo 6 metri; **6 months ~** che dura 6
mesi, di 6 mesi; **all night ~** tutta la notte;
~ before molto tempo prima; **before ~**
(+ future) presto, fra poco; (+ past) poco
tempo dopo; **at ~ last** finalmente; **~
-distance** a (race) di fondo; (call)
interurbano(a); **~hand** n scrittura
normale; **~ing** n desiderio, voglia, brama
// a di desiderio; pieno(a) di nostalgia.

longitude ['lɔŋgɪtju:d] n longitudine f.

long: **~ jump** n salto in lunghezza;
~-lost a perduto(a) da tempo;
~-playing a: **~-playing record (L.P.)**
n (disco) 33 giri m inv; **~-range** a a lunga
portata; **~-sighted** a presbite; (fig)
lungimirante; **~-standing** a di vecchia
data; **~-suffering** a estremamente
paziente; infinitamente tollerante;
~-term a a lungo termine; **~ wave** n
onde fpl lunghe; **~-winded** a prolisso(a),
interminabile.

loo [lu:] n (col) W.C. m inv, cesso.

look [luk] vi guardare; (seem) sembrare,
parere; (building etc): **to ~ south/on to
the sea** dare a sud/sul mare // n sguardo;
(appearance) aspetto, aria; **~s** npl aspetto;
bellezza; **to ~ like** assomigliare a; **to ~
after** vt fus occuparsi di, prendere cura di;
guardare, badare a; **to ~ at** vt fus
guardare; **to ~ down on** vt fus (fig)
guardare dall'alto, disprezzare; **to ~ for**
vt fus cercare; **to ~ forward to** vt fus non
veder l'ora di; **to ~ on** vi fare da
spettatore; **to ~ out** vi (beware): non c'è;
out (for) stare in guardia (per); **to ~ out
for** vt fus stare in aspetto per; cercare; **to
~ to** vt fus stare attento(a) a; (rely on,)
contare su; **to ~ up** vi alzare gli occhi;
(improve) migliorare // vt (word) cercare;
(friend) andare a trovare; **to ~ up to** vt
fus avere rispetto per; **~-out** n posto
d'osservazione; guardia; **to be on the
~-out (for)** stare in guardia (per).

loom [lu:m] n telaio // vi sorgere; (fig)
minacciare.

loop [lu:p] n cappio; **~hole** n via d'uscita;
scappatoia.

loose [lu:s] a (knot) sciolto(a); (screw)
allentato(a); (stone) cadente; (clothes)
ampio(a), largo(a); (animal) in libertà,
scappato(a); (life, morals) dissoluto(a);
(discipline) allentato(a); (thinking) poco
rigoroso(a), vago(a); **to be at a ~ end**
non saper che fare; **~ly** ad lentamente;
approssimativamente; **~n** vt sciogliere.

loot [lu:t] n bottino // vt saccheggiare;
~ing n saccheggio.

lop [lɔp]: **to ~ off** vt tagliare via, recidere.

lop-sided ['lɔp'saɪdɪd] a non
equilibrato(a), assimetrico(a).

lord [lɔ:d] n signore m; **L~** Smith lord

Smith; **the L~** il Signore; **the (House of)
L~s** la Camera dei Lord; **~ly** a nobile,
maestoso(a); (arrogant) altero(a); **~ship**
n: **your L~ship** Sua Eccellenza.

lore [lɔ:*] n tradizioni fpl.

lorry ['lɔrɪ] n camion m inv; **~ driver** n
camionista m.

lose [lu:z], pt,pp **lost** [lu:z, lɔst] vt perdere;
(pursuers) distanziare // vi perdere; **to ~
(time)** (clock) ritardare; **~r** n perdente
m/f.

loss [lɔs] n perdita; **to be at a ~** essere
perplesso(a).

lost [lɔst] pt,pp of **lose** // a perduto(a); **~
property** n oggetti mpl smarriti.

lot [lɔt] n (at auctions) lotto; (destiny)
destino, sorte f; **the ~** tutto(a) quanto(a);
tutti(e) quanti(e); **a ~** molto; **a ~ of** una
gran quantità di, un sacco di; **~s of**
molto(a); **to draw ~s (for sth)** tirare a
sorte (per qc).

lotion ['ləuʃən] n lozione f.

lottery ['lɔtərɪ] n lotteria.

loud [laud] a forte, alto(a); (gaudy)
vistoso(a), sgargiante // ad (speak etc)
forte; **~hailer** n portavoce m inv; **~ly** ad
fortemente, ad alta voce; **~speaker** n
altoparlante m.

lounge [laundʒ] n salotto, soggiorno // vi
oziare; starsene colle mani in mano; **~
suit** n abito completo; abito da passeggio.

louse, pl **lice** [laus, laɪs] n pidocchio.

lousy ['lauzɪ] a (fig) orrendo(a),
schifoso(a).

lout [laut] n zoticone m.

lovable ['lʌvəbl] a simpatico(a), carino(a),
amabile.

love [lʌv] n amore m // vt amare; voler
bene a; **to ~ to do:** **I ~ to do** mi piace
fare; **to be in ~ with** essere
innamorato(a) di; **to make ~** fare
l'amore; **'15 ~'** (TENNIS) '15 a zero'; **~
affair** n intrigo amoroso; **~ letter** n
lettera d'amore.

lovely ['lʌvlɪ] a bello(a); incantevole;
gradevole, piacevole.

lover ['lʌvə*] n amante m/f; (amateur): **a ~ of** un(un')amante di;
un(un')appassionato(a) di.

loving ['lʌvɪŋ] a affettuoso(a), amoroso(a),
tenero(a).

low [ləu] a basso(a) // ad in basso // n
(METEOR) depressione f // vi (cow)
muggire; **to feel ~** sentirsi giù; **he's very
~** (ill) è molto debole; **to turn (down) ~**
vt abbassare; **~-cut** a (dress) scollato(a);
~ly a umile, modesto(a); **~-lying** a a
basso livello; **~-paid** a mal pagato(a).

loyal ['lɔɪəl] a fedele, leale; **~ty** n fedeltà,
lealtà.

lozenge ['lɔzɪndʒ] n (MED) pastiglia;
(GEOM) losanga.

L.P. n abbr see **long-playing**.

Ltd abbr see **limited**.

lubricant ['lu:brɪkənt] n lubrificante m.

lubricate ['lu:brɪkeɪt] vt lubrificare.

lucid ['lu:sɪd] a lucido(a); **~ity** [-'sɪdɪtɪ] n
lucidità.

luck [lʌk] n fortuna, sorte f; **bad ~** sfortuna, mala sorte; **~ily** ad fortunatamente, per fortuna; **~y** a fortunato(a); (number etc) che porta fortuna.

lucrative ['luːkrətɪv] a lucrativo(a), lucroso(a), profittevole.

ludicrous ['luːdɪkrəs] a ridicolo(a), assurdo(a).

lug [lʌg] vt trascinare.

luggage ['lʌgɪdʒ] n bagagli mpl; **~ rack** n portabagagli m inv.

lukewarm ['luːkwɔːm] a tiepido(a).

lull [lʌl] n intervallo di calma // vt (child) cullare; (person, fear) acquietare, calmare.

lullaby ['lʌləbaɪ] n ninnananna.

lumbago [lʌm'beɪgəu] n lombaggine f.

lumber ['lʌmbə*] n roba vecchia; **~jack** n boscaiolo.

luminous ['luːmɪnəs] a luminoso(a).

lump [lʌmp] n pezzo; (in sauce) grumo; (swelling) gonfiore m // vt (also: **~ together**) riunire, mettere insieme; **a ~ sum** somma globale; **~y** a (sauce) grumoso(a).

lunacy ['luːnəsɪ] n demenza, follia, pazzia.

lunar ['luːnə*] a lunare.

lunatic ['luːnətɪk] a, n pazzo(a), matto(a).

lunch [lʌntʃ] n pranzo.

luncheon ['lʌntʃən] n pranzo; **~ voucher** n buono m pasto inv.

lung [lʌŋ] n polmone m.

lunge [lʌndʒ] vi (also: **~ forward**) fare un balzo in avanti.

lurch [lɜːtʃ] vi vacillare, barcollare // n scatto improvviso.

lure [luə*] n richiamo; lusinga // vt allettare.

lurid ['luərɪd] a sgargiante; (details etc) impressionante.

lurk [lɜːk] vi stare in agguato.

luscious ['lʌʃəs] a succulento(a); delizioso(a).

lush [lʌʃ] a lussureggiante.

lust [lʌst] n lussuria; cupidigia; desiderio; (fig): **~ for** sete f di; **to ~ after** vt fus bramare, desiderare; **~ful** a lascivo(a), voglioso(a).

lustre ['lʌstə*] n lustro, splendore m.

lusty ['lʌstɪ] a vigoroso(a), robusto(a).

lute [luːt] n liuto.

Luxembourg ['lʌksəmbɔːg] n Lussemburgo.

luxuriant [lʌg'zjuərɪənt] a lussureggiante.

luxurious [lʌg'zjuərɪəs] a sontuoso(a), di lusso.

luxury ['lʌkʃərɪ] n lusso // cpd di lusso.

lying ['laɪɪŋ] n mentire m.

lynch [lɪntʃ] vt linciare.

lynx [lɪŋks] n lince f.

lyre ['laɪə*] n lira.

lyric ['lɪrɪk] a lirico(a); **~s** npl (of song) parole fpl; **~al** a lirico(a).

M

m. abbr of **metre, mile, million**.

M.A. abbr see **master**.

mac [mæk] n impermeabile m.

macaroni [mækə'rəunɪ] n maccheroni mpl.

mace [meɪs] n mazza; (spice) macis m or f.

machine [mə'ʃiːn] n macchina // vt (dress etc) cucire a macchina; **~ gun** n mitragliatrice f; **~ry** n macchinario, macchine fpl; (fig) macchina; **machinist** n macchinista m/f.

mackerel ['mækrl] n, pl inv sgombro.

mackintosh ['mækɪntɔʃ] n impermeabile m.

mad [mæd] a matto(a), pazzo(a); (foolish) sciocco(a); (angry) furioso(a).

madam ['mædəm] n signora.

madden ['mædn] vt fare infuriare.

made [meɪd] pt, pp of **make**; **~-to-measure** a fatto(a) su misura.

madly ['mædlɪ] ad follemente; (love) alla follia.

madman ['mædmən] n pazzo, alienato.

madness ['mædnɪs] n pazzia.

magazine [mægə'ziːn] n (PRESS) rivista; (MIL: store) magazzino, deposito; (of firearm) caricatore m.

maggot ['mægət] n baco, verme m.

magic ['mædʒɪk] n magia // a magico(a); **~al** a magico(a); **~ian** [mə'dʒɪʃən] n mago/a.

magistrate ['mædʒɪstreɪt] n magistrato; giudice m/f.

magnanimous [mæg'nænɪməs] a magnanimo(a).

magnate ['mægneɪt] n magnate m.

magnet ['mægnɪt] n magnete m, calamita; **~ic** [-'netɪk] a magnetico(a); **~ism** n magnetismo.

magnification [mægnɪfɪ'keɪʃən] n ingrandimento.

magnificence [mæg'nɪfɪsns] n magnificenza.

magnificent [mæg'nɪfɪsnt] a magnifico(a).

magnify ['mægnɪfaɪ] vt ingrandire; **~ing glass** n lente f d'ingrandimento.

magnitude ['mægnɪtjuːd] n grandezza; importanza.

magnolia [mæg'nəulɪə] n magnolia.

magpie ['mægpaɪ] n gazza.

mahogany [mə'hɔgənɪ] n mogano // cpd di or in mogano.

maid [meɪd] n domestica; (in hotel) cameriera; **old ~** (pej) vecchia zitella.

maiden ['meɪdn] n fanciulla // a (aunt etc) nubile; (speech, voyage) inaugurale; **~ name** n nome m nubile or da ragazza.

mail [meɪl] n posta // vt spedire (per posta); **~box** n (US) cassetta per la posta; **~ing list** n elenco d'indirizzi; **~-order** n vendita (or acquisto) per corrispondenza.

maim [meɪm] vt mutilare.

main [meɪn] a principale // n (pipe)

conduttura principale; **the ~s** (ELEC) la linea principale; **~s operated** a che funziona a elettricità; **in the ~** nel complesso, nell'insieme; **~land** n continente m; **~stay** n (fig) sostegno principale.

maintain [mein'tein] vt mantenere; (affirm) sostenere; **maintenance** ['meintənəns] n manutenzione f; (alimony) alimenti mpl.

maisonette [meizə'nɛt] n appartamento a due piani.

maize [meiz] n granturco, mais m.

majestic [mə'dʒɛstik] a maestoso(a).

majesty ['mædʒisti] n maestà f inv.

major ['meidʒə*] n (MIL) maggiore m // a (greater, MUS) maggiore; (in importance) principale, importante.

majority [mə'dʒɔriti] n maggioranza.

make [meik] vt (pt, pp **made** [meid]) fare; (manufacture) fare, fabbricare; (cause to be): **to ~ sb sad** etc rendere qd triste etc; (force): **to ~ sb do sth** costringere qd a fare qc, far fare qc a qd; (equal): **2 and 2 ~ 4** 2 più 2 fa 4 // n fabbricazione f; (brand) marca; **to ~ do with** arrangiarsi con; **to ~ for** vt fus (place) avviarsi verso; **to ~ out** vt (write out) scrivere; (understand) capire; (see) distinguere; (: numbers) decifrare; **to ~ up** vt (invent) inventare; (parcel) fare // vi conciliarsi; (with cosmetics) truccarsi; **to ~ up for** vt fus compensare; ricuperare; **~believe** a immaginario(a); **~r** n fabbricante m/f; creatore/trice, autore/trice; **~shift** a improvvisato(a); **~up** n trucco; (articles) cosmetici mpl.

making ['meikiŋ] n (fig): **in the ~** in formazione.

maladjusted [mælə'dʒʌstid] a incapace di adattarsi.

malaise [mæ'leiz] n malessere m.

malaria [mə'lɛəriə] n malaria.

Malaysia [mə'leiziə] n Malaysia.

male [meil] n (BIOL, ELEC) maschio // a maschile; maschio(a); **~ and female students** studenti e studentesse; **~ sex** sesso maschile.

malevolent [mə'lɛvələnt] a malevolo(a).

malfunction [mæl'fʌŋkʃən] n funzione f difettosa.

malice ['mælis] n malevolenza; **malicious** [mə'liʃəs] a malevolo(a); (LAW) doloso(a).

malign [mə'lain] vt malignare su; calunniare.

malignant [mə'lignənt] a (MED) maligno(a).

malingerer [mə'liŋgərə*] n scansafatiche m/f inv.

malleable ['mæliəbl] a malleabile.

mallet ['mælit] n maglio.

malnutrition [mælnju:'triʃən] n denutrizione f.

malpractice [mæl'præktis] n prevaricazione f; negligenza.

malt [mɔːlt] n malto.

Malta ['mɔːltə] n Malta; **Maltese** [-'tiːz] a, n (pl inv) maltese (m/f).

maltreat [mæl'triːt] vt maltrattare.

mammal ['mæml] n mammifero.

mammoth ['mæməθ] n mammut m inv // a enorme, gigantesco(a).

man, pl **men** [mæn, mɛn] n uomo; (CHESS) pezzo; (DRAUGHTS) pedina // vt fornire d'uomini; stare a; essere di servizio a.

manage ['mænidʒ] vi farcela // vt (be in charge of) occuparsi di; gestire; **~able** a maneggevole; fattibile; **~ment** n amministrazione f, direzione f; (of artist) manager m inv; (COMM) gerente m; (of artist) manager m inv; **~ress** [-ə'rɛs] n direttrice f; gerente f; **~rial** [-ə'dʒiəriəl] a dirigenziale; **managing** a: **managing director** amministratore m delegato.

mandarin ['mændərin] n mandarino.

mandate ['mændeit] n mandato.

mandatory ['mændətəri] a obbligatorio(a); (powers etc) mandatorio(a).

mandolin(e) ['mændəlin] n mandolino.

mane [mein] n criniera.

maneuver [mə'nuːvə*] etc (US) = **manoeuvre** etc.

manful ['mænful] a coraggioso(a), valoroso(a).

mangle ['mæŋgl] vt straziare; mutilare // n mangano.

mango, **~es** ['mæŋgəu] n mango.

mangy ['meindʒi] a rognoso(a).

manhandle ['mænhændl] vt malmenare.

manhole ['mænhəul] n botola stradale.

manhood ['mænhud] n età virile; virilità.

manhunt ['mænhʌnt] n caccia all'uomo.

mania ['meiniə] n mania; **~c** ['meiniæk] n maniaco/a.

manicure ['mænikjuə*] n manicure f inv; **~ set** n trousse f inv della manicure.

manifest ['mænifɛst] vt manifestare // a manifesto(a), palese; **~ation** [-'teiʃən] n manifestazione f.

manifesto [mæni'fɛstəu] n manifesto.

manipulate [mə'nipjuleit] vt manipolare.

mankind [mæn'kaind] n umanità, genere m umano.

manly ['mænli] a virile; coraggioso(a).

man-made ['mæn'meid] a sintetico(a); artificiale.

manner ['mænə*] n maniera, modo; **~s** npl maniere fpl; **~ism** n vezzo, tic m inv.

manoeuvre [mə'nuːvə*] vt manovrare // vi far manovre // n manovra.

manor ['mænə*] n (also: ~ **house**) maniero.

manpower ['mænpauə*] n manodopera.

mansion ['mænʃən] n casa signorile.

manslaughter ['mænslɔːtə*] n omicidio preterintenzionale.

mantelpiece ['mæntlpiːs] n mensola del caminetto.

mantle ['mæntl] n mantello.

manual ['mænjuəl] a manuale // n manuale m.

manufacture [mænju'fæktʃə*] vt fabbricare // n fabbricazione f, manifattura; **~r** n fabbricante m.

manure [mə'njuə*] n concime m.
manuscript ['mænjuskrɪpt] n manoscritto.
many ['mɛnɪ] det molti(e) // pronoun molti(e), un gran numero; **a great ~** moltissimi(e), un gran numero (di); **~ a...** molti(e)..., più di un(a)... .
map [mæp] n carta (geografica) // vt fare una carta di; **to ~ out** vt tracciare un piano di.
maple ['meɪpl] n acero.
mar [mɑ:*] vt sciupare.
marathon ['mærəθən] n maratona.
marauder [mə'rɔ:də*] n saccheggiatore m; predatore m.
marble ['mɑ:bl] n marmo; (toy) pallina, bilia; **~s** n (game) palline, bilie.
March [mɑ:tʃ] n marzo.
march [mɑ:tʃ] vi marciare; sfilare // n marcia; (demonstration) dimostrazione f; **~-past** n sfilata.
mare [mɛə*] n giumenta.
margarine [mɑ:dʒə'ri:n] n margarina.
margin ['mɑ:dʒɪn] n margine m; **~al** a marginale.
marigold ['mærɪɡəuld] n calendola.
marijuana [mærɪ'wɑːnə] n marijuana.
marina [mə'ri:nə] n marina.
marine [mə'ri:n] a (animal, plant) marino(a); (forces, engineering) marittimo(a) // n fante m di marina; (US) marine m inv.
marital ['mærɪtl] a maritale, coniugale.
maritime ['mærɪtaɪm] a marittimo(a).
mark [mɑ:k] n segno; (stain) macchia; (of skid etc) traccia; (SCOL) voto; (SPORT) bersaglio; (currency) marco // vt segnare; (stain) macchiare; (SCOL) dare un voto a; correggere; **to ~ time** segnare il passo; **to ~ out** vt delimitare; **~ed** a spiccato(a), chiaro(a); **~er** n (sign) segno; (bookmark) segnalibro.
market ['mɑ:kɪt] n mercato // vt (COMM) mettere in vendita; **~ day** n giorno di mercato; **~ garden** n (Brit) orto industriale; **~ing** n marketing m; **~ place** n piazza del mercato.
marksman ['mɑ:ksmən] n tiratore m scelto; **~ship** n abilità nel tiro.
marmalade ['mɑ:məleɪd] n marmellata d'arance.
maroon [mə'ru:n] vt (fig): **to be ~ed (in or at)** essere abbandonato(a) (in) // a bordeaux inv.
marquee [mɑ:'ki:] n padiglione m.
marquess, marquis ['mɑ:kwɪs] n marchese m.
marriage ['mærɪdʒ] n matrimonio; **~ bureau** n agenzia matrimoniale.
married ['mærɪd] a sposato(a); (life, love) coniugale, matrimoniale.
marrow ['mærəu] n midollo; (vegetable) zucca.
marry ['mærɪ] vt sposare, sposarsi con; (subj: father, priest etc) dare in matrimonio // vi (also: **get married**) sposarsi.
Mars [mɑ:z] n (planet) Marte m.

marsh [mɑ:ʃ] n palude f.
marshal ['mɑ:ʃl] n maresciallo; (US: fire) capo; (: police) capitano // vt adunare.
marshy ['mɑ:ʃɪ] a paludoso(a).
martial ['mɑ:ʃl] a marziale; **~ law** n legge f marziale.
Martian ['mɑ:ʃɪən] n marziano/a.
martyr ['mɑ:tə*] n martire m/f // vt martirizzare; **~dom** n martirio.
marvel ['mɑ:vl] n meraviglia // vi: **to ~ (at)** meravigliarsi (di); **~lous** a meraviglioso(a).
Marxism ['mɑ:ksɪzəm] n marxismo; **Marxist** a, n marxista (m/f).
marzipan ['mɑ:zɪpæn] n marzapane m.
mascara [mæs'kɑ:rə] n mascara m.
mascot ['mæskət] n mascotte f inv.
masculine ['mæskjulɪn] a maschile // n genere m maschile; **masculinity** [-'lɪnɪtɪ] n mascolinità.
mashed [mæʃt] a: **~ potatoes** purè m di patate.
mask [mɑ:sk] n maschera // vt mascherare.
masochist ['mæsəukɪst] n masochista m/f.
mason ['meɪsn] n (also: **stone~**) scalpellino; (also: **free~**) massone m; **~ry** n muratura.
masquerade [mæskə'reɪd] n ballo in maschera; (fig) mascherata // vi: **to ~ as** farsi passare per.
mass [mæs] n moltitudine f, massa; (PHYSICS) massa; (REL) messa // vi ammassarsi; **the ~es** le masse.
massacre ['mæsəkə*] n massacro // vt massacrare.
massage ['mæsɑ:ʒ] n massaggio // vt massaggiare.
masseur [mæ'sə:*] n massaggiatore m; **masseuse** [-'sə:z] n massaggiatrice f.
massive ['mæsɪv] a enorme, massiccio(a).
mass media ['mæs'mi:dɪə] npl mass media mpl.
mass-produce ['mæsprə'dju:s] vt produrre in serie.
mast [mɑ:st] n albero.
master ['mɑ:stə*] n padrone m; (ART etc, teacher: in primary school) maestro; (: in secondary school) professore m; (title for boys): **M~ X** Signorino X // vt domare; (learn) imparare a fondo; (understand) conoscere a fondo; **M~'s degree** n titolo accademico superiore al 'Bachelor'; **~ key** n chiave f maestra; **~ly** a magistrale; **~mind** n mente f superiore // vt essere il cervello di; **~piece** n capolavoro; **~ plan** n piano generale; **~ stroke** n colpo maestro; **~y** n dominio; padronanza.
masturbate ['mæstəbeɪt] vi masturbare; **masturbation** [-'beɪʃən] n masturbazione f.
mat [mæt] n stuoia; (also: **door~**) stoino, zerbino // a = **matt**.
match [mætʃ] n fiammifero; (game) partita, incontro; (fig) uguale m/f; matrimonio; partito // vt intonare; (go well with) andare benissimo con; (equal) uguagliare // vi combaciare; **to be a good**

~ andare bene; to ~ up vt intonare; ~box n scatola di fiammiferi; ~ing a ben assortito(a); ~less a senza pari.

mate [meɪt] n compagno/a di lavoro; (col) amico/a; (animal) compagno/a; (in merchant navy) secondo // vi accoppiarsi // vt accoppiare.

material [məˈtɪərɪəl] n (substance) materiale m, materia; (cloth) stoffa // a materiale; (important) essenziale; ~s npl materiali mpl; ~istic [-əˈlɪstɪk] a materialistico(a); ~ize vi realizzarsi.

maternal [məˈtɜːnl] a materno(a).

maternity [məˈtɜːnɪtɪ] n maternità // cpd di maternità; (clothes) pre-maman inv; ~ hospital n ≈ clinica ostetrica.

mathematical [mæθəˈmætɪkl] a matematico(a).

mathematician [mæθəməˈtɪʃən] n matematico/a.

mathematics [mæθəˈmætɪks] n matematica.

maths [mæθs] n matematica.

matinée [ˈmætɪneɪ] n matinée f inv.

mating [ˈmeɪtɪŋ] n accoppiamento; ~ call n chiamata all'accoppiamento; ~ season n stagione f degli amori.

matriarchal [meɪtrɪˈɑːkl] a matriarcale.

matriculation [mətrɪkjuˈleɪʃən] n immatricolazione f.

matrimonial [mætrɪˈməʊnɪəl] a matrimoniale, coniugale.

matrimony [ˈmætrɪmənɪ] n matrimonio.

matron [ˈmeɪtrən] n (in hospital) capoinfermiera; (in school) infermiera; ~ly a matronale; dignitoso(a).

matt [mæt] a opaco(a).

matted [ˈmætɪd] a ingarbugliato(a).

matter [ˈmætə*] n questione f; (PHYSICS) materia, sostanza; (content) contenuto; (MED: pus) pus m // vi importare; it doesn't ~ non importa; (I don't mind) non fa niente; what's the ~? che cosa c'è?; no ~ what qualsiasi cosa accada; that's another ~ quello è un altro affare; as a ~ of course come cosa naturale; as a ~ of fact in verità; ~-of-fact a prosaico(a).

matting [ˈmætɪŋ] n stuoia.

mattress [ˈmætrɪs] n materasso.

mature [məˈtjʊə*] a maturo(a); (cheese) stagionato(a) // vi maturare; stagionare; (COMM) scadere; **maturity** n maturità.

maudlin [ˈmɔːdlɪn] a lacrimoso(a).

maul [mɔːl] vt lacerare.

mausoleum [mɔːsəˈlɪəm] n mausoleo.

mauve [məʊv] a malva inv.

mawkish [ˈmɔːkɪʃ] a sdolcinato(a); insipido(a).

max. abbr of maximum.

maxim [ˈmæksɪm] n massima.

maximum [ˈmæksɪməm] a massimo(a) // n (pl maxima [ˈmæksɪmə]) massimo.

May [meɪ] n maggio.

may [meɪ] vi (conditional: might) (indicating possibility): he ~ come può darsi che venga; (be allowed to): ~ I smoke? posso fumare?; (wishes): ~ God

bless you! Dio la benedica!; he might be there può darsi che ci sia; I might as well go potrei anche andarmene; you might like to try forse le piacerebbe provare.

maybe [ˈmeɪbɪ] ad forse, può darsi; ~ he'll... può darsi che lui... +sub, forse lui... .

mayday [ˈmeɪdeɪ] n S.O.S. m.

May Day [ˈmeɪdeɪ] n il primo maggio.

mayhem [ˈmeɪhem] n cagnara.

mayonnaise [meɪəˈneɪz] n maionese f.

mayor [mɛə*] n sindaco; ~ess n sindaca; moglie f del sindaco.

maze [meɪz] n labirinto, dedalo.

me [miː] pronoun mi, m' + vowel; (stressed, after prep) me.

meadow [ˈmedəʊ] n prato.

meagre [ˈmiːgə*] a magro(a).

meal [miːl] n pasto; (flour) farina; ~time n l'ora di mangiare; ~y-mouthed a che parla attraverso eufemismi.

mean [miːn] a (with money) avaro(a), gretto(a); (unkind) meschino(a), maligno(a); (average) medio(a) // vt (pt, pp meant [ment]) (signify) significare, voler dire; (intend): to ~ to do aver l'intenzione di fare // n mezzo; (MATH) media; ~s npl mezzi mpl; by ~s of per mezzo di; (person) a mezzo di; by all ~s ma certo, prego; to be meant for essere destinato(a) a; what do you ~? che cosa vuol dire?

meander [mɪˈændə*] vi far meandri; (fig) divagare.

meaning [ˈmiːnɪŋ] n significato, senso; ~ful a significativo(a); ~less a senza senso.

meanness [ˈmiːnnɪs] n avarizia; meschinità.

meant [ment] pt, pp of **mean**.

meantime [ˈmiːntaɪm] ad, **meanwhile** [ˈmiːnwaɪl] ad (also: in the ~) nel frattempo.

measles [ˈmiːzlz] n morbillo.

measly [ˈmiːzlɪ] a (col) miserabile.

measure [ˈmɛʒə*] vt, vi misurare // n misura; (ruler) metro; ~d a misurato(a); ~ments npl misure fpl; **chest/hip** ~ment giro petto/fianchi.

meat [miːt] n carne f; ~y a che sa di carne; (fig) sostanzioso(a).

Mecca [ˈmekə] n Mecca.

mechanic [mɪˈkænɪk] n meccanico; ~s n meccanica // npl meccanismo; ~al a meccanico(a).

mechanism [ˈmekənɪzəm] n meccanismo.

mechanization [mekənaɪˈzeɪʃən] n meccanizzazione f.

medal [ˈmedl] n medaglia; ~lion [mɪˈdælɪən] n medaglione m; ~list (SPORT) vincitore/trice di medaglia.

meddle [ˈmedl] vi: to ~ in immischiarsi in, mettere le mani in; to ~ with toccare.

media [ˈmiːdɪə] npl media mpl.

mediaeval [medɪˈiːvl] a = **medievale**.

mediate [ˈmiːdɪeɪt] vi interporsi; fare da mediatore/trice; **mediation** [-ˈeɪʃən] mediazione *f*; **mediator** *n* mediatore/trice.

medical ['mɛdɪkl] *a* medico(a); ~ **student** *n* studente/essa di medicina.

medicated ['mɛdɪkeɪtɪd] *a* medicato(a).

medicinal [mɛ'dɪsɪnl] *a* medicinale.

medicine ['mɛdsɪn] *n* medicina; ~ **chest** *n* armadietto farmaceutico.

medieval [mɛdɪ'iːvl] *a* medievale.

mediocre [miːdɪ'əukə*] *a* mediocre; **mediocrity** [-'ɔkrɪtɪ] *n* mediocrità.

meditate ['mɛdɪteɪt] *vi*: **to ~ (on)** meditare (su); **meditation** [-'teɪʃən] *n* meditazione *f*.

Mediterranean [mɛdɪtə'reɪnɪən] *a* mediterraneo(a); **the ~ (Sea)** il (mare) Mediterraneo.

medium ['miːdɪəm] *a* medio(a) // *n* (*pl* **media**: *means*) mezzo; (*pl* **mediums**: *person*) medium *m inv*; **the happy ~** il giusto medio.

medley ['mɛdlɪ] *n* selezione *f*.

meek [miːk] *a* dolce, umile.

meet [miːt], *pt*, *pp* **met** [miːt, mɛt] *vt* incontrare; (*for the first time*) fare la conoscenza di; (*go and fetch*): **I'll ~ you at the station** verrò a prenderla alla stazione; (*join*: *objects*) unirsi; **to ~ with** *vt fus* incontrare; ~**ing** *n* incontro; (*session*: *of club etc*) riunione *f*; (*interview*) intervista; **she's at a** ~**ing** (*COMM*) è in riunione.

megaphone ['mɛgəfəun] *n* megafono.

melancholy ['mɛlənkəlɪ] *n* malinconia // *a* malinconico(a).

mellow ['mɛləu] *a* (*wine, sound*) ricco(a); (*person, light*) dolce; (*colour*) caldo(a); (*fruit*) maturo(a) // *vi* (*person*) addolcirsi.

melodious [mɪ'ləudɪəs] *a* melodioso(a).

melodrama ['mɛləudrɑːmə] *n* melodramma *m*.

melody ['mɛlədɪ] *n* melodia.

melon ['mɛlən] *n* melone *m*.

melt [mɛlt] *vi* (*gen*) sciogliersi, struggersi; (*metals*) fondersi; (*fig*) intenerirsi // *vt* sciogliere, struggere; fondere; (*person*) commuovere; **to ~ away** *vi* sciogliersi completamente; **to ~ down** *vt* fondere; ~**ing point** *n* punto di fusione.

member ['mɛmbə*] *n* membro; ~ **country/state** *n* paese *m*/stato membro; **M~ of Parliament (M.P.)** *n* deputato; ~**ship** *n* iscrizione *f*; (*numero d'*)iscritti *mpl*, membri *mpl*.

membrane ['mɛmbreɪn] *n* membrana.

memento [mə'mɛntəu] *n* ricordo, souvenir *m inv*.

memo ['mɛməu] *n* appunto; (*COMM etc*) comunicazione *f* di servizio.

memoir ['mɛmwɑː*] *n* memoria; ~**s** *npl* memorie *fpl*, ricordi *mpl*.

memorable ['mɛmərəbl] *a* memorabile.

memorandum, *pl* **memoranda** [mɛmə'rændəm, -də] *n* appunto; (*COMM etc*) comunicazione *f* di servizio; (*DIPLOMACY*) memorandum *m inv*.

memorial [mɪ'mɔːrɪəl] *n* monumento

commemorativo // *a* commemorativo(a).

memorize ['mɛməraɪz] *vt* imparare a memoria.

memory ['mɛmərɪ] *n* memoria; (*recollection*) ricordo; **in ~ of** in memoria di.

men [mɛn] *npl of* **man**.

menace ['mɛnəs] *n* minaccia // *vt* minacciare; **menacing** *a* minaccioso(a).

menagerie [mɪ'nædʒərɪ] *n* serraglio.

mend [mɛnd] *vt* aggiustare, riparare; (*darn*) rammendare // *n* rammendo; **on the ~** in via di guarigione.

menial ['miːnɪəl] *a* da servo, domestico(a); umile.

meningitis [mɛnɪn'dʒaɪtɪs] *n* meningite *f*.

menopause ['mɛnəupɔːz] *n* menopausa.

menstruate ['mɛnstrueɪt] *vi* mestruare; **menstruation** [-'eɪʃən] *n* mestruazione *f*.

mental ['mɛntl] *a* mentale.

mentality [mɛn'tælɪtɪ] *n* mentalità *f inv*.

mention ['mɛnʃən] *n* menzione *f* // *vt* menzionare, far menzione di; **don't ~ it!** non c'è di che!, prego!

menu ['mɛnjuː] *n* (*set* ~) menu *m inv*; (*printed*) carta.

mercantile ['məːkəntaɪl] *a* mercantile; (*law*) commerciale.

mercenary ['məːsɪnərɪ] *a* venale // *n* mercenario.

merchandise ['məːtʃəndaɪz] *n* merci *fpl*.

merchant ['məːtʃənt] *n* mercante *m*, commerciante *m*; **timber/wine** ~ negoziante *m* di legno/vino; ~ **bank** *n* banca d'affari; ~ **navy** *n* marina mercantile.

merciful ['məːsɪful] *a* pietoso(a), clemente.

merciless ['məːsɪlɪs] *a* spietato(a).

mercury ['məːkjurɪ] *n* mercurio.

mercy ['məːsɪ] *n* pietà; (*REL*) misericordia; **to have ~ on sb** aver pietà di qd; **at the ~ of** alla mercè di.

mere [mɪə*] *a* semplice; **by a ~ chance** per mero caso; ~**ly** *ad* semplicemente, non ... che.

merge [məːdʒ] *vt* unire // *vi* fondersi, unirsi; (*COMM*) fondersi; ~**r** *n* (*COMM*) fusione *f*.

meridian [mə'rɪdɪən] *n* meridiano.

meringue [mə'ræŋ] *n* meringa.

merit ['mɛrɪt] *n* merito, valore *m* // *vt* meritare.

mermaid ['məːmeɪd] *n* sirena.

merriment ['mɛrɪmənt] *n* gaiezza, allegria.

merry ['mɛrɪ] *a* gaio(a), allegro(a); ~**-go-round** *n* carosello.

mesh [mɛʃ] *n* maglia; rete *f* // *vi* (*gears*) ingranarsi.

mesmerize ['mɛzməraɪz] *vt* ipnotizzare; affascinare.

mess [mɛs] *n* confusione *f*, disordine *m*; (*fig*) pasticcio; (*MIL*) mensa; **to ~ about** *vi* (*col*) trastullarsi; **to ~ about with** *vt fus* (*col*) gingillarsi con; (*: plans*) fare un pasticcio di; **to ~ up** *vt* sporcare; fare un pasticcio di; rovinare.

message ['mɛsɪdʒ] *n* messaggio.

messenger ['mɛsɪndʒə*] *n* messaggero/a.

messy ['mɛsɪ] *a* sporco(a); disordinato(a).

met [mɛt] *pt, pp* of **meet**.

metabolism [mɛ'tæbəlɪzəm] *n* metabolismo.

metal ['mɛtl] *n* metallo // *vt* massicciare; **~lic** [-'tælɪk] *a* metallico(a); **~lurgy** [-'tælədʒɪ] *n* metallurgia.

metamorphosis, *pl* **phoses** [mɛtə'mɔːfəsɪs, -iːz] *n* metamorfosi *f inv.*

metaphor ['mɛtəfə*] *n* metafora.

metaphysics [mɛtə'fɪzɪks] *n* metafisica.

mete [miːt]: **to ~ out** *vt fus* infliggere.

meteor ['miːtɪə*] *n* meteora.

meteorology [miːtɪə'rɔlədʒɪ] *n* meteorologia.

meter ['miːtə*] *n* (*instrument*) contatore *m*; (*US*) = **metre**.

method ['mɛθəd] *n* metodo; **~ical** [mɪ'θɔdɪkl] *a* metodico(a).

methylated spirit ['mɛθɪleɪtɪd'spɪrɪt] *n* (*also*: **meths**) alcool *m* denaturato.

meticulous [mɛ'tɪkjʊləs] *a* meticoloso(a).

metre ['miːtə*] *n* metro.

metric ['mɛtrɪk] *a* metrico(a); **~al** *a* metrico(a); **~ation** [-'keɪʃən] *n* conversione *f* al sistema metrico.

metronome ['mɛtrənəʊm] *n* metronomo.

metropolis [mɪ'trɔpəlɪs] *n* metropoli *f inv.*

mettle ['mɛtl] *n* coraggio.

mew [mjuː] *vi* (*cat*) miagolare.

Mexican ['mɛksɪkən] *a, n* messicano(a).

Mexico ['mɛksɪkəʊ] *n* Messico; **~ City** Città del Messico.

mezzanine ['mɛtsəniːn] *n* mezzanino.

miaow [miː'aʊ] *vi* miagolare.

mice [maɪs] *npl* of **mouse**.

microbe ['maɪkrəʊb] *n* microbio.

microfilm ['maɪkrəʊfɪlm] *n* microfilm *m inv* // *vt* microfilmare.

microphone ['maɪkrəfəʊn] *n* microfono.

microscope ['maɪkrəskəʊp] *n* microscopio; **microscopic** [-'skɔpɪk] *a* microscopico(a).

mid [mɪd] *a*: **~ May** metà maggio; **~ afternoon** metà pomeriggio; **in ~ air** a mezz'aria; **~day** *n* mezzogiorno.

middle ['mɪdl] *n* mezzo; centro; (*waist*) vita // *a* di mezzo; **~aged** *a* di mezza età; **the M~ Ages** *npl* il Medioevo; **~class** *a* ≈ borghese; **the ~ class(es)** ≈ la borghesia; **M~ East** *n* Medio Oriente *m*; **~man** *n* intermediario; agente *m* rivenditore.

middling ['mɪdlɪŋ] *a* medio(a).

midge [mɪdʒ] *n* moscerino.

midget ['mɪdʒɪt] *n* nano/a.

Midlands ['mɪdləndz] *npl* contee del centro dell'Inghilterra.

midnight ['mɪdnaɪt] *n* mezzanotte *f.*

midriff ['mɪdrɪf] *n* diaframma *m.*

midst [mɪdst] *n*: **in the ~ of** in mezzo a.

midsummer [mɪd'sʌmə*] *n* mezza *or* piena estate *f.*

midway [mɪd'weɪ] *a, ad*: **~ (between)** a mezza strada (fra).

midwife, midwives ['mɪdwaɪf, -vz] *n* levatrice *f*; **~ry** [-'wɪfərɪ] *n* ostetrica.

midwinter [mɪd'wɪntə*] *n* pieno inverno.

might [maɪt] *vb see* **may** // *n* potere *m*, forza; **~y** *a* forte, potente // *ad* (*col*) molto.

migraine ['miːgreɪn] *n* emicrania.

migrant ['maɪgrənt] *n* (*bird, animal*) migratore *m*; (*person*) migrante *m/f*; nomade *m/f* // *a* migratore(trice); nomade; (*worker*) emigrato(a).

migrate [maɪ'greɪt] *vi* migrare; **migration** [-'greɪʃən] *n* migrazione *f.*

mike [maɪk] *n* (*abbr of* **microphone**) microfono.

mild [maɪld] *n* a mite; (*person, voice*) dolce; (*flavour*) delicato(a); (*illness*) leggero(a) // *n* birra leggera.

mildew ['mɪldjuː] *n* muffa.

mildly ['maɪldlɪ] *ad* mitemente; dolcemente; delicatamente; leggermente; **to put it ~** a dire poco.

mile [maɪl] *n* miglio; **~age** *n* distanza in miglia, ≈ chilometraggio; **~ometer** *n* = **milometer**; **~stone** *n* pietra miliare.

milieu ['miːljəː] *n* ambiente *m.*

militant ['mɪlɪtnt] *a, n* militante (*m/f*).

military ['mɪlɪtərɪ] *a* militare // *n*: **the ~** i militari, l'esercito.

militate ['mɪlɪteɪt] *vi*: **to ~ against** essere d'ostacolo a.

militia [mɪ'lɪʃə] *n* milizia.

milk [mɪlk] *n* latte *m* // *vt* (*cow*) mungere; (*fig*) sfruttare; **~ chocolate** *n* cioccolato al latte; **~ing** *n* mungitura; **~man** *n* lattaio; **~ shake** *n* frappé *m inv*; **~y** *a* lattiginoso(a); (*colour*) latteo(a); **M~y Way** *n* Via Lattea.

mill [mɪl] *n* mulino; (*small: for coffee, pepper etc*) macinino; (*factory*) fabbrica; (*spinning ~*) filatura // *vt* macinare // *vi* (*also*: **~ about**) formicolare.

millennium, *pl* **~s** *or* **millennia** [mɪ'lɛnɪəm, -'lɛnɪə] *n* millennio.

miller ['mɪlə*] *n* mugnaio.

millet ['mɪlɪt] *n* miglio.

milli... ['mɪlɪ] *prefix*: **~gram(me)** *n* milligrammo; **~litre** *n* millilitro; **~metre** *n* millimetro.

milliner ['mɪlɪnə*] *n* modista; **~y** *n* modisteria.

million ['mɪljən] *n* milione *m*; **~aire** *n* milionario, ≈ miliardario.

millstone ['mɪlstəʊn] *n* macina.

milometer [maɪ'lɔmɪtə*] *n* ≈ contachilometri *m inv.*

mime [maɪm] *n* mimo // *vt, vi* mimare.

mimic ['mɪmɪk] *n* imitatore/trice // *vt* fare la mimica di // *vi* fare la mimica; **~ry** *n* mimica; (*ZOOL*) mimetismo.

min. *abbr of* **minute(s), minimum**.

minaret [mɪnə'rɛt] *n* minareto.

mince [mɪns] *vt* tritare, macinare // *vi* (*in walking*) camminare a passettini // *n* (*CULIN*) carne *f* tritata *or* macinata; **he**

does not ~ (his) words parla chiaro e tondo; **~meat** n frutta secca tritata per uso in pasticceria; **~ pie** n specie di torta con frutta secca; **~r** n tritacarne m inv.

mind [maɪnd] n mente f // vt (attend to, look after) badare a, occuparsi di; (be careful) fare attenzione a, stare attento(a) a; (object to): **I don't ~ the noise** il rumore non mi dà alcun fastidio; **do you ~ if ...?** le dispiace se ...?; **I don't ~** non m'importa; **it is on my ~** mi preoccupa; **to my ~** secondo me, a mio parere; **to be out of one's ~** essere uscito(a) di mente; **never ~** non importa, non fa niente; **to keep sth in ~** non dimenticare qc; **to make up one's ~** decidersi; **'~ the step'** 'attenzione allo scalino'; **to have in ~ to do** aver l'intenzione di fare; **~ful** a: **~ful of** attento(a) a; memore di; **~less** a idiota.

mine [maɪn] pronoun il(la) mio(a), pl i(le) miei(mie); **this book is ~** questo libro è mio // n miniera; (explosive) mina // vt (coal) estrarre; (ship, beach) minare; **~ detector** n rivelatore m di mine; **~field** n campo minato; **~r** n minatore m.

mineral ['mɪnərəl] a minerale // n minerale m; **~s** npl (soft drinks) bevande fpl gasate; **~ogy** [-'rælədʒɪ] n mineralogia; **~ water** n acqua minerale.

minesweeper ['maɪnswiːpə*] n dragamine m inv.

mingle ['mɪŋgl] vt mescolare, mischiare // vi: **to ~ with** mescolarsi a, mischiarsi con.

miniature ['mɪnətʃə*] a in miniatura // n miniatura.

minibus ['mɪnɪbʌs] n minibus m inv.

minim ['mɪnɪm] n (MUS) minima.

minimal ['mɪnɪml] a minimo(a).

minimize ['mɪnɪmaɪz] vt minimizzare.

minimum ['mɪnɪməm] n (pl: minima ['mɪnɪmə]) minimo // a minimo(a).

mining ['maɪnɪŋ] n industria mineraria // a minerario(a); di minatori.

minion ['mɪnjən] n (pej) caudatario; favorito/a.

miniskirt ['mɪnɪskəːt] n minigonna.

minister ['mɪnɪstə*] n (POL) ministro; (REL) pastore m; **~ial** [-'tɪərɪəl] a (POL) ministeriale.

ministry ['mɪnɪstrɪ] n ministero; (REL): **to go into the ~** diventare pastore.

mink [mɪŋk] n visone m; **~ coat** n pelliccia di visone.

minnow ['mɪnəu] n pesciolino d'acqua dolce.

minor ['maɪnə*] a minore, di poca importanza; (MUS) minore // n (LAW) minorenne m/f.

minority [maɪ'nɔrɪtɪ] n minoranza.

minstrel ['mɪnstrəl] n' giullare m, menestrello.

mint [mɪnt] n (plant) menta; (sweet) pasticca di menta // vt (coins) battere; **the (Royal) M~** la Zecca; **~ condition** come nuovo(a) di zecca; **~ sauce** n salsa di menta.

minuet [mɪnjuˈɛt] n minuetto.

minus ['maɪnəs] n (also: ~ **sign**) segno meno // prep meno.

minute a [maɪˈnjuːt] minuscolo(a); (detail) minuzioso(a) // n ['mɪnɪt] minuto; (official record) processo verbale, resoconto sommario; **~s** npl verbale m, verbali mpl.

miracle ['mɪrəkl] n miracolo; **miraculous** [mɪˈrækjuləs] a miracoloso(a).

mirage ['mɪrɑːʒ] n miraggio.

mirror ['mɪrə*] n specchio // vt rispecchiare, riflettere.

mirth [məːθ] n gaiezza.

misadventure [mɪsədˈvɛntʃə*] n disavventura; **death by ~** morte f accidentale.

misanthropist [mɪˈzænθrəpɪst] n misantropo/a.

misapprehension ['mɪsæprɪˈhɛnʃən] n malinteso.

misappropriate [mɪsəˈprəuprɪeɪt] vt appropriarsi indebitamente di.

misbehave [mɪsbɪˈheɪv] vi comportarsi male; **misbehaviour** n comportamento scorretto.

miscalculate [mɪsˈkælkjuleɪt] vt calcolare male; **miscalculation** [-ˈleɪʃən] n errore m di calcolo.

miscarriage [mɪsˈkærɪdʒ] n (MED) aborto spontaneo; **~ of justice** errore m giudiziario.

miscellaneous [mɪsɪˈleɪnɪəs] a (items) vario(a); (selection) misto(a).

miscellany [mɪˈsɛlənɪ] n raccolta.

mischief ['mɪstʃɪf] n (naughtiness) birichineria; (harm) male m, danno; (maliciousness) malizia; **mischievous** a (naughty) birichino(a); (harmful) danno-so(a).

misconception ['mɪskənˈsɛpʃən] n idea sbagliata.

misconduct [mɪsˈkɔndʌkt] n cattiva condotta; **professional ~** reato professionale.

misconstrue [mɪskənˈstruː] vt interpretare male.

miscount [mɪsˈkaunt] vt,vi contare male.

misdemeanour [mɪsdɪˈmiːnə*] n misfatto; infrazione f.

misdirect [mɪsdɪˈrɛkt] vt mal indirizzare.

miser ['maɪzə*] n avaro.

miserable ['mɪzərəbl] a infelice; (wretched) miserabile.

miserly ['maɪzəlɪ] a avaro(a).

misery ['mɪzərɪ] n (unhappiness) tristezza; (pain) sofferenza; (wretchedness) miseria.

misfire [mɪsˈfaɪə*] vi far cilecca; (car engine) dare accensione irregolare.

misfit ['mɪsfɪt] n (person) spostato/a.

misfortune [mɪsˈfɔːtʃən] n sfortuna.

misgiving(s) [mɪsˈgɪvɪŋ(z)] n(pl) dubbi mpl, sospetti mpl.

misguided [mɪsˈgaɪdɪd] a sbagliato(a); poco giudizioso(a).

mishandle [mɪsˈhændl] vt (treat roughly) maltrattare; (mismanage) trattare male.

mishap ['mɪshæp] n disgrazia.

misinform [misin'fɔːm] vt informare male.

misinterpret [misin'tɔːprit] vt interpretare male.

misjudge [mis'dʒʌdʒ] vt giudicare male.

mislay [mis'lei] vt irg smarrire.

mislead [mis'liːd] vt irg sviare; ~ing a ingannevole.

mismanage [mis'mænidʒ] vt gestire male; trattare male; ~ment n cattiva amministrazione f.

misnomer [mis'nəumə*] n termine m sbagliato or improprio.

misplace [mis'pleis] vt smarrire; collocare fuori posto.

misprint ['misprint] n errore m di stampa.

mispronounce [mispra'nauns] vt pronunciare male.

misread [mis'riːd] vt irg leggere male.

misrepresent [misrepri'zent] vt travisare.

miss [mis] vt (fail to get) perdere; (regret the absence of): **I ~ him/it** sento la sua mancanza, lui/esso mi manca // vi mancare // n (shot) colpo mancato; (fig): **that was a near ~** c'è mancato poco; **to ~ out** vt omettere.

Miss [mis] n Signorina.

missal ['misl] n messale m.

misshapen [mis'ʃeipən] a deforme.

missile ['misail] n (AVIAT) missile m; (object thrown) proiettile m.

missing ['misiŋ] a perso(a), smarrito(a); (after escape, disaster: person) mancante; **to go ~** sparire.

mission ['miʃən] n missione f; ~ary n missionario/a.

misspent ['mis'spent] a: **his ~ youth** la sua gioventù sciupata.

mist [mist] n nebbia, foschia // vi (also: ~ over, ~ up) annebbiarsi; (windows) appannarsi.

mistake [mis'teik] n sbaglio, errore m // vt (irg: like **take**) sbagliarsi di; fraintendere; **to ~ for** prendere per; ~n a (idea etc) sbagliato(a); **to be ~n** sbagliarsi; ~n **identity** n errore m di persona.

mister ['mistə*] n (col) signore m; see **Mr**.

mistletoe ['misltəu] n vischio.

mistook [mis'tuk] pt of **mistake**.

mistranslation [mistræns'leiʃən] n traduzione f errata.

mistreat [mis'triːt] vt maltrattare.

mistress ['mistris] n padrona; (lover) amante f; (in primary school) maestra; see **Mrs**.

mistrust [mis'trʌst] vt diffidare di.

misty ['misti] a nebbioso(a), brumoso(a).

misunderstand [misʌndə'stænd] vt, vi irg capire male, fraintendere; ~ing n malinteso, equivoco.

misuse n [mis'juːs] cattivo uso; (of power) abuso // vt [mis'juːz] far cattivo uso di; abusare di.

mitigate ['mitigeit] vt mitigare.

mitre ['maitə*] n mitra; (CARPENTRY) ugnatura.

mitt(en) ['mit(n)] n mezzo guanto; manopolo.

mix [miks] vt mescolare // vi mescolarsi // n mescolanza; preparato; **to ~ up** vt mescolare; (confuse) confondere; ~ed a misto(a); ~ed **grill** n misto alla griglia; ~ed-up a (confused) confuso(a); ~er n (for food) sbattitore m; (person): **he is a good ~er** è molto socievole; ~ture n mescolanza; (blend: of tobacco etc) miscela; (MED) sciroppo; ~-up n confusione f.

moan [məun] n gemito // vi gemere; (col: complain): **to ~ (about)** lamentarsi (di); ~ing n gemiti mpl.

moat [məut] n fossato.

mob [mob] n folla; (disorderly) calca; (pej): **the ~** la plebaglia // vt accalcarsi intorno a.

mobile ['məubail] a mobile; ~ **home** n grande roulotte f inv (utilizzata come domicilio).

mobility [məu'biliti] n mobilità.

moccasin ['mɔkəsin] n mocassino.

mock [mɔk] vt deridere, burlarsi di // a falso(a); ~ery n derisione f; ~ing a derisorio(a); ~-up n modello dimostrativo; abbozzo.

mod [mɔd] a see **convenience**.

mode [məud] n modo.

model ['mɔdl] n modello; (person: for fashion) indossatore/trice; (: for artist) modello/a // vt modellare // vi fare l'indossatore (or l'indossatrice) // a (railway: toy) modello inv in scala; (child, factory) modello inv; **to ~ clothes** presentare degli abiti.

moderate a, n ['mɔdərət] moderato(a) // vb ['mɔdəreit] vi moderarsi, placarsi // vt moderare; **moderation** [-'reiʃən] n moderazione f, misura.

modern ['mɔdən] a moderno(a); ~ize vt modernizzare.

modest ['mɔdist] a modesto(a); ~y n modestia.

modicum ['mɔdikəm] n: **a ~ of** un minimo di.

modification [mɔdifi'keiʃən] n modificazione f.

modify ['mɔdifai] vt modificare.

module ['mɔdjuːl] n modulo.

mohair ['məuhɛə*] n mohair m.

moist [mɔist] a umido(a); ~en ['mɔisn] vt inumidire; ~ure ['mɔistʃə*] n umidità; (on glass) goccioline fpl di vapore; ~urizer ['mɔistʃəraizə*] n idratante f.

molar ['məulə*] n molare m.

molasses [məu'læsiz] n molassa.

mold [məuld] n, vt (US) = **mould**.

mole [məul] n (animal) talpa; (spot) neo.

molecule ['mɔlikjuːl] n molecola.

molest [məu'lest] vt molestare.

mollusc ['mɔləsk] n mollusco.

mollycoddle ['mɔlikɔdl] vt coccolare, vezzeggiare.

molt [məult] *vi* (*US*) = **moult**.

molten ['məultən] *a* fuso(a).

moment ['məumənt] *n* momento, istante *m*; importanza; ~**ary** *a* momentaneo(a), passeggero(a); ~**ous** [-'mentəs] *a* di grande importanza.

momentum [məu'mentəm] *n* velocità acquisita, slancio; (*PHYSICS*) momento; **to gather** ~ aumentare di velocità.

monarch ['mɔnək] *n* monarca/chessa; ~**ist** *n* monarchista *m/f*; ~**y** *n* monarchia.

monastery ['mɔnəstəri] *n* monastero.

monastic [mə'næstik] *a* monastico(a).

Monday ['mʌndi] *n* lunedì *m inv*.

monetary ['mʌnitəri] *a* monetario(a).

money ['mʌni] *n* denaro, soldi *mpl*; ~**lender** *n* prestatore *m* di denaro; ~ **order** *n* vaglia *m inv*.

mongol ['mɔngəl] *a,n* (*MED*) mongoloide (*m/f*).

mongrel ['mʌngrəl] *n* (*dog*) cane *m* bastardo.

monitor ['mɔnitə*] *n* (*SCOL*) capoclasse *m/f*; (*also:* **television** ~) monitor *m inv* // *vt* controllare.

monk [mʌŋk] *n* monaco.

monkey ['mʌŋki] *n* scimmia; ~ **nut** *n* nocciolina americana; ~ **wrench** *n* chiave *f* a rullino.

mono... ['mɔnəu] *prefix*: ~**chrome** *a* monocromo(a).

monocle ['mɔnəkl] *n* monocolo.

monogram ['mɔnəgræm] *n* monogramma *m*.

monologue ['mɔnəlɔg] *n* monologo.

monopolize [mə'nɔpəlaiz] *vt* monopolizzare.

monopoly [mə'nɔpəli] *n* monopolio.

monosyllabic [mɔnəusi'læbik] *a* monosillabico(a); (*person*) che parla a monosillabi.

monotone ['mɔnətəun] *n* pronunzia (*or* voce *f*) monotona.

monotonous [mə'nɔtənəs] *a* monotono(a).

monotony [mə'nɔtəni] *n* monotonia.

monsoon [mɔn'su:n] *n* monsone *m*.

monster ['mɔnstə*] *n* mostro.

monstrosity [mɔns'trɔsiti] *n* mostruosità *f inv*.

monstrous ['mɔnstrəs] *a* mostruoso(a).

montage [mɔn'tɑ:ʒ] *n* montaggio.

month [mʌnθ] *n* mese *m*; ~**ly** *a* mensile // *ad* al mese; ogni mese // *n* (*magazine*) rivista mensile.

monument ['mɔnjumənt] *n* monumento; ~**al** [-'mentl] *a* monumentale; (*fig*) colossale.

moo [mu:] *vi* muggire, mugghiare.

mood [mu:d] *n* umore *m*; **to be in a good/bad** ~ essere di buon/cattivo umore; **to be in the** ~ **for** essere disposto(a) a, aver voglia di; ~**y** *a* (*variable*) capriccioso(a), lunatico(a); (*sullen*) imbronciato(a).

moon [mu:n] *n* luna; ~**beam** *n* raggio di luna; ~**light** *n* chiaro di luna; ~**lit** *a* illuminato(a) dalla luna.

moor [muə*] *n* brughiera // *vt* (*ship*) ormeggiare // *vi* ormeggiarsi.

moorings ['muəriŋz] *npl* (*chains*) ormeggi *mpl*; (*place*) ormeggio.

moorland ['muələnd] *n* brughiera.

moose [mu:s] *n, pl inv* alce *m*.

moot [mu:t] *vt* sollevare // *a*: ~ **point** punto discutibile.

mop [mɔp] *n* lavapavimenti *m inv* // *vt* lavare con lo straccio; **to** ~ **one's brow** asciugarsi la fronte; **to** ~ **up** *vt* asciugare con uno straccio; ~ **of hair** *n* zazzera.

mope [məup] *vi* fare il broncio.

moped ['məuped] *n* (*Brit*) ciclomotore *m*.

moral ['mɔrl] *a* morale // *n* morale *f*; ~**s** *npl* moralità.

morale [mɔ'rɑ:l] *n* morale *m*.

morality [mə'ræliti] *n* moralità.

morass [mə'ræs] *n* palude *f*, pantano.

morbid ['mɔ:bid] *a* morboso(a).

more [mɔ:*] *det* più // *ad* più, di più; ~ **people** più gente; **I want** ~ ne voglio ancora *or* di più; ~ **dangerous than** più pericoloso di (*or* che); ~ **or less** più *or* meno; ~ **than ever** più che mai.

moreover [mɔ:'rəuvə*] *ad* inoltre, di più.

morgue [mɔ:g] *n* obitorio.

morning ['mɔ:niŋ] *n* mattina, mattino; mattinata; **in the** ~ la mattina; **7 o'clock in the** ~ le 7 di *or* della mattina.

Morocco [mə'rɔkəu] *n* Marocco.

moron ['mɔ:rɔn] *n* deficiente *m/f*; ~**ic** [mə'rɔnik] *a* deficiente.

morose [mə'rəus] *a* cupo(a), tetro(a).

morphine ['mɔ:fi:n] *n* morfina.

Morse [mɔ:s] *n* (*also:* ~ **code**) alfabeto Morse.

morsel ['mɔ:sl] *n* boccone *m*.

mortal ['mɔ:tl] *a, n* mortale (*m*); ~**ity** [-'tæliti] *n* mortalità.

mortar ['mɔ:tə*] *n* (*CONSTR*) malta; (*dish*) mortaio.

mortgage ['mɔ:gidʒ] *n* ipoteca; (*loan*) prestito ipotecario // *vt* ipotecare.

mortified ['mɔ:tifaid] *a* umiliato(a).

mortuary ['mɔ:tjuəri] *n* camera mortuaria; obitorio.

mosaic [məu'zeiik] *n* mosaico.

Moscow ['mɔskəu] *n* Mosca.

Moslem ['mɔzləm] *a, n* = **Muslim**.

mosque [mɔsk] *n* moschea.

mosquito, ~**es** [mɔs'ki:təu] *n* zanzara; ~ **net** *n* zanzariera.

moss [mɔs] *n* muschio; ~**y** *a* muscoso(a).

most [məust] *det* la maggior parte di; il più di // *pronoun* la maggior parte // *ad* più; (*work, sleep etc*) di più; (*very*) molto, estremamente; **the** (*also:* + *adjective*) il(la) più; ~ **fish** la maggior parte dei pesci; ~ **of** la maggior parte dei pesci; **at the** (*very*) ~ al massimo; **to make the** ~ **of** trarre il massimo vantaggio da; ~**ly** *ad* per lo più.

MOT *n* (*abbr of Ministry of Transport*): **the**

~ **(test)** *revisione annuale obbligatoria degli autoveicoli.*

motel [məʊ'tɛl] *n* motel *m inv.*

moth [mɔθ] *n* farfalla notturna; tarma; ~**ball** *n* palla di canfora; ~-**eaten** *a* tarmato(a).

mother ['mʌðə*] *n* madre *f* // *vt (care for)* fare da madre a; ~**hood** *n* maternità; ~-**in-law** *n* suocera; ~**ly** *a* materno(a); ~-**of-pearl** *n* madreperla; ~-**to-be** *n* futura mamma; ~ **tongue** *n* madrelingua.

mothproof ['mɔθpru:f] *a* antitarmico(a).

motif [məʊ'ti:f] *n* motivo.

motion ['məʊʃən] *n* movimento, moto; *(gesture)* gesto; *(at meeting)* mozione *f* // *vt, vi:* **to ~ (to) sb to do** fare cenno a qd di fare; ~**less** *a* immobile; ~ **picture** *n* film *m inv.*

motivated ['məʊtɪveɪtɪd] *a* motivato(a).

motivation [məʊtɪ'veɪʃən] *n* motivazione *f.*

motive ['məʊtɪv] *n* motivo // *a* motore(trice).

motley ['mɔtlɪ] *a* eterogeneo(a), molto vario(a).

motor ['məʊtə*] *n* motore *m; (col: vehicle)* macchina // *a* motore(trice); ~**bike** *n* moto *f inv;* ~**boat** *n* motoscafo; ~**car** *n* automobile *f;* ~**cycle** *n* motocicletta; ~**cyclist** *n* motociclista *m/f;* ~**ing** *n* turismo automobilistico // *a:* ~**ing holiday** *n* vacanza in macchina; ~**ist** *n* automobilista *m/f;* ~ **racing** *n* corse *fpl* automobilistiche; ~ **scooter** *n* motorscooter *m inv;* ~ **vehicle** *n* autoveicolo; ~**way** *n (Brit)* autostrada.

mottled ['mɔtld] *a* chiazzato(a), marezzato(a).

motto, ~**es** ['mɔtəʊ] *n* motto.

mould [məʊld] *n* forma, stampo; *(mildew)* muffa // *vt* formare; *(fig)* foggiare; ~**er** *vi (decay)* ammuffire; ~**y** *a* ammuffito(a).

moult [məʊlt] *vi* far la muta.

mound [maʊnd] *n* rialzo, collinetta.

mount [maʊnt] *n* monte *m,* montagna; *(horse)* cavalcatura; *(for jewel etc)* montatura // *vt* montare; *(horse)* montare a // *vi* salire, montare; *(also:* ~ **up)** aumentare.

mountain ['maʊntɪn] *n* montagna // *cpd* di montagna; ~**eer** [-'nɪə*] *n* alpinista *m/f;* ~**eering** [-'nɪərɪŋ] *n* alpinismo; **to go** ~**eering** fare dell'alpinismo; ~**ous** *a* montagnoso(a); ~**side** *n* fianco della montagna.

mourn [mɔːn] *vt* piangere, lamentare // *vi:* **to ~ (for)** piangere, lamentarsi (di); ~**er** *n* parente *m/f* or amico/a del defunto; persona venuta a rendere omaggio al defunto; ~**ful** *a* triste, lugubre; ~**ing** *n* lutto // *cpd (dress)* da lutto; **in** ~**ing** in lutto.

mouse, *pl* **mice** [maʊs, maɪs] *n* topo; ~**trap** *n* trappola per i topi.

moustache [məs'tɑːʃ] *n* baffi *mpl.*

mousy ['maʊsɪ] *a (person)* timido(a); *(hair)* marrone indefinito(a).

mouth, ~**s** [maʊθ, -ðz] *n* bocca; *(of river)* bocca, foce *f; (opening)* orifizio; ~**ful** *n*

boccata; ~ **organ** *n* armonica; ~-**watering** *a* che fa venire l'acquolina in bocca.

movable ['mu:vəbl] *a* mobile.

move [mu:v] *n (movement)* movimento; *(in game)* mossa; *(: turn to play)* turno; *(change of house)* trasloco // *vt* muovere, spostare; *(emotionally)* commuovere; *(POL: resolution etc)* proporre // *vi (gen)* muoversi, spostarsi; *(traffic)* circolare; *(also:* ~ **house)** cambiar casa, traslocare; **to ~ towards** andare verso; **to ~ sb to do sth** indurre or spingere qd a fare qc; **to get a ~ on** affrettarsi, sbrigarsi; **to ~ about** *vi (fidget)* agitarsi; *(travel)* viaggiare; **to ~ along** *vi* muoversi avanti; **to ~ away** *vi* allontanarsi, andarsene; **to ~ back** *vi* indietreggiare; *(return)* ritornare; **to ~ forward** *vi* avanzare // *vt* avanzare, spostare in avanti; *(people)* far avanzare; **to ~ in** *vi (to a house)* entrare (in una nuova casa); **to ~ on** *vi* riprendere la strada // *vt (onlookers)* far circolare; **to ~ out** *vi (of house)* sgombrare; **to ~ up** *vi* avanzare.

movement ['mu:vmənt] *n (gen)* movimento; *(gesture)* gesto; *(of stars, water, physical)* moto.

movie ['mu:vɪ] *n* film *m inv;* **the ~s** il cinema; ~ **camera** *n* cinepresa.

moving ['mu:vɪŋ] *a* mobile; commovente.

mow, *pt* **mowed,** *pp* **mowed** or **mown** [məʊ, -n] *vt* falciare; *(lawn)* mietere; **to ~ down** *vt* falciare; ~**er** *n* falciatore/trice.

M.P. *n abbr see* **member.**

m.p.g. *abbr* = *miles per gallon (30 m.p.g. = 9.5 l. per 100 km).*

m.p.h. *abbr* = *miles per hour (60 m.p.h. = 96 km/h).*

Mr ['mɪstə*] *n*: ~ **X** Signor X, Sig. X.

Mrs ['mɪsɪz] *n*: ~ **X** Signora X, Sig.ra X.

Ms [mɪz] *n (= Miss or Mrs):* ~ **X** ≈ Signora X, Sig.ra X.

much [mʌtʃ] *det* molto(a) // *ad, n* or *pronoun* molto; ~ **milk** molto latte; **how ~ is it?** quanto costa?

muck [mʌk] *n (mud)* fango; *(dirt)* sporcizia; **to ~ about** *vi (col)* fare lo stupido; *(waste time)* gingillarsi; ~**y** *a (dirty)* sporco(a), lordo(a).

mucus ['mju:kəs] *n* muco.

mud [mʌd] *n* fango.

muddle ['mʌdl] *n* confusione *f,* disordine *m;* pasticcio // *vt (also:* ~ **up)** impasticciare; **to be in a ~** *(person)* non riuscire a raccapezzarsi; **to get in a ~** *(while explaining etc)* imbrogliarsi; **to ~ through** *vi* cavarsela alla meno peggio.

mud: ~**dy** *a* fangoso(a); ~**guard** *n* parafango; ~-**slinging** *n (fig)* infangamento.

muff [mʌf] *n* manicotto.

muffin ['mʌfɪn] *n* specie di pasticcino soffice da tè.

muffle ['mʌfl] *vt (sound)* smorzare, attutire; *(against cold)* imbaccuccare; ~**d** *a* smorzato(a), attutito(a).

mufti ['mʌftɪ] *n*: **in ~** in borghese.

mug [mʌg] *n* (*cup*) tazzone *m*; (: *for beer*) boccale *m*; (*col: face*) muso; (: *fool*) scemo/a // *vt* (*assault*) assalire; **~ging** *n* assalto.

muggy ['mʌgɪ] *a* afoso(a).

mule [mju:l] *n* mulo.

mull [mʌl]: **to ~ over** *vt* rimuginare.

mulled [mʌld] *a*: **~ wine** vino caldo.

multi... ['mʌltɪ] *prefix* multi...; **~coloured** *a* multicolore, variopinto(a).

multiple ['mʌltɪpl] *a* multiplo(a); molteplice // *n* multiplo; **~ sclerosis** *n* sclerosi *f* a placche.

multiplication [mʌltɪplɪ'keɪʃən] *n* moltiplicazione *f*.

multiply ['mʌltɪplaɪ] *vt* moltiplicare // *vi* moltiplicarsi.

multitude ['mʌltɪtju:d] *n* moltitudine *f*.

mum [mʌm] *n* mamma // *a*: **to keep ~** non aprire bocca; **~'s the word!** acqua in bocca!

mumble ['mʌmbl] *vt, vi* borbottare.

mummy ['mʌmɪ] *n* (*mother*) mamma; (*embalmed*) mummia.

mumps [mʌmps] *n* orecchioni *mpl*.

munch [mʌntʃ] *vt, vi* sgranocchiare.

mundane [mʌn'deɪn] *a* terra a terra *inv*.

municipal [mju:'nɪsɪpl] *a* municipale; **~ity** [-'pælɪtɪ] *n* municipio.

munitions [mju:'nɪʃənz] *npl* munizioni *fpl*.

mural ['mjuərl] *n* dipinto murale.

murder ['mɔ:də*] *n* assassinio, omicidio // *vt* assassinare; **~er** *n* omicida *m*, assassino; **~ous** *a* micidiale.

murk [mɔ:k] *n* oscurità, buio; **~y** *a* tenebroso(a), buio(a).

murmur ['mɔ:mə*] *n* mormorio // *vt, vi* mormorare.

muscle ['mʌsl] *n* muscolo; **to ~ in** *vi* immischiarsi.

muscular ['mʌskjulə*] *a* muscolare; (*person, arm*) muscoloso(a).

muse [mju:z] *vi* meditare, sognare // *n* musa.

museum [mju:'zɪəm] *n* museo.

mushroom ['mʌʃrum] *n* fungo // *vi* (*fig*) svilupparsi rapidamente.

music ['mju:zɪk] *n* musica; **~al** *a* musicale // *n* (*show*) commedia musicale; **~al box** *n* scatola armonica; **~al instrument** *n* strumento musicale; **~ hall** *n* teatro di varietà; **~ian** [-'zɪʃən] *n* musicista *m/f*.

musket ['mʌskɪt] *n* moschetto.

Muslim ['mʌzlɪm] *a, n* musulmano(a).

muslin ['mʌzlɪn] *n* mussolina.

mussel ['mʌsl] *n* cozza.

must [mʌst] *auxiliary vb* (*obligation*): **I ~ do it** devo farlo; (*probability*): **he ~ be there by now** dovrebbe essere arrivato ormai; **I ~ have made a mistake** devo essermi sbagliato // *n* cosa da non mancare; cosa d'obbligo.

mustard ['mʌstəd] *n* senape *f*, mostarda.

muster ['mʌstə*] *vt* radunare.

mustn't ['mʌsnt] = **must not**.

musty ['mʌstɪ] *a* che sa di muffa *or* di rinchiuso.

mute [mju:t] *a, n* muto(a).

mutilate ['mju:tɪleɪt] *vt* mutilare; **mutilation** [-'leɪʃən] *n* mutilazione *f*.

mutinous ['mju:tɪnəs] *a* (*troops*) ammutinato(a); (*attitude*) ribelle.

mutiny ['mju:tɪnɪ] *n* ammutinamento // *vi* ammutinarsi.

mutter ['mʌtə*] *vt, vi* borbottare, brontolare.

mutton ['mʌtn] *n* carne *f* di montone.

mutual ['mju:tʃuəl] *a* mutuo(a), reciproco(a).

muzzle ['mʌzl] *n* muso; (*protective device*) museruola; (*of gun*) bocca // *vt* mettere la museruola a.

my [maɪ] *a* il(la) mio(a), *pl* i(le) miei(mie).

myself [maɪ'sɛlf] *pronoun* (*reflexive*) mi; (*emphatic*) io stesso(a); (*after prep*) me.

mysterious [mɪs'tɪərɪəs] *a* misterioso(a).

mystery ['mɪstərɪ] *n* mistero; **~ story** *n* racconto del mistero.

mystic ['mɪstɪk] *n* mistico // *a* (*mysterious*) esoterico(a); **~al** *a* mistico(a).

mystify ['mɪstɪfaɪ] *vt* mistificare; (*puzzle*) confondere.

mystique [mɪs'ti:k] *n* fascino.

myth [mɪθ] *n* mito; **~ology** [mɪ'θɒlədʒɪ] *n* mitologia.

N

nab [næb] *vt* (*col*) beccare, acchiappare.

nag [næg] *n* (*pej: horse*) ronzino; (: *person*) brontolone/a // *vt* tormentare // *vi* brontolare in continuazione; **~ging** *a* (*doubt, pain*) persistente.

nail [neɪl] *n* (*human*) unghia; (*metal*) chiodo // *vt* inchiodare; **to ~ sb down to a date/price** costringere qd a un appuntamento/ad accettare un prezzo; **~brush** *n* spazzolino da *or* per unghie; **~file** *n* lima da *or* per unghie; **~ polish** *n* smalto da *or* per unghie; **~ scissors** *npl* forbici *fpl* da *or* per unghie; **~ varnish** *n* = **~ polish**.

naïve [naɪ'i:v] *a* ingenuo(a).

naked ['neɪkɪd] *a* nudo(a).

name [neɪm] *n* nome *m*; (*reputation*) nome, reputazione *f* // *vt* (*baby etc*) chiamare; (*plant, illness*) nominare; (*person, object*) identificare; (*price, date*) fissare; **in the ~ of** in nome di; **~ dropping** *n* menzionare qd o qc per fare bella figura; **~less** *a* senza nome; **~ly** *ad* cioè; **~sake** *n* omonimo.

nanny ['nænɪ] *n* bambinaia.

nap [næp] *n* (*sleep*) pisolino; (*of cloth*) peluria; **to have a ~** schiacciare un pisolino; **to be caught ~ping** essere preso alla sprovvista.

napalm ['neɪpɑ:m] *n* napalm *m*.

nape [neɪp] *n*: **~ of the neck** nuca.

napkin ['næpkɪn] *n* tovagliolo; (*Brit: for baby*) pannolino.

nappy ['næpɪ] *n* pannolino.

narcotic [nɑ:'kɒtɪk] *n* narcotico.

nark [nɑ:k] *vt* (*col*) scocciare.

narrate [nəˈreɪt] vt raccontare, narrare.

narrative [ˈnærətɪv] n narrativa // a narrativo(a).

narrow [ˈnærəu] a stretto(a); (fig): **to take a ~ view of** avere una visione limitata di // vi restringersi; **to have a ~ escape** farcela per un pelo; **to ~ sth down to** ridurre qc a; **~ly** ad per un pelo; (time) per poco; **~-minded** a meschino(a).

nasal [ˈneɪzl] a nasale.

nasty [ˈnɑːstɪ] a (person, remark) cattivo(a); (smell, wound, situation) brutto(a).

nation [ˈneɪʃən] n nazione f.

national [ˈnæʃənl] a nazionale // n cittadino/a; **~ dress** n costume m nazionale; **~ism** n nazionalismo; **~ist** a,n nazionalista (m/f); **~ity** [-ˈnælɪtɪ] n nazionalità f inv; **~ization** [-aɪˈzeɪʃən] n nazionalizzazione f; **~ize** vt nazionalizzare; **~ly** ad a livello nazionale.

nation-wide [ˈneɪʃənwaɪd] a diffuso(a) in tutto il paese // ad in tutto il paese.

native [ˈneɪtɪv] n abitante m/f del paese; (in colonies) indigeno/a // a indigeno(a); (country) natio(a); (ability) innato(a); **a ~ of Russia** un nativo della Russia; **a ~ speaker of French** una persona di madrelingua francese; **~ language** madrelingua.

natter [ˈnætə*] vi chiacchierare.

natural [ˈnætʃrəl] a naturale; (ability) innato(a); (manner) semplice; **~ gas** n gas m metano; **~ist** n naturalista m/f; **~ize** vt naturalizzare; **~ly** ad naturalmente; (by nature: gifted) di natura.

nature [ˈneɪtʃə*] n natura; (character) carattere m; **by ~** di natura.

naught [nɔːt] n zero.

naughty [ˈnɔːtɪ] a (child) birichino(a), cattivello(a); (story, film) spinto(a).

nausea [ˈnɔːsɪə] n (MED) nausea; (fig: disgust) schifo; **~te** [ˈnɔːsɪeɪt] vt nauseare; far schifo a.

nautical [ˈnɔːtɪkl] a nautico(a).

naval [ˈneɪvl] a navale; **~ officer** n ufficiale m di marina.

nave [neɪv] n navata centrale.

navel [ˈneɪvl] n ombelico.

navigable [ˈnævɪgəbl] a navigabile.

navigate [ˈnævɪgeɪt] vt percorrere navigando // vi navigare; **navigation** [-ˈgeɪʃən] n navigazione f; **navigator** n (NAUT, AVIAT) ufficiale m di rotta; (explorer) navigatore m; (AUT) copilota m/f.

navvy [ˈnævɪ] n manovale m.

navy [ˈneɪvɪ] n marina; **~(-blue)** a blu scuro inv.

near [nɪə*] a vicino(a); (relation) prossimo(a) // ad vicino // prep (also: **~ to**) vicino a, presso; (time) verso // vt avvicinarsi a; **to come ~ to** avvicinarsi; **~by** [nɪəˈbaɪ] a vicino(a) // ad vicino; **N~ East** n Medio Oriente m; **~ly** ad quasi; **~ miss** n: **that was a ~ miss** c'è mancato poco; **~ness** n vicinanza; **~side** n (AUT: right-hand drive) lato

sinistro; **~-sighted** a miope.

neat [niːt] a (person, room) ordinato(a); (work) pulito(a); (solution, plan) ben indovinato(a), azzeccato(a); (spirits) liscio(a); **~ly** ad con ordine; (skilfully) abilmente.

nebulous [ˈnɛbjuləs] a nebuloso(a); (fig) vago(a).

necessarily [ˈnɛsɪsrɪlɪ] ad necessariamente.

necessary [ˈnɛsɪsrɪ] a necessario(a).

necessitate [nɪˈsɛsɪteɪt] vt rendere necessario(a).

necessity [nɪˈsɛsɪtɪ] n necessità f inv.

neck [nɛk] n collo; (of garment) colletto; **~ and ~** testa a testa.

necklace [ˈnɛklɪs] n collana.

neckline [ˈnɛklaɪn] n scollatura.

née [neɪ] a: **~ Scott** nata Scott.

need [niːd] n bisogno // vt aver bisogno di.

needle [ˈniːdl] n ago // vt punzecchiare.

needless [ˈniːdlɪs] a inutile.

needlework [ˈniːdlwəːk] n cucito.

needy [ˈniːdɪ] a bisognoso(a).

negation [nɪˈgeɪʃən] n negazione f.

negative [ˈnɛgətɪv] n negativo // a negativo(a).

neglect [nɪˈglɛkt] vt trascurare // n (of person, duty) negligenza; (state of) ~ stato di abbandono.

negligee [ˈnɛglɪʒeɪ] n négligé m inv.

negligence [ˈnɛglɪdʒəns] n negligenza.

negligent [ˈnɛglɪdʒənt] a negligente; **~ly** ad con negligenza.

negligible [ˈnɛglɪdʒɪbl] a insignificante, trascurabile.

negotiable [nɪˈgəuʃɪəbl] a negoziabile; (cheque) trasferibile; (road) transitabile.

negotiate [nɪˈgəuʃɪeɪt] vi negoziare // vt (COMM) negoziare; (obstacle) superare; **negotiation** [-ˈeɪʃən] n negoziato, trattativa; **negotiator** n negoziatore/trice.

Negress [ˈniːgrɪs] n negra.

Negro [ˈniːgrəu] a, n (pl: ~es) negro(a).

neighbour [ˈneɪbə*] n vicino/a; **~hood** n vicinato; **~ing** a vicino(a); **~ly** a: **he is a ~ly person** ha da buon vicino.

neither [ˈnaɪðə*] a, pronoun né l'uno(a) né l'altro(a), nessuno(a) dei(delle) due // cj neanche, nemmeno, neppure // ad: **~ good nor bad** né buono né cattivo; **I didn't move and ~ did Claude** io non mi mossi e nemmeno Claude.

neon [ˈniːɔn] n neon m; **~ light** n luce f al neon; **~ sign** n insegna al neon.

nephew [ˈnevjuː] n nipote m.

nerve [nəːv] n nervo; (fig) coraggio; (impudence) faccia tosta; **a fit of ~s** una crisi di nervi; **~-racking** a che spezza i nervi.

nervous [ˈnəːvəs] a nervoso(a); **~ breakdown** n esaurimento nervoso; **~ness** n nervosismo.

nest [nɛst] n nido.

nestle [ˈnɛsl] vi accoccolarsi.

net [nɛt] n rete f // a netto(a); ~**ball** n specie di pallacanestro.

Netherlands ['nɛðələndz] npl: **the** ~ i Paesi Bassi.

nett [nɛt] a = **net**.

netting ['nɛtɪŋ] n (for fence etc) reticolato.

nettle ['nɛtl] n ortica.

network ['nɛtwɔːk] n rete f.

neurosis, pl **neuroses** [njuə'rəusɪs, -siːz] n nevrosi f inv.

neurotic [njuə'rɔtɪk] a, n nevrotico(a).

neuter ['njuːtə*] a neutro(a) // n neutro // vt (cat etc) castrare.

neutral ['njuːtrəl] a neutro(a); (person, nation) neutrale // n (AUT) // **in** ~ **in** folle; ~**ity** [-'trælɪtɪ] n neutralità.

never ['nɛvə*] ad (non...) mai; ~ **again** mai più; **I'll** ~ **go there again** non ci vado più; ~-**ending** a interminabile; ~**theless** [nɛvəðə'lɛs] ad tuttavia, ciò nonostante, ciò nondimeno.

new [njuː] a nuovo(a); (brand new) nuovo(a) di zecca; ~**born** a neonato(a); ~**comer** ['njuːkʌmə*] n nuovo(a) venuto(a); ~**ly** ad di recente; ~ **moon** n luna nuova.

news [njuːz] n notizie fpl; (RADIO) giornale m radio; (TV) telegiornale m; **a piece of** ~ una notizia; ~ **agency** n agenzia di stampa; ~ **agent** n giornalaio; ~ **flash** n notizia f lampo inv; ~ **paper** n giornale m; ~ **stand** n edicola.

New Year ['njuː'jɪə*] n Anno Nuovo; ~'s **Day** n il Capodanno; ~'s **Eve** n la vigilia di Capodanno.

New Zealand [njuː'ziːlənd] n Nuova Zelanda.

next [nɛkst] a prossimo(a) // ad accanto; (in time) dopo; **when do we meet** ~? quando ci rincontriamo?; ~ **door** ad accanto; ~-**of-kin** n parente m/f prossimo(a); ~ **time** ad la prossima volta; ~ **to** prep accanto a; ~ **to nothing** quasi niente.

N.H.S. n abbr of National Health Service.

nib [nɪb] n (of pen) pennino.

nibble ['nɪbl] vt mordicchiare.

nice [naɪs] a (holiday, trip) piacevole; (flat, picture) simpatico(a); (person) simpatico(a), gentile; (distinction, point) sottile; ~-**looking** a bello(a); ~-**ly** ad bene.

niceties ['naɪsɪtɪz] npl finezze fpl.

nick [nɪk] n tacca f; vt (col) rubare; **in the** ~ **of time** appena in tempo.

nickel ['nɪkl] n nichel m; (US) moneta da cinque centesimi di dollaro.

nickname ['nɪkneɪm] n soprannome m // vt soprannominare.

nicotine ['nɪkətiːn] n nicotina.

niece [niːs] n nipote f.

Nigeria [naɪ'dʒɪərɪə] n Nigeria.

niggling ['nɪglɪŋ] a insignificante.

night [naɪt] n notte f; (evening) sera; **at** ~ la sera; **by** ~ di notte; ~**cap** n bicchierino prima di andare a letto; ~ **club** n locale m; ~**dress** n camicia da notte; ~**fall** n crepuscolo; ~**ie** ['naɪtɪ] n camicia da notte.

nightingale ['naɪtɪŋgeɪl] n usignolo.

night life ['naɪtlaɪf] n vita notturna.

nightly ['naɪtlɪ] a di ogni notte or sera; (by night) notturno(a) // ad ogni notte or sera.

nightmare ['naɪtmɛə*] n incubo.

night school ['naɪtskuːl] n scuola serale.

night-time ['naɪttaɪm] n notte f.

night watchman ['naɪt'wɔtʃmən] n guardiano notturno.

nil [nɪl] n nulla m; (SPORT) zero.

nimble ['nɪmbl] a agile.

nine [naɪn] num nove; ~**teen** num diciannove; ~**ty** num novanta.

ninth [naɪnθ] a nono(a).

nip [nɪp] vt pizzicare.

nipple ['nɪpl] n (ANAT) capezzolo.

nippy ['nɪpɪ] a (weather) pungente; (car, person) svelto(a).

nitrogen ['naɪtrədʒən] n azoto.

no [nəu] det nessuno(a), non; **I have** ~ **money** non ho soldi; **there is** ~ **reason to believe...** non c'è nessuna ragione per credere...; **I have** ~ **books** non ho libri // ad non; **I have** ~ **more wine** non ho più vino // excl, n no (m inv); ~ **entry** vietata l'entrata.

nobility [nəu'bɪlɪtɪ] n nobiltà.

noble ['nəubl] a, n nobile (m).

nobody ['nəubədɪ] pronoun nessuno.

nod [nɔd] vi accennare col capo, fare un cenno; (sleep) sonnecchiare // a cenno; **to** ~ **off** vi assopirsi.

noise [nɔɪz] n rumore m; (din, racket) chiasso; **noisy** a (street, car) rumoroso(a); (person) chiassoso(a).

nomad ['nəumæd] n nomade m/f.

no man's land ['nəumænzlænd] n terra di nessuno.

nominal ['nɔmɪnl] a nominale.

nominate ['nɔmɪneɪt] vt (propose) proporre come candidato; (elect) nominare.

nomination [nɔmɪ'neɪʃən] n nomina; candidatura.

nominee [nɔmɪ'niː] n persona nominata; candidato.

non... [nɔn] prefix non...; ~-**alcoholic** a analcolico(a).

nonchalant ['nɔnʃələnt] a incurante, indifferente.

non-committal ['nɔnkə'mɪtl] a evasivo(a).

nondescript ['nɔndɪskrɪpt] a qualunque inv.

none [nʌn] pronoun (not one thing) niente; (not one person) nessuno(a).

nonentity [nɔ'nɛntɪtɪ] n persona insignificante.

non: ~-**fiction** n saggistica; ~-**flammable** a ininfiammabile.

nonplussed [nɔn'plʌst] a sconcertato(a).

nonsense ['nɔnsəns] n sciocchezze fpl.

non: ~-**smoker** n non fumatore/trice; ~-**stick** a antiaderente, antiadesivo(a); ~-**stop** a continuo(a); (train, bus) direttissimo(a) // ad senza sosta.

noodles ['nuːdlz] npl taglierini mpl.

nook [nuk] *n*: ~s **and crannies** angoli *mpl*.

noon [nu:n] *n* mezzogiorno.

no one ['nəuwʌn] *pronoun* = **nobody**.

nor [nɔ:*] *cj* = **neither** // *ad see* **neither**.

norm [nɔ:m] *n* norma.

normal ['nɔ:ml] *a* normale; ~**ly** *ad* normalmente.

north [nɔ:θ] *n* nord *m*, settentrione *m* // *a* nord *inv*, del nord, settentrionale // *ad* verso nord; **N~ America** *n* America del Nord; ~**-east** *n* nord-est *m*; ~**ern** ['nɔ:ðən] *a* del nord, settentrionale; **N~ern Ireland** *n* Irlanda del Nord; **N~ Pole** *n* Polo Nord; **N~ Sea** *n* Mare *m* del Nord; ~**ward(s)** ['nɔ:θwəd(z)] *ad* verso nord; ~**-west** *n* nord-ovest *m*.

Norway ['nɔ:weɪ] *n* Norvegia.

Norwegian [nɔ:'wi:dʒən] *a* norvegese // *n* norvegese *m/f*; (LING) norvegese *m*.

nose [nəuz] *n* naso; (of animal) muso; ~**-dive** *n* picchiata; ~**y** *a* curioso(a).

nostalgia [nɔs'tældʒɪə] *n* nostalgia; **nostalgic** *a* nostalgico(a).

nostril ['nɔstrɪl] *n* narice *f*; (of horse) frogia.

nosy ['nəuzɪ] *a* = **nosey**.

not [nɔt] *ad* non; ~ **at all** niente affatto; **you must** ~ **or mustn't do this** non deve fare questo; **he isn't...** egli non è... .

notable ['nəutəbl] *a* notevole.

notably ['nəutəblɪ] *ad* notevolmente.

notch [nɔtʃ] *n* tacca.

note [nəut] *n* nota; (letter, banknote) biglietto // *vt* prendere nota di; **to take** ~**s** prendere appunti; ~**book** *n* taccuino; ~**d** ['nəutɪd] *a* celebre; ~**paper** *n* carta da lettere.

nothing ['nʌθɪŋ] *n* nulla *m*, niente *m*; ~ **new** niente di nuovo; **for** ~ (free) per niente.

notice ['nəutɪs] *n* avviso; (of leaving) preavviso // *vt* notare, accorgersi di; **to take** ~ **of** fare attenzione a; **to bring sth to sb's** ~ fare notare qc a qd; ~**able** *a* evidente; ~ **board** *n* (Brit) tabellone *m* per affissi.

notify ['nəutɪfaɪ] *vt*: **to** ~ **sth to sb** far sapere qc a qd; **to** ~ **sb of sth** avvisare qd di qc.

notion ['nəuʃən] *n* idea; (concept) nozione *f*.

notorious [nəu'tɔ:rɪəs] *a* famigerato(a).

notwithstanding [nɔtwɪθ'stændɪŋ] *ad* nondimeno // *prep* nonostante, malgrado.

nougat ['nu:ga:] *n* torrone *m*.

nought [nɔ:t] *n* zero.

noun [naun] *n* nome *m*, sostantivo.

nourish ['nʌrɪʃ] *vt* nutrire; ~**ing** *a* nutriente; ~**ment** *n* nutrimento.

novel ['nɔvl] *n* romanzo // *a* nuovo(a); ~**ist** *n* romanziere/a; ~**ty** *n* novità *f inv*.

November [nəu'vɛmbə*] *n* novembre *m*.

novice ['nɔvɪs] *n* principiante *m/f*; (REL) novizio/a.

now [nau] *ad* ora, adesso; ~ **and then**, ~ **and again** ogni tanto; **from** ~ **on** da ora in poi; ~**adays** ['nauədeɪz] *ad* oggidì.

nowhere ['nəuwɛə*] *ad* in nessun luogo, da nessuna parte.

nozzle ['nɔzl] *n* (of hose) boccaglio.

nuance ['nju:ã:ns] *n* sfumatura.

nuclear ['nju:klɪə*] *a* nucleare.

nucleus, *pl* **nuclei** ['nju:klɪəs, 'nju:klɪaɪ] *n* nucleo.

nude [nju:d] *a* nudo(a) // *n* (ART) nudo; **in the** ~ tutto(a) nudo(a).

nudge [nʌdʒ] *vt* dare una gomitata a.

nudist ['nju:dɪst] *n* nudista *m/f*.

nudity ['nju:dɪtɪ] *n* nudità.

nuisance ['nju:sns] *n*: **it's a** ~ è una seccatura; **he's a** ~ lui dà fastidio.

null [nʌl] *a*: ~ **and void** nullo(a); ~**ify** ['nʌlɪfaɪ] *vt* annullare.

numb [nʌm] *a* intormentito(a).

number ['nʌmbə*] *n* numero // *vt* numerare; (include) contare; **a** ~ **of** un certo numero di; **the staff** ~**s 20** gli impiegati sono in 20; ~ **plate** *n* targa.

numeral ['nju:mərəl] *n* numero, cifra.

numerical [nju:'merɪkl] *a* numerico(a).

numerous ['nju:mərəs] *a* numeroso(a).

nun [nʌn] *n* suora, monaca.

nurse [nɜ:s] *n* infermiere/a // *vt* (patient, cold) curare; (hope) nutrire; ~**(maid)** *n* bambinaia.

nursery ['nɜ:sərɪ] *n* (room) camera dei bambini; (institution) asilo; (for plants) vivaio; ~ **rhyme** *n* filastrocca; ~ **school** *n* scuola materna; ~ **slope** *n* (SKI) pista per principianti.

nursing ['nɜ:sɪŋ] *n* (profession) professione *f* di infermiere (or di infermiera); ~ **home** *n* casa di cura.

nut [nʌt] *n* (of metal) dado; (fruit) noce *f*; **he's** ~**s** (col) è matto; ~**case** *n* (col) mattarello/a; ~**crackers** *npl* schiaccianoci *m inv*; ~**meg** ['nʌtmɛg] *n* noce *f* moscata.

nutrition [nju:'trɪʃən] *n* nutrizione *f*.

nutritious [nju:'trɪʃəs] *a* nutriente.

nutshell ['nʌtʃɛl] *n* guscio di noce; **in a** ~ in poche parole.

nylon ['naɪlɔn] *n* nailon *m*; ~**s** *npl* calze *fpl* di nailon.

O

oaf [əuf] *n* zoticone *m*.

oak [əuk] *n* quercia.

O.A.P. *abbr see* **old**.

oar [ɔ:*] *n* remo.

oasis, *pl* **oases** [əu'eɪsɪs, əu'eɪsi:z] *n* oasi *f inv*.

oath [əuθ] *n* giuramento; (swear word) bestemmia; **on** ~ sotto giuramento; giurato(a).

oatmeal ['əutmi:l] *n* farina d'avena.

oats [əuts] *n* avena.

obedience [ə'bi:dɪəns] *n* ubbidienza; **in** ~ **to** conformemente a.

obedient [ə'bi:dɪənt] *a* ubbidiente.

obelisk ['ɔbɪlɪsk] *n* obelisco.

obesity [əu'bi:sɪtɪ] *n* obesità.

obey [ə'beɪ] *vt* ubbidire a; (instructions,

regulations) osservare // *vi* ubbidire.
obituary [ə'bɪtjuərɪ] *n* necrologia.
object *n* ['ɔbdʒɪkt] oggetto; (*purpose*) scopo, intento; (*LING*) complemento oggetto // *vi* [əb'dʒɛkt]: **to ~ to** (*attitude*) disapprovare; (*proposal*) protestare contro, sollevare delle obiezioni contro; **I ~!** mi oppongo!; **he ~ed that ... obiettò che ...;** **~ion** [əb'dʒɛkʃən] *n* obiezione *f*; (*drawback*) inconveniente *m*; **~ionable** [əb'dʒɛkʃənəbl] *a* antipatico(a); (*smell*) sgradevole; (*language*) scostumato(a); **~ive** *n* obiettivo // *a* obiettivo(a); **~ivity** [ɔbdʒɪk'tɪvɪtɪ] *n* obiettività; **~or** *n* oppositore/trice.
obligation [ɔblɪ'geɪʃən] *n* obbligo, dovere *m*; (*debt*) obbligo (di riconoscenza).
obligatory [ə'blɪgətərɪ] *a* obbligatorio(a).
oblige [ə'blaɪdʒ] *vt* (*force*): **to ~ sb to do** costringere qd a fare; (*do a favour*) fare una cortesia a; **to be ~d to sb for sth** essere grato a qd per qc; **obliging** *a* servizievole, compiacente.
oblique [ə'bliːk] *a* obliquo(a); (*allusion*) indiretto(a).
obliterate [ə'blɪtəreɪt] *vt* cancellare.
oblivion [ə'blɪvɪən] *n* oblio.
oblivious [ə'blɪvɪəs] *a*: **~ of** incurante di; inconscio(a) di.
oblong ['ɔblɔŋ] *a* oblungo(a) // *n* rettangolo.
obnoxious [əb'nɔkʃəs] *a* odioso(a); (*smell*) disgustoso(a), ripugnante.
oboe ['əubəu] *n* oboe *m*.
obscene [əb'siːn] *a* osceno(a).
obscenity [əb'sɛnɪtɪ] *n* oscenità *f inv*.
obscure [əb'skjuə*] *a* oscuro(a) // *vt* oscurare; (*hide: sun*) nascondere; **obscurity** *n* oscurità.
obsequious [əb'siːkwɪəs] *a* ossequioso(a).
observable [əb'zə:vəbl] *a* osservabile; (*appreciable*) notevole.
observance [əb'zə:vns] *n* osservanza.
observant [əb'zə:vnt] *a* attento(a).
observation [ɔbzə'veɪʃən] *n* osservazione *f*; (*by police etc*) sorveglianza.
observatory [əb'zə:vətrɪ] *n* osservatorio.
observe [əb'zə:v] *vt* osservare; (*remark*) fare osservare; **~r** *n* osservatore/trice.
obsess [əb'sɛs] *vt* ossessionare; **~ion** [əb'sɛʃən] *n* ossessione *f*; **~ive** *a* ossessivo(a).
obsolescence [ɔbsə'lɛsns] *n* obsolescenza.
obsolete ['ɔbsəliːt] *a* obsoleto(a); (*word*) desueto(a).
obstacle ['ɔbstəkl] *n* ostacolo; **~ race** *n* corsa agli ostacoli.
obstetrics [ɔb'stɛtrɪks] *n* ostetrica.
obstinacy ['ɔbstɪnəsɪ] *n* ostinatezza.
obstinate ['ɔbstɪnɪt] *a* ostinato(a).
obstreperous [əb'strɛpərəs] *a* turbolento(a).
obstruct [əb'strʌkt] *vt* (*block*) ostruire, ostacolare; (*halt*) fermare; (*hinder*) impedire; **~ion** [əb'strʌkʃən] *n* ostruzione *f*; ostacolo; **~ive** *a* ostruttivo(a).
obtain [əb'teɪn] *vt* ottenere // *vi* essere in uso; **~able** *a* ottenibile.

obtrusive [əb'truːsɪv] *a* (*person*) importuno(a); (*smell*) invadente; (*building etc*) imponente e invadente.
obtuse [əb'tjuːs] *a* ottuso(a).
obviate ['ɔbvɪeɪt] *vt* ovviare a, evitare.
obvious ['ɔbvɪəs] *a* ovvio(a), evidente; **~ly** *ad* ovviamente; certo.
occasion [ə'keɪʒən] *n* occasione *f*; (*event*) avvenimento // *vt* cagionare; **~al** *a* occasionale; **I smoke an ~al cigarette** ogni tanto fumo una sigaretta.
occupation [ɔkju'peɪʃən] *n* occupazione *f*; (*job*) mestiere *m*, professione *f*; **~al hazard** *n* rischio del mestiere.
occupier ['ɔkjupaɪə*] *n* occupante *m/f.*
occupy ['ɔkjupaɪ] *vt* occupare; **to ~ o.s. by doing** occuparsi a fare.
occur [ə'kə:*] *vi* accadere; (*difficulty, opportunity*) capitare; (*phenomenon, error*) trovarsi; **to ~ to sb** venire in mente a qd; **~rence** *n* caso, fatto; presenza.
ocean ['əuʃən] *n* oceano; **~-going** *a* d'alto mare.
ochre ['əukə*] *n* ocra *inv*.
o'clock [ə'klɔk] *ad*: **it is 5 ~** sono le 5.
octagonal [ɔk'tægənl] *a* ottagonale.
octane ['ɔkteɪn] *n* ottano.
octave ['ɔktɪv] *n* ottava.
October [ɔk'təubə*] *n* ottobre *m*.
octopus ['ɔktəpəs] *n* polpo, piovra.
odd [ɔd] *a* (*strange*) strano(a), bizzarro(a); (*number*) dispari *inv*; (*left over*) in più; (*not of a set*) spaiato(a); **60~~** 60 e oltre; **at ~ times** di tanto in tanto; **the ~ one out** l'eccezione *f*; **~ity** *n* bizzarria; (*person*) originale *m*; **~-job man** *n* tuttofare *m inv*; **~ jobs** *npl* lavori *mpl* occasionali; **~ly** *ad* stranamente; **~ments** *npl* (*COMM*) rimanenze *fpl*; **~s** *npl* (*in betting*) quota; **the ~s are against his coming c'è** poca probabilità che venga; **it makes no ~s** non importa; **at ~s** in contesa.
ode [əud] *n* ode *f*.
odious ['əudɪəs] *a* odioso(a), ripugnante.
odour ['əudə*] *n* odore *m*; **~less** *a* inodoro(a).
of [ɔv, əv] *prep* di; **a friend ~ ours** un nostro amico; **3 ~ them went** 3 di loro sono andati; **the 5th ~ July** il 5 luglio; **a boy ~ 10** un ragazzo di 10 anni.
off [ɔf] *a,ad* (*engine*) spento(a); (*tap*) chiuso(a); (*food: bad*) andato(a) a male; (*absent*) assente; (*cancelled*) sospeso(a) // *prep* da; a una distanza di; **to be ~** (*to leave*) partire, andarsene; **to be ~ sick** essere assente per malattia; **a day ~** un giorno di vacanza; **to have an ~ day** non essere in forma; **he had his coat ~** si era tolto il cappotto; **10% ~** (*COMM*) con uno sconto di 10%; **5 km ~ (the road)** a 5 km (dalla strada); **~ the coast** al largo della costa; **a house ~ the main road** una casa fuori della strada maestra; **I'm ~ meat** la carne non mi va più; non mangio più la carne; **on the ~ chance** a caso.
offal ['ɔfl] *n* (*CULIN*) frattaglie *fpl*.
offbeat ['ɔfbiːt] *a* eccentrico(a).

off-colour ['ɔf'kʌlə*] *a* (*ill*) malato(a), indisposto(a).
offence, offense (*US*) [ə'fɛns] *n* (*LAW*) contravvenzione *f*; (: *more serious*) reato; **to take ~ at** offendersi per.
offend [ə'fɛnd] *vt* (*person*) offendere; **~er** *n* delinquente *m/f*; (*against regulations*) contravventore/trice.
offensive [ə'fɛnsɪv] *a* offensivo(a); (*smell etc*) sgradevole, ripugnante // *n* (*MIL*) offensiva.
offer ['ɔfə*] *n* offerta, proposta // *vt* offrire; 'on ~' (*COMM*) 'in offerta speciale'; **~ing** *n* offerta.
offhand [ɔf'hænd] *a* disinvolto(a), noncurante // *ad* all'impronto.
office ['ɔfɪs] *n* (*place*) ufficio; (*position*) carica; **to take ~** entrare in carica; **~ block** *n* complesso di uffici; **~ boy** *n* garzone *m*; **~r** *n* (*MIL etc*) ufficiale *m*; (*of organization*) funzionario; (*also:* **police ~r**) agente *m* di polizia; **~ worker** *n* impiegato/a d'ufficio.
official [ə'fɪʃl] *a* (*authorized*) ufficiale // *n* ufficiale *m*; (*civil servant*) impiegato/a statale; funzionario; **~ly** *ad* ufficialmente.
officious [ə'fɪʃəs] *a* invadente.
offing ['ɔfɪŋ] *n*: **in the ~** (*fig*) in vista.
off: **~-licence** *n* (*Brit: shop*) spaccio di bevande alcoliche; **~-peak** *a* (*ticket etc*) a tariffa ridotta; (*time*) non di punta; **~-season** *a*, *ad* fuori stagione.
offset ['ɔfsɛt] *vt irg* (*counteract*) controbilanciare, compensare.
offshore [ɔf'ʃɔ:*] *a* (*breeze*) di terra; (*island*) vicino alla costa; (*fishing*) costiero(a).
offside ['ɔf'saɪd] *a* (*SPORT*) fuori gioco // *n* (*AUT: with right-hand drive*) lato destro.
offspring ['ɔfsprɪŋ] *n* prole *f*, discendenza.
off: **~stage** *ad* nelle quinte; **~-white** *a* bianco sporco *inv*.
often ['ɔfn] *ad* spesso; **as ~ as not** quasi sempre.
ogle ['əʊgl] *vt* occhieggiare.
oil [ɔɪl] *n* olio; (*petroleum*) petrolio; (*for central heating*) nafta // *vt* (*machine*) lubrificare; **~can** *n* oliatore *m* a mano; (*for storing*) latta da olio; **~field** *n* giacimento petrolifero; **~-fired** *a* a nafta; **~ level** *n* livello dell'olio; **~ painting** *n* quadro a olio; **~ refinery** *n* raffineria di petrolio; **~ rig** *n* derrick *m inv*; (*at sea*) piattaforma per trivellazioni subacquee; **~skins** *npl* indumenti *mpl* di tela cerata; **~ slick** *n* chiazza d'olio; **~ tanker** *n* petroliera; **~ well** *n* pozzo petrolifero; **~y** *a* unto(a), oleoso(a); (*food*) untuoso(a).
ointment ['ɔɪntmənt] *n* unguento.
O.K., okay ['əʊ'keɪ] *excl* d'accordo! // *vt* approvare; **is it ~?**, **are you ~?** tutto bene?
old [əʊld] *a* vecchio(a); (*ancient*) antico(a), vecchio(a); (*person*) vecchio(a), anziano(a); **how ~ are you?** quanti anni ha?; **he's 10 years ~** ha 10 anni; **~ age** *n* vecchiaia; **~-age pensioner (O.A.P.)** *n*

pensionato/a; **~er brother/sister** fratello/sorella maggiore; **~-fashioned** *a* antiquato(a), fuori moda; (*person*) all'antica.
olive ['ɔlɪv] *n* (*fruit*) oliva; (*tree*) olivo // *a* (*also:* **~-green**) verde oliva *inv*; **~ oil** *n* olio d'oliva.
Olympic [əʊ'lɪmpɪk] *a* olimpico(a); **the ~ Games, the ~s** i giochi olimpici, le Olimpiadi.
omelet(te) ['ɔmlɪt] *n* omelette *f inv*.
omen ['əʊmən] *n* presagio, auguro.
ominous ['ɔmɪnəs] *a* minaccioso(a); (*event*) di malauguro.
omission [əʊ'mɪʃən] *n* omissione *f*.
omit [əʊ'mɪt] *vt* omettere.
on [ɔn] *prep* su; (*on top of*) sopra // *ad* (*machine*) in moto; (*light, radio*) acceso(a); (*tap*) aperto(a); **is the meeting still ~?** terrà sempre luogo la riunione?; la riunione è ancora in corso?; **when is this film ~?** quando c'è questo film?; **~ the train** in treno; **~ the wall** sul or al muro; **~ television** alla televisione; **~ learning this** imparando questo; **~ arrival** all'arrivo; **~ the left** sulla or a sinistra; **~ Friday** venerdì; **~ Fridays** di or il venerdì; **a week ~ Friday** venerdì fra otto giorni; **put your coat ~** mettiti il cappotto; **to walk etc ~** continuare a camminare *etc*; **it's not ~!** non è possibile!; **~ and off** ogni tanto.
once [wʌns] *ad* una volta // *cj* non appena, quando; **at ~** subito; (*simultaneously*) a un tempo; **all at ~** *ad* (*tutto*) ad un tratto; **~ a week** una volta alla settimana; **~ more** ancora una volta; **~ and for all** una volta per sempre.
oncoming ['ɔnkʌmɪŋ] *a* (*traffic*) che viene in senso opposto.
one [wʌn] *det*, *num* un(uno) *m*, una(un') *f* // *pronoun* uno(a); (*impersonal*) si; **this ~** questo(a) qui; **that ~** quello(a) là; **the ~ book which...** l'unico libro che...; **~ by ~** a uno(a) a uno(a); **~ never knows** non si sa mai; **to express ~'s opinion** esprimere la propria opinione; **~ another** l'un(a) l'altro(a); **~-man** *a* (*business*) diretto(a) *etc* da un solo uomo; **~self** *pronoun* si; (*after prep, also emphatic*) sé, se stesso(a); **~-way** *a* (*street, traffic*) a senso unico.
ongoing ['ɔngəʊɪŋ] *a* in corso; in attuazione.
onion ['ʌnjən] *n* cipolla.
onlooker ['ɔnlʊkə*] *n* spettatore/trice.
only ['əʊnlɪ] *ad* solo, soltanto // *a* solo(a), unico(a) // *cj* solo che, ma; **an ~ child** un figlio unico; **not ~** non solo; **I ~ took one** ne ho preso soltanto uno, non ne ho preso che uno.
onset ['ɔnsɛt] *n* inizio; (*of winter, old age*) approssimarsi *m*.
onshore ['ɔnʃɔ:*] *a* (*wind*) di mare.
onslaught ['ɔnslɔ:t] *n* attacco, assalto.
onto ['ɔntu] *prep* = **on to**.
onus ['əʊnəs] *n* onere *m*, peso.
onward(s) ['ɔnwəd(z)] *ad* (*move*) in

avanti; **from this time** ~ d'ora in poi.
onyx ['ɒnɪks] n onice f.
ooze [uːz] vi stillare.
opal ['əupl] n opale m or f.
opaque [əu'peɪk] a opaco(a).

open ['əupn] a aperto(a); (road) libero(a); (meeting) pubblico(a); (admiration) evidente, franco(a); (question) insoluto(a); (enemy) dichiarato(a) // vt aprire // vi (eyes, door, debate) aprirsi; (flower) sbocciare; (shop, bank, museum) aprire; (book etc: commence) cominciare; **to ~ on to** vt fus (subj: room, door) dare su; **to ~ out** vt aprire // vi aprirsi; **to ~ up** vt aprire; (blocked road) sgombrare // vi aprirsi; **in the ~ (air)** all'aperto; **~-air** a all'aperto; **~ing** n apertura; (opportunity) occasione f, opportunità f inv; sbocco; (job) posto vacante; **~ly** ad apertamente; **~-minded** a che ha la mente aperta; **~ sandwich** n canapè m inv; **the ~ sea** il mare aperto, l'alto mare.
opera ['ɒpərə] n opera; **~ glasses** npl binocolo da teatro; **~ house** n opera.
operate ['ɒpəreɪt] vt (machine) azionare, far funzionare; (system) usare // vi funzionare; (drug) essere efficace; **to ~ on sb (for)** (MED) operare qd (di).
operatic [ɒpə'rætɪk] a dell'opera, lirico(a).
operating ['ɒpəreɪtɪŋ] a: **~ table** tavolo operatorio; **~ theatre** sala operatoria.
operation [ɒpə'reɪʃən] n operazione f; **to be in ~** (machine) essere in azione or funzionamento; (system) essere in vigore; **~al** a in funzione; d'esercizio.
operative ['ɒpərətɪv] a (measure) operativo(a) // n (in factory) operaio/a.
operator ['ɒpəreɪtə*] n (of machine) operatore/trice; (TEL) centralinista m/f.
operetta [ɒpə'rɛtə] n operetta.
opinion [ə'pɪnɪən] n opinione f, parere m; **in my ~** secondo me, a mio avviso; **~ated** a dogmatico(a).
opium ['əupɪəm] n oppio.
opponent [ə'pəunənt] n avversario/a.
opportune ['ɒpətjuːn] a opportuno(a); **opportunist** [-'tjuːnɪst] n opportunista m/f.
opportunity [ɒpə'tjuːnɪtɪ] n opportunità f inv, occasione f.
oppose [ə'pəuz] vt opporsi a; **~d to** a contrario(a) a; **as ~d to** in contrasto con; **opposing** a opposto(a); (team) avversario/a.
opposite ['ɒpəzɪt] a opposto(a); (house etc) di fronte // ad di fronte, dirimpetto // prep di fronte a // n opposto, contrario; (of word) contrario; **his ~ number** il suo corrispondente.
opposition [ɒpə'zɪʃən] n opposizione f.
oppress [ə'prɛs] vt opprimere; **~ion** [ə'prɛʃən] n oppressione f; **~ive** a oppressivo(a).
opt [ɒpt] vi: **to ~ for** optare per; **to ~ to do** scegliere di fare; **to ~ out of** ritirarsi da.
optical ['ɒptɪkl] a ottico(a).
optician [ɒp'tɪʃən] n ottico.
optimism ['ɒptɪmɪzəm] n ottimismo.

optimist ['ɒptɪmɪst] n ottimista m/f; **~ic** [-'mɪstɪk] a ottimistico(a).
optimum ['ɒptɪməm] a ottimale.
option ['ɒpʃən] n scelta; (SCOL) materia facoltativa; (COMM) opzione f; **to keep one's ~s open** (fig) non impegnarsi; **~al** a facoltativo(a); (COMM) a scelta.
opulence ['ɒpjuləns] n opulenza; abbondanza.
or [ɔː*] cj o, oppure; (with negative): **he hasn't seen** ~ **heard anything** non ha visto né sentito niente; ~ **else** se no, altrimenti; oppure.
oracle ['ɒrəkl] n oracolo.
oral ['ɔːrəl] a orale // n esame m orale.
orange ['ɒrɪndʒ] n (fruit) arancia // a arancione.
oration [ɔː'reɪʃən] n orazione f.
orator ['ɒrətə*] n oratore/trice.
oratorio [ɒrə'tɔːrɪəu] n oratorio.
orb [ɔːb] n orbe m.
orbit ['ɔːbɪt] n orbita // vt orbitare intorno a.
orchard ['ɔːtʃəd] n frutteto.
orchestra ['ɔːkɪstrə] n orchestra; **~l** [-'kɛstrəl] a orchestrale; (concert) sinfonico(a).
orchid ['ɔːkɪd] n orchidea.
ordain [ɔː'deɪn] vt (REL) ordinare; (decide) decretare.
ordeal [ɔː'diːl] n prova, travaglio.
order ['ɔːdə*] n ordine m; (COMM) ordinazione f // vt ordinare; **in ~** in ordine; (of document) in regola; **in ~ of size** in ordine di grandezza; **in ~ to do** per fare; **in ~ that** affinché +sub; **to ~ sb to do** ordinare a qd di fare; **the lower ~s** (pej) i ceti inferiori; ~ **form** n modulo d'ordinazione; **~ly** n (MIL) attendente m // a (room) in ordine; (mind) metodico(a); (person) ordinato(a), metodico(a).
ordinal ['ɔːdɪnl] a (number) ordinale.
ordinary ['ɔːdnrɪ] a normale, comune; (pej) mediocre.
ordination [ɔːdɪ'neɪʃən] n ordinazione f.
ore [ɔː*] n minerale m grezzo.
organ ['ɔːgən] n organo; **~ic** [ɔː'gænɪk] a organico(a).
organism ['ɔːgənɪzəm] n organismo.
organist ['ɔːgənɪst] n organista m/f.
organization [ɔːgənaɪ'zeɪʃən] n organizzazione f.
organize ['ɔːgənaɪz] vt organizzare; **~r** n organizzatore/trice.
orgasm ['ɔːgæzəm] n orgasmo.
orgy ['ɔːdʒɪ] n orgia.
Orient ['ɔːrɪənt] n: **the ~** l'Oriente m; **oriental** [-'entl] a, n orientale (m/f).
orientate ['ɔːrɪənteɪt] vt orientare.
orifice ['ɒrɪfɪs] n orifizio.
origin ['ɒrɪdʒɪn] n origine f.
original [ə'rɪdʒɪnl] a originale; (earliest) originario(a) // n originale m; **~ity** [-'nælɪtɪ] n originalità; **~ly** ad (at first) all'inizio.
originate [ə'rɪdʒɪneɪt] vi: **to ~ from**

venire da, essere originario(a) di; (*suggestion*) provenire da.

ornament ['ɔːnəmənt] *n* ornamento; (*trinket*) ninnolo; **~al** [-'mɛntl] *a* ornamentale.

ornate [ɔː'neɪt] *a* molto ornato(a).

ornithologist [ɔːnɪ'θɔlədʒɪst] *n* ornitologo/a.

ornithology [ɔːnɪ'θɔlədʒɪ] *n* ornitologia.

orphan ['ɔːfn] *n* orfano/a // *vt:* **to be ~ed** diventare orfano; **~age** *n* orfanotrofio.

orthodox ['ɔːθədɔks] *a* ortodosso(a).

orthopaedic [ɔːθə'piːdɪk] *a* ortopedico(a).

oscillate ['ɔsɪleɪt] *vi* oscillare.

ostensible [ɔs'tɛnsɪbl] *a* preteso(a); apparente; **ostensibly** *ad* all'apparenza.

ostentation [ɔstɛn'teɪʃən] *n* ostentazione *f*.

ostentatious [ɔstɛn'teɪʃəs] *a* pretenzioso(a); ostentato(a).

osteopath ['ɔstɪəpæθ] *n* specialista *m/f* di osteopatia.

ostracize ['ɔstrəsaɪz] *vt* dare l'ostracismo a.

ostrich ['ɔstrɪtʃ] *n* struzzo.

other ['ʌðə*] *a* altro(a); **~ than** altro che; *a* parte; **~wise** *ad,cj* altrimenti.

otter ['ɔtə*] *n* lontra.

ought, *pt* **ought** [ɔːt] *auxiliary vb:* **I ~ to do it** dovrei farlo; **this ~ to have been corrected** questo avrebbe dovuto essere corretto; **he ~ to win** dovrebbe vincere.

ounce [auns] *n* oncia (= 28.35 *g*; 16 in a pound).

our ['auə*] *a* il(la) nostro(a), *pl* il(e) nostri(e); **~s** *pronoun* il(la) nostro(a), *pl* i(le) nostri(e); **~selves** *pronoun pl* (*reflexive*) ci; (*after preposition*) noi; (*emphatic*) noi stessi(e).

oust [aust] *vt* cacciare, espellere.

out [aut] *ad* fuori; (*published, not at home etc*) uscito(a); (*light, fire*) spento(a); **~ here** qui fuori; **~ there** là fuori; **he's ~** è uscito; (*unconscious*) ha perso conoscenza; **to be ~ in one's calculations** essersi sbagliato nei calcoli; **to run/back etc ~** uscire di corsa/a marcia indietro *etc*; **~ loud** *ad* ad alta voce; **~ of** (*outside*) fuori di; (*because of:* anger *etc*) per; (*from among:*) **~ of 10** su 10; (*without:*) **~ of petrol** senza benzina, a corto di benzina; **made ~ of wood** di *or* in legno; **~ of order** (*machine etc*) guasto(a).

outboard ['autbɔːd] *n:* **~ (motor)** (motore *m*) fuoribordo.

outbreak ['autbreɪk] *n* scoppio; epidemia.

outbuilding ['autbɪldɪŋ] *n* dipendenza.

outburst ['autbəːst] *n* scoppio.

outcast ['autkɑːst] *n* esule *m/f*, (*socially*) paria *m inv*.

outclass [aut'klɑːs] *vt* surclassare.

outcome ['autkʌm] *n* esito, risultato.

outcry ['autkraɪ] *n* protesta, clamore *m*.

outdated [aut'deɪtɪd] *a* (*custom, clothes*) fuori moda; (*idea*) sorpassato(a).

outdo [aut'duː] *vt irg* sorpassare.

outdoor [aut'dɔː*] *a* all'aperto; **~s** *ad* fuori; all'aria aperta.

outer ['autə*] *a* esteriore; **~ space** *n* spazio cosmico.

outfit ['autfɪt] *n* equipaggiamento; (*clothes*) abito; **'~ter's'** 'confezioni da uomo'.

outgoings ['autgəuɪŋz] *npl* (*expenses*) spese *fpl*.

outgrow [aut'grəu] *vt irg* (*clothes*) diventare troppo grande per.

outing ['autɪŋ] *n* gita; escursione *f*.

outlandish [aut'lændɪʃ] *a* strano(a).

outlaw ['autlɔː] *n* fuorilegge *m/f* // *vt* (*person*) mettere fuori della legge; (*practice*) proscrivere.

outlay ['autleɪ] *n* spese *fpl*; (*investment*) sborsa, spesa.

outlet ['autlɛt] *n* (*for liquid etc*) sbocco, scarico; (*for emotion*) sfogo; (*for goods*) sbocco; (*also:* **retail ~**) punto di vendita.

outline ['autlaɪn] *n* contorno, profilo; (*summary*) abbozzo, grandi linee *fpl*.

outlive [aut'lɪv] *vt* sopravvivere a.

outlook ['autluk] *n* prospettiva, vista.

outlying ['autlaɪɪŋ] *a* periferico(a).

outmoded [aut'məudɪd] *a* passato(a) di moda; antiquato(a).

outnumber [aut'nʌmbə*] *vt* superare in numero.

outpatient ['autpeɪʃənt] *n* paziente *m/f* ambulatoriale.

outpost ['autpəust] *n* avamposto.

output ['autput] *n* produzione *f*.

outrage ['autreɪdʒ] *n* oltraggio; scandalo // *vt* oltraggiare; **~ous** [-'reɪdʒəs] *a* oltraggioso(a); scandaloso(a).

outrider ['autraɪdə*] *n* (*on motorcycle*) battistrada *m inv*.

outright *ad* ['autraɪt] completamente; schiettamente; apertamente; sul colpo // *a* ['autraɪt] completo(a); schietto(a) e netto(a).

outset ['autsɛt] *n* inizio.

outside [aut'saɪd] *n* esterno, esteriore *m* // *a* esterno(a), esteriore // *ad* fuori, all'esterno // *prep* fuori di, all'esterno di; **at the ~** (*fig*) al massimo; **~ lane** *n* (*AUT*) corsia di sorpasso; **~r** *n* (*in race etc*) outsider *m inv*; (*stranger*) straniero/a.

outsize ['autsaɪz] *a* enorme; (*clothes*) per taglie forti.

outskirts ['autskəːts] *npl* sobborghi *mpl*.

outspoken [aut'spəukən] *a* molto franco(a).

outstanding [aut'stændɪŋ] *a* eccezionale, di rilievo; (*unfinished*) non completo(a); non evaso(a); non regolato(a).

outstay [aut'steɪ] *vt:* **to ~ one's welcome** diventare un ospite sgradito.

outstretched [aut'strɛtʃt] *a* (*hand*) teso(a); (*body*) disteso(a).

outward ['autwəd] *a* (*sign, appearances*) esteriore; (*journey*) d'andata; **~ly** *ad* esteriormente; in apparenza.

outweigh [aut'weɪ] *vt* avere maggior peso di.

outwit [aut'wɪt] *vt* superare in astuzia.

oval ['əuvl] *a,n* ovale (*m*).

ovary ['ǝuvǝrɪ] n ovaia.

ovation [ǝu'veɪʃǝn] n ovazione f.

oven ['ʌvn] n forno; ~**proof** a da forno.

over ['ǝuvǝ*] ad al di sopra // a (or ad) (finished) finito(a), terminato(a); (too) troppo; (remaining) che avanza // prep su; sopra; (above) al di sopra di; (on the other side of) di là di; (more than) più di; (during) durante; ~ **here** qui; ~ **there** là; **all** ~ (everywhere) dappertutto; (finished) tutto(a) finito(a); ~ **and** ~ (again) più e più volte; ~ **and above** oltre a (a); **to ask sb** ~ invitare qd (a passare).

over... ['ǝuvǝ*] prefix: ~**abundant** sovrabbondante.

overact [ǝuvǝr'ækt] vi (THEATRE) esagerare or strafare la propria parte.

overall a,n ['ǝuvǝrɔːl] a totale // n (Brit) grembiule m // ad [ǝuvǝr'ɔːl] nell'insieme, complessivamente; ~**s** npl tuta (da lavoro).

overawe [ǝuvǝr'ɔː] vt intimidire.

overbalance [ǝuvǝ'bælǝns] vi perdere l'equilibrio.

overbearing [ǝuvǝ'bɛǝrɪŋ] a imperioso(a), prepotente.

overboard ['ǝuvǝbɔːd] ad (NAUT) fuori bordo, in mare.

overcast ['ǝuvǝkɑːst] a coperto(a).

overcharge [ǝuvǝ'tʃɑːdʒ] vt: **to** ~ **sb for sth** far pagare troppo caro a qd per qc.

overcoat ['ǝuvǝkǝut] n soprabito, cappotto.

overcome [ǝuvǝ'kʌm] vt irg superare; sopraffare.

overcrowded [ǝuvǝ'kraudɪd] a sovraffollato(a).

overcrowding [ǝuvǝ'kraudɪŋ] n sovraffollamento; (in bus) calca.

overdo [ǝuvǝ'duː] vt irg esagerare; (overcook) cuocere troppo.

overdose ['ǝuvǝdǝus] n dose f eccessiva.

overdraft ['ǝuvǝdrɑːft] n scoperto (di conto).

overdrawn [ǝuvǝ'drɔːn] a (account) scoperto(a).

overdue [ǝuvǝ'djuː] a in ritardo; (recognition) tardivo(a).

overestimate [ǝuvǝr'ɛstɪmeɪt] vt sopravvalutare.

overexertion [ǝuvǝrɪg'zɑːʃǝn] n logorio (fisico).

overexpose [ǝuvǝrɪk'spǝuz] vt (PHOT) sovraesporre.

overflow [ǝuvǝ'flǝu] vi traboccare.

overgrown [ǝuvǝ'grǝun] a (garden) ricoperto(a) di vegetazione.

overhaul vt [ǝuvǝ'hɔːl] revisionare // n ['ǝuvǝhɔːl] revisione f.

overhead ad [ǝuvǝ'hɛd] di sopra // a ['ǝuvǝhɛd] aereo(a); (lighting) verticale; ~**s** npl spese fpl generali.

overhear [ǝuvǝ'hɪǝ*] vt irg sentire (per caso).

overjoyed [ǝuvǝ'dʒɔɪd] a pazzo(a) di gioia.

overland ['ǝuvǝlænd] a, ad per via di terra.

overlap [ǝuvǝ'læp] vi sovrapporsi.

overload [ǝuvǝ'lǝud] vt sovraccaricare.

overlook [ǝuvǝ'luk] vt (have view of) dare su; (miss) trascurare; (forgive) passare sopra a.

overnight [ǝuvǝ'naɪt] ad (happen) durante la notte; (fig) tutto ad un tratto // a di notte; fulmineo(a); **he stayed there** ~ ci ha passato la notte; **if you travel** ~... se viaggia di notte... .

overpass ['ǝuvǝpɑːs] n cavalcavia m inv.

overpower [ǝuvǝ'pauǝ*] vt sopraffare; ~**ing** a irresistibile; (heat, stench) soffocante.

overrate [ǝuvǝ'reɪt] vt sopravvalutare.

overreact [ǝuvǝriː'ækt] vi reagire in modo esagerato.

override [ǝuvǝ'raɪd] vt (irg: like **ride**) (order, objection) passar sopra a; (decision) annullare; **overriding** a preponderante.

overrule [ǝuvǝ'ruːl] vt (decision) annullare; (claim) respingere.

overseas [ǝuvǝ'siːz] ad oltremare; (abroad) all'estero // a (trade) estero(a); (visitor) straniero(a).

overseer ['ǝuvǝsiːǝ*] n (in factory) caposquadra m.

overshadow [ǝuvǝ'ʃædǝu] vt (fig) eclissare.

overshoot [ǝuvǝ'ʃuːt] vt irg superare.

oversight ['ǝuvǝsaɪt] n omissione f, svista.

oversimplify [ǝuvǝ'sɪmplɪfaɪ] vt rendere troppo semplice.

oversleep [ǝuvǝ'sliːp] vi irg dormire troppo a lungo.

overspill ['ǝuvǝspɪl] n eccedenza di popolazione.

overstate [ǝuvǝ'steɪt] vt esagerare; ~**ment** n esagerazione f.

overt [ǝu'vǝːt] a palese.

overtake [ǝuvǝ'teɪk] vt irg sorpassare; **overtaking** n (AUT) sorpasso.

overthrow [ǝuvǝ'θrǝu] vt irg (government) rovesciare.

overtime ['ǝuvǝtaɪm] n (lavoro) straordinario.

overtone ['ǝuvǝtǝun] n (also: ~**s**) sottinteso.

overture ['ǝuvǝtʃuǝ*] n (MUS) ouverture f inv; (fig) approccio.

overturn [ǝuvǝ'tǝːn] vt rovesciare // vi rovesciarsi.

overweight [ǝuvǝ'weɪt] a (person) troppo grasso(a); (luggage) troppo pesante.

overwhelm [ǝuvǝ'wɛlm] vt sopraffare; sommergere; schiacciare; ~**ing** a (victory, defeat) schiacciante; (desire) irresistibile.

overwork [ǝuvǝ'wǝːk] vt far lavorare troppo // vi lavorare troppo, strapazzarsi.

overwrought [ǝuvǝ'rɔːt] a molto agitato(a).

owe [ǝu] vt dovere; **to** ~ **sb sth, to** ~ **sth to sb** dovere qc a qd.

owing to ['ǝuɪŋtuː] prep a causa di, a motivo di.

owl [aul] n gufo.

own [ǝun] vt possedere // a proprio(a); **a**

room of my ~ la mia propria camera; **to get one's ~ back** vendicarsi; **on one's ~** tutto(a) solo(a); **to ~ up** *vi* confessare; **~er** *n* proprietario/a; **~ership** *n* possesso.

ox, *pl* **oxen** [ɔks, 'ɔksn] *n* bue *m*.

oxide ['ɔksaɪd] *n* ossido.

oxtail ['ɔksteɪl] *n*: **~ soup** minestra di coda di bue.

oxygen ['ɔksɪdʒən] *n* ossigeno; **~ mask/tent** *n* maschera/tenda ad ossigeno.

oyster ['ɔɪstə*] *n* ostrica.

oz. *abbr of* **ounce(s)**.

ozone ['əuzəun] *n* ozono.

P

p [pi:] *abbr of* **penny, pence**.

p.a. *abbr of* **per annum**.

pa [pɑ:] *n* (*col*) papà *m inv*, babbo.

pace [peɪs] *n* passo; (*speed*) passo; velocità // *vi*: **to ~ up and down** camminare su e giù; **to keep ~ with** camminare di pari passo a; (*events*) tenersi al corrente di; **~maker** *n* (*MED*) segnapasso.

pacific [pə'sɪfɪk] *n*: **the P~** (*Ocean*) il Pacifico, l'Oceano Pacifico.

pacifist ['pæsɪfɪst] *n* pacifista *m/f*.

pacify ['pæsɪfaɪ] *vt* pacificare; (*soothe*) calmare.

pack [pæk] *n* pacco; balla; (*of hounds*) muta; (*of thieves etc*) banda; (*of cards*) mazzo // *vt* (*goods*) impaccare, imballare; (*in suitcase etc*) mettere; (*box*) riempire; (*cram*) stipare, pigiare; (*press down*) tamponare; turare; **to ~ (one's bags)** fare la valigia.

package ['pækɪdʒ] *n* pacco; balla; (*also: ~ deal*) pacchetto; forfait *m inv*; **~ tour** *n* viaggio organizzato.

packet ['pækɪt] *n* pacchetto.

pack ice ['pækaɪs] *n* banchisa.

packing ['pækɪŋ] *n* imballaggio; **~ case** *n* cassa da imballaggio.

pact [pækt] *n* patto, accordo; trattato.

pad [pæd] *n* blocco; (*for inking*) tampone *m*; (*col: flat*) appartamentino // *vt* imbottire; **~ding** *n* imbottitura; (*fig*) riempitivo.

paddle ['pædl] *n* (*oar*) pagaia // *vi* sguazzare; **~ steamer** *n* vapore *m* con ruote a pala; **paddling pool** *n* piscina per bambini.

paddock ['pædɔk] *n* recinto; paddock *m inv*.

paddy ['pædɪ] *n*: **~ field** *n* risaia.

padlock ['pædlɔk] *n* lucchetto.

padre ['pɑːdrɪ] *n* cappellano.

paediatrics [pi:dɪ'ætrɪks] *n* pediatria.

pagan ['peɪgən] *a n* pagano(a).

page [peɪdʒ] *n* pagina; (*also: ~ boy*) fattorino; (*at wedding*) paggio // *vt* (*in hotel etc*) (far) chiamare.

pageant ['pædʒənt] *n* spettacolo storico; grande cerimonia; **~ry** *n* pompa.

paid [peɪd] *pt*, *pp of* **pay** // *a* (*work, official*)

rimunerato(a); **to put ~ to** mettere fine a.

pail [peɪl] *n* secchio.

pain [peɪn] *n* dolore *m*; **to be in ~** soffrire, aver male; **to have a ~ in** aver male *or* un dolore a; **to take ~s to** do mettercela tutta per fare; **~ed** *a* addolorato(a), afflitto(a); **~ful** *a* doloroso(a), che fa male; difficile, penoso(a); **~killer** *n* antalgico, antidolorifico; **~less** *a* indolore; **~staking** ['peɪnzteɪkɪŋ] *a* sollecito(a).

paint [peɪnt] *n* vernice *f*, colore *m* // *vt* dipingere; (*walls, door etc*) verniciare; **to ~ the door blue** verniciare la porta di azzurro; **~brush** *n* pennello; **~er** *n* pittore *m*; imbianchino; **~ing** *n* pittura; verniciatura; (*picture*) dipinto, quadro; **~-stripper** *n* prodotto sverniciante.

pair [pɛə*] *n* (*of shoes, gloves etc*) paio; (*of people*) coppia; duo *m inv*; **a ~ of scissors** delle forbici.

pajamas [pɪ'dʒɑ:məz] *npl* (*US*) pigiama *m*.

Pakistan [pɑ:kɪ'stɑ:n] *n* Pakistan *m*; **~i** *a*, *n* pakistano(a).

pal [pæl] *n* (*col*) amico/a, compagno/a.

palace ['pæləs] *n* palazzo.

palatable ['pælɪtəbl] *a* gustoso(a).

palate ['pælɪt] *n* palato.

palaver [pə'lɑ:və*] *n* chiacchiere *fpl*; storie *fpl*.

pale [peɪl] *a* pallido(a); **~ blue** *a* azzurro *or* blu pallido *inv*; **~ness** *n* pallidezza.

Palestine ['pælɪstaɪn] *n* Palestina; **Palestinian** [-'tɪnɪən] *a*, *n* palestinese (*m/f*).

palette ['pælɪt] *n* tavolozza.

palisade [pælɪ'seɪd] *n* palizzata.

pall [pɔ:l] *n* (*of smoke*) cappa // *vi*: **to ~ (on)** diventare noioso(a) (a).

pallid ['pælɪd] *a* pallido(a), smorto(a).

pally ['pælɪ] *a* (*col*) amichevole.

palm [pɑ:m] *n* (*ANAT*) palma, palmo; (*also: ~ tree*) palma // *vt*: **to ~ sth off on sb** (*col*) rifilare qc a qd; **~ist** *n* chiromante *m/f*; **P~ Sunday** *n* la Domenica delle Palme.

palpable ['pælpəbl] *a* palpabile.

palpitation [pælpɪ'teɪʃən] *n* palpitazione *f*.

paltry ['pɔ:ltrɪ] *a* derisorio(a); insignificante.

pamper ['pæmpə*] *vt* viziare, accarezzare.

pamphlet ['pæmflət] *n* dépliant *m inv*.

pan [pæn] *n* (*also: saucepan ~*) casseruola; (*also: frying ~*) padella // *vi* (*CINEMA*) fare una panoramica.

panacea [pænə'sɪə] *n* panacea.

Panama ['pænəmɑ:] *n* Panama *m*; **~ canal** *n* canale *m* di Panama.

pancake ['pænkeɪk] *n* frittella.

panda ['pændə] *n* panda *m inv*.

pandemonium [pændɪ'məunɪəm] *n* pandemonio.

pander ['pændə*] *vi*: **to ~ to** lusingare; concedere tutto a.

pane [peɪn] *n* vetro.

panel ['pænl] *n* (*of wood, cloth etc*)

pannello; (RADIO, TV) giuria; ~ling n rivestimento a pannelli.

pang [pæŋ] n: ~s of hunger spasimi mpl della fame; ~s of conscience morsi mpl di coscienza.

panic ['pænɪk] n panico // vi perdere il sangue freddo; ~ky a (person) pauroso(a).

pannier ['pænɪə*] n (on animal) bisaccia; (on bicycle) borsa.

panorama [pænə'rɑːmə] n panorama m.

pansy ['pænzɪ] n (BOT) viola del pensiero, pensée f inv; (col) femminuccia.

pant [pænt] vi ansare.

panther ['pænθə*] n pantera.

panties ['pæntɪz] npl slip m, mutandine fpl.

pantomime ['pæntəmaɪm] n pantomima.

pantry ['pæntrɪ] n dispensa.

pants [pænts] npl mutande fpl, slip m; (US: trousers) pantaloni mpl.

papacy ['peɪpəsɪ] n papato.

papal ['peɪpəl] a papale, pontificio(a).

paper ['peɪpə*] n carta; (also: wall~) carta da parati, tappezzeria; (also: news~) giornale m; (study, article) saggio; (exam) prova scritta // a di carta // vt tappezzare; (identity) ~s npl carte fpl, documenti mpl; ~back n tascabile m; edizione f economica; ~ bag n sacchetto di carta; ~ clip n graffetta, clip f inv; ~ mill n cartiera; ~weight n fermacarte m inv; ~work n lavoro amministrativo.

papier-mâché ['pæpɪeɪ'mæʃeɪ] n cartapesta.

paprika ['pæprɪkə] n paprica.

par [pɑː*] n parità, pari f; (GOLF) norma; on a ~ with alla pari con.

parable ['pærəbl] n parabola.

parachute ['pærəʃuːt] n paracadute m inv // vi scendere col paracadute; **parachutist** n paracadutista m/f.

parade [pə'reɪd] n parata; (inspection) rivista, rassegna // vt (fig) fare sfoggio di // vi sfilare in parata.

paradise ['pærədaɪs] n paradiso.

paradox ['pærədɔks] n paradosso; ~ical [-'dɔksɪkl] a paradossale.

paraffin ['pærəfɪn] n: ~ (oil) paraffina.

paragraph ['pærəɡrɑːf] n paragrafo.

parallel ['pærəlel] a parallelo(a); (fig) analogo(a) // n (line) parallela; (fig, GEO) parallelo.

paralysis [pə'rælɪsɪs] n paralisi f inv.

paralyze ['pærəlaɪz] vt paralizzare.

paramount ['pærəmaunt] a: of ~ importance di capitale importanza.

paranoia [pærə'nɔɪə] n paranoia.

paraphernalia [pærəfə'neɪlɪə] n attrezzi mpl, roba.

paraphrase ['pærəfreɪz] vt parafrasare.

paraplegic [pærə'pliːdʒɪk] n paraplegico(a).

parasite ['pærəsaɪt] n parassita m.

paratrooper ['pærətruːpə*] n paracadutista m (soldato).

parcel ['pɑːsl] n pacco, pacchetto // vt (also: ~ up) impaccare.

parch [pɑːʃ] vt riardere; ~ed a (person) assetato(a).

parchment ['pɑːtʃmənt] n pergamena.

pardon ['pɑːdn] n perdono; grazia // vt perdonare; (LAW) graziare; ~! scusi! ~ me! mi scusi!; I beg your ~! scusi!; I beg your ~? prego?

parent ['pɛərənt] n genitore m; ~s npl genitori mpl; ~al [pə'rɛntl] a dei genitori.

parenthesis, pl **parentheses** [pə'rɛnθɪsɪs, -siːz] n parentesi f inv.

Paris ['pærɪs] n Parigi.

parish ['pærɪʃ] n parrocchia; (civil) ≈ municipio // a parrocchiale; ~ioner [pə'rɪʃənə*] n parrocchiano/a.

parity ['pærɪtɪ] n parità.

park [pɑːk] n parco // vt, vi parcheggiare; ~ing n parcheggio; ~ing lot n (US) posteggio, parcheggio; ~ing meter n parchimetro; ~ing place n posto di parcheggio.

parliament ['pɑːləmənt] n parlamento; ~ary [-'mɛntərɪ] a parlamentare.

parlour ['pɑːlə*] n salotto.

parochial [pə'rəukɪəl] a parrocchiale; (pej) provinciale.

parody ['pærədɪ] n parodia.

parole [pə'rəul] n: on ~ lasciato(a) libero(a) sulla parola.

parquet ['pɑːkeɪ] n: ~ floor(ing) parquet m.

parrot ['pærət] n pappagallo; ~ fashion ad in modo pappagallesco.

parry ['pærɪ] vt parare.

parsimonious [pɑːsɪ'məunɪəs] a parsimonioso(a).

parsley ['pɑːslɪ] n prezzemolo.

parsnip ['pɑːsnɪp] n pastinaca.

parson ['pɑːsn] n prete m; (Church of England) parroco.

part [pɑːt] n parte f; (of machine) pezzo; (MUS) voce f; parte f // a in parte // ad = **partly** // vt separare // vi (people) separarsi; (roads) dividersi; to take ~ in prendere parte a; on his ~ da parte sua; for my ~ per parte mia; for the most ~ in generale; nella maggior parte dei casi; to ~ with vt fus separarsi da; rinunciare a; (take leave) lasciare; in ~ exchange in pagamento parziale.

partial ['pɑːʃl] a parziale; to be ~ to avere un debole per.

participate [pɑː'tɪsɪpeɪt] vi: to ~ (in) prendere parte a, partecipare (a); **participation** [-'peɪʃən] n partecipazione f.

participle ['pɑːtɪsɪpl] n participio.

particle ['pɑːtɪkl] n particella.

particular [pə'tɪkjulə*] a particolare; speciale; (fussy) difficile; meticoloso(a); ~s npl particolari mpl, dettagli mpl; (information) informazioni fpl; ~ly ad particolarmente; in particolare.

parting ['pɑːtɪŋ] n separazione f; (in hair) scriminatura // a d'addio.

partisan [pɑːtɪ'zæn] n partigiano/a // a partigiano(a); di parte.

partition [pɑː'tɪʃən] n (POL) partizione f; (wall) tramezzo.

partly ['pɑːtlɪ] ad parzialmente; in parte.

partner ['pɑːtnə*] n (COMM) socio/a; (SPORT) compagno/a; (at dance) cavaliere/dama; ~**ship** n associazione f; (COMM) società f inv.

partridge ['pɑːtrɪdʒ] n pernice f.

part-time ['pɑːt'taɪm] a,ad a orario ridotto.

party ['pɑːtɪ] n (POL) partito; (team) squadra; gruppo; (LAW) parte f; (celebration) ricevimento; serata; festa.

pass [pɑːs] vt (gen) passare; (place) passare davanti a; (exam) passare, superare; (candidate) promuovere; (overtake, surpass) sorpassare, superare; (approve) approvare // vi passare // n (permit) lasciapassare m inv; permesso; (in mountains) passo, gola; (SPORT) passaggio; (SCOL: also: ~ mark): **to get a ~** prendere la sufficienza; **could you ~ the vegetables round?** potrebbe far passare i contorni?; **to ~ away** vi morire; **to ~ by** vi passare // vt trascurare; **to ~ for** passare per; **to ~ out** vi svenire; ~**able** a (road) praticabile; (work) accettabile.

passage ['pæsɪdʒ] n (gen) passaggio; (also: ~way) corridoio; (in book) brano, passo; (by boat) traversata.

passenger ['pæsɪndʒə*] n passeggero/a.

passer-by [pɑːsə'baɪ] n passante m/f.

passing ['pɑːsɪŋ] a (fig) fuggevole; **a ~ reference** un accenno; **in ~** incidentalmente.

passion ['pæʃən] n passione f; amore m; ~**ate** a appassionato(a).

passive ['pæsɪv] a (also LING) passivo(a).

passport ['pɑːspɔːt] n passaporto.

password ['pɑːswəːd] n parola d'ordine.

past [pɑːst] prep (further than) oltre, di là di; dopo; (later than) dopo // a passato(a); (president etc) ex inv // n passato; **he's ~ forty** ha più di quarant'anni; **for the ~ few days** da qualche giorno; in questi ultimi giorni; **to run ~** passare di corsa.

pasta ['pæstə] n pasta.

paste [peɪst] n (glue) colla; (CULIN) pâté m inv; pasta // vt collare.

pastel ['pæstl] a pastello(a).

pasteurized ['pæstəraɪzd] a pastorizzato(a).

pastille ['pæstl] n pastiglia.

pastime ['pɑːstaɪm] n passatempo.

pastoral ['pɑːstərl] a pastorale.

pastry ['peɪstrɪ] n pasta.

pasture ['pɑːstʃə*] n pascolo.

pasty n ['pæstɪ] pasticcio di carne // a ['peɪstɪ] pastoso(a); (complexion) pallido(a).

pat [pæt] vt accarezzare, dare un colpetto (affettuoso) a // n: **a ~ of butter** un panetto di burro.

patch [pætʃ] n (of material) toppa; (spot) macchia; (of land) pezzo // vt (clothes) rattoppare; **a bad ~** un brutto periodo; **to**

~ **up** vt rappezzare; ~**work** n patchwork m; ~**y** a irregolare.

pâté ['pæteɪ] n pâté m inv.

patent ['peɪtnt] n brevetto // vt brevettare // a patente, manifesto(a); ~ **leather** n cuoio verniciato.

paternal [pə'təːnl] a paterno(a).

paternity [pə'təːnɪtɪ] n paternità.

path [pɑːθ] n sentiero, viottolo; viale m; (fig) via, strada; (of planet, missile) traiettoria.

pathetic [pə'θetɪk] a (pitiful) patetico(a); (very bad) penoso(a).

pathologist [pə'θɒlədʒɪst] n patologo/a.

pathology [pə'θɒlədʒɪ] n patologia.

pathos ['peɪθɒs] n pathos m.

pathway ['pɑːθweɪ] n sentiero, viottolo.

patience ['peɪʃns] n pazienza; (CARDS) solitario.

patient ['peɪʃnt] n paziente m/f; malato/a // a paziente.

patio ['pætɪəʊ] n terrazza.

patriot ['peɪtrɪət] n patriota m/f; ~**ic** [pætrɪ'ɒtɪk] a patriottico(a).

patrol [pə'trəʊl] n pattuglia // vt pattugliare; ~ **car** n autoradio f inv (della polizia); ~**man** n (US) poliziotto.

patron ['peɪtrən] n (in shop) cliente m/f; (of charity) benefattore/trice; ~**age** ['pætrənɪdʒ] n patronato; ~**ize** ['pætrənaɪz] vt essere cliente abituale di; (fig) trattare con condiscendenza; ~ **saint** n patrono.

patter ['pætə*] n picchiettio; (sales talk) propaganda di vendita // vi picchiettare.

pattern ['pætən] n modello; (design) disegno, motivo; (sample) campione m.

paunch [pɔːntʃ] n pancione m.

pauper ['pɔːpə*] n indigente m/f.

pause [pɔːz] n pausa // vi fare una pausa, arrestarsi.

pave [peɪv] vt pavimentare; **to ~ the way for** aprire la via a.

pavement ['peɪvmənt] n (Brit) marciapiede m.

pavilion [pə'vɪlɪən] n padiglione m; tendone m.

paving ['peɪvɪŋ] n pavimentazione f; ~**stone** n lastra di pietra.

paw [pɔː] n zampa // vt dare una zampata a; (subj: person: pej) palpare.

pawn [pɔːn] n pegno; (CHESS) pedone m; (fig) pedina // vt dare in pegno; ~**broker** n prestatore m su pegno; ~**shop** n monte m di pietà.

pay [peɪ] n stipendio; paga // vb (pt,pp paid [peɪd]) vt pagare // vi pagare; (be profitable) rendere; **to ~ attention (to)** fare attenzione (a); **to ~ back** vt rimborsare; **to ~ for** vt fus pagare; **to ~ in** vt versare; **to ~ up** vt saldare; ~**able** a pagabile; ~ **day** n giorno di paga; ~**ee** n beneficiario/a; ~**ment** n pagamento; versamento; saldamento; ~ **packet** n busta f paga inv; ~**roll** n ruolo (organico).

p.c. abbr per **per cent**.

pea [piː] n pisello.

peace [pi:s] *n* pace *f*; (*calm*) calma, tranquillità; ~**able** *a* pacifico(a); ~**ful** *a* pacifico(a), calmo(a); ~-**keeping** *n* mantenimento della pace.

peach [pi:tʃ] *n* pesca.

peacock ['pi:kɔk] *n* pavone *m*.

peak [pi:k] *n* (*of mountain*) cima, vetta; (*mountain itself*) picco; (*fig*) massimo; (: *of career*) acme *f*; ~ **period** *n* periodo di punta.

peal [pi:l] *n* (*of bells*) scampanio, carillon *m inv*; ~**s of laughter** scoppi *mpl* di risa.

peanut ['pi:nʌt] *n* arachide *f*, nocciolina americana; ~ **butter** *n* burro di arachidi.

pear [pɛə*] *n* pera.

pearl [pə:l] *n* perla.

peasant ['pɛznt] *n* contadino/a.

peat [pi:t] *n* torba.

pebble ['pɛbl] *n* ciottolo.

peck [pɛk] *vt* (*also:* ~ **at**) beccare; (*food*) mangiucchiare // *n* colpo di becco; (*kiss*) bacetto; ~**ish** *a* (*col*): **I feel** ~**ish** ho un languorino.

peculiar [pɪ'kju:lɪə*] *a* strano(a), bizzarro(a); peculiare; ~ **to** peculiare di; ~**ity** [pɪkju:lɪ'ærɪtɪ] *n* peculiarità *f inv*; (*oddity*) bizzarria.

pecuniary [pɪ'kju:nɪərɪ] *a* pecuniario(a).

pedal ['pɛdl] *n* pedale *m* // *vi* pedalare.

pedantic [pɪ'dæntɪk] *a* pedantesco(a).

pedestal ['pɛdəstl] *n* piedestallo.

pedestrian [pɪ'dɛstrɪən] *n* pedone/a // *a* pedonale; (*fig*) prosaico(a), pedestre.

pediatrics [pi:dɪ'ætrɪks] *n* (*US*) = **paediatrics**.

pedigree ['pɛdɪgri:] *n* stirpe *f*; (*of animal*) pedigree *m inv* // *cpd* (*animal*) di razza.

pedlar ['pɛdlə*] *n* venditore *m* ambulante.

peek [pi:k] *vi* guardare furtivamente.

peel [pi:l] *n* buccia; (*of orange, lemon*) scorza // *vt* sbucciare // *vi* (*paint etc*) staccarsi.

peep [pi:p] *n* (*look*) sguardo furtivo, sbirciata; (*sound*) pigolio // *vi* guardare furtivamente; **to** ~ **out** *vi* mostrarsi furtivamente; ~**hole** *n* spioncino.

peer [pɪə*] *vi*: **to** ~ **at** scrutare // *n* (*noble*) pari *m inv*; (*equal*) pari *m/f inv*, uguale *m/f*; ~**age** *n* dignità di pari; pari *mpl*.

peeved [pi:vd] *a* stizzito(a).

peevish ['pi:vɪʃ] *a* stizzoso(a).

peg [pɛg] *n* -caviglia; (*for coat etc*) attaccapanni *m inv*; (*also:* **clothes** ~) molletta; **off the** ~ *ad* confezionato(a).

pejorative [pɪ'dʒɔrətɪv] *a* peggiorativo(a).

pekingese [pi:kɪ'ni:z] *n* pechinese *m*.

pelican ['pɛlɪkən] *n* pellicano.

pellet ['pɛlɪt] *n* pallottola, pallina.

pelmet ['pɛlmɪt] *n* mantovana; cassonetto.

pelt [pɛlt] *vt*: **to** ~ **sb** (**with**) bombardare qd (con) // *vi* (*rain*) piovere a dirotto // *n* pelle *f*.

pelvis ['pɛlvɪs] *n* pelvi *f inv*, bacino.

pen [pɛn] *n* penna; (*for sheep*) recinto.

penal ['pi:nl] *a* penale; ~**ize** *vt* punire; (*SPORT*) penalizzare; (*fig*) svantaggiare.

penalty ['pɛnltɪ] *n* penalità *f inv*; sanzione *f* penale; (*fine*) ammenda; (*SPORT*) penalizzazione *f*; ~ (**kick**) *n* (*FOOTBALL*) calcio di rigore.

penance ['pɛnəns] *n* penitenza.

pence [pɛns] *npl of* **penny**.

pencil ['pɛnsl] *n* matita; ~ **sharpener** *n* temperamatite *m inv*.

pendant ['pɛndnt] *n* pendaglio.

pending ['pɛndɪŋ] *prep* in attesa di // *a* in sospeso.

pendulum ['pɛndjʊləm] *n* pendolo.

penetrate ['pɛnɪtreɪt] *vt* penetrare; **penetrating** *a* penetrante; **penetration** [-'treɪʃən] *n* penetrazione *f*.

penfriend ['pɛnfrɛnd] *n* corrispondente *m/f*.

penguin ['pɛŋgwɪn] *n* pinguino.

penicillin [pɛnɪ'sɪlɪn] *n* penicillina.

peninsula [pə'nɪnsjʊlə] *n* penisola.

penis ['pi:nɪs] *n* pene *m*.

penitence ['pɛnɪtns] *n* penitenza.

penitent ['pɛnɪtnt] *a* penitente.

penitentiary [pɛnɪ'tɛnʃərɪ] *n* (*US*) carcere *m*.

penknife ['pɛnnaɪf] *n* temperino.

pennant ['pɛnənt] *n* banderuola.

penniless ['pɛnɪlɪs] *a* senza un soldo.

penny, *pl* **pennies** *or* **pence** ['pɛnɪ, 'pɛnɪz, pɛns] *n* penny *m* (*pl* pence).

pension ['pɛnʃən] *n* pensione *f*; ~**able** *a* che ha diritto a una pensione; ~**er** *n* pensionato/a.

pensive ['pɛnsɪv] *a* pensoso(a).

pentagon ['pɛntəgən] *n* pentagono.

Pentecost ['pɛntɪkɔst] *n* Pentecoste *f*.

penthouse ['pɛnthaus] *n* appartamento (di lusso) nell'attico.

pent-up ['pɛntʌp] *a* (*feelings*) represso(a).

penultimate [pɛ'nʌltɪmət] *a* penultimo(a).

people ['pi:pl] *npl* gente *f*; persone *fpl*; (*citizens*) popolo // *n* (*nation, race*) popolo // *vt* popolare; **4/several** ~ **came** 4/parecchie persone sono venute; **the room was full of** ~ la stanza era piena di gente; ~ **say that...** si dice *or* la gente dice che... .

pep [pɛp] *n* (*col*) dinamismo; **to** ~ **up** *vt* vivacizzare; (*food*) rendere più gustoso(a).

pepper ['pɛpə*] *n* pepe *m*; (*vegetable*) peperone *m* // *vt* pepare; ~**mint** *n* (*plant*) menta peperita; (*sweet*) pasticca di menta.

peptalk ['pɛptɔ:k] *n* (*col*) discorso di incoraggiamento.

per [pə:*] *prep* per; a; ~ **hour** all'ora; ~ **kilo** il chilo *etc*; ~ **day** al giorno; ~ **cent** per cento; ~ **annum** all'anno.

perceive [pə'si:v] *vt* percepire; (*notice*) accorgersi di.

percentage [pə'sɛntɪdʒ] *n* percentuale *f*.

perceptible [pə'sɛptɪbl] *a* percettibile.

perception [pə'sɛpʃən] *n* percezione *f*; sensibilità; perspicacia.

perceptive [pə'sɛptɪv] *a* percettivo(a); perspicace.

perch [pə:tʃ] *n* (*fish*) pesce *m* persico; (*for*

bird) sostegno, ramo // *vi* appollaiarsi.
percolator ['pɔːkəleitə*] *n* caffettiera a pressione; caffettiera elettrica.
percussion [pəˈkʌʃən] *n* percussione *f*.
peremptory [pəˈremptəri] *a* perentorio(a).
perennial [pəˈreniəl] *a* perenne // *n* pianta perenne.
perfect *a,n* ['pɔːfikt] *a* perfetto(a) // *in* (*also:* ~ **tense**) perfetto, passato prossimo // *vt* [pɔˈfekt] perfezionare; mettere a punto; ~**ion** [-ˈfekʃən] *n* perfezione *f*; ~**ionist** *n* perfezionista *m/f*.
perforate ['pɔːfəreit] *vt* perforare; ~**ion** [-ˈreiʃən] *n* perforazione *f*; (*line of holes*) dentellatura.
perform [pəˈfɔːm] *vt* (*carry out*) eseguire, fare; (*symphony etc*) suonare; (*play, ballet*) dare; (*opera*) fare // *vi* suonare; recitare; ~**ance** *n* esecuzione *f*; (*at theatre etc*) rappresentazione *f*, spettacolo; (*of an artist*) interpretazione *f*; (*of player etc*) performance *f*; (*of car, engine*) prestazione *f*; ~**er** *n* artista *m/f*; ~**ing** *a* (*animal*) ammaestrato(a).
perfume ['pɔːfjuːm] *n* profumo.
perfunctory [pəˈfʌŋktəri] *a* superficiale, per la forma.
perhaps [pəˈhæps] *ad* forse.
peril ['peril] *n* pericolo; ~**ous** *a* pericoloso(a).
perimeter [pəˈrimitə*] *n* perimetro; ~ **wall** *n* muro di cinta.
period ['piəriəd] *n* periodo; (*HISTORY*) epoca; (*SCOL*) lezione *f*; (*full stop*) punto; (*MED*) mestruazioni *fpl* // *a* (*costume, furniture*) d'epoca; ~**ic** [-ˈɔdik] *a* periodico(a); ~**ical** [-ˈɔdikl] *a* periodico(a) // *n* periodico.
peripheral [pəˈrifərəl] *a* periferico(a).
periphery [pəˈrifəri] *n* periferia.
periscope ['periskəup] *n* periscopio.
perish ['periʃ] *vi* perire, morire; (*decay*) deteriorarsi; ~**able** *a* deperibile; ~**ing** *a* (*col: cold*) da morire.
perjure ['pɔːdʒə*] *vt*: **to** ~ **o.s.** spergiurare; **perjury** *n* spergiuro.
perk [pɔːk] *n* vantaggio; **to** ~ **up** *vi* (*cheer up*) rianimarsi; ~**y** *a* (*cheerful*) vivace, allegro(a).
perm [pɔːm] *n* (*for hair*) permanente *f*.
permanence ['pɔːmənəns] *n* permanenza.
permanent ['pɔːmənənt] *a* permanente.
permeate ['pɔːmieit] *vi* penetrare // *vt* permeare.
permissible [pəˈmisibl] *a* permissibile, ammissibile.
permission [pəˈmiʃən] *n* permesso.
permissive [pəˈmisiv] *a* tollerante; **the** ~ **society** la società permissiva.
permit *n* ['pɔːmit] permesso // *vt* [pəˈmit] permettere; **to** ~ **sb to do** permettere a qd di fare, dare il permesso a qd di fare.
permutation [pɔːmjuˈteiʃən] *n* permutazione *f*.
pernicious [pɔːˈniʃəs] *a* pernicioso(a). nocivo(a).

perpendicular [pɔːpənˈdikjulə*] *a,n* perpendicolare (*f*).
perpetrate ['pɔːpitreit] *vt* perpetrare, commettere.
perpetual [pəˈpetjuəl] *a* perpetuo(a).
perpetuity [pɔːpiˈtjuːiti] *n*: **in** ~ in perpetuo.
perplex [pəˈpleks] *vt* rendere perplesso(a); (*complicate*) imbrogliare.
persecute ['pɔːsikjuːt] *vt* perseguitare; **persecution** [-ˈkjuːʃən] *n* persecuzione *f*.
persevere [pɔːsiˈviə*] *vi* perseverare.
Persian ['pɔːʃən] *a* persiano(a) // *n* (*LING*) persiano; **the** (~) **Gulf** *n* il Golfo Persico.
persist [pəˈsist] *vi*: **to** ~ (**in doing**) persistere (nel fare); ostinarsi (a fare); ~**ence** *n* persistenza; ostinazione *f*; ~**ent** *a* persistente; ostinato(a).
person ['pɔːsn] *n* persona; ~**able** *a* di bell'aspetto; ~**al** *a* personale; individuale; ~**ality** [-ˈnæliti] *n* personalità *f inv*; ~**ally** *ad* personalmente; ~**ify** [-ˈsɔnifai] *vt* personificare.
personnel [pɔːsəˈnel] *n* personale *m*; ~ **manager** *n* direttore/trice del personale.
perspective [pəˈspektiv] *n* prospettiva.
perspicacity [pɔːspiˈkæsiti] *n* perspicacia.
perspiration [pɔːspiˈreiʃən] *n* traspirazione *f*, sudore *m*.
perspire [pɔːsˈpaiə*] *vi* traspirare.
persuade [pəˈsweid] *vt* persuadere.
persuasion [pəˈsweiʒən] *n* persuasione *f*.
persuasive [pəˈsweisiv] *a* persuasivo(a).
pert [pɔːt] *a* (*bold*) sfacciato(a), impertinente.
pertaining [pɔːˈteiniŋ]: ~ **to** *prep* che riguarda.
pertinent ['pɔːtinənt] *a* pertinente.
perturb [pəˈtɔːb] *vt* turbare.
Peru [pəˈruː] *n* Perù *m*.
perusal [pəˈruːzl] *n* attenta lettura.
Peruvian [pəˈruːvjən] *a, n* peruviano(a).
pervade [pəˈveid] *vt* pervadere.
perverse [pəˈvɔːs] *a* perverso(a).
perversion [pəˈvɔːʃn] *n* pervertimento, perversione *f*.
perversity [pəˈvɔːsiti] *n* perversità.
pervert *n* ['pɔːvɔːt] pervertito/a // *vt* [pəˈvɔːt] pervertire.
pessimism ['pesimizəm] *n* pessimismo.
pessimist ['pesimist] *n* pessimista *m/f*; ~**ic** [-ˈmistik] *a* pessimistico(a).
pest [pest] *n* animale *m* (*or* insetto) pestifero; (*fig*) peste *f*.
pester ['pestə*] *vt* tormentare, molestare.
pesticide ['pestisaid] *n* pesticida *m*.
pestle ['pesl] *n* pestello.
pet [pet] *n* animale *m* domestico; (*favourite*) favorito/a // *vt* accarezzare // *vi* (*col*) fare il petting; ~ **lion** *n* leone *m* ammaestrato.
petal ['petl] *n* petalo.
peter ['piːtə*]: **to** ~ **out** *vi* esaurirsi; estinguersi.
petite [pəˈtiːt] *a* piccolo(a) e aggraziato(a).
petition [pəˈtiʃən] *n* petizione *f*.

petrified ['petrɪfaɪd] *a* (*fig*) morto(a) di paura.

petrol ['petrəl] *n* (*Brit*) benzina.

petroleum [pə'trəʊlɪəm] *n* petrolio.

petrol: ~ **pump** *n* (*in car, at garage*) pompa di benzina; ~ **station** *n* stazione *f* di rifornimento; ~ **tank** *n* serbatoio della benzina.

petticoat ['petɪkəʊt] *n* sottana.

pettiness ['petɪnɪs] *n* meschinità.

petty ['petɪ] *a* (*mean*) meschino(a); (*unimportant*) insignificante; ~ **cash** *n* piccola cassa; ~ **officer** *n* sottufficiale *m* di marina.

petulant ['petjʊlənt] *a* irritabile.

pew [pju:] *n* panca (di chiesa).

pewter ['pju:tə*] *n* peltro.

phallic ['fælɪk] *a* fallico(a).

phantom ['fæntəm] *n* fantasma *m*.

Pharaoh ['feərəʊ] *n* faraone *m*.

pharmacist ['fɑːməsɪst] *n* farmacista *m/f*.

pharmacy ['fɑːməsɪ] *n* farmacia.

phase [feɪz] *n* fase *f*, periodo // *vt*: to ~ **sth in/out** introdurre/eliminare qc progressivamente.

Ph.D. (*abbr* = *Doctor of Philosophy*) *n* (*degree*) dottorato di ricerca.

pheasant ['feznt] *n* fagiano.

phenomenon, ** *pl* **phenomena [fə'nɒmɪnən, -nə] *n* fenomeno.

phew [fju:] *excl* uff!

phial ['faɪəl] *n* fiala.

philanthropic [fɪlən'θrɒpɪk] *a* filantropico(a).

philanthropist [fɪ'lænθrəpɪst] *n* filantropo.

philately [fɪ'lætəlɪ] *n* filatelia.

Philippines ['fɪlɪpiːnz] *npl* (*also*: **Philippine Islands**) Filippine *fpl*.

philosopher [fɪ'lɒsəfə*] *n* filosofo/a.

philosophical [fɪ'lɒsɪfɪk] *a* filosofico(a).

philosophy [fɪ'lɒsəfɪ] *n* filosofia.

phlegm [flem] *n* flemma; ~**atic** [fleg'mætɪk] *a* flemmatico(a).

phobia ['fəʊbjə] *n* fobia.

phone [fəʊn] *n* telefono // *vt* telefonare; to ~ **back** *vt*, *vi* richiamare.

phonetics [fə'netɪks] *n* fonetica.

phon(e)y ['fəʊnɪ] *a* falso(a), fasullo(a) // *n* (*person*) ciarlatano.

phonograph ['fəʊnəgrɑːf] *n* (*US*) giradischi *m*.

phosphate ['fɒsfeɪt] *n* fosfato.

phosphorus ['fɒsfərəs] *n* fosforo.

photo ['fəʊtəʊ] *n* foto *f inv*.

photo... ['fəʊtəʊ] *prefix*: ~**copier** *n* fotocopiatrice *f*; ~**copy** *n* fotocopia // *vt* fotocopiare; ~**genic** [-'dʒɛnɪk] *a* fotogenico(a); ~**graph** *n* fotografia // *vt* fotografare; ~**grapher** [fə'tɒgrəfə*] *n* fotografo; ~**graphic** [-'græfɪk] *a* fotografico(a); ~**graphy** [fə'tɒgrəfɪ] *n* fotografia.

phrase [freɪz] *n* espressione *f*, (*LING*) locuzione *f*; (*MUS*) frase *f* // *vt* esprimere; ~ **book** *n* vocabolarietto.

physical ['fɪzɪkl] *a* fisico(a); ~**ly** *ad* fisicamente.

physician [fɪ'zɪʃən] *n* medico.

physicist ['fɪzɪsɪst] *n* fisico.

physics ['fɪzɪks] *n* fisica.

physiology [fɪzɪ'ɒlədʒɪ] *n* fisiologia.

physiotherapist [fɪzɪəʊ'θerəpɪst] *n* fisioterapista *m/f*.

physiotherapy [fɪzɪəʊ'θerəpɪ] *n* fisioterapia.

physique [fɪ'ziːk] *n* fisico; costituzione *f*.

pianist ['piːənɪst] *n* pianista *m/f*.

piano [pɪ'ænəʊ] *n* pianoforte *m*.

piccolo ['pɪkələʊ] *n* ottavino.

pick [pɪk] *n* (*tool*: *also*: ~-**axe**) piccone *m* // *vt* scegliere; (*gather*) cogliere; **take your** ~ scelga; **the** ~ **of** il fior fiore di; to ~ **one's teeth** stuzzicarsi i denti; to ~ **pockets** borseggiare; to ~ **on** *vt fus* (*person*) avercela con; to ~ **out** *vt* scegliere; (*distinguish*) distinguere; to ~ **up** *vi* (*improve*) migliorarsi // *vt* raccogliere; (*collect*) passare a prendere; (*AUT*: *give lift to*) far salire; (*learn*) imparare; to ~ **up speed** acquistare velocità; to ~ **o.s. up** rialzarsi.

picket ['pɪkɪt] *n* (*in strike*) scioperante *m/f* che fa parte di un picchetto; picchetto // *vt* picchettare; ~ **line** *n* controllo del picchetto.

pickle ['pɪkl] *n* (*also*: ~**s**: *as condiment*) sottaceti *mpl* // *vt* mettere sottaceto; mettere in salamoia.

pick-me-up ['pɪkmiːʌp] *n* tiramisù *m inv*.

pickpocket ['pɪkpɒkɪt] *n* borsaiolo.

pickup ['pɪkʌp] *n* (*on record player*) pick-up *m inv*; (*small truck*) camioncino.

picnic ['pɪknɪk] *n* picnic *m inv* // *vi* fare un picnic.

pictorial [pɪk'tɔːrɪəl] *a* illustrato(a).

picture ['pɪktʃə*] *n* quadro; (*painting*) pittura; (*photograph*) foto(grafia); (*drawing*) disegno; (*film*) film *m inv* // *vt* raffigurarsi; **the** ~**s** il cinema; ~ **book** *n* libro illustrato.

picturesque [pɪktʃə'resk] *a* pittoresco(a).

piddling ['pɪdlɪŋ] *a* (*col*) insignificante.

pidgin ['pɪdʒɪn] *a*: ~ **English** *n* inglese semplificato misto ad elementi indigeni.

pie [paɪ] *n* torta; (*of meat*) pasticcio.

piebald ['paɪbɔːld] *a* pezzato(a).

piece [piːs] *n* pezzo; (*of land*) appezzamento; (*item*): **a** ~ **of furniture/advice** un mobile / consiglio // *vt*: to ~ **together** mettere insieme; **in** ~**s** (*broken*) in pezzi; (*not yet assembled*) smontato(a); **to take to** ~**s** smontare; ~**meal** *ad* pezzo a pezzo, a spizzico; ~**work** *n* (lavoro a) cottimo.

pier [pɪə*] *n* molo; (*of bridge etc*) pila.

pierce [pɪəs] *vt* forare; (*with arrow etc*) trafiggere.

piercing ['pɪəsɪŋ] *a* (*cry*) acuto(a).

piety ['paɪətɪ] *n* pietà, devozione *f*.

pig [pɪg] *n* maiale *m*, porco.

pigeon ['pɪdʒən] *n* piccione *m*; ~**hole** *n*

casella; ~-**toed** a che cammina con i piedi in dentro.

piggy bank ['pɪgɪbæŋk] n salvadanaro.

pigheaded ['pɪg'hedɪd] a caparbio(a), cocciuto(a).

piglet ['pɪglɪt] n porcellino.

pigment ['pɪgmənt] n pigmento.

pigmy ['pɪgmɪ] n = **pygmy.**

pigsty ['pɪgstaɪ] n porcile m.

pigtail ['pɪgteɪl] n treccina.

pike [paɪk] n (spear) picca; (fish) luccio.

pilchard ['pɪltʃəd] n specie di sardina.

pile [paɪl] n (pillar, of books) pila; (heap) mucchio; (of carpet) pelo // vb (also: ~ **up**) vt ammucchiare // vi ammucchiarsi.

piles [paɪlz] npl emorroidi fpl.

pileup ['paɪlʌp] n (AUT) tamponamento a catena.

pilfering ['pɪlfərɪŋ] n rubacchiare m.

pilgrim ['pɪlgrɪm] n pellegrino/a; ~**age** n pellegrinaggio.

pill [pɪl] n pillola; **the ~** la pillola.

pillage ['pɪlɪdʒ] vt saccheggiare.

pillar ['pɪlə*] n colonna; ~ **box** n (Brit) cassetta postale.

pillion ['pɪljən] n (of motor cycle) sellino posteriore.

pillory ['pɪlərɪ] n berlina // vt mettere alla berlina.

pillow ['pɪləu] n guanciale m; ~**case** n federa.

pilot ['paɪlət] n pilota m/f // cpd (scheme etc) pilota inv // vt pilotare; ~ **boat** n battello pilota; ~ **light** n fiamma pilota.

pimp [pɪmp] n mezzano.

pimple ['pɪmpl] n foruncolo.

pin [pɪn] n spillo; (TECH) perno // vt attaccare con uno spillo; ~**s and needles** formicolio; **to ~ sb down** (fig) obbligare qd a pronunziarsi.

pinafore ['pɪnəfɔ:*] n grembiule m (senza maniche); ~ **dress** n scamiciato.

pincers ['pɪnsəz] npl pinzette fpl.

pinch [pɪntʃ] n pizzicotto, pizzico // vt pizzicare; (col: steal) grattare // vi (shoe) stringere; **at a ~** in caso di bisogno.

pincushion ['pɪnkuʃən] n puntaspilli m inv.

pine [paɪn] n (also: ~ **tree**) pino // vi: **to ~ for** struggersi dal desiderio di; **to ~ away** vi languire.

pineapple ['paɪnæpl] n ananas m inv.

ping [pɪŋ] n (noise) tintinnio; ~-**pong** ® n ping-pong m ®.

pink [pɪŋk] a rosa inv // n (colour) rosa m inv; (BOT) garofano.

pinnacle ['pɪnəkl] n pinnacolo.

pinpoint ['pɪnpɔɪnt] vt indicare con precisione.

pinstripe ['pɪnstraɪp] n stoffa gessata.

pint [paɪnt] n pinta (= 0.56 l).

pinup ['pɪnʌp] n pin-up girl f inv.

pioneer [paɪə'nɪə*] n pioniere/a.

pious ['paɪəs] a pio(a).

pip [pɪp] n (seed) seme m; (time signal on radio) segnale m orario.

pipe [paɪp] n tubo; (for smoking) pipa; (MUS) piffero // vt portare per mezzo di

tubazione; ~**s** npl (also: **bag~s**) cornamusa (scozzese); **to ~ down** vi (col) calmarsi; ~ **dream** n vana speranza; ~**line** n conduttura; (for oil) oleodotto; ~**r** n piffero; suonatore/trice di cornamusa.

piping ['paɪpɪŋ] ad: ~ **hot** caldo bollente.

pique [pi:k] n picca.

piracy ['paɪərəsɪ] n pirateria.

pirate ['paɪərət] n pirata m; ~ **radio** n radio pirata f inv.

pirouette [pɪru'et] n piroetta // vi piroettare.

Pisces ['paɪsi:z] n Pesci mpl.

pistol ['pɪstl] n pistola.

piston ['pɪstən] n pistone m.

pit [pɪt] n buca, fossa; (also: **coal ~**) miniera; (also: **orchestra ~**) orchestra // vt: **to ~ sb against sb** opporre qd a qd; ~**s** npl (AUT) box m; **to ~ o.s. against** opporsi a.

pitch [pɪtʃ] n (throw) lancio; (MUS) tono; (of voice) altezza; (SPORT) campo; (NAUT) beccheggio; (tar) pece f // vt (throw) lanciare // vi (fall) cascare; (NAUT) beccheggiare; **to ~ a tent** piantare una tenda; ~-**black** a nero(a) come la pece; ~**ed battle** n battaglia campale.

pitcher ['pɪtʃə*] n brocca.

pitchfork ['pɪtʃfɔ:k] n forcone m.

piteous ['pɪtɪəs] a pietoso(a).

pitfall ['pɪtfɔ:l] n trappola.

pith [pɪθ] n (of plant) midollo; (of orange) parte f interna della scorza; (fig) essenza, succo; vigore m.

pithy ['pɪθɪ] a conciso(a); vigoroso(a).

pitiable ['pɪtɪəbl] a pietoso(a).

pitiful ['pɪtɪful] a (touching) pietoso(a); (contemptible) miserabile.

pitiless ['pɪtɪlɪs] a spietato(a).

pittance ['pɪtns] n miseria, magro salario.

pity ['pɪtɪ] n pietà // vt aver pietà di; **what a ~!** che peccato!; ~**ing** a compassionevole.

pivot ['pɪvət] n perno // vi imperniarsi.

pixie ['pɪksɪ] n folletto.

placard ['plækɑ:d] n affisso.

placate [plə'keɪt] vt placare, calmare.

place [pleɪs] n posto, luogo; (proper position, rank, seat) posto; (house) casa, alloggio; (home): **at/to his ~** a casa sua // vt (object) posare, mettere; (identify) riconoscere; individuare; **to take ~** aver luogo; succedere; **to ~ an order** dare un'ordinazione; **out of ~** (not suitable) inopportuno(a); **in the first ~** in primo luogo; ~ **mat** n sottopiatto.

placid ['plæsɪd] a placido(a), calmo(a).

plagiarism ['pleɪdʒjərɪzm] n plagio.

plagiarize ['pleɪdʒjəraɪz] vt plagiare.

plague [pleɪg] n piaga; (MED) peste f.

plaice [pleɪs] n, pl inv pianuzza.

plaid [plæd] n plaid m inv.

plain [pleɪn] a (clear) chiaro(a), palese; (simple) semplice; (frank) franco(a), aperto(a); (not handsome) bruttino(a); (without seasoning etc) scondito(a);

naturale; (*in one colour*) tinta unita *inv* // *ad* francamente, chiaramente // *n* pianura; **in ~ clothes** (*police*) in borghese; **~ly** *ad* chiaramente; (*frankly*) francamente; **~ness** *n* semplicità.

plaintiff ['pleɪntɪf] *n* attore/trice.

plait [plæt] *n* treccia.

plan [plæn] *n* pianta; (*scheme*) progetto, piano // *vt* (*think in advance*) progettare; (*prepare*) organizzare // *vi* far piani *or* progetti; **to ~ to do** progettare di fare.

plane [pleɪn] *n* (*AVIAT*) aereo; (*tree*) platano; (*tool*) pialla; (*ART, MATH etc*) piano // *a* piano(a), piatto(a) // *vt* (*with tool*) piallare.

planet ['plænɪt] *n* pianeta *m*.

planetarium [plænɪ'tɛərɪəm] *n* planetario.

plank [plæŋk] *n* tavola, asse *f.*

plankton ['plæŋktən] *n* plancton *m*.

planner ['plænə*] *n* pianificatore/trice.

planning ['plænɪŋ] *n* progettazione *f*; **family ~** pianificazione *f* delle nascite.

plant [plɑːnt] *n* pianta; (*machinery*) impianto; (*factory*) fabbrica // *vt* piantare; (*bomb*) mettere.

plantation [plæn'teɪʃən] *n* piantagione *f.*

plaque [plæk] *n* placca.

plasma ['plæzmə] *n* plasma *m*.

plaster ['plɑːstə*] *n* intonaco; (*also:* **~ of Paris**) gesso; (*also:* **sticking ~**) cerotto // *vt* intonacare; ingessare; (*cover*) **to ~ with** coprire di; **in ~** (*leg etc*) ingessato(a); **~ed** *a* (*col*) ubriaco(a) fradicio(a); **~er** *n* intonacatore *m.*

plastic ['plæstɪk] *n* plastica // *a* (*made of plastic*) di *or* in plastica; (*flexible*) plastico(a), malleabile; (*art*) plastico(a).

plasticine ['plæstɪsiːn] *n* ® plastilina ®.

plastic surgery ['plæstɪk'sədʒərɪ] *n* chirurgia plastica.

plate [pleɪt] *n* (*dish*) piatto; (*sheet of metal*) lamiera; (*PHOT*) lastra; (*in book*) tavola; **gold ~** (*dishes*) vasellame *m* d'oro; **silver ~** (*dishes*) argenteria.

plateau, **~s** *or* **~x** ['plætəu, -z] *n* altipiano.

plateful ['pleɪtful] *n* piatto.

plate glass [pleɪt'glɑːs] *n* vetro piano.

platform ['plætfɔːm] *n* (*at meeting*) piattaforma; (*stage*) palco; (*RAIL*) marciapiede *m*; **~ ticket** *n* biglietto d'ingresso ai binari.

platinum ['plætɪnəm] *n* platino.

platitude ['plætɪtjuːd] *n* luogo comune.

platoon [plə'tuːn] *n* plotone *m.*

platter ['plætə*] *n* piatto.

plausible ['plɔːzɪbl] *a* plausibile, credibile; (*person*) convincente.

play [pleɪ] *n* gioco; (*THEATRE*) commedia // *vt* (*game*) giocare a; (*team, opponent*) giocare contro; (*instrument, piece of music*) suonare; (*play, part*) interpretare // *vi* giocare; suonare; recitare; **to ~ down** *vt* minimizzare; **to ~ up** *vi* (*cause trouble*) fare i capricci; **to ~act** *vi* fare la commedia; **~ed-out** *a* spossato(a); **~er** *n* giocatore/trice; (*THEATRE*) attore/trice; (*MUS*) musicista *m/f*; **~ful** *a* gioioso(a);

~ground *n* campo di ricreazioni; **~group** *n* giardino d'infanzia; **~ing card** *n* carta da gioco; **~ing field** *n* campo sportivo; **~mate** *n* compagno/a di gioco; **~-off** *n* (*SPORT*) bella; **~ on words** *n* gioco di parole; **~pen** *n* box *m inv*; **~thing** *n* giocattolo; **~wright** *n* drammaturgo/a.

plea [pliː] *n* (*request*) preghiera, domanda; (*excuse*) scusa; (*LAW*) (argomento di) difesa.

plead [pliːd] *vt* patrocinare; (*give as excuse*) addurre a pretesto // *vi* (*LAW*) perorare la causa; (*beg*): **to ~ with sb** implorare qd.

pleasant ['plɛznt] *a* piacevole, gradevole; **~ly** *ad* piacevolmente; **~ness** *n* (*of person*) amabilità; (*of place*) amenità; **~ry** *n* (*joke*) scherzo.

please [pliːz] *vt* piacere a // *vi* (*think fit*): **do as you ~** faccia come le pare; **~!** per piacere!; **my bill, ~** il conto, per piacere; **~ yourself!** come ti (*or* le) pare!; **~d** *a*: **~d** (*with*) contento(a) di; **pleasing** *a* piacevole, che fa piacere.

pleasurable ['plɛʒərəbl] *a* molto piacevole, molto gradevole.

pleasure ['plɛʒə*] *n* piacere *m*; **'it's a ~'** 'prego'; **~ steamer** *n* vapore *m* da diporto.

pleat [pliːt] *n* piega.

plebiscite ['plɛbɪsɪt] *n* plebiscito.

plectrum ['plɛktrəm] *n* plettro.

pledge [plɛdʒ] *n* pegno; (*promise*) promessa // *vt* impegnare; promettere.

plentiful ['plɛntɪful] *a* abbondante, copioso(a).

plenty ['plɛntɪ] *n* abbondanza; **~ of** tanto(a), molto(a); un'abbondanza di.

pleurisy ['pluərɪsɪ] *n* pleurite *f.*

pliable ['plaɪəbl] *a* flessibile; (*person*) malleabile.

pliers ['plaɪəz] *npl* pinza.

plight [plaɪt] *n* situazione *f* critica.

plimsolls ['plɪmsəlz] *npl* scarpe *fpl* da tennis.

plinth [plɪnθ] *n* plinto; piedistallo.

plod [plɔd] *vi* camminare a stento; (*fig*) sgobbare; **~der** *n* sgobbone *m.*

plonk [plɔŋk] (*col*) *n* (*wine*) vino da poco // *vt*: **to ~ sth down** buttare giù qc bruscamente.

plot [plɔt] *n* congiura, cospirazione *f*; (*of story, play*) trama; (*of land*) lotto // *vt* (*mark out*) fare la pianta di; rilevare; (*: diagram etc*) tracciare; (*conspire*) congiurare, cospirare // *vi* congiurare; **~ter** *n* cospiratore/trice.

plough, plow (*US*) [plau] *n* aratro // *vt* (*earth*) arare; **to ~ back** *vt* (*COMM*) reinvestire; **to ~ through** *vt fus* (*snow etc*) procedere a fatica in.

ploy [plɔɪ] *n* stratagemma *m.*

pluck [plʌk] *vt* (*fruit*) cogliere; (*musical instrument*) pizzicare; (*bird*) spennare // *n* coraggio, fegato; **to ~ up courage** farsi coraggio; **~y** *a* coraggioso(a).

plug [plʌg] *n* tappo; (*ELEC*) spina; (*AUT*)

candela // vt (hole) tappare; (col: advertise) spingere.

plum [plʌm] n (fruit) susina // a: ~ **job** n (col) impiego ottimo or favoloso.

plumb [plʌm] a verticale // n piombo // ad (exactly) esattamente // vt sondare.

plumber ['plʌmə*] n idraulico.

plumbing ['plʌmɪŋ] n (trade) lavoro di idraulico; (piping) tubature fpl.

plumbline ['plʌmlaɪn] n filo a piombo.

plume [pluːm] n piuma, penna; (decorative) pennacchio.

plummet ['plʌmɪt] vi cadere a piombo.

plump [plʌmp] a grassoccio(a); to ~ **for** vt fus (col: choose) decidersi per.

plunder ['plʌndə*] n saccheggio // vt saccheggiare.

plunge [plʌndʒ] n tuffo // vt immergere // vi (fall) cadere, precipitare; to take the ~ saltare il fosso; **plunging** a (neckline) profondo(a).

pluperfect [pluː'pəːfɪkt] n piucchepperfetto.

plural ['pluərl] a, n plurale (m).

plus [plʌs] n (also: ~ **sign**) segno più // prep più; **ten/twenty** ~ più di dieci/venti; ~ **fours** npl calzoni mpl alla zuava.

plush [plʌʃ] a lussuoso(a).

ply [plaɪ] n (of wool) capo; (of wood) strato // vt (tool) maneggiare; (a trade) esercitare // vi (ship) fare il servizio; to ~ sb with drink dare da bere continuamente a qd; ~**wood** n legno compensato.

P.M. abbr see prime.

p.m. ad (abbr of post meridiem) del pomeriggio.

pneumatic [njuː'mætɪk] a pneumatico(a).

pneumonia [njuː'məʊnɪə] n polmonite f.

P.O. abbr see post office.

poach [pəʊtʃ] vt (cook) affogare; (steal) cacciare (or pescare) di frodo // vi fare il bracconiere; ~**ed** a (egg) affogato(a); ~**er** n bracconiere m; ~**ing** n caccia (or pesca) di frodo.

pocket ['pɒkɪt] n tasca // vt intascare; to be out of ~ rimetterci; ~**book** n (wallet) portafoglio; (notebook) taccuino; ~ **knife** n temperino; ~ **money** n paghetta, settimana.

pockmarked ['pɒkmɑːkt] a (face) butterato(a).

pod [pɒd] n guscio // vt sgusciare.

podgy ['pɒdʒɪ] a grassoccio(a).

poem ['pəʊɪm] n poesia.

poet ['pəʊɪt] n poeta/essa; ~**ic** [-'ɛtɪk] a poetico(a); ~ **laureate** n poeta m laureato (nominato dalla Corte Reale); ~**ry** n poesia.

poignant ['pɔɪnjənt] a struggente; (sharp) pungente.

point [pɔɪnt] n (gen) punto; (tip: of needle etc) punta; (in time) punto, momento; (SCOL) voto; (main idea, important part) nocciolo; (also: decimal ~): **2 ~ 3 (2.3)** 2 virgola 3 (2,3) // vt (show) indicare; (gun etc): to ~ sth at puntare qc contro // vi

mostrare a dito; ~**s** npl (AUT) puntine fpl; (RAIL) scambio; to make a ~ fare un'osservazione; to get the ~ capire; to come to the ~ venire al fatto; there's no ~ (in doing) è inutile (fare); good ~**s** vantaggi mpl; (of person) qualità fpl; to ~ out vt far notare; to ~ to indicare; (fig) dimostrare; ~**-blank** ad (also: at ~-blank range) a bruciapelo; (fig) categoricamente; ~**ed** a (shape) aguzzo(a), appuntito(a); (remark) specifico(a); ~**edly** ad in maniera inequivocabile; ~**er** n (stick) bacchetta, (needle) lancetta; (dog) pointer m, cane m da punta; ~**less** a inutile, vano(a); ~ of view n punto di vista.

poise [pɔɪz] n (balance) equilibrio; (of head, body) portamento; (calmness) calma // vt tenere in equilibrio; to be ~**d** for (fig) essere pronto(a) a.

poison ['pɔɪzn] n veleno // vt avvelenare; ~**ing** n avvelenamento; ~**ous** a velenoso(a).

poke [pəʊk] vt (fire) attizzare; (jab with finger, stick etc) punzecchiare; (put): to ~ **sth in(to)** spingere qc dentro; to ~ **about** vi frugare.

poker ['pəʊkə*] n attizzatoio; (CARDS) poker m; ~**-faced** a dal viso impassibile.

poky ['pəʊkɪ] a piccolo(a) e stretto(a).

Poland ['pəʊlənd] n Polonia.

polar ['pəʊlə*] a polare; ~ **bear** n orso bianco.

polarize ['pəʊləraɪz] vt polarizzare.

pole [pəʊl] n (of wood) palo; (ELEC, GEO) polo.

Pole [pəʊl] n polacco/a.

polecat ['pəʊlkæt] n (US) puzzola.

polemic [pɒ'lɛmɪk] n polemica.

pole star ['pəʊlstɑː*] n stella polare.

pole vault ['pəʊlvɔːlt] n salto con l'asta.

police [pə'liːs] n polizia // vt mantenere l'ordine in; ~ **car** n macchina della polizia; ~**man** n poliziotto, agente m di polizia; ~ **station** n posto di polizia; ~**woman** n donna f poliziotto inv.

policy ['pɒlɪsɪ] n politica; (also: **insurance** ~) polizza (d'assicurazione).

polio ['pəʊlɪəʊ] n polio f.

Polish ['pəʊlɪʃ] a polacco(a) // n (LING) polacco.

polish ['pɒlɪʃ] n (for shoes) lucido; (for floor) cera; (for nails) smalto; (shine) lucentezza, lustro; (fig: refinement) raffinatezza // vt lucidare; (fig: improve) raffinare; to ~ off vt (work) sbrigare; (food) mangiarsi; ~**ed** a (fig) raffinato(a).

polite [pə'laɪt] a cortese; ~**ly** ad cortesemente; ~**ness** n cortesia.

politic ['pɒlɪtɪk] a diplomatico(a); ~**al** [pə'lɪtɪkl] a politico(a); ~**ian** [-'tɪʃən] n politico; ~**s** npl politica.

polka ['pɒlkə] n polca; ~ **dot** n pois m inv.

poll [pəʊl] n scrutinio; (votes cast) voti mpl; (also: **opinion** ~) sondaggio (d'opinioni) // vt ottenere.

pollen ['pɒlən] n polline m.

pollination [pɔlɪˈneɪʃən] *n* impollinazione *f*.

polling [ˈpəʊlɪŋ]: ~ **booth** *n* cabina elettorale; ~ **day** *n* giorno delle elezioni; ~ **station** *n* sezione *f* elettorale.

pollute [pəˈluːt] *vt* inquinare.

pollution [pəˈluːʃən] *n* inquinamento.

polo [ˈpəʊləʊ] *n* polo; ~-**neck** *a* a collo alto risvoltato.

polyester [pɔlɪˈɛstə*] *n* poliestere *m*.

polygamy [pɔˈlɪgəmɪ] *n* poligamia.

Polynesia [pɔlɪˈniːzɪə] *n* Polinesia.

polytechnic [pɔlɪˈtɛknɪk] *n* (*college*) istituto superiore di tendenza tecnologica.

polythene [ˈpɔlɪθiːn] *n* politene *m*; ~ **bag** *n* sacco di plastica.

pomegranate [ˈpɔmɪgrænɪt] *n* melagrana.

pommel [ˈpɔml] *n* pomo.

pomp [pɔmp] *n* pompa, fasto.

pompous [ˈpɔmpəs] *a* pomposo(a).

pond [pɔnd] *n* pozza/ stagno.

ponder [ˈpɔndə*] *vt* ponderare, riflettere su; ~**ous** *a* ponderoso(a), pesante.

pontiff [ˈpɔntɪf] *n* pontefice *m*.

pontificate [pɔnˈtɪfɪkeɪt] *vi* (*fig*): **to** ~ (**about**) pontificare (su).

pontoon [pɔnˈtuːn] *n* pontone *m*.

pony [ˈpəʊnɪ] *n* pony *m inv*; ~**tail** *n* coda di cavallo.

poodle [ˈpuːdl] *n* barboncino, barbone *m*.

pooh-pooh [ˈpuːˈpuː] *vt* deridere.

pool [puːl] *n* (*of rain*) pozza; (*pond*) stagno; (*artificial*) vasca; (*also:* **swimming** ~) piscina; (*US: shared*) fondo comune; (*billiards*) specie di biliardo a buca // *vt* mettere in comune.

poor [puə*] *a* povero(a); (*mediocre*) mediocre, cattivo(a) // *npl:* **the** ~ i poveri; ~**ly** *ad* poveramente; *male* // *a* indisposto(a), malato(a).

pop [pɔp] *n* (*noise*) schiocco; (*MUS*) musica pop; (*US: col: father*) babbo // *vt* (*put*) mettere (in fretta) // *vi* scoppiare; (*cork*) schioccare; **to** ~ **in** *vi* passare; **to** ~ **out** *vi* fare un salto fuori; **to** ~ **up** *vi* apparire, sorgere; ~ **concert** *n* concerto *m* pop *inv*; ~**corn** *n* pop-corn *m*.

pope [pəʊp] *n* papa *m*.

poplar [ˈpɔplə*] *n* pioppo.

poplin [ˈpɔplɪn] *n* popeline *f*.

poppy [ˈpɔpɪ] *n* papavero.

populace [ˈpɔpjʊləs] *n* popolo.

popular [ˈpɔpjʊlə*] *a* popolare; (*fashionable*) in voga; ~**ity** [-ˈlærɪtɪ] *n* popolarità; ~**ize** *vt* divulgare; (*science*) volgarizzare.

population [pɔpjʊˈleɪʃən] *n* popolazione *f*.

populous [ˈpɔpjʊləs] *a* popolato(a).

porcelain [ˈpɔːslɪn] *n* porcellana.

porch [pɔːtʃ] *n* veranda.

porcupine [ˈpɔːkjupaɪn] *n* porcospino.

pore [pɔː*] *n* poro // *vi:* **to** ~ **over** essere immerso(a) in.

pork [pɔːk] *n* carne *f* di maiale.

pornographic [pɔːnəˈgræfɪk] *a* pornografico(a).

pornography [pɔːˈnɔgrəfɪ] *n* pornografia.

porous [ˈpɔːrəs] *a* poroso(a).

porpoise [ˈpɔːpəs] *n* focena.

porridge [ˈpɔrɪdʒ] *n* porridge *m*.

port [pɔːt] *n* porto; (*opening in ship*) portello; (*NAUT: left side*) babordo; (*wine*) porto.

portable [ˈpɔːtəbl] *a* portatile.

portal [ˈpɔːtl] *n* portale *m*.

portcullis [pɔːtˈkʌlɪs] *n* saracinesca.

portent [ˈpɔːtent] *n* presagio.

porter [ˈpɔːtə*] *n* (*for luggage*) facchino, portabagagli *m inv*; (*doorkeeper*) portiere *m*, portinaio.

porthole [ˈpɔːthəʊl] *n* oblò *m inv*.

portico [ˈpɔːtɪkəʊ] *n* portico.

portion [ˈpɔːʃən] *n* porzione *f*.

portly [ˈpɔːtlɪ] *a* corpulento(a).

portrait [ˈpɔːtreɪt] *n* ritratto.

portray [pɔːˈtreɪ] *vt* fare il ritratto di; (*character on stage*) rappresentare; (*in writing*) ritrarre; ~**al** *n* ritratto; rappresentazione *f*.

Portugal [ˈpɔːtjugl] *n* Portogallo.

Portuguese [pɔːtjuˈgiːz] *a* portoghese // *n*, *pl inv* portoghese *m/f*; (*LING*) portoghese *m*.

pose [pəʊz] *n* posa // *vi* posare; (*pretend*): **to** ~ **as** atteggiarsi a, posare a // *vt* porre.

posh [pɔʃ] *a* (*col*) elegante; (*family*) per bene.

position [pəˈzɪʃən] *n* posizione *f*; (*job*) posto // *vt* mettere in posizione, collocare.

positive [ˈpɔzɪtɪv] *a* positivo(a); (*certain*) sicuro(a), certo(a); (*definite*) preciso(a); definitivo(a).

posse [ˈpɔsɪ] *n* (*US*) drappello.

possess [pəˈzɛs] *vt* possedere; ~**ion** [pəˈzɛʃən] *n* possesso; (*object*) bene *m*; ~**ive** *a* possessivo(a); ~**or** *n* possessore/posseditrice.

possibility [pɔsɪˈbɪlɪtɪ] *n* possibilità *f inv*.

possible [ˈpɔsɪbl] *a* possibile; **if** ~ se possibile; **as big as** ~ il più grande possibile.

possibly [ˈpɔsɪblɪ] *ad* (*perhaps*) forse; **if you** ~ **can** se le è possibile; **I cannot** ~ **come** proprio non posso venire.

post [pəʊst] *n* posta; (*collection*) levata; (*job, situation*) posto; (*pole*) palo // *vt* (*send by post*) impostare; (*MIL*) appostare; (*appoint*): **to** ~ **to** assegnare a; (*notice*) affiggere; ~**age** *n* affrancatura; ~**al** *a* postale; ~**al order** *n* vaglia *m inv* postale; ~**box** *n* cassetta postale; ~**card** *n* cartolina.

postdate [ˈpəʊstˈdeɪt] *vt* (*cheque*) postdatare.

poster [ˈpəʊstə*] *n* manifesto, affisso.

poste restante [pəʊstˈrɛstãnt] *n* fermo posta *m*.

posterity [pɔsˈtɛrɪtɪ] *n* posterità.

postgraduate [ˈpəʊstˈgrædjuət] *n* ≈ laureato/a che continua gli studi.

posthumous [ˈpɔstjuməs] *a* postumo(a); ~**ly** *ad* dopo la mia (*or* sua *etc*) morte.

postman ['pəustmən] *n* postino.
postmark ['pəustmɑ:k] *n* bollo *or* timbro postale.
postmaster ['pəustmɑ:stə*] *n* direttore *m* d'un ufficio postale.
post-mortem [pəust'mɔ:təm] *n* autopsia.
post office ['pəustɔfɪs] *n* (*building*) ufficio postale; (*organization*) poste *fpl*; ~ **box** (**P.O. box**) *n* casella postale (C.P.).
postpone [pəs'pəun] *vt* rinviare; ~**ment** *n* rinvio.
postscript ['pəustskrɪpt] *n* poscritto.
postulate ['pɔstjuleɪt] *vt* postulare.
posture ['pɔstʃə*] *n* portamento; (*pose*) posa, atteggiamento // *vi* posare.
postwar ['pəust'wɔ:*] *a* del dopoguerra.
posy ['pəuzɪ] *n* mazzetto di fiori.
pot [pɔt] *n* (*for cooking*) pentola; casseruola; (*for plants, jam*) vaso; (*col: marijuana*) erba // *vt* (*plant*) piantare in vaso; **to go to** ~ andare in malora.
potash ['pɔtæʃ] *n* potassa.
potato, ~**es** [pə'teɪtəu] *n* patata.
potency ['pəutnsɪ] *n* potenza; (*of drink*) forza.
potent ['pəutnt] *a* potente, forte.
potentate ['pəutnteɪt] *n* potentato.
potential [pə'tɛnʃl] *a* potenziale // *n* possibilità *fpl*; ~**ly** *ad* potenzialmente.
pothole ['pɔthəul] *n* (*in road*) buca; (*underground*) marmitta; ~**r** *n* speleologo/a; **potholing** *n*: **to go potholing** fare la speleologia.
potion ['pəuʃən] *n* pozione *f*.
potluck [pɔt'lʌk] *n*: **to take** ~ tentare la sorte.
potshot ['pɔtʃɔt] *n*: **to take** ~**s at** tirare a vanvera contro.
potted ['pɔtɪd] *a* (*food*) in conserva; (*plant*) in vaso.
potter ['pɔtə*] *n* vasaio // *vi*: **to** ~ **around**, ~ **about** lavoracchiare; ~**y** *n* ceramiche *fpl*.
potty ['pɔtɪ] *a* (*col: mad*) tocco(a) // *n* (*child's*) vasino.
pouch [pautʃ] *n* borsa; (*ZOOL*) marsupio.
pouf(fe) [pu:f] *n* (*stool*) pouf *m inv*.
poultice ['pəultɪs] *n* impiastro, cataplasma.
poultry ['pəultrɪ] *n* pollame *m*.
pounce [pauns] *vi*: **to** ~ (**on**) balzare addosso a, piombare su // *n* balzo.
pound [paund] *n* (*weight*) libbra; (*money*) (*lira*) sterlina; (*for dogs*) canile *m* municipale // *vt* (*beat*) battere; (*crush*) pestare, polverizzare // *vi* (*beat*) battere, martellare.
pour [pɔ:*] *vt* versare // *vi* riversarsi; (*rain*) piovere a dirotto; **to** ~ **away** *vt* vuotare; **to** ~ **in** *vi* (*people*) entrare a flotti; **to** ~ **out** *vt* vuotare; versare; (*serve: a drink*) mescere; ~**ing** *a*: ~**ing rain** pioggia torrenziale.
pout [paut] *vi* sporgere le labbra; fare il broncio.
poverty ['pɔvətɪ] *n* povertà, miseria;

~**-stricken** *a* molto povero(a), misero(a).
powder ['paudə*] *n* polvere *f* // *vt* spolverizzare; (*face*) incipriare; ~ **room** *n* toilette *f inv* (per signore); ~**y** *a* polveroso(a).
power ['pauə*] *n* (*strength*) potenza, forza; (*ability, POL: of party, leader*) potere *m*; (*MATH*) potenza; (*ELEC*) corrente *f* // *vt* fornire di energia; **mental** ~**s** capacità *fpl* mentali; ~ **cut** *n* interruzione *f or* mancanza di corrente; ~**ed** *a*: ~**ed by** azionato(a) da; ~**ful** *a* potente, forte; ~**less** *a* impotente, senza potere; ~ **point** *n* presa di corrente; ~ **station** *n* centrale *f* elettrica.
powwow ['pauwau] *n* riunione *f*.
pox [pɔks] *n see* **chicken**.
p.p. *abbr*: ~ **J. Smith** per il Signor J. Smith.
P.R. *abbr of* **public relations**.
practicability [præktɪkə'bɪlɪtɪ] *n* praticabilità.
practicable ['præktɪkəbl] *a* (*scheme*) praticabile.
practical ['præktɪkl] *a* pratico(a); ~ **joke** *n* beffa; ~**ly** *ad* (*almost*) quasi.
practice ['præktɪs] *n* pratica; (*of profession*) esercizio; (*at football etc*) allenamento; (*business*) gabinetto; clientela // *vt,vi* (*US*) = **practise**; **in** ~ (*in reality*) in pratica; **out of** ~ fuori esercizio; **2 hours' piano** ~ 2 ore di esercizio al pianoforte.
practise, (*US*) **practice** ['præktɪs] *vt* (*work at: piano, one's backhand etc*) esercitarsi a; (*train for: skiing, running etc*) allenarsi a; (*a sport, religion*) praticare; (*method*) usare; (*profession*) esercitare // *vi* esercitarsi; (*train*) allenarsi; **practising** *a* (*Christian etc*) praticante; (*lawyer*) che esercita la professione.
practitioner [præk'tɪʃənə*] *n* professionista *m/f*.
pragmatic [præg'mætɪk] *a* prammatico(a).
prairie ['prɛərɪ] *n* prateria.
praise [preɪz] *n* elogio, lode *f* // *vt* elogiare, lodare; ~**worthy** *a* lodevole.
pram [præm] *n* carrozzina.
prance [prɑ:ns] *vi* (*horse*) impennarsi.
prank [præŋk] *n* burla.
prattle ['prætl] *vi* cinguettare.
prawn [prɔ:n] *n* gamberetto.
pray [preɪ] *vi* pregare.
prayer [prɛə*] *n* preghiera; ~ **book** *n* libro di preghiere.
preach [pri:tʃ] *vt,vi* predicare; ~**er** *n* predicatore/trice.
preamble [prɪ'æmbl] *n* preambolo.
precarious [prɪ'kɛərɪəs] *a* precario(a).
precaution [prɪ'kɔ:ʃən] *n* precauzione *f*; ~**ary** *a* (*measure*) precauzionale.
precede [prɪ'si:d] *vt,vi* precedere.
precedence ['prɛsɪdəns] *n* precedenza; **to take** ~ **over** avere la precedenza su.
precedent ['prɛsɪdənt] *n* precedente *m*.
preceding [prɪ'si:dɪŋ] *a* precedente.

precept ['priːsɛpt] n precetto.
precinct ['priːsɪŋkt] n (round cathedral) recinto; ~s npl (neighbourhood) dintorni mpl, vicinanze fpl; **pedestrian** ~ n zona pedonale.
precious ['prɛʃəs] a prezioso(a).
precipice ['prɛsɪpɪs] n precipizio.
precipitate [prɪ'sɪpɪtɪt] a (hasty) precipitoso(a); **precipitation** [-'teɪʃən] n precipitazione f.
precipitous [prɪ'sɪpɪtəs] a (steep) erto(a), ripido(a).
précis, pl **précis** ['preɪsiː, -z] n riassunto.
precise [prɪ'saɪs] a preciso(a); ~ly ad precisamente; ~ly! appunto!
preclude [prɪ'kluːd] vt precludere, impedire; **to** ~ **sb from doing** impedire a qd di fare.
precocious [prɪ'kəʊʃəs] a precoce.
preconceived [priːkən'siːvd] a (idea) preconcetto(a).
precondition [priːkən'dɪʃən] n condizione f necessaria.
precursor [priː'kɜːsə*] n precursore m.
predator ['prɛdətə*] n predatore m; ~y a predatore(trice).
predecessor ['priːdɪsɛsə*] n predecessore/a.
predestination [priːdɛstɪ'neɪʃən] n predestinazione f.
predetermine [priːdɪ'tɜːmɪn] vt predeterminare.
predicament [prɪ'dɪkəmənt] n situazione f difficile.
predicate ['prɛdɪkɪt] n (LING) predicativo m.
predict [prɪ'dɪkt] vt predire; ~**ion** [-'dɪkʃən] n predizione f.
predominant [prɪ'dɒmɪnənt] a predominante; ~ly ad in maggior parte; soprattutto.
predominate [prɪ'dɒmɪneɪt] vi predominare.
pre-eminent [priː'ɛmɪnənt] a preminente.
pre-empt [priː'ɛmt] vt acquistare per diritto di prelazione.
preen [priːn] vt: **to** ~ **itself** (bird) lisciarsi le penne.
prefab ['priːfæb] n casa prefabbricata.
prefabricated [priː'fæbrɪkeɪtɪd] a prefabbricato(a).
preface ['prɛfəs] n prefazione f.
prefect ['priːfɛkt] n (Brit: in school) studente/essa con funzioni disciplinari; (in Italy) prefetto.
prefer [prɪ'fɜː*] vt preferire; ~**able** ['prɛfrəbl] a preferibile; ~**ably** ['prɛfrəbl] ad preferibilmente; ~**ence** ['prɛfrəns] n preferenza; ~**ential** [prɛfə'rɛnʃəl] a preferenziale.
prefix ['priːfɪks] n prefisso.
pregnancy ['prɛgnənsɪ] n gravidanza.
pregnant ['prɛgnənt] a incinta af.
prehistoric ['priːhɪs'tɒrɪk] a preistorico(a).
prejudge [priː'dʒʌdʒ] vt pregiudicare.
prejudice ['prɛdʒʊdɪs] n pregiudizio; (harm) torto, danno // vt pregiudicare,

ledere; ~**d** a (person) pieno(a) di pregiudizi; (view) prevenuto(a).
prelate ['prɛlət] n prelato.
preliminary [prɪ'lɪmɪnərɪ] a preliminare; **preliminaries** npl preliminari mpl.
prelude ['prɛljuːd] n preludio.
premarital ['priː'mærɪtl] a prematrimoniale.
premature ['prɛmətʃʊə*] a prematuro(a).
premeditated [priː'mɛdɪteɪtɪd] a premeditato(a).
premier ['prɛmɪə*] a primo(a) // n (POL) primo ministro.
première ['prɛmɪɛə*] n première f inv.
premise ['prɛmɪs] n premessa; ~**s** npl locale m; **on the** ~**s** sul posto.
premium ['priːmɪəm] n premio.
premonition [prɛmə'nɪʃən] n premonizione f.
preoccupation [priːɔkjʊ'peɪʃən] n preoccupazione f.
preoccupied [priː'ɔkjʊpaɪd] a preoccupato(a).
prep [prɛp] n (SCOL: study) studio; ~ **school** n = **preparatory school.**
prepaid [priː'peɪd] a pagato(a) in anticipo.
preparation [prɛpə'reɪʃən] n preparazione f; ~**s** npl (for trip, war) preparativi mpl.
preparatory [prɪ'pærətərɪ] a preparatorio(a); ~ **school** n scuola elementare privata.
prepare [prɪ'pɛə*] vt preparare // vi: **to** ~ **for** prepararsi a; ~**d for** preparato(a) a; ~**d to** pronto(a) a.
preponderance [prɪ'pɒndərns] n preponderanza.
preposition [prɛpə'zɪʃən] n preposizione f.
preposterous [prɪ'pɒstərəs] a assurdo(a).
prerequisite [priː'rɛkwɪzɪt] n requisito indispensabile.
prerogative [prɪ'rɒgətɪv] n prerogativa.
presbytery ['prɛzbɪtərɪ] n presbiterio.
prescribe [prɪ'skraɪb] vt prescrivere; (MED) ordinare.
prescription [prɪ'skrɪpʃən] n prescrizione f; (MED) ricetta.
presence ['prɛzns] n presenza; ~ **of mind** n presenza di spirito.
present ['prɛznt] a presente; (wife, residence, job) attuale // n regalo; (also: ~ **tense**) tempo presente // vt [prɪ'zɛnt] presentare; (give): **to** ~ **sb with sth** offrire qc a qd; **at** ~ al momento; ~**able** [prɪ'zɛntəbl] a presentabile; ~**ation** [-'teɪʃən] n presentazione f; (gift) regalo, dono; (ceremony) cerimonia per il conferimento di un regalo; ~**day** a attuale, d'oggigiorno; ~**ly** ad (soon) fra poco, presto; (at present) al momento.
preservation [prɛzə'veɪʃən] n preservazione f, conservazione f.
preservative [prɪ'zɜːvətɪv] n conservante m.
preserve [prɪ'zɜːv] vt (keep safe) preservare, proteggere; (maintain) conservare; (food) mettere in conserva //

n (*for game, fish*) riserva; (*often pl: jam*) marmellata; (: *fruit*) frutta sciroppata.

preside [prɪ'zaɪd] *vi* presiedere.

presidency ['prɛzɪdənsɪ] *n* presidenza.

president ['prɛzɪdənt] *n* presidente *m*; ~**ial** [-'dɛnʃl] *a* presidenziale.

press [prɛs] *n* (*tool, machine*) pressa; (*for wine*) torchio; (*newspapers*) stampa; (*crowd*) folla // *vt* (*push*) premere, pigiare; (*squeeze*) spremere; (: *hand*) stringere; (*clothes: iron*) stirare; (*pursue*) incalzare; (*insist*): **to ~ sth on sb** far accettare qc da qd // *vi* premere; accalcare; **we are ~ed for time** ci manca il tempo; **to ~ for sth** insistere per avere qc; **to ~ on** *vi* continuare; ~ **agency** *n* agenzia di stampa; ~ **conference** *n* conferenza stampa; ~ **cutting** *n* ritaglio di giornale; ~**ing** *a* urgente // *n* stiratura; ~ **stud** *n* bottone *m* a pressione.

pressure ['prɛʃə*] *n* pressione *f*; ~ **cooker** *n* pentola a pressione; ~ **gauge** *n* manometro; ~ **group** *n* gruppo di pressione; **pressurized** *a* pressurizzato(a).

prestige [prɛs'tiːʒ] *n* prestigio.

prestigious [prɛs'tɪdʒəs] *a* prestigioso(a).

presumably [prɪ'zjuːməblɪ] *ad* presumibilmente.

presume [prɪ'zjuːm] *vt* supporre; **to ~ to do** (*dare*) permettersi di fare.

presumption [prɪ'zʌmpʃən] *n* presunzione *f*; (*boldness*) audacia.

presumptuous [prɪ'zʌmpʃəs] *a* presuntuoso(a).

presuppose [priːsə'pəuz] *vt* presupporre.

pretence, pretense (*US*) [prɪ'tɛns] *n* (*claim*) pretesa; **to make a ~ of doing** far finta di fare.

pretend [prɪ'tɛnd] *vt* (*feign*) fingere // *vi* (*feign*) far finta; (*claim*): **to ~ to sth** pretendere a qc; **to ~ to do** far finta di fare.

pretentious [prɪ'tɛnʃəs] *a* pretenzioso(a).

preterite ['prɛtərɪt] *n* preterito.

pretext ['priːtɛkst] *n* pretesto.

pretty ['prɪtɪ] *a* grazioso(a), carino(a) // *ad* abbastanza, assai.

prevail [prɪ'veɪl] *vi* (*win, be usual*) prevalere; (*persuade*): **to ~ (up)on sb to do** persuadere qd a fare; ~**ing** *a* dominante.

prevalent ['prɛvələnt] *a* (*belief*) predominante; (*customs*) diffuso(a); (*fashion*) corrente; (*disease*) comune.

prevarication [prɪværɪ'keɪʃən] *n* tergiversazione *f*.

prevent [prɪ'vɛnt] *vt* prevenire; **to ~ sb from doing** impedire a qd di fare; ~**able** *a* evitabile; ~**ative** *a* preventivo(a); ~**ion** [-'vɛnʃən] *n* prevenzione *f*; ~**ive** *a* preventivo(a).

preview ['priːvjuː] *n* (*of film*) anteprima.

previous ['priːvɪəs] *a* precedente; anteriore; ~**ly** *ad* prima.

prewar ['priː'wɔː*] *a* anteguerra *inv*.

prey [preɪ] *n* preda // *vi*: **to ~ on** far

preda di; **it was ~ing on his mind** gli rodeva la mente.

price [praɪs] *n* prezzo // *vt* (*goods*) fissare il prezzo di; valutare; ~**less** *a* inapprezzabile.

prick [prɪk] *n* puntura // *vt* pungere; **to ~ up one's ears** drizzare gli orecchi.

prickle ['prɪkl] *n* (*of plant*) spina; (*sensation*) pizzicore *m*.

prickly ['prɪklɪ] *a* spinoso(a); (*fig: person*) permaloso(a); ~ **heat** *n* sudamina.

pride [praɪd] *n* orgoglio; superbia // *vt*: **to ~ o.s. on** essere orgoglioso(a) di; vantarsi di.

priest [priːst] *n* prete *m*, sacerdote *m*; ~**ess** *n* sacerdotessa; ~**hood** *n* sacerdozio.

prig [prɪg] *n*: **he's a ~** è compiaciuto di se stesso.

prim [prɪm] *a* pudico(a); contegnoso(a).

primarily ['praɪmərɪlɪ] *ad* principalmente, essenzialmente.

primary ['praɪmərɪ] *a* primario(a); (*first in importance*) primo(a); ~ **school** *n* scuola elementare.

primate *n* (*REL*: ['praɪmɪt], *ZOOL*: ['praɪmeɪt]) primate *m*.

prime [praɪm] *a* primario(a), fondamentale; (*excellent*) di prima qualità // *vt* (*gun*) innescare; (*pump*) adescare; (*fig*) mettere al corrente; **in the ~ of life** nel fiore della vita; ~ **minister (P.M.)** *n* primo ministro; ~**r** *n* (*book*) testo elementare.

primeval [praɪ'miːvl] *a* primitivo(a).

primitive ['prɪmɪtɪv] *a* primitivo(a).

primrose ['prɪmrəuz] *n* primavera.

primus (stove) ['praɪməs(stəuv)] *n* fornello a petrolio.

prince [prɪns] *n* principe *m*.

princess [prɪn'sɛs] *n* principessa.

principal ['prɪnsɪpl] *a* principale // *n* (*headmaster*) preside *m*.

principality [prɪnsɪ'pælɪtɪ] *n* principato.

principle ['prɪnsɪpl] *n* principio.

print [prɪnt] *n* (*mark*) impronta; (*letters*) caratteri *mpl*; (*fabric*) tessuto stampato; (*ART, PHOT*) stampa // *vt* imprimere; (*publish*) stampare, pubblicare; (*write in capitals*) scrivere in stampatello; **out of ~** esaurito(a); ~**ed matter** *n* stampe *fpl*; ~**er** *n* tipografo; ~**ing** *n* stampa; ~**ing press** *n* macchina tipografica; ~**-out** *n* tabulato.

prior ['praɪə*] *a* precedente // *n* priore *m*; ~ **to doing** prima di fare.

priority [praɪ'ɔrɪtɪ] *n* priorità *f inv*; precedenza.

priory ['praɪərɪ] *n* monastero.

prise [praɪz] *vt*: **to ~ open** forzare.

prism ['prɪzəm] *n* prisma *m*.

prison ['prɪzn] *n* prigione *f*; ~**er** *n* prigioniero/a.

pristine ['prɪstiːn] *a* originario(a); intatto(a); puro(a).

privacy ['prɪvəsɪ] *n* solitudine *f*, intimità.

private ['praɪvɪt] *a* privato(a); personale

// n soldato semplice; '~' (*on envelope*)
'riservata'; **in** ~ in privato; ~ **eye** n
investigatore m privato; ~**ly** ad in
privato; (*within oneself*) dentro di sé.
privet ['prɪvɪt] n ligustro.
privilege ['prɪvɪlɪdʒ] n privilegio; ~**d** a
privilegiato(a).
privy ['prɪvɪ] a: **to be** ~ **to** essere al
corrente di; **P~ Council** n Consiglio della
Corona.
prize [praɪz] n premio // a (*example, idiot*)
perfetto(a); (*bull, novel*) premiato(a) // vt
apprezzare, pregiare; ~ **fight** n incontro
di pugilato tra professionisti; ~ **giving** n
premiazione f; ~**winner** n premiato/a.
pro [prəu] n (*SPORT*) professionista m/f; **the**
~**s and cons** il pro e il contro.
probability [prɔbə'bɪlɪtɪ] n probabilità f
inv.
probable ['prɔbəbl] a probabile; **probably**
ad probabilmente.
probation [prə'beɪʃən] n (*in employment*)
periodo di prova; (*LAW*) libertà vigilata; **on**
~ (*employee*) in prova; (*LAW*) in libertà
vigilata.
probe [prəub] n (*MED, SPACE*) sonda;
(*enquiry*) indagine f, investigazione f // vt
sondare, esplorare; indagare.
probity ['prəubɪtɪ] n probità.
problem ['prɔbləm] n problema m; ~**atic**
[-'mætɪk] a problematico(a).
procedure [prə'si:dʒə*] n (*ADMIN, LAW*)
procedura; (*method*) metodo,
procedimento.
proceed [prə'si:d] vi (*go forward*)
avanzare, andare avanti; (*go about it*)
procedere; (*continue*): **to** ~ (**with**)
continuare; **to** ~ **to** andare a; passare a;
to ~ **to do** mettersi a fare; ~**ing** n
procedimento, modo d'agire; ~**ings** npl
misure fpl; (*LAW*) procedimento; (*meeting*)
riunione f; (*records*) rendiconti mpl; atti
mpl; ~**s** ['prəusi:dz] npl profitto, incasso.
process ['prəuses] n processo; (*method*)
metodo, sistema m // vt trattare;
(*information*) elaborare; ~**ing** n
trattamento; elaborazione f.
procession [prə'seʃən] n processione f,
corteo.
proclaim [prə'kleɪm] vt proclamare,
dichiarare.
proclamation [prɔklə'meɪʃən] n
proclamazione f.
procrastination [prəukræstɪ'neɪʃən] n
procrastinazione f.
procreation [prəukrɪ'eɪʃən] n
procreazione f.
procure [prə'kjuə*] vt (*for o.s.*) procurarsi;
(*for sb*) procurare.
prod [prɔd] vt pungolare // n (*push, jab*)
pungolo.
prodigal ['prɔdɪgl] a prodigo(a).
prodigious [prə'dɪdʒəs] a prodigioso(a).
prodigy ['prɔdɪdʒɪ] n prodigio.
produce n ['prɔdju:s] (*AGR*) prodotto,
prodotti mpl // vt [prə'dju:s] produrre; (*to
show*) esibire, mostrare; (*cause*)
cagionare, causare; (*THEATRE*) mettere in

scena; ~**r** n (*THEATRE*) direttore/trice;
(*AGR, CINEMA*) produttore m.
product ['prɔdʌkt] n prodotto.
production [prə'dʌkʃən] n produzione f;
(*THEATRE*) messa in scena; ~ **line** n
catena di lavorazione.
productive [prə'dʌktɪv] a produttivo(a).
productivity [prɔdʌk'tɪvɪtɪ] n produttività.
profane [prə'feɪn] a profano(a); (*language*)
empio(a).
profess [prə'fes] vt professare.
profession [prə'feʃən] n professione f;
~**al** n (*SPORT*) professionista m/f // a (*professional*); (*work*) da professionista;
~**alism** n professionismo.
professor [prə'fesə*] n professore m
(*titolare di una cattedra*).
proficiency [prə'fɪʃənsɪ] n competenza,
abilità.
proficient [prə'fɪʃənt] a competente, abile.
profile ['prəufaɪl] n profilo.
profit ['prɔfɪt] n profitto; beneficio // vi: **to**
~ (**by** *or* **from**) approfittare (di);
~**ability** [-'bɪlɪtɪ] n redditività; ~**able** a
redditizio(a).
profiteering [prɔfɪ'tɪərɪŋ] n (*pej*)
affarismo.
profound [prə'faund] a profondo(a).
profuse [prə'fju:s] a infinito(a),
abbondante; ~**ly** ad con grande effusione;
profusion [-'fju:ʒən] n profusione f,
abbondanza.
progeny ['prɔdʒɪnɪ] n progenie f;
discendenti mpl.
programme, **program** (*US*)
['prəugræm] n programma m // vt
programmare; **programming**, **pro-
graming** (*US*) n programmazione f.
progress n ['prəugres] progresso // vi
[prə'gres] avanzare, procedere; **in** ~ in
corso; **to make** ~ far progressi; ~**ion**
[-'greʃən] n progressione f; ~**ive** [-'gresɪv]
a progressivo(a); (*person*) progressista
m/f; ~**ively** [-'gresɪvlɪ] ad progressivamente.
prohibit [prə'hɪbɪt] vt proibire, vietare;
~**ion** [prəuɪ'bɪʃən] n (*US*) proibizionismo;
~**ive** a (*price etc*) proibitivo(a).
project n ['prɔdʒekt] (*plan*) piano;
(*venture*) progetto; (*SCOL*) studio // vb
[prə'dʒekt] vt proiettare // vi (*stick out*)
sporgere.
projectile [prə'dʒektaɪl] n proiettile m.
projection [prə'dʒekʃən] n proiezione f;
sporgenza.
projector [prə'dʒektə*] n proiettore m.
proletarian [prəulɪ'teərɪən] a, n
proletario(a).
proletariat [prəulɪ'teərɪət] n proletariato.
proliferate [prə'lɪfəreɪt] vi proliferare;
proliferation [-'reɪʃən] n proliferazione f.
prolific [prə'lɪfɪk] a prolifico(a).
prologue ['prəulɔg] n prologo.
prolong [prə'lɔŋ] vt prolungare.
prom [prɔm] n abbr of **promenade**; (*US:
ball*) ballo studentesco.
promenade [prɔmə'nɑ:d] n (*by sea*)

lungomare *m*; ~ **concert** *n* concerto di musica classica.

prominence ['prɔmɪnəns] *n* prominenza; importanza.

prominent ['prɔmɪnənt] *a* (*standing out*) prominente; (*important*) importante.

promiscuity [prɔmɪs'kjuːɪti] *n* (*sexual*) rapporti *mpl* multipli.

promiscuous [prə'mɪskjuəs] *a* (*sexually*) di facili costumi.

promise ['prɔmɪs] *n* promessa // *vt,vi* promettere; **promising** *a* promettente.

promontory ['prɔmǝntri] *n* promontorio.

promote [prə'məut] *vt* promuovere; (*venture, event*) organizzare; ~**r** *n* (*of sporting event*) organizzatore/trice; **promotion** [-'məuʃǝn] *n* promozione *f*; (*of new product*) promotion *m*.

prompt [prɔmpt] *a* rapido(a), svelto(a); puntuale; (*reply*) sollecito(a) // *ad* (*punctually*) in punto // *vt* incitare; provocare; (*THEATRE*) suggerire a; **to** ~ **sb to do** spingere qd a fare; ~**er** *n* (*THEATRE*) suggeritore *m*; ~**ly** *ad* prontamente; puntualmente; ~**ness** *n* prontezza; puntualità.

prone [prəun] *a* (*lying*) prono(a); ~ **to** propenso(a) a, incline a.

prong [prɔŋ] *n* rebbio, punta.

pronoun ['prəunaun] *n* pronome *m*.

pronounce [prə'nauns] *vt* pronunziare // *vi*: **to** ~ **(up)on** pronunziare su; ~**d** *a* (*marked*) spiccato(a); ~**ment** *n* dichiarazione *f*.

pronunciation [prǝnʌnsɪ'eɪʃǝn] *n* pronunzia.

proof [pruːf] *n* prova; (*of book*) bozza; (*PHOT*) provino; (*of alcohol*) grado // *a*: ~ **against** a prova di.

prop [prɔp] *n* sostegno, appoggio // *vt* (*also*: ~ **up**) sostenere, appoggiare; (*lean*): **to** ~ **sth against** appoggiare qc contro *or* a.

propaganda [prɔpǝ'gændǝ] *n* propaganda.

propagation [prɔpǝ'geɪʃǝn] *n* propagazione *f*.

propel [prə'pɛl] *vt* spingere (in avanti), muovere; ~**ler** *n* elica; ~**ling pencil** *n* matita a mina.

propensity [prə'pɛnsɪti] *n* tendenza.

proper ['prɔpǝ*] *a* (*suited, right*) adatto(a), appropriato(a); (*seemly*) decente; (*authentic*) vero(a); (*col: real*) noun + vero(a) e proprio(a); ~**ly** *ad* decentemente; proprio, dei tutto; ~ **noun** *n* nome *m* proprio.

property ['prɔpǝti] *n* (*things owned*) beni *mpl*; proprietà *fpl*; (*land*) beni *m* immobile; tenuta, terra; (*CHEM etc*: *quality*) proprietà *f inv*; ~ **owner** *n* proprietario/a.

prophecy ['prɔfɪsi] *n* profezia.

prophesy ['prɔfɪsaɪ] *vt* predire.

prophet ['prɔfɪt] *n* profeta *m*; ~**ic** [prǝ'fɛtɪk] *a* profetico(a).

proportion [prə'pɔːʃǝn] *n* proporzione *f*; (*share*) parte *f* // *vt* -proporzionare, commisurare; ~**al** *a* proporzionale; ~**ate** *a* proporzionato(a).

proposal [prə'pǝuzl] *n* proposta; (*plan*) progetto; (*of marriage*) proposta di matrimonio.

propose [prə'pǝuz] *vt* proporre, suggerire // *vi* fare una proposta di matrimonio; **to** ~ **to do** proporsi di fare, aver l'intenzione di fare.

proposition [prɔpǝ'zɪʃǝn] *n* proposizione *f*.

propound [prə'paund] *vt* proporre, presentare.

proprietor [prə'praɪǝtǝ*] *n* proprietario/a.

propulsion [prə'pʌlʃǝn] *n* propulsione *f*.

prosaic [prǝu'zeɪɪk] *a* prosaico(a).

prose [prǝuz] *n* prosa; (*SCOL: translation*) traduzione *f* dalla madrelingua.

prosecute ['prɔsɪkjuːt] *vt* processare; **prosecution** [-'kjuːʃǝn] *n* processo; (*accusing side*) accusa; **prosecutor** *n* accusatore/trice; (*also*: **public** ~) pubblico ministero.

prospect *n* ['prɔspɛkt] prospettiva; (*hope*) speranza // *vb* [prǝ'spɛkt] *vt* fare assaggi in // *vi* fare assaggi; ~**s** *npl* (*for work etc*) prospettive *fpl*; **prospecting** *n* prospezione *f*; **prospective** *a* possibile; futuro(a); **prospector** *n* prospettore *m*.

prospectus [prǝ'spɛktǝs] *n* prospetto, programma *m*.

prosper [prǝ'spɔ*] *vi* prosperare; ~**ity** [-'spɛrɪti] *n* prosperità; ~**ous** *a* prospero(a).

prostitute ['prɔstɪtjuːt] *n* prostituta.

prostrate ['prɔstreɪt] *a* prostrato(a).

protagonist [prǝ'tægǝnɪst] *n* protagonista *m/f*.

protect [prǝ'tɛkt] *vt* proteggere, salvaguardare; ~**ion** *n* protezione *f*; ~**ive** *a* protettivo(a); ~**or** *n* protettore/trice.

protégé ['prǝutǝʒeɪ] *n* protetto; ~**e** *n* protetta.

protein ['prǝutiːn] *n* proteina.

protest *n* ['prǝutɛst] protesta // *vi* [prǝ'tɛst] protestare.

Protestant ['prɔtɪstǝnt] *a,n* protestante (*m/f*).

protocol ['prǝutǝkǝl] *n* protocollo.

prototype ['prǝutǝtaɪp] *n* prototipo.

protracted [prǝ'træktɪd] *a* tirato(a) per le lunghe.

protrude [prǝ'truːd] *vi* sporgere.

protuberance [prǝ'tjuːbǝrǝns] *n* sporgenza.

proud [praud] *a* fiero(a), orgoglioso(a); (*pej*) superbo(a).

prove [pruːv] *vt* provare, dimostrare // *vi*: **to** ~ **correct** *etc* risultare vero(a) *etc*; **to** ~ **o.s.** mostrare le proprie capacità; **to** ~ **o.s./itself (to be) useful** *etc* mostrarsi *or* rivelarsi utile *etc*.

proverb ['prɔvǝːb] *n* proverbio; ~**ial** [prǝ'vǝːbɪǝl] *a* proverbiale.

provide [prǝ'vaɪd] *vt* fornire, provvedere; **to** ~ **sb with sth** fornire *or* provvedere qd di qc; **to** ~ **for** *vt* provvedere a; ~**d** (**that**) *cj* purché + *sub*, a condizione che + *sub*.

Providence ['prɔvɪdəns] n Provvidenza.
providing [prə'vaɪdɪŋ] cj purché + sub, a condizione che + sub.
province ['prɔvɪns] n provincia; **provincial** [prə'vɪnʃəl] a provinciale.
provision [prə'vɪʒən] n (supply) riserva; (supplying) provvista; rifornimento; (stipulation) condizione f; **~s** npl (food) provviste fpl; **~al** a provvisorio(a).
proviso [prə'vaɪzəu] n condizione f.
provocation [prɔvə'keɪʃən] n provocazione f.
provocative [prə'vɔkətɪv] a (aggressive) provocatorio(a); (thought-provoking) stimolante; (seductive) provocante.
provoke [prə'vəuk] vt provocare; incitare.
prow [prau] n prua.
prowess ['prauɪs] n prodezza.
prowl [praul] vi (also: **~ about, ~ around**) aggirarsi furtivamente; **~er** n tipo sospetto (che s'aggira con l'intenzione di rubare, aggredire etc).
proximity [prɔk'sɪmɪtɪ] n prossimità.
proxy ['prɔksɪ] n procura; **by ~** per procura.
prudence ['pru:dns] n prudenza.
prudent ['pru:dnt] a prudente.
prudish ['pru:dɪʃ] a puritano(a).
prune [pru:n] n prugna secca // vt potare.
pry [praɪ] vi: **to ~ into** ficcare il naso in.
psalm [sɑ:m] n salmo.
pseudo- ['sju:dəu] prefix pseudo...; **~nym** n pseudonimo.
psyche ['saɪkɪ] n psiche f.
psychiatric [saɪkɪ'ætrɪk] a psichiatrico(a).
psychiatrist [saɪ'kaɪətrɪst] n psichiatra m/f.
psychiatry [saɪ'kaɪətrɪ] n psichiatria.
psychic ['saɪkɪk] a (also: **~al**) psichico(a); (person) dotato(a) di qualità telepatiche.
psychoanalyse [saɪkəu'ænəlaɪz] vt psicanalizzare.
psychoanalysis, pl lyses [saɪkəu-'nælɪsɪs, -sɪːz] n psicanalisi f inv.
psychoanalyst [saɪkəu'ænəlɪst] n psicanalista m/f.
psychological [saɪkə'lɔdʒɪkl] a psicologico(a).
psychologist [saɪ'kɔlədʒɪst] n psicologo/a.
psychology [saɪ'kɔlədʒɪ] n psicologia.
psychopath ['saɪkəupæθ] n psicopatico/a.
psychotic [saɪ'kɔtɪk] a,n psicotico(a).
P.T.O. abbr (= please turn over) v.r. (vedi retro).
pub [pʌb] n (abbr of public house) pub m inv.
puberty ['pju:bətɪ] n pubertà.
public ['pʌblɪk] a pubblico(a) // n pubblico; **the general ~** il pubblico.
publican ['pʌblɪkən] n proprietario di un pub.
publication [pʌblɪ'keɪʃən] n pubblicazione f.
public: ~ company n società f inv per azioni (costituita tramite pubblica

sottoscrizione); **~ convenience** n gabinetti mpl; **~ house** n pub m inv.
publicity [pʌb'lɪsɪtɪ] n pubblicità.
publicly ['pʌblɪklɪ] ad pubblicamente.
public: ~ opinion n opinione f pubblica; **~ relations** n pubbliche relazioni fpl; **~ school** n (Brit) scuola privata; **~-spirited** a che ha senso civico.
publish ['pʌblɪʃ] vt pubblicare; **~er** n editore m; **~ing** n (industry) editoria; (of a book) pubblicazione f.
puce [pju:s] a color pulce inv.
puck [pʌk] n (ICE HOCKEY) disco.
pucker ['pʌkə*] vt corrugare.
pudding ['pudɪŋ] n budino; (dessert) dolce m.
puddle ['pʌdl] n pozza, pozzanghera.
puerile ['pjuəraɪl] a puerile.
puff [pʌf] n sbuffo; (also: **powder ~**) piumino // vt: **to ~ one's pipe** tirare sboccate di fumo // vi uscire a sbuffi; (pant) ansare; **to ~ out smoke** mandar fuori sbuffi di fumo; **~ed** a (col: out of breath) senza fiato.
puffin ['pʌfɪn] n puffino.
puff pastry ['pʌf'peɪstrɪ] n pasta sfoglia.
puffy ['pʌfɪ] a gonfio(a).
pugnacious [pʌg'neɪʃəs] a combattivo(a).
pull [pul] n (tug): **to give sth a ~** tirare su qc; (fig) influenza // vt tirare; (muscle) strappare // vi tirare; **to ~ to pieces** fare a pezzi; **to ~ one's punches** (BOXING) risparmiare l'avversario; **not to ~ one's punches** (fig) non avere peli sulla lingua; **to ~ one's weight** dare il proprio contributo; **to ~ o.s. together** ricomporsi, riprendersi; **to ~ sb's leg** prendere in giro qd; **to ~ apart** vt (break) fare a pezzi; **to ~ down** vt (house) demolire; (tree) abbattere; **to ~ in** vi (AUT: at the kerb) accostarsi; (RAIL) entrare in stazione; **to ~ off** vt (deal etc) portare a compimento; **to ~ out** vi partire; (AUT: come out of line) spostarsi sulla mezzeria // vt staccare; far uscire; (withdraw) ritirare; **to ~ through** vi farcela; **to ~ up** vi (stop) fermarsi // vt (uproot) sradicare; (stop) fermare.
pulley ['pulɪ] n puleggia, carrucola.
pullover ['puləuvə*] n pullover m inv.
pulp [pʌlp] n (of fruit) polpa; (for paper) pasta per carta.
pulpit ['pulpɪt] n pulpito.
pulsate [pʌl'seɪt] vi battere, palpitare.
pulse [pʌls] n polso.
pulverize ['pʌlvəraɪz] vt polverizzare.
puma ['pju:mə] n puma m inv.
pummel ['pʌml] vt dare pugni a.
pump [pʌmp] n pompa; (shoe) scarpetta // vt pompare; (fig: col) far parlare; **to ~ up** vt gonfiare.
pumpkin ['pʌmpkɪn] n zucca.
pun [pʌn] n gioco di parole.
punch [pʌntʃ] n (blow) pugno; (fig: force) forza; (tool) punzone m; (drink) ponce m // vt (hit): **to ~ sb/sth** dare un pugno a qd/qc; **to ~ a hole (in)** fare un buco (in); **~-up** n (col) rissa.

punctual ['pʌŋktjuəl] a puntuale; ~**ity** [-'æliti] n puntualità.

punctuate ['pʌŋktjueit] vt punteggiare; **punctuation** [-'eiʃən] n interpunzione f, punteggiatura.

puncture ['pʌŋktʃə*] n foratura // vt forare.

pundit ['pʌndit] n sapientone/a.

pungent ['pʌndʒənt] a piccante; (fig) mordace, caustico(a).

punish ['pʌniʃ] vt punire; ~**able** a punibile; ~**ment** n punizione f.

punt [pʌnt] n (boat) barchino; (FOOTBALL) colpo a volo.

puny ['pju:ni] a gracile.

pup [pʌp] n cucciolo/a.

pupil ['pju:pl] n allievo/a; alunno/a.

puppet ['pʌpit] n burattino.

puppy ['pʌpi] n cucciolo/a, cagnolino/a.

purchase ['pɔːtʃis] n acquisto, compera // vt comprare; ~**r** n compratore/trice.

pure [pjuə*] a puro(a).

purge [pɔːdʒ] n (MED) purga; (POL) epurazione f // vt purgare; (fig) epurare.

purification [pjuərifi'keiʃən] n purificazione f.

purify ['pjuərifai] vt purificare.

purist ['pjuərist] n purista m/f.

puritan ['pjuəritən] n puritano/a; ~**ical** [-'tænikl] a puritano(a).

purity ['pjuəriti] n purità.

purl [pɔːl] n punto rovescio.

purple ['pɔːpl] a di porpora; viola inv.

purport [pɔː'pɔːt] vi: **to** ~ **to be/do** pretendere di essere/fare.

purpose ['pɔːpəs] n intenzione f, scopo; **on** ~ apposta; ~**ful** a deciso(a), risoluto(a); ~**ly** ad apposta.

purr [pɔː*] vi fare la fusa.

purse [pɔːs] n borsellino // vt contrarre.

purser ['pɔːsə*] n (NAUT) commissario di bordo.

pursue [pə'sjuː] vt inseguire; ~**r** n inseguitore/trice.

pursuit [pə'sjuːt] n inseguimento; (occupation) occupazione f, attività f inv; **scientific** ~**s** ricerche fpl scientifiche.

purveyor [pə'veiə*] n fornitore/trice.

pus [pʌs] n pus m.

push [puʃ] n spinta; (effort) grande sforzo; (drive) energia // vt spingere; (button) premere; (thrust): **to** ~ **sth (into)** ficcare qc (in); (fig) fare pubblicità a // vi spingere; premere; **to** ~ **aside** vt scostare; **to** ~ **off** vi (col) filare; **to** ~ **on** vi (continue) continuare; **to** ~ **through** vt (measure) far approvare; **to** ~ **up** vt (total, prices) far salire; ~**chair** n passeggino; ~**over** n (col): **it's a** ~**over** è un lavoro da bambini; ~**y** a (pej) opportunista.

puss, pussy(-cat) [pus, 'pusi(kæt)] n micio.

put, pt, pp **put** [put] vt mettere, porre; (say) dire, esprimere; (a question) fare; (estimate) stimare; **to** ~ **about** vi (NAUT) virare di bordo // vt (rumour) diffondere;

to ~ **across** vt (ideas etc) comunicare; far capire; **to** ~ **away** vt (return) mettere a posto; **to** ~ **back** vt (replace) rimettere (a posto); (postpone) rinviare; (delay) ritardare; **to** ~ **by** vt (money) mettere da parte; **to** ~ **down** vt (parcel etc) posare, mettere giù; (pay) versare; (in writing) mettere per iscritto; (suppress: revolt etc) reprimere, sopprimere; (attribute) attribuire; **to** ~ **forward** vt (ideas) avanzare, proporre; (date) anticipare; **to** ~ **in** vt (application, complaint) presentare; **to** ~ **off** vt (postpone) rimandare, rinviare; (discourage) dissuadere; **to** ~ **on** vt (clothes, lipstick etc) mettere; (light etc) accendere; (play etc) mettere in scena; (food, meal) servire; (brake) mettere; **to** ~ **on weight** ingrassare; **to** ~ **on airs** darsi delle arie; **to** ~ **out** vt mettere fuori; (one's hand) porgere; (light etc) spegnere; (person: inconvenience) scomodare; **to** ~ **up** vt (raise) sollevare, alzare; (pin up) affiggere; (hang) appendere; (build) costruire, erigere; (increase) aumentare; (accommodate) alloggiare; **to** ~ **up with** vt fus sopportare.

putrid ['pjuːtrid] a putrido(a).

putt [pʌt] vt (ball) colpire leggermente // n colpo leggero; ~**er** n (GOLF) putter m inv; ~**ing green** n green m inv; campo da putting.

putty ['pʌti] n stucco.

put-up ['putʌp] a: ~ **job** n montatura.

puzzle ['pʌzl] n enigma m, mistero; (jigsaw) puzzle m // vt confondere, rendere perplesso(a) // vi scervellarsi; **puzzling** a sconcertante, inspiegabile.

pygmy ['pigmi] n pigmeo/a.

pyjamas [pi'dʒɑːməz] npl pigiama m.

pylon ['pailən] n pilone m.

pyramid ['pirəmid] n piramide f.

python ['paiθən] n pitone m.

Q

quack [kwæk] n (of duck) qua qua m inv; (pej: doctor) dottoruccio/a.

quad [kwɔd] abbr of **quadrangle**, **quadruplet**.

quadrangle ['kwɔdræŋgl] n (MATH) quadrilatero; (courtyard) cortile m.

quadruped ['kwɔdruped] n quadrupede m.

quadruple [kwɔ'druːpl] a quadruplo(a) // n quadruplo // vt quadruplicare // vi quadruplicarsi; ~**t** [-'druːplit] n uno/a di quattro gemelli.

quagmire ['kwægmaiə*] n pantano.

quail [kweil] n (ZOOL) quaglia.

quaint [kweint] a bizzarro(a); (old-fashioned) antiquato(a); grazioso(a), pittoresco(a).

quake [kweik] vi tremare // n abbr of **earthquake**.

Quaker ['kweikə*] n quacchero/a.

qualification [kwɔlifi'keiʃən] n (degree etc) qualifica, titolo; (ability) competenza, qualificazione f; (limitation) riserva, restrizione f.

qualified ['kwɔlɪfaɪd] a qualificato(a); (able) competente, qualificato(a); (limited) condizionato(a).

qualify ['kwɔlɪfaɪ] vt abilitare; (limit: statement) modificare, precisare // vi: to ~ (as) qualificarsi (come); to ~ (for) acquistare i requisiti necessari (per); (SPORT) qualificarsi (per or a).

qualitative ['kwɔlɪtətɪv] a qualitativo(a).

quality ['kwɔlɪtɪ] n qualità f inv.

qualm [kwɑːm] n dubbio; scrupolo.

quandary ['kwɔndrɪ] n: in a ~ in un dilemma.

quantitative ['kwɔntɪtətɪv] a quantitativo(a).

quantity ['kwɔntɪtɪ] n quantità f inv; ~ surveyor n geometra m (specializzato nel calcolare la quantità e il costo del materiale da costruzione).

quarantine ['kwɔrəntiːn] n quarantena.

quarrel ['kwɔrl] n lite f, disputa // vi litigare; ~some a litigioso(a).

quarry ['kwɔrɪ] n (for stone) cava; (animal) preda // vt (marble etc) estrarre.

quart [kwɔːt] n ≈ litro (= 2 pints).

quarter ['kwɔːtə*] n quarto; (of year) trimestre m; (district) quartiere m // vt dividere in quattro; (MIL) alloggiare; ~s npl alloggi mpl, quadrato; a ~ of an hour un quarto d'ora; ~ final n quarto di finale; ~ly a trimestrale // ad trimestralmente; ~master n (MIL) furiere m.

quartet(te) [kwɔːˈtɛt] n quartetto.

quartz [kwɔːts] n quarzo; ~ watch n orologio al quarzo.

quash [kwɔʃ] vt (verdict) annullare.

quasi- ['kweɪzaɪ] prefix quasi + noun; quasi, pressoché + adjective.

quaver ['kweɪvə*] n (MUS) croma // vi tremolare.

quay [kiː] n (also: ~side) banchina.

queasy ['kwiːzɪ] a (stomach) delicato(a); to feel ~ aver la nausea.

queen [kwiːn] n (gen) regina; (CARDS etc) regina, donna; ~ mother n regina madre.

queer [kwɪə*] a strano(a), curioso(a); (suspicious) dubbio(a), sospetto(a); (sick): I feel ~ mi sento poco bene // n (col) finocchio.

quell [kwɛl] vt domare.

quench [kwɛntʃ] vt (flames) spegnere; to ~ one's thirst dissetarsi.

query ['kwɪərɪ] n domanda, questione f; (doubt) dubbio // vt mettere in questione.

quest [kwɛst] n cerca, ricerca.

question ['kwɛstʃən] n domanda, questione f // vt (person) interrogare; (plan, idea) mettere in questione or in dubbio; it's a ~ of doing si tratta di fare; beyond ~ fuori di dubbio; out of the ~ fuori discussione, impossibile; ~able a discutibile; ~ing a interrogativo(a) // n interrogatorio; ~ mark n punto interrogativo.

questionnaire [kwɛstʃəˈnɛə*] n questionario.

queue [kjuː] n coda, fila // vi fare la coda.

quibble ['kwɪbl] vi cavillare.

quick [kwɪk] a rapido(a), veloce; (reply) pronto(a); (mind) pronto(a), acuto(a) // ad rapidamente, presto // n: cut to the ~ (fig) toccato(a) sul vivo; be ~! fai presto!; ~en vt accelerare, affrettare; (rouse) animare, stimolare // vi accelerare, affrettarsi; ~ly ad rapidamente, velocemente; ~ness n rapidità; prontezza; acutezza; ~sand n sabbie fpl mobili; ~step n (dance) fox-trot m inv; ~-witted a pronto(a) d'ingegno.

quid [kwɪd] n, pl inv (Brit: col) sterlina.

quiet ['kwaɪət] a tranquillo(a), quieto(a); (ceremony) semplice; (colour) discreto(a) // n tranquillità, calma; keep ~! sta zitto!; on the ~ di nascosto; ~en (also: ~en down) vi calmarsi, chetarsi // vt calmare, chetare; ~ly ad tranquillamente, calmamente; sommessamente; discretamente; ~ness n tranquillità, calma; silenzio.

quill [kwɪl] n penna d'oca.

quilt [kwɪlt] n piumino; (continental) ~ n soffiocone m imbottito.

quin [kwɪn] abbr of quintuplet.

quinine [kwɪˈniːn] n chinino.

quintet(te) [kwɪnˈtɛt] n quintetto.

quintuplet [kwɪnˈtjuːplɪt] n uno/a di cinque gemelli.

quip [kwɪp] n frizzo.

quirk [kwəːk] n ghiribizzo.

quit, pt, pp quit or quitted [kwɪt] vt lasciare, partire da // vi (give up) mollare; (resign) dimettersi; notice to ~ preavviso (dato all'inquilino).

quite [kwaɪt] ad (rather) assai; (entirely) completamente, del tutto; I ~ understand capisco perfettamente; ~ a few of them non pochi di loro; ~ (so)! esatto!

quits [kwɪts] a: ~ (with) pari (con).

quiver ['kwɪvə*] vi tremare, fremere // n (for arrows) faretra.

quiz [kwɪz] n (game) quiz m inv; indovinello // vt interrogare; ~zical a enigmatico(a).

quoits [kwɔɪts] npl gioco degli anelli.

quorum ['kwɔːrəm] n quorum m.

quota ['kwəʊtə] n quota.

quotation [kwəʊˈteɪʃən] n citazione f; (of shares etc) quotazione f; (estimate) preventivo; ~ marks npl virgolette fpl.

quote [kwəʊt] n citazione f // vt (sentence) citare; (price) dare, fissare; (shares) quotare // vi: to ~ from citare; to ~ for a job dare un preventivo per un lavoro.

R

rabbi ['ræbaɪ] n rabbino.

rabbit ['ræbɪt] n coniglio; ~ hutch n conigliera.

rabble ['ræbl] n (pej) canaglia, plebaglia.

rabid ['ræbɪd] a rabbioso(a); (fig) fanatico(a).

rabies ['reɪbiːz] n rabbia.

RAC n abbr of Royal Automobile Club.

raccoon [rə'kuːn] n procione m.

race [reɪs] n corsa; (competition) gara, corsa // vt (person) gareggiare (in corsa) con; (horse) far correre; (engine) imballare // vi correre; ~**course** n campo di corse, ippodromo; ~**horse** n cavallo da corsa; ~ **relations** npl rapporto fra le razze.

racial ['reɪʃl] a razziale; ~ **discrimination** n discriminazione f razziale; ~**ism** n razzismo; ~**ist** a, n razzista (m/f).

racing ['reɪsɪŋ] n corsa; ~ **car** n macchina da corsa; ~ **driver** n corridore m automobilista.

racist ['reɪsɪst] a,n (pej) razzista (m/f).

rack [ræk] n rastrelliera; (also: **luggage** ~) rete f, portabagagli m inv; (also: **roof** ~) portabagagli // vt torturare, tormentare; **toast** ~ n portatoast m inv.

racket ['rækɪt] n (for tennis) racchetta; (noise) fracasso; baccano; (swindle) imbroglio, truffa; (organized crime) racket m inv.

racoon [rə'kuːn] n = **raccoon**.

racquet ['rækɪt] n racchetta.

racy ['reɪsɪ] a brioso(a); piccante.

radar ['reɪdɑː*] n radar m // cpd radar inv.

radiance ['reɪdɪəns] n splendore m, radiosità.

radiant ['reɪdɪənt] a raggiante; (PHYSICS) radiante.

radiate ['reɪdɪeɪt] vt (heat) irraggiare, irradiare // vi (lines) irradiarsi.

radiation [reɪdɪ'eɪʃən] n irradiamento; (radioactive) radiazione f.

radiator ['reɪdɪeɪtə*] n radiatore m; ~ **cap** n tappo del radiatore.

radical ['rædɪkl] a radicale.

radii ['reɪdɪaɪ] npl of **radius**.

radio ['reɪdɪəu] n radio f inv; **on the** ~ alla radio; ~ **station** n stazione f radio inv.

radio... ['reɪdɪəu] prefix: ~**active** a radioattivo(a); ~**activity** n radioattività; ~**grapher** [-'ɔgrəfə*] n radiologo/a; ~**graphy** [-'ɔgrəfi] n radiografia; ~**logy** [-'ɔlədʒi] n radiologia.

radish ['rædɪʃ] n ravanello.

radium ['reɪdɪəm] n radio.

radius, pl **radii** ['reɪdɪəs, -aɪ] n raggio; (ANAT) radio.

raffia ['ræfɪə] n rafia.

raffle ['ræfl] n lotteria.

raft [rɑːft] n zattera.

rafter ['rɑːftə*] n trave f.

rag [ræg] n straccio, cencio; (pej: newspaper) giornalaccio, bandiera; (for charity) iniziativa studentesca a scopo caritativo // vt prendere in giro; ~**s** npl stracci mpl, brandelli mpl; ~**-and-bone man** n straccivendolo; ~**bag** n (fig) guazzabuglio.

rage [reɪdʒ] n (fury) collera, furia // vi (person) andare su tutte le furie; (storm) infuriare; **it's all the** ~ fa furore.

ragged ['rægɪd] a (edge) irregolare; (cuff) logoro(a); (appearance) pezzente.

raid [reɪd] n (MIL) incursione f; (criminal) rapina; (by police) irruzione f // vt fare un'incursione in; rapinare; fare irruzione in; ~**er** n rapinatore/trice; (plane) aeroplano da incursione.

rail [reɪl] n (on stair) ringhiera; (on bridge, balcony) parapetto; (of ship) battagliola; (for train) rotaia; ~**s** npl binario, rotaie fpl; **by** ~ per ferrovia; ~**ing(s)** n(pl) ringhiere fpl; ~**road** n (US), ~**way** n ferrovia; ~**wayman** n ferroviere m; ~**way station** n stazione f ferroviaria.

rain [reɪn] n pioggia // vi piovere; **in the** ~ sotto la pioggia; ~**bow** n arcobaleno; ~**coat** n impermeabile m; ~**drop** n goccia di pioggia; ~**fall** n pioggia; (measurement) piovosità; ~**proof** a impermeabile; ~**y** a piovoso(a).

raise [reɪz] n aumento // vt (lift) alzare; sollevare; (build) erigere; (increase) aumentare; (a protest, doubt, question) sollevare; (cattle, family) allevare; (crop) coltivare; (army, funds) raccogliere; (loan) ottenere; **to** ~ **one's voice** alzare la voce.

raisin ['reɪzn] n uva secca.

rajah ['rɑːdʒə] n ragià m inv.

rake [reɪk] n (tool) rastrello; (person) libertino // vt (garden) rastrellare; (with machine gun) spazzare.

rakish ['reɪkɪʃ] a dissoluto(a); disinvolto(a).

rally ['rælɪ] n (POL etc) riunione f; (AUT) rally m inv; (TENNIS) scambio // vt riunire, radunare // vi raccogliersi, radunarsi; (sick person, Stock Exchange) riprendersi; **to** ~ **round** vt fus raggrupparsi intorno a; venire in aiuto di.

ram [ræm] n montone m; (also: device) ariete m // vt conficcare; (crash into) cozzare, sbattere contro; percuotere; speronare.

ramble ['ræmbl] n escursione f // vi (pej: also: ~ **on**) divagare; ~**r** n escursionista m/f; (BOT) rosa rampicante; **rambling** a (speech) sconnesso(a); (BOT) rampicante.

ramification [ræmɪfɪ'keɪʃən] n ramificazione f.

ramp [ræmp] n rampa.

rampage [ræm'peɪdʒ] n: **to be on the** ~ scatenarsi in modo violento // vi: **they went rampaging through the town** si sono scatenati in modo violento per la città.

rampant ['ræmpənt] a (disease etc) che infierisce.

rampart ['ræmpɑːt] n bastione m.

ramshackle ['ræmʃækl] a (house) cadente; (car etc) sgangherato(a).

ran [ræn] pt of **run**.

ranch [rɑːntʃ] n ranch m inv; ~**er** n proprietario di un ranch; cowboy m inv.

rancid ['rænsɪd] a rancido(a).

rancour ['ræŋkə*] n rancore m.
random ['rændəm] a fatto(a) or detto(a) per caso // n: **at ~** a casaccio.
randy ['rændı] a (col) arrapato(a); lascivo(a).
rang [ræŋ] pt of **ring**.
range [reındʒ] n (of mountains) catena; (of missile, voice) portata; (of products) gamma; (MIL: also: **shooting ~**) campo di tiro; (also: **kitchen ~**) fornello, cucina economica // vi: **to ~ over** coprire; **to ~ from ... to** andare da ... a; **~r** n guardia forestale.
rank [ræŋk] n fila; (MIL) grado; (also: **taxi ~**) posteggio di taxi // vi: **to ~ among** essere nel numero di // a puzzolente; vero(a) e proprio(a); **the ~s** (MIL) la truppa; **the ~ and file** (fig) la gran massa.
rankle ['ræŋkl] vi bruciare.
ransack ['rænsæk] vt rovistare; (plunder) saccheggiare.
ransom ['rænsəm] n riscatto; **to hold sb to ~** (fig) esercitare pressione su qd.
rant [rænt] vi vociare; **~ing** n vociare m.
rap [ræp] n colpo secco e lievo; picchio // vt bussare a; picchiare su.
rape [reıp] n violenza carnale, stupro // vt violentare.
rapid ['ræpıd] a rapido(a); **~s** npl (GEO) rapida.
rapist ['reıpıst] n violentatore m.
rapport [ræ'pɔː] n rapporto.
rapture ['ræptʃə*] n estasi f inv: **to go into ~s over** andare in solluchero per; **rapturous** a estatico(a).
rare [rɛə*] a raro(a); (CULIN: steak) al sangue.
rarefied ['rɛərıfaıd] a (air, atmosphere) rarefatto(a).
rarely ['rɛəlı] ad raramente.
rarity ['rɛərıtı] n rarità f inv.
rascal ['rɑːskl] n mascalzone m.
rash [ræʃ] a imprudente, sconsiderato(a) // n (MED) eruzione f.
rasher ['ræʃə*] n fetta sottile (di lardo or prosciutto).
rasp [rɑːsp] n (tool) lima.
raspberry ['rɑːzbərı] n lampone m.
rasping ['rɑːspıŋ] a stridulo(a).
rat [ræt] n ratto.
ratchet ['rætʃıt] n (TECH) dente m d'arresto.
rate [reıt] n (proportion) tasso, percentuale f; (speed) velocità f inv; (price) tariffa // vt giudicare; stimare; **to ~ sb/sth as** valutare qd/qc come; **to ~ sb/sth among** annoverare qd/qc tra; **~s** npl (Brit) imposte fpl comunali; (fees) tariffe fpl; **~able** value n valore m imponibile or locativo (di una proprietà); **~ of exchange** n corso dei cambi; **~payer** n contribuente m/f (che paga le imposte comunali).
rather ['rɑːðə*] ad piuttosto; **it's ~ expensive** è piuttosto caro; (too much) è un po' caro; **I would** or **I'd ~ go** preferirei andare.

ratification [rætıfı'keıʃən] n ratificazione f.
ratify ['rætıfaı] vt ratificare.
rating ['reıtıŋ] n classificazione f; punteggio di merito; (NAUT: sailor) marinaio semplice.
ratio ['reıʃıəu] n proporzione f.
ration ['ræʃən] n (gen pl) razioni fpl // vt razionare.
rational ['ræʃənl] a razionale, ragionevole; (solution, reasoning) logico(a); **~e** [-'nɑːl] n fondamento logico; giustificazione f; **~ize** vt razionalizzare; **~ly** ad razionalmente; logicamente.
rat race ['rætreıs] n mondo cane.
rattle ['rætl] n tintinnio; (louder) strepito; (object: of baby) sonaglino; (: of sports fan) raganella // vi risuonare, tintinnare; fare un rumore di ferraglia // vt scuotere (con strepito); **~snake** n serpente m a sonagli.
raucous ['rɔːkəs] a rauco(a).
ravage ['rævıdʒ] vt devastare; **~s** npl danni mpl.
rave [reıv] vi (in anger) infuriarsi; (with enthusiasm) andare in estasi; (MED) delirare.
raven ['reıvən] n corvo.
ravenous ['rævənəs] a affamato(a).
ravine [rə'viːn] n burrone m.
raving ['reıvıŋ] a: **~ lunatic** n pazzo(a) furioso(a).
ravioli [rævı'əulı] n ravioli mpl.
ravish ['rævıʃ] vt (delight) estasiare; **~ing** a incantevole.
raw [rɔː] a (uncooked) crudo(a); (not processed) greggio(a); (sore) vivo(a); (inexperienced) inesperto(a); **~ material** n materia prima.
ray [reı] n raggio.
rayon ['reıən] n raion m.
raze [reız] vt radere, distruggere.
razor ['reızə*] n rasoio; **~ blade** n lama di rasoio.
Rd abbr of **road**.
re [riː] prep con riferimento a.
reach [riːtʃ] n portata; (of river etc) tratto // vt raggiungere; arrivare a // vi stendersi; **out of/within ~** (object) fuori a portata di mano; **within easy ~ (of)** (place) a breve distanza (di), vicino (a); **to ~ out** vi: **to ~ out for** stendere la mano per prendere.
react [riː'ækt] vi reagire; **~ion** [-'ækʃən] n reazione f; **~ionary** [-'ækʃənrı] a,n reazionario(a).
reactor [riː'æktə*] n reattore m.
read, pt,pp **read** [riːd, rɛd] vi leggere // vt leggere; (understand) intendere, interpretare; (study) studiare; **to ~ out** vt leggere ad alta voce; **~er** n lettore/trice; (book) libro di lettura; (at university) professore con funzioni preminenti di ricerca; **~ership** n (of paper etc) numero di lettori.
readily ['rɛdılı] ad volentieri; (easily) facilmente.
readiness ['rɛdınıs] n prontezza; **in ~** (prepared) pronto(a).

reading ['ri:dɪŋ] n lettura; (*understanding*) interpretazione f; (*on instrument*) indicazione f; ~ **lamp** n lampada da studio; ~ **room** n sala di lettura.

readjust [ri:ə'dʒʌst] vt raggiustare // vi (*person*): **to** ~ **(to)** riadattarsi (a).

ready ['rɛdɪ] a pronto(a); (*willing*) pronto(a), disposto(a); (*quick*) rapido(a); (*available*) disponibile // ad: ~-**cooked** già cotto(a) // n: **at the** ~ (*MIL*) pronto a sparare; (*fig*) tutto(a) pronto(a); ~ **cash** n denaro in contanti; ~-**made** a prefabbricato(a); (*clothes*) confezionato(a).

real [rɪəl] a reale; vero(a); **in** ~ **terms** in realtà; ~ **estate** n beni mpl immobili; ~**ism** n (*also ART*) realismo; ~**ist** n realista m/f; ~**istic** [-'lɪstɪk] a realistico(a).

reality [rɪ'ælɪtɪ] n realtà f inv; **in** ~ in realtà, in effetti.

realization [rɪəlaɪ'zeɪʃən] n presa di coscienza; realizzazione f.

realize ['rɪəlaɪz] vt (*understand*) rendersi conto di; (*a project, COMM: asset*) realizzare.

really ['rɪəlɪ] ad veramente, davvero.

realm [rɛlm] n reame m, regno.

ream [ri:m] n risma.

reap [ri:p] vt mietere; (*fig*) raccogliere.

reappear [ri:ə'pɪə*] vi ricomparire, riapparire; ~**ance** n riapparizione f.

rear [rɪə*] a di dietro; (*AUT: wheel etc*) posteriore // n didietro, parte f posteriore // vt (*cattle, family*) allevare // vi (*also*: ~ **up**) (*animal*) impennarsi; ~**guard** n retroguardia.

rearm [ri:'ɑ:m] vt, vi riarmare; ~**ament** n riarmo.

rearrange [ri:ə'reɪndʒ] vt riordinare.

rear-view ['rɪəvju:] a: ~ **mirror** n (*AUT*) specchio retrovisivo.

reason ['ri:zn] n ragione f; (*cause, motive*) ragione, motivo // vi: **to** ~ **with sb** far ragionare qd; **to have** ~ **to think** avere motivi per pensare; **it stands to** ~ **that** è ovvio che; ~**able** a ragionevole; (*not bad*) accettabile; ~**ably** ad ragionevolmente; ~**ed** a (*argument*) ponderato(a); ~**ing** n ragionamento.

reassert [ri:ə'sə:t] vt riaffermare.

reassure [ri:ə'ʃuə*] vt rassicurare; **to** ~ **sb of** rassicurare qd di o su; **reassuring** a rassicurante.

rebate ['ri:beɪt] n (*on product*) ribasso; (*on tax etc*) sgravio; (*repayment*) rimborso.

rebel n ['rɛbl] ribelle m/f // vi [rɪ'bɛl] ribellarsi; ~**lion** n ribellione f; ~**lious** a ribelle.

rebirth [ri:'bə:θ] n rinascita.

rebound vi [rɪ'baund] (*ball*) rimbalzare // n ['ri:baund] rimbalzo.

rebuff [rɪ'bʌf] n secco rifiuto // vt respingere.

rebuild [ri:'bɪld] vt irg ricostruire.

rebuke [rɪ'bju:k] n rimprovero // vt rimproverare.

rebut [rɪ'bʌt] vt rifiutare; ~**tal** n rifiuto.

recall [rɪ'kɔ:l] vt richiamare; (*remember*)

ricordare, richiamare alla mente // n richiamo; **beyond** ~ a irrevocabile.

recant [rɪ'kænt] vi ritrattarsi; (*REL*) fare abiura.

recap ['ri:kæp] n ricapitolazione f // vt ricapitolare // vi riassumere.

recapture [ri:'kæptʃə*] vt riprendere; (*atmosphere*) ricreare.

recede [rɪ'si:d] vi allontanarsi; ritirarsi; calare; **receding** a (*forehead, chin*) sfuggente; **he's got a receding hairline** sta stempiando.

receipt [rɪ'si:t] n (*document*) ricevuta; (*act of receiving*) ricevimento; ~**s** npl (*COMM*) introiti mpl.

receive [rɪ'si:v] vt ricevere; (*guest*) ricevere, accogliere.

receiver [rɪ'si:və*] n (*TEL*) ricevitore m; (*of stolen goods*) ricettatore/trice; (*LAW*) curatore m fallimentare.

recent ['ri:snt] a recente; ~**ly** ad recentemente.

receptacle [rɪ'sɛptɪkl] n recipiente m.

reception [rɪ'sɛpʃən] n ricevimento; (*welcome*) accoglienza; (*TV etc*) ricezione f; ~ **desk** n ricevimento; ~**ist** n receptionist m/f inv.

receptive [rɪ'sɛptɪv] a ricettivo(a).

recess [rɪ'sɛs] n (*in room*) alcova; (*POL etc: holiday*) vacanze fpl.

recharge [ri:'tʃɑ:dʒ] vt (*battery*) ricaricare.

recipe ['rɛsɪpɪ] n ricetta.

recipient [rɪ'sɪpɪənt] n beneficiario/a; (*of letter*) destinatario.

reciprocal [rɪ'sɪprəkl] a reciproco(a).

reciprocate [rɪ'sɪprəkeɪt] vt ricambiare, contraccambiare.

recital [rɪ'saɪtl] n recital m inv.

recite [rɪ'saɪt] vt (*poem*) recitare.

reckless ['rɛkləs] a (*driver etc*) spericolato(a).

reckon ['rɛkən] vt (*count*) calcolare; (*consider*) considerare, stimare; (*think*): **I** ~ **that ...** penso che ...; **to** ~ **on** vt fus contare su; ~**ing** n conto; stima; **the day of** ~ **ing** il giorno del giudizio.

reclaim [rɪ'kleɪm] vt (*land*) bonificare; (*demand back*) richiedere, reclamare; **reclamation** [rɛklə'meɪʃən] n bonifica.

recline [rɪ'klaɪn] vi stare sdraiato/a; **reclining** a (*seat*) ribaltabile.

recluse [rɪ'klu:s] n eremita m, appartato/a.

recognition [rɛkəg'nɪʃən] n riconoscimento; **to gain** ~ essere riconosciuto(a); **transformed beyond** ~ irriconoscibile.

recognizable ['rɛkəgnaɪzəbl] a riconoscibile.

recognize ['rɛkəgnaɪz] vt: **to** ~ **(by/as)** riconoscere (a o da/come).

recoil [rɪ'kɔɪl] vi (*gun*) rinculare; (*spring*) balzare indietro; (*person*): **to** ~ **(from)** indietreggiare (davanti a) // n rinculo; contraccolpo.

recollect [rɛkə'lɛkt] vt ricordare; ~**ion** [-'lɛkʃən] n ricordo.

recommend [rɛkə'mɛnd] vt raccomandare; (advise) consigliare; ~ation [-'deɪʃən] n raccomandazione f; consiglio.

recompense ['rɛkəmpɛns] vt ricompensare; (compensate) risarcire.

reconcile ['rɛkənsaɪl] vt (two people) riconciliare; (two facts) conciliare, quadrare; to ~ o.s. to rassegnarsi a; **reconciliation** [-sɪlɪ'eɪʃən] n riconciliazione f; conciliazione f.

recondition [ri:kən'dɪʃən] vt rimettere a nuovo; rifare.

reconnaissance [rɪ'kɔnɪsns] n (MIL) ricognizione f.

reconnoitre [rɛkə'nɔɪtə*] (MIL) vt fare una ricognizione di // vi fare una ricognizione.

reconsider [ri:kən'sɪdə*] vt riconsiderare.

reconstruct [ri:kən'strʌkt] vt ricostruire; ~ion [-kʃən] n ricostruzione f.

record n ['rɛkɔːd] ricordo, documento; (of meeting etc) nota, verbale m; (register) registro; (file) pratica, dossier m inv; (also: **police** ~) fedina penale sporca; (MUS: disc) disco; (SPORT) record m inv, primato // vt [rɪ'kɔːd] (set down) prendere nota di, registrare; (relate) raccontare; (MUS: song etc) registrare; **in** ~ **time** a tempo di record; **to keep a** ~ **of** tener nota di; **off the** ~ a ufficioso(a); ~ **card** n (in file) scheda; ~**er** n avvocato che funge da giudice; (MUS) flauto diritto; ~ **holder** n (SPORT) primatista m/f; ~**ing** n (MUS) registrazione f; ~ **library** n discoteca; ~ **player** n giradischi m inv.

recount [rɪ'kaunt] vt raccontare, narrare.

re-count ['ri:kaunt] n (POL: of votes) nuovo computo.

recoup [rɪ'ku:p] vt ricuperare.

recourse [rɪ'kɔːs] n ricorso; rimedio; **to have** ~ **to** ricorrere a.

recover [rɪ'kʌvə*] vt ricuperare // vi (from illness) rimettersi (in salute), ristabilirsi; (country, person: from shock) riprendersi.

re-cover [ri:'kʌvə*] vt (chair etc) ricoprire.

recovery [rɪ'kʌvərɪ] n ricupero; ristabilimento; ripresa.

recreate [ri:krɪ'eɪt] vt ricreare.

recreation [rɛkrɪ'eɪʃən] n ricreazione f; svago; ~**al** a ricreativo(a).

recrimination [rɪkrɪmɪ'neɪʃən] n recriminazione f.

recruit [rɪ'kru:t] n recluta // vt reclutare; ~**ment** n reclutamento.

rectangle ['rɛktæŋgl] n rettangolo; **rectangular** [-'tæŋgjulə*] a rettangolare.

rectify ['rɛktɪfaɪ] vt (error) rettificare; (omission) riparare.

rector ['rɛktə*] n (REL) parroco (anglicano); **rectory** n presbiterio.

recuperate [rɪ'kju:pəreɪt] vi ristabilirsi.

recur [rɪ'kə:*] vi riaccadere; (idea, opportunity) riapparire; (symptoms) ripresentarsi; ~**rence** n recrudescenza; riapparizione f; rinnovo; ~**rent** a

ricorrente, periodico(a); ~**ring** a (MATH) periodico(a).

red [rɛd] n rosso; (POL: pej) rosso/a // a rosso(a); **in the** ~ (account) scoperto; (business) in deficit; ~ **carpet treatment** n cerimonia col gran pavese; **R** ~ **Cross** n Croce f Rossa; ~**currant** n ribes m inv; ~**den** vt arrossare // vi arrossire; ~**dish** a rossiccio(a).

redeem [rɪ'di:m] vt (debt) riscattare; (sth in pawn) ritirare; (fig, also REL) redimere; ~**ing** a (feature) che salva.

redeploy [ri:dɪ'plɔɪ] vt (resources) riorganizzare.

red-haired [rɛd'hɛəd] a dai capelli rossi.

red-handed [rɛd'hændɪd] a: **to be caught** ~ essere preso(a) in flagrante or con le mani nel sacco.

redhead ['rɛdhɛd] n rosso/a.

red herring ['rɛd'hɛrɪŋ] n (fig) falsa pista.

red-hot [rɛd'hɔt] a arrovente.

redirect [ri:daɪ'rɛkt] vt (mail) far seguire.

redistribute [ri:dɪ'strɪbju:t] vt ridistribuire.

red light ['rɛd'laɪt] n: **to go through a** ~ (AUT) passare col rosso; **red-light district** n quartiere m luce rossa inv.

redness ['rɛdnɪs] n rossore m; (of hair) rosso.

redo [ri:'du:] vt irg rifare.

redolent ['rɛdəulnt] a: ~ **of** che sa di; (fig) che ricorda.

redouble [ri:'dʌbl] vt: **to** ~ **one's efforts** raddoppiare gli sforzi.

redress [rɪ'drɛs] n riparazione f.

red tape ['rɛd'teɪp] n (fig) burocrazia.

reduce [rɪ'dju:s] vt ridurre; (lower) ridurre, abbassare; **reduction** [rɪ'dʌkʃən] n riduzione f; (of price) ribasso; (discount) sconto.

redundancy [rɪ'dʌndənsɪ] n licenziamento.

redundant [rɪ'dʌndnt] a (worker) licenziato(a); (detail, object) superfluo(a); **to make** ~ licenziare.

reed [ri:d] n (BOT) canna; (MUS: of clarinet etc) ancia.

reef [ri:f] n (at sea) scogliera.

reek [ri:k] vi: **to** ~ (**of**) puzzare (di).

reel [ri:l] n bobina, rocchetto; (TECH) aspo; (FISHING) mulinello; (CINEMA) rotolo // vt (TECH) annaspare; (also: ~ **up**) avvolgere // vi (sway) barcollare.

re-election [ri:ɪ'lɛkʃən] n rielezione f.

ref [rɛf] n (col: abbr of referee) arbitro.

refectory [rɪ'fɛktərɪ] n refettorio.

refer [rɪ'fə:*] vt: **to** ~ **sb** (or **sth**) **to** (dispute, decision) deferire qc a; (inquirer: for information) indirizzare qd a; (reader: to text) rimandare qd a; **to** ~ **to** vt fus (allude to) accennare a; (apply to) riferire a; (consult) rivolgersi a; ~**ring to your letter** (COMM) in riferimento alla Vostra lettera.

referee [rɛfə'ri:] n arbitro; (for job application) referenza // vt arbitrare.

reference ['rɛfrəns] n riferimento;

(*mention*) menzione *f*, allusione *f*; (*for job application: letter*) referenza; lettera di raccomandazione; (: *person*) referenza; **with ~ to** a riguardo; (*COMM: in letter*) in *or* con riferimento a; **~ book** *n* libro di consultazione.

referendum, -da]-*n* referendum *m inv*. [refə'rendəm, -də]-*n* referendum *m inv*.

refill *vt* [riː'fɪl] riempire di nuovo; (*pen, lighter etc*) ricaricare // *n* ['riːfɪl] (*for pen etc*) ricambio.

refine [rɪ'faɪn] *vt* raffinare; **~d** *a* (*person, taste*) raffinato(a); **~ment** *n* (*of person*) raffinatezza; **~ry** *n* raffineria.

reflect [rɪ'flɛkt] *vt* (*light, image*) riflettere; (*fig*) rispecchiare // *vi* (*think*) riflettere, considerare; **to ~ on** *vt fus* (*discredit*) rispecchiarsi su; **~ion** [-'flɛkʃən] *n* riflessione *f*; (*image*) riflesso; (*criticism*): **~ion on** giudizio su; **on ~ion** pensandoci sopra; **~or** *n* (*also AUT*) catarifrangente *m*.

reflex ['riːflɛks] *a* riflesso(a) // *n* riflesso; **~ive** [rɪ'flɛksɪv] *a* (*LING*) riflessivo(a).

reform [rɪ'fɔːm] *n* riforma // *vt* riformare; **the R~ation** [refə'meɪʃən] *n* la Riforma; **~ed** *a* cambiato(a) (per il meglio); **~er** *n* riformatore/trice.

refrain [rɪ'freɪn] *vi*: **to ~ from doing** trattenersi dal fare // *n* ritornello.

refresh [rɪ'frɛʃ] *vt* rinfrescare; (*subj: food, sleep*) ristorare; **~er course** *n* corso di aggiornamento; **~ment room** *n* posto di ristoro; **~ments** *npl* rinfreschi *mpl*.

refrigeration [rifrɪdʒə'reɪʃən] *n* refrigerazione *f*.

refrigerator [rɪ'frɪdʒəreɪtə*] *n* frigorifero.

refuel [riː'fjuəl] *vt* rifornire (di carburante) // *vi* far rifornimento (di carburante).

refuge ['rɛfjuːdʒ] *n* rifugio; **to take ~ in** rifugiarsi in.

refugee [rɛfju'dʒiː] *n* rifugiato/a, profugo/a.

refund *n* ['riːfʌnd] rimborso // *vt* [rɪ'fʌnd] rimborsare.

refurbish [riː'fɔːbɪʃ] *vt* rimettere a nuovo.

refusal [rɪ'fjuːzəl] *n* rifiuto.

refuse *n* ['rɛfjuːs] rifiuti *mpl* // *vt, vi* [rɪ'fjuːz] rifiutare; **~ collector** *n* netturbino.

refute [rɪ'fjuːt] *vt* confutare.

regain [rɪ'geɪn] *vt* riguadagnare; riacquistare, ricuperare.

regal ['riːgl] *a* regio(a); **~ia** [rɪ'geɪlɪə] *n* insegne *fpl* regie.

regard [rɪ'gɑːd] *n* riguardo, stima // *vt* considerare, stimare; **to give one's ~s to** porgere i suoi saluti a; **~ing, as ~s, with ~ to** riguardo a; **~less** *ad* lo stesso; **~less of** a dispetto di, nonostante.

regatta [rɪ'gætə] *n* regata.

regency ['riːdʒənsɪ] *n* reggenza.

regent ['riːdʒənt] *n* reggente *m*.

régime [reɪ'ʒiːm] *n* regime *m*.

regiment ['rɛdʒɪmənt] *n* reggimento; **~al**

[-'mɛntl] *a* reggimentale; **~ation** [-'teɪʃən] *n* irreggimentazione *f*.

region ['riːdʒən] *n* regione *f*; **in the ~ of** (*fig*) all'incirca di; **~al** *a* regionale.

register ['rɛdʒɪstə*] *n* registro; (*also: electoral ~*) lista elettorale // *vt* registrare; (*vehicle*) immatricolare; (*luggage*) spedire assicurato(a); (*letter*) raccomandare; (*subj: instrument*) segnare // *vi* iscriversi; (*at hotel*) firmare il registro; (*make impression*) entrare in testa; **~ed** *a* (*design*) depositato(a); (*letter*) raccomandato(a).

registrar ['rɛdʒɪstrɑː*] *n* ufficiale *m* di stato civile; segretario.

registration [rɛdʒɪs'treɪʃən] *n* (*act*) registrazione *f*; iscrizione *f*; (*AUT: also: ~ number*) numero di targa.

registry ['rɛdʒɪstrɪ] *n* ufficio del registro; **~ office** *n* anagrafe *f*.

regret [rɪ'grɛt] *n* rimpianto, rincrescimento // *vt* rimpiangere; **I ~ that I/he cannot help** mi rincresce di non poter aiutare/che lui non possa aiutare; **~fully** *ad* con rincrescimento; **~table** *a* deplorevole.

regroup [riː'gruːp] *vt* raggruppare // *vi* raggrupparsi.

regular ['rɛgjulə*] *a* regolare; (*usual*) abituale, normale; (*soldier*) dell'esercito regolare; (*COMM: size*) normale // *n* (*client etc*) cliente *m/f* abituale; **~ity** [-'lærɪtɪ] *n* regolarità *f inv*; **~ly** *ad* regolarmente.

regulate ['rɛgjuleɪt] *vt* regolare; **regulation** [-'leɪʃən] *n* (*rule*) regola, regolamento; (*adjustment*) regolazione *f*.

rehabilitation ['riːhəbɪlɪ'teɪʃən] *n* (*of offender*) riabilitazione *f*; (*of disabled*) riadattamento.

rehash [riː'hæʃ] *vt* (*col*) rimaneggiare.

rehearsal [rɪ'həːsəl] *n* prova.

rehearse [rɪ'həːs] *vt* provare.

reign [reɪn] *n* regno // *vi* regnare; **~ing** *a* (*monarch*) regnante; (*champion*) attuale.

reimburse [riːɪm'bəːs] *vt* rimborsare.

rein [reɪn] *n* (*for horse*) briglia.

reincarnation [riːɪnkɑː'neɪʃən] *n* reincarnazione *f*.

reindeer ['reɪndɪə*] *n, pl inv* renna.

reinforce [riːɪn'fɔːs] *vt* rinforzare; **~d concrete** *n* cemento armato; **~ment** *n* (*action*) rinforzamento; **~ments** *npl* (*MIL*) rinforzi *mpl*.

reinstate [riːɪn'steɪt] *vt* reintegrare.

reissue [riː'ɪʃuː] *vt* (*book*) ristampare, ripubblicare; (*film*) distribuire di nuovo.

reiterate [riː'ɪtəreɪt] *vt* reiterare, ripetere.

reject *n* ['riːdʒɛkt] (*COMM*) scarto // *vt* [rɪ'dʒɛkt] rifiutare, respingere; (*COMM: goods*) scartare; **~ion** [rɪ'dʒɛkʃən] *n* rifiuto.

rejoice [rɪ'dʒɔɪs] *vi*: **to ~** (**at** *or* **over**) provare diletto in.

rejuvenate [rɪ'dʒuːvəneɪt] *vt* ringiovanire.

rekindle [riː'kɪndl] *vt* riaccendere.

relapse [rɪ'læps] *n* (*MED*) ricaduta.

relate [rɪ'leɪt] *vt* (*tell*) raccontare; (*connect*) collegare; **~d** *a* imparentato(a);

collegato(a), connesso(a); ~**d to** imparentato(a) con; collegato(a) or connesso(a) con; **relating**: **relating to** prep che riguarda, rispetto a.

relation [rı'leıʃən] n (person) parente m/f; (link) rapporto, relazione f; ~**ship** n rapporto; (personal ties) rapporti mpl, relazioni fpl.

relative ['relətıv] n parente m/f // a relativo(a); (respective) rispettivo(a); ~**ly** ad relativamente.

relax [rı'læks] vi rilasciarsi; (person: unwind) rilassarsi // vt rilasciare; (mind, person) rilassare; ~**ation** [ri:læk'seıʃən] n rilasciamento; rilassamento; (entertainment) ricreazione f, svago; ~**ed** a rilasciato(a); rilassato(a); ~**ing** a rilassante.

relay ['ri:leı] n (SPORT) corsa a staffetta // vt (message) trasmettere.

release [rı'li:s] n (from prison) rilascio; (from obligation) liberazione f; (of gas etc) emissione f; (of film etc) distribuzione f; (record) disco; (device) disinnesto // vt (prisoner) rilasciare; (from obligation, wreckage etc) liberare; (book, film) fare uscire; (news) rendere pubblico(a); (gas etc) emettere; (TECH: catch, spring etc) disinnestare; (let go) rilasciare; lasciar andare; sciogliere; **to** ~ **one's grip** mollare la presa; **to** ~ **the clutch** (AUT) staccare la frizione.

relegate ['relɔgeıt] vt relegare.

relent [rı'lent] vi cedere; ~**less** a implacabile.

relevance ['relɔvəns] n pertinenza; ~ **of sth to sth** rapporto tra qc e qc.

relevant ['relɔvənt] a pertinente; (chapter) in questione; ~ **to** pertinente a.

reliability [rılaıɔ'bılıtı] n fidabilità; affidabilità.

reliable [rı'laıɔbl] a (person, firm) fidato(a), che dà affidamento; (method) sicuro(a); (machine) affidabile; **reliably** ad: **to be reliably informed** sapere da fonti sicure.

reliance [rı'laıɔns] n: ~ (**on**) fiducia (in); bisogno (di).

relic ['relık] n (REL) reliquia; (of the past) resto.

relief [rı'li:f] n (from pain, anxiety) sollievo; (help, supplies) soccorsi mpl; (of guard) cambio; (ART, GEO) rilievo.

relieve [rı'li:v] vt (pain, patient) sollevare; (bring help) soccorrere; (take over from: gen) sostituire; (: guard) rilevare; **to** ~ **sb of sth** alleggerire qd di qc.

religion [rı'lıdʒən] n religione f; **religious** a religioso(a).

relinquish [rı'lıŋkwıʃ] vt abbandonare; (plan, habit) rinunziare a.

relish ['relıʃ] n (CULIN) condimento; (enjoyment) gran piacere m // vt (food etc) godere; **to** ~ **doing** adorare fare.

relive [ri:'lıv] vt rivivere.

reload [ri:'lɔud] vt ricaricare.

reluctance [rı'lʌktəns] n riluttanza.

reluctant [rı'lʌktənt] a riluttante, mal

disposto(a); ~**ly** ad di mala voglia, a malincuore.

rely [rı'laı]: **to** ~ **on** vt fus contare su; (be dependent) dipendere da.

remain [rı'meın] vi restare, rimanere; ~**der** n resto; (COMM) rimanenza; ~**ing** a che rimane; ~**s** npl resti mpl.

remand [rı'mɑ:nd] n: **on** ~ in detenzione preventiva // vt: **to** ~ **in custody** rinviare in carcere; trattenere a disposizione della legge.

remark [rı'mɑ:k] n osservazione f // vt osservare, dire; (notice) notare; ~**able** a notevole; eccezionale.

remedial [rı'mi:dıəl] a (tuition, classes) di riparazione.

remedy ['remɔdı] n: ~ (**for**) rimedio (per) // vt rimediare a.

remember [rı'membɔ*] vt ricordare, ricordarsi di; ~ **me to** (in letter) ricordami a; **remembrance** n memoria; ricordo.

remind [rı'maınd] vt: **to** ~ **sb of sth** ricordare qc a qd; **to** ~ **sb to do** ricordare a qd di fare; ~**er** n richiamo; (note etc) promemoria m inv.

reminisce [remı'nıs] vi: **to** ~ (**about**) abbandonarsi ai ricordi (di).

reminiscences [remı'nısnsız] npl reminiscenze fpl, memorie fpl.

reminiscent [remı'nısnt] a: ~ **of** che fa pensare a, che richiama.

remission [rı'mıʃən] n remissione f; (of fee) esonero.

remit [rı'mıt] vt (send: money) rimettere; ~**tance** n rimessa.

remnant ['remnɔnt] n resto, avanzo; ~**s** npl (COMM) scampoli mpl; fine f serie.

remorse [rı'mɔ:s] n rimorso; ~**ful** a pieno(a) di rimorsi; ~**less** a (fig) spietato(a).

remote [rı'mɔut] a remoto(a), lontano(a); (person) distaccato(a); ~ **control** n telecomando; ~**ly** ad remotamente; (slightly) vagamente; ~**ness** n lontananza.

remould ['ri:mɔuld] n (tyre) gomma rivestita.

removable [rı'mu:vɔbl] a (detachable) staccabile.

removal [rı'mu:vɔl] n (taking away) rimozione f; soppressione f; (from house) trasloco; (from office: sacking) destituzione f; (MED) ablazione f; ~ **van** n furgone m per traslochi.

remove [rı'mu:v] vt togliere, rimuovere; (employee) destituire; (stain) far sparire; (doubt, abuse) sopprimere, eliminare.

remuneration [rımju:nɔ'reıʃən] n rimunerazione f.

rend, pt, pp **rent** [rend, rent] vt lacerare.

render ['rendɔ*] vt rendere; (CULIN: fat) struggere; ~**ing** n (MUS etc) interpretazione f.

rendez-vous ['rɔndıvu:] n appuntamento; (place) luogo d'incontro; (meeting) incontro.

renegade ['renıgeıd] n rinnegato/a.

renew [rɪ'nju:] vt rinnovare; (*negotiations*) riprendere; ~**al** n rinnovamento; ripresa.

renounce [rɪ'nauns] vt rinunziare a; (*disown*) ripudiare.

renovate ['rɛnɔveɪt] vt rinnovare; (*art work*) restaurare; **renovation** [-'veɪʃən] n rinnovamento; restauro.

renown [rɪ'naun] n rinomanza; ~**ed** a rinomato(a).

rent [rɛnt] pt, pp of **rend** // n affitto // vt (*take for rent*) prendere in affitto; (*also*: ~ **out**) dare in affitto; ~**al** n (*for television, car*) fitto.

renunciation [rɪnʌnsɪ'eɪʃən] n rinnegamento; (*self-denial*) rinunzia.

reopen [ri:'əupən] vt riaprire; ~**ing** n riapertura.

reorder [ri:'ɔ:də*] vt ordinare di nuovo; (*rearrange*) riorganizzare.

reorganize [ri:'ɔ:gənaɪz] vt riorganizzare.

rep [rɛp] n (*COMM: abbr of* **representative**) rappresentante m/f; (*THEATRE: abbr of* **repertory**) teatro di repertorio.

repair [rɪ'pɛə*] n riparazione f // vt riparare; **in good/bad** ~ **in** buona/cattiva condizione; ~ **kit** n corredo per riparazioni; ~ **shop** n (*AUT etc*) officina.

repartee [rɛpɑ:'ti:] n risposta pronta.

repay [ri:'peɪ] vt irg (*money, creditor*) rimborsare, ripagare; (*sb's efforts*) ricompensare; ~**ment** n rimborsamento; ricompensa.

repeal [rɪ'pi:l] n (*of law*) abrogazione f; (*of sentence*) annullamento // vt abrogare; annullare.

repeat [rɪ'pi:t] n (*RADIO, TV*) replica // vt ripetere; (*pattern*) riprodurre; (*promise, attack, also COMM: order*) rinnovare; ~**edly** ad ripetutamente, spesso.

repel [rɪ'pɛl] vt respingere; ~**lent** a repellente // n: **insect** ~**lent** prodotto m anti-insetti inv.

repent [rɪ'pɛnt] vi: **to** ~ (**of**) pentirsi (di); ~**ance** n pentimento.

repercussion [ri:pə'kʌʃən] n (*consequence*) ripercussione f.

repertoire ['rɛpətwɑ:*] n repertorio.

repertory ['rɛpətərɪ] n (*also*: ~ **theatre**) teatro di repertorio.

repetition [rɛpɪ'tɪʃən] n ripetizione f; (*COMM: order etc*) rinnovo.

repetitive [rɪ'pɛtɪtɪv] a (*movement*) che si ripete; (*work*) monotono(a); (*speech*) pieno(a) di ripetizioni.

replace [rɪ'pleɪs] vt (*put back*) rimettere a posto; (*take the place of*) sostituire; (*TEL*): '~ **the receiver**' 'riattaccare'; ~**ment** n rimessa; sostituzione f; (*person*) sostituto/a; ~**ment part** n pezzo di ricambio.

replenish [rɪ'plɛnɪʃ] vt (*glass*) riempire; (*stock etc*) rifornire.

replete [rɪ'pli:t] a ripieno(a); (*well-fed*) sazio(a).

replica ['rɛplɪkə] n replica, copia.

reply [rɪ'plaɪ] n risposta // vi rispondere.

report [rɪ'pɔ:t] n rapporto; (*PRESS etc*)

cronaca; (*also*: **school** ~) pagella // vt riportare; (*PRESS etc*) fare una cronaca su; (*bring to notice: occurrence*) segnalare; (: *person*) denunciare // vi (*make a report*) fare un rapporto (*or* una cronaca); (*present o.s.*): **to** ~ (**to sb**) presentarsi (a qd); **it is** ~**ed that** si dice che; ~**ed speech** n (*LING*) discorso indiretto; ~**er** n reporter m inv.

reprehensible [rɛprɪ'hɛnsɪbl] a riprensibile.

represent [rɛprɪ'zɛnt] vt rappresentare; ~**ation** [-'teɪʃən] n rappresentazione f; ~**ations** npl (*protest*) protesta; ~**ative** n rappresentativo/a; (*US: POL*) deputato/a // a rappresentativo(a), caratteristico(a).

repress [rɪ'prɛs] vt reprimere; ~**ion** [-'prɛʃən] repressione f; ~**ive** a repressivo(a).

reprieve [rɪ'pri:v] n (*LAW*) sospensione f dell'esecuzione della condanna; (*fig*) dilazione f // vt sospendere l'esecuzione della condanna a; accordare una dilazione a.

reprimand ['rɛprɪmɑ:nd] n rampogna // vt rampognare.

reprisal [rɪ'praɪzl] n rappresaglia.

reproach [rɪ'prəutʃ] n rimprovero // vt: **to** ~ **sb with sth** rimproverare qd di qc; **beyond** ~ irreprensibile; ~**ful** a di rimprovero.

reproduce [ri:prə'dju:s] vt riprodurre // vi riprodursi; **reproduction** [-'dʌkʃən] n riproduzione f; **reproductive** [-'dʌktɪv] a riproduttore(trice); riproduttivo(a).

reprove [rɪ'pru:v] vt (*action*) disapprovare; (*person*): **to** ~ (**for**) biasimare (per); **reproving** a di disapprovazione.

reptile ['rɛptaɪl] n rettile m.

republic [rɪ'pʌblɪk] n repubblica; ~**an** a,n repubblicano(a).

repudiate [rɪ'pju:dɪeɪt] vt ripudiare.

repugnant [rɪ'pʌgnənt] a ripugnante.

repulse [rɪ'pʌls] vt respingere.

repulsion [rɪ'pʌlʃən] n ripulsione f.

repulsive [rɪ'pʌlsɪv] a ripugnante, ripulsivo(a).

reputable ['rɛpjutəbl] a di buona reputazione; (*occupation*) rispettabile.

reputation [rɛpju'teɪʃən] n reputazione f.

repute [rɪ'pju:t] n reputazione f; ~**d** a reputato(a); ~**dly** ad secondo che si dice.

request [rɪ'kwɛst] n domanda; (*formal*) richiesta // vt: **to** ~ (**of** or **from sb**) chiedere a (qd).

requiem ['rɛkwɪəm] n requiem m or f inv.

require [rɪ'kwaɪə*] vt (*need: subj: person*) aver bisogno di; (: *thing, situation*) richiedere; (*want*) volere; esigere; (*order*) obbligare; ~**d** a richiesto(a); **if** ~**d in** caso di bisogno; ~**ment** n esigenza; bisogno; requisito.

requisite ['rɛkwɪzɪt] n cosa necessaria // a necessario(a); **toilet** ~**s** articoli mpl da toletta.

requisition [rɛkwɪ'zɪʃən] n: ~ (**for**) richiesta (di) // vt (*MIL*) requisire.

rescind [rɪ'sɪnd] vt annullare; (law) abrogare; (judgment) rescindere.

rescue ['rɛskju:] n salvataggio; (help) soccorso // vt salvare; ~ **party** n squadra di salvataggio; ~**r** n salvatore/trice.

research [rɪ'sə:tʃ] n ricerca, ricerche fpl // vt fare ricerche su; ~**er** n ricercatore/trice; ~ **work** n ricerche fpl.

resemblance [rɪ'zɛmbləns] n somiglianza.

resemble [rɪ'zɛmbl] vt assomigliare a.

resent [rɪ'zɛnt] vt risentirsi di; ~**ful** a pieno(a) di risentimento; ~**ment** n risentimento.

reservation [rɛzə'veɪʃən] n (booking) prenotazione f; (doubt) dubbio; (protected area) riserva; (on road: also: **central** ~) spartitraffico m inv; **to make a** ~ (**in an hotel/a restaurant/on a plane**) prenotare una camera/una tavola/un posto.

reserve [rɪ'zə:v] n riserva // vt (seats etc) prenotare; ~**s** npl (MIL) riserve fpl; **in** ~ in serbo; ~**d** a (shy) riservato(a); (seat) prenotato(a).

reservoir ['rɛzəvwa:*] n serbatoio.

reshape [ri:'ʃeɪp] vt (policy) ristrutturare.

reshuffle [ri:'ʃʌfl] n: **Cabinet** ~ (POL) rimpasto governativo.

reside [rɪ'zaɪd] vi risiedere.

residence ['rɛzɪdəns] n residenza; ~ **permit** n permesso di soggiorno.

resident ['rɛzɪdənt] n residente m/f; (in hotel) cliente m/f fisso(a) // a residente.

residential [rɛzɪ'dɛnʃl] a di residenza; (area) residenziale.

residue ['rɛzɪdju:] n resto; (CHEM, PHYSICS) residuo.

resign [rɪ'zaɪn] vt (one's post) dimettersi da // vi dimettersi; **to** ~ **o.s. to** rassegnarsi a; ~**ation** [rɛzɪg'neɪʃən] n dimissioni fpl; rassegnazione f; ~**ed** a rassegnato(a).

resilience [rɪ'zɪlɪəns] n (of material) elasticità, resilienza; (of person) capacità di recupero.

resilient [rɪ'zɪlɪənt] a (person) che si riprende facilmente.

resin ['rɛzɪn] n resina.

resist [rɪ'zɪst] vt resistere a; ~**ance** n resistenza.

resolute ['rɛzəlu:t] a risoluto(a).

resolution [rɛzə'lu:ʃən] n risoluzione f.

resolve [rɪ'zɒlv] n risoluzione f // vt (decide): **to** ~ **to do** decidere di fare; ~**d** a risoluto(a).

resonant ['rɛzənənt] a risonante.

resort [rɪ'zɔ:t] n (town) stazione f; (recourse) ricorso // vi: **to** ~ **to** aver ricorso a; **as a last** ~ come ultimo ricorso.

resound [rɪ'zaund] vi: **to** ~ (**with**) risonare (di); ~**ing** a risonante.

resource [rɪ'sɔ:s] n risorsa; ~**s** npl risorse fpl; ~**ful** a pieno(a) di risorse, intraprendente.

respect [rɪs'pɛkt] n rispetto // vt rispettare; **with** ~ **to** rispetto a, riguardo a; **in this** ~ per questo riguardo;

~**ability** [-ə'bɪlɪtɪ] n rispettabilità; ~**able** a rispettabile; ~**ful** a rispettoso(a).

respective [rɪs'pɛktɪv] a rispettivo(a); ~**ly** ad rispettivamente.

respiration [rɛspɪ'reɪʃən] n respirazione f.

respite ['rɛspaɪt] n respiro, tregua.

resplendent [rɪs'plɛndənt] a risplendente.

respond [rɪs'pɒnd] vi rispondere.

response [rɪs'pɒns] n risposta.

responsibility [rɪspɒnsɪ'bɪlɪtɪ] n responsabilità f inv.

responsible [rɪs'pɒnsɪbl] a (liable): ~ (**for**) responsabile (di); (trustworthy) fidato(a); (job) di (grande) responsabilità; **responsibly** ad responsabilmente.

responsive [rɪs'pɒnsɪv] a che reagisce.

rest [rɛst] n riposo; (stop) sosta, pausa; (MUS) pausa; (support) appoggio, sostegno; (remainder) resto, avanzi mpl // vi riposarsi; (be supported): **to** ~ **on** appoggiarsi su; (remain) rimanere, restare // vt (lean): **to** ~ **sth on/against** appoggiare qc su/contro; **the** ~ **of them** gli altri; **it** ~**s with him to decide** sta a lui decidere.

restart [ri:'sta:t] vt (engine) rimettere in marcia; (work) ricominciare.

restaurant ['rɛstərɒŋ] n ristorante m; ~ **car** n vagone m ristorante.

restful ['rɛstful] a riposante.

rest home ['rɛsthəum] n casa di riposo.

restitution [rɛstɪ'tju:ʃən] n (act) restituzione f; (reparation) riparazione f.

restive ['rɛstɪv] a agitato(a), impaziente; (horse) restio(a).

restless ['rɛstlɪs] a agitato(a), irrequieto(a).

restock [ri:'stɒk] vt rifornire.

restoration [rɛstə'reɪʃən] n restauro; restituzione f.

restore [rɪs'stɔ:*] vt (building) restaurare; (sth stolen) restituire; (peace, health) ristorare.

restrain [rɪs'treɪn] vt (feeling) contenere, frenare; (person): **to** ~ (**from doing**) trattenere (dal fare); ~**ed** a (style) contenuto(a), sobrio(a); (manner) riservato(a); ~**t** n (restriction) limitazione f; (moderation) ritegno.

restrict [rɪs'trɪkt] vt restringere, limitare; ~**ed area** n (AUT) zona a velocità limitata; ~**ion** [-kʃən] n restrizione f, limitazione f; ~**ive** a restrittivo(a).

rest room ['rɛstrum] n (US) toletta.

result [rɪ'zʌlt] n risultato // vi: **to** ~ **in** avere per risultato.

resume [rɪ'zju:m] vt, vi (work, journey) riprendere.

resumption [rɪ'zʌmpʃən] n ripresa.

resurgence [rɪ'sə:dʒəns] n rinascita.

resurrection [rɛzə'rɛkʃən] n risurrezione f.

resuscitate [rɪ'sʌsɪteɪt] vt (MED) risuscitare; **resuscitation** [-'teɪʃən] n rianimazione f.

retail ['ri:teɪl] n (vendita al) minuto // cpd al minuto // vt vendere al minuto; ~**er** n commerciante m/f al minuto, dettagliante *m*; ~ **price** *n* prezzo al minuto.

retain [rɪ'teɪn] *vt* (*keep*) tenere, serbare; ~**er** *n* (*servant*) servitore *m*; (*fee*) onorario.

retaliate [rɪ'tælɪeɪt] *vi*: **to ~ (against)** vendicarsi (di); **retaliation** [-'eɪʃən] *n* vendetta, rappresaglie *fpl*.

retarded [rɪ'tɑːdɪd] *a* ritardato(a); (*also: mentally ~*) ritardato(a) (di mente).

retch [retʃ] *vi* aver conati di vomito.

rethink ['riː'θɪŋk] *vt* ripensare.

reticence ['retɪsns] *n* reticenza.

reticent ['retɪsnt] *a* reticente.

retina ['retɪnə] *n* retina.

retinue ['retɪnjuː] *n* seguito, scorta.

retire [rɪ'taɪə*] *vi* (*give up work*) andare in pensione; (*withdraw*) ritirarsi, andarsene; (*go to bed*) andare a letto, ritirarsi; ~**d** *a* (*person*) pensionato(a); ~**ment** *n* pensione *f*; **retiring** *a* (*person*) riservato(a).

retort [rɪ'tɔːt] *n* (*reply*) rimbecco; (*container*) storta // *vi* rimbeccare.

retrace [riː'treɪs] *vt* ricostruire; **to ~ one's steps** tornare sui passi.

retract [rɪ'trækt] *vt* (*statement*) ritrattare; (*claws, undercarriage, aerial*) ritrarre, ritirare // *vi* ritrarsi; ~**able** *a* retrattile.

retrain [riː'treɪn] *vt* (*worker*) riaddestrare; ~**ing** *n* riaddestramento.

retreat [rɪ'triːt] *n* ritirata; (*place*) rifugio // *vi* battere in ritirata; (*flood*) ritirarsi.

retrial [riː'traɪəl] *n* nuovo processo.

retribution [retrɪ'bjuːʃən] *n* castigo.

retrieval [rɪ'triːvəl] *n* ricupero, riparazione *f*.

retrieve [rɪ'triːv] *vt* (*sth lost*) ricuperare, ritrovare; (*situation, honour*) salvare; (*error, loss*) riparare; (*COMPUTERS*) ricuperare; ~**r** *n* cane *m* da riporto.

retrospect ['retrəspekt] *n*: **in ~** guardando indietro; ~**ive** [-'spektɪv] *a* retrospettivo(a); (*law*) retroattivo(a).

return [rɪ'tɜːn] *n* (*going or coming back*) ritorno; (*of sth stolen etc*) restituzione *f*; (*recompense*) ricompensa; (*FINANCE: from land, shares*) profitto, reddito; (*report*) rapporto // *cpd* (*journey, match*) di ritorno; (*ticket*) di andata e ritorno // *vi* tornare, ritornare // *vt* rendere, restituire; (*bring back*) riportare; (*send back*) mandare indietro; (*put back*) rimettere; (*POL: candidate*) eleggere; ~**s** *npl* (*COMM*) incassi *mpl*; profitti *mpl*; **many happy ~s (of the day)!** auguri!, buon compleanno!

reunion [riː'juːnɪən] *n* riunione *f*.

reunite [riːjuː'naɪt] *vt* riunire.

rev [rev] *n* (*abbr of* **revolution**: *AUT*) giro // *vb* (*also: ~ up*) *vt* imballare // *vi* imballarsi.

revamp ['riː'væmp] *vt* rinnovare; riorganizzare.

reveal [rɪ'viːl] *vt* (*make known*) rivelare, svelare; (*display*) rivelare, mostrare; ~**ing** *a* rivelatore(trice); (*dress*) scollato(a).

reveille [rɪ'vælɪ] *n* (*MIL*) sveglia.

revel ['revl] *vi*: **to ~ in sth/in doing** dilettarsi di qc/a fare.

revelation [revə'leɪʃən] *n* rivelazione *f*.

reveller ['revlə*] *n* crapulone/a, festaiolo/a.

revelry ['revlrɪ] *n* crapula, baldoria.

revenge [rɪ'vendʒ] *n* vendetta; (*in game etc*) rivincita // *vt* vendicare; **to take ~** vendicarsi; ~**ful** *a* vendicatore(trice); vendicativo(a).

revenue ['revənjuː] *n* reddito.

reverberate [rɪ'vɜːbəreɪt] *vi* (*sound*) rimbombare; (*light*) riverberarsi; **reverberation** [-'reɪʃən] *n* (*of light, sound*) riverberazione *f*.

reverence ['revərəns] *n* venerazione *f*, riverenza.

reverent ['revərənt] *a* riverente.

reverie ['revərɪ] *n* fantasticheria.

reversal [rɪ'vɜːsl] *n* capovolgimento.

reverse [rɪ'vɜːs] *n* contrario, opposto; (*back*) rovescio; (*AUT: also: ~ gear*) marcia indietro // *a* (*order, direction*) contrario(a), opposto(a) // *vt* (*turn*) invertire, rivoltare; (*change*) capovolgere, rovesciare; (*LAW: judgment*) cassare // *vi* (*AUT*) fare marcia indietro; ~**d charge call** *n* (*TEL*) telefonata con addebito al ricevente.

reversion [rɪ'vɜːʃən] *n* ritorno.

revert [rɪ'vɜːt] *vi*: **to ~ to** tornare a.

review [rɪ'vjuː] *n* rivista; (*of book, film*) recensione *f* // *vt* passare in rivista; fare la recensione di; ~**er** *n* recensore/a.

revise [rɪ'vaɪz] *vt* (*manuscript*) rivedere, correggere; (*opinion*) emendare, modificare; (*study: subject, notes*) ripassare; **revision** [rɪ'vɪʒən] *n* revisione *f*; ripasso.

revitalize [riː'vaɪtəlaɪz] *vt* ravvivare.

revival [rɪ'vaɪvl] *n* ripresa; ristabilimento; (*of faith*) risveglio.

revive [rɪ'vaɪv] *vt* (*person*) rianimare; (*custom*) far rivivere; (*hope, courage*) ravvivare; (*play, fashion*) riesumare // *vi* (*person*) rianimarsi; (*hope*) ravvivarsi; (*activity*) riprendersi.

revoke [rɪ'vəuk] *vt* revocare; (*promise, decision*) rinveire su.

revolt [rɪ'vəult] *n* rivolta, ribellione *f* // *vi* rivoltarsi, ribellarsi; ~**ing** *a* ripugnante.

revolution [revə'luːʃən] *n* rivoluzione *f*; (*of wheel etc*) rivoluzione, giro; ~**ary** *a, n* rivoluzionario(a); ~**ize** *vt* rivoluzionare.

revolve [rɪ'vɔlv] *vi* girare.

revolver [rɪ'vɔlvə*] *n* rivoltella.

revolving [rɪ'vɔlvɪŋ] *a* girevole.

revue [rɪ'vjuː] *n* (*THEATRE*) rivista.

revulsion [rɪ'vʌlʃən] *n* ripugnanza.

reward [rɪ'wɔːd] *n* ricompensa, premio // *vt*: **to ~ (for)** ricompensare (per); ~**ing** *a* (*fig*) soddisfacente.

rewind [riː'waɪnd] *vt irg* (*watch*) ricaricare; (*ribbon etc*) riavvolgere.

rewire [riː'waɪə*] *vt* (*house*) rifare l'impianto elettrico di.

reword [ri:'wə:d] *vt* formulare *or* esprimere con altre parole.

rewrite [ri:'rait] *vt irg* riscrivere.

rhapsody ['ræpsədi] *n* (*MUS*) rapsodia; (*fig*) elogio stravagante.

rhetoric ['retərik] *n* retorica; ~al [ri'tɔrikl] *a* retorico(a).

rheumatic [ru:'mætik] *a* reumatico(a).

rheumatism ['ru:mətizəm] *n* reumatismo.

Rhine [rain] *n*: the ~ il Reno.

rhinoceros [rai'nɔsərəs] *n* rinoceronte *m*.

rhododendron [rəudə'dendrn] *n* rododendro.

Rhone [rəun] *n*: the ~ il Rodano.

rhubarb ['ru:bɑ:b] *n* rabarbaro.

rhyme [raim] *n* rima; (*verse*) poesia.

rhythm ['riðm] *n* ritmo; ~ic(al) *a* ritmico(a); ~ically *ad* con ritmo.

rib [rib] *n* (*ANAT*) costola // *vt* (*tease*) punzecchiare.

ribald ['ribəld] *a* licenzioso(a), volgare.

ribbed [ribd] *a* (*knitting*) a coste.

ribbon ['ribən] *n* nastro; **in** ~**s** (*torn*) a brandelli.

rice [rais] *n* riso; ~**field** *n* risaia; ~ **pudding** *n* budino di riso.

rich [ritʃ] *a* ricco(a); (*clothes*) sontuoso(a); **the** ~ i ricchi; ~**es** *npl* ricchezze *fpl*; ~**ness** *n* ricchezza.

rickets ['rikits] *n* rachitismo.

rickety ['rikiti] *a* zoppicante.

rickshaw ['rikʃɔ:] *n* risciò *m inv*.

ricochet ['rikəʃei] *n* rimbalzo // *vi* rimbalzare.

rid, *pt*, *pp* **rid** [rid] *vt*: **to** ~ **sb of** sbarazzare *or* liberare qd di; **to get** ~ **of** sbarazzarsi di; **good riddance!** che liberazione!

ridden ['ridn] *pp of* **ride.**

riddle ['ridl] *n* (*puzzle*) indovinello // *vt*: **to be** ~**d with** essere crivellato(a) di.

ride [raid] *n* (*on horse*) cavalcata; (*outing*) passeggiata; (*distance covered*) cavalcata; corsa // *vi* (*pt* **rode**, *pp* **ridden** [rəud, 'ridn]) *vi* (*as sport*) cavalcare; (*go somewhere*: *on horse, bicycle*) andare (a cavallo *or* in bicicletta *etc*); (*journey*: *on bicycle, motor cycle, bus*) andare, viaggiare // *vt* (*a horse*) montare, cavalcare; **we rode all day** abbiamo cavalcato tutto il giorno; **to** ~ **a horse/bicycle/camel** montare a cavallo/in bicicletta/in groppa a un cammello; **to** ~ **at anchor** (*NAUT*) essere alla fonda; **horse** ~ cavalcata; **car** ~ passeggiata in macchina; **to take sb for a** ~ (*fig*) prendere in giro qd; fregare qd; ~**r** *n* cavalcatore/trice; (*in race*) fantino; (*on bicycle*) ciclista *m/f*; (*on motorcycle*) motociclista *m/f*; (*in document*) clausola addizionale, aggiunta.

ridge [ridʒ] *n* (*of hill*) cresta; (*of roof*) colmo; (*of mountain*) giogo; (*on object*) riga (in rilievo).

ridicule ['ridikju:l] *n* ridicolo; scherno // *vt* mettere in ridicolo.

ridiculous [ri'dikjuləs] *a* ridicolo(a).

riding ['raidin] *n* equitazione *f*; ~ **school** *n* scuola d'equitazione.

rife [raif] *a* diffuso(a); **to be** ~ **with** abbondare di.

riffraff ['rifræf] *n* canaglia.

rifle ['raifl] *n* carabina // *vt* vuotare; ~ **range** *n* campo di tiro; (*indoor*) tiro al bersaglio.

rift [rift] *n* fessura, crepatura; (*fig: disagreement*) incrinatura, disaccordo.

rig [rig] *n* (*also*: **oil** ~: *on land*) derrick *m inv*; (: *at sea*) piattaforma per trivellazioni subacquee // *vt* (*election etc*) truccare; **to** ~ **out** *vt* attrezzare; (*pej*) abbigliare, agghindare; **to** ~ **up** *vt* allestire; ~**ging** *n* (*NAUT*) attrezzatura.

right [rait] *a* giusto(a); (*suitable*) appropriato(a); (*not left*) destro(a) // *n* (*title, claim*) diritto; (*not left*) destra // *ad* (*answer*) correttamente; (*not on the left*) a destra // *vt* raddrizzare; (*fig*) riparare // *excl* bene!; **to be** ~ (*person*) aver ragione; (*answer*) essere giusto(a) *or* corretto(a); ~ **now** proprio adesso; subito; ~ **against the wall** proprio contro il muro; ~ **ahead** sempre diritto; proprio davanti; ~ **in the middle** proprio nel mezzo; ~ **away** subito; **by** ~**s** di diritto; **on the** ~ a destra; ~ **angle** *n* angolo retto; ~**eous** ['raitʃəs] *a* retto(a), virtuoso(a); (*anger*) giusto(a), giustificato(a); ~**eousness** ['raitʃəsnis] *n* rettitudine *f*, virtù *f*; ~**ful** *a* (*heir*) legittimo(a); ~**handed** (*person*) che adopera la mano destra; ~**hand man** *n* braccio destro; **the** ~**hand side** il lato destro; ~**ly** *ad* bene, correttamente; (*with reason*) a ragione; ~**minded** *a* sensato(a); ~ **of way** *n* diritto di passaggio; (*AUT*) precedenza; ~**wing** *n* (*MIL, SPORT*) ala destra; (*POL*) destra; ~**wing** *a* (*POL*) di destra.

rigid ['ridʒid] *a* rigido(a); (*principle*) rigoroso(a); ~**ity** [ri'dʒiditi] *n* rigidità; ~**ly** *ad* rigidamente.

rigmarole ['rigmərəul] *n* tiritera; commedia.

rigorous ['rigərəs] *a* rigoroso(a).

rigour ['rigə*] *n* rigore *m*.

rim [rim] *n* orlo; (*of spectacles*) montatura; (*of wheel*) cerchione *m*; ~**less** *a* (*spectacles*) senza montatura; ~**med** *a* bordato(a); cerchiato(a).

rind [raind] *n* (*of bacon*) cotenna; (*of lemon etc*) scorza.

ring [riŋ] *n* anello; (*also*: **wedding** ~) fede *f*; (*of people, objects*) cerchio; (*of spies*) giro; (*of smoke etc*) spirale *m*; (*arena*) pista, arena; (*for boxing*) ring *m inv*; (*sound of bell*) scampanio; (*telephone call*) colpo di telefono // *vb* (*pt* **rang**, *pp* **rung** [ræŋ, rʌŋ]) *vi* (*person, bell, telephone*) suonare; (*also*: ~ **out**: *voice, words*) risuonare; (*TEL*) telefonare // *vt* (*TEL*: *also*: ~ **up**) telefonare a; **to** ~ **the bell** suonare; **to** ~ **back** *vt*, *vi* (*TEL*) richiamare; **to** ~ **off** *vi* (*TEL*) mettere giù, riattaccare; ~**leader** *n* (*of gang*) capobanda *m*.

ringlets ['riŋlits] *npl* boccoli *mpl*.

ring road ['rɪŋrəud] n raccordo anulare.

rink [rɪŋk] n (also: **ice ~**) pista di pattinaggio.

rinse [rɪns] n risciacquatura; (hair tint) colorito // vt sciacquare; darsi il colorito a.

riot ['raɪət] n sommossa, tumulto // vi tumultuare; **a ~ of colours** un'orgia di colori; **to run ~** creare disordine; **~ous** a tumultuoso(a); che fa crepare dal ridere; **~ously funny** che fa crepare dal ridere.

rip [rɪp] n strappo // vt strappare // vi strapparsi; **~cord** n cavo di sfilamento.

ripe [raɪp] a (fruit) maturo(a); (cheese) stagionato(a); **~n** vt maturare // vi maturarsi; stagionarsi; **~ness** n maturità.

ripple ['rɪpl] n increspamento, ondulazione f; mormorio // vi incresparsi.

rise [raɪz] n (slope) salita, pendio; (hill) altura; (increase: in wages) aumento; (: in prices, temperature) rialzo, aumento; (fig: to power etc) ascesa // vi (pt **rose**, pp **risen** [rəuz, 'rɪzn]) alzarsi, levarsi; (prices) aumentarsi; (waters, river) crescere; (sun, wind, person: from chair, bed) levarsi; (also: **~ up**: rebel) insorgere; ribellarsi; **to give ~ to** provocare, dare origine a; **to ~ to the occasion** essere all'altezza.

risk [rɪsk] n rischio; pericolo // vt rischiare; **to take** or **run the ~ of doing** correre il rischio di fare; **at ~** in pericolo; **~y** a rischioso(a).

risqué ['riːskeɪ] a (joke) spinto(a).

rissole ['rɪsəul] n crocchetta.

rite [raɪt] n rito.

ritual ['rɪtjuəl] a, n rituale (m).

rival ['raɪvl] n rivale m/f; (in business) concorrente m/f // a rivale; che fa concorrenza // vt essere in concorrenza con; **to ~ sb/sth** in competere con qd/qc in; **~ry** n rivalità; concorrenza.

river ['rɪvə*] n fiume m // cpd (port, traffic) fluviale; **~bank** n argine m; **~bed** n alveo (fluviale); **~side** n sponda del fiume.

rivet ['rɪvɪt] n ribattino, rivetto // vt ribadire; (fig) concentrare, fissare.

Riviera [rɪvɪ'ɛərə] n: **the (French) ~** la Costa Azzurra.

RN abbr of Royal Navy.

road [rəud] n strada; (small) cammino; (in town) via; **~block** n blocco stradale; **~hog** n guidatore m egoista e spericolato; **~ map** n carta stradale; **~side** n margine m della strada; **~sign** n cartello stradale; **~way** n carreggiata; **~worthy** a in buono stato di marcia.

roam [rəum] vi errare, vagabondare // vt vagare per.

roar [rɔː*] n ruggito; (of crowd) tumulto; (of thunder, storm) muggito // vi ruggire; tumultuare; muggire; **to ~ with laughter** scoppiare dalla risa; **a ~ing fire** un bel fuoco; **to do a ~ing trade** fare affari d'oro.

roast [rəust] n arrosto // vt (meat) arrostire.

rob [rɔb] vt (person) rubare; (bank) svaligiare; **to ~ sb of sth** derubare qd di qc; (fig: deprive) privare qd di qc; **~ber** n ladro; (armed) rapinatore m; **~bery** n furto; rapina.

robe [rəub] n (for ceremony etc) abito; (also: **bath ~**) accappatoio // vt vestire.

robin ['rɔbɪn] n pettirosso.

robot ['rəubɔt] n robot m inv.

robust [rəu'bʌst] a robusto(a); (material) solido(a).

rock [rɔk] n (substance) roccia; (boulder) masso; roccia; (in sea) scoglio; (sweet) zucchero candito // vt (swing gently: cradle) dondolare; (: child) cullare; (shake) scrollare, far tremare // vi dondolarsi; scrollarsi, tremare; **on the ~s** (drink) col ghiaccio; (ship) sugli scogli; (marriage etc) in crisi; **~-bottom** n (fig) stremo; **~ery** n giardino roccioso.

rocket ['rɔkɪt] n razzo; (MIL) razzo, missile m.

rock face ['rɔkfeɪs] n parete f della roccia.

rock fall ['rɔkfɔːl] n caduta di massa.

rocking chair ['rɔkɪŋtʃɛə*] n sedia da dondolo.

rocking horse ['rɔkɪŋhɔːs] n cavallo a dondolo.

rocky ['rɔkɪ] a (hill) roccioso(a); (path) sassoso(a); (unsteady: table) traballante.

rod [rɔd] n (metallic, TECH) asta; (wooden) bacchetta; (also: **fishing ~**) canna da pesca.

rode [rəud] pt of **ride**.

rodent ['rəudnt] n roditore m.

rodeo ['rəudɪəu] n rodeo.

roe [rəu] n (species: also: **~ deer**) capriolo; (of fish) uova fpl di pesce; **soft ~** latte m di pesce.

rogue [rəug] n mascalzone m; **roguish** a birbantesco(a).

role [rəul] n ruolo.

roll [rəul] n rotolo; (of banknotes) mazzo; (also: **bread ~**) panino; (register) lista; (sound: of drums etc) rullo; (movement: of ship) rullio // vt rotolare; (also: **~ up**: string) aggomitolare; (also: **~ out**: pastry) stendere // vi rotolare; (wheel) girare; **to ~ in** vi (mail, cash) arrivare a bizzeffe; **to ~ over** vi rivoltarsi; **to ~ up** vi (col: arrive) arrivare // vt (carpet) arrotolare; **~ call** n appello; **~ed gold** a d'oro laminato; **~er** n rullo; (wheel) rotella; **~er skates** npl pattini mpl a rotelle.

rolling ['rəulɪŋ] a (landscape) ondulato(a); **~ pin** n matterello; **~ stock** n (RAIL) materiale m rotabile.

Roman ['rəumən] a, n romano(a); **~ Catholic** a, n cattolico(a).

romance [rə'mæns] n storia (or avventura or film m inv) romantico(a); (charm) poesia; (love affair) idillio.

Romanesque [rəumə'nɛsk] a romanico(a).

Romania [rəu'meɪnɪə] n Romania; **~n** a, n romeno(a).

romantic [rə'mæntɪk] a romantico(a); sentimentale.

romanticism [rə'mæntisizəm] n
romanticismo.
Rome [rəum] n Roma.
romp [rɔmp] n gioco rumoroso // vi (also:
~ **about**) far chiasso, giocare in un modo
rumoroso.
rompers ['rɔmpəz] npl pagliaccetto.
roof [ru:f] n tetto; (of tunnel, cave) volta //
vt coprire (con un tetto); ~ **garden** n
giardino pensile; ~**ing** n materiale m per
copertura; ~ **rack** n (AUT) portabagagli
m inv.
rook [ruk] n (bird) corvo nero; (CHESS)
torre f // vt (cheat) truffare, spennare.
room [ru:m] n (in house) stanza, camera;
(in school etc) sala; (space) posto, spazio;
~**s** npl (lodging) alloggio; ~**ing house** n
(US) casa in cui si affittano camere o
appartamentini ammobiliati; ~**mate** n
compagno/a di stanza; ~ **service** n
servizio da camera; ~**y** a spazioso(a);
(garment) ampio(a).
roost [ru:st] n appollaiato // vi
appollaiarsi.
rooster ['ru:stə*] n gallo.
root [ru:t] n radice f // vt (plant, belief) far
radicare; **to** ~ **about** vi (fig) frugare; **to**
~ **for** vt fus fare il tifo per; **to** ~ **out** vt
estirpare.
rope [rəup] n corda, fune f; (NAUT) cavo //
vt (box) legare; (climbers) legare in
cordata; **to** ~ **sb in** (fig) coinvolgere qd;
to know the ~**s** (fig) conoscere i trucchi
del mestiere; ~ **ladder** n scala di corda.
rosary ['rəuzəri] n rosario; roseto.
rose [rəuz] pt of **rise** // n rosa; (on watering
can) rosetta // a rosa inv.
rosé ['rəuzei] n vino rosato.
rose: ~**bed** n roseto; ~**bud** n bocciolo di
rosa; ~**bush** n rosaio.
rosemary ['rəuzməri] n rosmarino.
rosette [rəu'zet] n rosetta; (larger)
coccarda.
roster ['rɔstə*] n: **duty** ~ ruolino di
servizio.
rostrum ['rɔstrəm] n tribuna.
rosy ['rəuzi] a roseo(a).
rot [rɔt] n (decay) putrefazione f; (fig: pej)
stupidaggini fpl // vt, vi imputridire,
marcire.
rota ['rəutə] n ruolino di servizio.
rotary ['rəutəri] a rotante.
rotate [rəu'teit] vt (revolve) far girare;
(change round: crops) avvicendare; (: jobs)
fare a turno // vi (revolve) girare;
rotating a (movement) rotante; **rotation**
[-'teiʃən] n rotazione f.
rotor ['rəutə*] n rotore m.
rotten ['rɔtn] a (decayed) putrido(a),
marcio(a); (dishonest) corrotto(a); (col:
bad) brutto(a); (: action) vigliacco(a); **to**
feel ~ (ill) sentirsi proprio male.
rotund [rəu'tʌnd] a grassoccio(a);
tondo(a).
rouble ['ru:bl] n rublo.
rouge [ru:ʒ] n rossetto.
rough [rʌf] a aspro(a); (person, manner:
coarse) rozzo(a), aspro(a); (: violent)

brutale; (district) malfamato(a); (weather)
cattivo(a); (plan) abbozzato(a); (guess)
approssimativo(a) // n (GOLF) macchia;
(person) duro; **to** ~ **it** far vita dura; **to**
play ~ far il gioco pesante; **to sleep** ~
dormire all'addiaccio; **to feel** ~ sentirsi
male; **to** ~ **out** vt (draft) abbozzare; ~**en**
vt (a surface) rendere ruvido(a); ~**ly** ad
(handle) rudemente, brutalmente; (make)
grossolanamente; (approximately) approssimativamente; ~**ness** n asprezza;
rozzezza; brutalità; ~ **work** n (at school
etc) brutta copia.
roulette [ru:'let] n roulette f.
Roumania [ru:'meiniə] n = **Romania**.
round [raund] a rotondo(a) // n tondo,
cerchio; (of toast) fetta; (duty: of policeman,
milkman etc) giro; (: of doctor) visite fpl;
(game: of cards, in competition) partita;
(BOXING) round m inv; (of talks) serie f inv
// vt (corner) girare; (bend) prendere;
(cape) doppiare // prep intorno a // ad:
right ~, **all** ~ tutt'attorno; **all the year**
~ tutto l'anno; **it's just** ~ **the corner**
(also fig) è dietro l'angolo; **to go** ~ fare il
giro; **to go** ~ **an obstacle** aggirare un
ostacolo; **to go** ~ **a house** visitare una
casa; **to** ~ **off** vt (speech etc) finire; **to** ~
up vt radunare; (criminals) fare una retata
di; (prices) arrotondare; ~**about** n (AUT)
rotatoria; (at fair) giostra // a (route,
means) indiretto(a); ~ **of ammunition** n
cartuccia; ~ **of applause** n applausi mpl;
~ **of drinks** n giro di bibite; ~ **of**
sandwiches n sandwich m inv; ~**ed** a
arrotondato(a); (style) armonioso(a); ~**ly**
ad (fig) chiaro e tondo; ~**-shouldered** a
dalle spalle tonde; ~ **trip** n (viaggio di)
andata e ritorno; ~**up** n raduno; (of
criminals) retata.
rouse [rauz] vt (wake up) svegliare; (stir
up) destare; provocare; risvegliare;
rousing a (speech, applause)
entusiastico(a).
rout [raut] n (MIL) rotta // vt mettere in
rotta.
route [ru:t] n itinerario; (of bus) percorso;
(of trade, shipping) rotta.
routine [ru:'ti:n] a (work) corrente,
abituale; (procedure) solito(a) // n (pej)
routine f, tran tran m; (THEATRE) numero;
daily ~ orario quotidiano.
roving ['rəuviŋ] a (life) itinerante.
row [rəu] n (line) riga, fila; (KNITTING)
ferro; (behind one another: of cars, people)
fila // vi (in boat) remare; (as sport)
vogare // vt (boat) manovrare a remi; **in**
a ~ (fig) di fila.
row [rau] n (noise) baccano, chiasso; (dispute) lite f // vi litigare.
rowdiness ['raudinis] n baccano;
(fighting) zuffa.
rowdy ['raudi] a chiassoso(a);
turbolento(a) // n teppista m/f.
rowing ['rəuiŋ] n canottaggio; ~ **boat** n
barca a remi.
rowlock ['rɔlək] n scalmo.

royal ['rɔɪəl] *a* reale; ~**ist** *a, n* realista (*m/f*).

royalty ['rɔɪəltɪ] *n* (*royal persons*) (membri *mpl* della) famiglia reale; (*payment: to author*) diritti *mpl* d'autore; (: *to inventor*) diritti di brevetto.

r.p.m. *abbr* (= *revs per minute*) giri/min. (giri/minuto).

R.S.V.P. *abbr* (= *répondez s'il vous plaît*) R.S.V.P.

Rt Hon. *abbr* (= *Right Honourable*) ≈ Onorevole.

rub [rʌb] *n* (*with cloth*) fregata, strofinata; (*on person*) frizione *f,* massaggio // *vt* fregare, strofinare; frizionare; **to ~ sb up the wrong way** lisciare qd contro pelo; **to ~ off** *vi* andare via; **to ~ off on** lasciare una traccia su.

rubber ['rʌbə*] *n* gomma; ~ **band** *n* elastico; ~ **plant** *n* ficus elastica *m inv;* ~ **stamp** *n* timbro di gomma; ~**y** *a* gommoso(a).

rubbish ['rʌbɪʃ] *n* (*from household*) immondizie *fpl,* rifiuti *mpl;* (*fig: pej*) cose *fpl* senza valore; robaccia; sciocchezze *fpl;* ~ **bin** *n* pattumiera; ~ **dump** *n* (*in town*) immondezzaio.

rubble ['rʌbl] *n* macerie *fpl;* (*smaller*) pietrisco.

ruble ['ru:bl] *n* (*US*) = **rouble**.

ruby ['ru:bɪ] *n* rubino.

rucksack ['rʌksæk] *n* zaino.

rudder ['rʌdə*] *n* timone *m.*

ruddy ['rʌdɪ] *a* (*face*) fresco(a); (*col: damned*) maledetto(a).

rude [ru:d] *a* (*impolite: person*) scortese, rozzo(a); (: *word, manners*) grossolano(a), rozzo(a); (*shocking*) indecente; ~**ly** *ad* scortesemente; grossolanamente; ~**ness** *n* scortesia; grossolanità.

rudiment ['ru:dɪmənt] *n* rudimento; ~**ary** [-'mentərɪ] *a* rudimentale.

rueful ['ru:ful] *a* mesto(a), triste.

ruff [rʌf] *n* gorgiera.

ruffian ['rʌfɪən] *n* briccone *m,* furfante *m.*

ruffle ['rʌfl] *vt* (*hair*) scompigliare; (*clothes, water*) increspare; (*fig: person*) turbare.

rug [rʌg] *n* tappeto; (*for knees*) coperta.

rugby ['rʌgbɪ] *n* (*also:* ~ **football**) rugby *m.*

rugged ['rʌgɪd] *a* (*landscape*) aspro(a); (*features, determination*) duro(a); (*character*) brusco(a).

rugger ['rʌgə*] *n* (*col*) rugby *m.*

ruin ['ru:ɪn] *n* rovina // *vt* rovinare; (*spoil: clothes*) sciupare; ~**s** *npl* rovine *fpl,* ruderi *mpl;* ~**ation** [-'neɪʃən] *n* rovina; ~**ous** *a* rovinoso(a); (*expenditure*) inverosimile.

rule [ru:l] *n* regola; (*regulation*) regolamento, regola; (*government*) governo // *vt* (*country*) governare; (*person*) dominare; (*decide*) decidere // *vi* regnare; decidere; (*LAW*) dichiarare; **as a ~** normalmente, di ~ **d** *a* (*paper*) vergato(a); ~**r** *n* (*sovereign*) sovrano/a; (*leader*) capo (dello Stato); (*for measuring*) regolo, riga; **ruling** *a* (*party*) al potere;

(*class*) dirigente // *n* (*LAW*) decisione *f.*

rum [rʌm] *n* rum *m* // *a* (*col*) strano(a).

Rumania [ru:'meɪnɪə] *n* = **Romania**.

rumble ['rʌmbl] *n* rimbombo; brontolio // *vi* rimbombare; (*stomach, pipe*) brontolare.

rummage ['rʌmɪdʒ] *vi* frugare.

rumour ['ru:mə*] *n* voce *f* // *vt*: **it is ~ed that** corre voce che.

rump [rʌmp] *n* (*of animal*) groppa; ~ **steak** *n* bistecca di girello.

rumpus ['rʌmpəs] *n* (*col*) baccano; (: *quarrel*) rissa.

run [rʌn] *n* corsa; (*outing*) gita (in macchina); (*distance travelled*) percorso, tragitto; (*series*) serie *f;* (*THEATRE*) periodo di rappresentazione; (*SKI*) pista // *vb* (*pt ran, pp run* [ræn, rʌn]) *vt* (*operate: business*) gestire, dirigere; (: *competition, course*) organizzare; (: *hotel*) gestire; (: *house*) governare; (*force through: rope, pipe*): **to ~ sth through** far passare qc attraverso; (*to pass: hand, finger*): **to ~ sth over** passare qc su; (*water, bath*) far scorrere // *vi* correre; (*pass: road etc*) passare; (*work: machine, factory*) funzionare, andare; (*bus, train: operate*) far servizio; (: *travel*) circolare; (*continue: play, contract*) durare; (*slide: drawer; flow: river, bath*) scorrere; (*colours, washing*) stemperarsi; (*in election*) presentarsi candidato; **there was a ~ on ...** c'era una corsa a ...; **in the long ~** alla lunga; in fin dei conti; **on the ~** in fuga; **I'll ~ you to the station** la porto alla stazione; **to ~ a risk** correre un rischio; **to ~ about** *vi* (*children*) correre qua e là; **to ~ across** *vt fus* (*find*) trovare per caso; **to ~ away** *vi* fuggire; **to ~ down** *vi* (*clock*) scaricarsi // *vt* (*AUT*) investire; (*criticize*) criticare; **to be ~ down** essere esausto(a) *or* a zero; **to ~ off** *vi* fuggire; **to ~ out** *vi* (*person*) uscire di corsa; (*liquid*) colare; (*lease*) scadere; (*money*) esaurirsi; **to ~ out of** *vt fus* rimanere a corto di; **to ~ over** *vt sep* (*AUT*) investire, arrotare // *vt fus* (*revise*) rivedere; **to ~ through** *vt fus* (*instructions*) dare una scorsa a; **to ~ up** *vt* (*debt*) lasciar accumulare; **to ~ up against** (*difficulties*) incontrare; ~**away** *a* (*person*) fuggiasco(a); (*horse*) in libertà; (*truck*) fuori controllo; (*inflation*) galoppante.

rung [rʌŋ] *pp of* **ring** // *n* (*of ladder*) piolo.

runner ['rʌnə*] *n* (*in race*) corridore *m;* (*on sledge*) pattino; (*for drawer etc, carpet: in hall etc*) guida; ~ **bean** *n* (*BOT*) fagiolo rampicante; ~**up** *n* secondo(a) arrivato(a).

running ['rʌnɪŋ] *n* corsa; direzione *f;* organizzazione *f;* funzionamento // *a* (*water*) corrente; (*commentary*) simultaneo(a); **6 days ~** 6 giorni di seguito.

runny ['rʌnɪ] *a* che cola.

run-of-the-mill ['rʌnəvðə'mɪl] *a* solito(a), banale.

runt [rʌnt] *n* (*also: pej*) omuncolo; (*ZOOL*)

animale m più piccolo del normale.
run-through ['rʌnθru:] n prova.

runway ['rʌnweɪ] n (AVIAT) pista (di decollo).

rupture ['rʌptʃə*] n (MED) ernia // vt: **to ~ o.s.** darsi un'ernia.

rural ['ruərl] a rurale.

ruse [ru:z] n trucco.

rush [rʌʃ] n corsa precipitosa; (of crowd) afflusso; (hurry) furia, fretta; (current) flusso // vt mandare or spedire velocemente; (attack: town etc) prendere d'assalto // vi precipitarsi; **don't ~ me!** non mi affrettare!; **~es** npl (BOT) giunchi mpl; **~ hour** n ora di punta.

rusk [rʌsk] n biscotto.

Russia ['rʌʃə] n Russia; **~n** a russo(a) // n russo/a; (LING) russo.

rust [rʌst] n ruggine f // vi arrugginirsi.

rustic ['rʌstɪk] a rustico(a) // n (pej) cafone/a.

rustle ['rʌsl] vi frusciare // vt (paper) far frusciare; (US: cattle) rubare.

rustproof ['rʌstpru:f] a inossidabile.

rusty ['rʌstɪ] a arrugginito(a).

rut [rʌt] n solco; (ZOOL) fregola.

ruthless ['ru:θlɪs] a spietato(a).

rye [raɪ] n segale f.

S

Sabbath ['sæbəθ] n (Jewish) sabato; (Christian) domenica.

sabbatical [sə'bætɪkl] a: **~ year** n anno sabbatico.

sabotage ['sæbətɑ:ʒ] n sabotaggio // vt sabotare.

saccharin(e) ['sækərɪn] n saccarina.

sack [sæk] n (bag) sacco // vt (dismiss) licenziare, mandare a spasso; (plunder) saccheggiare; **to get the ~** essere mandato a spasso; **a ~ful** of un sacco di; **~ing** n tela di sacco; (dismissal) licenziamento.

sacrament ['sækrəmənt] n sacramento.

sacred ['seɪkrɪd] a sacro(a).

sacrifice ['sækrɪfaɪs] n sacrificio // vt sacrificare.

sacrilege ['sækrɪlɪdʒ] n sacrilegio.

sacrosanct ['sækrəusæŋkt] a sacrosanto(a).

sad [sæd] a triste; **~den** vt rattristare.

saddle ['sædl] n sella // vt (horse) sellare; **to be ~d with sth** (col) avere qc sulle spalle; **~bag** n bisaccia; (on bicycle) borsa.

sadism ['seɪdɪzm] n sadismo; **sadist** n sadico/a; **sadistic** [sə'dɪstɪk] a sadico(a).

sadness ['sædnɪs] n tristezza.

safari [sə'fɑ:rɪ] n safari m inv.

safe [seɪf] a sicuro(a); (out of danger) salvo(a), al sicuro; (cautious) prudente // n cassaforte f; **~ from** al sicuro da; **~ and sound** sano(a) e salvo(a); **(just) to be on the ~ side** per non correre rischi; **~guard** n salvaguardia // vt salvaguardare; **~keeping** n custodia;

~ly ad sicuramente; sano(a) e salvo(a); prudentemente.

safety ['seɪftɪ] n sicurezza; **~ belt** n cintura di sicurezza; **~ pin** n spilla di sicurezza.

saffron ['sæfrən] n zafferano.

sag [sæg] vi incurvarsi; afflosciarsi.

sage [seɪdʒ] n (herb) salvia; (man) saggio.

Sagittarius [sædʒɪ'tɛərɪəs] n Sagittario.

sago ['seɪgəu] n sagù m.

said [sɛd] pt, pp of **say**.

sail [seɪl] n (on boat) vela; (trip): **to go for a ~** fare un giro in barca a vela // vt (boat) condurre, governare // vi (travel: ship) navigare; (: passenger) viaggiare per mare; (set off) salpare; (SPORT) fare della vela; **they ~ed into Genoa** entrarono nel porto di Genova; **to ~ through** (fig) vt fus superare senza difficoltà // vi farcela senza difficoltà; **~boat** n (US) barca a vela; **~ing** n (SPORT) vela; **to go ~ing** fare della vela; **~ing boat** n barca a vela; **~ing ship** n veliero; **~or** n marinaio.

saint [seɪnt] n santo/a.

sake [seɪk] n: **for the ~ of** per, per amore di, per il bene di; **for pity's ~** per pietà.

salad ['sæləd] n insalata; **~ bowl** n insalatiera; **~ cream** n (tipo di) maionese f; **~ dressing** n condimento per insalata; **~ oil** n olio da tavola.

salary ['sælərɪ] n stipendio.

sale [seɪl] n vendita; (at reduced prices) svendita, liquidazione f; **'for ~'** 'in vendita'; **on ~ or return** da vendere o rimandare; **~room** n sala delle aste; **~sman** n commesso; (representative) rappresentante m; **~swoman** n commessa.

salient ['seɪlɪənt] a saliente.

saliva [sə'laɪvə] n saliva.

sallow ['sæləu] a giallastro(a).

salmon ['sæmən] n, pl inv salmone m.

saloon [sə'lu:n] n (US) saloon m inv, bar m inv; (AUT) berlina; (ship's lounge) salone m.

salt [sɔlt] n sale m // vt salare; (CULIN) salato(a); **~ cellar** n saliera; **~y** a salato(a).

salutary ['sæljutərɪ] a salutare.

salute [sə'lu:t] n saluto // vt salutare.

salvage ['sælvɪdʒ] n (saving) salvataggio; (things saved) beni mpl salvati o recuperati // vt salvare, mettere in salvo.

salvation [sæl'veɪʃən] n salvezza; **S~ Army** n Esercito della Salvezza.

salvo ['sælvəu] n salva.

same [seɪm] a stesso(a), medesimo(a) // pronoun: **the ~** lo/la stesso(a), gli(le) stessi(e); **the ~ book as** lo stesso libro di (or che); **all or just the ~** tuttavia; **to do the ~** fare la stessa cosa; **to do the ~ as sb** fare come qd.

sample ['sɑ:mpl] n campione m // vt (food) assaggiare; (wine) degustare.

sanatorium, pl **sanatoria** [sænə'tɔ:rɪəm, -rɪə] n sanatorio.

sanctimonious [sæŋktɪ'məunɪəs] a bigotto(a), bacchettone(a).

sanction ['sæŋkʃən] n sanzione f // vt sancire, sanzionare.

sanctity ['sæŋktɪtɪ] n santità.

sanctuary ['sæŋktjuərɪ] n (holy place) santuario; (refuge) rifugio; (for wildlife) riserva.

sand [sænd] n sabbia // vt cospargere di sabbia; ~s npl spiaggia.

sandal ['sændl] n sandalo.

sandcastle ['sændkɑ:sl] n castello di sabbia.

sand dune ['sænddju:n] n duna di sabbia.

sandpaper ['sændpeɪpə*] n carta vetrata.

sandpit ['sændpɪt] n (for children) buca di sabbia per i giochi dei bambini.

sandstone ['sændstəun] n arenaria.

sandwich ['sændwɪtʃ] n tramezzino, panino, sandwich m inv // vt (also: ~ in) intramezzare, interporre; **cheese/ham** ~ **sandwich** al formaggio/prosciutto; ~ **course** n corso di formazione professionale.

sandy ['sændɪ] a sabbioso(a); (colour) color sabbia inv, biondo(a) rossiccio(a).

sane [seɪn] a (person) sano(a) di mente; (outlook) sensato(a).

sang [sæŋ] pt of **sing**.

sanguine ['sæŋgwɪn] a ottimista.

sanitary ['sænɪtərɪ] a (system, arrangements) sanitario(a); (clean) igienico(a); ~ **towel**, ~ **napkin** (US) n assorbente m (igienico).

sanitation [sænɪ'teɪʃən] n (in house) impianti mpl sanitari; (in town) fognature fpl.

sanity ['sænɪtɪ] n sanità mentale; (common sense) buon senso.

sank [sæŋk] pt of **sink**.

Santa Claus [sæntə'klɔ:z] n Babbo Natale.

sap [sæp] n (of plants) linfa // vt (strength) fiaccare.

sapling ['sæplɪŋ] n alberello.

sapphire ['sæfaɪə*] n zaffiro.

sarcasm ['sɑ:kæzm] n sarcasmo.

sarcastic [sɑ:'kæstɪk] a sarcastico(a).

sardine [sɑ:'di:n] n sardina.

Sardinia [sɑ:'dɪnɪə] n Sardegna.

sash [sæʃ] n fascia; ~ **window** n finestra a ghigliottina.

sat [sæt] pt,pp of **sit**.

Satan ['seɪtən] n Satana m.

satchel ['sætʃl] n cartella.

satellite ['sætəlaɪt] a, n satellite (m).

satin ['sætɪn] n raso, satin m // a di or in satin.

satire ['sætaɪə*] n satira; **satirical** [sə'tɪrɪkl] a satirico(a).

satisfaction [sætɪs'fækʃən] n soddisfazione f.

satisfactory [sætɪs'fæktərɪ] a soddisfacente.

satisfy ['sætɪsfaɪ] vt soddisfare; (convince) convincere; ~**ing** a soddisfacente.

saturate ['sætʃəreɪt] vt: to ~ (with) saturare (di).

Saturday ['sætədɪ] n sabato.

sauce [sɔ:s] n salsa; (containing meat, fish) sugo; ~**pan** n casseruola.

saucer ['sɔ:sə*] n sottocoppa m, piattino.

saucy ['sɔ:sɪ] a impertinente.

saunter ['sɔ:ntə*] vi andare a zonzo, bighellonare.

sausage ['sɔsɪdʒ] n salsiccia; ~ **roll** n rotolo di pasta sfoglia ripiena di salsiccia.

savage ['sævɪdʒ] a (cruel, fierce) selvaggio(a), feroce; (primitive) primitivo(a) // n selvaggio/a // vt attaccare selvaggiamente; ~**ry** n crudeltà, ferocia.

save [seɪv] vt (person, belongings) salvare; (money) risparmiare, mettere da parte; (time) risparmiare; (food) conservare; (avoid: trouble) evitare // vi (also: ~ up) economizzare // n (SPORT) parata // prep salvo, a eccezione di.

saving ['seɪvɪŋ] n risparmio // a: **the ~ grace of** l'unica cosa buona di; ~**s** npl risparmi mpl; ~**s bank** n cassa di risparmio.

saviour ['seɪvjə*] n salvatore m.

savour ['seɪvə*] n sapore m, gusto // vt gustare; ~**y** a saporito(a); (dish: not sweet) salato(a).

saw [sɔ:] pt of **see** // n (tool) sega // vt (pt **sawed**, pp **sawed** or **sawn** [sɔ:n]) segare; ~**dust** n segatura; ~**mill** n segheria.

saxophone ['sæksəfəun] n sassofono.

say [seɪ] n: **to have one's** ~ fare sentire il proprio parere; **to have a** ~ avere voce in capitolo // vt (pt, pp **said** [sɛd]) dire; **could you** ~ **that again?** potrebbe ripeterlo?; **that is to** ~ cioè, vale a dire; **to** ~ **nothing of** per non parlare di; **that ...** mettiamo or diciamo che ...; **that goes without** ~**ing** va da sé; ~**ing** n proverbio, detto.

scab [skæb] n crosta; (pej) crumiro/a; ~**by** a crostoso(a).

scaffold ['skæfəuld] n impalcatura; (gallows) patibolo; ~**ing** n impalcatura.

scald [skɔ:ld] n scottatura // vt scottare.

scale [skeɪl] n scala; (of fish) squama // vt (mountain) scalare; ~**s** npl bilancia; **on a large** ~ su vasta scala; ~ **model** n modello in scala; **small**-~ **model** n modello in scala ridotta.

scallop ['skɔləp] n pettine m.

scalp [skælp] n cuoio capelluto // vt scotennare.

scalpel ['skælpl] n bisturi m inv.

scamper ['skæmpə*] vi: **to** ~ **away,** ~ **off** darsela a gambe.

scan [skæn] vt scrutare; (glance at quickly) scorrere, dare un'occhiata a; (poetry) scandire; (TV) analizzare; (RADAR) esplorare.

scandal ['skændl] n scandalo; (gossip) pettegolezzi mpl; ~**ize** vt scandalizzare; ~**ous** a scandaloso(a).

Scandinavia [skændɪ'neɪvɪə] n Scandinavia; ~**n** a, n scandinavo(a).

scant [skænt] a scarso(a); ~**y** a insufficiente; (swimsuit) ridotto(a).

scapegoat ['skeɪpgəut] n capro espiatorio.

scar [skɑː] n cicatrice f // vt sfregiare.

scarce [skɛəs] a scarso(a); (copy, edition) raro(a); ~**ly** ad appena; **scarcity** n scarsità, mancanza.

scare [skɛə*] n spavento; panico // vt spaventare, atterrire; **to** ~ **sb stiff** spaventare a morte qd; ~**crow** n spaventapasseri m inv; ~**d** a: **to be** ~**d** aver paura; ~**monger** n allarmista m/f.

scarf, scarves [skɑːf, skɑːvz] n (long) sciarpa; (square) fazzoletto da testa, foulard m inv.

scarlet ['skɑːlɪt] a scarlatto(a); ~ **fever** n scarlattina.

scarves [skɑːvz] npl of **scarf**.

scathing ['skeɪðɪŋ] a aspro(a).

scatter ['skætə*] vt spargere; (crowd) disperdere // vi disperdere; ~**brained** a scervellato(a), sbadato(a); ~**ed** a sparso(a), sparpagliato(a).

scatty ['skætɪ] a (col) scervellato(a), sbadato(a).

scavenger ['skævəndʒə*] n spazzino.

scene [siːn] n (THEATRE, fig etc) scena; (of crime, accident) scena, luogo; (sight, view) vista, veduta; ~**ry** n (THEATRE) scenario; (landscape) panorama m; **scenic** a scenico(a); panoramico(a).

scent [sɛnt] n odore m, profumo; (fig: track) pista; (sense of smell) olfatto, odorato.

sceptic ['skɛptɪk] n scettico/a; ~**al** a scettico(a); ~**ism** ['skɛptɪsɪzm] n scetticismo.

sceptre ['sɛptə*] n scettro.

schedule ['ʃɛdjuːl] n programma m, piano; (of trains) orario; (of prices etc) lista, tabella // vt stabilire; **as** ~**d** come stabilito; **on** ~ in orario; in regola con la tabella di marcia; **to be ahead of/behind** ~ essere in anticipo/ritardo sul previsto.

scheme [skiːm] n piano, progetto; (method) sistema m; (dishonest plan, plot) intrigo, trama; (arrangement) disposizione f, sistemazione f // vt progettare; (plot) ordire // vi fare progetti; (intrigue) complottare; **scheming** a intrigante // n intrighi mpl, macchinazioni fpl.

schism ['skɪzəm] n scisma m.

schizophrenic [skɪtsə'frɛnɪk] a schizofrenico(a).

scholar ['skɔlə*] n erudito/a; ~**ly** a dotto(a), erudito(a); ~**ship** n erudizione f; (grant) borsa di studio.

school [skuːl] n scuola; (in university) scuola, facoltà f inv // vt (animal) addestrare; ~**book** n libro scolastico; ~**boy** n scolaro; ~**days** npl giorni mpl di scuola; ~**girl** n scolara; ~**ing** n istruzione f; ~**leaving age** n età dell'adempimento dell'obbligo scolastico; ~**master** n (primary) maestro; (secondary) insegnante m; ~**mistress** n maestra; insegnante f; ~**teacher** n insegnante m/f, docente m/f; (primary) maestro/a.

schooner ['skuːnə*] n (ship) goletta,

schooner m inv; (glass) bicchiere m alto da sherry.

sciatica [saɪ'ætɪkə] n sciatica.

science ['saɪəns] n scienza; ~ **fiction** n fantascienza; **scientific** [-'tɪfɪk] a scientifico(a); **scientist** n scienziato/a.

scintillating ['sɪntɪleɪtɪŋ] a scintillante.

scissors ['sɪzəz] npl forbici fpl; **a pair of** ~ un paio di forbici.

scoff [skɔf] vt (col: eat) trangugiare, ingozzare // vi: **to** ~ (**at**) (mock) farsi beffe (di).

scold [skəʊld] vt rimproverare.

scone [skɔn] n focaccia da tè.

scoop [skuːp] n mestolo; (for ice cream) cucchiaio dosatore; (PRESS) colpo giornalistico, notizia (in) esclusiva; **to** ~ **out** vt scavare; **to** ~ **up** vt tirare su, sollevare.

scooter ['skuːtə*] n (motor cycle) motoretta, scooter m inv; (toy) monopattino.

scope [skəʊp] n (capacity: of plan, undertaking) portata; (: of person) competenza; (opportunity) opportunità; **within the** ~ **of** entro la competenza di.

scorch [skɔːtʃ] vt (clothes) strinare, bruciacchiare; (earth, grass) seccare, bruciare; ~**er** n (col: hot day) giornata torrida; ~**ing** a cocente, scottante.

score [skɔː*] n punti mpl, punteggio; (MUS) partitura, spartito; (twenty) venti // vt (goal, point) segnare, fare; (success) ottenere // vi segnare; (FOOTBALL) fare un gol; (keep score) segnare i punti; **on that** ~ a questo riguardo; ~**board** n tabellone m segnapunti; ~**card** n (SPORT) cartoncino segnapunti; ~**r** n marcatore/trice; (keeping score) segnapunti m inv.

scorn [skɔːn] n disprezzo // vt disprezzare.

Scorpio ['skɔːpɪəʊ] n Scorpione m.

scorpion ['skɔːpɪən] n scorpione m.

Scot [skɔt] n scozzese m/f.

scotch [skɔtʃ] vt (rumour etc) soffocare; **S**~ n whisky m scozzese, scotch m.

scot-free ['skɔt'friː] a impunito(a).

Scotland ['skɔtlənd] n Scozia.

Scots [skɔts] a scozzese; ~**man/woman** n scozzese m/f.

Scottish ['skɔtɪʃ] a scozzese.

scoundrel ['skaundrl] n farabutto/a; (child) furfantello/a.

scour ['skauə*] vt (clean) pulire strofinando; raschiare via; ripulire; (search) battere, perlustrare.

scourge [skəːdʒ] n flagello.

scout [skaut] n (MIL) esploratore m; (also: **boy** ~) giovane esploratore, scout m inv; **to** ~ **around** vi cercare in giro.

scowl [skaul] vi accigliarsi, aggrottare le sopracciglia; **to** ~ **at** guardare torvo.

scraggy ['skrægɪ] a scarno(a), molto magro(a).

scram [skræm] vi (col) filare via.

scramble ['skræmbl] n arrampicata // vi inerpicarsi; **to** ~ **for** azzuffarsi per; ~**d eggs** npl uova fpl strapazzate.

scrap [skræp] *n* pezzo, pezzetto; *(fight)* zuffa; *(also:* ~ **iron)** rottami *mpl* di ferro, ferraglia // *vt* demolire; *(fig)* scartare; ~**s** *npl (waste)* scarti *mpl*; ~**book** *n* album *m inv* di ritagli.

scrape [skreɪp] *vt,vi* raschiare, grattare // *n*: **to get into a** ~ cacciarsi in un guaio; ~**r** *n* raschietto.

scrap: ~ **heap** *n* mucchio di rottami; ~ **merchant** *n* commerciante *m* di ferraglia; ~ **paper** *n* cartaccia; ~**py** *a* frammentario(a), sconnesso(a).

scratch [skrætʃ] *n* graffio // *a:* ~ **team** *n* squadra raccogliticcia // *vt* graffiare, rigare // *vi* grattare, graffiare; **to start from** ~ cominciare or partire da zero; **to be up to** ~ essere all'altezza.

scrawl [skrɔːl] *n* scarabocchio // *vi* scarabocchiare.

scrawny ['skrɔːnɪ] *a* scarno(a), pelle e ossa *inv*.

scream [skriːm] *n* grido, urlo // *vi* urlare, gridare.

scree [skriː] *n* ghiaione *m*.

screech [skriːtʃ] *n* strido; *(of tyres, brakes)* stridore *m* // *vi* stridere.

screen [skriːn] *n* schermo; *(fig)* muro, cortina, velo // *vt* schermare, fare schermo a; *(from the wind etc)* riparare; *(film)* proiettare; *(book)* adattare per lo schermo; *(candidates etc)* selezionare; ~**ing** *n (MED)* dépistage *m inv*.

screw [skruː] *n* vite *f*; *(propeller)* elica // *vt* avvitare; ~**driver** *n* cacciavite *m*; ~**y** *a (col)* svitato(a).

scribble ['skrɪbl] *n* scarabocchio // *vt* scribacchiare in fretta // *vi* scarabocchiare.

script [skrɪpt] *n (CINEMA etc)* copione *m*; *(in exam)* elaborato or compito d'esame.

Scripture ['skrɪptʃə*] *n* sacre Scritture *fpl*.

scriptwriter ['skrɪptraɪtə*] *n* soggettista *m/f*.

scroll [skrəʊl] *n* rotolo di carta.

scrounge [skraʊndʒ] *vt (col):* **to** ~ **sth (off** *or* **from sb)** scroccare (qc a qd) // *vi:* **to** ~ **on sb** vivere alle spalle di qd; ~**r** *n* scroccone/a.

scrub [skrʌb] *n (clean)* strofinata; *(land)* boscaglia // *vt* pulire strofinando; *(reject)* annullare.

scruff [skrʌf] *n*: **by the** ~ **of the neck** per la collottola.

scruffy ['skrʌfɪ] *a* sciatto(a).

scrum(mage) ['skrʌm(ɪdʒ)] *n* mischia.

scruple ['skruːpl] *n* scrupolo.

scrupulous ['skruːpjuləs] *a* scrupoloso(a).

scrutinize ['skruːtɪnaɪz] *vt* scrutare, esaminare attentamente.

scrutiny ['skruːtɪnɪ] *n* esame *m* accurato.

scuff [skʌf] *vt (shoes)* consumare strasciando.

scuffle ['skʌfl] *n* baruffa, tafferuglio.

scullery ['skʌlərɪ] *n* retrocucina *m or f*.

sculptor ['skʌlptə*] *n* scultore *m*.

sculpture ['skʌlptʃə*] *n* scultura.

scum [skʌm] *n* schiuma; *(pej: people)* feccia.

scurrilous ['skʌrɪləs] *a* scurrile, volgare.

scurry ['skʌrɪ] *vi* sgambare, affrettarsi.

scurvy ['skɜːvɪ] *n* scorbuto.

scuttle ['skʌtl] *n (NAUT)* portellino; *(also:* **coal** ~) secchio del carbone // *vt (ship)* autoaffondare // *vi (scamper):* **to** ~ **away,** ~ **off** darsela a gambe, scappare.

scythe [saɪð] *n* falce *f*.

sea [siː] *n* mare *m* // *cpd* marino(a), del mare; *(ship, sailor, port)* marittimo(a), di mare; **on the** ~ *(boat)* in mare; *(town)* di mare; **to be all at** ~ *(fig)* non sapere che pesci pigliare; ~ **bird** *n* uccello di mare; ~**board** *n* costa; ~ **breeze** *n* brezza di mare; ~**farer** *n* navigante *m*; ~**food** *n* frutti *mpl* di mare; ~ **front** *n* lungomare *m*; ~**going** *a (ship)* d'alto mare; ~**gull** *n* gabbiano.

seal [siːl] *n (animal)* foca; *(stamp)* sigillo; *(impression)* impronta del sigillo // *vt* sigillare.

sea level ['siːlɛvl] *n* livello del mare.

sea lion ['siːlaɪən] *n* leone *m* marino.

seam [siːm] *n* cucitura; *(of coal)* filone *m*.

seaman ['siːmən] *n* marinaio.

seamy ['siːmɪ] *a* orribile.

seance ['seɪɒns] *n* seduta spiritica.

seaplane ['siːpleɪn] *n* idrovolante *m*.

seaport ['siːpɔːt] *n* porto di mare.

search [sɜːtʃ] *n (for person, thing)* ricerca; *(of drawer, pockets)* esame *m* accurato; *(LAW: at sb's home)* perquisizione *f* // *vt* perlustrare, frugare; *(examine)* esaminare minuziosamente // *vi:* **to** ~ **for** ricercare; **to** ~ **through** *vt fus* frugare; **in** ~ **of** alla ricerca di; ~**ing** *a* minuzioso(a); penetrante; ~**light** *n* proiettore *m*; ~ **party** *n* squadra di soccorso; ~ **warrant** *n* mandato di perquisizione.

seashore ['siːʃɔː*] *n* spiaggia.

seasick ['siːsɪk] *a* che soffre il mal di mare.

seaside ['siːsaɪd] *n* spiaggia; ~ **resort** *n* stazione *f* balneare.

season ['siːzn] *n* stagione *f* // *vt* condire, insaporire; ~**al** *a* stagionale; ~**ing** *n* condimento; ~ **ticket** *n* abbonamento.

seat [siːt] *n* sedile *m*; *(in bus, train: place)* posto; *(PARLIAMENT)* seggio; *(buttocks)* didietro; *(of trousers)* fondo // *vt* far sedere; *(have room for)* avere or essere fornito(a) di posti a sedere per; ~ **belt** *n* cintura di sicurezza.

sea water ['siːwɔːtə*] *n* acqua di mare.

seaweed ['siːwiːd] *n* alga.

seaworthy ['siːwɜːðɪ] *a* atto(a) alla navigazione.

sec. *abbr of* **second(s).**

secluded [sɪ'kluːdɪd] *a* isolato(a), appartato(a).

seclusion [sɪ'kluːʒən] *n* isolamento.

second ['sɛkənd] *num* secondo(a) // *ad (in race etc)* al secondo posto; *(RAIL)* in seconda // *n (unit of time)* secondo; *(in series, position)* secondo/a; *(AUT: also:* ~ **gear)** seconda; *(COMM: imperfect)* scarto

// vt (*motion*) appoggiare; ~**ary** a secondario(a); ~**ary school** n scuola secondaria; ~**class** a di seconda classe; ~**er** n sostenitore/trice; ~**hand** a di seconda mano, usato(a); ~ **hand** n (*on clock*) lancetta dei secondi; ~**ly** ad in secondo luogo; ~**-rate** a scadente; ~ **thoughts** npl ripensamenti mpl; **on** ~ **thoughts** ripensandoci bene.

secrecy ['si:krəsɪ] n segretezza.

secret ['si:krɪt] a segreto(a) // n segreto.

secretariat [sɛkrɪ'tɛərɪət] n segretariato.

secretary ['sɛkrətərɪ] n segretario/a; **S**~ **of State (for)** (*Brit*: POL) ministro (di).

secretive ['si:krətɪv] a riservato(a).

sect [sɛkt] n setta; ~**arian** [-'tɛərɪən] a settario(a).

section ['sɛkʃən] n sezione f // vt sezionare, dividere in sezioni.

sector ['sɛktə*] n settore m.

secular ['sɛkjulə*] a secolare.

secure [sɪ'kjuə*] a (*free from anxiety*) sicuro(a); (*firmly fixed*) assicurato(a), ben fermato(a); (*in safe place*) al sicuro // vt (*fix*) fissare, assicurare; (*get*) ottenere, assicurarsi.

security [sɪ'kjuərɪtɪ] n sicurezza; (*for loan*) garanzia.

sedate [sɪ'deɪt] a posato(a); calmo(a) // vt calmare.

sedation [sɪ'deɪʃən] n (MED) l'effetto dei sedativi.

sedative ['sɛdɪtɪv] n sedativo, calmante m.

sediment ['sɛdɪmənt] n sedimento.

seduce [sɪ'dju:s] vt sedurre; **seduction** [-'dʌkʃən] n seduzione f; **seductive** [-'dʌktɪv] a seducente.

see [si:] vb (pt **saw**, pp **seen** [sɔ:, si:n]) vt vedere; (*accompany*): **to** ~ **sb to the door** accompagnare qd alla porta // vi vedere; (*understand*) capire // n sede f vescovile; **to** ~ **that** (*ensure*) badare che + sub, fare in modo che + sub; **to** ~ **off** vt salutare alla partenza; **to** ~ **through** vt portare a termine // vt fus non lasciarsi ingannare da; **to** ~ **to** vt fus occuparsi di.

seed [si:d] n seme m; (*fig*) germe m; (TENNIS) testa di serie; **to go to** ~ fare seme; (*fig*) scadere; ~**ling** n piantina di semenzaio; ~**y** a (*shabby: person*) sciatto(a); (: *place*) cadente.

seeing ['si:ɪŋ] cj: ~ (**that**) visto che.

seek, pt,pp **sought** [si:k, sɔ:t] vt cercare.

seem [si:m] vi sembrare, parere; **there seems to be ...** sembra che ci sia ...; ~**ingly** ad apparentemente.

seen [si:n] pp of **see**.

seep [si:p] vi filtrare, trapelare.

seer [sɪə*] n profeta/essa, veggente m/f.

seesaw ['si:sɔ:] n altalena a bilico.

seethe [si:ð] vi ribollire; **to** ~ **with anger** fremere di rabbia.

see-through ['si:θru:] a trasparente.

segment ['sɛgmənt] n segmento.

segregate ['sɛgrɪgeɪt] vt segregare, isolare.

seismic ['saɪzmɪk] a sismico(a).

seize [si:z] vt (*grasp*) afferrare; (*take possession of*) impadronirsi di; (LAW) sequestrare; **to** ~ (**up)on** vt fus ricorrere a; **to** ~ **up** vi (TECH) grippare.

seizure ['si:ʒə*] n (MED) attacco; (LAW) confisca, sequestro.

seldom ['sɛldəm] ad raramente.

select [sɪ'lɛkt] a scelto(a) // vt scegliere, selezionare; ~**ion** [-'lɛkʃən] n selezione f, scelta; ~**ive** a selettivo(a).

self [sɛlf] n (pl **selves** [sɛlvz]): **the** ~ l'io m // prefix auto...; ~**-assured** a sicuro(a) di sé; ~**-catering** a in cui ci si cucina da sé; ~**-centred** a egocentrico(a); ~**-coloured** a monocolore; ~**-confidence** n sicurezza di sé; ~**-conscious** a timido(a); ~**-contained** a (*flat*) indipendente; ~**-control** n autocontrollo; ~**-defence** n autodifesa; (LAW) legittima difesa; ~**-discipline** n autodisciplina; ~**-employed** a che lavora in proprio; ~**-evident** a evidente; ~**-explanatory** a ovvio(a); ~**-indulgent** a indulgente verso se stesso(a); ~**-interest** n interesse m personale; ~**-ish** a egoista; ~**-ishness** n egoismo; ~**-less** ad altruisticamente; ~**-pity** n autocommiserazione f; ~**-portrait** n autoritratto; ~**-possessed** a controllato(a); ~**-preservation** n istinto di conservazione; ~**-respect** n rispetto di sé, amor proprio; ~**-respecting** a che ha rispetto di sé; ~**-righteous** a soddisfatto(a) di sé; ~**-sacrifice** n abnegazione f; ~**-satisfied** a compiaciuto(a) di sé; ~**-seal** a autosigillante; ~**-service** n autoservizio, self-service m; ~**-sufficient** a autosufficiente; ~**-supporting** a economicamente indipendente.

sell, pt,pp **sold** [sɛl, səuld] vt vendere // vi vendersi; **to** ~ **at** or **for 1000 lire** essere in vendita a 1000 lire; **to** ~ **off** vt svendere, liquidare; ~**er** n venditore/trice; ~**ing price** n prezzo di vendita.

sellotape ['sɛləuteɪp] n ® nastro adesivo, scotch m ®.

sellout ['sɛlaut] n tradimento; (*of tickets*): **it was a** ~ registrò un tutto esaurito.

selves [sɛlvz] npl of **self**.

semantic [sɪ'mæntɪk] a semantico(a); ~**s** n semantica.

semaphore ['sɛməfɔ:*] n segnali mpl con bandiere; (RAIL) semaforo.

semen ['si:mən] n sperma m.

semi ['sɛmɪ] prefix semi...; ~**-breve** n semibreve f; ~**circle** n semicerchio; ~**colon** n punto e virgola; ~**conscious** a parzialmente cosciente; ~**detached (house)** n casa gemella; ~**final** n semifinale f.

seminar ['sɛmɪnɑ:*] n seminario.

semiquaver ['sɛmɪkweɪvə*] n semicroma.

semiskilled ['sɛmɪ'skɪld] a: ~ **worker** n operaio(a) non specializzato(a).

semitone ['sɛmɪtəun] n (MUS) semitono.

semolina [sɛmə'li:nə] *n* semolino.

senate ['sɛnɪt] *n* senato; **senator** *n* senatore/trice.

send, *pt,pp* **sent** [sɛnd, sɛnt] *vt* mandare; **to ~ sb to Coventry** dare l'ostracismo a qd; **to ~ away** *vt* (*letter, goods*) spedire; (*person*) mandare via; **to ~ away for** *vt fus* richiedere per posta, farsi spedire; **to ~ back** *vt* rimandare; **to ~ for** *vt fus* mandare a chiamare, far venire; **to ~ off** *vt* (*goods*) spedire; (*SPORT: player*) espellere; **to ~ out** *vt* (*invitation*) diramare; **to ~ up** *vt* (*person, price*) far salire; (*parody*) mettere in ridicolo; **~er** *n* mittente m/f.

senile ['si:naɪl] *a* senile.

senior ['si:nɪə*] *a* (*older*) più vecchio(a); (*of higher rank*) di grado più elevato // *n* persona più anziana; (*in service*) persona con maggiore anzianità; **~ity** [-'ɔrɪtɪ] *n* anzianità.

sensation [sɛn'seɪʃən] *n* sensazione f; **to create a ~** fare scalpore; **~al** *a* sensazionale; (*marvellous*) eccezionale.

sense [sɛns] *n* senso; (*feeling*) senso, sensazione f; (*meaning*) senso, significato; (*wisdom*) buonsenso // *vt* sentire, percepire; **it makes ~** ha senso; **~s** *npl* ragione f; **~less** *a* sciocco(a); (*unconscious*) privo(a) di sensi.

sensibility [sɛnsɪ'bɪlɪtɪ] *n* sensibilità; **sensibilities** *npl* sensibilità *sg*.

sensible ['sɛnsɪbl] *a* sensato(a), ragionevole.

sensitive ['sɛnsɪtɪv] *a*: **~ (to)** sensibile (a); **sensitivity** [-'tɪvɪtɪ] *n* sensibilità.

sensual ['sɛnsjuəl] *a* sensuale.

sensuous ['sɛnsjuəs] *a* sensuale.

sent [sɛnt] *pt,pp of* **send**.

sentence ['sɛntns] *n* (*LING*) frase f; (*LAW: judgment*) sentenza; (*: punishment*) condanna // *vt*: **to ~ sb to death/to 5 years** condannare qd a morte/a 5 anni.

sentiment ['sɛntɪmənt] *n* sentimento; (*opinion*) opinione f; **~al** [-'mɛntl] *a* sentimentale.

sentry ['sɛntrɪ] *n* sentinella.

separate *a* ['sɛprɪt] separato(a) // *vb* ['sɛpəreɪt] *vt* separare // *vi* separarsi; **~ly** *ad* separatamente; **~s** *npl* (*clothes*) coordinati *mpl*; **separation** [-'reɪʃən] *n* separazione f.

September [sɛp'tɛmbə*] *n* settembre m.

septic ['sɛptɪk] *a* settico(a); (*wound*) infettato(a).

sequel ['si:kwl] *n* conseguenza; (*of story*) seguito.

sequence ['si:kwəns] *n* (*series*) serie f; (*order*) ordine m.

sequin ['si:kwɪn] *n* lustrino, paillette f inv.

serenade [sɛrə'neɪd] *n* serenata.

serene [sɪ'ri:n] *a* sereno(a), calmo(a); **serenity** [sə'rɛnɪtɪ] *n* serenità, tranquillità.

sergeant ['sɑ:dʒənt] *n*. sergente m; (*POLICE*) brigadiere m.

serial ['sɪərɪəl] *n* (*PRESS*) romanzo a puntate; (*RADIO, TV*) trasmissione f a puntate // *a* (*number*) di serie; **~ize** *vt* pubblicare a puntate; trasmettere a puntate.

series ['sɪərɪ:s] *n* serie f inv; (*PUBLISHING*) collana.

serious ['sɪərɪəs] *a* serio(a), grave; **~ly** *ad* seriamente; **~ness** *n* serietà, gravità.

sermon ['sə:mən] *n* sermone m.

serrated [sɪ'reɪtɪd] *a* seghettato(a).

serum ['sɪərəm] *n* siero.

servant ['sə:vənt] *n* domestico/a.

serve [sə:v] *vt* (*employer etc*) servire, essere a servizio di; (*purpose*) servire a; (*customer, food, meal*) servire; (*apprenticeship*) fare; (*prison term*) scontare // *vi* (*also TENNIS*) servire; (*be useful*): **to ~ as/for/to do** servire da/per/per fare // *n* (*TENNIS*) servizio; **it ~s him right** ben gli sta, se l'èmeritata; **to ~ out, ~ up** *vt* (*food*) servire.

service ['sə:vɪs] *n* servizio; (*AUT: maintenance*) assistenza, revisione f // *vt* (*car, washing machine*) revisionare; **the S~s** le forze armate; **to be of ~ to sb, to do sb a ~** essere d'aiuto a qd; **to put one's car in for (a) ~** portare la macchina in officina per una revisione; **dinner ~** *n* servizio da tavola; **~able** *a* pratico(a), utile; **~ area** *n* (*on motorway*) area di servizio; **~man** *n* militare m; **~ station** *n* stazione f di servizio.

serviette [sə:vɪ'ɛt] *n* tovagliolo.

servile ['sə:vaɪl] *a* servile.

session ['sɛʃən] *n* (*sitting*) seduta, sessione f; (*SCOL*) anno scolastico (*or* accademico); **to be in ~** essere in seduta.

set [sɛt] *n* serie f inv; (*RADIO, TV*) apparecchio; (*TENNIS*) set m inv; (*group of people*) mondo, ambiente m; (*CINEMA*) scenario; (*THEATRE: stage*) scene fpl; (*: scenery*) scenario; (*MATH*) insieme m; (*HAIRDRESSING*) messa in piega // *a* (*fixed*) stabilito(a), determinato(a); (*ready*) pronto(a) // *vb* (*pt, pp* **set**) (*place*) posare, mettere; (*fix*) fissare; (*adjust*) regolare; (*decide: rules etc*) stabilire, fissare; (*TYP*) comporre // *vi* (*sun*) tramontare; (*jam, jelly*) rapprendersi; (*concrete*) fare presa; **to be ~ on doing** essere deciso a fare; **to be (dead) ~ against** essere completamente contrario a; **to ~ (to music)** mettere in musica; **to ~ on fire** dare fuoco a; **to ~ free** liberare; **to ~ sail** prendere il mare; **to ~ about** *vt fus* (*task*) intraprendere, mettersi a; **to ~ aside** *vt* mettere da parte; **to ~ back** *vt* (*in time*): **to ~ back (by)** mettere indietro (di); **to ~ off** *vi* partire // (*bomb*) far scoppiare; (*cause to start*) mettere in moto; (*show up well*) dare risalto a; **to ~ out** *vi*: **to ~ out to do** proporsi di fare // *vt* (*arrange*) disporre; (*state*) esporre, presentare; **to ~ up** *vt* (*organization*) fondare, costituire; (*record*) stabilire; (*monument*) innalzare; **~back** *n* (*hitch*) contrattempo, inconveniente m.

settee [sɛ'ti:] *n* divano, sofà m inv.

setting ['sɛtɪŋ] n ambiente m; (of jewel) montatura.

settle ['sɛtl] vt (argument, matter) appianare; (problem) risolvere; (MED: calm) calmare // vi (bird, dust etc) posarsi; (sediment) depositarsi; (also: ~ **down**) sistemarsi, stabilirsi; calmarsi; **to ~ to sth** applicarsi a qc; **to ~ for sth** accontentarsi di qc; **to ~ in** vi sistemarsi; **to ~ on sth** decidersi per qc; **to ~ up with sb** regolare i conti con qd; **~ment** n (payment) pagamento, saldo; (agreement) accordo; (colony) colonia; (village etc) villaggio, comunità f inv; **~r** n colonizzatore/trice.

setup ['sɛtʌp] n (arrangement) situazione f; sistemazione f; (situation) situazione f.

seven ['sɛvn] num sette; **~teen** num diciassette; **~th** num settimo(a); **~ty** num settanta.

sever ['sɛvə*] vt recidere, tagliare; (relations) troncare.

several ['sɛvərl] a, pronoun alcuni(e), diversi(e); **~ of us** alcuni di noi.

severe [sɪ'vɪə*] a (serious) serio(a), grave; (hard) duro(a); (plain) semplice, sobrio(a); **severity** [sɪ'vɛrɪtɪ] n severità; gravità; (of weather) rigore m.

sew, pt **sewed**, pp **sewn** [səu, səud, səun] vt, vi cucire; **to ~ up** vt ricucire.

sewage ['su:dʒ] n acque fpl di scolo.

sewer ['su:ə*] n fogna.

sewing ['səuɪŋ] n cucitura; cucito; **~ machine** n macchina da cucire.

sewn [səun] pp of **sew**.

sex [sɛks] n sesso; **to have ~ with** avere rapporti sessuali con; **~ act** n atto sessuale.

sexual ['sɛksjuəl] a sessuale.

sexy ['sɛksɪ] a provocante, sexy inv.

shabby ['ʃæbɪ] a malandato(a); (behaviour) vergognoso(a).

shack [ʃæk] n baracca, capanna.

shackles ['ʃæklz] npl ferri mpl, catene fpl.

shade [ʃeɪd] n ombra; (for lamp) paralume m; (of colour) tonalità f inv; (small quantity): **a ~ of** un po' or un'ombra di // vt ombreggiare, fare ombra a; **in the ~** all'ombra; **a ~ smaller** un tantino più piccolo.

shadow ['ʃædəu] n ombra // vt (follow) pedinare; **~ cabinet** n (POL) governo m ombra inv; **~y** a ombreggiato(a), ombroso(a); (dim) vago(a), indistinto(a).

shady ['ʃeɪdɪ] a ombroso(a); (fig: dishonest) losco(a), equivoco(a).

shaft [ʃɑ:ft] n (of arrow, spear) asta; (AUT, TECH) albero; (of mine) pozzo; (of lift) tromba; (of light) raggio.

shaggy ['ʃægɪ] a ispido(a).

shake [ʃeɪk] vb (pt **shook**, pp **shaken** [ʃuk, 'ʃeɪkn]) vt scuotere; (bottle, cocktail) agitare // vi tremare // n scossa; **to ~ hands with sb** stringere or dare la mano a qd; **to ~ off** vt scrollare (via); (fig) sbarazzarsi di; **to ~ up** vt scuotere; **~up** n riorganizzazione f drastica; **shaky** a

(hand, voice) tremante; (building) traballante.

shale [ʃeɪl] n roccia scistosa.

shall [ʃæl] auxiliary vb: **I ~ go** andrò.

shallow ['ʃæləu] a poco profondo(a); (fig) superficiale.

sham [ʃæm] n finzione f, messinscena; (jewellery, furniture) imitazione f // a finto(a) // vt fingere, simulare.

shambles ['ʃæmblz] n confusione f, baraonda, scompiglio.

shame [ʃeɪm] n vergogna // vt far vergognare; **it is a ~ (that/to do)** è un peccato (che + sub/fare); **what a ~!** che peccato!; **~faced** a vergognoso(a); **~ful** a vergognoso(a); **~less** a sfrontato(a); (immodest) spudorato(a).

shampoo [ʃæm'pu:] n shampoo m inv // vt fare lo shampoo a.

shamrock ['ʃæmrɔk] n trifoglio (simbolo nazionale dell'Irlanda).

shandy ['ʃændɪ] n birra con gassosa.

shanty ['ʃæntɪ] n baracca, capanna; **~ town** n bidonville f inv.

shape [ʃeɪp] n forma // vt formare; (statement) formulare; (sb's ideas) condizionare // vi (also: ~ **up**) (events) andare, mettersi; (person) cavarsela; **to take ~** prendere forma; **-shaped** suffix: **heart-shaped** a a forma di cuore; **~less** a senza forma, informe; **~ly** a ben proporzionato(a).

share [ʃɛə*] n (thing received, contribution) parte f; (COMM) azione f // vt dividere; (have in common) condividere, avere in comune; **to ~ out (among or between)** dividere (tra); **~holder** n azionista m/f.

shark [ʃɑ:k] n squalo, pescecane m.

sharp [ʃɑ:p] a (razor, knife) affilato(a); (point) acuto(a), acuminato(a); (nose, chin) aguzzo(a); (outline) netto(a); (cold, pain) pungente; (MUS) diesis; (voice) stridulo(a); (person: quick-witted) sveglio(a), (: unscrupulous) disonesto(a) // n (MUS) diesis m inv // ad: **at 2 o'clock ~** alle due in punto; **~en** vt affilare; (pencil) fare la punta a; (fig) aguzzare; **~ener** n (also: **pencil ~ener**) temperamatite m inv; (also: **knife ~ener**) affilacoltelli m inv; **~eyed** a dalla vista acuta.

shatter ['ʃætə*] vt mandare in frantumi, frantumare; (fig: upset) distruggere; (: ruin) rovinare // vi frantumarsi, andare in pezzi.

shave [ʃeɪv] vt radere, rasare // vi radersi, farsi la barba // n: **to have a ~** farsi la barba; **~n** a (head) rasato(a), tonsurato(a); **~r** n (also: **electric ~r**) rasoio elettrico.

shaving ['ʃeɪvɪŋ] n (action) rasatura; **~s** npl (of wood etc) trucioli mpl; **~ brush** n pennello da barba; **~ cream** n crema da barba; **~ soap** n sapone m da barba.

shawl [ʃɔ:l] n scialle m.

she [ʃi:] pronoun ella, lei, essa; **~-cat** n gatta; **~-elephant** n elefantessa; NB: for ships, countries follow the gender of your translation.

sheaf, sheaves [ʃi:f, ʃi:vz] n covone m.

shear [ʃiə*] vt (pt ~ed, pp ~ed or shorn [ʃɔ:n]) (sheep) tosare; to ~ off vt tosare; (branch) tagliare; ~s npl (for hedge) cesoie fpl.

sheath [ʃi:θ] n fodero, guaina; (contraceptive) preservativo.

sheaves [ʃi:vz] npl of sheaf.

shed [ʃɛd] n capannone m // vt (pt,pp shed) (leaves, fur etc) perdere; (tears) versare.

sheep [ʃi:p] n, pl inv pecora; ~dog n cane m da pastore; ~ish a vergognoso(a), timido(a); ~skin n pelle f di pecora.

sheer [ʃiə*] a (utter) vero(a) (e proprio(a)); (steep) a picco, perpendicolare; (almost transparent) sottile // ad a picco.

sheet [ʃi:t] n (on bed) lenzuolo; (of paper) foglio; (of glass) lastra; (of metal) foglio, lamina; ~ lightning n lampo diffuso.

sheik(h) [ʃeik] n sceicco.

shelf, shelves [ʃelf, ʃelvz] n scaffale m, mensola.

shell [ʃel] n (on beach) conchiglia; (of egg, nut etc) guscio; (explosive) granata; (of building) scheletro // vt (peas) sgranare; (MIL) bombardare, cannoneggiare.

shellfish [ʃelfiʃ] n, pl inv (crab etc) crostaceo; (scallop etc) mollusco; (pl: as food) crostacei; molluschi.

shelter [ʃeltə*] n riparo, rifugio // vt riparare, proteggere; (give lodging to) dare rifugio or asilo a // vi ripararsi, mettersi al riparo; ~ed a (life) ritirato(a); (spot) riparato(a), protetto(a).

shelve [ʃelv] vt (fig) accantonare, rimandare; ~s npl of shelf.

shepherd [ʃepəd] n pastore m // vt (guide) guidare.

sheriff [ʃerif] n sceriffo.

sherry [ʃeri] n sherry m.

shield [ʃi:ld] n scudo // vt: to ~ (from) riparare (da), proteggere (da or contro).

shift [ʃift] n (change) cambiamento; (of workers) turno // vt spostare, muovere; (remove) rimuovere // vi spostarsi, muoversi; ~ work n lavoro a squadre; ~y a ambiguo(a); (eyes) sfuggente.

shilling [ʃiliŋ] n scellino (= 12 old pence; 20 in a pound).

shilly-shally [ʃiliʃæli] vi tentennare, esitare.

shimmer [ʃimə*] vi brillare, luccicare.

shin [ʃin] n tibia.

shine [ʃain] n splendore m, lucentezza // vb (pt, pp shone [ʃɔn]) vi (ri)splendere, brillare // vt far brillare, far risplendere; (torch): to ~ sth on puntare qc verso.

shingle [ʃiŋgl] n (on beach) ciottoli mpl; (on roof) assicella di copertura; ~s n (MED) erpete m.

shiny [ʃaini] a lucente, lucido(a).

ship [ʃip] n nave f // vt trasportare (via mare); (send) spedire (via mare); (load) imbarcare, caricare; ~building n costruzione f navale; ~ment n carico; ~ping n (ships) naviglio; (traffic)

navigazione f; ~shape a in perfetto ordine; ~wreck n relitto; (event) naufragio; ~yard n cantiere m navale.

shire [ʃaiə*] n contea.

shirk [ʃə:k] vt sottrarsi a, evitare.

shirt [ʃə:t] n (man's) camicia; in ~ sleeves in maniche di camicia; ~y a (col) incavolato(a).

shiver [ʃivə*] n brivido // vi rabbrividire, tremare.

shoal [ʃəul] n (of fish) banco.

shock [ʃɔk] n (impact) urto, colpo; (ELEC) scossa; (emotional) colpo, shock m inv; (MED) shock // vt colpire, scioccare; scandalizzare; ~ absorber n ammortizzatore m; ~ing a scioccante, traumatizzante; scandaloso(a), oltraggioso(a); ~proof a antiurto inv.

shod [ʃɔd] pt, pp of shoe.

shoddy [ʃɔdi] a scadente.

shoe [ʃu:] n scarpa; (also: horse~) ferro di cavallo // vt (pt,pp shod [ʃɔd]) (horse) ferrare; ~brush n spazzola per le scarpe; ~horn n calzante m; ~lace n stringa; ~ polish n lucido per scarpe; ~shop n calzoleria; ~tree n forma per scarpe.

shone [ʃɔn] pt,pp of shine.

shook [ʃuk] pt of shake.

shoot [ʃu:t] n (on branch, seedling) germoglio // vb (pt,pp shot [ʃɔt]) vt (game) cacciare, andare a caccia di; (person) sparare a; (execute) fucilare; (film) girare // vi (with gun): to ~ (at) sparare (a), fare fuoco (su); (with bow): to ~ (at) tirare (su); (FOOTBALL) sparare, tirare (forte); to ~ down vt (plane) abbattere; to ~ in/out vi entrare/uscire come una freccia; to ~ up vi (fig) salire alle stelle; ~ing n (shots) sparatoria; (HUNTING) caccia; ~ing range n poligono (di tiro), tirassegno; ~ing star n stella cadente.

shop [ʃɔp] n negozio; (workshop) officina // vi (also: go ~ping) fare spese; ~ assistant n commesso/a; ~ floor n officina; (fig) operai mpl, maestranza fpl; ~keeper n negoziante m/f, bottegaio/a; ~lifting n taccheggio; ~per n compratore/trice; ~ping n (goods) spesa, acquisti mpl; ~ping bag n borsa per la spesa; ~ping centre n centro commerciale; ~soiled a sciupato(a) a forza di stare in vetrina; ~ steward n (INDUSTRY) rappresentante m sindacale; ~ window n vetrina.

shore [ʃɔ:*] n (of sea) riva, spiaggia; (of lake) riva // vt: to ~ (up) puntellare.

shorn [ʃɔ:n] pp of shear.

short [ʃɔ:t] a (not long) corto(a); (soon finished) breve; (person) basso(a); (curt) brusco(a), secco(a); (insufficient) insufficiente // n (also: ~ film) cortometraggio; (a pair of) ~s (i) calzoncini; to be ~ of sth essere a corto di or mancare di qc; I'm 3 ~ me ne mancano 3; in ~ in breve; ~ of doing a meno che non si faccia; everything ~ of tutto fuorché; it is ~ for è l'abbreviazione or il diminutivo di; **to cut ~** (*speech, visit*) accorciare, abbreviare; (*person*) interrompere; **to fall ~ of** non essere all'altezza di; **to stop ~** fermarsi di colpo; **to stop ~ of** non arrivare fino a; **~age** n scarsezza, carenza; **~bread** n biscotto di pasta frolla; **~circuit** n cortocircuito // vt cortocircuitare // vi fare cortocircuito; **~coming** n difetto; **~(crust) pastry** n pasta frolla; **~cut** n scorciatoia; **~en** vt accorciare, ridurre; **~hand** n stenografia; **~hand typist** n stenodattilografo/a; **~ list** n (*for job*) rosa dei candidati; **~-lived** a effimero(a), di breve durata; **~ly** ad fra poco; **~-sighted** a miope; **~ story** n racconto, novella; **~-tempered** a irascibile; **~-term** a (*effect*) di or a breve durata; **~wave** n (RADIO) onde fpl corte.

shot [ʃɔt] pt,pp of **shoot** // n sparo, colpo; (*person*) tiratore m; (*try*) prova; (*injection*) iniezione f; (PHOT) foto f inv; **like a ~** come un razzo; (*very readily*) immediatamente; **~gun** n fucile m da caccia.

should [ʃud] auxiliary vb: **I ~ go now** dovrei andare ora; **he ~ be there now** dovrebbe essere arrivato ora; **I ~ go if I were you** se fossi in te andrei; **I ~ like to** mi piacerebbe.

shoulder ['ʃəuldə*] n spalla; (*of road*): **hard ~** banchina // vt (*fig*) addossarsi, prendere sulle proprie spalle; **~ bag** n borsa a tracolla; **~ blade** n scapola; **~ strap** n bretella, spallina.

shout [ʃaut] n urlo, grido // vt gridare // vi urlare, gridare; **to give sb a ~** chiamare qd gridando; **to ~ down** vt zittire gridando; **~ing** n urli mpl.

shove [ʃʌv] vt spingere; (*col: put*): **to ~ sth in** ficcare qc in; **to ~ off** vi (NAUT) scostarsi.

shovel ['ʃʌvl] n pala // vt spalare.

show [ʃəu] n (*of emotion*) dimostrazione f, manifestazione f; (*semblance*) apparenza; (*exhibition*) mostra, esposizione f; (THEATRE, CINEMA) spettacolo // vb (pt **~ed**, pp **shown** [ʃəun]) vt far vedere, mostrare; (*courage etc*) dimostrare, dar prova di; (*exhibit*) esporre // vi vedersi, essere visibile; **to ~ sb in** far entrare qd; **to ~ off** vi (*pej*) esibirsi, mettersi in mostra // vt (*display*) mettere in risalto; (*pej*) mettere in mostra; **to ~ sb out** accompagnare qd alla porta; **to ~ up** vi (*stand out*) essere ben visibile; (*col: turn up*) farsi vedere // vt mettere in risalto; (*unmask*) smascherare; **~ business** n industria dello spettacolo; **~down** n prova di forza.

shower ['ʃauə*] n (*rain*) acquazzone m; (*of stones etc*) pioggia; (*also:* **~bath**) doccia // vi fare la doccia // vt: **to ~ sb with** (*gifts, abuse etc*) coprire qd di; (*missiles*) lanciare contro qd una pioggia di.

showground ['ʃəugraund] n terreno d'esposizione.

showing ['ʃəuiŋ] n (*of film*) proiezione f.

show jumping ['ʃəudʒʌmpiŋ] n concorso ippico (di salto ad ostacoli).

showmanship ['ʃəumənʃip] n abilità d'impresario.

shown [ʃəun] pp of **show**.

show-off ['ʃəuɔf] n (*col: person*) esibizionista m/f.

showroom ['ʃəurum] n sala d'esposizione.

shrank [ʃræŋk] pt of **shrink**.

shrapnel ['ʃræpnl] n shrapnel m.

shred [ʃrɛd] n (*gen pl*) brandello // vt fare a brandelli; (CULIN) sminuzzare, tagliuzzare.

shrewd [ʃru:d] a astuto(a), scaltro(a).

shriek [ʃri:k] n strillo // vt, vi strillare.

shrift [ʃrift] n: **to give sb short ~** sbrigare qd.

shrill [ʃril] a acuto(a), stridulo(a), stridente.

shrimp [ʃrimp] n gamberetto.

shrine [ʃrain] n reliquario; (*place*) santuario.

shrink [ʃriŋk] vb (pt **shrank** [ʃræŋk, ʃrʌŋk]) vi restringersi; (*fig*) ridursi // vt (*wool*) far restringere // n (*col: pej*) psicanalista m/f; **~age** n restringimento.

shrivel ['ʃrivl] vt (*also: ~ up*) vi raggrinzare, avvizzire // vi raggrinzirsi, avvizzire.

shroud [ʃraud] n sudario // vt: **~ed in mystery** avvolto(a) nel mistero.

Shrove Tuesday ['ʃrəuv'tju:zdi] n martedì m grasso.

shrub [ʃrʌb] n arbusto; **~bery** n arbusti mpl.

shrug [ʃrʌg] n scrollata di spalle // vt,vi: **to ~ (one's shoulders)** alzare le spalle, fare spallucce; **to ~ off** vt passare sopra a.

shrunk [ʃrʌŋk] pp of **shrink**; **~en** a rattrappito(a).

shudder ['ʃʌdə*] n brivido // vi rabbrividire.

shuffle ['ʃʌfl] vt (*cards*) mescolare; **to ~ (one's feet)** strascicare i piedi.

shun [ʃʌn] vt sfuggire, evitare.

shunt [ʃʌnt] vt (RAIL: direct) smistare; (: divert) deviare // vi: **to ~ (to and fro)** fare la spola.

shut, pt, pp shut [ʃʌt] vt chiudere // vi chiudersi, chiudere; **to ~ down** vt, vi chiudere definitivamente; **to ~ off** vt fermare, bloccare; **to ~ up** vi (*col: keep quiet*) stare zitto(a), fare silenzio // vt (*close*) chiudere; (*silence*) far tacere; **~ter** n imposta; (PHOT) otturatore m.

shuttle ['ʃʌtl] n spola, navetta; (*also:* **~ service**) servizio m navetta inv.

shuttlecock ['ʃʌtlkɔk] n volano.

shy [ʃai] a timido(a).

Siamese [saiə'mi:z] a: **~ cat** gatto siamese.

Sicily ['sisili] n Sicilia.

sick [sik] a (*ill*) malato(a); (*vomiting*): **to be ~** vomitare; (*humour*) macabro(a); **to feel ~** avere la nausea; **to be ~ of** (*fig*) averne abbastanza di; **~ bay** n infermeria; ~**en** vt nauseare; ~**ening** a (fig) disgustoso(a), rivoltante.

sickle ['sɪkl] n falcetto.

sick: ~ **leave** n congedo per malattia; ~**ly** a malaticcio(a); (causing nausea) nauseante; ~**ness** n malattia; (vomiting) vomito; ~ **pay** n sussidio per malattia.

side [saɪd] n lato; (of lake) riva // cpd (door, entrance) laterale // vi: **to ~ with sb** parteggiare per qd, prendere le parti di qd; **by the ~ of** a fianco di; (road) sul ciglio di; ~ **by ~** fianco a fianco; **to take ~s (with)** schierarsi (con); ~**board** n credenza; ~**boards**, ~**burns** npl (whiskers) basette fpl; ~ **effect** n (MED) effetto collaterale; ~**light** n (AUT) luce f di posizione; ~**line** n (SPORT) linea laterale; (fig) attività secondaria; ~**long** a obliquo(a); ~ **road** n strada secondaria; ~**saddle** ad all'amazzone; ~ **show** n attrazione f; ~**track** vt (fig) distrarre; ~**walk** n (US) marciapiede m; ~**ways** ad di traverso.

siding ['saɪdɪŋ] n (RAIL) binario di raccordo.

sidle ['saɪdl] vi: **to ~ up (to)** avvicinarsi furtivamente (a).

siege [siːdʒ] n assedio.

sieve [sɪv] n setaccio // vt setacciare.

sift [sɪft] vt passare al crivello; (fig) vagliare.

sigh [saɪ] n sospiro // vi sospirare.

sight [saɪt] n (faculty) vista; (spectacle) spettacolo; (on gun) mira // vt avvistare; **in ~** in vista; **out of ~** non visibile; ~**seeing** n giro turistico; **to go ~seeing** visitare una località; ~**seer** n turista m/f.

sign [saɪn] n segno; (with hand etc) segno, gesto; (notice) insegna, cartello // vt firmare; **to ~ in/out** vi firmare il registro (all'arrivo/alla partenza); **to ~ up** (MIL) vt arruolare // vi arruolarsi.

signal ['sɪɡnl] n segnale m // vt (person) fare segno a; (message) segnalare.

signature ['sɪɡnətʃə*] n firma; ~ **tune** n sigla musicale.

signet ring ['sɪɡnətrɪŋ] n anello con sigillo.

significance [sɪɡ'nɪfɪkəns] n significato; importanza.

significant [sɪɡ'nɪfɪkənt] a significativo(a).

signify ['sɪɡnɪfaɪ] vt significare.

signpost ['saɪnpəust] n cartello indicatore.

silence ['saɪlns] n silenzio // vt far tacere, ridurre al silenzio; ~**r** n (on gun, AUT) silenziatore m.

silent ['saɪlnt] a silenzioso(a); (film) muto(a).

silhouette [sɪluː'ɛt] n silhouette f inv.

silicon chip ['sɪlɪkən'tʃɪp] n piastrina di silicio.

silk [sɪlk] n seta // cpd di seta; ~**y** a di seta.

silly ['sɪlɪ] a stupido(a), sciocco(a).

silt [sɪlt] n limo.

silver ['sɪlvə*] n argento; (money) monete da 5, 10 o 50 pence; (also: ~**ware**) argenteria // cpd d'argento; ~ **paper** n

carta argentata, (carta) stagnola; ~**-plated** a argentato(a); ~**smith** n argentiere m; ~**y** a (colour) argenteo(a); (sound) argentino(a).

similar ['sɪmɪlə*] a: ~ **(to)** simile (a); ~**ity** [-'lærɪtɪ] n somiglianza, rassomiglianza.

simile ['sɪmɪlɪ] n similitudine f.

simmer ['sɪmə*] vi cuocere a fuoco lento.

simple ['sɪmpl] a semplice; **simplicity** [-'plɪsɪtɪ] n semplicità; **simplify** ['sɪmplɪfaɪ] vt semplificare; **simply** ad semplicemente.

simulate ['sɪmjuleɪt] vt fingere, simulare.

simultaneous [sɪməl'teɪnɪəs] a simultaneo(a).

sin [sɪn] n peccato // vi peccare.

since [sɪns] ad da allora // prep da // cj (time) da quando; (because) poiché, dato che; ~ **then** da allora.

sincere [sɪn'sɪə*] a sincero(a); **sincerity** [-'serɪtɪ] n sincerità.

sine [saɪn] n (MATH) seno.

sinew ['sɪnjuː] n tendine m; ~**s** npl muscoli mpl.

sinful ['sɪnful] a peccaminoso(a).

sing, pt **sang**, pp **sung** [sɪŋ, sæŋ, sʌŋ] vt,vi cantare.

singe [sɪndʒ] vt bruciacchiare.

singer ['sɪŋə*] n cantante m/f.

single ['sɪŋɡl] a solo(a), unico(a); (unmarried: man) celibe; (: woman) nubile; (not double) semplice // n (also: ~ **ticket**) biglietto di (sola) andata; (record) 45 giri m; ~**s** npl (TENNIS) singolo; **to ~ out** vt scegliere; (distinguish) distinguere; ~**-breasted** a a un petto; **in ~ file** in fila indiana; ~**-handed** ad senza aiuto, da solo(a); ~**-minded** a tenace, risoluto(a); ~ **room** n camera singola.

singlet ['sɪŋɡlɪt] n canottiera.

singly ['sɪŋɡlɪ] ad separatamente.

singular ['sɪŋɡjulə*] a (exceptional, LING) singolare; (unusual) strano(a) // n (LING) singolare m.

sinister ['sɪnɪstə*] a a sinistro(a).

sink [sɪŋk] n lavandino, acquaio // vb (pt **sank**, pp **sunk** [sæŋk, sʌŋk]) vt (ship) (fare) affondare, colare a picco; (foundations) scavare; (piles etc) to ~ **sth into** conficcare qc in // vi affondare, andare a fondo; (ground etc) cedere, avvallarsi; **to ~ in** vi conficcarsi, penetrare.

sinner ['sɪnə*] n peccatore/trice.

sinuous ['sɪnjuəs] a sinuoso(a).

sinus ['saɪnəs] n (ANAT) seno.

sip [sɪp] n sorso // vt sorseggiare.

siphon ['saɪfən] n sifone m; **to ~ off** vt travasare (con un sifone).

sir [sə*] n signore m; S~ **John Smith** Sir John Smith; **yes** ~ sì, signore.

siren ['saɪərn] n sirena.

sirloin ['səːlɔɪn] n lombata di manzo.

sirocco [sɪ'rɔkəu] n scirocco.

sissy ['sɪsɪ] n (col) femminuccia.

sister ['sɪstə*] n sorella; (nun) suora;

(*nurse*) infermiera *f* caposala *inv*; ~-**in-law** *n* cognata.

sit, *pt,pp* **sat** [sɪt, sæt] *vi* sedere, sedersi; (*assembly*) essere in seduta // *vt* (*exam*) sostenere, dare; **to** ~ **down** *vi* sedersi; **to** ~ **up** *vi* tirarsi su a sedere; (*not go to bed*) stare alzato(a) fino a tardi.

site [saɪt] *n* posto; (*also:* **building** ~) cantiere *m* // *vt* situare.

sit-in [ˈsɪtɪn] *n* (*demonstration*) sit-in *m inv*, manifestazione *f* di protesta con occupazione.

sitting [ˈsɪtɪŋ] *n* (*of assembly etc*) seduta; (*in canteen*) turno; ~ **room** *n* soggiorno.

situated [ˈsɪtjueɪtɪd] *a* situato(a).

situation [sɪtjuˈeɪʃən] *n* situazione *f*.

six [sɪks] *num* sei; ~**teen** *num* sedici; ~**th** *a* sesto(a); ~**ty** *num* sessanta.

size [saɪz] *n* dimensioni *fpl*; (*of clothing*) taglia, misura; (*of shoes*) numero; (*glue*) colla; **to** ~ **up** *vt* giudicare, farsi un'idea di; ~**able** *a* considerevole.

sizzle [ˈsɪzl] *vi* sfrigolare.

skate [skeɪt] *n* pattino; (*fish: pl inv*) razza // *vi* pattinare; ~**board** *n* skateboard *m inv*; ~**r** *n* pattinatore/trice; **skating** *n* pattinaggio; **skating rink** *n* pista di pattinaggio.

skeleton [ˈskɛlɪtn] *n* scheletro; ~ **staff** *n* personale *m* ridotto.

sketch [skɛtʃ] *n* (*drawing*) schizzo, abbozzo; (*THEATRE*) scenetta comica, sketch *m inv* // *vt* abbozzare, schizzare; ~ **book** *n* album *m inv* per schizzi; ~ **pad** *n* blocco per schizzi; ~**y** *a* incompleto(a), lacunoso(a).

skewer [ˈskjuːə*] *n* spiedo.

ski [skiː] *n* sci *m inv* // *vi* sciare; ~ **boot** *n* scarpone *m* da sci.

skid [skɪd] *n* slittamento // *vi* slittare.

skier [ˈskiːə*] *n* sciatore/trice.

skiing [ˈskiːɪŋ] *n* sci *m*.

skilful [ˈskɪlful] *a* abile.

ski lift [ˈskiːlɪft] *n* sciovia.

skill [skɪl] *n* abilità *f inv*, capacità *f inv*; ~**ed** *a* esperto(a); (*worker*) qualificato(a), specializzato(a).

skim [skɪm] *vt* (*milk*) scremare; (*soup*) schiumare; (*glide over*) sfiorare // *vi*: **to** ~ **through** (*fig*) scorrere, dare una scorsa a.

skimp [skɪmp] *vt* (*work*) fare alla carlona; (*cloth etc*) lesinare; ~**y** *a* misero(a), striminzito(a); frugale.

skin [skɪn] *n* pelle *f* // *vt* (*fruit etc*) sbucciare; (*animal*) scuoiare, spellare; ~-**deep** *a* superficiale; ~ **diving** *n* nuoto subacqueo; ~ **graft** *n* innesto epidermico; ~**ny** *a* molto magro(a), pelle e ossa *inv*; ~ **test** *n* prova di reazione cutanea.

skip [skɪp] *n* saltello, balzo; (*container*) benna // *vi* saltare; (*with rope*) saltare la corda // *vt* (*pass over*) saltare.

skipper [ˈskɪpə*] *n* (*NAUT, SPORT*) capitano.

skipping rope [ˈskɪpɪŋrəup] *n* corda per saltare.

skirmish [ˈskəːmɪʃ] *n* scaramuccia.

skirt [skəːt] *n* gonna, sottana // *vt*

fiancheggiare, costeggiare; ~**ing board** *n* zoccolo.

skit [skɪt] *n* parodia; scenetta satirica.

ski tow [ˈskiːtəu] *n* = **ski lift**.

skittle [ˈskɪtl] *n* birillo; ~**s** *n* (*game*) (gioco dei) birilli *mpl*.

skive [skaɪv] *vi* (*Brit: col*) fare il lavativo.

skulk [skʌlk] *vi* muoversi furtivamente.

skull [skʌl] *n* cranio, teschio.

skunk [skʌŋk] *n* moffetta.

sky [skaɪ] *n* cielo; ~-**light** *n* lucernario; ~**scraper** *n* grattacielo.

slab [slæb] *n* lastra.

slack [slæk] *a* (*loose*) allentato(a); (*slow*) lento(a); (*careless*) negligente // *n* (*in rope etc*) parte *f* non tesa; ~**s** *npl* pantaloni *mpl*; ~**en** (*also:* ~**en off**) *vi* rallentare, diminuire // *vt* allentare.

slag [slæg] *n* scorie *fpl*; ~ **heap** *n* ammasso di scorie.

slam [slæm] *vt* (*door*) sbattere; (*throw*) scaraventare; (*criticize*) stroncare // *vi* sbattere.

slander [ˈslɑːndə*] *n* calunnia; diffamazione *f* // *vt* calunniare; diffamare.

slang [slæŋ] *n* gergo; slang *m*.

slant [slɑːnt] *n* pendenza, inclinazione *f*; (*fig*) angolazione *f*, punto di vista; ~**ed** *a* tendenzioso(a); ~**ing** *a* in pendenza, inclinato(a).

slap [slæp] *n* manata, pacca; (*on face*) schiaffo // *vt* dare una manata a; schiaffeggiare // *ad* (*directly*) in pieno; ~**dash** *a* abborracciato(a); ~**stick** *n* (*comedy*) farsa grossolana; **a** ~-**up meal** un pranzo (*or* una cena) coi fiocchi.

slash [slæʃ] *vt* squarciare; (*face*) sfregiare; (*fig: prices*) ridurre drasticamente, tagliare.

slate [sleɪt] *n* ardesia // *vt* (*fig: criticize*) stroncare, distruggere.

slaughter [ˈslɔːtə*] *n* strage *f*, massacro // *vt* (*animal*) macellare; (*people*) trucidare, massacrare; ~**house** *n* macello, mattatoio.

Slav [slɑːv] *a* slavo(a).

slave [sleɪv] *n* schiavo/a // *vi* (*also:* ~ **away**) lavorare come uno schiavo; ~**ry** *n* schiavitù *f*.

sleazy [ˈsliːzɪ] *a* trasandato(a).

sledge [slɛdʒ] *n* slitta; ~**hammer** *n* mazza, martello da fabbro.

sleek [sliːk] *a* (*hair, fur*) lucido(a), lucente; (*car, boat*) slanciato(a), affusolato(a).

sleep [sliːp] *n* sonno // *vi* (*pt, pp* **slept** [slɛpt]) dormire; **to go to** ~ addormentarsi; **to** ~ **in** *vi* (*lie late*) alzarsi tardi; (*oversleep*) dormire fino a tardi; ~**er** *n* (*person*) dormiente *m/f*; (*RAIL: on track*) traversina; (*: train*) treno di vagoni letto; ~**ing** *a* addormentato(a); ~**ing bag** *n* sacco a pelo; ~**ing car** *n* vagone *m* letto *inv*, carrozza *f* letto *inv*; ~**ing pill** *n* sonnifero; ~**lessness** *n* insonnia; **a** ~-**less night** una notte in bianco; ~**walker** *n* sonnambulo/a; ~**y** *a* assonnato(a), sonnolento(a); (*fig*) addormentato(a).

sleet [sli:t] n nevischio.
sleeve [sli:v] n manica; ~less a (garment) senza maniche.
sleigh [slei] n slitta.
sleight [slait] n: ~ of hand gioco di destrezza.
slender ['slɛndə*] a snello(a), sottile; (not enough) scarso(a), esiguo(a).
slept [slɛpt] pt,pp of **sleep**.
slice [slais] n fetta // vt affettare, tagliare a fette.
slick [slik] a (clever) brillante; (insincere) untuoso(a), falso(a) // n (also: oil ~) chiazza di petrolio.
slid [slid] pt,pp of **slide**.
slide [slaid] n (in playground) scivolo; (PHOT) diapositiva; (also: hair ~) fermaglio (per capelli); (in prices) caduta // vb (pt,pp slid [slid]) vt far scivolare // vi scivolare; ~ rule n regolo calcolatore; **sliding** a (door) scorrevole; **sliding scale** n scala mobile.
slight [slait] a (slim) snello(a), sottile; (frail) delicato(a), fragile; (trivial) insignificante; (small) piccolo(a) // n offesa, affronto // vt (offend) offendere, fare un affronto a; the ~est il minimo (or la minima); not in the ~est affatto, neppure per sogno; ~ly ad lievemente, un po'.
slim [slim] a magro(a), snello(a) // vi dimagrire; fare (or seguire) una dieta dimagrante.
slime [slaim] n limo, melma; viscidume m.
sling [sliŋ] n (MED) benda al collo // vt (pt,pp slung [slʌŋ]) lanciare, tirare.
slip [slip] n scivolata, scivolone m; (mistake) errore m, sbaglio; (underskirt) sottoveste f; (of paper) striscia di carta; tagliando, scontrino // vt (slide) far scivolare // vi (slide) scivolare; (move smoothly): to ~ into/out of scivolare in/via da; (decline) declinare; to give sb the ~ sfuggire qd; a ~ of the tongue un lapsus linguae; to ~ away vi svignarsela; to ~ in vt introdurre casualmente; to ~ out vi uscire furtivamente; ~ped disc n spostamento delle vertebre.
slipper ['slipə*] n pantofola.
slippery ['slipəri] a scivoloso(a).
slip road ['slipprəud] n (to motorway) rampa di accesso.
slipshod ['slipʃɔd] a sciatto(a), trasandato(a).
slip-up ['slipʌp] n granchio.
slipway ['slipwei] n scalo di costruzione.
slit [slit] n fessura, fenditura; (cut) taglio; (tear) squarcio; strappo // vt (pt,pp slit) tagliare; (make a slit) squarciare; strappare.
slither ['sliðə*] vi scivolare, sdrucciolare.
slog [slɔg] n faticata // vi lavorare con accanimento, sgobbare.
slogan ['sləugən] n motto, slogan m inv.
slop [slɔp] vi (also: ~ over) traboccare; versarsi // vt spandere; versare; ~s npl acqua sporca; sbobba.
slope [sləup] n pendio; (side of mountain) versante m; (of roof) pendenza; (of floor) inclinazione f // vi: to ~ down declinare; to ~ up essere in salita.
sloppy ['slɔpi] a (work) tirato(a) via; (appearance) sciatto(a); (film etc) sdolcinato(a).
slot [slɔt] n fessura // vt: to ~ into introdurre in una fessura; ~ machine n distributore m automatico.
slouch [slautʃ] vi ciondolare.
slovenly ['slʌvənli] a sciatto(a), trasandato(a).
slow [sləu] a lento(a); (watch): to be ~ essere indietro // ad lentamente // vt,vi (also: ~ down, ~ up) rallentare; ' ~ ' (road sign) 'rallentare'; ~ly ad lentamente; in ~ motion al rallentatore.
sludge [slʌdʒ] n fanghiglia.
slug [slʌg] n lumaca; (bullet) pallottola; ~gish a lento(a).
sluice [slu:s] n chiusa.
slum [slʌm] n catapecchia.
slumber ['slʌmbə*] n sonno.
slump [slʌmp] n crollo, caduta; depressione f, crisi f inv // vi crollare.
slung [slʌŋ] pt,pp of **sling**.
slur [slə:*] n pronuncia indistinta; (stigma) diffamazione f, calunnia; (smear): ~ (on) macchia (su); (MUS) legatura // vt pronunciare in modo indistinto.
slush [slʌʃ] n neve mista a fango.
slut [slʌt] n donna trasandata, sciattona.
sly [slai] a furbo(a), scaltro(a); on the ~ di soppiatto.
smack [smæk] n (slap) pacca; (on face) schiaffo // vt schiaffeggiare; (child) picchiare // vi: to ~ of puzzare di; to ~ one's lips fare uno schiocco con le labbra.
small [smɔ:l] a piccolo(a); ~ ads npl piccola pubblicità; in the ~ hours alle ore piccole; ~pox n vaiolo; ~ talk n chiacchiere fpl.
smarmy ['smɑ:mi] a (col) untuoso(a), strisciante.
smart [smɑ:t] a elegante; (clever) intelligente; (quick) sveglio(a) // vi bruciare; to ~en up vt farsi bello(a) // vt (people) fare bello(a); (things) abbellire.
smash [smæʃ] n (also: ~-up) scontro, collisione f // vt frantumare, fracassare; (opponent) annientare, schiacciare; (hopes) distruggere; (SPORT: record) battere // vi frantumarsi, andare in pezzi; ~ing a (col) favoloso(a), formidabile.
smattering ['smætəriŋ] n: a ~ of un'infarinatura di.
smear [smiə*] n macchia; (MED) striscio // vt ungere; (fig) denigrare, diffamare.
smell [smɛl] n odore m; (sense) olfatto, odorato // vb (pt,pp smelt or smelled [smɛlt, smɛld]) vt sentire (l')odore di // vi (food etc): to ~ (of) avere odore (di); (pej) puzzare, avere un cattivo odore; ~y a puzzolente.
smile [smail] n sorriso // vi sorridere.
smirk [smə:k] n sorriso furbo; sorriso compiaciuto.

smith [smɪθ] n fabbro; **~y** n fucina.
smitten ['smɪtn] a: **~ with** colpito(a) da.
smock [smɔk] n grembiule m, camice m.
smog [smɔg] n smog m.
smoke [sməuk] n fumo // vt, vi fumare; **to have a ~** fumarsi una sigaretta; **~d** a (bacon, glass) affumicato(a); **~r** n (person) fumatore/trice; (RAIL) carrozza per fumatori; **smoking** n: 'no smoking' (sign) 'vietato fumare'; **smoky** a fumoso(a); (surface) affumicato(a).
smooth [smu:ð] a liscio(a); (sauce) omogeneo(a); (flavour, whisky) amabile; (movement) regolare; (person) melliluo(a) // vt lisciare, spianare; (also: **~ out**: difficulties) appianare.
smother ['smʌðə*] vt soffocare.
smoulder ['sməuldə*] vi covare sotto la cenere.
smudge [smʌdʒ] n macchia; sbavatura // vt imbrattare, sporcare.
smug [smʌg] a soddisfatto(a), compiaciuto(a).
smuggle ['smʌgl] vt contrabbandare **~r** n contrabbandiere/a; **smuggling** n contrabbando.
smutty ['smʌtɪ] a (fig) osceno(a), indecente.
snack [snæk] n spuntino; **~ bar** n tavola calda, snack bar m inv.
snag [snæg] n intoppo, ostacolo imprevisto.
snail [sneɪl] n chiocciola.
snake [sneɪk] n serpente m.
snap [snæp] n (sound) schianto, colpo secco; (photograph) istantanea; (game) rubamazzo // a improvviso(a) // vt (far) schioccare; (break) spezzare di netto; (photograph) scattare un'istantanea di // vi spezzarsi con un rumore secco; **to ~ open/shut** aprirsi/chiudersi di scatto; **to ~ at** vt fus (subj: dog) cercare di mordere; **to ~ off** vt (break) schiantare; **to ~ up** vt afferrare; **~py** a rapido(a); **~shot** n istantanea.
snare [snɛə*] n trappola.
snarl [snɑ:l] vi ringhiare.
snatch [snætʃ] n (fig) furto con strappo, scippo; (small amount): **~es** of frammenti mpl di // vt strappare (con violenza); (steal) rubare.
sneak [sni:k] vi: **to ~ in/out** entrare/uscire di nascosto; **~y** a falso(a), disonesto(a).
sneer [snɪə*] n ghigno, sogghigno // vi ghignare, sogghignare.
sneeze [sni:z] n starnuto // vi starnutire.
snide [snaɪd] a malignо(a).
sniff [snɪf] n fiutata, annusata // vi fiutare, annusare; tirare su col naso; (in contempt) arricciare il naso // vt fiutare, annusare.
snigger ['snɪgə*] n riso represso // vi ridacchiare, ridere sotto i baffi.
snip [snɪp] n pezzetto; (bargain) (buon) affare m, occasione f // vt tagliare.
sniper ['snaɪpə*] n (marksman) franco tiratore m, cecchino.
snippet ['snɪpɪt] n frammento.

snivelling ['snɪvlɪŋ] a (whimpering) piagnucoloso(a).
snob [snɔb] n snob m/f inv; **~bery** n snobismo; **~bish** a snob inv.
snooker ['snu:kə*] n tipo di gioco del biliardo.
snoop ['snu:p] vi: **to ~ on sb** spiare qd.
snooty ['snu:tɪ] a borioso(a), snob inv.
snooze [snu:z] n sonnellino, pisolino // vi fare un sonnellino.
snore [snɔ:*] vi russare.
snorkel ['snɔ:kl] n (of swimmer) respiratore a tubo.
snort [snɔ:t] n sbuffo // vi sbuffare.
snout [snaut] n muso.
snow [snəu] n neve f // vi nevicare; **~ball** n palla di neve; **~bound** a bloccato(a) dalla neve; **~drift** n cumulo di neve (ammucchiato dal vento); **~drop** n bucaneve m inv; **~fall** n nevicata; **~flake** n fiocco di neve; **~man** n pupazzo di neve; **~plough** n spazzaneve m inv; **~storm** n tormenta.
snub [snʌb] vt snobbare // n offesa, affronto; **~-nosed** a dal naso camuso.
snuff [snʌf] n tabacco da fiuto.
snug [snʌg] a comodo(a); (room, house) accogliente, comodo(a).
so [səu] ad (degree) così, tanto; (manner: thus) così, in questo modo // cj perciò; **~ as to do** in modo da or così da fare; **~ that** (purpose) affinché + sub; (result) così che; **~ do I**, **~ am I** etc anch'io etc; **if ~** se è così; **I hope ~** spero di sì; **10 or ~** circa 10; **~ far** fin qui, finora; (in past) fino ad allora; **~ long!** arrivederci!; **~ many** tanti(e); **~ much** ad tanto // det tanto(a); **~ and ~** n tale m/f dei tali.
soak [səuk] vt inzuppare; (clothes) mettere a mollo // vi inzupparsi; (clothes) essere a mollo; **to be ~ed through** essere fradicio(a); **to ~ in** vi penetrare; **to ~ up** vt assorbire.
soap [səup] n sapone m; **~ powder** n detersivo; **~y** a insaponato(a).
soar [sɔ:*] vi volare in alto.
sob [sɔb] n singhiozzo // vi singhiozzare.
sober ['səubə*] a non ubriaco(a); (sedate) serio(a); (moderate) moderato(a); (colour, style) sobrio(a); **to ~ up** vt far passare la sbornia a // vi farsi passare la sbornia.
Soc. abbr of **society**.
so-called ['səu'kɔ:ld] a cosiddetto(a).
soccer ['sɔkə*] n calcio.
sociable ['səuʃəbl] a socievole.
social ['səuʃl] a sociale // n festa, serata; **~ club** n club m inv sociale; **~ism** n socialismo; **~ist** a,n socialista (m/f); **~ science** n scienze fpl sociali; **~ security** n previdenza sociale; **~ welfare** n assistenza sociale; **~ work** n servizio sociale; **~ worker** n assistente m/f sociale.
society [sə'saɪətɪ] n società f inv; (club) società, associazione f; (also: **high ~**) alta società.
sociology [səusɪ'ɔlədʒɪ] n sociologia.

sock [sɔk] n calzino // vt (hit) dare un pugno a.

socket ['sɔkɪt] n cavità f inv; (of eye) orbita; (ELEC: also: **wall** ~) presa di corrente; (: for light bulb) portalampada m inv.

sod [sɔd] n (of earth) zolla erbosa; (col!) bastardo/a (!).

soda ['səʊdə] n (CHEM) soda; (also: ~ **water**) acqua di seltz.

sodden ['sɔdn] a fradicio(a).

sodium ['səʊdɪəm] n sodio.

sofa ['səʊfə] n sofà m inv.

soft [sɔft] a (not rough) morbido(a); (not hard) soffice; (not loud) sommesso(a); (kind) gentile; (weak) debole; (stupid) stupido(a); ~ **drink** n analcolico; ~**en** ['sɔfn] vt ammorbidire; addolcire; attenuare // vi ammorbidirsi; addolcirsi; attenuarsi; ~-**hearted** a sensibile; ~**ly** ad dolcemente; morbidamente; ~**ness** n dolcezza; morbidezza; ~**ware** n software m.

soggy ['sɔgi] a inzuppato(a).

soil [sɔil] n (earth) terreno, suolo // vt sporcare; (fig) macchiare.

solar ['səʊlə*] a solare.

sold [səʊld] pt,pp of **sell**; ~ **out** a (COMM) esaurito(a).

solder ['səʊldə*] vt saldare // n saldatura.

soldier ['səʊldʒə*] n soldato, militare m.

sole [səʊl] n (of foot) pianta (del piede); (of shoe) suola; (fish: pl inv) sogliola // a solo(a), unico(a).

solemn ['sɔləm] a solenne; grave; serio(a).

solicitor [sə'lɪsɪtə*] n (for wills etc) ≈ notaio; (in court) ≈ avvocato.

solid ['sɔlɪd] a (not hollow) pieno(a); (strong, sound, reliable, not liquid) solido(a); (meal) sostanzioso(a) // n solido.

solidarity [sɔlɪ'dærɪti] n solidarietà.

solidify [sə'lɪdɪfaɪ] vi solidificarsi // vt solidificare.

solitaire [sɔlɪ'tɛə*] n (game, gem) solitario.

solitary ['sɔlɪtəri] a solitario(a).

solitude ['sɔlɪtju:d] n solitudine f.

solo ['səʊləʊ] n assolo; ~**ist** n solista m/f.

solstice ['sɔlstɪs] n solstizio.

soluble ['sɔljʊbl] a solubile.

solution [sə'lu:ʃən] n soluzione f.

solve [sɔlv] vt risolvere.

solvent ['sɔlvənt] a (COMM) solvibile // n (CHEM) solvente m.

sombre ['sɔmbə*] a scuro(a); (mood, person) triste.

some [sʌm] det (a few) alcuni(e), qualche; (certain) certi(e); (a certain number or amount) see phrases below; (unspecified) un(a)... qualunque // pronoun alcuni(e); un po' // ad: ~ **10 people** circa 10 persone; **I have** ~ **books** ho qualche libro o alcuni libri; **have** ~ **tea/ice-cream/water** prendi un po' di tè/gelato/acqua; **there's** ~ **milk in the fridge** c'è un po' di latte nel frigo; ~ **(of it) was left** ne è rimasto un po'; **I've got** ~ (i.e. books etc) ne ho

alcuni; (i.e. milk, money etc) ne ho un po'; ~**body** pronoun qualcuno; ~ **day** ad uno di questi giorni, un giorno o l'altro; ~**how** ad in un modo o nell'altro, in qualche modo; (for some reason) per qualche ragione; ~**one** pronoun = **somebody**; ~**place** ad (US) = **somewhere**.

somersault ['sʌməsɔ:lt] n capriola; salto mortale // vi fare una capriola (or un salto mortale); (car) cappottare.

something ['sʌmθɪŋ] pronoun qualcosa; ~ **interesting** qualcosa di interessante.

sometime ['sʌmtaɪm] ad (in future) una volta o l'altra; (in past): ~ **last month** durante il mese scorso.

sometimes ['sʌmtaɪmz] ad qualche volta.

somewhat ['sʌmwɔt] ad piuttosto.

somewhere ['sʌmwɛə*] ad in or da qualche parte.

son [sʌn] n figlio.

song [sɔŋ] n canzone f; ~**book** n canzoniere m.

sonic ['sɔnɪk] a (boom) sonico(a).

son-in-law ['sʌnɪnlɔ:] n genero.

sonnet ['sɔnɪt] n sonetto.

sonny ['sʌni] n (col) ragazzo mio.

soon [su:n] ad presto, fra poco; (early) presto; ~ **afterwards** subito dopo; see also **as**; ~**er** ad (time) prima; (preference): **I would** ~**er do** preferirei fare; ~**er or later** prima o poi.

soot [sʊt] n fuliggine f.

soothe [su:ð] vt calmare.

sop [sɔp] n: **that's only a** ~ è soltanto un'offa.

sophisticated [sə'fɪstɪkeɪtɪd] a sofisticato(a); raffinato(a); altamente perfezionato(a); complesso(a).

sopping ['sɔpɪŋ] a (also: ~ **wet**) bagnato(a) fradicio(a).

soppy ['sɔpi] a (pej) sentimentale.

soprano [sə'prɑːnəʊ] n (voice) soprano; (singer) soprano m/f.

sorcerer ['sɔːsərə*] n stregone m, mago.

sordid ['sɔːdɪd] a sordido(a).

sore [sɔ:*] a (painful) dolorante; (col: offended) offeso(a) // n piaga; ~**ly** ad (tempted) fortemente.

sorrow ['sɔrəʊ] n dolore m; ~**ful** a triste.

sorry ['sɔri] a spiacente; (condition, excuse) misero(a); ~! scusa! (or scusi! or scusate!); **to feel** ~ **for sb** rincrescersi per qd.

sort [sɔ:t] n specie f, genere m // vt (also: ~ **out**: papers) classificare; ordinare; (: letters etc) smistare; (: problems) risolvere; ~**ing office** n ufficio m smistamento inv.

SOS n (abbr of save our souls) S.O.S. m inv.

so-so ['səʊsəʊ] ad così così.

soufflé ['su:fleɪ] n soufflé m inv.

sought [sɔ:t] pt,pp of **seek**.

soul [səʊl] n anima; ~-**destroying** a demoralizzante; ~**ful** a pieno(a) di sentimento.

sound [saʊnd] a (healthy) sano(a); (safe, not damaged) solido(a), in buono stato; (reliable, not superficial) solido(a); (sensible) giudizioso(a), di buon senso //

ad: ~ **asleep** profondamente addormentato // n (noise) suono; rumore m; (GEO) stretto // vt (alarm) suonare; (also: ~ **out**: opinions) sondare // vi suonare; (fig: seem) sembrare; **to** ~ **like** rassomigliare a; ~ **barrier** n muro del suono; ~**ing** n (NAUT etc) scandagliamento; ~**ly** ad (sleep) profondamente; (beat) duramente; ~**proof** vt insonorizzare, isolare acusticamente // a insonorizzato(a), isolato(a) acusticamente; ~**track** n (of film) colonna sonora.

soup [su:p] n minestra; brodo; zuppa; **in the** ~ (fig) nei guai; ~**spoon** n cucchiaio da minestra.

sour ['sauə*] a aspro(a); (fruit) acerbo(a); (milk) acido(a), fermentato(a); (fig) arcigno(a); acido(a); **it's** ~ **grapes** è soltanto invidia.

source [sɔ:s] n fonte f, sorgente f; (fig) fonte.

south [sauθ] n sud m, meridione m, mezzogiorno // a del sud, sud inv, meridionale // ad verso sud; **S~ Africa** n Sudafrica m; **S~ African** a, n sudafricano(a); **S~ America** n Sudamerica, America del sud; **S~ American** a, n sudamericano(a); ~**east** n sud-est m; ~**erly** ['sʌðəlɪ] a dal sud, meridionale; ~**ern** ['sʌðən] a del sud, meridionale; esposto(a) a sud; **S~ Pole** n Polo Sud; ~**ward(s)** ad verso sud; ~**-west** n sud-ovest m.

souvenir [su:və'nɪə*] n ricordo, souvenir m inv.

sovereign ['sɔvrɪn] a,n sovrano(a); ~**ty** n sovranità.

soviet ['səuvɪət] a sovietico(a); **the S~ Union** l'Unione f Sovietica.

sow n [sau] scrofa // vt [səu] (pt ~**ed**, pp **sown** [səun]) seminare.

soya bean ['sɔɪəbi:n] n seme m di soia.

spa [spɑ:] n (resort) stazione f termale.

space [speɪs] n spazio; (room) posto; spazio; (length of time) intervallo // cpd spaziale // vt (also: ~ **out**) distanziare; ~**craft** n veicolo spaziale; ~**man/woman** n astronauta m/f, cosmonauta m/f; **spacing** n spaziatura.

spacious ['speɪʃəs] a spazioso(a), ampio(a).

spade [speɪd] n (tool) vanga; pala; (child's) paletta; ~**s** npl (CARDS) picche fpl; ~**work** n (fig) duro lavoro preparatorio.

Spain [speɪn] n Spagna.

span [spæn] pt of **spin** // n (of bird, plane) apertura alare; (of arch) campata; (in time) periodo; durata // vt attraversare; (fig) abbracciare.

Spaniard ['spænjəd] n spagnolo/a.

spaniel ['spænjəl] n spaniel m inv.

Spanish ['spænɪʃ] a spagnolo(a) // n (LING) spagnolo.

spank [spæŋk] vt sculacciare.

spanner ['spænə*] n chiave f inglese.

spare [spɛə*] a di riserva, di scorta; (surplus) in più, d'avanzo; (part) pezzo di ricambio // vt (do without) fare a meno di; (afford to give) concedere; (refrain from hurting, using) risparmiare; **to** ~ (surplus) d'avanzo; ~ **part** n pezzo di ricambio; ~ **time** n tempo libero.

sparing ['spɛərɪŋ] a (amount) scarso(a); (use) parsimonioso(a); ~ **of words** che risparmia le proprie parole; ~**ly** ad moderatamente.

spark [spɑ:k] n scintilla; ~**(ing) plug** n candela.

sparkle ['spɑ:kl] n scintillio, sfavillio // vi scintillare, sfavillare; (bubble) spumeggiare, frizzare; **sparkling** a scintillante, sfavillante; (wine) spumante.

sparrow ['spærəu] n passero.

sparse [spɑ:s] a sparso(a), rado(a).

spasm ['spæzəm] n (MED) spasmo; (fig) accesso, attacco; ~**odic** [spæz'mɔdɪk] a spasmodico(a); (fig) intermittente.

spastic ['spæstɪk] n spastico/a.

spat [spæt] pt,pp of **spit**.

spate [speɪt] n (fig): ~ **of** diluvio or fiume m di; **in** ~ (river) in piena.

spatter ['spætə*] vt, vi schizzare.

spatula ['spætjulə] n spatola.

spawn [spɔ:n] vt deporre // vi deporre le uova // n uova fpl.

speak, pt spoke, pp spoken [spi:k, spəuk, 'spəukn] vt (language) parlare; (truth) dire // vi parlare; **to** ~ **to sb/of or about sth** parlare a qd/di qc; ~ **up!** parla più forte!; ~**er** n (in public) oratore/trice; (also: **loud~er**) altoparlante m; (POL): **the S~er** il presidente della Camera dei Comuni; **to be on** ~**ing terms** parlarsi.

spear [spɪə*] n lancia.

spec [spɛk] n (col): **on** ~ sperando bene.

special ['spɛʃl] a speciale; **take** ~ **care** siate particolarmente prudenti; ~**ist** n specialista m/f; ~**ity** [spɛʃɪ'ælɪtɪ] n specialità f inv; ~**ize**: **to** ~**ize** (**in**) specializzarsi (in); ~**ly** ad specialmente, particolarmente.

species ['spi:ʃi:z] n, pl inv specie f inv.

specific [spə'sɪfɪk] a specifico(a); preciso(a); ~**ation** [spɛsɪfɪ'keɪʃən] n specificazione f.

specify ['spɛsɪfaɪ] vt specificare, precisare.

specimen ['spɛsɪmən] n esemplare m, modello; (MED) campione m.

speck [spɛk] n puntino, macchiolina; (particle) granello.

speckled ['spɛkld] a macchiettato(a).

specs [spɛks] npl (col) occhiali mpl.

spectacle ['spɛktəkl] n spettacolo; ~**s** npl occhiali mpl; **spectacular** [-'tækjulə*] a spettacolare // n (CINEMA etc) film m inv etc spettacolare.

spectator [spɛk'teɪtə*] n spettatore m.

spectre ['spɛktə*] n spettro.

spectrum, pl spectra ['spɛktrəm, -rə] n spettro; (fig) gamma.

speculate ['spɛkjuleɪt] vi speculare; (try to guess): **to** ~ **about** fare ipotesi su; **speculation** [-'leɪʃən] n speculazione f;

congettura; **speculative** [-lǝtiv] a speculativo(a).

speech [spi:tʃ] n (faculty) parola; (talk) discorso; (manner of speaking) parlata; (enunciation) elocuzione f; ~**less** a ammutolito(a), muto(a); ~ **therapy** n cura dei disturbi del linguaggio.

speed [spi:d] n velocità f inv; (promptness) prontezza; **at full** or **top** ~ a tutta velocità; **to** ~ **up** vi, vt accelerare; ~**boat** n motoscafo; fuoribordo m inv; ~**ily** ad velocemente; prontamente; ~**ing** n (AUT) eccesso di velocità; ~ **limit** n limite m di velocità; ~**ometer** [spɪ'dɔmɪtǝ*] n tachimetro; ~**way** n (SPORT) pista per motociclismo; ~**y** a veloce, rapido(a); pronto(a).

spell [spɛl] n (also: **magic** ~) incantesimo; (period of time) (breve) periodo // vt (pt,pp spelt or ~ed [spɛlt, spɛld]) (in writing) scrivere (lettera per lettera); (aloud) dire il nome delle lettere di; (fig) significare; **to cast a** ~ **on sb** fare un incantesimo a qd; **he can't** ~ lui fa errori di ortografia; ~**bound** a incantato(a); affascinato(a); ~**ing** n ortografia.

spelt [spɛlt] pt,pp of **spell**.

spend [spɛnd] pt,pp **spent** [spɛnd, spɛnt] vt (money) spendere; (time, life) passare; ~**ing money** n denaro per le piccole spese; ~**thrift** n spendaccione/a.

spent [spɛnt] pt,pp of **spend** // a (patience) esaurito(a).

sperm [spǝ:m] n spermatozoo; (semen) sperma m; ~ **whale** n capodoglio.

spew [spju:] vt vomitare.

sphere [sfɪǝ*] n sfera.

spice [spaɪs] n spezia // vt aromatizzare.

spick-and-span ['spɪkǝn'spæn] a impeccabile.

spicy ['spaɪsɪ] a piccante.

spider ['spaɪdǝ*] n ragno.

spike [spaɪk] n punta.

spill [spɪl] pt,pp **spilt** or ~**ed** [spɪl, -t, -d] vt versare, rovesciare // vi versarsi, rovesciarsi.

spin [spɪn] n (revolution of wheel) rotazione f; (AVIAT) avvitamento; (trip in car) giretto // vb (pt **spun, span,** pp **spun** [spʌn, spæn]) vt (wool etc) filare; (wheel) far girare // vi girare; **to** ~ **a yarn** raccontare una storia; **to** ~ **out** vt far durare.

spinach ['spɪnɪtʃ] n spinacio; (as food) spinaci mpl.

spinal ['spaɪnl] a spinale; ~ **cord** n midollo spinale.

spindly ['spɪndlɪ] a lungo(a) e sottile, filiforme.

spin-drier [spɪn'draɪǝ*] n centrifuga.

spine [spaɪn] n spina dorsale; (thorn) spina; ~**less** a invertebrato(a), senza spina dorsale; (fig) smidollato(a).

spinning ['spɪnɪŋ] n filatura; ~ **top** n trottola; ~ **wheel** n filatoio.

spinster ['spɪnstǝ*] n nubile f; zitella.

spiral ['spaɪǝrl] n spirale f // a a spirale //

vi (fig) salire a spirale; ~ **staircase** n scala a chiocciola.

spire ['spaɪǝ*] n guglia.

spirit ['spɪrɪt] n (soul) spirito, anima; (ghost) spirito, fantasma m; (mood) stato d'animo, umore m; (courage) coraggio; ~**s** npl (drink) alcolici mpl; **in good** ~**s** di buon umore; **in low** ~**s** triste, abbattuto(a); ~**ed** a vivace, vigoroso(a); (horse) focoso(a); ~ **level** n livella a bolla (d'aria).

spiritual ['spɪrɪtjʊǝl] a spirituale // n (also: **Negro** ~) spiritual m inv; ~**ism** n spiritismo.

spit [spɪt] n (for roasting) spiedo // vi (pt, pp **spat** [spæt]) sputare; (fire, fat) scoppiettare.

spite [spaɪt] n dispetto // vt contrariare, far dispetto a; **in** ~ **of** nonostante, malgrado; ~**ful** a dispettoso(a).

spittle ['spɪtl] n saliva; sputo.

splash [splæʃ] n spruzzo; (sound) ciac m inv; (of colour) schizzo // vt spruzzare // vi (also: ~ **about**) sguazzare.

spleen [spli:n] n (ANAT) milza.

splendid ['splɛndɪd] a splendido(a), magnifico(a).

splendour ['splɛndǝ*] n splendore m.

splice [splaɪs] vt (rope) impiombare; (wood) calettare.

splint [splɪnt] n (MED) stecca.

splinter ['splɪntǝ*] n scheggia // vi scheggiarsi.

split [splɪt] n spaccatura; (fig: POL) scissione f // vb (pt, pp **split**) vt spaccare; (party) dividere; (work, profits) spartire, ripartire // vi (divide) dividersi; **to** ~ **up** vi (couple) separarsi, rompere; (meeting) sciogliersi; ~**ting headache** n mal m di testa da impazzire.

splutter ['splʌtǝ*] vi farfugliare; sputacchiare.

spoil [spɔɪl] pt,pp **spoilt** or ~**ed** [spɔɪl, -t, -d] vt (damage) rovinare, guastare; (mar) sciupare; (child) viziare; ~**s** npl bottino; ~**sport** n guastafeste m/f inv.

spoke [spǝʊk] pt of **speak** // n raggio.

spoken ['spǝʊkn] pp of **speak**.

spokesman ['spǝʊksmǝn] n portavoce m inv.

sponge [spʌndʒ] n spugna // vt spugnare, pulire con una spugna // vi: **to** ~ **on** scroccare a; ~ **cake** n pan m di Spagna; ~**r** n (pej) parassita m/f, scroccone/a; **spongy** a spugnoso(a).

sponsor ['spɔnsǝ*] n (RADIO, TV) finanziatore/trice (a scopo pubblicitario) // vt sostenere; patrocinare; ~**ship** n finanziamento (a scopo pubblicitario); patrocinio.

spontaneous [spɔn'teɪnɪǝs] a spontaneo(a).

spooky ['spu:kɪ] a che fa accapponare la pelle.

spool [spu:l] n bobina.

spoon [spu:n] n cucchiaio; ~**-feed** vt nutrire con il cucchiaio; (fig) imboccare; ~**ful** n cucchiaiata.

sporadic [spə'rædɪk] a sporadico(a).
sport [spɔ:t] n sport m inv; (person) sportivo/a // vt sfoggiare; ~ing a sportivo(a); **to give sb a ~ing chance** dare a qd una possibilità (di vincere); ~s **car** n automobile f sportiva; ~s **jacket** n giacca sportiva; ~sman n sportivo; ~smanship n spirito sportivo; ~s **page** n pagina sportiva; ~swear n abiti mpl sportivi; ~swoman n sportiva; ~y a sportivo(a).
spot [spɔt] n punto; (mark) macchia; (dot: on pattern) pallino; (pimple) foruncolo; (place) posto; (small amount): **a ~ of** un po' di // vt (notice) individuare, distinguere; **on the ~** sul posto; su due piedi; ~ **check** n controllo senza preavviso; ~less a immacolato(a); ~light n proiettore m; (AUT) faro ausiliario; ~ted a macchiato(a); a puntini, a pallini; ~ted **with** punteggiato(a) di; ~ty a (face) foruncoloso(a).
spouse [spauz] n sposo/a.
spout [spaut] n (of jug) beccuccio; (of liquid) zampillo, getto // vi zampillare.
sprain [spreɪn] n storta, distorsione f // vt: **to ~ one's ankle** storcersi una caviglia.
sprang [spræŋ] pt of **spring**.
sprawl [sprɔ:l] vi sdraiarsi (in modo scomposto).
spray [spreɪ] n spruzzo; (container) nebulizzatore m, spray m inv; (of flowers) mazzetto // vt spruzzare; (crops) irrorare.
spread [sprɛd] n diffusione f; (distribution) distribuzione f; (CULIN) pasta (da spalmare) // vb (pt,pp **spread**) vt (cloth) stendere, distendere; (butter etc) spalmare; (disease, knowledge) propagare, diffondere // vi stendersi, distendersi; spalmarsi; propagarsi, diffondersi.
spree [spri:] n: **to go on a ~** fare baldoria.
sprig [sprɪg] n ramoscello.
sprightly ['spraɪtlɪ] a vivace.
spring [sprɪŋ] n (leap) salto, balzo; (coiled metal) molla; (season) primavera; (of water) sorgente f // vi (pt **sprang**, pp **sprung** [spræŋ, sprʌŋ]) saltare, balzare; **to ~ from** provenire da; **to ~ up** vi (problem) presentarsi; ~board n trampolino; ~clean n (also: ~cleaning) grandi pulizie fpl di primavera; ~time n primavera; ~y a elastico(a).
sprinkle ['sprɪŋkl] vt spruzzare; spargere; **to ~ water etc on, ~ with water etc** spruzzare dell'acqua etc su; **to ~ sugar etc on, ~ with sugar etc** spolverizzare di zucchero etc; ~d **with** (fig) cosparso(a) di.
sprint [sprɪnt] n volata, scatto // vi correre di volata, scattare; ~er n velocista m/f.
sprite [spraɪt] n elfo, folletto.
sprout [spraut] vi germogliare; **(Brussels) ~s** npl cavolini mpl di Bruxelles.

spruce [spru:s] n abete m rosso // a lindo(a); azzimato(a).
sprung [sprʌŋ] pp of **spring**.
spry [spraɪ] a arzillo(a), sveglio(a).
spun [spʌn] pt, pp of **spin**.
spur [spə:*] n sperone m; (fig) sprone m, incentivo // vt (also: ~ **on**) spronare; **on the ~ of the moment** lì per lì.
spurious ['spjuərɪəs] a falso(a).
spurn [spə:n] vt rifiutare con disprezzo, sdegnare.
spurt [spə:t] n getto; (of energy) esplosione f // vi sgorgare; zampillare.
spy [spaɪ] n spia // vi: **to ~ on** spiare // vt (see) scorgere; ~ing n spionaggio.
sq. (MATH), **Sq.** (in address) abbr of **square**.
squabble ['skwɔbl] vi bisticciarsi.
squad [skwɔd] n (MIL) plotone m; (POLICE) squadra.
squadron ['skwɔdrn] n (MIL) squadrone m; (AVIAT, NAUT) squadriglia.
squalid ['skwɔlɪd] a sordido(a).
squall [skwɔ:l] n raffica; burrasca.
squalor ['skwɔlə*] n squallore m.
squander ['skwɔndə*] vt dissipare.
square [skwɛə*] n quadrato; (in town) piazza; (instrument) squadra // a quadrato(a); (honest) onesto(a); (col: ideas, tastes) di vecchio stampo // vt (arrange) regolare; (MATH) elevare al quadrato // vi (agree) accordarsi; **all ~** pari; **a ~ meal** un pasto abbondante; **2 metres ~** di 2 metri per 2; **1 ~ metre** 1 metro quadrato; ~ly ad diritto; fermamente.
squash [skwɔʃ] n (drink): **lemon/orange ~** sciroppo di limone/arancia; (SPORT) squash m // vt schiacciare.
squat [skwɔt] a tarchiato(a), tozzo(a) // vi accovacciarsi; ~ter n occupante m/f abusivo(a).
squawk [skwɔ:k] vi emettere strida rauche.
squeak [skwi:k] vi squittire.
squeal [skwi:l] vi strillare.
squeamish ['skwi:mɪʃ] a schizzinoso(a); disgustato(a).
squeeze [skwi:z] n pressione f; (also ECON) stretta // vt premere; (hand, arm) stringere; **to ~ out** vt spremere.
squelch [skwɛltʃ] vi fare ciac; sguazzare.
squib [skwɪb] n petardo.
squid [skwɪd] n calamaro.
squint [skwɪnt] vi essere strabico(a) // n: **he has a ~** è strabico.
squire ['skwaɪə*] n proprietario terriero.
squirm [skwə:m] vi contorcersi.
squirrel ['skwɪrəl] n scoiattolo.
squirt [skwə:t] n schizzo // vi schizzare; zampillare.
Sr abbr of **senior**.
St abbr of **saint**, **street**.
stab [stæb] n (with knife etc) pugnalata; (col: try): **to have a ~ at (doing) sth** provare a fare qc // vt pugnalare.
stability [stə'bɪlɪtɪ] n stabilità.
stabilize ['steɪbəlaɪz] vt stabilizzare.

stable ['steɪbl] n (for horses) scuderia; (for cattle) stalla // a stabile.

stack [stæk] n catasta, pila // vt accatastare, ammucchiare.

stadium ['steɪdɪəm] n stadio.

staff [stɑ:f] n (work force) personale m; (: SCOL) personale insegnante; (: servants) personale di servizio; (MIL) stato maggiore; (stick) bastone m // vt fornire di personale.

stag [stæg] n cervo.

stage [steɪdʒ] n palcoscenico; (profession): **the ~** il teatro, la scena; (point) punto; (platform) palco // vt (play) allestire, mettere in scena; (demonstration) organizzare; (fig: perform: recovery etc) effettuare; **in ~s** per gradi; a tappe; **~ coach** n diligenza; **~ door** n ingresso degli artisti; **~ fright** n paura del pubblico; **~ manager** n direttore m di scena.

stagger ['stægə*] vi barcollare // vt (person) sbalordire; (hours, holidays) scaglionare; **~ing** a (amazing) incredibile, sbalorditivo(a).

stagnant ['stægnənt] a stagnante.

stagnate [stæg'neɪt] vi stagnare.

stag party ['stægpɑ:tɪ] n festa di addio al celibato.

staid [steɪd] a posato(a), serio(a).

stain [steɪn] n macchia; (colouring) colorante m // vt macchiare; (wood) tingere; **~ed glass window** n vetrata; **~less** a (steel) inossidabile; **~ remover** n smacchiatore m.

stair [stɛə*] n (step) gradino; **~s** npl scale fpl, scala; **on the ~s** sulle scale; **~case, ~way** n scale fpl, scala.

stake [steɪk] n palo, piolo; (BETTING) puntata, scommessa // vt (bet) scommettere; (risk) rischiare; **to be at ~** essere in gioco.

stalactite ['stæləktaɪt] n stalattite f.

stalagmite ['stæləgmaɪt] n stalagmite f.

stale [steɪl] a (bread) raffermo(a), stantio(a); (beer) svaporato(a); (smell) di chiuso.

stalemate ['steɪlmeɪt] n stallo; (fig) punto morto.

stalk [stɔ:k] n gambo, stelo // vt inseguire // vi camminare con sussiego.

stall [stɔ:l] n bancarella; (in stable) box m inv di stalla // n (AUT) far spegnere // vi (AUT) spegnersi, fermarsi; (fig) temporeggiare; **~s** npl (in cinema, theatre) platea.

stalwart ['stɔ:lwət] n membro fidato.

stamina ['stæmɪnə] n vigore m, resistenza.

stammer ['stæmə*] n balbuzie f // vi balbettare.

stamp [stæmp] n (postage ~) francobollo; (implement) timbro; (mark, also fig) marchio, impronta; (on document) bollo; timbro // vt battere il piede // vt battere; (letter) affrancare; (mark with a ~) timbrare; **~ album** n album m inv per francobolli; **~ collecting** n filatelia.

stampede [stæm'pi:d] n fuggi fuggi m inv.

stance [stæns] n posizione f.

stand [stænd] n (position) posizione f; (MIL) resistenza; (structure) supporto, sostegno; (at exhibition) stand m inv; (in shop) banco; (at market) bancarella; (booth) chiosco; (SPORT) tribuna // vb (pt,pp **stood** [stud]) vi stare in piedi; (rise) alzarsi in piedi; (be placed) trovarsi // vt (place) mettere, porre; (tolerate, withstand) resistere, sopportare; **to make a ~** prendere posizione; **to ~ for parliament** presentarsi come candidato (per il parlamento); **it ~s to reason** è logico; **to ~ by** vi (be ready) tenersi pronto // vt fus (opinion) sostenere; **to ~ for** vt fus (signify) rappresentare, significare; (tolerate) sopportare, tollerare; **to ~ in for** vt fus sostituire; **to ~ out** vi (be prominent) spiccare; **to ~ up** vi (rise) alzarsi in piedi; **to ~ up for** vt fus difendere; **to ~ up to** vt fus tener testa a, resistere a.

standard ['stændəd] n modello; standard m inv; (level) livello; (flag) stendardo // a (size etc) normale, standard inv; **~s** npl (morals) principi mpl, valori mpl; **~ize** vt normalizzare, standardizzare; **~ lamp** n lampada a stelo; **~ of living** n livello di vita.

stand-by ['stændbaɪ] n riserva, sostituto; **~ ticket** n (AVIAT) biglietto senza garanzia.

stand-in ['stændɪn] n sostituto/a; (CINEMA) controfigura.

standing ['stændɪŋ] a diritto(a), in piedi // n rango, condizione f, posizione f; **of many years' ~** che esiste da molti anni; **~ committee** n commissione f permanente; **~ order** n (at bank) ordine m permanente (di pagamento periodico); **~ orders** npl (MIL) regolamento; **~ room** n posto all'impiedi.

stand-offish [stænd'ɔfɪʃ] a scostante, freddo(a).

standpoint ['stændpɔɪnt] n punto di vista.

standstill ['stændstɪl] n: **at a ~** alla fermata; (fig) a un punto morto; **to come to a ~** fermarsi; giungere a un punto morto.

stank [stæŋk] pt of **stink**.

staple ['steɪpl] n (for papers) graffetta // a (food etc) di base // vt cucire; **~r** n cucitrice f.

star [stɑ:*] n stella; (celebrity) divo/a; (principal actor) vedette f inv // vi: **to ~ (in)** essere il (or la) protagonista (di) // vt (CINEMA) essere interpretato/a da.

starboard ['stɑ:bəd] n dritta; **to ~ a** dritta.

starch [stɑ:tʃ] n amido; **~ed** a (collar) inamidato(a).

stardom ['stɑ:dəm] n celebrità.

stare [stɛə*] n sguardo fisso // vi: **to ~ at** fissare.

starfish ['stɑ:fɪʃ] n stella di mare.

stark [stɑ:k] a (bleak) desolato(a) // ad: **~ naked** completamente nudo(a).

starling ['stɑ:lɪŋ] n storno.

start [stɑːt] *n* inizio; (*of race*) partenza; (*sudden movement*) sobbalzo // *vt* cominciare, iniziare // *vi* partire, mettersi in viaggio; (*jump*) sobbalzare; **to ~ doing sth** (in)cominciare a fare qc; **to ~ off** *vi* cominciare; (*leave*) partire; **to ~ up** *vi* cominciare; (*car*) avviarsi // *vt* iniziare; (*car*) avviare; **~er** *n* (*AUT*) motorino d'avviamento; (*SPORT: official*) starter *m inv*; (: *runner, horse*) partente *m/f*; (*CULIN*) primo piatto; **~ing point** *n* punto di partenza.

startle ['stɑːtl] *vt* far trasalire; **startling** *a* sorprendente, sbalorditivo(a).

starvation [stɑːˈveɪʃən] *n* fame *f*, inedia.

starve [stɑːv] *vi* morire di fame; soffrire la fame // *vt* far morire di fame, affamare; **I'm starving** muoio di fame.

state [steɪt] *n* stato // *vt* dichiarare, affermare; annunciare; **the S~s** gli Stati Uniti; **to be in a ~** essere agitato(a); **~d** *a* fissato(a), stabilito(a); **~ly** *a* maestoso(a), imponente; **~ment** *n* dichiarazione *f*; (*LAW*) deposizione *f*; **~sman** *n* statista *m*.

static ['stætɪk] *n* (*RADIO*) scariche *fpl* // *a* statico(a); **~ electricity** *n* elettricità statica.

station ['steɪʃən] *n* stazione *f*; (*rank*) rango, condizione *f* // *vt* collocare, disporre.

stationary ['steɪʃənrɪ] *a* fermo(a), immobile.

stationer ['steɪʃənə*] *n* cartolaio/a; **~'s (shop)** *n* cartoleria; **~y** *n* articoli *mpl* di cancelleria.

station master ['steɪʃənmɑːstə*] *n* (*RAIL*) capostazione *m*.

station wagon ['steɪʃənwægən] *n* (*US*) giardinetta.

statistic [stəˈtɪstɪk] *n* statistica; **~s** *npl* (*science*) statistica; **~al** *a* statistico(a).

statue ['stætjuː] *n* statua.

stature ['stætʃə*] *n* statura.

status ['steɪtəs] *n* posizione *f*, condizione *f* sociale; prestigio; stato; **the ~ quo** lo statu quo; **~ symbol** *n* simbolo di prestigio.

statute ['stætjuːt] *n* legge *f*; **~s** *npl* (*of club etc*) statuto; **statutory** *a* stabilito(a) dalla legge, statutario(a).

staunch [stɔːntʃ] *a* fidato(a), leale.

stave [steɪv] *n* (*MUS*) rigo // *vt*: **to ~ off** (*attack*) respingere; (*threat*) evitare.

stay [steɪ] *n* (*period of time*) soggiorno, permanenza // *vi* rimanere; (*reside*) alloggiare, stare; (*spend some time*) trattenersi, soggiornare; **to ~ put** non muoversi; **to ~ with friends** stare presso amici; **to ~ the night** passare la notte; **to ~ behind** *vi* restare indietro; **to ~ in** *vi* (*at home*) stare in casa; **to ~ on** *vi* restare, rimanere; **to ~ out** *vi* (*of house*) rimanere fuori (di casa); **to ~ up** *vi* (*at night*) rimanere alzato(a).

STD *n* (*abbr of Subscriber Trunk Dialling*) teleselezione *f*.

steadfast ['stedfɑːst] *a* fermo(a), risoluto(a).

steadily ['stedɪlɪ] *ad* continuamente; (*walk*) con passo sicuro.

steady ['stedɪ] *a* stabile, solido(a), fermo(a); (*regular*) costante; (*person*) calmo(a), tranquillo(a) // *vt* stabilizzare; calmare; **to ~ oneself** ritrovare l'equilibrio.

steak [steɪk] *n* (*meat*) bistecca; (*fish*) trancia.

steal, *pt* **stole**, *pp* **stolen** [stiːl, stəʊl, 'stəʊln] rubare.

stealth [stelθ] *n*: **by ~** furtivamente; **~y** *a* furtivo(a).

steam [stiːm] *n* vapore *m* // *vt* trattare con vapore; (*CULIN*) cuocere a vapore // *vi* fumare; (*ship*): **to ~ along** filare; **~ engine** *n* macchina a vapore; (*RAIL*) locomotiva a vapore; **~er** *n* piroscafo, vapore *m*; **~roller** *n* rullo compressore.

steel [stiːl] *n* acciaio // *cpd* di acciaio; **~works** *n* acciaieria.

steep [stiːp] *a* ripido(a), scosceso(a); (*price*) eccessivo(a) // *vt* inzuppare; (*washing*) mettere a mollo.

steeple ['stiːpl] *n* campanile *m*; **~chase** *n* corsa a ostacoli, steeplechase *m inv*.

steer [stɪə*] *n* manzo // *vt* (*ship*) governare; (*car*) guidare // *vi* (*NAUT: person*) governare; (: *ship*) rispondere al timone; (*car*) guidarsi; **~ing** *n* (*AUT*) sterzo; **~ing column** *n* piantone *m* dello sterzo; **~ing wheel** *n* volante *m*.

stem [stem] *n* (*of flower, plant*) stelo; (*of tree*) fusto; (*of glass*) gambo; (*of fruit, leaf*) picciolo; (*NAUT*) prua, prora // *vt* contenere, arginare; **to ~ from** *vt fus* provenire da, derivare da.

stench [stentʃ] *n* puzzo, fetore *m*.

stencil ['stensl] *n* (*of metal, cardboard*) stampino, mascherina; (*in typing*) matrice *f*.

step [step] *n* passo; (*stair*) gradino, scalino; (*action*) mossa, azione *f* // *vi*: **to ~ forward** fare un passo avanti; **~s** *npl* = **stepladder**; **to ~ down** *vi* (*fig*) ritirarsi; **to ~ off** *vt fus* scendere da; **to ~ up** *vt* aumentare; intensificare; **~brother** *n* fratellastro; **~child** *n* figliastro/a; **~father** *n* patrigno; **~ladder** *n* scala a libretto; **~mother** *n* matrigna; **stepping stone** *n* pietra di un guado; (*fig*) trampolino; **~sister** *n* sorellastra.

stereo ['stɛrɪəʊ] *n* (*system*) sistema *m* stereofonico; (*record player*) stereo *m inv* // *a* (*also*: **~phonic**) stereofonico(a).

stereotype ['stɪərɪətaɪp] *n* stereotipo.

sterile ['sterail] *a* sterile; **sterilize** ['sterɪlaɪz] *vt* sterilizzare.

sterling ['stɜːlɪŋ] *a* (*gold, silver*) di buona lega; (*fig*) autentico(a), genuino(a); *n* (*ECON*) (lira) sterlina; **a pound ~** una lira sterlina.

stern [stɜːn] *a* severo(a) // *n* (*NAUT*) poppa.

stethoscope ['steθəskəʊp] *n* stetoscopio.

stew [stjuː] *n* stufato // *vt*, *vi* cuocere in umido.

steward ['stjuːəd] *n* (*AVIAT, NAUT, RAIL*)

steward *m inv*; (*in club etc*) dispensiere *m*; **~ ess** *n* assistente *f* di volo, hostess *f inv*.

stick [stik] *n* stecco; bastone *m* // *vb* (*pt, pp* **stuck** [stʌk]) *vt* (*glue*) attaccare; (*thrust*): **to ~ sth into** conficcare *or* piantare *or* infiggere qc in; (*col: put*) ficcare; (*col: tolerate*) sopportare // *vi* conficcarsi; tenere; (*remain*) restare, rimanere; **to ~ out, to ~ up** *vi* sporgere, spuntare; **to ~ up for** *vt fus* difendere; **~er** *n* cartellino adesivo.

stickler ['stiklə*] *n*: **to be a ~ for** essere pignolo(a) su, tenere molto a.

sticky ['stiki] *a* attaccaticcio(a), vischioso(a); (*label*) adesivo(a).

stiff [stif] *a* rigido(a), duro(a); (*muscle*) legato(a), indolenzito(a); (*difficult*) difficile, arduo(a); (*cold*) freddo(a), formale; (*strong*) forte; (*high: price*) molto alto(a); **~en** *vt* irrigidire; rinforzare // *vi* irrigidirsi; indurirsi; **~ neck** *n* torcicollo.

stifle ['staifl] *vt* soffocare; **stifling** *a* (*heat*) soffocante.

stigma ['stigmə] *n* (*BOT, fig*) stigma *m*; **~ta** [stig'maːtə] *npl* (*REL*) stigmate *fpl*.

stile [stail] *n* cavalcasiepe *m*; cavalcasteccato.

stiletto [sti'letəu] *n* (*also: ~ heel*) tacco a spillo.

still [stil] *a* fermo(a); silenzioso(a) // *ad* (*up to this time, even*) ancora; (*nonetheless*) tuttavia, ciò nonostante; **~born** *a* nato(a) morto(a); **~ life** *n* natura morta.

stilt [stilt] *n* trampolo; (*pile*) palo.

stilted ['stiltid] *a* freddo(a), formale; artificiale.

stimulate ['stimjuleit] *vt* stimolare; **stimulating** *a* stimolante.

stimulus, *pl* **stimuli** ['stimjuləs, 'stimjulai] *n* stimolo.

sting [stiŋ] *n* puntura; (*organ*) pungiglione *m* // *vt* (*pt, pp* **stung** [stʌŋ]) pungere.

stingy ['stindʒi] *a* spilorcio(a), tirchio(a).

stink [stiŋk] *n* fetore *m*, puzzo // *vi* (*pt* **stank**, *pp* **stunk** [stæŋk, stʌŋk]) puzzare; **~er** *n* (*col*) porcheria; fetente *m/f*; **~ing** *a* (*col*): **a ~ing...** uno schifo di..., un(a) maledetto(a)...

stint [stint] *n* lavoro, compito // *vi*: **to ~ on** lesinare su.

stipulate ['stipjuleit] *vt* stipulare.

stir [stəː*] *n* agitazione *f*, clamore *m* // *vt* rimescolare; (*move*) smuovere, agitare // *vi* muoversi; **to ~ up** *vt* provocare, suscitare; **~ring** *a* eccitante; commovente.

stirrup ['stirəp] *n* staffa.

stitch [stitʃ] *n* (*SEWING*) punto; (*KNITTING*) maglia; (*MED*) punto (di sutura); (*pain*) fitta // *vt* cucire, attaccare; suturare.

stoat [stəut] *n* ermellino.

stock [stɔk] *n* riserva, provvista; (*COMM*) giacenza, stock *m inv*; (*AGR*) bestiame *m*; (*CULIN*) brodo; (*FINANCE*) titoli *mpl*, azioni *fpl* // *a* (*fig: reply etc*) consueto(a); classico(a) // *vt* (*have in stock*) avere, vendere; **well-~ed** ben fornito(a); **to**

take ~ (*fig*) fare il punto; **to ~ up with** *vt fus* fare provvista di.

stockade [stɔ'keid] *n* palizzata.

stockbroker ['stɔkbrəukə*] *n* agente *m* di cambio.

stock exchange ['stɔkikstʃeindʒ] *n* Borsa (Valori).

stocking ['stɔkiŋ] *n* calza.

stockist ['stɔkist] *n* fornitore *m*.

stock market ['stɔkmaːkit] *n* Borsa, mercato finanziario.

stock phrase ['stɔk'freiz] *n* cliché *m inv*.

stockpile ['stɔkpail] *n* riserva // *vt* accumulare riserve.

stocktaking ['stɔkteikiŋ] *n* (*COMM*) inventario.

stocky ['stɔki] *a* tarchiato(a), tozzo(a).

stodgy ['stɔdʒi] *a* pesante, indigesto(a).

stoical ['stəuikəl] *a* stoico(a).

stoke [stəuk] *vt* alimentare; **~r** *n* fochista *m*.

stole [stəul] *pt of* **steal** // *n* stola.

stolen ['stəuln] *pp of* **steal**.

stolid ['stɔlid] *a* impassibile.

stomach ['stʌmək] *n* stomaco; (*abdomen*) ventre *m* // *vt* sopportare, digerire; **~ache** *n* mal *m* di stomaco.

stone [stəun] *n* pietra; (*pebble*) sasso, ciottolo; (*in fruit*) nocciolo; (*MED*) calcolo; (*weight*) misura di peso = 6.348 kg.; 14 libbre // *cpd* di pietra // *vt* lapidare; **~-cold** *a* gelido(a); **~-deaf** *a* sordo(a) come una campana; **~work** *n* muratura; **stony** *a* pietroso(a), sassoso(a).

stood [stud] *pt,pp of* **stand**.

stool [stuːl] *n* sgabello.

stoop [stuːp] *vi* (*also: have a ~*) avere una curvatura; (*bend*) chinarsi, curvarsi.

stop [stɔp] *n* arresto; (*stopping place*) fermata; (*in punctuation*) punto // *vt* arrestare, fermare; (*break off*) interrompere; (*also: put a ~ to*) porre fine a // *vi* fermarsi; (*rain, noise etc*) cessare, finire; **to ~ doing sth** cessare *or* finire di fare qc; **to ~ dead** fermarsi di colpo; **to ~ off** *vi* sostare brevemente; **to ~ up** *vt* (*hole*) chiudere, turare; **~lights** *npl* (*AUT*) stop *mpl*; **~over** *n* breve sosta; (*AVIAT*) scalo.

stoppage ['stɔpidʒ] *n* arresto, fermata; (*of pay*) trattenuta; (*strike*) interruzione *f* del lavoro.

stopper ['stɔpə*] *n* tappo.

stop-press ['stɔp'pres] *n* ultimissime *fpl*.

stopwatch ['stɔpwɔtʃ] *n* cronometro.

storage ['stɔːridʒ] *n* immagazzinamento; (*COMPUTERS*) memoria.

store [stɔː*] *n* provvista, riserva; (*depot*) deposito; (*large shop*) grande magazzino // *vt* immagazzinare; **to ~ up** *vt* mettere in serbo, conservare; **~room** *n* dispensa.

storey ['stɔːri] *n* piano.

stork [stɔːk] *n* cicogna.

storm [stɔːm] *n* tempesta, temporale *m*, burrasca; uragano // *vi* (*fig*) infuriarsi // *vt* prendere d'assalto; **~y** *a* tempestoso(a), burrascoso(a).

story ['stɔːrɪ] n storia; favola; racconto; (US) = **storey**; ~**book** n libro di racconti.

stout [staut] a solido(a), robusto(a); (brave) coraggioso(a); (fat) corpulento(a), grasso(a) // n birra scura.

stove [stəuv] n (for cooking) fornello; (: small) fornelletto; (for heating) stufa.

stow [stəu] vt mettere via; ~**away** n passeggero(a) clandestino(a).

straddle ['strædl] vt stare a cavalcioni di.

strafe [strɑːf] vt mitragliare.

straggle ['strægl] vi crescere (or estendersi) disordinatamente; trascinarsi; rimanere indietro; ~**d along the coast** disseminati(e) lungo la costa; ~**r** n sbandato/a; **straggling, straggly** a (hair) in disordine.

straight [streɪt] a dritto(a); (frank) onesto(a), franco(a) // ad diritto; (drink) liscio // n: **the** ~ la linea retta; (RAIL) il rettilineo; (SPORT) la dirittura d'arrivo; **to put** or **get** ~ mettere in ordine, mettere ordine in; ~ **away**, ~**off** (at once) immediatamente; ~ **off**, ~ **out** senza esitare; ~**en** vt (also: ~**en out**) raddrizzare; ~**forward** a semplice; onesto(a), franco(a).

strain [streɪn] n (TECH) sollecitazione f; (physical) sforzo; (mental) tensione f; (MED) strappo; distorsione f; (streak, trace) tendenza; elemento // vt tendere; (muscle) sforzare; (ankle) storcere; (friendship, marriage) mettere a dura prova; (filter) colare, filtrare // vi sforzarsi; ~**s** npl (MUS) motivo; ~**ed** a (laugh etc) forzato(a); (relations) teso(a); ~**er** n passino, colino.

strait [streɪt] n (GEO) stretto; ~ **jacket** n camicia di forza; ~‧**laced** a bacchettone(a).

strand [strænd] n (of thread) filo; ~**ed** a nei guai; senza mezzi di trasporto.

strange [streɪndʒ] a (not known) sconosciuto(a); (odd) strano(a), bizzarro(a); ~**r** n sconosciuto/a; estraneo/a.

strangle ['stræŋgl] vt strangolare; ~**hold** n (fig) stretta (mortale).

strap [stræp] n cinghia; (of slip, dress) spallina, bretella // vt legare con una cinghia; (child etc) punire (con una cinghia).

strapping ['stræpɪŋ] a ben piantato(a).

strata ['strɑːtə] npl of **stratum**.

strategic [strə'tiːdʒɪk] a strategico(a).

strategy ['strætɪdʒɪ] n strategia.

stratum, pl **strata** ['strɑːtəm, 'strɑːtə] n strato.

straw [strɔː] n paglia.

strawberry ['strɔːbərɪ] n fragola.

stray [streɪ] a (animal) randagio(a) // vi perdersi; ~ **bullet** n proiettile m vagante.

streak [striːk] n striscia; (fig: of madness etc): **a** ~ **of** una vena di // vt striare, screziare // vi: **to** ~ **past** passare vicino(a) come un fulmine; ~**y** a

screziato(a), striato(a); ~**y bacon** n ≈ pancetta.

stream [striːm] n ruscello; corrente f; (of people) fiume m // vt (SCOL) dividere in livelli di rendimento // vi scorrere; **to** ~ **in/out** entrare/uscire a fiotti.

streamer ['striːmə*] n (flag) fiamma; (of paper) stella filante.

streamlined ['striːmlaɪnd] a aerodinamico(a), affusolato(a); (fig) razionalizzato(a).

street [striːt] n strada, via; ~**car** n (US) tram m inv; ~ **lamp** n lampione m.

strength [streŋθ] n forza; (of girder, knot etc) resistenza, solidità; ~**en** vt rinforzare; fortificare; consolidare.

strenuous ['strenjuəs] a vigoroso(a), energico(a); (tiring) duro(a), pesante.

stress [strɛs] n (force, pressure) pressione f; (mental strain) tensione f; (accent) accento // vt insistere su, sottolineare.

stretch [strɛtʃ] n (of sand etc) distesa // vi stirarsi; (extend): **to** ~ **to/as far as** estendersi fino a // vt tendere, allungare; (spread) distendere; (fig) spingere (al massimo); **at a** ~ ininterrottamente; **to** ~ **out** vi allungarsi, estendersi // vt (arm etc) allungare, tendere; (: to spread) distendere; **to** ~ **out for sth** allungare la mano per prendere qc.

stretcher ['strɛtʃə*] n barella, lettiga.

strewn [struːn] a: ~ **with** cosparso(a) di.

stricken ['strɪkən] a provato(a); affranto(a); ~ **with** colpito(a) da.

strict [strɪkt] a (severe) rigido(a), severo(a); (precise) preciso(a), stretto(a); ~**ly** ad severamente; strettamente, assolutamente.

stride [straɪd] n passo lungo // vi (pt **strode**, pp **stridden** [strəud, 'strɪdn]) camminare a grandi passi.

strident ['straɪdnt] a stridente.

strife [straɪf] n conflitto; litigi mpl.

strike [straɪk] n sciopero; (of oil etc) scoperta; (attack) attacco // vb (pt,pp **struck** [strʌk]) vt colpire; (oil etc) scoprire, trovare // vi far sciopero, scioperare; (attack) attaccare; (clock) suonare; **to** ~ **a match** accendere un fiammifero; **to** ~ **down** vt (fig) atterrare; **to** ~ **out** vt depennare; **to** ~ **up** vt (MUS) attaccare; **to** ~ **up a friendship with** fare amicizia con; ~**breaker** n crumiro/a; ~**r** n scioperante m/f; (SPORT) attaccante m; **striking** a impressionante.

string [strɪŋ] n spago; (row) fila; sequenza; catena; (MUS) corda // vt (pt,pp **strung** [strʌŋ]): **to** ~ **out** disporre di fianco; **the** ~**s** npl (MUS) gli archi; ~ **bean** n fagiolino; ~(**ed**) **instrument** n (MUS) strumento a corda; ~ **of pearls** filo di perle.

stringent ['strɪndʒənt] a rigoroso(a); (need) stringente, impellente.

strip [strɪp] n striscia // vt spogliare; (also: ~ **down**: machine) smontare // vi spogliarsi; ~ **cartoon** n fumetto.

stripe [straɪp] *n* striscia, riga; ~**d** *a* a strisce *or* righe.

strip light ['strɪplaɪt] *n* tubo al neon.

stripper ['strɪpə*] *n* spogliarellista.

striptease ['strɪptiːz] *n* spogliarello.

strive, *pt* **strove**, *pp* **striven** [straɪv, strəuv, 'strɪvn] *vi*: **to** ~ **to do** sforzarsi di fare.

strode [strəud] *pt of* **stride.**

stroke [strəuk] *n* colpo; (*MED*) colpo apoplettico; (*caress*) carezza // *vt* accarezzare; **at a** ~ in un attimo; **on the** ~ **of 5** alle 5 in punto, allo scoccare delle 5.

stroll [strəul] *n* giretto, passeggiatina // *vi* andare a spasso.

strong [strɔŋ] *a* forte; vigoroso(a); solido(a); vivo(a); **they are 50** ~ sono in 50; ~**hold** *n* fortezza, roccaforte f; ~**ly** *ad* fortemente, con forza; energicamente; vivamente; ~**room** *n* camera di sicurezza.

strove [strəuv] *pt of* **strive.**

struck [strʌk] *pt,pp of* **strike.**

structural ['strʌktʃərəl] *a* strutturale; (*CONSTR*) di costruzione; di struttura.

structure ['strʌktʃə*] *n* struttura; (*building*) costruzione f, fabbricato.

struggle ['strʌgl] *n* lotta // *vi* lottare.

strum [strʌm] *vt* (*guitar*) strimpellare.

strung [strʌŋ] *pt,pp of* **string.**

strut [strʌt] *n* sostegno, supporto // *vi* pavoneggiarsi.

stub [stʌb] *n* mozzicone m; (*of ticket etc*) matrice f, talloncino; **to** ~ **out** *vt* schiacciare.

stubble ['stʌbl] *n* stoppia; (*on chin*) barba ispida.

stubborn ['stʌbən] *a* testardo(a), ostinato(a).

stuck [stʌk] *pt,pp of* **stick** // *a* (*jammed*) bloccato(a); ~-**up** *a* presuntuoso(a).

stud [stʌd] *n* bottoncino; borchia; (*of horses*) scuderia, allevamento di cavalli; (*also*: ~ **horse**) stallone m // *vt* (*fig*): ~**ded with** tempestato(a).

student ['stjuːdənt] *n* studente/essa // *cpd* studentesco(a); universitario(a); degli studenti.

studied ['stʌdɪd] *a* studiato(a), calcolato(a).

studio ['stjuːdɪəu] *n* studio.

studious ['stjuːdɪəs] *a* studioso(a); (*studied*) studiato(a), voluto(a); ~**ly** *ad* (*carefully*) deliberatamente, di proposito.

study ['stʌdɪ] *n* studio // *vt* studiare; esaminare // *vi* studiare.

stuff [stʌf] *n* cosa, roba; (*belongings*) cose *fpl*, roba; (*substance*) sostanza, materiale m // *vt* imbottire; (*CULIN*) farcire; ~**ing** *n* imbottitura; (*CULIN*) ripieno; ~**y** *a* (*room*) mal ventilato(a), senz'aria; (*ideas*) antiquato(a).

stumble ['stʌmbl] *vi* inciampare; **to** ~ **across** (*fig*) imbattersi in; **stumbling block** *n* ostacolo, scoglio.

stump [stʌmp] *n* ceppo; (*of limb*) moncone m.

stun [stʌn] *vt* stordire; sbalordire.

stung [stʌŋ] *pt, pp of* **sting.**

stunk [stʌŋk] *pp of* **stink.**

stunning ['stʌnɪŋ] *a* (*piece of news etc*) sbalorditivo(a); (*girl, dress*) favoloso(a), stupendo(a).

stunt [stʌnt] *n* bravata; trucco pubblicitario; (*AVIAT*) acrobazia // *vt* arrestare; ~**ed** *a* stentato(a), rachitico(a); ~**man** *n* cascatore m.

stupefy ['stjuːpɪfaɪ] *vt* stordire; intontire; (*fig*) stupire.

stupendous [stjuː'pɛndəs] *a* stupendo(a), meraviglioso(a).

stupid ['stjuːpɪd] *a* stupido(a); ~**ity** [-'pɪdɪtɪ] *n* stupidità f *inv*, stupidaggine f.

stupor ['stjuːpə*] *n* torpore m.

sturdy ['stəːdɪ] *a* robusto(a), vigoroso(a); solido(a).

sturgeon ['stəːdʒən] *n* storione m.

stutter ['stʌtə*] *n* balbuzie f // *vi* balbettare.

sty [staɪ] *n* (*of pigs*) porcile m.

stye [staɪ] *n* (*MED*) orzaiolo.

style [staɪl] *n* stile m; (*distinction*) eleganza, classe f; **stylish** *a* elegante.

stylized ['staɪlaɪzd] *a* stilizzato(a).

stylus ['staɪləs] *n* (*of record player*) puntina.

suave [swɑːv] *a* untuoso(a).

sub... [sʌb] *prefix* **sub...**, **sotto...**; **subconscious** *a, n* subcosciente (m); **subdivide** *vt* suddividere.

subdue [səb'djuː] *vt* sottomettere, soggiogare; ~**d** *a* pacato(a); (*light*) attenuato(a); (*person*) poco esuberante.

subject *n* ['sʌbdʒɪkt] soggetto; (*citizen etc*) cittadino/a; (*SCOL*) materia // *vt* [səb'dʒɛkt]: **to** ~ **to** sottomettere a; esporre a; **to be** ~ **to** (*law*) essere sottomesso(a) a; (*disease*) essere soggetto(a) a; ~**ive** *a* soggettivo(a); ~ **matter** *n* argomento; contenuto.

subjunctive [səb'dʒʌŋktɪv] *a* congiuntivo(a) // *n* congiuntivo.

sublime [sə'blaɪm] *a* sublime.

submachine gun ['sʌbmə'ʃiːngʌn] *n* mitra m *inv.*

submarine [sʌbmə'riːn] *n* sommergibile m.

submerge [səb'məːdʒ] *vt* sommergere; immergere // *vi* immergersi.

submission [səb'mɪʃən] *n* sottomissione f.

submissive [səb'mɪsɪv] *a* remissivo(a).

submit [səb'mɪt] *vt* sottomettere // *vi* sottomettersi.

subordinate [sə'bɔːdɪnət] *a,n* subordinato(a).

subscribe [səb'skraɪb] *vi* contribuire; **to** ~ **to** (*opinion*) approvare, condividere; (*fund*) sottoscrivere; (*newspaper*) abbonarsi a; essere abbonato(a) a; ~**r** *n* (*to periodical, telephone*) abbonato/a.

subscription [səb'skrɪpʃən] *n* sottoscrizione f; abbonamento.

subsequent ['sʌbsɪkwənt] *a* successivo(a),

seguente; conseguente; ~ly *ad* in seguito, successivamente.

subside [səb'saɪd] *vi* cedere, abbassarsi; (*flood*) decrescere; (*wind*) calmarsi; ~**nce** [-'saɪdns] *n* cedimento, abbassamento.

subsidiary [səb'sɪdɪərɪ] *a* sussidiario(a); accessorio(a) // *n* filiale *f.*

subsidize ['sʌbsɪdaɪz] *vt* sovvenzionare.

subsidy ['sʌbsɪdɪ] *n* sovvenzione *f.*

subsistence [səb'sɪstəns] *n* esistenza; mezzi *mpl* di sostentamento.

substance ['sʌbstəns] *n* sostanza; (*fig*) essenza.

substantial [səb'stænʃl] *a* solido(a); (*amount, progress etc*) notevole; (*meal*) sostanzioso(a).

substantiate [səb'stænʃɪeɪt] *vt* comprovare.

substitute ['sʌbstɪtjuːt] *n* (*person*) sostituto/a; (*thing*) succedaneo, surrogato // *vt*: **to ~ sth/sb for** sostituire qc/qd con; **substitution** [-'tjuːʃən] *n* sostituzione *f.*

subtitle ['sʌbtaɪtl] *n* (*CINEMA*) sottotitolo.

subtle ['sʌtl] *a* sottile; ~**ty** *n* sottigliezza.

subtract [səb'trækt] *vt* sottrarre; ~**ion** [-'trækʃən] *n* sottrazione *f.*

suburb ['sʌbəːb] *n* sobborgo; **the ~s** la periferia; ~**an** [sə'bəːbn] *a* suburbano(a).

subversive [sʌb'vəːsɪv] *a* sovversivo(a).

subway ['sʌbweɪ] *n* (*US*) metropolitana; (*Brit*) sottopassaggio.

succeed [sək'siːd] *vi* riuscire; avere successo // *vt* succedere a; **to ~ in doing** riuscire a fare; ~**ing** *a* (*following*) successivo(a).

success [sək'sɛs] *n* successo; ~**ful** *a* (*venture*) coronato(a) da successo, riuscito(a); **to be ~ful (in doing)** riuscire (a fare).

succession [sək'sɛʃən] *n* successione *f.*

successive [sək'sɛsɪv] *a* successivo(a); consecutivo(a).

successor [sək'sɛsə*] *n* successore *m.*

succinct [sək'sɪŋkt] *a* succinto(a), breve.

succulent ['sʌkjulənt] *a* succulento(a).

succumb [sə'kʌm] *vi* soccombere.

such [sʌtʃ] *a, det* tale; (*of that kind*): ~ **a book** un tale libro, un libro del genere; ~ **books** tali libri, libri del genere; (*so much*): ~ **courage** tanto coraggio; ~ **a long trip** un viaggio così lungo; ~ **good books** libri così buoni; ~ **a lot of** talmente o così tanto(a); **making** ~ **a noise that** facendo un rumore tale che; ~ **as** (*like*) come; **a noise** ~ **as** to un rumore tale da; **as** ~ *ad* come *or* in quanto tale; ~-**and**-~ *det* tale (*after noun*).

suck [sʌk] *vt* succhiare; (*breast, bottle*) poppare; ~**er** *n* (*zool, tech*) ventosa; (*bot*) pollone *m*; (*col*) gonzo/a, babbeo/a.

suckle ['sʌkl] *vt* allattare.

suction ['sʌkʃən] *n* succhiamento; (*tech*) aspirazione *f.*

sudden ['sʌdn] *a* improvviso(a); **all of a** ~ improvvisamente, all'improvviso; ~**ly**

ad bruscamente, improvvisamente, di colpo.

suds [sʌdz] *npl* schiuma (di sapone).

sue [suː] *vt* citare in giudizio.

suede [sweɪd] *n* pelle *f* scamosciata // *cpd* scamosciato(a).

suet ['suɪt] *n* grasso di rognone.

suffer ['sʌfə*] *vt* soffrire, patire; (*bear*) sopportare, tollerare // *vi* soffrire; ~**ing** *n* sofferenza.

suffice [sə'faɪs] *vi* essere sufficiente, bastare.

sufficient [sə'fɪʃənt] *a* sufficiente; ~ **money** abbastanza soldi; ~**ly** *ad* sufficientemente, abbastanza.

suffix ['sʌfɪks] *n* suffisso.

suffocate ['sʌfəkeɪt] *vi* (*have difficulty breathing*) soffocare; (*die through lack of air*) asfissiare; **suffocation** [-'keɪʃən] *n* soffocamento; (*MED*) asfissia.

sugar ['ʃugə*] *n* zucchero // *vt* zuccherare; ~ **beet** *n* barbabietola da zucchero; ~ **cane** *n* canna da zucchero; ~**y** *a* zuccherino(a), dolce; (*fig*) sdolcinato(a).

suggest [sə'dʒɛst] *vt* proporre, suggerire; indicare; ~**ion** [-'dʒɛstʃən] *n* suggerimento, proposta; ~**ive** *a* suggestivo(a).

suicide ['suɪsaɪd] *n* (*person*) suicida *m/f*; (*act*) suicidio.

suit [suːt] *n* (*man's*) vestito; (*woman's*) completo, tailleur *m inv*; (*cards*) seme *m*, colore *m* // *vt* andar bene a *or* per; essere adatto(a) a *or* per; (*adapt*): **to ~ sth to** adattare qc a; ~**able** *a* adatto(a); appropriato(a).

suitcase ['suːtkeɪs] *n* valigia.

suite [swiːt] *n* (*of rooms*) appartamento; (*MUS*) suite *f inv*; (*furniture*): **bedroom/dining room** ~ arredo *or* mobilia per la camera da letto/sala da pranzo.

sulk [sʌlk] *vi* fare il broncio; ~**y** *a* imbronciato(a).

sullen ['sʌlən] *a* scontroso(a); cupo(a).

sulphur ['sʌlfə*] *n* zolfo; ~**ic** [-'fjuərɪk] *a*: ~**ic acid** acido solforico.

sultana [sʌl'tɑːnə] *n* (*fruit*) uva (secca) sultanina.

sultry ['sʌltrɪ] *a* afoso(a).

sum [sʌm] *n* somma; (*scol etc*) addizione *f*; **to ~ up** *vt,vi* ricapitolare.

summarize ['sʌməraɪz] *vt* riassumere, riepilogare.

summary ['sʌmərɪ] *n* riassunto // *a* (*justice*) sommario(a).

summer ['sʌmə*] *n* estate *f* // *cpd* d'estate, estivo(a); ~**house** *n* (*in garden*) padiglione *m*; ~**time** *n* (*season*) estate *f*; ~ **time** *n* (*by clock*) ora legale (estiva).

summit ['sʌmɪt] *n* cima, sommità; vertice *m*; ~ (**conference**) *n* (conferenza al) vertice.

summon ['sʌmən] *vt* chiamare, convocare; **to ~ up** *vt* raccogliere, fare appello a; ~**s** *n* ordine *m* di comparizione // *vt* citare.

sump [sʌmp] *n* (*AUT*) coppa dell'olio.

sumptuous ['sʌmptjuəs] *a* sontuoso(a).

sun [sʌn] *n* sole *m*; **in the ~** al sole; **~bathe** *vi* prendere un bagno di sole; **~burnt** *a* abbronzato(a); (*painfully*) scottato(a) dal sole; **~ cream** *n* crema solare.

Sunday ['sʌndɪ] *n* domenica.

sundial ['sʌndaɪəl] *n* meridiana.

sundry ['sʌndrɪ] *a* vari(e), diversi(e); **all and ~** tutti quanti; **sundries** *npl* articoli diversi, cose diverse.

sunflower ['sʌnflauə*] *n* girasole *m*.

sung [sʌŋ] *pp of* **sing**.

sunglasses ['sʌnglɑːsɪz] *npl* occhiali *mpl* da sole.

sunk [sʌŋk] *pp of* **sink**; **~en** *a* sommerso(a); infossato(a).

sun: ~light *n* (luce *f* del) sole *m*; **~lit** *a* assolato(a), soleggiato(a); **~ny** *a* assolato(a), soleggiato(a); (*fig*) allegro(a), felice; **~rise** *n* levata del sole, alba; **~set** *n* tramonto; **~shade** *n* parasole *m*; **~shine** *n* (luce *f* del) sole *m*; **~stroke** *n* insolazione *f*, colpo di sole; **~tan** *n* abbronzatura; **~tan oil** *n* olio solare; **~trap** *n* luogo molto assolato, angolo pieno di sole.

super ['su:pə*] *a* (col) fantastico(a).

superannuation [su:pərænjuˈeɪʃən] *n* contributi *mpl* pensionistici; pensione *f*.

superb [su:ˈpɔ:b] *a* magnifico(a).

supercilious [su:pəˈsɪlɪəs] *a* sprezzante, sdegnoso(a).

superficial [su:pəˈfɪʃəl] *a* superficiale.

superfluous [su:ˈpɔ:fluəs] *a* superfluo(a).

superhuman [su:pəˈhju:mən] *a* sovrumano(a).

superimpose ['su:pərɪmˈpəuz] *vt* sovrapporre.

superintendent [su:pərɪnˈtɛndənt] *n* direttore/trice; (*POLICE*) ≈ commissario (capo).

superior [suˈpɪərɪə*] *a,n* superiore (*m/f*); **~ity** [-ˈɔrɪtɪ] *n* superiorità.

superlative [suˈpɔːlətɪv] *a* superlativo(a), supremo(a) // *n* (*LING*) superlativo.

superman ['su:pəmæn] *n* superuomo.

supermarket ['su:pəmɑːkɪt] *n* supermercato.

supernatural [su:pəˈnætʃərəl] *a* soprannaturale.

superpower ['su:pəpauə*] *n* (*POL*) superpotenza.

supersede [su:pəˈsi:d] *vt* sostituire, soppiantare.

supersonic ['su:pəˈsɔnɪk] *a* supersonico(a).

superstition [su:pəˈstɪʃən] *n* superstizione *f*.

superstitious [su:pəˈstɪʃəs] *a* superstizioso(a).

supervise ['su:pəvaɪz] *vt* (*person etc*) sorvegliare; (*organization*) soprintendere a; **supervision** [-ˈvɪʒən] *n* sorveglianza; supervisione *f*; **supervisor** *n* sorvegliante *m/f*; soprintendente *m/f*; (*in shop*) capocommesso/a.

supper ['sʌpə*] *n* cena.

supple ['sʌpl] *a* flessibile; agile.

supplement *n* ['sʌplɪmənt] supplemento // *vt* [sʌplɪˈmɛnt] completare, integrare; **~ary** [-ˈmɛntərɪ] *a* supplementare.

supplier [səˈplaɪə*] *n* fornitore *m*.

supply [səˈplaɪ] *vt* (*provide*) fornire; (*equip*): **to ~ (with)** approvvigionare (di); attrezzare (con) // *n* riserva, provvista; (*supplying*) approvvigionamento; (*TECH*) alimentazione *f* // *cpd* (*teacher etc*) supplente; **supplies** *npl* (*food*) viveri *mpl*; (*MIL*) sussistenza; **~ and demand** la domanda e l'offerta.

support [səˈpɔːt] *n* (*moral, financial etc*) sostegno, appoggio; (*TECH*) supporto // *vt* sostenere; (*financially*) mantenere; (*uphold*) sostenere, difendere; **~er** *n* (*POL etc*) sostenitore/trice, fautore/ trice; (*SPORT*) tifoso/a.

suppose [səˈpəuz] *vt, vi* supporre; immaginare; **to be ~d to do** essere tenuto(a) a fare; **~dly** [səˈpəuzɪdlɪ] *ad* presumibilmente; (*seemingly*) apparentemente; **supposing** *cj* se, ammesso che + *sub*; **supposition** [sʌpəˈzɪʃən] *n* supposizione *f*, ipotesi *f inv*.

suppress [səˈprɛs] *vt* reprimere; sopprimere; tenere segreto(a); **~ion** [səˈprɛʃən] *n* repressione *f*; soppressione *f*; **~or** *n* (*ELEC etc*) soppressore *m*.

supremacy [suˈprɛməsɪ] *n* supremazia.

supreme [suˈpri:m] *a* supremo(a).

surcharge ['sɔːtʃɑːdʒ] *n* supplemento; (*extra tax*) soprattassa.

sure [ʃuə*] *a* sicuro(a); (*definite, convinced*) sicuro(a), certo(a); **~!** (*of course*) senz'altro!, certo!; **~ enough** infatti; **to make ~ of** assicurarsi di; **~-footed** *a* dal passo sicuro; **~ly** *ad* sicuramente; certamente.

surety ['ʃuərətɪ] *n* garanzia.

surf [sɔːf] *n* risacca; cresta dell'onda; frangenti *mpl*.

surface ['sɔːfɪs] *n* superficie *f* // *vt* (*road*) asfaltare // *vi* risalire alla superficie; (*fig: person*) venire a galla, farsi vivo(a); **~ mail** *n* posta ordinaria.

surfboard ['sɔːfbɔːd] *n* tavola per surfing.

surfeit ['sɔːfɪt] *n*: **a ~ of** un eccesso di; un'indigestione di.

surfing ['sɔːfɪŋ] *n* surfing *m*.

surge [sɔːdʒ] *n* (*strong movement*) ondata; (*of feeling*) impeto // *vi* (*waves*) gonfiarsi; (*ELEC: power*) aumentare improvvisamente; (*fig*) sollevarsi.

surgeon ['sɔːdʒən] *n* chirurgo.

surgery ['sɔːdʒərɪ] *n* chirurgia; (*room*) studio *or* gabinetto medico, ambulatorio; **~ hours** *npl* orario delle visite o di consultazione.

surgical ['sɔːdʒɪkl] *a* chirurgico(a); **~ spirit** *n* alcool denaturato.

surly ['sɔːlɪ] *a* scontroso(a), burbero(a).

surmise [sɔːˈmaɪz] *vt* supporre, congetturare.

surmount [sɔːˈmaunt] *vt* sormontare.

surname ['sɔːneɪm] *n* cognome *m*.

surpass [sɔːˈpɑːs] *vt* superare.

surplus ['sɔːpləs] n eccedenza; (ECON) surplus m inv // a eccedente, d'avanzo.

surprise [sə'praɪz] n sorpresa; (astonishment) stupore m // vt sorprendere; stupire; **surprising** a sorprendente, stupefacente.

surrender [sə'rɛndə*] n resa, capitolazione f // vi arrendersi.

surreptitious [sʌrəp'tɪʃəs] a furtivo(a).

surround [sə'raund] vt circondare; (MIL etc) accerchiare; **~ing** a circostante; **~ings** npl dintorni mpl; (fig) ambiente m.

surveillance [sɔː'veɪləns] n sorveglianza, controllo.

survey n ['sɔːveɪ] vista; (study) esame m; (in housebuying etc) perizia; (of land) rilevamento, rilievo topografico // vt [sɔː'veɪ] osservare; esaminare; valutare; rilevare; **~ing** n (of land) agrimensura; **~or** n perito; geometra m; (of land) agrimensore m.

survival [sə'vaɪvl] n sopravvivenza; (relic) reliquia, vestigio.

survive [sə'vaɪv] vi sopravvivere // vt sopravvivere a; **survivor** n superstite m/f, sopravvissuto(a).

susceptible [sə'sɛptəbl] a: **~ (to)** sensibile (a); (disease) predisposto(a) (a).

suspect a, n ['sʌspɛkt] a sospetto(a) // n persona sospetta // vt [səs'pɛkt] sospettare; (think likely) supporre; (doubt) dubitare.

suspend [səs'pɛnd] vt sospendere; **~ed sentence** n condanna con la condizionale; **~er belt** n reggicalze m inv; **~ers** npl giarrettiere fpl; (US) bretelle fpl.

suspense [səs'pɛns] n apprensione f; (in film etc) suspense m.

suspension [səs'pɛnʃən] n (gen AUT) sospensione f; (of driving licence) ritiro temporaneo; **~ bridge** n ponte m sospeso.

suspicion [səs'pɪʃən] n sospetto.

suspicious [səs'pɪʃəs] a (suspecting) sospettoso(a); (causing suspicion) sospetto(a).

sustain [səs'teɪn] vt sostenere; sopportare; (LAW: charge) confermare; (suffer) subire; **~ed** a (effort) prolungato(a).

sustenance ['sʌstɪnəns] n nutrimento; mezzi mpl di sostentamento.

swab [swɔb] n (MED) tampone m.

swagger ['swægə*] vi pavoneggiarsi.

swallow ['swɔləu] n (bird) rondine f // vt inghiottire; (fig: story) bere; **to ~ up** vt inghiottire.

swam [swæm] pt of **swim**.

swamp [swɔmp] n palude f // vt sommergere.

swan [swɔn] n cigno.

swap [swɔp] n scambio // vt: **to ~ (for)** scambiare (con).

swarm [swɔːm] n sciame m // vi formicolare; (bees) sciamare.

swarthy ['swɔːðɪ] a di carnagione scura.

swastika ['swɔstɪkə] n croce f uncinata, svastica.

swat [swɔt] vt schiacciare.

sway [sweɪ] vi (building) oscillare; (tree) ondeggiare; (person) barcollare // vt (influence) influenzare, dominare.

swear, pt **swore**, pp **sworn** [swɛə*, swɔː*, swɔːn] vi (witness etc) giurare; (curse) bestemmiare, imprecare; **to ~ to sth** giurare qc; **~ word** n parolaccia.

sweat [swɛt] n sudore m, traspirazione f // vi sudare; **in a ~** in un bagno di sudore.

sweater ['swɛtə*] n maglione m.

sweaty ['swɛtɪ] a sudato(a); bagnato(a) di sudore.

swede [swiːd] n rapa svedese.

Swede [swiːd] n svedese m/f.

Sweden ['swiːdn] n Svezia.

Swedish ['swiːdɪʃ] a svedese // n (LING) svedese m.

sweep [swiːp] n spazzata; (curve) curva; (expanse) distesa; (range) portata; (also: **chimney ~**) spazzacamino // vb (pt, pp **swept** [swɛpt]) vt spazzare, scopare // vi camminare maestosamente; precipitarsi, lanciarsi; (e)stendersi; **to ~ away** vt spazzare via; trascinare via; **to ~ past** vi sfrecciare accanto; passare accanto maestosamente; **to ~ up** vt, vi spazzare; **~ing** a (gesture) largo(a); circolare; **a ~ing statement** una affermazione generica.

sweet [swiːt] n dolce m; (candy) caramella // a dolce; (fresh) fresco(a); (fig) piacevole; delicato(a), grazioso(a); gentile; **~bread** n animella; **~corn** n granturco dolce; **~en** vt addolcire; zuccherare; **~heart** n innamorato/a; **~ness** n sapore m dolce; dolcezza; **~pea** n pisello odoroso; **to have a ~ tooth** avere un debole per i dolci.

swell [swɛl] n (of sea) mare m lungo // a (col: excellent) favoloso(a) // vb (pt **~ed**, pp **swollen**, **~ed** ['swəulən]) vt gonfiare, ingrossare; aumentare // vi gonfiarsi, ingrossarsi; (sound) crescere; (MED) gonfiarsi; **~ing** n (MED) tumefazione f, gonfiore m.

sweltering ['swɛltərɪŋ] a soffocante.

swept [swɛpt] pt,pp of **sweep**.

swerve [swɔːv] vi deviare; (driver) sterzare; (boxer) scartare.

swift [swɪft] n (bird) rondone m // a rapido(a), veloce.

swig [swɪg] n (col: drink) sorsata.

swill [swɪl] n broda // vt (also: **~ out**, **~ down**) risciacquare.

swim [swɪm] n: **to go for a ~** andare a fare una nuotata // vb (pt **swam**, pp **swum** [swæm, swʌm]) vi nuotare; (SPORT) fare del nuoto; (head, room) girare // vt (river, channel) attraversare or percorrere a nuoto; (length) nuotare; **~mer** n nuotatore/trice; **~ming** n nuoto; **~ming baths** npl piscina; **~ming cap** n cuffia; **~ming costume** n costume m da bagno; **~ming pool** n piscina; **~suit** n costume m da bagno.

swindle ['swɪndl] n truffa // vt truffare; **~r** n truffatore/trice.

swine [swaɪn] *n*, *pl inv* maiale *m*, porco; (*col!*) porco.

swing [swɪŋ] *n* altalena; (*movement*) oscillazione *f*; (*MUS*) ritmo; swing *m* // *vb* (*pt*, *pp* **swung** [swʌŋ]) *vt* dondolare, far oscillare; (*also*: ~ **round**) far girare // *vi* oscillare, dondolare; (*also*: ~ **round**) (*object*) roteare; (*person*) girarsi, voltarsi; **to be in full** ~ (*activity*) essere in piena attività; (*party etc*) essere nel pieno; ~ **bridge** *n* ponte *m* girevole; ~ **door** *n* porta battente.

swingeing ['swɪndʒɪŋ] *a* (*defeat*) violento(a); (*price increase*) enorme.

swinging ['swɪŋɪŋ] *a* (*step*) cadenzato(a), ritmico(a); (*rhythm, music*) trascinante.

swipe [swaɪp] *n* forte colpo; schiaffo // *vt* (*hit*) colpire con forza; dare uno schiaffo a; (*col: steal*) sgraffignare.

swirl [swəːl] *n* turbine *m*, mulinello // *vi* turbinare, far mulinello.

swish [swɪʃ] *a* (*col: smart*) all'ultimo grido, alla moda // *vi* sibilare.

Swiss [swɪs] *a*, *n*, *pl inv* svizzero(a); ~ **German** *a* svizzero(a) tedesco(a).

switch [swɪtʃ] *n* (*for light, radio etc*) interruttore *m*; (*change*) cambiamento // *vt* (*change*) cambiare; scambiare; **to** ~ **off** *vt* spegnere; **to** ~ **on** *vt* accendere; (*engine, machine*) mettere in moto, avviare; ~**back** *n* montagne *fpl* russe; ~**board** *n* (*TEL*) centralino; ~**board operator** centralinista *m/f*.

Switzerland ['swɪtsəlɛnd] *n* Svizzera.

swivel ['swɪvl] *vi* (*also*: ~ **round**) girare.

swollen ['swəʊlən] *pp of* **swell** // *a* (*ankle etc*) gonfio(a).

swoon [swuːn] *vi* svenire.

swoop [swuːp] *n* (*by police etc*) incursione *f* // *vi* (*also*: ~ **down**) scendere in picchiata, piombare.

swop [swɔp] *n*, *vt* = **swap**.

sword [sɔːd] *n* spada; ~**fish** *n* pesce *m* spada *inv*.

swore [swɔː*] *pt of* **swear**.

sworn [swɔːn] *pp of* **swear**.

swot [swɔt] *vt* sgobbare su // *vi* sgobbare.

swum [swʌm] *pp of* **swim**.

swung [swʌŋ] *pt*, *pp of* **swing**.

sycamore ['sɪkəmɔː*] *n* sicomoro.

syllable ['sɪləbl] *n* sillaba.

syllabus ['sɪləbəs] *n* programma *m*.

symbol ['sɪmbl] *n* simbolo; ~**ic(al)** [-'bɔlɪk(l)] *a* simbolico(a); ~**ism** *n* simbolismo; ~**ize** *vt* simbolizzare.

symmetrical [sɪ'mɛtrɪkl] *a* simmetrico(a).

symmetry ['sɪmɪtrɪ] *n* simmetria.

sympathetic [sɪmpə'θɛtɪk] *a* (*showing pity*) compassionevole; (*kind*) comprensivo(a); ~ **towards** ben disposto(a) verso.

sympathize ['sɪmpəθaɪz] *vi*: **to** ~ **with sb** compatire qd; partecipare al dolore di qd; ~**r** *n* (*POL*) simpatizzante *m/f*.

sympathy ['sɪmpəθɪ] *n* compassione *f*; **in** ~ **with** d'accordo con; (*strike*) per solidarietà con; **with our deepest** ~ con

le nostre più sincere condoglianze.

symphony ['sɪmfənɪ] *n* sinfonia.

symposium [sɪm'pəʊzɪəm] *n* simposio.

symptom ['sɪmptəm] *n* sintomo; indizio.

synagogue ['sɪnəgɔg] *n* sinagoga.

synchronize ['sɪŋkrənaɪz] *vt* sincronizzare // *vi*: **to** ~ **with** essere contemporaneo(a) a.

syncopated ['sɪŋkəpeɪtɪd] *a* sincopato(a).

syndicate ['sɪndɪkɪt] *n* sindacato.

syndrome ['sɪndrəʊm] *n* sindrome *f*.

synonym ['sɪnənɪm] *n* sinonimo; ~**ous** [sɪ'nɒnɪməs] *a*: ~**ous (with)** sinonimo(a) (di).

synopsis, *pl* **synopses** [sɪ'nɒpsɪs, -siːz] *n* sommario, sinossi *f inv*.

syntax ['sɪntæks] *n* sintassi *f inv*.

synthesis, *pl* **syntheses** ['sɪnθəsɪs, -siːz] *n* sintesi *f inv*.

synthetic [sɪn'θɛtɪk] *a* sintetico(a).

syphilis ['sɪfɪlɪs] *n* sifilide *f*.

syphon ['saɪfən] *n*, *vb* = **siphon**.

Syria ['sɪrɪə] *n* Siria; ~**n** *a*, *n* siriano(a).

syringe [sɪ'rɪndʒ] *n* siringa.

syrup ['sɪrəp] *n* sciroppo; (*also*: **golden** ~) melassa raffinata.

system ['sɪstəm] *n* sistema *m*; (*order*) metodo; (*ANAT*) organismo; ~**atic** [-'mætɪk] *a* sistematico(a); metodico(a); ~**s analyst** *n* analista programmatore *m*.

T

ta [tɑː] *excl* (*Brit: col*) grazie!

tab [tæb] *n* (*loop on coat etc*) laccetto; (*label*) etichetta; **to keep** ~**s on** (*fig*) tenere d'occhio.

tabby ['tæbɪ] *n* (*also*: ~ **cat**) (gatto) soriano, gatto tigrato.

table ['teɪbl] *n* tavolo, tavola // *vt* (*motion etc*) presentare; **to lay** *or* **set the** ~ apparecchiare *or* preparare la tavola; ~ **of contents** *n* indice *m*; ~**cloth** *n* tovaglia; ~ **d'hôte** [tɑːbl'dəʊt] *a* (*meal*) a prezzo fisso; ~ **lamp** *n* lampada da tavolo; ~**mat** *n* sottopiatto; ~ **salt** *n* sale *m* fino or da tavola; ~**spoon** *n* cucchiaio da tavola; (*also*: ~**spoonful**: *as measurement*) cucchiaiata.

tablet ['tæblɪt] *n* (*MED*) compressa; (: *for sucking*) pastiglia; (*for writing*) blocco; (*of stone*) targa.

table: ~ **tennis** *n* tennis *m* da tavolo, ping-pong *m* ®; ~ **wine** *n* vino da tavola.

taboo [tə'buː] *a*, *n* tabù (*m inv*).

tabulate ['tæbjuleɪt] *vt* (*data, figures*) tabulare, disporre in tabelle.

tacit ['tæsɪt] *a* tacito(a).

taciturn ['tæsɪtəːn] *a* taciturno(a).

tack [tæk] *n* (*nail*) bulletta; (*stitch*) punto d'imbastitura; (*NAUT*) bordo, bordata // *vt* imbullettare; imbastire // *vi* bordeggiare; **to change** ~ virare di bordo; **on the wrong** ~ (*fig*) sulla strada sbagliata.

tackle ['tækl] *n* attrezzatura, equipaggiamento; (*for lifting*) paranco; (*RUGBY*) placcaggio // *vt* (*difficulty*) affrontare; (*RUGBY*) placcare.

tacky ['tækı] *a* colloso(a), appiccicaticcio(a); ancora bagnato(a).

tact [tækt] *n* tatto; ~**ful** *a* delicato(a), discreto(a).

tactical ['tæktıkl] *a* tattico(a).

tactics ['tæktıks] *n,npl* tattica.

tactless ['tæktlıs] *a* che manca di tatto.

tadpole ['tædpəʊl] *n* girino.

tag [tæg] *n* etichetta; **to ~ along** *vi* seguire.

tail [teıl] *n* coda; (*of shirt*) falda // *vt* (*follow*) seguire, pedinare; **to ~ away, ~ off** *vi* (*in size, quality etc*) diminuire gradatamente; ~**back** *n* ingorgo; ~ **coat** *n* marsina; ~ **end** *n* (*of train, procession etc*) coda; (*of meeting etc*) fine *f*.

tailor ['teılə*] *n* sarto; ~**ing** *n* (*cut*) stile *m*; ~**-made** *a* (*also fig*) fatto(a) su misura.

tailwind ['teılwınd] *n* vento di coda.

tainted ['teıntıd] *a* (*food*) guasto(a); (*water, air*) infetto(a); (*fig*) corrotto(a).

take, *pt* **took,** *pp* **taken** [teık, tuk, 'teıkn] *vt* prendere; (*gain: prize*) ottenere, vincere; (*require: effort, courage*) occorrere, volerci; (*tolerate*) accettare, sopportare; (*hold: passengers etc*) contenere; (*accompany*) accompagnare; (*bring, carry*) portare; (*exam*) sostenere, presentarsi a; **it ~s a lot of time/courage** occorre *or* ci vuole molto tempo/coraggio; **I ~ it that** suppongo che; **to ~ for a walk** (*child, dog*) portare a fare una passeggiata; **to ~ after** *vt fus* assomigliare a; **to ~ apart** *vt* smontare; **to ~ away** *vt* portare via; togliere; **to ~ back** *vt* (*return*) restituire; riportare; (*one's words*) ritirare; **to ~ down** *vt* (*building*) demolire; (*letter etc*) scrivere; **to ~ in** *vt* (*deceive*) imbrogliare, abbindolare; (*understand*) capire; (*include*) comprendere, includere; (*lodger*) prendere, ospitare; **to ~ off** *vi* (*AVIAT*) decollare // *vt* (*remove*) togliere; (*imitate*) imitare; **to ~ on** *vt* (*work*) accettare, intraprendere; (*employee*) assumere; prendere; (*opponent*) sfidare, affrontare; **to ~ out** *vt* portare fuori; (*remove*) togliere; (*licence*) prendere, ottenere; **to ~ sth out of** tirare qc fuori da; estrarre qc da; **to ~ over** *vt* (*business*) rilevare // *vi*: **to ~ over from sb** prendere le consegne *or* il controllo da qd; **to ~ to** *vt fus* (*person*) prendere in simpatia; (*activity*) prendere gusto a; **to ~ up** *vt* (*one's story*) riprendere; (*dress*) accorciare; (*occupy: time, space*) occupare; (*engage in: hobby etc*) mettersi a; ~**away** *a* (*food*) da portar via; ~**-home pay** *n* stipendio netto; ~**off** *n* (*AVIAT*) decollo; ~**over** *n* (*COMM*) rilevamento.

takings ['teıkıŋz] *npl* (*COMM*) incasso.

talc [tælk] *n* (*also:* ~**um powder**) talco.

tale [teıl] *n* racconto, storia; (*pej*) fandonia.

talent ['tælnt] *n* talento.

talk [tɔːk] *n* discorso; (*gossip*) chiacchiere *fpl*; (*conversation*) conversazione *f*; (*interview*) discussione *f* // *vi* (*chatter*)

chiacchierare; **to ~ about** parlare di; (*converse*) discorrere *or* conversare su; **to ~ sb out of/into doing** dissuadere qd da/convincere qd a fare; **to ~ shop** parlare del lavoro *or* degli affari; **to ~ over** *vt* discutere; ~**ative** *a* loquace, ciarliero(a).

tall [tɔːl] *a* alto(a); **to be 6 feet ~** ≈ essere alto 1 metro e 80; ~**boy** *n* cassettone *m* alto; ~ **story** *n* panzana, frottola.

tally ['tælı] *n* conto, conteggio // *vi*: **to ~ (with)** corrispondere (con).

tambourine [tæmbə'riːn] *n* tamburello.

tame [teım] *a* addomesticato(a); (*fig: story, style*) insipido(a), scialbo(a).

tamper ['tæmpə*] *vi*: **to ~ with** manomettere.

tampon ['tæmpɔn] *n* assorbente *m* interno.

tan [tæn] *n* (*also:* **sun~**) abbronzatura // *vt* abbronzare // *vi* abbronzarsi // *a* (*colour*) marrone rossiccio *inv*.

tandem ['tændəm] *n* tandem *m inv*.

tang [tæŋ] *n* odore *m* penetrante; sapore *m* piccante.

tangent ['tændʒənt] *n* (*MATH*) tangente *f*.

tangerine [tændʒə'riːn] *n* mandarino.

tangible ['tændʒəbl] *a* tangibile.

tangle ['tæŋgl] *n* groviglio // *vt* aggrovigliare; **to get in(to) a ~** finire in un groviglio.

tango ['tæŋgəʊ] *n* tango.

tank [tæŋk] *n* serbatoio; (*for processing*) vasca; (*for fish*) acquario; (*MIL*) carro armato.

tankard ['tæŋkəd] *n* boccale *m*.

tanker ['tæŋkə*] *n* (*ship*) nave *f* cisterna *inv*; (*truck*) autobotte *f*, autocisterna *f*.

tantalizing ['tæntəlaızın] *a* allettante.

tantamount ['tæntəmaunt] *a*: ~ **to** equivalente a.

tantrum ['tæntrəm] *n* accesso di collera.

tap [tæp] *n* (*on sink etc*) rubinetto; (*gentle blow*) colpetto // *vt* dare un colpetto a; (*resources*) sfruttare, utilizzare; ~**-dancing** *n* tip tap *m*.

tape [teıp] *n* nastro; (*also:* **magnetic ~**) nastro (magnetico) // *vt* (*record*) registrare (su nastro); ~ **measure** *n* metro a nastro.

taper ['teıpə*] *n* candelina // *vi* assottigliarsi.

tape recorder ['teıprıkɔːdə*] *n* registratore *m* (a nastro).

tapestry ['tæpıstrı] *n* arazzo; tappezzeria.

tapioca [tæpı'əʊkə] *n* tapioca.

tar [tɑː] *n* catrame *m*.

tarantula [tə'ræntjulə] *n* tarantola.

tardy ['tɑːdı] *a* tardo(a); tardivo(a).

target ['tɑːgıt] *n* bersaglio; (*fig: objective*) obiettivo; ~ **practice** *n* tiro al bersaglio.

tariff ['tærıf] *n* (*COMM*) tariffa; (*taxes*) tariffe *fpl* doganali.

tarmac ['tɑːmæk] *n* macadam *m* al catrame; (*AVIAT*) pista di decollo.

tarnish ['tɑːnıʃ] *vt* offuscare, annerire; (*fig*) macchiare.

tarpaulin [tɑː'pɔːlɪn] n tela incatramata.
tart [tɑːt] n (CULIN) crostata; (col: pej: woman) sgualdrina // a (flavour) aspro(a), agro(a).
tartan ['tɑːtn] n tartan m inv.
tartar ['tɑːtə*] n (on teeth) tartaro; ~ **sauce** n salsa tartara.
task [tɑːsk] n compito; **to take to** ~ rimproverare; ~ **force** n (MIL, POLICE) unità operativa.
Tasmania [tæz'meɪnɪə] n Tasmania.
tassel ['tæsl] n fiocco.
taste [teɪst] n gusto; (flavour) sapore m, gusto; (fig: glimpse, idea) idea // vt gustare; (sample) assaggiare // vi: **to** ~ **of** (fish etc) sapere or avere sapore di; **it** ~**s like fish** sa di pesce; **can I have a** ~ **of this wine?** posso assaggiare un po' di questo vino?; **to have a** ~ **of sth** assaggiare qc; **to have a** ~ **for sth** avere un'inclinazione per qc; ~**ful** a di buon gusto; ~**less** a (food) insipido(a); (remark) di cattivo gusto; **tasty** a saporito(a), gustoso(a).
tatters ['tætəz] npl: **in** ~ (also: **tattered**) a brandelli, sbrindellato(a).
tattoo [tə'tuː] n tatuaggio; (spectacle) parata militare // vt tatuare.
tatty ['tætɪ] a (col) malandato(a).
taught [tɔːt] pt,pp of **teach**.
taunt [tɔːnt] n scherno // vt schernire.
Taurus ['tɔːrəs] n Toro.
taut [tɔːt] a teso(a).
tavern ['tævən] n taverna.
tawdry ['tɔːdrɪ] a pacchiano(a).
tawny ['tɔːnɪ] a fulvo(a).
tax [tæks] n (on goods) imposta; (on services) tassa; (on income) imposte fpl, tasse fpl // vt tassare; (fig: strain: patience etc) mettere alla prova; ~**ation** [-'seɪʃən] n tassazione f; tasse fpl, imposte fpl; ~ **avoidance** n l'evitare legalmente il pagamento di imposte; ~ **collector** n esattore m delle imposte; ~ **evasion** n evasione f fiscale; ~ **exile** n chi ripara all'estero per evadere le imposte; ~**free** a esente da imposte.
taxi ['tæksɪ] n taxi m inv // vi (AVIAT) rullare; ~ **driver** n tassista m/f; ~ **rank**, ~ **stand** n posteggio dei taxi.
tax: ~ **payer** n contribuente m/f; ~ **return** n dichiarazione f dei redditi.
TB abbr of **tuberculosis**.
tea [tiː] n tè m inv; (snack: for children) merenda; **high** ~ cena leggera (presa nel tardo pomeriggio); ~ **bag** n bustina di tè; ~ **break** n intervallo per il tè.
teach, pt, pp **taught** [tiːtʃ, tɔːt] vt: **to** ~ **sb sth**, ~ **sth to sb** insegnare qc a qd // vi insegnare; ~**er** n insegnante m/f; (in secondary school) professore/essa; (in primary school) maestro/a; ~**ing** n insegnamento; ~**ing staff** n insegnanti mpl, personale m insegnante.
tea cosy ['tiːkəʊzɪ] n copriteiera m inv.
teacup ['tiːkʌp] n tazza da tè.
teak [tiːk] n teak m.
tea leaves ['tiːliːvz] npl foglie fpl di tè.

team [tiːm] n squadra; (of animals) tiro; ~ **games/work** giochi mpl/lavoro di squadra.
tea party ['tiːpɑːtɪ] n tè m inv (ricevimento).
teapot ['tiːpɔt] n teiera.
tear n [tɛə*] strappo; [tɪə*] lacrima // vb [tɛə*] (pt **tore**, pp **torn** [tɔː*, tɔːn]) vt strappare // vi strapparsi; **in** ~**s** in lacrime; **to burst into** ~**s** scoppiare in lacrime; **to** ~ **along** vi (rush) correre all'impazzata; ~**ful** a piangente, lacrimoso(a); ~ **gas** n gas m lacrimogeno.
tearoom ['tiːruːm] n sala da tè.
tease [tiːz] vt canzonare; (unkindly) tormentare.
tea set ['tiːsɛt] n servizio da tè.
teaspoon ['tiːspuːn] n cucchiaino da tè; (also: ~**ful**: as measurement) cucchiaino.
tea strainer ['tiːstreɪnə*] n colino da tè.
teat [tiːt] n capezzolo.
teatime ['tiːtaɪm] n l'ora del tè.
tea towel ['tiːtauəl] n strofinaccio (per i piatti).
technical ['tɛknɪkl] a tecnico(a); ~**ity** [-'kælɪtɪ] n tecnicità; (detail) dettaglio tecnico.
technician [tɛk'nɪʃən] n tecnico/a.
technique [tɛk'niːk] n tecnica.
technological [tɛknə'lɔdʒɪkl] a tecnologico(a).
technology [tɛk'nɔlədʒɪ] n tecnologia.
teddy (bear) ['tɛdɪ(bɛə*)] n orsacchiotto.
tedious ['tiːdɪəs] a noioso(a), tedioso(a).
tedium ['tiːdɪəm] n noia, tedio.
tee [tiː] n (GOLF) tee m inv.
teem [tiːm] vi abbondare, brulicare; **to** ~ **with** brulicare di; **it is** ~**ing (with rain)** piove a dirotto.
teenage ['tiːneɪdʒ] a (fashions etc) per giovani, per adolescenti; ~**r** n adolescente m/f.
teens [tiːnz] npl: **to be in one's** ~ essere adolescente.
tee-shirt ['tiːʃəːt] n = **T-shirt**.
teeter ['tiːtə*] vi barcollare, vacillare.
teeth [tiːθ] npl of **tooth**.
teethe [tiːð] vi mettere i denti.
teething ['tiːðɪŋ] a: ~ **ring** n dentaruolo; ~ **troubles** npl (fig) difficoltà fpl iniziali.
teetotal ['tiː'təʊtl] a astemio(a).
telecommunications ['tɛlɪkəmjuːnɪ'keɪʃənz] n telecomunicazioni fpl.
telegram ['tɛlɪgræm] n telegramma m.
telegraph ['tɛlɪgrɑːf] n telegrafo; ~**ic** [-'græfɪk] a telegrafico(a); ~ **pole** n palo del telegrafo.
telepathy [tə'lɛpəθɪ] n telepatia.
telephone ['tɛlɪfəun] n telefono // vt (person) telefonare a; (message) telefonare; ~ **booth**, ~ **box** n cabina telefonica; ~ **call** n telefonata; ~ **directory** n elenco telefonico; ~ **exchange** n centralino telefonico; ~ **number** n numero di telefono;

telephonist [tə'lefənɪst] n telefonista m/f.
telephoto ['tɛlɪ'fəutəu] a: ~ **lens** n teleobiettivo.
teleprinter ['tɛlɪprɪntə*] n telescrivente f.
telescope ['tɛlɪskəup] n telescopio // vi incastrare a cannocchiale.
televise ['tɛlɪvaɪz] vt teletrasmettere.
television ['tɛlɪvɪʒən] n televisione f; ~ **programme** n programma m televisivo; ~ **set** n televisore m.
tell, pt, pp **told** [tɛl, təuld] vt dire; (relate: story) raccontare; (distinguish): **to ~ sth from** distinguere qc da // vi (have effect) farsi sentire, avere effetto; **to ~ sb to do** dire a qd di fare; **to ~ on** vt fus (inform against) denunciare; **to ~ off** vt rimproverare, sgridare; **~er** n (in bank) cassiere/a; **~ing** a (remark, detail) rivelatore(trice); **~tale** a (sign) significativo(a) // n malalingua, pettegolo/a.
telly ['tɛlɪ] n (col: abbr of **television**) tivù f inv.
temerity [tə'mɛrɪtɪ] n temerarietà.
temp [tɛmp] n (abbr of **temporary**) segretaria temporanea.
temper ['tɛmpə*] n (nature) carattere m; (mood) umore m; (fit of anger) collera // vt (moderate) temperare, moderare; **to be in a ~** essere in collera; **to lose one's ~** andare in collera.
temperament ['tɛmprəmənt] n (nature) temperamento; **~al** [-'mɛntl] a capriccioso(a).
temperance ['tɛmpərns] n moderazione f; (in drinking) temperanza nel bere.
temperate ['tɛmprət] a moderato(a); (climate) temperato(a).
temperature ['tɛmprətʃə*] n temperatura; **to have or run a ~** avere la febbre.
tempered ['tɛmpəd] a (steel) temprato(a).
tempest ['tɛmpɪst] n tempesta.
tempi ['tɛmpi:] vt **tempo**.
template ['tɛmplɪt] n sagoma.
temple ['tɛmpl] n (building) tempio; (ANAT) tempia.
tempo, ~s or **tempi** ['tɛmpəu, 'tɛmpi:] n tempo; (fig: of life etc) ritmo.
temporal ['tɛmpərl] a temporale.
temporary ['tɛmpərərɪ] a temporaneo(a); (job, worker) avventizio(a), temporaneo(a); ~ **secretary** n segretaria temporanea.
tempt [tɛmpt] vt tentare; **to ~ sb into doing** indurre qd a fare; **~ation** [-'teɪʃən] n tentazione f; **~ing** a allettante, seducente.
ten [tɛn] num dieci.
tenacious [tə'neɪʃəs] a tenace.
tenacity [tə'næsɪtɪ] n tenacia.
tenancy ['tɛnənsɪ] n affitto; condizione f di inquilino.
tenant ['tɛnənt] n inquilino/a.
tend [tɛnd] vt badare a, occuparsi di // vi: **to ~ to do** tendere a fare; (colour): **to ~ to** tendere a.
tendency ['tɛndənsɪ] n tendenza.

tender ['tɛndə*] a tenero(a); (delicate) fragile; (sore) dolorante; (affectionate) affettuoso(a) // n (COMM: offer) offerta; (money): **legal ~** valuta (a corso legale) // vt offrire; **~ize** vt (CULIN) far intenerire.
tendon ['tɛndən] n tendine m.
tenement ['tɛnəmənt] n casamento.
tenet ['tɛnət] n principio.
tennis ['tɛnɪs] n tennis m; ~ **ball** n palla da tennis; ~ **court** n campo da tennis; ~ **racket** n racchetta da tennis.
tenor ['tɛnə*] n (MUS, of speech etc) tenore m.
tense [tɛns] a teso(a) // n (LING) tempo.
tension ['tɛnʃən] n tensione f.
tent [tɛnt] n tenda.
tentacle ['tɛntəkl] n tentacolo.
tentative ['tɛntətɪv] a esitante, incerto(a); (conclusion) provvisorio(a).
tenterhooks ['tɛntəhuks] npl: **on ~** sulle spine.
tenth [tɛnθ] num decimo(a).
tent: ~ **peg** n picchetto da tenda; ~ **pole** n palo da tenda, montante m.
tenuous ['tɛnjuəs] a tenue.
tenure ['tɛnjuə*] n (of property) possesso; (of job) permanenza; titolarità.
tepid ['tɛpɪd] a tiepido(a).
term [tə:m] n (limit) termine m; (word) vocabolo, termine; (SCOL) trimestre m; (LAW) sessione f // vt chiamare, definire; **~s** npl (conditions) condizioni fpl; (COMM) prezzi mpl, tariffe fpl; ~ **of imprisonment** periodo di prigionia; **in the short/long ~** a breve/lunga scadenza; **to be on good ~s with** essere in buoni rapporti con; **to come to ~s with** (person) arrivare a un accordo con; (problem) affrontare.
terminal ['tə:mɪnl] a finale, terminale; (disease) nella fase terminale // n (ELEC) morsetto; (for oil, ore etc) terminal m inv; (also: **air ~**) aerostazione f; (also: **coach ~**) capolinea m.
terminate ['tə:mɪneɪt] vt mettere fine a // vi: **to ~ in** finire in or con.
terminology [tə:mɪ'nɔlədʒɪ] n terminologia.
terminus, pl **termini** ['tə:mɪnəs, 'tə:mɪnaɪ] n (for buses) capolinea m; (for trains) stazione f terminale.
termite ['tə:maɪt] n termite f.
terrace ['tɛrəs] n terrazza; (row of houses) fila di case (unite); **the ~s** (SPORT) le gradinate; **~d** a (garden) a terrazze.
terrain [tɛ'reɪn] n terreno.
terrible ['tɛrɪbl] a terribile; (weather) bruttissimo(a); (work) orribile; **terribly** ad terribilmente; (very badly) spaventosamente male.
terrier ['tɛrɪə*] n terrier m inv.
terrific [tə'rɪfɪk] a incredibile, fantastico(a); (wonderful) formidabile, eccezionale.
terrify ['tɛrɪfaɪ] vt terrorizzare.
territory ['tɛrɪtərɪ] n territorio.

terror ['tɛrə*] n terrore m; **~ism** n terrorismo; **~ist** n terrorista m/f; **~ize** vt terrorizzare.

terse [tə:s] a (style) conciso(a); (reply) laconico(a).

test [tɛst] n (trial, check, of courage etc) prova; (: of goods in factory) controllo, collaudo; (MED) esame m; (CHEM) analisi f inv; (exam: of intelligence etc) test m inv; (: in school) saggio; (also: **driving ~**) esame m di guida // vt provare; controllare, collaudare; esaminare; analizzare; saggiare; sottoporre ad esame.

testament ['tɛstəmənt] n testamento; **the Old/New T~** il Vecchio/Nuovo testamento.

test: ~ case n (LAW, fig) caso da annali or che farà testo; **~ flight** n volo di prova.

testicle ['tɛstɪkl] n testicolo.

testify ['tɛstɪfaɪ] vi (LAW) testimoniare, deporre.

testimonial [tɛstɪ'məunɪəl] n (reference) benservito; (gift) testimonianza di stima.

testimony ['tɛstɪmənɪ] n (LAW) testimonianza, deposizione f.

test: ~ match n (CRICKET, RUGBY) partita internazionale; **~ paper** n (SCOL) interrogazione f scritta; **~ pilot** n pilota m collaudatore; **~ tube** n provetta.

testy ['tɛstɪ] a irritabile.

tetanus ['tɛtənəs] n tetano.

tether ['tɛðə*] vt legare, impastoiare // n: **at the end of one's ~** al limite (della pazienza).

text [tɛkst] n testo; **~book** n libro di testo.

textile ['tɛkstaɪl] n tessile m.

texture ['tɛkstʃə*] n tessitura; (of skin, paper etc) struttura.

Thai [taɪ] a tailandese // n tailandese m/f; (LING) tailandese m; **~land** n Tailandia.

Thames [tɛmz] n: **the ~** il Tamigi.

than [ðæn, ðən] cj che; (with numerals, pronouns, proper names): **more ~ 10/me/Maria** più di 10/me/Maria; **you know her better ~ I do** la conosce meglio di me or di quanto non la conosca io; **she has more apples ~ pears** ha più mele che pere.

thank [θæŋk] vt ringraziare; **~ you (very much)** grazie (tante); **~s** npl ringraziamenti mpl, grazie fpl // excl grazie!; **~s to** prep grazie a; **~ful:** **~ful (for)** riconoscente (per); **~less** a ingrato(a); **T~sgiving (Day)** n giorno del ringraziamento.

that [ðæt, ðət] cj che // det quel (quell', quello) m; quella(quell') f // pronoun ciò; (the one, not 'this one') quello(a); (relative) che; prep + il(la sogg.; (with time): **on the day ~ he came** il giorno in cui or quando venne // ad: **~ high** così alto; alto così; **~ one** quello(a) (là); **what's ~?** cos'è?; **who's ~?** chi è?; **is ~ you?** sei tu?; **~'s what he said** questo è or ecco quello che ha detto; **~ is...** cioè è..., vale a dire...; **I can't work ~ much** non posso lavorare così tanto.

thatched [θætʃt] a (roof) di paglia; **~**

cottage n cottage m inv col tetto di paglia.

thaw [θɔ:] n disgelo // vi (ice) sciogliersi; (food) scongelarsi // vt (food) (fare) scongelare; **it's ~ing** (weather) sta sgelando.

the [ði:, ðə] det il(lo, l') m; la(l') f; i(gli) mpl; le fpl.

theatre ['θɪətə*] n teatro; **~-goer** n frequentatore/trice di teatri.

theatrical [θɪ'ætrɪkl] a teatrale.

theft [θɛft] n furto.

their [ðɛə*] a il(la) loro, pl i(le) loro; **~s** pronoun il(la) loro, pl i(le) loro; **it is ~s** è loro; **a friend of ~s** un loro amico.

them [ðɛm, ðəm] pronoun (direct) li(le); (indirect) gli, loro (after vb); (stressed, after prep: people) loro; (: people, things) essi(e); **I see ~** li vedo; **give ~ the book** dà loro or dagli il libro.

theme [θi:m] n tema m; **~ song/tune** n tema musicale.

themselves [ðəm'sɛlvz] pl pronoun (reflexive) si; (emphatic) loro stessi(e); (after prep) se stessi(e); **between ~** tra (di) loro.

then [ðɛn] ad (at that time) allora; (next) poi, dopo; (and also) e poi // cj (therefore) perciò, dunque, quindi // a: **the president** il presidente di allora; **from ~ on** da allora in poi.

theologian [θɪə'ləudʒən] n teologo/a.

theology [θɪ'ɔlədʒɪ] n teologia.

theorem ['θɪərəm] n teorema m.

theoretical [θɪə'rɛtɪkl] a teorico(a).

theorize ['θɪəraɪz] vi teorizzare.

theory ['θɪərɪ] n teoria.

therapeutic(al) [θɛrə'pju:tɪk(l)] a terapeutico(a).

therapy ['θɛrəpɪ] n terapia.

there [ðɛə*] ad là, lì; **~, ~!** su, su!; **it's ~** è lì; **he went ~** ci è andato; **~ is c'è; ~ are** ci sono; **~ he is** eccolo; **~ has been** c'è stato; **on/in ~** lassù/lì dentro; **to go ~ and back** andarci e ritornare; **~abouts** ad (place) nei pressi, da quelle parti; (amount) giù di lì, all'incirca; **~after** ad da allora in poi; **~fore** ad perciò, quindi.

thermal ['θə:ml] a termico(a).

thermometer [θə'mɔmɪtə*] n termometro.

thermonuclear ['θə:məu'nju:klɪə*] a termonucleare.

Thermos ['θə:məs] n ® (also: **~ flask**) thermos m inv ®.

thermostat ['θə:məstæt] n termostato.

thesaurus [θɪ'sɔ:rəs] n dizionario dei sinonimi.

these [ði:z] pl pronoun, det questi(e).

thesis, pl theses ['θi:sɪs, 'θi:si:z] n tesi f inv.

they [ðeɪ] pl pronoun essi(esse); (people only) loro; **~ say that...** (it is said that) si dice che...

thick [θɪk] a spesso(a); (crowd) compatto(a); (stupid) ottuso(a), lento(a) // n: **in the ~ of** nel folto di; **it's 20 cm ~** ha uno spessore di 20 cm; **~en** vi ispessire // vt (sauce etc) ispessire, rendere più denso(a); ~ness n spessore m; ~set a tarchiato(a), tozzo(a); ~skinned a (fig) insensibile.

thief, thieves [θi:f, θi:vz] n ladro/a.

thigh [θaɪ] n coscia; ~bone n femore m.

thimble ['θɪmbl] n ditale m.

thin [θɪn] a sottile; (person) magro(a); (soup) brodoso(a); (hair, crowd) rado(a); (fog) leggero(a) // vt (hair) sfoltire; to ~ (down) (sauce, paint) diluire.

thing [θɪŋ] n cosa; (object) oggetto; (contraption) aggeggio; ~s npl (belongings) cose fpl; for one ~ tanto per cominciare; the best ~ would be to la cosa migliore sarebbe di; how are ~s? come va?

think, pt, pp **thought** [θɪŋk, θɔ:t] vi pensare, riflettere // vt pensare, credere; (imagine) immaginare; to ~ of pensare a; what did you ~ of them? cosa ne ha pensato?; to ~ about sth/sb pensare a qc/qd; I'll ~ about it ci penserò; to ~ of doing pensare di fare; I ~ so penso di sì; to ~ well of avere una buona opinione di; to ~ over vt riflettere su; to ~ up vt ideare.

third [θɔ:d] num terzo(a) // n terzo(a); (fraction) terzo, terza parte f; (scol: degree) ≈ laurea col minimo dei voti; ~ly ad in terzo luogo; ~ party insurance n assicurazione f contro terzi; ~-rate a di qualità scadente; the T~ World n il Terzo Mondo.

thirst [θɔ:st] n sete f; ~y a (person) assetato(a), che ha sete.

thirteen ['θɔ:'ti:n] num tredici.

thirty ['θɔ:tɪ] num trenta.

this [ðɪs] det, pronoun questo(a); ~ one questo(a) (qui); ~ is what he said questo è quello or ciò che ha detto.

thistle ['θɪsl] n cardo.

thong [θɒŋ] n cinghia.

thorn [θɔ:n] n spina; ~y a spinoso(a).

thorough ['θʌrə] a (search) minuzioso(a); (knowledge, research) approfondito(a), profondo(a); coscienzioso(a); (cleaning) a fondo; ~bred n (horse) purosangue m/f inv; ~fare n strada transitabile; 'no ~fare' 'divieto di transito'; ~ly ad minuziosamente; in profondità; a fondo; he ~ly agreed fu completamente d'accordo.

those [ðəuz] pl pronoun quelli(e) // pl det quei(quegli) mpl; quelle fpl.

though [ðəu] cj benché, sebbene // ad comunque.

thought [θɔ:t] pt, pp of **think** // n pensiero; (opinion) opinione f; (intention) intenzione f; ~ful a pensieroso(a), pensoso(a); ponderato(a); (considerate) premuroso(a); ~less a irriguardoso(a).

thousand ['θauzənd] num mille; ~th num millesimo(a); one ~ mille; ~s of migliaia di.

thrash [θræʃ] vt picchiare; bastonare; (defeat) battere; to ~ about vi dibattersi; to ~ out vt dibattere, sviscerare.

thread [θrɛd] n filo; (of screw) filetto // vt

(needle) infilare; to ~ one's way between infilarsi tra; ~bare a consumato(a). logoro(a).

threat [θrɛt] n minaccia; ~en vi (storm) minacciare // vt: to ~en sb with sth/to do minacciare qd con qc/di fare.

three [θri:] num tre; ~-dimensional a tridimensionale; (film) stereoscopico(a); ~-piece suit n completo (con gilè); ~-piece suite n salotto comprendente un divano e due poltrone; ~-ply a (wool) a tre strati; (wool) a tre fili; ~-wheeler n (car) veicolo a tre ruote.

thresh [θrɛʃ] vt (AGR) trebbiare; ~ing machine n trebbiatrice f.

threshold ['θrɛʃhəuld] n soglia.

threw [θru:] pt of **throw**.

thrifty ['θrɪftɪ] a economico(a).

thrill [θrɪl] n brivido // vi eccitarsi, tremare // vt (audience) elettrizzare; to be ~ed (with gift etc) essere commosso(a); ~er n film m inv (or dramma m or libro) del brivido.

thrive, pt **thrived, throve** pp **thrived, thriven** [θraɪv, θrəuv, 'θrɪvn] vi crescere or svilupparsi bene; (business) prosperare; he ~s on it gli fa bene, ne gode.

throat [θrəut] n gola; to have a sore ~ avere (un or il) mal di gola.

throb [θrɒb] n (of heart) battito; (of engine) vibrazione f; (of pain) fitta // vi (heart) palpitare; (engine) vibrare; (with pain) pulsare.

throes [θrəuz] npl: in the ~ of alle prese con; in preda a; in the ~ of death in agonia.

thrombosis [θrɒm'bəusɪs] n trombosi f.

throne [θrəun] n trono.

throttle ['θrɒtl] n (AUT) valvola a farfalla // vt strangolare.

through [θru:] prep attraverso; (time) per, durante; (by means of) per mezzo di; (owing to) a causa di // a (ticket, train, passage) diretto(a) // ad attraverso; to put sb ~ to sb (TEL) passare qd a qd; to be ~ (TEL) ottenere la comunicazione; (have finished) avere finito; 'no ~ way' 'strada senza sbocco'; ~out prep (place) dappertutto in; (time) per or durante tutto(a) // ad dappertutto; sempre.

throve [θrəuv] pt of **thrive**.

throw [θrəu] n tiro, getto; (SPORT) lancio // vt (pt **threw,** pp **thrown** [θru:, θrəun]) tirare, gettare; (SPORT) lanciare; (rider) disarcionare; (fig) confondere; (pottery) formare al tornio; to ~ a party dare una festa; to ~ away vt gettare or buttare via; to ~ off vt sbarazzarsi di; to ~ out vt buttare fuori; (reject) respingere; to ~ up vi vomitare; ~away a da buttare; ~-in n (SPORT) rimessa in gioco.

thru [θru:] prep, a, ad (US) = **through.**

thrush [θrʌʃ] n tordo.

thrust [θrʌst] n (TECH) spinta // vt (pt, pp **thrust**) spingere con forza; (push in) conficcare.

thud [θʌd] n tonfo.

thug [θʌg] n delinquente m.

thumb [θʌm] *n* (ANAT) pollice *m* // *vt* (*book*) sfogliare; **to ~ a lift** fare l'autostop; **~ index** *n* indice *m* a rubrica; **~tack** *n* (*US*) puntina da disegno.

thump [θʌmp] *n* colpo forte; (*sound*) tonfo // *vt* battere su // *vi* picchiare, battere.

thunder ['θʌndə*] *n* tuono // *vi* tuonare; (*train etc*): **to ~ past** passare con un rombo; **~clap** *n* rombo di tuono; **~ous** *a* fragoroso(a); **~storm** *n* temporale *m*; **~y** *a* temporalesco(a).

Thursday ['θə:zdɪ] *n* giovedì *m inv*.

thus [ðʌs] *ad* così.

thwart [θwɔ:t] *vt* contrastare.

thyme [taɪm] *n* timo.

thyroid ['θaɪrɔɪd] *n* tiroide *f*.

tiara [tɪ'ɑ:rə] *n* (*woman's*) diadema *m*.

Tiber ['taɪbə*] *n*: **the ~** il Tevere.

tic [tɪk] *n* tic *m inv*.

tick [tɪk] *n* (*sound: of clock*) tic tac *m inv*; (*mark*) segno; spunta; (*ZOOL*) zecca; (*col*): **in a ~** in un attimo // *vi* fare tic tac // *vt* spuntare; **to ~ off** *vt* spuntare; (*person*) sgridare.

ticket ['tɪkɪt] *n* biglietto; (*in shop: on goods*) etichetta; (: *from cash register*) scontrino; (*for library*) scheda; **~ collector** *n* bigliettaio; **~ holder** *n* persona munita di biglietto; **~ office** *n* biglietteria.

tickle ['tɪkl] *n* solletico // *vt* fare il solletico a, solleticare; (*fig*) stuzzicare; piacere a; far ridere; **ticklish** *a* che soffre il solletico.

tidal ['taɪdl] *a* di marea.

tiddlywinks ['tɪdlɪwɪŋks] *n* gioco della pulce.

tide [taɪd] *n* marea; (*fig: of events*) corso.

tidy ['taɪdɪ] *a* (*room*) ordinato(a), lindo(a); (*dress, work*) curato(a), in ordine; (*person*) ordinato(a) // *vt* (*also: ~ up*) riordinare, mettere in ordine; **to ~ o.s. up** rassettarsi.

tie [taɪ] *n* (*string etc*) legaccio; (*also: neck~*) cravatta; (*fig: link*) legame *m*; (*SPORT: draw*) pareggio // *vt* (*parcel*) legare; (*ribbon*) annodare // *vi* (*SPORT*) pareggiare; **'black/white ~'** 'smoking/abito di rigore'; **to ~ sth in a bow** annodare qc; **to ~ a knot in sth** fare un nodo a qc; **to ~ down** *vt* fissare con una corda; (*fig*): **to ~ sb down to** costringere qd a accettare; **to ~ up** *vt* (*parcel, dog*) legare; (*boat*) ormeggiare; (*arrangements*) concludere; **to be ~d up** (*busy*) essere occupato or preso.

tier [tɪə*] *n* fila; (*of cake*) piano, strato.

tiff [tɪf] *n* battibecco.

tiger ['taɪgə*] *n* tigre *f*.

tight [taɪt] *a* (*rope*) teso(a), tirato(a); (*clothes*) stretto(a); (*budget, programme, bend*) stretto(a); (*control*) severo(a), fermo(a); (*col: drunk*) sbronzo(a) // *ad* (*squeeze*) fortemente; (*shut*) ermeticamente; **~s** *npl* collant *m inv*; **~en** *vt* (*rope*) tendere; (*screw*) stringere; (*control*) rinforzare // *vi* tendersi; stringersi; **~-fisted** *a* avaro(a); **~ly** *ad*

(*grasp*) bene, saldamente; **~-rope** *n* corda (da acrobata).

tile [taɪl] *n* (*on roof*) tegola; (*on wall or floor*) piastrella, mattonella.

till [tɪl] *n* registratore *m* di cassa // *vt* (*land*) coltivare // *prep, cj* = **until**.

tiller ['tɪlə*] *n* (NAUT) barra del timone.

tilt [tɪlt] *vt* inclinare, far pendere // *vi* inclinarsi, pendere.

timber ['tɪmbə*] *n* (*material*) legname *m*; (*trees*) *mpl* da legname.

time [taɪm] *n* tempo; (*epoch: often pl*) epoca, tempo; (*by clock*) ora; (*moment*) momento; (*occasion, also* MATH) volta; (MUS) tempo // *vt* (*race*) crònometrare; (*programme*) calcolare la durata di; (*remark etc*) dire (*or* fare) al momento giusto; **a long ~** molto tempo; **for the ~ being** per il momento; **from ~ to ~** ogni tanto; **in ~** (*soon enough*) in tempo; (*after some time*) col tempo; (MUS) a tempo; **in a week's ~** fra una settimana; **on ~** puntualmente; **5 ~ s 5 5** volte *or* per 5; **what ~ is it?** che ora è?, che ore sono?; **to have a good ~** divertirsi; **~'s up!** è (l')ora!; **~ bomb** *n* bomba a orologeria; **~keeper** *n* (SPORT) cronometrista *m/f*; **~ lag** *n* intervallo, ritardo; (*in travel*) differenza di fuso orario; **~less** *a* eterno(a); **~ limit** *n* limite *m* di tempo; **~ly** *a* opportuno(a); **~ off** *n* tempo libero; **~r** *n* (*in kitchen*) contaminuti *m inv*; **~-saving** *a* che fa risparmiare tempo; **~ switch** *n* interruttore *m* a tempo; **~table** *n* orario; **~ zone** *n* fuso orario.

timid ['tɪmɪd] *a* timido(a); (*easily scared*) pauroso(a).

timing ['taɪmɪŋ] *n* sincronizzazione *f*; (*fig*) scelta del momento opportuno, tempismo; (SPORT) cronometraggio.

timpani ['tɪmpənɪ] *npl* timpani *mpl*.

tin [tɪn] *n* stagno; (*also: ~ plate*) latta; (*can*) barattolo (di latta), lattina, scatola; (*for baking*) teglia; **~ foil** *n* stagnola.

tinge [tɪndʒ] *n* sfumatura // *vt*: **~d with** tinto(a) di.

tingle ['tɪŋgl] *vi* pizzicare.

tinker ['tɪŋkə*] *n* calderaio ambulante; (*gipsy*) zingaro/a; **to ~ with** *vt fus* armeggiare intorno a; cercare di riparare.

tinkle ['tɪŋkl] *vi* tintinnare.

tinned [tɪnd] *a* (*food*) in scatola.

tinny ['tɪnɪ] *a* metallico(a).

tin opener ['tɪnəupnə*] *n* apriscatole *m inv*.

tinsel ['tɪnsl] *n* decorazioni *fpl* natalizie (argentate).

tint [tɪnt] *n* tinta.

tiny ['taɪnɪ] *a* minuscolo(a).

tip [tɪp] *n* (*end*) punta; (*protective: on umbrella etc*) puntale *m*; (*gratuity*) mancia; (*for coal*) discarica; (*for rubbish*) immondezzaio; (*advice*) suggerimento // *vt* (*waiter*) dare la mancia a; (*tilt*) inclinare; (*overturn: also:* **~ over**) capovolgere; (*empty: also:* **~ out**) scaricare; **~-off** *n* (*hint*) soffiata; **~ped** *a* (*cigarette*) col

filtro; **steel-~ped** con la punta d'acciaio.
tipple ['tɪpl] vi sbevazzare // n: **to have a ~** prendere un bicchierino.
tipsy ['tɪpsɪ] a brillo(a).
tiptoe ['tɪptəu] n: **on ~** in punta di piedi.
tiptop ['tɪp'tɔp] a: **in ~ condition** in ottime condizioni.
tire ['taɪə*] vt stancare // vi stancarsi; **~d a** stanco(a); **to be ~d** di essere stanco or stufo di; **~less** a instancabile; **~some** a noioso(a); **tiring** a faticoso(a).
tissue ['tɪʃu:] n tessuto; (paper handkerchief) fazzoletto di carta; **~ paper** n carta velina.
tit [tɪt] n (bird) cinciallegra; **to give ~ for tat** rendere pan per focaccia.
titbit ['tɪtbɪt] n (food) leccornia; (news) notizia ghiotta.
titillate ['tɪtɪleɪt] vt titillare.
titivate ['tɪtɪveɪt] vt agghindare.
title ['taɪtl] n titolo; **~ deed** n (LAW) titolo di proprietà; **~ role** n ruolo or parte f principale.
titter ['tɪtə*] vi ridere scioccamente.
tittle-tattle ['tɪtltætl] n chiacchiere fpl, pettegolezzi mpl.
tizzy ['tɪzɪ] n: **to be in a ~** essere in agitazione.
to [tu:, tə] prep a; (towards) verso; **give it ~ me** dammelo; **the key ~ the front door** la chiave della porta d'ingresso; **the main thing is ~ ...** l'importante è di...; **to go ~ France/Portugal** andare in Francia/Portogallo; **I went ~ Claudia's** sono andato da Claudia; **to go ~ town/school** andare in città/a scuola; **to pull/push the door ~** tirare/spingere la porta; **to go ~ and fro** andare e tornare.
toad [təud] n rospo; **~stool** n fungo (velenoso); **~y** vi adulare.
toast [təust] n (CULIN) toast m, pane m abbrustolito; (drink, speech) brindisi m inv // vt (CULIN) abbrustolire; (drink to) brindare a; **a piece or slice of ~** una fetta di pane abbrustolito; **~er** n tostapane m inv; **~master** n direttore m dei brindisi.
tobacco [tə'bækəu] n tabacco; **~nist** n tabaccaio/a; **~nist's (shop)** n tabaccheria.
toboggan [tə'bɔgən] n toboga m inv; (child's) slitta.
today [tə'deɪ] ad,n (also fig) oggi (m).
toddler ['tɔdlə*] n bambino/a che impara a camminare.
toddy ['tɔdɪ] n grog m inv.
to-do [tə'du:] n (fuss) storie fpl.
toe [təu] n dito del piede; (of shoe) punta; **to ~ the line** (fig) stare in riga, conformarsi; **~nail** n unghia del piede.
toffee ['tɔfɪ] n caramella.
toga ['təugə] n toga.
together [tə'geðə*] ad insieme; (at same time) allo stesso tempo; **~ with** prep insieme a; **~ness** n solidarietà; intimità.
toil [tɔɪl] n travaglio, fatica // vi affannarsi; sgobbare.
toilet ['tɔɪlət] n (lavatory) gabinetto // cpd

(bag, soap etc) da toletta; **~ bowl** n vaso or tazza del gabinetto; **~ paper** n carta igienica; **~ries** npl articoli mpl da toletta; **~ roll** n rotolo di carta igienica; **~ water** n colonia.
token ['təukən] n (sign) segno; (voucher) buono; **book/record ~** n buono-libro/disco.
told [təuld] pt, pp of **tell**.
tolerable ['tɔlərəbl] a (bearable) tollerabile; (fairly good) passabile.
tolerance ['tɔlərns] n (also: TECH) tolleranza.
tolerant ['tɔlərnt] a: **~ (of)** tollerante (nei confronti di).
tolerate ['tɔləreɪt] vt sopportare; (MED, TECH) tollerare; **toleration** [-'reɪʃən] n tolleranza.
toll [təul] n (tax, charge) pedaggio // vi (bell) suonare; **the accident ~ on the roads** il numero delle vittime della strada; **~bridge** n ponte m a pedaggio.
tomato, **~es** [tə'mɑ:təu] n pomodoro.
tomb [tu:m] n tomba.
tombola [tɔm'bəulə] n tombola.
tomboy ['tɔmbɔɪ] n maschiaccio.
tombstone ['tu:mstəun] n pietra tombale.
tomcat ['tɔmkæt] n gatto.
tomorrow [tə'mɔrəu] ad,n (also fig) domani (m inv); **the day after ~** dopodomani; **~ morning** domani mattina.
ton [tʌn] n tonnellata (=1016 kg; 20 cwt); (NAUT: also: **register ~**) tonnellata di stazza (=2.83 cu.m; 100 cu. ft); **~s of** (col) un mucchio or sacco di.
tone [təun] n tono // vi intonarsi; **to ~ down** vt (colour, criticism, sound) attenuare; **to ~ up** vt (muscles) tonificare; **~-deaf** a che non ha orecchio (musicale).
tongs [tɔŋz] npl tenaglie fpl; (for coal) molle fpl; (for hair) arricciacapelli m inv.
tongue [tʌŋ] n lingua; **~ in cheek** ad ironicamente; **~-tied** a (fig) muto(a); **~-twister** n scioglilingua m inv.
tonic ['tɔnɪk] n (MED) tonico; (MUS) nota tonica; (also: **~ water**) acqua tonica.
tonight [tə'naɪt] ad stanotte; (this evening) stasera // n questa notte; questa sera.
tonnage ['tʌnɪdʒ] n (NAUT) tonnellaggio, stazza.
tonne [tʌn] n (metric ton) tonnellata.
tonsil ['tɔnsl] n tonsilla; **~litis** [-'laɪtɪs] n tonsillite f.
too [tu:] ad (excessively) troppo; (also) anche; **~ much** ad troppo // det troppo(a); **~ many** det troppi(e); **~ bad!** tanto peggio!, peggio così!
took [tuk] pt of **take**.
tool [tu:l] n utensile m, attrezzo // vt lavorare con un attrezzo; **~ box/kit** n cassetta f portautensili/attrezzi inv.
toot [tu:t] vi suonare; (with car-horn) suonare il clacson.
tooth, pl **teeth** [tu:θ, ti:θ] n (ANAT, TECH) dente m; **~ache** n mal m di denti; **~brush** n spazzolino da denti; **~paste**

dentifricio (in pasta); ~**pick** n stuzzicadenti m inv.

top [tɔp] n (of mountain, page, ladder) cima; (of box, cupboard, table) sopra m inv, parte f superiore; (lid: of box, jar) coperchio; (: of bottle) tappo; (toy) trottola // a più alto(a); (in rank) primo(a); (best) migliore // vt (exceed) superare; (be first in) essere in testa a; **on ~ of** sopra, in cima a; (in addition to) oltre a; **from ~ to toe** dalla testa ai piedi; **to ~ up** vt riempire; ~**floor** n ultimo piano; ~ **hat** n cilindro; ~**-heavy** a (object) con la parte superiore troppo pesante.

topic [ˈtɔpɪk] n argomento; ~**al** a d'attualità.

top: ~**less** a (bather etc) col seno scoperto; ~**less swimsuit** n topless m inv; ~**-level** a (talks) ad alto livello; ~**most** a il(la) più alto(a).

topple [ˈtɔpl] vt rovesciare, far cadere // vi cadere; traballare.

topsy-turvy [ˈtɔpsɪˈtɜːvɪ] a,ad sottosopra.

torch [tɔːtʃ] n torcia; (electric) lampadina tascabile.

tore [tɔː*] pt of **tear**.

torment n [ˈtɔːment] tormento // vt [tɔːˈment] tormentare; (fig: annoy) infastidire.

torn [tɔːn] pp of **tear** // a: ~ **between** (fig) combattuto(a) tra.

tornado, ~**es** [tɔːˈneɪdəu] n tornado.

torpedo, ~**es** [tɔːˈpiːdəu] n siluro.

torpor [ˈtɔːpə*] n torpore m.

torque [tɔːk] n coppia di torsione.

torrent [ˈtɔrnt] n torrente m; ~**ial** [-ˈrenʃl] a torrenziale.

torso [ˈtɔːsəu] n torso.

tortoise [ˈtɔːtəs] n tartaruga; ~**shell** [ˈtɔːtəʃel] a di tartaruga.

tortuous [ˈtɔːtjuəs] a tortuoso(a).

torture [ˈtɔːtʃə*] n tortura // vt torturare.

Tory [ˈtɔːrɪ] a dei tories, conservatore/trice // n tory m inv, conservatore/trice.

toss [tɔs] vt gettare, lanciare; (pancake) far saltare; (head) scuotere; **to ~ a coin** fare a testa o croce; **to ~ up for sth** fare a testa o croce per qc; **to ~ and turn** (in bed) girarsi e rigirarsi.

tot [tɔt] n (drink) bicchierino; (child) bimbo/a.

total [ˈtəutl] a totale // n totale m // vt (add up) sommare; (amount to) ammontare a.

totalitarian [təutælɪˈtɛərɪən] a totalitario(a).

totem pole [ˈtəutəmpəul] n totem m inv.

totter [ˈtɔtə*] vi barcollare.

touch [tʌtʃ] n tocco; (sense) tatto; (contact) contatto; (FOOTBALL) fuori gioco m // vt toccare; **a ~ of** (fig) un tocco di; un pizzico di; **in ~ with** in contatto con; **to get in ~ with** mettersi in contatto con; **to lose ~** (friends) perdersi di vista; **to ~ on** vt fus (topic) sfiorare, accennare a; **to ~ up** vt (paint) ritoccare; ~**-and-go** a incerto(a); **it was ~-and-go whether**

we did it c'è mancato poco che non lo facessimo; ~**down** n atterraggio; (on sea) ammaraggio; ~**ed** a commosso(a); (col) tocco(a), toccato(a); ~**ing** a commovente; ~**line** n (SPORT) linea laterale; ~**y** a (person) suscettibile.

tough [tʌf] a duro(a); (resistant) resistente; (meat) duro(a), tiglioso(a); ~ **luck!** che disdetta!; peggio per me (or te etc)!; ~**en** vt indurire, rendere più resistente.

toupee [ˈtuːpeɪ] n parrucchino.

tour [ˈtuə*] n viaggio; (also: package ~) viaggio organizzato or tutto compreso; (of town, museum) visita; (by artist) tournée f inv // vt visitare; ~**ing** n turismo.

tourism [ˈtuərɪzəm] n turismo.

tourist [ˈtuərɪst] n turista m/f // ad (travel) in classe turistica // cpd turistico(a); ~ **office** n pro loco f inv.

tournament [ˈtuənəmənt] n torneo.

tousled [ˈtauzld] a (hair) arruffato(a).

tout [taut] vi: **to ~** procacciare, raccogliere; cercare clienti per; **to ~ sth (around)** cercare di (ri)vendere qc.

tow [təu] vt rimorchiare; **'on ~'** (AUT) 'veicolo rimorchiato'.

toward(s) [təˈwɔːd(z)] prep verso; (of attitude) nei confronti di; (of purpose) per.

towel [ˈtauəl] n asciugamano; (also: tea ~) strofinaccio; ~**ling** n (fabric) spugna; ~ **rail** n portasciugamano.

tower [ˈtauə*] n torre f; ~ **block** n palazzone m; ~**ing** a altissimo(a), imponente.

town [taun] n città f inv; **to go to ~** andare in città; (fig) mettercela tutta; ~ **clerk** n segretario comunale; ~ **council** n consiglio comunale; ~ **hall** n ≈ municipio; ~ **planner** n urbanista m/f; ~ **planning** n urbanistica.

towpath [ˈtəupɑːθ] n alzaia.

towrope [ˈtəurəup] n (cavo da) rimorchio.

toxic [ˈtɔksɪk] a tossico(a).

toy [tɔɪ] n giocattolo; **to ~ with** vt fus giocare con; (idea) accarezzare, trastullarsi con; ~**shop** n negozio di giocattoli.

trace [treɪs] n traccia // vt (draw) tracciare; (follow) seguire; (locate) rintracciare.

track [træk] n (mark) traccia; (on tape, SPORT, path: gen) pista; (: of bullet etc) traiettoria; (: of suspect, animal) pista, tracce fpl; (RAIL) binario, rotaie fpl // vt seguire le tracce di; **to keep ~ of** seguire; **to ~ down** vt (prey) scovare; snidare; (sth lost) rintracciare; ~**er dog** n cane m poliziotto inv; ~ **suit** n tuta sportiva.

tract [trækt] n (GEO) tratto, estensione f; (pamphlet) opuscolo, libretto; **respiratory ~** (ANAT) apparato respiratorio.

tractor [ˈtræktə*] n trattore m.

trade [treɪd] n commercio; (skill, job) mestiere m // vi commerciare; **to ~ with/in** commerciare con/in; **to ~ in** vt (old car etc) dare come pagamento parziale; ~**mark** n marchio di fabbrica.

~name n marca, nome m depositato; **~r** n commerciante m/f; **~sman** n (shopkeeper) negoziante m; **~ union** n sindacato; **~ unionist** sindacalista m/f; **trading** n commercio; **trading estate** n zona industriale.

tradition [trə'dɪʃən] n tradizione f; **~s** npl tradizioni, usanze fpl; **~al** a tradizionale.

traffic ['træfɪk] n traffico // vi: **to ~ in** (pej: liquor, drugs) trafficare in; **~ circle** n (US) isola rotatoria; **~ jam** n ingorgo (del traffico); **~ lights** npl semaforo; **~ warden** n addetto/a al controllo del traffico e del parcheggio.

tragedy ['trædʒədɪ] n tragedia.

tragic ['trædʒɪk] a tragico(a).

trail [treɪl] n (tracks) tracce fpl, pista; (path) sentiero; (of smoke etc) scia // vt trascinare, strascicare; (follow) seguire // vi essere al traino; (dress etc) strusciare; (plant) arrampicarsi; strisciare; **to ~ behind** vi essere al traino; **~er** n (AUT) rimorchio; (US) roulotte f inv; (CINEMA) prossimamente m inv.

train [treɪn] n treno; (of dress) coda, strascico // vt (apprentice, doctor etc) formare; (sportsman) allenare; (dog) addestrare; (memory) esercitare; (point: gun etc): **to ~ sth on** puntare qc contro // vi formarsi; allenarsi; **one's ~ of thought** il filo dei propri pensieri; **~ed** a qualificato(a); allenato(a); addestrato(a); **~ee** [treɪ'niː] n allievo/a; (in trade) apprendista m/f; **~er** n (SPORT) allenatore/trice; (of dogs etc) addestratore/trice; **~ing** n formazione f; allenamento; addestramento; **in ~ing** (SPORT) in allenamento; (fit) in forma; **~ing college** n istituto professionale; (for teachers) ≈ istituto magistrale.

traipse [treɪps] vi girovagare, andare a zonzo.

trait [treɪt] n tratto.

traitor ['treɪtə*] n traditore m.

tram [træm] n (also: ~car) tram m inv; **~line** n linea tranviaria.

tramp [træmp] n (person) vagabondo/a // vi camminare con passo pesante // vt (walk through: town, streets) percorrere a piedi.

trample ['træmpl] vt: **to ~ (underfoot)** calpestare.

trampoline ['træmpəliːn] n trampolino.

trance [trɑːns] n trance f inv; (MED) catalessi f inv.

tranquil ['træŋkwɪl] a tranquillo(a); **~lity** n tranquillità; **~lizer** n (MED) tranquillante m.

transact [træn'zækt] vt (business) trattare; **~ion** [-'zækʃən] n transazione f; **~ions** npl (minutes) atti mpl.

transatlantic ['trænzət'læntɪk] a transatlantico(a).

transcend [træn'sɛnd] vt trascendere; (excel over) superare.

transcript ['trænskrɪpt] n trascrizione f; **~ion** [-'skrɪpʃən] n trascrizione f.

transept ['trænsɛpt] n transetto.

transfer n ['trænsfə*] (gen, also SPORT) trasferimento; (POL: of power) passaggio; (picture, design) decalcomania; (: stick-on) autoadesivo // vt [træns'fɜː*] trasferire; passare; decalcare; **to ~ the charges** (TEL) telefonare con addebito al ricevente; **~able** [-'fɔːrəbl] a trasferibile.

transform [træns'fɔːm] vt trasformare; **~ation** [-'meɪʃən] n trasformazione f; **~er** n (ELEC) trasformatore m.

transfusion [træns'fjuːʒən] n trasfusione f.

transient ['trænzɪənt] a transitorio(a), fugace.

transistor [træn'zɪstə*] n (ELEC) transistor m inv; (also: ~ radio) radio f inv a transistor.

transit ['trænzɪt] n: **in ~** in transito; **~ lounge** n sala di transito.

transition [træn'zɪʃən] n passaggio, transizione f; **~al** a di transizione.

transitive ['trænzɪtɪv] a (LING) transitivo(a).

transitory ['trænzɪtərɪ] a transitorio(a).

translate [trænz'leɪt] vt tradurre; **translation** [-'leɪʃən] n traduzione f; (SCOL: as opposed to prose) versione f; **translator** n traduttore/trice.

transmission [trænz'mɪʃən] n trasmissione f.

transmit [trænz'mɪt] vt trasmettere; **~ter** n trasmettitore m.

transparency [træns'pɛərnsɪ] n (PHOT) diapositiva.

transparent [træns'pærnt] a trasparente.

transplant vt [træns'plɑːnt] trapiantare // n ['trænsplɑːnt] (MED) trapianto.

transport n ['trænspɔːt] trasporto // vt [træns'pɔːt] trasportare; **~ation** [-'teɪʃən] n (mezzo di) trasporto; (of prisoners) deportazione f; **~ café** n trattoria per camionisti.

transvestite [trænz'vɛstaɪt] n travestito/a.

trap [træp] n (snare, trick) trappola; (carriage) calesse m // vt prendere in trappola, intrappolare; (immobilize) bloccare; (jam) chiudere, schiacciare; **~door** n botola.

trapeze [trə'piːz] n trapezio.

trapper ['træpə*] n cacciatore m di animali da pelliccia.

trappings ['træpɪŋz] npl ornamenti mpl; indoratura, sfarzo.

trash [træʃ] n (pej: goods) ciarpame m; (: nonsense) sciocchezze fpl; **~ can** n (US) secchio della spazzatura.

trauma ['trɔːmə] n trauma m; **~tic** [-'mætɪk] a traumatico(a).

travel ['trævl] n viaggio; viaggi mpl // vi viaggiare; (move) andare, spostarsi // vt (distance) percorrere; **~ler** n viaggiatore/trice; **~ler's cheque** n assegno turistico; **~ling** n viaggi mpl // cpd (bag, clock) da viaggio; (expenses) di viaggio; **~ sickness** n mal m d'auto (or di mare or d'aria).

travesty ['trævəstɪ] n parodia.

trawler ['trɔːlə*] *n* peschereccio (a strascico).

tray [treɪ] *n* (*for carrying*) vassoio; (*on desk*) vaschetta.

treacherous ['tretʃərəs] *a* traditore(trice).

treachery ['tretʃərɪ] *n* tradimento.

treacle ['triːkl] *n* melassa.

tread [trɛd] *n* passo; (*sound*) rumore *m* di passi; (*of tyre*) battistrada *m inv //* (*pt trod*, *pp trodden* [trɔd, 'trɔdn]) camminare; **to ~ on** *vt fus* calpestare.

treason ['triːzn] *n* tradimento.

treasure ['treʒə*] *n* tesoro // *vt* (*value*) tenere in gran conto, apprezzare molto; (*store*) custodire gelosamente.

treasurer ['treʒərə*] *n* tesoriere/a.

treasury ['treʒərɪ] *n* tesoreria; **the T~** (*POL*) il ministero del tesoro.

treat [triːt] *n* regalo // *vt* trattare; (*MED*) curare; **it was a ~** mi (*or ci etc*) ha fatto veramente piacere; **to ~ sb to sth** offrire qc a qd.

treatise ['triːtɪz] *n* trattato.

treatment ['triːtmənt] *n* trattamento.

treaty ['triːtɪ] *n* patto, trattato.

treble ['trɛbl] *a* triplo(a), triplice // *n* (*MUS*) soprano *m/f* // *vt* triplicare // *vi* triplicarsi; **~ clef** *n* chiave *f* di violino.

tree [triː] *n* albero; **~ trunk** *n* tronco d'albero.

trek [trɛk] *n* viaggio; camminata; (*tiring walk*) tirata a piedi // *vi* (*as holiday*) fare dell'escursionismo.

trellis ['trɛlɪs] *n* graticcio, pergola.

tremble ['trɛmbl] *vi* tremare; (*machine*) vibrare.

tremendous [trɪ'mɛndəs] *a* (*enormous*) enorme; (*excellent*) meraviglioso(a), formidabile.

tremor ['trɛmə*] *n* tremore *m*, tremito; (*also*: **earth ~**) scossa sismica.

trench [trɛntʃ] *n* trincea.

trend [trɛnd] *n* (*tendency*) tendenza; (*of events*) corso; (*fashion*) moda; **~y** *a* (*idea*) di moda; (*clothes*) all'ultima moda.

trepidation [trɛpɪ'deɪʃən] *n* trepidazione *f*, agitazione *f*.

trespass ['trɛspəs] *vi*: **to ~ on** entrare abusivamente in; (*fig*) abusare di; **'no ~ing'** 'proprietà privata', 'vietato l'accesso'.

trestle ['trɛsl] *n* cavalletto; **~ table** *n* tavolo su cavalletti.

trial ['traɪəl] *n* (*LAW*) processo; (*test: of machine etc*) collaudo; (*hardship*) prova, difficoltà *f inv*; (*worry*) cruccio; **to be on ~** essere sotto processo; **by ~ and error** a tentoni.

triangle ['traɪæŋgl] *n* (*MATH, MUS*) triangolo.

tribe [traɪb] *n* tribù *f inv*; **~sman** *n* membro della tribù.

tribulation [trɪbjuː'leɪʃən] *n* tribolazione *f*.

tribunal [traɪ'bjuːnl] *n* tribunale *m*.

tributary ['trɪbjuːtərɪ] *n* (*river*) tributario, affluente *m*.

tribute ['trɪbjuːt] *n* tributo, omaggio; **to**

pay ~ to rendere omaggio a.

trice [traɪs] *n*: **in a ~** in un attimo.

trick [trɪk] *n* trucco; (*clever act*) stratagemma *m*; (*joke*) tiro; (*CARDS*) presa // *vt* imbrogliare, ingannare; **to play a ~ on sb** giocare un tiro a qd; **~ery** *n* inganno.

trickle ['trɪkl] *n* (*of water etc*) rivolo; gocciolio // *vi* gocciolare; **to ~ in/out** (*people*) entrare/uscire alla spicciolata.

tricky ['trɪkɪ] *a* difficile, delicato(a).

tricycle ['traɪsɪkl] *n* triciclo.

trifle ['traɪfl] *n* sciocchezza; (*CULIN*) ≈ zuppa inglese // *ad*: **a ~ long** un po' lungo; **trifling** *a* insignificante.

trigger ['trɪgə*] *n* (*of gun*) grilletto; **to ~ off** *vt* dare l'avvio a.

trigonometry [trɪgə'nɔmətrɪ] *n* trigonometria.

trim [trɪm] *a* ordinato(a); (*house, garden*) ben tenuto(a); (*figure*) snello(a) // *n* (*haircut etc*) spuntata, regolata; (*embellishment*) finiture *fpl*; (*on car*) guarnizioni *fpl* // *vt* spuntare; (*decorate*): **to ~ (with)** decorare (con); (*NAUT: a sail*) orientare; **~mings** *npl* decorazioni *fpl*; (*extras: gen CULIN*) guarnizione *f*.

Trinity ['trɪnɪtɪ] *n*: **the ~** la Trinità.

trinket ['trɪŋkɪt] *n* gingillo; (*piece of jewellery*) ciondolo.

trio ['triːəu] *n* trio.

trip [trɪp] *n* viaggio; (*excursion*) gita, escursione *f*; (*stumble*) passo falso // *vi* inciampare; (*go lightly*) camminare con passo leggero; **on a ~** in viaggio; **to ~ up** *vi* inciampare // *vt* fare lo sgambetto a.

tripe [traɪp] *n* (*CULIN*) trippa; (*pej: rubbish*) sciocchezze *fpl*, fesserie *fpl*.

triple ['trɪpl] *a* triplo(a).

triplets ['trɪplɪts] *npl* bambini(e) trigemini(e).

triplicate ['trɪplɪkət] *n*: **in ~** in triplice copia.

tripod ['traɪpɔd] *n* treppiede *m*.

trite [traɪt] *a* banale, trito(a).

triumph ['traɪʌmf] *n* trionfo // *vi*: **to ~ (over)** trionfare (su); **~al** [-'ʌmfl] *a* trionfale; **~ant** [-'ʌmfənt] *a* trionfante.

trivia ['trɪvɪə] *npl* banalità *fpl*.

trivial ['trɪvɪəl] *a* insignificante; (*commonplace*) banale.

trod [trɔd] *pt of* tread; **~den** *pp of* tread.

trolley ['trɔlɪ] *n* carrello; **~ bus** *n* filobus *m inv*.

trollop ['trɔləp] *n* prostituta.

trombone [trɔm'bəun] *n* trombone *m*.

troop [truːp] *n* gruppo, truppa; **~s** *npl* (*MIL*) truppe *fpl*; **to ~ in/out** *vi* entrare/uscire a frotte; **~er** *n* (*MIL*) soldato di cavalleria; **~ing the colour** (*ceremony*) sfilata della bandiera.

trophy ['trəufɪ] *n* trofeo.

tropic ['trɔpɪk] *n* tropico; **in the ~s** ai tropici; **T~ of Cancer/Capricorn** *n* tropico del Cancro/Capricorno; **~al** *a* tropicale.

trot [trɔt] *n* trotto // *vi* trottare; **on the ~**

(*fig: col*) di fila, uno(a) dopo l'altro(a).

trouble ['trʌbl] *n* difficoltà *f inv*, problema *m*; difficoltà *fpl*, problemi; (*worry*) preoccupazione *f*; (*bother, effort*) sforzo; (*POL*) conflitti *mpl*, disordine *m*; (*MED*): **stomach** *etc* ~ disturbi *mpl* gastrici *etc* // *vt* disturbare; (*worry*) preoccupare // *vi*: **to** ~ **to do** disturbarsi a fare; ~**s** *pl* (*POL etc*) disordini *mpl*; **to be in** ~ avere dei problemi; **to go to the** ~ **of doing** darsi la pena di fare; **it's no** ~! di niente!; **what's the** ~? cosa c'è che non va?; ~**d** *a* (*person*) preoccupato(a), inquieto(a); (*epoch, life*) agitato(a), difficile; ~**-free** *a* senza problemi; ~**maker** *n* elemento disturbatore, agitatore/trice; ~**shooter** *n* (*in conflict*) conciliatore *m*; ~**some** *a* fastidioso(a), seccante.

trough [trɔf] *n* (*also:* **drinking** ~) abbeveratoio; (*also:* **feeding** ~) trogolo, mangiatoia; (*channel*) canale *m*; ~ **of low pressure** *n* (*GEO*) depressione *f*.

trounce [traunts] *vt* (*defeat*) sgominare.

troupe [tru:p] *n* troupe *f inv*.

trousers ['trauzəz] *npl* pantaloni *mpl*, calzoni *mpl*; **short** ~ *npl* calzoncini *mpl*.

trousseau, *pl* ~**x** *or* ~**s** ['tru:səu, -z] *n* corredo da sposa.

trout [traut] *n*, *pl inv* trota.

trowel ['trauəl] *n* cazzuola.

truant ['truənt] *n*: **to play** ~ marinare la scuola.

truce [tru:s] *n* tregua.

truck [trʌk] *n* autocarro, camion *m inv*; (*RAIL*) carro merci aperto; (*for luggage*) carrello *m* portabagagli *inv*; ~ **driver** *n* camionista *m/f*.

trudge [trʌdʒ] *vi* arrancare.

true [tru:] *a* vero(a); (*accurate*) accurato(a), esatto(a); (*genuine*) reale; (*faithful*) fedele.

truffle ['trʌfl] *n* tartufo.

truly ['tru:lɪ] *ad* veramente; (*truthfully*) sinceramente; (*faithfully*) fedelmente.

trump [trʌmp] *n* briscola; ~**ed-up** *a* inventato(a).

trumpet ['trʌmpɪt] *n* tromba.

truncated [trʌŋ'keɪtɪd] *a* tronco(a).

truncheon ['trʌntʃən] *n* sfollagente *m inv*.

trundle ['trʌndl] *vt*, *vi*: **to** ~ **along** rotolare rumorosamente.

trunk [trʌŋk] *n* (*of tree, person*) tronco; (*of elephant*) proboscide *f*; (*case*) baule *m*; ~**s** *npl* (*also:* **swimming** ~**s**) calzoncini *mpl* da bagno; ~ **call** *n* (*TEL*) (telefonata) interurbana.

truss [trʌs] *n* (*MED*) cinto erniario; **to** ~ (**up**) *vt* (*CULIN*) legare.

trust [trʌst] *n* fiducia; (*LAW*) amministrazione *f* fiduciaria; (*COMM*) trust *m inv* // *vt* (*rely on*) contare su; (*entrust*): **to** ~ **sth to sb** affidare qc a qd; ~**ed** *a* fidato(a); ~**ee** [trʌs'ti:] *n* (*LAW*) amministratore(trice) fiduciario/trice; (*of school etc*) amministratore/trice; ~**ful**, ~**ing** *a* fiducioso(a); ~**worthy** *a* fidato(a), degno(a) di fiducia; ~**y** *a* fidato(a).

truth, ~**s** [tru:θ, tru:ðz] *n* verità *f inv*; ~**ful** *a* (*person*) sincero(a); (*description*) veritiero(a), esatto(a).

try [traɪ] *n* prova, tentativo; (*RUGBY*) meta // *vt* (*LAW*) giudicare; (*test: sth new*) provare; (*strain*) mettere alla prova // *vi* provare; **to** ~ **to do** provare a fare; (*seek*) cercare di fare; **to** ~ **on** *vt* (*clothes*) provare; **to** ~ **it on** (**with sb**) (*fig*) cercare di farla a qd); **to** ~ **out** *vt* provare, mettere alla prova; ~**ing** *a* (*day, experience*) logorante, pesante; (*child*) difficile, insopportabile.

tsar [zɑ:*] *n* zar *m inv*.

T-shirt ['ti:ʃəːt] *n* maglietta.

T-square ['ti:skwɛə*] *n* riga a T.

tub [tʌb] *n* tinozza; mastello; (*bath*) bagno.

tuba ['tju:bə] *n* tuba.

tubby ['tʌbɪ] *a* grassoccio(a).

tube [tju:b] *n* tubo; (*underground*) metropolitana; (*for tyre*) camera d'aria.

tuberculosis [tjubə:kju'ləusɪs] *n* tubercolosi *f*.

tubing ['tju:bɪŋ] *n* tubazione *f*; **a piece of** ~ un tubo.

tubular ['tju:bjulə*] *a* tubolare.

TUC *n* (*abbr of Trades Union Congress*) confederazione *f* dei sindacati britannici.

tuck [tʌk] *n* (*SEWING*) piega // *vt* (*put*) mettere; **to** ~ **away** *vt* riporre; **to** ~ **in** *vt* mettere dentro; (*child*) rimboccare // *vi* (*eat*) mangiare di buon appetito; abbuffarsi; **to** ~ **up** *vt* (*child*) rimboccare; ~ **shop** *n* negozio di pasticceria (*in una scuola*).

Tuesday ['tju:zdɪ] *n* martedì *m inv*.

tuft [tʌft] *n* ciuffo.

tug [tʌg] *n* (*ship*) rimorchiatore *m* // *vt* tirare con forza; ~**-of-war** *n* tiro alla fune.

tuition [tju:'ɪʃən] *n* lezioni *fpl*.

tulip ['tju:lɪp] *n* tulipano.

tumble ['tʌmbl] *n* (*fall*) capitombolo // *vi* capitombolare, ruzzolare; (*somersault*) fare capriole // *vt* far cadere; ~**down** *a* cadente, diroccato(a); ~ **dryer** *n* asciugatrice *f*.

tumbler ['tʌmblə*] *n* bicchiere *m* (*senza piede*); acrobata *m/f*.

tummy ['tʌmɪ] *n* (*col*) pancia.

tumour ['tju:mə*] *n* tumore *m*.

tumult ['tju:mʌlt] *n* tumulto; ~**uous** [-'mʌltjuəs] *a* tumultuoso(a).

tuna ['tju:nə] *n*, *pl inv* (*also:* ~ **fish**) tonno.

tune [tju:n] *n* (*melody*) melodia, aria // *vt* (*MUS*) accordare; (*RADIO, TV, AUT*) regolare, mettere a punto; **to be in/out of** ~ (*instrument*) essere accordato(a)/scordato(a); (*singer*) essere intonato(a)/stonato(a); **to** ~ **in** (**to**) (*RADIO, TV*) sintonizzarsi (su); **to** ~ **up** *vi* (*musician*) accordare lo strumento; ~**ful** *a* melodioso(a); ~**r** *n* (*radio set*) sintonizzatore *m*; **piano** ~**r** accordatore/trice di pianoforte.

tungsten ['tʌŋstn] *n* tungsteno.

tunic ['tju:nɪk] *n* tunica.

tuning ['tju:nɪŋ] n messa a punto; ~ **fork** n diapason m inv.

Tunisia [tju:'nɪzɪə] n Tunisia.

tunnel ['tʌnl] n galleria // vi scavare una galleria.

tunny ['tʌnɪ] n tonno.

turban ['tɔ:bən] n turbante m.

turbine ['tɔ:baɪn] n turbina.

turbojet ['tɔ:bəu'dʒɛt] n turboreattore m.

turbot ['tɔ:bət] n, pl inv rombo gigante.

turbulence ['tɔ:bjuləns] n (AVIAT) turbolenza.

turbulent ['tɔ:bjulənt] a turbolento(a); (sea) agitato(a).

tureen [tə'ri:n] n zuppiera.

turf [tɔ:f] n terreno erboso; (clod) zolla // vt coprire di zolle erbose; **the T~** n l'ippodromo; **to ~ out** vt (col) buttar fuori.

turgid ['tɔ:dʒɪd] a (speech) ampolloso(a), pomposo(a).

Turk [tɔ:k] n turco/a.

turkey ['tɔ:kɪ] n tacchino.

Turkey ['tɔ:kɪ] n Turchia.

Turkish ['tɔ:kɪʃ] a turco(a) // n (LING) turco; ~ **bath** n bagno turco.

turmoil ['tɔ:mɔɪl] n confusione f, tumulto.

turn [tɔ:n] n giro; (in road) curva; (tendency: of mind, events) tendenza; (performance) numero; (MED) crisi f inv, attacco // vt girare, voltare; (milk) far andare a male; (change): **to ~ sth into** trasformare qc in // vi girare; (person: look back) girarsi, voltarsi; (reverse direction) girarsi indietro; (change) cambiare; (become) diventare; **to ~ into** trasformarsi in; **a good ~** un buon servizio; **a bad ~** un brutto tiro; **it gave me quite a ~** mi ha fatto prendere un bello spavento; **'no left ~'** (AUT) 'divieto di svolta a sinistra'; **it's your ~** tocca a lei; **in ~** a sua volta; a turno; **to take ~s (at sth)** fare (qc) a turno; **to ~ about** vi girarsi indietro; **to ~ away** vi girarsi (dall'altra parte); **to ~ back** vi ritornare, tornare indietro; **to ~ down** vt (refuse) rifiutare; (reduce) abbassare; (fold) ripiegare; **to ~ in** vi (col: go to bed) andare a letto // vt (fold) voltare in dentro; **to ~ off** vi (from road) girare, voltare // vt (light, radio, engine etc) spegnere; **to ~ on** vt (light, radio etc) accendere; (engine) avviare; **to ~ out** vt (light, gas) chiudere, spegnere // vi: **to ~ out to be...** rivelarsi..., risultare ...; **to ~ up** vi (person) arrivare, presentarsi; (lost object) saltar fuori // vt (collar, sound) alzare; ~**ed-up a** (nose) all'insù; ~**ing n** (in road) curva; ~**ing point n** (fig) svolta decisiva.

turnip ['tɔ:nɪp] n rapa.

turnout ['tɔ:naut] n presenza, affluenza.

turnover ['tɔ:nəuvə*] n (COMM) giro di affari.

turnpike ['tɔ:npaɪk] n (US) autostrada a pedaggio.

turnstile ['tɔ:nstaɪl] n tornella.

turntable ['tɔ:nteɪbl] n (on record player) piatto.

turn-up ['tɔ:nʌp] n (on trousers) risvolto.

turpentine ['tɔ:pəntaɪn] n (also: **turps**) acqua ragia.

turquoise ['tɔ:kwɔɪz] n (stone) turchese m // a color turchese; di turchese.

turret ['tʌrɪt] n torretta.

turtle ['tɔ:tl] n testuggine f; ~**neck (sweater)** n maglione m con il collo alto.

tusk [tʌsk] n zanna.

tussle ['tʌsl] n baruffa, mischia.

tutor ['tju:tə*] n (in college) docente m/f (responsabile di un gruppo di studenti); (private teacher) precettore m; ~**ial** [-'tɔ:rɪəl] n (SCOL) lezione f con discussione (a un gruppo limitato).

tuxedo [tʌk'si:dəu] n (US) smoking m inv.

T.V. [ti:'vi:] n (abbr of **television**) tivù f inv.

twang [twæŋ] n (of instrument) suono vibrante; (of voice) accento nasale.

tweed [twi:d] n tweed m inv.

tweezers ['twi:zəz] npl pinzette fpl.

twelfth [twelfθ] num dodicesimo(a).

twelve [twelv] num dodici; **at ~** alle dodici, a mezzogiorno; (midnight) a mezzanotte.

twentieth ['twɛntɪɪθ] num ventesimo(a).

twenty ['twɛntɪ] num venti.

twice [twaɪs] ad due volte; ~ **as much** due volte tanto.

twig [twɪg] n ramoscello // vt, vi (col) capire.

twilight ['twaɪlaɪt] n crepuscolo.

twill [twɪl] n spigato.

twin [twɪn] a,n gemello(a).

twine [twaɪn] n spago, cordicella // vi (plant) attorcigliarsi; (road) serpeggiare.

twinge [twɪndʒ] n (of pain) fitta; **a ~ of conscience/regret** un rimorso/rimpianto.

twinkle ['twɪŋkl] n scintillio; guizzo // vi scintillare; (eyes) brillare.

twirl [twɔ:l] n mulinello; piroetta // vt mulinare // vi roteare.

twist [twɪst] n torsione f; (in wire, flex) storta; (in story) colpo di scena // vt attorcigliare; (weave) intrecciare; (roll around) arrotolare; (fig) deformare // vt attorcigliarsi; arrotolarsi; (road) serpeggiare.

twit [twɪt] n (col) minchione/a.

twitch [twɪtʃ] n strattone m; (nervous) tic m inv // vi contrarsi; avere un tic.

two [tu:] num due; **to put ~ and ~ together** (fig) trarre le conclusioni; ~**-door a** (AUT) a due porte; ~**-faced a** (pej: person) falso(a); ~**-piece (suit)** n due pezzi m inv; ~**-piece (swimsuit)** n (costume m da bagno a) due pezzi m inv; ~**-seater** n (plane) biposto; (car) macchina a due posti; ~**some** n (people) coppia; ~**-way** a (traffic) a due sensi.

tycoon [taɪ'ku:n] n: **(business) ~** magnate m.

type [taɪp] n (category) genere m; (model) modello; (example) tipo; (TYP) tipo, carattere m // vt (letter etc) battere (a macchina), dattilografare; ~cast a (actor) a ruolo fisso; ~script n dattiloscritto; ~writer n macchina da scrivere.

typhoid ['taɪfɔɪd] n tifoidea.

typhoon [taɪ'fuːn] n tifone m.

typhus ['taɪfəs] n tifo.

typical ['tɪpɪkl] a tipico(a).

typify ['tɪpɪfaɪ] vt essere tipico(a) di.

typing ['taɪpɪŋ] n dattilografia.

typist ['taɪpɪst] n dattilografo/a.

tyranny ['tɪrənɪ] n tirannia.

tyrant ['taɪərnt] n tiranno.

tyre ['taɪə*] n pneumatico, gomma; ~ pressure n pressione f (delle gomme).

tzar [zɑː*] n = tsar.

U

ubiquitous [juː'bɪkwɪtəs] a onnipresente.

udder ['ʌdə*] n mammella.

UFO ['juːfəu] n (abbr of unidentified flying object) UFO m inv.

ugh [əːh] excl puah!

ugliness ['ʌglɪnɪs] n bruttezza.

ugly ['ʌglɪ] a brutto(a).

UHF abbr of ultra-high frequency.

U.K. n abbr see united.

ulcer ['ʌlsə*] n ulcera.

Ulster ['ʌlstə*] n Ulster m.

ulterior [ʌl'tɪərɪə*] a ulteriore; ~ motive n secondo fine m.

ultimate ['ʌltɪmət] a ultimo(a), finale; (authority) massimo(a), supremo(a); ~ly ad alla fine; in definitiva, in fin dei conti.

ultimatum [ʌltɪ'meɪtəm] n ultimatum m inv.

ultraviolet ['ʌltrə'vaɪəlɪt] a ultravioletto(a).

umbilical [ʌm'bɪlɪkl] a: ~ cord cordone m ombelicale.

umbrage ['ʌmbrɪdʒ] n: to take ~ offendersi, impermalirsi.

umbrella [ʌm'brelə] n ombrello.

umpire ['ʌmpaɪə*] n arbitro.

umpteen [ʌmp'tiːn] a non so quanti(e); for the ~th time per l'ennesima volta.

UN, UNO abbr see united.

unabashed [ʌnə'bæʃt] a imperturbato(a).

unabated [ʌnə'beɪtɪd] a non diminuito(a).

unable [ʌn'eɪbl] a: to be ~ to non potere, essere nell'impossibilità di; essere incapace di.

unaccompanied [ʌnə'kʌmpənɪd] a (child, lady) non accompagnato(a).

unaccountably [ʌnə'kauntəblɪ] ad inesplicabilmente.

unaccustomed [ʌnə'kʌstəmd] a insolito(a); to be ~ to sth non essere abituato a qc.

unanimity [juːnə'nɪmɪtɪ] n unanimità.

unanimous [juː'nænɪməs] a unanime; ~ly ad all'unanimità.

unashamed [ʌnə'ʃeɪmd] a sfacciato(a); senza vergogna.

unassuming [ʌnə'sjuːmɪŋ] a modesto(a), senza pretese.

unattached [ʌnə'tætʃt] a senza legami, libero(a).

unattended [ʌnə'tɛndɪd] a (car, child, luggage) incustodito(a).

unattractive [ʌnə'træktɪv] a privo(a) di attrattiva, poco attraente.

unauthorized [ʌn'ɔːθəraɪzd] a non autorizzato(a).

unavoidable [ʌnə'vɔɪdəbl] a inevitabile.

unaware [ʌnə'wɛə*] a: to be ~ of non sapere, ignorare; ~s ad di sorpresa, alla sprovvista.

unbalanced [ʌn'bælənst] a squilibrato(a).

unbearable [ʌn'bɛərəbl] a insopportabile.

unbeatable [ʌn'biːtəbl] a imbattibile.

unbeknown(st) [ʌnbɪ'nəun(st)] ad: ~ to all'insaputa di.

unbelievable [ʌnbɪ'liːvəbl] a incredibile.

unbend [ʌn'bend] vb (irg) vi distendersi // vt (wire) raddrizzare.

unbreakable [ʌn'breɪkəbl] a infrangibile.

unbridled [ʌn'braɪdld] a sbrigliato(a).

unbroken [ʌn'brəukən] a intero(a); continuo(a).

unburden [ʌn'bɔːdn] vt: to ~ o.s. sfogarsi.

unbutton [ʌn'bʌtn] vt sbottonare.

uncalled-for [ʌn'kɔːldfɔː*] a (remark) fuori luogo inv; (action) ingiustificato(a).

uncanny [ʌn'kænɪ] a misterioso(a), strano(a).

unceasing [ʌn'siːsɪŋ] a incessante.

uncertain [ʌn'sɜːtn] a incerto(a); dubbio(a); ~ty n incertezza.

unchanged [ʌn'tʃeɪndʒd] a immutato(a).

uncharitable [ʌn'tʃærɪtəbl] a duro(a), severo(a).

uncharted [ʌn'tʃɑːtɪd] a inesplorato(a).

unchecked [ʌn'tʃekt] a incontrollato(a).

uncle ['ʌŋkl] n zio.

uncomfortable [ʌn'kʌmfətəbl] a scomodo(a); (uneasy) a disagio, agitato(a); fastidioso(a).

uncommon [ʌn'kɔmən] a raro(a), insolito(a), non comune.

uncompromising [ʌn'kɔmprəmaɪzɪŋ] a intransigente, inflessibile.

unconditional [ʌnkən'dɪʃənl] a incondizionato(a), senza condizioni.

unconscious [ʌn'kɔnʃəs] a privo(a) di sensi, svenuto(a); (unaware) inconsapevole, inconscio(a) // n: the ~ l'inconscio; ~ly ad inconsciamente.

uncontrollable [ʌnkən'trəuləbl] a incontrollabile; indisciplinato(a).

uncouth [ʌn'kuːθ] a maleducato(a), grossolano(a).

uncover [ʌn'kʌvə*] vt scoprire.

unctuous ['ʌŋktjuəs] a untuoso(a).

undaunted [ʌn'dɔːntɪd] a intrepido(a).

undecided [ʌndɪ'saɪdɪd] a indeciso(a).

undeniable [ʌndɪ'naɪəbl] a innegabile, indiscutibile.

under ['ʌndə*] prep sotto; (less than) meno di; al disotto di; (according to) secondo, in

conformità a // ad (al) disotto; **from ~
sth** da sotto a *or* dal disotto di qc; ~
there là sotto; ~ **repair** in riparazione.

under... ['ʌndə*] *prefix* sotto..., sub...;
~**age** a minorenne; ~**carriage** *n*
carrello (d'atterraggio); ~**clothes** *npl*
biancheria (intima); ~**coat** *n* (paint)
mano *f* di fondo; ~**cover** a segreto(a),
clandestino(a); ~**current** *n* corrente *f*
sottomarina; ~**cut** *vt irg* vendere a prezzo
minore di; ~**developed** a sottosvilup-
pato(a); ~**dog** *n* oppresso/a; ~**done** a
(CULIN) al sangue; (pej) poco cotto(a); ~
estimate *vt* sottovalutare; ~**exposed**
a (PHOT) sottoesposto(a); ~**fed** a
denutrito(a); ~**foot** da sotto i piedi; ~**go**
vt irg subire; (treatment) sottoporsi a;
~**graduate** *n* studente(essa)
universitario(a); ~**ground** *n* metropolitana; (POL) movimento clandestino // *ad*
sottoterra; clandestinamente; ~**growth** *n*
sottobosco; ~**hand(ed)** a (fig) furtivo(a),
subdolo(a); ~**lie** *vt irg* essere alla base di;
~**line** *vt* sottolineare; ~**ling** ['ʌndəlɪŋ] *n*
(pej) subalterno/a, tirapiedi *m/f inv*;
~**mine** *vt* minare; ~**neath** [ʌndə'niːθ] *ad*
sotto, disotto // *prep* sotto, al di sotto di;
~**paid** a mal pagato(a); ~**pants** *npl*
(Brit) mutande *fpl*, slip *m inv*; ~**pass** *n*
sottopassaggio; ~**play** *vt* minimizzare;
~**privileged** a non abbiente; meno
favorito(a); ~**rate** *vt* sottovalutare;
~**shirt** *n* (US) maglietta; ~**shorts** *npl*
(US) mutande *fpl*, slip *m inv*; ~**side** *n*
disotto; ~**skirt** *n* sottoveste *f*.

understand [ʌndə'stænd] *vb* (irg: like
stand) *vt, vi* capire, comprendere; **I ~
that...** sento che...; credo di capire che...;
~**able** a comprensibile; // *n* comprensione *f*;
(agreement) accordo.

understatement [ʌndə'steɪtmənt] *n*:
that's an ~! a dire poco!

understood [ʌndə'stud] *pt, pp* of **understand** // a inteso(a); (implied)
sottinteso(a); **to make o.s. ~** farsi capire.

understudy ['ʌndəstʌdɪ] *n* sostituto/a,
attore/trice supplente.

undertake [ʌndə'teɪk] *vt irg*
intraprendere; impegnarsi a.

undertaker ['ʌndəteɪkə*] *n* impresario di
pompe funebri.

undertaking [ʌndə'teɪkɪŋ] *n* impresa;
(promise) promessa.

underwater [ʌndə'wɔːtə*] *ad* sott'acqua
// a subacqueo(a).

underwear ['ʌndəwɛə*] *n* biancheria
(intima).

underworld ['ʌndəwəːld] *n* (of crime)
malavita.

underwriter ['ʌndəraɪtə*] *n* (INSURANCE)
sottoscrittore/trice.

undesirable [ʌndɪ'zaɪərəbl] a
indesiderabile; sgradito(a).

undies ['ʌndɪz] *npl* (col) robina, biancheria
intima da donna.

undisputed [ʌndɪs'pjuːtɪd] a indiscusso(a).

undistinguished [ʌndɪs'tɪŋgwɪʃt] a
mediocre, qualunque.

undo [ʌn'duː] *vt irg* disfare; ~**ing** *n* rovina,
perdita.

undoubted [ʌn'dautɪd] a sicuro(a),
certo(a); ~**ly** *ad* senza alcun dubbio.

undress [ʌn'drɛs] *vi* spogliarsi.

undue [ʌn'djuː] a eccessivo(a).

undulating ['ʌndjuleɪtɪŋ] a ondeggiante;
ondulato(a).

unduly [ʌn'djuːlɪ] *ad* eccessivamente.

unearth [ʌn'əːθ] *vt* dissotterrare; (fig)
scoprire.

unearthly [ʌn'əːθlɪ] a soprannaturale;
(hour) impossibile.

uneasy [ʌn'iːzɪ] a a disagio; (worried)
preoccupato(a).

uneconomic(al) ['ʌniːkə'nɒmɪk(l)] a non
economico(a); antieconomico(a).

unemployed [ʌnɪm'plɔɪd] a
disoccupato(a) // *n*: **the ~** i disoccupati.

unemployment [ʌnɪm'plɔɪmənt] *n*
disoccupazione *f*.

unending [ʌn'endɪŋ] a senza fine.

unerring [ʌn'əːrɪŋ] a infallibile.

uneven [ʌn'iːvn] a ineguale; irregolare.

unexpected [ʌnɪk'spektɪd] a inatteso(a),
imprevisto(a).

unfailing [ʌn'feɪlɪŋ] a inesauribile;
infallibile.

unfair [ʌn'fɛə*] a: ~ **(to)** ingiusto(a) (nei
confronti di).

unfaithful [ʌn'feɪθful] a infedele.

unfamiliar [ʌnfə'mɪlɪə*] a sconosciuto(a),
strano(a).

unfasten [ʌn'fɑːsn] *vt* slacciare; sciogliere.

unfavourable [ʌn'feɪvərəbl] a
sfavorevole.

unfeeling [ʌn'fiːlɪŋ] a insensibile, duro(a).

unfinished [ʌn'fɪnɪʃt] a incompiuto(a).

unfit [ʌn'fɪt] a inadatto(a); (ill) malato(a),
in cattiva salute; (incompetent): ~ **(for)**
incompetente (in); (: work, service) inabile
(a); ~ **for habitation** inabitabile.

unflagging [ʌn'flægɪŋ] a instancabile.

unflappable [ʌn'flæpəbl] a calmo(a),
composto(a).

unflinching [ʌn'flɪntʃɪŋ] a che non
indietreggia, risoluto(a).

unfold [ʌn'fəuld] *vt* spiegare; (fig) rivelare
// *vi* (view, countryside) distendersi; (story,
plot) svelarsi.

unforeseen ['ʌnfɔː'siːn] a imprevisto(a).

unforgivable [ʌnfə'gɪvəbl] a
imperdonabile.

unfortunate [ʌn'fɔːtʃnət] a sfortunato(a);
(event, remark) infelice; ~**ly** *ad*
sfortunatamente, purtroppo.

unfounded [ʌn'faundɪd] a infondato(a).

unfriendly [ʌn'frendlɪ] a poco
amichevole, freddo(a).

ungainly [ʌn'geɪnlɪ] a goffo(a),
impacciato(a).

ungodly [ʌn'gɒdlɪ] a empio(a); **at an ~
hour** a un'ora impossibile.

unguarded [ʌn'gɑːdɪd] a: ~ **moment** *n*

momento di distrazione *or* di disattenzione.

unhappiness [ʌnˈhæpɪnɪs] *n* infelicità.

unhappy [ʌnˈhæpɪ] *a* infelice; ~ **with** (*arrangements etc*) insoddisfatto(a) di.

unharmed [ʌnˈhɑːmd] *a* incolume, sano(a) e salvo(a).

unhealthy [ʌnˈhɛlθɪ] *a* (*gen*) malsano(a); (*person*) malaticcio(a).

unheard-of [ʌnˈhəːdɔv] *a* inaudito(a), senza precedenti.

unhook [ʌnˈhuk] *vt* sganciare; sfibbiare.

unhurt [ʌnˈhəːt] *a* incolume, sano(a) e salvo(a).

unicorn [ˈjuːnɪkɔːn] *n* unicorno.

unidentified [ʌnaɪˈdɛntɪfaɪd] *a* non identificato(a).

uniform [ˈjuːnɪfɔːm] *n* uniforme *f*, divisa // *a* uniforme; ~**ity** [-ˈfɔːmɪtɪ] *n* uniformità.

unify [ˈjuːnɪfaɪ] *vt* unificare.

unilateral [juːnɪˈlætərəl] *a* unilaterale.

unimaginable [ʌnɪˈmædʒɪnəbl] *a* inimmaginabile, inconcepibile.

uninhibited [ʌnɪnˈhɪbɪtɪd] *a* senza inibizioni; senza ritegno.

unintentional [ʌnɪnˈtɛnʃənəl] *a* involontario(a).

union [ˈjuːnjən] *n* unione *f*; (*also:* **trade** ~) sindacato // *cpd* sindacale, dei sindacati; **U**~ **Jack** *n* bandiera nazionale britannica.

unique [juːˈniːk] *a* unico(a).

unison [ˈjuːnɪsn] *n*: **in** ~ all'unisono.

unit [ˈjuːnɪt] *n* unità *f inv*; (*section: of furniture etc*) elemento; (*team, squad*) reparto, squadra.

unite [juːˈnaɪt] *vt* unire // *vi* unirsi; ~**d** a unito(a); unificato(a); (*efforts*) congiunto(a); **U**~**d Kingdom (U.K.)** *n* Regno Unito; **U**~**d Nations (Organization) (UN, UNO)** *n* (Organizzazione *f* delle) Nazioni Unite (O.N.U.); **U**~**d States (of America) (US, USA)** *n* Stati *mpl* Uniti (d'America) (USA).

unit trust [ˈjuːnɪttrʌst] *n* (*Brit*) fondo d'investimento.

unity [ˈjuːnɪtɪ] *n* unità.

universal [juːnɪˈvəːsl] *a* universale.

universe [ˈjuːnɪvəːs] *n* universo.

university [juːnɪˈvəːsɪtɪ] *n* università *f inv*.

unjust [ʌnˈdʒʌst] *a* ingiusto(a).

unkempt [ʌnˈkɛmpt] *a* trasandato(a); spettinato(a).

unkind [ʌnˈkaɪnd] *a* scortese; crudele.

unknown [ʌnˈnəun] *a* sconosciuto(a).

unladen [ʌnˈleɪdn] *a* (*ship, weight*) a vuoto.

unlawful [ʌnˈlɔːful] *a* illecito(a), illegale.

unleash [ʌnˈliːʃ] *vt* sguinzagliare; (*fig*) scatenare.

unleavened [ʌnˈlɛvnd] *a* non lievitato(a), azzimo(a).

unless [ʌnˈlɛs] *cj* a meno che (non) + *sub*; ~ **otherwise stated** salvo indicazione contraria.

unlicensed [ʌnˈlaɪsənst] *a* senza licenza per la vendita di alcolici.

unlike [ʌnˈlaɪk] *a* diverso(a) // *prep* a differenza di, contrariamente a.

unlikely [ʌnˈlaɪklɪ] *a* improbabile; inverosimile.

unlimited [ʌnˈlɪmɪtɪd] *a* illimitato(a).

unload [ʌnˈləud] *vt* scaricare.

unlock [ʌnˈlɔk] *vt* aprire.

unlucky [ʌnˈlʌkɪ] *a* sfortunato(a); (*object, number*) che porta sfortuna, di malaugurio.

unmarried [ʌnˈmærɪd] *a* non sposato(a); (*man only*) scapolo, celibe; (*woman only*) nubile; ~ **mother** *n* ragazza *f* madre *inv*.

unmask [ʌnˈmɑːsk] *vt* smascherare.

unmistakable [ʌnmɪsˈteɪkəbl] *a* indubbio(a); facilmente riconoscibile.

unmitigated [ʌnˈmɪtɪgeɪtɪd] *a* non mitigato(a), assoluto(a), vero(a) e proprio(a).

unnatural [ʌnˈnætʃrəl] *a* innaturale; contro natura.

unnecessary [ʌnˈnɛsəsərɪ] *a* inutile, superfluo(a).

unobtainable [ʌnəbˈteɪnəbl] *a* (*TEL*) non ottenibile.

unofficial [ʌnəˈfɪʃl] *a* non ufficiale; (*strike*) non dichiarato(a) dal sindacato.

unorthodox [ʌnˈɔːθədɔks] *a* non ortodosso(a).

unpack [ʌnˈpæk] *vi* disfare la valigia (*or le valigie*).

unpalatable [ʌnˈpælətəbl] *a* (*truth*) sgradevole.

unparalleled [ʌnˈpærəlɛld] *a* incomparabile, impareggiabile.

unpleasant [ʌnˈplɛznt] *a* spiacevole.

unplug [ʌnˈplʌg] *vt* staccare.

unpopular [ʌnˈpɔpjulə*] *a* impopolare.

unprecedented [ʌnˈprɛsɪdəntɪd] *a* senza precedenti.

unpredictable [ʌnprɪˈdɪktəbl] *a* imprevedibile.

unpretentious [ʌnprɪˈtɛnʃəs] *a* senza pretese.

unqualified [ʌnˈkwɔlɪfaɪd] *a* (*teacher*) non abilitato(a); (*success*) assoluto(a), senza riserve.

unravel [ʌnˈrævl] *vt* dipanare, districare.

unreal [ʌnˈrɪəl] *a* irreale.

unreasonable [ʌnˈriːznəbl] *a* irragionevole.

unrelated [ʌnrɪˈleɪtɪd] *a*: ~ **(to)** senza rapporto (con); non imparentato(a) (con).

unrelenting [ʌnrɪˈlɛntɪŋ] *a* implacabile; accanito(a).

unreliable [ʌnrɪˈlaɪəbl] *a* (*person, machine*) che non dà affidamento; (*news, source of information*) inattendibile.

unrelieved [ʌnrɪˈliːvd] *a* (*monotony*) uniforme.

unremitting [ʌnrɪˈmɪtɪŋ] *a* incessante, infaticabile.

unrepentant [ʌnrɪˈpɛntənt] *a* impenitente.

unrest [ʌnˈrɛst] *n* agitazione *f*.

unroll [ʌnˈrəul] *vt* srotolare.

unruly [ʌnˈruːlɪ] *a* indisciplinato(a).

unsafe [ʌnˈseɪf] *a* pericoloso(a), rischioso(a).

unsaid [ʌn'sɛd] a: **to leave sth ~** passare qc sotto silenzio.

unsatisfactory ['ʌnsætɪs'fæktərɪ] a che lascia a desiderare, insufficiente.

unsavoury [ʌn'seɪvərɪ] a (fig: person) losco(a); (: reputation, subject) disgustoso(a), ripugnante.

unscathed [ʌn'skeɪðd] a incolume.

unscrew [ʌn'skruː] vt svitare.

unscrupulous [ʌn'skruːpjuləs] a senza scrupoli.

unseemly [ʌn'siːmlɪ] a sconveniente.

unsettled [ʌn'sɛtld] a turbato(a); instabile; indeciso(a).

unsightly [ʌn'saɪtlɪ] a brutto(a), sgradevole a vedersi.

unskilled [ʌn'skɪld] a: **~ worker** n manovale m.

unsophisticated [ʌnsə'fɪstɪkeɪtɪd] a semplice, naturale.

unspeakable [ʌn'spiːkəbl] a (bad) abominevole.

unsteady [ʌn'stɛdɪ] a instabile, malsicuro(a).

unstuck [ʌn'stʌk] a: **to come ~** scollarsi; (fig) fare fiasco.

unsuccessful [ʌnsək'sɛsful] a (writer, proposal) che non ha successo; (marriage, attempt) mal riuscito(a), fallito(a); **to be ~** (in attempting sth) non riuscire; non avere successo; (application) non essere considerato(a); **~ly** ad senza successo.

unsuitable [ʌn'suːtəbl] a inadatto(a); inopportuno(a); sconveniente.

unsuspecting [ʌnsə'spɛktɪŋ] a che non sospetta niente.

unswerving [ʌn'swɜːvɪŋ] a fermo(a).

untangle [ʌn'tæŋgl] vt sbrogliare.

untapped [ʌn'tæpt] a (resources) non sfruttato(a).

unthinkable [ʌn'θɪŋkəbl] a impensabile, inconcepibile.

untidy [ʌn'taɪdɪ] a (room) in disordine; (appearance, work) trascurato(a); (person, writing) disordinato(a).

untie [ʌn'taɪ] vt (knot, parcel) disfare; (prisoner, dog) slegare.

until [ən'tɪl] prep fino a; (after negative) prima di // cj finché, fino a quando; (in past, after negative) prima che + sub, prima di + infinitive.

untimely [ʌn'taɪmlɪ] a intempestivo(a), inopportuno(a); (death) prematuro(a).

untold [ʌn'təuld] a incalcolabile; indescrivibile.

untoward [ʌntə'wɔːd] a sfortunato(a), sconveniente.

unused [ʌn'juːzd] a nuovo(a).

unusual [ʌn'juːʒuəl] a insolito(a), eccezionale, raro(a).

unveil [ʌn'veɪl] vt scoprire; svelare.

unwavering [ʌn'weɪvərɪŋ] a fermo(a), incrollabile.

unwell [ʌn'wɛl] a indisposto(a).

unwieldy [ʌn'wiːldɪ] a poco maneggevole.

unwilling [ʌn'wɪlɪŋ] a: **to be ~ to do** non voler fare; **~ly** ad malvolentieri.

unwind [ʌn'waɪnd] vb (irg) vt svolgere, srotolare // vi (relax) rilassarsi.

unwitting [ʌn'wɪtɪŋ] a involontario(a).

unworthy [ʌn'wɜːðɪ] a indegno(a).

unwrap [ʌn'ræp] vt disfare; aprire.

unwritten [ʌn'rɪtn] a (agreement) tacito(a).

up [ʌp] prep: **to go/be ~ sth** salire/essere su qc // ad su, (di) sopra; in alto; **~ there** lassù; **~ above** al di sopra; **~ to** fino a; **to be ~** (out of bed) essere alzato(a) or in piedi; **it is ~ to you** tocca a lei decidere; **what is he ~ to?** cosa sta tramando?; **he is not ~ to it** non ne è capace; **~-and-coming** a pieno(a) di promesse, promettente; **~s and downs** npl (fig) alti e bassi mpl.

upbringing ['ʌpbrɪŋɪŋ] n educazione f.

update [ʌp'deɪt] vt aggiornare.

upgrade [ʌp'greɪd] vt promuovere; (job) rivalutare.

upheaval [ʌp'hiːvl] n sconvolgimento; tumulto.

uphill [ʌp'hɪl] a in salita; (fig: task) difficile // ad: **to go ~** andare in salita, salire.

uphold [ʌp'həuld] vt irg approvare; sostenere.

upholstery [ʌp'həulstərɪ] n tappezzeria.

upkeep ['ʌpkiːp] n manutenzione f.

upon [ə'pɔn] prep su.

upper ['ʌpə*] a superiore // n (of shoe) tomaia; **the ~ class** = l'alta borghesia; **~-class** a dell'alta borghesia; **~most** a il(la) più alto(a); predominante.

upright ['ʌpraɪt] a diritto(a); verticale; (fig) diritto(a), onesto(a) // n montante m.

uprising ['ʌpraɪzɪŋ] n insurrezione f, rivolta.

uproar ['ʌprɔː*] n tumulto, clamore m.

uproot [ʌp'ruːt] vt sradicare.

upset n ['ʌpsɛt] turbamento // vt [ʌp'sɛt] (irg: like set) (glass etc) rovesciare; (plan, stomach) scombussolare; (person: offend) contrariare; (: grieve) addolorare; scovolgere // a [ʌp'sɛt] contrariato(a); addolorato(a); (stomach) scombussolato(a), disturbato(a).

upshot ['ʌpʃɔt] n risultato.

upside ['ʌpsaɪd]: **~-down** ad sottosopra; **to turn ~-down** capovolgere; (fig) mettere sottosopra.

upstairs [ʌp'stɛəz] ad, a di sopra, al piano superiore.

upstart ['ʌpstɑːt] n nuovo(a) ricco(a).

upstream [ʌp'striːm] ad a monte.

uptake ['ʌpteɪk] n: **he is quick/slow on the ~** è pronto/lento di comprendonio.

up-to-date ['ʌptə'deɪt] a moderno(a); aggiornato(a).

upturn ['ʌptɜːn] n (in luck) svolta favorevole.

upward ['ʌpwəd] a ascendente; verso l'alto; **~(s)** ad in su, verso l'alto.

uranium [juə'reɪnɪəm] n uranio.

urban ['ɜːbən] a urbano(a).

urbane [ɜː'beɪn] a civile, urbano(a), educato(a).

urchin ['ɔːtʃin] *n* monello; **sea ~** *n* riccio di mare.

urge [ɔːdʒ] *n* impulso; stimolo; forte desiderio // *vt*: **to ~ sb to do** esortare qd a fare, spingere qd a fare; raccomandare a qd di fare; **to ~ on** *vt* spronare.

urgency ['ɔːdʒənsi] *n* urgenza; (*of tone*) insistenza.

urgent ['ɔːdʒənt] *a* urgente.

urinate ['juərineit] *vi* orinare.

urn [ɔːn] *n* urna; (*also*: **tea ~**) bollitore *m* per il tè.

us [ʌs] *pronoun* ci; (*stressed, after prep*) noi.

US, USA *n abbr see* **united**.

usage ['juːzidʒ] *n* uso.

use *n* [juːs] uso; impiego, utilizzazione *f* // *vt* [juːz] usare, utilizzare, servirsi di; **she ~d to do it** lo faceva (una volta), era solita farlo; **in ~** in uso; **out of ~** fuori uso; **it's no ~** non serve, è inutile; **to be ~d to** avere l'abitudine di; **to ~ up** *vt* consumare; esaurire; **~d** *a* (*car*) d'occasione; **~ful** *a* utile; **~fulness** *n* utilità; **~less** *a* inutile; **~r** *n* utente *m/f*.

usher ['ʌʃə*] *n* usciere *m*; (*in cinema*) maschera; **~ette** [-'rɛt] *n* (*in cinema*) maschera.

USSR *n*: **the ~** l'URSS *f*.

usual ['juːʒuəl] *a* solito(a); **~ly** *ad* di solito.

usurer ['juːʒərə*] *n* usuraio/a.

usurp [juːˈzɔːp] *vt* usurpare.

utensil [juːˈtɛnsl] *n* utensile *m*.

uterus ['juːtərəs] *n* utero.

utilitarian [juːtiliˈtɛəriən] *a* utilitario(a).

utility [juːˈtiliti] *n* utilità; (*also*: **public ~**) servizio pubblico.

utilization [juːtilaiˈzeiʃən] *n* utilizzazione *f*.

utilize ['juːtilaiz] *vt* utilizzare; sfruttare.

utmost ['ʌtməust] *a* estremo(a) // *n*: **to do one's ~** fare il possibile *or* di tutto.

utter ['ʌtə*] *a* assoluto(a), totale // *vt* pronunciare, proferire; emettere; **~ance** *n* espressione *f*; parole *fpl*.

U-turn ['juːˈtɔːn] *n* inversione *f* a U.

V

v. *abbr of* **verse, versus, volt**; (*abbr of* **vide**) vedi, vedere.

vacancy ['veikənsi] *n* (*job*) posto libero; (*room*) stanza libera; **'no vacancies'** 'completo'.

vacant ['veikənt] *a* (*job, seat etc*) libero(a); (*expression*) assente.

vacate [vəˈkeit] *vt* lasciare libero(a).

vacation [vəˈkeiʃən] *n* vacanze *fpl*; **~ course** *n* corso estivo.

vaccinate ['væksineit] *vt* vaccinare; **vaccination** [-ˈneiʃən] *n* vaccinazione *f*.

vaccine ['væksiːn] *n* vaccino.

vacuum ['vækjum] *n* vuoto; **~ cleaner** *n* aspirapolvere *m inv*; **~ flask** *n* thermos *m inv* ®.

vagina [vəˈdʒainə] *n* vagina.

vagrant ['veigrnt] *n* vagabondo/a.

vague [veig] *a* vago(a); (*blurred: photo, memory*) sfocato(a); **~ly** *ad* vagamente.

vain [vein] *a* (*useless*) inutile, vano(a); (*conceited*) vanitoso(a); **in ~** inutilmente, invano.

valentine ['væləntain] *n* (*also*: **~ card**) cartolina *or* biglietto di San Valentino.

valiant ['væliənt] *a* valoroso(a), coraggioso(a).

valid ['vælid] *a* valido(a), valevole; (*excuse*) valido(a); **~ity** [-ˈliditi] *n* validità.

valley ['væli] *n* valle *f*.

valuable ['væljuəbl] *a* (*jewel*) di (grande) valore; (*time*) prezioso(a); **~s** *npl* oggetti *mpl* di valore.

valuation [væljuˈeiʃən] *n* valutazione *f*, stima.

value ['væljuː] *n* valore *m* // *vt* (*fix price*) valutare, dare un prezzo a; (*cherish*) apprezzare, tenere a; **~ added tax (VAT)** *n* imposta sul valore aggiunto (I.V.A.); **~d** *a* (*appreciated*) stimato(a), apprezzato(a).

valve [vælv] *n* valvola.

van [væn] *n* (*AUT*) furgone *m*; (*RAIL*) vagone *m*.

vandal ['vændl] *n* vandalo/a; **~ism** *n* vandalismo.

vanguard ['væŋgɑːd] *n* avanguardia.

vanilla [vəˈnilə] *n* vaniglia // *cpd* (*ice cream*) alla vaniglia.

vanish ['væniʃ] *vi* svanire, scomparire.

vanity ['væniti] *n* vanità; **~ case** *n* valigetta per cosmetici.

vantage ['vɑːntidʒ] *n*: **~ point** *n* posizione *f* or punto di osservazione; (*fig*) posizione vantaggiosa.

vapour ['veipə*] *n* vapore *m*.

variable ['vɛəriəbl] *a* variabile; (*mood*) mutevole.

variance ['vɛəriəns] *n*: **to be at ~ (with)** essere in disaccordo (con); (*facts*) essere in contraddizione (con).

variant ['vɛəriənt] *n* variante *f*.

variation [vɛəriˈeiʃən] *n* variazione *f*; (*in opinion*) cambiamento.

varicose ['værikəus] *a*: **~ veins** *npl* varici *fpl*.

varied ['vɛərid] *a* vario(a), diverso(a).

variety [vəˈraiəti] *n* varietà *f inv*; (*quantity*) quantità, numero; **~ show** *n* varietà *m inv*.

various ['vɛəriəs] *a* vario(a), diverso(a); (*several*) parecchi(e), molti(e).

varnish ['vɑːniʃ] *n* vernice *f* // *vt* verniciare.

vary ['vɛəri] *vt, vi* variare, mutare; **~ing** *a* variabile

vase [vɑːz] *n* vaso.

vast [vɑːst] *a* vasto(a); (*amount, success*) enorme; **~ly** *ad* enormemente.

vat [væt] *n* tino.

VAT [væt] *n abbr see* **value**.

Vatican ['vætikən] *n*: **the ~** il Vaticano.

vault [vɔːlt] *n* (*of roof*) volta; (*tomb*) tomba; (*in bank*) camera blindata; (*jump*) salto // *vt* (*also*: **~ over**) saltare (d'un balzo).

vaunted ['vɔːntɪd] a: **much-~** tanto celebrato(a).

VD n abbr see **venereal**.

veal [viːl] n vitello.

veer [vɪə*] vi girare; virare.

vegetable ['vedʒtəbl] n verdura, ortaggio // a vegetale.

vegetarian [vedʒɪ'tɛərɪən] a, n vegetariano(a).

vegetate ['vedʒɪteɪt] vi vegetare.

vegetation [vedʒɪ'teɪʃən] n vegetazione f.

vehemence ['viːɪməns] n veemenza, violenza.

vehicle ['viːɪkl] n veicolo.

veil [veɪl] n velo // vt velare.

vein [veɪn] n vena; (on leaf) nervatura; (fig: mood) vena, umore m.

velocity [vɪ'lɒsɪtɪ] n velocità.

velvet ['vɛlvɪt] n velluto.

vending machine ['vɛndɪŋməʃiːn] n distributore m automatico.

vendor ['vɛndə*] n venditore/trice.

veneer [və'nɪə*] n impiallacciatura; (fig) vernice f.

venerable ['vɛnərəbl] a venerabile.

venereal [vɪ'nɪərɪəl] a: **~ disease (VD)** n malattia venerea.

Venetian [vɪ'niːʃən] a veneziano(a); **~ blind** n (tenda alla) veneziana.

Venezuela [vɛne'zweɪlə] n Venezuela m; **~n** a, n venezuelano(a).

vengeance ['vɛndʒəns] n vendetta; **with a ~** (fig) davvero; furiosamente.

Venice ['vɛnɪs] n Venezia.

venison ['vɛnɪsn] n carne f di cervo.

venom ['vɛnəm] n veleno; **~ous** a velenoso(a).

vent [vɛnt] n foro, apertura; (in dress, jacket) spacco // vt (fig: one's feelings) sfogare, dare sfogo a.

ventilate ['vɛntɪleɪt] vt (room) dare aria a, arieggiare; **ventilation** [-'leɪʃən] n ventilazione f; **ventilator** n ventilatore m.

ventriloquist [vɛn'trɪləkwɪst] n ventriloquo/a.

venture ['vɛntʃə*] n impresa (rischiosa) // vt rischiare, azzardare // vi arrischiarsi, azzardarsi.

venue ['vɛnjuː] n luogo di incontro; (SPORT) luogo (designato) per l'incontro.

veranda(h) [və'rændə] n veranda.

verb [vəːb] n verbo; **~al** a verbale; (translation) letterale.

verbose [vəː'bəus] a verboso(a).

verdict ['vəːdɪkt] n verdetto.

verge [vəːdʒ] n bordo, orlo; **on the ~ of doing** sul punto di fare; **to ~ on** vt fus rasentare.

verger ['vəːdʒə*] n (REL) sagrestano.

verification [vɛrɪfɪ'keɪʃən] n verifica.

verify ['vɛrɪfaɪ] vt verificare.

vermin ['vəːmɪn] npl animali mpl nocivi; (insects) insetti mpl parassiti.

vermouth ['vəːməθ] n vermut m inv.

vernacular [və'nækjulə*] n vernacolo.

versatile ['vəːsətaɪl] a (person) versatile;

(machine, tool etc) (che si presta) a molti usi.

verse [vəːs] n versi mpl; (stanza) stanza, strofa; (in bible) versetto.

versed [vəːst] a: **(well-)~ in** versato(a) in.

version ['vəːʃən] n versione f.

versus ['vəːsəs] prep contro.

vertebra, pl **~e** ['vəːtɪbrə, -briː] n vertebra.

vertebrate ['vəːtɪbrɪt] n vertebrato.

vertical ['vəːtɪkl] a, n verticale (m); **~ly** ad verticalmente.

vertigo ['vəːtɪgəu] n vertigine f.

verve [vəːv] n brio; entusiasmo.

very ['vɛrɪ] ad molto // a: **the ~ book which** proprio il libro che; **at the ~ end** proprio alla fine; **the ~ last** proprio l'ultimo; **at the ~ least** almeno; **~ much** moltissimo.

vespers ['vɛspəz] npl vespro.

vessel ['vɛsl] n (ANAT) vaso; (NAUT) nave f; (container) recipiente m.

vest [vɛst] n maglia; (sleeveless) canottiera; (US: waistcoat) gilè m inv // vt: **to ~ sb with sth, to ~ sth in sb** conferire qc a qd; **~ed interests** npl (COMM) diritti mpl acquisiti.

vestibule ['vɛstɪbjuːl] n vestibolo.

vestige ['vɛstɪdʒ] n vestigio.

vestment ['vɛstmənt] n (REL) paramento liturgico.

vestry ['vɛstrɪ] n sagrestia.

vet [vɛt] n (abbr of **veterinary surgeon**) veterinario // vt esaminare minuziosamente; (text) rivedere.

veteran ['vɛtərn] n veterano; (also: **war ~**) reduce m; **~ car** n auto f inv d'epoca.

veterinary ['vɛtrɪnərɪ] a veterinario(a); **~ surgeon** n veterinario.

veto ['viːtəu] n, pl **~es** veto // vt opporre il veto a.

vex [vɛks] vt irritare, contrariare; **~ed** a (question) controverso(a), dibattuto(a).

VHF abbr of very high frequency.

via ['vaɪə] prep (by way of) via; (by means of) tramite.

viable ['vaɪəbl] a attuabile; vitale.

viaduct ['vaɪədʌkt] n viadotto.

vibrate [vaɪ'breɪt] vi: **to ~ (with)** vibrare (di); (resound) risonare (di); **vibration** [-'breɪʃən] n vibrazione f.

vicar ['vɪkə*] n pastore m; **~age** n presbiterio.

vice [vaɪs] n (evil) vizio; (TECH) morsa.

vice- [vaɪs] prefix vice...; **~chairman** n vicepresidente m.

vice squad n (vaɪsskwɔd) n (squadra del) buon costume f.

vice versa ['vaɪsɪ'vəːsə] ad viceversa.

vicinity [vɪ'sɪnɪtɪ] n vicinanze fpl.

vicious ['vɪʃəs] a (remark) maligno(a), cattivo(a); (blow) violento(a); **~ness** n malignità, cattiveria; ferocia.

vicissitudes [vɪ'sɪsɪtjuːdz] npl vicissitudini fpl.

victim ['vɪktɪm] n vittima; **~ization**

[-aɪzeɪʃən] n persecuzione f; rappresaglie fpl; **~ize** vt perseguitare; compiere delle rappresaglie contro.

victor ['vɪktə*] n vincitore m.

Victorian [vɪk'tɔːrɪən] a vittoriano(a).

victorious [vɪk'tɔːrɪəs] a vittorioso(a).

victory ['vɪktərɪ] n vittoria.

video ['vɪdɪəu] cpd video...; **~(-tape) recorder** n videoregistratore m.

vie [vaɪ] vi: **to ~ with** competere con, rivaleggiare con.

Vienna [vɪ'enə] n Vienna.

view [vjuː] n vista, veduta; (opinion) opinione f // vt (situation) considerare; (house) visitare; **on ~** (in museum etc) esposto(a); **in my ~** a mio avviso, secondo me; **in ~ of the fact that** considerato che; **~er** n (viewfinder) mirino; (small projector) visore m; (TV) telespettatore/trice; **~finder** n mirino; **~point** n punto di vista.

vigil ['vɪdʒɪl] n veglia; **~ance** n vigilanza; **~ant** a vigile.

vigorous ['vɪgərəs] a vigoroso(a).

vigour ['vɪgə*] n vigore m.

vile [vaɪl] a (action) vile; (smell) disgustoso(a), nauseante; (temper) pessimo(a).

villa ['vɪlə] n villa.

village ['vɪlɪdʒ] n villaggio; **~r** n abitante m/f di villaggio.

villain ['vɪlən] n (scoundrel) canaglia; (criminal) criminale m; (in novel etc) cattivo.

vindicate ['vɪndɪkeɪt] vt comprovare; giustificare.

vindictive [vɪn'dɪktɪv] a vendicativo(a).

vine [vaɪn] n vite f; (climbing plant) rampicante m.

vinegar ['vɪnɪgə*] n aceto.

vineyard ['vɪnjɑːd] n vigna, vigneto.

vintage ['vɪntɪdʒ] n (year) annata, produzione f; **~ wine** n vino d'annata.

vinyl ['vaɪnl] n vinile m.

viola [vɪ'əulə] n viola.

violate ['vaɪəleɪt] vt violare; **violation** [-'leɪʃən] n violazione f.

violence ['vaɪələns] n violenza; (POL etc) incidenti mpl violenti.

violent ['vaɪələnt] a violento(a); **~ly** ad violentemente; estremamente.

violet ['vaɪələt] a (colour) viola inv, violetto(a) // n (plant) violetta.

violin [vaɪə'lɪn] n violino; **~ist** n violinista m/f.

VIP n (abbr of very important person) V.I.P. m/f inv.

viper ['vaɪpə*] n vipera.

virgin ['vɜːdʒɪn] n vergine f // a vergine; **the Blessed V~** la Beatissima Vergine; **~ity** [-'dʒɪnɪtɪ] n verginità.

Virgo ['vɜːgəu] n (sign) Vergine f.

virile ['vɪraɪl] a virile.

virility [vɪ'rɪlɪtɪ] n virilità.

virtually ['vɜːtjuəlɪ] ad (almost) praticamente.

virtue ['vɜːtjuː] n virtù f inv; (advantage)

pregio, vantaggio; **by ~ of** grazie a.

virtuoso [vɜːtju'əuzəu] n virtuoso.

virtuous ['vɜːtjuəs] a virtuoso(a).

virus ['vaɪərəs] n virus m inv.

visa ['viːzə] n visto.

vis-à-vis [viːzə'viː] prep rispetto a, nei riguardi di.

viscount ['vaɪkaunt] n visconte m.

visibility [vɪzɪ'bɪlɪtɪ] n visibilità.

visible ['vɪzəbl] a visibile.

vision ['vɪʒən] n (sight) vista; (foresight, in dream) visione f; **~ary** a visionario/a.

visit ['vɪzɪt] n visita; (stay) soggiorno // vt (person) andare a trovare; (place) visitare; **~ing card** n biglietto da visita; **~or** n visitatore/trice; (guest) ospite m/f; (in hotel) cliente m/f; **~ors' book** n libro d'oro; (in hotel) registro.

visor ['vaɪzə*] n visiera.

vista ['vɪstə] n vista, prospettiva.

visual ['vɪzjuəl] a visivo(a); visuale; ottico(a); **~ aid** n sussidio visivo.

visualize ['vɪzjuəlaɪz] vt immaginare, figurarsi; (foresee) prevedere.

vital ['vaɪtl] a vitale; **~ity** [-'tælɪtɪ] n vitalità; **~ly** ad estremamente; **~ statistics** npl (fig) misure fpl.

vitamin ['vɪtəmɪn] n vitamina.

vivacious [vɪ'veɪʃəs] a vivace.

vivacity [vɪ'væsɪtɪ] n vivacità.

vivid ['vɪvɪd] a vivido(a); **~ly** ad (describe) vividamente; (remember) con precisione.

vivisection [vɪvɪ'sekʃən] n vivisezione f.

vocabulary [vəu'kæbjulərɪ] n vocabolario.

vocal ['vəukl] a (MUS) vocale; (communication) verbale; (noisy) rumoroso(a); **~ist** n cantante m/f di musica vocale, vocalist m/f inv.

vocation [vəu'keɪʃən] n vocazione f; **~al** a professionale.

vociferous [və'sɪfərəs] a rumoroso(a).

vodka ['vɔdkə] n vodka f inv.

vogue [vəug] n moda; (popularity) popolarità, voga.

voice [vɔɪs] n voce f // vt (opinion) esprimere.

void [vɔɪd] n vuoto // a: **~ of** privo(a) di.

volatile ['vɔlətaɪl] a volatile; (fig) volubile.

volcanic [vɔl'kænɪk] a vulcanico(a).

volcano [vɔl'keɪnəu] n, **~es** [vɔl'keɪnəuz] n vulcano.

volition [və'lɪʃən] n: **of one's own ~** di sua volontà.

volley ['vɔlɪ] n (of gunfire) salva; (of stones etc) raffica, gragnola; (TENNIS etc) volata; **~ball** n pallavolo f.

volt [vəult] n volt m inv; **~age** n tensione f, voltaggio.

voluble ['vɔljubl] a loquace, ciarliero(a).

volume ['vɔljuːm] n volume m; **~ control** n (RADIO, TV) regolatore m or manopola del volume.

voluntarily ['vɔləntrɪlɪ] ad volontariamente; gratuitamente.

voluntary ['vɔləntərɪ] a volontario(a); (unpaid) gratuito(a), non retribuito(a).

volunteer [vɔlən'tɪə*] n volontario/a // vi

(MIL) arruolarsi volontario; **to ~ to do** offrire (volontariamente) di fare.

voluptuous [vəˈlʌptjuəs] *a* voluttuoso(a).

vomit [ˈvɔmɪt] *n* vomito // *vt, vi* vomitare.

vote [vəut] *n* voto, suffragio; *(cast)* voto; *(franchise)* diritto di voto // *vi* votare; **~ of thanks** *n* discorso di ringraziamento; **~r** *n* elettore/trice; **voting** *n* scrutinio.

vouch [vautʃ]: **to ~ for** *vt* farsi garante di.

voucher [ˈvautʃə*] *n (for meal, petrol)* buono; *(receipt)* ricevuta.

vow [vau] *n* voto, promessa solenne // *vi* giurare.

vowel [ˈvauəl] *n* vocale *f*.

voyage [ˈvɔɪdʒ] *n* viaggio per mare, traversata.

vulgar [ˈvʌlgə*] *a* volgare; **~ity** [-ˈgærɪtɪ] *n* volgarità.

vulnerable [ˈvʌlnərəbl] *a* vulnerabile.

vulture [ˈvʌltʃə*] *n* avvoltoio.

W

wad [wɔd] *n (of cotton wool, paper)* tampone *m*; *(of banknotes etc)* fascio.

wade [weɪd] *vi*: **to ~ through** camminare a stento in // *vt* guadare.

wafer [ˈweɪfə*] *n (CULIN)* cialda; *(REL)* ostia.

waffle [ˈwɔfl] *n (CULIN)* cialda; *(col)* ciance *fpl*; riempitivo // *vi* cianciare; parlare a vuoto.

waft [wɔft] *vt* portare // *vi* diffondersi.

wag [wæg] *vt* agitare, muovere // *vi* agitarsi.

wage [weɪdʒ] *n* salario, paga // *vt*: **to ~ war** fare la guerra; **~s** *npl* salario, paga.

wager [ˈweɪdʒə*] *n* scommessa.

waggle [ˈwægl] *vt* dimenare, agitare // *vi* dimenarsi, agitarsi.

wag(g)on [ˈwægən] *n (horse-drawn)* carro; *(truck)* furgone *m*; *(RAIL)* vagone *m* (merci).

wail [weɪl] *n* gemito; *(of siren)* urlo // *vi* gemere; urlare.

waist [weɪst] *n* vita, cintola; **~coat** *n* panciotto, gilè *m inv*; **~line** *n* (giro di) vita.

wait [weɪt] *n* attesa // *vi* aspettare, attendere; **to lie in ~ for** stare in agguato a; **I can't ~ to** *(fig)* non vedo l'ora di; **to ~ behind** *vi* rimanere (ad aspettare); **to ~ for** aspettare; **to ~ on** *vt fus* servire; **~er** *n* cameriere *m*; **'no ~ing'** *(AUT)* 'divieto di sosta'; **~ing list** *n* lista di attesa; **~ing room** *n* sala d'aspetto or d'attesa; **~ress** *n* cameriera.

waive [weɪv] *vt* rinunciare a, abbandonare.

wake [weɪk] *vb (pt woke, ~d, pp woken, ~d)* [wəuk, ˈwəukn] *vt (also: ~ up)* svegliare // *vi (also: ~ up)* svegliarsi // *n (for dead person)* veglia funebre; *(NAUT)* scia; **~n** *vt, vi* = **wake**.

Wales [weɪlz] *n* Galles *m*.

walk [wɔːk] *n* passeggiata // *n* giretto; *(short)* giretto; *(gait)* passo, andatura; *(path)* sentiero; *(in*

park etc) sentiero, vialetto // *vi* camminare; *(for pleasure, exercise)* passeggiare // *vt (distance)* fare or percorrere a piedi; *(dog)* accompagnare, portare a passeggiare; **10 minutes' ~ from** 10 minuti di cammino or a piedi da; **from all ~s of life** di tutte le condizioni sociali; **~er** *n (person)* camminatore/trice; **~ie-talkie** [ˈwɔːkɪˈtɔːkɪ] *n* radiotelefono portatile; **~ing** *n* camminare *m*; **~ing stick** *n* bastone *m* da passeggio; **~out** *n (of workers)* sciopero senza preavviso or a sorpresa; **~over** *n (col)* vittoria facile, gioco da ragazzi.

wall [wɔːl] *n* muro; *(internal, of tunnel, cave)* parete *f*; **~ed** *a (city)* fortificato(a).

wallet [ˈwɔlɪt] *n* portafoglio.

wallflower [ˈwɔːlflauə*] *n* violacciocca; **to be a ~** *(fig)* fare da tappezzeria.

wallop [ˈwɔləp] *vt (col)* pestare.

wallow [ˈwɔləu] *vi* sguazzare, voltolarsi.

wallpaper [ˈwɔːlpeɪpə*] *n* carta da parati.

walnut [ˈwɔːlnʌt] *n* noce *f*; *(tree)* noce *m*.

walrus [ˈwɔːlrəs], *pl* **~** or **~es** [ˈwɔːlrəs] *n* tricheco.

waltz [wɔːlts] *n* valzer *m inv* // *vi* ballare il valzer.

wan [wɔn] *a* pallido(a), smorto(a); triste.

wand [wɔnd] *n (also: magic ~)* bacchetta (magica).

wander [ˈwɔndə*] *vi (person)* girare senza meta, girovagare; *(thoughts)* vagare; *(river)* serpeggiare; **~er** *n* vagabondo/a.

wane [weɪn] *vi (moon)* calare; *(reputation)* declinare.

want [wɔnt] *vt* volere; *(need)* aver bisogno di; *(lack)* mancare di // *n*: **for ~ of** per mancanza di; **~s** *npl (needs)* bisogni *mpl*; **to ~ to do** volere fare; **to ~ sb to do** volere che qd faccia; **to be found ~ing** non risultare all'altezza.

wanton [ˈwɔntn] *a* sfrenato(a); senza motivo.

war [wɔː*] *n* guerra; **to go to ~** entrare in guerra.

ward [wɔːd] *n (in hospital: room)* corsia; (: *section)* reparto; *(POL)* circoscrizione *f*; *(LAW: child)* pupillo/a; **to ~ off** *vt* parare, schivare.

warden [ˈwɔːdn] *n (of institution)* direttore/trice; *(of park, game reserve)* guardiano/a; *(also:* **traffic ~)** addetto/a al controllo del traffico e del parcheggio.

warder [ˈwɔːdə*] *n* guardia carceraria.

wardrobe [ˈwɔːdrəub] *n (cupboard)* guardaroba *m inv*, armadio; *(clothes)* guardaroba; *(THEATRE)* costumi *mpl*.

warehouse [ˈwɛəhaus] *n* magazzino.

wares [wɛəz] *npl* merci *fpl*.

warfare [ˈwɔːfɛə*] *n* guerra.

warhead [ˈwɔːhed] *n (MIL)* testata, ogiva.

warily [ˈwɛərɪlɪ] *ad* cautamente, con prudenza.

warlike [ˈwɔːlaɪk] *a* guerriero(a).

warm [wɔːm] *a* caldo(a); *(thanks, welcome, applause)* caloroso(a); **it's ~** fa caldo; **I'm ~** ho caldo; **to ~ up** *vi* scaldarsi, riscaldarsi; *(athlete, discussion)* riscaldarsi

// *vt* scaldare, riscaldare; (*engine*) far scaldare; ~-**hearted** *a* affettuoso(a); ~**ly** *ad* caldamente; calorosamente; vivamente; ~**th** *n* calore *m*.

warn [wɔːn] *vt* avvertire, avvisare; ~**ing** *n* avvertimento; (*notice*) avviso; ~**ing light** *n* spia luminosa.

warp [wɔːp] *vi* deformarsi // *vt* deformare; (*fig*) corrompere.

warrant ['wɔrnt] *n* (*LAW: to arrest*) mandato di cattura; (: *to search*) mandato di perquisizione.

warranty ['wɔrənti] *n* garanzia.

warrior ['wɔriə*] *n* guerriero/a.

warship ['wɔːʃip] *n* nave *f* da guerra.

wart [wɔːt] *n* verruca.

wartime ['wɔːtaim] *n*: **in** ~ in tempo di guerra.

wary ['weəri] *a* prudente.

was [wɔz] *pt of* **be**.

wash [wɔʃ] *vt* lavare // *vi* lavarsi // *n*: **to give sth a** ~ lavare qc, dare una lavata a qc; **to have a** ~ lavarsi; **to** ~ **away** *vt* (*stain*) togliere lavando; (*subj: river etc*) trascinare via; **to** ~ **down** *vt* lavare; **to** ~ **off** *vi* andare via con il lavaggio; **to** ~ **up** *vi* lavare i piatti; (*fig: story*) ~**basin** *n* lavabo; ~**er** *n* (*TECH*) rondella; ~**ing** *n* (*linen etc*) bucato; ~**ing machine** *n* lavatrice *f*; ~**ing powder** *n* detersivo (in polvere); ~**ing-up** *n* rigovernatura, lavatura dei piatti; ~**out** *n* (*col*) disastro; ~**room** *n* gabinetto.

wasn't ['wɔznt] = **was not**.

wasp [wɔsp] *n* vespa.

wastage ['weistidʒ] *n* spreco; (*in manufacturing*) scarti *mpl*.

waste [weist] *n* spreco; (*of time*) perdita; (*rubbish*) rifiuti *mpl* // *a* (*material*) di scarto; (*food*) avanzato(a) // *vt* sprecare; (*time, opportunity*) perdere; ~**s** *npl* distesa desolata; **to** ~ **away** *vi* deperire; ~**bin** *n* bidone *m* or secchio della spazzatura; ~ **disposal unit** *n* eliminatore *m* di rifiuti; ~**ful** *a* sprecone(a); (*process*) dispendioso(a); ~ **ground** *n* terreno incolto or abbandonato; ~**paper basket** *n* cestino per la carta straccia.

watch [wɔtʃ] *n* orologio; (*act of watching*) sorveglianza; (*guard: MIL, NAUT*) guardia; (*NAUT: spell of duty*) quarto // *vt* (*look at*) osservare; (: *match, programme*) guardare; (*spy on, guard*) sorvegliare, tenere d'occhio; (*be careful of*) fare attenzione a // *vi* osservare, guardare; (*keep guard*) fare or montare la guardia; **to** ~ **out** *vi* fare attenzione; ~**dog** *n* cane *m* da guardia; ~**ful** *a* attento(a), vigile; ~**maker** *n* orologiaio/a; ~**man** *n* guardiano; (*also*: **night ~man**) guardiano notturno; ~**strap** *n* cinturino da orologio.

water ['wɔːtə*] *n* acqua // *vt* (*plant*) annaffiare; **in British** ~**s** nelle acque territoriali britanniche; **to** ~ **down** *vt* (*milk*) diluire; (*fig: story*) edulcorare; ~**closet** *n* W.C. *m inv*, gabinetto; ~**colours** *npl* colori *mpl* per acquarello; ~**cress** *n* crescione *m*; ~**fall** *n* cascata; ~**ing can**

n annaffiatoio; ~ **level** *n* livello dell'acqua; (*of flood*) livello delle acque; ~ **lily** *n* ninfea; ~**line** *n* (*NAUT*) linea di galleggiamento; ~**logged** *a* saturo(a) d'acqua; imbevuto(a) d'acqua; (*football pitch etc*) allagato(a); ~ **main** *n* conduttura dell'acqua; ~**mark** *n* (*on paper*) filigrana; ~**melon** *n* anguria, cocomero; ~ **polo** *n* pallanuoto *f*; ~**proof** *a* impermeabile; ~**shed** *n* (*GEO, fig*) spartiacque *m*; ~-**skiing** *n* sci *m* acquatico; ~**tight** *a* stagno(a); ~**works** *npl* impianto idrico; ~**y** *a* (*colour*) slavato(a); (*coffee*) acquoso(a).

watt [wɔt] *n* watt *m inv*.

wave [weiv] *n* onda; (*of hand*) gesto, segno; (*in hair*) ondulazione *f* // *vi* fare un cenno con la mano; (*flag*) sventolare // *vt* (*handkerchief*) sventolare; (*stick*) brandire; (*hair*) ondulare; ~**length** *n* lunghezza d'onda.

waver ['weivə*] *vi* vacillare; (*voice*) tremolare.

wavy ['weivi] *a* ondulato(a); ondeggiante.

wax [wæks] *n* cera // *vt* dare la cera a; (*car*) lucidare // *vi* (*moon*) crescere; ~**works** *npl* cere *fpl*; museo delle cere.

way [wei] *n* via, strada; (*path, access*) passaggio; (*distance*) distanza; (*direction*) parte *f*, direzione *f*; (*manner*) modo, stile *m*; (*habit*) abitudine *f*; (*condition*) condizione *f*; **which** ~? — **this** ~ da che parte *or* in quale direzione? — da questa parte, per di qua; **to be on one's** ~ essere in cammino *or* sulla strada; **to be in the** ~ bloccare il passaggio; (*fig*) essere tra i piedi *or* d'impiccio; **to go out of one's** ~ **to do** (*fig*) mettercela tutta *or* fare di tutto per fare; **in a** ~ in un certo senso; **in some** ~**s** sotto certi aspetti; '~ **in**' 'entrata', 'ingresso'; '~ **out**' 'uscita'; **the** ~ **back** la via del ritorno.

waylay [wei'lei] *vt irg* tendere un agguato a; attendere al passaggio.

wayward ['weiwəd] *a* capriccioso(a); testardo(a).

W.C. ['dʌblju'siː] *n* W.C. *m inv*, gabinetto.

we [wiː] *pl pronoun* noi.

weak [wiːk] *a* debole; (*health*) precario(a); (*beam etc*) fragile; ~**en** *vi* indebolirsi // *vt* indebolire; ~**ling** ['wiːkliŋ] *n* smidollato/a; debole *m/f*; ~**ness** *n* debolezza; (*fault*) punto debole, difetto.

wealth [wɛlθ] *n* (*money, resources*) ricchezza, ricchezze *fpl*; (*of details*) abbondanza, profusione *f*; ~**y** *a* ricco(a).

wean [wiːn] *vt* svezzare.

weapon ['wɛpən] *n* arma.

wear [wɛə*] *n* (*use*) uso; (*deterioration through use*) logorio, usura; (*clothing*): **sports/baby~** abbigliamento sportivo/per neonati // *vb* (*pt wore, pp worn* [wɔː*, wɔːn]) *vt* (*clothes*) portare; mettersi; (*damage: through use*) consumare // *vi* (*last*) durare; (*rub etc through*) consumarsi; **town/evening** ~ *n* abiti *mpl* *or* tenuta da città/sera; ~ **and tear** *n* usura, consumo; **to** ~ **away** *vt* consumare; erodere // *vi* consumarsi; essere eroso(a); **to ~ down** *vt* consumare; (*strength*) esaurire; **to ~ off** *vi* sparire lentamente; **to ~ on** *vi* passare; **to ~ out** *vt* consumare; (*person, strength*) esaurire.

weariness ['wɪərɪnɪs] *n* stanchezza.

weary ['wɪərɪ] *a* stanco(a); (*tiring*) faticoso(a) // *vi:* **to ~ of** stancarsi di.

weasel ['wiːzl] *n* (ZOOL) donnola.

weather ['wɛðə*] *n* tempo // *vt* (*wood*) stagionare; (*storm, crisis*) superare; **~-beaten** *a* (*person*) segnato(a) dalle intemperie; (*building*) logorato(a) dalle intemperie; **~ cock** *n* banderuola; **~ forecast** *n* previsioni *fpl* del tempo, bollettino meteorologico.

weave, *pt* **wove**, *pp* **woven** [wiːv, wəuv, 'wəuvn] *vt* (*cloth*) tessere; (*basket*) intrecciare; **~r** *n* tessitore/trice; **weaving** *n* tessitura.

web [wɛb] *n* (*of spider*) ragnatela; (*on foot*) palma; (*fabric, also fig*) tessuto; **~bed** *a* (*foot*) palmato(a).

wed [wɛd] *vt* (*pt, pp* **wedded**) sposare // *n:* **the newly-~s** gli sposi novelli.

we'd [wiːd] = **we had, we would**.

wedding ['wɛdɪŋ] *n* matrimonio; **silver/golden ~** *n* nozze *fpl* d'argento/d'oro; **~ day** *n* giorno delle nozze *or* del matrimonio; **~ dress** *n* abito nuziale; **~ present** *n* regalo di nozze; **~ ring** *n* fede *f*.

wedge [wɛdʒ] *n* (*of wood etc*) cuneo; (*under door etc*) zeppa; (*of cake*) spicchio, fetta // *vt* (*fix*) fissare con zeppe; (*push*) incuneare.

wedlock ['wɛdlɔk] *n* vincolo matrimoniale.

Wednesday ['wɛdnzdɪ] *n* mercole-dì *m inv*.

wee [wiː] *a* (*Scottish*) piccolo(a); piccolissimo(a).

weed [wiːd] *n* erbaccia // *vt* diserbare; **~-killer** *n* diserbante *m*.

week [wiːk] *n* settimana; **~-day** *n* giorno feriale; (COMM) giornata lavorativa; **~-end** *n* fine settimana *m or f inv*, weekend *m inv*; **~ly** *ad* ogni settimana, settimanalmente // *a,n* settimanale (*m*).

weep, *pt, pp* **wept** [wiːp, wɛpt] *vi* (*person*) piangere; **~ing willow** *n* salice *m* piangente.

weigh [weɪ] *vt,vi* pesare; **to ~ anchor** salpare *or* levare l'ancora; **to ~ down** *vt* (*branch*) piegare; (*fig: with worry*) opprimere, caricare; **to ~ up** *vt* valutare.

weight [weɪt] *n* peso; **sold by ~** venduto(a) a peso; **~lessness** *n* mancanza di peso; **~ lifter** *n* pesista *m*; **~y** *a* pesante; (*fig*) importante, grave.

weir [wɪə*] *n* diga.

weird [wɪəd] *a* strano(a), bizzarro(a); (*eerie*) soprannaturale.

welcome ['wɛlkəm] *a* benvenuto(a) // *n* accoglienza, benvenuto // *vt* accogliere cordialmente; (*also:* **bid ~**) dare il benvenuto a; (*be glad of*) rallegrarsi di; **to**

be ~ essere il(la) benvenuto(a); **welcoming** *a* accogliente.

weld [wɛld] *n* saldatura // *vt* saldare; **~er** *n* (*person*) saldatore *m*; **~ing** *n* saldatura (autogena).

welfare ['wɛlfɛə*] *n* benessere *m*; **~ state** *n* stato assistenziale; **~ work** *n* assistenza sociale.

well [wɛl] *n* pozzo // *ad* bene // *a:* **to be ~** andare bene; (*person*) stare bene // *excl* allora!; ma!; ebbene!; **~ done!** bravo(a)!; **get ~ soon!** guarisci presto!; **to do ~ in sth** riuscire in qc.

we'll [wiːl] = **we will, we shall**.

well: ~-behaved *a* ubbidiente; **~-being** *n* benessere *m*; **~-built** *a* (*person*) ben fatto(a); **~-developed** *a* (*girl*) sviluppata; **~-earned** *a* (*rest*) meritato(a); **~-groomed** *a* curato(a), azzimato(a); **~-heeled** *a* (*col: wealthy*) agiato(a), facoltoso(a).

wellingtons ['wɛlɪŋtənz] *npl* (*also:* **wellington boots**) stivali *mpl* di gomma.

well: ~-known *a* (*person*) ben noto(a); (*: famous*) famoso(a); **~-meaning** *a* ben intenzionato(a); **~-off** *a* benestante, danaroso(a); **~-read** *a* colto(a); **~-to-do** *a* abbiente, benestante.

Welsh [wɛlʃ] *a* gallese // *n* (LING) gallese *m*; **~man/woman** *n* gallese *m/f*; **~ rarebit** *n* crostino al formaggio.

went [wɛnt] *pt of* **go**.

wept [wɛpt] *pt, pp of* **weep**.

were [wəː*] *pt of* **be**.

we're [wɪə*] = **we are**.

weren't [wəːnt] = **were not**.

west [wɛst] *n* ovest *m*, occidente *m*, ponente *m* // *a* (a) ovest *inv*, occidentale // *ad* verso ovest; **the W~** *n* l'Occidente *m*; **the W~ Country** *n* il sud-ovest dell'Inghilterra; **~erly** *a* (*wind*) occidentale, da ovest; **~ern** *a* occidentale, dell'ovest // *n* (CINEMA) western *m inv*; **W~ Germany** *n* Germania occidentale *or* ovest; **W~ Indies** *npl* Indie *fpl* occidentali; **~ward(s)** *ad* verso ovest.

wet [wɛt] *a* umido(a), bagnato(a); (*soaked*) fradicio(a); (*rainy*) piovoso(a); **to get ~** bagnarsi; **~ blanket** *n* (*fig*) guastafeste *m/f*; **'~ paint'** 'vernice fresca'; **~ suit** *n* tuta da sub.

we've [wiːv] = **we have**.

whack [wæk] *vt* picchiare, battere; **~ed** *a* (*col: tired*) sfinito(a), a pezzi.

whale [weɪl] *n* (ZOOL) balena.

wharf, wharves [wɔːf, wɔːvz] *n* banchina.

what [wɔt] *excl* cosa!, come! // *det* quale // *pronoun* (*interrogative*) che cosa, cosa, che; (*relative*) quello che, ciò che; **~ a mess!** che disordine!; **~ is it called?** come si chiama?; **~ about doing ...?** cosa ne diresti di fare ...?; **~ about me?** e io?; **~ever** *det:* **~ever book** qualunque *or* qualsiasi libro + *sub* // *pronoun:* **do ~ever is necessary/you want** faccia qualunque *or* qualsiasi cosa sia necessaria/lei voglia; **~ever happens**

qualunque cosa accada; **no reason
~ever** or **~soever** nessuna ragione
affatto or al mondo.

wheat [wi:t] n grano, frumento.

wheel [wi:l] n ruota; (AUT: also: **steering
~**) volante m; (NAUT) (ruota del) timone
m // vt spingere // vi (also: ~ **round**)
girare; **~barrow** n carriola; **~chair** n
sedia a rotelle.

wheeze [wi:z] n respiro affannoso // vi
ansimare.

when [wɛn] ad quando // cj quando, nel
momento in cui; (whereas) mentre;
~ever ad quando mai // cj quando;
(every time that) ogni volta che.

where [wɛə*] ad,cj dove; **this is ~** è qui
che; **~abouts** ad dove // n: **sb's
~abouts** luogo dove qd si trova; **~as** cj
mentre; **~ver** [-'ɛvə*] ad dove mai // cj
dovunque + sub.

whet [wɛt] vt (tool) affilare; (appetite etc)
stimolare.

whether ['wɛðə*] cj se; **I don't know ~
to accept or not** non so se accettare o no;
it's doubtful ~ è poco probabile che; **~
you go or not** che lei vada o no.

which [wɪtʃ] det (interrogative) che, quale;
~ one of you? chi di voi?; **tell me ~
one you want** mi dica quale vuole //
pronoun (interrogative, indirect) quale;
(relative: subject) che; (: object) che, prep +
cui, il(la) quale; **I don't mind ~** non mi
importa quale; **the apple ~ you ate/~
is on the table** la mela che ha
mangiato/che è sul tavolo; **the chair on
~** la sedia sulla quale o su cui; **the book
of ~** il libro del quale or di cui; **he said
he knew, ~ is true/I feared** disse che
lo sapeva, il che è vero/ciò che temevo;
after ~ dopo di che; **in ~ case** nel qual
caso; **~ever** det: **take ~ever book you
prefer** prenda qualsiasi libro che
preferisce; **~ever book you take**
qualsiasi libro prenda.

whiff [wɪf] n soffio; sbuffo; odore m.

while [waɪl] n momento // cj mentre; (as
long as) finché; (although) sebbene + sub;
per quanto + sub; **for a ~** per un po'.

whim [wɪm] n capriccio.

whimper ['wɪmpə*] n piagnucolio // vi
piagnucolare.

whimsical ['wɪmzɪkl] a (person)
capriccioso(a); (look) strano(a).

whine [waɪn] n gemito // vi gemere;
uggiolare; piagnucolare.

whip [wɪp] n frusta; (for riding) frustino;
(Brit: POL: person) capogruppo (che
sovrintende alla disciplina dei colleghi di
partito) // vt frustare; (snatch) sollevare
(or estrarre) bruscamente; **~ped cream**
n panna montata; **~-round** n colletta.

whirl [wə:l] n turbine m // vt (far) girare
rapidamente; (far) turbinare // vi
turbinare; **~pool** n mulinello; **~wind** n
turbine m.

whirr [wə:*] vi ronzare; rombare; frullare.

whisk [wɪsk] n (CULIN) frusta; frullino // vt
sbattere, frullare; **to ~ sb away** or **off**

portar via qd a tutta velocità.

whisker ['wɪskə*] n: **~s** npl (of animal)
baffi mpl; (of man) favoriti mpl.

whisk(e)y ['wɪskɪ] n whisky m inv.

whisper ['wɪspə*] n sussurro; (rumour)
voce f // vi,vt sussurrare.

whist [wɪst] n whist m.

whistle ['wɪsl] n (sound) fischio; (object)
fischietto // vi fischiare.

white [waɪt] a bianco(a); (with fear)
pallido(a) // n bianco; (person) bianco/a;
~-collar worker n impiegato; **~ lie** n
bugia pietosa; **~ness** n biancherza;
~wash n (paint) bianco di calce // vt
imbiancare; (fig) coprire.

Whitsun ['wɪtsn] n la Pentecoste.

whittle ['wɪtl] vt: **to ~ away, ~ down**
ridurre, tagliare.

whizz [wɪz] vi sfrecciare; **~ kid** n (col)
ragazzo/a prodigio.

WHO n (abbr of World Health Organization)
O.M.S. f (Organizzazione mondiale della
sanità).

who [hu:] pronoun (interrogative) chi;
(relative) che; **~dunit** [hu:'dʌnɪt] n (col)
giallo; **~ever** pronoun: **~ever finds it**
chiunque lo trovi; **ask ~ever you like** lo
chieda a chiunque vuole; **~ever told you
that?** chi mai gliel'ha detto?

whole [həʊl] a (complete) tutto(a),
completo(a); (not broken) intero(a),
intatto(a) // n (total) totale m; (sth not
broken) tutto; **the ~ of the time** tutto il
tempo; **on the ~, as a ~** nel complesso,
nell'insieme; **~hearted** a sincero(a);
~sale n commercio or vendita
all'ingrosso // a all'ingrosso; (destruction)
totale; **~saler** n grossista m/f; **~some** a
sano(a); salutare; **wholly** ad
completamente, del tutto.

whom [hu:m] pronoun che, prep + il(la)
quale; (interrogative) chi.

whooping cough ['hu:pɪŋkɔf] n pertosse f.

whopping ['wɒpɪŋ] a (col: big) enorme.

whore [hɔ:*] n (pej) puttana.

whose [hu:z] det: **~ book is this?** di chi è
questo libro?; **~ pencil have you taken?**
di chi è la matita che ha preso?; **the man
~ son you rescued** l'uomo di cui or del
quale ha salvato il figlio; **the girl ~
sister you were speaking to** la ragazza
alla sorella di cui or della quale stava
parlando // pronoun: ~ di chi è
questo?; **I know ~ it is** so di chi è.

why [waɪ] ad perché // excl oh!; ma come!;
the reason ~ la ragione perché or per la
quale; **~ever** ad perché mai.

wick [wɪk] n lucignolo, stoppino.

wicked ['wɪkɪd] a cattivo(a), malvagio(a);
maligno(a); perfido(a); (mischievous) mali-
zioso(a).

wicker ['wɪkə*] n vimine m; (also:
~work) articoli di vimini.

wicket ['wɪkɪt] n (CRICKET) porta; area tra
le due porte.

wide [waɪd] a largo(a); (region, knowledge)
vasto(a); (choice) ampio(a) // ad: **to open
~** spalancare; **to shoot ~** tirare a vuoto

or fuori bersaglio; ~**-angle lens** *n* grandangolare *m*; ~**-awake** *a* completamente sveglio(a); ~**ly** *ad* (*different*) molto, completamente; (*believed*) generalmente; ~**ly spaced** molto distanziati(e); ~**n** *vt* allargare, ampliare; ~ **open** *a* spalancato(a); ~**spread** *a* (*belief etc*) molto *or* assai diffuso(a).

widow ['wɪdəu] *n* vedova; ~**ed** *a* (che è rimasto(a)) vedovo(a)); ~**er** *n* vedovo.

width [wɪdθ] *n* larghezza.

wield [wɪːld] *vt* (*sword*) maneggiare; (*power*) esercitare.

wife, wives [waɪf, waɪvz] *n* moglie *f*.

wig [wɪg] *n* parrucca.

wiggle ['wɪgl] *vt* dimenare, agitare // *vi* (*loose screw etc*) traballare; (*worm*) torcersi.

wild [waɪld] *a* selvatico(a); selvaggio(a); (*sea*) tempestoso(a); (*idea, life*) folle; stravagante; ~**s** *npl* regione *f* selvaggia; ~**erness** ['wɪldənɪs] *n* deserto; ~**-goose chase** *n* (*fig*) pista falsa; ~**life** *n* natura; ~**ly** *ad* (*applaud*) freneticamente; (*hit, guess*) a casaccio; (*happy*) follemente.

wilful ['wɪlful] *a* (*person*) testardo(a), ostinato(a); (*action*) intenzionale; (*crime*) premeditato(a).

will [wɪl] *auxiliary vb*: **he** ~ **come** verrà // *vt* (*pt, pp* ~**ed**): **to** ~ **sb to do** volere che qd faccia; **he** ~**ed himself to go on** continuò grazie a un grande sforzo di volontà // *n* volontà; testamento; ~**ing** *a* volonteroso(a); ~**ing to do** disposto(a) a fare; ~**ingly** *ad* volentieri; ~**ingness** *n* buona volontà.

willow ['wɪləu] *n* salice *m*.

will power ['wɪlpauə*] *n* forza di volontà.

wilt [wɪlt] *vi* appassire.

wily ['waɪlɪ] *a* furbo(a).

win [wɪn] *n* (*in sports etc*) vittoria // *vb* (*pt, pp* **won** [wʌn]) *vt* (*battle, prize*) vincere; (*money*) guadagnare; (*popularity*) conquistare // *vi* vincere; **to** ~ **over,** ~ **round** *vt* convincere.

wince [wɪns] *n* trasalimento, sussulto // *vi* trasalire.

winch [wɪntʃ] *n* verricello, argano.

wind *n* [wɪnd] vento; (*MED*) flatulenza, ventosità // *vb* [waɪnd] (*pt, pp* **wound** [waund]) *vt* attorcigliare; (*wrap*) avvolgere; (*clock, toy*) caricare; (*take breath away*: [wɪnd]) far restare senza fiato // *vi* (*road, river*) serpeggiare; **to** ~ **up** *vt* (*clock*) caricare; (*debate*) concludere; ~**break** *n* frangivento; ~**fall** *n* colpo di fortuna; ~**ing** ['waɪndɪŋ] *a* (*road*) serpeggiante; (*staircase*) a chiocciola; ~ **instrument** *n* (*MUS*) strumento a fiato; ~**mill** *n* mulino a vento.

window ['wɪndəu] *n* finestra; (*in car, train*) finestrino; (*in shop etc*) vetrina; (*also:* ~**pane**) vetro; ~ **box** *n* cassetta da fiori; ~ **cleaner** *n* (*person*) pulitore *m* di finestre; ~ **ledge** *n* davanzale *m*; ~ **pane** *n* vetro; ~ **sill** *n* davanzale *m*.

windpipe ['wɪndpaɪp] *n* trachea.

windscreen, windshield (*US*) ['wɪndskriːn, 'wɪndʃiːld] *n* parabrezza *m inv*; ~ **washer** *n* lavacristallo; ~ **wiper** *n* tergicristallo.

windswept ['wɪndswɛpt] *a* spazzato(a) dal vento.

windy ['wɪndɪ] *a* ventoso(a); **it's** ~ c'è vento.

wine [waɪn] *n* vino; ~ **cellar** *n* cantina; ~ **glass** *n* bicchiere *m* da vino; ~ **list** *n* lista dei vini; ~ **tasting** *n* degustazione *f* dei vini; ~ **waiter** *n* sommelier *m inv*.

wing [wɪŋ] *n* ala; ~**s** *npl* (*THEATRE*) quinte *fpl*; ~**er** *n* (*SPORT*) ala.

wink [wɪŋk] *n* ammiccamento // *vi* ammiccare, fare l'occhiolino.

winner ['wɪnə*] *n* vincitore/trice.

winning ['wɪnɪŋ] *a* (*team*) vincente; (*goal*) decisivo(a); ~**s** *npl* vincite *fpl*; ~ **post** *n* traguardo.

winter ['wɪntə*] *n* inverno; ~ **sports** *npl* sport *mpl* invernali.

wintry ['wɪntrɪ] *a* invernale.

wipe [waɪp] *n* pulita, passata // *vt* pulire (strofinando); (*dishes*) asciugare; **to** ~ **off** *vt* cancellare; (*stains*) togliere strofinando; **to** ~ **out** *vt* (*debt*) pagare, liquidare; (*memory*) cancellare; (*destroy*) annientare; **to** ~ **up** *vt* asciugare.

wire ['waɪə*] *n* filo; (*ELEC*) filo elettrico; (*TEL*) telegramma *m*.

wireless ['waɪəlɪs] *n* telegrafia senza fili; (*set*) (apparecchio *m*) radio *f inv*.

wiry ['waɪərɪ] *a* magro(a) e nerboruto(a).

wisdom ['wɪzdəm] *n* saggezza; (*of action*) prudenza; ~ **tooth** *n* dente *m* del giudizio.

wise [waɪz] *a* saggio(a); prudente; giudizioso(a).

...wise [waɪz] *suffix*: **time**~ per quanto riguarda il tempo, in termini di tempo.

wisecrack ['waɪzkræk] *n* battuta spiritosa.

wish [wɪʃ] *n* (*desire*) desiderio; (*specific desire*) richiesta // *vt* desiderare, volere; **best** ~**es** (*on birthday etc*) i migliori auguri; **with best** ~**es** (*in letter*) cordiali saluti, con i migliori saluti; **to** ~ **sb goodbye** dire arrivederci a qd; **he** ~**ed me well** mi augurò di riuscire; **to** ~ **to do/sb to do** desiderare *or* volere fare/che qd faccia; **to** ~ **for** desiderare; **it's** ~**ful thinking** è prendere i desideri per realtà.

wisp [wɪsp] *n* ciuffo, ciocca; (*of smoke, straw*) filo.

wistful ['wɪstful] *a* malinconico(a).

wit [wɪt] *n* (*gen pl*) intelligenza; presenza di spirito; (*wittiness*) spirito, arguzia; (*person*) bello spirito; **to be at one's** ~**s' end** (*fig*) non sapere più cosa fare; **to** ~ *ad* cioè.

witch [wɪtʃ] *n* strega; ~**craft** *n* stregoneria.

with [wɪð, wɪθ] *prep* con; **red** ~ **anger** rosso dalla *or* per la rabbia; **covered** ~ **snow** coperto di neve; **the man** ~ **the grey hat** l'uomo dal cappello grigio; **to be** ~ **it** (*fig*) essere al corrente; essere sveglio(a); **I am ~ you** (*I understand*) la seguo.

withdraw [wɪθ'drɔː] *vb* (*irg*) *vt* ritirare; (*money from bank*) ritirare; prelevare // *vi* ritirarsi; (*go back on promise*) ritrattarsi; **~al** *n* ritiro; prelievo; (*of army*) ritirata; (*MED*) stato di privazione.

wither ['wɪðə°] *vi* appassire; **~ed** *a* appassito(a); (*limb*) atrofizzato(a).

withhold [wɪθ'həuld] *vt irg* (*money*) trattenere; (*decision*) rimettere, rimandare; (*permission*): **to ~ (from)** rifiutare (a); (*information*): **to ~ (from)** nascondere (a).

within [wɪð'ɪn] *prep* all'interno, (*in time, distances*) entro // *ad* all'interno, dentro; **~ sight of** in vista di; **~ a mile of** entro un miglio da; **~ the week** prima della fine della settimana.

without [wɪð'aut] *prep* senza.

withstand [wɪθ'stænd] *vt irg* resistere a.

witness ['wɪtnɪs] *n* (*person*) testimone *m/f* // *vi* (*event*) essere testimone di; (*document*) attestare l'autenticità di; **to bear ~ to sth** testimoniare qc; **~ box**, **~ stand** (*US*) *n* banco dei testimoni.

witticism ['wɪtɪsɪzm] *n* spiritosaggine *f*.

witty ['wɪtɪ] *a* spiritoso(a).

wives [waɪvz] *npl of* **wife**.

wizard ['wɪzəd] *n* mago.

wk *abbr of* **week**.

wobble ['wɔbl] *vi* tremare; (*chair*) traballare.

woe [wəu] *n* dolore *m*; disgrazia.

woke [wəuk] *pt of* **wake**; **~n** *pp of* **wake**.

wolf, wolves [wulf, wulvz] *n* lupo.

woman, pl women ['wumən, 'wɪmɪn] *n* donna; **~ doctor** *n* dottoressa; **~ly** *a* femminile.

womb [wuːm] *n* (*ANAT*) utero.

women ['wɪmɪn] *npl of* **woman**.

won [wʌn] *pt,pp of* **win**.

wonder ['wʌndə°] *n* meraviglia // *vi*: **to ~ whether** domandarsi se; **to ~ at** essere sorpreso(a) di; meravigliarsi di; **to ~ about** domandarsi di; pensare a; **it's no ~ that** c'è poco *or* non c'è da meravigliarsi che + *sub*; **~ful** *a* meraviglioso(a); **~fully** *ad* (+ *adjective*) meravigliosamente; (+ *vb*) a meraviglia.

wonky ['wɔŋkɪ] *a* (*col*) traballante.

won't [wəunt] = **will not**.

woo [wuː] *vt* (*woman*) fare la corte a.

wood [wud] *n* legno; (*timber*) legname *m*; (*forest*) bosco; **~ carving** *n* scultura in legno, intaglio; **~ed** *a* boschivo(a); boscoso(a); **~en** *a* di legno; (*fig*) rigido(a); inespressivo(a); **~pecker** *n* picchio; **~wind** *n* (*MUS*) strumento a fiato in legno; **the ~wind** (*MUS*) i legni; **~work** *n* parti *fpl* in legno; (*craft, subject*) falegnameria; **~worm** *n* tarlo del legno.

wool [wul] *n* lana; **to pull the ~ over sb's eyes** (*fig*) imbrogliare qd; **~len** *a* di lana; **~lens** *npl* indumenti *mpl* di lana; **~ly** *a* lanoso(a); (*fig: ideas*) confuso(a).

word [wɔːd] *n* parola; (*news*) notizie *fpl* // *vt* esprimere, formulare; **in other ~s** in

altre parole; **to break/keep one's ~** non mantenere/mantenere la propria parola; **I'll take your ~ for it** la crederò sulla parola; **~ing** *n* formulazione *f*; **~y** *a* verboso(a).

wore [wɔː°] *pt of* **wear**.

work [wɔːk] *n* lavoro; (*ART, LITERATURE*) opera // *vi* lavorare; (*mechanism, plan etc*) funzionare; (*medicine*) essere efficace // *vt* (*clay, wood etc*) lavorare; (*mine etc*) sfruttare; (*machine*) far funzionare; **to be out of ~** essere disoccupato(a); **~s** *n* (*factory*) fabbrica // *npl* (*of clock, machine*) meccanismo; **to ~ loose** *vi* allentarsi; **to ~ on** *vt fus* lavorare a; (*principle*) basarsi su; **to ~ out** *vi* (*plans etc*) riuscire, andare bene // *vt* (*problem*) risolvere; (*plan*) elaborare; **it ~s out at £100** fa 100 sterline; **to get ~ed up** andare su tutte le furie; eccitarsi; **~able** *a* (*solution*) realizzabile; **~er** *n* lavoratore/trice, operaio/a; **~ing class** *n* classe *f* operaia *or* lavoratrice; **~ing-class** *a* operaio(a); **~ing man** *n* lavoratore *m*; **in ~ing order** funzionante; **~man** *n* operaio; **~manship** *n* abilità; lavoro; fattura; **~shop** *n* officina; **~-to-rule** *n* sciopero bianco.

world [wɔːld] *n* mondo // *cpd* (*champion*) del mondo; (*power, war*) mondiale; **to think the ~ of sb** (*fig*) pensare un gran bene di qd; **out of this ~** a formidabile; **~ly** *a* di questo mondo; **~-wide** *a* universale.

worm [wɔːm] *n* verme *m*.

worn [wɔːn] *pp of* **wear** // *a* usato(a); **~-out** *a* (*object*) consumato(a), logoro(a); (*person*) sfinito(a).

worried ['wʌrɪd] *a* preoccupato(a).

worrier ['wʌrɪə°] *n* ansioso/a.

worry ['wʌrɪ] *n* preoccupazione *f* // *vt* preoccupare // *vi* preoccuparsi; **~ing** *a* preoccupante.

worse [wɔːs] *a* peggiore // *ad, n* peggio; **a change for the ~** un peggioramento; **~n** *vt, vi* peggiorare; **~ off** *a* in condizioni (economiche) peggiori.

worship ['wɔːʃɪp] *n* culto // *vt* (*God*) adorare, venerare; (*person*) adorare; **Your W~** (*to mayor*) signor sindaco; (*to judge*) signor giudice; **~per** *n* adoratore/trice; (*in church*) fedele *m/f*, devoto/a.

worst [wɔːst] *a* il(la) peggiore // *ad, n* peggio; **at ~** al peggio, per male che vada.

worsted ['wustɪd] *n*: **(wool) ~** lana pettinata.

worth [wɔːθ] *n* valore *m* // *a*: **to be ~** valere; **it's ~ it** vale la pena; **50 pence ~ of apples** 50 pence di mele; **~less** *a* di nessun valore; **~while** *a* (*activity*) utile; (*cause*) lodevole; **a ~while book** un libro che vale la pena leggere.

worthy ['wɔːðɪ] *a* (*person*) degno(a); (*motive*) lodevole; **~ of** degno di.

would [wud] *auxiliary vb*: **she ~ come** verrebbe; **he ~ have come** sarebbe venuto; **~ you like a biscuit?** vuole *or* vorrebbe un biscotto?; **he ~ go there on Mondays** ci andava il lunedì; **~-be** *a* (*pej*) sedicente.

wound *vb* [waund] *pt, pp of* **wind** // *n,vt* [wu:nd] *n* ferita // *vt* ferire; **~ed in the leg** ferito(a) alla gamba.

wove [wəuv] *pt of* **weave**; **~n** *pp of* **weave**.

wrangle ['ræŋgl] *n* litigio // *vi* litigare.

wrap [ræp] *n* (*stole*) scialle *m*; (*cape*) mantellina // *vt* (*also*: **~ up**) avvolgere; (*parcel*) incartare; **~per** *n* (*of book*) copertina; **~ping paper** *n* carta da pacchi; (*for gift*) carta da regali.

wrath [rɔθ] *n* collera, ira.

wreath, ~s [ri:θ, ri:ðz] *n* corona.

wreck [rɛk] *n* (*sea disaster*) naufragio; (*ship*) relitto; (*pej: person*) rottame *m* // *vt* demolire; (*ship*) far naufragare; (*fig*) rovinare; **~age** *n* rottami *mpl*; (*of building*) macerie *fpl*; (*of ship*) relitti *mpl*.

wren [rɛn] *n* (*ZOOL*) scricciolo.

wrench [rɛntʃ] *n* (*TECH*) chiave *f*; (*tug*) torsione *f* brusca; (*fig*) strazio // *vt* strappare; storcere; **to ~ sth from** strappare qc a *or* da.

wrestle ['rɛsl] *vi*: **to ~ (with sb)** lottare (con qd); **to ~ with** (*fig*) combattere *or* lottare contro; **~r** *n* lottatore/trice; **wrestling** *n* lotta; (*also*: **all-in wrestling**) catch *m*, lotta libera.

wretched ['rɛtʃid] *a* disgraziato(a); (*col: weather, holiday*) orrendo(a), orribile; (: *child, dog*) pestifero(a).

wriggle ['rɪgl] *n* contorsione *f* // *vi* dimenarsi; (*snake, worm*) serpeggiare, muoversi serpeggiando.

wring, *pt, pp* wrung [rɪŋ, rʌŋ] *vt* torcere; (*wet clothes*) strizzare; (*fig*): **to ~ sth out of** strappare qc a.

wrinkle ['rɪŋkl] *n* (*on skin*) ruga; (*on paper etc*) grinza // *vt* corrugare; raggrinzire // *vi* corrugarsi; raggrinzirsi.

wrist [rɪst] *n* polso; **~ watch** *n* orologio da polso.

writ [rɪt] *n* ordine *m*; mandato.

write, *pt* wrote, *pp* written [raɪt, rəut, 'rɪtn] *vt, vi* scrivere; **to ~ down** *vt* annotare; (*put in writing*) mettere per iscritto; **to ~ off** *vt* (*debt*) cancellare; (*depreciate*) deprezzare; **to ~ out** *vt* scrivere; (*copy*) ricopiare; **to ~ up** *vt* redigere; **~-off** *n* perdita completa; **the car is a ~-off** la macchina va bene per il demolitore; **~r** *n* autore/trice, scrittore/trice.

writhe [raɪð] *vi* contorcersi.

writing ['raɪtɪŋ] *n* scrittura; (*of author*) scritto, opera; **in ~** per iscritto; **~ paper** *n* carta da scrivere.

written ['rɪtn] *pp of* **write**.

wrong [rɔŋ] *a* sbagliato(a); (*not suitable*) inadatto(a); (*wicked*) cattivo(a); (*unfair*) ingiusto(a) // *ad* in modo sbagliato, erroneamente // *n* (*evil*) male *m*;

(*injustice*) torto // *vt* fare torto a; **you are ~ to do it** ha torto a farlo; **you are ~ about that** si sbaglia; **to be in the ~** avere torto; **what's ~?** cosa c'è che non va?; **to go ~** (*person*) sbagliarsi; (*plan*) fallire, non riuscire; (*machine*) guastarsi; **~ful** *a* illegittimo(a); ingiusto(a); **~ly** *ad* a torto.

wrote [rəut] *pt of* **write**.

wrought [rɔːt] *a*: **~ iron** ferro battuto.

wrung [rʌŋ] *pt, pp of* **wring**.

wry [raɪ] *a* storto(a).

wt. *abbr of* **weight**.

X Y Z

Xmas ['ɛksməs] *n abbr of* **Christmas**.

X-ray ['ɛks'reɪ] *n* raggio X; (*photograph*) radiografia // *vt* radiografare.

xylophone ['zaɪləfəun] *n* xilofono.

yacht [jɔt] *n* panfilo, yacht *m inv*; **~ing** *n* yachting *m*, sport *m* della vela; **~sman** *n* yachtsman *m inv*.

Yank [jæŋk] *n* (*pej*) yankee *m/f inv*.

yap [jæp] *vi* (*dog*) guaire, abbaiare.

yard [jɑːd] *n* (*of house etc*) cortile *m*; (*measure*) iarda (= 914 mm; 3 feet); **~stick** *n* (*fig*) misura, criterio.

yarn [jɑːn] *n* filato; (*tale*) lunga storia.

yawn [jɔːn] *n* sbadiglio // *vi* sbadigliare; **~ing** *a* (*gap*) spalancato(a).

yd. *abbr of* **yard(s)**.

year [jɪə*] *n* anno; (*referring to harvest, wine etc*) annata; **~ly** *a* annuale // *ad* annualmente.

yearn [jəːn] *vi*: **to ~ for sth/to do** desiderare ardentemente qc/di fare; **~ing** *n* desiderio intenso.

yeast [ji:st] *n* lievito.

yell [jɛl] *n* urlo // *vi* urlare.

yellow ['jɛləu] *a* giallo(a).

yelp [jɛlp] *n* guaito, uggiolio // *vi* guaire, uggiolare.

yes [jɛs] *ad*, *n* sì (*m inv*).

yesterday ['jɛstədɪ] *ad*,*n* ieri (*m inv*).

yet [jɛt] *ad* ancora; già // *cj* ma, tuttavia; **it is not finished ~** non è ancora finito; **the best ~** finora il migliore; **as ~** finora.

yew [ju:] *n* tasso.

Yiddish ['jɪdɪʃ] *n* yiddish *m*.

yield [ji:ld] *n* produzione *f*, resa; reddito // *vt* produrre, rendere; (*surrender*) cedere // *vi* cedere.

yodel ['jəudl] *vi* cantare lo jodel *or* alla tirolese.

yoga ['jəugə] *n* yoga *m*.

yog(h)ourt, yog(h)urt ['jəugət] *n* iogurt *m inv*.

yoke [jəuk] *n* giogo.

yolk [jəuk] *n* tuorlo, rosso d'uovo.

yonder ['jɔndə*] *ad* là.

you [ju:] *pronoun* tu; (*polite form*) lei; (*pl*) voi; (: *very formal*) loro; (*complement direct*) ti; la; vi; li; (: *indirect*) ti; le; vi; gli; (*stressed*) te; lei; voi; loro; (*one*): **fresh air**

does ~ **good** l'aria fresca fa bene; ~
never know non si sa mai.

you'd [ju:d] = **you had; you would**.

you'll [ju:l] = **you will; you shall**.

young [jʌŋ] a giovane // npl (of animal)
piccoli mpl; (people): **the** ~ i giovani, la
gioventù; ~**ster** n giovanotto, ragazzo;
(child) bambino/a.

your [jɔ:*] a il(la) tuo(a), pl i(le) tuoi(tue);
il(la) suo(a), pl i(le) suoi(sue); il(la)
vostro(a), pl i(le) vostri(e); il(la) loro, pl
i(le) loro.

you're [juə*] = **you are**.

yours [jɔ:z] pronoun il(la) tuo(a), pl i(le)
tuoi(tue); (polite form) il(la) suo(a), pl i(le)
suoi(sue); (pl) il(la) vostro(a), pl i(le)
vostri(e); (: very formal) il(la) loro, pl i(le)
loro; ~ **sincerely/faithfully** cordiali/
distinti saluti.

yourself [jɔ:'sɛlf] pronoun (reflexive) ti; si;
(after prep) te; sé; (emphatic) tu stesso(a);
lei stesso(a); **yourselves** pl pronoun
(reflexive) vi; si; (after prep) voi; loro;
(emphatic) voi stessi(e); loro stessi(e).

youth [ju:θ] n gioventù f; (young man: pl ~**s**
[ju:ðz]) giovane m, ragazzo; ~**ful** a
giovane; da giovane; giovanile; ~ **hostel**
n ostello della gioventù.

you've [ju:v] = **you have**.

Yugoslav ['ju:gəu'sla:v] a, n jugoslavo(a).

Yugoslavia ['ju:gəu'sla:vɪə] n Jugoslavia.

zany ['zeɪnɪ] a un po' pazzo(a).

zeal [zi:l] n zelo; entusiasmo; ~**ous** ['zɛləs]
a zelante; premuroso(a).

zebra ['zi:brə] n zebra; ~ **crossing** n
(passaggio pedonale a) strisce fpl, zebre
fpl.

zero ['zɪərəu] n zero; ~ **hour** n l'ora zero.

zest [zɛst] n gusto; (CULIN) buccia.

zigzag ['zɪgzæg] n zigzag m inv // vi
zigzagare.

zinc [zɪŋk] n zinco.

zip [zɪp] n (also: ~ **fastener,** ~**per**)
chiusura f or cerniera f lampo inv // vt
(also: ~ **up**) chiudere con una cerniera
lampo.

zither ['zɪðə*] n cetra.

zodiac ['zəudɪæk] n zodiaco.

zombie ['zɔmbɪ] n (fig): **like a** ~ come un
morto che cammina.

zone [zəun] n zona; (subdivision of town)
quartiere m.

zoo [zu:] n zoo m inv.

zoologist [zu:'ɔlədʒɪst] n zoologo/a.

zoology [zu:'ɔlədʒɪ] n zoologia.

zoom [zu:m] vi: **to** ~ **past** sfrecciare; ~
lens n zoom m inv, obiettivo a focale
variabile.

ITALIAN VERBS

NB: **Verbi inglesi:** le forme irregolari di verbi inglesi si trovano in ordine alfabetico nella nomenclatura con rimando alla forma di base.

1 Gerundio *2* Participio passato *3* Presente *4* Imperfetto *5* Passato remoto *6* Futuro *7* Condizionale *8* Congiuntivo presente *9* Congiuntivo passato *10* Imperativo

andare *3* vado, vai, va, andiamo, andate, vanno *6* andrò *etc 8* vada *10* va'!, vada!, andate!, vadano!

apparire *2* apparso *3* appaio, appari *o* apparisci, appare *o* apparisce, appaiono *o* appariscono *5* apparvi *o* apparsi, apparisti, apparve *o* appari *o* apparse, apparvero *o* apparirono *o* apparsero *8* appaia *o* apparisca

aprire *2* aperto *3* apro *5* aprii *o* apersi, apristi *8* apra

AVERE *3* ho, hai, ha, abbiamo, avete, hanno *5* ebbi, avesti, ebbe, avemmo, aveste, ebbero *6* avrò *etc 8* abbia *etc 10* abbi!, abbia!, abbiate!, abbiano!

bere *1* bevendo *2* bevuto *3* bevo *etc 4* bevevo *etc 5* bevvi *o* bevetti, bevesti *6* berrò *etc 8* beva *etc 9* bevessi *etc*

cadere *5* caddi, cadesti *6* cadrò *etc*

cogliere *2* colto *3* colgo, colgono *5* colsi, cogliesti *8* colga

correre *2* corso *5* corsi, corresti

cuocere *2* cotto *3* cuocio, cociamo, cuociono *5* cossi, cocesti

dare *3* do, dai, da, diamo, date, danno *5* diedi *o* detti, desti *6* darò *etc 8* dia *etc 9* dessi *etc 10* da'!, dia!, date!, diano!

dire *1* dicendo *2* detto *3* dico, dici, dice, diciamo, dite, dicono *4* dicevo *etc 5* dissi, dicesti *6* dirò *etc 8* dica, diciamo, diciate, dicano *9* dicessi *etc 10* di'!, dica!, dite!, dicano!

dolere *3* dolgo, duoli, duole, dolgono *5* dolsi, dolesti *6* dorrò *etc 8* dolga

dovere *3* devo *o* debbo, devi, deve, dobbiamo, dovete, devono *o* debbono *6* dovrò *etc 8* debba, dobbiamo, dobbiate, devano *o* debbano

ESSERE *2* stato *3* sono, sei, è, siamo, siete, sono *4* ero, eri, era, eravamo, eravate, erano *5* fui, fosti, fu, fummo, foste, furono *6* sarò *etc 8* sia *etc 9* fossi, fossi, fosse, fossimo, foste, fossero *10* sii!, sia!, siate!, siano!

fare *1* facendo *2* fatto *3* faccio, fai, fa, facciamo, fate, fanno *4* facevo *etc 5* feci, facesti *6* farò *etc 8* faccia *etc 9* facessi *etc 10* fa'!, faccia!, fate!, facciano!

FINIRE *1* finendo *2* finito *3* finisco, finisci, finisce, finiamo, finite, finiscono *4* finivo, finivi, finiva, finivamo, finivate, finivano *5* finii, finisti, finì, finimmo, finiste, finirono *6* finirò, finirai, finirà, finiremo, finirete, finiranno *7* finirei, finiresti, finirebbe, finiremmo, finireste, finirebbero *8* finisca, finisca, finisca, finiamo, finiate, finiscano *9* finissi, finissi, finisse, finissimo, finiste, finissero *10* finisci!, finisca!, finite!, finiscano!

giungere *2* giunto *5* giunsi, giungesti

leggere *2* letto *5* lessi, leggesti

mettere *2* messo *5* misi, mettesti

morire *2* morto *3* muoio, muori, muore, moriamo, morite, muoiono *6* morirò *o* morrò *etc 8* muoia

muovere *2* mosso *5* mossi, movesti

nascere *2* nato *5* nacqui, nascesti

nuocere *2* nuociuto *3* nuoccio, nuoci, nuoce, nociamo *o* nuociamo, nuocete, nuocciono *4* nuocevo *etc 5* nocqui, nuocesti *6* nuocerò *etc 7* nuoccia

offrire *2* offerto *3* offro *5* offersi *o* offrii, offristi *8* offra

parere *2* parso *3* paio, paiamo, paiono *5* parvi *o* parsi, paresti *6* parrò *etc 8* paia, paiamo, pariate, paiano

PARLARE *1* parlando *2* parlato *3* parlo, parli, parla, parliamo, parlate, parlano *4* parlavo, parlavi, parlava, parlavamo, parlavate, parlavano *5* parlai, parlasti, parlò, parlammo, parlaste, parlarono *6* parlerò, parlerai, parlerà, parleremo, parlerete, parleranno *7* parlerei, parleresti, parlerebbe, parleremmo, parlereste, parlerebbero *8* parli, parli, parli, parliamo, parliate, parlino *9* parlassi, parlassi, parlasse, parlassimo, parlaste, parlassero *10* parla!, parli!, parlate!, parlino!

piacere *2* piaciuto *3* piaccio, piacciamo, piacciono *5* piacqui, piacesti *8* piaccia *etc*

porre *1* ponendo *2* posto *3* pongo, poni, pone, poniamo, ponete, pongono *4* ponevo *etc* *5* posi, ponesti *6* porrò *etc* *8* ponga, poniamo, poniate, pongano *9* ponessi *etc*

potere *3* posso, puoi, può, possiamo, potete, possono *6* potrò *etc* *8* possa, possiamo, possiate, possano

prendere *2* preso *5* presi, prendesti

ridurre *1* riducendo *2* ridotto *3* riduco *etc* *4* riducevo *etc* *5* ridussi, riducesti *6* ridurrò *etc* *8* riduca *etc* *9* riducessi *etc*

riempire *1* riempiendo *3* riempio, riempi, riempie, riempiono

rimanere *2* rimasto *3* rimango, rimangono *5* rimasi, rimanesti *6* rimarrò *etc* *8* rimanga

rispondere *2* risposto *5* risposi, rispondesti

salire *3* salgo, sali, salgono *8* salga

sapere *3* so, sai, sa, sappiamo, sapete, sanno *5* seppi, sapesti *6* saprò *etc* *8* sappia *etc* *10* sappi!, sappia!, sappiate!, sappiano!

scrivere *2* scritto *5* scrissi, scrivesti

sedere *3* siedo, siedi, siede, siedono *8* sieda

spegnere *2* spento *3* spengo, spengono *5* spensi, spegnesti *8* spenga

stare *2* stato *3* sto, stai, sta, stiamo, state, stanno *5* stetti, stesti *6* starò *etc* *8* stia *etc* *9* stessi *etc* *10* sta'!, stia!, state!, stiano!

tacere *2* taciuto *3* taccio, tacciono *5* tacqui, tacesti *8* taccia

tenere *3* tengo, tieni, tiene, tengono *5* tenni, tenesti *6* terrò *etc* *8* tenga

trarre *1* traendo *2* tratto *3* traggo, trai, trae, traiamo, traete, traggono *4* traevo *etc* *5* trassi, traesti *6* trarrò *etc* *8* tragga *9* traessi *etc*

udire *3* odo, odi, ode, odono *8* oda

uscire *3* esco, esci, esce, escono *8* esca

valere *2* valso *3* valgo, valgono *5* valsi, valesti *6* varrò *etc* *8* valga

vedere *2* visto *o* veduto *5* vidi, vedesti *6* vedrò *etc*

VENDERE *1* vendendo *2* venduto *3* vendo, vendi, vende, vendiamo, vendete, vendono *4* vendevo, vendevi, vendeva, vendevamo, vendevate, vendevano *5* vendei *o* vendetti, vendesti, vendé *o* vendette, vendemmo, vendeste, venderono *o* vendettero *6* venderò, venderai, venderà, venderemo, venderete, venderanno *7* venderei, venderesti, venderebbe, venderemmo, vendereste, venderebbero *8* venda, venda, venda, vendiamo, vendiate, vendano *9* vendessi, vendessi, vendesse, vendessimo, vendeste, vendessero *10* vendi!, venda!, vendete!, vendano!

venire *2* venuto *3* vengo, vieni, viene, vengono *5* venni, venisti *6* verrò *etc* *8* venga

vivere *2* vissuto *5* vissi, vivesti

volere *3* voglio, vuoi, vuole, vogliamo, volete, vogliono *5* volli, volesti *6* vorrò *etc* *8* voglia *etc* *10* vogli!, voglia!, vogliate!, vogliano!

VERBI INGLESI

present	pt	pp	present	pt	pp
arise	arose	arisen	eat	ate	eaten
awake	awoke	awaked	fall	fell	fallen
be (am,	was,	been	feed	fed	fed
is, are;	were		feel	felt	felt
being)			fight	fought	fought
bear	bore	born(e)	find	found	found
beat	beat	beaten	flee	fled	fled
become	became	become	fling	flung	flung
befall	befell	befallen	fly	flew	flown
begin	began	begun	forbid	forbade	forbidden
behold	beheld	beheld	forecast	forecast	forecast
bend	bent	bent	forget	forgot	forgotten
beset	beset	beset	forgive	forgave	forgiven
bet	bet,	bet,	forsake	forsook	forsaken
	betted	betted	freeze	froze	frozen
bid	bid	bid	get	got	got, (US)
bind	bound	bound			gotten
bite	bit	bitten	give	gave	given
bleed	bled	bled	go	went	gone
blow	blew	blown	(goes)		
break	broke	broken	grind	ground	ground
breed	bred	bred	grow	grew	grown
bring	brought	brought	hang	hung,	hung,
build	built	built		hanged	hanged
burn	burnt,	burnt,	have	had	had
	burned	burned	hear	heard	heard
burst	burst	burst	hide	hid	hidden
buy	bought	bought	hit	hit	hit
can	could	(been able)	hold	held	held
cast	cast	cast	hurt	hurt	hurt
catch	caught	caught	keep	kept	kept
choose	chose	chosen	kneel	knelt,	knelt,
cling	clung	clung		kneeled	kneeled
come	came	come	know	knew	known
cost	cost	cost	lay	laid	laid
creep	crept	crept	lead	led	led
cut	cut	cut	lean	leant,	leant,
deal	dealt	dealt		leaned	leaned
dig	dug	dug	leap	leapt,	leapt,
do (3rd	did	done		leaped	leaped
person;			learn	learnt,	learnt,
he/she/				learned	learned
it/does)			leave	left	left
draw	drew	drawn	lend	lent	lent
dream	dreamed,	dreamed,	let	let	let
	dreamt	dreamt	lie	lay	lain
drink	drank	drunk	(lying)		
drive	drove	driven	light	lit,	lit,
dwell	dwelt	dwelt		lighted	lighted

present	pt	pp	present	pt	pp
lose	lost	lost	speed	sped,	sped,
make	made	made		speeded	speeded
may	might	—	spell	spelt,	spelt,
mean	meant	meant		spelled	spelled
meet	met	met	spend	spent	spent
mistake	mistook	mistaken	spill	spilt,	spilt,
mow	mowed	mown,		spilled	spilled
		mowed	spin	spun	spun
must	(had to)	(had to)	spit	spat	spat
pay	paid	paid	split	split	split
put	put	put	spoil	spoiled,	spoiled,
quit	quit,	quit,		spoilt	spoilt
	quitted	quitted	spread	spread	spread
read	read	read	spring	sprang	sprung
rend	rent	rent	stand	stood	stood
rid	rid	rid	steal	stole	stolen
ride	rode	ridden	stick	stuck	stuck
ring	rang	rung	sting	stung	stung
rise	rose	risen	stink	stank	stunk
run	ran	run	stride	strode	strode
saw	sawed	sawn	strike	struck	struck,
say	said	said			stricken
see	saw	seen	strive	strove	striven
seek	sought	sought	swear	swore	sworn
sell	sold	sold	sweep	swept	swept
send	sent	sent	swell	swelled	swollen,
set	set	set			swelled
shake	shook	shaken	swim	swam	swum
shall	should	—	swing	swung	swung
shear	sheared	shorn,	take	took	taken
		sheared	teach	taught	taught
shed	shed	shed			
shine	shone	shone	tear	tore	torn
shoot	shot	shot	tell	told	told
show	showed	shown	think	thought	thought
shrink	shrank	shrunk	throw	threw	thrown
shut	shut	shut	thrust	thrust	thrust
sing	sang	sung	tread	trod	trodden
sink	sank	sunk	wake	woke,	woken,
sit	sat	sat		waked	waked
slay	slew	slain			
sleep	slept	slept	wear	wore	worn
slide	slid	slid	weave	wove,	woven,
sling	slung	slung		weaved	weaved
slit	slit	slit	wed	wedded,	wedded,
smell	smelt,	smelt,		wed	wed
	smelled	smelled	weep	wept	wept
sow	sowed	sown,	win	won	won
		sowed	wind	wound	wound
			wring	wrung	wrung
speak	spoke	spoken	write	wrote	written

405

NUMBERS

I NUMERI

one/first	uno(a)/primo(a)
two/second	due/secondo(a)
three/third	tre/terzo(a)
four/fourth	quattro/quarto(a)
five/fifth	cinque/quinto(a)
six/sixth	sei/sesto(a)
seven/seventh	sette/settimo(a)
eight/eighth	otto/ottavo(a)
nine/ninth	nove/nono(a)
ten/tenth	dieci/decimo(a)
eleven/eleventh	undici/undicesimo(a)
twelve/twelfth	dodici/dodicesimo(a)
thirteen/thirteenth	tredici/tredicesimo(a)
fourteen/fourteenth	quattordici/quattordicesimo(a)
fifteen/fifteenth	quindici/quindicesimo(a)
sixteen/sixteenth	sedici/sedicesimo(a)
seventeen/seventeenth	diciassette/diciassettesimo(a)
eighteen/eighteenth	diciotto/diciottesimo(a)
nineteen/nineteenth	diciannove/diciannovesimo(a)
twenty/twentieth	venti/ventesimo(a)
twenty-one/twenty-first	ventuno/ventunesimo(a)
twenty-two/twenty-second	ventidue/ventiduesimo(a)
twenty-three/twenty-third	ventitré/ventitreesimo(a)
twenty-eight/twenty-eighth	ventotto/ventottesimo(a)
thirty/thirtieth	trenta/trentesimo(a)
forty	quaranta
fifty	cinquanta
sixty	sessanta
seventy	settanta
eighty .	ottanta
ninety	novanta
a hundred, one hundred/hundredth	cento/centesimo(a)
a hundred and one/hundred-and-first	cento uno/centunesimo(a)
two hundred	duecento
a thousand, one thousand/thousandth	mille/millesimo(a)
one thousand two hundred and two	milleduecentodue
five thousand	cinquemila
a million, one million/millionth	un milione/milionesimo(a)

THE TIME	L'ORA
what time is it? it's o it is ...	*che ora è?, che ore sono?* *è/sono ...*
midnight	mezzanotte, le dodici di sera
one (o'clock) (a.m. *o* in the morning), 1 a.m.	l'una
ten past one	l'una e dieci
a quarter past one, one fifteen	l'una e un quarto, l'una e quindici
half past one, one thirty	l'una e mezzo *o* mezza, l'una e trenta
a quarter to two, one forty-five	le due meno un quarto, l'una e quarantacinque
ten to two, one fifty	le due meno dieci, l'una e cinquanta
twelve (o'clock), midday, noon	mezzogiorno, le dodici
one (o'clock) (p.m. *o* in the afternoon), 1 p.m.	l'una, il tocco, le tredici
seven (o'clock) (p.m. *o* at night)	le sette (di sera), le diciannove
(at) what time?	*a che ora?*
at midnight	a mezzanotte
at one (o'clock)	all'una
at seven (o'clock)	alle sette